CHARLES O. GINGERICH

THE
SECRET
DOCTRINE

VOL. 6

OTHER WORKS BY H. P. BLAVATSKY

THE SECRET DOCTRINE

THE SYNTHESIS OF SCIENCE, RELIGION AND PHILOSOPHY

by

H. P. BLAVATSKY

Volume 6

INDEX AND GLOSSARY

THE ADYAR EDITION

————— 1 9 7 1 —————

THE THEOSOPHICAL PUBLISHING HOUSE

ADYAR   MADRAS   INDIA

68, Great Russell Street, London, W.C.I., England

Post Box 270, Wheaton, Illinois 60187, U.S.A.

9-86

	Volumes I, II	Volume III
First Edition	1888	1897
Second Edition	1888	
Third Edition	1893	
Reprinted	1902	
Reprinted	1905	
Reprinted	1908	
Reprinted	1911	1910
Reprinted	1913	1913
Reprinted	1918	1918
Reprinted	1921	1921
Reprinted	1928	1928

	Volumes 1-6
Fourth (Adyar) Edition	1938
Reprinted London	1950
Fifth (Adyar) Edition	1962
Reprinted	1971

SBN   7229-7176-1 (U.K.)

ISBN   0-8356-7176-3 (U.S.A.)

PRINTED IN INDIA

AT THE VASANTA PRESS, THE THEOSOPHICAL SOCIETY, ADYAR, MADRAS 20

PAGING IN THE FIVE EDITIONS

PAGING IN THE FIVE EDITIONS

	ED. 1 & 2 VOL. I Page	ED. 3 VOL. I Page	ED. 4 & 5 VOL. I Page
Fly Leaf	I		1
Portriat of H. P. B.	—	—	3
Title Page, Volume I. Cosmogenesis	III	III	3
Copyright	IV	IV	4
Dedication	V	V	5
Preface to the First Edition	VII	XIX	7
Preface to the Third and Revised Edition	—	XXIII	9
Preface to the Fourth (Adyar) Edition	—	—	10
Preface to the Fifth (Adyar) Edition	—	—	12
H. P. Blavatsky: A Sketch of her Life	—	—	13
How the Secret Doctrine was written	—	—	18
Table of Contents	IX	VII	37
Introductory	XVII	1	41
The Need of such a Book	XIX	2	42
The Antiquity of Documents and MSS.	XXIII	6	46
What the Book is intended to do	XXVIII	11	51
Proem			
Pages from a Prehistoric Period	1	31	69
The Oldest MS. in the World and its Symbolism ...	2	32	70
The One Life, Active and Passive	4	33	71
The Secret Doctrine—Pantheism—Atheism ...	6	35	73
" Space " in all Religions and in Occultism ...	9	38	75
Seven Cosmic Elements—Seven Races of Mankind ...	12	40	78
The Three Postulates of the Secret Doctrine ...	14	42	79
MS. Leaf of *The Secret Doctrine*	—	—	79
Description of the Stanzas from the Book of Dzyan ...	20	47	84
BOOK I. PART I. COSMIC EVOLUTION.			
Seven Stanzas translated with Commentaries from the Secret Book of Dzyan	25	53	89
Verses from the Rig Veda	26	54	90
Stanza I. The Night of the Universe	27	55	91
,, II. The Idea of Differentiation	28	56	92
,, III. The Awakening of Kosmos	28	57	92
,, IV. The Septenary Hierarchies	30	60	94
,, V. Fohat: The Child of the Septenary Hierarchies	31	61	95
,, VI. Our World, its Growth and Development ...	32	63	96
,, VII. The Parents of Man on Earth	33	65	97

		ED. 1 & 2 VOL. I Page	ED. 3 VOL. I Page	ED. 4 & 5 VOL. I Page
The Stanzas of Dzyan from the 1886 M.S.	... ...	—	—	101
Commentaries on the Seven Stanzas and their terms, according to their numeration in Stanzas and Shlokas	... ...	35	67	109
Stanza I.				
Verse 1.	The Seven Eternities	35	67	109
Verse 2.	Time	36	68	110
	Time and Universal Mind	37	69	110
Verse 3.	The Universal Mind and the Dhyan Chohans	38	69	111
Verse 4.	Nidana and Maya: The Causes of Misery ...	39	70	112
	The Causes of being	39	70	112
Verse 5.	Darkness	40	72	113
	What is Darkness in Philosophy?	40	72	113
Verse 6.	The Great Breath	42	73	114
	The Seven Sublime Lords	42	73	114
	Motion, The Great Breath	43	74	115
Verse 7.	Being and Non-Being. The Causes of Existence	44	75	116
Verse 8.	The Eye of Dangma. The One form of Existence	46	77	118
Verse 9.	Ālaya, the Universal Soul	47	78	119
	Can the Finite Conceive the Infinite? ...	51	81	122
Stanza II.				
Verse 1.	The State of Paranirvāna. The Builders ...	53	83	123
Verse 2.	The Absolute Knows Itself Not ...	54	84	124
Verse 3.	The Germ of Life Was Not Yet	57	87	127
Verse 4.	Astral Light is not the Anima Mundi ...	58	88	128
Verse 5.	Svābhāvat	60	90	130
Verse 6.	The Universe Was Still Concealed in the Divine Thought	61	91	130
	Divine Thought, Divine thinkers ...	61	91	130
Stanza III.				
Verse 1.	The Great Vibration	62	91	131
	The Universe, a Flitting Shadow	63	92	131
Verse 2.	... ...	63	93	132
Verse 3.	... ...	64	94	133
	Nature's Symbols	65	94	133
Verse 4.	... ...	66	95	134
	The Power of Numbers	67	96	135
	The Churning of the Ocean	67	97	135
Verse 5.	... ...	68	97	136
	The Blossom of the Root of Life ...	69	98	137
Verse 6.	... ...	69	98	137

		ED. 1 & 2 VOL. I Page	ED. 3 VOL. I Page	ED. 4 & 5 VOL. I Page
	Darkness and Light	70	99	137
	Light emerges from Darkness	71	100	138
Verse 7.	...	71	100	138
	Androgynous Deities	72	101	139
	The Dragon and the Logoi	73	102	139
	The Serpent Symbol	74	103	141
	Noumenal and Phenomenal Light. The Astral Light	75	104	142
	The Magical Agent	76	105	143
	Deity in Space and Time	77	106	143
Verse 8.	...	77	106	143
	I Am that I am	78	107	144
	Primeval Radiations from the Unity	79	107	144
Verse 9.	...	81	109	146
	Primeval Differentiations	81	109	146
Verses 10, 11.	...	83	111	148
	The Web of Being	83	111	148
	Conscious Electricity: Fohat	85	113	150
Verse 12.	...	85	113	150
Stanza IV.				
Verse 1.	The Son of the Fire	86	113	150
	The Seven Mystic Senses	87	115	151
Verse 2.	...	88	115	152
Verse 3.	...	88	116	152
	The Vehicle of the Universe—the Dhyan Chohans	89	117	153
	The Immaculate Conceptions	91	119	155
Verse 4.	The Army of the Voice	93	120	156
	The Potency of Speech and Sound	93	120	157
	Speech and Mind	95	121	157
	The Seven Senses	96	123	158
	Nature, the Perpetual Motion	97	124	160
Verse 5.	...	98	125	160
	The Boundless Circle	98	125	160
	The Ogdoad and the Heptad	99	126	162
	Fire, the Great Symbol of Deity	101	127	163
	The Stellar " Sons of Light "	103	129	164
Verse 6.	...	103	129	165
	The Divine Recorders	105	131	166
Stanza V.				
Verse 1.	The Fiery Whirlwind and the Primordial Seven	106	131	166

		ED. 1 & 2 VOL. I Page	ED. 3 VOL. I Page	ED. 4 & 5 VOL. I Page
	No Man—No God	107	132	167
Verse 2.	They Produce Fohat	107	133	168
	Celestial Buddhas	108	133	168
	The Theogony of the Creators	109	135	169
	The Protean Spirit-Substance	112	137	171
	The Correlation of the Gods	113	138	171
	Manifested Symbols	114	139	173
	The Seven Worlds	116	141	175
Verse 3.	... ...	116	141	175
	The Antiquity of Physical Sciences ...	117	143	176
Verse 4.	... ...	118	144	177
	The Evolution of the Principles of Nature ...	119	144	177
	The One Flame	120	145	179
	The Mystery of the Fire	121	146	179
Verse 5.	... ...	122	147	180
	The Winged Wheels	122	147	180
	The Secret of the Elements	123	147	180
	Monism and Materialism ...	124	149	183
	The Square [or the] Real Meaning of the Tabernacle	125	150	184
	The Four Celestial Beings	126	151	184
	The Dragons of Secret Wisdom ...	127	152	185
	The Planetary Spirits and the Lipika ...	128	153	186
Verse 6.	... ...	129	153	187
	The Ring " Pass Not "	130	155	188
	The Sidereal Book of Life	131	156	189
	The God of Man and the God of the Ant ...	133	157	190
	The Day of " Come to Us " ...	134	159	192
	The Soul's Pilgrimage and its Rest ...	135	159	192
Stanza VI.	...			
Verse 1.	The Logos	136	160	193
	The Mystery of the Female Logos ...	137	161	194
Verse 2.	The Seven Laya Centres	138	162	195
	From No-number to Number Seven. The Elementary Germs ...	139	163	195
Verse 3.	The Evolution of the Elements ...	140	163	196
	Were the Ancients Ignorant of the Physical Sciences?	141	165	197
	The Sleep of the Eternal Mother	143	167	199
Verse 4.	The Building of the Worlds ...	144	168	200
	The Cosmic Plane, an Illusion ...	145	169	201
	Primordial Substance, a Reality ...	147	171	202
	A Neutral Centre	148	171	203

	ED. 1 & 2 VOL. I Page	ED. 3 VOL. I Page	ED. 4 & 5 VOL. I Page
Dead Planets. The Moon is not Dead, but			
Only Sleepeth	149	172	204
Laplace's Mistake ...	150	173	205
Nature can Never Cease	151	174	206
Theosophical Misconceptions. A Digression	151	174	206
A Few Early Misconceptions Concerning Planets, Rounds, and Man	152	176	207
Descending and Re-ascending States	153	177	208
The Planetary Divisions and the Human Principles	153	177	208
Exchange of Life-principles. The Moon	155	178	209
Opinions Differ and yet Agree	157	181	211
Septenary Division in Different Indian Systems	157	181	212
The Transmigrations of the Ego ...	159	183	213
A Re-adjustment of Facts. The Septenary Chain	161	185	215
Like Questions, like Answers. Relation of the other Planets to the Earth	163	187	217
An Authoritative Letter	165	188	219
Priceless Advice Neglected	167	190	221
The Number 777 ...	168	191	221
The Seven Branches of the Tree of Knowledge	168	192	222
The Monadic Evolutions	169	192	222
Additional Facts and Explanations Concerning the Globes and the Monads	170	193	223
The Mystery of the Moon Unveiled	171	194	224
The Lunar Chain and the Earth Chain. Transfer of Life-elements.	171	195	225
The Earth, the Child of the Moon	172	195	225
The Monadic Host ...	174	197	227
The Classification of the Monads ...	174	197	227
The Elemental Kingdoms	176	199	229
As Above, so Below, is the Law ...	177	200	230
Monads and Atoms. The Monad Defined	177	200	230
The Lunar Monads. The Pitris	179	202	231
The Lunar Ancestors	180	203	232
A Triple Evolution in Nature	181	203	233
The Fourth Globe ...	182	205	234
Man, the Oldest Son of the Earth	183	206	235
Man or Ape; which was First? ...	185	207	236
An Erroneous Opinion	186	209	237
A Master's Letter ...	189	211	239
Stanza VI. (Continued).			
Verse 5. (First half). Creation in the Fourth Round	191	213	242
The Preliminary Creation of Man	191	213	242

		ED. 1 & 2 VOL. I Page	ED. 3 VOL. I Page	ED. 4 & 5 VOL. I Page
	(Second half). The Curse, the First Cause of Sin, and War	193	215	243
	The Codex Nazaræus Repeats the Allegory ...	195	216	245
	Ilda-Baoth-Jehovah	197	219	247
Verse 6.	... ...	199	220	248
	No Shadow, no Light	201	222	250
	The Struggle for Life	202	223	250
	The War in Heaven	202	223	251
	The Birth of the Worlds	203	225	252
	Seeing Sound, Hearing Colours	205	226	253
Verse 7.	... ...	205	226	254
	The Seven Grades of Initiation ...	206	227	255
	The Tree from which the Adepts Grow ...	207	228	256
	The Lost Canon of Proportion	208	229	257
	The Sacred Island	209	230	258
	The Origin of Devotion	210	231	258
	The Sons of Wisdom	211	232	259
Stanza VII.				
Verse 1.	The Creative Powers	213	233	260
	Divisions of the Hierarchies	213	233	260
	One Parent Flame, Countless Flames ...	215	235	262
	Teachings Contrasted	217	237	264
	The Hierarchies of Spirits	219	239	266
	Nature-spirits, or Elementals, Correlation of Beings	221	241	268
Verse 2.	... ...	222	242	269
	The Mystery of Being	223	243	269
	The Ancestry of Man	224	245	271
	Spirit Falling into Matter	225	246	272
	The Egyptian System. The " Seven Souls " in Egyptology	227	247	273
	The Moon God	227	248	274
	Many Streams, but One Source	229	250	276
	Jehovah a Female Sephira	230	251	277
Verse 3.	The Differentiation of the " One " ...	231	251	277
	The Origin of Man	231	252	277
	What Incarnates in Animal Man ...	233	254	279
	Dii Sunt Demones Inversi	235	255	280
Verse 4.	The Immortal Root	237	257	282
Verse 5.	Formation of Man the Thinker	238	258	283
	Chaldean Metaphysics	239	259	284
	The True and the False Kabalah ...	241	261	286
	Occult and Kabalistic Pneumatics [or] Doctrines	243	263	288

	ED. 1 & 2 VOL. I Page	ED. 3 VOL. I Page	ED. 4 & 5 VOL. I Page
Occultists and Kabalists Differ	244	264	289
Spirit alone is Helpless on Earth	247	267	292
Matter, Life and Substance	248	268	293
The " Devourers "	250	269	294
The Four Dimensions of Space	251	271	295
Oceans of Carbonic Acid	252	273	297
The Great Archæus	253	275	299
The Great Magic Agent	253	275	299
But why Slander the Indian Hierophants?	255	276	299
Ākāsha is not Ether	257	277	300
Atoms are Invisible Lives	259	279	302
The Occult Vital Chemistry and Bacteriology	261	281	305
The Fiery Lives	262	283	306
Paracelsus died too early	263	284	307
Verse 6.	264	285	308
Man, the Shadow of His Prototype, the Watcher	265	285	308
Verse 7.	265	286	309
Earth Peopled by the Shadows of the Gods from Heaven	267	287	310
The " Second Advent "	268	289	311
Summing Up.			
The First Chapter of Creation	269	290	312
The Upanishads	269	290	313
Occultism in the Upanishads	270	291	314
A Recapitulation	272	293	316
The Pith and Marrow of The Secret Doctrine [or] Occultism	273	293	316
The Guiding Intelligence of the Universe	274	295	317
The Nature of the Celestial Men	275	295	318
The Unity of All in Nature	276	297	319
Many Bodies but one Soul	277	297	320
The Three Universes	278	298	320
Hermes, or Aristotle?	279	300	322
Matter is the Shadow of Spirit	281	301	323
The Yliaster of Paracelsus	283	303	325
Paracelsus Anticipated Tyndall	283	304	325
Hermes in Christian Garb	285	305	326
The Eternal Alone is Real. Alone the Eternal is Rest	287	307	238
Extracts from an Eastern Private Commentary, hitherto Secret.			
A Few Occult Aphorisms	289	309	330
Occult Aphorisms	291	311	332
Yoga Powers	292	312	333
The Seven Powers of Nature	293	313	333

		ED. 1 & 2 VOL. I Page	ED. 3 VOL. I Page	ED. 4 & 5 VOL. 1 Page
Universal Illusion	... ...	295	314	335
Ākāsha	... ...	296	315	336
Nothing New Under the Sun	... ...	297	317	337
Men Welcome Error, and Crucify the Truth	...	299	318	338
Additional Notes	... ...	—	—	340
Bibliography	... ...	—	—	341

VOL. 2

BOOK I. PART II. THE EVOLUTION OF SYMBOLISM IN ITS APPROXIMATE ORDER. EXPLANATORY

SECTIONS		301	319	1
Contents		302	XI	5
Section I. Symbolism and Ideographs		303	321	15
The Egyptian Cat-Symbol		304	322	16
Emblem and Symbol Differ		305	324	17
Magic Potency of Sound		307	325	19
The Mystery Language		308	327	20
Section II. The Mystery Language and its Keys		310	329	22
Egypt's Many Religions		311	330	23
The Jews, and their System		312	332	25
The Great Pyramid Measures		314	333	26
Piazzi Smyth and Petrie Disagree		315	334	27
The Quadrature of the Circle		315	335	28
The Truth must Prevail at Last		317	337	29
Moses and the Ark of Bulrushes copied from Sargon ...		319	339	31
Occult Numbers		321	341	33
The Cross, a Phallic Symbol		321	342	34
Identity of the Ancient Symbols		322	342	34
The " Satanic " Races		324	345	37
The Impartiality of Scientific Denials		325	346	38
Section III. Primordial Substance and Divine Thought ...		325	347	39
Divine Thought, or Cineritious Matter		327	348	41
The Universal Illusion		329	351	42
Ether, as its Noumenon, Intelligence		330	352	44
Pater Omnipotens Aether		331	353	44
What Manu says of this		333	355	46
The Cosmogenesis of Manu		333	355	47
The Seven Prakritis		335	357	49
The God of " Genesis "		336	359	50
Darkness is Light		337	359	51
The Mystic Fire		339	361	52

	ED. 1 & 2 VOL. I Page	ED. 3 VOL. I Page	ED. 4 & 5 VOL. 2 Page
Aether	339	362	53
One Tree of Knowledge	341	364	55
Section IV. Chaos-Theos-Kosmos	342	365	56
The Union of Chaos and Spirit	343	366	57
The Soul of the World	343	367	58
The Birth of Mind	345	368	59
The Mystic Elements	347	371	61
Section V. On the Hidden Deity, its Symbols and Glyphs. The			
Many are One	349	373	64
The Gnostic Idea	351	375	65
The Gnosis of Marcus	351	375	65
The Egyptian Version. The Great Mind	353	377	68
The Symbols of the Creative Powers	354	378	69
International Correlation of Gods	355	380	70
Orinthological Symbols	357	382	72
Ancient Symbology	358	382	72
Section VI. The Mundane Egg. The Egg-born God ...	359	384	74
Egg and Ark	360	385	75
Whence our Figures?	361	386	76
Lunar and Solar Deities	362	387	77
Egg-born Logoi	363	389	79
Fiery Serpents	364	389	79
The Winged Globe	365	391	81
Two Aspects of " God "	366	393	82
The Scandinavian Logos	367	394	83
Section VII. The Days and Nights of Brahma	368	395	84
Human Gods and Divine Men	369	396	85
Three Kinds of Pralaya	370	397	86
The Rebirth of Gods	371	398	87
The Re-absorption of All	371	398	87
The Dissolution of the Egg	373	400	88
A Kabalistic Key	374	401	90
Archaic Symbolism	375	402	90
The Coming of Night	376	403	91
The Purānic Prophecy	377	404	92
The Return of Moru	378	405	93
Section VIII. The Lotus as a Universal Symbol. Lotus and Lily	379	406	94
The Ideal Becoming Material	379	407	95
The Exoteric and the Esoteric	381	408	96

	ED. 1 & 2 VOL. I Page	ED. 3 VOL. I Page	ED. 4 & 5 VOL. 2 Page
Hebrew Anthropomorphism ...	381	409	96
The Purity of Early Phallicism	383	410	97
Brahman and Semite	383	411	98
The Letter M ...	384	412	99
The Egyptian Lotus	385	413	100
Section IX. *The Moon, Deus Lunus, Phoebe.* A Glance at the			
Lunar Myth	386	415	102
The Christian Lunar God	387	416	103
A Key Note to the Moon	389	418	105
The Physiological Key to the Moon Symbol	390	419	105
The Time Periods	391	420	106
The " Double Womb "	392	421	107
Copies and Originals	393	422	108
An Allegory from the Zohar	393	423	109
Solar-lunar Worship in the Church	395	424	110
Hecate-luna the Counterpart of Jehovah	395	425	111
The Moon Bi-sexual	396	426	112
The Dignity of Saïs	399	429	114
Ante-historical Catholicism	401	431	116
Identity of Typology	402	432	118
Section X. *Tree, Serpent, and Crocodile Worship*	403	434	120
The Serpent, the Symbol of Initiation	404	435	120
The Degeneration [or] Degradation of the Symbol	405	436	121
Ashvattha Tree	406	437	123
The Seven-headed Dragons ...	407	438	124
" Sevening " ...	408	439	124
Dragon and Crocodile	409	440	126
The Dual-logos	410	441	126
The Mystery of the Seven Thunders	411	442	127
Section XI. *Demon est Deus Inversus*	411	443	129
Death is Life. No Life without Death	413	445	131
Theological Etymologies	414	446	132
The Angels Slandered	417	449	135
The Fall of the Angels	418	450	135
The War of the Gods	418	450	135
Wilson's Criticism Criticized ...	420	452	138
The Deception of the Gods. Transformation of the			
Legend ...	421	454	140
The Deception, an Allegory ...	423	455	140
Section XII. *The Theogony of the Creative Gods*	424	457	142
Myth is Oral Tradition	425	458	143

	ED. 1 & 2 VOL. I Page	ED. 3 VOL. I Page	ED. 4 & 5 VOL. 2 Page
Jehovah not the Supreme Deity. The Point within the Circle	426	459	144
The Creative Logoi, Androgynous	427	461	146
The Primeval Theogony of the Vedantins	428	461	146
The One is Known by the Many	429	462	147
Synonyms of the Logos or Verbum	429	462	147
The Female Logoi	431	465	150
The Factors of Creation	432	465	150
The Pythagorean Idea	433	467	151
Antiquity of the Pyramids	435	469	153
Cosmic Gods	436	470	154
Identity of the Hierarchies in all Religions	438	472	156
Incredible, but True	439	473	157
The Same Idea in Confucianism	440	474	158
The Mystery of Blackness	443	477	161
Difference between the Aryan and Semitic Systems ...	444	479	162
God is our Higher Self	445	479	162
Section XIII. *The Seven Creations*	445	480	164
The Seven Creations of the Purānas ...	446	481	165
The Order of the Evolution	446	481	165
The Ogdoad	448	483	167
The Six Stellar Gods. The Gnostics and the Hindu Versions	449	484	167
Primary and Secondary Creations	450	485	169
Many Versions of the One Truth	451	487	170
The Seven Purānic Creations...	452	488	171
Creations Continued	455	491	174
Who the Kumaras are	457	493	176
The " Virgin Ascetics "	458	495	178
The Patron-guide of Israel	459	496	179
Importance of the Number Seven	460	496	180
Section XIV. *The Four Elements*	460	498	181
On the Elements	460	498	181
The Cosmic Gods	463	501	183
St. Paul Believed in Cosmic Gods. The Language of the Elements	464	503	185
A Confession of Science	465	503	186
Jehovah, a God of the Elements	466	504	187
The Fighting Gods. Pagan and Christian Worship of the Elements	467	506	188
Astarte and the Virgin Mary	468	507	189
Prayer is often Sorcery	468	507	190
Physical Forces the Vehicles of the Elements ...	470	509	191

VI–2

	ED. 1 & 2 VOL. I Page	ED. 3 VOL. I Page	ED. 4 & 5 VOL. 2 Page
Section XV. On Kwan-Shi-Yin and Kwan-Yin ...	470	510	192
Diseased Imagination. Kwan-Shi-Yin and Phallicism ...	471	511	193
The Real Meaning	472	512	193
Snobs or Dragons? Crinolines, or the Dragon-garb	473	513	195

BOOK I. PART III. ADDENDA. SCIENCE AND
   THE SECRET DOCTRINE CONTRASTED.

On Occult and Modern Science ...	475	515	197
Contents ...	476	XIV	8
Addenda to Book I ...	477	517	199

Section I. Reasons for these Addenda			
Mutual Position Defined ...	477	517	199
Forces are Devas and Genii	478	519	201
Dual Nature of the Sun. Occultism versus Materialism	479	520	201
Light is both Spirit and Matter. The Sabbath of the			
Mystic ...	481	521	203
The Sons of Light	481	522	204

| Section II.   Modern Physicists are Playing at Blind Man's Buff   ... | 482 | 523 | 205 |
| No Agreement among Scientists | 483 | 524 | 206 |

Section III.[1] " An Lumen Sit Corpus, Nec Non? " " Is Light			
a Body, or not? " ...	483	525	206
The Metaphysics of Physical Science. The Hypotheti-			
cal Ether ...	485	526	207
A Selection of Contradictory Hypotheses ...	485	527	208
Scientific Imagination	487	528	209
Actio In Distans	487	529	211
Scientific Theories of the Constitution of Ether. The			
Physical " Phantom " ...	489	530	211
Cauchy's Views	489	531	212

Section IV. Is Gravitation a Law? ...	490	532	213
Gravity or what?	491	533	213
Jehovah, one of the Elohim ...	492	535	215
The Triple Sidereal Force. Intelligences or Blind			
Force? ...	493	535	216
Newton Then and Newton Now	494	536	217
New Bottles for Old Wine. Perpetual Motion	497	539	220
The Cause of Attraction ...	498	540	221
Chronic Negation	498	541	222

[1] In the Third and subsequent Editions this section has not been separately numbered, so that the following sections in those Editions are numbered one fewer than in the older Editions.

	ED. 1 & 2 VOL. I Page	ED. 3 VOL. I Page	ED. 4 & 5 VOL. 2 Page
Kepler's Ideas	498	541	222
The Cause of Rotation	499	543	223
Section V. The Theories of Rotation in Science	500	544	224
Current Hypotheses explaining the Origin of Rotation ...	500	544	224
Hypotheses of the Origin of the Seven Planets and Comets ...	500	544	224
Conflicting [or] Contradictory Hypotheses ...	501	545	224
Scientific Aberrations	503	547	227
The Paradoxes of Science. More Hypotheses ...	505	549	229
Forces are Realities	506	551	230
Section VI. The Masks of Science. Physics or Metaphysics? ...	506	552	231
Academical Misnomers	507	553	231
What are the Forces?	508	553	232
The Fixing of Light	509	555	233
The View of the Occultists	509	555	234
What is Force?	511	557	235
They Agree to Disagree	513	559	238
The Mystic Rays. Scientific and Occult Theories on Heat	515	561	240
The Causes and the Effects	517	563	242
The Atoms of Science. What is an Atom? ...	519	565	243
The Vicious Circle	519	566	244
Chemical Gods	521	567	245
The Vishishtādvaita System	522	569	246
Suggestive Allegories	523	569	247
Section VII. An Attack on the Scientific Theory of Force by a Man of Science	523	571	248
Dr. Richardson's Heresy on Nervous Ether ...	524	572	249
We Disagree. Ether and Atoms	527	574	251
The Spirit and Soul of Kosmos	527	575	251
Section VIII. Life, Force, or Gravity	529	577	253
Mysterious Sun Fluid	529	578	254
Sun-force and Earth-force	531	579	255
Pantheism or Monotheism	533	581	257
The Seven Physical Senses and their Action ...	535	583	258
The Tree of Life	536	585	260
What is Nervous Ether?	537	586	261
The Life-principle. Too much Life may Kill ...	539	588	263
Section IX. The Solar Theory	540	590	264
The Heart of the Solar System	541	590	264
The Primordial Element	542	592	266

	ED. 1 & 2 VOL. I Page	ED. 3 VOL. I Page	ED. 4 & 5 VOL. 2 Page
The Quintessence of Kosmos	543	593	267
The Original Base	545	595	269
Elements and Meta-elements [or] Non-elements ...	546	596	270
Occult Chemistry	547	596	270
What is the Directive Force? The Tree of Life and Being. Monads and Atoms	549	599	272
A Scientific Caduceus	550	600	273
The Caduceus of Life	551	601	274
Occultism in Chemistry. Professor Crookes on the Elements	552	603	275
True Signs of the Times	554	605	278
Section X. The Coming Force. Its Possibilities and Impossibilities	554	605	278
Divine, Infernal, or Terrestrial Force	554	605	278
Mr. Keeley, An Unconscious Occultist	557	608	281
Occult Mysteries and Society	558	609	281
The First-born of Ether	559	610	283
Limits to Discoveries	560	611	284
Inter-etheric Waves	561	612	285
Keely's Ether	562	613	285
A Premature Discovery	563	615	287
The Secrets of Sound and Odour	565	616	288
What is the New Force?	565	617	289
Section XI. On the Elements and Atoms	566	619	290
Metaphysical Chemistry	567	619	290
The Whirling of the Soul	568	621	292
Pantheism versus Materialism	569	622	292
The Eternal Pilgrim	570	623	293
The Diamond Heart	571	624	295
Buddhas of the Three Worlds	572	625	296
The Crest-jewel of Wisdom	573	627	297
What are the Seven Planets?	575	628	298
Uranus and Neptune	575	629	299
The Cyclic Fall of the Gods	577	631	301
Section XII. Ancient Thought in Modern Dress	579	633	303
Antiquity our Great Master	579	633	303
Chemistry and Occult Science	580	635	305
A Chase after the Primal Matter	581	635	305
The Trinity in Unity	582	637	306
All-Potential Unity	583	637	307
Genesis of the Elements	584	639	308

			ED. 1 & 2 VOL. I Page	ED. 3 VOL. I Page	ED. 4 & 5 VOL. 2 Page
The " Seventh " in Chemistry	...	...	585	640	309
Purānas versus Royal Society	...	...	587	641	311
Section XIII. *Scientific and Esoteric Evidence for, and Objections*					
to the Modern Nebular Theory	...	...	588	643	312
" So far shalt Thou go . . . ."	...	...	589	644	313
Modern Science and Occultism	...	...	589	644	313
Forces are Emanations	...	...	591	647	315
Unanswerable Queries	...	...	593	649	317
What are the Nebulae?	...	...	595	651	319
Cometary Matter	...	...	596	653	321
The Meta-elements of Physical Science	...	...	597	654	322
What is Primitive Matter?	...	...	599	655	323
The Nebular Theory a Romance	...	...	599	656	323
The Future Synthesis	...	...	600	656	324
Section XIV. *Forces—Modes of Motion or Intelligences?*		...	601	658	325
Hermes and Kant	...	...	601	658	325
Kant and Occultism	...	...	602	659	326
The Vital Principle	...	...	603	660	327
Mind in Nature	...	...	604	661	328
Occult and Physical Sciences	...	...	605	662	329
Plurality of Worlds	...	...	607	665	331
The Geology of Enoch	...	...	609	667	333
Section XV. *Gods, Monads, and Atoms*	...	...	610	669	335
Which of the Two is Blind?	...	...	611	670	336
Who are the Blind?	...	...	611	670	336
The Mathematical Point. The Gods of the Ancients—					
the Monads	...	...	613	672	338
Space, Force and Matter	...	...	615	674	340
Phantoms of the Mind. The Monad and the Duad	...		617	676	342
Atomic Souls	...	...	619	679	344
The Monad of Leibnitz	...	...	619	680	345
The Chemistry of the Future. The Genesis of the					
Elements	...	...	621	681	346
Aryan and Western Science	...	...	622	683	347
The Genesis of Atoms	...	...	623	683	349
Hermes or Huxley?	...	...	625	685	350
The Teaching of Leibnitz and Occultism	...	...	627	687	352
Spinoza and Leibnitz	...	...	629	689	353
The Nature of the Monad	...	...	630	691	355
Māyā and Mahāmāyā	...	...	631	692	356
The Monads according to Occultism	...	...	632	692	356

	ED. 1 & 2 VOL. I Page	ED. 3 VOL. I Page	ED. 4 & 5 VOL. 2 Page
Spirit and Matter One	633	693	357
The Wheels of Life	633	694	358
Section XVI. Cyclic Evolution and Karma ...	634	695	359
The Roots and Causes	635	695	359
Is Man a God or a Beast?	636	697	361
The Swing of Karma. Karmic Cycles and Universal Ethics	637	698	362
The Network of Destiny and Karma	639	701	364
Cyclic Wheels within Wheels	641	703	366
Karma-Nemesis	642	704	367
Ancient and Modern Prophecies	645	707	370
Astrology a Science	647	709	371
Section XVII. The Zodiac and its Antiquity ...	647	710	373
The Zodiac in the Bible	647	710	373
Antiquity of Zodiac	650	713	376
The Jewish Patriarchs and the Zodiacal Signs ...	651	714	377
The Zodiac and the Patriarchs	651	714	377
The Sign of Jonas	653	717	380
Chaldeo-Judean Gods	655	718	381
Zodiacal Cycles	656	719	382
The Dragon and the Bull	657	720	383
Bailly's Conclusions	659	723	384
The Beginning of Kali Yuga. Hindu Astronomy ...	662	725	387
The Eye of Taurus	663	726	388
Hindu Astronomical Methods	664	727	389
The Aryan Hindus Vindicated	667	729	391
Section XVIII. Summary of the Mutual Position	668	731	393
Science Confesses her Ignorance. The Exact Sciences of Negation	669	732	394
No Void Possible	671	734	396
Forces are Gods	672	735	397
The Aliases of Fohat	673	736	398
The Gods of Egypt. Materialism is Leading Europe towards a Catastrophe	675	739	399
Legend and History	676	739	400
Additional Notes	—	—	403
Bibliography	—	—	404

	ED. 1 & 2 VOL. II. Page	ED. 3 VOL. II. Page	ED. 4 & 5 VOL. 3 Page
Fly-leaf	I	I	1
Title Page. Volume II. Anthropogenesis	III	III	3
Dedication	V	—	—
Table of Contents	VII	V	5
Preliminary Notes			
On the Archaic Stanzas and the Four Prehistoric Continents	1	1	15
The Lemnos-born Kabiri	3	3	17
The Secrets of Kouyunjik	5	5	18
I. The Imperishable Sacred Land ...	6	6	19
II. Hyperborean Continent ...	7	6	20
III. Lemuria	7	7	20
IV. Atlantis	8	7	21
V. America and Europe ...	8	7	21
Pre-tertiary Giants	9	8	22
Geological Periods	9	9	22
The Tropics at the Pole	11	11	23
Note	12	11	24

BOOK II. PART I. ANTHROPOGENESIS

Twelve Stanzas translated with commentaries from the Secret Book of Dzyan	13	13	25
Verses from the Kalevala	14	14	26
Stanza I. Beginnings of Sentient Life	15	15	27
,, II. Nature Unaided Fails ...	15	16	28
,, III. Attempts to Create Man ...	16	17	29
,, IV. Creation of the First Race ...	17	18	29
,, V. The Evolution of the Second Race	17	19	30
,, VI. The Evolution of the Sweat-Born ...	18	20	30
,, VII. From the Seven Divine down to the First Human Race	18	20	31
,, VIII. Evolution of the Animal Mammalian—the First Fall	19	21	31
,, IX. The Final Evolution of Man ...	20	22	32
,, X. The History of the Fourth Race ...	20	23	32
,, XI. The Civilization and Destruction of the Third and Fourth Races ...	20	23	33
,, XII. The Fifth Race and its Divine Instructors	21	24	33
Commentaries			
Stanza I. The Beginnings of Sentient Life	22	25	35
Verse 1. The Lha, or Spirit of the Earth	22	25	35

		ED. 1 & 2 VOL. II Page	ED. 3 VOL. II Page	ED. 4 & 5 VOL. 3 Page
	The Action of the Great Breath	23	26	36
	Cosmic Ultimates	24	27	37
	Man, The Third Logos	25	28	38
	Dragon and Serpent	25	29	39
	Man's Dual and Triple Nature	27	30	40
Verse 2.	Invocation of the Earth to the Sun	27	31	40
	Mercury and the Sun	27	31	40
	The Celestial Governors of Humanity	29	33	41
	The Horses of Shukra's Car	31	34	44
	Shukra (Venus) and the Earth	31	35	44
	Parent Stars and Sister Planets	33	36	45
	The One and the Many	34	37	46
	The " Seven " Mystery	35	39	47
	The Three Kinds of Light	37	41	49
	The Numbers of Creation	39	43	51
	The Emanations of Ain Soph	41	44	52
	Evolution, not Creation	42	45	53
	Adam-Adami, Adam-Kadmon	43	46	55
Verse 3.	What the Sun Answers	44	48	56
	The First War in Heaven	45	49	57
Verse 4.	Transformation of the Earth	46	50	58
Two Antediluvian Astronomers		47	51	59
	Nārada and Asuramāya	47	51	59
	The Mirror of Futurity	49	53	61
Verse 5.	After Enormous Periods the Earth Creates Monsters	52	55	63
Stanza II.	Nature Unaided Fails	52	55	63
	What the Earth-Whirl Produced [1]	52	55	63
	The Monsters of Chaos	53	56	63
Verse 6.	The " Creators " are Displeased	55	58	65
	Unaided Physical Nature Fails	56	59	66
Verse 7.	They Dry the Earth	57	60	67
	The Double Dragon	57	60	67
Creation of Divine Beings in the Exoteric Accounts		58	61	68
	The Bodies of Brahmā	58	61	68
	The Four Classes of Creative Powers	60	63	70
	What the Gnostics say	61	65	72
Verse 8.	The Forms are Destroyed by Them	63	66	74
	Who are the Flames?	63	66	74
Verse 9.	The First Great Tides	64	67	74
Verse 10.	The Beginning of Incrustation	65	68	75
	Divine Will becomes Eros	65	69	76

[1] In the 1st and 2nd editions this heading is wrongly placed over p. 51. It relates to p. 52. Possibly " earth-whirl " should read " earth-wheel."

	ED. 1 & 2 VOL. II Page	ED. 3 VOL. II Page	ED. 4 & 5 VOL. 3 Page
The Chronology of the Brahmins	66	69	76
The Race that Never Dies	67	71	78
The Various Pralāyas	69	72	78
Yugas and Kalpas	69	73	79
Scientific Self-complacence	71	74	80
Variations of Exact Science	71	75	81
Cosmogony an Intelligent Plan ...	73	77	83
Stanza III. Attempts to Create Man	75	78	84
Verse 11. The Descent of the Demiurge	75	78	84
The Secret of the Fall of the Angels ...	75	78	85
Verse 12. The Lunar Gods Ordered to Create	75	79	85
The Lords of the Moon	75	79	85
Verse 13. The Higher Gods Refuse	77	81	86
The Various Classes of Creators	77	81	86
The Living Spiritual Fire	79	83	88
Man, a God in Animal Form	81	85	90
" Fires," " Sparks," and " Flames " ...	83	87	92
The Son of YaH	85	89	94
Stanza IV. Creation of the First Races	86	90	95
Verse 14. Creation of Men	86	90	95
Man not Created Perfect	87	91	95
On the Identity and Differences of the Incarnating Powers ...	88	92	97
Pitris of the Gods and Demons	89	93	98
Verse 15. They are Empty Shadows	90	95	99
Progenitors of Men	91	95	100
Seven Classes of Pitris	91	96	100
The Refusal to Create	92	97	101
A Grand Apocalyptic Metaphor	93	98	102
What Prometheus Symbolized	95	99	103
Records of Ancient Races	96	101	103
The Trees of Life	97	102	106
The Swastika	98	103	107
The Hammer of Thor	99	104	107
The Prophecy of the Seventh Race ...	100	105	109
The Divine Babe, Agni	101	106	109
Verse 16. The Creators are Perplexed how to Create a Thinking Man	102	107	110
Primitive Man a Failure	102	107	110
The Divine Rebels...	103	108	111
Perplexity of the Assyriologists	104	109	112
Verse 17. What is Needed for the Formation of a Perfect Man ...	105	110	113
Man's Father, the Sun	105	110	113

	ED. 1 & 2 VOL. II Page	ED. 3 VOL. II Page	ED. 4 & 5 VOL. 3 Page
What Hydrogen Really is	105	111	114
Bath-kol, Daughter of the Divine Voice ...	107	112	115
The Evolution of the Senses	107	113	116
Stanza V. The Evolution of the Second Races	109	115	117
Verse 18. The Sons of Yoga	109	115	117
The Tabula Smaragdina	109	115	117
The " Shells " of Sheba Hachaloth ...	111	117	120
The Secret Work of Chiram	113	119	122
The Fire Diety	114	121	122
Sons of Yoga	115	122	124
Verse 19. The Sexless Second Race	116	122	124
Modes of Reproduction	116	123	124
The Outgrowth of Races	117	124	126
Darwin on Androgynous Forms	118	125	126
The Blastema of Science	119	126	128
Naudin's Primordial Blastema ...	119	127	128
Verse 20. The Sons of the Sons of Twilight	120	127	129
Verse 21. The " Shadow," or the Astral Man, Retires within and Man Develops a Physical Body ...	121	128	129
Leda, Castor and Pollux	121	128	130
The Allegory of Castor and Pollux ...	122	129	131
The Divine Hermaphrodite	124	131	132
The Riddle of the Sphinx	124	131	133
Jah-Hovah Androgynous	125	133	133
Seth our Progenitor. The Esoteric Cain ...	127	135	136
The Jewish God-name	129	137	138
Stanza VI. The Evolution of the " Sweat-born "	131	139	139
Verse 22. The Evolution of the Three Races continued ...	131	139	139
The Swan and the Egg	131	139	139
Bi-sexual Reproduction	133	141	141
The Virgin Third Race	135	143	144
The Bi-sexual Third Race	135	143	144
Egyptian Belief	137	145	145
The Shadow Image of Elohim ...	137	145	145
Verse 23. The Second Race Creates the Third and Perishes ...	138	146	146
A Few Words about " Deluges and Noahs " ...	138	147	146
The Ark of Manu	139	147	147
What the Flood means	139	147	147
The " Deluge " a Universal Tradition ...	141	149	149
Various Deluges	141	149	149
The Arkite Symbols	143	151	151
The Jewish Noah and the Chaldean Nuah ...	145	153	153

	ED. 1 & 2 VOL. II Page	ED. 3 VOL. II Page	ED. 4 & 5 VOL. 3 Page
The " White Island "	147	155	154
Agreement of Dates	147	155	155
Could Men exist 18,000,000 years ago?	148	157	156
How old is Humanity?	149	157	157
Adam-Galatea	150	159	158
Spontaneous Generation	151	159	158
What is Evolution?	152	161	159
Aristotle denied Heliocentricism	153	162	160
An " Organism without Organs "	154	163	162
The Solar System in the Purānas	155	164	162
Science is Silent	155	165	163
The Sleight-of-hand of Science	157	166	164
" Spontaneous Generation "	157	167	165
Oceans of Carbonic Acid?	159	169	167
Stanza VII. *From the Semi-divine down to the First Human Races*	161	170	168
Verse 24. *The Higher Creators Reject in their Pride the Forms evolved by the " Sons of Yoga "*	161	170	168
A Suggestive Stanza	161	171	169
The " Black Fire " of the " Zohar "	162	171	169
Creators and Sub-creators	163	172	170
The " Adversaries " of the Gods	163	173	171
To the Moneron, the Creator	165	175	173
Primal Modes of Reproduction	166	175	173
Monads and Rounds	167	177	174
Monogenism or Polygenism	169	178	176
How the First Mammals were produced	170	179	177
Verse 25. *They will not Incarnate in the Early " Egg-born "*	171	180	178
A Suggestive Explanation	171	180	178
The Gods are Deified Men	172	181	179
Verse 26. *They Select the Androgynes*	172	182	179
Verse 27. *The First Man Endowed with Mind*	172	182	179
The Sons of Kriyāshakti	173	182	179
Chhāyā-birth	174	183	181
A Saint Hypnotized	175	184	181
The Story of Kandu and Pramlocha explained	175	185	182
" Sweat-born " and Androgynes	177	187	183
The Birth-days of the Dhyānis	179	189	186
Stanza VIII. *Evolution of the Animal Mammalians.—The First Fall*	180	190	186
Verse 28. *How the First Mammals were produced*	180	190	187
Men, the Progenitors of Animals	181	191	187

	ED. 1 & 2 VOL. II Page	ED. 3 VOL. II Page	ED. 4 & 5 VOL. 3 Page
Archaic Zoology	183	193	190
Verse 29. A quasi-Darwinian Evolution	183	193	190
Verse 30. The Animals get Solid Bodies	183	194	190
Verse 31. Their Separation into Sexes	184	194	190
Verse 32. The First Sin of the Mindless Men	184	194	190
The Sin of the Mindless Men	185	195	190
What may be the Objections to the Foregoing	185	195	191
The Darwinists mistaken	187	197	193
The Real Primeval man	189	199	195
Naturalists inventing Links	189	200	195
Stanza IX. The Final Evolution of Man	191	201	196
Verse 33. The Creators Repent	191	201	197
Verse 34. They Atone for their Neglect	191	201	197
Verse 35. Men become Endowed with Minds	191	201	197
The Cause of Degeneration	191	201	197
The Boneless Race	193	203	199
The Hairy Men of China	195	205	200
Hybridization	195	205	200
The Separation of Sexes	197	207	202
Verse 36. The Fourth Race develops Perfect Speech	198	208	203
Primeval Language	198	209	204
The Transformation of the Earth	201	211	206
Verse 37. Every Androgynous Unit is separated and becomes Bi-sexual	201	211	206
Edens, Serpents, and Dragons	202	212	207
The Garden of Eden, a College	203	213	208
Flying Camels	205	215	210
Kircher's Dragon	207	217	211
Has Satan any Reality?	209	219	213
Cobras as Symbols	209	220	214
Two Schools of Magic	211	221	216
The Seventh Son of the Seventh Son	213	223	217
Buddha's Great Mountain	215	225	219
Scientific Belief in " Dragons "	217	227	221
" Mythical " Monsters a Reality	217	228	221
The Flying Dragons	219	229	223
The " Sons of God " and the " Sacred Island "	220	230	223
The Continent of the Gods	221	231	225
The Testimony of Jacolliot	222	233	226
The Magicians of Atlantis	223	234	227
The Colossi of Bamian	224	235	228
Cook and Bull Hypotheses	225	236	229

	ED. 1 & 2 VOL. II Page	ED. 3 VOL. II Page	ED. 4 & 5 VOL. 3 Page
Stranza X. The History of the Fourth Race	227	237	230
Verse 38. The Birth of the Fourth, Atlantean Race ...	227	237	230
Verses 39. The Sub-races of the Fourth Humanity begin to divide and interblend; they form the First mixed Races of Various Colours	227	237	230
The Moon-Coloured Race	227	237	230
The Mysteries among the Mayas	229	239	232
Satanic Myths	231	241	234
Holy Satan	233	243	236
The Shadow of God	235	245	238
Caput Angelorum	237	247	240
Mahāsura and Satan	237	247	240
Theological Snuffers	239	249	241
" Principles " explained	241	251	244
Man, the Pale Shadow of God	243	253	245
Satan, a Centripetal Force	245	255	247
The Sacrifice of the Fiery Angels	246	257	249
The Curse of Vasishtha	247	258	250
The " Conscious Entity "	248	259	251
Scientific Anthropology in the Purānas ...	249	259	251
Answers to Objections	251	261	253
Archaic Teachings in the Purānas and Genesis. Physical Evolution	251	262	254
Mr. Gladstone kills Genesis	253	263	254
A Lesson in Natural History	254	265	256
From Worm to Man	255	266	257
The Contradictions of Science	257	267	259
The " absolute rule " of Science not borne out by facts	258	269	260
Identity of Human and Animal Embryos ...	259	270	261
The Inherent Law of Progressive Development ...	260	271	262
Nature is Uniform	261	273	263
A Panoramic View of the Early Races ...	263	275	265
Millions of years hence	263	275	265
Bailly and Faber	265	277	267
The Natural " Fall "	267	279	269
The Symbolism of Cronus	269	281	271
The Races in Greek Mythology	271	283	273
Verse 40. The Superiority of the Atlantean over other Races ...	271	284	273
Verse 41. They fall into sin and beget Children and Monsters ...	271	284	273
Verse 42. The First Germs of Anthropomorphism and Sexual Religion. They lose their " Third Eye " ...	271	284	273
The Golden Age	273	285	275

	ED. 1 & 2 VOL. II Page	ED. 3 VOL. II Page	ED. 4 & 5 VOL. 3 Page
No Devils outside Humanity	275	287	277
Are Giants a Fiction?	277	289	278
The Giants	277	289	278
The Testimony of Antiquity	278	291	280
Christendom is Idolatrous	279	292	281
Fourth Race Giants	280	293	282
The Seven Virgin-youths	281	294	283
The Sacred Four	282	295	283
The Serpent of Eternity	283	296	284
The Children of Brahmā	284	297	286
The Tibetan Lilith ...	285	298	286
Human and Animal Cross-breeding	286	299	287
The Races of Men not all human	286	300	288
The Dumb Man who walks on all Fours	288	301	289
The Races with the " Third Eye "	289	302	290
The " Third Eye " ...	289	302	290
Man, the Storehouse of all the Seeds of Life	289	303	291
Mazdean Symbolism	291	305	292
Angels called Birds ...	293	306	294
" Three-eyed " Mortals	293	307	295
Occult Physiology ...	295	309	296
The Cyclops no Myth	296	310	297
The Seat of the Soul	298	311	299
The Evolution of the Eye	299	313	300
Evolution of Root Races in the Fourth Round	300	314	301
The Third [or] Odd Eye is now a Gland	301	315	302
The Number of Monads is Limited	303	317	304
The Law of Retribution	305	319	306
The Primeval Manus of Humanity	307	321	308
The Seven and Fourteen Manus ...	307	321	308
The " Blinds " of Exotericism	309	323	309
The Four Earlier Races	311	325	312
The Esoteric meaning of " Fish "	313	327	313
The Inner Man in the Zohar	315	329	315
Stanza XI. The Civilization and Destruction of the Third and Fourth Races	316	330	316
Verse 43. The Lemuro-Atlanteans Build Cities and Spread Civilization	316	330	316
Presentments of Truths	317	331	317
Degeneration of Mankind	319	333	319
The Hindu Symbolization	321	335	320
The Magi in the Days of Krishna	323	337	323
Atlantis now Ocean Floor	325	339	325

	ED. 1 & 2 VOL. II Page	ED. 3 VOL. II Page	ED. 4 & 5 VOL. 3 Page
On Foot Across the Oceans	327	341	327
Changes of Climate	329	343	328
Cycles within Cycles	330	345	330
Verse 44. *Their Statues, Witnesses to the Size of the*			
Lemuro-Atlanteans	331	346	331
Prehistoric Statues	331	346	331
The Old Continents	333	347	332
The Secret Annals	335	349	334
How to read Symbols	335	350	335
Standing Witnesses to Submerged Continents ...	336	351	336
The Mystery of Easter Island	337	351	336
The Bamian Statues	337	353	337
The Antediluvian Buddhas ...	339	354	338
The Handiwork of Initiates	339	355	339
Cyclopean Ruins and Colossal Stones as Witnesses to Giants ...	341	356	340
The Materialism of the Bible	341	356	340
Animated Stones	341	357	340
The " Rocking-stones " in Europe ...	343	358	342
Living, Speaking, and Moving Stones ...	345	361	345
Universal Witnesses	347	363	346
It takes a God to become a Man	349	365	348
Verse 45. *Lemuria Destroyed by Fire, Atlantis by Water.*			
The Flood	349	365	349
Verse 46. *The Destruction of the Fourth Race and of the Last*			
Antediluvian Monster-animals	349	365	349
Stanza XII. *The Fifth Race and its Divine Instructors* ...	351	366	350
Verse 47. *The Remnants of the First Two Races Disappear for*			
ever. Groups of the Various Atlantean Races			
saved from the Deluge along with the Forefathers			
of the Fifth	351	366	350
Verse 48. *The Origins of our Present Race, the Fifth. The*			
First Divine Dynasties	351	366	350
Verse 49. *The Earliest Glimmerings in History, now pinned*			
to the Allegorical Chronology of the Bible, and			
" Universal " History slavishly following it.—			
The Nature of the First Instructors and			
Civilizers of Mankind	351	366	350
The " Great Dragons " and Serpents ...	351	367	350
The Astronomical Dragon	353	368	351
The Poles have been Thrice Inverted ...	353	369	352
Serpents and Dragons under Different Symbolisms ...	354	370	353
The Naasenian Gnostics	355	371	354
The Sidereal and Cosmic Glyphs	356	371	355

	ED. 1 & 2 VOL. II Page	ED. 3 VOL. II Page	ED. 4 & 5 VOL. 3 Page
The Two Mystic Poles	357	373	356
God and Nature Anthropomorphized ...	359	375	359
Who were Enoch and the others? ...	361	377	360
The Poles, the "Heavenly Measure" ...	363	379	362
The Dragon, Human yet Divine	365	381	364
Our Divine Instructors	365	381	364
The Various Noahs	365	382	364
Hermes in Astronomy and elsewhere ...	366	383	366
What the Priests told Herodotus ...	369	385	368
What are Spirits?	370	387	369
A Universal Corroboration	371	387	370
Plato's Idea of Evil	373	389	371
Wheat brought down by the Gods ...	373	391	372
"Sons of God" Perfect and Imperfect ...	375	391	373
The Mystery of Azazel	376	393	375
The Fallacies of the Two Churches ...	377	394	376
Drunken Indra	378	395	377
The Origin of the Satanic Myth	378	395	377
The Secret of the Dragon	379	396	378
The Theft of Rāhu	381	398	380
Agni, the Fire-god	381	399	380
The Gods, the Facets of one Gem ...	383	400	381
Merodach-Michael	384	401	383
The Builders of the Material World ...	385	402	384
The Sun-gods, Creative Powers	386	403	385
Who first created Woman?	387	405	386
Jehovah Ophiomorphos	389	407	388
Noah was a Kabir, hence he must have been a Demon ...	390	408	389
The Flood Legends	391	409	390
The Oldest Persian Traditions about the Polar and the Sub-merged Continents	393	411	392
The Legends of Iran	393	411	392
Esoteric Chronology	395	413	393
The Persian Phoenix	397	415	396
The Arctic Continent	399	417	397
The Unreachable Land	401	419	400
Western Speculations, founded on the Greek and Purānic Traditions	402	420	401
Orientalists in the Wrong Box ...	403	421	401
Future Continents Symbolized ...	405	423	403
The Puzzles of Antiquity	407	425	405
What Marcellus says	409	427	407
The "Curse" from a Philosophical point of view ...	409	428	408
The Ancient and the Modern Man ...	411	429	409

	ED. 1 & 2 VOL. II Page	ED. 3 VOL. II Page	ED. 4 & 5 VOL. 3 Page
The Travesty of Prometheus	413	431	412
Christ connected with Epaphos	415	433	413
The Mistake of Arrian explained	417	435	415
Was Aeschylus Initiated?	419	437	417
The Gift of Prometheus	420	438	418
One of the Functions of Zeus	421	440	419
Additional Fragments from a Commentary on the Verses of Stanzas XII	423	441	421
The " Buddhas of Confession " [1]	423	441	421
The Oldest Records about Atlantis	425	443	424
The Doom of Atlantis	427	445	425
The " Eastern Aethiopians "	429	447	427
Shadowy Mementoes of the Past	429	448	427
The Egyptian Zodiacs	431	449	429
Mistakes of the Egyptologists	431	450	429
Theories of a self-made Adept	433	451	431
The Races, Sub-races, and Family-races	434	453	432
Illustration of the Races	435	454	433
The Egyptian Labyrinth	436	455	433
Conclusion	437	455	434
More in the forhcoming volumes	437	456	434
History " written in the Stars "	438	457	436
Modern Science mistrusted	439	458	437
A Wholesale Denial	440	459	437
Historical Liars	442	461	440
Paradoxes of Science	443	462	440
The Coming New Race	445	463	442
The Future Mankind	446	465	444
Additional Notes	—	—	445
Bibliography	—	—	448
			VOL. 4
BOOK II. PART II. THE ARCHAIC SYMBOLISM OF THE WORLD-RELIGIONS	447	467	13
Table of Contents	448	11	5
Esoteric Tenets Corroborated in Every Scripture	449	469	15
The Vedas written by Initiates	451	471	17
XVI.[2] Adam-Adami	452	473	19
" Nabathean Agriculture "	453	475	20

[1] Possibly this should read " The Buddhas of Compassion."

[2] This section-numbering is continued from Book I, Part, II, in the 1st and 2nd editions. In subsequent editions these sections have been numbered anew from II-XI, number I having been assigned to the introductory section, " Esoteric Tenets Corroborated in Every Scripture."

			ED. 1 & 2 VOL. II Page	ED. 3 VOL. II Page	ED. 4 & 5 VOL. 4 Page
Many Views of Many Minds	...	...	455	476	22
Nebo, the God of Wisdom	...	...	456	477	23
The Kabalistic Four Adams	...	...	457	479	24
XVII. *The " Holy of Holies ". Its Degradation*	...	...	459	481	27
The " God " Sub Rosa	...	...	459	481	27
What was the Circle-dance	...	...	461	483	28
Christian Symbolism	...	...	463	485	31
The God IAO	...	...	465	487	33
The " Four-faced " Brahmā	...	...	465	488	33
The Etymology of " Sacrament "	...	...	467	489	35
I Am that I Am	...	...	468	491	36
The Old and the New Jehovah	...	...	469	492	37
Who the Jews Really are	...	...	470	493	38
The Craft of the Rabbins	...	...	471	494	39
Jehovah a Substitute	...	...	472	495	40
The Elohistic and Jehovistic Texts	...	...	473	496	41
Who was Abraxas?	...	...	474	497	42
XVII. *On the Myth of the " Fallen Angels " in its Various*					
Aspects	...	...	475	498	43
A. *The Evil Spirit: Who and What?*	...	...	475	498	43
Nature, a Stone-cold Mother	...	...	475	498	43
The " Monkey of God "	...	...	476	499	44
The Genesis of the Devil	...	...	477	501	45
God and Devil, both Metatrons	...	...	479	503	47
The Angel of the Face	...	...	479	503	48
Fraudulent Translation of the Bible	...	...	481	505	49
The Vedas, once Universal	...	...	483	507	51
B. *The Gods of Light proceed from the Gods of Darkness*	...		483	507	52
The Sons of Eternity	...	...	485	509	53
The Shadows of the Shadows	...	...	487	511	55
Who the Ādityas are	...	...	489	513	57
The One Passive Deity	...	...	489	514	58
The " Zohar " on the " Fallen Ones "	...	...	491	515	59
C. *The Many Meanings of the " War in Heaven "*	...		492	516	60
Reminders of the Fate of the Atlanteans	...	...	492	517	61
The Real Meaning of the Cherub	...	...	493	518	61
Various Names for Initiates	...	...	495	519	63
The Symbol of the " Tree "	...	...	496	521	64
Traces of Pre-historic Strifes	...	...	497	522	65
The Tāraka war	...	...	497	523	66
Allegories on the " War in Heaven "	...	...	499	525	67
The War of the Titans	...	...	500	525	68
Sarpas—Serpents—Nāgas	...	...	501	527	69

			ED. 1 & 2 VOL. II Page	ED. 3 VOL. II Page	ED. 4 & 5 VOL. 4 Page
The Myth of Bel and Merodach	...	...	503	528	71
The Origin of Exoteric Religions	...	...	503	529	71
The Sacredness of the Serpent	...	...	505	531	73
XIX. *Is Pleroma Satan's Lair?*	...	...	506	532	75
The Living Devils	...	...	507	533	76
Jehovah, a Personating Spirit	...	...	509	535	78
Ākāsha, the " Mysterium Magnum "	...	...	511	537	80
The Soul, and Heart of the Great Mother	...	...	512	539	81
Mind, the Quickening Spirit ...	...	...	513	540	82
The Logos and Satan are One	...	...	515	541	84
The Seventh Mystery of Creation	...	...	516	543	85
Baresma, the Divine Twig	...	...	517	544	86
The Number 888	...	...	518	545	87
XX. *Prometheus, the Titan. His Origin in Ancient India*		...	519	546	88
The " Father of Mortals "	...	...	519	547	88
The Ash Yggdrasil	...	...	520	547	89
The Poetry of Modern Orientalists	...	...	521	549	90
The Boon given by Prometheus	...	...	523	551	92
Greek Ideas Misunderstood	...	...	525	553	93
The Six Brothers of Krishna	...	...	527	555	96
XXI. *Enoïchion-Henoch*	...	...	529	557	98
Who Invented Writing?	...	...	529	557	98
The Adept Dies but to Live	...	...	531	559	100
What Enoch is, Esoterically	...	...	533	561	102
The Secret Power of the Satans	...	...	534	563	104
St. Augustine and Enoch	...	...	535	564	105
XXII. *The Symbolism of the Mystery-Names Iao and Jehovah, with their Relation to the Cross and Circle*	...	...	536	565	106
The Jews alone the Heirloom of Jehovah	...	...	537	569	107
A Grotesque Verse Explained	...	...	539	569	109
The Antiquity of the Cross	...	...	541	571	111
A Personal is a Finite God	...	...	543	573	114
A Plagiarism by Pascal	...	...	545	575	115
A. *Cross and Circle*	...	...	545	575	115
Variations of the Cross-symbolism	...	...	547	577	116
The Heavenly " Porpoise "	...	...	549	579	119
" Guha," the Mysterious	...	...	549	580	119
The Rishis and the Pleiades	...	...	551	581	120
" Deus Enim et Circulus est	...	...	552	583	122
The Degradation of the Symbol	...	...	553	583	123
B. *The Fall of the Cross into Matter*	...	...	553	584	123
The Supreme Good of Plato ?	...	...	554	585	124

		ED. 1 & 2 VOL. II Page	ED. 3 VOL. II Page	ED. 4 & 5 VOL. 4 Page
The Law of Retribution	...	555	585	125
The Riddle of the Cross	...	556	587	126
The Primitive Cross	...	557	587	126
Its Early Significance. The Sleep of Siloam	...	558	589	128
The Meaning of the Crucifixion ...	...	561	591	131
The Real Paternoster	...	562	593	132
XXIII. *The Upanishads in Gnostic Literature* ...	...	563	594	133
The Seven Thunders	...	563	595	133
When Time be no Longer	...	565	597	136
Pistis Sophia	...	566	597	136
Truth between two Contrasts ...	...	567	599	137
The Divine Self's Wisdom	...	569	601	139
The Antiquity of the Kapilas ...	...	571	603	141
XXIV. *The Cross and the Pythagorean Decad* ...	...	573	605	144
The Gnostics and Pythagoras ...	...	573	605	144
The Three Sciences	...	575	607	146
The Mystic Meaning of Makara ...	...	576	609	148
Poseidon's Five Ministers	...	577	611	149
The Puzzles of Symbolism	...	579	613	150
The Master Mason's Grip	...	581	614	152
The " Golden Candlestick "	...	581	615	153
The Mystery of the Number Six ...	...	583	616	154
The Root of Wisdom	...	584	617	155
Seeming Contradictions	...	585	618	156
The Hosts of the Blessed Ones ...	...	586	619	157
The Cross, a Christian After-thought ...	...	587	620	158
The "Worm that never dies" ...	...	588	621	160
Man, the Reviler of God	...	589	623	161
XXV. *The Mysteries of the Hebdomad* ...	...	590	624	162
A. *Saptaparna*	...	590	625	162
The " Hieroglyphical Senary " ...	...	591	625	163
The Meaning of the Double Triangle ...	...	591	625	163
Spiritual and Physical Correspondences ...	...	593	627	165
Noah, an Aspect of the Creator ...	...	595	629	167
The Theogonic Key	...	595	629	167
Noah in a New Dress	...	596	630	168
B. *The Tetraktis in Relation to the Heptagon* ...	...	598	632	169
The Roots of Things	...	599	633	169
The Music of the Spheres	...	601	635	172
The " Voice of Nature "	...	601	635	172
The Septenary Demonstrated ...	...	603	637	174
Proofs from a Gnostic Gospel ...	...	604	639	175

	ED. 1 & 2 VOL. II Page	ED. 3 VOL. II Page	ED. 4 & 5 VOL. 4 Page
C. *The Septenary Element in the Vedas. It Corroborates the Occult Teaching Concerning the Seven Globes and the Seven Races* ...	605	640	176
The Vedic Teachings ...	605	641	176
The Seven Earths and the Seven Races ...	607	642	178
The Zoroastrian Septenary ...	609	643	180
The " Breaths " of the " One Breath " ...	610	645	181
D. *The Septenary in the Exoteric Works* ...	611	646	182
The Septenate in the Purānas ...	611	647	182
Who are the Maruts? ...	613	648	184
The Doom of Continual Rebirth ...	615	651	187
Persian Symbology ...	617	653	188
E. *Seven in Astronomy, Science, and Magic* ...	618	654	190
The Cycle of the Naros ...	619	655	190
Various Cyclic Calculations ...	621	657	193
The Septenate in Physiology ...	623	659	194
The Hairy Symbol ...	625	661	196
The Number Seven in Chemistry ...	627	663	198
The Seven Priests of the Zunis ...	629	665	199
F. *The Seven Souls of the Egyptologists* ...	630	666	201
The Septenary in Egypt ...	631	667	202
The Sidereal Seven ...	631	667	202
The " Principles " in the Egyptian Metaphysics ...	633	669	203
The " Watermen " of the " Bundahish " ...	634	671	206
Man, the Parent of all the Mammals ...	635	672	206
The Trans- and Cis-Himālayan Esoteric Doctrine ...	636	673	207
An Allegory in the Anugītā ...	637	674	209
The Allegory Explained ...	639	675	210
Endless is the Search for Truth ...	640	677	211
Hypnotism is—Satanism ...	641	678	212
BOOK II. PART III. ADDENDA, SCIENCE AND THE SECRET DOCTRINE CONTRASTED ...	643	679	213
Table of Contents ...	644	XV	9
Section I. Archaic, or Modern Anthropology ...	645	681	215
The New Masters of Protestantism ...	645	681	215
The Fallacies of Modern Scientists ...	647	683	217
" Physiological " versus " Natural " Selection ...	647	683	217
The Occult and the Modern Doctrines ...	649	685	219
" The Testimonium Paupertatis of Natural Science " ...	651	687	221
An Exchange of Mutual Compliments ...	651	687	221
" Almighty Evolution " ...	652	689	222

	ED. 1 & 2 VOL. II Page	ED. 3 VOL. II Page	ED. 4 & 5 VOL. 4 Page
Science is Silent on every Problem	653	690	223
Physical and Spiritual Evolution Reconciled	654	691	224
The One Unpardonable Sin	655	692	225
Section II. The Ancestors Mankind is offered by Science	656	693	226
An Unverified Charge against the Ancients	657	694	227
Various Modes of Reproduction	659	697	228
Where are the " Missing Links?"	661	698	230
Ready-made Materials of Speech	662	699	232
Proofs of our " Noble Descent "	663	700	233
Scientific Trespassers	664	701	233
Mr. Huxley applies an " Extinguisher "	665	703	235
A Walker or a Climber	667	704	236
An Absolutely Theoretical Pithecoid Man	669	707	239
A Pithecoid Man Wanted	669	707	239
The Sozura a Creature Entirely Unknown to Science	669	707	239
Plastidular Souls, and Conscious Nerve-cells	670	708	240
Haeckel Creates Souls	671	708	240
A Cautious move towards " Magic "	671	709	241
The meaning of Soul with Haeckel	672	710	242
The Atoms of our " Father-Bathybius "	674	712	243
Section III. The Fossil Relics of Man and the Anthropoid Ape	675	713	245
A. Geological Facts bearing on the Question of their Relationship	675	713	245
Dryopithecus, the missing link	675	713	245
Insurmountable Difficulties for the Darwinians	677	715	247
Materialism is Puzzled	679	717	249
" Blurred Copies " of their Bestial Sires	679	717	249
B. Western Evolutionism. The Comparative Anatomy of Man and the Anthropoid in no Way a Confirmation of Darwinism	680	719	250
Hanumān, the Monkey-God	680	719	250
Huxley calls the Darwinists to Order	681	719	251
The Gorilla's Addresses to the Evolutionist	682	721	252
The Darwinists and their Opponents. The Argument of Rudimentary Organs	683	723	253
Epitomized History in the Fœtus	684	723	254
Reversion from the Wrong End	685	723	255
C. Darwinism and the Antiquity of Man: The Anthropoids and their Ancestry	685	724	255
The Evidence of Skulls	687	725	256
Huxley's Bold Speculations	687	725	256
Grant Allen's Illusions	687	726	257
The Pedigree of the Apes	688	727	258
The Incubus of Ethnology	689	727	259

	ED. 1 & 2 VOL. II Page	ED. 3 VOL. II Page	ED. 4 & 5 VOL. 4 Page
Section IV. Duration of the Geological Periods, Cycles, and the Antiquity of Man	690	729	260
Professor Sayce Sketches out Chronology	691	730	261
Babylonian Dates	692	731	262
No Agreement between Scientists	693	733	263
Contradictory Hypothesis	694	733	264
A. Modern Scientific Speculations about the Ages of the Globe, Animal Evolution, and Man	694	733	264
Materialists at Loggerheads	695	735	264
Mivart's Billions of Years	697	736	266
Planetary Life-impulses	697	737	267
The Adept-astronomer	699	738	268
B. On Chains of Planets and their Plurality	699	739	269
Of other Worlds besides our Own	699	739	269
States of Consciousness	701	741	271
Worlds mentioned in the Bible	703	743	272
Who are the Kings of Edom?	705	745	274
What Flammarion tells us	707	747	277
Science and Occultism may yet agree	709	749	278
C. Supplementary Remarks on Esoteric Geological Chronology	709	749	278
Seceders from Darwinism	711	751	280
Parallelism of Life	711	752	281
The two Sciences Contrasted	711	752	281
The Sufficiency of the " Animalists "	715	755	284
One Salvation for Science	717	757	285
Between two Voids	719	759	287
The Palaeolithic Landseer	721	761	289
The Risings and Falls of Civilization	723	763	291
Entrapped by the Reindeer	723	763	291
Strange Confession of Science	725	765	293
A once Tropical Pole	726	766	295
No " Missing Link " anywhere	727	767	296
Astral Man—the Solution	728	768	296
Palaeolithic man, a Calligraphist	729	769	297
The Kabalists and Science	730	770	298
Herbert Spencer on special Creations	730	771	299
Section V. Organic Evolution and Creative Centres	731	772	300
Still Greater Difficulties	731	772	300
Dhyān Chohans and these Centres	732	773	301
The " Ground-plan " and " Designers "	732	773	301
The " to be or not to be " of Science	733	774	302
The " Meganthropus "	734	775	303

	ED. 1 & 2 VOL. II Page	ED. 3 VOL. II Page	ED. 4 & 5 VOL. 4 Page
A. *The Origin and Evolution of the Mammalia. Science and the*			
Esoteric Phylogeny	734	775	303
Conjectures are not Facts	735	776	304
Schmidt's Diagram	735	777	305
The Unity of Type	737	778	306
Factors in the Origin of Species	737	779	307
B. *The European Palaeolithic Races—Whence, and How Distri-*			
buted	738	779	307
Africa in Europe	739	781	308
A Tardy Admission	741	783	310
Section VI. *Giants, Civilizations, and Submerged Continents*			
Traced in History	742	784	311
A Mysterious Nation	743	785	312
The Associates of the Apes and the Angels ...	745	787	314
Remarkable " Coincidences."	745	788	315
The Occult Interpretation of the " Bible " ...	747	789	316
The Seven Sabbaths	747	790	317
Revelation and the Secret Doctrine ...	748	790	317
The Symbols of Soul-killing Churchianity ...	748	790	317
The Ape later than Man	749	791	318
The Age of Egypt	750	793	319
Darwinians Reject the Truth	751	793	320
The Tombs of the Giants, Druidic Stones ...	752	795	321
Still more Astounding Contradictions ...	753	795	322
Races of Giants	754	797	323
Who were the Druids?	756	799	325
Paganism and Christianity agree	757	800	326
The Mazdean View of the Seven Earths ...	758	801	328
The Druidical Belief in Rebirth	760	803	329
A. *Some Statements about the Sacred Islands and Continents in*			
the Classics, Explained Esoterically	760	804	330
Who or What will be denied next?	761	804	330
The men, " whose Sleep was never disturbed by			
Dreams "	761	805	331
The Heirloom of Atlantis	763	807	333
The God-bearing Land	765	809	335
" The Greater Gods of Olympos "	766	809	335
The Power of Names	767	811	336
The Sons of Coelus and Terra	769	813	338
Southern and Northern Atlantis	770	813	339
The Children of Niobe	771	815	340
The Cycles of Time	773	816	341
The " Island of the Divine Kings "	773	817	342

			ED. 1 & 2 VOL. II Page	ED. 3 VOL. II Page	ED. 4 & 5 VOL. 4 Page
Who were the Nephilim?	...	...	775	819	344
The Titans in Prison	...	...	776	820	345
Mythology built on History	...	...	777	821	346
Section VII. Scientific and Geological Proofs of the Existence of Several Submerged Continents	...	...	778	822	347
Geology corroborates Occultism	...	...	779	823	347
Evidence of the Flora	...	...	781	823	350
Tradition as True as History	...	...	781	825	350
Atlantis, necessary to Ethnology	...	...	783	827	351
Astræa falls on her head	...	...	785	829	353
Ingenious Explanations	...	...	787	831	356
Communications between South Sea Islands	...	788	832	356
Haeckel for once is right	...	...	789	833	357
Evidence of Language	...	...	790	834	358
Final and irrefutable Evidence	...	...	791	835	359
Recent Suggestive Discoveries	...	...	793	837	361
Enough has now been said	...	...	793	837	361
Hear both Sides	...	...	794	839	362
Old Masonic Symbolism explained by Ragon	...	795	840	363
The Prologue to Esoteric Truth	...	...	797	841	365
The End a Fitting Prelude to Truth	...	...	798	842	366
Additional Notes	...	...	...	—	367
Bibliography	...	...	...	—	367

					ED. 3 VOL. III Page	ED. 4 & 5 VOL. 5 Page
Fly-leaf	...	...	..	...	... I	1
Title Page	...	...	...	...	... III	3
Table of Contents	...	...	...	...	VII	9
Preface	...	...	...	...	... XIX	7
Introductory	...	...	...	...	... 1	25
One Key to all Sacred Books		...	...	...	3	26
Assumptions have to be proven		...	...	...	5	29
The Spirit of Plato's Teaching		...	...	...	7	30
Self-contradiction of the Critic		...	...	...	9	32
The Character of Ammonius Saccas		...	...	...	11	34
Plato a Follower of Pythagoras		...	...	...	13	36

[*BOOK III.   THE ADEPTS OF HISTORY AND THE DOWNFALL OF THE MYSTERIES*] [1]

Section I. Preliminary Survey	...	...	...	....	14	37
The Protectors of China	...	...	...	...	15	38
The A. B. C. of Magic	...	...	...	...	17	40
Magic as old as Man	...	...	...	...	19	42
The Tree of Knowledge	...	...	...	...	21	43
Occultism must Win the Day	...	...	...	...	23	45
Black Magic at Work	...	...	...	...	25	47
Black Magic and Hypnotism	...	...	...	...	27	48
The Philosophy stands on its own Merits		...	...	...	29	50
Section II. Modern Criticism and the Ancients	...	...	...	...	30	51
All Honour to genuine Scientists	...	...	...	...	31	52
What is a Myth	...	...	...	...	33	53
Chladean Oracles	...	...	...	...	35	55
Section III. The Origin of Magic	...	...	...	...	36	57
The Books of Hermes	...	...	...	...	37	58
What is the Origin of Magic?	...	...	...	...	39	59
Pherecydes of Syros	...	...	...	...	41	61
Cain, Mathematical and Anthropomorphic		...	...	...	43	63
Section IV. The Secrecy of Initiates	...	...	...	...	44	64
Exoteric and Esoteric Teachings	...	...	...	...	45	65
Origen on " Genesis "	...	...	...	...	47	66
The " Dark Sayings " of the " Testaments "		...	...	...	49	69
The Greatest Crime ever Perpetrated	...	...	...	...	51	70
Asiatic Religions Proclaim their Esoterism openly		...	...	...	53	72
The Wisdom-Religion	...	...	...	...	55	74

[1] H.P.B. had planned to write a IIIrd and IVth Book to her great work, but these were never finished. Annie Besant published posthumously a substitute for them in one volume, compiled from H.P.B.'s scattered and unpublished MSS. For the tentative titles of these two Books given here see *S. D.* [1] I xl; II 437.

	ED. 3 VOL. III Page	ED. 4 & 5 VOL. 5 Page
Section V. Some Reasons for Secrecy	56	75
The Key of Practical Theurgy	57	76
The Ladder of Being	59	78
Three Ways open to the Adept	61	80
Man is God	63	81
Jesus taught Reincarnation	65	83
Section VI. The Dangers of Practical Magic	67	85
Names are Symbols	69	86
The Three Mothers	71	88
The Bible and Word-juggling	73	90
Moses and the Jews	75	92
Section VII. Old Wine in New Bottles	76	93
Copies that Ante-dated Originals	77	94
Which were the Thieves?	79	94
Character of the Bible	81	97
Section VIII. The Book of Enoch, the Origin and the Foundation of		
Christianity	82	99
The Book of Enoch and Christianity	83	100
Enoch Records the Races	85	101
The Book of Enoch Symbolical	87	104
Occultists do not reject the Bible	89	105
Section IX. Hermetic and Kabalistic Doctrines	91	107
The Kabalah and the Book of Enoch	93	109
Numbers and Measures	95	111
The Doctrine belongs to all	97	112
Section X. Various Occult Systems of Interpretations of Alphabets and		
Numerals	98	113
Numbers and Magic	99	114
Gods and Numbers	101	116
The Universal Language	103	118
Section XI. The Hexagon with the Central Point, or the Seventh Key ...	105	120
Occult Weapons	107	121
Section XII. The Duty of the True Occultist toward Religions	109	124
Christian and Non-Christian Adepts	111	125
Section XIII. Post-Christian Adepts and their Doctrines	112	126
Unfair Criticism	113	127
The Two Eternal Principles	115	129
Section XIV. Simon and his Biographer Hippolytus	117	131
Uneven Balances	119	132
Stones as " Evidences "	121	134

	ED. 3 VOL. III Page	ED. 4 & 5 VOL. 5 Page
Section XV. St. Paul the real Founder of present Christianity	122	136
Abrogation of Law by Initiates	123	137
Paul changed to Simon	125	138
Section XVI. Peter a Jewish Kabalist, not an Initiate	126	138
The Seat of Peter	127	140
Section XVII. Apollonius of Tyana	129	142
The Mysterious Teacher	131	144
Apollonius cannot be Destroyed	133	145
De Mirville on Apollonius	135	147
Apollonius no Fiction	137	149
Section XVIII. Facts underlying Adept Biographies	138	150
Jesus and Apollonius	139	151
Biographies of Initiates	141	152
Similarity of Legends	143	155
Nature of Christ	145	157
A Serious Mistranslation	147	158
Secret Doctrine of Jesus	149	160
The Cross and Crucifix	151	161
The Story of Jesus	153	163
The Primitive Woman	155	165
Kabalistic reading of Gospels	157	167
Universal Teachings	159	168
Section XIX. St. Cyprian of Antioch	160	170
Magic in Antioch	161	170
Sorcerer becomes Saint	163	173
Section XX. The Eastern Gupta Vidya and the Kabalah	164	174
A Mystery within a Mystery	165	174
Authorship of the Zohar	167	177
Chaldaic and Hebrew	169	178
The First Men	171	180
Many Events not Historical	173	182
The Real Hebrew Characters lost	175	184
Hebrew Esotericism not Primitve	177	186
The Concealed of all the Concealed	179	188
Three-in-one and Four	181	189
The Septenary Sephira	183	191
The Blind Leading the Blind	185	193
Section XXI. Hebrew Allegories	186	194
The Hebrew Bible does not exist	187	195
Some Hebrews were Initiates	189	197
The Seven Creative Gods	191	199
Seven Keys to all Allegories	193	200

					ED. 3 VOL. III Page	ED. 4 & 5 VOL. 5 Page
Gerald Massey on the Seven Creators	...		...	...	195	201
The Father and Mother	...	...	...	...	197	204
Section XXII. The " Zohar " on Creation and the Elohim		...		...	199	205
Angels as Builders	...	...	...	...	201	207
Who are the Elohim?	...	...	...	...	203	208
Monad, Duad, and Triad...	...	...	...	...	205	210
The Creative Gods	...	...	...	...	207	212
God the Host	...	...	...	...	209	214
Section XXIII. What the Occultists and Kabalists have to say	...			...	211	216
The Mystery of the Sun	...		...	...	213	217
Section XXIV. Modern Kabalists in Science and Occult Astronomy			...		215	221
The place of Neptune	...	...	...	...	217	222
Self-generation Ex-nihilo?	...	...	...	...	219	223
Are there Angels in Stars?	...	...	...	...	221	225
Section XXV. Eastern and Western Occultism	...	...		...	222	226
Primordial Matter	...	...	...	...	223	227
The Great Deep	...	...	...	...	225	228
The Chaos of Genesis	...	...	...	...	227	230
The Bible of Humanity	...	...	...	...	229	232
Chaos is Theos or Kosmos	...	...	...	...	231	234
One Hundred and Eight	...	...	...	...	233	236
Section XXVI. The Idols and the Teraphim	...	...			234	237
Divining by Teraphim	...	...	...	...	235	238
Jehovah and Teraphim	...	...	...	...	237	240
Idol of the Moon	...	...	...	...	239	242
Section XXVII. Egyptian Magic	...	...		...	241	243
Evidence of Papyri	...	...	...	...	243	244
Symbols and their Reading	...	...	...	...	245	246
Rebirth and Transmigration	...	...	...	...	247	248
The Egyptian Khous	...	...	...	...	249	250
Obsession in Egypt	...	...	...	...	251	251
Two Rituals of Magic	...	...	...	...	253	254
Magical Statues	...	...	...	...	255	255
Romances—but True	...	...	...	...	257	257
Section XXVIII. The Origin of the Mysteries	...	...			258	258
An Instant in Heaven	...	...	...	...	259	259
Growth of Popular Beliefs	...	...	...	...	261	260
A true Priesthood	...	...	...	...	263	262
The Egyptian Priests	...	...	...	...	265	263
Revealing and Reveiling	...	...	...	...	267	266
Atlanteans Degenerating	...	...	...	...	269	268

	ED. 3 VOL. III Page	ED. 4 & 5 VOL. 5 Page
Section XXIX. *The Trial of the Sun Initiate*	270	269
Vishvakarma and Vikartana	271	270
The Transmission of Light	273	272
Masonry and the Jesuits	275	273
Section XXX. *The Mystery " Son of Initiation "*	277	275
The Sun as God	279	276
Section XXXI. *The Objects of the Mysteries*	281	279
Mysteries and Theophany	283	281
The Mysteries of Masonry	285	282
Section XXXII. *Traces of the Mysteries*	287	284
Christos and Chrestos	289	285
The Symbolism of Nārada	291	287
Egyptian Initiation	293	290
The Self-sacrificing Victim	295	291
Orpheus	297	293
Section XXXIII. *The Last of the Mysteries in Europe*	298	294
Alesia and Bibractis	299	295
The Learning of Egypt	301	297
Section XXXIV. *The Post-Christian Successors to the Mysteries* ...	303	298
The Root Races	305	300
The " False Gnosis "	307	301
Teachings of Ammonius	309	302
Difficulties and Dangers	311	305
The Neo-Platonic School	313	306
Section XXXV. *Symbolism of Sun and Stars*	315	309
The Circle Dance	317	310
Christian Astrolatry	319	313
Michael the Conqueror	321	314
The Christian Sun-God	323	316
Section XXXVI. *Pagan Sidereal Worship, or Astrology*	325	318
The Planetary Angels	327	320
Celestial Wheels	329	321
The Promethean Mystery	331	323
Section XXXVII. *The Souls of the Stars—Universal Heliolatry* ...	332	324
Christian Star-worship	333	325
A Singular Confession	335	326
Section XXXVIII. *Astrology and Astrolatry*	337	329
The Defence of Astrology	339	330
Its Later Deterioration	341	333
Its Prominent Disciples	343	334

	ED. 3 VOL. III Page	ED. 4 & 5 VOL, 5 Page
Section XXXIX. Cycles and Avatāras	345	336
An Unfulfilled Prophecy	347	338
Secret Cycles	349	339
Section XL. Secret Cycles	350	340
The Naros	351	341
Age of the Vedas	353	342
Testimony of the Song Celestial	355	345
Mackey's Arguments	357	345
Title Page. The Mystery of Buddha	359	—
Section XLI. The Doctrine of Avatāras	361	349
All Avatāras Identical	363	351
Voluntary Incarnations	365	353
Cardinal de Cusa	367	355
The Seven Rays	369	356
Special Cases	371	358
The Higher Astral	373	359
Section XLII. The Seven Principles	374	361
The Purified Self	375	361
Section XLIII. The Mystery of Buddha	376	363
Shankarāchārya	377	364
The Buddha cannot Reincarnate	379	366
A Fuller Explanation	381	368
Sacrifice	383	370
Shankarāchārya still living	385	371
Section XLIV. " Reincarnations " of Buddha	386	373
Vajradhara	387	374
Living Buddhas	389	376
An Obscure Passage	391	378
Section XLV. An Unpublished Discourse of Buddha	393	379
A Mistaken View	395	380
Section XLVI. Nirvāna-Moksha	396	381
The Ākāsha	397	381
Matter is Ever Living	399	384
Blind Faith not Expected	401	386
What Annihilation means	403	387
Section XLVII. The Secret Books of " Lam Rin " and Dzyan	405	389
Section XLVIII. Amita Buddha, Kwan-Shai-Yin, and Kwan-yin.—What the " Book of Dzyan " and the Lamaseries of Tsong-Kha-pa say	407	391
Section XLIX. Tsong-Kha-pa—Lohans in China	409	393
The Lost Word	411	395
Tibetan Prophecies	413	396

	ED. 3 VOL. III Page	ED. 4 & 5 VOL. 5 Page
Section L. A few more Misconceptions Corrected	414	397
Misrepresentations of Buddhism	415	398
A Mysterious Land	417	400
Absurd Conclusions	419	402
Materialistic Orientalists	421	404
Introduction of Buddhism into Tibet	423	405
Section LI. The " Doctrine of the Eye " and the " Doctrine of the Heart," or the " Heart's Seal "	424	406
Swedenborg's Claims	425	406
The God " Who "	427	408
More Misrepresentations	429	410
Aryāsanga	431	412
[BOOK IV. OCCULT TEACHINGS] [1]		
Title Page. Some Papers on the Bearing of Occult Philosophy on Life ...	433	415
Note by Annie Besant	434	416
Paper I. A Warning	435	417
Om	436	418
The Jewel in the Lotus	437	419
The Pythagorean Tetrad	439	420
Seven Correspondential Contents	441	422
Correspondences between Races and Man ...	443	425
Diagram I.	444	426
Man and the Logos	445	426
Cosmic, Spiritual and Physical Centres	447	428
Woman and Alchemy	449	430
Sound and Colour	451	431
The Planets, the Days of the Week and their Corresponding Colours and Metals ...	452	432
Diagram II.	452	432
The Days of the Week	453	432
Paper II. An Explanation	455	435
Astrology and Lunar Weeks	457	437
Seeing Sounds and Hearing Colours	459	439
Planetary and Human Bodies	461	441
Planets and Faculties	463	442
What Magic is in Reality	465	444
Simon Magus the Magician	465	444
Series of Aeons	467	446
The Triple Aeon	469	448
Magic and Miracles	471	450

[1] See footnote p. xlii.

	ED. 3 VOL. III Page	ED. 4 & 5 VOL. 5 Page
Magic a Divine Science	473	451
The Seven Hierarchies	475	453
Colours, Sounds and Forms	477	455
Origines	477	455
Colours and Principles	479	456
The Primordial Seven	481	459
The Roots of Colour and Sound	481	459
Diagram III.	482	460
The Hierarchies and Man	483	460
The Unity of Deity	483	462
Wisdom and Truth	485	463
Paper III. A Word Concerning the Earlier Papers	486	464
Concerning Secrecy	487	465
Occult Secrecy	487	465
The Light and Dark Sides of Nature	489	466
Is the Practice of Concentration Beneficent?	490	468
Nature's Finer Forces	491	469
About "Principles" and "Aspects"	493	471
The "Seven Principles"	493	471
The Auric Egg	495	472
The Tāttvic Correlations and Meaning	497	474
Five or Seven Tattvas	497	474
The Tattvas	499	475
Diagram IV. Esoteric and Tāntra Tables of the Tattvas	501	478
Hatha and Rāja Yoga	503	479
The Awakening of the Seventh Sense	505	482
The Master Chakras	507	483
The Human Harp	509	485
On Exoteric "Blinds" and "the Death of the Soul"	510	486
The Duality of Manas	512	488
The Living and the Dead	513	488
Gaining Immortality	515	490
The Philosophical Rationale of the Tenet	517	492
Light and Life	517	492
The Two Egos	519	495
Death of the Soul	521	496
Reincarnation of Lower Soul	523	498
The Dweller on the Threshold	525	500
The Word	527	502
The Divine Witness	529	503

VI–4

	ED. 3 VOL. III Page	ED. 4 & 5 VOL. 5 Page
Appendix. Notes on Papers I, II, and III	530	505
A Mantra Operative	531	505
Colour and Spiritual Sound	533	508
Musical Table	535	509
[*Papers IV, V, VI*]. *Notes on Some Oral Teachings* ...	537	510
The Three Vital Airs. The Auric Egg	537	510
The Dweller on the Threshold. Intellect	539	512
Karma. The Turīya State. Mahat	540	513
How to advance. Fear and Hatred. The Triangle	541	514
Psychic Vision	542	515
Triangle and Quaternary	543	516
Nidānas. Manas. The Spinal Cord	544	517
Prāna—Antahkarana	545	518
Miscellaneous	546	519
Sacred Centres of the Body. Nādis	547	520
Sevens	548	521
Ākāsha Nature's Sounding-board. Sounds	549	522
Prāna. The Second Spinal Cord	550	523
Kosmic Consciousness. Initiates	551	524
Terrestrial	552	525
Divisions of the Astral plane	553	526
Kosmic Planes. General Notes	555	528
Differentiation. Manvantaric Aspect of Parabrahman and Mūlaprakriti. Objective Consciousness	557	530
Astral Consciousness. Kāma-Prānic Consciousness. Kāma-Manasic Consciousness. Manasic Consciousness. Buddhic Consciousness	558	531
Men and Pitris. Miscellaneous	559	532
The Human Principles	560	533
Power of Imagination. Notes	561	534
Suns and Planets. The Moon	562	535
Why Cycles return. The Solar System. Precious Stones. Time. ...	563	536
Death. Atoms	563	537
Talas and Lokas	565	538
Explanation of the States of Consciousness Corresponding to the Vedāntic Classification of Lokas	565	539
States of Consciousness. Further Explanations of the same Classifications	567	540
Lokas	568	541
Man and Lokas	568	542
Diagram V.	569	543
Yogis in Svarloka. Forms in the Astral Light. States of Consciousness	571	544
Mother-love	572	545
Consciousness and Self-consciousness	573	546
Scales of Consciousness	575	548
The Ego. Bhūrloka	576	549

	ED. 3 VOL. III Page	ED. 4 & 5 VOL. 5 Page
Vibrations and Impressions. Pineal Gland	577	549
The Heart. Astral and Ego. Individuality	577	550
Lower Manas. Kāma. Self-hood	578	551
The Crucifixion of the Christos	579	552
Kāmpa Rūpa	580	553
Heart	581	553
Rising above the Brain. The Fires. Perception	581	554
Christ and Apollonius	583	556
Will and Desire	584	557
The Beginnings. Origines	585	557
Dreams. Nidānas	585	558
Karmic Effects. Skandhas	587	560
Subtle Bodies	588	561
Fire is Kriyāshakti	589	562
Hints on the future	590	562
The Egos	590	563
Responsibility and the Ego	591	563
Monadic Evolution	592	565
Functions of the Astral body	593	565
Additional Notes	—	568
Bibliography	—	574

INDEX

VOLS. 1—5

INDEX

Corresponding pages of the Adyar Edition with earlier editions:

	Adyar	1893	1888
Vol.	1	Vol. i to p. 318	to p. 299
„	2	„ „ pp. 321-740	pp. 303-676
„	3	Vol. ii to p. 466	to p. 446
„	4	„ „ pp. 468-842	pp. 449-798
„	5	Vol. iii	
„	6	Index, and new Glossary	

A

AAM, Toom is, ii. 398
AANROO, Deceased allotted land in, i. 282
  Domain of Osiris in, ii. 398
  Khem, who gleans in, i. 268
  Wheat in field of, iii. 373
AANROO-FIELD, domain of Amenti, i. 282
AARON, v. 166, 182
AB, the Father, iii. 93
ABABEL, the mystical Tree, iv. 188
ABACUS, the Pythagorean, ii. 76
ABAHU, Rabbi, iii. 64
ABAMMON, v. 58
ABARBANEL, iv. 23; v. 163
ABBA Father, ii. 70; v. 211
ABBA, Rabbi, iv. 196, 199; v. 176
ABD ALLATIF, on Sabaeans, iii. 361
ABDERA, Democritus of, i. 176
ABDI of Muhammadans, iv. 173
ABEL, Cain and, i. 292; ii. 368; iii. 133, 143;
  iv. 37; v. 86, 164, 165, 166, 190
  Hebel or, a female, iii. 136
  Jesus, is, v. 161
  Sacrifice of, iii. 275
  Soil, life-bearing, iii. 275
  Woman, first, iii. 387
AB HATI, Animal Soul, iv. 205
ABHAYAM, iii. 404
ABHIDHARMA, v. 81
ABHIJNAS, v. 399
ABHIMANIN, iii. 249; iv. 90
  Sons of, ii. 245
ABHRA, a wisdom deity, v. 111
ABHUTARAJASAS, or Rajasas, iii. 98
ABJAYONI, or Padmayoni, ii. 87
ABRACADABRA, i. 87
ABRAHAM, v. 65, 111, 112, 177, 179, 180
  Bosom of, ii. 291
  El Elion of, iii. 379
  God of, iv. 79
  Jehovah to, iv. 77
  Kabalistic books and, v. 211
  Language of, v. 181, 197
  Lord God of, ii. 188; iv. 107
  Palestine, coming to, ii. 91
  Pillars of, Lingams, iv. 40
  Puranic MSS., in, i. 53
  Race-father, iii. 52
  Sarah and, iii. 181
  Saturn identical with, ii. 301
  Seed of, ii. 301
  Sepher Yetzireh, and, i. 64
  Ur, came from, iii. 148
  Woman of, freed and bond, iii. 86
A-BRAHMS, Brahms and, iii. 139
A-BRA(H)M becomes Abraham, iii. 148; v. 110
ABRAM, v. 110, 111, 165
  Abraham and, iii. 52
  Arba derived from, ii. 51
  Circumcized servants of, ii. 35
  Lamp of, ii. 52
  No-Brahman, or, iii. 205
  Sarai, or SRI, and, iii. 86
ABRASAX, Gnostic sects, iv. 41
  Sun Eternal, iii. 218
  Supreme God, ii. 64

ABRAXAS, Generative Deity, a, iv. 42
  Gnostic sects and, iv. 41
  Ievo antagonistic to, iv. 111
  Osiris on, gems, iv. 135
  Priapus, one with, iv. 25
  Supreme Unknown, v. 129
ABRAYANTI, one of the Pleiades, iv. 121
ABSOLUTE, Ain Soph, the, iv. 110
  All, the, i. 74; v. 210
  Aspects of the, i. 80
  Atyantika, or, iii. 79, 310
  Being, i. 112, 122, 130, 311; iv. 16; v. 552
  Be-ness, One, i. 80
  Brahma, the, Cause, ii. 165
  Breath of the, i. 292; v. 387
  Cause, the, i. 74; ii. 399; iii. 87; v. 351
  Chit or Intelligence, i. 73
  Circle, v. 129, 455
  " Concealed Lord," the, i. 123
  Consciousness, i. 70, 80, 119, 122, 126, 127,
    263, 309, 320; ii. 360
  Contains the Universe in Itself, v. 233
  Creative Power, the, and, iii. 87
  Crookes on the, ii. 305
  Darkness, i. 126, 138; ii. 204
  Definition of, no, iii. 46
  Deity, i. 128, 224, 293; ii. 257, 338; iii. 166,
    241; v. 387, 462, 471
  Dissolution, iii. 310
  Éliphas Lévi and, v. 230
  Emanation from the, i. 335; v. 77
  Essence, i. 73, 126, 317
  Eternal, v. 425
  Existence, the one, i. 113, 116; ii. 39
  First cannot be, i. 80
  God as, ii. 129
  Hegel on, i. 81
  Human Intellect and, v. 353
  Intelligence, i. 149
  Itself, stands by, iv. 169
  Kabalists' mistakes as to, i. 262
  Law, iii. 96
  Life, i. 302, 319; ii. 262; iii. 47; v. 455
  Light, i. 137, 250; iii. 49, 104, 169, 218;
    v. 227, 492
  Mahamaya of the Is, iii. 444
  Mahat, an aspect of, i. 122
  Man becoming one with, iii. 88
  Manas, and, i. 233
  Monad becomes, i. 193
  Motion, i. 80, 115, 126; v. 515, 557
  Non-Being, i. 119, 124, 243
  No-Number is, i. 152
  No-thing, the, i. 262; iv. 123
  Nucleoles form part of, iii. 46
  One, i. 300; ii. 192; iv. 113; v. 430
  Oulom, the, ii. 68
  Parabrahman, the, i. 80, 131
  Parinirvana, Perfection, i. 114
  Paranishpanna is the, i. 115, 120, 124
  Perfection of the, All, i. 140; iii. 411; iv.125
  " Perpetual Motion," i. 125
  Personified Powers, aspects of, ii. 65
  Planes too near the, first two, i. 228
  Plenum, the, container, i. 75
  Point, the, ii. 60
  Pralaya, the, i. 77

ABSOLUTE (*Contd.*)
　Pre-cosmic Root-Substance, aspect of, i. 80
　Principle, i. 73, 122
　Protestant conception of, v. 78
　Ray of the One, i. 178, 278
　Reality, One, i. 79, 124
　Rest, i. 137; iii. 90
　Secret Mystery Name of, v. 408
　Self identical with the, Higher, i. 319
　Self-Consciousness attained by the, i. 122
　Silent All, ii. 60
　Sound of, v. 455
　Spinoza on the, All, ii. 353
　Spirit, i. 73; ii. 51, 165; v. 408
　Spiritual world of the, v. 435
　Substance, Divine, ii. 166
　THAT which is the, All, iii. 166
　Thought, i. 111; iv. 58.
　Time, ii. 136
　Unity, v. 198
　Universal Cosmos symbolized by, v. 436
　Unknowable, the, iv. 297
　Unmanifested, or, i. 152
　Veil shrouding the, i. 122
　Wisdom, i. 43, 69; iii. 106, 383
　Wisdom, Ideation mirrored in, ii. 41
　Word, manifesting in the, iv. 123
ABSOLUTENESS, Breath of the, i. 292, 331
　All-pervading, v. 434
　Conditioned, cannot be, i. 74
　Emanation from, v. 539
　God, the, of, ii. 131
　Incomprehensible, i. 309
　Infinity, the, of, i. 189
　Non-being, of, ii. 204
　Parabrahman is, i. 181
　Plane of, the, i. 188
　Principle, of the One, i. 83
　State of, indescribable, i. 86
　Thought in its, Divine, iv. 107
ABSOLUTER GEIST, i. 122
ABSOLUTES, Two, impossible, i. 74
AB SOO, Space called, iv. 70
ABSTRACT, Knowledge, v. 373
　Nature, v. 187
　Unity, v. 206
ABSTRACTION, Absolute, ii. 53
　Atom an, ii. 237
　Causeless Cause an, the, ii. 293
　Concretion follows the lines of, i. 230
　Deity of the Pagans an, ii. 370
　Elohim not an, i. 276
　Ever-Present, an, i. 70
　Holy of Holies an, iv. 40
　Ideal, ii. 63
　Incomprehensible, ii. 341
　Jehovah not an, ii. 344
　Logos as an, ii. 65
　Mathematical, a, ii. 394
　Matter as an, ii. 41; ii. 290
　Metaphysical, i. 117
　Mūlaprakriti, as an, iii. 37
　Plane of, i. 110
　Reality to, giving, i. 296
　Sephiroth not, ii. 357
　Shekinah, the purest, ii. 343
　Spirit *per se* an, i. 243

Universal, a, iv. 40, 169
ABYDOS, Osiris worshipped at, ii. 155; iii. 399
　Synchronistic table at, iii. 367
ABYSS, Arg floating on the, iv. 28
　Beginning, a great, in the, ii. 145
　Boundless and Void, ii. 83
　Chaos, the, or, i. 193; iv. 71; v. 198, 228
　Chaotic, Fountains of the, iii. 150
　Creation, the, of primordial, iii. 75
　Darkness, the, of, iii. 64
　Demiourgos reflected in the, looks of the, iii.246
　Destruction in the, iii. 66
　Gate of the, iv. 159
　Infinite, ii. 60
　Lady of the Nether iv. 30
　Learning, of, iv. 70
　Male unit, dug by the, iv. 125
　Manifested World, the, iii. 238
　Matter, the, of, i. 245
　Mentality, the, of, iii. 90
　Noot the celestial, i. 274
　Space, the, of, ii. 90; iii. 64
　Spirit of the, iii. 112
　Waters, the, of primordial, iv. 151
　Watery, iii. 64, 150; iv. 71, 223, 283
ABYSSINIA, *Book of Enoch* in, iv. 101
　Formation of, iv. 316
　Island, formerly an, iii. 367
　Pistis Sophia brought from, iv. 136
ACADEMY, French, v. 51, 57, 94
　Royal, v. 51, 89
ACCAD, or ACCADIA, Sargon of, iv. 261
ACCADIAN calendar, iv. 263
ACCIDENT, Karma and, iii. 304
　Lives, no, in our, ii. 368
ACCUMULATORS, Faure's, ii. 304
ACCUSER, *Book of the Dead*, in the, iii. 384
　Soul, of the, i. 166
ACHAMŌTH, Ilda-baoth mother of, iii. 246
　Sophia, or, i. 190; v. 74, 204
ACHAR, Jehovah, the, iv. 78
ACHATH, Creator of, i. 188
ACHER, v. 305
ACHERON, iii. 356
ACHILLES, Heel of, iv. 208
　Shield of, iii. 393
ACHIT, Anātmā and Parabrahman, i. 128
ACHYUTA, Chyuta, became the, iii. 58
　Immutable, the, ii. 266
　Vishnu, a name of, i. 84
ACOSMISM, i. 209
ACOSTA, i. 257
ACRANIA, iv. 227
ACROPOLIS, Argos, the, iii. 295
　Temple on the, ii. 52
ACTIO IN DISTANS, ii. 210, 214
ACTION, Ākāsha exists because of, ii. 46
　Divine, kingdom of, iii. 244
　Fatalism of blind, ii. 368
　Forces, Design in, of, i. 320
　Fruit of our, i. 282
　Independent, falsely so-called, ii. 289
　Karma or, i. 317; ii. 359; iii. 303, 306
　Marshalling of, i. 363
　Matter and, ii. 370; iii. 47
　Molecular, ii. 220
　Nature of a God known by, ii. 139

ACTION (*Contd.*)
 Organs of, v. 538
 Personal and impersonal, iii. 306
 Priests, good, the only, i. 323
 Psychic, v. 515
 Seed of, i. 282
 Spheres of, iv. 192
 Spirits of, i. 303
 Spiritual sphere of, iv. 192
 Thought and, i. 332
 Unity in thought and, ii. 369
 Vital, developing all forces, ii. 315
 Whirlwind raised by, ii. 364
 Will determines, ii. 364
 With and without, i. 130
 World of, the third, iii. 119
 Worshipped, of the, iv. 67
ACTIVITY, Cycles of, i. 309; iii. 116
 Periods of, i. 131, 209
 Plane of, i. 232
 Stages of, iv. 317
 Vital, i. 325
ACTOR, Dress of an, ii. 294
 Characters played by an, iii. 307
ACTS, Consequences of, i. 330
 Nature's, are cyclic, ii. 365
AD, Assyrian is " Father," in, iii. 55
 Sons of, i. 255
AD-AD, Aramaean means " only one," in,
  iii. 54, 55
AD-AH, Sons of, iii. 208
ADAM, iii. 223; v. 86, 167, 180, 181, 190
 Adept, first, v. 297
 Ādi-Nāth Sanskrit for, iv. 19
 Admi or Adami, iii. 17
 Androgyne, iii. 136, 187; iv. 24
 Apple, and the, i. 187; ii. 18
 Ark, body of, in the, iv. 35
 A-sexual, the, iii. 128
 Athamas or Thomas, iii. 143
 Barhishad became the, of dust, iii. 87
 Bible, in the, iii. 382
 Biblical, the, iii. 22, 81
 Book of Enoch and, iii. 133
 Cain not son of, iii. 136
 Chaldean, the, iii. 110
 Children of, ii. 166
 Church, a, iii. 54
 Clergy on descent from, ii. 35
 Collective name, a, iii. 18
 Creation of, iii. 392
 Dead-letter sense, in the, iii. 158
 Discovery of, (s), v. 222
 Dust, the, of, i. 287; iii. 87, 91, 95, 121; v. 157,
  190, 199
 Earth, the, of, iii. 134; v. 190
 Eden, in, iii. 121
 Elohim and, v. 208
 Elohim were, i. 287; iii. 145, 381
 Enos and, iv. 37
 Essence, emanating from Divine, i. 64
 Eve, and, i. 194; ii. 37, 175; iii. 73, 155,199,268,
  275, 281; iv. 67, 226, 269, v. 165, 206, 291
 Fall of, iii. 177; iv. 80; v. 180, 203
 Family of, human, iii. 288
 First, the, ii. 67
 First man, not, ii. 36

Formation of, from clay, iv. 216
 Garden, in, ii. 121
 Generations of, iv. 102
 Generic name, a, iv. 21
 Genesis, and, iii. 15, 182, 386; iv. 231
 Gnostic tradition in, v. 203
 Heavenly, v. 188
 Highest, the, and, iv. 72
 Humanity, collective, iii. 142
 Initiating an, iii. 207
 Jehovah or, ii. 62; iii. 134; iv. 35
 Jehovah, Cain male part of, iii. 387
 Jews, obtained from Chaldea, iii. 54
 Kaimurath identical with, iii. 393, 395, 396
 Lifthrasir the coming, iii. 109
 Lilith, and, iii. 181, 264
 Mādim, Mars and, iii. 152; v. 166
 Maimonides on, iv. 34
 Mankind, is, iii. 128
 Mosaic *Bible*, and the, iii. 54
 Noah, period from, to, iii. 424
 Personification, as a, iii. 391
 Pūranic MSS. in forged, i. 53
 Planet, formed long after our, ii. ii. 37
 Priapean monster represents fourth, iv. 25
 Primitive Race, stands for, iii. 134
 Protoplastic androgyne, iv. 24
 Races, of the different, iii. 409; iv. 249
 Raphael to, ii. 347
 Red, the, iii. 122
 Reincarnation, and, i. 67
 Rib of, v. 199
 Rishoon is the Lunar Spirit, iii. 396
 Second, iii. 15
 Sevenfold, v. 202, 203
 Sons of, iii. 315; iv. 37, 107
 Soul, the first living, iv. 82
 Soul of life requires, i. 292; v. 154
 Spirit, a quickening, iv. 82
 Square, v. 166
 Swaddling clothes, in, iv. 261
 Tailless, iii. 328
 Terrestrial, first, iii. 169
 Theology, in Christian, iii. 104
 Tree of Knowledge and, ii. 120
 Tree of Life, and, iii. 220
 True, is, iv. 24
 White, the, ii. 36
 Woman from the second, iii. 137
 Yima, or, iv. 182
ADAM-ADAMI, ii. 70; iii. 54, 55; iv. 19,
  21, 23
AD-AM-AK-AD-MON, iii. 55
ADAMAS, Kabir, named, iii. 17
 Ophite, the, iv. 25
ADAM-EVE, Jehovah or, iii. 136
 Race, the Second, ii. 123; iii. 143
ADAM-GALATEA, iii. 158
ADAMI, Adam, Admi or, iii. 17
 Red earth, the, iv. 21
 Symbol, the manifold, iv. 19
ADAMIC, Humanity, i. 63
 Man, iii. 315; v. 199
 Orthodox, 6,000 years, iv. 245
 Race, the, iii. 19, 100; iv. 278
ADAM-JEHOVAH, iii. 55
ADAM-JEHOVAH-EVE, iii. 133

ADAM KADMON, v. 116, 157, 190
  Adam-Adami or, ii. 70
  Ad-am-ak-ad-mon or, iii. 55
  Adonis or, iii. 55
  Ain Soph, vehicle of, ii. 151; iv. 298
  Ain-Soph Shekinah, ii. 344
  Ancient of Days and, i. 129
  Androgyne, iii. 49, 137; iv. 34
  Anu preceded, iii. 152
  Archetypal Man, the, ii. 107, 161
  Body of, i. 284
  Brahmā and, iii. 133
  Dual-Man, generic name of, iii. 49
  Elohim framed, i. 284
  Emanations of, v. 291
  Female portion of, i. 263; iii. 272
  Genesis, of, iii. 16, 121
  Heavenly Man or, i. 194; iii. 57, 237; iv. 114, 167, 196, 274; v. 215
  Jehovah and, iv. 35
  Kabalah, in the, iii. 17
  Kabalists and, i. 231; iii. 137
  Light, is Spiritual, ii. 50
  Logoi as, the, i. 291
  Logos, the, i. 262; ii. 147; iii. 136, 237; iv. 114
  Lord, is the, iii. 136
  Mind-born son of, iii. 135
  Orgin of, iv. 107
  Paradigmatic, iv. 23
  Primitive Man, v. 299
  Sephira and, i. 161, 263; ii. 146, 148
  Sephiroth and, iii. 237; iv. 274
  Sephirothic Tree, personifies, the, ii. 67; iii. 18, 294
  Seventh Creation, v. 199
  Symbol, the four-lettered, iii. 38
  Twofold man, the, ii. 169
  Universe symbolized by, v. 419
  Yodcheva or, iii. 137
ADAM-KDM, the Heavenly Man, iii. 49
ADAMS, Animal, iii. 264
  Creation of the human, iii. 57
  Four, the, iv. 24, 71
  Kabalistic four, iv. 24
  Nebo and Budha both, iv. 23, 24
  Prediction of, iii. 439
  Primitive men or, iii. 17
  Primordial seven, iii. 57
  Two, v. 199
ADAM'S EARTH, or primordial matter, i. 76; ii. 267
ADAM'S PEAK, v. 134
ADAMU, or Dark Race, iii. 18
ADAN, the city of, iii. 40
AD-ARGAT, the Syrian Goddess, iii. 55
AD-AR-GAT or Aster't, iii. 54
ADBHITANYA, iii. 319
ADBHŪTAM in *Rig Veda*, iv. 193
ADDER, Dan described as an, ii. 377; iii. 216
ADDRESS of the Gods to Vishnu, ii. 139
ADELAIDE, Natives near, iii. 201
ADEPT (see also Adepts, Initiates, Rishis, Masters, etc.)
  Aerial body of an, v. 360
  Ālaya the Self of an, i. 121
  Angel, iv. 197

Ape theory, an, rejects the, i. 241
Āryan, v. 418
Aryāsanga, a pre-Christian, i. 121
Astral Ego of, v. 168, 361, 427
Astronomers, iv. 268
Atlantis, an, on, iii. 406
Bacon, Roger, an, ii. 276
Chaldean, Bible of the, iv. 22
Chela to a higher Initiate, the, i. 255
Christos, becoming the full, iv. 152; v. 105
Correlation of Elements, and, ii. 18
Cross at Initiation, attached to a, iv. 128
Divine, v. 97
Dragon a symbol of the, iii. 282
Ego of an, iii. 220
Enoïchion, is, v. 102
Form, an, changing his, iv. 174
" G " and the, the letter, iv. 146
Galilean, iii. 234
Good Law, of the, v. 125
Guru, v. 282
History of every, v. 65, 168
Initiated, iii. 39
Invisible, becoming, iv. 340
Jīvanmukta, the highest, i. 118
Magic of the, White, iii. 425
Matter, on, ii. 268
Mayavi Rupa, His, v. 472, 561
Monad, reading all in the, ii. 356
Mysteries of Nature known to the, iv. 119
Occultist, the, i. 201
Perfect, or, v. 82
Personalities of an, i. 318
Principality after death, v. 172
Quoted, iii. 405
Rāja Yogi, every, a, i. 213
Returns no more, v. 354, 539
Revelation to an, iv. 22
Right Hand, of the, v. 49, 419
Secret Wisdom, in, iv. 101
Self-made, a, iii. 361, 429
Serpent a symbol of the, iii. 363
Son of God, v. 276
Spiritual faculties of the, ii. 289
Student, reveals to the, ii. 18
Sufferings of, v. 153
Third Eye of the, iv. 186
Three Ways open to, v. 80
Trance of the, ii. 240
Tyana, of, v. 142
Upādhis separated by the, i. 213
Vision of the, ii. 212
White, v. 512
Will of an, born through the, iii. 129
Work without fault must be written by an, v. 211
ADEPTS, Abode of, iv. 63
  Age, in every, ii. 207
  Ākāsha of the, ii. 52
  Alchemists, and, iii. 348
  Anāgamins, v. 410
  Ancient, the, great, iii. 423
  Apes, hope for the, iii. 265
  Āryan, iii. 383
  Astral body of, v. 80, 354, 427
  Atlantean and Āryan, iv. 63
  Authority of the, ii. 315

ADEPTS (*Contd.*)
  Balaam taught by, iii. 407
  Beings perceived by, ii. 329
  Black Art, of the, v. 47
  Books, existence of, recorded in the Sacred, i. 57
  Buddhahood, reached by, ii. 298
  Celibate, the, iii. 92
  China, in, v. 39
  Cis-Himālayan, iii. 373
  Civilize, tarry to, iii. 207
  Classes of, seven, ii. 298
  Commentaries compiled by, iii. 36
  Coptic, iii. 430
  Cross used by, sign of the, iv. 132
  Cyclic laws, and the, iv. 194
  Death of, iv. 100; v. 80, 427
  Degrees of, v. 399
  Dhyāni-Buddha, have each their, ii. 296; v. 370
  Difficulties encountered by, i. 223; iv. 271
  Dragons, named, iii. 219
  Earliest known, iv. 70; v. 75, 262
  Egos of great, iv. 186
  Egyptian, iii. 430
  Fifth Race, of the, ii. 137
  Firm ground, on, ii. 152
  Forefather of all, iv. 70
  Forces of the Moon, on the, ii. 111
  Generic title of, iii. 215
  Good Law, of the, iv. 64; v. 125
  Greek, iii. 430
  Heathen, v. 61
  Heavenward aspirations of, iii. 220
  Hierophants, and, iii. 366; v. 395
  Hindu, iv. 202
  History, known to, i. 61
  Incarnations of, v. 263, 352, 354
  Indian, ii. 23
  Initiates and, i. 335; ii. 337
  Initiation, and, ii. 120; v. 373
  Israelites, of the, v. 185
  Karma and, v. 49, 376, 378, 467, 512
  Knowledge, cannot communicate, iv. 271
  Life of the, iv. 64
  Light known to, properties of, ii. 241
  Lipika, do not know all orders of, i. 186
  Mankind will be composed of, iii. 444
  Manvantaras, of previous, iii. 103
  Mental vision of, i. 220
  Miracles of, v. 125, 394
  Moon, knowledge of the, i. 211
  Multiply again, the, will, iii. 277
  Mystery of the Lunar Chain known to, i. 231
  Mystics of antiquity, and, iv. 99
  Nāgas of the, ii. 121
  Nebo starts a new race of, iv. 23
  Nebular Theory and, ii. 252, 312, 314, 318
  Nirmānakāya of, v. 168, 453
  Nursery for future, i. 255
  Occult Fraternity preserve the teaching of, i. 56
  Perfection of, i. 316; v. 79
  Personality of, v. 151
  Phraseology of, iii. 355
  Planetary system, on, ii. 318
  Post-Christian, v. 124, 125
  Post-diluvian, ii. 135
  Powers of, v. 354, 419

  Principles, Lower, of, v. 359
  Pyramids, living under, iii. 350
  Researches of, ii. 337
  Revelations not made by, ii. 18
  Right Path, of the, iii. 215; iv. 63, 70; v. 64, 122, 419
  Saints, and, iii. 421
  Scarce, v. 297
  Science known to, iv. 17
  Seed for future, iii. 231
  Serpent symbolical of, iii. 103; v. 75
  Serpent-holes, from, iv. 317
  Seventh Race, will return in the, iv. 100
  Shiva, the patron of, iii. 283
  Solar System, cannot go beyond, v. 532
  Solar System, known to, iv. 271
  Sun's nature known to, iv. 167
  Sword of Knowledge used by, ii. 260
  Third Race, of the, iii. 214
  True, nearly died out, v. 276
  Truths, concealed by, i. 41
  Vidyā, of the Sacred, iii. 436
  Visions of, i. 316
  War between, iv. 70
  "Wondrous Being" governs, i. 255
  World, efforts of, i. 66
ADEPTSHIP, Criterion of, v. 148
  Cycle of, v. 155
  Degrees of, v. 354, 399
  Embryo of divine, iv. 186
  Jesus, and, v. 155
  Higher, v. 359
  In Kali-yuga, v. 396
  Practical, v. 467
  Tests of, v. 263
  Way to, v. 544
ADERENOSA, v. 293
ADHI BUDHA, Supreme Wisdom, i. 43
ADHIVĀHIKAS, bearers in transit, i. 190
ĀDI, First, in Sanskrit is, i. 187; iii. 54; iv. 19; v. 180
  One, the, i. 43
  Race called, first speaking, iv. 19
ĀDIBHŪTA, or prīmeval cause of all, i. 43
ĀDI-BUDDHA, Correlation of, i. 193
  Decrees of, iii. 59
  First or Primeval Wisdom, i. 124; v. 350, 352, 366, 368, 374, 391
  Supreme Wisdom, or, i. 43; v. 365
  Unknown, the one, ii. 294
  Wisdom of, concealed, i. 170
ĀDI-BUDDHI, or Absolute Consciousness, ii. 360; v. 391, 392
ĀDI-BUDDHIC MONAD, ii. 296
ĀDIKRIT, Creator, ii. 87
ĀDI-NĀTH, or First Lord, iv. 19
ĀDI-NIDĀNA Svabhāvat, i. 160
ĀDI-PARVA of the *Mahābhārata*, iii. 235
ĀDI-SANAT, the number, i. 160
ĀDI-SHAKTI, Mūlaprakriti emanation from, i. 76
ADI, Tattva, v. 475
ĀD-ĪSHVARA, iv. 19
ADITI, Ākāsha or, ii. 46, 251; v. 381
  Ambā or, ii. 179
  Cosmic Space or, i. 124
  Daksha and, i. 198; ii. 348; iii. 249

ADITI (*Contd.*)
  Depth of, unfathomable, iii. 218
  Diti is, iv. 184, 185
  Dyaus or, i. 162
  Gaea one with, iii. 271
  Gaia metaphysically, iii. 75
  Light, Primordial, iii. 54, 115
  Mother, ii. 350; iv. 96; v. 233
  Mūlaprakriti called, ii. 148
  Sephira is, ii. 69, 72, 149; iii. 54; v. 107
  Sons of, i. 139, 161; ii. 276; iii. 215
  Sophia and, v. 199
  Space, is Infinite, i. 161
  Spirit, and the, iv. 25
  Sun, Mother of the, ii. 254
  Surārani, called, iv. 96
  THAT, in, i. 72
  Vāch or, i. 194; ii. 149, 152; v. 165
  Vaidic, v. 192
ADITI-GAEA, Prakriti materialized is, iii. 76
ADITI-PRAKRITI, i. 326
ADITI-VĀCH, ii. 70, 150; iii. 55
ADITYA, Adhivāhikas, a name of, i. 190
  Planetary God, the, iii. 76
ĀDITYAS, Ashvins, or Sacrificers, iv. 177
  Devas, are real, iii. 99
  Gods, the eight, or, i. 163
  Planets, the, the seven, i. 162
  Rudras who are, iii. 188; iv. 156
  Secret Doctrine, in, i. 155
  Sustainers of life, iv. 57
  Vaivasvata period, in, iii. 99
  Varuna, chief of, iii. 271
  Vedas, in, iii. 250
  Vedic deities, the, i. 138
  Vedic times, of, iv. 96
ADI-VARSHA, the primitive Eden, iii. 206, 208
ADJUSTMENT, Harmony, is universal, iii. 306
  Sphere of final, i. 234
  Struggles and wars of, i. 244
  Work of, intelligent, ii. 221
AD-M, appellation of, iii. 54
ADMI, Adam or Adami, iii. 17
AD-ON, or Lord of Syria, iii. 54
ADON, Adonai and Adonim, iv. 19; v. 201, 203
  Baal or, a Phallic God, iv. 28
  Hiram's temple to, iv. 111
ADONAI, Adonim and, iv. 19; v. 203
  Footstool of, iii. 238
  Iao-Jehovah, a name of, iii. 388
  Israelites, of the, iv. 19
  Iurbo-Adonaï, or, ii. 84
  Jehovah, a title of, ii. 156; iv. 33, 78
  Jewish, the, iii. 55
  Star, the, six-pointed, iv. 102
  Sun, genius of the, ii. 301; iv. 108
A Do Na Y, or Lord, iv. 19
ADONEUS, a stellar spirit, ii. 167
ADONI, Jews' reading of, iii. 138
ADONIM and Adonai, iv. 19
ADONIS, Adam-Kadmon or, iii. 55
  First Lord, the, iv. 19
  Lunar God, a, ii. 111
  Mysteries of, iii. 216
  Osiris and, iv. 338
  Ptah, identical with, ii. 68
ADRASTEIA, the inevitable, iii. 306

ADRIAN, Emperor, v. 148, 334
ADULTERER, Seed of the, iv. 160
ADVAITA, Brāhman of the, Sect, ii. 361
  Doctrine, i. 131, 145
  Philosophy, i. 74, 124; ii. 247; iv. 208; v. 402
  Vedāntists, (or Vedāntins) the, i. 126; ii. 247
  Without a Second, i. 124
ADVAITI and the Vishishthādvaita Philosophy, i. 128
ADVAITIN, Brāhmans, opposed to orthodox, i. 74
  Doctrines, i. 122
  Occultists are not Atheists, i. 73
  Philosophy, the, Vedāntic, iv. 168
ADVAITIS, Purusha and Prakriti, on, iv. 170
  Vedāntins, and, i. 123; v. 383
ADVENT of Christ, Enoch and Elijah, iv. 100
  Second, the, i. 311
ADVENTURES of an Atom, i. 199
ADVERSARIES, Christianity, in iii. 388
  Gods, of the; iii. 171
ADVERSARY, Anthropomorphic God, of the, iii. 377
  Azazel, not the, of Jehovah, iii. 375
  Demon, the, iv. 56
  God and, iv. 76
  Human form, in, ii. 130
  Jehovah the first, iii. 3 86
  Law on the, the, iv. 46
  Lucifer as the, iii. 170
  Matter, the, of Spirit, iii. 237
  Nature, the, in, ii. 129
  Satan as the, ii. 129; iii. 71, 238, 246, 374, 386, 388
  Theology, the, in, iii. 71
ADYAR, i. 190
ADYTA, Documents stored in the, i. 58
  First Principle beyond the, ii. 144
  Initiation Halls of the, iv. 26; v. 321
  Secrecy of the, i. 177
ADYTUM, Sacred, of Occult Mysteries, ii, 35; v. 265
Sanctum Sanctorum or, iv. 27
Serapeum of, v. 161
ÆACHUS, v. 61
AED-EN, Eden or, iii. 54
A, E, I, O, U denote the Five Races, iv. 26
ÆLIAN, quoted, iii. 417; iv. 329
ÆNEAS, Astral double of, iv. 340
AEOLIAN, Harp, v. 485
  Kronos, form of, i. 173; iii. 391
  Mars, the, the name of, iii. 391
AEOLUS, Typhōeus chained by, ii. 187
ÆON, Adam, the Patriarch, ii. 366
  Eternity, sometimes denoting, i. 132
  Intermediate, an, iv. 56
  Logos, or First, ii. 66
  Lower, v. 446, 449
  Sunrise of another, i. 242
ÆONS, Angels, created by, ii. 65; v. 161, 445
  Archaic, the, i. 211
  Beingless, the, ii. 66
  Brahmā and, Days of, ii. 160
  Chief of the, i. 245
  Differentiation, of, slow, iv. 306
  Divine Man, or, v. 449
  Evolution of, duration of, iv. 116

ÆONS (*Contd.*)
Falling down of, ii. 134
Female, v. 447
First of the, iii. 380
Genii or, i. 245
Gnostic, v. 462
Higher, v. 445, 448
Highest of, iv. 58; v. 449
Kalpas or, of Life, i. 176
Manvantaras, in former, i. 320
Material History, of, ii. 363
Nirvāna, of suffering before, iii. 90
Pairs of, iv. 139; v. 446
Pantheist, of, v. 215
Primordial, v. 446
Seven, v. 128
Six, v. 447
Spheres, rebellious, of, iv, 176
Stellar spirits, v. 170
Time, of, ii. 123; iv. 243
Tree of Life and, v. 446
Triple, v. 448
Universal, v. 446
AERIFORM, Primeval man, iii. 89
Transformations of the, globes, i. 254
AERIUS, or Pan, ii. 184
ÆROBES, i. 294, 302, 304
AEROLITES, Howard on, iv. 352
AEROLITHS, v. 225
AERONAUTICS, Vimāna Vidyā or, iii. 424
ÆSAR, an Etruscan God, iii. 123
Irish Gods, one of the, iii. 123
ÆSCHYLUS, Initiate, an, iii. 417; iv. 93
Prometheus of, iii. 411; iv. 90, 92, 332
quoted, iii, 273, 410, 412
Tragedies of, iv. 243
Trilogy of, iii. 412
ÆSCULAPIUS v. 294 (see also Esculapius and
  Asclepios)
Apollo, son of, iii. 115
Asclepios or, iii. 213
Embryo, and the human, iii. 261
Ptah, identical, with, ii. 68
Saviour of All, called, ii. 68
Serpent, and the, iii. 214
Sun-God, iv. 31
ÆSERS of the Scandinavian Eddas, iii. 40
ÆSIR, Scandinavian or, iv. 323
ÆSWAR, Ishvara or, iii. 123
ÆTHER, (see Ether, etc.), Aditi, is, ii. 46
Aditi the principle higher than, i. 194
Ākāsha the primary of, ii. 260
Ancients, of the, ii. 45
Astronomy, in modern, ii. 208
Being of another Plane, a, ii. 211
Breath of the Father, is the, 1, 141
Chaos, and, ii. 144.
Deified by Ancients, ii. 44
Elasticity of the, ii. 209
Element, the fifth, ii. 57, 81
Elements, the synthesis of all, ii. 57, 184
Energy, the quintessence of all, ii. 233
Ether and, of the Ancients, ii. 45
Father, Omnipotent, ii. 181
Father-Mother, is, i. 78
Fire is, i. 151; v. 562
Fiery Waters of Space, the, iii. 399

Forces, the cause of, ii. 233
Gravitation, Father, and, ii. 218
Greeks, the sacred, of the, ii. 210
Hemera and, i. 170
Imponderable aspect of, ii. 45
Lodge on, ii. 211
Logoi, related to, ii. 150
Magnus, ii. 44
Mochus on, ii. 81
Nervous, ii. 233, 257, 327
Noumenon of, Ether the, ii. 232
Occultist, of the, ii. 240
Osiris representing, ii. 54
Pater, v. 476
Personifications of, i. 197
Phenomena, in world of, ii. 61
Prima Materia, Soul of, ii. 54
Richardson on Aith-ur or, ii. 251
Science, unknown to, i. 163
Sons of, ii. 283
Spiller on, ii. 232
Sub-division of, ii. 56, 57
Synonyms of, iv. 80
Ulom and, ii. 81
Universal, ii. 205
Zeus-Zēn, or, ii. 54; iii. 139
ÆTHERIC vibrations, ii. 286
ÆTHIOP river, iii. 415
ÆTHIOPIANS, Eastern, iii. 427
Pioneer race of, iii. 416
ÆTNA, the celestial pillar, iv. 332
ÆVUM, v. 108
AFFINITY, Atoms, of the, i. 70; iv. 241
Caloric, of, ii. 249
Chemical, v. 531
Cohesion, laws of, and, i. 302
Electric power of, i. 178
Spiritual, v. 551
AFGHĀNISTĀN, Arabs in, iii. 205
Khorasān came from, tribe of, i. 55
AFGHĀNS, Ben-Israel, children of, iii. 205
Israelites, and, iii. 205
Jews, will not call themselves, iii. 205
AFRICA, America and, iii. 327
Asia formed after, iv. 177
Atlantes of Western, iv. 331
Atlanteans and, iv. 310
Atlantis and, iii. 266; iv. 358
Continent of, iii. 205; iv. 332
Emergence of, iii. 266
Ethiopian of, iv. 39
Europe and, iii. 21, 327, 367; iv. 309
Gigantic men in, iii. 423
Irish stones in, origin of, iii. 343
Karma of, iii. 175
Lemuria included part of, iii. 20
Migrations to, iii. 328
Negro of, iii. 441
Nīla in Western, iii. 402
Northern, iv. 293
Pushkara will form part of, iii. 403
Races of, iii. 198
Root-stocks of, iii. 178
Shāka will form part of, iii. 403
Shveta-Dvīpa and, iii. 401
Sicily joined to, iv. 320
Skulls of races in, iii. 175

AFRICA (Contd.)
  Stones of, iv. 321
  Tribes of, iii. 169, 419, 423, 431
  Types in, variability of, iii. 423
  Western, the first men lived in, iv. 249
AGADI, Akkad, called, ii. 32
  Sargon, capital of, ii. 32
AGASSIZ, iii. 142, 177, 178; iv. 182, 216, 221
AGASTYA, the sage, i. 24; iii. 235
AGATHODÆMON, Archangel or, the highest,
    iii. 71
  Christ the, iii. 282
  Christos, the, iii. 376
  Egypt, called a king of, iii. 365
  Genius, the Good, ii. 194
  Gnostic Saviour, the, iv. 25
  Hermes Anubis or, iii. 41
  Legend of, iv. 87
  Light, Shadow of the, iii. 218
  Mercury as, iii. 41
  Pyramid tomb of, iii. 361
  Seth, was, iii. 361
  Serpent, the good, ii. 126, 159; iii. 214
  Tree of Being, and the, ii. 129
AGATHODAIMON, the good Spirit, ii. 58
AGE, (see Ages) Argonauts, of the, iii. 18
  Āryan Brāhmanical nation, of the, iv. 180
  Augustan, the, i. 256
  Azoic, of Science, i. 302
  Black, i. 65; ii. 192; iii. 433; iv. 96
  Brahmā, of, i. 74, 124, 225, 254, 330; ii. 84,
    123, 275; iii. 80; v. 493
  Bronze, the, of, iii. 204, 272; iv. 341
  Cambrian, the, iii. 23
  Chipped-stone, iv. 310
  Devonian, i. 297
  Earth, of our, iii. 59, 76
  Elephas primigenius, of, iv. 257
  Eocene, iii. 431; iv. 247, 260
  Fourth Race, of the, iii. 296
  Globe, geological, of the, iii. 157, 162, 253, 309
  Golden, ii. 369, 375; iii. 130, 204, 272, 275,
    371; iv. 89, 290, 346; v. 337, 338, 339
  Great, i. 252, 291; ii. 380; iii. 87
  Horror, the, of, iii. 332
  Human race, of, iv. 189
  Humanity, of, i. 205; iii. 441; iv. 256
  Ice, so-called, iii. 81
  Iron, ii. 369; iii. 204, 272; v. 338, 339
  Kali, of sin and sorrow, iv. 120
  Kali Yuga, of, ii. 389; iv. 96, 120
  Kalpa or, great, i. 150; iii. 308
  Mahākalpa or great, i. 110
  Mammalia, of, iv. 166, 282
  Man of, iii. 76, 289, 330; iv. 256
  Materialistic, v. 25
  Meanings, of, several, iii. 320
  Miocene, iii. 23, 24, 431; iv. 253
  Moon, of the, iii. 76
  Mythopoeic, the, i. 310
  Palaeolithic, the, i. 256
  Pigmies, of, iv. 283
  Primary, the, iii. 167
  Pyrolithic, the, iii. 167
  Reptiles, of, iv. 282
  Satya Yuga, the, of, i. 136; ii. 92, iii. 153
  Secondary, man in, iii. 22, 23

  Silver, iii. 204, 272
  Silurian, i. 297
  Sin and Sorrow, of, iv. 120
  Stone, iii. 439; iv. 251
  Tertiary, iii. 22; iv. 249
  Third, the, i. 255
  Third Race, of, iv. 282
  Titan of the Secondary, iii. 22
  Titanic, the first, iii. 410
  Tradition of the Christian, iv. 21
  Wheel of the small, i. 254
  World, of the, iv. 104
AGED, Form of the, iv. 274
AGENT, Architect, Creator, for the, iii. 55
  Ether an, i. 302
  Gravity acting through an, ii. 214
  Lapis Philosophorum, or Universal, iii. 122
  Magic, great, iv. 80, 81
  Provocateur, the Lord an, iii. 386
  Spirit, an, of God, i. 244
AGENTS, Creation, of, ii. 174
  Forces on this Plane or, ii. 216
  Harmony, of Universal, iii. 107
  Karma, of, iv. 45
  Kosmos, Active, in, iii. 116
  Monads not merely, ii. 356
  Senses, caused by, ii. 259
AGES (see Age) Archaic, i. 45; iii. 78, 108; iv.127
  Azoic, the, iii. 167
  Babylonian divine, iv. 190
  Dark, the, iii. 427
  Day of Brahmā, of a, i. 132
  Duration of, iii. 76, 77, 89
  Geology, in, iii. 23, 164
  Globe, of the, iv. 264
  Great, the four, ii. 169
  Mahāyugas or Great, i. 132
  Man, seven, of, iii. 312
  Middle, the, ii. 336; iv. 26
  Minor, the, ii. 380
  Periods of four, ii. 86
  Post-diluvian, iii. 435
  Pre-diluvian, iii. 168
  Pre-historic, iii. 77, 275; iv. 20
  Primary, of Geology, iii. 164
  Primitive, the, iii. 357
  Quaternary, the, iv. 237
  Reptiles, of the, iii. 66
  Science, of, iii. 81
  Secondary, of Geology, iii. 164
  Shakespeare, seven, of, 126, 312
  Signification of the four, iii. 273
  Years, meant by, ii. 54
AGGLUTINATIVE, Language in the, stage,
    iv. 232
  Speech, iii. 204
AGRUERUS, great Phoenician God, iii. 150
ĀGNEYA, a synonym for Krittikā, iv. 120
ĀGNEYĀSTRA, also Agneyastra, fiery weapon,
    iv. 129, 200
  Magic, the, iv, 129
  Origin of, iv. 201
AGNI, Abhimānin, iii. 249; iv. 90
  Āryan God, the, iii. 123
  Asura, an, iii. 101; iv. 68
  Bhūranyu, an epithet of, iv. 89
  Brahmā, eldest son of, ii. 245

AGNI (*Contd.*)
  Dhruva and, iv. 119
  Father of the three Fires, iii. 67
  Fire-god, the, iii. 380; iv. 150, 184
  Friends of, the seven, iv. 177
  God of Fire, the, ii. 183; iv. 135
  Hebdomad, and, the second, ii. 167
  Hindu, the, ii. 54
  Hymn to, iv. 95
  Indian, the, iii. 382
  Kālī and, ii. 161
  Kāma, identified with, iii. 183
  Kārtikeya and, iv. 120
  Sanskrit, in, iii. 109
  Sons of, v. 517
  Titans, sons of, iii. 150
  Vaishvānara, a name of, iii. 311; iv. 138
  Vedas, in the, iii. 412
  Vedic Trimūrti, a, i. 153
AGNIBĀHU, Priyavrata, son of, iii. 369
AGNIBHŪ, Kārtikeya called, iii. 381; iv. 120, 190
AGNIDHRA of Jambu-dvipa, iii. 320
AGNIHOTRIS, or Fire-priests, iv. 67
AGNI-PUTRA in India, the, iii. 362
AGNI-RATHA, Force from an, ii. 286
AGNIS of the Āryas, iii. 95
AGNISHVĀTTA, Ancestors, the, iii. 87
  Barhishads and, iii. 97
  Boon of the, iv. 94
  Dhyānīs and the, Fire, iii. 100
  Fires, the, devoid of, iii. 87
  Flames, or, iii. 89
  Kumāras and, iii. 97
  Marīchi, father of the, iii. 98
  Pitris, the, i. 233; iii. 98, 282
  Progenitors, the, iii. 87
  Saviours, the, our, iii. 410
  Solar Deities are, i, 151
AGNISHVĀTTA-KUMĀRA, iii. 360; v. 539
AGNI-VISHNU-SŪRYA, iv. 179
AGNOSTIC, v. 88, 247
  Carelessness of the, iv. 160
  First Cause, speculation on, ii. 40; iv. 160
  Mytholators, and, iv. 158
  Speculative thinkers, iii. 165
AGNOSTICISM, Geological problems and,
      iv. 347
  Janus-faced, ii. 252
  Nescience and, i. 74
  Philosophy and, ii. 361
  Science and, ii. 244
  Spencer's, i. 80
  Sterile, v. 28
AGNUS DEI, iii. 382
AGNYASTRA, or fire-weapons, iii. 425
AGRAE, v. 276, 279
AGRASANDHĀNI and the soul's Life, i. 166
AGRICULTURE, Ceres and, iii. 389
  Discovery of, iii. 372
  Huschenk, in days of, iii. 395
  Isis and, iii. 389
  Isis-Osiris invented, iii. 365
  Operations of, ii. 366
  Nabatheans, of, iv. 23
  Revelation of, iii. 363
AGRIPPA, ii. 172, 336; iv. 55; v. 116, 174
AH, root of verb " to be," iv. 180

AHAM=I, ii. 172; iv. 33
AHAMKĀRA, v. 494, 497, 553
  Ahamship or, ii. 260
  Being, the origin of all, ii. 172
  Body of Desires of, i. 304
  Egoship or, ii. 260
  Egotism, or the feeling of, iv. 185
  Element, the, i. 247; iii. 243
  Indriya Creation and, ii. 172
  Manas springs from, ii. 47, 48
  Origin of the Elements, the, iv. 187
  Prakritis, one of the seven, i. 300
  Sānkhya philosophy, in, ii. 48
  Spiritual ascension, opposed to, iv. 210
  Triple aspect of, ii. 48, 172
  Vishnu Purāna, in the, i. 134
AHAM-SA, or " I am He," iv. 33
A-HAMSA, Brahmā is, i. 85
A-HAM-SA or Hamsa, i. 144
AHAM-SHIP or Ahamkāra, ii. 260
  Mahat becomes, i. 142
AHAN or Day, iii. 68
AHAZ reproved by Isaiah, iv. 60
AH-HI, Army, like an, i. 111
  Celestial Beings or, i. 111
  Chohanic, i. 124
  Dhyān Chohans or, i. 111
  Individuality of the, i. 112
  Laws, act according to, i. 111
  Powers of Nature and, i. 111
  Responsibilities of the, i. 112
AHI, Indra and, i. 251
  Nāga called, iii. 188
  Vritra or, iii. 381
AHI-VITRA, Indra and, iii. 383
AHIYÉ ASHER AHIYÉ, iv. 36, 109
AHMED Ben Yusouf Eltiphas, iii. 365
A'HOOR, *i.e.*, back, iv. 109
AHRIMAN, Ahura Mazda, and, iv. 56
  Angels, were primordial, iv. 57
  Conqueror of, v. 47
  Dethroned, will be, iii. 418
  Depths of, v. 215
  Divine aspect of, iv. 86
  Evil thought of, iv. 58
  Fire, surrounded with, iv. 85
  Ministers of, ii. 301
  Ormazd, and the Bull of, iii. 102; v. 315
  Osiris and, iii. 284; v. 285
AHTI the Dragon, iii. 39
AHU, Achad, the Eka, the, i. 172
AHURA, Asura and, iii. 71; iv. 178
  Mazda, i. 170; iii. 101, 106, 236, 292, 293, **357,**
      379, 383, 418; iv. 44, 46, 48, 56, 85, **179,**
      181, 273; v. 214
  Supreme Spirit or, iii. 69
  Zoroastrians', iv. 68
AI, crucifixion of King of, iv. 128
AIDONEUS of the Subterranean World,
      ii. 184
AILANTHUS is bi-sexual, iii. 142
AIMA the Great Mother, iii. 93, 383; v. 211
AIN, Aiōr, En or, i. 262
  En-Soph, or, v. 191
  Non-being or, iv. 197
  No-thing, or, iii. 137
AINDRĪ, Indrānī or, iv. 185

AINDRIYAKA, Aindrī the personification of, iv. 185
　Creation, the third, ii. 165
　Organic creation or, ii. 172
　Senses or, ii. 172
AIN SOPH, Absolute Endless no-thing, i. 262; ii. 342; iv. 110
　Adam Kadmon and, i. 231; ii. 151; iv. 298
　Boudless All, the, i. 169; v. 386
　Boundless Time, or, iii. 236; v. 391
　Christians have ignored, ii. 106
　Concealed, the, iii. 119
　Deity, the Nameless, iv. 110
　Delight of, in itself, iii. 135
　Descent, allegorical, of, iv. 298
　Fiery Soul of the Pelican, the, i. 146
　Forms of, ii. 151
　Head of, ii. 71
　Jehovah blended with, iii. 385; iv. 168
　Jewish, the, iv. 123; v. 188
　Kabalists, of the, iii. 137; iv. 27, 40; v. 198
　Kāla or, iii. 236
　Left-hand of, ii. 339
　Manifestation of, iii. 51
　Mystery name of, iii. 134
　Negation, a term of, ii. 147
　Nothingness, the great, ii. 57
　One, is, iii. 291
　Parabrahman and, i. 124, 172; ii. 141; iii. 236; v. 187, 227
　Ray from, i. 262; ii. 294
　Sephirothic aspects of, ii. 65
　Seven letters, manifests through, ii. 49
　Shekinah-Adam-Kadmon, ii. 344
　Unity, the concealed, ii. 64, 68
　Unity, infinite, or, v. 189
　Unknowable, the, i. 124; iii. 52
　Unknown of the Infinite, v. 215
　Unnameable, the, iii. 52
　Vehicle of, ii. 151; iv. 298
　Veil of, iii. 219; v. 191
　Zeruāna Akerne and, iii. 236
　Zohar on the, iv. 106; v. 191
AIŌN, before Bythos, ii. 64
　Time or, iv. 58
AIŌR, En, Ain or, i. 262
AIR, Akāsha and, i. 253; v. 510
　Ancients' knowledge of, ii. 246
　Body, the cosmic gross, ii. 249
　Breath of all, born from, i. 295
　Chemical constituents of, i. 179
　Composition of, ii. 311
　Coruscations in, ii. 358
　Creation of, i. 298
　Eagle and, iii. 123
　Element, as an, i. 303, 326; ii. 51, 72, 152, 166; iv. 154, 187
　Ether and, i. 78, 301; ii. 44, 258
　Fire and, i. 297, iii. 122
　Gases and, ii. 186
　God of the, ii. 183
　Hydrogen and, iii. 114, 123
　John and, St., iii. 123
　Kabbalists of the, v. 230
　Monsters of the, iii. 22
　Mothers, one of the Three, v. 107
　Nature of, ii. 88

Nitrogen and, i. 298
Number Two, v. 189
Occultism, the, of, i. 265
Personifications of, i. 197
Prince of the, iv. 53, 84
Quaternary of matter, one of the, iv. 171
Race that could live in Fire or, iii. 224
Rudimentary man nursed by, iii. 121
Seven layers, in, v. 425
Space, spreads over, ii. 88
Spirit and, i. 303; ii. 56, 177, 181
Upādhi of, iii. 114
Vibration breaks up, ii. 287
Walking in the, iii. 286
AIR PLANE, iii. 290
AIRY BODIES, Lords of the, iii. 85
AIRY, Sir George, quoted, ii. 308
AIRYAMA-ISHYŌ, iv. 86
AIRYAMAN, the holy, iv. 86
AIRYANA VAĒJŌ, iii. 19, 209, 355, 414
AIRYANA-VARSEDYA, iii. 414
AISH, Asr, Osiris or, iii. 123
　Man, Hebrew for, iv. 130
AITH-UR, Solar Fire, Ether, ii. 251
AJA, Hindu, the, iii. 354
　Kāma is, iii. 183; iv. 150
　Krishna is, iii. 79
　Logos, as the, iv. 150
　Rig Veda, in the, iv. 150
　Unborn, the, iii. 79, 183; v. 370
　Vedāntins, the, of the, iv. 174
AJITAS refused to create, iii. 99
AJNA-PLEXUS, v. 480
AJUNTA, Labyrinths of, iii. 224
AK or Creator, iii, 54
AK-AD or Father-Creator, iii. 54
AKAROT, iii. 256
ĀKĀSHA, Adepts and, ii. 52
　Aditi and, iii. 54; iv. 185; v. 381
　Æther and, i. 142; ii. 45, 57
　Ambā means, ii. 179
　Aura, v. 472
　Bridge, a, v. 523
　Centres, and, v. 556
　Celestial Virgin, the, ii. 46
　Chaos, proceeds from, ii. 260
　Crystallized, v. 483
　Definition of, iv. 81
　Diathermanous Matter, is, i. 78
　Differentiation of elements in, ii. 172; v. 511
　Element not, the One, i. 78
　Ether and, i. 78, 130, 142, 159, 253, 298, 300, 301, 336; ii. 45, 208, 250; v. 512
　Fire and, i. 297
　First born of the One, ii. 261
　Fohat acts through, i. 170
　Forces and, ii. 310; v. 475
　Heat, and radiant, i. 78
　Higher planes and, v. 423
　Inter-etheric force and, ii. 285
　Kant and, ii. 326
　Logos, and, v. 475
　Magic, Agent, v. 120
　Materialist, and the, i. 336
　Mother, the, ii. 46
　Mother-Father, the, iii. 399
　Mūlaprakriti and, i. 76, 109; v. 475, 519

ĀKĀSHA (*Contd.*)
Nārāyana concealed in, i. 277
Nirvāna and eternal, ii. 360; v. 381
Noumenon of Ether, i. 298; ii. 258
Occultism and, ii. 216
Pairs of opposites and, iv. 139
Pater Æther or, ii. 211
Plastic, i. 83
Pradhāna synonym for, i. 300; v. 519
Prakriti and, i. 300; ii. 232
Pure, v. 471, 510
Seven degrees of, v. 475
Sophia Achamôth or, i. 247
Soul, the Universal, ii. 67
Sound, and, ii. 88; v. 475
Space Divine, v. 379, 382
Spirit of, ii. 177
Substance, primordial, ii. 39
Supersubstantial essence of, ii. 240
Sthūla Sharira of, iv. 186
Synonyms of, i. 300; iv. 80
Tattva, v. 475, 479
Terrestrial, v. 230
Universally present, v. 475
Universe, limited to, v. 475
Vāch, a form of, i. 194
Vibrations of, v. 505
Water, symbol of, ii. 177
AKĀSHIC, Jesus, Garment of, iv. 152
Aura, v. 470
Essence, v. 474
Fire, v. 482
Light, v. 80
Photographs of worlds, i. 83
Plane, v. 522
Primal Natures, i. 147
Principle, the, i. 303
Shell, v. 80
Universal Soul, the, i. 76
AKBAR, the Emperor, i. 47, 56, 136
AKER, Apap slain by, iii. 217
God, the, iv. 159
Set's serpent, iii. 217
AKHU, intelligence or perception, iv. 203
AKIBEEL reveals meaning of portents, iii. 375
AKKAD (see Accad), City of, iv. 261
Nimrod, capital of, ii. 32
AKKADIANS, Ak-ad or, iii. 54
Ancestors of the, ii. 108
Ancient, v. 436
Brāhmans and, iii. 207
Cosmic powers conceived by, iv. 45
Creative God of the, iii. 365
Ea of the, iii. 71
Emigrants, were, iii. 208
Genesis of the, ii. 72; iii. 207
Hymns of, v. 202
Lord of Ghosts of the, iii. 147
Months named by the, ii. 375
Silik-Muladag of the, iv. 45
Serpent of the, ii. 124
Zi or Spirit with the, iii. 65
AKKADS, the Great Deep of the, iii. 64
AKSHA or latitude, iii. 400
AKSHONNATI, or elevation of the pole, iii. 400
AKTA or anointed, iii. 109
" ALAHIM, of lives," the spirit of, v. 116

ALAIM, Seven, v. 206
ALAIS, meteorites of, iv. 276
AL-AIT, the God of Fire, iii. 150
ALALUS, Pithecanthropus, iv. 231, 249
ALASKAN PENINSULA, the iii. 327
ĀLAYA, Anima Mundi, the " Heart " of the, i. 128
Atmic State, v. 539
Brahma, an aspect of, i. 121
Existence of, absolute, i. 121
Mahat and, v. 499, 519, 558
Pāramārtha and, i. 119
Root of all, v. 402
Threefold meaning of, i. 121
Universal Soul, v. 471, 494, 499
Universe, of the, i. 119
Vijnān, v. 390
ĀLAYIC state, v. 540
ALBATH, v. 113, 116
ALBATROSS, magical properties of, ii. 77
ALBERTUS MAGNUS and Roger Bacon, ii. 306
ALBUS McGALDUS, skeleton of, iv. 319
ALCAMENES, statuary of, ii. 103
AL-CHAZARI, the Prince, iii. 51
ALCHEMICAL, Chemical or, ii. 256
Metaphors conceal, meanings, ii. 245
Progeny of Fire, description of the, iii. 75
Solvent of life, the, i. 302
Svastika an, sign, iii. 108
Test for pure air, ii. 351
Transmutations, Nature's, iii. 177
Trinity, the, iii. 114
ALCHEMISTIC, mysteries, iv. 201
ALCHEMISTS, v. 60, 227
Adam's Earth of, i. 76
Adepts and, iii. 348
Athanor of the, i. 147
Celestial Virgin of the, ii. 178
Chemists and, iii. 348
Christian, ii. 156
Cosmic Matter to the, ii. 267
Ether on, iv. 166
Exact Science and, i. 200
Fictions of, ii. 239
Fires and the, iii. 115
Heirs of the, ii. 336
Jehovah and Christian, ii. 156
Language of, v. 174
Matter on, ii. 267, 268
Mediaeval, i. 64, 146; v. 85, 88
Miracles of, i. 64
Mystic Watchers of, i. 178
Occultists and, Eastern, iv. 164
Phraseology, v. 73
Psychology of the, v. 73
Reveries of, v. 335
Spiritual secretion, and, ii. 234
Sun in the Ship, on the, ii. 126
Tetragram of the, iv. 127
Transformations, on, ii. 59
Women, and, v. 430
Writings of, v. 174
ALCHEMY, Arabian, v. 297
Birthplace of, iv. 333; v. 297
Books on, ancient, ii. 306
Chaldeans, of, v. 297
Chemistry, the new, ii. 348

ALCHEMY (Contd.)
  Compromise with, ii. 219
  Cradle of, v. 297
  Egypt in, v. 297
  Elements in, i. 148; ii. 308
  Fourth Race taught, iii. 424
  Hermeticism, or Western, iii. 122
  Hydrogen in, iii. 114
  Mercury in, iv. 112
  Occult, iii. 123
  Ozone in, ii. 279
  Phenomena and, Occult, i. 197
  Primordial substance of, ii. 43
  Sciences, and ancient, i. 306
  Spiritual, v. 297
ALCYONE in Pleiades, ii. 225; iii. 430; iv. 121, 337
ALDEBARAN, iv. 353, 354
ALEI, v. 325
ALEIM, Astrologers, the, iii. 208; v. 318
  Elohim, iii. 207
  Magi or, iii. 208
ALEPH, symbol of the Bull, ii. 383; iv. 121, 146; v. 206
ALESIA, v. 294, 295, 306
ALETAE, Planets, the seven, iii. 360
  Titans, the, iii. 150, 360
ALETHEIA or Truth, iv. 145; v. 462, 463
ALEUTIAN Islands, iii. 322, 327
ALEXANDER Jannaeus, iv. 72
  Polyhistor, i. 49; iii. 63
  Prof. ii. 312
  The Great, i. 49, 178; ii. 376; iii. 19, 415, 416; iv. 329; v. 54, 58
  Severus, v. 147, 149, 407
ALEXANDRIA, Bishop Cyril of, v. 307
  Caesar and the burning of, iv. 333
  Founded, v. 297
  Gnostics of, ii. 134
  Greeks of, ii. 384
  Indian figures and, ii. 76
  Initiates of, iv. 145
  Library in, i. 46, 56; iii. 65; iv. 262; v. 295, 307
  Neo-Platonists of, i. 65; ii. 125
  Orphio-Christos of Mystics of, ii. 79
  Theosophists of, v. 299
ALFURAS, skulls of, iv. 92
ALGAE, ii. 230; iv. 281
ALGATH, v. 113
ALGEBRA, ii. 340; iv. 125
ALGERIA, iv. 321
ALHIM, Creator, the, ii. 56
  Elohim or, i. 172, 174; iii. 50
  God, the, iii. 50
  Hebrew, i. 154
  Kosmos fashioned by, ii. 60
  Life, of, iii. 51
  Light, creates, iii. 50
  Wisdom, of, hidden, iii. 51
  Words of, iii. 53
ALHIM-NESS, iii. 52
ALKAHEST proper, the, ii. 59
ALKALOID, Ptomaine, the, poison, i. 305
  Saliva contains venomous, i. 305
ALL, Absolute, the, i. 75, 140, 278; ii. 60, 353; iii. 166, 383; iv. 123; v. 354
  Abstract, i. 80

Ain Soph, the, i. 169
  Boundless, i. 114, 169
  Breath of the, i. 141
  Causeless Cause, the, i. 80
  Circle, the, iv. 193
  Darkness filled the, i. 113
  Divine, the, ii. 169
  Emanation concealed in the, i. 74
  Eternal, the, i. 75
  Germ becoming the, i. 69
  God, the, i. 135
  Golden Egg not created by, i. 74
  Infinite, i. 75
  Life, is, i. 293
  Nature, in the, i. 156; ii. 43
  No-Thing is the, Absolute, iv. 123
  Nothing yet the, ii. 146
  Number, is One, i. 150
  One, the, i. 75; ii. 170; iv. 113
  Pan the Great, iv. 153
  Primordial Substance, the, ii. 43
  Ray of the, i. 278
  Root of the, i. 203, 300
  Rootless Root of, i. 136
  Self, v. 269
  Spinoza, the, of, ii. 353
  Unconditioned, the One, i. 311
  Unconscious, the, i. 132
  Unit merged in the, ii. 43
  Unknowable, the, iv. 58
  Unknown, the, i. 167
ALLA of the Arabs, iv. 173
ALLAHABĀD, ii. 108; iii. 224
ALL-BEING, Brahmā, is, i. 125
  Rootless Root of, ii. 123
ALL-BE-NESS, i. 125
ALL-CAUSE, Parabrahman the, iii. 116
ALL-DEITY, Circle or, iv. 167
  Science and the, iii. 107
ALLAN KARDEC School, v. 82
ALLANTOIS, v. 422, 424
ALLEGORICAL, Adam, permutations of, iii.134
  Animals, references to Sacred, iii. 187
  Āryan writing, ii. 22
  Chaldean tablets are, iii. 16
  Cosmogony, accounts of, i. 286
  Descriptions, iv. 206
  Drama of Initiation, iii. 417
  Flood meaning of the, iii. 153
  Forms of belief, iv. 134
  Genesis is, iii. 244
  Half-man, the, iv. 134
  Interpretation, the, ii. 89
  Monsters, iv. 135
  Plato, language of, iii. 268
  Purānas are, iii. 320
  Ra, assimilation to, i. 274
  Racial events, iii. 415
  Religion, form of, iv. 24, 228
  Rig Vedic hymns are, iv. 176
  Scriptures are, ancient, iii. 86
  Secret Doctrine teachings are, iii. 16
  Symbol, the, iii. 380
  Systems, the, dual, i. 246
  War in Heaven, the, iii. 270, 383
ALLEGORIES, Anthropomorphic, i. 189
  Āryan, iii. 382; iv. 147

ALLEGORIES (*Contd.*)
Astronomical, iii. 381; iv. 147
Atlantis, of, iv. 337
Cain, of, iii. 225
Conceptions in the shape of ii. 231
Cosmic, iii. 131, 381
Creation, of, iii. 66
Cube of the perfect, ii. 58
Cycles, of the, ii. 85
Earth, of the, iii. 56
Egyptian, iii. 379
Esoteric truths given as, iv. 354
Fatherhood in, v. 204
Flood, of the, iii. 18, 152
Fohat, the key to the, ii. 397
Greek, iv. 337
Hidden meaning of, iii. 434
Hindu, ii. 62; iv. 121
Homer's, iii. 382
Isis-Osiris, of iii. 151
Kabalah, in the, iv. 195
Manvantaras, of, ii. 85
Matter and Purusha, of, ii. 81
Meaning of, iii. 112
Moon, of the, iii. 56
Mosaic, iii. 132
Nāgas in the, iii. 188
Nārada, of, iv. 138, 156
Noah, of, iii. 225
Oriental traditions full of, ii. 134
Purānic, iii. 145, 182
Powers, concealing the nature of the, ii. 186
Purānas, of the, ii. 245; iii. 24, 68
Semi-esoteric,, iii. 89
Sons of the Seven, ii. 276
Testaments, in both, ii. 152
Vāch, veil, ii. 152
Veil of, iii. 156
ALLEGORY, Abel, of, iv. 37
Adam, of, iii. 182, 220
Agnishvātta, of the, iii. 87
Androgynes in every, iii. 133
Angels, of the Fall of the, i. 244
Ape's origin, of the, i. 241
Archaic mysteries, of the, iii. 232
Āryan, the, iii. 91, 102
Astronomical, iii. 352, 385; iv. 111; 273
Asuras, of the fallen, i. 239
Brahmā, of, iii. 88
Brazen Serpent, of the, ii. 79
Cain, of, iii. 225; iv. 37
Candidate's awakening of the, iv. 128
Castor and Pollux, of, iii. 132
Chaldean account of Creation not, iii. 63
Cosmic, i. 251; iii. 130, 181
Cosmogonical, iii. 385
Creation, of, iii. 49, 63, 66
Cross, of the, iv. 111
Deluge, of the, iii. 18
Eastern, phraseology of, i. 166, 216
Edom, of Kings of, iii. 64
Egyptian, i. 282
Enoch, of, iv. 102
Esoteric, ii. 253
Eve, of, iii. 199
Existence, in, the Absolute, ii. 39
Fall, of the, i. 244; iii. 73

Fancies of, iii. 102
Gandharva, of, ii. 247
Genesis, in, i. 291; iii. 182
Gnostic, of Satan, iii. 246
Greek, iii. 112, 158
Hanumān, of, iii. 171
Hindu, iii. 45
Indian, iii. 18
Indra's Soma-drinking, of, iii. 377
Io, of, iii. 416
Ischins, of the, iii. 375
Isis Unveiled, in, i. 293
Israelites' deluge, of the, iii. 18
Jacob, of the sons of, iii. 216
Jupiter, of, iii. 203
Rāma, of, iii. 183
Kandū, of, iii. 178
Keys of, seven, iii. 35
Kings of Edom, of the, iii. 64
Kronos and, ii. 136; iii. 419
Kumāras in, iv. 149
Leda, of, iii. 130, 203
Linga Purāna, in the, iii. 251
Manus, of the, iii. 155, 309; iv. 188
Maruts, of the, iv. 184
Matsya Avatāra, iii. 79
Moses an, history of, iv. 33
Nature's inability to create, of, iii. 111
Palestine, concerning burial in, ii. 292
Personification for purposes of, ii. 302
Poetical, iii. 108
Pralayas, of two, iv. 340
Prometheus, iii. 88, 112, 412, 414
Purānas, in the, iii. 69, 181
Purūravas, of the, ii. 247
Pygmalion, of, iii. 158
Raumas, of the, iii. 189
Religion, in every, iii. 107
Religious mysteries, in, iii. 132
Satan, of, iii. 246
Science rejects, i. 250
Scrolls of Wisdom, of the, iii. 108
Secret Meaning of, ii. 140
Serpent, of the Brazen, ii. 79
Shukra, an, of, iii. 44
Solomon's Temple, of, ii. 26
Sounds, etc., of, v. 420
Spirit of, ii. 141; iii. 73; iv. 140
Suggestive, is, ii. 247
Sweat-born, of the, iii. 183
Temple, of the, ii. 27
Tien-Hoang, of the, iii. 40
Titans, of the Western, iii. 44
Tradition, and, iii. 238
Tree of Life, iii. 220
Universes, of the three, i. 321
Uranus, of, ii. 136
Vaivasvata, of, iii. 147
Vishnu, of, iii. 50
Vishvakarman, of, iv. 129
War in Heaven, of the, iii. 73, 378
Yima, of, iv. 181
Zeus, of, iii. 131, 419
ALL-EMBRACER, the, iii. 271
ALL-EMBRACING DEITY, the, iii. 388
ALLEN, Grant, quoted, iii. 289; iv. 249, 255, 257, 260, 309

ALL-FATHER, Abyss, dwelt in the, ii. 145
  Darkness wherein dwells the, ii. 145
  Divinities in the house of, iii. 109
ALLIGATOR MOUND, iv. 322
ALL-IN-ALL, i. 85; ii. 61
ALL-knowing Lord, the, iii. 101
ALLNESS of the world, iii. 50
ALL NYUG, i. 87
ALM, Mahomet's mystic word, iv. 31
ALMANAC, ii. 366
ALMEH, the Egyptian dancing girls, iv. 31
ALMIGHTY, Deity, iv. 174
  Lord God, iv. 78
  Matter, the creating, ii. 347
  Prayers to the, ii. 188
  Satan first-born of the, iii. 241
  Throne of the, iii. 74
  Triune, the, i. 343
AL-OM-JAH, v. 290
AL-ORIT, the God of Fire, iii. 360
ALORUS, Adam, iv. 21
ALPHA, Christ, the, ii. 383
  Creation, the, of, iii. 108
  Dhruva now, the Pole Star, iv. 183
  Draconis, ii. 123; iii. 430
  Esotericism, of Eastern, iv. 15
  Omega, and, i. 70, 311; ii. 39, 192, 340;
    iii. 54; iv. 15, 152; v. 356
  Polaris, ii. 153
  Tau the, of Secret Divine Wisdom, iv. 152
ALPHABET, Chaldean, v. 114
  Chinese, v. 118
  Egyptian, i. 310; iv. 153
  Gods, of the, iii. 363
  Greek, the, iv. 135; v. 211
  Hebrew, the, i. 157; iv. 121, 146; v. 114, 118,
    178, 197, 211, 505
  Hermetic, v. 211
  Mayas, of the, i. 310
  Philosophical meaning of ancient, i. 157;
    iv. 145
  Russian, iv. 117
  Sanskrit, i. 157; v. 114, 197, 505
  Senzar, v. 114, 117, 505
  Slavonian, iv. 117
  Thoth, of, ii. 19; v. 123
ALPHONSO, tables of, ii. 391
ALPINE, Ice-age in, valleys, iii. 81
  Path of knowledge, iii. 428
ALPS, iv. 320, 347, 355
ALTAR, Christian churches, in, ii. 182
  Horns of the, iii. 416
  Kārana, of, i. 323
  Mithra, of, iv. 175
  Proportions of the, i. 257
ALTER EGO, Satan transformed into the
    Divine, iv. 44
  Venus-Lucifer the, of the Earth, ii. 17
ALTRUISM, Law of Harmony depends on,
    iii. 303
ALTYN-TAG, subterranean libraries of, i. 47, 55
ALUMINUM, ii. 274, 276
ALWAYS-EXISTING, the, iv. 125
AM means divine or deity, iii. 55
AMALTHAEA, Jupiter's foster-mother, iv. 150
AMĀNASA or mindless, iii. 100, 197
AMANUENSES of Eternal Ideation, i. 165

AMASIS, year of, v. 258, 297
AMAZARAK, teacher of sorcerers, iii. 375
AMAZONS, Aphides keep house like the, iii. 142
  Circle-dance of the, iv. 28; v. 310
AMBĀ one of the Pleiades, iv. 121
  Aditi, or, ii. 179
AMBER, Tears become, iv. 340
AMBHĀMSI, Suggestiveness of the term, ii. 178
  Waters, or, ii. 177, 179
AMBROSE, St., quoted, v. 312
AMBROSIA, Dragon and forbidden, iv. 85
  Ūrdhvasrotas who feed on, iii. 170
AMDO, district of, i. 169
AME no ani naka nushi no Kami, i. 261
AMENOPHES, King, ii. 114
AMENTI, Assessors in, i. 166
  Corn of, i. 282
  Counsellor of Osiris in, iv. 49
  Devachan or, v. 247
  Egyptian, Initiate descended into, iv. 128
  Justice conferred in, ii. 24
  Osiris and, ii. 24; iv. 49, 151
  Region of, i. 166; v. 257
  Soul in, ii. 80
  Spirit in, one becomes pure, ii. 398
  Thot, Scribe in, ii. 100
AMENTIAN region, the, iii. 378
AMERICA, Aborigines of, iii. 205, iv. 360
  Atlanta, called, iii. 225
  Atlantis called, iii. 154
  Basque language akin to that of, iv. 358
  Central, ruins in, v. 283
  Cities in, ruined, ii. 400
  Colossal stones in, iv. 321
  Continent, the fifth, iii. 21
  Dolichocephalae of, iv. 360
  Europe and, iii. 333, 405
  Forests of, iv. 246
  Giant-skeletons in, iii. 294
  Horse in, origin of the, iv. 360
  Human stocks in, iv. 249
  Idealists of, iv. 235
  Iguana lizard of South, iii. 161
  India, thought to be part of, iii. 326
  Kabalists in, i. 72
  Miocene period in, iv. 350, 352
  Myth by Europeans, regarded as a, ii. 336
  Nāgas, peopled by descendants of, iii. 188
  Nargals of, iii. 217
  North and South, iii. 402
  Pampas of, ii. 183, 200
  Pātāla is, iii. 141, 218, 443; iv. 200
  Philosophers in, iv. 235
  Primeval man in, iii. 178
  Pushkara is, iii. 402, 403
  Pyramids in, iii. 350
  Root Race in, Fifth, ii. 200
  Sanskritists in, ii. 373
  Savages of, iii. 437
  Seven in ancient, number, iii. 447
  Shāka, will form part of, iii. 403
  Skeletons in, giant, iii. 95
  South, iii. 402
  Spiritualists in, iii. 95
  Substantialists in, i. 201; ii. 289
  Symbols of tribes of, ii. 82, 106, 183
  Transformations in, iii. 442

AMERICA (*Contd.*)
Tribes of, i. 180
Upheaval of, iii. 405
Zuni Indians of, iv. 200
AMERICAN, Ancient, cross of, v. 162
Anglo-Saxons, people were pure, iii. 442
Archaeologists, iii. 421
Kabalist, an, i. 154
Noah, the, iii. 149
Primary Race, the, iii. 442
Race will not be, the Sixth, iii. 443
Zone, the, iii. 443
AMERICAS, Cataclysm will destroy both, iii.442
Europe, portions of, the, older than, iv. 177
AMERS taught the solution of magic, iii. 375
AMESHA SPENTAS, Amshaspends, or, iii. 357,
383; iv. 86, 179
AMEYĀTMAN, ii. 140
AMIDA or Buddha, i. 169; v. 391, 410
Sutra, v. 410
AMITĀBHA, A-mi-to Fo, is, iii. 186
Avatāra of, i. 169
Buddha, or, ii. 193; v. 391, 410, 420
Dhyāni-Buddha, a, i. 168
Dhyānis, or, iii. 186
Tien and, ii. 71
AMITA Buddha, v. 391
A-MI-TO FO, or Amitābha, iii. 186; v. 391
AMMIANUS Marcellinus, quoted, ii. 110;
iii. 427
AMMON, Creative God, the, ii. 80
Egyptian God, the, ii. 82
Exclusion, of, the, ii. 399
Horus, becomes, iv. 32
Mon, or, ii. 82
Moot and, ii. 148; iv. 32
Mout, mother and wife of, i. 155
Mystic eyes of, iii. 217
Neïth, was the Goddess, iii. 143
Spirit of, v. 246, 331
Theban Triad, one of the, iv. 32
AMMONIA, elements of, ii. 307
AMMONITES, Moloch of the, ii. 113
AMMONIUS Saccas, v. 33, 34, 64, 65, 68, 145,
299, 302, 303, 304, 307, 308
AMMON-RA, Amenophes, to, ii. 114
Generator, the, ii. 82
Mother's husband, his, ii. 108
AMNION, v. 422, 423, 424
AMOEBA, Division of, iv. 231
Man, from, to, iii. 257
Reproduction of the, iii. 125
AMOEBIAN souls, iv. 220
AMONA, Mother, ii. 70
AMOORLAND, iv. 352
AMOURA, iv. 266
AMPÈRE, Law of, ii. 237
AMPHAIN-ESSUMEN, iv. 25
AMPHIBIA, iii. 172; iv. 227, 254
AMPHIBIAN, Ancestors, iii. 127; iv. 255
Fauna, iv. 254
Mammalia traced to an, ancestor, iii. 172
AMPHION, iv. 363
AMPHIOXUS, iii. 369; iv. 233
AMPHITRITE, iv. 150
AMPSIU-OURAAN, iv. 139
AMRITA, Guna, beyond any, ii. 62

Immortality, i. 135, 137; ii. 62; iii. 380; v. 287
Water of Life, or, i. 135; 375
AMRUS, v. 295
AMSHASPENDS, iii. 357, 365, 384; iv. 56, 85, 179
Archangels, the, are, ii. 155
Asuras, and, iii. 101
Dual nature of the, iv. 44
Manvantaric emanations, are, ii. 147
One in Many are, the, i. 172
Osiris the chief, ii. 155
Rishis or, v. 333
Seven, v. 198, 315
Synthesis standing for, the veiled, ii. 53
Zoroastrians, of the, i. 186, 281; v. 214, 386
AMSHUMANT, Sagara's grandson, iv. 141
AMULETS, Mandrake, of, iii. 40
Psammite, made of, iv. 313
AMUN, the source of light, iii. 139; v. 253, 299
AM-SMEN, Paradise of Eight, v. 200
AMYOT, Father, quoted, ii. 194
AN, Basin of Persaea in, iv. 116
Chief of, ii. 398
ANA, Belita, and, iv. 30
Chaldean, i. 155
ANAKTES, Kabiri identified with the, iii. 359
Vulcan's progeny and the, iii. 114
ANAEROBES, Human body, in, i. 304
Scientists and, i. 294
ANAEL, regent of Venus, the, v. 310
ANĀGĀMIN path to Nirvāna, i. 255; v. 399, 410
ANAGRAM, Kumāra an, iv. 149
Mystic, a, iv. 33
Temura, and, v. 115
ANAGRAMMATICAL significance of Makara,
iv. 151
ANAGRANĪYAS, ii. 72
ANAITIA, wife of Shiva, i. 155
ANAÏTIS of the Medes and Persians, ii. 111
ANAK, Sons of, iv. 325
ANAKIM, iii. 336, 340; v. 309
ANALOGIES, False, ii. 194
Gentiles and Jews, between, iv. 39
Greek words, of, iv. 90
Inferior races, of, ii. 171
Sequence of, ii. 336
ANALOGUES of the inferior races, iii. 169
ANALOGY, Comparative, indisputable, iv. 134
Cosmos and man, between, i. 226
Doctrine of, i. 239
Elements, between chemical, iv. 198
Esotericisms, between various, i. 274
Evolution, Law of, in, i. 206, 239, 265; iii. 76
Law of, i. 205, 206, 239, 265, 304; ii. 266, 309,
328; iii. 76, 161, 257; iv. 188, 270
Life of man and Universe, between, i. 306
Matter an, of invisible worlds, ii. 330
Nature judged by, everything in, i. 176
Ovum, in segmentation of the human, iv. 254
Universe follows, i. 230
ĀNANDA, Disciple of Buddha, v. 407
ĀNANDAMAYA Sheath, the, ii. 294
ĀNANDAMAYAKOSHA or Spiritual Soul,
i. 212; v. 271
ANANIA, John Lorenzo, quoted, iv. 173
ANANTA, Serpent of Eternity, the, ii. 124
Shesha or, i. 140; iii. 60
Svastika and, iii. 109

ANANTA-SHESHA, Eternity, the Great Serpent, of, ii. 58
   Vishnu, a form of, iv. 73
ANASTASI, Magic of, v. 254
   Papyri of, v. 332
ANASTASIUS, quoted, v. 134
ANATHEMA, iii. 407
ANĀTMA, i. 129
ANATOMISTS, Embryo, studied by the, iii. 194
   Rudimentary organs, the, and, iv. 253
ANATOMY, Anthropoid, of the, iv. 250
   Aspirations not explained by, i. 223
   Body, of the human, iv. 223
   Brain, of the, iii. 302
   Comparative, iii. 96
   Love not explained by, i. 223
   Man, the, of, ii. 312
   Monkey, of the, iv. 250
   Pineal gland, of the, iii. 298
ANAXAGORAS of Clazomenæ, i. 121, 177; ii. 45, 170, 215, 291, 303, 310, 319, 348
ANAXIMENES, i. 143; ii. 314
ANCESTOR, Amphibian, an, iii. 12.
   Animal, or man, iii. 176
   Anthropoid, iii. 159, 195; iv. 217
   Ape, of the, iii. 96, 193, 291, 441; iv. 248, 252
   Catarrhini, of the, iv. 259
   Common, a, iv. 236, 259
   Darwinists on common, iv. 259
   Deucalion as, of race, iv. 88
   Divine, man's, iv. 289
   Dryopithecus, of the, iv. 247, 249
   Homo primigenius, of the, iii. 195
   Human races, of, iv. 88
   Hypothetical, our, iv. 238
   Palaeolithic man, of, iv. 245
   Pithecoid, a, i. 237; iii. 22; iv. 206, 250, 285
   Pithecoid-like, of man, i. 280
   Plastidules, of our common, iv. 243
   Primitive, the, iii. 168; iv. 239
   Protyle, of the, just-born, i. 325
   Sacrificers, iv. 177
   Science and human, iv. 247
   Seth, a semi-divine, iii. 91
   Taht-Esmun, first human, i. 274
ANCESTORS, Akkadians, of the, ii. 108
   Ancient peoples, of the most, iii. 328
   Anthropoids, of the, iii. 200
   Apes, of the, i. 241; iv. 237, 238, 252
   Arboreal, hairy, iv. 260
   Arhats, of, iii. 179
   Arūpa Pitris our, i. 266
   Atlanteans of, i. 241
   Australian tribes, Lemurians, of, iii. 202
   Autochthonous, iii. 17
   Basques, of, iv. 358
   Belief of savages concerning, ii. 120
   Brāhmans, of Pānini, iii. 437
   Breathed out man, the, iii. 95
   Celestial, i. 293
   Discoveries of our, ii. 183
   Divine, our, i. 147; iv. 316
   Divine man, of, iii. 91
   Dual-sexed, iii. 139
   Fashioners or, iii. 103
   Fishes, of, iv. 254
   Giant, iii. 351

Hall of, Totmes, iv. 129
Human race, of, iii. 150, 217, 322
Indo-Iranians, of, iv. 178
Isanagi and Isanami, i. 286
Lunar, i. 211, 214, 232, 274, 307; iii. 56, 85, 100, 150
Mankind is offered by Science, the, iv. 220, 226
Materialists, of the, iii. 369
Monera their own, iii. 159
Nahualts, of, iii. 47
Occultists, of, i. 269
Parsīs, of, iii. 397
Philosophy of our, ii. 231
Pitris are our, i. 151, 232, 266; iii. 56, 100
Progenitors or, of men, iii. 57, 87, 100
Progeny of the, i. 271
Prophecies of our, iii. 109
Quadrumanic, iv. 231
Race, of the, i. 53; iii. 150, 217
Science offers to man, the, iv. 220, 226
Spiritual, iii. 180
Tales of Northern, ii. 142
Terrene, i. 233
Trojans were Āryans, of, iii. 110
Unicellular classes, of, iv. 227
Wisdom of our, ii. 201; iii. 109
ANCESTRAL, Bodies, iv. 241
   Features, reversion to, iv. 255
   Germinal cell, the, i. 270
   Heart, the, i. 267
   Missing link, iv. 248
   Organisms, history of, iv. 226
   Series of Man, the, iv. 237
   Soul, Seb, or the, iv. 203
   Spirits, the, iii. 17
   Trees of our Race, iv. 226
   Types, iv. 219, 306
ANCESTRY, Androgyne, ii. 31
   Animal, of man, iv. 253
   Anthropoids, of the, iv. 255
   Mammals, of the, iii. 191
   Man, of, iii. 196
   Nations with no common, ii. 308
   Pithecoid, iii. 160
   Simian, a, iv. 249
   Unknown, the, iii. 191
ANCH (see Ankh) or Vital Force, etc., iv. 205
ANCHITHERIUM, iv. 285, 305
ANCIENT, Ancients, of, iii. 93; iv. 275
   Ādi-Sanat the Primeval, i. 161
   Books, v. 142
   Days, the, of, i. 129, 161, 169, 284; ii. 109, 179; iii. 93; v. 175
   One, the, iv. 196
ANCIENTS, Astronomy known by the, iv. 104
   Builders, Host of the, called the, ii. 58
   Chaos, the, of, ii. 58
   Charge against the, iv. 228
   Chronological computations of the, iv. 190
   Confucius on the, i. 59
   Cosmic Circle of, iv. 115
   Cosmography of the, iv. 104
   Cycles of the, iii. 395
   Cyclic Æons of the, ii. 135
   Dhyān Chohans, and the, iv. 155
   Elements of the, i. 197; ii. 19, 190, 201, 264
   Evil defined by, ii. 131

ANCIENTS (*Contd.*)
Evolution known to, ii. 46
Forces, understood, i. 159
Geognosy of, iv. 104
Gods of, i. 161; ii. 338; iii. 35
Hermaphrodites, and the, iii. 126
Imagination of, iii. 436
Kabiri, Gods of, v. 309
Knowledge of, i. 256, 257; v. 42
Kyriel of, iii. 35
Machinery of, i. 257
Matter and Spirit, idea of, ii. 291
Moderns, and, v. 28
Moons of the, seven, i. 231
Mysteries of, v. 54
Ogdoad of, v. 221
Philosophy of, iii. 115
Physical sciences, and, i. 197; ii. 150
Planets of, i. 207; iv. 173
Polar circles of, i. 253
Powers known to, ii. 186
Quaternary with, iv. 153
Religion of, iii. 115
Sanctum Sanctorum of, iv. 27
Science, the, and, i. 197; 150; iii. 115, 153
Septenary constitution known to, iv. 132
Sevening of, ii. 125
Six with, number, iv. 164
Sound to, iii. 115
Speculations of, iv. 191
Speech with, iii. 115
Spirit and Matter, view of, ii. 291
Symbologists and, ii. 15
Theos of, iv. 115
Thought known to, the power of, iii. 180
Traditions of, iii. 371
Wisdom of, ii. 310; iii. 199; v. 51
World-stuff of, i. 149
Zodiac known to, ii. 372
ANCYRA, Council of, v. 157
ANDAKATĀHA, iv. 187
ANDAMAN ISLANDERS, iii. 201
ANDERSON, J.A., v. 449
ANDES, iv. 314
ANDHRA dynasty of Magadha, iii. 224
ANDREWS, Dr., iii. 144
ANDROGYNE, Adam, the, iii. 133, 136, 187;
    iv. 24, 25, 72
Adam Kadmon the, iv. 34
Ancestry, ii. 31
Angels, the, iii. 49
Being, an, divided his, iii. 155
Creative Gods were, ii. 146
Creators, the, iii. 387
Deity, the, ii. 113; iii. 76; iv. 114
Deus Lunus, the, ii. 112
Divine, the, iii. 133, 365, 414
Dual, iii. 218
Genesis, man of, iii. 137
Goat of Mendes, the, i. 297
Gods, series of, iv. 173
Heavenly, v. 190
Hermaphrodite or, iii. 184; v. 438
Humanity, the, iii. 177
Jehovah is, i. 129
M is, the letter, ii. 99
Mammals and man, iv. 282

Moon an, deity, iii. 76
Mother, the, the Great, i. 263
Nature, iv. 40
Neptune, ministers of, iv. 148
Noah the, man, ii. 162
Number ten, representation of, ii. 108
Ophis the, iii. 219
Potential, the i. 292
Races, the, ii. 162; iii. 172, 179, 184, 202
Ray, the, iv. 58
Result, the, ii. 155
Sephira is, ii. 69, 151
Sephiroth, synthesis of, i. 160
Sexes or, opposite, i. 291
Stanzas on the, iii. 206
Stock, a prior, iii. 127
Symbol of, v. 129
Unity, ii. 68
Upper Adam is, iv. 25
Virgo-Scorpio, the, ii. 131
ANDROGYNES, Bi-sexual Race reincarnated in
    the, iii. 16
Creators incarnate in the, iii. 168
Egos, v. 77
Humanity were, the third, iii. 37
Jod-Heva inactive, iii. 143
Root Race, the, the third, iii. 172, 178
Scientists deny, iv. 314
Separation of, iii. 170
Sweat-born and, iii. 182
Symbology of the, iii. 132
ANDROGYNOUS, Aristophanes, race of, iii. 184
Bi-sexual or, iv. 346
Deity, an, i. 139; ii. 57
Dual-sexed or, i. 264
Eloha, the, iii. 70
Elohim, the, i. 188
Energy, the, i. 194
Gods held to be, iii. 139
Hermaphrodite or, iii. 127
Jah-Hovah, iii. 134
Jehovah is, i. 72
Lemurian race was, iv. 346
Logos, the, i. 155
Manifested beings become, i. 194
Nature becomes, iii. 43, 142
Principle, the, i. 83; ii. 70
Race, the, iii. 105, 133, 141, 187, 202, 283;
    iv. 102
Second Self, the, ii. 114
Separation of the, iii. 134, 203
Substance the, ii. 346
Unit, the, iii. 196
Word, the, iv. 107
ANEMOS, Pneuma or Wind, i. 273; ii. 56
ANGEL, Animal and, iii. 347
Atom and, i. 167
Avenging, the, ii. 368
Bird a synonym of, iii. 294
Cherub or, ii. 78
Companion, iv. 197
Counsel of the great, iii. 240
Darkness, an, of, iv. 151
Death, the, of, iii. 120, 384, 387
Deva or, i. 255
Deva-lokas or, spheres, ii. 330
Dhyān Chohan as, i. 268

ANGEL (*Contd.*)
Elohim a fighting, iii. 378
Face, of the, ii. 179; iv. 48
Fallen, myth of the, iii. 180; iv. 85
Gabriel, the, iv. 108
God or, iii. 358
Guardian, iv. 46
Hierarchies, of the, iii. 36
Immaculate on earth, no, iv. 52
Incarnated, an, iii. 97, 285
Initiates define an, ii. 292
Intransitive, nature of the, iii. 120
Jews, patron, of, ii. 179
Karmic law, under, i. 244
Lucifer, the Bright, iii. 120, 387
-Man, i. 240; iii. 123
Messenger or, iii. 358
Metatron or, iii. 119
Michael, the, iii. 380, 381
-Monad, ii. 298
Myth of the Fallen, iii. 180; iv. 43
-Names in *Bible*, iv. 106
Nemesis a Fury or an, ii. 367
Planet, of a, iii. 93
Rebellious, the, i. 244
Recording, iv. 85
Revelation, the, of, iv. 136, 189
Samaël, the, iii. 120
Satan, the, iii. 236, 387; iv. 45
Spheres, the, ii. 330
Star, of the, ii. 296
Sun, of the, iii. 381
Worlds, of the, iii. 237
ANGEL-FORCE, iv. 297
ANGELIC beings, i. 178, 265; ii. 134, 177; iii. 88
Fall, the, iii. 284
Form of Jehovah, iii. 381
Heart, the, iii. 100
Heaven, the, iv. 56
Hierarchy, the, i. 187, ii. 168
Host, i. 111, 178, 271
Jehovah, form of, iii. 381
Light of Truth, entity presiding over the, iv. 81
Man, iii. 248, 284, 387
Nārada, form of, iii. 91
Nirvāna, an entity and, iii. 90
Planes, seven, iii. 243
Virtues, i. 181; ii. 110
ANGELOLOGIES, ii. 337
ANGELOLOGY, Christian, iv. 69
Hebrew, i. 155
Jewish, iii. 72; iv. 69; v. 319
Roman Catholic, v. 326
ANGELOS, the Greek, iii. 59
ANGELS, Adonai, of the, iv. 19
Androgyne, iii. 49
Apes or, iv. 314
Asuras and, iv. 69
Azazel, one of the transgressing, iii. 375
Believers in, ii. 328, 336
Bible, in the, iii. 357; iv. 156
Birds, the glyph of, iv. 340
B'ne Aleim or, iii. 374
Bodies of, iii. 225
Cherubim, and, i. 185
Christians, of, i. 161, 268; ii. 328

Company of, iv. 182
Cosmic Forces, as, ii. 222
Creations of, iii. 53, 72, 239, 245; v. 127
Creative, the seven, iii. 17, 104
Darkness, the, ii. 177; iv. 57
De Mirville on, v. 94
Demons and, iii. 69
Devils, and, i. 329; iii. 393
Dhyān Chohans or, i. 318
Divine Breath, of, iii. 104
Dragon, and, i. 244; iii. 39; iv. 66
Elect, v. 109
Elements, as, ii. 88
Enoch's, ii. 247; iv. 156
Esoteric teachings as to, iv. 220
Ever-subjective, iii. 115
Face, of the, ii. 152
Fall of the, i. 244; iii. 169, 178, 231, 270, 284; iv. 55
Fallen, i. 50, 244, 246, 248, 267; iii. 71, 102, 112, 232, 276, 381, 388; iv. 11, 59, 61, 69, 76, 78, 79, 85, 95, 98, 105
Father, see the face of the, ii. 66
Fiery, iii. 249
Forces, Intelligent, i. 280; ii. 222
Four, v. 104
Genii or, i. 245
Germ of the, iii. 156
Glyph of the, iv. 340
Gods called, ii. 335
God's messages, doing, i. 259
Great Council, of, v. 213
Guardian, i. 268; v. 76, 357, 439
Habitat of, iii. 119
Hallelujahs of, ii. 337
Heavens as, the seven, ii. 167
Hierarchies of, v. 453
Hierarchy of, ii. 309; iii. 39, 105
Higher, iii. 90
Host of the, iii. 38
Humanity and, i. 273
Ideal Light, and the, i. 327
Incarnating, iii. 235, 360; iv. 55
Independent, iii. 318
Ischins, the lower, iii. 374
Jews, of, i. 161
Kabalah and, iii. 285
Karmic law affects, i. 319
Kings of the, iii. 316
Legends of, iii. 103
Light, of, iii. 102
Lord of, iii. 65
Lotus, and, ii. 94
Lower, iii. 111, 158, 374; v. 168, 210
Lunar Spirits, and, i. 248
Man-God above, iii. 376
Masters of, v. 60
Material, the, iii. 73
Men, are, i. 319
Men, aspire to become, i. 290
Men appeal to, iii. 206
Messenger or, i. 259; ii. 366
Michael and his, i. 244; v. 326
Milton's, iv. 75
Ministering, i. 155, 156
Myth of the Fallen, iv. 43
Nature, of, iii. 275

ANGELS (*Contd.*)
　Occultists do not worship, ii. 222
　Orders of, iii. 294
　Pagan Gods, and, v. 325
　Patriarchs or, the seven, iii. 365
　Pentateuch, in, v. 319
　Perfect, no, iii. 169
　Planetary, i. 248; iii. 360; v. 129, 253, 309
　Planets, identified with, iii. 98, 124, 318
　Powers or, ii. 65; iii. 275
　Presence, of the, i. 165; iii. 240; iv. 145; v. 207, 208, 333, 356, 386
　Primordial, iv. 57
　Principalities, or, ii. 64
　Rebellious, i. 246; ii. 301
　Regents or, i. 181
　Religion, of Western, i. 268
　Revelation, of, iv. 133
　Rishis, of the, i. 248
　Rope of the, i. 154
　Rūpa, i. 265
　Sadducees knew no, iii. 71
　Satan, of, iii. 71
　Science and, ii. 336; iii. 66; iv. 225
　Secondary Cause, v. 207
　Secret of, iv. 104
　Sephiroth or, ii. 65
　Septenary group of, i. 277; ii. 309
　Seraphim or, i. 156
　Seven, v. 129
　Sidereal Beings, i. 182
　Solar, iii. 97
　Souls and, iii. 294
　Space and Time, act in, ii. 136
　Spheres, of, i. 176; iii. 238
　Stars, of, iii. 357; v. 320
　Sun, in, v. 315
　Theodice of the Fallen, iii. 102
　Terrestrial, v. 168
　Third Order of, v. 129
　Universality of, v. 191
　Wisdom of, v. 102
　Worlds of, iii. 92
ANGELUS Rector, Kepler's, ii. 201
ANGER, Desire and, are obstructors, iv. 209
　Fools, the passion of, ii. 133
　Secretion, called a, ii. 234
ANGIRAS, Brahmā, a mind-born son of, iii. 88
　Shankara, Guru of, iv. 66
ANGIRASAS, Gods and Men, intermediate between, iv. 177
ANGLE, axial, of inclination, iii. 335, 359
ANGLO-SAXONS, Americans were pure, ii. 442
ANGRA MAINYU, iii. 379, 384; iv. 85, 86
ANGUINUM of the Pagan Druid, the, ii. 83
ANGUIPEDAL monster, the, iii. 80
ANGULA, or finger's breadth, i. 330
ANI, God, v. 462
ANIMAL Ærobes transform, matter, i. 302
　Angel, and, iii. 347
　Ancestry of man, the, iv. 253
　Bi-sexuality in the, kingdom, iii. 142
　Brain, the, iii. 84
　Breath of Life in the, i. 260, 287
　Centre, the real, i. 304
　Conception easy in, creation, iii. 409
　Consciousness, i. 280; v. 546, 549, 555

Creation, iii. 409
　Desire, Kāma, or, i. 287; iv. 165
　Development of, forms, iii. 195; iv. 267
　Divine Man in, iii. 277
　Divine within the, iv. 44
　Double-sexed, the kingdom, iii. 105
　Element, the, iii. 358, 410, 420
　Embryo an, the physical, i. 235
　Evolution, i. 239; iii. 78, 187, 255; iv. 223, 257, 264
　Flaming sword of, passions, iii. 73
　Fohat, Soul of Nature, i. 171
　Forms, perfecting of, iv. 298
　God in the, iii. 90, 376
　Gratification, iii. 409
　Instinct, Shuchi the fire of, iii. 113
　Jīva in the, i. 271
　Kāma in the, i. 287; iii. 411
　Kingdom, the, i. 227, 228, 278, 310; iii. 15, 78, 105, 142, 167; 243, 291; iv. 146, 206, 254, 256, 266
　Life, i. 260, 287, 294, 311; ii. 332; iii. 50, 63, 67, 158, 169, 246, 302
　Lunar Pitris and the, kingdom, i. 227
　Mac-benah, symbolized by, iv. 146
　Macrocosm to the, man a, iii. 184
　Man, the, i. 167, 292, 304; ii. 376; iii. 53, 192, 193, 298; iv. 239, 247, 303
　Manas of the, iii. 411
　Matter in the, body, ii. 256
　Mechanical, iii. 425
　Monad, the, i. 230; iii. 53, 111, 158, 192; iv. 94
　Nervous ether an, product, ii. 261
　Parents, monsters from, iii. 190
　Passions, iii. 73
　Plant, and, i. 283; ii. 179; iv. 162, 287
　Principles, iii. 269
　Product, nervous ether an, ii. 261
　Progenitor, an, iv. 251
　Propensities, ii. 334
　Protoplasm, iii. 159
　Psychic guided by the, iii. 411
　Races, iii. 93, 330
　Remains, the, iii. 65
　Root-types, primeval, iv. 219
　Round, impulse stops at the Fourth, i. 229
　Science and the, ii. 361
　Serpents with, bodies, iii. 66
　Soul, i. 208, 278, 289; iii. 242; iv. 168, 203, 205; v. 208, 456, 491, 565
　Sounds, iv. 231
　Species, iv. 257
　Spirits, iii. 299
　Symbol, the, ii. 106
　Tamed, the, will be, iii. 270
　Theorists, iv. 237
　Tiamat, the, of, iii. 383
　Type, the, iv. 252
　Vitality, v. 565
　World, the, iii. 278
ANIMAL-ELECTRIC Fires, the, iii. 111
ANIMAL LIKE, Embryo develops into the foetus, iii. 194
　Human forms, iii. 103
　Structures of organism, iv. 252
　Zeus wished to have men, iii. 412

ANIMALISM, Ascent from, iv. 355
  Chronic, iii. 411
  Satan our Saviour from, iv. 82
ANIMALISTIC THEORY, v. 26
ANIMALITY, Development in, ii. 334
ANIMALIZED Fourth Root Race, iv. 253
ANIMAL-MAN, Cross of Initiation, on the,
  iv. 13,
  Transformation of the, iii. 131
ANIMAL-MEN, Blue and red-faced, iii. 198
ANIMALS, Adam created before, in *Genesis*,
  iii. 187
  Alkaloids generated by, i. 305
  Annulose, the, iv. 194
  Antediluvian, iii. 206, 386
  Aquatic, ii. 68
  Astral shadows of, iii. 193
  Atoms, composed of living, i. 304
  Blind, iii. 298
  Boneless, iii. 190
  Bones, with, iii. 190
  Breeding with, iii. 287, 288
  Chipped-stone age, in the, iv. 284
  Consciousness of, iv. 271; v. 531, 547
  Creation of, ii. 165, 174; iii. 64, 187
  Daksha gave birth to, iii. 190
  Domestication of, iii. 372; iv. 284
  Elementals of, v. 540
  Esoteric meaning of expression, ii. 165
  Evangelists, representing the, ii. 78
  Evolution of, iii. 176
  Ezekiel, of, iv. 102
  Feeling of, v. 549
  Genesis, and man in, iii. 187
  Germs for higher, iv. 286
  Gigantic, iv. 329
  Heaven's Belt or sacred, iii. 36
  Hermaphroditism in, iii. 179
  Huge, destroyed, iii. 349
  Human heads, with, iii. 66
  Life in, iii. 257
  Man, contemporary with, iv. 320
  Man generated by, iii. 269
  Man precedes, iv. 314
  Marsupial, the, iii. 202
  Moon's influence on, iii. 113
  Mythical, iii. 221
  Occult powers of, iii. 84
  Pets, v. 565
  Planets, in other, ii. 326
  Potentialities of, v. 547
  Powers of, iii. 84
  Procreation of, iv. 83
  Production of, iii. 349; iv. 326
  Progenitors, iii. 188
  Propagation of, iv. 229
  Psychic vision in, v. 515
  Revelation, in, iv. 102
  Sacred, ii. 68, 160; iii. 36
  Science on, iii. 168
  Self, in, v. 546
  Senses of, ii. 331
  Sin committed with, iii. 197
  Soul of, i. 246; iv. 240
  Sweat of the earth, produced from the, iii. 349
  Ternaries only, were, iv. 147
  Three-eyed, iii. 297

  Unclean, ii. 70
  Will in, iv. 240
  Worlds, of the Old and New, iv. 360
  Zoology, unknown to, iii. 197
ANIMAL-THEORY of Haeckel and Huxley,
  ii. 18
ANIMA MUNDI, Adi Buddhi and, v. 391
  Ākāsha and the, i. 247
  Ālaya or, i. 119, 120
  Ana is Chaldean for, i. 155
  Astral Light or, i. 129, 155
  Bi-sexual, is. i. 246
  Buddha, or, v. 374
  Dual, is. i. 246
  Ishvara or, i. 336
  Life or, i. 121; ii. 303
  Light in the, iii. 247
  Logos the, i. 128; ii. 296
  Mother of Cosmos, the, i. 159
  Over-Soul or, i. 119
  Ptah as, ii. 68
  Science dare not whisper, i. 121
  Solar system, of the, iv. 241
  Soul or, i. 119
  Space, v. 382
  Spiritual Soul or, iv. 144
  Svabhāvat a synonym for, i. 161
  Universal Soul or, i. 121; ii. 81, 182; iv. 131;
    v. 383
ANIMA-SUPRA-MUNDI, i. 189
ANIMATE, Inanimate, and, ii. 173; iii. 269
  Matter, ii. 352
  Monadic principle, iv. 238
ANIMATION of the Third Race, iii. 233
ANIMUS, Soul or, i. 273
ANĪYĀMSAM ANĪYASĀM, ii. 72, 266; iii. 58;
  iv. 301
ANJANĀ, wife of Kesari, i. 241
ANKH, the sign of life, iii. 43; iv. 117
ANKH-CROSS, iv. 117
ANKH-SIGN, iv. 117
ANKH-TIE, iv. 116, 118
ANNA, Chaldean Ana, derived from the, i. 155
  Virgin Mary, mother of the, i. 155
ANNALISTS, History destroyed by, ii. 400
  Lipika are, the, i. 165
ANNALS, Astronomy, the, of, ii. 391
  Babylonia, the, of, iv. 261
  China, of, iii. 303
  Civilization, of, i. 54
  Divine kings, of, iii. 366
  Heroes and giants in, of every nation, i. 310
  Secret, iii. 334; iv. 362
ANNAMAYAKOSHA, or Sthūla Sharīra, i. 212
ANNAPURNA, wife of Shiva, i. 155
ANNEDOTI, the Chaldean, iii. 365
ANNIHILATION, of form, v. 387
  Nirvana is not, i. 309
  Personal, v. 486
  Void of Final, ii. 345
ANNIHILATIONISTS, iii. 164
ANNUNCIATION, Lily of the, ii. 94, v. 117
ANNUS MAGNUS, iv. 353, 354
ANOINTED, Akta, or, iii. 110
  Christos, the, iii. 36
  Hermes-Mercury, Termini of, iv. 112
  Jehovah, the, has become, iii. 236

ANOINTED (*Contd.*)
Keys of the Sanctuary given to the, iii. 236
Sanctuary entered by the, iii. 236
Wisdom of the, iii. 236
ANOMALY in Nature, i. 268
ANOMOEANS, v. 156
ANOPLOTHERIDAE, iv. 305
ANOUKA-NOAH, iv. 21
ANOUKI, Ankh derived from, iii. 43
ANQUETIL DU PERRON, triumph of, iii. 440
ANSATED Cross, Astronomical sign of Venus, iii. 43
Dragon with, ii. 383
Easter Island statues, on, ii. 34
Egyptian, ii. 383; iv. 118, 157, 171
Form of the, ii. 34
Life, the symbol of, iii. 43
Phallic symbol, the, a, iv. 154
Pharaohs, of the, iv. 113
Sexual aspect of, iii. 220
Sun on the, disk of, iv. 129
Venus, the, a sign of, iii. 43
AMSHĀMSHĀVATĀRA, iii. 358
ANSON, W.S.W., quoted, ii. 142
ANT, Consciousness of the, iii. 129
God to, we appear as, i. 190
ANTAHKARANĀ, v. 487, 488, 496, 529, 530, 551, 553, 554
Bridge between Higher and Lower Manas, v.495
Consciousness of, v. 497
Destruction of, v. 498, 502
Imaginary, is. v. 518
Path, is, v. 497, 519
Pituitary Body, and, v. 521
Sattva, or, i. 136
Seven steps of, v. 519, 543
ANTAEUS, the Giant, Tomb of, iii. 280
ANTARCTIC regions, the, iii. 356; iv. 345
ANT-EATERS, iv. 357
ANTE-CHRISTIAN Gnostic symbol, iv. 25
ANTEDILUVIAN, Animals, iii. 206
Astronomers, two, iii. 59
Dragon, an, animal, iii. 386
Earth, the, iii. 405
Fathers, the, iii. 408
Giants, the, ii. 135; iii. 80, 273; iv. 331
Mammals, skeletons of men and, iv. 309
Monsters, iii. 159, 316
Nations, iii. 334
Records, iv. 105
Sciences, iii. 334
Titans, iii. 389
Wisdom, misunderstood, iv. 52
Women, iii. 286
Zodiac is, ii. 374
ANTEDILUVIANS, Belief of the, i. 280
Bible, of the, iii. 392
Gigantic, iii. 409
ANTEGENETIC period, the, ii. 72
ANTELOPE, Makara the head of an, iv. 148, 150
ANTELOPES, iv. 305
ANTE-SEXUAL reproduction, iv. 229
ANTETYPES, Types and, ii. 309
ANTHIMES, v. 173
ANTHROPO-COSMOGENESIS, i. 261
ANTHROPOGENESIS, Cosmogenesis precedes, i. 261

Esoteric, iii. 276; iv. 221
Evolutionist, of the, iii. 165
Explanations in the, i. 242
Lunar Ancestors and, i. 211
Millennium of, ii. 91
Nature in our, i. 233
Races, of the prehistoric, iii. 19
Scriptures and, the ancient, iii. 176
Treatment of, in this book, iv. 365
Veil over, iii. 93
ANTHROPOGONY, Androgynes in every, iii. 133
Cosmotheogony to, from, iii. 107
Theogony, in relation to, ii. 79
ANTHROPOGRAPHY, i. 276
ANTHROPOID APE, Anatomy of man and, iv. 250
Ancestor, the, i. 241; iii. 159, 193, 195, 200; iv. 267
Atlanteans and the, iv. 259
Australian savages not descended from, iii. 198
Descendant of man, the, i. 234; iii. 289
Developed, a highly, iv. 248
Evolution of the, iv. 250
Fossil relics of the, iv. 245, 260
Man, the, half-descended from, i. 234
Man, the, next to, iii. 264
Man could live at time of the, iv. 247
Man not traced from, iv. 257
Monads of, i. 236
Monsters of Third Race not, iii. 191
Mythical iv. 246
Parent of modern, iv. 298
Races represented by, iii. 374
Retrogression of the, iv. 252
Savage, gulf between the, and, iv. 248
Science and the, iii. 287
Species of, iii. 191
Transformation of the, iii. 178
ANTHROPOIDS, Ancestry of the, iv. 255
Glacial period, of the, iv. 248
Higher, the, i. 238
Imaginary, iii. 315
Lords of Wisdom and, iii. 206
Man and, iii. 15, 96; iv. 216
Origin of, iii. 206
Schweinfurth on, iv. 235
Skulls of, and man, iv. 216
ANTHROPOLOGICAL, Biblical figures, ii. 371
Chaldeans, notions of, iii. 18
Discoveries, ii. 362
Evolution, iii. 215
Form of man, ii. 290
Institute, iv. 39
Key, an, ii. 106; iii. 92, 118
Moon symbol, an, key to, ii. 106
Nārada, a key to, mysteries, iii. 92
Record of an, fact, ii. 134
Society, iv. 224, 309
Svastika, an, sign, iii. 108
Symbols, iv. 130
System, the, ii. 78; iv. 221
Titans founded on an, fact, iii. 161
ANTHROPOLOGISTS, Age of man, on, iv. 256
Agnosticism of, iv. 215
Animal ancestry and, iv. 253

ANTHROPOLOGISTS (*Contd.*)
  Antiquity of man, on the, iv. 314
  Ariadne, and the thread of, iii. 77
  Chronology of, iii. 163
  Conclusions of, iv. 38
  Differences of, iii. 178
  European Science of, the, iv. 249
  Evolution, and esoteric, iv. 257
  Missing link of, iii. 191
  Modern, iii. 22
  Physiological proofs of the, iii. 193
  Tibetan extinct nations not classed by, i. 55
ANTHROPOLOGY, Antiquity of man, and the,
    ii. 35; iii. 435
  Ape, on our descent from the, ii. 35
  Archaic Science and modern, iii. 315; iv. 215
  Bible chronology and, iii. 200
  Chronology and, iii. 77, 200
  Cross in, the, iv. 131
  Darwinian, iii. 22; iv. 239, 259, 290
  Divine Revelation, and, ii. 36
  French School of, iii. 290
  Genesis, in, i. 291
  Gnostics of the, iv. 182
  Max Müller on, iv. 290
  Modern, and Esotericism, iii. 81
  Occult, iii. 296, 441; iv. 245, 258
  Orthodox, iv. 246
  Practical, iv. 219
  Problems of, ii. 210
  Scientific systems and, ii. 31; iv. 260
  Secret volumes, of the, iv. 259
ANTHROPO-MONOTHEISTIC conceptions,
    iii. 53
ANTHROPOMORPHIC, Allegories, i. 189
  Apes called, iv. 235
  Being, Prayer to an, i. 328
  Conceptions, gross, iii. 50
  Creation, i. 76
  Creator, the, iii. 52, 166
  Deity, an, ii. 137; iii. 305; iv. 125
  God, an, i. 319, 322; ii. 21, 89, 189, 204, 222,
    269, 328; iii. 377, 414; iv. 40, 113, 173
  Jehovah, the, ii. 187, 344
  Kabalists, the, God of the, ii. 89
  Kronos will swallow the, fiction, iii. 414
  Occultists deny an, God, ii. 222
  Phallic God, an, iv. 40
  Powers, worship of, iii. 275
  Prayer to an, God, i. 328
  Satan's shape, ii. 130
  Scriptures, element in the old, iv. 228
  Supreme Being, an, i. 327
  Theology, i. 120
ANTHROPOMORPHISM, v. 77, 78, 90
  Exoteric, iii. 271
  Germs of, iii. 230
  Greeks, among the, ii. 39
  Incipient stage of, iii. 316
  Jewish, ii. 97
  Progress of, rapid, iv. 71
  Revelation and, v. 207
  Symbology, of Jewish, ii. 97
  Theology, of current, i. 70, 120
ANTHROPOMORPHISTS, form and matter
    worshipped by, iii. 275
  Later age of, v. 284

Mediaeval, iii. 108
ANTHROPOMORPHIZED, Arcanum has
    been, iii. 236
  Divine Power of Nature has been, ii. 73
  Gods, the, iii. 54
  Powers, the Divine, iii. 54
  Religions become, iv. 178
  Satan, iv. 77
  Symbol, the, generative, iv. 77
  Systems, the, ii. 344
  Trinity, the, ii. 166
ANTHROPOMORPHIZING, Divine, the,
    iv. 177
  Ever-spiritual, the, iv. 85
ANTHROPOMORPHOUS, Ape, the,
    iv. 251, 297
  Archangel, the, iii. 376
ANTHRŌPOS, ii. 168; v. 204
ANTHROPOSOPHY, terrestrial, iii. 292
ANTI-CARTESIAN, ii. 352
ANTICHRIST, ii. 337; iii. 232; iv. 100
ANTI-CHRISTIAN churches, iii. 232
ANTI-DARWINISTS, iii. 200; iv. 266
ANTIGONUS, Saccho, v. 185
ANTILEGOMENA, v. 160
ANTILLES, the seven, iii. 47
ANTIMONY, ii. 274
ANTINOMY, ii. 339
ANTIOCH, v. 136, 171
  Bishop of, v. 173
  Council of, v. 156
ANTIPHRASIS, metaphysical, i. 83
ANTIPODES, America at the, iii. 21;
    v. 286
  Lands of the, iii. 426
  Pātāla or, iii. 188, 401, 405, 443; iv. 200
ANTIQUARIANS, iv. 135
ANTIQUITIES, Gnostic, iv. 135
ANTITYPES of Prometheus, iii. 418
ANTONIUS, quoted, v. 351
ANU, Atom, the primordial, i. 204
  Babylonian God, a, iii. 147
  Bel and, iii. 152
  Brahmā and, ii. 266, 290
  Deity, the concealed, ii. 71
  Messengers of the God, iii. 72
  Nature became, ii. 246
  Noah and, iii. 152
ANUBIS, God, v. 246
  Horus and, iii. 384; v. 247
  Science and, v. 239
  Scroll, holding a, ii. 127
  Temples of, v. 295
ANUBIS-SYRIUS of the Egyptians, iv. 49
ANUGRAHA the Eighth Creation, ii. 167, 175
ANŪNAKĪ, or Angels of Earth, iii. 250
ANUPĀDAKA, Brahman, one with, i. 131
  Circle called, i. 154
  Essence, born of the Divine, i. 169
  Hierarchy of, i. 123
  Kāla Chakra explains the, i. 123
  Parentless, is, i. 123, 169; ii. 295; v. 202, 291,
    476
  Soul-endowed man, in a latent state, i. 123
  Space, the eternal, i. 77
  Tattva, v. 476
  Wheel, was the Great, i. 119

ANUVATSARA, v. 339, 340
AOAI, one of Poseidon's Ministers, iv. 149
AOUR, Od and Ob, i. 142
APĀM-NAPĀT or Fohat, iii. 399
APĀNA, Breath or, iv. 137
 Inspirational breath or, i. 157
 Mind opened in state of, i. 157
 Offering, the, a portion of the, iv. 137
 Prāna and the, i. 158; iv. 137
 Udāna, subject to, iv. 139
APAP (See Apophis), Akar slain by, iii. 217
 Serpent of Evil, iv. 159
 Serpent, the, ii. 399
APARINĀNIM, ii. 306
ĀPAS, v. 475, 476, 479, 486
APE, Aboriginal tribes, and some, iv. 256
 Ancestor of real, i. 241; iii. 96, 195, 441;
  iv. 206
 Anthropoid, iii. 200; iv. 245
 Anthropology and, ii. 35
 Brains of man and, iv. 231
 Catarrhine, iv. 235
 -Creature, Primitive man an, iv. 231
 Darwin and the, i. 236
 Degenerated man, a, iv. 285
 Descendant of man, a, iv. 289
 Descended from, man not, i. 241
 Descent of man, and, iv. 237
 Deva, Third Race more, than, i. 240
 Dog-headed, ii. 103
 Evolution of the, iii. 264; iv. 249
 Evolutionist on the, iv. 244
 Family, the, iii. 289
 India, sacred in, i. 241
 Link between man and, no, iii. 265
 Lowest human race and highest, iv. 247
 Man and, i. 237, 240, 241; iii. 96, 191, 195,
  265, 289, 441; iv. 206, 235, 237, 247, 249,
  252, 257, 259, 267, 285, 297
 Mental barrier between, and man, iv. 235
 Pithecoid, iii. 347
 Resemblance between, and man, iv. 259
 Structure of, and man, iv. 252
 Tailless, the, iv. 225
 Third Round man, like, i. 232, 240
APE-ANCESTOR theory, iii. 191, 193, 328;
 iv. 232, 250, 258, 355
APE-LIKE, Cave-dwellers, iv. 256
 Forms of men, i. 232; iii. 67, 192; iv. 258
 Jaws of Palaeolithic men, iv. 256
 Mammal of an, organization, iv. 216
 Man may have been, i. 238
 Men, i. 241; iii. 264
 Theory of Vogt and Darwin, iv. 235
 Third Round man, i. 232; iii. 67
APE-MAN, iii. 199, 317; iv. 239, 298
APE-MEN, the dumb, iv. 250
APES, Age of the, iii. 264
 Ancestors of the, iv. 237, 238
 Angels and, iv. 314
 Anthropoid and other, i. 234, 236; iii. 191,
  198, 287, 374; iv. 247, 250, 252
 Blurred copies of men, iii. 264
 Evolution of, iii. 263; iv. 250
 Extinction of, iii. 265
 Fifth Round will be men, in, iii. 264
 Fossil, iv. 260

 Lower, iv. 258
 Mammalian, iii. 206
 Men and, i. 234, 238; iii. 172, 174, 265, 315,
  327; iv. 297
 Mesozoic times, in, iv. 246
 Miocene period, of the, iv. 259
 Monads of the, i. 236
 Origin of, iii. 206
 Pedigree of the, iv. 258
 Platyrrhine, the, iii. 178
 Race of, a new, iv. 285
 Rudimentary men, raised into, i. 238
 Transformation of the, iii. 264
 Types up to the, iii. 195
APE-STOCK, iv. 248
APE-THEORY, Lucae on the, iv. 216
 Science and the, iv. 257
APHARIDES, iii. 131
APHELION, ii. 397
APHIDES or plant-lice, iii. 142
APHORISM, Kabalistic, i. 291
 Zoroaster, of, iii. 440
APHRODITE, v. 212, 438
APIS, Bull of, sacred, i. 192
 Egyptians, of the, iii. 416
 Pacis, ii. 383
APOGEE, Moon in, ii. 390
 Motions of the, ii. 385
APOLLO, Aesculapius, ii. 68; iii. 115
 Antichrist, v. 312
 Aspects of, iv. 340
 Banquet, referred to in the, iii. 142
 Birth of, iv. 339
 Birthplace of, iv. 343
 Bi-sexual, originally, i. 139
 Creative powers, assumes, iv. 340
 Cyclops, and, iv. 339
 Diana, and, iv. 340
 God of Four Races, the, iv. 343
 God of Light, iii. 20
 God of the Seers, iv. 339
 Greek, the, iii. 380, 381
 Helios, or, iii. 382
 Heptachord of, i. 220
 Hermaphrodite, ii. 112
 Hyperborean, iii. 20; iv. 338
 Karneios, a title of, iii. 55
 Krishna and, etc., v. 96, 288
 Latona, and, ii. 81
 Lyre, of, v. 276
 Mason after the manner of, a, iv. 363
 Plato on, iii. 142
 Python and, iii. 378; v. 289
 Reign of, v. 312
 Root Race, and, Third, iii. 184
 Seers, God of the, iv. 339, 340
 Septenary sacred to, iv. 174
 Sun, or the, iii. 130
 Sun-God, the, iii. 215, 382
 Swans and, ii. 73
 Temples of, v. 295
 Torch of, ii. 52
 Traditions of, iii. 24
 Trinity, and the Christian, ii. 111
 Troy, at, iii. 280
APOLLODORUS, Dioskouroi of, iii. 131
 Fourth Race and, iv. 340

APOLLODORUS (*Contd.*)
  Fragments left by, iii. 63
  Golden Apples, on the, iv. 339
  Quoted, iv. 88
APOLLONIUS, Buddhist Nāgas, met, iii. 215
  Rhodius, iii. 342, 361
APOLLONIUS OF TYANA, ii. 169; v. 61, 142
    143, 144, 145, 146, 147, 148, 149, 152, 153,
  Adept, an, v. 124, 305
  Buddha, and, v. 377
  Christ compared, and, v. 556
  Healer, a, v. 263
  Nirmanakaya, a, v. 76
  Personality of, v. 151
  Prevision of, v. 298
  Tortures of, v. 282
APOLLO-PYTHON, iii. 213
APOLLYON, iii. 232
APOPHIS (See Apap), Dragon, the, ii. 179;
    iii. 384; v. 489, 491, 499, 502
  Serpent of Evil, the, iv. 159
  Typhon the same as, iii. 379
APOSTATE, Julian called, v. 218
APOSTATES to the Vedas, Daityas are, ii. 140
APOSTLE, Gentiles of, v. 130, 138, 215, 327
  Initiate, God of the, i. 75
  Judas the, iii. 388
  Philip the, iv. 136
  Rishi and, agree, i. 75
APOSTLES, Cherubs of the, iii. 123
  Evangelists and, v. 100, 101
  Jesus, of, v. 69, 82, 83, 84, 124, 139
  Holy Ghost descends on the, i. 151
  Miracles, of, v. 450
  Numbers of, v. 104
  Simon and, v. 132
  Twelve, the, ii. 115
  Western religion, of, iv. 126
  Zodiac and the, ii. 375
APPERCEPTION, Clearness of, ii. 352
  Leibnitz invented the term, i. 231
  Nascent, ii. 174
  Perception from, i. 228; ii. 354
  Sensitive plants, of, ii. 174
  Spiritual, v. 549
APPERCEPTIVE BEINGS; Hierarchies of,
    ii. 354
APPLE, Adam and the, ii. 18
  Dangerous fruit, a, ii. 228
  Newton's, ii. 207
  Pippala Haoma, iii. 106
  Serpent and Tree, iii. 354
  Tree of Knowledge, from the, i. 187
APPLES, Apollodorus on the Golden, iv. 339
  Hercules and the Golden, iv. 339
APPLE-TREE of the Hesperides, i. 187
APSARASES, Kāma, the king of the, iii. 182
  Kandū and, iii. 182
  Qualities and Quantities, are, iv. 157
  Sun's attendants the, iii. 215
APSIS, iii. 330
APTERYX of Australia, iv. 251
APULEIUS, iv. 60
AQUA, iii. 122
AQUATIC, iii. 167
AQUARIUS, Degree of, ii. 386, 388
  Ganymedes or, iv. 353, 354

Sphere of Reuben in, ii. 377
  Zodiac, eleventh sign of the, iii. 352
AQUEDUCTS, Cement of the ancient, iii. **428**
AQUEOUS element, the, iii. 358
AQUILA, v. 165
AQUINAS, Thomas, ii. 306
AQUITAINE, Bone caves of, iv. 313
ARAB figures, ii. 76
  Seth, belief about, iii. 365
  Thebith, the, ii. 388
ARABIA, Ad in ancient, Sons of, iii. 54
  Arabs in, iii. 205
  Arva-st'hān or, iii. 404
  Commerce of, iv. 263
  Egyptians passed from, iv. 316
  Hierophants of, v. 74
  Sinai in, Mount, iii. 86
  Sons of Ad in, iii. 54
  Winged serpents from, ii. 77
ARABIAN, Caesar Philippus, the, ii. 23
  Historian, Masoudi the, iv. 20
  Job, the, ii. 374
  Legend, the, iii. 153
  Nomadic tribes, the, ii. 373
  Prophet, the, iv. 21
  Zodiac, ii. 273
ARABIANS, Fanes of the, iv. 175
  Primal cause of later, ii. 343
ARABIC, Chaldaean works in, i. 329
  Cifron, the, ii. 76
  Figures, ii. 22; iv. 124
  Language, v. 197
  Numerical System, v. 342
  Records in, iii. 428
ARABS, Allah of the, iv. 173
  Āryans, the, are later, iii. 205
  Astronomy among, ii. 384, 385
  Descent of, iii. 205
  Divisions of year, iv. 192
  Numeration of, v. 342
  Purānas, spoken of in the, iii. 405
  Upper Egypt, of, v. 180
ARACHNIDA, iii. 259
ARAEA or red earth, iii. 199
ARAGO, ii. 254
  Quoted v. 225, 330
ARAMEAN, iii. 54; v. 165
ARAMAIC, iv. 169; v. 99
ARANĪ, Arani and, v. 93
  Mistress of the Race, iv. 96
  Vase of Election, the, iv. 97
ARANI, Aranī, and, iv. 93
  Pramantha and, iii. 109
  Svastika identified with, iii. 109
ARARAT, Biblical narrative, of, iii. 153
  Deity descending on, ii. 162
  Mount of descent, or, iv. 169
  Noah and, iv. 169
ARASA-MARAM or Banyan tree, iii. 219
ARATH derivation of Ararat, iv. 169
ARAUCARIA, iii. 259
ARBA, Abraham descended from, ii. 51
ARBO-AL or Mystic Four, ii. 51, 166
ARC, Ascending, the, i. 278, 295; iii. 187, 253,
    301
  Descending, the, i. 295; iii. 187, 301
  Opposite, of the cycle, iii. 413

ARC (Contd.)
  Oviform curve, an, of, iv. 117
  Physical, the, iv. 196
  Satan's name and the, iii. 44
  Spiritual, the, i. 295; iv. 196
ARCA, Arg or, iv. 28
ARCADIAN, v. 61, 238
ARCANA, Being, the, of, ii. 199, 316
  Knowledge, of, iv. 68
  Nature's unravelling, ii. 337
  Rabbi Schimeon revealed the, iv. 197
  Sanctuaries, the, of the, iv. 365
  Veil, behind the, iii. 335
ARCANE, Arche, Arke, iv. 31
  Deity is an, fire, i. 70
  Doctrines, i. 61
  Teachings, ii. 128
ARCANUM, Hermes, the, of, iii. 236
  Magic, i. 299; iv. 127
  Phallicized, has been, iii. 236
  Secret, a most, iii. 283
  Sôd explained as, iii. 216
ARCA, Archagetas born from the, iv. 31
ARCHÆOLOGICAL discoveries, iii. 436;
  iv. 356
  Evidences of former continents, iv. 356
ARCHAEOLOGIST, Civilizations, and relics of
  ancient, iv. 291
  Demands of the, iv. 21
  Ideographic productions and the, iii. 436
  King, the, iv. 175
  Secret cycle and, v. 341
ARCHAEOLOGISTS, v. 47
  American, iii. 421
  Antiquity, dwarf, ii. 400
  Babylonian civilization, and, iv. 261
  Cheta Cave, and the, i. 44
  Sabeanism rendered by, i. 77
ARCHAEOLOGY, Discoveries of, iii. 336, 428;
  v. 93, 161, 257
  Fossil man, and, iii. 279
  Horus, on, iii. 384
ARCHAEOPTERYX, the, iii. 190
ARCHÆUS, Anch or, iv. 205
  Father-Æther, is, i. 123
  Great the, i. 299
  Greek, the, ii. 52
  Human body, the, in the, ii. 256
  Life-principle, the, and the, iv. 224
  Liquor vitæ or, ii. 256
  Magnetic nature, the, is of a, ii. 262
  Nervous ether identical with the, ii. 256, 262
  Paracelsus and the, i. 123
  Self-moving, ii. 395
ARCHAGETAS, Æsculapius called, iv. 31
ARCHAI of Plato, v. 215
ARCHAIC, Cosmogony, v. 107
  Esoteric System, v. 197
  Inscriptions, v. 257
  Initiations, v. 340
  Mysteries, v. 271, 274
  Science, v. 45, 93
  Telephone, v. 240
  Wisdom, v. 215, 331
ARCHANGEL, Agathodaemon, the, iii. 71
  Anthropomorphous, the, iii. 376
  Buddhi and, i. 82

Christ, the, v. 277
Churches, the, of the, ii. 363
Gabriel, the, ii. 94; iii. 248; iv. 40; v. 117
Greek churches, of the, ii. 363
Highest, the, i. 320
Latin churches, of the, ii. 363
Lux or Lucifer, the, first, called, v. 309,
  310, 312
Michael the, ii. 178, 336; iii. 102, 232, 248,
  383; iv. 47
Mineral to, i. 82
Moon, named from, ii. 109
Plant to, i. 82
Raphael the, ii. 347
Satan an, ii. 132; iii. 71
Secret, whose name was, ii. 155
Virgin Mary and the, ii. 94, 99
ARCHANGELS, Amshaspends are, ii. 155
  Archontes and, i. 281
  Christian theology, of, i. 81, 152, 248; ii. 328
  Church, of, iii. 245
  Conqueror of, iii. 73
  Create, refusing to, iii. 248
  Deities, the highest, i. 176
  Dhyan Chohans and, v. 214
  Elements standing for, ii. 53
  Fall of the, iii. 73
  Hierarchy of, i. 114
  Host of, iii. 381
  Mercury ruled by, ii. 153
  Moon, one of, named from the, ii. 109
  Nabatheans believed in seven, iv. 22
  Philo, of, v. 215
  Planetary, v. 325
  Prototypes of the, iv. 155
  Rebellion of the, iii. 73
  Roman Church, of the, i. 281
  Science and, ii. 336
  Seven, the, ii. 156; v. 122
  Spirits of the Face, the, iii. 123
  Theology, of, i. 81; iii. 250; iv. 44
ARCHE, Arca or, iv. 31
  Ark, Rek or, iv. 117
  Hebrew Rasit and the, iv. 28
ARCHEBIOSIS or Life-origination, ii. 174, 266;
  iii. 172
ARCHETYPAL Forms upon which Logoi
  build, ii. 95
  Ideas of the Neeo-Platonists, i. 324
  Man, the, ii. 107; v. 233
  Man, the Protologos or, ii. 70
  Man, symbols of the, ii. 161
  Universe, the, i. 207
  World, the, i. 161, 230 249, 261; iii. 15; v. 73
ARCHETYPE, Goethe, the, of, iv. 306
  Humanity, the, of, iv. 88
  Males, of the first, iii. 17
  Man, of, v. 78
ARCHETYPES, World of the, iii. 48
ARCH-FORGERS, Brāhamans as, iii. 440
ARCHI, name of Adhivāhīkas, i. 190
ARCHIMEDES, i. 176
ARCHIS are pure souls, the, i. 190
ARCHISATRAP of the Sacred Militia, iv. 47;
  v. 325
ARCHISTRATEGUS, iv. 66; v. 325
ARCHITECT, Brahmā, the, ii. 59

ARCHITECT (*Contd.*)
Builder, the, not, ii. 143
Cause of the, ii. 144
Deity or, superior, iii. 55
Demiurge not yet the, ii. 95
Hammer of the Great, i. 248
Invisible, v. 306
Logos, an, the, i. 322
Planetary Chain, of our, i. 186
Universe, great, of the, ii. 338; iii. 110
World, of the, ii. 59, 157, 160; iv. 129
ARCHITECTS, Creators or, i. 187
Demiurge and the, the, ii. 60
Dhyān Chohans the, i. 81
Divine Will of the, ii. 303
Globe, of the, i. 70
Group of, i. 279
Intelligent, ii. 357
Modern, i. 257
Mountain ranges, of the, iii. 159
Planets called the, i. 163
Priests and, iii. 379
Watchers or the, i. 310
Will of the, divine, ii. 303
World, of the, i. 81; iv. 85
Zodiac, of the, ii. 382
ARCHITECTURE, Books on, ancient, i. 256
China, of, iii. 312
Ephemeral, iii. 312
Geometry and, v. 420
Greeks, and, v. 41
Hindus, of the, iii. 229
Invention, of, iii. 363
Lemuro-Atlanteans, of the, iii. 317
Mars the Lord of, iii. 391
Vitruvius on, i. 256
ARCHONS, Christian belief in, ii. 328; v. 130
Darkness, of, v. 223
Hosts of the, or powers, i. 246
ARCHONTES, Air of, v. 215
Archangels, i. 281; v. 315
Cosmocratores and, v. 329
ARCHYTAS, Disciple of Pythagoras, v. 524
ARCH-PROPHETS of the Temples, iii. 368
ARCTIC circle, iii. 293, 397
Ocean, iii. 398
Pole, iii. 328
Region, iii. 329, 356
Traveller, speculations of an, iii. 398
Winter, tempests of an, ii. 332
Year, the length of the, iii. 293
ARCTURUS, making of, ii. 373
ARDAN or Jordan, ii. 107
ARDHANĀRĪ, the Hindu, iv. 102
Īshvara, the Isis of the Hindus, ii. 107
ARDIS, the top of Mount Armon, iii. 375
ARELIM, Father, v. 191
ARES, Greek, the, iii. 391
Power, the dividing, i. 326
ARETIA or Titaea Magna, iii. 151
ARETS, Earth means, iii. 151; iv. 35
AREUS, Mars was named, iii. 391
ARG or Arca, iv. 28
Arka or, iii. 414
ARGEAK, the giant, iii. 395
ARGEN slain by Tahmurath, iii. 396
ARGHA, Ark or, iii. 150, 153; iv. 29, 35

Crescent form of the, iv. 30
Greeks, of the, iv. 30
Hindus, the, of the, iv. 29, 41
Moon or, iii. 150, 153, 414; iv. 35
Mysteries, the, of the, iv. 414; iv. 28
Naviformed, iii. 414
Seed of Life, the, and the, ii. 75; iii. 72
Ship or, v. 163
Vehicle, an, or, iii. 292
ARGHYA or libation cup, iii. 414
ARGHYANĀTH, title of the Mahā Chohan, iii. 414
ARGHYAVARSHA, Argos is, iii. 414, 416
ARG-IANS, dialect of the, iii. 414; iv. 31
ARGIANS, Io means the Moon among the, iv. 31
ARGOLIANS, Phoroneus father of, iv. 90
ARGOLIS, Phoroneus in, iv. 88
ARGONAUTS, Expedition of, ii. 378
Onamacritus attributed to, v. 293
Stone left at Cyzicum, by, iii. 345
ARGOS, Arghyavarsha is, iii. 416
Castor at, iii. 131
Kingly race at, iii. 414, 416
Labours of Hercules at, v. 259
ARGUS, Death of, iii. 366
Hermes and, iii. 366
Mercury the Earth's, iii. 41
ARGYLE, quoted, iii. 372
ARHAT, Body of an, i. 73
Conception of an, i. 294
Esoteric School, i. 212
Knowledge, absolute, of an, i. 120
Para-nirvāna attained by the, i. 120
Prasanga School and, v. 402
Siddhis of the, i. 160
Third eye of the, iii. 296
ARHATS, Ancestors of the, iii. 179, 180
Bas-pa, and, v. 379
Buddha, of, i. 44; v. 145, 349, 368, 379, 400, 405, 411
Buddhist, i. 51; iii. 339; v. 395, 399
Cosmogony of, iv. 16
Esotericism of, iv. 207
Exodus of, i. 51
Fire-Mist, of, i. 255
Forefathers of present, iii. 180
Hatha Yoga discountenanced by, i. 158
Heart of the Law and, v. 407
Initiation of the, i. 44
India, no more in, v. 395
Lohans or, v. 393, 394
Magic Powers of, v. 27
Nirvana, in, v. 401
Persecution of, v. 395
Preservation of the great, iii. 185
Proselytism by, i. 44
Sages or, iii. 174
Seven seen by the, i. 162
Sons of Wisdom become, iii. 168
Truths, of the four, ii. 125
ARHATSHIP, v. 349, 396
ladder of, i. 255
ARIA or Iran, iii. 205
ARIADNE, the thread of, iii. 77, 161
ARIES, Beginning of, v. 344
Degree of, iii. 434
Mars and, iii. 391

ARIES (*Contd.*)
  Vernal equinox, and the, iv. 263
  Volney on, ii. 384
ARIMASPES, Atlanteans, the, were not, iv. 343
  One-eyed, the, were, iv. 338
ARIMASPI, Herodotus, the, of, iii. 414
ARIMASPIAN Host, iii. 414
ARION progeny of Poseidon and Ceres, iii. 398
ARIOSTO, v. 73
ARISTARCHUS and revolution of earth, i. 176
ARISTÆAS or ARISTEAS, v. 61, 183
ARITOBULUS forger, ii. 374; v. 302
ARISTOPHANES, quoted, ii. 75; iii. 105, 142, 184; v. 255, 266
ARISTOPHYLI, Ptolemy on the, iii. 205
ARISTOTELEAN, Method, the inductive, or, i. 208
ARISTOTLE, Few Adepts in the days of, v. 276
  Bacon and, ii. 203
  Creation, on direct, iii. 166
  Date of, ii. 74
  Deity, on the Triple, i. 128
  Elements of, ii. 182
  Ethics, v. 302
  Geometry, and, ii. 340
  Greek, the, i. 270
  History begins with, v. 275
  Inductive method of, iv. 144
  Initiate, not an, v. 464
  Method of, iv. 208
  Moden Science and, i. 322; iii. 160
  Numbers, on, ii. 77
  Plato, etc., and, i. 182; v. 53, 60
  Psychology of, iii. 287
  Pupil of, swept away religion, v. 294
  Rulers, on the, ii. 216
  Space, on, ii. 50
  Sphericity of the Earth taught by, i. 176
  Substantial forms of, ii. 356
  Teaching of, v. 53, 78, 445
  Thales and, ii. 59
  Weissmann and, i. 270
  Zodiac and, v. 241
ARISTOTLE-BACONIAN method, iii. 160
ARITHMOMANCY, Science of, iv. 147
ARIUS, doctrines of, v. 156
ARJUNA, Krishna, on, ii. 123
  Pātāla, descended to, iii. 218
  Ulūpī, marries, iv. 200
ARJUNA MISHRA, quoted, i. 158, 159; iv. 137, 139, 209, 210
ARK, Allegory of the, iii. 292
  Ararat, the, on, iv. 169
  Argha or, iii. 150; iv. 28
  Building of the, iv. 103
  Covenant, the, of the, iii. 52; iv. 27, 28, 31, 32, 41, 87; v. 186
  David's dance before the, ii. 49; iv. 28
  Deucalion, the, of, iii. 272
  Face of the Waters, on, iii. 153
  Female Principle, or, iv. 283
  Hindus, of the, iv. 29
  Humanity saved in an, iv. 283
  Isis-Osiris and the, iii. 151
  Istar shut in the, iii. 153
  Life survives in the, iv. 29
  Manu, the, of, iii. 147

  Measurements of, ii. 28; iv. 32, 113
  Moon or, iii. 150
  Moses and, of rushes, ii. 32
  Noah's, ii. 75; iii. 48, 79, 398; iv. 35, 113, 181; v. 197
  Noëtic, iii. 359
  Osiris enters, iii. 150
  Parkhurst on, iii. 313
  Salvation, the, of, iii. 313
  Seed saved in an, iii. 308
  Ship or, iv. 343
  Solar Boat or, iii. 150
  Symbolism of, iii. 292
  Table of Stone in, iv. 41
  Typhon of the, iv. 117
  Vaivasvata Manu and, iii. 79; iv. 181
  Vara, or, iii. 292
  Womb of Nature, or, ii. 162
  Worship in the, iv. 37
  Yima, of, iv. 181
ARKA, Arche or, iv. 31
  Arg or, the female generative power, iii. 414
ARKITE Symbols, iii. 150, 151
  Titans, and, iii. 150, 343
ARK-TIE or cross of the North, iv. 117
ARLIS, destruction of, v. 595
ARMAITA SPENTA or Spirit of Earth, iv. 86
ARMIES, Celestial, iv. 119
  God, of, ii. 238
  Holy Ones, of the Four, i. 181
  Trees, called, iv. 64
ARMON, Ardis the top of Mount, iii. 375
  Hermon said to be Mount, iii. 407
ARMY, Ah-hi like an, i. 111
  Sons of Light, of, i. 177
  Spiritual beings, of, i. 184
  Voice, of the, i. 156, 157, 159
ARNAUD and Alkaloids, i. 305
ARNOBIUS, quoted, iii. 151, 341, v. 42
ARNOLD, Edwin, not an Initiate, v. 218
AROMA, Spiritual, of all lives, iv. 203
ARRHETOS or the Ineffable, ii. 164
ARRIAN, Alexander slandered by, iii. 416
  quoted, iii. 415
ARTEMIS, Human victims sacrificed to, ii. 111
  Luna in Heaven, was, ii. 102
  Moon connected with, i. 275
  Soteira and Apollo, ii. 112
ARTEMIS-LOCHIA, Goddess of childbirth, ii. 111
ARTES, the Egyptian Mars, iii. 151
ARTHA or comprehension, i. 120
ARTHUR, King, iii. 392, 397; iv. 323
ARTIFICER, Gods, of the, iii. 344; iv. 113
  Tubal Cain, an, iii. 389
  Vishvakarman, the, iv. 113
ART (S), Ancients, of the, iii. 428
  Architects taught the, i. 310
  Aryan, v. 41
  Atlanteans, of the, iii. 424
  Bailly on, the origin of the, iv. 311
  Beginning of the, iii. 363
  Black, v. 46
  Demi-gods taught the, iii. 225
  Enchantment, of, iv. 212
  Fourth Race of the, ii. 185; iii. 428
  Inventor of the, iv. 98

ART (S) (Contd.)
　Lemuro-Atlanteans, of the, iii. 317
　Lost, the, iii. 428
　Magic, ii. 190; v. 62, 132
　Mars the Lord of, iii. 391
　Masters in the, i. 66
　Occult, v. 62
　Origin of the, iv. 99; v. 41
　Prehistoric Ages, of the, iv. 20
　Progress in the, ii. 386
　Prometheus brought the, iii. 411, 412
　Secret, i. 61
　Sons of God taught the, i. 256; iv. 143
　Third Race, of the, iii. 200, 427
ART-SPEECH, ii. 25, 104
ARTUFAS or Initiation Caves, iii. 188
ARUNA, Jatāyu son of, iv. 141
ARŪPA, Astral body, and, iii. 103; v. 370
　Bodiless or, i. 266
　Devas, iv. 156
　Divine, the, i. 178
　Formless or, i. 160, 179, 249; ii. 357; iii. 100; v. 356
　Gods, iii. 318
　Incorporeal or, i. 247; iii. 200
　No-Form or, i. 124
　Pitris, i. 266; iii. 100, 102
　Plane, the, iii. 118; v. 515
　Pralaya not for the, world, iii. 79
　Pure, v. 401
　Rūpa and, i. 177, 180, 187
　Seven Lights of, v. 363
　Square, the Formless, i. 160
　Stanzas on, i. 152
　Ten are the, i. 161
　Triad, the, i. 261
　Worlds, the, i. 179; ii. 154, 295; v. 380
ARVĀKSROTA, Man, the, iii. 170
ARVĀKSROTAS, Brahmā's seventh creation the, ii. 165; iii. 170
　Creation of the, ii. 164; iii. 170
ĀRYABHATTA of India, i. 176; iv. 68; v. 341
ĀRYAN, Adam, the, iii. 182
　Adami an, symbol, iv. 19
　Adepts, iii. 383; iv. 63; v. 431
　Age of the, Race, iii. 23
　Agni the, God, iii. 123
　Allegory, the, iii. 91, 102; iv. 147
　Asiatic, the, i. 259
　Astronomical Records, v. 342
　Astronomy, ii. 376
　Brāhmans, v. 390
　Castes, orthodox, iii. 409
　Cataclysms will destroy the, Race, iii. 442
　Chronology, iii 82
　Civilization. i. 57; iii. 334; v. 342
　Cosmogony, ii. 57; iii. 243; iv 56
　Creation, views of iii. 65, 135; iv. 56
　Dvijas, iv. 37; v. 390
　Element,the, iii. 442
　Era, the, iii. 79
　Esotericism, i. 174, 175, 273, 274; ii. 99
　Faiths, ii. 104
　Fifth Race, the, or, i. 173; iii. 23, 205, 426, 439; iv. 102, 186
　Genius Loci of the, ii. 183
　God, the, iii. 123

Hermes, i. 328
Hierophant, iv. 39
Hindu, ii. 39, 103, 104, 376; iii. 68, 338, 369, 405; iv. 38, 177
Humanity, iii. 408
Initiates, iv. 68
Invasion, iv. 284, 310
Jehovah, prototype of, iii. 133
Language, iii. 205
Literature, the oldest, i. 50
Mātarishvan, the, iii. 412
Mathematics, v. 342
Max Müller's theory, iv. 323
Music, Hindu, v. 197
Mystics, iii. 102
Mysteries, v. 165, 269
Mythology, iii. 138
Myths, iv. 147; v. 185
Nations, iii. 318
Occultists, iii. 162
Origin of the, Race, iv. 268
People, the, iv. 19
Period, the, iii. 431
Philosophers, the, i. 121; iii. 166
Philosophy, ii. 103; iii. 77, 369
Psychology, the old, i. 273
Qubbalah, Sources of the, ii. 91
Race, the, i. 52, 173, 175; ii. 39; iii. 23, 114, 130, 152, 173, 205, 252, 351, 394, 426, 431, 439, 442, 443; iv. 16, 102, 186, 268, 312, 338
Religion, i. 52, 58; ii. 98
Rishis, ii. 286
Root Race, iii. 21; iv. 268
Sages, v. 382
Science, and Western, ii. 348
Scriptures, iv. 184; v. 195
South Sea Islanders, and, iii. 419
Stock, iv. 312
Supreme All of the, i. 327
Symbolism, iv. 37
Symbologists, iv. 121
Symbology, ii. 97; v. 195
Symbols, ii. 99; iv. 19, 117
Systems, ii. 162; iii. 380
Theo-anthropographies, iii. 137
Theogony, iii. 69; iv. 16
Thought and Esotericism, i. 175
Traditions, and Teachings, iii. 130; v. 197
Vedic Race, the, iii. 173
Wisdom, iv. 16; v. 306
ĀRYAN-ASIATICS, iii. 431
ĀRYAN-HINDŪS, iii. 328
ĀRYANISM in the Rig Veda, iii. 377
ĀRYANISTS, Ignorance of, ii. 114
　Max Müller, and, iii. 423
ĀRYANS, Ādam descends from the yellow, iii. 423
　Ādi unknown Deity of the, i. 43
　Allegories of the, iii. 382
　Archaic, iii. 47
　Astronomy of the, ii. 391
　Atlanteans and, iii. 393; iv. 345; v. 66
　Christian week and, v. 333
　Circle a symbol of the, iv. 107
　Cosmogony of the, iii. 36
　Cosmographies of the, iv. 175

ĀRYANS (*Contd.*)
Decimal notation, the, and, ii. 76
Deity of the, i. 43; iv. 108
Early, the, i. 43, 173; iii. 108, 370; iv. 179
Egyptians and the, iv. 203
Esoteric Doctrine of the, iii. 47; iv. 179
Ether, the, on, ii. 208
Europeans the latest, ii. 143
Fifth Race, the, i. 173; v. 268
Forces believed in intelligent, ii. 143
Hindu, iv. 175
Holy of Holies and the, iv. 37
Indian, v. 107, 109
Jews and, v. 87
Knowledge of the ancient, ii. 246
Mahābhāratan, v. 121
Max Müller on the, iii. 423
Mêlée of Atlanteans and, iv. 345
Mongols and, iv. 178
Mystery-God of, v. 286
Mythology of the, ii. 16; iv. 66
Negroes and, iv. 178
Noah of the, iii. 307
Peris and, iii. 392
Primitive, v. 104, 269
Race, the fifth, i. 173; iv. 329
Religion of the, ii. 28
Science of computation and, ii. 348; v. 342
Secret Doctrine of the, iii. 242; v. 91, 180
Semites and, ii. 381; iii. 150, 268; iv. 108
Seven among the, number, iii. 47, 150
Supreme All of the, i. 327
Svastika and the early, iii. 108
Symbols of the, i. 174, ii. 28; iv. 107
Teachings of old, i. 270
Tenets of, v. 268
Trojans were, iii. 110
Vaidic, iv. 66; v. 217
Veddhas, said to be, iii. 201
Western, ii. 369
Zoroastrian, v. 315
ĀRYA SAMĀJ, Figures of the, school, iii. 78
Founder of, iii. 79
ĀRYAS, Agnis of ancient, iii. 95
Prophecy concerning the, ii. 92
ĀRYĀSANGA, Adept, a pre-Christian, i. 121;
v. 369, 400, 412, 489
Adept of the, school, an, i. 213
Ritual of; v. 168
School, the, i. 119, 136, 213
Treatises of, i. 43
Yogāchārya school of, i. 119; v. 399, 400, 412
ĀRYĀVARTA, Asuramaya an astronomer in,
iii. 61
Astronomy in, iii. 61
Gnosis in, v. 305
India is, iii. 416
Myth of Prometheus came from, iv. 93
Primeval Occultism of, iv. 135
Prometheus, produced the myth of, iv. 93
Sacred land of, iv. 155
ĀRYO-ATLANTEANS, iii. 431
ARZAHI or west, iv. 328
ASAM or Easam, an Irish word, iii. 123
ASARADEL, iii. 375
ASAT, Mūlaprakriti or, iv. 168
Sat and, iv. 16

ASATHOR, iii. 385
AS-BURJ (see also Ashburj and Az-burj)
Mountain of, iii. 401, 405
Teneriffe may be, iii. 406
ASCETIC, Ceremonies, iv. 211
Daityas, ii. 140
Divine Soul in, iv. 185
Dragon, a, iii. 364
Goal of, iv. 138
Grand, the, iii. 171
Great, the, iv. 184
John the Baptist an, iv. 136
Kārtikeya an, iv. 190
Kings led an, life, iv. 70
Life, the, iv. 70
Mahā Yogī the great, iv. 184
Moses an, iv. 33
Nārada the strife-making, iii. 178
Penances, ii. 140
Shiva an, iii. 283; iv. 118
Third Eye of the, iv. 186
Yogi and, the grand, iii. 171
ASCETICISM, Chaste, incarnates, iii. 283
Opponent of, an, iv. 185
ASCETICS, Allegory relating to, iii. 88
Āryan Race, of the, iv. 186
Buddhist, i. 226
Celestial, iv. 142
Chinese, i. 226
Circle of, enchanted, i. 45
Egyptian, i. 62
Gods strive with the, iii. 181
Initiated, iii. 277
Japanese, i. 226
Race of fruitless, iii. 277
Sons of Brahma as, iii. 91
Spinal Column and, v. 520
Sword of Knowledge of the, ii. 260
Third age, of the, iii. 319
Tibet, of, v. 38
ASCHMOGH a huge serpent, iii. 209
ASCIDIANS and Medusae, iii. 128
ASCLEPIADES, iii. 341; v. 54
ASCLEPIAS Acida or soma plant, iv. 67
ASCLEPIOS or Asklepios (See Æsculapius)
Apollo and, iii. 215
Definitions of, i. 329, 335
Demi-god, a, iii. 363
Indian, the, i. 328
King and, the, ii. 289
Maitreya the Indian, i. 328
Quoted, i. 327
Supernal Gods of, ii. 325
ASCLEPIUS, Apollo, son of, iv. 339
ASENATH, Daughter of Petephre, v. 266
ASES, Creative powers, were, ii. 145
Holy gods, were, iii. 107
Norse Legends, iii. 105
Scandinavia, of, iii. 105
War of the, iii. 385
A-SEXUAL, Adam, the, iii. 128
Humanity originally, iii. 141
Multiplication, iii. 141
Reproduction, iv. 228
Second race, iii. 125
Sexless, from the, iii. 124
ASGARD, Gods, the habitat of the, iii. 105

ASHA is fire, iii. 123
ASHER, Libra the Balance in, ii. 377
ASHMOLE, Elias, v. 282
ASHOKA, Cave-temples in the time of, iii. 224
   Chandragupta and, iv. 120; v. 260
   Missionaries of, v. 271
ASHRAMS, v. 390, 400
ASHTADISHA, iv. 148
ASHTAR Vidiā, iii. 425
ASHTEROTH or Venus, iii. 153
ASH-TREE, ask or, iii. 106
   Bronze Race from the, iv. 89
   Celestial, the, iv. 89
   Hesiodic, the, iii. 106
   Third Race from the, iii. 188
   Yggdrasil, iv. 89
   Zeus and the, iii. 188
ASHVAMEDHA PARVAN, i. 157
   Sacrifice, iv. 141
ASHVATTHA-TREE, ii. 273; iii. 106
   Being, of, ii. 123
   Bodhi, the holy, of, iv. 160
   Bo-tree, or, ii. 247
   Hindu, the, iii. 106
   Life, of, ii. 123, 260; iv. 210
   Symbol of the, iv. 210
ASHVINI, v. 344
ASHVINS, Adityas and, iv. 177
   Sacrificers and, iv. 177
   Sky and Sun, twin sons of, i. 138
ASH-WOOD men made by Jupiter, iv. 341
ASHOKA, king, v. 260, 271
ASIA, America, united to, iii. 322
   Āryan emigration to, iv. 338
   Atlantis, issued after destruction of, iv. 177
   Atmosphere of Central, iii. 356
   Brāhmans in Central, iv. 135
   Civilization of Central, i. 54
   Contemporary with man, iii. 400
   Cross in Central, iv. 127
   Dhyān Chohan in, ii. 363
   Elevation of, iv. 264
   Events in, succession of, ii. 384
   Flora of, iv. 350
   Fourth race, the refuge of the, iv. 292
   Human stocks in, origin of, iv. 249
   Hercules, origin of, v. 258
   Io in, iii. 414
   Island in Central, sacred, i. 258
   Jewish Kabalists in, v. 305
   Khamism is from Western, i. 175
   Lemuria, a prolongation of, iv. 338
   Light of, v. 27
   Men of, early, iii. 328
   Mongolian of, iv. 39
   Mysteries brought from, v. 71, 276
   Nations of, Central, v. 40
   Northern, iv. 345
   Occultists in, v. 381
   Perpetual Land, the, iv. 345
   Plateaux of Central, iv. 180, 313
   Present, iii. 327
   Protector of, the, iii. 815
   Sanctuaries of Central, v. 59
   Sea in middle, iii. 224
   Sea to north of, iv. 346
   Sons of Light in Central, i. 64

Stones in, iii. 345; iv. 321
Tanais and, iv. 342
Tradition, the source of, iv. 356
Two-horned, an epithet used in, iii. 397
ASIA-MINOR, Akkadians in, iii. 207
   America coeval with, iii. 21
   Europe coeval with, iii. 21
   Initiates of, iv. 128
   Mandrake in, iii. 40
   Priests in, iii. 370
ASIAH, iv. 176; v. 299, 300
ASIAN root-stocks, the, iii. 178
ASITA the Dark, iii. 42
ASK or Ash tree, iii. 106
ASP, Crown formed of an, iii. 39
ĀSPHUJIT, Venus or, iii. 45
ASR and Aish, Osiris, iii. 123
ASSESSORS, Agrasandhāni, the, i. 166
ASSOCIATION, laws of, i. 116
ASSUR, Īshvara, seen in, ii. 380
ASSYRIAN (see also Syrian), Ad or Adi in, iii. 54, 55
   Adam, the, iii. 18, 110
   Armies called trees, iv. 64
   Arts, iv. 20
   Astronomy, ii. 376
   Bulls, the, iii. 123
   Carvings, v. 436
   Chaos, emblems of, iii. 385
   Chronology, iv. 261
   Civilization, iii. 334
   Cuneiform inscriptions, iii. 17
   Cylinders, iii. 229
   Demon, an, iii. 344
   Egypt under, dominion, ii. 23
   Emblems of Chaos, iii. 385
   Exoteric mob, v. 438
   Exoteric teaching, v. 437
   Inscriptions, iii. 17
   Knowledge of the Planets, v. 437
   Lumazi, seven of, v. 202
   Nebo, adoration of, iv. 23
   Priest, the, iii. 379
   Records, ii. 126
   Relics, and, pre-Mosaic, v. 94
   Sciences, iv. 20
   Shemite or, iii. 207
   Seven in the, tiles, number, iii. 47
   Svastika an, symbol, iv. 158
   Tablets, iii. 207, 352
   Tiles, iii. 47, 72, 426, 436; iv. 45; v. 193, 199
   Turanian and, iii. 207
ASSYRIOLOGISTS, v. 436
   Anu and the, iii. 73
   Chronology of the, iv. 261
   Dragon, on the, iii. 353
   Nipur, and the northern, iii. 148
   Perplexity of, iii. 112
   Seven, and the number, iii. 17
ASTANPHAEUS, primordial power, v. 201
ASTAPHÆUS, a Stellar Spirit, ii. 167
ASTAPHAI, Genius of Mercury, ii. 301; iv. 108
ASTARTE, Hiram's temple to, iv. 111
   Lunar God, a, ii. 111
   Phœnician prayer to, ii. 189
   Temple to, iv. 111
   Worship of, iv. 28

ASTERIA, Delos or, iv. 340, 342
  Golden star island of, iii. 382
ASTERISM(S) iv. 157; v. 344
  Cyclical progress of, iii. 255
  Lunar, iv. 120
ASTERIUS, tomb of, iii. 280
ASTEROIDS, the Earth's influence on, iv. 270
ASTEROPE, one of the Pleiades, iv. 337
ASTER'T the Syrian Goddess, iii. 54, 55
ASTORETH, Jews worshipped, iv. 30
  Moon or, ii. 112, 113
  Symbol of Nature, an impersonal, iv. 30
ASTRA, Sanskrit, in, iv. 201
  Destructive engines, v. 121
  Vidyā the highest magical knowledge, ii. 286; iii. 425
ASTRÆA, Golden Age, renews the, iv. 353
  Justice, goddess of, iv. 353
  Venus-Lucifer or, iv. 354
  Virgin, v. 337
ASTRAKHĀN on the Caspian Sea, iii. 414
ASTRAL, iii. 253; v. 208, 524, 525
  Action comes from the North, iii. 399
  Barhishad, Doubles of the, iii. 98
  Ego of Gautama, v. 365
  Earth, iii. 253
  Envelope, the, i. 280; iv. 282
  Evolution, i. 228; iii. 165, 259; iv. 219, 304
  Figures of the First Race, iii. 304
  Fire, i. 148; iii. 247
  Gods, sons of Ildabaoth, ii. 167
  Humanity, First or, iii. 121
  Ideation, iv. 168
  Influences i. 262
  Inner Man, ii. 363
  Kingdom, evolution of the, iii. 78
  Life, Races revert to the, iii. 250, 265
  Models, bodies inferior to their, iii. 88, 231
  Mould of physical man, iv. 296
  Phantom, Ābhūtarajasas without an, iii. 98
  Phenomena, Occult, iv. 198
  Photographs, i. 83
  Plane, the, i. 181, 183, 266; ii. 369; iii. 99; iv. 258; v. 456, 516, 524, 526, 527, 531
  Powers, Genii classed below, i. 334
  Progenitors of the Mammalia, iv. 254
  Prototypes, i. 228, 325; iii. 78, 193, 259, 297; iv. 196, 306
  Races, iii. 126, 165, 281
  Radiation, iv. 132
  Realms, Primaries in, ii. 202
  Records, Lipika and the, i. 166; v. 546
  Reflects, i. 288
  Regions, i. 228
  Relics, iv. 298
  Revolution, v. 316
  Root-types, iv. 219
  Rulers of the Spheres, ii. 310
  Selves, the human, iii. 119
  Seven Divisions of, v. 522
  Shadows, i. 274, 278; iii. 57, 113, 117, 119, 130, 171, 193
  Shells or Form, iii. 120
  Sons of Yoga, iii. 126, 203
  Soul, the, i. 288; iii. 292; v. 387
  Spheres, ii. 150, 301
  Spirit, the, i. 245

Statues, iii. 103
  Tablets, iii. 204
  Types, iv. 230
  Universe, super, v. 220
  Waves, Dragon slain in the, iii. 64
  World, the, i. 128; iii. 45; v. 418
Bodies, Linga Sharīra, v. 491
  Mankind, the, of, ii. 349
  Moon, symbol of, v. 535
  Perceptive life, and, v. 530
  Progenitors, of the, iii. 121, 146
  Shadows, iii. 95
Body, v. 244, 249, 354, 486, 518, 566
  Adept, the, of an, iv. 100; v. 545
  Animal, the, of an, iii. 201
  Atoms of the, iv. 241
  Birth of the, iii. 15
  Capacities, iii. 302
  Chhāyā or, iii. 181
  Children of Brahmā, iii. 286
  Colour of, v. 555
  Communication of Planets with the Earth, ii. 299
  Consciousness, v. 526, 527, 531
  Consolidation of the, iv. 223
  Constitution of man, iv. 288
  Creation of, iii. 17
  Creation of the seven Adams, iii. 17
  Desires, the, of, i. 304
  Development, Process of, iii. 165; iv. 253
  Double or, iii. 88; v. 565
  Elementary, or, ii. 398
  Esotericism, of, iv. 203
  Flesh covers the, iii. 130
  Image of Man or, i. 287; v. 561
  Initiate lives in his, iv. 67
  Ka or the, iv. 205
  Kosmos, the, of the, i. 221
  Linga Sharīra or, i. 212, 287; iv. 168; v. 561
  Lower, of man, v. 78
  Māyāvi or, iii. 244
  Molecular, is, v. 550
  Personal Self, the lower, or the, iii. 118; v. 78
  Physical, the, within the, iii. 156
  Progenitors, the, of the, iv. 230
  Projection of, v. 561
  Red-Violet, v. 458
  Spirit, action in, and, v. 452
  Upādhi of Life, the, i. 208
  Vital, v. 472
Double, Æneas, the, of, iv. 340
  Barhishad, of the, iii. 98
  Bhūta or, iii. 111
  Body, or, iii. 88, 208
  Divine, the, i. 235
  Fathers, of the, iii. 124
  Lunar Monads, of the, i. 232
  Nature, of, v. 456
Fluid, Athanor of Alchemists or, i. 147; iii. 194
  Ether, universal, iii. 194
  Kabalist, or Light of the, ii. 248
  Thought on the, sign of, i. 156
Form, v. 471, 472, 473
  Ethereal, within an, iii. 67, 300
  Fossil, iv. 254
  Human, i. 236; iii. 912
  Monad, the, clothing the, iii. 126

ASTRAL *form* (*Contd.*)
  Pitris, of the, i. 293
  Prototype, of, i. 325
  Shadow, or, i. 274, 278
  Shells, or, iii. 120
  Soul-less, a, iv. 287
Image, Chhāya or, iii. 110, 145
  Fatal, the, i. 290
Light, v. 120, 424, 546, 550, 551, 558, 559, 566
  Ākāsha and, i. 142, 298, 301
  Ākāshic principle not the, i. 303
  Ana, the Chaldean, i. 155
  Anima Mundi and, i. 129, 245; ii. 182; v. 382
  Ante-natal life traced in the, i. 166
  Bhagavad Gītā on the, i. 150
  Bi-sexual, the, is, i. 246
  Christian Kabalists, the, of the, i. 246
  Cosmic Soul or, iii. 122
  Creative properties of the, ii. 59
  Currents of the, iii. 84
  Definition of the, iv. 80
  Destructive properties of the, ii. 59
  Devil and, iv. 53
  Divine, of Occultism, i. 196
  Dragon, a glyph for the, i. 140
  Dual, the, is, i. 246; ii. 194
  Earth, and, v. 512
  Elemental forms in the, v. 544
  Éliphas Lévi on the, i. 299; ii. 52; iii. 408
  Entities, the, full of, ii. 45
  Entity, the, an, iv. 81
  Ether is the, ii. 39
  Forces represented by the, i. 334
  Glyph for the, i. 140
  Human body and the, ii. 250
  Lower, the, i. 247
  Kabalists, the, of the, i. 140, 246; ii. 57, 81; v. 192, 383
  Karma of Humanity, the, iv. 82
  Lotus the prototype of the, iv. 132
  Martinists, of the, iii. 408; iv. 80
  Motion of the, vibratory, ii. 62
  Nebular mist-place in the, ii. 83
  Occultism, the, of, i. 196
  Old Book on the, iii. 250
  Potency of the, dual, ii. 194
  Prakriti and the, i. 299
  Prima Materia and the, ii. 54
  Prototypes in the, i. 129, 132
  Psychic, v. 542
  Reading in the, iii. 239
  Reality obscured by the, i. 130
  Secrets of the, i. 336
  Serpent, the, called a, iii. 355
  Shadow of the, ii. 54
  Skandhas in the, v. 560
  Soul of the, is divine, ii. 141
  Synonyms of the, iv. 80
  Tablets of the, i. 165
  Terrestrial, v. 477, 521
  Universal, v. 521
  Universal Cause, the, is, the, iv. 81
  Universal Soul and, ii. 68
  Universal Soul, material aspect of, ii. 139
  Visions in the, i. 215; v. 429, 453
Man, v. 457
  Animals preceded, iii. 193

  Ego or, v. 359
  Ethereal or, iii. 159
  Physical, the, is model of, i. 235; ii. 364; iii. 88, 111
  Primeval, iv. 258
  Round began with the, this, iii. 177
  Shadow or, iii. 117
Matter, v. 566
  Clouds of, i. 220
  Cosmic Substance becomes, i. 142
  Forms of men woven of, iv. 306
ASTRAL (S), Instruments, cut, v. 561
  Living men, of, v. 453
  Semi-divine, iii. 433
ASTRO-DHYĀNIC figures, the, i. 276
ASTRO-ETHEREAL sphere of action, iv. 192
ASTROLATRY, Astrological, v. 329
  Chaldean, iv. 24, 194; v. 329, 331
  Christian, iii. 52; v. 313
  Esoteric, v. 319
  Heliolatry and, ii. 108
  Monotheism and, iii. 52
  Ogdoad in, ii. 167
  Sabaeanism, ii. 117; v. 98, 318
  Tree of, iii. 36
ASTROLOGER, Asuramaya the, iii. 62
  Brāhman, regulated connubial life, iii. 409
ASTROLOGERS, v. 331, 334, 335, 435
  Astronomers and, ii. 371
  Calculations of, ii. 367
  Chaldean, v. 333
  Christian, ii. 379; v. 437
  Correspondences of, v. 433
  Days of the week and, v. 432
  Egyptian, v. 327
  Esoteric, v. 435
  India, in, i. 275
  Kasdim and Gazzim, v. 333
  Magi, and, v. 333
  Modern, v. 433, 436
  Occultists and, ii. 371
  Pagan, v. 325
  Sun, replace Uranus by the, i. 162
  Uranus, the, and, i. 162
  Western, v. 436
ASTROLOGICAL, Babylonians, magic of, iv. 136
  Constellations, aspect of the, iii. 186
  Correspondences, v. 441
  Mediaeval Mysteries, phase of, iv. 201
  Mercury as an, planet, iii. 41
  Numbers, v. 151
  Saturday, v. 326
  Sign, Scorpio an, iii. 138
  Star, the, ii. 296
  Symbols, i. 276
  Theogony, keys to, iii. 36
ASTROLOGY, v. 219, 331, 334, 335, 442
  Accepted though derided, ii. 370
  Antiquity of, v. 331
  Astronomy and, ii. 104, 370; v. 151, 314, 318
  Bailly on, v. 330, 331
  Barkayal taught, iii. 375
  Ceremonial, v. 327, 335
  Chaldean, iv. 194; v. 327, 329, 334
  Earth in, the, iii. 42
  Exoteric, v. 330

ASTROLOGY (Contd.)
 Heavenly bodies and mankind connected by,
  iv. 68
 Indian, i. 266
 Initiation and, iv. 68
 Judicial, ii. 298
 Judiciary, ii. 371; v. 250, 330, 332, 334
 Kabalistic, v. 332, 443
 Lebas discovers root of, v. 330
 Magic and, v. 219
 Materialism and, v. 335
 Mythology and, ii. 104
 Occult, v. 333
 Occult mysteries and, iv. 68
 Physical plane, on the, iv. 202
 Primitive, v. 332
 Primitive Gods in, v. 333
 Principles of, iii. 393
 Pyramid, illustrated by the Great, ii. 29
 Real, v. 460
 Reform of, v. 438
 Ritualistic, v. 335
 Roman School, of, v. 334
 Science of, i. 166
 Sorcery, and, iv. 21
 Superstitious, v. 327
 Symbology, and, v. 325
 Systems, v. 435
 Tree of, iii. 36
 Venus in, iii. 42
 Western, v. 443
 White and black, v. 331
ASTRO-MAGIANS of India, iv. 184
ASTRONOMER(S), Beliefs of, v. 224
 Chaldean, v. 27
 Egyptian, v. 27
 French, v. 221
 Hypotheses of, v. 222
 Indian, v. 342, 343
 Learned, v. 54
 Mathematical proof of, v. 222
 Modern, v. 224
 Neptune and, v. 536
ASTRONOMIC character of diluvian tragedy,
 iii. 362
ASTRONOMICAL, Adept's calculation, iii. 405
 Allegory, ii. 17; iii. 57, 73, 381, 383, 385;
  iv. 111, 157
 Āryans, symbols of the, ii. 28
 Aspect, ii. 17; iii. 35, 197; iv. 117
 Astraea, significance of, iv. 353
 Atlantis, demonstrations of, iii. 406
 Bible, symbols in the, ii. 377
 Book of the oldest, iii. 325
 Book of Enoch, knowledge in the, iv. 104
 Calculations, ii. 390; iii. 405; iv. 102
 Cat, symbolism of the, ii. 103
 Chaldeans, notions (and observations) of the,
  iii. 18; iv. 191
 Chinese, knowledge of the, ii. 384; iv. 192
 Christian Trinity, iii. 357
 Christians, ignorance of the early, iv. 278
 Christos, meaning of, iv. 110
 Cross, iv. 102, 111, 117, 122, 127
 Cycles, iii. 60, 80, 330
 Deluge is, allegory of the, ii. 162
 Dynasties, iii. 433

 Earth in, tables, iii. 42
 Egyptians and the, cross, iv. 113, 127
 Elements, ii. 385
 Epoch, the true, ii. 387
 Esotericism, mysteries of, iv. 202
 Events, iii. 383; iv. 104
 Fact, record of an, ii. 134
 Flood, an, iii. 352
 Formula, an, iv. 130
 Generation from an, standpoint, i. 275
 Genesis, character of, iii. 151
 Glyph, aspect of double, iv. 117
 Hermes, meaning of, iv. 112
 Hindu, methods, etc., ii. 389
 Job, references in, ii. 374
 Kalpa, an, iii. 308
 Keys, iii. 36; iv. 118, 138
 Legend, iii. 213
 Limits of date, iv 263
 Lunar Mythos, aspect of the, ii. 17
 Measure of time, i. 232
 Methods, iv. 169
 Moon from the standpoint, i. 211, 274
 Mysteries, i. 274; ii. 121; iv. 118, 202
 Myth, iv. 202
 Observations for 630,000, years, ii. 376
 Occultism and, theories, iii. 81
 Periods, ii. 107; iii. 390
 Pesh-Hun and the, cycles, iii. 61
 Phenomena, iii. 83, 276
 Pi, the, i. 174
 Records, i. 205; iii. 352
 Rig Veda in its, aspect, iii. 197
 Shesha's, knowledge, iii. 60
 Sidereal bodies, ii. 70
 Societies, Royal, ii. 391
 Speculations, i. 216; ii. 316
 Stones used for, purposes, iii. 344, 345
 Struggles, i. 244, 251
 Symbolism, ii. 28, 103, 162, 377; iii. 130, 390;
  iv. 108, 118, 154, 190
 System, the, ii. 78
 Tables, ii. 385; iii. 42
 Tārakā-Maya full of, truth, iii. 57
 Tau or, cross, iv. 113
 Theories, Facts, not, iii. 81
 Trinity an, triad, iv. 110
 Truth concealed, iii. 102
 Twins an, symbol, iii. 130
 Value, an, iv. 130
 Venus in, tables, iii. 42
 Virgin, meaning of the, ii. 384
 War in Heaven, iii. 378; iv. 67
 Wars, i. 244
 Work, this not an, ii. 312
ASTRONOMY, Accurate, known 2,400 B.C.,
 ii. 376
 Allegories of, iii. 379
 Ancient, iii. 293, 332; iv. 104
 Anticipated, iii. 255
 Arabs, of, ii. 384
 Archaic, ii. 303
 Archaic, Science and, v. 98
 Āryans, of, ii. 391
 Astrolatry and, iii. 52
 Astrology and, ii. 104, 370; v. 151, 314, 318
 Atlanteans, of, iv. 331

ASTRONOMY (Contd.)
Atlas fond of, iv. 62
Aztec remains, and, ii. 35
Bentley on Hindu, iv. 68
Birth of, the, iii. 42
Chemistry and, ii. 305
Cosmolatry and, iii. 86
Cross in, iii. 220
Dragon in, ii. 118
Earth according to, iii. 75
Eclipses, and, iii. 379
Egyptians, of the, iv. 192
Esoteric, 435
Exact science, as an, ii. 320
Fixed Stars and, v. 222
Foreign, borrowing a, ii. 385
Fourth race, of the, iii. 424
Geology and, iii. 81, 82; iv. 233
Glyphs connected with, ii. 33
Gods teaching, iii. 365
Grecian, ii. 303
Hebrews of the, iii. 85
Hindus, of the, ii. 384, 386, 390; iii. 332; iv. 68
Indian, ii. 303
Inductive science, as an, ii. 310
Inventor of, iii. 365; iv. 98
Isis-Osiris and, iii. 365
Jyotis taught, iv. 335
Kabiri-Titans in, iii. 360
Kārtikeya in, iv. 190
Kepler's mystical, ii. 379
Kumāras in, iv. 149
Latona in, iv. 339
Lemuro-Atlanteans, of the, iii. 317
Lunar eclipses, and, iii. 379
Mercury in, iv. 112
Meru and, iii. 356
Modern, attitude of, ii. 313, 314
Moon in, ii. 109
Most High, the sun in, iv. 108
Mysteries, connected with, iii. 132
Mystic, ii. 379; iii. 59
Mythology and, ii. 104
Nebular theory of, ii. 312
Noah in, Sydic, iii. 391
Occult teachings concerning, ii. 229
Œdipus of, i. 211
Ouranos taught, iv. 335
Pātāla and, iii. 356
Physical, ii. 208; iv. 202; v. 424
Physiology and, v. 151
Planets in, i. 204, 217; ii. 109
Pleiades in, iv. 121
Proctor on, ii. 375
Purānic, iii. 255
Pyramid, in the Great, ii. 25, 29
Pythagoras studied, v. 322
Sanskrit MSS. on, iv. 121
Science of, ii. 310, 320, 371; iv. 233; v. 222
Secret books teach, i. 252
Seven in, number, iv. 190
Shell of, ii. 370
Shesha the great teacher of, iii. 60
Solar eclipses, and the, iii. 379
Sun-Gods in, iii. 55
Swedenborg, and, v. 406
Symbolism in, ii. 33; iii. 428

Tamiel taught, iii. 375
Teachings of, iii. 253, 330
Theology and, ii. 33; v. 220
Third Race, in the, v. 341
Tien taught, iv. 335
Treatise on, v. 341
Uranus taught, iv. 331, 335
Wolf on, ii 325
ASTRONOMUS, Hierophant in Egypt, v. 318, 332
ASTRO-SYMBOLOGY, ii. 301
ASTRO-THEOGONICAL, ii. 298
ASTRO-THEOSOPHIC, iv. 29
ASU or breath, iii. 69, 95; iv. 68
ASURA, Aesar derived from, iii. 123
Ahura or, iv. 178, 180
Asurendra the great, iv. 56
Demon Deity or, iii. 57
Divine means, spiritual, iii. 101
Origin of the name, iv. 56
Sura became, iii. 230, 240
ASURA DEVATĀ, iii. 250
ASURAMAYA, Astronomer, the earliest, iii. 61
Atlantean Astrologer and Astronomer, iii. 62, 325, 434
Calculations of, iii. 80
Fragments from, iii. 78
Magician, iii. 61
Nārada and, iii. 59
Zodiacs of, iii. 434
ASURA MAZDHĀ, iii. 101; iv. 56
ASURAS, Ahura restores the, iii. 71
Allegory of the, i. 185, 239
Angelic Fall, the, and the, iii. 284
Arūpa Gods or, iii. 318
Asu breath from, iii. 95
Battle between, and Gods, iv. 66
Body of Night, created from the, iii. 170
Brahmā, issuing from, iii. 69
Brāhmans, the, of the, iii. 301
Creation of, ii. 295; iii. 170; iv. 68
Daityas and, ii. 137
Deceiver, deluded by the, ii. 140
Demons and, ii. 62
Devas, the, are real, iii. 99, 169
Earth, peopling the, iv. 85
Enemies of the Gods, iii. 233
Fallen Angels or, iv. 94
Fire of the, ii. 245; iii. 68
Flames or, iii. 250
Gods and, iii. 71, 88, 383, 389; iv. 66, 68; v. 287
Group of the Septenary Host, the, i. 266
Hindūism, the, of, ii. 62
Human pioneers become, iii. 323
Indian, Pantheon, of the, iv. 94
Indra conqueror of the, i. 251; iii. 377
Intermediate state of, iii. 249
Kumāras and, iii. 98, 115, 172
Law, followed the, iv. 55
Manu produced the, iii. 156
Nāgas and, ii. 62
Pioneers, become human, iii. 323
Pitris, form the spiritual, iii. 100
Pre-Brāhmanical, iii. 171
Primordial Angels, the, are, iv. 57
Rākshasas identified with, iii. 171

ASURAS (*Contd.*)
Rig Veda, in the, iv. 68
Rudras were, iv. 156
Secret Doctrine, in the, i. 155
Septenary Host, the highest of the, i. 266
Shankha-dvīpa, of, iii. 403
Shukra, the pupils of, iii. 45
Suras and, ii. 130, 136; iii. 102
Synonyms for, i. 155
Tempting demons, called, iii. 181
Titans, copied from, ii. 136
Vishnu Purāna, in the, iii. 235
War of, ii. 136; iii. 73, 88, 383, 389; iv. 68
ASURENDRA, the great Asura, iv. 56
ATABUTOS, Simoon called, iii. 384
ATALA, v. 538, 542
Hell, a, iii. 403, 406
Purānas, of the, iii. 401
Sin, the Land of, iii. 322
Southern Pole, at the, iii. 403
White Devil, and the, iii. 154
White Island, or the, iii. 401
AT-AL-AS the Divine Sun, iii. 360
ATASH-BEHRAM of the Parsīs, ii. 52
ATAVISM, Atlantean culture, and, iv. 310
Cave-men and, iv. 310
Evidence of, iv. 319
Law of, i. 305; iv. 319
ATHAMAS or Adam, iii. 143
ATHAMAZ or Adam-Kadmon, iii. 55
ATHANOR of the Alchemists, i. 147
ATHAT-ashamaim, v. 231
ATHEISM, Divine order protested against by,
i. 234
Idiotic, based on lethal materiality, iii. 166
Mechanical; iv. 232
Negations of, iv. 221
Paranirvāna and, i. 309
Secret Doctrine teaches no, i. 322
Speculative, iv. 125
Unscientific, v. 70
ATHEIST, a model, ii. 292
ATHEISTICAL systems, foundation of, ii. 331
ATHEISTS, Advaitins are not, i. 73, 74
Anatomy, must be insane, knowing, iv. 223
Believers in Karma not, iii. 306
Buddhists called, i. 73, 74
Dryden on the, of mankind, ii. 369
Epicurus, like, ii. 336; v. 78
Esotericism, and, v. 462
Kabala, v. 384
Karma and, ii.369; iii. 306
Occultists are not, i. 73
Pantheists and, v. 384
Pantheists called, i. 74
Vedāntins cannot be called, i. 74
ATHENA and Prometheus, iv. 88
ATHENÆUS and Satan's name, iii. 44
ATHENAGORAS, v. 34, 36, 302, 303, 304
ATHENE, Apollo and, iv. 340
Gladstone on, iv. 339
ATHENIAN sentiment, iii. 410
Week, v. 433
ATHENIANS, Æschylus condemned by the,
iii. 417
Boreas, sacrificing to, ii. 188
Moon Goddess of, ii. 115

Unknown God of, ii. 40
ATHENS, Ancient, submerged, iii. 272
Monkey fossils near, iv. 292
Theatres of, iii. 411
ATHOTIS an ancient physician, iii. 334
ATHTOR or Mother Night, ii. 60
ATIRMA, stonemason, v. 252
ATKINSON, quoted, ii. 394
ATLANTA, America called, iii. 225
ATLANTEAN, Affinities, iv. 360
Age, Bailly on the, iii. 267
Astronomer, the, iii. 62, 325
Asuramaya the, iii. 59, 78, 434
Bodies, produced by us in, iii. 304
British Islands, an, survivor saw, iii. 343
Buddhas, eleven, iii. 421
Chipped-stone men, ancestry of, iv. 284
Civilization, iii. 204, 265, 424; iv. 291;
v. 258
Continents, iii. 307, 421; iv. 177, 309, 310
Culture, reappearance of, iv. 310
Cycle, Jupiter belongs to the, iii. 272
Deluge, the, iii. 18, 79; iv. 103
Divisions of the Earth, seven, iii. 365
Fourth or, race, i. 240, 242, 243; ii. 112, 334,
377; iii. 154, 230, 323, 333, 439; iv. 102
Giants, ii. 135; iii. 80, 102, 235, 273, 281, 392,
422, 431, 443; v. 260
Heirloom, iii. 428
Humanities, iii. 431
Images, iii. 331
Initiates, i. 257
Karma and the race, iii. 304, 409; iv. 310
Languages, iii. 204
Law of offering, the, iv. 317
Legend, Pharaoh and the, iv. 62
Libraries destroyed, iv. 262
Magic symbol, iii. 355
Memory of, gigantic, iii. 273
Mysteries, and, v. 258, 269
Nations, iii. 268, 424
Niobe the, race, iv. 340
Noah an, iii. 389
Offshoots, savage tribes are, iv. 290
Palæolithic men, iv. 309
Part-cycle, the, iv. 280
Period, the, ii. 334; iii. 190, 268
Pre-Adamic races were, ii. 37
Progress, iii. 266
Prototypes, iii. 22
Prowess, iv. 323
Races, i. 240, 242, 243; ii. 37, 112, 334, 377;
iii. 132, 154, 230, 251, 274, 275, 288, 295,
319, 323, 333, 409, 421, 439, 442; iv. 102,
175, 283, 312
Records, iii. 352
Relics, iii. 326, 343, 346
Savage tribes, offshoots, iv. 290
Skeleton of an, iv. 244
Sorcerers, iii. 102; iv. 61, 208; v. 256, 299
Sorcery, iii. 287; iv. 71
Submersion, iii. 148, 307
Sub-race in Europe, seventh, iv. 312
Symbol of, magic, iii. 355
Titans, iii. 295
Traditions of the Moon, ii. 112
Zodiacs, iii. 434

ATLANTEANS, Adepts of Left Hand, v 262
  Ancestors of the, i. 241
  Ancestors of Fourth Race, v. 268
  Animality of the, iv. 353
  Āryans and, iii. 393; iv. 345; v. 66
  Battles between two classes of, iv. 341
  Boasts of the, iv. 331
  Classes of, two, iv. 341
  Cursing the sun, iv. 331
  Degradation of, iv. 340
  Descendants of, iv. 325, 343
  Description of, iii. 426
  Destruction of, iii. 331
  Doom of, iii. 431, 433
  Dragons, called the Great, iv. 325
  Druid priests descendants of, iv. 325
  Egyptians and, iv. 319
  Elements, and the four, ii. 185
  End of, untimely, iii. 185
  Eocene age, of, iv. 285
  Extermination of, iii. 309
  Ezekiel on fate of the, iv. 61
  Features of the, iii. 228
  Figures current among, v. 336
  Force called by, Mash Mak, sidereal, ii. 286
  Geburim, or Giants were, ii. 133
  Greeks and, iv. 312, 319
  Groups of, saved, iii. 350
  Guanches an offshoot of the, iv. 248, 359
  Iranians on the, iv. 341
  Kumāras connected with the, iv. 156
  Lankā, the, of, iii. 239, 278
  Left-hand adepts, v. 262
  Mêlée of, and Āryans, iv. 345
  Monads came with the last, iii. 304
  Monsters bred by, iv. 249
  Moon, subjected by, v. 533
  Moses and, iii. 424
  Mysteries, of, v. 261, 269, 283
  Powers of, Superhuman, iv. 333
  Race overlapped the, third, iii. 443
  Rākshasas and, iii. 278
  Remnants of, iv. 313
  Rishis and, the, iv. 70
  Romans and, iv. 312
  Sanskrit not spoken by, i. 87
  Senzar understood by, i. 64
  Sin of the, iii. 303; iv. 259; v. 258
  Sons of Night, called, iv. 341
  Sons of the Sun, called, iv. 341
  Sorcery of the, v. 91
  South Pole, gravitated toward the, iii. 276
  Speech of the, iii. 204
  Submersion of, v. 185
  Tenets of, v. 268
  Ungodly, perished, iii. 349
  War, and, v. 300
  Wives of the, iii. 288
  Work ascribed to, iii. 61
  Writing invented by, iii. 437
  Yasna on the, iv. 341
ATLANTES, Diodorus on, iv. 335
  History and mythology of, iv. 330
  Titans called, iii. 360
  Uranus first king of, iv. 334
ATLANTIC, Elevated ridge in the, iii. 333
  Flood, the great, iii. 352

  Great Waters, the, and the, iv. 345
  Islands, iii. 22, 402, 407; iv. 358
  Land and White Island, iii. 154
  Lemuria, the, portion of, iii. 333
  North and South, iii. 404
  Ocean, ii. 137; iii. 154, 405
  Pillars of Hercules in the, iii. 154
  Plato's island, iii. 22, 406
  Proserpine, islands in the, sacred to, iii. 407
  Steamers on the, iii. 163
ATLANTIDES, Atlas, the seven daughters of, iv. 62
  Diodorus, accused by, iii. 406
  History, the, of, iv. 330
  Mythology, the, of, iv. 330
  Symbols of the Fourth Race, the, were, iv. 62
ATLANTIS, Africa not so old as, iii. 367
  Anthropoids and, iii. 198
  Atala or, iii. 401
  Atlas is, iv. 332
  Bailly believed in, iv. 311
  Biological Evidence of, iv. 356
  Botany points to, iv. 308, 350
  Catastrophe of, iv. 344
  Continent of, ii. 85, 377; iii. 21, 252, 267, 349, 370
  Countries in, two, iii. 370
  Deluge of, i. 136
  Derivation of, iii. 218
  Description of, iii. 322
  Destruction of, iii. 21, 152, 316; iv. 177; v. 104, 109
  Division of, iii. 405; iv. 334
  Donnelly on, iii. 269, 278, 333; iv. 351, 361
  Doom of, iii. 425
  Duppa Crotch on, iv. 350
  Ethnology, necessary to, iv. 351
  Events of, prehistoric, iii. 392
  Evidences of, iv. 350, 352, 355, 358, 360
  Ezekiel on the fate of, iv. 62
  Flood, the sinking of, or the, iv. 179
  Geological basis of, iii. 333
  Giants of, iii. 277, 345
  Greeks, of the, iii. 403
  History of, iii. 314
  Initiates of, v. 263
  Inscriptions of, iv. 361
  Insular continents, one of the seven, iii. 326
  Islands of, the, iii. 78, 267, 404, 405, 431; iv. 334
  Land of sin, iii. 322
  Legends of, iv. 344
  Lemuria, and, iii. 21, 47, 333, 400; iv. 345, 348
  Lost, the, i. 50, 64; iii. 224
  Lyell on, iv. 295, 355
  Magicians of, iii. 227
  Manu of the sunken, iii. 310
  Marcellus on, iii. 407
  Mayas coeval with Plato's, iii. 47
  Miocene period and, iii. 21; iv. 309, 347
  Mysteries of, v. 261
  Name, under another, iv. 336
  Neptune's division of, iv. 334
  Nereus and, iv. 335
  Niobe and, iv. 341
  Ocean floors, part of, iii. 323

ATLANTIS (*Contd.*)
Ogygia identified with, iv. 339
Palmy days of, iii. 188
Peninsula of, iii. 23, 149
Period of, iii. 266
Phlegyan Island said to be, iii. 152, 364
Plato, of, iii. 21, 47, 223, 266, 314, 322, 323, 370, 406, 427; iv. 312, 330; v. 73
Pliocene portion of the great, iii. 394
Poseidon and, iv. 335
Poseidonis or, iii. 323, 406
Position of, iii. 323, 333
Races of, iii. 370
Reappearance of, iii. 325
Records of, iii. 422
Remnants of, iii. 252
Romaka-pura part of, iii. 62
Rulers of, iv. 335
Science and, iv. 285
Senzar understood by inhabitants of, i. 64
Shāka-dvīpa or, iii. 322, 406
Sinking of, iii. 315, 325
Solon and, iv. 354
Sorcerers of, ii. 137; iii. 383
Submersion of, ii. 157; iii. 268, 351, 393; iv. 332
Taurus vertical to, iii. 406
Traditions of, iii. 226; iv. 350, 355
Uranus, first king of, iv. 335
Wilford on, iii. 405
ATLANTIS Hypothesis in Botanical Aspect, iv. 295
ATLANTO-ĀRYAN races, iii. 423, 434; iv. 315, 319, 320
ATLANTO-LEMURIANS, Apes, sires of, iv.258
Veda and the, iv. 51
Wives of the, iii. 284
ATLANTOSAURUS Immanis, iii. 222
ATLAS, Atlantis named from, iii. 370
Daughters of, iv. 190
Hero, the, iv. 62
Lemuria in the days of, iv. 332
Madagascar and, iii. 266
Meru is not on, iii. 400
Mount, iii. 402, 405; iv. 62, 331, 335
Nila, mountains of the, range, iii. 404
Noah and, iii. 268
Orion and, iiiī. 279
Parents of, iv. 334
Region surrounding Mount, iv. 335
Relic, the sole Western, iv. 333
Story of, iv. 331
Tartarus, in, iv. 332
Titan, and, iii. 268
Tradition of, esoteric, iv. 333
World, supporting the, iii. 279; iv. 359
ĀTMĀ, Absolute knowledge, is, ii. 294
All-Spirit, iii. 118
Aspects of, ii. 294
Atom, and, v. 537
Bird of immortality, iii. 48
Breath of Life not, i. 273
Buddhi, and, v. 77, 487
Buddhi informed by, ii. 291
Buddhi in relation to, i. 231; ii. 291
Buddhi inseparable from, i. 231; ii. 291
Buddhi the vehicle of, i. 43, 178, 231, 291; iii. 234; iv. 152, 176

Buddhi-Manas, i. 83, 243, 267, 282; ii. 293; iii. 68, 121; v. 497
Chit or, i. 128
Christos, and, i. 190; iii. 234; iv. 49
Definitions of, ii. 294
Deity, essence of, iv. 49
Dhyāni has to be, -Buddhi, an, i. 243
Esoteric Buddhism in, v. 426
Etymology, v. 479
Father in Heaven, v. 532
Garments of, i. 290
God, v. 488
Great Mother, first principle of the, i. 332
Human, v. 487
Human principle, the seventh, iv. 165
Illusive body of, ii. 294
Immortality, bird of, iii. 48
Impersonal principle, the, i. 190; iv. 49
Individual Principle, not, v. 426
Īshvara, beyond, ii. 297
Jīva, v. 471
Kshetrajna, the, ii. 294
Light, a ray of, i. 289
Manas and, iii. 121; iv. 150; v. 515
Marai, and the higher, ii. 293; iii. 68
Māyā surrounding, ii. 297
Monad rendered as, ii. 293
Mould of the garments of, i. 290
Neshamah or, i. 287, 290
Not-Spirit, is, ii. 297
Occultists' view of, i. 273
One reality, the, i. 233
Only witness, ii. 294
Parabrahman and, i. 128, 188; ii. 146
Pavilion of, ii. 297
Physical body, and, abyss between, iv. 96
Plane, does not belong to this, i. 289
Principle, as a, i. 190, 209, 230, 332; ii. 48; iv. 96, 165
Pure spirit, or, iv. 203
Radiance of, v. 427
Radiation, iii. 243; v. 534
Ray of light, i. 289
Reflections of, i. 233
Region of, pure soul, iii. 402
Self is, ii. 48
Sixth principle, v. 427
Seventh Principle, v. 361, 426
Soul and, i. 190; iii. 402
Spirit or, i. 178, 179, 273, 287, 332; ii. 291, 294, 335, 344; iii. 48, 69, 121; iv. 152, 168, 203
Spiritual vivifying principle or, i. 230
Substratum, the one real, ii. 294
Super-Spirit, v. 408
Synthesis, the eternal immortal, i. 213
Systems, in the various, i. 212
Triad, part of the human, i. 267, 282
Unity, is synthesized by, ii. 294
Universal soul, inseparable from the, v. 497
Universal spirit, the, iii. 234; iv. 168
Upādhis of, i. 213
Vehicle of, i. 43, 178, 231, 290; iii. 69, 234; iv. 176; v. 545
Vidyā, spirit-knowledge or, i. 249
Vidyā or spiritual divine wisdom, i. 222
Zoroaster, the, of, iv. 49

ĀTMABHŪ the Self-existent, iii. 183; iv. 150
ĀTMĀ-BUDDHI, v. 76, 203, 530, 531, 532, 556
  Devachan and, ii. 47
  Dhyāni has to be an, i. 243
  Divine, Instructor or Guru, iii. 122
  Dual soul, the, i. 230
  First race, of, iii. 257
  Flame, the, i. 284
  Guru, the divine, iii. 122
  Highest Self, v. 362
  Indiscrete, is one and, i. 274
  Instructor, the divine, iii. 122
  Irrational on this plane without Manas, i. 288
  Manas and, i. 267, 274, 288, 289
  Monad, the dual, i. 136, 231
  Personality merged in, i. 123
  Pudding-bags had, v. 532
  Second race of the, iii. 257
  Soul and spirit or, i. 263, 274
  Spirit-Soul or, i. 260, 263
  Universal Soul, v. 499
ĀTMĀ-BUDDHI-MANAS, i. 265, 282, 288; ii. 52; iii. 68, 121; v. 364, 489, 503, 514, 515, 519, 533, 555
ĀTMAMĀTRĀSU, ii. 47, 48
ĀTMAN, Breath or spirit, v. 269
  Buddhi and the apperception of, i. 229
  Christos the, of the universe, i. 190
  Communion with Brahman, v. 145
  Divine Fire, v. 451
  Divine ray, the, i. 269
  Ego not the, the human, iii. 89
  Ego taking refuge in the, iii. 118
  Higher Self, v. 365, 421
  Human Ego not the, iii. 89
  Inner man warmed by, iii. 119
  Living spirit of nature or, iii. 117
  Man, in, v. 451
  Mother-spirit or, i. 260
  Non-Being, passes into, i. 243
  Principle, the seventh, ii. 193; v. 423
  Protologos or, iii. 117
  Pūrvaja, is, iii. 117
  Ray, the divine, i. 269
  Self, luminous, or iv. 210
  Spirit or i. 274; iii. 117; v. 421
  Sun compared with, iii. 118
  Superphysical, v. 423
  Uncreate Power, v. 448
  Unit-ray, or, v. 421
  Universal self or, iv. 210
  Universal spirit, one with the, i. 308; ii. 294
  Universe, Christos, of, i. 190
  Vedāntins, of the, i. 170
ĀTMANAH, from self, ii. 47
ĀTMIC Aura, v. 507
  Ray, the vehicle of the, i. 229; v. 427
  Sense, v. 540
  State, v. 539, 540
ATMOSPHERE, Atoms changed in our, ii. 307
  Blood, of the, ii. 256
  Effect of vibrations in our, ii. 278
  Globe, the, of every, i. 198, 200; iv. 186
  Heaven the first, iii. 84
  Humanity needed no, primitive, ii. 333

Indra the personified, iv. 185
Intelligent beings in our, ii. 330
Mars, of, iv. 276
Māyāvic veil, the, our, ii. 153
Mercury, of, iv. 276
Monads, ablaze with, ii. 358
Planetary, the, i. 199
Stars, of the, ii. 320
Suns, the, ii. 320
Tenuity of the, ii. 287
Terrestrial, iv. 186
Vibrations in the, ii. 278
ATMOSPHERIC, changed Conditions of the globe, iii. 64
  Dust of terrestrial origin, ii. 370
  Fluid, a solar, ii. 226
  Laws, present, ii. 333
  Molecules, impact of, ii. 278
  Vul, the, iii. 385
ATMU a divine or eternal soul, iv. 203; v. 412
ATOM, Absolute intelligence thrills through every, i. 320
  Absolute life cannot produce an inorganic, i. 320
  Æons, do not become man after, i. 230
  Alive, every, is, i. 305
  Angel, and, i. 167
  Anu means, ii. 72, 266, 290
  Ātma and, v. 537
  Ātman, is, v. 537
  Atoms, of, i. 306
  Brahmā called Anu, the, ii. 290
  Breath of life in every, the, i. 260
  Chemist, of the, ii. 236
  Consciousness in every, iv. 271
  Contradictions about the, ii. 208
  Cosmic, the, i. 311, ii. 360
  Deity contained in every, i. 128
  Differentiation of every, i. 199
  Etheric, the, ii. 281
  Evolution of the, i. 235
  Fohat in every, of matter, i. 196
  Force, apart from ii. 234
  Germ in every, i. 127; v. 558
  God, every, tends to become, i. 214
  Heart beating in every, of Nature, iv. 160
  Heat in every, i. 149
  Infinite world, the smallest, in the, ii. 368
  Inorganic, no, is, i. 302; iii. 173
  Intelligence in every, i. 320
  Involution of, i. 235
  Jīva in the mineral, i. 271
  Kosmos, spirit in every, in, ii. 51
  Life in every, i. 106, 260, 272, 293, 294, 302, 304
  Living, or life-giving, i. 305
  Lost, no, iv. 297
  Man produced from the, i. 230
  Meaning of the term, ii. 292
  Memory in every, iv. 241
  Mineral, i. 260, 271, 293
  Molecule, Soul of, v. 537
  Monad and the, i. 86, 230; ii. 355
  Motion pulsates in every, i. 176
  Nature, in every, of, iv. 160
  Noumenon of the, ii. 241
  Occultism and the, i. 294; ii. 267

ATOM (Contd.)
Periodical, the, is, ii. 269
Physical eye cannot perceive an, i. 127
Potentiality of every, i. 167
Power directing the, ii. 272
Primordial, the, i. 204; ii. 174; iv. 300
Protyle in every, ii. 42
Purusha, the, inseparable from, ii. 306
Qualities of the, ii. 205
Reality of the chemists', ii. 236
Science and the, ii. 42, 206
Self-consciousness and, i. 167
Sentient life shown in the, desire for, i. 116
Slumbering, the, i. 176
Spirit pervades every, ii. 51
Spiritual, the, ii. 48, 267
Substance-principle latent in every, i. 317
Ultimate living, or life, i. 304
Universe is alive, every, in the, i. 305
Velocity of each etheric, ii. 281
Vital fires in every, iii. 269
Watery abysses, of the, iv. 223
What is an?, ii. 237
ATOM-CELLS of Haeckel, iv. 240
ATOMIC, Anu or, ii. 246, 266
Atoms, the most, of, iii. 58
Constitution of matter, ii. 212
Differentiation, ii. 207
Ego is, v. 550
Electricity is, i. 171; ii. 304, 396
Elements, iv. 145
Emanations, iv. 227
Energy, iv. 242
Evolution, theory of, ii. 349
Expansion, i. 269
Forces, v. 383
Forms or Rūpas, i. 265
Helmholtz and, electricity, ii. 304
Leucippus, theory of, i. 70
Matter becomes, ii. 275
Occult, theory, i. 305
Organisms, i. 268
Souls, ii. 344
Theory, i. 70, 305; ii. 243, 291, 303, 349
Transformations of matter, i. 254
Vibration, ii. 175, 286
Vortices, ii. 292
Weight, ii. 271, 308, 350
ATOMICITIES, dominant, ii. 275
ATOMISM a graphic system, ii. 206
ATOMISTS, ii. 292, 303, 338
ATOMO-MECHANICAL Laws, ii. 208
Masks, ii. 268
Theory, ii. 237
ATOMO-MECHANICALISTS, ii. 209
ATOMS, actual identical, iv. 241
Aggregation of, ii. 349, 397
Alike, are, ii. 355
Allegory of the, Jewish, ii. 292
Animal, ii. 174
Animated, ii. 291
Assemblage of ultimate, ii. 271
Atmosphere, changed in our, ii. 307
Atomic of, the most, iii. 58
Birth of, ii. 306, 308
Bodies of the hierarchies are the, ii. 354
Body, the, of the, ii. 292

Centres of force, or, i. 147; ii. 231
Chemical, i. 198, 265; ii. 347, 351; iii. 116
Combinations of, iii. 168
Condensation of the, ii. 316
Conscious, iv. 240
Cosmic, ii. 397
Death, the, after, ii. 262
Death of, ii. 275
Decay of, ii. 275
Development of, progressive, i. 115
Differentiation of the, i. 302; ii. 246; iii. 93
Dimensions of the, ii. 353
Divine, ii. 291
Divisibility of matter into, ii. 353
Elastic, ii. 251
Elemental, the, i. 170; ii. 290
Elementary substances composed of, i. 171
Elements and, ii. 290
Elements of Leibnitz and, ii. 355
Energy of, ii. 275
Essence of the, i. 160
Ether the envelope of, ii. 287
Evolution of, i. 265; ii. 273, 307, 350
Exchange of, perpetual, i. 198
Fire, differentiated, i. 302
Fire-mist, of the, i. 302
Fohat shapes the, i. 150, 171
Ghost of the, iv. 243
Gods and, ii. 335, 344, 348, 349
Groups of, ii. 276
Gyratory movement of the, i. 176
Hierarchies and the, ii. 354
Hypothesis of, iv. 225
Innumerable sparks, the, i. 168
Intelligent rulers of, ii. 276
Interaction of, ii. 327
Interstellar, ii. 357
Laya, issuing from, ii. 172
Leibnitz, of, ii. 355, 356
Life-principle, and, iv. 241, 242
Lucretius, of, ii. 318
Mahāpralaya and, i. 206
Manvantara, at every, ii. 268
Marshalling of, ii. 395
Material, contrary to reason, ii. 355
Material molecules or, ii. 357
Materialists and, ii. 338, 395
Mineral, i. 175
Mirrors of the, ii. 348
Molecules, of, ii. 278, 349, 357
Monads and, ii. 335, 344, 346, 348, 349, 355, 356
Movement of, i. 176
Nature of, ii, 174, 244
Noumenal essence of the, i. 160
Nyāya, of the, ii. 49
Occultism, of, ii. 244
Organic units, chemical, are, ii. 351
Permanent, iv. 241
Physical, are countless, i. 230
Physicists cannot see, ii. 330
Plane of matter, seven, on the, ii. 360
Points, as material, ii. 212
Powers setting in action the, i. 331
Pregenetic matter separated into, i. 142
Primaries the shadows of, ii. 202
Primeval, the, ii. 316

ATOMS (Contd.)
  Primordial, the, i. 165
  Primordial Choas, in, i. 205
  Pure, ii. 291
  Rulers of groups of, ii. 276
  Science and, i. 196; ii. 51
  Self-moving, ii. 395
  Shapes, sizes, etc., ii. 220
  Souls and, ii. 291, 344
  Space filled with, i. 70
  Spiritual, are, v. 550
  Spirits of, i. 268
  Svabhāvat sends Fohat to harden, i. 150
  Total, of the universal, iii. 90
  Transformation of, i. 203; iv. 242
  Transmission of the identical, iv. 242
  Ultimate, ii. 205
  Unconscious, iv. 240
  Universal total, of the, iii. 90
  Universal vibration of, i. 149
  Universe, and the, ii. 57
  Vibration of, i. 149; ii. 358
  Views of, ancient and modern, ii. 243
  Vortical, ii. 215, 303
  Waves of science produced by, ii. 358
  Worlds linked with, i. 115; ii. 328
ATOM-SOULS, Haeckel's, iv, 240, 242
  One, Differentiations from the, ii. 291
ATONEMENT, Blood, through, iv, 269
  Buddha, of, v. 371
  Christ as the victim of, iv. 65
  Christian, iv. 74, 272
  Creators, of the, iii. 196
  Dogma of, v. 271
  Fall and, of the Christians, iv. 74
  Goat the victim of, iv. 79
  Metaphorical, iv. 52
  Origin of, v. 272
  Vicarious, v. 499
  Victim of the, iv. 65, 79
ATRI, Barhishad as sons of, iii 98
  Brahmā, a mind-born son of, iii. 88
ATROPHIED, Divine power in will, iii. 180
  Eye of Shiva, iii. 303
  Inner senses, iii. 295
  Odd eye, iii. 299
  Organs in man, iv. 251
ATROPHY, Physical senses in mediumship, of, iii. 370
  Spiritual eye, of the, iii. 307
  Temporary, of a physical sense, iii. 370
  Third eye, of the, iii. 298; iv. 338
AT-TEE-'KAH D'At-tee'keen or ancient of ancients, iii. 93
ATTEEKAH Kaddosha, the ancient, iv. 97
ATTICA, antiquity of the people of, iii. 351
ATTOCK, Alexander and, iii. 415
  India and, iii. 416
  Sind to, iii. 415
ATTRACTION, Atom, and repulsion of, ii. 212
  Caloric, of, ii. 249
  Cause of, ii. 213
  Centre of, motion round the, iii. 243
  Contraries, of, ii. 122
  Equilibrium and, ii. 227
  Force of, i. 78; ii. 213
  Gravitation, alias, ii. 219
  Law of, i. 201; iii. 369
  Love or, ii. 220
  Molecular, ii. 394
  Occultists and, ii. 328
  Planetary motion not explained by, ii. 253
  Principia defines, ii. 213
  Rays of light, for different, ii. 304
  Repulsion, and, i. 78, 165, 333, ii. 212, 238, 328
  Spirits guiding so-called, ii. 214
ATTRACTIVE force of contrasts, iii. 112
ATTRIBUTE, Matter, the one, of, i. 296
ATTRIBUTELESS divine essence, ii. 354
ATTRIBUTES, Absolute is devoid of, the, i. 262
  Body, origin of the, of a, ii. 235
  Brahma, of, iii. 117
  Brahmā, of, i. 114; iii. 117
  Causeless Cause, abstract, of the, ii. 143
  Deity, of the incognizable, ii. 151, 156
  Devil, of the, iii. 397
  Divine, iv. 118
  Gods, of the, iii. 54, 111, 240; iv. 116
  Isis, of, iii. 43; iv. 127
  Kabiri, of the, iii. 360
  Matter, the, of, ii. 365
  Names, mystic, or, ii. 67
  Nemesis without, ii. 367
  Nirupādhi, without, ii. 306
  Outlines of, shadowy, iii. 104
  Personified, of God, iii. 240
  Pillar, of a, ii. 146
  Providence, finite of, ii. 367
  Space, of, i. 295
  Spiritual, iii. 281
  Universal Unity, of one, ii. 353
ATUM, Egyptian, and Adam, v. 203
ATWATER on Aztec remains, ii. 35
ATYANTIKA, Absolute, or, iii. 79, 310
  Individualities, concerned with some, ii. 86
  Pralaya, the third, ii. 86
ATYS, a lunar goddess, iii 111
ATZILATIC world, the, iii. 119
AUB or Ob a serpent, ii. 80
AUDLANG or Heaven, iii. 109
AUDUBON, iii. 438
AUDUMLA, ii. 83, 145
AUGMENTATION of energy, ii. 283
AUGOEIDES, Zanoni and his, ii. 296; v. 427; 515
AUGUR questions the serpent, iii. 214
AUGURS, the, iv. 87
AUGUSTAN age, the, i. 256
AUGUSTINE, St., i. 182; iii. 44; iv. 105, 160; v. 71, 207
AUGUSTUS Emperor, vi. 218, 334
AUM, ii. 150; iii. 406; v. 108, 395, 418, 421, 431, 479, 502, 505, 514, 519
AUPHANIM or wheels, i. 155, 176; v. 192, 213, 214
AUR or light, ii. 69
AURA, Ātmic, v. 507, 543
  Augoeides and, v. 427
  Colours in, v. 453, 457, 458, 459, 460, 485
  Egg-shaped sphere of, iii. 126
  Everything has an, v. 562
  Force, and vital, ii. 262
  Generators of human beings, of, i. 305
  Heart, of, v. 550

AURA (Contd.)
Masters on the, ii. 239
Objects, of, v. 562
Planet of the, i. 280
Pure, v. 429, 531
Sphere of, iii. 126
Terrestrial, v. 501
Vital Force, and, ii. 262
World, of a nascent, iii. 235
AURELIAN (US) Emperor, v. 147, 148
AURIC Egg, v. 472, 485, 486, 508, 510, 511, 512
519, 534, 546
Blue, v. 427, 458
Body, v. 427, 440, 441, 458
Envelope, v. 429, 454, 456, 457, 473, 517,
527, 528, 533, 551
Fluid, v. 533
Light, v. 533
AURNAVĀBHA, quoted, i. 172
AUROCHS antediluvian mammals, iv. 309
AURORA Australis, i. 253
Borealis, i. 253; ii. 346, 358; iv. 200
AURVA and his Chela Sagara, iv. 200
AUSTRALIA, Apteryx of, iv. 251
Eastern continent, part of the, iv. 333
Europe one with, iii. 333; iv. 350
Lemuria and, iii. 20
Relic, a, iii. 314
Retardation of, iii. 202
Southern continent, remnant of, iv. 357
Tertiary periods of, iii. 21
AUSTRALIAN aborigines, iii. 199
Anthropologists on the, Race, iv. 293
Brain of the, native, iii. 199; iv. 251
Civilization of the, iv. 231
Dying out, native, iii. 331; iv. 349
Esoteric view of the, iv. 290
Flat-headed, iv. 231, 348
Half-animal, tribes, iii. 201
Inferior races, iii. 169
Karma of the, iii. 175
Lemurians, the, descended from the, iii. 318
Malay, and, iv. 348
Native, the, iii. 198, 201
Savages, iii. 198
Tribes, iii. 198, 201, 327
AUSTRALIS, the Aurora, i. 253
AUSTRALOIDS, supposed descent from
Anthropoids, iii. 315
AUSTRIA, large bones found in, iii. 280
AUTHORITY, Archaic symbol of an, ii. 339
Bible as an, ii. 374
Cyclic recurrences, of, ii. 371
Ephemeral, ii. 362
Kabalists, of the Western, i. 299
Manu, the, of, iii. 98
Pope of Rome as an, iii. 317
Rig Veda, of the, iii. 101
Sages of, ii. 336
AUTOCHTHONOUS ancestors, iii. 17
Civilizations, system of, ii. 378
AUTO-GENERATION of the Gods, ii. 114
AUTOMATA, incorporeal, ii. 356
AUTOMATON, Free-will, Man an, without,
ii. 131
Jehovah, the, created by, iii. 246
Man an, making, ii. 131; iii. 347

AUTUN, the old Bibractis, v. 295
AUVERGNAT, cranial capacity of the, iii. 175
AVABODHA=mother of knowledge, iv. 97
AVALOKITESHVARA, Ādi-Buddha, a cor-
relation of, i. 191, 193
Buddha, the first, i. 169; v. 368
Buddhists, of the, i. 141, 188; ii. 146
Chenresi in Tibetan, is, iii. 185
China, in, iii. 186
Esotericism, the, of, i. 139, 141
First Lord or, i. 260
Īshvara or, manifested, i. 170
Kwan-Shai-Yin or, i. 139; ii. 193
Kwan-Yin in China is, iii. 186
Logos or, the, i. 169, 188; ii. 147; iv. 208
Manifestation of, i. 43
Padmapāni or, iii. 185, 186
Transformations of, ii. 192
Universal principle, or the, ii. 193
Verbum or, ii. 147
AVARA=inferior, iii. 170, 190
AVASTHĀS, the three divine (hypostases), i. 84
AVATĀRA, Amitābha, the, of, i. 169
Boar, the, iii. 321; v. 105
Buddha an, of Vishnu, iv. 149
Crucified in space, v. 270
Dionysus one with the coming, iii. 418
Fall of a God, the, iv. 52
Faultless book could only be written by an,
iv. 211
Fish, the, ii. 100; iii. 147, 308
Incarnation of, God, v. 253
Jīvanmukta, a, v. 352
Kalki, the, i. 311; iii. 414; v. 337
Keshin slain by, iii. 59
Matsya, the, ii. 100; iii. 147, 308
Nara-simha, the, iii. 229
Present, the, ii. 84
Shankara, an, v. 365, 366, 367
Vishnu, of, i. 83, 151, 307; ii. 380; iii. 147;
iv. 150; v. 311, 349
AVATĀRAS, Buddhas and, ii. 192; iii. 421
Divine-human, ii. 64
Hindus, of the, iv. 125; v. 157
Incarnations, or, divine, iv. 46; v. 351, 357
Indian, ii. 114
Krishna an, iv. 120
Pantheistic, conception of, i. 123
Periodical, i. 123
Saviour and, ii. 363; v. 232
True and False, v. 95, 358
Vishnu, of, iii. 45, 406
AVATĀRAS or manifestations to man, ii. 391
AVATĀRISM, v. 350, 358
AVELING, E.B., quoted, iii. 96; iv. 220, 222, 238
AVENGERS, Laws of life their own, ii. 368
Winged Wheels, the, and the, i. 185
AVESTAIC, Amshaspends, the, iii. 383
Apāmnapāt the, name for Fohat, iii. 399
AVICEBRON'S Qabbalah, quoted, ii. 156
AVIDYĀ of the Vedāntins, i. 74
Ignorance, irresponsibility and, v. 503
Nidanas, Vedana and, v. 517, 559
AVIKĀRA, the changeless, iii. 58
AVĪTCHI, v. 411, 486, 489, 496, 498, 501,
502, 504
AVOGADRO, ii. 237, 347

AVYAKTA=causality, ii. 246; iii. 58
AVYAKTĀNUGRAHENA or indiscrete principle, ii. 246
AVYAYA, Aparināmin and, ii. 306
Scriptures on the, exoteric, iii. 79
Vishnu the eternal, ii. 86
AXES, Parallel, no more, iii. 355
Planets, of the, ii. 317
Polar, iii. 429
Svastika and the world's, iii. 108
AXIAL disturbances, iii. 314, 329
Humanity, the, point of, i. 240
Motions, ii. 229
AXIEROS, AXIOKERSA, Cabir named, iii. 361
Demeter, female aspect of, iii. 361
Kumāras, and the, iii. 114
AXIOKERSOS, iii. 114, 361
AXIS, Displacement of the, of rotation, iv. 104
Disturbance of the, ii. 85; iii. 276
Earth's, ii. 85, 366; iii. 63, 153, 293, 315, 329; iv. 103, 104, 294, 340
Inclination of, iii. 63, 293, 329, 359; iv. 103, 104, 276
Jupiter's, iv. 276
Neutral, the, i. 203; ii. 276
Planet, the, of a, ii. 316
Sun, the, of the, ii. 225
AYANA, the abode of Vishnu, iv. 163
AYANAM, Hindus, of the, iv. 192
Rūdūs make an, three, iv. 191
AYIN=nothing, ii. 65
AZA, to illuminate, iii. 123
AZAEL, the hosts of, iv. 59
AZAL, Azazel derived from, iii. 375
AZARA, v. 182
AZAZEL, Azazyel, or, iii. 375; v. 180
Church dogma, of the, iii. 375
Ischins, chief of the, iii. 375
Mystery of, ii. 159
Scapegoat of Israel, the, iii. 388, 407
Serpent, a prototype of, iii. 386
AZHI-DAHAKA and Thraetaona, War between, iii. 389
AZILUTH, Chaiah obtained from, iv. 176; v. 299
AZOIC ages, i. 302; iii. 167
AZORES are remnants of an old continent, iii. 226; iv. 359, 361
AZTALAN, the country of the Aztecs, ii. 35
AZTECS, ii. 35; iii. 149, 443; v. 43

B

BA or the soul of breath, iv. 203; v. 357
BAAL, Æsculapius identical with, ii. 68
Common origin of, v. 195
Incense to, ii. 375
Israelites, of the, ii. 113
Mysteries of, iii. 216
Phallic God, a, iv. 28
Phœnicians, of the, iv. 110
Priests of, iii. 216
Prophets of, iv. 28
Saturn the same as, ii. 179
Worship of, v. 194
BAAL-ADONIS, ii. 184
BAAL-BEC, temples of, v. 217

BABBAGE, DR., quoted, i. 166
BABE, the divine, iii. 109
BABEL, builders of, iii. 374
Tower of, iii. 16, 274; iv. 331; v. 185
BABIAN, Ruins of, iv. 175
BABIES, Dog-headed, iii. 60
BABINET, v. 221, 225
BABOON, Catarrhine, iv. 232
Physiologically regenerated, iii. 265
BABOONS in the Pliocene periods, iv. 246
BABYLON, Arrow-headed inscriptions of, iv. 361
Divinities of, iii. 378
Foundation cylinder of, iv. 261
Hierophants of, iii. 378, 379
Huschenk built the city of, iii. 395
Inscriptions of, iv. 361
Magians of, v. 74
Mythology of, iii. 138
Nabatheans founded, iv. 20
Planetary temple of, iv. 23
Religion of, i. 49
BABYLONIA, Archaic statues of, iv. 262
Brāhman learning had a seat in, i. 54
Excavations in, v. 55
Gandunia was, iii. 54
Gan-duniyas a name of, iii. 207
Nebo of, iv. 23
Niffer or Nipur in northern, iii. 147
Pharisees' tenets came from, iii. 71
Sanskrit learning had a seat in, i. 54
Secret wisdom in, ii. 67
Semi-demon of, iii. 196
Statues of, iv. 262
BABYLONIAN, Anu a, God, iii. 147
Bel a, God, iii. 147
Captivity, Genesis a reminiscence of the, iii. 207
Captivity, iv. 41, 189; v. 103, 179, 181
Civilization, iii. 207; iv. 261
Creation, legend of, iii. 16, 72; v. 200
Cuneiform inscriptions, iii. 17
Cylinders, iii. 17, 112, 229, 250; v. 123
Dag Oannes the, iv. 150
Deluge, the, iii. 18
Divine ages, iv. 190
Dragons on, tiles, iii. 210
Ea, a, God, iii. 147
Ezra, the, iii. 151
Flood, the, iii. 225
Fragments, iii. 18
Gods, i. 173; ii. 381; iii. 147, 285
Inscriptions, iii. 17
Landowner, iv. 20
Lateres Coctiles or, tiles, ii. 72
Legend, iii. 16, 153, 382
Magism, i. 77
Moses, ii. 32
Naros and, v. 341
Oannes the, Dag, iv. 150
Qū-tāmy a, landowner, iv. 20
Religion, iv. 261
Sargon was the, Moses, ii. 37
Sin the, God, ii. 104
Talmud, i. 64
Tiles, ii. 32, 72; iii. 210; v. 176
Zu the, God, iii. 285

BABYLONIANS, Cycles of the, iv. 136
  Fall, and the, iii. 18
  Messiah of the, ii. 380
BAB-EL-ON-YA, v. 180
BACCHANTE, Serpent in hair of the, iii. 214
BACCHIC frenzy, Circle dance a, iv. 29
  Mysteries, v. 412
BACCHUS, ii. 49, 111
  Birth of, iii. 362
  Celestial Priapus born from Venus and, iv. 25
  Fish, as a, iii. 314
  Identity of, v. 277, 278
  Jupiter and, iii. 362
  Lord, ii. 184
  Mysteries of, iii. 216; v. 161, 255
  Phallic God, a, iv. 28
  Sabasius called, iii. 417
  Semele, mother of, ii. 116
  Solar, the, iii. 418
  Synonyms of, v. 316, 317
BACON, Roger, i. 219; ii. 203, 306, 336; iii. 437, 440; v. 28, 464
BACON, Lord (Francis), ii. 308; v. 28
BACTERIA, iii. 174
  Living, pass through boiling water, ii. 332
  Microbes, etc., i. 294
  Organisms, in human, i. 304
  Science, the, of, i. 271
BACTERIUM, Microscopical, i. 272
BADÁONI, quoted, i. 47
BADHAS, Imperfections, or, iii. 170
BAER, von de, quoted, iv. 219
BAFFIN'S Bay, iii. 400
BAHAK-ZIVO, Father of Genii, the, i. 245
  Nazaraean Gnostics, of, iii. 158
BAHTI, v. 41
BAI, the intellectual soul, iv. 205
BAIBHAR, Mount, i. 44
BAILLY, Age of human race, and, iv. 189
  Astrology and, v. 330, 331
  Astronomers, on ancient, ii. 384, 391; iv. 311
  Atlantis, believed in, iii. 370
  Atlantis, mistake of, about, iii. 268, 393, 401
  Atlantis, on influence of, iv. 341
  Atlantis of Plato, on, iii. 267
  Computation of, iii. 433
  Conclusions of, ii. 385
  Ecliptic, on the, iv. 104
  Hindus, on learning of the, iv. 311
  Horse of, the fabled, iii. 398
  Measure of time in Antiquity, on, iv. 192
  Plurality of Worlds, on, iv. 275
  Prehistoric nations, on, iv. 312
  Quoted on Astrology, v. 330
  Theogony, on Hesiod's, iv. 346
  Traditions, on, iii. 368, 392
  Voltaire, letter to, iv. 311
  Zodiac, on the, ii. 374
BAIN, Prof., quoted, i. 180, 183, 296; ii. 39, 252; iii. 164
BAISSAC, Jules, *Satan ou le Diable* of, iv. 78
BAIT-OXLY, Tomb of, iv. 129
BAKHAN-ALEARE, Adoration of, iv. 129
BAKHATEN, chief of, v. 252, 253
BALAAM, Prophet, iii. 407
BALADEVA, v. 258, 260

BALA-RĀMA, Krishna's elder brother, iv. 185; v. 258
BALANCE, Good and evil, light and darkness, between, i. 246
  Mars, Lord of the, iii. 391
  Qabbalists, the, of the, iv. 25
  Satan beareth the, and sword, iii. 237
BAL-I-LU (Martānda), i. 162
BALKH in Central Asia, iii. 337
BALL, Sir R.S., referred to, iii. 75
BALLANCHE, quoted, v. 272
BALLS, Fire, of, i. 105, 200
  Primordial dust in the shape of, i. 250
BALTHAZAR, one of the Magi, ii. 380
BALTIC, Amber only found in, iv. 340
  Level of the, iv. 320
BALTISTĀN, iii. 414
BALZAC, quoted, i. 135
BAMBOO BOOKS, the, iii. 303
BAMIAN, Colossal statues of, iii. 228, 336, 337
BANDHA, or bondage, i. 189
BANNER of Kāma-deva, iv. 150
BANNERS, of the twelve tribes, ii. 377
  Zodiacal signs on, of the twelve tribes, ii. 377
BANYAN, Ever-living human, i. 255
  Tree the, iii. 219
BAOTH Chaos, i. 247
BAPHOMET, Éliphas Lévi, the, of, i. 297
  Satan, the goat-headed, iii. 388
BAPTISM, of Blood, v. 271
  Christian, v. 83
  Devil said to possess man till his, iii. 213
  Fire, by, v. 323
  Infants, of, v. 157
  Jesus, of, v. 168
  Messiah connected with water in, ii. 100
  Rite of Initiation, a, v. 168
  Smoke, of, iv. 136
  Spirit of Holy Light, of the, iv. 136
  Waters of Grace of modern, ii. 178
BAPTIST, John the, i. 245; v. 83
  Pymander and St. John the, iii. 123
BARAHIEL, Rabbi, quoted, ii. 343
BARBARADESA, iii. 404
BARBARAS, Purānas, spoken of in, iii. 405
BARBARIANS, Indus, Masters of the banks of the, ii. 92
  Mediterranean, iv. 323
  Mlechchhas, or, ii. 92; iii. 60
BARBARISM, Dark ages of, iii. 427
  Deluges of, iv. 312
BARBARY, Spain, joined to, iv. 320
BARBELO, one of the three Invisible Gods, iv. 140
BARESMA, Mystic and Mysterious, iii. 384
  Twig, or the divine, iv. 86
BAR-HEBRAEUS on Enoch, iv. 98
BARHISHAD, Fashioners identical with the, Pitris, iii. 103
  Fathers or, the, iii. 110
  Fires, the, possessed of, iii. 87
  Pitris or, iii. 98
  Progenitors or ancestors, the, iii. 87
BARHISHADS, Kumāras, Agnishvāttas and, iii. 97
BARIUM, ii. 276
BARKAYAL taught Astrology, iii. 375

BARNABAS at Lystra, iv. 49
BARNANG, i. 87
BARNI, quoted, ii. 339
BARONIUS quoted, v. 62, 93
BARTH, quoted, iv. 16, 17
BARTHELEMY St. Hilaire referred to, iii. 209
BARTLETT, quoted, iv. 167
BARUCH, the prophet, v. 313
BASES, Upādhis or, i. 213; iv. 164
BASHAN, Tall men of, iv. 325
BASHT or PASHT, a Goddess, iv. 122
BASILEA, Royal, Asteria called, or, iv. 342
BASILEUS, v. 130
BASILICA, St. John Lateran, v. 173
BASILIDEAN gems, ii. 194
    Stones, iii. 214
BASILIDEANS, the, ii. 64
BASILIDES, ii. 65; v. 93, 128, 169, 207, 351, 462
BASIN of Persæa, iv. 116
BASIS, Hydrogen, the spiritual and material
    iii. 121
    Kosmos, of the manifested, ii. 339
    Manifested, Being, the, of, iii. 37
    Noumenal basis of second triangle, ii. 339
    Noumenon requires, to become a pheno-
        menon, i. 111
    Phenomenon, of a, i. 111
    Perfection, the corruptible, of, iii. 104
    Principle, of the, i. 212
    Second Triangle, the, noumenal of the, ii. 339
    Upādhi or physical, i. 163, 323
" BASKETS " of writings on palm leaves,
    iii. 421
BASLE, Map published at, iii. 326
BAS-PA, v. 379
BASQUES, Ancestors of the, iv. 358
    Canary Islands, the, allied to the men of the,
        iv. 310
    Guanches, and, iv. 360
    Isolated language of the, iv. 358
    Remote Ancestors of the, iv. 358
BASTIAN, Dr., iii. 262; iv. 322
BAT-WINGED men, iv. 206
BATH-KOL, Daughter of the Divine voice,
    iii. 115; v. 240
    Hebrew, the, i. 194; v. 237
BATHYBIUS HAECKELII, ii. 266; iii. 172, 196
    iv. 226, 240, 243
BATHYBIUS, the gelatinous, iv. 220
BATOO, Noom sends a girl to, iii. 272
BATTLE, Flames the, of the, i. 251
    Gods and Asuras, between, iv. 66
    Good and evil, the great, between, iv. 63
    Life, of, iii. 274; iv. 218
BATTLES, Creators and Destroyers, fought
    between, i. 105, 248
    Planets, of the, i. 163
    Sons of Darkness, between Sons of Light and,
        iv. 341
    Space, fought for, i. 105
BATYLOS, the Grecian, iii. 94
BAUDDHISTS, Seventh zone of, iii. 401
BAUDRY, F., iv. 93, 95
BAUMGARTNER, Prof., Germs for higher ani-
    mals, on, iv. 286
BE WITH US, Great Day, the, i. 104, 106, 187,
    188, 192, 195, 309

BEACHES, Scotland, raised, in, iv. 355
    Pliocene raised, iv. 324
BEALE, Prof., Life, on, ii. 264
    Referred to, ii. 359
BEAM, Parent-Sun, of the, ii. 363
    Uncreated, the, i. 319
BEAMS, Moon, the, and sparks of one, i. 282
    Symbol of our spiritual Egos, i. 283
    Universal Sun, one of the, of, i. 271
BEAR, Great, the, i. 260, 274; iv. 117, 119
    Lesser, the, ii. 128
    Thot-Sabaoth, the, iii. 124
    Typhon of the Great, iv. 117
BEAST, Apocalyptic great, the, ii. 381
    Artificially-made, an, iii. 425
    God or a, is man a, ii. 361
    Woman and the, meaning of, iv. 317
BEASTS, Magic watchers or speaking, iii. 425
BEAUMETZ, Dr. D., referred to, iii. 161
BEAVER, Consciousness of the, iii. 129
BECOMING, Creation or, i. 324
    Nature ever, not simply being, i. 301
    Sacred number of, nine, iv. 193
    Science ever, ii. 240
    Universe an eternal, the, iv. 16
BEDE, Chronology, and church, iii. 394
    Cosmogonical essay of the Venerable, ii. 159
    Referred to, v. 71
BEELZEBUB, iii. 388
BEER, the well of, ii. 80
BEES, Civilization of, iv. 220
    Parthenogenesis, and, iv. 229
    Reproduction of, iii. 142
BEGER, Inscription discovered by, ii. 116
BEGLOR, discoverer of the Cheta Cave, i. 44
BEHEMOTH, Darkness, the principle of, iv. 54;
    v. 202
BEHRING'S Straits, iii. 326, 329
BEING, Absolute, i. 130, 243, 311; iv. 16; v. 552
    Absolute, and non-being of Hegel, i. 81
    Absolute, the awful mystery of, i. 122
    Absolute, and consciousness, i. 119
    Active periods of, iii. 241
    Arcana of, ii. 199, 316
    Basis of manifested, iii. 37
    Centres of, iii. 46
    Collectivity, in its, i. 124
    Conditioned, the two aspects of, i. 80
    Conscious and unconscious, i. 124
    Consciousness and, iii. 282
    Cycle of, and forms, i. 192
    Deity not a, but Be-ness, i. 129
    Divine, v. 88, 299
    Egg, the secret of, represented by the, ii. 74
    Eternal non-being, the one, i. 116
    Evolution of, ii. 336
    Forms of, ii. 363
    Gana or classes of, i. 331
    Genealogical Tree of, iv. 160
    Generation, descended into, iii. 236
    Hierarchy of, the, i. 190, ii. 337
    Immortal, ii. 123
    Intelligent, v. 224
    Intermediate, v. 129
    Ladder of, the, i. 308; v. 356
    Life and, every form of, i. 311
    Life and, revolution of, i. 242

BEING (*Contd.*)
Lords of, iii. 410; iv. 145
Lords of, the seven, i. 153
Mahākalpa, cycle of, or, i. 113
Manifested illusive, i. 294
Manvantara, or period of sentient, ii. 90
Monadic, ladder of, ii. 358
Moon as disposer of, ii. 102
Mysteries of, i. 44; iv. 157
Mystery of the last word of, i. 315
Mystery of, the, i. 265; ii. 53, 369
Neutral centre of, iv. 300
Nidānas, or causes of, i. 112
Non-being is absolute, i. 124
Non-being a more real, i. 125.
Non-being and, i. 220; v. 384, 486, 400
Non-existence or absolute, i. 112
One number or, i. 152
Passivity of, i. 323
Plane of, after Nirvāna, i. 309
Planes of, i. 152, 181, 240, 298; iii. 243, 282; iv. 204
Planetary, v. 466
Poles of, the opposite, ii. 319
Pure, ii. 219
Root of all, ii. 354
Rootless Root, not related to finite, i. 79
Sacred number of, nine the, iv. 193
Sat not in itself, iv. 16
Secret of, and Non-being, i. 220
Self of, the, i. 157
Serpent and tree a divine glyph, of Immortal, ii. 123
Seven Planes of, iii. 243
Seven Worlds of, i. 179
Spheres of, the, iii. 46; iv. 187
Subhāva, or, i. 130
Supreme, v. 299
Svabhāvat, the Synonym of, i. 130
Thread of, i. 282
Two planes of consciousness and, iii. 282
Ultimate substance root of all, iv. 124
Universal, i. 327
World of, i. 155, 179
World of, one law in the, ii. 359
BEINGLESS, Æon, the, ii. 66
BEINGS, Divine, v. 219
BEL, Anu, and Noah, iii. 152
Bible and, the, iii. 382
Creator, the, ii. 72
Dragon, and, i. 50; iii. 378; iv. 45, 71
God and Planet, iii. 36
Jupiter, or, ii. 153
Mansions of God, and, v. 199
Mercury was the God, iv. 110
Moon, the eldest son of, iii. 385
Mulil, the older, iii. 147
Primeval Babylonian God, the, iii. 147
Saturn the same as, ii. 179
Sidereal Sovereignty of, v. 332
Sun, the, iii. 73
BEL-BELITANUS, iii. 215
BEL-MERODACH, Nebo son of, iii. 215
BEL-MOLOCH or Jupiter, ii. 184
BEL-SHEMESH Lord of the Sun, ii. 112
BELA, son of Beor, iv. 275
BELGAMER, the Swedish, iv. 344

BELGIUM, iv. 313
BELITA ANA and Davkina, iv. 30
BELL-SOUNDS in space, ii. 280
BELOS, temple of, v. 180
BELOW, i. 138
Above so, as, i. 266, 317
Above or, not known to occultist, ii. 396
BELSHAZZAR, palace of, v. 245
BELT, Thomas, quoted, iv. 265, 294
BELUS, Thalatth conquered by, the male principle, iii. 65
Temple the, of, i. 49
BENARES, v. 340, 363
Astronomical observations at, ii. 390
BE-NESS, Absolute abstract space one aspect of, i. 79
Absolute Being or, iv. 16
Aspects, of, in Secret Doctrine, two, i. 79
Being, from, into, iii. 37
Ideal Abstraction of, i. 243
Life itself or, i. 129
Non-Being is Absolute, iv. 197
One Absolute, first fundamental doctrine of Secret Doctrine, i. 80
Rootless Root, is the, i. 79
Sat, or, i. 178, 199, 330; ii. 280; iii. 311
That is the One, i. 74
Thought or speculation, is beyond all, i. 79
Trinity symbol of One Absolute, theological, ii. 80
BEN-ASAI, v. 305
BEN-ISSRAÉL, Afghans call themselves, iii. 205
BEN YaH, son of YaH, iii. 94
BEN ZOMA, v. 305
BENFEY, referred to, iii. 101
BENGAL, Dwarfed races in, iii. 409
Sāgara the name of Bay of, iv. 142
Tāntrikas of, i. 211
BENI-ELOHIM, Sons of God, iii. 389
BENI-SHAMASH, Vatican tradition of the, iv. 75
BENJAMIN, Cancer in sphere of, ii. 377
BENNOO or Phœnix, ii. 24
BENTLEY, John, referred to, ii. 85, 391; iii. 73, 85, 428; v. 201, 344, 347
Chronology of, iii. 85
Great War, on the date of the, ii. 85
Newton correspondence of, and, ii. 214, 217
Precession of the equinoxes, on, iv. 120
Purānic Astronomy, on, iii. 255
War in Heaven, on, iv. 67
BENT ROSH, v. 252, 253
BEOR, Bela the son of, iv. 275
BERGERAC, de, New World of, iv. 272
BERIAH, v. 299
BERKELEY, Copyist, only a, i. 159
BERNARD, Claude, i. 294
BERNARDIN de St. Pierre on Plurality of Worlds, iv. 275
BERNOUILLI, Attraction, on, ii. 214
Plurality of worlds, and, iv. 275
BEROSUS, Chaldean Cosmogony of, iv. 72
Chronological errors of, supposed, iv. 21
Creation, account of, iii. 271
Cosmogony of, ii. 57; iii. 63
Ea, obtained information from, iii. 124
Fragments left by, i. 49
Generations of Kings given by, iii. 393

BEROSUS (*Contd.*)
 Genesis, knew the source of, iii. 151
 Ilus, the, of, ii. 53
 Keys extant in the days of, ii. 23
 Legend in, iii. 143
 Monsters described by, iii. 66
 Oannes of, iii. 196, 229
 Primordial Principle of, iv. 283
 Prophecy, taught, ii. 375
 Quoted, v. 57, 62, 180, 332
 Saroses, on the, ii. 381
 Thalatth of, ii. 109; iii. 71, 75
BERTHOLLET, Canaries, on the races of the, iv. 359
BERYLLIUM, ii. 274
BES, the God, ii. 100
BESTIALITY, Generations of, iii. 318
 Human, iv. 298
 Primeval mindless races, of, iv. 259
 Sterility present result of, iii. 200
BESTLA, daughter of the Frost-Giants, ii. 145
BETH, abode, v. 206
BETHEL, the Jewish, iv. 40
BETHLEHEM, the Star of, iv. 191
BETYLI and magic stones, iii. 345
BHĀDRAPADĀ, v. 343, 344, 345
BHAGAVĀN appealed to, iii. 404
 Brahma hurled to earth by, iv. 52
 Vishnu or, iii. 59
BHAGAVAT, Brahma directs his thoughts to, ii. 59; v. 345
BHAGULPORE, Round Tower of, iii. 94
BHANTE, " the brothers," v. 389
BHANTE Yul, " Seat of the Brothers," v. 390
BHĀRATA, India, generally means, iii. 368
 India, or, iii. 405
 Nandi brought from iii. 406
BHĀRATA-VARSHA, iii. 141, 188, 321, 322, 368, 392, 402, 403; iv. 69
BHĀRATEANS and Rākshasas, war between, iv. 345
BHĀRGĀVAS, Race of, iii. 45
BHĀSHYA, or commentary, i. 315
BHĀSHYĀCHĀRYA, N., quoted, i. 190
BHĀSKARA, the light maker, i. 161, 164
BHĀSKARA Āchārya, iii. 320
BHĀVA, Being or states of being, i. 130; v. 559
 Logos called, i. 301
BHAVĀNI, v. 412
BHRĀNTIDARSHNATAH, false perception, i. 84; iii. 117
BHIKKUS, v. 411
BHOD Yul, v. 396
BHRIGU, Prajāpatis, one of the, iii. 86
 Rishi, the great, ii. 154; iii. 45, 86
 Shrī, the daughter of, iii. 86
 Shukra the son of, iii. 42
BHRIGU, quoted, iii. 309
BHRIGUS or consumers, iii. 86
BHŪH, ii. 150
BHŪJAM side, iv. 148
BHŪMI, Earth, or, i. 260, 282, 294; v. 322
 Fourth Principle, and, i. 304
 Sisters of, the six, i. 295
BHURANYU an epithet of Agni, iv. 89
BHŪR LOKA, iii. 321; v. 537, 541, 544, 545, 549

BHŪTA(S), v. 244, 538, 541
 Creation, the second, ii. 165, 171
 Doubles, or, i. 235
 Empty, senseless, man remained, an, iii. 30, 113
 Form or mind, without, ii. 29
 Primitive man, a, iii. 110
 Progeny of the boneless were, iii. 99
BHŪTĀDI, Bhūtas proceeded from, iii. 116
 Elements, the, origin, of, ii. 88, 172
BHŪTAS, Fierce beings called, iii. 170
BHŪTASARGA, Bhūtādi preceded, ii. 172
 Creation, the second, ii. 165
 Creation, the elemental, ii. 171
BHŪTĀTMAN, living or life soul, iii. 117
BHŪTESHA, Lord of the elements, Vishnu as, or, ii. 172
BHŪTS or the genii of Hermes, i. 335
BHUVAH, ii. 150
BHUVAR LOKA, iii. 321; v. 537, 541
BHUVO-LOKA (BHUVA-LOKA), the middle region, ii. 87
BIBLE, Abstract ideas made concrete in, iv. 40
 Adept of the Chaldean, iv. 22
 Adonai in, iv. 19
 Allegory, of, v. 67, 192
 Androgyne deity in, ii. 113
 Archaic, our, iii. 424
 Astronomical symbols in, ii. 377
 Basis of, v. 192
 Bel and, iii. 382
 Blinds in, i. 186; iv. 40
 B'ne Aleim in, iii. 373
 Brahmans said to have plagiarized, i. 54
 Breath of life in, i. 260
 Carpenter of, iii. 110
 Celestial beings in, v. 212
 Cherubim of, i. 185
 Christian, v. 174
 Chronologists and, facts, iv. 260
 Chronology of, ii. 378, 382; iii. 81, 394; iv. 194; v. 181, 200
 Circle and, the, iv. 115
 Civilization, on stages of human, iv. 318
 Covenants of, three, iii. 51
 Creation, ii. 37; iii. 15
 Creations of, iii. 19
 Cross and the, iv. 115
 Dark sayings in, iv. 104
 Dead letter of, ii. 17, 28, 31; iii. 16, 104, 158
 Deluge of, v. 103
 Devil in, i. 138
 Divine origin of, v. 201
 Eliazar on, iii. 143
 Elohim in, ii. 60; v. 128
 Elohistic portions of, v. 196
 Emblems in, ii. 18
 Enos, Enochs, in, iii. 135; v. 106
 Esoteric interpretation of, ii. 28; iii. 232; v. 66, 97
 Esoteric statements in, iv. 55
 Esoteric work, an, ii. 33; v. 181
 Esotericism in, i. 308; v. 66, 97, 278
 Evolution and, iv. 230
 Exoteric, iv. 227
 Expressions of circumference to diameter in, iv. 114

BIBLE (Contd.)
Ezra's adjusted, v. 185
Fables of, ii. 50; v. 66
Fall in, iii. 285
Fiat lux of, the, i. 291
Flood in, ii. 54; iii. 153
Geometrical figures in, i. 134
Giants in, iii. 161, 279; iv. 69
Gibborim of, iii. 339
God of, ii. 344; v. 97, 167
God-names in, iv. 106
Great flood, records of, ii. 54
Hebrew, the, ii. 97; v. 178, 195, 197
Hermaphrodites in, ii. 37
Hermes Bel and Homer, the, way to the, through, iii. 382
Homer and, iii. 382
Humanity, of, v. 232
Inconsistencies in, iv. 103
Indian symbolism connected with, ii. 33, 133
Inspiration of, v. 200, 201
Interpretation of, ii. 32; iv. 316
Jehovah of, i. 308; ii. 300; iii. 135; iv. 32, 167; v. 187
Jewish, v. 41, 195
Joseph in, iii. 110
Kabalah explains, i. 314; ii. 58; iii. 232; iv. 195
Kedeshim of, iv. 28
Key to, iv. 39
Legendary form of records are, iii. 238
Letters, contains, 3, 567, 180; i. 50
Living Soul, of the, i. 284
Logograms in, iii. 335
Lord God in, v. 234
Male and female of, iv. 34
Man in, synonym for, i. 284
Mandrake of, iii. 40
Mary in, iii. 110
Mathematics and Metrology in, v. 89
Matzebah explained in, v. 237
Mighty men of, iii. 281
Miracles, iii. 200
Mosaic, the, iii. 54
Mysteries of, v. 68, 86
Mystery language, and, ii. 30
Nabathean agriculture and, iv. 22
Natural history, at variance with, iii. 256
Nephesh in, i. 260
No first man except in, iii. 272
Noah of, iii. 307
Numerical method of reading, iv. 113; v. 194
Occult book, an, v. 105, 136
Occult teaching explains the, iii. 376
Paracelsus and, i. 334
Patriarchs, ii. 171; iii. 365
Phallic element in, iv. 228
Plurality of worlds and, ii. 331; iv. 277
Pre-Adamic races in, ii. 37; iii. 254
Purānas compared with, iii. 134
Qū-tāmy, of, iv. 23
Records of, iii. 238
Revelation, a divine, ii. 109
Revisers of, v. 158
Roman Catholics and, ii. 188
Sacred animals in, i. 155; ii. 159
Satan in, iii. 377
Science and, iv. 316

Secret Doctrine of, v. 68, 72, 91
Secret Wisdom in, ii. 28
Seraphim of, i. 185
Serpent worship on, iii. 214
Septuagint, and, v. 183
Seven in, iv. 175, 182
Seven periods in, ii. 165
Solar years of, ii. 382
Solomon and, iii. 395
Spirit in, iii. 49
Spiritual elements of, v. 194, 195
Sunday schools, in, i. 275
Symbolism of organs of generation in, ii. 97; v. 71, 72
Symbols in, ii. 377; v. 208
Translations of, erroneous, iv. 49; v. 183, 209, 231, 317
Zodiac in, ii. 374
Zohar and, i. 261
BIBLICAL Adam, iii. 22
Adam chronology, iii. 81
Ararat, iii. 153
Azazel and, scholars, iii. 375
Chronology, v. 102, 200, 201
Cosmogony, iv. 215
Cross and, scholars, ii. 383
Dagon, iii. 147
Deluge, iii. 18; v. 102
Glyphs, ii. 33; v. 73, 137
I am the I am, i. 144
History, iii. 208
Jews, iv. 41
Names, symbolical, v. 86, 89
Numbers, ii. 33
Origin of man, iii. 165
Patriarchs, ii. 374; iv. 21; v. 357
Protestant, Society of Paris, iv. 108
Pseudo-personages, iii. 151
Pyramidalists, ii. 27
Teachings rejected, iii. 158
Theology, iii. 22
Writers, iii. 54
BIBLIOTHÈQUE ORIENTALE, referred to, iii. 393
BIBRACTIS, v. 295, 306
BIGANDET, Bishop, v. 365
BĪJA VIDYA, v. 396
BIMATER, iii. 362
BINAH, ii. 156; iii. 272
Chokmah and, ii. 156, 343; iii. 143; v. 192, 438
Divine names of, ii. 109
Female consciousness, iv. 97
Feminine word, i. 72
Heart or, ii. 67
Intelligence, i. 285; ii. 67
Jehovah in its best aspect is, ii. 108
Jehovah no better than, i. 262
Jehovah with, identification of, i. 277
Mother, v. 191
Nature, intelligent, iii. 94
Passive potency, or intelligence, a, ii. 70
Sephira, the third, iii. 383
Sephirothal triangle, one of, i. 161
Triangle of, i. 161; v. 213
Understanding, iii. 94; v. 211
Virāj and, v. 214
BINARIES and unities, i. 283, 284

BINARY, Chaos, the female, or, iv. 125
  Interlaced triangles, in, iv. 164
  Number five, in, ii. 99; iv. 147
  Pythagoreans hated, iv. 146
  Yin, the, iv. 124
BIOGENESIS, law of, iv. 241
BIOGENETIC law, iii. 194; iv. 229
BIOGRAPHER, of Mertz, French, ii. 354
BIOGRAPHIES, Gods, of the, iii. 179
  Planets, of all the, iii. 57
BIOGRAPHY, Devil, of the Christian, iv. 45
  Moses, the, of, iii. 426
BIOLOGICAL, Physical forces are, in their
    essence, ii. 190
  Sacrifice of Daksha, revelation in, iii. 189
  Speculations, modern, iii. 190
  Theories of Science, i. 269
BIOLOGIST, Mode of generation, and present,
    iii. 126
  Modern, v. 31
  Terra incognita of, i. 265
BIOLOGISTS, Antiquity of man not accepted
    by, iii. 22
  Difficulties of, i. 270
  Europe and America, of, v. 42, 47
  Evolution and Western, iv. 304
  Protoplasm, seeking for homogeneous, i. 118
BIOLOGY, Celestial bodies, and, ii. 31
  Materialistic views on, ii. 31
  Primitive, the, iv. 202
  Principles of, iii. 348
  Problems of, ii. 210
  Progress achieved in, iii. 361
  Science of, ii. 78
  Separation of sexes admitted by, iii. 191
  Vital principle, denies the, ii. 327
BIOURASP, delegate of Dzahhak, iv. 20
BIPED, Animals need not be either quadruped
    or, ii. 322
  Ape, a, type, iv. 247
  Evolution of man into a, iii. 441
BIPEDS, Daksha made, iii. 190
  Quadrupeds, created before, iii. 170
BIRCH, S., v. 252
BIRD, Angel, a symbol for, iii. 294
  Ash tree, divine, in the, iv. 89
  Constellations of the Vermilion, ii. 125
  First cause pictured as an invisible, ii. 74
  Immortality of, iii. 48
  Karshipta, the, iii. 293
  Leda is mythical, iii. 130
  Mammal, after reptile and before, ii. 120
  Phoenix, of Resurrection, iv. 24
  Rabbins' mythos of an enormous, iv. 189
  Soul, symbol of, iii. 294
  Space the nest of eternal, iii. 294
  Wisdom, of, iii. 294
BIRDS, Angels, glyph of higher divinities and,
    iv. 340
  Apollo and Athene as, iv. 340
  Balaam, which inspired, iii. 407
  Desert, human beings with bodies of, of the,
    iii. 66
  Divinities, glyphs of, iv. 340
  Giant, iii. 32
  Lizards with, wings, iii. 66
  Septenary law, and the, iv. 193

Shell-heads, with, iii. 206
  South, of the, iii. 438
  Third round, resultant of the, iv. 254
BIRD'S NEST, heaven, iii. 294
BIRTH, Astral, of the, iii. 15
  Astronomy, of, iii. 42
  Atoms, of, ii. 306, 308
  Christ, of, ii. 384; iv. 191, 261
  Cross represents, iv. 126
  Death, destiny from, to, ii. 364
  Elements, of the, i. 326
  Form, of every, ii. 303, 304
  Four modes of, v. 559
  Function, ii. 105
  Garuda, of, iv. 135
  Globes of, i. 222
  Immaculate, ii. 114
  Inequalities of, iii. 169, 304
  Initiates giving, to themselves, iv. 129
  Krita age, given to race who shall follow laws
    of, ii. 92
  Law of, universal, i. 200
  Life, and, ii. 61
  Man, of, iii. 276
  Mars Lord of, iii. 391
  Microcosm, of, iv. 151
  Miraculous, iv. 120
  Moses, of, iii. 426
  New Sun, of, ii. 126
  Number seven and, ii. 34
  Pentateuch, and origin of, iv. 115
  Race, of new, iii. 443
  Saviour, Oracles as to, of, ii. 383
  Septenary law, controlled by, iv. 193
  Seventh round, in the, v. 563
  Spiritual, iv. 37, 151
  Zodiac and, of Jesus, ii. 382
BIRTHDAY of world, number seven, ii. 124
BIRTHDAYS of Dhyānis, iii. 186
BIRTH-HOUR of Jesus, ii. 379
BIRTH-ORIGIN, iv. 35
BIRTH-ORIGINATOR, Jehovah as, iv. 35
BIRTH-SHELL, ii. 308
BIRTHS, Gautama on previous, iii. 358
  Second, several, for every, iii. 304
BISCHOF, Coal formation, on, iv. 265
  Experiments of, iii. 167
BI-SEXUAL, Androgynous, iii. 196; iv. 346
  Element, iii. 133
  Emblem, Jehovah, a, iv. 28
  Hermaphrodite or, iii. 141
  Mammalia, all life, before, iv. 166
  Man, iii. 141
  Primitive humanity, iii. 139
  Reproduction, iii. 141
  Root-types, iv. 305
  Second race, potentially, iii. 16
  Third race, iii. 144, 202
BI-SEXUALITY, Vegetable, iii. 142
BI-UNE magnetism, creative, ii. 122
BJERREGAARD, C.H.A., quoted, ii. 355, 357
BLACK, age, i. 65; ii. 192; iii. 433; iv. 96;
    v. 396
  Art, v. 46, 249
  Atlanteans, iii. 431
  Birds, inner meaning of, ii. 161
  Cosmic symbols, ii. 161

BLACK (*Contd.*)
Face, iii. 425
Fire, iii. 169
Land, iii. 319
Magic, *q. v.*
Magician, iii. 425
Men, and yellow, iii. 226
Race, iii. 251
Races, iii. 350, 422; iv. 265, 313
Saved, some, iii. 33
Sin, with, iii. 33, 230, 319, 406
Sins of, faced, iii. 424
Water, ii. 134
Waters, iii. 405
BLAKE, Dr. Carter, Article by, iv. 324
Naulette jaw, on the, iv. 313
Pacificus, named by, iv. 351
BLANCHARD, Opinion of, iii. 167
Origin of Life, on, i. 297
Pasteur rejected by, iii. 158
BLASTEMA, primordial, iii. 128
Protoplasm, or, iii. 128
BLASTODERM, Formation of, iv. 254
BLASTODERMIC Vesicle, v. 424
BLESSED, Hū, the Holy and, ii. 343
Island of the, iii. 370
Ones, the, i. 271; iv. 157
Seats of the, iii. 422
Virgin, rosary of the, iii. 50
BLIND, Anagrammatic, an, iv. 152
Forces, v. 223, 225
Ogdoad a, ii. 167
BLINDS, dead-letter in Gnostic Gospel, iv. 140
Esoteric, iii. 309; v. 435, 444, 469
Jewish Kabalists, of, iv. 134
BLISS, Absolute, ii. 294
Attainment of, v. 81
Humanity, final, of, iv. 185
Land of, iii. 355, 423
Non-Being, the, of, i. 124
Paranirvāna, of, i. 311
Seven ways to, i. 112
BLOCHMAN, Dr., Translation by, i. 47
BLOOD, Atmosphere of, ii. 256
Baptism of, v. 271, 272
Circulation of, ii. 265, 282; v. 31
Kāma Rūpa is, v. 553
Primitive humanity needed no, ii. 333
Shedding of, iii. 55
Spirit, water and, ii. 294
Vital force may poison, ii. 262
BLOODSHED, Sexual, the first, iii. 389
BLUMENBACH'S Malay race, iii. 327
B'NE Aleim, iii. 232
Jewish *Bible*, of, iii. 373
Sons of God, iii. 374; v. 299
B'NE Alhim, ii. 158
Children of God, ii. 130
Sons of the Gods, iii. 36
BO-TREE of Wisdom, ii. 247
BO-TREES, v. 49
BOAR, Avatara, the, ii. 84, 85; iii. 64, 85, 254, 321
BOAT, Solar, i. 274; iii. 150; iv. 99
BOATS, Third race built, iii. 398
BOAZ, Jakin and, iv. 65
Pillar of Solomon's temple, left, iv. 29

BOCHART, v. 184
BODHA, i. 43
BODHIDHARMA, v. 409, 410
BODHI, Samadhi or, i. 43
Tree of, iv. 160
Wisdom, v. 399
BODHIMŪR, quoted, i. 73
BODHISATTVA, v. 365, 366, 369, 376
Amitabha for his, v. 368
Astral principles of, v. 359
Buddha, and, v. 369
Candidate becomes a, i. 169
Chenresi a, iii. 186
Choice of a, iv. 374
Death, after, v. 374
Dhyan-Chohan, or, iii. 185
Gautama's mother, gives lotus to, ii. 94
Kwan-Shi-Yin, a, ii. 193
Shankaracharya, of, v. 376
Ultimate tenuity conceivable to, i. 137
Way to his Father, a, v. 369
BODHISATTVAS, v. 82, 168, 291, 393, 399, 401 539
Buddhas or, human, i. 123
Dhyāni-Buddhas, human correspondents of, i. 115
Human, worship of, iii. 46
Intelligences, as informing, iii. 46
Living, v. 388
Signs of, v. 392
Superhuman, ii. 295
Super-terrestrial, ii. 296
Worship of, iii. 46
BODIES, Animal, Monads in, ii. 355
Appearance, only human in, iii. 286
Atlantean, or, iii. 304
Atoms, of, ii. 349, 354
Brahmā, of, iii. 68
Buddhi, v. 366
Devas in illusive, iii. 270
Easily accessible, iii. 349
Elementary, ii. 350
Entities of forces denied to be, ii. 396
Ether, formed of, ii. 288
Formation of sidereal, ii. 292
Four, i. 261
Generation of, iv. 146
Hierarchies, of the, ii. 354
Inorganic, Monads in, ii. 355
Intelligence, the local fitting of, ii. 332
Invisible powers clothe themselves in, ii. 212
Lords, of the, iii. 30
Masters, of, v. 545
Monads create for themselves, ii. 357
Monads in every cell, ii. 355
Phenomenal, are only, ii. 356
Physical, in Pralaya, i. 309
Powers, of, ii. 212; iii. 54
Radiations of the seven, i. 303
Seven groups furnished with, iii. 304
Shadows of, sinless, iv. 181
Sidereal, i. 220; ii. 292
Simple or elementary, ii. 350
Sons of the Twilight, of, iii. 30
Vishnu in all, ii. 137
BODLEIAN Library, MS. in the, iv. 50

BODY, Adam Kadmon, of, i. 284
  Adam in the ark, of, iv. 35
  Adept, of, iv. 100
  Animal, the, ii. 256
  Astral Light, of, ii. 141
  Atoms of, ii. 292
  Auric, v. 427, 440
  Brahmā, of, iii. 168
  Building of the physical, iii. 243
  Correspondences of, v. 441
  Dawn of, iii. 170
  Day, of, iii. 170
  Deity, of, i. 285
  Desires, of, iii. 244; iv. 24
  Egypt of, the, ii. 127
  Fire and water, of, i. 137
  First, the, i. 240
  Force, and, ii. 226
  Formation of, ii. 395
  God needed a conscious, iii. 236
  Gods, of, iii. 170
  Growth, of, iii. 258
  Holy Ghost, the, of, i. 297
  Human, the, i. 304
  Illusion, of, iii. 67; v. 472
  Infernal, of Astral Light, ii. 141
  Inner man changes his, iii. 283
  Invisible, ii. 256
  Kosmos, the, Astral, of, i. 221
  Light, a, is? ii. 205
  Manifested, the, ii. 69
  Mastery over, iii. 274
  Matter, in animal, finely diffused form of, ii. 256
  Molecules of, v. 557
  Moon and human, i. 276
  Nephesh, mould of, i. 290
  Night, iii. 100, 170, 172
  Physical, i. 208, 287; iii. 243; v. 473, 518
  Procreation, used as means of, iii. 285
  Psychic man, tool of the, iii. 303
  Shell, the, i. 304
  Soul, built by the, iv. 296
  Soul and spirit inform, ii. 335
  Soul in every part of, iii. 299
  Spirit, soul and, i. 114, 172, 181, 272; iii. 249; iv. 174
  Sthūla Sharīra or external, i. 269
  Sun and moon in connection with, i. 276
  Temple of, the, i. 260; iii. 273
  Universal forces, cannot be detached from relation to, ii. 235
  Universe, of, ii. 56, 57
  Upādhi, an, v. 521
  Vehicle of the soul-substance, i. 205
BODY-VEHICLE, Soul, the astral envelope, of, i. 280
  World, of, i. 173
  Worship, iii. 281, 286
BŒOTIA submerged, iii. 272
BŒOTIANS Deucalion of the, iv. 88
  Futurity, prediction of, by, v. 334
  Zeus written Deus by the, iv. 154
BOETHIUS'S De Arithmetica, referred to, ii. 76
BOGATEREY, giants, of Russia, iv. 324
BOGOLUBOF, Prof., on anærobes, i. 294
BÖHME, Jacob, Genii, the nursling of the, ii. 217
  Newton derived knowledge from, ii. 217

Occultist an, iv. 167
  Theosophy of, iv. 201
BOHN'S Classical Library, referred to, iii. 410
BOHU, v. 165
BOIS-REYMOND, du, Hæckel criticized by, iv. 220, 221
  Hæckel and, iv. 233, 234
  Hæckel, versus, iv. 227
  Value of pedigree, on, iv. 226
BOKER, dawn or morning, iii. 254
BOLIDES, theory of, v. 225
BOLIVIA, Chulpas of, iv. 321
  Early man, traditions in, iv. 314
BONELESS animals, iii. 32
  Ethereal man, iii. 157
  Fathers, iii. 99
  Life to men with bones, the, gave, iii. 29, 30, 113
  Mind-born, iii. 164
  Primeval man projected by, iii. 244
  Race, iii. 199
  Self-born, or, iii. 178
  Sweat-born or, iii. 172
  Third race, animals in, iii. 190
BONES, Animals with, iii. 32
  Beings with, iii. 29
  Boneless gave life to men with, iii. 113
  Dauphiné, in Lower, iii. 279
  Enormous, iii. 279, 337, 346
  First race with solid, iii. 328
  Giant, iii. 295
  Giants, of, iii. 407
  Gorilla and man, of the, iv. 251
  Human, iii. 351
  Men with, iii. 30
  Phosphorus for, iii. 82
  Powerful with, iii. 31
BÖNS, iv. 157; v. 39, 393, 398
BOOK, Black age, written at beginning of, i. 65
BOOKS ancient anatomical, iii. 334
  Brahmanical, the sacred, i. 314
  Destruction of Chinese, iv. 262
  Enoch said to have concealed his, iv. 99
  Henoch author of thirty, iii. 366
  Hermes, concealment of the, of, iv. 99
  Hermes, the, of, iii. 38
  Hermetic, i. 329
  Inventor of, iv. 98
  Secret, teach astronomy, the, i. 252
BOPADEVA, iv. 162
BOPP, i. 54
BÖR, son of Buri, ii. 145
BORDJ, Mithras son of, ii. 54
  Suggestive myth of, ii. 54
BOREALIS, Aurora, and Australis, i. 253
BOREAS, Astarte, and, ii. 189
  Athenians sacrificed to, ii. 188
  God, the frozen-hearted, iii. 20
  Hesiodic, ii. 187
  Hyper-borean land beyond the reach of, iii. 2
  Son of, iv. 340
BORLASE, Dr., on the Druids, iv. 325
BORNEO, Fragments of, iii. 226
  Part of Australian continent, iv. 357
  Wild men of, iii. 201
BORRICHIUS, Olaus, v. 297

BORSIPPA, Temple of Nebo at, iv. 23
BORY de St. Vincent, iv. 216
BOS, Frontosus, iii. 289
  Longifrons, iii. 289
  Primigenius, iii. 289
BOSCOVITCH on centres of force, ii. 231
BOSOM, Aditi, of, ii. 350
  Breath returning to eternal, iii. 54
  Earth, of, iii. 17
  Eternal, i. 200; iii. 54
  Eternal mother, of, i. 199
  Eternal one, of, ii. 291
  Mother, the, i. 149, 201
  Space, of inner, i. 200
BOSSUET, Fallen angels, on the, ii. 44
  Idolatry, on, iii. 281
  Quoted, v. 330
  Speculations of, iv. 53
BOTANY, Atlantis, points to, iv. 308
  Esoteric teachings confirmed by, iii. 202
  Nodes, uses the terms, ii. 33
  Occult, i. 306
  Triangle, and the, iv. 166
  Zoology, and, iii. 125
BOTTOMLESS, Pit, ii. 52, iii. 240
  Space, in its, depths, ii. 340
BOUCHEPORN, de, Speculations of, iii. 329
BOUCHER De Perthes, Discoveries of, iv. 245
  Fossil man, on, iii. 279
BOUH, Sarmatian God, iv. 173
BOUILLAUD, ii. 390
BOULANGER, quoted, iii. 371
BOULAQ or Bulak, Discoveries of mummies at, i. 52
  Museum, ii. 101
  Papyri, v. 243
  Theban Triad represented at, iv. 32
BOUNDLESS, Absolutely, ii. 69
  Aditi the, i. 161
  Age, v. 391
  Ain Soph, the, iii. 134
  All, Ain Soph, the, i. 169
  All, darkness filled the, i. 113
  Being, v. 191
  Bounded and conditioned, i. 126
  Circle, i. 160, 173; iii. 339; iv. 56
  Darkness, the, i. 160; ii. 41
  Divine substance, ii. 166
  Kosmos, periodical, i. 69
  Light, ii. 300
  Limit, gave birth to, iii. 236
  Manifestation, cannot be limited to one, iv. 126
  Monad is, the, i. 230
  One Cause, iii. 195
  Principle, i. 79
  Space, i. 173
  Space in the, i. 330
  Spiritual Monad, i. 230
  Time, iv. 119
  Unity, iii. 54
  Whole, ii. 107
BOURBOURG, de, Abbé Brasseur, Mexican demi-god in the book of, iii. 378
  Referred to, iii. 105, 110, 168, 218, 379
BOURDIN, Jules, ii. 310
BOURGEOIS, Abbé, quoted, iv. 245, 318

BOURGES, Dr., on Evolutionary Psychology, iv. 224
BOVEY TRACEY, Extinct lake of, iv. 295
BRĀHMANS, Dual system of, iv. 144
BRAHM, derived from root brih, i. 75
  Lotus, enthroned above, ii. 94
BRAHMA (neuter), Absolute Cause of all Causes, ii. 165
  Aspects of, i. 84, 121
  Brahmā confused with, iv. 33
  Energies of, iii. 124
  Incognizable, i. 121, iii. 117
  One Deity, iv. 209
  Pradhānika, spirit, one, i. 300; ii. 164
  Pums, and, ii. 164
  Supreme, i. 84
  Vishnu as, ii. 137; iii. 154
BRAHMĀ, Abode of, iii. 402
  Abraham, and, v. 110
  Activity of, ii. 174
  Adam-jehovah identical with, iii. 55
  Aditi, a form of, ii. 348
  Age of, i. 124, 254, 330; iii. 80; v. 493, 534
  Agni abhimānin son of, iii. 249
  All Being is, i. 125
  Allegory of, i. 153
  Anu the atom called, ii. 290
  Asleep, falls, ii. 92
  Astral children of, iii. 286
  Asuras and, i. 266
  Atom, called Anu the, ii. 290
  Beings from various parts of, iv. 196
  Birth of, v. 422
  Boar, in form of, iii. 254
  Bodies of, iii. 68
  Body of, iii. 70, 168
  Body of Twilight of, iii. 129
  Born of, iii. 174
  Brahman, distinct from, i. 262; ii. 266
  Brahman, vehicle of, i. 83
  Brāhmanas, of the, v. 190
  Brāhmans from mouth of, i. 258
  Cause of potencies for creation, i. 125
  Centaurs created by, iii. 75
  Chaos and, ii. 58, 59
  Create, does not, ii. 60
  Created deity, iii. 117
  Creates the world anew, ii. 175
  Creates four orders of beings, ii. 175
  Creation and, i. 125; ii. 173; iii. 172; iv. 114, 195
  Creation of, seventh, i. 264; iii. 170
  Creation of, third, iv. 114
  Creative cause, i. 76; v. 188, 233
  Creative power of, ii. 170
  Creator, i. 75, 84, 148, 161; iii. 56, 313
  Daksha to create, commands, iii. 190
  Darkness, sprung from, ii. 59
  Daughter of, i. 194
  Day of, i. 78, 278, 285, 291; ii. 136, 165, 275, 382; iii. 20, 79, 154, 308; iv. 73, 230; v. 353, 543
  Day and night of, iii. 80
  Days of, ii. 160; iv. 73; v. 327
  Days and nights of, i. 71, 131; ii. 84, 89
  Demons by, creation of, iii. 172
  Desire to create, moved by, i. 167

BRAHMĀ (Contd.)
  Dionysos, contrasted with, ii. 49
  Dissolution of, ii. 86
  Dyaus, merges back into, ii. 92
  Earth, hurled down on, iv. 52
  Earth, regions of, not our, ii. 113
  Egg, born from an, ii. 81; v. 188, 233
  Egg of, i. 301; ii. 46, 49, 83; iv. 123, 203;
    v. 456, 475, 486
  Egg, produced from, i. 146; ii. 65
  Emepht is, ii. 82
  Father-Mother-Son, in esoteric parlance, i. 114
  Female Logos of, iii. 115
  Fiery Javelin of, iv. 201
  Fire-god, ii. 54
  First gods of all nations, representative of,
    iv. 150
  First son of, ii. 245
  Five words of, iv. 152
  Four-faced, i. 125, 170; ii. 58, 184; v. 530
  Generative power, symbol of, iii. 133
  Golden egg of, ii. 49, 83; iv. 123
  Hair of, iii. 188
  Hamsa-vāhana, i. 144
  Hari in the form of, ii. 87
  Head of, i. 201; iv. 70, 150
  Heat, evolved from, ii. 95
  Hindu deity, iii. 418
  Hiranyagarbha is, i. 153
  Jewish, v. 192
  Jyotisha, name of, iv. 335
  Kabalist view of, iii. 136
  Kāla, emanation of, ii. 145
  Kāla form of, ii. 179
  Kālahamsa called, i. 84; ii. 74
  Kalpa, in a past, ii. 173
  Kāma born from heart of, iii. 183
  Karma, attributes defeat to, iv. 185
  Kashyapa's relation to, iii. 256
  Kinnaras created by, iii. 75
  Kumāras, creates, ii. 176
  Kumāras, reputed father of, iii. 114
  Kwan-Shi-Yin or, ii. 171
  Legends of, iii. 86
  Logoi, one of the, i. 129
  Logos, male-female, i. 74, 75
  Logos of, i. 194, 301; iii. 115
  Lords of being, creates ten, iv. 145
  Lord Prajāpati, ii. 295
  Lotus, issuing from, ii. 96
  Mahā-Ātma or, ii. 81
  Mahāsura rebelled against, iii. 240
  Mahat, is, i. 141, 263; ii. 170; iii. 171
  Mahesha and, i. 53
  Male called, i. 145; ii. 47
  Male Power, v. 165, 233
  Male-female, i. 130
  Manifestation of the ever-unmanifested, iii. 236
  Manifestations, or Brahman in its highest, ii. 123
  Manu-Svayambhuva is, iii. 137
  Manus created, iii. 240
  Manus, in day of, fourteen, i. 132
  Marichi son of, iii. 98
  Mars identical with, iii. 55
  Meru, seat of, iv. 354
  Mind-born sons of, i. 152; ii. 154, 295; iii. 56,
    141, 183; iv. 195; v. 78, 356

  Mortals, sons of, reborn as, iv. 345
  Nāgas, connected with, ii. 155
  Nārada at feud with, iv. 70
  Nārada cursed by, iv. 156
  Nārada son of, ii. 130; iii. 59; v. 287
  Nārada, teaches, iii. 60
  Naras created by, iii. 75
  Night and Day of, equal, i. 285
  Night of, i. 71, 79, 110, 114, 125, 131, 165;
    ii. 84, 89; iii. 80, 90, 308
  Night's rest of, iii. 247
  Origin of Gods from, ii. 175
  Origin of name of, i. 179
  Padma represents half life of, iii. 186
  Padmapāni, or, iv. 208
  Panchāsya, and, i. 261
  Parabrahman, and, i. 85, 262; ii. 170
  Parabrahman, with, iv. 168
  Pitris sons of, iii. 100
  Planetary principle, supreme, ii. 82
  Poetical description of night of, ii. 91
  Potencies of creation and, i. 125
  Pradhāna, superior to, ii. 86
  Prajāpati=, i. 146, 153, 158; ii. 144, 295
  Prajāpati-Vāch or, ii. 150; v. 439
  Prajāpatis, one of the, ii. 70
  Prakriti and spirit, essentially, ii. 269
  Prakriti, aspect of, ii. 266
  Prakriti, in womb of, iv. 96
  Prakritika at end of age of, ii. 86
  Pralaya, Mahā, or, i. 225
  Primary period of activity of, ii. 174
  Progeny of, first, iii. 87
  Propator, as, i. 262
  Ra and, i. 277
  Rebels against, ii. 177; iii. 381
  Recoalescence of, iii. 310
  Rig Veda, not named in, ii. 144, 162
  Rudra and, iv. 118
  Rudra, creates progeny in, iv. 185
  Rudra from head of, i. 201
  Sanandana son of, iii. 87
  Sarasvatī wife of, iii. 86
  Sarpas from hair of, iii. 188
  Saviours of, iii. 171
  Sephirotic tree, personifies, ii. 67
  Seven creations of, iv. 195; v. 199
  Shiva precipitated by, iv. 84
  Shiva springs from, iii. 251
  Shiva, Vishnu and, i. 328
  Six creations work of, ii. 172, 173
  Son (s) of, i. 152, 175, 282; ii. 130, 154, 176,
    245, 295; iii. 56, 59, 87, 98, 100, 102, 141,
    180, 183, 249; iv. 195, 345; v. 111, 291,
    356
  Sons of, rebellious, iii. 92
  Soul of world, evolved from, ii. 95
  Sound of names answering to, ii. 168
  Spirit and Prakriti, essentially, ii. 269
  Spirit of life, ii. 81
  Supreme, every, iii. 358
  Suras, breathed out, iii. 95
  Svar-loka abode of, iii. 402
  Swan, assumes form of, ii. 72
  Symbol of generative power, iii. 133
  Symbol of Seven Universal Forces, v. 472
  THAT, an aspect of, ii. 89, 170

BRAHMĀ (Contd.)
Theogony and, ii. 152
Theos, is, ii. 58
Universal soul, Akashic form of, i. 76
Universe and, i. 148; ii. 148, 165; iii. 43, 310; iv. 187
Vāch, and, ii. 148; iii. 155; iv. 40
Vāch, daughter of, i. 194; iii. 416
Vāch, female Logos of, iii. 115
Vāhan of, i. 145
Vaivasvata, preceded, iii. 152
Vedas, not found in, i. 43
Vedhas and sons of, iii. 87
Virāj and, i. 194; iii. 98
Vishnu and, i. 53, 75, 328
Vishnu as, ii. 138; iii. 154
Will or desire of, i. 170
Wrathful, said to be, iii. 87
Year of, i. 110
Years of, ii. 54
Yoga or union with, iii. 124
Zones produced by, seven, iv. 188
BRAHMĀTMĀ, v. 162, 395
BRAHMACHĀRI BAWA, iii. 425
BRAHMACARYA, Life of, iv. 25
BRAHMADANDA, v. 480, 520
BRAHMĀDICAS, Wilford's, iii. 150
BRAHMA-KĀLAHAMSA or divine Swan, iii. 130
BRAHMA-LOKA, the denizens of, ii. 87; v. 353, 537
BRAHMAN, Absorption in, i. 192
Anthropomorphic reflections of, i. 130
Anupadaka one with, i. 131
Atom, in every, i. 83
Brahm or, derived from root brih, i. 75
Communion of, v. 145
Divine unity, or, i. 309
Hamsa and A-hamsa, is, i. 85
Hamsa-vāhana, and, i. 84, 144
Impersonal, v. 188
Initiations, three of, v. 520
Ka, and, v. 408
Kālahamsa, called, i. 84, 145
Krishna greater than, ii. 123
Kshetrajna, or, iv. 210
Lord of all creatures, i. 159
Mahā-Ātmā or, ii. 182
Manifestations of, ii. 123
Meaning of, v. 269
Mysterium Magnum of Paracelsus, the, i. 130
Noumenon, the, ii. 89
One Self merges into, ii. 293, 294
Reality, the only, i. 83
Reflection of, i. 130
Root, the undecaying supreme, i. 73
Self, the, iv. 210
Spirit of life or, ii. 182
Supreme, v. 81
Swan, the eternal, i. 84, 145
THAT or, ii. 296
There is but one, ii. 138
Unity, or the divine, i. 309
Universal soul is not, ii. 138
Unmanifested, the, i. 75
Vehicle of, Brahmā the, i. 83

BRĀHMANA (BRĀHMAN), Advaita sect, of the, ii. 361
Āryan, iv. 39
Astrologer, the, iii. 409
Babylonia seat of, learning, i. 54
Caste of, v. 261, 263
Cosmogony explained to, ii. 269
Dvija, iii. 80
Grihasta or family man, iii. 409
Hotris and the, i. 158
Initiates, ii. 141
Initiations, three, of, v. 520
Kailāsa, and, v. 110
Key to Puranas, Initiates and, ii. 141
Mahat explained by, i. 142
Occultist and, iii. 82
Origin of true, i. 258
Sacrifice officiated by, iii. 155
Teaching of, v. 306
Upanishads, learned in the, iv. 162
Yogi. iii. 409
BRĀHMANAS, Āryan, v. 390
Bodhisattvas and, ii. 296
Creation, on first, ii. 169, 170
Earth, reborn on, ii. 295, 296
Knowledge of fire among, iv. 137
Orientalists, reproached by the, i. 136
Personnel of, iii. 286
Rishis, descended from, v. 41
Udāna as understood by, iv. 137
BRAHMANASPATI, or Brihaspati, i. 179; iv. 67
Brihaspati, Jupiter or, iii. 57
Exoteric worship, represents, iv. 67
BRAHMANDIKA or Solar and Lunar Pitris, ii. 160
BRAHMANICAL, Age of humanity, teachings as to, i. 205
Allegory, v. 199
Ambition, iii. 71
Aryan, nation, iv. 180
Books, sacred, i. 314; iii. 135, 154, 290; v. 178
Calculations, i. 200
Calendar faultless from, standpoint, iii. 62
Chronology, iv. 281
Cord, v. 520
Creation in, books, iii. 135
Esotericism, i. 274
Figments, ii. 86
Figures, iii. 78, 80
Forgeries, i. 53
Golden egg, the, iv. 123
Greed of power, iii. 71
Heresy, v. 366
Kosmos, doctrine of the, i. 204
Legends, iii. 418
Literature, i. 46; v. 91, 176
Logos, iv. 207
Mysteries, v. 105
Mystic phrase, ii. 296
Nārāyana, i. 132
Pitris of the, system, iii. 129
Philosophy, v. 358
Popular writings, iii. 80
Rāja Yoga, division of, i. 211
Sacred science of numbers, i. 153
Secret code, i. 315

BRAHMANICAL (*Contd.*)
Secret schools, v. 400
Septenary in the, system, iv. 207; v. 199
Temple literature, i. 46
Theo-mythology, iii. 101
Thread, v. 510
Vaidic Rites, v. 138
Wisdom in the Rahasyas, i. 314
Works, stored in a cave, i. 53
Writers, iii. 54
Yugas, doctrine of the, ii. 382
BRĀHMANISM, Buddhism, compared with, iv. 208
Demons of, iii. 102
Exoteric, iii. 42
Four a sacred number in, i. 153
Hinduism or early, ii. 60
Infinite Essence, teaching of, regarding, i. 71
Isis Unveiled said to be plagiarized from, i. 67
Venus in, iii. 42
BRĀHMANS, Akkad tribes and, iii. 207
Animus of, iv. 69
Arch-forgers and liars, declared to be, iii. 440
Aryan, iii, 389, 434
Brahma is for, alone, iii. 172
Brahmaputras, claim descent from, i. 258
Buddhism, enemies of, ii. 84
Buddhism, esoteric teachings of, i. 43
Buddhist canon possibly not lost to, i. 51
Calculations of, iii. 61
Calendar of, iii. 62, 77
Caste among, i. 314, 315
Asia, primeval, initiated in, iv. 135
Chaldeans instructed by, i. 54, 176; ii. 384
Chandālas and ex-, iii. 205
Chandragupta, arrayed against, iv. 120
Chronology of, ii. 380; iii. 63, 76, 203; iv. 166
Cycles of, i. 251
Deity, called after, iii. 135
Druids and, iv. 325
Dvijas or, i. 44
Eggs, do not eat, ii. 81
Family ties and, ii. 98
Figures of, iii. 162
Forefathers of, iii. 434
Gautama a disciple of, i. 314
Grihastha, iii. 87
Hells of, i. 253
India by, occupation of, iv. 179, 337
Initiated, i. 44; iii. 320; iv. 135
Instructors of, iv. 311
Kali Yuga, testimony of, regarding, ii. 387
Kalki Avatāra of the, ii. 99
Kshatriya kings, pupils to, i. 314
Life-cycle of, i. 277
Logoi, on, iii. 41
Lord of, iii. 57
Magas caste and, iii. 322
Mantras chanted by, i. 157
Manu contradicts orthodox, i. 74
Manuscripts of, i. 47
Messiah of, ii. 380
Moon's position determined by, ii. 390
Occultists differ from, iii. 308
Original sin, do not believe in, ii. 98
Orthodox, iii. 102
Pitris sacred with, iii. 100

Power of, over storms, ii. 189
Purānas of, iv. 136
Religion of, in relation to *Bible*, i. 54
Rishis and, ii. 301; iv. 70
Sacred books of, i. 53, 60; ii. 81
Secret Philosophy, and, iv. 207
Septenary division, and, iv. 164
Sevenfold classification of, iv. 212
Shramana and, i. 47
Shri-Antara of, i. 177
Soma drunk by, iv. 67
Teaching and, our, iii. 156
Tirvaloor, ii. 386, 390
Twice-born i. 44; iii. 120
Udāna as understood by, iv. 137
Upanishads of the, iv. 136
Upper India, land of, iii. 326
Vedas, keep original text of, i. 47
Wilford and modern, iii. 402
Zodiac, and the, ii. 384
BRAHMĀ-PRAJĀPATI, Alive, breath of, became, iv. 68
Creative God, iv. 39
First-born of, iv. 33
Jehovah-Sephiroth, identity between, and, iii. 134
Kālahamsa not vehicle of, i. 145
Male and female, i. 153
Virāj, creates, iii. 56
BRAHMA-PURUSHA, ii. 64
BRAHMAPUTRAS, Hindu, iii. 373
BRAHMARANDRA, in the crown of the head, i. 190; v. 520
BRAHMĀ-RUDRA, Mind-born sons of, ii. 178
BRAHMARISHIS, iii. 183; iv. 70
BRAHMAS, Buddhas, and, ii. 51
Five, i. 261
BRAHMA-VĀCH, Androgyne God, iv. 173
Aryan prototype of Jehovah, iii. 133
Manu, bi-sexual in, i. 139
Prajāpati, female half of, i. 146
BRAHMĀ-VĀCH-VIRĀJ, iii. 135
BRAHMA VAIVARTA, ii. 84
BRAHMA VIDYA, v. 434
BRAHMĀ-VIRĀJ, Adam, Mars and, are red, iii. 55
Androgynous principle and, ii. 70
Jehovah-Adam, identity between, and, iii. 134
Male-aspect of, iii. 137
Prajāpati becomes, i. 146
Vāch and, v. 190
BRAHMĀ-VIRĀJ-VĀCH, iii. 133
BRAHMĀ-VISHNU = infinite space, i. 75
Shiva, transformed into, ii. 262
BRAHMĀ-VISHNU-SHIVA, or three heads on one neck, ii. 103
BRAHMO-BUDDHISTIC system, v. 384
BRAHMS and A-BRAHMS in days of old, iii. 139
BRAIN, Anatomy, ii. 302
Anthropoids, of, iv. 252
Apes of, iii. 199; iv. 250, 252
Cavities, v. 556
Cell-tissue, iv. 243
Chokmah, number of the, or, ii. 67
Consciousness, v. 546
Convolutions of, v. 556
Dryopithecus, of, iv. 246

BRAIN (*Contd.*)
Eyes grow out of, iii. 296
Father, of the, i. 201
Grey matter, iv. 243
Heart, in the, v. 553
Illusion of our physical, i. 322
Impression, i. 309; ii. 289
Intellect, iii. 302
Mammalian, iii. 302
Memory, organ of, iii. 303
Mind and, ii. 327; iv. 247; v. 547
Negro, of the, iv. 248
Nerve fibrils, i. 337
Normal or abnormal state of, iii. 297
Palaeolithic man, of, iv. 256
Paralysis of, v. 557
Phosphorus for, ii. 307
Physical, v. 79, 487, 488, 527
Physics, of, iv. 243
Prolongation of, iii. 298
Seven faculties of, v. 442
Solar world, of, ii. 264
Speech, and, iv. 231
Vibrations of sound and, ii. 278
BRAINLESS, Sin of the, iii. 191
BRAIN-STUFF furnished by third principle of
Great Mother, i. 332
B'RAISHEETH, Construction, stands over the
six Sephiroth of, ii. 90
Logos, the first emanation or, ii. 90
BRANCHIOSTOMA, Materialists, may be an-
cestors of our, iii. 369
BRASS, symbolizes nether world, ii. 79
BRAUN, quoted, iv. 219
BRAYE, Dr., Statues discovered by, iv. 292
BRAZEN, Feminine principle, ii. 79
Serpent, i. 299; ii. 70, 79, 132, 194; iii. 212,
364, 386; iv. 40
BRAZIL, Fauna of, iv. 360
BRÉAL, quoted, iii. 271
BREATH, Absolute, Monad a, of, i. 292
Absoluteness, of, i. 331
Æther or, i. 141
All, of the, i. 132, 141
Angels of the first divine, iii. 104
Animal life, of, iii. 67
Asu or, iii. 69
Asuras, of God, iii. 69
Brahmā Prajāpati, of, iv. 68
Ceaseless, eternal, i. 124
Cool, i. 78
Cosmos, organizes, i. 135
Creative, i. 170, 177
Darkness, i. 132
Day of the great, iii. 20
Divine, i. 77, 114, 115, 245; iv. 121
Elements, first, of the differentiation of, ii. 171
Elohim, of, ii. 90; v. 228
Eternal, i. 124, 126, 132, 141
Eternal bosom, returning to, iii. 54
Eternal, which is, i. 77
Father, of the, i. 141
Father, spirit the, of the, i. 149
Father-Mother, of, i. 200
Film from a divine, i. 330
Fire of, i. 148, 149
First the, iii. 244

Fohat of, i. 193; ii. 360
Form, needed a, iii. 29
God, of, i. 135; ii. 297; iii. 69, 97
Great, i. 77, 80, 115, 203; ii. 174; iii. 20, 36
Heat, i. 165
Heaven of, i. 260
Hot, i. 78
Human Monad or, iii. 113
Intra-cosmic, i. 302
Kneph, concealed, of, ii. 68
Kneph, Snake-emblem incubates waters with,
ii. 68
Lha, of the, iii. 27
Life, the, of, i. 260, 272, 273, 287, 288; ii. 56,
351; iii. 91, 169, 182; iv. 23, 160, 203; v. 439
Light-maker or, i. 161
Mārtānda, dead, given back by, i. 164
Mother, of the, i. 149
Motion or, i. 70, 160; ii. 220; v. 229
Mystery of, i. 176
Nephesh or, iii. 169; iv. 23, 176
Nostril, from right, iii. 398
Number is a, i. 135
One existence of, i. 125
Perpetual motion, i. 125
Pneuma, iii. 121
Pralayic eternities, does not cease during, i. 125
Prāna, or, of life, iv. 203
Progeny, Fohat, of their, i. 105
Seven, gave life to, iii. 36
Soul of, iv. 203
Stone, becomes a, i. 167
Substance, divine, of the soul of, ii. 244
Supporters, of the, i. 298
Suppression of, v. 479, 486
Universal soul, of the, i. 163
Universe and great, i. 115
Vishnu, of, ii. 87
Voice, self or wind, i. 159
Voltaire on the, iii. 97
Word, crystallized into the, i. 145
BREATHS, Asuras the highest, iii. 101
Dhyan Chohans, never-resting, i. 165
Direction, which blow in every, ii. 219
Five, v. 486
Formless fiery, i. 261
Hieroglyph of the, ii. 398
Holy circumgyrating, i. 166
Intellectual, iii. 318
Nārada on the, iv. 137
One breath, of the, iv. 181
Seven, v. 357
Smaller, ii. 219
Understanding, had no, iii. 118
Worlds becoming as, ii. 330
BREE, Dr. C. R., on Darwin, iv. 266
BRETAGNE, Carnac of, iii. 379
BREWSTER, Sir D., quoted, iv. 271; v. 255
BRIAH, iv. 176
BRIAREUS not a myth, iii. 80; iv. 344
BRIATIC WORLD, the, iii. 119; v. 375
BRIDE, Christ, of, iii. 376
Christian Kabalists, of the, i. 263
Lamb, of the, iii. 234
Malkuth, of the heavenly man, iv. 167
Tetragrammaton, of, i. 285
Triangle, represented the left side of, ii. 340

BRIDGE, Celestial, the, i. 264
BRIGHU, 1st sub-race, 3rd race, v. i. 22
BRIHASPATI (see Brahmanaspati), i. 179;
  iii 57; iv. 66, 67; v. 339, 340
  Cycle, v. 339
  God and planet, iii. 36
  Gold-coloured, the, iv. 66
  Jupiter or, iii. 42, 147; iv. 23, 66; v. 340
  Religion, representative of exoteric, iv. 69
  Rig Veda, in the, iv. 66
  Rishi, v. 165
  Shukra foe of, iii. 57
BRIMHAM, Rocking stones of, iii. 346
BRITISH ASSOCIATION, Anti-Darwinists in,
  iv. 266
  Birmingham meeting of the, ii. 269
  Referred to, ii. 305; iii. 176
  Strobic-circles, and the, iv. 161
BRITISH COLUMBIA Antiquities in, iii. 428
BRITISH ISLES, ISLANDS, Birth of the,
  iii. 326, 343; iv. 320
  Elevation and depression of the, iv. 355
  Referred to, iii. 333; iv. 315
  White Island, said to be the, iii. 401
BRITISH MUSEUM, Archaic statues in, iii. 331
  Corroborative evidence in, iii. 340
  Could not contain all books in library at
    Altyntag, i. 48
  Dragons in, iii. 353
  Easter Island statues in, iii. 337; iv. 250
  Referred to, i. 190; ii. 115; iii. 426
BRITTANY, Menhirs of, iii. 351
BROBDINGNAGIANS, referred to, iv. 325
BROCA, Prof., quoted, iii. 252; iv. 251, 358
BRONZE, Age, iii. 204, 272, 273; iv. 89, 341
  Birth of the race of, iv. 90
  Periods, iv. 310
  Race of, iv. 90
  Wall of, iv. 345
BROTHERHOOD (S), i. 47
  Adepts, of, ii. 298; iv. 208
  Black, v. 46
  Esoteric, v. 400
  Freemasonic, v. 273
  Les Trinosophes, v. 296
  Nabatheans were an Occult, iv. 22
  Palliative, a, ii. 369
  Pledges demanded of Chelas by the, i. 218
  Rosicrucians of, v. 292
  Serpent, of the, iii. 385
  Shamballa, of, v. 372
BROTHERS, of Himālaya Āshrama, v. 390
  Light and Darkness, of, v. 467
  Shadow, of, v. 466, 502
BROWN, Atlanteans, iii. 431
  Black with sin, race became, iii. 230
  Races, iii. 230, 350, 422; iv. 265, 313
  Saved from the Fourth Race, iii. 33
  Zone was, fourth on every, iii. 33
BRUCE, iii. 438; iv. 101, 136; v. 99
BRÜCKER, quoted, ii. 171
BRUSSELS, Prehistoric Congress at, iv. 321
BRYANT, Jacob, quoted, ii. 74, 161; iii. 363, 390
B-S'PH-R, iii. 51
BUBASTIS, City of, ii. 103
BUCK, Brahma under form of a, ii. 149
BUCKLE, H. T., quoted, i. 337

BUDDHA, Adept, v. 79
  Æons elapsed before term could be applied
    to mortals, i. 43
  Age of, v. 377
  Aim of, v. 397
  Art of writing and, v. 27
  Aryan, i. 44; iii. 338
  Atonement of, v. 371
  Avalokiteshvara the first, i. 169
  Avatāra of Vishnu, iv. 149; v. 349, 352
  Dakinī, iii. 286
  Darshanas and, i. 119
  Death of, v. 105
  Dhammapada, in the, iii. 119
  Dionysus is one with, iii. 418
  Disciples of, iii. 46
  Discourse of, v. 379, 411
  Divine intellect, acquirement of, i. 43
  Divine prototype of the human, i. 168
  Doctrines of, v. 82, 349, 371, 411
  Dvijas and, i. 44
  Enlightened, i. 41
  Esoteric philosophy of, v. 363
  Eternals, two of, v. 381
  Gautama, iii. 338, 421; v. 125, 400
  Gautama or Amitābha, ii. 193
  Gautama, origins of the teachings of, i. 118
  Gautama, a Sixth-Rounder, i. 216
  Higher Self of, v. 365
  Hindu, a, i. 44; iii. 338
  Initiation, at his last, ii. 298; v. 363, 373
  King-Initiate, a, v. 263
  Knowledge not revealed since the days of, i.314
  Kshatriya, i. 44
  Law, the good, of, i. 51; v. 387
  Mahāyāna originated after death of, i. 112
  Maitreya, ii. 99, 192; v. 412
  Maitreya, secret book of, v. i. 23
  Manifestations of, v. 365
  Māyāmoha attributed to, ii. 136
  Melha with the personality of a, iii. 74
  Mistakes of, v. 363, 561
  Mystery of, v. 361, 363
  Neo-Platonists and, period between, i. 66
  Nirvana on earth, who reached, iv. 101; v. 350,
    366, 373
  Principles of, v. 366, 368
  Prohibition of the Lord, ii. 360
  Protectors of Law of, iii. 39
  Reincarnation, iii. 358; v. 373, 376, 378, 391
  Religion of, not contained in Esoteric Buddhism,
    i. 41
  Sacrifice of, v. 370
  Samādhi, in position of, iii. 338
  Saviour, the world's, ii. 94
  Shankarāchārya, successor of, i. 65; v. 364,
    378, 381
  Siddārtha, v. 357
  Spirit of, i. 169; ii. 193
  Supreme, ii. 295; v. 374, 420
  Svastika on statues of, iv. 157
  Threefold manifestation of every, ii. 296
  Tibet, perfect, to incarnate in, iii. 185
  Tradition of the life of, i. 314
  Unable to teach all imparted to him, i. 45
  Upanishads appealed to against, i. 315
  Wisdom of, i. 42

BUDDHA (*Contd.*)
  Worship of some disciples of, iii. 46
BUDDHA GAYA, i. 44
BUDDHAHOOD, Great Adepts who have reached, ii. 298
BUDDHAISM, correct spelling, i. 42
BUDDHAIST, correct spelling, i. 42
BUDDHA-LHA, iii. 421
BUDDHA-LIKE children, iii. 413
BUDDHAS, Anupādaka, designated, i. 123
  Bodhisattvas, or, i. 123; v. 393, 539
  Brahmās and, ii. 51
  Celestial, i. 168; v. 393
  Church, spirit of, present in the, ii. 193
  Colossal statues not, iii. 337
  Confession, of, iii. 421
  Contemplation of, i. 169
  Dhyāni, i. 32; v. 366
  Easter Island statues, contrasted with, iii. 228
  Enlightened, or, iii. 421
  Human, i. 123, 168; ii. 295
  Last of the, ii. 192
  Link between the, connecting, ii. 363
  Mahātmās or, iii. 421
  Mānushi (human), i. 32, 123, 225; v. 365
  Odin and, two different personages, i. 52
  Odin or Woden is one of the thirty-five, iii. 421
  Perfect, v. 399, 401
  Pratyeka, v. 390, 399
  Precursors of, iii. 206
  Prototypes of the, eternal, i. 168
  Race of, iii. 413; iv. 51
  Seven, v. 368, 409
  Shākyamuni, who preceded, iii. 421
  Statues of, of previous Manvantaras, iii. 228
  Succession of, v. 349, 376
  Twenty-five, v. 393
  World has had four, i. 115
BUDDHI, v. 427, 531
  Akasha, of, iv. 185
  Arūpa, v. 545
  Atmā and, v. 362, 451
  Ātmā, Manas, i. 267, 282; iii. 68, 121; v. 533
  Ātmā, Manas of the manifested universe, i. 83
  Ātmā inseparable from, i. 231
  Ātmā, spiritual vehicle of, iii. 234
  Ātmā, the vehicle of, i. 243; v. 451, 487
  Ātman and, iii. 243; v. 448
  Chit, quality of Manas in conjunction with, i. 330
  Conscience and, iv. 176
  Cosmic monad, the, i. 229
  Devamātri, Sun the, of, ii. 251
  Divine Soul, i. 82, 163, 178, 264; ii. 291; v. 362
  Ego, not, the human, iii. 89
  Ego-tism destroyed by, i. 43
  Faculty of cognizing, i. 43
  Functions of, v. 494
  Great Mother, second principle of, i. 332
  Human principle, sixth, iv. 165
  Indiscrete, neither discrete nor, ii. 172
  Individuality, acquires by impulse and effort, i. 82
  Intelligence or, ii. 88
  Manas as connected with, v. 427, 482, 533
  Manas, Ātmā, the human Triad, i. 267
  Manas attracted towards, iv. 64
  Manas becomes conscious through, i. 289
  Manas, liberated from its terrestrial, ii. 88
  Manas, manifesting by, iii. 277
  Manas merging into, iii. 417
  Manas, the fire which is the union between, and, iii. 250
  Manas, the Upādhi, of, i. 163
  Manas, union of, and, iii. 234
  Mahat, characteristic property of, i. 301
  Mirror, ii. 294,
  Monad, the cosmic, i. 229
  Operation of, v. 506
  Plane of, ii. 298; iv. 306
  Plastic mediator, the, i. 288
  Prakriti, a spiritual modification of, ii. 294
  Principles of, v. 427
  Ray of Ālaya, v. 471
  Ruach or, i. 290
  Sattva rendered, i. 136
  Senses and, iv. 209
  Seventh sense, iv. 210
  Shankara on, i. 136
  Sixth principle, ii. 193
  Solar Rays and, v. 423
  Soul divine in connection with, iii. 91
  Soul of Ātmā, iii. 69
  Spiritual intuition, and, ii. 43
  Spiritual soul or, i. 209, 322; iv. 152, 168, 203; v. 438, 471, 496
  Understanding or, iv. 209
  Union between Manas and, iii. 244
  Universal, ii. 296
  Upādhi of, i. 163
  Vāhan of Ātman, the, i. 308
  Vehicle of Atma, iii. 69, 234; v. 487
  Vitala, and v. 539
BUDDHI-MANAS, Atma, the, breaks loose from, i. 243; v. 494, 497
BUDDHIC Bodies, v. 366
  Consciousness, v. 532, 539
  Sense, v. 540
BUDDHIS, Divine Souls, or formless, i. 179
BUDDHISM, Army of spiritual beings to protect, i. 184
  Bhagavad Gītā, and, ii. 136
  Book of the Dead confirms, i. 267
  Brāhmanism compared with, iv. 208
  Buddhism and, difference between, i. 42
  China, in A.D. 51, i. 51; v. 406, 407, 409
  Chinese, compared with the Vision of *Ezekiel*, i. 184
  Chinese, i. 44; ii. 124
  Christianity and, symbolism in, ii. 263
  Darshanas said to be taken from, i. 119
  Dogmas, no, v. 385, 386
  Esoteric Philosophy and, iii. 164; v. 398, 402, 403, 407
  Exoteric, ii. 149
  Founder of, v. 72
  Four a sacred number in, i. 153
  Gautama Buddha, and, i. 118
  Genii of Chinese, ii. 124
  Hatred of, i. 43
  Hinduism, outcome of, ii. 392
  Infinite essence, on the, i. 71
  Isis Unveiled said to be plagiarism from, i. 67
  Key-note of, v. 397

BUDDHISM (*Contd.*)
  Max Muller on, iii. 255
  Monier Williams on, i. 119
  North, of, ii. 294
  Orthodox, and esoteric Buddhism, i. 44
  Pantheism and, v. 410
  Philosophers of, i. 71
  Pythagorean philosophy and, v. 387
  Religious system of, i. 42
  Sacred doctrine of, iii. 422
  Sacred number in, i. 153
  Schools of, v. 405, 409, 410
  Swedenborg and esoteric, i. 177; v. 406, 407
  Theosophy not confined to, i. 41
  Tibet, in, v. 39, 375, 392, 398, 404, 405, 406
BUDDHIST, Arhats, i. 51
  Āryāsanga, esoteric school of, i. 121
  Ascetics, i. 226
  Beginnings of, sects, i. 261
  Books of antiquity, v. 392
  Canon, sacred, i. 50; v. 390
  Chinese, i. 226; v. 410
  Chinese and, philosophy, i. 280
  Classification, i. 212
  Discipline, v. 413
  Dragon temples in, countries, iii. 378
  Esoteric and exoteric, iv. 157; v. 410
  Esoteric philosopher, Fohat of the, i. 70
  Esoteric traditions, ii. 84
  Esotericism, v. 406 to 413
  God and creation, denies, ii. 361
  God, recognizes no personal, ii. 360
  Hermits, v. 410
  Japanese, i. 226
  Literature, i. 50
  Logos, iv. 207
  Monastery in Kailās, i. 51; v. 405
  Mongolian, iv. 126
  Mystics in Japan, i. 135
  Nāgas, of the Exoteric, iii. 39
  Reform, i. 44
  Religion, Northern, iii. 421
  Religion in relation to the *Bible*, i. 54
  Rite during an eclipse, iii. 103
  Schools, so-called esoteric, i. 44
  St. Michael, a, iii. 74
  Sects, v. 399
  Svabhāvat, i. 118, 161; ii. 395
  System, i. 261
  Teachings, i. 201
  Tradition, i. 50
  Vedāntic teachers, and, i. 212
BUDDHISTIC, Philosophy, i. 237
  Legends, iii. 418
  Occultism, i. 44
  Svabhāvat, the, aspect of Mūlaprakriti, i. 130
  Theosophy, ii. 391
BUDDHISTS, Ālaya has a threefold meaning
    for esoteric, i. 121
  Atheists, not, i. 73
  Avalokiteshvara of, i. 188; ii. 146
  Canon, sacred, i. 50
  China, sacred island of, in, ii. 193
  Creator denied by, i. 71
  Founder, ii. 81
  Four truths according to, i. 115
  Island believed in by, mythical, iv. 208

  Island of, sacred, ii. 193
  Kanjur of Northern, i. 50
  Kwan-Yin, ii. 149, 192, 193
  Logos of the, i. 188
  Lotus held sacred by, ii. 94
  Mystical minds, iv. 126
  Northern, i. 43, 50; ii. 192
  Personal God, introduced no, ii. 158
  Positivists, of Archaic age, i. 71
  Sacred Books, i. 60
  Secret books, tradition as to, i. 57
  Seven-leaved plant sacred among, i. 282
  Tanjur of Northern, i. 50
  Tarim, visit the remains at, i. 48
  Vedānta and Uttara Maimāmsa, i. 118
BUDDING, Reproduction by, iii. 125, 174
BUDH, Male organ, said by Phallicists to signify,
    ii. 194
  Mercury is, ii. 195
  Sanskrit root, to know, i. 42
BUDHA, Birth of, iv. 67
  Esoteric Wisdom or, iv. 67
  Ida, wife of, iii. 147, 148
  Men of, iii. 56
  Mercury, or, iii. 40, 42, 366, 373; iv. 22, 110
  Mother of Mercury, i. 54
  Planet, a, iii. 366
  Sirius the star of, iii. 373
  Soma, son of, ii. 108
  Soma, father of, i. 275
  Wisdom, i. 42, 275; iii. 147, 148, 236; iv. 67
  Wise, iv. 66
BUDHA-SOMA of India, Thot-Lunus the, ii.112
BUDHISM, Buddhism and, Difference between,
    i. 42; ii. 263
  Esoteric, doctrines of, iii. 109
  Esoteric Wisdom or, i. 192
BUFFON, Fauna, on African and American,
    iv. 360
  Geological dates, on, iv. 268
  Plurality of worlds, on, iv. 275
  Referred to, ii. 321; iv. 216
BUILDER, Architect not the, ii. 143
  Conscious, last, i. 320
  Divine, iii. 199; v. 44
  Fohat the, i. 195
  Gods, of the, iii. 344
  Nature of v. 460.
BUILDERS, Architects or, v. 210
  Babel, of the Tower of, iii. 274
  Collective Deity manifested in, v. 309
  Creative Angels or, v. 449
  Creators, or, i. 70
  Dhyan Chohans called, iii. 177; v. 320
  Divine, ii. 315
  Divine thought, following the plan of, ii. 53
  Dolmen, iv. 322
  Earth, descend on radiant, i. 106
  Eastern Doctrine of, v. 208
  Elohim or, i. 284
  Fiery lives as, i. 306
  Groups of, i. 186
  Heavenly orbs, iv. 122
  Host of the, ii. 58
  Initiators of, iii. 344
  Logoi or, i. 146
  Luminous sons, the, i. 124

BUILDERS (*Contd.*)
Magnum Opus of, i. 297
Masons or, iv. 301
Men, were all, i. 167
Mound, iv. 322
Mountain ranges, of our, iii. 159
Nārada and, v. 287
Occultists believe in, i. 166
One, called, ii. 303
Osiris the synthesis of the group of, ii. 155
Planetary spirits and Lipika, difference between, i. 168
Powers, could only gradually obtain their, iii. 318
Prajāpatis called, ii. 90
Priests called, iii. 379
Pyramid, iv. 262
St. Denys and, v. 207
Seven, i. 152; ii. 154, 202; v. 171
Shining seven or, i. 260
Sons of God styled, i. 257
Stanzas, of the, i. 152; ii. 90; iii. 365
Supervision and guidance of, i. 279
Tree of Life planted by, v. 154
Universe fashioned by, i. 123, 165; v. 74
Watchers or, the, iii. 357
World, of the, iv. 83; v. 215
BULL, Adoration, of, i. 135
Aleph or, iv. 121, 146
Apis the sacred, i. 192
Dragon and, ii. 383
Eye of the, ii. 388
Fifth race, symbol of, iv. 102
Fire, principle of, ii. 105
Head of, ii. 383
Mendes, of, ii. 100
Nandi, the sacred, iii. 406
One of four sacred animals, ii. 78
Ormazd, of, iii. 102
Osiris, sacred to, ii. 105
Phallic symbol, a, iv. 154
Pleiades beyond the, ii. 374
Ruling daimon, v. 439
St. Luke and the, iii. 123
Six-pointed star, in the, iv. 102
Symbol, as a, iii. 416; iv. 102, 154
Taurus or, ii. 383
Uriel the, i. 185; iii. 124
BULLS, Assyrian, iii. 123
Men, with the heads of, iii. 65
BULSTRODE, W., quoted, v. 388
BUMI haptāita, iv. 327
BUNSEN, Baron, Deluge traced by, iii. 149
Egypt, on antiquity of, ii. 153
Eusebius and, i. 50
Great Pyramid, on, iv. 319
Menes, on antiquity of iii. 373
Prometheus, on, iii. 411
Referred to, i. 175; ii. 252; iii. 44, 91; v. 58, 140, 249, 296, 502
BUNYAN, referred to, v. 70
BURATS, v. 398, 403
BURGESS referred to, ii. 391
BURGUNDY, Dukes of, v. 264
BURI, the Producer, ii. 145
BURMA, Nirvāna, Neibban in, i. 112
Philosophical teaching in, i. 44

BURMEISTER, Antiquity of man, on the, iv. 319
Development of the earth, on the, ii. 364
Opinions of, iii. 162
BURNELL'S translations referred to, ii. 46, 47; iv. 145
BURNES on statues at Bamian, iii. 337
BURNOUF, quoted, ii. 95; iii. 389; iv. 119, 141; v. 380, 398, 408
BURNS, Robert, referred to, ii. 16
BUSHMAN, Low intellectuality of, iii. 175
BUSHMEN, Arrowheads of, iv. 91
Culture cannot raise, iii. 419
Inferior race, an, iii. 288; iv. 290
Lemuro-Atlanteans, iii. 201
Palaeolithic men, iv. 91
Pigmy, iv. 291
BUTLEROF, Prof., quoted, referred to, i. 295; ii. 241, 244, 305; iv. 221
BUTO, v. 165
BUTTERFLY, Ego-Soul free as a, iv. 131
Grub becoming chrysalis then, i. 213
Soul symbolized by, iii. 294
BYBLINE HEIGHTS, iii. 415
BYBLUS and Tyre, v. 279
BYTHOS, Aion existed before, ii. 64
Depth, iii. 218; iv. 139, 144, 145, 146; v. 165
Ennoia of, iv. 58
Gnostics, of, i. 262; iv. 58
Sigē and, iv. 145, 146
BYZANTINE style of painting, iii. 339

C

CABBALAH, iii. 49, 50, 51, 86
CABBALISTIC value of name of Christ, iv. 110
CABAR ZIO, mighty lord of splendour, i. 246
CABIRI, Faber's, iii. 359
Mysteries of, iii. 267
Races of, iii. 392
Sanchoniathon of, iii. 392
Titans or, iii. 150
CACTUS-PLANT, Races illustrated by, iii. 432
CADIZ Atlantis located beyond, iii. 370
CADMUS, Alphabet of, i. 46
Demi-God, a, iii. 363
Generic name, a, iii. 270
CADUCEUS, Cynocephalus represented with, ii. 104
Mercury, of, ii. 273; iii. 213, 363
Serpent, of, i. 299
Symbolized by ogdoad, iv. 152
CÆCUM, Vermiform appendix, of, iv. 251
CÆNOZOIC AGES, iv. 166
CÆSAR, v. 295
CÆSAR PHILIPPUS the Arabian, ii. 23
CÆSAREA, Bishop of, i. 49; v. 157
CÆSIUM, Seeds of, ii. 276
CAGLIOSTRO and St. Germain classed as impostors, iii. 164; v. 46, 282
CAHERMAN, Simorgh instructs, iv. 188
CAICAUS fights the Divsefid, iii. 401
CAIN, Abel and, ii. 130; iii. 133, 143; v. 37, 62, 63, 71, 72, 86, 161, 164, 166, 190, 291
Abel's blood, shedding, iv. 37
Allegory of, iii. 225
Esoteric, the, iii. 136

CAIN (*Contd.*)
  Genealogy of, iii. 390
  Human Race, of, ii. 282
  Jehovah identical with, ii. 132, 302; iii. 386, 387
  Jewish myth of, iii. 393
  Kain, or, iii. 136
  Lord God, iii. 272
  Mars, is, iii. 389
  Nod, took wife from land of, iii. 288
  Personification of, iii. 391
  Prototype, symbol of, iii. 275
  Pulastya and identity of, ii. 133
  Sacrificer, the, iii. 275
  Samael or Satan, generated by, iii. 388
  Tiller of soil, iii. 275
CAIN-JEHOVAH, Eve giving birth to, iv. 37
  Jehovah-Eve and, iii. 136
CAIN-JEHOVAH-ABEL, iii. 133
CAIN-VULCAIN, iii. 391
CAINAN, Enoch begets, iii. 390
CAINITE (S), Kenite or, iv. 111
  Jehovah, becomes the name of, i. 72
  Phallic, and, i. 72
  Races, iii. 179
  Creator, call the serpent, iii. 214
  Degraded, iii. 388
  Deluge, and the, ii. 133; iii. 390
  Fourth root-race, the, iii. 153
CAINOZOIC times, iii. 211
CAIRNS, Proportions of, i. 257
CAIRO, Frog goddesses in museum, ii. 101
  Theban triad represented at, iv. 32
CAJETAN, Cardinal, iv. 100
CALCULATIONS, Astrologers of, ii. 367
  Asuramaya, attributed to, iii. 59, 62, 80
  Cyclic seven, of the, iv. 136
  Cyclic, various, iii. 192, 194
  Early Aryan, iii. 269
  Egyptian zodiacal, iii. 352
  Esoteric, iv. 364
  Esoteric, system, basis of, iii. 80
  Figures belonging to occult, i. 224
  Geological, iii. 81
  Heavenly bodies, concerning the, of, ii. 385
  Hindu, ii. 386, 389
  Nārada, of, iii. 80
  Sods, of the, iii. 394
  Temples and monuments, as to, iii. 379
CALENDAR, Arcadian, iv. 263
  Atlantean works, of, iii. 62
  Authority of, v. 250
  Hindu, iii. 77
  Tamil, iii. 77, 79
  Vedic, iv. 121
CALENDAR-FORMS of Mayas of Yucatan, ii. 106
CALENDARS, Nations, of various, ii. 106
  Ptolemy's, ii. 388
  Theogonies and religions, ii. 378
CALF, Allegory of the cow, and, ii. 113
  Golden, the, ii. 302; v. 71
  Puranas, in the, ii. 113
CALIFORNIA, iii. 328
CALIFORNIA SEQUOIA, Species of, iii. 24
CALLISTHENES quoted, iv. 191
CALORIC, Equalization of, ii. 250
  Luminous, i. 299

Material particles, not a motion of, ii. 206
  Motion not a mere form of, ii. 248
  Solids and liquids, influence on, ii. 250
  Sun force or, ii. 248, 249
  Vital, i. 299
CALORIFIC sun, energy of the, ii. 242
CALORIMETRY, ii. 207
CALPE, Strait of, iii. 370
CALVARY, Cross of, in Egypt, iv. 129
  Sacrifice of, v. 292
  Tragedy on, solemn, ii. 337
CALVIN, v. 60, 561
  On Michael, iv. 47
CALVINISTS, Theology of, iii. 305; v. 104
CALYPSO, Atlas, daughter of, iv. 331
  Ogygia, island of, iv. 339
CAMBODIA, Angkor-Vat, iii. 428
CAMBRIAN, Age, iii. 23
  Life, iv. 281
  Period, iii. 23; iv. 257
CAMBRIDGE, v. 51
CAMBRY, Recantation, of, iii. 344
  Rocking Stones, on, iii. 343
CAMBYSES, Sais, at, ii. 114
  Temple of the Kabirim, in the, iii. 359
CAMEL, Flying, iii. 210
  Llama and, iv. 360
CAMPANILE, column of San Marco, iii. 94
CANAAN, Descendants of, iii. 379
  Tall men of, iv. 325
CANAANITES, Arts and Sciences of, iv. 20
  Nebo adored by, iv. 23
CANARIES, the, iii. 226; iv. 358
CANARY- ISLANDS, Guanches of, iv. 248, 310, 358, 359
  Origin of, iv. 359, 360
  Sculptured stones of, iv. 359
CANCER, Benjamin in sphere of, ii. 377
  South Pole at, iii. 429
  Tropic of, iii. 355, 401
CANDAULES, Gyges successor of, iv. 345
CANDIDATE, Cruciform couches used by, iv. 129
  Dragon fought the, iii. 380
  Initiation for, iii. 380; iv. 29, 34, 113, 129
  Maruts represent passions in, iv. 186
  Pythagoras and school of, ii. 151
  Sun awakens the entranced, iv. 128
  Tau, and, iv. 113
CANDIDATES, Reincarnation revealed to, iv. 122
CANDLESTICK, Golden, iv. 153; v. 314, 316, 320
CANES VENATICI, Nebula of, ii. 322
CANNIBALISM, Neolithic, iv. 292
CANON, Buddhist sacred, i. 50, 53
  Christian, i. 248; iv. 107
  Hebrew, ii. 373
  Jehovah in the Christian, iv. 107
  Monochord, of, iv. 172
  Proportion lost, of, i. 257
CANSTADT Man of, iv. 257, 313, 314
CANTON, Descendants of the Miao-tse, near, iii. 282
CAPE DE VERDE, Elevation near, iv. 361
  Islands, iii. 226; iv. 359
CAPE OF GOOD HOPE, Meteorites at, iv. 276

CAPELLINI, Discoveries by, iii. 290
CAPRICORN(US), Constellation of, i. 279; iv. 147
  Dhyānis, abode of, in, i. 266
  Dolphin became, iv. 150
  Goat and, iv. 150
  Naphtali, in, ii. 377
  North Pole at, iii. 429
  Tropic of, iii. 355
CAPTIVITY, the Babylonian, iv. 41, 189; v. 216
CAPUT ANGELORUM, iii. 240
CARBON, Atoms in Benzol ring, ii. 349
  Element, an, iv. 164
  Elements saturated with, iii. 167
  Gigantic masses of, i. 297
  Groupings of, ii. 274
  Meteorites, in, iv. 276
  Molecules of, iii. 165
  Nature of Intelligence and, ii. 332
  Physical body, and, iv. 165
  Protoplasm, contained in, ii. 362
CARBONIC Acid, Experiment with, iii. 144
  Importance of, i. 306; ii. 307
  Oceans of, i. 297; iii. 167
  Plants dependent on, iii. 291
  Vapours charged with, iii. 165
  Waves of, iii. 253
CARBONIFEROUS Age, iii. 158; iv. 282
  Period, i. 297; iii. 278
CARDINAL POINTS, Cross pointing to, iv. 126
  Cube and the, ii. 83
  Four, ii. 60, 183, 341; iv. 148, 163
  Genii of the, ii. 124
  Mars held the, iii. 391
  Zodiacal circle, ii. 78
CARIBBEAN SEA, the, iii. 422
CARLYLE quoted, i. 259, 260; ii. 15; iv. 38; v. 45
CARMEL, v. 65
CARNAC, Brittany, in, iii. 341, 342, 346
  Initiates at (Morbihan), iv. 319, 323
  Serpent's Mount, means, iii. 379
  Stones of, iv. 321, 323
CARNELLY, Dr., referred to, ii. 308
CARPENTER, St. Joseph, the, iii. 110
  Vishvakarman, of the Gods, iv. 113
CARPENTER, Dr., on Foraminiferae, iii. 260
CARPOCRATES, v. 93, 128
CARSON (Nevada), Gigantic footprints at, vi. 324
CARTAS, quoted, iii. 379
CARTHAGE, Giant's bones at, iii. 280
  Joly on, iv. 320
CASKET, fallen from Heaven, v. 404
CASPIAN Sea, Astrakhan on the, iii. 414
  Indian Ocean, and, iv. 180
CASSELL, Rev. Dr., quoted, i. 173; iii. 50, 51
CASSIAN, v. 297
CASSINI, ii. 386, 389, 390
CASSIOPEIA, New Star in, ii. 314
CASSIUS, Hermone, on Kabirim, iii. 363
CASTE, Brāhman, i. 315; v. 261
  Chaldees, a, iv. 317
  Gotras of Brāhmans, iv. 70
  Initiates, of, i. 259
  Levites, a priestly, iii. 139
  Magas, of, iii. 322
  Nebo, devoted to, iv. 22

One Veda, one Deity, one, i. 145
  Races, iv. 70
  Upanishads written before, system, i. 314
CASTES, Evolution of Sacerdotal, iv. 71
CASTOR and Pollux, Dioscuri were, iii. 362
  Born from Leda's egg, ii. 81
  Greeks, of the, iii. 360
  Leda, sons of, iii. 130
  Moon and, iii. 132
  Semi-immortality of, iii. 131
  Sun and, iii. 132
CAT, Basht with head of, iv. 122
  Basin of Persaea in An, of, iv. 116
  Egypt, sacred in, iv, 122
  Genus Felis, iv. 301
  Lunar orb, sign of, ii. 16
  Lunar symbol, a, ii. 103
  Moon, symbol of, ii. 16, 17
  Sun also called, ii. 17
CAT-MYTH of the Egyptians, ii. 16
CAT-SYMBOL, ii. 17
CATACLYSM, Atlantis of, iv. 181
  Book of Enoch, of, iii. 314
  Cosmogonical, a, iii. 153
  Deluge, and, iv. 320, 353
  Europe on the eve of, ii. 371
  Final, iii. 443
  Geological, iii. 154, 265
  Hindu tradition of, iii. 152
  Mid-Miocene, iv. 75
  Next, iii. 332
  Orphic hymn on, iv. 354
  Stock reserved from last, i. 316
  Zodiac used to foretell every, ii. 375
CATACLYSMS, Archaic scientists and, iv. 269
  Cosmic, ii. 85
  Ecclesiastes, in, iv. 273
  Europe, will destroy, iii. 442
  Final geological, iii. 227
  Fourth Round, iii. 157
  Future, iii. 403
  Geological, i. 66
  Globe, iii. 146
  Nations saved during, iv. 343
  Periodical, iii. 310, 332, 435
  Political, i. 66
  Racial, iii. 325
  Stanza 22, on, Commentary on, iii. 312
CATACOMBS, Chaldea, in, iii. 378
  Egypt, in, iii. 378
  Iconography of, iv. 158
  Ozimandyas, of, ii. 34
  Svastika in, iv. 158
CATARRHINE Apes, descendants of, iii. 266
  Baboon, iv. 232
CATARRHINES, Man and the long-tailed, iv. 236
CATARRHINI, Ancestors of, iv. 249
  Anthropoids, iii. 198
CATARRHINIANS, Old-world, iii. 178
CATARRHINIDES, iii. 328
CATECHISM, Calvinist, iii. 305
  Commentaries on, iii. 67
  Druses, of, iii. 40
  Esoteric, i. 338
  Inner Schools, of, iii. 283
  Occult, i. 77, 203

CATECHISM (Contd.)
    Quoted, i. 179; ii. 351
    Senzar, i. 75
    Southern India, of, iii. 43
    Vishishthādvaita Vedāntins, of, ii. 246
CATERPILLAR, emblem of Psyche, i. 141
CATHOLIC(S) Christian, iii. 102
    Church, Roman, ii. 179
    Dogmatic beliefs of, ii. 222
    Writer quoted, a, iii. 94
CATHOLICISM, and Magic, v. 45
    Ante-historical, Roman, ii. 116
    Spiritualism, and, v. 48
    Secret Symbology, and, v. 46
CAUCASIAN Aryan race, iv. 38
    Mountains, iii. 247, 397
CAUCASUS, Arctic circle and, iii. 397
    Mountains of, iii. 414
    Prometheus chained on Mount, iii. 412
    Songsters of the, iii. 398
CAUCHY, Atoms, on, ii. 205, 209, 212
    Velocity of chromatic rays, on, ii. 209
CAUSAL, Buddhas, v. 366
    Body, v. 77
    Consciousness, v. 356
    Soul, v. 77, 83, 351
CAUSALITY, Avyakta or, iii. 58
    Immaterial, ii. 121
    Latent, is, iii. 241
    Primal cause of the, iii. 129
    Unknowable, i. 196
CAUSATION, Effects, and, iv. 56
    Finite, ii. 363
    Intelligent, iv. 307
    Material, ii. 165
    Physical forces, of, ii. 186
CAUSATIVE, effects became, ii. 143
    Generation, Moon the, of, iv. 32
    Number 9, male, i. 174
    Womb of world, ii. 306
CAUSE, Absolute, i. 74; ii. 165, 399; iii. 87; v. 351
    Abstract thought of, i. 161
    All-Father, of all, ii. 145
    All things, of, i. 301
    Architect, of the, ii. 144
    Attraction, of, ii. 213, 253
    Being, of, v. 445
    Beginningless, ii. 269
    Brahma, the, ii. 165; iii. 117
    Causeless, i. 76, 80, 109, 125, 153, 302, 323;
        ii. 143, 293; iii. 244; iv. 160
    Causes of, ii. 292
    Concatenation of, iv. 233
    Conscious, ii. 241
    Creation not work of highest, ii. 138
    Creative, i. 76; iii. 220
    Definitions of a, ii. 230
    Deity the highest, iv. 183
    Divine thought the, i. 156
    Effect, and, i. 118; ii. 141, 158, 170, 234,
        293; iii. 250; iv. 170; v. 558
    Efficient, ii. 86; iv. 124
    Electricity not a, ii. 241
    Emancipation of, i. 328
    Endless, ii. 269
    Eternal, i. 80, 109, 114, 118, 156; ii. 170;
        iii. 306

Existence of a natural, ii. 326
First, i. 80, 81, 262; ii. 224, 324; iii. 128, 129;
    iv. 79; v. 187
First and efficient, iv. 124
Generated, i. 243
Great Unknown, iii. 116
Idea, the manifestation, ii. 347
Ideal, the, i. 125
Impossible to conceive anything without,
    i. 117
Incognizable, iv. 55
Infinite, i. 79
Karana or, i. 114, 118, 156
Karma and, ii. 359
Kosmos merging in the one, iii. 195
Life of, i. 274
Material, i. 118
Mechanical, ii. 318
Misery, of, iii. 383
Monad, of unity, ii. 343
Nature, of, ii. 169, 252
One Causeless, the, i. 80, 125
One, the, ii. 343; iii. 306
Pagan philosophers sought for, iv. 160
Parabrahman not first, iii. 116
Perpetual, ii. 269
Phenomena of, ii. 278, 328
Phenomenon, and, ii. 215
Primal, i. 114; ii. 343
Radical, i. 316
Seasons, of, ii. 334
Sorrow, of, v. 397
Space, the, i. 109
Suffering, of, iii. 383
Undifferentiated, ii. 47
Universal, ii. 379; iv. 81; v. 261
Unknowable, iii. 55
Unknown, i. 76; iv. 56; v. 218, 227
Variations of, iv. 218
CAUSELESS Cause, the (see CAUSE,
    Causless) Force, one, ii. 165
    Heat, breath of fire, or, i. 149
    World, v. 403
CAUSES, Absolute cause of all, ii. 165
    Agents, of meaning of, ii. 259
    Attraction and primary physical, ii. 214
    Being, of, i. 112
    Conscious, i. 201
    Developing, ii. 360
    Dynamical effect of, ii. 368
    Dzyu deals with primal, i. 168
    Effects, and, i. 224; ii. 234, 318; iii. 84
    Elementals are secondary, i. 202
    Endexoteric, are, iii. 84
    Existence of, i. 91, 116
    Heavenly orbs, of, iv. 122
    Human units can produce good, iv. 81
    Light, of, ii. 239
    Man creates, iii. 306
    Māyāvic, ii. 211
    Mechanical, iv. 222
    Misery, of, i. 91, 112
    Phenomena, of, ii. 207
    Primal, ii. 200
    Primary, iv. 164
    Qualities, of knowledge of, ii. 258
    Real, i. 201

CAUSES (Contd.)
  Science meddles with, ii. 186
  Second, iii. 128
  Sinful lives produced by, iv. 81
  Sphere of primal, ii. 200
  Transcendental set of, ii. 289
CAVE, Cro-Magnon, of, iv. 248
  Devon, in, iv. 290
  Gimil, of, iii. 109
  Hor-eb, the, of, iv. 111
  Initiation, of, iii. 240; iv. 128
  Malta, deposits of, iv. 291
  Sepulchral, iv. 248
CAVE-Dwellers, Ape-like, iv. 256
CAVE-LIBRARIES in Lamaseries, i. 47
CAVE-MEN, i. 256; iii. 319; iv. 284, 309, 310
CAVE-TEMPLES, i. 257; iii. 224
CAVERN, Fossils of Kent's, iv. 292
CAVES, Ancestors of the Nualts, of, iii. 47
  Aquitaine bone, iv. 313
  Hindustān, of, ii. 34
  Implements found in, iv. 91
  Initiate-Hermits, of, iv. 70
  Initiation, of, iii. 188
  Neolithic, iii. 351
  Race which retired to rocky, iii. 282
  Rishis, of, iii. 380
  Zoroastrian, i. 184
CAZOTTE, v. 282
CEDAR, Initiate called a, iv. 63
CELÆNO, daughter of Atlas, iv. 337
CELESTIAL, Abyss, ii. 75
  Ancestors, i. 293
  Armies, iv. 119
  Ascetics, iv. 142
  Ash tree, iv. 89
  Beings, i. 178, 184, 250, 263; iii. 99; v. 356, 368
  Beings, Ah-hi or, i. 111
  Beings, or Anupādaka, i. 123
  Beings, Avatāras of, iii. 421
  Beings, double of, iv. 46
  Beings, Dhyān-Chohans or, iii. 236
  Beings, happy, iv. 170
  Beings, group of, i. 268
  Beings, hosts of, i. 190
  Beings, Lha or, iii. 35
  Bodies, ii. 207, 304; iv. 196, 334; v. 201, 223, 224
  Bridge, i. 264
  Buddhas, i. 168; v. 393
  Calculations, ii. 390
  Chemistry, Hunt's, ii. 218
  Deities, numbers revealed by, ii. 151
  Demons, female, iv. 185
  Earths, iv. 187
  Fires, iv. 90
  Fruits, iii. 48
  Garment of primeval man, iii. 121
  Genii, iii. 373
  Gods, ii. 184; iii. 215; iv. 181
  Hierarchies, i. 319; v. 212, 368
  Hierarchy, i. 268; v. 368
  Host, leader of, iii. 381; iv. 185
  Hosts, leader of, iii. 73; iv. 119
  Logos, i. 291
  Maidens, v. 293

  Man, one, i. 277
  Men, i. 214, 277; iii. 57
  Messengers, iii. 311
  Militia, iii. 41
  Movements, ii. 385
  Musicians, iv. 156
  Nile, iv. 40, 151
  Numbers of China, iii. 48
  Phantasmagoria, ii. 378
  Pole, iv. 354
  Power of the essence of gods, iii. 101
  Priapus, iv. 25
  Prototype of man, ii. 364
  River, Noon, the, ii. 24
  Selves, ii. 295
  Serpent, iii. 44
  Singers, iv. 156
  Sons of Dhyāni-Buddhas, iii. 124
  Space, ii. 318
  Sphere, v. 201
  Spirits, ii. 87; iii. 369; iv. 54
  Stones, ii. 157
  Teachers, iii. 283
  Tetraktys iv. 175
  Thrones, iii. 422
  Virgin, i. 129, 263; ii. 46, 178; iii. 213; iv. 55, 81
  Virgin-Mother, ii. 179
  Wheels, v. 214, 321
  Worlds, v. 321
CELESTIALS, Human intercourse with, ii. 357
CELIBACY, condition of chelaship, iii. 297
CELIBATE, Adepts, iii. 92
  Eternal, the, iii. 204, 251
  Invisible, i. 264
  Kumāra, the eternal, iii. 204
  Sons of Brahmā, i. 282
CELL, Embryological, i. 270
  Infinitesimal, i. 270
  Monad in every, ii. 355, 357
  Nucleated, iii. 173, 257; iv. 228
  Nucleus, iii. 173
  Physical, i. 265
  Psychic, iii. 243
CELL-SOUL, Bathybius, iv. 220
  Hæckel, of, iv. 243
  Simple, iv. 240
CELL-SOULS and soul-cells, iv. 220, 240
CELL THEORY of botany and zoology, iii. 125
CELLS, blind indifferent, iv. 218
  Buddhist, iii. 339
  Formation of, iii. 258
  Fruit, i. 294
  Material body, i. 306
  Organic, i. 294
  Organs, of, i. 307
CELSUS, Origen against, ii. 164
CELTIC giants, iv. 323
  Mysteries, v. 306
CELTO-Britannic regions, Druids of the, iii. 379
CELTS, Apollo of the, iii. 55
  Stone, iv. 291
CENOZOIC monsters, iii. 295
CENSORINUS, quoted, ii. 151
CENTAURS or Naras, iii. 75

CENTRAL AMERICA, Early man in traditions of, iv. 314
  Le Plongeon explorer in, iii. 47
  Monuments of, iv. 358
  Ruins in, iii. 428
CENTRAL AMERICAN history, iii. 278
CENTRAL ASIA, Atmosphere of, iii. 356
  Brahmans initiated in, iv. 135
  Buddhist monks of, iii. 339
  Bunsen's deluge in, iii. 149
  Caves of, ii. 34
  Civilization in, i. 54
  Colossal status of, iii. 337
  Cross in, iv. 127
  Crypts in, i. 58
  Grotto in, ii. 185
  Mountains of, iii. 397
  Mysteries engraved on rocks in, i. 276
  Plateaux of, iv. 180
  Pushkara and, iii. 403
  Rock temples in, ii. 34
  Rocks in, iii. 437
  Sacred island in, i. 258
  Shaka and, iii. 403
  Sons of light in, i. 64
  Table-lands of, iv. 292
  Wisdom-Religions in, ii. 91
  Yellow-hue fled to, iii. 423
CENTRAL POINT, Atoms emanated from the, ii. 360
  Circle with a, ii. 79; iv. 123; v. 455
  Infinite space, in, iv. 40
  Inward, turned, ii. 53
  Monad or, v. 186
  Mystic system, of the, iii. 48
  Pleiades, a, iv. 121
  Svastika and the, iv. 126
  Unit denoted by the, iv. 164
  Vishnu's navel, or, v. 233
  White, ii. 41
CENTRAL STAR, v. 219, 277, 439, 441
CENTRAL SUN, Aditi and the, v. 218, 219, 277
  Creative light, emits, iii. 241
  Fohat, and, i. 250
  Great, i. 319
  Kabalists', iii. 218
  Mysterious, ii. 397
  Secondary and, iii. 242
  Shadow of the, ii. 363
  Solar systems separated from, i. 79
  Suns emanating from, ii. 251
  Universe evolving from, ii. 95
  Universe, of the spiritual, ii. 53
  Word of, i. 277
CENTRE, Animal, i. 304
  Astronomical cross, of the, iii. 102
  Being, of, iv. 300
  Circle, of a, iv. 115, 123
  Circle whose, is everywhere, i. 133
  Circumference, and, iv. 115
  Creative force, of, ii. 274
  Draco, the, iii. 44
  Empyrean, ii. 338
  Energy, i. 77; ii. 360
  Eternal, v. 325
  Force of, iii. 312

Human stocks from a common, iv. 315
Keely on a neutral, ii. 280
Laya or sleeping, i. 202; v. 536
Life, of, iii. 263
Logos a, ii. 151
Luminosity, of, i. 114
Macrocosmic, iii. 197
Mysterious, ii. 277
Neutral, i. 203; iii. 263
Rest of, iii. 242
Solar, the, ii. 325
Spiritual energy, of, i. 188
Sun the, iii. 161
Sun's, ii. 390
System, of our, iii. 157, 161
Triad, a, ii. 341
Unity, of, ii. 151
Vitality, of, ii. 291
CENTRES, Atoms of force, i. 147; ii. 353
  Being, of, iii. 46
  Caves stand for seven, iii. 47
  Creative, iv. 300
  Emanations of the, ii. 360
  Energy of, ii. 146; iv. 176
  Esoteric learning of Asiatic, iv. 15
  Etheric, i. 203
  Evolution of, iii. 46
  Fohat, of, i. 203
  Force, of, i. 176, 200; ii. 174, 231, 355; iv. 301; v. 474
  Forces, of, i. 165, 229
  Form of, ii. 352
  Imperishable, i. 200
  Laya, i. 200
  Laya, seven, i. 195, 203, 210
  Life, of, iii. 46
  Living, ii. 264
  Man in, v. 555
  Men born on seven different, iii. 251
  Monads, of, ii. 357
  Neutral, i. 203, 210
  Parabrahman, innumerable, of energy in, i. 192
  Religion, ancient, of, i. 52
  Ring, of the, i. 77
  Spiritual, i. 170
  Three, Seven and Ten, v. 435
  Vortices of, i. 255
  Wheels, of force, i. 176, 200
CENTRIFUGAL, Evolution, i. 310
  Force, ii. 223, 316; iii. 37, 177
  Forces, ii. 134, 328
  Matter, iii. 264
  Spirit, for, iii. 264
  Tendency equal to gravity, iii. 75
  Theory, ii. 317
CENTRIPETAL, Evolution, i. 310
  Force, ii. 318; iii. 37, 177
  Forces, i. 324; ii. 134, 328
  Matter, descending arc, for, iii. 264
  Spirit will become, iii. 264
CEREALS, Development of, iii. 372
  Neolithic, iv. 284
CEREBRAL hemispheres, the, iii. 298
CEREBRATION, and chylification, i. 337
CEREMONIAL Astrology, v. 335
  Magic, i. 73, 280; iv. 241, 317

CEREMONIAL (*Contd.*)
  Mysteries, v. 271
  Worship, Egypt, of, i. 52
  Profitless, iii. 102
CEREMONIES, Egyptian, iii. 427; v. 289
  Hindu, ii. 384
  Palestine, of nations remote from, iv. 39
  Purification, of, v. 271
  Worship, of primitive, iii. 366
CEREMONY, Holy of Holies, of passing
    through, iv. 37
  Priest at the marriage, ii. 340
  Sacrificial, iii. 109
  Sarvamedha, iv. 177
  Yima, of, iv. 181
CERES, Agriculture, and, iii. 389
  Diana, daughter of, iii. 417
  Ierna, worshipped at, iv. 329; v. 267
  Mysteries, of, v. 171
  Poseidon and, iii. 398; iv. 344
  Saturn and, ii. 226
  Sicily, in, iii. 363
CERINTHUS and the Gnostic sects, iv. 77;
    v. 351
CETACEA, the, iv. 238
CEYLON, Atlantis, a remnant of, iii. 226, 314
  Eclipses explained in, iii. 380
  Giants of, iii. 335
  Lankā or, iii. 332, 433
  Lemuria and, iii. 20
  Leo vertical to, iii. 406
  Veddhas of, iii. 201, 419; iv. 291
CHABAS, M., quoted, v. 244, 249, 251, 252, 256
CHABIR, v. 311
CHADYĀTANA, v. 559
CHAIAH, or principle of spiritual life, iv. 176
CHAIN, Cosmic, of universes, i. 115
  Earth lowest of the, i. 286; ii. 85, 166; iii. 107;
    iv. 72
  Earth, of spheres beyond our, iv. 271
  Globes, of, i. 113, 124, 206, 217, 224, 225,
    232, 248, 278; iii. 35, 87, 109; iv. 179,
    317, 327
  Humanity on our own, i. 224; iii. 79
  Links in one, i. 229; iii. 36
  Lunar the, i. 224, 225, 231, 247
  Lunar Pitris and the newly formed, i. 227
  Mount Rhipaeus, of, iii. 20
  Objective little, our, ii. 382
  Planet, of our, iv. 328
  Planetary, i. 86, 114, 172, 186, 207, 209, 210,
    278, 295; iii. 79, 236, 309, 320, 383; iv. 176,
    187, 267, 272; v. 529
  Planets, of, i. 85
  Pralaya, new, after, i. 234
  Septenary, i. 175, 195, 247; ii. 90, 309, 380,
    382; iii. 309; iv. 327
  Spheres, of, i. 254; iv. 135, 178
  Stanzas occupied with the planetary, i. 130
  String or, i. 217
  Terrene, i. 210
  Terrestrial, our, i. 217, 255; iv. 135, 275
  Wheel or planetary, i. 278
  World-planets, ii. 380
  Worlds, of, iii. 259; iv. 73, 176
CHAINS, Angels in the, of matter, iv. 59
  Circular, of globes, i. 215

Globes, of, i. 214, 218; ii. 299
Mars and Mercury are septenary, i. 219
Planetary, the, i. 206, 213, 224; iii. 311
Planets of, iv. 108, 269
Strings, or, i. 220
System, in our, ii. 299; iii. 312
Worlds, of, i. 207, 213
CHAITANYA, i. 73; v. 153
CHAKNA Padma Karpo, iii. 186
CHAKRA, Circle or, i. 173; iv. 33
  Disk of Vishnu, the, or, iv. 33, 116
  Mūlādhāra, v. 480
  Trans-Himālayan, i. 173
  Wheel, the, or, i. 262
CHAKRAS, seven, v. 483
CHAKRAVARTIN, the everlasting king, iv. 51
CHĀKSHUSHA Manu of the sixth period,
    iv. 186
CHALDAIC, Language, v. 184
  Letters, v. 163
  Phonographs, v. 178
CHALDEA, Adam of the Jews came from, iii. 54
  Berosus, in the days of, ii. 23
  Catacombs in, iii. 378
  Christian legends come from India via, i. 248
  Chronologies of, iii. 223, 427
  Dragon in, iii. 353
  Elohim came to the Jews from, i. 154
  Emblems of chaos in, iii. 385
  Ghosts of old, iii. 229
  Giants of, iii. 335
  Gods of, iii. 101
  Israelites' captivity in, ii. 25
  Kabiri or Kabarium received name in, ii. 153
  Magi of, i. 49; iii. 323, 393
  Measures of, ii. 25
  Rabbins brought calculations from, iv. 136
  Refugees of, iii. 205
  Religion of, i. 321
  Scriptures of, i. 49
  Sorcerers of, iii. 216
CHALDEAN, Account of Genesis, i. 49; ii. 32,
    72; iii. 16, 18, 19, 72, 112, 383
  Adam, iii. 110
  Adept, iv. 22; v. 242
  Alchemy, v. 297
  Allegory, iii. 292
  Alphabet, v. 114
  Ana, Anna derived from the, i. 155
  Annedoti, iii. 365
  Anu belongs to the, Trinity, ii. 71; iii. 72
  Arets earth, in, iii. 151
  Ark, allegory of the, iii. 292
  Astrolatry and Astrology, iv. 194; v. 329 to 335
  Biblical figures, and, iv. 195
  Bower of Voluptuousness, iii. 209
  Brahman, v. 110
  Civilization, iii. 229
  Cosmas Indicopleustes and a, iii. 398
  Cosmogony, ii. 44, 71; iii. 64; iv. 72, 188;
    v. 208
  Creation, account of, iii. 63, 112
  Curse, account of, iii. 284
  Cylinders, v. 123
  Dagon, iii. 64, 147
  Deluge, iii. 18
  Division of ether, v. 172

CHALDEAN (*Contd.*)
  Dynasties, ii. 381; iii. 316, 426; iv. 54; v. 236
  Fragments, iii. 64, 113, 124, 188
  Gnostics, Christian, i. 261
  Gods, the seven, ii. 298; iii. 106; v. 333
  Heptakis, the seven rays of, i. 274
  Hieratic texts, v. 57
  Hierophants, ii. 67
  Initiation, and Initiates, v. 137, 173, 242
  Jews borrowed, gods, ii. 381
  Kabalah, i. 249; ii. 344; iv. 29; v. 189, 208, 226
  Kings, ii. 32
  Legends, iii. 303; iv. 227
  Literature, i. 50
  Magi not, names of, ii. 380
  Man-fish, iii. 64, 147
  Manuscript, ii. 110
  Moon worship, ii. 104
  Moses, source of, iii. 426
  MSS., v. 102
  Mythology, v. 110
  Necropolis, iv. 30
  Noah, iii. 149
  Nuah, iii. 153
  Numerical system, i. 153
  Oannes, i. 307
  Oracles, i. 281; ii. 62, 183
  Philosophy, ii. 343, 397
  Qū-tāmy, iv. 24
  Records, i. 54
  Religion, i. 76
  Sanctuaries, v. 176
  Scriptures, i. 49, ii, 180; iii. 55; iv. 23
  Septenary, iv. 184
  Sin, i. 293; ii. 110
  Soma, worship of, ii. 108
  Star-worshippers, iv. 20
  Sun=El, in, iv. 110
  Symbology, ii. 33
  Symbols, iii. 382; iv. 22
  Tablets, iii. 16, 63, 71
  Teraphim, v. 242
  Theogony, iii. 250; v. 326
  Theurgists, v. 137
  Third eye, legends of the, iii. 303
  Tiles, v. 177
  Traditions, iii. 393
  Triad, iii. 39
  Trinity, iii. 72
  Works, i. 329
  Xisuthrus, iii. 147
CHALDEANS, Ain Soph of, v. 188
  Akkadians and, ii. 375
  Arts of, iv. 20
  Astronomical observations of, iv. 191
  Belief of, ii. 58
  Brāhmans and, i. 54
  Chronology of, iv. 261
  Circle, a symbol with, iv. 107
  Civilizations of, iii. 334
  Cosmogony of, iii. 36
  Druids akin to, iv. 325
  Ea changed into Tiamat by later, iii. 64
  Egyptians taught by, i. 176
  Esotericism of, i. 173
  Fairy tales of, i. 310

Genii of, i. 247
Greeks and, ii. 384
Jews borrowed from, ii. 381; iii. 150
Kabalah of, iii. 242
Moon, Nānak or Nanar among, iii. 147
Mystery gods of, iii. 17
Names in Genesis traced to, iii. 207
Numeration of, v. 341
Observations of, iii. 385, 388
Planets of, v. 242
Religion of, iv. 111
Sciences of, iv. 20
Svastika found with, iv. 158
Symbols of, iv. 107
Worlds of, iv. 175
Zodiac of, ii. 384
CHALDEO-Akkadian acount of creation, iii. 17
CHALDEO-Assyrian, Accounts of, iii. 17
  Tiles, iv. 45
CHALDEO-Hebrews, iv. 110
  Mythology, iv. 45
CHALDEES, Ancestors of, iii. 328
  Astrology of, v. 163
  Discoveries by, ii. 310
  Hebrews and, iv. 317
  Initiation of, iii. 354
  Legends of, iii. 153
  Magi or, ii. 125
  Meaning of, iv. 317
  Modern, i. 189
  Mysteries, iii. 47
  Symbology of, iii. 123
  Taurus sacred to, ii. 383
  Tiamat or Tisalet of the later, iii. 71
  Worship of, iv. 329
CHALLENGER, the, iii. 333; iv. 350, 351, 361
CHAM, Flood, v. 62
CHAMBER, King's, in Pyramid, i. 308; iv. 29, 34, 38, 128
  Tomb, Cheops's, of perfections, ii. 30
CHAMBERS, J.D. quoted, iii. 16
CHAMBERS, Seven planetary, ii. 292
CHAMELEON, Third eye in, iii. 298
CHAMMAIM, Name of Pyramids, v. 62
CHAMP Dolent, near St. Malo, iv. 321
CHAMPLAIN, epoch of North polar submersion, iii. 327
CHAMPOLLION, quoted, ii. 154, 195; iii. 367; v. 58, 214, 245, 249, 332
CHANANEA, the Rabbi, i. 64
CHĀNADĀLAS, Jews descended from, ii. 25; iii. 205
CHANDRABHĀGĀ, Barbarians masters of, ii. 92
CHANDRAGUPTA, Brāhmans arrayed against, iv. 120; v. 260
CHANDRAKIRTI, v. 402
CHANDRAVANSHAS, dynasties and kings, ii. 104, 108
CHANDRĀYANA, or lunar year, i. 110
CHANG, the Supreme Wisdom, v. 374
CHANG CHUB, v. 389
CHANG-TY, the Lord, iii. 282
CH'ANOCH, Enos or Hanoch, iii. 390
CHANTONG or He of the thousand eyes, iii. 186
CHAOS, Abyss of, i. 193; ii. 90; v. 227, 475
  Aether, and, ii. 144
  Ancients, of the, ii. 57

CHAOS (Contd.)
Atoms in Primordial, i. 205
Baoth, child born in egg of, i. 247
Binary or, iv. 125
Bythos and, iv. 146
Con-ton (kon-ton) or, i. 261, 286
Cosmic powers at feud with, iv. 45
Creation from, i. 245; ii. 171
Darkness of, ii. 59, 382; v. 233
Deep or, the, i. 134, 294; ii. 24, 50, 398; iii. 147; iv. 96
Deluge and monsters generated in, iii. 63, 313
Depths, the rayless, i. 264
Divine ray, and, i. 137
Divine thought and, i. 133; iv. 273
Egg dropped into, ii. 74
Energy reflected in, i. 50
Erebus born out of, i. 170
Eternal Element, v. 230
Evil or, ii. 24; iii. 383
Feminine symbol, v. 129, 192
Flood of waters in, iii. 152
Great deep and, iv. 96
Harmony and, ii. 151
Ideos or, i. 325
Kabalistic trinity, and the, i. 169
Kronos, and, ii. 307
Light in darkness or, iii. 115
Matter or, i. 154, 190; ii. 303; iii. 152
Moist principle or, iv. 163
Monsters of, iii. 63
Mother, i. 146; ii. 323; iv. 71; v. 129, 235
Mūlaprakriti, primary aspect of, ii. 260
Non-being, and, ii. 365
Noon or, ii. 24
Nux born out of, i. 170
Personifications of, ii. 149
Phanes and, ii. 307
Primeval, i. 164; iii. 94; iv. 73
Primeval deep, or, i. 134
Primeval space, or, iv. 45
Primeval waters, or, ii. 52
Primitive, the, ii. 323
Primordial, i. 205; ii. 24, 43
Principles confused in, iii. 384
Ray, causes to cease, i. 277
Secondary, iv. 54
Sense, to the, i. 70
Senseless, was, ii. 54
Shape, takes, ii. 69
Sigē and, iv. 146
Sound called world out of, ii. 151
Space or, i. 169; ii. 90, 179; iv. 45; v. 234
Spirit and, i. 137, 141; ii. 182; iii. 76, 112, 383; iv. 73, 227
Symbolism of, i. 132
Symbols of, ii. 149
Thalatth presides over, ii. 109
Tohu-vah-bohu, v. 189, 227, 228, 230, 234
Undifferentiated substance, v. 448
Universal form not mirrored in, iv. 274
Universe emerges from, i. 194; ii. 319
Vacuity, or, ii. 172
Virgin-Mother, i. 134
Void or, ii. 57

Waters or, i. 132; ii, 24, 52; iii. 152; v. 206, 228, 233, 234
Wisdom of, i. 140
CHAOS-THEOS-KOSMOS, triple deity, the, ii. 61.
Section, referred to, ii. 82, 87
Unknown First Cause, or, ii. 56
CHAOTIC, Antegenetic, or, period, ii. 72
Earth, ii. 54; iii. 139
Principle, iv. 168
CHAPPE, the Abbé, iv. 192
CHARĀCHARA or locomotive or fixed, ii. 173
CHARACTERISTICS Akāsha, of, i. 300
Animating principle, of the, ii. 363
Cell, in the germ, i. 270
Cometary matter of, ii. 321
Earthly, i. 318
Gases, of, ii. 348
Genii and gods, of, i. 329
Human organism, of, iii. 67
Kali Yuga, of, ii. 92
Karma, of law of, ii. 359
Matter, of, ii. 354
Races, of, iii. 442
Zodiac, of signs of, ii. 377
CHARACTERIZATION, Law of permanent, iv. 236
CHARCOT, Mesmer, vindicates, iii. 164
Referred to, iii. 370; v. 48
CHARIOT, Heavenly form used as a, ii. 71
Ray, used by the, i. 262
Vehicle, or, i. 262
CHARIOTS, Dhruva, attached to, iv. 57
Lha, of the, iii. 27
Planets, of the, iii. 44
CHARLES, Law of, i. 149; v. 122
CHARMERS, Serpents are, ii. 126
CHARMS, Fruit, on, ii. 190
Magic shield destroyed, iii. 393
CHART, Cyclopaedia, from a Japanese, iii. 208
Origen's ii. 167
Primitive and symbolic, ii. 41.
CHĀRVĀKA materialists, ii. 136
School of, v. 402
CHASTITY, Condition of chelaship, a, iii. 297
Gods of, ii. 193
CHAT or elementary body, iv. 205
CHATEAUBRIAND, De, on the Serpent, ii. 120
CHĀTTAM-PARAMBU the Field of Death, iii. 346
CHATUR, Eka is, i. 93
Four, is, i. 138
Tri, takes to itself, i. 93
Vidya, v. 519
Yugas, v. 259
CHATUR-MUKHAM or perfect cube, iv. 33
CHATVĀRAH in connection with Mānavah, iii. 148
CHAUBARD, the astronomer, ii. 230
CHAU-YAN, v. 411
CHAVAH, Eve a European transformation of, iii. 199
Hebrew, v. 202
CHĀYĀH in the Kabalah, iv. 205; v. 191
CHEBEL or conception, Abel is, iii. 133
CHEIRON, Brazen columns of, iv. 184

CHELA, v. 519
  Accepted, an, i. 218
  Eastern, v. 228
  Initiation of, v. 282
  Lanoo, or, i. 138
  Need fear no danger, iii. 296
  Probationary, v. 353
  Pupil or, i. 255
  Sagara, to Aurva, iv. 200
  Third degree of initiation, v. 172, 282
CHELAS, Circle of pledged, i. 224
  Diet of, v. 171
  Eastern, v. 74, 97, 228
  Master and his, i. 87, 221
  Meaning of dragon not given to, iv. 72
  Outer or semi-lay, i. 181
  Pledged, v. 85, 172
  Secrecy of, v. 97, 305
  Silence, Law, of, v. 74, 282
  Upanishads used formally by, i. 314
  Visions of, v. 172, 482
  Vow of poverty, v. 82
  Warning to, who fail, iii. 247
CHELASHIP, Conditions of, iii. 297; v. 305
CHELONIANS, iv. 266
CHEMI or ancient Egypt, ii. 83
CHEMICAL, Action, ii. 46
  Actions peculiar to different orbs, ii. 321
  Affinity, laws of, iv. 193; v. 531
  Agent, iv. 165
  Atoms, i. 198, 265; ii. 347, 351; iii. 116; iv. 242
  Combination, ii. 327
  Constituents, i. 305
  Death, action in, ii. 250
  Element, ii. 349
  Elements, ii. 51, 182, 348; iv. 198
  Evolution, i. 271
  Force, ii. 233
  Investigations, ii. 394
  Light, action of terrestrial, ii. 321
  Manifestations, i. 204
  Molecules, compound, ii. 350
  Natural philosophy, branch of, ii. 398
  Organism, structure in an, i. 302
  Particle, a, ii. 345
  Physical and, ii. 270
  Trinity, iii. 114
  Variety and numerical relations, iv. 198
CHEMIS (Chemi) Phantom form of the, ii. 83
CHEMIST, Atom of the, ii. 206
  Occultist-Alchemist and, i. 199
  Psychometer ought to be a, i. 250
  Zero-point of matter, stops at, i. 189
CHEMISTRY, Aryans learned, iii. 424
  Atomic mechanics, must be, ii. 238
  Atoms of, i. 265; ii. 205
  Chain and, v. 62
  Crookes a specialist in, ii. 346
  Discoveries, i. 197
  Elements, ii. 181, 271, 346
  Ether in, ii. 208
  Father of modern, iv. 226
  Hydrogen in, iii. 114
  Inductive science, an, ii. 310
  Magicians of the future, the, i. 304
  Mechanics and, ii. 237

  Mediaeval ages and, iii. 428
  Missing links of, i. 148
  Modern, i. 265; ii. 241
  Nature, and occult, ii. 268
  New, ii. 34
  Number seven in, iv. 198
  Problem of, ii. 320
  Protyle, and, i. 325; ii. 53
  Revolutions in old, ii. 347
  Sub-elements, ii. 61
  Terms, War in, about, ii. 51
  Vital, ii. 256
CHEMISTS, Adepts, alchemists and, iii. 348
  Atom of the, ii. 236
  Cometary matter not known to, ii. 321
  Discoveries, of, v. 467
  Element, view of the, ii. 347
  Ozone of modern, i. 303
  Protyle, searching for, i. 118; ii. 342
  Zero, use of the term, i. 195
CHEMNU ' lovely spectre,' v. 49
CHENRESI, Dhyāni, iii. 185, 186
  Padmapāni or, iii. 180
  Tibetan, v. 420
CHENRESI VANCHUG, the powerful, all-seeing, iii. 185
CHEOPS, Pyramid of, i. 174; ii. 30; v. 296
CHERCHEN DASYA, vol. i, 54-5
CHERUBIM, Ark, over the, iv. 87
  Bible of the, i. 185
  Cherubs, or, iv. 69
  Immortality, conferring, iii. 246
CHERUBIMS, Cunning work of the, i. 184
CHERUB(S), v. 325
  Apostles, and the, iii. 123
  Ark, on the, iv. 28
  Christian Hierarchy, in, i. 155
  Derivation of, ii. 80
  Eighth world is the abode of, ii. 153
  Elohim, sparks and, iii. 95
  Garden of Eden, at the gate of, i. 185
  Jews of the, iii. 123
  Lord God rode upon a, ii. 197
  Seraph, or, ii. 78
  Serpent or, ii. 80
  Tetragrammaton, standing beside the, iii. 360
  Wings of the two, ii. 377
CHESED, corresponds to Globe G., i. 249
CHETA Cave of Fa-hian, i. 44
CHEU, v. 393
CHEVALIER DRACH, v. 216, 219
CHEYBI or Spiritual soul, iv. 205
CH'AN or Dan a term for Esoteric Schools, i. 44
CHHANDAJAS or will-born, iv. 156
CHHĀYĀ, Astral image, body, or, iii. 110, 181; v. 565, 566
  Double of the Pitris, or iii. 128; v. 472
  Linga Sharīra or, iv. 165
  Lower Manas and, v. 533
  Pitris, of the, iv. 55
  Race, iii. 29, 99
  Seed, v. 565
  Self-born, iii. 110, 181; iv. 55
  Spleen and, v. 565
CHHĀYĀ-birth, a mode of sexless procreation, iii. 181

CHHĀYĀ Loka, Divine Arūpa reflects itself in,
i. 96, 178
CHHĀYĀS, Boneless animals, of, iii. 190
Fathers, of the, iii. 217
First race formed from, iii. 145
Images or, iii. 236
Inferior, iii. 231
Lords entered the, iii. 168
Lunar Pitris, of, i. 233; v. 472
Men, of, iii. 193
Self-born were, iii. 146
Seven of the third, iv. 162
Shadow-Adam of our doctrine, iv. 72
Shadows, or, i. 243; ii. 296; iii. 99; iv. 102
Solid, became, iii. 32
CHIDĀKĀSHAM, field of universal conscious-
ness iv. 168, 170
CHIIM, Elohim identical with, i. 188
CHILD, Earth, of, iii. 285
Egg of chaos, born in the, i. 247
Lotus-flowers seated on the, ii. 96
Present is, of past, iii. 444
Radiant, i. 93, 138
Receiving the kingdom of God as a little, iv. 72
CHILD, Mrs. L. M. quoted, ii. 73
CHILD-birth, Artemis-Lochia goddess of, ii. 111
Diana presided over, ii. 102
Dragon and, iii. 382
Grecian moon-goddesses and, i. 307
Woman in, iii. 382
CHILDHOOD, Humanity, of, i. 316
Languages of, iii. 204
Lemurians, of the, iii. 274
Mankind, of, i. 271
Moses, of, iii. 426
CHILDREN, birth of, iii. 230
Earth and mankind become, ii. 333
Earth, of, iii. 101
God, of, ii. 130
Inertness, of, v. 200
Israel, of, iv. 107, 109
Jesus on, iv. 72
Kronus, swallowed his, iii. 414
Mary, of, iv. 96
Men, of, iv. 108
Niobe, of, iv. 341
Rebellion, of, ii. 24, 80
Rebellious, iii. 216
Reincarnations of young, iii. 304
Sun, of the, iv. 75
Yellow father and white mother, of the, iii. 30
CHIM-NANG, the Chinese, iii. 365
CHIMPANZEE, Anthropoid mammal and,
iii. 198
Brain, size of, iv. 251
Creation of the, iv. 248
Dryopithecus and, iv. 246
Fossils of the, iii. 265
Human descent of, iv. 253
Intelligence of, iv. 245, 248
Nergo separated from the, iv. 248
CHINA, Ancient annals of, iii. 303
Architecture of, iii. 312
Buddhism in, v. 406, 409
Buddhist Arhats reach, i. 51
Celestial numbers of, iii. 48
Chronologies of, iii. 427

Confucius, and, iv. 124
Contemplative school of, v. 410
Cosmogony, i. 158
Dragon temples in, iii. 378
Esoteric schools of, i. 46
Falling demon of, iv. 54
Fohi in, men of, iii. 39
Garden of Eden in, iii. 208
Gautama called Amida in, i. 169
Kwan-Shai-Yin in, i. 139; ii. 193
Kwan-Yin in, i. 193; iii. 186
Lotus revered in, ii. 94
Lung-Shu of, i. 130
Monstrous reptiles in, iv. 282
Mountain tribe in, iii. 201
Nāgārjuna of, i. 130
Planetary conjunctions important in, ii. 382
Protectors of, v. 38
P'u-to (Puto) in, island of, i. 139; ii. 193
Shu-king, primitive Bible of, i. 64
Tao-ists of, iv. 124
Tradition in, i. 56
CHINAMEN, Japanese and, ii. 19; iii. 441
Oratorios to, iv. 220
Svastika and, iv. 157
CHINAMEN, Lineage of the inland, iii. 282
Offshoots of, iii. 185
Year of, iv. 192
CHINESE, Adepts, v. 38, 39
Alphabet, ii. 19; v. 118
Amitabha, v. 392
Ancestors, iii. 139
Astronomical sphere, ii. 384
Astronomical work, iv. 192
Astronomy, iv. 335
Atlantis in teachings, iii. 371
Autumn, ii. 125
Books, iv. 262
Buddhist ascetics, i. 226
Buddhist philosophy, i. 280
Buddhist rite, iii. 103
Buddhists, ii. 158
Characters, iii. 437; v. 118
Chronology, iii. 223, 434
Civilizations of, iii. 334
Cosmogonies, ii. 71; iv. 55
Cosmographies, iv. 175
Cycle, v. 341
Dragon, iii. 210, 214, 281, 364
Emperors, iii. 364
Exoteric worship, i. 184
Fifth race, and the, iii. 364
First man, ii. 81
Fohi, ii. 374
Forefathers, iii. 423
Giants on, iii. 282
Great tone, v. 443
Language, ii. 19
Legends, iii. 303, 368
Logograms, iii. 335
Lunar month, ii. 124
Magic, v. 40
Mystics, i. 130
Nests, ii. 329
Nirvana in, Nippang, i. 112
Philosophy, i. 280
Records, i. 314

CHINESE (Contd.)
  Riddle, iv. 33
  Scholars, i. 45; ii. 194
  Senzar commentaries, translations of, i. 87
  Temple literature, i. 46
  Text of Stanza VI, i. 193
  Third eye, legends of the, iii. 303
  Traditions, iii. 65, 188
  Turanian class, belong to the, i. 52
  Wisdom Religions among, ii. 91
  Works known to Orientalists, i. 46
  Writer, referred to, iii. 422
  Yao, iii. 150
  Zodiac, iv. 191
CHINMĀTRA or Parabrahman, iv. 168
CHINSREG, Magical circles, v. 398
CHINTAMANY, Raghanaracharya referred to, iii. 62
CHIOR-gaur or dance of giants, iii. 342
CHIPPED-stone age, the, iv. 310
CHIRAM or Hiram, Secret work of, iii. 122
CHIT, Achit, Ātmā, Mahat, etc., i. 128; v. 530
CHITKALĀ, the Kwan-Yin of the Buddhists, i. 329
CHITON, a coat, iii. 207
CHITONUTH-our, iii. 207
CHITRAGUPTA, the register of, i. 166
CHITRA SHIKHANDINAS, Bright-crested, or, ii. 172; v. 324
  Great Bear, the, i. 274; iv. 202; v. 202
CHLORINE, ii. 270, 274, 308, 309
CHNOUPHIS or Agathodaemon, solar, iii. 214, 215, 376
CHNUMIS sun of universe, iv. 87
CHOD, rite of, v. 377
CHOEMNIS, v. 62
CHOGĪ Dangpoi Sangye, ii. 294
CHOHAN, the Mahā, iii. 414
CHOHANIC, Dhyāni-Buddhic, i. 124
  Host, Dhyān, i. 214
CHOHANS, Dhyānis, Gods, ii. 344
  Five-fold, iv. 149
  Intelligences, informing, iii. 46
  Lords of the Moon, or, iii. 29, 85
CHOIR, Gods, of, iii. 146
  Planets, of, ii. 380
CHOIRS, Genii, of, i. 334
  Spirits, of, iv. 54
CHOKMAH, Binah and, ii. 70, 156, 343; iv. 197; v. 191, 192, 211, 213, 438
  Brain, or the, ii. 67
  Kether or, ii. 156
  Male wisdom, iii. 93; iv. 97
  Sephirothal triad, i. 160; iii. 272; v. 191
  Wisdom, or, i. 284; ii. 70; iii. 93, 143; iv. 273
CHOKMAH-Binah, the male-female, iv. 197
CHOKRA or servant, ii. 92
CHOLULA, Great pyramid of, iii. 278; v. 283
CHOM-DEN-DA, v. 396
CHONS, v. 251, 253, 256
CHORD, Magnetic or odic, ii. 279
CHORDS, Etheric, ii. 288
  Universal consciousness, of, i. 220
CHOSEN people, of God, ii. 377
  Israel, of, iv. 111
  Jacob, sons of, iii. 426
  Jehovah's, iv. 168

  Laws of the, iii. 115
  Lord's portion, the, iv. 108
  Phallic symbols degraded by the, ii. 31
  Traditions of the, iii. 115
CHOSKU, v. 401
CHOSROES, King, v. 322
CHOW dynasty, iii. 303
CHOW KUNG, iii. 303
CHOZZAR, Dragon, iii. 355
  Male-female, iv. 149
  Neptune or, iv. 149
CHRESTOS, v. 104, 105, 108, 137, 159, 164, 292
  Christos incarnating in, iv. 144
  Mankind the, iii. 418
  Meaning of, v. 285
  Tribulation and sorrow, the man of, iv. 132
CHRESTS, Neophytes were called, iv. 132; v. 288
CHRIST, Agathodaemon or, iii. 282
  Agni suggestive of, iii. 110
  Angel man and, iii. 123
  Ascension of, iv. 277
  Birth of, ii. 384; iv. 191, 261
  Bride of, iii. 376
  Buddhi, not, iii. 234
  Central Figure of Gospels, v. 71, 72
  Christendom, and, iv. 216
  Christians, the, iv. 72
  Coming of, v. 276
  Cornerstone, the, iv. 198
  Cross is the, iv. 158
  Curicified by his Church, v. 84, 360
  Divinity of, v. 160
  Epaphos, connected with, iii. 413
  Ferouer of, iv. 49
  Gnostic Cabbalistic value of, iv. 110
  Gnostic, ii. 35; v. 351
  Gnostics and, i. 245; iii. 282; iv. 206
  Horus or, iv. 158, 206
  Hosts of angels and, iii. 240
  Jehovah or, iii. 85
  Joseph's dream, star in, ii. 375
  Light of, ii. 189
  Logos or, iii. 239
  Lucifer as, iv. 110
  Mercury the Ferouer of, iv. 49
  Mikael and, v. 315
  Myth, v. 556
  Nature of, iii. 170
  Nazarenes before, iii. 105
  Occult teachings of, iii. 234
  Ophites, and, ii. 194
  Paul's idea of, v. 137
  Pisces refer to, ii. 379
  Planetary conjunctions and, ii. 382
  Prometheus and, iii. 411
  Resurrection of, v. 150
  Roman Catholics and, ii. 337
  Satan, and, iv. 65
  Serpent, the, iii. 282
  Sibylline prophecy of, v. 337, 338
  Spirit of the teaching of, iv. 126
  Stars in the hand of, iv. 204
  Sun, ii. 104, 108; v. 216, 217, 317
  Taurus and, ii. 383
CHRIST-JUDAS one of lunar twins, ii. 108
CHRIST-Man, the, i. 123

CHRIST-state or Krishna, iv. 176
CHRIST-stone, iii. 340
CHRIST-Sun, Defender of the, iv. 47
CHRISTENDOM, Ignorance of, iv. 44
CHRISTIAN, Altar, ii. 182
  Angelology, iii. 71
  Apostle's view of deity, i. 75
  Astrolatry, v. 313
  Astrologers, v. 437
  Bible, ii. 374, 382; iv. 228
  Bishop, blessing of, iv. 127
  Canon, i. 248; iv. 107
  Catholics, iii. 102
  Chronologers, ii. 382
  Church, i. 89; v. 156, 157
  Churches, i. 63; ii. 182
  Circumcision, view of, iv. 160
  Clergy, iii. 266
  Computations, iii. 83
  Creation, i. 301
  Creed, iv. 227
  Cross, ii. 34, 383; iii. 107; iv. 127, 158
  Demons, iv. 45
  Devil, ii. 131; iii. 248
  Dogmas, i. 136; ii. 24, 116-7; iii. 112; iv. 44, 65; v. 95, 156, 157, 175
  Dogmatic, a, i. 139
  Era, i. 57, 61, 307; ii. 96, 134, 373, 381-2; iii. 233, 427; iv. 121
  Fall of the angels, idea, i. 136; iii. 178
  Fallen angels, dogma of, iii. 112
  Fathers, i. 62, 113, 140; ii. 51; v. 327
  Fire-worshipper, i. 180
  Generals, iii. 80
  Gnostics, i. 261; iv. 29, 133
  God of wind, sacrifices to the, ii. 187
  Heathen, hatred of, iv. 39
  Heaven, v. 319
  Hebrew Bible, and, ii. 97
  Hermetic books, editor of, ii. 399
  Hierarchy, i. 155
  Holy of Holies, iv. 34
  Interpretation, iii. 50
  Judaism, iv. 40
  Kabala, i. 286; iii. 44, 49
  Kabalists, the, i. 65; 178, 246, 263, 277, 324; iii. 123
  Lunar symbology, ii. 103
  Magna Mater, ii. 108
  Matter to the, ii. 361
  Melchizedek, writers on, iii. 390
  Monks, iv. 101; v. 413
  Mysteries, i. 65; iv. 130; v. 274
  Mystics, i. 83, 84, 262; ii. 65, 379; iii. 106; iv. 24; v. 198
  Nations, ii. 131; iv. 160
  Noah cannot be monopolized by, iii. 389
  Occultists, i. 83
  One law of the, iv. 124
  Orientalists, i. 74
  Orthodox, creed, iv. 227
  Pagan and, i. 335; ii. 189; v. 94, 95
  Persecutors, v. 60
  Phallic symbols, iii. 94
  Phallicism, ii. 171
  Philosophy, iii. 388
  Prophets, v. 277

Religion, ii. 104, 171; iii. 35, 235; v. 336
Revelation, iv. 189; v. 176
Roman Catholics, iii. 98
Sacerdotalism, iv. 130
Satan of theology, iii. 71, 235
Saviour, the, ii. 383; iii. 233, 413; v. 312
Scheme, the, iv. 65
Schemers, iv. 130
Scientists, v. 428, 468
Scripture, i. 308; v. 32, 132
Sectarianism, iv. 29
Septenary, iv. 184
Seraphim, i. 185
Serpent, symbolism of the, iii. 353
Smaragdine Tablet, disfigurement of, iii. 122
" Smoothing ", i. 327
Soul, teaching of, ii. 293
Symbolism, iii. 353; iv. 31; v. 94, 162, 288, 370
Symbologists, iv. 379
System, iii. 102
Teachings, iii. 418; iv. 202
Temples, iii. 94
Theogony, archangels, of, i. 114
Theologians, i. 71
Theological prejudice, iii. 69
Theology, i. 81, 109, 114, 139, 329; ii. 97-8, 328; iii. 53, 57, 71, 80, 103, 104; v. 204, 315
Topography, iii. 398
Traducers, iv. 36
Triad anthropomorphized by the orthodox, i. 83
Trinity, i. 53, 83; iii. 357; v. 33, 156, 211
War in heaven, dogma of the, i. 136; iv. 65
Wars, ii. 188
Writers, modern, ii. 190
Zodiac and the, era, ii. 383
CHRISTIAN, P., referred to, i. 156
CHRISTIANITY, Angelic hosts of, i. 111
  Archangels of, i. 152
  " Blessings of ", ii. 189
  Book of Enoch and, v. 99-106
  Cross of, iv. 132
  Devil of, iv. 97
  Dissolution, on the great, iv. 326
  Dogmas of, ii. 24
  Dust of, i. 63
  Early, i. 62; v. 66, 132
  Ecclesiastical, i. 246
  Fire a symbol of spirit of, i. 127
  Genesis, a prologue in, i. 77
  Greece, in, ii. 40
  Holy spirit of early, ii. 343
  Intolerance of early, ii. 333
  Judaism, based on, i. 308
  Kabalah in, v. 176, 232
  Magic followed the beginning of, i. 62
  Marriage a symbol of, ii. 340
  Mediaeval, i. 62
  Messengers of, ii. 60
  Monotheism, of, iii. 52
  Neo-Platonism and, v. 302, 303
  Occultism and, v. 217
  Orientalists insult, iii. 109
  Origin of, v. 101, 336
  Paul, founder of, v. 125-138
  Rabbis' hatred of, iv. 107
  Religion, the latest, iii. 389
  Satan, and, ii. 129

CHRISTIANITY (*Contd.*)
  Scriptures of Chaldea the basis for, i. 49
  Secret Doctrine in, v. 160, 169
  Sempiternity invented by ecclesiastical, i. 109
  Truth and fact, iii. 71
CHRISTIANS, Absolute of the, iv. 110
  Ain Soph, and, iii. 385
  Angels of, i. 161, 268
  Archangels, i. 248; iii. 376
  Astronomical ignorance of, iv. 278
  Bunsen denounced by, iii. 373
  Creation as viewed by, i. 279
  Cross of, iii. 43
  Devil of, ii. 131
  Dogma of, iii. 385
  Dragon of, ii. 383
  Elect Messiah, ii. 379
  Frog, symbol of early, ii. 100
  Genii of, i. 247
  Gentiles and, iv. 39
  Gnostics, iv. 175
  God of, i. 248
  Greek, ii. 328, 336
  Initiates among, iii. 71
  Jehovah, and, iv. 77, 110
  Jewish, i. 247, 285
  Jews and, iv. 39
  Jordan, the, iv. 155
  Kosmos, idea of, iii. 157
  Last Judgment of, i. 192
  Latin, ii. 336
  Logos of, i. 188; ii. 126
  Lucifer and, iii. 45
  Mahārājahs, four, i. 181
  Messengers of, i. 196
  Monads of, ii. 354
  Morning Star of, iv. 329
  Mystic, i. 245
  Nazarenes and, i. 247
  Nemesis, ii. 367
  Non-initiated, iii. 72
  Old Testament and, iv. 41
  Pagan nations, and, ii. 118
  Prometheus and, iii. 411
  Protestant, ii. 359
  Rabbins and, iii. 387
  Rebellious angels of, ii. 301
  Roman Catholic, ii. 328
  Sacred birds, ii. 78
  Satan and, iii. 44
  Sectarian, i. 327
  Serpent, and the brazen, iii. 364
  Spirits of, i. 165; ii. 24
  Supersensuous beings believed in by, ii. 349
  Supreme deity of, iv. 125
  Svastika and early, iv. 158
  Tau, and, iv. 163; v. 162
  Venus-Lucifer and, iii. 44
  Verbum of, i. 188
  Water lily of, ii. 94; v. 417
  Worm that never dies of, iv. 159
CHRISTOLATRY, v. 285
CHRISTOLOGY is mummified mythology, ii, 109
CHRISTOS, Adept becoming, iv. 152
  Agathodæmon or, iii. 376
  Ātmā, or, iv. 49
  Buddhi-Manas, v. 499

Chnouphis the Gnostic, iii. 215
Chrestos and, iv. 144; v. 104, 108, 137, 164, 286
  Crucifixion of the, v. 552, 556
  Dionysus, or, iii. 418
  Divine, the, i. 188
  Divine wisdom or, ii. 179
  Esoteric sexless, i. 139
  Gnostics of, iv. 110, 273
  Higher Ego, the, v. 563
  Initiates of, i. 245
  Light of, iii. 50
  Logos is, i. 192; iii. 233
  Messiah or, iii. 36; v. 163
  Nazarenes followers of, i. 247
  Perfect, v. 168
  Sacrificial victim, v. 530
  Seventh principle, the, iii. 234
  Sophia and, i. 190
  Sun stands for, i. 192
CHRISTOS-SOPHIA, ii. 195
CHRISTS, race of, New, iii. 413
  Reincarnations of, ii. 364
CHROMOSPHERE of the Sun, ii. 252, 307
CHRONOLOGERS, Bible, ii. 382
  Kalpas of, ii. 84
CHRONOLOGICAL, Calculations, iii. 61, 82
  Computations of ancients, iv. 190
  Cycles, iv. 362
  Data as to age of our planet, i. 205
  Geology's speculations on, iv. 233
  Information, iii. 76
  Kapila's, meanings of, iv. 142
  Mysteries, iii. 92
  Order ignored, iii. 320
  Statements, iii. 156
  System in Hebrew scripture, iv. 195
CHRONOLOGIES, Chaldea and China, of iii. 223, 427
CHRONOLOGISTS, Bible facts, and, iv. 260
  Church, disputes among, iii. 394
CHRONOLOGY, Anthropologists, of, iii. 163
  Archæologists tamper with, ii. 400
  Aryan calculations, based upon, iii. 268
  Bentley, of, iii. 85
  Biblical, ii. 371, 378; iii. 267, 336, 389, 391; iv. 21, 41, 194, 260; v. 199, 201
  Christian, v. 102, 438
  Church, iii. 394
  Darwin's, iii. 23
  Deluges, of the, iii. 307
  Discrepancies in, iii. 308
  Divine dynasties, of, iii. 367
  Earth, of our, iii. 59
  Eastern nations, iii. 263
  Esoteric, iii. 22; iv. 348
  Esoteric geological, iv. 278
  Exoteric Jewish, iii. 395
  Genesis, of, iv. 20; v. 139
  Geologists, of, iii. 163; iv. 364
  Greeks, the, iv. 191
  Hindu, iii. 83, 394; iv. 121, 191
  Initiates, veiled by, iv. 283
  Jews, of, iii. 395
  Judæo-Christian, ii. 85
  Modern Science, ii. 371
  Modern scientific systems of, ii. 31

CHRONOLOGY (*Contd.*)
Occult, iv. 195
Orthodox teachings, of, iii. 62
Orthodox western, iv. 260
Purānas, of the, iii. 228, 229; iv. 141
Race-periods, of, iv. 348
Riddles, in, iii. 358
Secret Doctrine, The, of the, iv. 16
Theological, iii. 200; iv. 364
Unscientific, ii. 382
CHROUB, or Cherubs in animal form, iii. 123
CHRYSOSTOM, v. 138
CHTHONIA the chaotic earth, ii. 54; iii. 139
CHTHONIAN divinities, iii. 362
CHU = DIVINE SPIRIT, iv. 205
CHUANG a Chinese philosopher, iii. 223
CHULPAS, burial places of Peru and Bolivia, iv. 204, 321
CHUNG KU, historiographer, iii. 65
CHUPUNIKA, one of the Pleiades, iv. 121
CHURCH, Adam, a, iii. 54
Apostolic, v. 139, 157
Archangels of the Roman, i. 281
Catholic, i. 155
Christ, of, iii. 234
Chronologists, disputes of, iii. 394
Councils, iii. 281; v. 156, 157
Devil and the, i. 138; iii. 241; iv. 155
Dhyān Chohans called devils by, iv. 155
Dogmas, i. 129, 246; iii. 382; v. 95, 156, 157, 175, 327
Fallen angels, and, iv. 78
Fathers of the, i. 61, 65, 246; ii. 64, 65, 99, 164, 183; iii. 105, 107; iv. 108, 133, 140; v. 71, 96, 149, 159, 167, 307, 313, 336
First-born of, ii. 115
Great enemy of, ii. 177
Greek, i. 272, 335; ii. 99, 179, 340; v. 93, 117, 483
Immaculate conception, dogma of, i. 129
Interpretation, ii. 44
Jews, and, ii. 24
Kabalists in the, iv. 316
Latin, i. 65, 335; ii. 340, 363; iii. 42, 376; iv. 31, 100, 105, 132; v. 62, 71, 93, 95, 116, 117, 139, 239, 332
Militant, iv. 132
Monza, at, iv. 158
Nave in a, ii. 31
Official, iv. 132
Oriental, v. 139
Pagan, v. 88
Personal God, and a, iv. 43
Plato, and, iv. 160
Progress, iv. 269
Ritual, i. 182; ii. 23
Ritualism, iii. 382
Roman, the, i. 163, 182, 281; ii. 99; v. 37, 78, 121, 122, 313, 317, 320, 327
Rome, of, ii. 103; iii. 234, 341
St. John, of, iv. 158
Satan, and, iv. 78
Satanic legions, of, ii. 44
Sons of, iii. 80
Spirit of Buddha present in, ii. 193
Teachings, ii. 132
Temptation on, iii. 32

CHURCH-LAMPS, Frog on the lotus on, ii. 101
CHURCHES, Altar, in, ii. 182
Archangels of, ii. 363
Birth of, iii. 236
Divine truth, fighting, iii. 376
Egg-symbol of, ii. 83
Figures of, iii. 83
Frog-symbol, in, ii. 101
Karma of the, iii. 232
Marriage in, ii. 340
Personæ of, ii. 153
Satan and, i. 248
Sects, or creeds, no, ii. 55
Seven, iv. 204; v. 316
CHURCHIANISM, v. 54
CHURCHIANITY, ii. 202; iv. 317
CHURCHMEN on plurality of worlds, ii. 331
CHURNING of the ocean, i. 135; ii. 62, 95, 100, 113; iii. 380
CHWOLSOHN, ii. 110, 135; iv. 19, 20, 22
CHY FA-HIAN, author of Foe-Koue-ki, iii. 208
CHYLIFICATION and cerebration, i. 337
CHYUTA the fallen, iii. 58
CIBOLA, Cities of, iii. 47
Expedition to, iv. 313
CICERO, iii. 216, 417; iv. 18; v. 61, 254, 262, 333, 334
CICHEN-ITZA, Sepulchre at, iii. 47
CIDASTES, the genus, iii. 222
CIFRON an Arabic word, ii. 76
CIMMERIAN darkness, iii. 77
CIMMERIANS, iv. 342, 343
CIPHER, Hieroglyphic, iii. 437
Occult, i. 157
Sephrim, ii. 76; iii. 351
CIPHERING, First teachers of, ii. 76
CIPHERS, (Cyphers) Figures, or, iii. 237
Multiplied, iii. 308
CIRCASSIA, Raised stones in, iii. 345
CIRCE and the companions of Ulysses, iv. 339
Science of, v. 122
CIRCLE, Ain-Soph a boundless, ii. 147
All-Deity, iv. 167
All Presence of the boundless, iv. 160
Arctic pole, of, iii. 24
Area, natural basis of all, ii. 27
Area of, inscribed in square, iv. 114
Aristotle omitted the, ii. 340
Avalokiteshvara the great, ii. 147
Bible and the, iv. 115
Boundary of the great, i. 154
Boundless, the, i. 161, 284; ii. 147, 339; iv. 56, 119, 160
British liner measures, origin of, ii. 25
Central point with, iv. 123
Chakra or, i. 173
Chelās, of pledged, i. 224
Circumference of a, iii. 50
Concealed unity symbolized by, iv. 123
Cosmogony, ii. 161
Cross and, ii. 81; iv. 106, 115, 116, 117, 119, 120, 153, 160
Cube and, iv. 171
Dance, v. 310
Darkness, of, i. 256
Decussated, iv. 160
Deity and the, iv. 107

CIRCLE (*Contd.*)
Diameter of the, ii. 107, 114; iii. 43, 50, 220; iv. 123
Divine spiritual, iii. 43
Eastern esotericism, ii. 33
Egg, or, i. 187; ii. 74
Elohim, of the, i. 173
Endless, i. 284
Ever invisible, v. 188
Fiery, iii. 356
Four fold, i. 253
God is a, iv. 115
Heaven of, ii. 144
Hierogram within a, ii. 339
Iao and the, iv. 106
Infinite, ii. 58; iv. 33, 144
Infinitude of the, ii. 338
Infinity of, i. 172, 192
Jehovah and the, iv. 106
Kabalistic, i. 173
Life of, i. 268; iv. 126
Line, and, ii. 76, 107
Mandala, or, ii. 100
Manifestation of, iii. 53
Mathematical point within, ii. 338
Measures in relation to, ii. 25
Mundane, iv. 127
Mysticism of, the, iv. 123
Necessity of, iii. 304, 378
Nought or, iv. 145
Number of, i. 154; v. 87
One but the All, not the, iv. 193
One is an unbroken, i. 77
Parker on the, ii. 27
Pass not, of, i. 188
Perfect, iv. 122; v. 206
Perpetual motion in a, iv. 16
Pillar and, iv. 31
Plane of, i. 77, 83
Plato, of, iv. 160
Point in the, i. 84, 154; ii. 79, 144, 338; iv. 123; v. 186, 455
Primary, iii. 122
Primordial, iv. 117; v. 207
Quadrature of the infinite, ii. 58
Regents, of, iv. 57
Sacred four within the, i. 161
Sciences of, iv. 268
Srpent and, ii. 80, 127; iii. 355
Spirals, formed of, iii. 218
Spirit of life symbolized by a, iv. 122
Spirit, transformed into, i. 172
Square and, ii. 337
Starry cross, and, iv. 121
Stars, of the seven, ii. 124
Sun was the one, i. 173
Symbolical, i. 133; v. 129, 206, 455
Tau and, i. 72; iv. 113
Tetraktys within the, iv. 197
Time, of, iv. 56, 119
Tiphereth, of, iii. 218
Triad comprises a, ii. 341
Triangle and, ii. 337
Unity, of the divine, i. 69
Universe, symbol of the, i. 84; ii. 74
Unknown, time, of, i. 173
Upper, iv. 205

Veil over, ii. 341
Vishnu, of, iv. 33
Wisdom of, iv. 122
Yoni, or, iii. 134
Zero, or, ii. 47
Zodiacal, ii. 78; v. 273
CIRCLE-Dance round the ark, iv. 28
CIRCLES, Angels break through the, iv. 55
Dots, and, i. 159
Druidical, i. 257
Fiery sons of Fohat in the four, i. 253
Fire, of, ii. 134; iii. 112, 235, 277
Galilee, in, iv. 324
Greek, ii. 362
Imaginary, in the heavens, ii. 370
Lines, and, i. 159
Lokas called, i. 253
Map full of concentric, ii. 159
Perpetual of time, ii. 362
Planets, of the, iv. 57
Seven, iii. 90; iv. 57; v. 309, 321
Stone, iii. 346; iv. 324
Strobic, iv. 161
Year, of the sidereal, iii. 355
CIRCULAR, Dance, v. 310
Motion, i. 250
Sun, Path of, v. 313
Stone-monuments, v. 341
Zodiac, iii. 430
CIRCULATION, Blood, of the, ii. 282
Matter, between the two planes of, i. 203
Nerve, auric, iii. 299
Vital fluid of, ii. 265
CIRCUMCISION, Antitype of, iv. 160
Apostle of, v. 130
Paul and, v. 137
CIRCUMFERENCE, Circle and, ii. 144; iv. 115
Diameter and, i. 155; iii. 50; iv. 114
Disappears, i. 72
Honoured, dwells in the centre and, the, iv. 125
Presence, symbolizes the, i. 69
Sign of the, iv. 152
Triad, one of a, ii. 341
CIS-HIMĀLAYAN, Adepts, i. 213; iii. 373
Crypts in, regions, iv. 159
Esoteric doctrine, iv. 145, 208
India, i. 213
Occultism, iii. 59; iv. 174
Regions, iii. 327; iv. 159
Secret teachings, iii. 253, 309
CITIES, Americas, ruined, of both, ii. 400
Arts and, iii. 318
Atlantean, iii. 370
Cibola, of, iii. 47
Construction of the first, iii. 371
Dates of the foundation of, iv. 260
Divine dynasties, of, iii. 318
Egypt, of, iii. 429
Henoch built, iii. 366
Indian, iii. 224
Lemuro-Atlanteans of, iii. 316, 317
Phœnicians, iii. 437
Sciences and, iii. 318
Sites of archaic, lost, iii. 312
Tchertchen, near, i. 56
Third and fourth races, of the, iii. 33

CITY, Eight, of the, ii. 24
  Foundations of a, iv. 364
  God, of, ii. 383; v. 337
  Golden, iii. 381
  Good, iii. 229
  Holy, iii. 93
  Snakes, of, iii. 345
  Sun, of, v. 180
CIVIL calendar of Papantla, ii. 35
CIVILIZATION, Absence of certain vestige of,
  iii. 312
  Ancient, i. 54
  Atlantean, iii. 265, 424, 427, 439; iv. 291, 339
  Australians, of, iv. 231
  Babylonian, iii. 207; iv. 261
  Bushmen, and the, iii. 419
  Central Asia, in, i. 54
  Chaldean, iii. 229
  Continent, of the lost, iii. 226
  Cyclopean, iv. 339
  Darwinians, and, iv. 355
  Degraded, i. 242
  Eastern Iranians, of, iv. 327
  Egypt, of, iii. 429
  Eocene period, of, iv. 314
  European, iv. 310
  Evolution, of, iv. 220
  Germanic races, of, ii. 142
  Highest point of, i. 243
  India, from, iii. 207
  Kabiri gave first impulse to, iii. 363
  Lemuro-Atlanteans, of, iii. 431
  Nations, of archaic, iii. 334
  Papuans, of, iv. 231
  Prehistoric, i. 54; iii. 427
  Prehistoric men, of, iii. 427
  Primeval, iv. 355
  Races, of the fourth and fifth, iii. 316
  Rise and fall of, cyclic, iv. 292
  Seeds of, iii. 203
  Tertiary age of, iv. 249
  Third race, of, iii. 327
CIVILIZATIONS, Autochthonous, ii. 378
  Divine dynasties, and, iii. 318
CIVILIZED nations, Jehovah the God of, iv. 110
CIVILIZERS of mankind, the first, iii. 350
CLACHA-BRATH of the Celt, iii. 342
CLAIRAUDIENCE puzzling to physiologists,
  ii. 260
  Phenomena of, ii. 191
CLAIRVOYANCE, v. 155, 339, 459, 487, 557
  Eye of Dangma not, i. 118
  Jnānshakti, manifestation of, i. 333
  Normal, i. 296
  Retrospective, iii. 211; iv. 61
  Spiritual, v. 155
CLAIRVOYANT, Eye of, i. 114
  Faculties, ii. 345
  Jesus, powers of, iii. 234
  Perception, v. 457, 458, 481, 485, 557
  Phenomena, ii. 191
  Powers, v. 527
  Wisdom, i. 69
CLAIRVOYANTS, Spirits sensed by, iii. 369
CLAROS, Oracle, v. 316
CLASSES, Adepts, of, ii. 298
  Arūpa Pitris, of the, iii. 102

VI-9

  Being, of, i. 331
  Creators, of, iii. 87
  Dhyān Chohans, of, iii. 110
  Divinities, of, iv. 157
  Egyptian gods, ii. 154
  Elohim, of, iii. 387
  Kingdoms, of, seven, ii. 360
  Monadic hosts, of, i. 227
  Monads divide into seven, i. 224
  Pitris, of, i. 214, 231, 240, 266; ii. 175; iii. 98,
  100
  Rudras, of, iii. 188
  Theologians, of, ii. 141
CLASSIFICATION, Archaic, ii. 124
  Brahmans, of, iv. 212
  Continents, of, iii. 21
  Difficulty of, ii. 270
  Elements of, ii. 310
  Hierarchies, of the, ii. 182
  Human principles, of, iv. 229
  Septenary, the, iv. 182
  Sevenfold, the, iv. 207, 212
CLAUSIUS, Prof. referred to, ii. 238, 310
CLAVIGERO, the seven families of, iii. 47
CLAY, Figures of, iii. 39
  Human couple made of, iv. 334
  Idol with feet of, ii. 283, 302
  Man made of, iii. 293
  Potter and, iii. 292
  Prometheus kneads the moist, iv. 88
  Solid earth, for, ii. 307
  Spirits animate the man of, iii. 275
  Tabernacle of, i. 307
CLEANTHES, taught by Zeno, v. 60
CLEMENS ALEXANDRINUS, Bible, on the,
  iv. 106; v. 33, 58-62, 66, 71, 73, 92, 169,
  303, 313, 316, 321
  Dragon, on the, iii. 281
  Ex-initiate, an, iv. 129
  Kabalah, on the, iv. 106
  Magic, on, v. 59, 60
  Moon-symbol, and the, ii. 102
  Mysteries, i. 65; v. 266, 279
  Neo-Platonists, and the, iii. 281; v. 59
  Phoroneus, on, iv. 88
  Quoted, ii. 182; iii. 417; iv. 14
  Referred to, ii. 183; iii. 417; v. 106
CLEOPATRA, v. 244, 334
CLERK MAXWELL referred to, ii. 239,
  275
CLIMACTERIC year of humanity, ii. 382
CLIMATE, Greenland former, of, iii. 24
  Lemuria, of, iv. 346
  Miocene period, of, iv. 247
  Rākshasas from the seventh, iii. 319
  Seventh, iii. 319, 405
  Spitzbergen, former, of, iii. 23
CLIMATES, Change in, iii. 444
  Europe, of pre-historic, iv. 308
  Globe divided into seven, iii. 402
  Seven, iii. 402; iv. 188
  Zones, and, iii. 252
CLIMATIC, Causes of, variations, iv. 218
  Evolution, iv. 305
  Variations, iii. 265
  Vicissitudes, iii. 329
CLIMES of Hvaniratha, the seven, iv. 179

CLISSOLD'S translation of Swedenborg, quoted, i. 177
CLODD, Edward, quoted, i. 70; iv. 255, 280, 283
CLOTHES, Cast-off, iii. 292
CLOTHING, Builders, of the, i. 309
  Inner principle, of, i. 319
  Origin of, iii. 206
CLOVEN tongues, ii. 118
CO-ADUNITION of Globes, i. 220
COAGULA, on Smaragdine Tablet, iii. 108
COAL, Bituminous, i. 297
  Formation, iii. 163
  Mines, ii. 284
  Primary age, in, iv. 282
COAT of Skin of the primitive man, ii. 367; iii. 161
COATS of Matter, ii. 369
COATS of Skin, i. 240; ii. 331; iii. 67, 82, 207, 283, 300; iv. 306, 317
COBRAS, Indian beliefs as to, iii. 214
COCKER on the Supreme Good, iv. 124
CODE, Rishis, of law, iv. 183
  Rocking Stones, of the, iii. 346
CŒLUS, Mercury son of, iv. 112
  Terra, and, sons of, iv. 338
COFFIN of Mahomet, the, ii. 268
COGITO—ergo sum, iii. 244
COHESION, Affinity, and, i. 302
  Disturbed, ii. 283
  Entity, not an, i. 202
  Explanation of, ii. 211, 249
  Force of, ii. 316
  Law of, i. 302
  Seven radicals, one of, i. 201
  Substance, a cause, of, ii. 239
COHESIVE force, ii. 233
COINCIDENCE, Number seven not, constant occurrence of, iii. 47
COINCIDENCES, Numerical, ii. 364
  Prof. Alexander, of, ii. 312
COINCIDENTALIST, Mr. Proctor the champion, ii. 26, 36
CO-LATITUDE or Lambaka, iii. 400
COLD flame, Light called, i. 94, 147
COLD Mother, ii. 266
COLD VIRGIN, Hyle referred to as the, i. 147
COLEBROOKE, quoted, i. 90, 119; ii. 47; iv. 195; v. 36, 340
COLEMAN, quoted, iii. 162
COLENSO'S Elohistic and Jehovistic Writers, iv. 41
COLERIDGE quoted, i. 318; ii. 370, 379; iv. 42; v. 314
COLLECTIVITY of the Kosmos, unconditioned, i. 206
COLLEGE, Aleim, of priests called, iii. 207
  Astrologers, of, iii. 208
  Sacerdotal, iii. 219
  Temples, i. 222
COLLEGES, Initiated priests of, iv. 102
  Sacerdotal, iii. 224
COLLINGWOOD, J. F., referred to, iii. 162
COLOGNE Cathedral and the magi, ii. 380
COLONIES, Faunal, iii. 325
COLONISTS, India, from, iii. 416
  Native races, and, iv. 349

COLONIZATION, Roman, iv. 293
COLORADO, Remains of the Cidastes in, iii. 222
COLOSSAL, Buildings, Cyclopean, iv. 339
  Images in the British Museum, iii. 337
  Men, iii. 336
  Pre-tertiary giant, man a, iii. 22
  Rocks, iii. 341
  Statues, iii. 228, 336
  Stones, iii. 280
COLOSSI, Broken, iii. 265
  Drapery of, iii. 338
  Egyptian kings of, iii. 368
COLOSSUS, Acropolis of Argos, of, iii. 295
  Rhodes of, iii. 338
  Three-eyed, iii. 296
COLOUR, Air, from, i. 253
  Aspects of seven, iv. 60
  Earth, of, v. 543
  Electricity and, ii. 278
  Form, and, v. 455-459
  Genesis of, ii. 164
  Human race, of each, iii. 105
  Keeley on, ii. 287
  Men each of his own, iii. 29
  Planes, of, v. 441, 456, 457
  Populations of, iv. 360
  Races, of the Aryan, iii. 252
  Scale of, iv. 199
  Sense of sight, and, iii. 116
  Seven in the world of, iv. 60, 198
  Sound, and, v. 442, 459-483, 484-486
  Sun, of, 441, 456
COLOURS, Aura, in, v. 456-460, 485, 486
  Correspondences of, v. 433, 437, 441, 454-459, 507
  Curtain, of the Temple, ii. 182
  Eclipses, in, ii. 209
  Elements, of solutions of, ii. 270
  Letters, of, v. 505
  Life, of vegetable, ii. 304
  Luxor, of, iii. 428
  Planets, and, v. 432, 433
  Races of various, iii. 230
  Seven, v. 421, 442, 454-460
  Sounds, and, ii. 239; v. 452, 454, 485, 486
COLUBER TORTUOSUS, or tortuous snake, iii. 233
COLUMBUS, America, discoverer of, i. 337
  America prophesied 2000 years before, iii. 370
  Pacific and the, iv. 357
COLUMN, Cutha tablet, first, of the, iii. 16
  San Marco at Venice, of, iii. 94
COLUMNS, Brazen, iv. 184
  Tree of knowledge, round the, iii. 17
  World of the, iii. 294
COLURE, Summer tropical, iii. 406
COMA of organic units, ii. 351
COMBAT between Gods and Asuras, ii. 140
COMBATS of the Gods, iv. 323
COMBINATION, Chemical, ii. 327
  Ethernal, iii. 270
  Numbers of Occult cosmogonies and, ii. 33
  Protoplasm, in, ii. 362
COMBINATIONS, Atoms, of, iii. 168
  Molecular, ii. 327
  Planets, of, ii. 297

COMBINATIONS (*Contd.*)
Ternary, of the, iv. 146
Various animals, of, iii. 65
COME TO US, the great day, of the Egyptians, i. 192
COMET, Appulse of a, ii. 321
Buffon's, ii. 321
Germ dropped from a, ii. 82
Particulars of, 1811, ii. 228
Supposed collision with a, iii. 329
Tail of, ii. 330, 331
COMETARY, Matter, i. 163, 198; ii. 318, 321
COMETS, Course of, i. 252
Gravitation, and, ii. 229
Matter composing, ii. 326
Movements of, ii. 370
Origin of, ii. 225
Wanderers or, i. 250, 255, 294; v. 535
COMMANDER of the Celestial armies, iv. 119
COMMANDMENTS in the esoteric catechism, i. 338
COMMENTARIES, Adept, compiled by, iii. 36
Archaic doctrine, on the, iii. 274
Authority of, i. 242
Book VI of the, iii. 206
Brahmā as Hamsa explained in the, i. 85
Catechism on the, iii. 67
Confucius, on books of, i. 49
Continent in the, first, iii. 20
Creation, on, iii. 254
Cross-breeding, on, iii. 288
Cursing the sun, on, iv. 331
Destruction of the worlds, on, iv. 274
Evil, on spread of, iii. 217
Evolution, on, iv. 159
Father-Mother of the Gods in, i. 136
Fifth book of, quoted, iii. 180
First race, on the, iii. 203
Glosses on, iii. 46
Human race, on, iii. 105, 140
Kiu-te, Books of, v. 389, 391
Law of periodicity, on, iv. 192
Life, on human, iii. 398
Lords of Wisdom, on, iii. 372
Manuscript, quoted, i. 149
Nandi, on sacred bull, iii. 406
Oriental metaphor in, iii. 400
Polar lands, on, iv. 344
Referred to, iii. 146, 184, 434
Sacred books, on, i. 56
Senzar, on, i. 87
Stanzas and, i. 109, ii. 199; iii. 15, 35, 66
Symbolism and, i. 88
Vedas, to, i. 56
COMMENTARY, Angelic beings on, ii. 177
Apes, on, iii. 289
Bhāshya or, i. 315
Book of Dzyān, on, i. 163; ii. 330; iii. 58; v. 357
Cataclysms, on, iii. 312
Celibacy, on, iii. 297
Eastern, i. 330
Esoteric doctrine, on, ii. 273
Fifth race, the, iii. 301, 349
Four races, on the, iii. 283
Fragments from a, iii. 421
Gaudapādāchārya, of, ii. 176
Kāla Chakra, v. 366

Great flood, on the, iii. 330
Manubhasya, ii. 47
Modern, iii. 40
Nature, explains first law of, i. 159
Nilakantha's, iv. 138
Pentateuch, on the, iv. 29
Period mentioned in, ii. 157
Polar continent, on the, iii. 400
Primordial matter, on, i. 147
Shankara, of iv. 209
Third race, on the, iii. 173, 329
Three fires, on the, iii. 249
Tree of life and the tree of knowledge, on, iii. 220
Vishnu Purāna, on, ii. 179
COMMENTATOR, Bhāgavata Purāna, of the, iii. 380
Fire on, iv. 137
Kwoh P'oh, iii. 65
Vishnu Purāna, on the, i. 300
COMMENTATORS, Rabbinical, on Enoch, iv. 169
Sanskrit, iii. 320
COMMERCIAL Crises and sun-spots, ii. 265
COMMODUS, Emperor, v. 283
COMMUNICATION, Colours, through, ii. 239
Early mode of, iii. 204
Impossible, between islands, iii. 227
Outer world, with the, ii. 257
Sounds, through, ii. 239
Worlds, between two, iii. 282
COMMUNION, Adepts, of, ii. 298
Initiates, ii. 301
COMPANION, Globes, iii. 320
Sun of Wisdom, of the, iii. 41
COMPANIONS, Arcana, and the, iv. 197
Chelas called, iv. 72
Tetragrammaton, of, iv. 196, 197
Seven, v. 202
COMPARATIVE, Anatomy, iii. 96
Mythology, i. 53
Philology, i. 48
Religion, ii. 29; v. 55, 407
COMPASS, Deities presiding over points of the, i. 186
Loka-pālas points of the, iv. 148
COMPENSATION, Kārmic, i. 226
Law of, ii. 364
COMPLEXION of first seven human shoots, iii. 33, 230
COMPLEXIONS, Human beings with swarthy, iii. 16
Men with varied, iii. 251
Shiva, of, ii. 36
COMPOSITION, Chemical, analogy of, ii. 322
Living matter, of, ii. 394
COMPOUND, Celestial Hierarchies, form, i. 319
Elements, ii. 290, 308
Ether, ii. 258
Gadolinium a, ii. 350
Molecules, ii. 350
Souls, ii. 291
Unit of Logoi, i. 291
COMPOUNDS, Combine, ceased to, ii. 200
Dissociation point for, ii. 308
Elements and, ii. 275
Mixtures nor, neither, ii. 270

COMPREHENSION, Elements having, ii. 189
  Spiritualized mortals, of, iii. 358
COMTE, referred to, ii. 252
CONCARNEAU, Moving stones near, iii. 344
CONCATENATION, Causes and effects, of,
  i. 224; ii. 318; iv. 233
  Man, a, iii. 315
CONCEALED, Ain Soph the, iii. 119
  Concealed of the, ii. 51; iii. 119; iv. 97
  Deity, ii. 82, 118, 155
  Divine intellect of the, iii. 38
  Egyptians, God of the, ii. 82
  Final hope, v. 400
  Germ, ii. 95
  Good eternal only in the eternally, ii. 131
  Hū, ii. 343
  Land, iv. 345
  Lord, i. 123
  Man, iii. 110
  Meaning in Plato, v. 29, 30
  Mind of the, iii. 38
  Mystery, book of, iv. 195
  Point, ii. 171
  Sun, the, i. 331; v. 188
  Wisdom, i. 170
CONCENTRATION, v. 543, 545
  Practice of, v. 468
  Seven forms of, iv. 209
CONCENTRIC Circles of the Tao-ists, iv. 124
CONCEPTION, Absolute, of the, iii. 166
  Anthropomorphic, iii. 50
  Artemis-Lochia and, ii. 111
  Beginning, easy in the, iii. 409
  Being with a mind of man, of a, iv. 114
  Cross and circle a universal, iv. 125
  Eternal universe, of an, iv. 114
  Finite, iii. 70
  Foetus, of the, iii. 181
  Immaculate, i. 65, 128, 129; ii. 108
  Lunar influence causing, iii. 50
  Moon affects human, i. 307
  Mystical, ii. 340
  Nirvāna, of, i. 309
  Original in all religions, ii. 142
  Philosophies, in all, ii. 55
  Pythagorean triangle the grandest, ii. 342
  Spiritual, iv. 37
  Subjective, ii. 365
  System, of the, i. 317
  Terrestrial, iv. 37
  Third race Titan, of the, iii. 22
  Unit, of an indivisible, ii. 341
  Unity, of the, iii. 54
  Universal, i. 317
  Unknowable, of the, ii. 399
CONCEPTIONALISTS opposed to realism,
  etc., i. 70
CONCEPTIONS, Allegories and, ii. 231
  Anthropomorphic, iv. 125
  Aryans, of, iii. 108
  Deity, of, iii. 166; iv. 125
  Esoteric philosophy, of, iv. 221
  Fallen angels, about the, iii. 232
  German materialists, of, iii. 109
  Glyphs and, ii. 122
  Moon, and the, i. 275
  Mystical, iii. 108

Occult philosophy, of, i. 317
  Present mankind, of, iii. 441
  Pure, become impure, ii. 301
  Purely spiritual, iii. 91
  Spiritual, i. 258
  Universe, of the, ii. 348
CONCH and CHAKRA, v. 288
CONCRETE, Abstract to, from, ii. 95
  Actuality, ii. 365
  Divine ideation passing to the, ii. 95
  Form, ii. 53, 69, 95
  Mind, experiences of the, i. 296
  Organism, i. 229
  Symbols, ii. 363
  Universe, the, ii. 94
CONCRETION follows the line of abstraction,
  i. 230
CONCRETIONS, Causes of physical, i.117
CONCUPISCENCE, The demon of, i. 245
CONCUPISCENT matter, blind, i. 293
CONDENSATION, Atoms, of, ii. 316
  Matter of, ii. 314
  Nebulæ, of, ii. 320; iii. 255
  Nuclei, ii. 322
  Oceans, of, iii. 167
CONDILLAC on plurality of worlds, iv. 275
CONDITIONED, Boundless and, the, i. 126
  Deity, a, iii. 117
  Existence not, ii. 332
  Life, ii. 293
  Nature, iv. 302
  Space, ii. 329; iii. 245
CONDUCTORS of men, Lares or, iii. 360
CONFESSION, Buddhas of, iii. 421
  Church, Greek and Roman, of, v. 483, 511
CONFIGURATION, Upsala, of ancient, iii. 401
  Venus, of, iii. 44
CONFLAGRATION, Early terrestrial, iv. 54
  Ecpyrosis or, iv. 353
  General volcanic, iii. 308
  Inhabitants of Svar-Loka disturbed by, ii. 87
  World, ii. 375
CONFLAGRATIONS and Deluges, iv. 353
CONFLICT, Powers of nature in, iv. 29
  Religion and science, between, i. 165; ii. 393
CONFLICTS with the Sons of Will and Yoga,
  iii. 230
CONFUCIANISTS, v. 38
  Complaints of, i. 49
  Virtue for its own sake, ii. 158
CONFUCIUS, China had, iv. 124; v. 64, 265
  Canonization of, ii. 158
  Cosmogony unknown to, ii. 158
  Dragon of, iii. 364
  Future life, on, a, ii. 158
  Great extreme of, ii. 71, 158
  Higher planes of evolution, belonging to, i. 216
  Pythagoras a contemporary with, ii. 158
  Religion of, i. 49
  Teachings of, ii. 159
  Transmitter, a, i. 59
CONGREVE, quoted, iii. 305
CONIFERAE, iv. 282
CONJUNCTION, Constellations, of the same,
  ii. 371
  Epoch of 1491, at the, ii. 386
  Moon, earth and sun, of, iii. 85

CONJUNCTION (*Contd.*)
  Planets of, ii. 376, 380, 387
  Sun and moon, of the, iii. 85, 433; v. 339
CONJUNCTIONS, Moon regulate conceptions, of, i. 275
  Planetary, ii. 382
CONNUBIAL life, Laws of Manu on, iii. 409
CONQUEROR, Dragon of the, iii. 383
  Indra, a, iii. 377
  Kārtikeya, of Tāraka, iv. 190
  Spirit, of, iii. 73
CONQUERORS of the world, iii. 397
CONQUEST, Evil, of, v. 374
  Ignorance, of, i. 313
CONSCIENCE, Counterfeit of the Spirit, the, iv. 176
  Divine, Buddhi or, i. 43
  Prickings of, v. 555
  Soul or, i. 330
CONSCIOUS Angels a force, ii. 357
  Astral body, life of an Adept in his, iv. 100
  Being, existence as a, ii. 146
  Beings, i. 243, 317; ii. 173, 330, 354
  Body, God needed a, iii. 236
  Cause, ii. 241, 278
  Creative force, iv. 222
  Ego of man, iii. 97
  Egos, spiritual, ii. 357
  Entities inhabiting ether, i. 337
  Entity, i. 334; iii. 247, 251
  Force has a, entity at its head; i. 334
  Human or, being, i. 243
  I am, the, iii. 120
  Immortal spirit, iii. 106
  Intelligent powers, i. 156
  Law, cause of natural, ii. 278
  Man, iii. 347; iv. 148
  Maruts actual, existences, iv. 186
  Mind, ii. 169
  Monads, ii. 346
  Nerve-cells, iv. 240
  Noumenon, guiding, ii. 358
  Powers, i. 156; iv. 222
  Primordial man, i. 294
  Principle, the, iii. 119; iv. 224
  Soul, iv. 89
  Spirits, iii. 174
  Spiritual quality, i. 330
  Spirituality on earth, iii. 73
  Thinking unit, iii. 100
CONSCIOUSNESS, Absolute, i. 70, 80, 112, 113, 122, 126; ii. 360; v. 354, 400
  Adepts of, i. 200
  Animal, iii. 129; v. 546, 549, 555
  Animals, of, iv. 271; v. 531, 547, 549
  Annihilation, of, ii. 345
  Astral, v. 526, 527, 531
  Atom endowed with, iv. 241
  Atoms, the source of, i. 142
  Binah or female, iv. 97
  Bodies not necessary to, ii. 332
  Brain, v. 546, 547
  Buddhi is latent, iii. 277
  Buddhic, v. 532, 539
  Centres of, i. 297
  Chaitanya or, i. 73
  Clairvoyant wisdom superior to, i. 69

  Cosmic, i. 249, 322
  Dawn of human, iii. 411
  Degrees of, i. 318
  Dhyān-Chohanic, ii. 297
  Differentiating, action of, iii. 73
  Divine, of man, iii. 107; iv. 220; v. 494, 528, 552
  Dream foundations of our collective, iii. 295
  Dreamless sleep, of, i. 119
  Dreams, in, v. 362, 527
  Expression of, i. 161
  Facts of, iv. 243
  Female, iv. 97
  Field of, v. 549
  Germ awakening, ii. 174
  Globes belonging to other states of, i. 220; iv. 271
  Great Breath and, i. 80
  Hæckel's soul and, iv. 243
  Human, i. 122, 256, 320; iii. 411
  Inconceivable apart from change, i. 80
  Idiots, of, v. 531
  Individual, i. 81, 122, 123, 231; iv. 239
  Individual Ego, of the, ii. 43
  Individualized, i. 81; iii. 243
  Instinct or direct, i. 280
  Jiva of, iii. 244
  Kāmic, v. 531, 566
  Kosmic, v. 524
  Light of perfect, ii. 352
  Limitations, implies, i. 126
  Limitations to our, i. 117
  Man of, i. 324; ii. 267; iii. 107, 387; iv. 94, 220
  Mānasic, v. 531
  Materialism, perverted by, iv. 234
  Matter, and, ii. 40, 42, 239
  Mind and, i. 69
  Monad, of the, i. 228, 292; iii. 68
  Moral, iv. 222
  Mysterious nature of, iv. 220
  Nature of the " Highest Being," i. 260
  Nature, in, ii. 297
  Nerve-cells, of, iv. 240
  No atom without, iv. 271
  Non-existence or absolute, i. 112
  Objective, i. 154; v. 530
  One Self, of the, iv. 145
  Opening of, iii. 387
  Parabrahman not even, i. 188; ii. 146
  Perception of, ii. 147
  Personality, of the false, iii. 307
  Plane of our, i. 113, 330; ii. 266, 315, 327; iv. 168, 242
  Planes of, i. 181, 220, 248; ii. 306; iii. 277, 282; iv. 204; v. 529
  Plants, of, v. 531
  Possession of the animal element, of, iii. 410
  Possible emergence of, i. 81
  Prajnā or, iii. 41; iv. 207
  Pre-cosmic ideation and, i. 81
  Primary element, the, ii. 88
  Primeval, ii. 294
  Profane, of the, ii. 342
  Profound sleep during, iv. 270
  Races endowed with, first, i. 313
  Sanjnā or spiritual, iii. 110
  Scales, Seven, v. 557

CONSCIOUSNESS (*Contd.*)
Science of, i. 336
Self-analysing; i. 124
Self, i. 122; v. 546
Sensation, and, ii. 266
Senses, of, v. 557
Sevenfold, v. 547, 548
Soul, iv. 94
Source of, i. 161
Spirit, and, i. 80, 81; ii. 41; iii. 53
Spiritual, i. 323; iii. 110; v. 488, 494, 525, 555, 567
State of, i. 231, 309
States of, i. 69, 110, 158, 220, 249, 278; iii. 41; iv. 168, 170, 207, 212, 270; v. 362, 429, 537-545, 548
Subjective, i. 191
Theological, ii. 393
Unconditioned, i. 80
Undeveloped, i. 258
Universal, i. 122, 220; iv. 59, 168
Universe, of the, i. 263, 317
Worlds on other planes of, ii. 307
CONSECRATED, Inland sea, iv. 70
Place, a, ii. 302
CONSEQUENCE of acts, i. 330; ii. 133, 175
CONSERVATION of energy, i. 164; ii. 238, 242
CONSOLATION, Sorrows, for, iv. 52
CONSOLIDATION, Earth's crust, of the, iii. 22
Frame, of the human, iii. 307
Globe, of the, iii. 146
Man, of, iii. 252
Physical, iii. 300; iv. 230
CONSONANTS, Language mixed with hard, iii. 204
CONSORT, Aster't, of Ad-on, iii. 55
Brahmā, of, ii. 54
CONSORTS of the Rishis, Pleiades, iv. 121
CONSTANT, Abbe Louis (see Éliphas Lévi), iv.106
CONSTANTINE, Emperor, i. 65; ii. 190; v. 34, 161, 194, 295
CONSTANTINOPLE, Burning the rolls at, iv. 333
Council of, iii. 281
CONSTELLATION, Born, under which one is, ii. 363
Capricornus, i. 279; iv. 147; v. 151
Cygnus, ii. 320
Dog, iii. 373
Draco, iii. 44
Dragon, iii. 351, 352, 354; v. 202
Great Bear, i. 260, 274; iv. 202; v. 202, 324
Hyades, the rain, iv. 354
Hydra, iii. 430
Lion, iii. 430
Makara, iv. 148, 151
Messiah, of the, ii. 379
Pisces, i. 309; ii. 91, 379, 380; iv. 151
Pleiades, iii. 388; iv. 121
Saptarishis a, iii. 98; v. 202
Scorpio a, v. 286
Shishumāra a, iv. 184
Taurus, iii. 383; v. 267
Thigh, v. 202
Virgo, and Sagittarius, ii. 377
Zodiacal, i. 166

CONSTELLATIONS, Allegories about, iv. 157
Animals symbolize, i. 156; ii. 78, 165; iii. 36, 187
Astrological aspect of, ii. 186
Conjunction of, ii. 371
Deluge associated with, iii. 351
Dolphin placed among, iv. 150
Fantastic, ii. 382
Figurative relation with, ii. 378
Flocks of, iii. 384
Hesiod and Homer, of, iv. 175
Hindu, iii. 430
Influence of, ii. 391
Job, referred to in, ii. 374
King, of, v. 270
Occult influence of, ii. 125
Return of certain, ii. 370
Seven great, ii. 124; v. 200
Signs or, twelve, ii. 375
Spectra of, ii. 322
Spiritual powers of, iii. 85
Stars and, i. 251; v. 309, 318
Zodiac divided into, 27, ii. 389
Zodiacal, ii. 106; iii. 330; v. 164, 251
CONSTITUTION, Archaic belief in sevenfold, of man, i. 281
Astral, man's, iv. 288
Bodies, ether determines, of, ii. 251
Chain, of our, i. 278; iv. 327
Grain of sand, of a, ii. 395
Human body, of the, i. 276
Inner being, of the, iv. 44
Man, septenary, of, i. 212, 286; iv. 96, 147, 167, 197, 211; v. 353, 547, 548
Physical living, iii. 111
Physical, of the sun, stars and moon, ii. 318
Races, of the first two, iii. 291
Septenary, i. 222; iv. 327
Specialization is in man's astral, iv. 288
Venus, of, iii. 45
CONSTITUTIONS, Septenary division in cosmic and human, iv. 167; v. 529
CONSUBSTANTIALITY, Globes not in, i. 220
Natures of rulers and ruled, of, iii. 371
Spirit, of the, ii. 187, 339
CONSUMERS, Bhrigus the, iii. 86
CONTEMPLATION, Buddhas of, i. 169
Dhyāni-Buddhas of, ii. 295
Doubts leading to certainties in, iii. 440
Four degrees of, v. 373
Problem of the atoms, of the, ii. 395
Pythagoras on, iv. 122
CONTINENT, Africa, of, iii. 205, 423
America and Europe, between, iv. 358
America of, iii. 188
Arctic, iii. 24, 398
Atlantean, iv. 208
Atlantic, iv. 359
Atlantis, ii. 377; iii. 21, 62, 323, 370, 393; v. 73, 104, 109, 263
Atlas personifies a, iv. 332
Cataclysms will destroy our, iii. 442
Chinese story of a lost, iii. 364
Civilization of the lost, iii. 226
Dry Island, iii. 397
Dvīpas, divided into seven, iii. 403
Europe, of, iii. 21, 397; iv. 358

CONTINENTS (*Contd.*)
Fate of every, iii. 349
Fifth, iii. 21, 47
Fourth, iii. 339; iv. 263
Future, iii. 323
God-inhabited, iii. 225
Horse-shoe like, iii. 326, 400
Hyperborean, iii. 20, 24, 276; iv. 339
Islands of, iii. 327
Lemurian, iii. 20, 178, 202, 224, 276, 278, 324
New, appearance of, ii. 287; v. 267
North Pole the first, iii. 400; iv. 353
Polynesian, iii. 227
Poseidonis and the great, iv. 337
Pre-Lemurian, iv. 344
Remnants of the fifth, iii. 443
Romakapura part of the lost, iii. 62
Seas buried under, ii. 157
Second, ii. 85
Sinking of a, ii. 31; iii. 308
Southern, iv. 357
Submerged, iii. 315; v. 104, 267
Submersion of the fourth, iii. 339
Tasmania, extending from India to, iii. 225
Third, iii. 371; iv. 333
CONTINENTAL, Formations, iv. 358
Masses, iii. 333
Trends, iii. 324
CONTINENTS, Allegory of two, iv. 340
Appearance of, iv. 179
Aryan scriptures, of, iv. 184
Atlantean Race, of, iii. 421
Atlantis, before, iv. 334
Classics of the, iv. 330
Cumulative evidence of, v. 356
Destruction of, ii. 376; iv. 274; v. 73, 104, 109, 263, 267
Disappearance of, iv. 345
Dvīpas or, iii. 162
Elevation of, iv. 355
Equatorial, iii. 370
Fall of the old, iii. 329
Fifth race, iii. 441
Formation of, iii. 403
Four, iii. 15, 19; iv. 264
Geological order of, iii. 21
Geology and submerged, iii. 316
History of, iv. 311
Huxley on former, iv. 350
Hyperborean, iii. 370
Insular, iii. 320
Legends of, iv. 356
Lemuro-Atlantean, iii. 23
Lost, iii. 332, 408
Master on the lost, a, iii. 332
Mountains of the ancient, iv. 332
North Pole and later, iii. 146
North to south, formed from, iv. 346
Oceans, and, iv. 273
Overlapping, iii. 431
Periodical sinking of, iii. 325
Polar, iii. 392
Prehistoric, iii. 15
Priyavrata's division of, iii. 369
Proofs of submerged, iv. 296
Races and, iii. 19
Rise of, iii. 325

Seven, iii. 321, 326, 369, 403; iv. 188, 317
Shifting of, i. 316; iv. 269
Sinking of, iii. 152
Sixth and Seventh, iii. 403
Sixth root-race, new, for the, iv. 326; v. 267
Submerged, iii. 307, 316, 336, 392; iv. 296, 311, 347, 351, 352
Subsidence of, iii. 325
Suspected lost, iv. 294
Terrestrial, ii. 137
Third and fourth, iii. 266
Three, iv. 177
Tradition of sunken, iii. 268
Upheaval of, iii. 359
CONTINGENT recoalescence of Brahmā, iii. 310
CONTRARIES, Attraction of, ii. 122
Harmony, produce, ii. 134
Shells or demons called, iii. 120
Tutti quanti of, ii. 130
CONVERSION, v. 557
CONVULSION, Date of the last, iii. 313
Geological, iii. 325
CONVULSIONS, Geological, ii. 363; iii. 58
Globe, of the, iv. 298, 345
Nature, of, iii. 313
Subterranean, iii. 314
Unconscious. ii. 262
COOK, Capt., and Easter Island, iii. 317, 336
COOKE, Prof. J. P., on Light, ii. 304
COOL BREATH is the Mother, i. 78
COOLING, Earth, of the, ii. 225
Globe, of the, iv. 264
Sun, of the, ii. 252
COPE, Prof., of Philadelphia, iii. 210
COPERNICUS, v. 316, 355
Intuition of, i. 177
Mean motions of moon, on, ii. 391
Theories, iii. 40; v. 331
COPPER, ii. 276
COPTIC, Adepts, iii. 430
I. O. H., iv. 31
Khamism or old, i. 175
Manuscript, i. 190; iv. 136
Phoenician, and, i. 175
Ro., p., iv. 117
COPTS, Retzins on the, iv. 360
COR LEONIS, iii. 406
CORAL-producing family, iii. 142
CORALS and Millepores, iii. 259
CORDILLERAS the result of depositions, iv. 355
CORDS, Quarters bound by, iv. 159
CORE, Sanctuary of, iii. 363
CORINTHIAN, Horses, iv. 116
CORINTHIANS and the Delphic Temple, iv. 152; v. 82, 142
CORN, Adepts, buried with, iii. 373
Isis and, iii. 373
Life, of, ii. 398
Production of, iii. 363
Zuni priests, presented to, iv. 200
CORN-BIN, Porphyry sarcophagus compared to a, ii. 29
CORNELIUS à Lapide, quoted, ii. 116; v. 213, 319, 320
Agrippa, v. 113, 116
CORNUTUS, quoted, ii. 111; iv. 112

CORNWALL, Traditions of giants in, iv. 323
CORONADO, referred to, iii. 47
CORPORA Striata, iii. 302
CORPORA Quadrigemina, iii. 302
CORPOREAL, Atoms, principles of the Gods, ii. 357
  Brahma, nature of, iii. 183
  Coats of skin not necessary to a, being, ii. 331
  Incorporeal, cannot express the, i. 327
  Nature, elements in, ii. 184
  Pitaras, classes of, iii. 57, 97
  Pitris, iii. 98, 101, 392
  Vāsudeva, i. 328
  World, iv. 180
CORPOREALISM of positive philosophy, i. 244
CORPOREALITIES, Incorporeal, ii. 289
CORPOREALITY, Gods in visible, iv. 83
  Science and, ii. 331
CORPSE, Land turned into a, iii. 206
  Mummy, swathed like a, ii. 127
  Serpent, encircled by a, ii. 127
CORPSES, in Lapland, called Manee, iv. 343
  Ptomaine generated by decaying, i. 305
CORPUSCLE and the future man, iii. 194
CORPUSCULAR, Newton, hypothesis of, ii. 39
  Theory, ii. 207, 213, 217, 231, 252, 303
CORRELATION, Cosmic, ii. 88
  Force of, ii. 54, 232
  Forces, of, i. 236; ii. 186, 220, 358, 398; iv. 25
  Growth, of, iv. 307
  Monads and atoms with " Gods ", of, ii. 346
  Personality, of individuality and, iv. 46
  Spirit, force and matter, of, ii. 54
  Vibrations, of, ii. 239
  World-elements, of, ii. 88
CORRELATIONS, Atoms, of, ii. 338
  Forces, of, ii. 245
  Spiritual, iii. 152
  Tattvic, v. 474-486
CORRELATIVE forces and fires, iii. 115
CORRESPONDENCE, Human and divine consciousness, between, ii. 345
  Worlds, of upper and lower, ii. 343
  Zodiac and the twelve tribes, between, ii. 377
CORRESPONDENCES, Antahkarana and Lokas, v. 543
  Astrological, v. 441
  Colours, days, metals, planets, v. 432, 436, 437
  Colours, Principles, Numbers, Elements, v. 441, 454
  Colours and Letters, v. 505
  Colour, Sound, Number, Form, v. 421, 453-455, 474, 485, 505, 508
  Cosmos and Man, v. 421-425, 459
  Doctrine of, i. 239
  Esoteric, v. 438
  Eternal law of, ii. 309
  Hierarchies, Rays, Colours, v. 459
  Laws of, v. 331
  Physical, iii. 33; iv. 165
  Planets and Physical Organs, v. 428, 438, 441, 442
  Principles and Physical Organs, v. 521
  Principles and Tattvas, v. 474-477
  Science of, v. 86, 87
  Spiritual, iv. 165
  Types and ante-types, ii. 309

CORRIDORS, Labyrinth, of the, iii. 77
  Tombs with, iv. 321
CORRUPTIBLE, Perfection grows out of the, iii. 104
CORRUPTION (S) of physical purity a curse, iii. 285
  Phonetic, of, Language, iii. 205
CORTES, Report sent to the, iii. 188
CORUSCATION of a comet, ii. 331
CORUSCATIONS of monads, dazzling, ii. 358
COSMAS Indicopleustes, quoted, ii. 246; iii. 267, 398
COSMIC, See also Kosmic
  Active intelligence, iv. 168
  Activity, i. 188; iii. 311
  Ākāsha, ideation, ii. 39
  Akāsha, principle, i. 78
  Alchemist, matter of the, ii. 267
  Allegories, i. 251; ii. 149; iii. 130, 181
  Angels, i. 185
  Ansated cross, meaning of, iv. 118
  Aspects or principles, iv. 168
  Astronomical character of Genesis, iii. 151
  Asuras, demons, i. 251
  Atomic differentiation and, i. 207
  Atoms, i. 311; ii. 360
  Body, gross, ii. 249
  Centres, v. 428
  Changes, ii. 26
  Children, iii. 194
  Circle replaced by Theos., iv, 115
  Comets forms of, existence, ii. 323
  Conditions, iii. 158
  Consciousness, i. 249, 322; ii. 41
  Constitution, ii. 382
  Constitutions, septenary, iv. 167; v. 529
  Correlation of world elements, ii. 88
  Creation, ii. 79, 97, 147
  Cycles, ii. 366; iii. 61
  Deep, iii. 271
  Deities, i. 135; ii. 100
  Deity in, nature, ii. 344
  Demons, dragons, etc., i. 251; iii. 381
  Depths, i. 138
  Desire evolves into absolute light, i. 250
  Devas, i. 185
  Dhyān Chohans, ii. 328
  Dhyāni-Buddhas or, gods, i. 119
  Differentiation, i. 229
  Diluvian tragedy, iii. 362
  Division, iv. 188
  Divisions of time, iii. 83
  Daud, ii. 68, 346
  Dust, i. 141, 167, 196; ii. 333
  Electricity, i. 142, 150, 201; ii. 278
  Element, i. 163, 192; ii. 190
  Elements, i. 78, 147; ii. 318, 328, iii. 358
  Energy, i. 170; ii. 41, 360; iv. 168
  Essence, ii. 230
  Events, ii. 85; iii. 147
  Evolution, i. 63, 85, 91, 130, 147, 170; ii. 53, 145; iii. 78, 311; iv. 84, 207
  Existence, ii. 323
  Fact, i. 251; iii. 74
  Fire, ii. 155
  Flood, iii. 147, 154, 310, 352
  Focus, i. 77

COSMIC (Contd.)
Forces, i. 280; ii. 136, 222, 256; iii. 140, 212, 402; iv. 25, 184, 324, 334; v. 315, 428, 484
Forms, ii. 160
Generation, standpoint as to, i. 276
Geometry applied to, theogony, ii. 340
Glyphs, iii. 355
Gods, i. 119, 197, 332; ii. 181, 183, 184, 185; iii. 361; iv. 69
Gradation is septenary, ii. 182
Great body, ii. 351
Heat, i. 147
Heaven, iv. 69
Idealism, iv. 170
Ideation, i. 81, 170; ii. 39, 40, 41, 42, 43, 51, 52; iii. 37; iv. 131
Illusion, i. 233
Intelligence, iv. 168; v. 471
Kabiri were, iii. 363
Laws, i. 318, 319
Life, ii. 172
Light, ii. 320; iii. 53
Logos, iv. 219
Magnetism, i. 201; ii. 220
Mahat, principle, iv. 185
Manifestation, ii. 155
Maruts, character of, iv. 186
Matrix, i. 161
Matter, i. 109, 136, 141, 149, 159, 163, 176, 252; ii. 54, 146, 155, 229, 267, 316, 341, 397; iii. 167
Mists, i. 168
Monad (Buddhi), i. 229
Monads, ii. 344; iii. 311
Moon's, aspect, iii. 76
Motion, i. 70, 156
Mysteries, iii. 92
Nature, i. 334; iv. 166, 186
North, action comes from, iii. 399
Noumenon of matter, i. 82
Orbs, i. 173
Organization, i. 71
Parabrahman, aspect of, iii. 69
Passions, iii. 385
Patriarchs, symbols, iii. 390
Periods, i. 207
Phenomena, iv. 215
Philosophy, Fiske's, iv. 348
Physics, i. 206
Plane(s), i. 169, 195, 230; ii. 107; iii. 116, 249; v. 429, 484
Powers, ii. 70, 136, 161; iii. 275; iv. 45
Pralaya, i. 83; ii. 161; iii. 79
Principles, i. 78, 163, 180; ii. 45, 177; iv. 185, 211; v. 227
Processes, v. 422-424
Protoplasm, i. 253
Protyle, i. 129
Rebirths, iii. 90
Regents over, cycles, ii. 366
Rest, iii. 311
Resurrection, iv. 27
Riddles for scientists, i. 149
Rig Veda, aspect of the, iii. 197
Scale, ii. 349
Screen of illusion, i. 319

Seed v. 422, 424
Septenary law, iv. 194
Serpent, iii. 377
Solar body, i. 332
Soul, ii. 83, 254; iii. 122
Space, i. 73, 124, 163; ii. 313; iv. 183; v. 382, 429
Spirits, ii. 355, 356
Spirit-substance, polarity of, iv. 96
Substance, i. 81, 142, 203; ii. 40, 41, 42, 51, 52; iii. 37, 388
Symbolism, iii. 156
Symbols, ii. 182; iii. 390; iv. 130
Terrestrial man, iii. 116
Theogony, iii. 151
Trinity, iii. 115
Ultimates, iii. 37
Universes, i. 115
Veil, ii. 146, 147, 252
Vitality, i. 163, 253
War in heaven, a, event, iii. 378
Wheels, v. 192
Will, ii. 357
World, i. 169, 182; ii. 182
COSMICAL, Allegories, iii. 381
Duration, of periods, iii. 61
Elements, ii. 51, 61
Fact, a, iv. 67
Flood, iii. 352
Forces, i. 181
Generation, iii. 139
Key, iv. 138
Law of non-Intervention, v. 224
Meaning of the Sacred Four, iv. 159
Periods, iii. 61
Rishis, ii. 154
Symbol and emblem, significance of, ii. 18
System, elements of the, iv. 130
Tabernacle, significance of, i. 184
Wars or struggles, i. 244
COSMO-psychic powers, the, i. 151
COSMO-sidereal sense, Primitive human race in a, iii. 134
COSMO-theogony to, Anthropogony, from, iii. 107
COSMOCRATORES, (KOSMOKRATORES)
Fabricators of the Solar system, iii. 36; v. 534
Forces, v. 329
Greek, iii. 106
Higher ones, or, iii. 36
Rectores tenebrarum or, i. 182
Seven, v. 315, 562
World bearers, ii. 44
World pillars, i. 281
COSMOGENESIS, Anthropogenesis, precedes, i. 261
Mulaprakriti basis of, iii. 37
Occult portion of, i. 186
COSMOGONIC, Jewish, traditions, iii. 17
Myths, i. 147
Vision of St. Paul, ii. 357
COSMOGONICAL, Allegory, iii. 385
Cataclysm, iii. 153
Construction, iv. 107
Hypotheses, ii. 310
Legends, ii. 46, 323

COSMOGONICAL (*Contd.*)
　Problem, ii. 323
　Svastika a, sign, iii. 108
　Symbols, iii. 54
　System, esoteric, ii. 315
　Tablets, iii. 64
　Taraka-maya full of, truth, iii. 57
　Teaching, occult, ii. 380
　Theory, ii. 318
COSMOGONIES, Ancient, iii. 36, 105; iv. 55,
　　188
　Basis for, i. 313
　Cardinal Wiseman on, iv. 273
　Chinese, iv. 55
　Fifth race, of our, ii. 60
　Genetic, iv. 195
　Hindu exoteric, ii. 160
　Light comes from darkness in all, iv. 54
　Purānic, iv. 195
　Similar opening sentences in all, ii. 161
　Universal soul, on the, ii. 67
　Veneration in, ii. 143
　Volumes of description, ii. 337
　Water in, i. 133
COSMOGONY, Ancient, ii. 50; iii. 120
　Archaic, i. 200, 277; ii. 159; v. 107
　Arhats, of the, iv. 16
　Aryan, iii. 243
　Berosus, of, iii. 63
　Biblical, iv. 215
　Chaldean, iii. 64; iv. 72
　China, of, ii. 71, 158
　Circle in every, iv. 107
　Creators of every, iii. 139
　Cross in, iv. 131
　Deluge and, iii. 152
　Diameter symbol in, iv. 107
　Divine Thought, and, i. 69
　Egyptian, i. 262; ii. 60; iv. 353
　Emblematical, iii. 359
　Esoteric, i. 169, 176, 215; ii. 312, 321; iii. 46,
　　154; v. 107, 476
　Evolution in every, iii. 120
　General, i. 242
　Genesis, i. 77; v. 92
　Golden egg, and the, ii. 144
　Grecian, i. 169
　Hermes, of, v. 107
　Hesiod's, iv. 17
　Hindu, ii. 269, 348; iii. 56; iv. 195, 196;
　　v. 231
　Intelligent plan, in, iii. 83
　Japan of, i. 262, 264
　Jewish, iv. 227
　Kabalistic, v. 228
　Logos of every, iv. 273
　Manu, of, iv. 145
　Modern speculations in, ii. 303
　Mystic numbers in, iii. 48
　Norse, ii. 145
　Number nine in, ii. 33
　Number seven in, iii. 47
　Numerical facts relating to, i. 223
　Oannes, of, iii. 64
　Occult, i. 204, 320; ii. 313; v.31, 180,
　　227
　Pherecydes, of, i. 246

　Philosophy and, iii. 48
　Phoenician, i. 170; ii. 171
　Planetary system, and, i. 79
　Primitive, iii. 250
　Primordial, mysteries of, iv. 157
　Primordial substance and, ii. 42
　Purānas, and, ii. 62, 65
　Records of, iii. 254
　Related to Geometry and Architecture, v. 420
　Rishis, of the, iv. 16
　Sanchuniathon, of, ii. 54
　Scandinavian, ii. 83
　Science, of, iv. 234
　Secret Doctrine, of the, i. 316; ii. 398
　Semitic, iii. 243
　Seven builders in every, ii. 154
　Shinto accounts of, i. 286
　Spiritual aspect of, i. 125
　Stanzas on, i. 79; iii. 15; iv. 15
　Svastika and, iii. 110
　Swan myth and, ii. 73
　Swan-symbol and, ii. 72
　Symbol in, iv. 124
　Taurus sacred in, ii. 383
　Theories on, iv. 15
　Treatment of, iv. 365
　Triangle in, ii. 340
　Tyrrhenian, ii. 54
　Universal esoteric, ii. 321
　Universe, of, i. 206
　Unknown deity of, ii. 41
　Vaivasvata in, iii. 154
　Vedic, iii. 54
　Water in, i. 133
COSMOGRAPHIES of Hindu Āryans, etc.,
　　iv. 175
COSMOGRAPHY, Ancients' knowledge of,
　　iv. 104
　Numbers and, iv. 134
COSMOLATRY, Astronomy and, iii. 86
　Fetichism, not a, ii. 181
　Modern science, and, ii. 62
COSMOLOGICAL, Allegory, iii. 383
　Dragons, iii. 384
　Law, ii. 199
　Problems, ii. 316
　Serpents, iii. 384
COSMOLOGIES, Ancient, iv. 175
COSMOLOGY, Esoteric, ii. 338
　Modern, ii. 314
　Occult, i. 142
　Occult teachings concerning, ii. 229
　Root-idea of every, ii. 142
COSMOS, (See also Kosmos)
　Analogy between, and man, i. 226
　Awakening of, i. 324
　Chaos and, v. 228
　Cosmic heat and, i. 147
　Creation of, iv. 227
　Dual motion affects, i. 324
　Fire of, i. 151
　Fohat, in, i. 195; v. 484
　Foot-rules within the resources of, i. 296
　Formation of, i. 163
　Humboldt's, iv. 243
　Logoi in the, iv. 207
　Lotus, or Padma, symbol of the, i. 127

COSMOS (*Contd.*)
Mother of, i. 159
Mysteries beyond the visible, i. 176
Numbers in, i. 153; iv. 130
Phenomenal, i. 154
Physical, i. 135
Principles of, i. 195; v. 435, 436, 454, 471, 476
Protomateria, from, i. 325
Resources of, i. 296; ii. 332
Rope that hedges off, i. 154
Ruling of, i. 187
Septenary division of, iv. 187; v. 521, 542
Solar, i. 213
Svastika and, iii. 108
Time and, iii. 37
Universal science and, i. 154
Visible, i. 79, 176, 186, 187
COSTE, quoted, iii. 149
COTTUS, a giant iv. 344
COUCH, Torture, of, i. 140
Vishnu, of, i. 140
COUCHES used at initiation, Cruciform, iv. 129
COULOMB'S law, ii. 226
COUNCILS, Church, v. 156, 157
COUNSELLORS, Vigilant, ii. 158
COUNT DE MAISTRE Cuts the Gordian knot, ii. 227
COUNT HUGO Cestrensis and the Mona stone, iii. 345
COUNT St. Germain, iii. 207
COUNTERFEIT of the Spirit, iv. 176
COUNTERPART, Ferouer, the spiritual, iv. 48
Hebel, of Cain, iii. 136
Spirit, of, iv. 176
COUNTERPARTS, Objective, of the noumenal essences, i. 317
COVENANT, Ankh, or, iv. 117
Ark of the, iii. 52; iv. 27, 28, 31, 33, 41, 87
Bible, of, iii. 51
Jews, iv. 41
New Testament, or, iii. 49
COVER, Dr., on the Haliaetus Washingtonii, iii. 438
COVERING soul, Shade or, iv. 204
COW, Audumla, or, ii. 83, 145
Bull and, ii. 105
Earth assumes shape of a, ii. 113
Fifth Race symbolized by, iv. 102
Golden, iv. 30, 37; v. 291
Holy of Holies symbolized by, iv. 37
Isis represented by, iv. 154
Melodious, ii. 152
Moon, and, ii. 105
Surabhi, of plenty, i. 135
Symbol, as, iii. 416; iv. 37, 102
Woman, and, ii. 105
Woman with head of, ii. 105
COW-horned, Io, iii. 416
Maid, iii. 416
COW-symbol, Hindu, iv. 38
COWELL, Prof., quoted, i. 73, 314
COWPER, quoted, i. 219
COW'S horns, Isis, of, ii. 152
Symbol, a, iii. 44
COX on the solar myths, ii. 16
CRACACHA or Krauncha, iii. 404

CRADLE, First man, of the, iii. 19, 209
Humanity, of, iii. 208, 223
Mankind, of, iii. 178
Physical man, the of, iii. 422
Third Root Race, of the, iii. 332
CRADLES, Humanity, of, iii. 223, 324
CRANIAL capacity, Mankind, of, iii. 441
Neanderthal skull, of, iv. 257
CRANIUM, Gorilla, of a, iii. 199
Seven forms of, ii. 56, 90
CRATA NEPOA, v. 290
CRATERS, Extinct, iii. 336
CRAUNCHA-dvipa, King, of, iii. 404
CRAWFORD, Dr. J. M., quoted, iii. 14, 39, 176
CREATE, Angels commanded to, iii. 245
Beget not, man will, iii. 285
Brahmā's desire to, i. 170
Desire to, iii. 68
Divine desire of Gods to, iii. 237
Kumāras refused to, iv. 156; v. 203
Man's capacity to, iii. 284
Nature fails to, iii. 313
Power to, iii. 68
Progeny, ii. 177; iv. 156; v. 203
Refusal to, ii. 177, 179; iii. 204, 241, 248; iv. 57, 156; v. 203
Woman, Jehovah first to, iii. 386
CREATED, Aiōn through whom all is, ii. 64
Ancestors, were, iii. 180
Atom ever, no, ii. 306
Begotten, not, iii. 413
Beings, ii. 175
Bodies, iii. 53
Born, not, iii. 270
Deity, iii. 116
God, iii. 305
Light, from, ii. 148
Lights, iii. 293
Monads, ii. 356
Nothing has ever been, i. 325; ii. 293
Third race no longer, iii. 269
CREATING powers produce man, iii. 106
CREATION, Accidental, iii. 263
Activity, the period of, i. 323
Adam, of, iii. 392; v. 190
Adams, of, ii. 36; iii. 17; v. 199
Agitation of the principles at the season of, ii. 170
Allegorical description of, iii. 16; v. 194-204
Allegory, of, i. 291; iii. 255
Alpha of, iii. 108
Animal, i. 238; iii. 66, 255, 409
Aryan primary, iv. 56
Aspect of, ii. 269
Babylonian accounts of, iii. 16, 72, 382; v. 203
Balzac's view of, i. 135
Becoming or, i. 324
Beginning of, ii. 168, 377; iii. 143; v. 208
Beings, of living, ii. 246
Believers in, iii. 179
Berosus on, iii. 75
Bhūta the second, ii. 171
Bible, and the, i. 85; ii. 37; iv.105; v. 157, 158, 198, 234
Book of, ii. 166
Brahmā and, i. 125; iii. 99, 170; iiv. 114
Brahmans speculated on, i. 251

CREATION (Contd.)

Cause of, i. 328; ii. 138
Chaldean account of, iii. 63, 112
Cosmic flood, before, iii. 154
Cosmos, of, ii. 147; iv. 227
Creator and, ii. 361
Cutha tablet and, iii. 65
Cycle of, ii. 89
Date of, iv. 261, 364
Deity and, ii. 68; iii. 166
Desire principle of, i. 170
Deva-sarga or divine, iii. 183
Development of, iii. 271
Dhyāna, by, v. 365
Divine, iii. 137, 183
Divine beings, of, iii. 68
Divine desire, and, iii. 76
Divine thought, and, iv. 107
Drama of, i. 130; iv. 46
Dual, of man, iii. 91
Earth, of our, iii. 36
Eighth, ii. 175; iv. 199
Element of primary, i. 265
Elohim of the hour of, iii. 389
Elohistic, iii. 85; v. 199, 204, 205-215
Entities, of all, ii. 260
Ephemeral, iii. 310
Eros connected with, iii. 183
Esoteric philosophy, in, ii. 65
Evolution and, i. 263; iii. 53
Evolution of animal, iii. 255
Ex nihilo, i. 279; iv. 182
Factors of, three, ii. 150
Fifth, ii. 174; iv. 150
First, ii. 169, 350; iii. 88
First light in, i. 142
First races, of the, iii. 95, 181
Fourth Round, ii. 173; iii. 289
Frankenstein, of, iii. 425
Fravarshi and, iv. 48
Functions of, iv. 156
Genesis, in, i. 291; iii. 254; iv. 56; v. 198, 199
Globe, of our, ii. 53; iii. 239
Gods, of Hindu, i. 86
Hæckel's, iv. 239
Hammer of, iii. 108
Highest cause, and the, ii. 157
Hindu, iii. 56
History of, i. 313
Human, i. 242; iii. 219
Ilmatar and, ii. 39
Immortals, of, ii. 173
Indriya, ii. 172
Inert cause of, ii. 138
Intellectual, ii. 175
Interval from, to, iii. 308
Jayas assist Brahma in, iii. 99
Jewish ideas of, iii. 77; v. 194-204
Kabalistic account of, ii. 51, 89; v. 205-215
Kama propels to, iii. 183
Kashyapa and, iii. 381
Kaumāra, ii. 177; iii. 115
Kosmos, of, iii. 96; v. 213
Kriyashakti and, iii. 231, 284; v. 535
Lakshmi at, ii. 95
Law of, iv. 107, 113, 300

Logos and, ii. 147, 295; v. 187, 189, 214, 426, 476
Lords of, iii. 135, 170
Mahattattva, ii. 169
Man, of, iii. 89, 96, 163, 177; iv. 82
Man no special, iv. 297; v. 157, 158
Masons on the era of, iv. 265
Meanings of, iii. 310
Mental life, endowed with, ii. 352
Middle world, of the, iv. 173
Monadic principle in, iv. 238
Monads of, ii. 301
Monstrous, iii. 124
Moon, of the, iii. 153
Moot and, ii. 170
Mosaic, i. 286
Motion, by accelerated, iv. 121
Mukya, or, ii. 173
Mysteries, of, iv. 156, 157; v. 196
Mystery of, i. 167, ii. 350; iii. 88, 219; iv. 85
Mystic powers, by, ii. 295
Nativity, and, iv. 195
New, iv. 73
Ninth, ii. 176
Number of, iii. 51, 52
Numbers and, v. 189, 206, 207
Objective, iii. 177
Occult philosophy and, ii. 165
Omega of, iii. 108
Order of, i. 298
Origin or, i. 301
Patristic fancy, of the, iii. 377
Perpetual, iii. 310
Phenomenal universe, of the, iii. 388
Philosophy of, iii. 70
Physical, of the man, iii. 89; v. 198, 210, 291, 448, 532
Physical senses pertain to a lower, iii. 115
Point, of a, ii. 338
Positive pole of, iii. 69
Potentiality for, no, iii. 89
Prajāpati Vāch in, i. 194
Prerogative of, iii. 419
Primary, i. 142, 265; ii. 174; iv. 300; v. 209, 210, 211
Primeval, iii. 271
Primitive man, of, iii. 110
Primordial, ii. 59; iii. 66, 147; v. 187
Process of, iii. 129
Prologue to, iv. 56
Psycho-chemical principle of, ii. 54
Races, of the wretched, iii. 105
Roman Church and, ii. 185; v. 207
Second, v. 203, 204
Second Logos of, ii. 295
Secondary, i. 142, 263; ii. 168, 171, 266; iii. 70, 122, 312
Secrets, of, iv. 114
Sepher Yetzireh and number, iii. 51
Sevenfold, ii. 49
Seventh, the, i. 264; ii. 91, 175; iii. 236; iv. 85; v. 199
Shinto idea of, i. 286
Shu, Egyptian God of, i. 142
Six days of, iii. 254; iv. 56, 273
Sixth, ii. 175

CREATION (*Contd.*)
Sons of God, of men by, iii. 40
Souls, of, ii. 301
Special, iii. 165, 265; iv. 215, 248, 255
Species, of, iii. 66; iv. 301
Svastika summary of, iii. 107
Tairyagyonya, ii. 174
Theological date for, iv. 364
Theological legend of, iv. 259
Theology and its 6,000 years of, ii. 35
Third, ii. 172
Tiryaksrotas, ii. 174
Trimurti, v. 117
Universe, of the, ii. 60; v. 188, 208, 233, 530, 538, 539
Urdhvasrota, ii. 175
Vegetable, iii. 142
Vishnu and, i. 328; v. 188, 233
Vowels uttered at, iv. 151
War at, ii. 137
War with evil preceded, iii. 112
Water, of, ii. 46
Week of, iv. 195
Will, by, iii. 148, 180; iv. 335; v. 535
World, of the, i. 176, 323, 327; ii. 82, 378, 381; iii. 135; v. 207
Zohar on, v. 205-215
Zoroastrian, iv. 56
CREATIONS, Angels, of, iii. 53
Animals, of, iii. 65
Aryan scriptures, in, iv. 184
Continents, of new, iv. 325
Divine thought no concern in, iii. 166
Elohite, iii. 19; v. 209, 210
Esoteric teaching on, ii. 165; v. 199, 210, 215
Evolution, mean stages of, ii. 173
Formation of the globe, before the last, iii. 64
Herbert Spencer on, iv. 299
Heterogeneous, iii. 52
India, described in, ii. 169, 170; v. 188, 210
Jehovite, iii. 19; v. 198, 199
Kalpa, of each, iii. 64
Nature by, ii. 295
Padma, ii. 145
Periodical, iii. 364
Prakritic, ii. 145
Processes for two, i. 293
Purānic, ii. 172
Puranas, in the, ii. 165; iii. 64; v. 188, 199
Self-existent are called, iii. 245
Seven, i. 264; ii. 164, 165, 167, 173; iv. 182, 183; v. 198
Space and Time, in, iv. 119; v. 189
Three elemental, ii. 173
Two, i. 293; iii. 19
Vishnu Purana, of the, ii. 167; v. 188, 421, 422
Wilson, Prof., on, ii. 171
Wisdom before all, iv. 58; v. 192
CREATIVE, Agent, ii. 139
Air, element, ii. 166
Chaos, powers in, iii. 271; v. 233, 234, 235
Cosmic forces, iv. 25; v. 315, 507
Deity, i. 84; ii. 45, 64; v. 462
Dhyān Chohans, i. 170; iii. 360; v. 214, 228, 375
Effort, i. 324

Elohim, iii. 15, 87, 134; iv. 167; v. 209, 210, 228
Energy, ii. 276
Faculty, iii. 221
Function, i. 258
God, Bhrāntidarshanatah, the, i. 84
Gods, ii. 78, 79, 144; iii. 103, 203; iv. 39, 156, 177; v. 199, 213
Hierarchies, v. 448, 460
Instinct, iii. 277
Law, iii. 240
Light, iii. 236, 241
Logoi, ii. 95
Logos, the, i. 169, 170, 264; iii. 236; v. 187, 189, 214
Magnetism, ii. 122
Nature, i. 72, 157; iii. 416
Origin of all things, ii. 107
Passion, ii. 87
Plane, iii. 48
Planetary angels, iii. 135; v. 207, 208
Potency, iii. 161; v. 426
Principle of nature, ii. 29
Principles in the Gods, iii. 116
Progenitors, iii. 130; v. 233
Purposes, i. 203, 331
Soul, ii. 75
Source of the divine mind, ii. 348
Spirits, i. 114, 247; ii. 222; iii. 16
Triad, i. 321
Triangle, v. 507
Word, iv. 112; v. 228, 229
World, i. 249
CREATOR, Absolute ALL, an aspect only of, iii. 166
Adam-Kadmon the, iv. 23
Aditi as, ii. 348
Anthropomorphic, i. 76; ii. 130; iii. 52, 165
Bel the, ii. 72
Brahmā the, i. 74, 85, 148, 328; ii. 70, 96; iii. 64, 170
Budha a, iv. 23
Buddhists and a, i. 71; ii. 360
Creation and, impossible, iii. 361
Daksha the, ii. 348; iii. 189; v. 287, 288
Dark races, of, iii. 19
Demiurge, or, ii. 130; iii. 19, 38
Demiurgic, ii. 67
Demiourgos, v. 213, 214, 215
Destroyer, and, iii. 123
Devil and, ii. 131
Divine foresight of, iii. 386
Ethereal body of, iii. 95
Executive agent, an, iii. 55
Father and, iii. 339, 399; iii. 55, 99; v. 215
Female, i. 193 v. 426
Fetahil the, i. 245
Fire the, i. 147; iii. 122
Fohat, or, ii. 281
Genesis, of, iii. 91; v. 158, 181, 190, 198, 207, 208
Globe, of our, iv. 42
God the Host, v. 212, 214
Hari the, ii. 87
Holy Ghost, the, i. 139; v. 211
Humanity, of, iii. 312
Incorporeal, iii. 244

CREATOR (Contd.)
Jehovah the, iii. 388; iv. 42, 167; v. 198, 199
Kama, a, iii. 183
Karma-Nemesis, of nations, ii. 367
Kashyapa the, iii. 141
Light, of, iii. 218
Logos or, i. 322; iii. 65; v. 426, 476
Lord God or, iii. 91; v. 234
Male, i. 134; v. 233
Man a, iii. 113, 197, 248, 292
Michael, of, iii. 73
Nations, of, ii. 367
Nebo a, iv. 23
Noah the, iv. 169
One principle not the immediate, ii. 143
Osiris the, ii. 398
Pantheists do not deny a, i. 74
Personal, a, iii. 165
Reincarnated, iii. 197
Scientific human, ii. 319
Serpent called, iii. 214
Shadow inferior to his, iii. 105
Shiva, of Spiritual man, ii. 178
Supposed, iii. 305
Supreme, iii. 135
Tree of knowledge, of the, iii. 384
Vishnu the, ii. 96; v. 233
Wisdom, associate of, v. 74
Zeus the, ii. 412
CREATORS, Amshaspends, v. 214
Angels, v. 207, 208, 213
Androgyne, iii. 387
Architects, or, i. 187, 279; v. 210, 213
Battles of, i. 105, 248
Beings on the earth, of, iii. 88
Body of illusion, of the, iii. 67
Builders or, ii. 70, 95, 155; v. 192, 207, 208, 210, 213, 260, 287, 288
Classes of, the, iii. 70, 104
Destroyers, and, i. 248, 306
Dhyān Chohans our, iii. 46; v. 203
Displeased, iii. 63
Divine, iv. 82; v. 203
Divine mind or, i. 301
Double-sexed, first, iii. 139
Earth, of the, ii. 391; iii. 106
Elohim, or, i. 196; v. 205-215, 228
Enemies of the, i. 307
Female, ii. 81
Forces or, iii. 166
Forefathers or, ii. 162; iii. 251
Forms, reject the, iii. 168
Group of, i. 279
Heaven, of, ii. 391
Hierarchies of, ii. 144; v. 448, 460
Host of, ii. 130; v. 213, 214
Ideal, ii. 96
Kumāras the, iv. 155, 156; v. 203
Lunar fathers become, iii. 124
Magnum Opus of the, i. 297
Man, of, i. 244, 272; ii. 169; iii. 95, 104; v. 203
Manus the, iii. 311
Material world, of, iii. 112
Pitris are, iii. 97
Planetary, i. 130, 140; v. 460

Practical, ii. 96
Prajāpatis or, iii. 92; v. 203, 210, 214, 233
Progeny of, iii. 57
Pygmalions, were, iii. 111
Races, of the earliest, iii. 435
Repentance of, iii. 197
Rishis are, ii. 160; v. 203, 288
Sephiroth, v. 192, 214, 231
Septenary or planetary, i. 140; v. 207
Seven, ii. 70, 81, 295; iii. 269; v. 207
Spiritual, i. 258; iii. 419; 203
Thinking man, of, iii. 95
Thoughts, of ideal, i. 268
Will of, i. 243
World, ii. 81, 295
CREATURE, Immortal, ii. 361
Tiamat, of, iii. 112
CREATURES, Elementals sentient, i. 268
Four-armed human, iii. 295
Karma, of, ii. 360
Kārmic law, of, i. 319
Logos, first of, iii. 170
Mammalians, preceding, iii. 177
Reason, without, iii. 67
CREED Martyrs of every, i. 337
Pagan symbolical, iii. 390
CREEDS, Exoteric, iii. 199
Nations, of other, ii. 188
Popular, iii. 71
Sects, or, no churches, ii. 55
Traditions in exoteric, iii. 199
CREMATION once universal, iv. 322
CRESCENT, Argha, of the, iv. 30
Cow marked with, ii. 105
Mary represented on, iv. 32
Phallic symbol, a, iv. 154
Satan and, iii. 44
CRETACEOUS, Formation, iii. 325
Period, the, iii. 163
Rocks, iv. 249
CRETANS, Dictynna of the, ii. 111
CRETIN, an arrested man, not an ape, iv. 248
CREUZER, ii. 182, 184, 378; iii. 287, 344, 366, 369; v. 54, 59, 310
Beliefs, on primitive, ii. 182
CRO-Magnon, Cave men, iv. 310, 360
Men, iv. 358, 359
Palæolithic type, iv. 248
Sepulchral cave of, iv. 248
CROCODILE, Dhyānis, and, i. 266
Dragon and, ii. 126
Huschenk's horse begotten by a, iii. 396
Makara or, i. 279, ii. 99; 353; iv. 147
Mesozoic times, of, iii. 161
Pentagram and, i. 266
Progeny of, iii. 398
Sacred, ii. 68
Sacred because amphibious, ii. 126
Sacred Nile, of the, iv. 148
Sebekh, called, i. 267
Soul comes from men, whose, iv. 206
Symbol of, i. 267
Worship, ii. 120
CROCODILE-Dragon type of Sevekh-Kronos, ii. 125
CROCODILE-headed God of Egypt, iv. 151

CROCODILES, Celestial Nile, in the, iv. 151
  Winged, iii. 260
CROMLECHS, Perfect proportions of, i. 257
CROOK=Vau, iv. 28
  Referred to, ii. 244, 322, 346, 347, 350
CRORES, Kalpa, of the, iii. 312
  Pantheon, of deities in the Hindu, i. 138
  Wheel whirled for thirty, iii. 28, 63
  Years, of, iii. 76
CROSS, Used by Adepts, v. 159
  Ansated, ii. 34, 383; iii. 43, 220; iv. 129, 154
  Antiquity of, iv. 158
  Anubis holding out a, ii. 127
  Astronomical, iv. 102, 121
  Bible did not originate, iv. 115
  Christ, stood for the, iv. 158
  Christian symbol, iv. 127; v. 159
  Christians, of, iii. 43, 107; v. 162
  Circle, and, iv. 117, 119, 120, 122, 125, 160
  Creative cause, symbol of, iii. 220
  Cube unfolded, or, iv. 172
  Earth represented by, over globe, iii. 42
  Egyptian ansated, ii. 383; iv. 118; v. 161, 325
  Evolution of, iii. 220
  Flesh, of, iii. 48
  Four partitioned line a, iv. 171
  Four-footed, iv. 117, 159
  Globe over, iii. 42, 43
  Horizontal and vertical line form, iv. 164
  Human life, and, ii. 34
  Iao and, iv. 106
  Initiation, of, iv. 131; v. 161, 325
  Jaina, iii. 107
  Jews, of the, iv. 153
  Latin; v. 161, 162
  Love, of, iv. 131
  Man attached to, ii. 34, 35; iv. 131
  Meaning of, ii. 15; v. 152
  Mundane, i. 72
  Pagoda of Mathura in form of, iv. 159
  Palenque, i. 106
  Phallic symbolism v. 292
  Phallus, and, ii. 122
  Plato's, iv. 131
  Primeval form of, ii. 179
  Prometheus on the, iv. 131
  Pythagorean decad, and, iv. 144
  Rose and, i. 84; v. 292, 293
  Sevenfold, v. 132
  Shoo and, God, iv. 116
  Sun and, iv. 128
  Svastika or, iii. 107; iv. 116, 158
  Symbol of, i. 244; ii. 34, 99
  Tau or Egyptian, ii. 122; iv. 153, 171; v. 161, 325
  Typology of the, iv. 116
  Venus represented by, and globe, iii. 42, 43
CROSS-bones and skull, symbol of, v. 161, 164
CROSS-breed, Apes a, iii. 264
  Possibility of, iii. 287
CROSS-breeding, iii. 206, 288
CROSS-symbol, Phallic form of the, ii. 34; v. 292
  Variations of the, iv. 117
CROSS-worship of the Jews, iv. 160
CROSSES, Italy in, iv. 112
CROTCH, W. Duppa, quoted, iv. 350

CROWN, Kether the, i. 284; ii. 67, 70, 151; iv. 167, 196; v. 191, 211
  Sephira is, i. 263; iii. 51; v. 191
  Sephirothal tree, the, i. 229; v. 439
CROWNS, Dragon with seven, iv. 53
CRUCIBLES, Living animal, iii. 177
CRUCIFIED, Krishna, iv. 131; v. 288
  Mount Kajbee, of, iii. 55
  Prometheus, iii. 55, 412
  Rose, v. 292
  Sun, v. 289
  Titan, iii. 411, 412
CRUCIFIX, Final form of the, iv. 158
  Christian symbol, v. 162, 288
CRUCIFIXION, Christos of, v. 552, 556
  Initiate, of, iv. 130
  Jesus, of, by disciples, v. 84, 360
  Meaning of, iv. 130
  Metaphorical, iv. 52
  Mystery of, ii. 79; iv. 130
  Nails, iv. 131
  Roman, v. 162
  Theoretical use of, iv. 129
  Three Maries at, ii. 100
  Universe and, v. 289
CRUCIFORM, Couches, iv. 129; v. 288
  Hermes-Mercury were, symbols of, iv. 112
  Lathe, ii. 35; iv. 113
  Noose, iv. 118
  Symbols, iv. 112; v. 159, 161, 162, 164, 325
  Termini, iv. 112
CRUDEN, quoted, i. 185, 285; ii. 132
CRUSADERS and the Swan-symbol, ii. 72
CRUST, Earth of, i. 304; iii. 22, 254
  Planet of a, ii. 281
CRUSTACEA, iv. 166, 281
CRUSTACEAN, the hard-shelled, iii. 161
CRUX, Ansata, the, ii. 34, 81; iii. 361
CRYPT, Egyptian, iii. 379
  Temple, iv. 128
CRYPTS, Archaic, iii. 378
  Cis-Himalayan regions, in, iv. 159
  Lāmasaries, of, i. 47
  Libraries, in secret, i. 56
  Mysteries recorded in subterranean, i. 276
  Russian travellers, known to, i. 58
CRYSTALLINE, Life, i. 120
  Mother, abode of the great, iv. 45
  Waters of primeval wisdom, ii. 118
CRYSTALLIZATION, Process of, iii. 78
  Transformation through, iii. 258
CRYSTALS, Evolution of, iv. 267
  Origin of, iii. 258
CSOMA de Körös on Āryāsanga, i. 121
CTEIS or Yoni, iv. 34
CUBE, Atom not a, ii. 205
  Circle, and, iv. 167
  Creative plane, on the, iii. 48
  Cross and, iv. 131, 172
  Divine, v. 189, 191
  Fertile number and, iv. 171
  Man a, iii. 48
  Meanings of, ii. 83
  Nature, in, iv. 166
  Perfect, the, i. 84; ii. 58, 160, 169; iv. 33, 183
  Pythagorean triangle and, ii. 341

CUBE (Contd.)
Second one, the, i. 189
Sevenfold, iv. 197
Six-faced, i. 129
Symbols of, ii. 58
Unfolded, the, ii. 34; iii. 48; iv. 131, 165, 171, 172
CUBES, Angelic beings, symbolize the, iii. 88
Geometry of nature and, i. 159
Sparks called, i. 156
CUBITS, Inch the base of Egyptian, ii. 25
CUDWORTH, Hylozoism of, iii. 167, 267; v. 188
CUELAP, Cyclopean ruins at, iv. 315
CULTURE-God, Sea, comes from the, iii. 229
Worship of, iii. 148
CUMBERLAND, Bishop, iii. 391
CUMMING, Gordon, iii. 438
CUNEIFORM, Fragments, iii. 436
Inscriptions, iii. 17, 64
Texts, ii. 72
CUNNINGHAM, General, i. 51
CUP, Golden-winged, iii. 382
Illusion of, ii. 83
Retribution of, i. 239
CUP-marks are records, iii. 345
CUPID, Eros, and, i. 169; iii. 75, 76, 183
Venus mother of, iii. 75, 416
CURBATI, Curvati, or fallen angels, ii. 44; v. 95
CURD-like or nebulous, i. 254
CURDS, Cosmic matter, and, i. 136
Fohat, of, ii. 397
Luminous egg spreads in, the, i. 134
Mother, of the, ii. 266
Ocean (of space), in the, i. 160
OEAOHOO is One, remain and, i. 136
Sea of, iii. 320
Space, in, i. 160, 294
World-stuff or, i. 255
CURDY appearance in sun's envelope, ii. 254
CURETES identical with the Kabiri, iii. 359
CURRENTS, Astral light, iii. 84
Fluid, of the fiery, ii. 52
Matter, of nebulous, ii. 224
Vibrating, ii. 242
CURSE, Corruption of physical purity a temporary, iii. 285
Destiny, means doom or, ii. 90
Devil, of belief in a personal, iii. 376
Dragon, of the, iii. 113
Earth, of the, ii. 90
Fall, after the, iii. 284
Fire of Prometheus turned into a, iii. 410
Incarnation, of, iii. 248
Karma, of, iii. 408
Kārmic, iii. 113
Kronos, of, iii. 413
Life, of, iii. 247
Personal being, not pronounced by a, i. 243
Philosophical point of view, from a, iii. 408
Physiology, from the standpoint of, iii. 409
Prometheus, against, iii. 247, 410, 418
Pronounced, is, i. 105, 242
Retardation, of, iii. 202
Speech a, or a blessing, i. 157
Woman and, iii. 220
Satan, on, iii. 238; iv. 46

CURTAIN, Adytum, of the, iv. 27
Egyptian temples, in, i. 183; ii. 182
CURTIS, Geo. T., quoted, iv. 253
CUSA Cardinal de, Pascal and, iv. 115
Quoted, iii. 166
CUSH, Ham, son of, iv. 184
Nimord, son of, iv. 20
CUSHING, F. Hamilton, became a Zuni, iv. 200
CUTHA tablets, iii. 63, 65
CUTTLE fish, iii. 296, 438
CUZCO, Fortress of, i. 257
CYBELE, Lightning of, ii. 52
Lunar goddess, a, ii. 111, 115
Temples of, v. 295
CYCLE, (see also Age, Round, Kalpa, Yuga, etc.)
Adeptship, of, v. 154, 155
Ananta the, iii. 107
Ascending arc of, ii. 366; iii. 137, 301, 309, 444
Atlantean, iii. 272, 431; iv. 102; v. 341
Beginning of, i. 238; ii. 152
Brihaspati, v. 339, 340
Chaldean, v. 236
Chinese, v. 341
Creation, of, ii. 89
Downward, iii. 137
Emblem of the Solar, iv. 135
Evolution, of, i. 232; iii. 194
Fauna, and, iii. 67
First and Second Race, between, iii. 182
Fourth, iv. 203
Fourth Race, iii. 431; iv. 102
France, of, ii. 371
Garuda a, ii. 139; iii. 256
Globe, of our, i. 229
Gods of, v. 462
Grand, ii. 367; iii. 218
Great, i. 301; iv. 135; v. 339
Horse is a, iii. 398
Human, i. 320
Incarnations, of, i. 82, 234, 272; ii. 296; iii. 171, 192, 375
Indian, v. 236
Initiation, of, ii. 26; iv. 137
Kali Yuga, of, iii. 433
Karma worked out in every, i. 268
Life, of, v. 274
Lunar, iv. 339
Mahākalpa, i. 248; iv. 135
Mahāyuga or, ii. 366
Manu, of a, i. 132
Manvantara or, of activity, i. 132, 310; ii. 397
Manvantaric, i. 240; ii. 139; iii. 71, 107, 398
Metempsychosis, of, i. 237
Moon, of, iv. 353
Narada reborn in every, iii. 323
Naros, of the, iv. 190; v. 341
Nations, of, ii. 40
Necessity, of, i. 82, 274; v. 213, 248, 300
New, a, i. 65; ii. 161
Noah's deluge, of, ii. 161
Occultists, of, iii. 195
Probationary, v. 91, 92
Procreating, i. 235
Quinquennial, v. 339
Ra's phases, of, i. 277
Racial, ii. 135; iii. 279
Sacredness of, iii. 83

CYCLE (Contd.)
Sar and Saros, or, i. 173
Sidereal year, of the, ii. 375
Sun's, iv. 353
Symbolism, of, ii. 121
Tatar, v. 341
Transformations, of, i. 270
Transmigration, of, i. 235
Triple, i. 227
Tropical, years, of, iii. 86
Turning-point of the, i. 237
Universe, of our, i. 243
Vedas, of, v. 341
Years, of eleven, ii. 265
Years, of, iii. 430
CYCLES, v. 336-348
Adam, before, iii. 396
Ancients, of, iii. 395
Astronomical, ii. 370; iii. 59, 330; v. 339
Babylonians, of, iv. 136
Chronological, iv. 362
Close of, ii. 337
Consciousness, Measured by, v. 536
Cycles within, iii. 330
Cyclopes, sons of, i. 257
Disease, in, iv. 193
Energy of, ii. 350
Esoteric, iii. 80
Evolution, of, i. 78, 310; iii. 187, 440
Exoteric, ii. 369
Forces, of, ii. 273
Geological, iii. 84
Hindu, v. 339
Historical, iii. 373
History proceeds in, ii. 400
Human, iii. 322
Ideas, of, i. 78
Kalpas or, iii. 92
Karmic, i. 362
Kings, of, i. 310
Kronos and, ii. 136
Length of, iii. 61
Mahākalpas and, ii. 85
Matter, of, ii. 362; iii. 444
Māyā, of, iii. 154
Measured, by consciousness, v. 536
Minor, ii. 85, 367
Mosaic Jews, of, ii. 382
Mystic astronomy, of, iii. 59
Nations, iii. 302, 439
Obscuration, of, i. 228
Overlapping, iii. 431
Pantheists, ii. 366
Periodic, ii. 350, 396
Pesh-Hun regulator of, iii. 60
Precession, of, ii. 376
Psychic, iii. 157; iv. 362
Quinquennial, v. 339, 343
Races, and, iv. 303
Racial, iii. 84
Rebirths, of, iii. 248
Rounds or, i. 213; iv. 188
Sacred figures of, i. 222
Secret, iii. 92; v. 340-348
Septenary, iii. 310; iv. 194; v. 339
Series of, i. 230
Shesha, in the bosom of, iii. 61

Smaller, i. 301
Soli-lunar, v. 336
Sothiac, ii. 153
Spiritual, ii. 362; iii. 157
Spirituality, of, iii. 444
Subjective world, i. 110
Sub-races, of, iii. 302
Svabhāvat and, ii. 360
Symbols of, v. 341
Theogonic evolution of, ii. 107
Time, of, iii. 108
Various, i. 154
Vis generatrix in, ii. 274
Warren, Col., on, v. 340
Week of days, of, iv. 195
Yugas or, iii. 68
Zoology, of, iv. 302
CYCLIC Activity, ii. 357
Aeons, ii. 135
Aggregations, ii. 316
Attempts to enlighten world, v. 396
Brahmā, character of, ii. 155
Civilization, iv. 292
Descent, ii. 134
Destiny, iii. 444
Development, iii. 418
Disease, changes in, i. 232
Divine breath, i. 114
Divisions, iv. 193
Elements, curve of, ii. 291
Events, ii. 371
Evolution, i. 192, 278; ii. 135, 359; iii. 46, 204, 301, 418, 420; iv. 300
Globes, order of, i. 224
Gyration, ii. 257
Impulse, ii. 349
Intricacies, iii. 60
Languages, evolution of, iii. 204
Law, i. 82, 337; ii. 135, 349; iii. 84, 165, 299; iv. 292, 349, 354; v. 300
Matter, activity of, ii. 357
Motion, iii. 90
Mysteries, iii. 413
Nature's acts are, ii. 365
Pilgrimage, iii. 111, 444
Powers, i. 331
Pralayas, iv. 230
Precession, iii. 265
Progress, i. 334
Rebirths, iii. 235, 237
Records, v. 340
Religion, iv. 292
Saviours, iii. 413; v. 336-339
Seven, iv. 136
Task, i. 322
Time, iii. 414
Transformations, iii. 413
Wheels, ii. 366
Years, ii. 157, 381
CYCLICAL, Asterisms, progress of, iii. 255
Astronomy, iii. 330; v. 337, 339, 340-348
Cataclysms, iii. 153; v. 103
History, iii. 330
Law, ii. 310
Processes in Kosmos, iii. 83
Space, translation in, ii. 274
Time, ii. 370

CYCLONES of 1888, iv. 269
CYCLOPEAN, Buildings, iii. 317; iv. 158, 399
  Easter Island, remains on, ii. 34, 157
  Eye, iii. 300
  Lore, iv. 323
  Monuments, iii. 344
  Peru, erections in, iv. 314
  Remnants, ii. 157; iii. 295
  Ruins, iii. 331, 340
  Statues, ii. 34
  Structures, iii. 341; iv. 323
  Towns in Europe, origin of, i. 257
CYCLOPES, Apollo and, iv. 338
  Druids not, iii. 342
  Fourth race belonged to the, iii. 295
  Hyperborean, iv. 339
  Kabiri and, iii. 389
  One-eyed, iv. 338
  Science ignorant of, iii. 344
  Seven, v. 325
  Sons of cycles, the, i. 257
  Ulysses and, iv. 339
  Wisdom-eye of, iv. 338
  Work, of, iii. 337
CYCLOPS, Demi-god, a, iii. 80
  Man a, iii. 291
  One-eyed, iv. 335
  Perseus and, iii. 344
CYGNUS, Constellation of, ii. 320
CYLINDERS, Assyrian, iii. 229
  Babylonian, iii. 17, 112, 250; iv. 261; v. 123
  Chaldean, v. 123
CYLLENE, Mercury born on Mount, iv. 112
CYNOCEPHALUS the dog-headed ape, ii. 103;
  iii. 198; iv. 225
CYPRIANUS, St., v. 170, 171, 173
CYPRIOTER, the, iv. 117
CYPRUS, Sargon conquered, iv. 261
CYRIL and the cruciform couches, iv. 129
CYRIL, Bishop, v. 307
CYROPÉDIE quoted, ii. 378
CYRUS, the great, ii. 378; iii. 359; iv. 261
CYTOBLASTEMA, cell-germinating substance,
  iii. 258
CYZICANS and Argonaut's stone, iii. 345
CZOLBE repeats Occultists' saying, iii. 162

D

DABAR, Word or Logos, ii. 65; iii. 51
DACTYLI and the Kabiri, iii. 344, 359
DAEDALUS, Colossus attributed to, iii. 296
DAEMON, Jupiter, ii. 188
  Lightning, of, ii. 188
  Nargal, iii. 217
DAEMONS, Plato's elementary, ii. 290
DAEVA, Invocation of the, iv. 86
DAEVAS, Evil-doing, iv. 85
DAG, Oannes, the Babylonian, iv. 150
  Messiah, ii. 379
DAGOBA, v. 162
DAGON, Babylonian, ii. 380; v. 163
  Chaldean Xisuthrus, of, iii. 147
  Fish, ii. 59; iii. 64
  Oannes and, ii. 109; iii. 147, 196; iv. 63
  Saturn, etc., ii. 366
DAIMON of Socrates, iii. 417; v. 65, 333

DAIMONES and genii, i. 329
DAITYA, Atlantis and, iii. 149; iv. 309
  Island, ii. 377; iii. 314, 431
  Magicians of, iii. 426
  Rāhu a giant of, iii. 380
  River of, iii. 355
  Sinking of, iv. 280
DAITYA-GURU, iii. 42, 44
DAITYAS, Dānavas or, iii. 335; iv. 69
  Defeat of, ii. 137
  Devatās and, iii. 404, 405
  Dvipa and, iii. 319
  Dynasties of the, iii. 368
  Features of the, iii. 228
  Giants or, iii. 190, 404, 406
  Gibborim or, iii. 275
  Gods or, ii. 140
  Indra and, iii. 377
  Māyāmoha deludes, ii. 140
  Monarch of, iii. 229
  Orders of, ii. 137
  Penances of, ii. 140
  Secret Doctrine, in synonym, i. 155
  Shukra, pupils of, iii. 45
  Titans, or, iii. 289; iv. 69
  Worlds seized by, ii. 139
  Yogis were, ii. 132
DAIVIPRAKRITI, Bhagavad Gita on, ii. 148
  Light of the Logos, i. 193, 263, 334; ii. 148, 326
  One with Shekinah, v. 189
DĀKINI, Sanskrit for, Khado, iii. 273, 286
DAKSHA, Aditi and, i. 198; ii. 348
  Avalokiteshvara like, iii. 185
  Birth of, iii. 183
  Creator, the, ii. 348; iii. 197
  Curse of, v. 288
  Daughter of, iii. 59
  Female, iii. 277
  Intelligent, iii. 249
  Kalpas, in all the, ii. 149
  Mānasaputras of, iii. 374
  Mārishā mother of, iii. 184
  Modes of reproduction and, iv. 228
  Nārada and, iii. 178, 277; iv. 70; v. 288
  Patriarch, iii. 183
  Pishāchā daughter of, ii. 132
  Prajāpatis, chief of, iii. 91
  Progenitor, the, iii. 185
  Rishis, one of the, ii. 154
  Sacrifice of, iii. 78, 189
  Sambhūti daughter of, iii. 98
  Samnati, daughter of, iv. 97
  Sons of, iii. 148; v. 288
  Sons of daughters of, ii. 245
  Synthesis of terrestrial creators, iii. 170
  Vinatā daughter of, ii. 81
DALAI-LAMA an incarnation of Kwan-Shi-Yin,
  ii. 193; v. 325, 393
DALAI LAMAS, the, iii. 185; v. 393
DALILAH, v. 277
DALTON, v. 335
DAMAKHOSHA, a king Rishi, iii. 229
DAMARU, drum of Shiva, iv. 70
DAMASCIUS, quoted, i. 137, 281; ii. 57, 143;
  iii. 341; v. 202
DAMASCUS blade, properties of a, iii. 428
DAMAVEND, Mountains of, iii. 396, 397

DAMBHOBHI, a variant of Dattoli, iii. 235
DAMBHOLI, a variant of Dattoli, iii. 235
DAMIS, v. 142, 143, 146
DAMZE YUL, India or, v. 378
D'ANSELME, v. 310
DAN, Ch'han, or, i. 44
  Dhyāna or, i. 44
  Jacob's words to, ii. 216
  Janna or, i. 44
  Scorpio, the badge of, v. 161, 166
  Virgo in the sphere of, ii. 377
DANA, Prof. J. D., referred to, iii. 324
DĀNAVA a giant demon, iii. 380
DANAVAS, Daityas and, iii. 335; iv. 69
  Danu, descendants of, iii. 380
  Dynasties of the, iii. 368
  Giants or, iii. 198
  Secret Doctrine, in synonym, i. 155
  Titans are, iii. 190, 380; iv. 69
  Ushanas leader of the, iv. 66
  Yogis, great, ii. 132
DANCE, Circle or Planetary, v. 310, 311, 322
  David's, iv. 28; v. 311
  Giants of, iii. 342
DANCING-girls Egyptian, iv. 31
DANGER, Influence, of, v. 560
  Magic, of, v. 85 to 92
  Occultism, of, v. 106, 465
  Occult knowledge, of, v. 69, 70, 80, 92
DANGMA, Alaya of the universe and, i. 119
  Eye of, i. 118, 266
  Lha and, v. 379
  Purified soul or, i. 118; v. 381
DANIEL, Angel of the Jews, on the, ii. 179
  Book of, v. 184
  Chaldean Astrologer, v. 333
  Initiate, Jewish, v. 151, 333
  Michael the angel of, iv. 49
  Prophet, i. 276; v. 151
  Times of, iii. 85
DANIELO, referred to, iv. 103
DANILEVSKY, N. T., the Russian scientist, iv. 224
DANKMOE, quoted, i. 275
DANTE, v. 73
DANU, Danavas descendants of, iii. 380
DANUBE, Hyperborean country not near the, iii. 20
DANVILLE'S MEMOIRES referred to, iii. 393
DARDANUS, v. 238
DARIA, Sir, v. 404
DARK, Aspects of deities, iii. 418
  Brothers, v. 466
  Cloaked Pentateuch, the, iv. 55; v. 71
  Creation and world-cosmogonies, iii. 64
  Eye, Lords of the, iii. 425
  Face, Lords of the, iii. 425, 426
  Faces, Magicians of the, iii. 426
  Flame, rays of the, iii. 237
  Powers, Pagan wisdom and the, ii. 367
  Sayings, sacred books and, iv. 104; v. 71, 182, 192
  Side of the moon, ii. 77
  Space, son of, i. 138
  Swan, ii. 72
  Waters, depths of the, i. 138

Wisdom, Lords of the, iii. 31, 169
Wisdom, Sons of, iii. 250, 284
DARK AGES, Ignorance of, iii. 427
  Maitland on, iii. 439
DARK EPAPHOS, Christ, the, iii. 413
  Dionysus Bacchus or, iii. 414
  Fifth descent from, iii. 416
DARKNESS, Absolute, i. 138; ii. 204
  Absolute light, the, essence of, i. 137, 250; iii. 49, 104; iv. 57
  Abyss of, iii. 64; v. 228
  Age of, ii. 192
  Ain Soph is, ii. 69; v. 227
  Angel of, iii. 35
  Angels in, iv. 59
  Angels of, ii. 177; iv. 57, 151
  Boundless all, filled, i. 113, 114; v. 227
  Brahmā sprung from, ii. 59
  Breath of, i. 132
  Chaos and, ii. 59, 382; v. 227, 228
  Cimmerian, iii. 77
  Circle of, i. 256
  Cosmic powers beyond which is, ii. 161
  Cosmogonies, and, iv. 54
  Deep, on the, iii. 69; iv. 56; v. 228
  Deity or, i. 141; ii. 65; v. 227
  Disintegration of the universe followed by, i. 71
  Divine ray an emanation of, i. 146
  Dragon of, ii. 80, 129
  During Pralaya, i. 137
  Earth covered with, iv. 54
  Essence of, i. 137
  Eternal light and, iii. 70; v. 227, 229, 230
  Eternal matrix and, i. 113
  Eternal Thought concealed in, v. 230
  Fabric of, i. 164
  Father-Mother, i. 113, 130
  Fathers blaze in, iv. 134
  Fludd's explanation of, i. 137
  Genesis on, iv. 56; v. 227 to 230
  Germ of unknown, i. 148
  God giving light to the path of, ii. 118
  Gods of light and, iv. 52
  Hell the kingdom of, iii. 233
  Idea born in, ii. 82
  Ignorance and, iii. 172
  Immutable, ii. 359
  Kingdom of, v. 153
  Light, absolute, i. 137; iv. 57
  Light, adversary of, iii. 388
  Light and, i. 137; ii. 328; iii. 69, 70; v. 227, 229, 230
  Light divided from, i. 298
  Light, generates, i. 170; iv. 60
  Light in, i. 77; iii. 115
  Light, identical with, i. 137
  Light interchangeable with, i. 113
  Light of the one, i. 148
  Light, radiates, i. 93, 133
  Light shining in, ii. 157
  Matter a prison of, iii. 107, 359
  Mental, iii. 379
  Monad returns into, ii. 145
  Monas said to dwell in, i. 132
  Mother-Space coeval with, i. 161; v. 227
  Non-Ego and, i. 115

DARKNESS (Contd.)
　　Occult nature of, iii. 360
　　Oi-Ha-Hou which is, i. 160
　　One true actuality, i. 137
　　Ormazd lives in, iv. 56
　　Paranishapanna or, i. 124
　　Pre-cosmic, ii. 169
　　Primary Thought of, v. 210
　　Primordial light and, i. 113; v. 227, 228
　　Prince of, iii. 119, 284
　　Principle of all things is, iv. 54
　　Quality of, iii. 69; iv. 141
　　Ray of the ever-, i. 127; ii. 294
　　Salvation from mental, iii. 419
　　Satan called king of, iv. 78
　　Secondary creation is, ii. 169
　　Self-existent lord called, ii. 46
　　Serpent of, ii. 128
　　Set and, iii. 384
　　Son of, i. 247
　　Sons of, iii. 274; iv. 56, 341
　　Spheres in which our light is, ii. 169
　　Spirit is, i. 137
　　Spirit of unknown, ii. 81
　　Spirits of, iii. 73, 102, 169, 235; iv. 81
　　Swan in, ii. 275
　　Symbol, and the first, ii. 161
　　Tāmasa, spiritual, ii. 88
　　Theological fictions and, iv. 139
　　Theory that two lights make, ii. 393
　　Typhon the power of, iii. 102
　　Unfathomable, i. 144
　　Universal light which is, ii. 51
　　Unknown, i. 192; ii. 143
　　Unknown light which is, ii. 71
　　Voidness and, i. 115; v. 209
　　Waters and the ray of, ii. 68
　　Waters breathed over by, i. 132; v. 227, 228
　　Wisdom in, i. 145
　　Wolf who comes out of, iii. 385
　　World enveloped in, ii. 87
DARMESTETER, J., ii. 50
DARSHANAS or schools of philosophy, i. 119
DARWIN, quoted, See Book Index
DARWIN, G. H., Theory of, iii. 74
DARWINIAN, Anthropology, iii. 22; iv. 239, 259, 290
　　Claim for common ancestor, iv. 206
　　Descent, iii. 196
　　Dogmas, iv. 201
　　Evolution, i. 251; iii. 49; iv. 222, 257
　　Evolutionists, i. 270; iii. 294
　　Huxley, a, iii. 160
　　Hypothesis, a, i. 238; iv. 256
　　Law, iii. 178
　　Materialism, iii. 165
　　Occult evolution and, iii. 192
　　Period of the first man, iv. 225
　　Quasi-evolution, iii. 186
　　Scheme and esoteric theory, iv. 259
　　School, i. 251; iii. 126
DARWINIAN THEORY, i. 240, 265; iii. 177, 257; iv. 237, 248, 249, 251, 260
　　Deserters from the, iv. 217
　　Evolution and the, iii. 196
　　Expansions of the, iv. 219
　　Materialistic and the, iii. 369

Max Müller on the, iv. 232
Opponents of the, iii. 176
quoted, iv. 231
DARWINIANS, Dryopithecus of the, iv. 248
　　Hairy arboreal ancestors and, iv. 260
　　Mammals and, iv. 304
　　Naked truth and, iv. 225
　　Primeval civilisation and, iv. 355
　　Seed and, iv. 223
DARWINISM, Alternative theory to, iv. 215
　　Anatomy of anthropoid, and, iv. 250
　　Antiquity of man and, iv. 255
　　Bishop Temple on, iv. 215
　　Blow to, iii. 67
　　Danilevsky upsets, iv. 224
　　Evolution meets, iv. 219
　　Expanded, iv. 217
　　Facts of, ii. 324
　　Fallacies of, iv. 297
　　Fiske and Huxley defended, iv. 250
　　Fundamental principles of, iv. 216
　　Hæckel and, iv. 237
　　Language and, iv. 290
　　Occultists and, i. 239
　　Origin of man and, iv. 237
　　Seceders from, iv. 280
　　Secondary laws of, iv. 232
　　Structural evidence hostile to, iv. 247
DARWINIST, Brief, the, iv. 254
　　French, iii. 109
　　Quoted, a, iii. 191
DARWINISTS, Anthropoids and, iii. 96
　　Common ancestor and, iv. 259
　　De Quatrefages and, iv. 257
　　Great gulf and, iv. 247
　　Mechanical theory of, iv. 218
　　Opponents of the, iv. 254
　　Protoplasm of the, iii. 128
　　Western Africa and, iv. 249
DASEIN as the manifold existence, i. 324
D'ASSIER, Paul referred to, ii. 345; iii. 156
DATES, Anthropologists and, iv. 364
　　Babylonian, iv. 262
　　Curtailed, iv. 260
DATTOLI, Variants of, iii. 235
DÄUMLING or Tom Thumb, i. 219
DAVID, Dance of, ii. 49; iv. 27, 28; v. 311
　　Divination of, iv. 22
　　God in the Ark and, iv. 37
　　Hezekiah's faith and that of, ii. 33; iii. 386
　　Iao not known till the time of, iv. 111
　　Jews date from, iv. 41
　　King, v. 239, 242
　　Moses not recognized by, iv. 111
　　Psalms of, quoted, iii. 143, 216; iv. 28
　　Psalms of, referred to, v. 148, 179
　　Shield of, v. 120
　　Solomon and, v. 176
DAVIS, J. Barnard, the Craniologist, iv. 91
DAVKINA, Ana and Belita, iv. 30
DAVY, Sir Humphrey, ii. 203
DAWN, Æon, of a new, i. 242
　　Body of the, iii. 170
　　Day of the Great Breath, of a, iii. 20
　　Effulgent, iii. 372
　　Jyotsnā, or, iii. 68
　　Lucifer, son of manvantaric, i. 138

DAWN (*Contd.*)
Manvantaric, i. 78, 114, 124; ii. 251, 349; iii. 166, 235
Morning twilight or, iii. 70
Night, after that, ii. 86
Night continues till the future, ii. 92
Night to, i. 132
Period, of new, i. 324
Phoebe or, iii. 130
Pralaya, after, i. 114
Precursor of the, iii. 42
Ray dropped at the new, i. 138
Rebirth of the worlds at, iii. 171
System of the rebuilding of the, ii. 254
DAWNS, Seven, iii. 308
DAWSON, Sir W., on the origin of man, iv. 297
DAY, Age of humanity, in the, iii. 441
Ahan or, iii. 68
Be With Us, the great, i. 188, 192, 195, 309
Body of the, iii. 170
Brahma, of, see DAY OF BRAHMĀ
Eighth, v. 199
Globe, for each, iv. 326
Gods of the, iv. 191
Great Breath of the, iii. 20
Kosmos awakes to a new, i. 176
Last, of World, iv. 326
Māyā of the, ii. 360
Nirvāna has neither night nor, ii. 89
Planets, on, iv. 276
Polar, length of a, iii. 293; iv. 342
Pregenetic, ii. 113
Sixth, v. 199
Seventh, the, iii. 236, 254; iv. 56; v. 129, 198, 199
DAY AND NIGHT, Alternation of, i. 82; ii. 129
Germs of, iv. 76
Interval between, iii. 70
Pair, a, iv. 137
Periods marked as, ii. 104
Symbol of, iii. 130
DAY-FIRES, iii. 28, 74
DAY OF BRAHMĀ, Age or, i. 291; ii. 165; iii. 308
Duration of a, i. 110; ii. 382
End of a, ii. 86
Great Breath, or, iii. 20
Kalpa or, iii. 80
Length of a, ii. 54, 86, 87, 136
Life-cycle or, i. 278
Mahāpralaya after a, iii. 154
Mahāyuga, a, ii. 91
Manus in a, fourteen, i. 132; ii. 168
Manvantara or, i. 78; ii. 84
Manvantaric dawn, at, i. 114
Night and, i. 285
Period of a, iii. 79
Planet and a, iv. 230
Pralaya after, ii. 275
DAY-STAR, Lucifer the genius of the, iv. 69
Sun, the, i. 299
DAY-SUN, Osiris, the, iv. 151
DAYĀNAND SARASVATI, Svāmi, i. 53; iii. 79, 218
DAYANISI, Worship of, ii. 113
DAYS, Ancient of, i. 129; 284; ii. 179; iii. 93
Brahmā, of, i. 131; ii. 84, 89; iv. 73

Correspondences of, v. 432, 433, 434, 437, 441
Creation, of, i. 85; iii. 254; iv. 56, 273; v. 198
Deity, of the, iv. 115
Lucky and unlucky, v. 250
Natural measure of, iv. 110
Planetary chain, of the, i. 209
Planets and, v. 432, 506
Solar, ii. 105
Week, of the, iv. 153; v. 199, 333, 432-434
DAZZLING FACE, Great king of the, iii. 424, 425
DBRIM, ii. 65, 150; iii. 49, 51, 52
DEAD, the Festival of, v. 116
DEAD-LETTER, Allegory *versus*, iii. 375
Bible, of the, ii. 28, 31; iii. 16, 281; iv. 109
Blinds in the Gnostic gospel, iv. 140
Dogma and, iii. 200
Husk of the, iii. 335
Interpretations, iv. 139
Lingam worshippers, iv. 40
Orientalist, to the, iv. 16
Orthodox, iv. 136
Purānas, of the, iii. 319; iv. 156
Religions, iii. 376
Sameness of the, iv. 86
DEATH, Abode after, ii. 184
Adepts, of, iv. 100
Angel of, iii. 120, 384, 387
Buddha, of, v. 105
Change called, iv. 30
Children of, iii. 304
Cross represents, iv. 126
Fire is Life and, i. 180
First Lord of, iv. 42
Foreseeing, iv. 92
Girdle is, iii. 237
Ignorance is, iii. 219
Initiate, of an, iv. 152; v. 271, 272, 290
Jesus, of, ii. 382; iv. 112; v. 162, 168
Kosmos, of, ii. 89
Krishna's, iv. 96
Life and, i. 82; ii. 87, 131; iv. 43, 82
Life after, i. 275
Lipika not Deities of, i. 166
Mahā Pralaya and, iii. 310
Māra or, iv. 151
Mars the Lord of, iii. 391
Moon the Goddess of, ii. 102
Mysteries of, iv. 17
Nature of, ii. 250
Nidānas, first of, v. 559
Penalty, ii. 78
Periods of, i. 209
Personified wisdom and, iii. 363, 364
Phoenix, of the, iv. 188
Plane, a change of, ii. 235; iv. 82
Ptah, God of, ii. 82
Real, v. 488, 489
Red Sea of, ii. 127
Satan frees from, i. 248
Second, v. 360, 489, 491, 496, 498
Septenary law in, iv. 193
Socrates, of, v. 333
Soul after, iii. 363, 364
Soul, of the, v. 486, 489, 491, 492, 496, 499, 500
St. Peter, of, v. 140, 141

DEATH (*Contd.*)
Sudden, v. 564
Suffering not finished by, i. 112
Transformation, is, v. 537
Tree of, iv. 130
Universal life and, iv. 82
Universe, of the, iv. 151
Yama, God of, iii. 56
Yima's kingship and, iv. 180
DEBIR, or Kirjath-sepher, iv. 98
DECAD, Combinations of, ii. 33
Higher and Lower, v. 436
Interlaced triangles are, iv. 163
Monad, emerging from the, ii. 158
Mystic, v. 382
Perfect number, the, v. 506, 507
Pythagorean, i. 110; ii. 33, 341; iv. 123, 144;
v. 382, 420, 506, 507
Septenary and triad form, i. 284; iv. 154
Ten and, ii. 47; iv. 152; v. 420
Unities and binaries in, i. 284
Universe, contains the, i. 161; v. 382
DECADES, Week of, iv. 194
DECAN OF ZODIAC, iii. 431
DECCAN, Weakened races in the, iii. 409
DECEASED, Aanroo, in, i. 282
Egg, in the, ii. 75, 80
DECEMBER, Solar gods incarnated in, ii. 382
DECHARME, see Book Index
DECIDUA, iv. 237, 238
DECIMAL NOTATION, ii. 76, 77; iii. 49; v. 342
DECUSSATED, Circle, Plato's, 160
Cross, iv. 126, 131
DEEP, Aditi the great, iii. 271; v. 233
Chaos or the, i. 294; ii. 24, 50, 398; iii. 147,
153; v. 120, 228, 230, 233, 234
Cosmic, great, iii. 271
Darkness on the face of, iii. 70; iv. 56
Demons of, iii. 383
Dragons of, iii. 32, 190
Ea, the God of, iii. 147
Gaea the great, iii. 271
Great, ii. 68, 179, 350, 398; iii. 64, 239, 271;
iv. 96; v. 228, 233, 234, 235
Great face of, iv. 45
Mother Space, v. 225
Powers of, iii. 383
Pralaya and, ii. 350
Primordial waters of, i. 146
Ra issuing from, i. 277
Sages come forth from, iv. 63
Space or, ii. 398; v. 233, 235
Spirit of, iii. 112
Thalassa or, iii. 124
Universal matrix or, iii. 75
Virgin Mother or, i. 134
Wisdom, of, iii. 19, 64
DEER Naphtali likened to a, ii. 377
DEFINITIONS OF ASCLEPIOS, i. 329, 335
DEFUNCT, *Book of the Dead*, in, iv. 159;
v. 289
Dev possesses soul of, v. 94
Egypt, in, i. 266; v. 245
Heart of, i. 166
Journey of, i. 274; v. 245
Soul or self of, i. 273
Sun, iv. 151

Toom prayed to by, ii. 398
Transformations of every, i. 273
Wicks of the, i. 282
DEGREES, Adeptship, of, iv. 136; v. 399
Consciousness, of, i. 318
Contemplation, of, v. 373, 374
Devas, of, iv. 281
Elemental kingdom, of the, ii. 173
Initiation, of, v. 280, 281, 282, 292, 312, 399
Intellectuality, of, iii. 175
Lipika, of, i. 186
Manas and Kāma-Manas, of, v. 512, 513, 517
Masonic, iv. 146; v. 282, 283
Monads' perception, of, ii. 356
Occult, of fire, iii. 123
Progenitors, of, iv. 281
Spiritual beings, of, i. 281
Spirituality, of, iii. 96
Substance, of, ii. 347
Theosophic, of Peuvret, iv. 172
DEITIES, Christian and Pagan, v. 94
Chief, Seven, v. 233
Defunct appear before, v. 245
Heathen, v. 94
Invocations to, v. 246
Manifested, v. 408
Pantheon, v. 95
Seven, v. 233
Two, v. 319
DEITY, Abode of the, ii. 397
Absolute, i. 128, 224, 293; ii. 338; iii. 166;
v. 208, 387, 462, 471
Abstract sexless, i. 129
Abstraction of, ii. 370
Action the will of, iv. 97
Advaitis, of the, iv. 170
Ahura Mazda, iii. 418
All-wise, iii. 183
Almighty, iv. 174
Androgynous, i. 139; ii. 113; iii. 76; v. 162
Anthropomorphic, iii. 305; v. 81, 387
Architecture of, iv. 113
Assimilation with, v. 265
Aspects of, ii. 275
Attributes of, ii. 156
Beneficent, iv. 118
Body of, i. 285
Chaldea, in, v. 188, 462
Changeless, v. 210
Christian church, of the, i. 84; iv. 77
Christian idea of, i. 84; ii. 102, 144, 189;
v. 210
Circle and, iv. 115, 119; v. 87, 206, 383
Collective, iii. 142
Concealed, i. 141, 142; ii. 118, 155; iv. 107;
v. 214, 230
Conception of, i. 128
Cosmic nature and, ii. 344
Create, prepares to, i. 207
Created, iii. 117
Creation and, iii. 166
Creative, iii. 116, 133; iv. 114, 123
Cube and, i. 84; v. 189
Culmination of, iii. 48
Darkness, v. 227
Darkness of, iv. 83
Demiurge no personal, i. 322

DEITY (*Contd.*)
Demon, iii. 57
Development of, v. 209
Devil as, iv. 53
Dragon, symbol of, iii. 385
Eastern esotericism and, ii. 162
Egyptian, i. 142; v. 214, 462
Elohists, of, v. 187
Esoteric philosophy and, i. 43, 193; ii. 163
Eternal, iii. 107; v. 108
Eternal light or, iii. 270
Expansion, as boundless, i. 179
Father of all, v. 210
Feminine form of, v. 211
Finite, ii. 344
Fire as, i. 70, 127, 151
Four-lettered name of, iii. 313
Fourth race, iv. 345
Garment of, v. 187
Generative, iv. 42
Geometrizing, iii. 51; iv. 126; v. 87, 90
Giants doomed by, iv. 103
Glyphs of, ii. 64
Gnostic address to, iv. 42
God, not, ii. 65
Greco-Olympian, iii. 418; v. 462
Greek Delta, and, v. 117
Hades, in, v. 230
Hebrew, iv. 173
Hidden one or, ii. 68
Hindu, iii. 418
Human-like ways of, iv. 125
Hypothetical, iv. 215
Ideas of an anthropomorphic, ii. 137; v. 81, 319, 387
Ideas of, iii. 50
Image of, iii. 132
Immeasurable space is, iii. 76
Immutability in, ii. 89
Impersonal, iii. 50; iv. 49
Incarnation of, ii. 162
Incognizable, i. 75, 173; iii. 64; iv. 161
Incomprehensible, i. 109
Indian, i. 142; v. 188, 209, 387, 420, 462
Infinite, i. 128; iii. 166; v. 233
Intelligible, ii. 81
Intra-cosmic, iii. 53
Invisible, v. 87
Jewish, ii. 300; iv. 38, 111, 113; v. 188, 210, 241, 325
Kabalist view of, i. 128; iv. 171; v. 91, 191, 210, 227, 228, 230
Kabiric, iii. 362
Leibnitz on, ii. 354
Life, presiding over a, ii. 363
Logical, ii. 338
Male, iii. 42; v. 228
Male and Female, v. 209
Maleficent, iv. 118
Man is, ii. 163; iv. 83; v. 81
Manas, of, ii. 241; iv. 64
Manifestation of, i. 70; ii. 58; iii. 166; iv. 183
Manifested, i. 128; iv. 83, 197
Mavantaric periodic, i. 170
Mexican, iii. 379
Mikael and, v. 326
Mind of the, i. 249

Monotheist, of the, ii. 257
Most High, iv. 111
Motion, the abstract, v. 515
Mysterious, iv. 171
Name of, four-lettered, iii. 313
Nameless, i. 178; iv. 110
National, ii. 300; iv. 111
Nature and, i. 144; ii. 212, 344; iii. 258; iv. 19, 43; v. 70, 87
Nature of, i. 314
Night and day, and, iv. 76
Number and, i. 135; v. 87, 116, 191, 382, 420, 462
Occultism and, i. 84; v. 387, 471
Omnipresent, i. 128
One, the, i. 128, 254; iii. 274, 381; iv. 209; v. 70, 206, 214, 462
One in many, the, i. 172
One Veda, one caste, one, i. 145
Organ representing, iv. 41
Ormazd, iii. 418
Orphic, ii. 111
Pagan gods, among, a, i. 72
Passive, iii. 38
Permutation of, iv. 167
Personal, i. 84, 309, 322; ii. 354, 359, 363; iii. 412; iv. 77, 81; v. 70, 77, 81, 206
Personifications of the attributes of, ii. 156
Philosophers and, iv. 160
Plato's, iv. 124; v. 31, 90, 382, 383
Popular Gods and, ii. 49
Potency of the, v. 449
Power name of, iv. 36
Presence, the ever invisible, i. 284
Primordial, iv. 151
Principle, a, ii. 215; v. 382
Protestant and, v. 78
Rabbis knew the meaning of, iii. 135; v. 188
Realization of, iv. 114
Reflection of, iv. 125
Religion, in, ii. 155; v. 70, 87
Representation of, iv. 107
Root of the one element in, ii. 181; v. 227
Satan and, i. 247
Sea and, i. 284; ii. 71
Secondary manifested, iv. 197
Secrets revealed by, ii. 247
Semitic, iv. 108
Serpent, iii. 379
Seventh principle a personal, ii. 363
Sexless, i. 129; v. 408
Shadow of the unknown, iv. 81
Shemites, of the, iv. 111
Soul, is a, v. 316
Space, i. 109; ii. 50, 52; iii. 76, 166, 271; v. 227
Substance and, i. 180; ii. 257
Sun, the, Life-giving, v. 154
Supreme, iii. 148, 410; iv. 111
Syllable, sacred to, v. 418
Symbol(s) of, i. 172, 173; ii. 60, 64, 66; iii. 385; iv. 152; v. 87, 189, 462
Tetragrammaton, name of, iii. 313
Third, v. 129
Throne of, ii. 338
Tibet, of, i. 139; v. 420
Triangle and, i. 84; 173; v. 117

DEITY (Contd.)
  Tribal, iv. 38
  Trinity and, i. 84; v. 188, 210, 219
  Triple aspect of, i. 128; iv. 168
  Unconditioned, i. 335
  Unity of, v. 462, 463
  Universal, i. 335; ii. 338; iii. 166, 258; v. 70, 206, 528
  Universe and, i. 156, 231
  Unknowable, ii. 50, 61, 275; v. 471
  Unknown, i. 43, 114; iii. 411; iv. 40, 58, 81; v. 227
  Unmanifested, iii. 271
  Unrelated, i. 335
  Unrevealed, i. 70, 144
  Unseen, ii. 50
  Vaidic, v. 87, 98, 188
  Veil of, iv. 115; v. 91
  Whirlwind and, i. 176
  Will of, iii. 129
  Wisdom, of, iii. 124
  Zoroastrian, iii. 418
  Zunis, of the, iv. 200
DELAMBRE, see Book Index
DELGARME, see Book Index
DELHI the site of ancient cities, iii. 224, 395
DELIVERANCE, Path of, v. 374
DELICIÆ HUMANI GENERIS, ii. 328
DELIUS slayer of Python, iv. 340
DELLA PENNA, iii. 389
DELOS, Island of, iv. 340, 341
DELPHI, Oracle at, ii. 187; iii. 378; v. 417
DELPHIC, Commandments, ii. 361
  Injunction, v. 81, 82
  Oracular vapours, ii. 52
  Temple, the, iv. 152
DELPHOS, v. 334
DELTA, Age of the, iv. 316
  Egypt, of, iii. 21; iv. 315
  Emigrants to, iii. 367
  Greek, iv. 153; v. 117
  Population cf, iv. 319
  Sahara once fertile as, iii. 404
  Three-cornered land of, iii. 416
DELIRIUM, Astral and, v. 526
DELUGE, Actual geological, iii. 314
  Atlantean, iii. 383; iv. 103
  Avatāra Vishnu and, ii. 380
  Aztec tradition of, ii. 35
  Babel after, iii. 374
  Biblical, iii. 18; v. 102, 103, 109
  Buddha and, iii. 421
  Cain and, iii. 390
  Chaldean, iii. 18
  Chronology since, iii. 394
  Church and, i. 65
  Constellations and, iii. 351; iv. 354
  Cumberland on, iii. 391, 392
  Denial of, iv. 308
  Faber on, iii. 267
  Fourth great, iii. 349
  Geology and, iii. 152
  Gods, or Kabirim, iii. 359
  Great, i. 136; iii. 349; v. 91
  Great dragon or, iii. 350
  Ham and, iii. 389
  Heroes who escaped, iii. 48

India and her partial, iii. 425
Jebel Djudi mountains of, iii. 153
Klée on, iv. 104
Last, iii. 353; iv. 99; v. 103
Legend of, iii. 152
Men from the mire of, iv. 88
Nabatheans after, iv. 20
Nations after, iv. 20
Noachian, i. 136; ii. 133, 161; iii. 17, 45, 266. 391, 398; iv. 103 343
Noah's raven after, ii. 161
Panodorus on, iii. 368
Papyri hardly posterior to, ii. 116
Patriarch, iv. 167
Pre-adamites and, iii. 396
Primeval woman after, ii. 247
Prophecy about, v. 104
Punishment, no, iii. 409
Pyramids associated with, iii. 351
Records of, iii. 364
Samothracian, iii. 18
Satya Yuga the first after, i. 136
Sign of, iii. 186
Symbolism of, iii. 313; iv. 283
Tall men before, iii. 280
Terrestrial iii. 148
Theological date for, iv. 364
Thessalian, iv. 345
Third, iii. 350
Tit or, iii. 360
Traditions, of, iii. 149, 267
Universal, iv. 103
Vaivasvata Manu and, iii. 79, 313
Vaivasvata's, i. 136; ii. 85; iii. 147
Waters of, iv. 168
Watery, iii. 154; iv. 188
Zodiac foretold, ii. 375
DELUGES, iv. 269
  Atlantean, iii. 18
  Barbarians and, iv. 312
  Causes of, iv. 340
  Conflagrations and, iv. 353
  Fifth Race has confused the, iii. 149
  Noahs and, iii. 146, 307
  Periodical, iii. 276
  Traditions of, iv. 320
  Universal, iii. 18
  Waters of, iii. 108
DEMETER, iii. 361, 363, 413
  Mysteries of, v. 171, 271
DEMI-GOD, Antiquity, of, iii. 80
  Elohim robbed by, iii. 412
  Gyges as, iv. 344
  Man a, iii. 418
  Nārada more than, iii. 59
  Pollux a, iii. 132
  Prometheus a, iii. 412
  Rāhu a, iii. 380
  Votan the Mexican, iii. 378
DEMI-GODS, Bodies assumed by, iii. 225
  Chinese, iii. 365
  Devatās or, iii. 404
  Dynasties of, iii. 366, 368, 371
  Golden age, all men, in the, iii. 419
  Inventors were, iii. 372
  Nation, in every, iii. 365
  Pagans and, iv. 50

DEMI-GODS (*Contd.*)
Raumas translated, iii. 189
Sciences revealed by, iii. 363
Stories of, iii. 441
Third Race, iii. 319; iv. 89
DEMIOURGOI (DEMIURGI) Seven, v. 325
Great Gods or, v. 214, 218
Seven, v. 325
Symbols of the, iii. 386
Unknown Cause, v. 213
DEMIOURGOS (DEMIURGUS, DEMI-URGE), the, ii. 160; iii. 240
Abstract idea, an, ii. 95
Anthropomorphized, ii. 130
Architect and, ii. 60, 95; v. 327
Builder of world, v. 215
Chaldean esotericism and, iii. 102
Chaos and, iv. 273
Collective, ii. 88; v. 214, 321
Create, does not, ii. 160
Creative Logos, i, 170
Creator, iii. 19; v. 214
Descent of, iii. 84
First-born of any, iv. 33
Iao or, iv. 111
Jehovah, iii. 143
Logos and, i. 322; iii. 35, 38; iv. 46, 170; v. 214, 215, 270, 321
Nazarenes, of the, iii. 246
Primordial water and, ii. 24
Rage of the, iii. 246
Solar fire and, ii. 24
War in heaven and, iii. 240
DEMIURGIC, Creator, the, ii. 67
Mind, ii. 62, 82
DEMIURGICAL GODDESSES, ii. 115
DEMOCRITUS, v. 44, 147, 264, 335
Abdera, of, i. 176; v. 297
Alchemist, v. 297
Atomist, an, i. 70; ii. 57, 243, 303
Cosmogony of, i. 121
Deity, on, v. 316
Gods believed in by, ii. 243, 336
Gyratory movement taught by, i. 176
Leucippus instructor of, i. 132, 176; ii. 57
Prehistoric race, belief in, iii. 287
Primordial principles, on, i. 132, 133
DEMON, Adversary or, iv. 56
Air, of, ii. 189
Assyrian, iii. 344
Asura or, iii. 57
Bigotry, of, i. 62
Dānava a, iii. 380
Deus and, ii. 109
Drought, of, iii. 383, 384
Fallen, iv. 54
God, inverse of, i. 281
Goddesses, v. 89
Guardian spirit stands for, iv. 46
Intolerance, i. 62
Magicians and, iii. 190
Matter, of, iii. 276
Pride of, iii. 276
Python the, iii. 382
Seth treated as a, iii. 44
South, v. 147
South Pole the abode of, iii. 402

Spirit or, ii. 358
Terror, of, iii. 401
Typhon as a, iii. 44
Wind, of, ii. 189
DEMON EST DEUS INVERSUS, i. 138; ii. 129, 131, 141; iii. 276; iv. 82; v. 468
DEMONISM, v. 170
DEMONOLOGISTS, v. 147
Roman Catholic, iv. 79
Satan of the, iii. 374
DEMONOLOGY, Satan in, iii. 388; v. 62, 321
DEMONS, Angels of light made, iii. 102
Asuras degraded into, i. 251; iv. 69
Celestial female, iv. 185
Christianity and, i. 155; iii. 389; iv. 45
Cosmic, iii. 381
Daimones as, v. 171
Deep, of the, iii. 383
Devas and, iii. 69
Devils and, ii. 137
Dogmatic religions and, iii. 413
Elements as, ii. 88
Ethical meanings of, i. 174
Female, iii. 273
Forces taken for, ii. 182
Gods and, ii. 175
Gods degraded into, iii. 102, 235
Hinduism and, ii. 62; iii. 91
Historical meanings of, i. 174
Kumāras degraded into, ii. 179
Lankā, men of, iv. 321
Male, iii. 273
Necromancy and, ii. 116
Pagan, iv. 45
Pious, ii. 132
Pitris, of, iii. 98
Porphyry, of, v. 240
Positive pole of creation, are, iii. 69
Powers of, iv. 22
Progenitors and, ii. 175
Rākshasas regarded as, iii. 172, 235
Rebirth of, ii. 178
Samael chief of, ii. 135
Satan belongs to the fifth class of, iii. 388
Semele, and, ii. 116
Seth one with the Hindu, iii. 91
Shankhadvīpa, of, iii. 403
Shells or, iii. 120
Solar Gods made, v. 315, 317
Tempting, iii. 181
Universal plenum, within the, ii. 292
Wicked, iii. 33, 403
DEMRUSCH, Giant, iii. 397
DEN, Trophonius, of, v. 148
DENDERA, Stonehenge and, iii. 344
Temple of, iii. 373
Zodiac of, iii. 367, 428, 430; v. 332
DENMARK, iv. 321, 355
DENON, referred to, iii. 429, 430, 431
DENTON, Mrs. Elizabeth, quoted, i. 250
Prof., referred to, i. 250
DENYS, Saint, v. 207, 209, 312, 386
DEPTH(S) Bythos or, i. 262; iv. 144
Chaos and, i. 264; iv. 146
Circle issues from, iii. 218
Cosmic, i. 138
Dark waters of, i. 138

DEPTH(S) (Contd.)
Invisible, ii. 338
Mother, of, i. 134
Ocean of Life, of, i. 134
Rayless, i. 264
Sigē and, iv. 146
Space, of, i. 135, 291; ii. 340
Spiritual soul of, iv. 144
Universal soul of, iv. 145
World of matter, of, iv. 85
DERVISHES, in literature, Howling, i. 66
DERUM, Boreas called, ii. 187
DESBOSSES, Father, referred to, ii. 356
DESCARTES see Book Index
DESERT, Gobi, of, iii. 18, 319, 371; iv. 71
Hermon, of, iii. 407
Illusion, of, i. 256
Ischins in a, iii. 375
Jews in the, iv. 79
Sahara, of, iii. 345, 404, 422
Scorpio and, rains, ii. 374
Shamo, iii. 326, 404, 414; iv. 71
Spread of sandy, iii. 312
Wind of, iii. 384
DESIRE, Animal, iv. 165
Body of, iv. 24
Boehme, on, iv. 205
Brahmā's to create, i. 170
Ceaseless pulse of, iii. 236, 237
Cosmic, i. 250
Create, to, iii. 68, 237
Creation, principle of, i. 170
Divine, iii. 76
Freedom, for, iv. 52
It, first arose in, iv. 150
Kāma or, i. 290; iii. 168
Kāma Deva, God, of, iii. 181, 182
Kāma Rūpa and animal, iv. 165
Obstructor, and, iv. 209
Sanandana without, iii. 183
Separateness and, v. 557
Sons of Brahmā without, iii. 87
Thought and, v. 546
Vehicle of, iii. 125
Vulture of, iii. 411
Will and, v. 510, 532
World of, ii. 296
DESIRES, Astral body of, i. 304
Body of egotistical, iii. 244
Insatiability of the lower, iii. 411
Kāma or animal, i. 287; iv. 185
Seat of animal, iii. 257
Selfish and sensual, iv. 64
Vehicle of, i. 209; iii. 29, 113
DESNOYERS on Tertiary man, iv. 321
DESTINIES, Artificers of our, ii. 368
God of, iv. 32
Nations, of, ii. 369, 380; iv. 337, 338
DESTINY, Action of the agents and, ii. 154;
v. 323
Curse means, ii. 90
Cyclic, iii. 444
Fate or, iii. 239
Fortune and, ii. 396
Ideas of, iv. 153
Imperishable sacred land, of, iii. 19
Karma or, iv. 176

Khonsoo who executes, iv. 32
Kosmos, of, ii. 319
Nations, of, ii. 367
Network of, ii. 364
Patriarchs, of, ii. 377
Planets, and, ii. 396; v. 314, 335
Races, of, ii. 367
Rocks of, iii. 346
Ruling, ii. 364
Stars, written in, ii. 364
Stone of, iii. 342
Universe, of, ii. 314
Windings in our, ii. 368
Work of, ii. 133
World of fatal, iv. 57
DESTROYER, Shankara, the, v. 188
Shiva, the, ii. 82, 178; iii. 122, 251; v. 530
DESTROYERS, Creators and, i. 248, 306
Friends and helpers of, i. 307
DESTRUCTION, personified, v. 117
Alexandrian Library, of, v. 57, 295
Arles, of, v. 295, 296
Atlantis, of, v. 104
Bibractis, of, v. 295
MSS., of, v. 295, 307
Races, of, v. 102, 104, 267
DEUCALION, iii. 272, 310, 314, 335; iv. 88, 338
DEUS ENIM ET CIRCULUS EST, iv. 122
DEUS EST DEMON INVERSUS, ii. 109; iv. 46
DEUS, Explicitus, i. 323
Implicitus, i. 323
Latins, of the, ii. 61; iv. 173
Mundus, ii. 183
Zeus written, iv. 154
DEUS LUNUS, ii. 102, 104, 112
DEUS NON FECIT MORTEM, iii. 420
DEV, the Persian, iv. 108; v. 94
DEV-bend, conqueror of giants, iii. 396
DEV-sefid, Taradaitya or abode of, iii. 405
DEVA, Ancestor, iv. 239
Angel or, i. 255
Ape and, i. 240
Being becomes a, iii. 322
Bird a synonym of, iii. 294
Consciousness, ii. 345
Deva-Brahmā, Pesh-Hun called, iii. 60
Deva-hue, Celestial kings of the, iii. 423
Deva-instructors, Dhyānis or, iv. 177
Deva-loka worlds and firmaments, i. 189
Deva-lokas, Angel spheres or, ii. 330
Deva-man, Third race, iii. 303
Deva-mātri, Eve or, i. 161; ii. 70
Deva-putra, Rishaya, or the Sons of the Gods,
iv. 177
Deva-Rishi, Nārada the, iii. 59, 92
Deva-sarga, Divine creation or, ii. 173; iii. 183
Deva-vardhika the Builder of the Gods, iv. 129
Eye, the, iii. 296
Goddess mother or, iv. 96
Hindu, iv. 108
Immortals or, iii. 173
Incarnated, iii. 107
Infinity, cannot cross boundary within, i. 192
Instructors, iv. 177
Kingdom, ii. 230
Mother of the Gods, or, i. 124, 161; ii. 251
Nārada doomed to perish as a, iii. 91

DEVA (Contd.)
Prometheus, a, iv. 94
Vaivasvata Manu, a, iv. 283
DEVACHAN, v. 411, 490, 495, 514, 549, 563, 566
Aanroo and, i. 268
Amenti is, v. 247
Animal an, has no, iii. 201
Atma in, ii. 47, 294
Atma-Buddhi, of, i. 267; ii. 47
Avitchi and, v. 230
Bliss of, i. 112; ii. 80
Earth, threshold of, i. 112
Ego and, v. 472, 549, 563, 564
Fields of Bliss or, ii. 101, v. 255
Higher Triad, for the, i. 289
Kāmaloka and, v. 357
Manas in, ii. 47; iii. 68, 120
Nirmānakāyas and, iv. 186
Occult advance in, v. 514
Principles in, man's higher, i. 226
Samādhi leads to, v. 403
Second death and, v. 360
Shoo, Tefnut, and Seb in, iii. 373
Spiritual gestation, is, v. 473
Spurning, iii. 283
Sudden death and, v. 564
Sukhāvatī, v. 392
Third race, no, iv. 181
DEVACHANIC, Entity, v. 472, 518
Experiences, v. 563
Regions, v. 374
States, v. 473, 490, 567
DEVACHANS, Seven successive, ii. 398
DEVADATTA, Jesus an incarnation of, v. 369
DEVAKĪ, Goddess-mother or, iv. 96
Krishna and, iv. 96
Madonna and, iv. 96
Sons of, iv. 176
Vishnu, child of, iii. 59
DEVĀKSHA, v. 483
DEVAMATA, Dialogue between Nārada and,
    iv. 137
DEVANĀGARĪ, Alphabet of Cadmus, and,
    i. 46; iii. 363
Characters have special meaning, v. 114, 118
Speech of Gods, v. 197, 264
DEVANIKA, v. 110
DEVĀPI of the race of Kuru, ii. 93
DEVARISHIS, or the Sons of Dharma or Yoga,
    iv. 70
DEVAS, Ādityas are, iii. 99
Allegories of, ii. 134
Amrita reserved for, ii. 62
Ancient Religion, of the, v. 332
Asuras are rebel, iii. 169
Bhu, of the Earth, v. 110
Bodies (illusive) of, iii. 270
Brahmans and, iii. 120; v. 520
Buddhist Creators, v. 214
Chemical terms and, ii. 271
Cosmic, i. 185
Demons more material, iii. 69
Devils or, i. 140
Dhyān Chohans or, i. 156, 181; ii. 123, 172,
    178; iii. 116, 235, 308; v. 332, 358
Dynasty of living, iii. 225, 368
Elements or, ii. 53

Entities called, i. 329
Fire-Angels and, iii. 245
Form, the origin of, ii. 172
Gandha, of, v. 540
Gandharva, iv. 157
Generation, who fell into, iii. 419
Gods cr, ii. 62, 134, 330; iii. 99
Great kings of the, i. 184
Greece, symbolized in, iii. 103
Hierarchies of, v. 339
Hindu, i. 140; iii. 180
Hosts of, iii. 381
Illusion or, i. 335
Incarnate, compelled to, iv. 85
Incarnations of, iv. 63
Inventors were, iii. 372
Lands of the, iii. 266
Logos, aspects of the, ii. 147
Lords, Dhyānis or, iv. 177
Lunar, iv. 63
Metaphysical, ii. 201
Monads of Leibnitz and, ii. 355
Mystery of, i. 239
Pitris or, v. 559
Planetary Angels, v. 358
Primeval, iv. 281
Propitiating, i. 319
Purānic legend of the, iii. 73
Rasa, of, v. 540
Rebel, iii. 169
Rishis and, iii. 95
Rudras are, iv. 156
Rūpa, of, v. 540
Science and, ii. 336
Secret Doctrine, synonym in, i. 155
Senza handed down by, i. 64
Seven great divisions of, ii. 178
Shadows, have no, iii. 121
Solar, i. 233
Space and time, act in, ii. 136
Sparsha, of, v. 539
Sun's attendants, are, iii. 215
Third Root race, of, i. 257
Vanquished, iv. 85
Varuna chief of, iv. 177
Vedic nations of, iii. 378
Wisdom of, v. 102
Worship offered to, iii. 233
DEVASENĀ, an aspect of Sarasvatī, iii. 204
DEVATĀ, Asura, iii. 250
DEVATĀS, Daityas and, iii. 404, 405
Divine beings, demi-gods or, iii. 404
Pitri, iii. 156
DEVAYĀNA, the way to Paramapada, i. 190
DEVI-DURGĀ, the wife of Shiva, i. 155
DEVIL, Ahriman proclaimed, iii. 102; v. 315
Altar of, iv. 321
Attributes of, iii. 397
Azazel said to be, iii. 375
Biography of the Christian, iv. 45, 97
Castle of, iii. 211
Christian, v. 62, 94, 315
Church transforms Lucifer into, i. 138
Conqueror of, v. 325
Creator opposite aspect of, ii. 131
Creative force, a, iv. 79
Darkness, called, i. 138

DEVIL (*Contd.*)
Deity of every age, iv. 53
Diabolos the, iii. 384
Dragon a name for, i. 140; iii. 107
Drouk signifies, iii. 211
Electricity neither God nor, i. 171
Evil outside mankind no, to produce a, iii. 387
Fallacy of a personal, iii. 376; iv. 43
Ferouer not, v. 94
Genesis of, iv. 45
God and, i. 147; ii. 132; iv. 45, 53
Horned and tailed, iv. 45
Iblis or, iii. 393
Initiates and, iv. 79
Invention of, iii. 241
Jehovah and, i. 138
Jupiter called, iv. 49
Latin Church, and, v. 95
Leviathan the, iii. 210
Lucifer called, i. 138
Magic and, v. 62
Master of persecutors, v. 60
Mercury called a, iv. 49
Occultists do not believe in, v. 60
Omnipotency of, v. 95
Pagans and, iv. 39
Personal, iii. 376; iv. 43
Pharisees declare Jesus to have a, iii. 377
Prince of the air not a, iv. 53
Prototype of Christian, iii. 248
Reality of, iii. 340
Repentance of, iii. 240
Samael the, iii. 387
Saraph Mehophep and, iii. 211
Satan and, iii. 377, 388
Serpent a symbol of, ii. 109, 160
Sign of the, iii. 107
Son of God, is, i. 138
Svastika and, iii. 107
Tempted of, ii. 132
Thalatth and the, ii. 109
Theology and, ii. 58, 109; iii. 211, 353; iv. 53, 153
Tomb of, in Ireland, iii. 211
Vehicle of man, iii. 231
Venus called, iv. 49
White, iii. 154, 401
White Island, of the, iii. 405
Wilford, of, iii. 154
Worshippers, iv. 83
Ye are of your father the, ii. 301
DEVIL-FISH of Victor Hugo, iv. 438
DEVIL-WORSHIP, Nagalism called, iii. 189
D'EVIL, i. 140; ii. 129
DEVILISH, Even numbers are, iv. 146
Science said to be, iii. 57
Wisdom which is, iii. 277
DEVILLE, H. St., Claire, quoted, ii. 267
DEVILS, Angels and, i. 182, 329; ii. 393
Archangels and, i. 281
Christian hell, of the, iv. 76
Christians, of, iii. 235
Church, of the, ii. 44; iii. 282; iv. 155
Deities and, iv. 76
Demons are not, iii. 69; v. 332
Depraved, utterly, iii. 169
Devas transformed into, v. 315

Dhyān Chohans said to be, iv. 155
Elementals, or, iv. 203
Gods and, ii. 368; iii. 44; iv. 49
Hindu devas and, i. 140
Hosts, and the, iv. 55
Jack the Ripper compared with, iv. 76
Jesus on, iii. 234
Knowledge of Futurity, of, v. 94
Logos subject to the, iii. 233
Modern, iv. 76
Mother of, iv. 81
Occultists accused of worshipping, iii. 369
Pagans, of, i. 182
Planets or, iv. 49
Solar Gods made, v. 317
Sons of, iii. 213
Spirits of evil and, iii. 169
Theological fancy of, ii. 189
Theology of, iv. 76
Zoroastrians and, i. 140
DEVONIAN AGE, the, i. 297; iii. 256; iv. 282
DEVONSHIRE, Miocene times, in, iv. 295
Palaeolithic age, in the, iv. 91
DEVOURERS, earth built by, i. 302
Fiery lives, the, i. 294
Fire-atoms and, i. 302
DEVS, Devas transformed into, v. 315
Giants strong and wicked, iii. 392
Izeds or, iv. 345
Magi, of the, ii. 301
Metals concealed by, iii. 395
Ocean, iii. 398
Peris, and, iii. 397; iv. 345
Sorcery of, iii. 393
Tahmurath enemy of, iii. 396
Zoroastrians, of the, iii. 301
DE-ZHIN SHEGSPA, v. 373, 377
DHAIRYA the parent of fortitude, iv. 97
DHAIVATA and Nishāda (the Hindu gamut), ii. 258
DHARMA, Devarishis sons of, iv. 70
Great Bear, a star of the, iv. 119
Kāma as son of, iii. 183
Sons of, iii. 183; iv. 70
Thorah or, ii. 109
Yoga, or, iv. 70
DHARMAKĀYA, i. 87; v. 354, 359, 364, 369, 370, 371, 374, 378, 401, 402, 403, 539
DHĀTU in the human body, seven, i. 331
DHĪMAT or all-wise deity, iii. 183
DHRITARASHTRA, v. 359
DHRITI or patience, iv. 97
DHRUVA, Age of, iv. 338
Alpha, now, iv. 183
Chariots attached to, iv. 57
Commentaries on, iv. 338
Enos seen in the, ii. 380
Ex-pole star, iv. 119
Pole-star, the, ii. 153; iv. 57, 183
DHULKARNAYN, the two-horned, iii. 397
DHYĀNA, of the first element, iii. 114
Jana, or, i. 44
Meditation, v. 373, 389
Yoga same as, iii. 124
DHYAN-CHOHAN, Absolute being mystery to, i. 122
Archangel or, i. 320

DHYAN-CHOHAN (*Contd.*)
Bodhisattva or, iii. 185
Buddhist, v. 320
Cosmic evolution, and, iii. 311
Creating, iii. 245; iv. 297
Creator the, v. 214
Daimon and, v. 303
Deity or, ii. 363
Evolution of, i. 268; ii. 175
Fohat runs errands for, i. 132
Individuality of the, i. 308
Infinity not crossed, boundary within, i. 192
Informing, iii. 45
Infusorium to, from, i. 179
Man and, i. 243, 309; ii. 169
Manu or, i. 132; iii. 309; iv. 239
Monad a, i. 308
Orders of, v. 260
Progenitor of Manu, or, iv. 239
Races represented by, iii. 185
Riddle unread by, ii. 43
Root-Manu or, iii. 309
Sanaka a, ii. 87
Sevenfold nature of, v. 203
Spiritual, i. 334
Uranus a, iv. 335
Venus, of, iii. 45

DHYAN-CHOHANIC, Body, iii. 100; v. 510
Centres of force, iv. 301
Consciousness, ii. 297
Energy or Fohat, iv. 219
Essence, i. 308; iii. 128
Host, i. 214
Impulse, iv. 307
Intelligences, v. 456
Minds, ii. 303
Thought, iv. 219
Wisdom, iv. 219, 305

DHYĀN-CHOHANS, Aether, first born of, ii. 283
Agents for humanity, i. 276
Aggregate of, i. 320, 322; ii. 171, 193
Ah-hi or, ii. 111
Amshaspends or, iii. 357
Ancients, called Gods, iv. 155
Angelic beings or, i. 178
Angels or, i. 318; ii. 336; v. 83, 208, 356
Anupādaka, are, i. 123
Archangels or, ii. 336; v. 214
Ases or, ii. 145
Astral man the reflection of, iii. 177
Asuras connected with, iii. 101
Avalokiteshvara and, ii. 193
Breaths, never-resting, i. 165
Builders, or, i. 279; iii. 177; iv. 301; v. 208, 375
Celestial Buddhas or, v. 393
Celestial Men, v. 203
Chief of, v. 374
Classes of, i. 240; ii. 298; iii. 110, 235, 318
Constitution of, ii. 310
Cosmic, ii. 328
Create, refused to, iii. 248
Creative, i. 114, 170; ii. 161; iii. 70, 360; v. 214, 228
Creators, our, iii. 46
Darkness beyond, ii. 161
Deity and, i. 173

Demi urge, form the, i. 322
Devas and, i. 181; ii. 123; iii. 116, 235, 308; v. 332, 358, 517
Dhyani Buddhas or, v. 374
Divine intelligence and, ii. 171
Divine powers, are, i. 86
Divisions of, ii. 178
Dragons of wisdom or, iii. 282
Dual nature of, i. 322
Earth under charge of, ii. 160
Elements standing for, ii. 53
Elohim or, iv. 79; v. 209, 210
Energies, re-awakened, i. 152
Entities called, i. 329
Esoteric Buddhism, of, v. 326, 386
Ethereal races of, i. 239
Evolution of, iii. 117; iv. 270; v. 532
Existences up to, i. 113
Fohat and, i. 132
Genii of the planets, or, ii. 378
Gods or, ii. 152; iii. 69; iv. 155, 334
Governors or, ii. 325
Groups of, i. 86, 246; iii. 242, 283, 297, 360, 365
Heavenly man, the, iv. 253
Hierarchies of, i. 156, 240, 334; iii. 282, 318; iv. 33; v. 453, 538, 539
Hosts of, i. 170, 178; ii. 88
Human, ii. 200
Humanity and, i. 273, 276
Incarnating, iii. 99, 270, 277
Instructed Third Race, v. 341
Intelligences or, i. 202
Kabirim identical with, iii. 392
Knowledge limited of, iv. 270
Kumāras called, iv. 151
Kwan-Shi-Yin and, ii. 193
Leibnitz's Monads and, ii. 355
Light reflected in, ii. 360; iii. 49
Logos and, i. 320
Lord of Lords, title of highest of, v. 357
Lower, i. 239, 292; iii. 282
Lunar, ii. 167
Ly and Tchong are two, iii. 282
Manus or, ii. 90
Manvantaric emanations or, ii. 147
Mighty ones were, iii. 392
Mind or, i. 320; ii. 319
Mission of, v. 350
Monads and, ii. 355; iii. 154, 304
Nature of, v. 554
One light reflected by, ii. 360
Orders of, i. 155; iii. 110
Pitris and, i. 239, 240, 292; ii. 160, 336
Planetary spirits or, i. 320; ii. 193, 360; v. 358
Planets under charge of, ii. 160, 375
Populations of, ii. 307
Primal natures of, i. 147
Primary stuff used by, ii. 322
Primaries seen by, i. 331
Prajāpatis, v. 214
Progenitors were, iii. 110
Prototypes of, ii. 336; v. 78
Races evolved by, iii. 308
Races of, i. 239
Rays or, i. 188; ii. 297; v. 208, 356, 358
Reflection of, iii. 177

DHYĀN-CHOHANS (Contd.)
　Reflection of one light by, ii. 360
　Revelation by, i. 76
　Ruling, i. 202
　Science and, ii. 336
　Second Race, iv. 335
　Seven, v. 74, 375
　Sevenfold Nature of, v. 203, 350
　Solar system woven by, ii. 322
　Sons of Fire, v. 445
　Sons of Light, v. 350
　Sons of Wisdom or, iii. 269
　Spheres under charge of, ii. 160, 378
　Spirits or Angels of Presence or, v. 74, 170, 356
　Substance of, corporeal, i. 331
　Supra-mundane spheres of, ii. 378
　Third Race and, v. 341
　Vebum, the manifested, i. 320
　Watchers of, i. 279
DHYĀNI, Archangel or, iii. 35
　Atma-Buddhi, an, i. 243
　Chenresi, iii. 185, 186
　Devas and, ii. 300
　Father-Mother, from the bright, iii. 28, 65
　Lha, called, iii. 35
　Lunar, man a, i. 239
　Man as a, i. 239; iii. 259
　Paths and portals of, v. 542
　Planetary, iii. 41
　Reborn a, iii. 259
　Sixfold, i. 271
　Six-principled, i. 270
　Special, iii. 41
DHYĀNI-Bodhisattva, v. 373
　Sons of the Dhyāni-Buddhas, i. 169; iii. 124
DHYĀNI-BUDDHA, v. 365, 366, 368, 374, 376
　Adepts of, ii. 296
　Angel of the star or, ii. 296
　Amitābha a, i. 168
　Archangel or, i. 82
　Augoeides or, ii. 296
　Bodhisattva and, ii. 296; v. 365, 369
　Celestial son of a, i. 169
　Dharmakāyas or, v. 370
　Father or, ii. 298
　Father-soul or, ii. 296
　Gautama, and, i. 168; v. 366, 368
　Group belonging to a, ii. 298
　Initiation, seen at, ii. 296
　Monad's rebirth guided by his, ii. 296; v. 366
　Planetary spirit or, ii. 298
　Star or, ii. 193, 298
　Twin-soul, the elder, ii. 296
DHYĀNI-BUDDHAS, Aggregate of, ii. 193; v. 373, 374
　Ālaya one with, i. 119
　Anupādaka or, i. 123; ii. 295; v. 291
　Archangels or, i. 176
　Architects or, i. 310
　Bodhisattvas and, i. 115, 132; ii. 295; iii. 46
　Buddhist system, in the, i. 261
　Celestial sons of, iii. 124
　Chhāyās of, ii. 296
　Contemplation of, ii. 296
　Cosmic Gods or, i. 119
　Deities, highest, i. 176
　Dhyan-Chohans or, i. 123; v. 358

Elements of mankind called, ii. 295
Elixir of life and, ii. 193
Elohim of, i. 172
Groups of, i. 310
Hierarchies of, v. 539
Human Buddhas and, v. 366, 376
Heavenly, ii. 295
Intelligences, informing, iii. 46
Mānushi-Buddhas and, i. 123
Meaning of, hidden, i. 174
Mysteries unfathomed by, i. 176
One in many, the, i. 172
Orientalists' mistakes concerning, i. 123
Parentless, ii. 295
Primeval, i. 137
Revelation from, i. 76
Seven, v. 325, 539
Synthesis of, i. 169
Watchers or, i. 310
Wisdom of, i. 168
DHYĀNI-BUDDHIC, or Ah-hi Paranishpanna, i. 124
DHYANI-CHOHANS, Mysteries not known to, i. 79
　Nirvana, all in, i. 176
DHYANI-PITRIS, v. 111
DHYANIC sight, limitations of, iii. 46
DHYĀNIPĀSHA or Rope of the angels, i. 154
DHYĀNIS or Dhyānis, Agnishvattas and, iii. 100
　Ancestors, or, i. 269
　Angels, or, i. 268; iii. 39
　Arūpa Pitris, or, iii. 102
　Beings slain by, iii. 124
　Bhūta evolved by, i. 235
　Birthdays of, iii. 186
　Bodhisattvas of, i. 115
　Breath, and the, iii. 29
　Capricornus, abode is in, i. 266
　Celestial Buddhas or, i. 168
　Chohans or, ii. 344
　Classes of, iii. 102
　Clothing of, ii. 344
　Create, refusing to, iii. 231
　Crocodile, connected with the, i. 266
　Deva-instructors or, iv. 177
　Disciples of, iii. 214
　Egos, or, iii. 292
　Elohim or, i. 276; ii. 139; iii. 16
　Esoteric philosophy, of, iii. 102
　Esoteric system, in the, i. 114
　Essence of, i. 268
　Evolution of, i. 265
　Fire, iii. 100
　First, i. 272
　Flagae, called, i. 268
　Gods or, i. 274, 334; ii. 139, 344
　Good, not always, iii. 225
　Heavenly men, or, iii. 16, 292
　Hierarchies of, i. 190; iii. 39
　Highest, i. 255; iii. 278
　Host of, iii. 231
　Human monad and, iii. 113
　Incarnations of, i. 255, 310; ii. 176; iii. 102, 231
　Inferior, i. 190, 310
　Intellectual, had to become, iii. 174
　Logoi, or, i. 233
　Lords, or Devas, iv. 177

DHYĀNĪS (Contd.)
  Lowest, i. 271
  Man becomes as one of the, i. 319
  Mānasa, i. 233
  Manvantaras, from other, iii. 103
  Monad and, iii. 113
  Nirmānakāyas and, iii. 102
  Occultism and, i. 265
  Orders of, i. 303
  Orientalists and, i. 168
  Physical body, without, i. 280
  Pitris and, i. 233, 235, 269; iii. 89, 100
  Planetary, iii. 41
  Progenitors or, iii. 292
  Progeny of, i. 235
  Rays of wisdom or, iii. 197
  Root-races and, i. 114; iii. 172
  Seven heavens, of the, iii. 275
  Shadows, incarnated in empty, iv. 55
  Solar Devas, or, i. 233
  Spirits of the earth or, i. 271
  Spiritual, iii. 174
  Spiritual perception, real to, i. 276
DIABLE, Origin of word, i. 140
DIABOLOS, Origin of word, i. 140; iii. 384
DIAGRAM(S), and Tables, Apes, of pedigree of, iv. 258
  Correspondences, of, i. 208; v. 426, 432, 437, 441, 454, 455, 458, 461, 478, 506
  Earth chain, of the, iv. 328
  Evolution of primordial matter, of, ii. 349
  Evolution of races, iii. 301
  Explanation of some, v. 435 et seq.
  Formation of the soul, i. 287
  Genealogical tree of the fifth race, of, iii. 432
  Human principles, of, i. 209, 224; v. 533, 534
  Kosmos and Consciousness of, v. 524, 525, 526, 527, 528, 529, 530
  Occultists, of, i. 261-268
  Origin of species, of, iv. 307
  Planes, of the seven, i. 249
  Planetary divisions, of the, i. 208
  Schmidt's, iv. 305
  Septenary division, of the, iv. 205
  Ungulate mammals, of the, iv. 305
  Use of, v. 464, 465
  World chain of globes, of the, i. 225
DIAGRAMMA of the Ophites, iv. 108
DIAMOND, Heart, ii. 295
DIAMOND-souled or Vajrasattvas, i. 123
DIANA, Apollo and, iv. 340
  Bearded, ii. 112
  Cat-shaped, ii. 103
  Ceres, daughter of, iii. 417
  Chaste, ii. 102
  Child-birth presided over, ii. 102
  Child-son of, ii. 115
  Demiurgical Goddess, a, ii. 115
  Invisible, visible and, ii. 115
  Latona and, iii. 417; iv. 340
  Life, presided over, ii. 102
  Lunar Goddess, a, iii. 36
  Moon and, i. 275; ii. 102, 103, 115; iii. 132; iv. 30, 340
  Mother, iii. 36
  Niobe and, children of, iv. 340
  One Mother of God, the, ii. 115

DIANA-HECATE-LUNA, the Three in One, ii. 102
DIANA-LUNA, the beauteous Goddess, ii. 110
DIANOIA and Logos are synonymous, iii. 38
DIAPASON harmony, the, iv. 172
DIARBEK, a city founded by Tahmurath, iii.396
DIASTEMES, musical, ii. 151
DIASTOLIC and SYSTOLIC property of the Unity, iii. 54
DIATESSARON, Harmony of four parts, iv. 172
DIATHERMANOUS matter, Ākāsha is, i. 78
DIATOMIC, Atoms of chemistry, i. 265
  Elements, ii. 275
DIAVOLO or Devil, etc., i. 140
DIAZ, Bernard, de Castilla, v. 43
DICTYNNA, of the Cretans was Artemis, ii. 111
  Temple, the, of, v. 144
DIDEROT on plurality of worlds, iv. 275
DIDYMIUM an element, i. 197; ii. 270
DIFFERENTIATION, Æons of, iv. 306
  Atom, of the primordial, iv. 300
  Atomic, i. 207
  Atoms of, ii. 357
  Beginning of, i. 254
  Binary, the origin of, iv. 146
  Cosmic, i. 207, 229; ii. 322; iii. 388
  Creative agent, of the, ii. 139
  Dawn of, i. 69
  Evolving energy after, ii. 345
  First, i. 72, 291, 302; iii. 245, 388
  Homogeneous, of the, ii. 397; iii. 419
  Illusive, i. 318
  Light, of eternal, iii. 70
  Matter, of, ii. 267, 313, 397
  Monads, of, ii. 357
  Mysterious, iii. 152
  Palaeolithic man, of, iv. 257
  Physiological, iii. 129
  Plane of, i. 292; iii. 192; v. 493
  Primeval, i. 250; ii. 313, 325; iii. 192
  Primordial, ii. 349
  Sexes, of, iii. 128, 188
  Space, of and in, i. 302
  Spirit the first, i. 302
  Spirit-matter, of, ii. 41
  Substance, of, ii. 322; iii. 245, 388; v. 485
  Svabhāvat, of, ii. 360
  Unit, of the, iv. 85
  Universe, i. 224
  World-stuff, of, ii. 319
  Zero, begins from, i. 195
DIGAMBARA, ii. 140; iv. 70
DII MAGNI identical with Kabiri, iii. 359
DIMENSIONS, Atoms of, ii. 353
  Four, of space, i. 295
  Metaphysical, ii. 353
  Six, iv. 163
  Three, i. 295; ii. 274
DINAH, daughter of Jacob, ii. 377
DINGIR, the Akkadian creative God, iii. 365
DINAKARA, v. 283
DINOSAURIANS of gigantic proportions,iii. 222
DINOTHERIUM GIGANTEUM, fossil remains of, iii. 279
DIŌCLETIAN, Emperor, v. 173, 297
DIODORUS SICULUS, see Book Index
DIOGENES LAËRTIUS, see Book Index

DION CASSIUS, v. 432
DIONUSUS of Mnaseas, iii. 392
DIONYSIA, licentious, ii. 49
DIONYSIAC Mysteries and the orphic egg. ii. 75
DIONYSIUS, the Areopagite, v. 150
DIONYSOS compared with Brahmā, ii. 49
    First-born of the world, ii. 75
    Second only to Zeus, v. 278
DIONYSUS, Adonai, basis of, ii. 184
    Bacchus or, ii. 49; iii. 418
    Christian trinity and, ii. 111
    Chthonius, ii. 184
    Lunar God, a, ii. 111
    Man-Saviour or, iii. 418
DIONYSUS-BACCHUS, or the dark Epaphos,
    iii. 414
DIONYSUS-SABASIUS, son of Zeus, iii. 413
DIOSCURI, DIOSKOUROI, Apollodorus, of,
    iii. 131
    Great Gods, were, iii. 360
    Kabiri, were, iii. 359, 362
    Sparks on the caps of, ii. 52
    Vulcan's progeny, and, iii. 114
DIS, Disposer of all things, the, i. 137
    Light, called, ii. 57
DISCIPLES, Brāhmans, of the, i. 314
    Buddha, of, iii. 46
    Chelas or, i. 87
    Christian, v. 122
    Gods-Hierophants, of the, iv. 16
    Group of, ii. 298
    John Baptist, of, iv. 136
    Masters' names assumed by, iii. 270
    Pledged, v. 105, 440
    Sciences taught to, iii. 433
DISCIPLINE, Buddhist and Christian, v. 413
    Mysteries were a, i. 57
DISCO Island, Miocene plants in, iv. 295
DISCOID or discoplacentalia, iv. 283
DISCOIDAL placenta, iv. 220
DISCOPLACENTALIA (discoid), iv. 283
DISCRETE, Elements, iii. 245
    Indiscrete, and, ii. 88, 172; iii. 135
    Prakriti, ii. 88
    Quantities, i. 303
    Substance, iii. 135
DISCUS, Rama's horns, and, iii. 217
    Solar, Thoth with the, iv. 99
DISEASE, Cyclic changes in, i. 232
    Epidemics of, i. 181
    Mediumship and, iii. 370
    Messengers bring, i. 181
    Mythology said to be, of language, ii. 16
    Serpent brings, iii. 355
    Treatment of, ii. 283
    Unbelief a, iii. 84
DISEASES, constitutional, iii. 409
    Creators and destroyers, due to unseen, i. 306
    Hereditary, iii. 409
    Over-population and, iii. 409
    Septenary law in, iv. 193
    Sidereal motion and, ii. 370
DISEMBODIED, Man, i. 320; ii. 21
    Manes or, men, iii. 373
    Monad, iii. 68
    Principles of earth, ii. 21
    Soul, ii. 291

DISK, Chakra or, of Vishnu, iv. 116
    Lunar, iv. 32
    Sun, of, ii. 396; v. 313
    Symbology of, i. 72
    White, representing Kosmos, i. 72
DISRAELI on apes and angels, iv. 314
DISSOCIATION-POINT, for compounds,
    ii. 308
DISSOLUTION, Brahmā's, ii. 86
    Constant, ii. 87
    Cyclic, ii. 316; v. 336
    Elemental, i. 301
    Evolution and, i. 77, 78
    Mahāpralaya or, i. 196, 206
    Manvantara, at end of, iii. 308
    Matter, of, ii. 92, 316
    Meanings of, iii. 310
    Periodical, i. 77; iv. 136
    Periods of, ii. 175
    Planetary, i. 213
    Pralaya or, i. 109, 213; v. 336
    THAT can have no concern with, ii. 89
    Universal, i. 109, 196, 206; ii. 275; iii. 79, 514;
        iv. 151
    World's, iii. 308
DITI, Aditi, a form of, iv. 184
    Dvāpara Yuga, in, iv. 186
    Indra, and, i. 185
    Maruts, mother of, iv. 141
DIV-SEFID or white devil, iii. 401, 405
DIVINATION, Ancient, ii. 110; v. 241
    Birds, by, ii. 78
    Confucius and, ii. 158
    Delphos, v. 334
    Ephod, by, v. 237, 239
    Idol of the Moon and, iv. 22; v. 237-242
    Mode of, iv. 22
    Scientific, ii. 363
    Spirits of Elements, by, v. 242
    Stones, by, iii. 345, 346; v. 241
    Teraphim, by the, iv. 22; v. 237-242
DIVINE-HUMAN, Avatāras, ii. 64
    Monad, ii. 194; v. 349-360
DIVINE-SPIRITUAL, Evolution of the, i. 261
DIVINERS, Greek, ii. 110
DIVINING-STONE or stone of the ordeal,
    iii. 342
DIVINING-STRAWS of Confucius, ii. 158
DIVINING-WHEELS, v. 123
DIVINITIES, All-Father in house of, iii. 109
    Babylon, of, iii. 378
    Birds, glyph of, iv. 340
    Chthonian, iii. 362
    Creation of, ii. 165, 173
    Delphi, of, iii. 378
    False, iii. 281
    Hindu, iii. 403
    Life and nature, and, ii. 142
    Natural, ii. 184
    Progeny, refuse to create, ii. 177
    Prototypes, as, ii. 175
    Secondary, ii. 91
    Veil of, ii. 184
DIVINITY, Chaldeans, of, iv. 111
    Creation and, iii. 101
    Christ, of, v. 156, 161, 176
    Draco a, iii. 44

DIVINITY (Contd.)
Feminine, of Waters, v. 212
Indwelling in man, v. 137
Self-conscious, iii. 102
Sidereal, ii. 44
Sun, a symbol of, ii. 201
Universe, of, ii. 396
Virgin an ancient, ii. 384
DIVISIBILITY of matter and substance, ii. 243, 250, 305
DIVISIONS, Antahkarana, seven, of, v. 519
Atlantean, iii. 365
Circle, of the, ii. 124
Cosmic, iii. 83
Globe, of our, iii. 16
Heart, of the, iii. 100
Humanity, of, iii. 432
Jambu-dvîpa, of, iii. 368
Kalpa, of the, iii. 64
Kosmic, v. 542
Lemurian, iii. 365
Lemuro-Atlantis, of, iii. 370
Mysterious, ii. 362
Planes, of, v. 522, 524, 526
Principles, etc., ii. 399
Races, of, iii. 251
Root-races, of, iii. 431
Science, of, ii. 260
Seasons, of, iii. 83
Time, of, ii. 362; iii. 83, 433; v. 333
Zodiac, of the, iii. 374; v. 273
Zones and, ii. 399
DIVO RAJAH or the sky, iv. 193
DIXON, C., and Darwinism, iv. 217
DJAN or Dzan, i. 44
DJIN illusory, i. 335; iii. 425
DJOOLJOOL, Bamian a portion of city of, iii. 338
DR. JEKYLL and Mr. Hyde, iii. 317
DOCTRINE, Archaic, i. 60; iii. 72
Child of earth, communicated to, iii. 285
Cycles, of, iv. 303
Esoteric Buddhism, of, iii. 109
Evolution of, ii. 324; iii. 66
Eye, of the, v. 387, 406, 407, 411
Fallen angels, of the, iii. 276
Heart, of the, v. 387, 394, 405, 406, 407
Hebdomad, of the, iv. 162
Hegelian, iv. 16
Hermes, ii. 350
Kant and occult, ii. 326
Logos, of the, iii. 38
Parent, i. 66
Pythagorean, ii. 151
Secret, see SECRET DOCTRINE and Book Index
Septenary, iv. 201
Seven souls, of the, iv. 202
Seventh principle, of the, i. 83
Spirits, of, iii. 368
Thread, ii. 335
Universal, Secret, v. 50
Upanishad or esoteric, i. 313
Yugas, of the, ii. 382
DOCTRINES, Arcane, i. 61
Archaic wisdom of, i. 60
Ibn Gebirol, of, iv. 29

Nabatheans, of the, iv. 22
Occult, ii. 326
Qū'tāmy, of, iv. 24
Theosophy, of, iv. 202
DOCUMENTARY RECORD, date of, iii. 77
DOCUMENTS, Air and fire impermeable to, i. 69
Archaic, ii. 154
Egyptian, ii. 154
Hieroglyphic, i. 52
Phoenician, cities, in, iii. 437
DODECADS, or celestial beings, sub-groups of, i. 187
DODECAGONAL pyramid, iv. 148
DODECAHEDRON, cube, concealed in, ii. 169
Geometrical figure of, ii. 53
Plato, of, ii. 58
Universe, of, iii. 48
DODECAPOD found on the dry island, iii. 396
DODECAPODIAN horse of Huschenck, iii. 397
DODONA, Oaks of, ii. 161
Oracle of, v. 254
DODONEAN JUPITER, the, ii. 183
DOG, Constellation of, iii. 373
Embryo of a, iii. 261
Erataoth the, iii. 124
DOG-HEADED, Babies, iii. 66
Men, iii. 28, 74
DOG-STAR or Sirius, iii. 373
DOGMA, Asuras and, iii. 69
Azazeal, concerning, iii. 375
Christian, ii. 116; iii. 385
Fall, of the, iii. 73
Fallen angels, of, iii. 112
Falsification causes, i. 308
Latin Church and, v. 95
Lemurians had no, iii. 274
Pagan symbol, founded on, iv. 74
Religious, iii. 275
Resurrection, of the, ii. 101
Satan, of, iii. 376, 386, 389
Secret Doctrine not imposed as, iii. 264
Spiritualists deny, ii. 393
Supernatural belongs to, iii. 200
Theological, iii. 73, 102, 408; iv. 15
DOGMAS, Christian, ii. 24; iii. 270
Christianity, of, v. 95
Church, i. 246; iii. 382; v. 327
Darwinian, iv. 201
Egyptian priests, of, ii. 24
God of, iii. 305, 414
Hebdomad, of the, iv. 162
Human, iii. 305
Invisible intelligences, as to, ii. 336
Materialistic, ii. 338
Metaphysic, of, ii. 346
Mysteries, of ancient, iii. 132
Natural selection, of, iii. 192
Nature, in, ii. 132
Occult, iii. 54
Philosophies, of, ii. 78
Plato and Christian, iii. 270
Religious, ii. 78; iii. 15
Theological, ii. 338; iii. 408
Theosophy, of, iv. 202
Transcendental, ii. 346
Universal, ii. 132

DOGMATIC, Denial, i. 329
   Empyreans, ii. 339
   Faith, i. 329
   Religions, i. 246; ii. 96; iii. 113, 376, 413
   Spirit, iii. 377
DOGMATISM, Avowal of, iv. 232
   Devil of, i. 299
   Evolutionists, of, iii. 176
   Roman Catholic, iii. 44
DOGS, Celestial flock, watching over, the, iii. 41
   Fishes, with tails of, iii. 65
DOLICHOCEPHALAE of America, iv. 360
DOLICHOCEPHALIC, Human form was, iii. 175, 198
D'OLIVET, Fabre, v. 193
DOLLINGER, quoted, v. 240, 255
DOLMA, two virgins, v. 420
DOLMENS, Gang-griften called, iv. 321
   Initiates built, i. 257
   Priest-architects, the work of, i. 257
   Tombs or, iv. 321
DOLPHIN, Poseidon symbolized by the, iv. 148 150, 344
   Sea-soundings of the, iii. 333; iv. 361
   Zodiac, tenth sign of, iv. 148
DOMAIN, Cosmological law, of, ii. 199
   Nature, of, iii. 161
   Osiris, of, ii. 398
   Physical science, of, ii. 335; iii. 436
   Sekhem, of, i. 282
DOMAINS, Astral and physical evolution of, iii. 259
   Planets of various beings, ii. 302
DOME, Supporters of the heavenly, i. 298
DOMES are phallic symbols, iii. 94
DOMESTICATED ANIMALS, iii. 372; iv. 284
DOMINANT ATOMICITIES, ii. 275
DOMINION, Sacerdotal in Egypt, iii. 430
   Sphere, of the outermost, iii. 236
DOMINIONS, Bel ruled by the, ii. 153
   Christian dogma, of, i. 155; v. 332
   Jupiter ruled by the, ii. 153
DOMITIAN, Emperor, v. 147, 334
DONDAM-PAY-DEN-PA, Absolute Truth, v. 400
DON JUAN, Sidereal, i. 275
   Zeus, the Graeco-Olympian, iii. 418
DON JUANIC GODS of the Pantheon, iii. 182
DONNELLY, quoted, iii. 225, 269, 278, 333, 334; iv. 310, 330, 351, 355, 361
DOOR, Human kingdom, into the, i. 226
   Unknown, of the, ii. 351
DOOR-KEEPER of the temple of the king, iii. 236
DOORS of ancient dwellings, iii. 279
DORDOGNE, Arrowheads from caves of, iv. 91
DORJECHANG the supreme Buddha, ii. 295; v. 374, 375
DORJESEMPA or Vajrasattva, Diamond Heart, i. 123; ii. 295
DORMANT Faculties, ii. 200
DOSTOIEVSKY, v. 360
DOTS, lines, etc., Commentary on, i. 159
   Map, in archaic, ii. 159
DOTTED SIDE of upper triangle, ii. 69
DOUAY Version of the Bible, i. 186

DOUBLE, Aeneas, of, iv. 340
   Astral body or, iii. 88
   Celestial, iv. 46
   Chhāyā or, iii. 128; v. 477
   Divine, iv. 48
   Dragon, iii. 68
   Evolution, iii. 96, 174
   Face on pyramid, ii. 141
   Four, one becomes, iii. 293
   God, of, ii. 343; iii. 378
   Heaven, iv. 56
   Line of cube, iv. 172
   Michael, of God, iii. 378
   Ones or hermaphrodites, iii. 43
   Persons seen at a distance, of, i. 279; v. 561
   Pitris, of the, iii. 128
   Ray, iv. 58
   Shakti female, of any God, ii. 343
   Sign of Venus and earth, iii. 42
   Swan, ii. 72
   Triangle, i. 177; iv. 102; v. 120, 356
   Womb, ii. 107
DOUBLE-FACED, Binary, called, iv. 146
   One-faced, became, iii. 296
DOUBLE-SEXED, Animals, iii. 105
   Anu, iii. 72
   Creators, iii. 139; v. 426
   Jehovah, iii. 72, 133, 138
   Organ, iv. 41
   Primeval race, iii. 142
   Vishnu, iii. 43
DOUBLES, Archangels, of, i. 281
   Astral, iii. 124
   Dhyānīs, of, iii. 111
   Fathers, of, iii. 124
   Human, ii. 160
   Pitris, of, i. 293; iii. 18
   Rishis, of the, ii. 160
DOUGLAS, Bishop defamed Apollonius, v. 145
D'OURCHES, Count and occultist, iv. 45
DOVE, Ark, sent from the, iii. 153
   Holy Ghost, symbol of the, ii. 69, 78
   Raven, and, iv. 34
   Sacred animal, as a, ii. 99, 159
   Symbol, as a, ii. 69, 78
DOVES, Black, ii. 161
   Harmless as, iii. 364
DOWLER, Dr. Skeleton found by, iii. 351
DOWNWARD EVOLUTION, ii. 274
DOWSON, quoted, i. 145, 175; iii. 155, 256; iv. 67, 118, 129, 184
DOXOLOGY of the seven heavens, iv. 133
DRACH, Chevalier, (ex-Rabbi) and Zohar, v. 216, 217, 219, 270
DRACO, Constellation, iii. 44
   Lesser Bear, and the, ii. 128
   Messiah, symbol of, iii. 355
   Pole-star, once the, iii. 44
DRACONTIA, Dragon, temples sacred to, iii. 379
   Plans of the, iii. 346
   Theories of the, iii. 347
DRAGON, Ahti the, iii. 39
   Angels with, bodies, iii. 39
   Apocalypse, of the, iii. 44, 382
   Apollo and, v. 289
   Apophis, the, iii. 384; v. 489, 499, 502
   Aryan man, not imagined by, iii. 221

DRAGON (*Contd.*)
Astral light, glyph for, i. 140
Azure, ii. 125
Bel and the, i. 50; iv. 45, 71
Bull and the, ii. 383
Cherubim, as, i. 185
Chinese, iii. 281, 364
Chozzar the, iii. 355
Conqueror of, iii. 383
Constellation of the, iii. 351, 352
Creation, and, iii. 112
Cross, and, ii. 383
Cycle, symbol of, iv. 53
Darkness, of, ii. 80, 129
Deep, of the, iii. 382
Deity, symbol of manifested, iii. 385
Demon, iii. 382
Devil, or, iii. 107
Divine, human and, iii. 364
Double, iii. 68
Evil, iii. 64; iv. 73
Evil winds from mouth of, the, iii. 399, 400
Fafnir, the, ii. 121
Fall and the, iii. 113
Fallen angels, personifies the, i. 50
Fiery, i. 141, 252; iii. 211; iv. 82
Five-pointed star, a, i. 266
Flood, and the old, iii. 351
Four-mouthed, iii. 209
Glyph for astral light, a, i. 140
Golden, ii. 171
Good, of, iii. 39
Great, ii. 179; iii. 44, 102, 350
Hippopotamus and, v. 202
Hoang-ty, leader of sons of, iv. 85
Horus, slain by, iii. 379
Human, iii. 364
Initiate called a, ii. 125
Leviathan, the, v. 202
Life, of, v. 202
Light, of, ii. 129
Logoi, denoted the, i. 140, 141
Makara, tenth Zodiacal sign, is, iii. 353
Meaning of, iii. 212, 214, 385
Medea, of, i. 299
Merodach the, slayer, iii. 64
Michael and, i. 244, 251; iv. 47
Moon, enemy of the, ii. 118
Nidhogg, the, i. 259
Occultists and the, iii. 213
Ophis, or, ii. 179
Pole of, iv. 354; v. 202
Powers of evil and, iii. 383
Python or, iii. 382
Rahu had a, tail, iii. 380
Raphael, the, iii. 124
Red, v. 202
St. George and the, ii. 178
St. John, of, iii. 102
Satan becomes the, iii. 71, 377; v. 171, 289
Sea, iii. 71
Seat of the, iii. 364
Serpent or, i. 140; ii. 120; iii. 39; v. 171, 202
Sevekh, the, v. 202
Seven-headed, iv. 53; v. 202
Slayer of the, iii. 64, 379, 383, 384, 396
Solar, v. 202, 289

Sons of, iv. 99
Spirit, represents, iii. 376
Sun and, ii. 123; iii. 377
Symbol, as a, iii. 354, 385; iv. 53
Tahmurath slays the, iii. 396
Temples sacred to the, iii. 378; v. 171
Thalatth the, iii. 71
Tiamat, iii. 64, 236; iv. 45
Typhon, the old, v. 202
Ulysses Aldrovandus, embalmed by, iii. 212
Venus identified with the, iii. 44
Virgin and, ii. 384
Winged, i. 299
Wisdom, of, i. 138, 139, 166; ii. 192, 194; iii. 103, 236, 376
Zodiac, in the, iii. 213
DRAGON-DEVILS of De Mirville, iii. 212
DRAGON-GARB of the Kwan-Yins, ii. 195
DRAGON'S Angels, iv. 66
DRAGONS, Antiquity of man, prove, iii. 212
Atlanteans and, iv. 325
Bad, iii. 276
Christianity and, iii. 389
Deep, of the, iii. 32, 190
Edens and, iii. 207
Esoteric systems, in all, iii. 380
Evil, of, iii. 407
Existence of, iii. 221
Fiery, iii. 216, 282
Flying, iii. 210
Gods called, iii. 354
Good, iii. 276
Heads of the, iv. 73
Initiates or, iv. 70
Kwan-Shi-Yin crowned with, ii. 193
Lake of the, iii. 208
Middle ages, of, iii. 211
Nāgas or, iii. 381
Seat, iii. 364
Serpents and, iii. 207
Stories of, iii. 211, 441
Symbolism of, i. 187; iii. 353; v. 202
Veritable, iii. 210
Winged, iii. 407
Wisdom, of, i. 187; ii. 125; iii. 35, 208, 214, 216, 233, 282, 352, 423
DRAGON-SERPENT oracle, Python the, iii. 380; v. 202
DRAGON-SLAYER, Initiate called a, iii. 216, 379
DRAGON-SNAKE and Sons of Wisdom, iii. 426
DRAINER of WATERS, Shuchi the, iii. 29, 113
DRAMA, Æschylus, of, iii. 417
Being, of, iii. 152
Christ, of, iii. 411
Creation, of, i. 130
Genesis, in, iii. 386
Greek, iii. 411
Humanity, of, ii. 337; iii. 147, 386
Indian, iii. 411
Initiation, of, iii. 417
Manvantaric, iii. 92
Planet, in fourth act, of, i. 242
Prometheus, of, iii. 411, 420
DRAMATIS PERSONÆ of Heathen Pantheons, iv. 44

DRAPER, Dr., quoted, i. 165; ii. 72; iv. 319; v. 271, 307
DRAPERY of the Colossus, iii. 339
DRAUPADI, v. 378
DRAVIDIAN tongue, the, iv. 358
DRAVIDIANS, Indian, iv. 337
DREAM, Consciousness, foundation of our collective, iii. 295
  Ether a, of old, ii. 39
  Jacob, of, v. 357
  Joseph, of, ii. 375
  Mother-substance a, of science, i. 331
  Soul produces a, ii. 356
DREAMLAND of mysteries, i. 221
DREAMLESS Sleep, i. 118, 119, 309; iii. 188
DREAMLIKE, Feebleness, iii. 411
  Illusive body, Sūkshma Sharīra or, i. 190
DREAMS, Abstract forms in, ii. 289
  Antahkarana, and, v. 497
  Astral light cause of, i. 303
  Atlanteans and, iv. 331
  Brain in, iv. 270
  Chaotic, i. 222
  Experiences in, v. 558
  Lower Manas asleep in, v. 558
  Occult, iii. 317
  Occultists, of, ii. 208
  Past incarnations and, v. 558
  Premonitions in, v. 527
  Prometheus discriminated, iii. 412
DREGS, Æther, of, ii. 57
  Light, of, ii. 204
DRIFTS, Marine Weapons found in, iv. 256
DRIVER of a vehicle used as a symbol, i. 202
DROGHEDANUM SEPULCRUM or devil's tomb, Dragheda, Castle of, iii. 211
DROP, White Swan overshadowed the big, iii. 30
DROPS, Ocean of the, ii. 236
  Sweat of, iii. 30, 31
DROSS, Former rounds, iii. 65
  Water men created from, iii. 28
DROUGHT, Demon of, iii. 383
DROUGHTS, Prehistoric, iv. 71
  Producing, power of, iii. 281, 384
DROUK signifies devil in Bretagne, iii. 211
DRUID, Anguinum of the, ii. 83
  Bardesin on Noah, ii. 161
DRUIDIC stones, iv. 321
DRUIDICAL Circles, i. 257
  Graves, v. 306
  Remains, iv. 323
  Religion, v. 147
  Rites, v. 284
  Temple, iii. 342
DRUIDS, Ancient, v. 45
  British, iv. 203; 306
  Celto-Britannic regions, of, iii. 379
  Chaldeans akin to, iv. 325
  College of, v. 295
  Cyclopean lore, heirs to, iv. 323
  Cyclopes, not, iii. 342
  Indians, akin to iv. 325
  Last, v. 306
  Magic and, v. 306
  Massacre of, v. 296
  Oaks of, v. 45, 49
  Origin of, iv. 325

Rebirth, believed in, iv. 329; v. 267
  Religion of, iv. 325; v. 294
  Sacred fires of, iv. 329; v. 267
  Sun and, v. 378
DRUM of Rudra-Shiva, iv. 70
DRUMMOND, Sir William, v. 292
DRUNKARD, Indra a, iii. 377
DRUSES, Secret catechisms of the, iii. 40
  From Mount Lebanon, v. 162
DRY ISLAND of Tahmurath, iii. 397, 398
DRYDEN quoted, ii. 369
DRYOPITHECUS ape, the, iv. 245, 248, 257, 302
DU BOIS-REYMOND, Quoted, ii. 394
  Referred to, iv. 280
DU CHAILLU, referred to, iii. 438
DUAD, Cosmic, ii. 346
  Elohim from, ii. 344
  Formation of, v. 210
  Indeterminate, ii. 152
  Jewish deity manifested, iv. 113
  Logos, or double-sexed, ii. 70
  Microposopus and the, iv. 196
  Monad and, v. 382, 383, 498
  Mother or, ii. 339
  Pythagoras, of, ii. 144; v. 116
  Represented Matter, v. 116
  Scintillas proceeded from the, ii. 343
  State of, imperfect, iv. 146
  Tetrad and, iv. 172
  Triad and, iv. 172
  Unity and the, v. 210, 211
DUAL, Action of the cycles, ii. 367
  Adam, iv. 23
  Androgyne, iii. 218
  Aspect of Deities, v. 292
  Aspect of Manas, iv. 185
  Aspect of the One Reality, i. 82
  Aspect of Sun, v. 285
  Aspect of THAT, ii. 269
  Aspect of the Universe, v. 466
  Aspect of the Verbum, iv. 84
  Atma-Buddhi is, i. 231
  Consciousness, v. 545
  Cosmic entities, ii. 328
  Creative power, i. 127
  Deity, character of supreme, iii. 410
  Element, ii. 72, 75
  Entities, i. 281
  Evolution, ii. 185
  Force, ii. 68, 220, 398; iii. 177
  Gods, ii. 82; iii. 365; iv. 83
  Heaven, i. 298
  Jehovah, v. 291
  Magic is, v. 85
  Man, iii. 49, 131
  Manas, ii. 47; v. 77, 427, 441, 488, 489, 494, 529, 563
  Mazdean Gods, nature of, iv. 44
  Nature, i. 301; ii. 190, 328; v. 38
  Nature of Gods, iii. 179
  Nature of man, iii. 40, 276; iv. 102, 230
  Nature of Manas, iv. 185, 210
  Nature of the serpent, ii. 120
  Numeral, iv. 123
  Personality, iii. 244
  Potency, physiological, ii. 194

DUAL (*Contd.*)
Power of secret wisdom, iii. 363
Principle, iii. 156
Progenitors, group of, iii. 100
Sex, i. 264; ii. 95; iii. 139
Significance in Shiva, iv. 118
Soul, i. 230; v. 387
Symbols, ii. 126
Work of Ptah, ii. 82
DUALISM, Androgynous, v. 162
Chaldeans of, v. 55
Manes, of, iv. 78
Mazdean religion, in, iv. 86
DUALISTIC, Purānic a, system, i. 300
Philosophy, ii. 246
Religions, i. 246
DUALITY, Amshaspends, of the, i. 281
Emanations of, ii. 328
Idea, of the, ii. 107
Line corresponding with, ii. 341
Planets, of, v. 315
Sidereal Influence, of, v. 330
Spirit of, in man, iv. 86
Universe pervaded by, i. 81
DUCK, Eggs of the, iv. 167
Kalevala, of the, iii. 26
DUFFERIN, Lord, discoveries, iii. 428
DUGPAS or sorcerers, iv. 157; v. 47, 122, 403,
540, 561
DUGPASHIP, Power of, iii. 225
DUHALDE, quoted, v. 40
DUI, the " bright Lord of Heaven ", v. 305
DULĀ, a star in the Pleiades, iv. 121
DULAURE on date of Zodiac, ii. 378
DUMAS, referred to, ii. 267
DUMB, Man walking on all fours, iii. 289
Races, i. 234; iii. 32, 190
DUMB-BELL nebula, ii. 322
DUNCAN, P. Martin, quoted, i. 164
DUNLAP, quoted, i. 245; ii. 62, 68; iii. 216;
iv. 28
DUODENARY number held to be perfect, ii. 375
DUOMO of Milan, iii. 94
DUPLEX heavens, i. 298; ii. 69
DUPUIS, quoted, ii. 379; iii. 39, 44; iv. 191;
v. 94, 317, 346
DURATION, Ages of, iii. 76, 89
Babylonian ages, of, iv. 190
Bosom of, i. 110
Cosmical periods, of, iii. 61
Cycles, of, ii. 28, 366; iii. 182; iv. 192
Earth has, nothing on, i. 110
Eternal, i. 110
Eternities, constituted by two, i. 111
Fevers, of, iv. 167
Geological ages and periods, ii. 290; iii. 22,
61, 76, 77, 82; iv. 255, 260, 268, 314
Hindu people, of the, ii. 386
Incarnations, of successive, ii. 361
Kronos stands for endless, ii. 136
Life-cycle, of a, iii. 107
Osiris, king, of, ii. 155
Periods of incalculable, iii. 89
Pralaya, of, ii. 382
Quaternary age, of, iii. 169
Races, of, iii. 313
Round, of each, iv. 134

Sensations give ideas of, i. 116
Sexual physical man, of, iii. 169
Space and, i. 115, 125; iii. 366
Tertiary age, of, iii. 164
Time, universal and conditioned, divided into,
i. 131
Universe, of the, iv. 189
DURGĀ, Illusion or, ii. 112
Kālī, iv. 150
Virgin, the, ii. 384
DUS KYI KHORLO, "Wheel of Time ", v. 365,
403, 404
DUSK rises at the horizon, ii. 91
DUST, Adam the man of, i. 287; iii. 91, 95, 121;
iv. 24, 25; v. 190, 199
Animals produced from, iii. 187
Cosmic, i. 167; ii. 333
Primordial, i. 250
Terrestrial origin of, ii. 370
DUTI or dutica, ii. 194
DUTIES of the celibate Adepts, iii. 92
DUTY, Dharma or religious, iii. 183
Occultist, of the, ii. 313
Royal high road of, ii. 368
DUW, The ALL called, by the Briton, v. 305
DVĀDASHA-KARA, Kārttikeya called, iv. 190
DVAITA, Doctrine, i. 145
Sect, ii. 170
DVĀPARA Yuga, one principle and the, v. 229
Third or, iii. 79, 154, 309, 322; iv. 51, 89, 186
DVARAKA, v. 259
DVIJA or initiated, iii. 80; iv. 30; v. 152, 276,
279, 390
DVIJAS or initiated Brāhmans, i. 44, 258; iv. 37;
v. 393
DVĪPA or Zones, i. 301; ii. 88; iii. 162, 266, 319,
320, 400, 401, 402, 403, 405, 406, 407
White, iii. 289; iv. 328
DWARFED Living things, iii. 329
Races of the Pole, iii. 330
DWARFING chronology, ii. 381; iii. 323
DWARFISH races, iii. 423; iv. 323
DWARFS, Atlantean, iii. 431
Dwergar or, iv. 323
Stories of, iii. 441
Thor's hammer forged by, iii. 107
DWELLER on high, exalted, iii. 51
On the Threshold, v. 500, 501, 512, 567
DWELLING of the Monad, First, i. 293
DWELLINGS, Lives, for the, iii. 28, 67
Lake, iv. 284
DWERGAR or Dwarfs, iv. 323
DWIJA, " Twice-born ", v. 393
DWINDLING of Spheres, Cyclic, iv. 302
DYAUS, Brahmā merges into, ii. 92
God, unrevealed, ii. 92
Son of, i. 162
DYNAMIC power of light and heat, ii. 239
DYNAMICAL, Effect of causes, ii. 368
Force, ii. 190
Heat, theory of, ii. 209
Leibnitz, enquiries of, ii. 352
DYNAMICS, Law of Occult, ii. 369
DYNAMISM of Leibnitz, ii. 354
DYNASPHERIC force, ii. 283, 284
DYNASTIES, Astronomical, iii. 433
Chaldean, ii. 381

DYNASTIES (Contd.)
  Dates of, iv. 262
  Demi-gods, of, iii. 368
  Divine, i. 310; ii. 381; iii. 145, 200, 316, 318,
    328, 350, 358, 363, 364, 367, 370, 421, 422,
    426, 433; iv. 54, 55, 61, 70, 325, 342, 343;
    v. 75, 528
  Egyptian, i. 310; ii. 125; iii. 44
  Gods, of, iii. 366, 368
  Great, seven, ii. 377
  Heroes, of, i. 310; iii. 368
  Kings, of, iii. 236
  Lower spirits, of, iii. 349
  Lunar, ii. 104
  Solar, ii. 104
DYNASTY, Chow, iii. 303
  Devas, of, iii. 225
  Divine, the, iii. 42, 144, 282; iv. 63
  Egyptians, of older, iii. 434
  Fourth, iii. 429
  Hia, (B. C. 1818), iii. 65
  Huschenck, of, iii. 395
  Kaikobad, of, iii. 397
  Menes, of, iii. 429
  Ming, of, iii. 65
  Solar-Lunar, iv. 23
DYOOKNAH or divine phantom, iii. 270; iv. 24
DZAHHAK named Biourasp, iv. 20
DZAN or DZYAN, Path of, v. 373
DZENODOO or mysteries, i. 226
DZUNGARIAN, Mani Kumbum, i. 110
DZYAN, meaning of, v. 389
DZYU Fohat becomes, i. 168
DZYU-MI deals with illusions, i. 168

E

E. DELPHICUM, sacred symbol, iv. 152
EA, Father, first, v. 203
  Gods, mother of, and the, iv. 45
  Oannes, prototype of, iv. 71
  Space birthplace of, iii. 64
  Sevenfold, v. 202
  Sublime fish, iv. 63
  Wisdom, God of, iii. 71, 124, 147, 229
EAGLE, Abraxas gems, on, iv. 135
  Evangelical, ii. 78
  Gabriel, i. 185; iii. 124
  Sacred animal, ii. 159
  St. John, air and, iii. 123
  Six-pointed star and, iv. 102
EAR OF WHEAT, iii. 431
EARS, Distorted, iii. 339
  Large hanging, iii. 338
EARTH, Adam of, iii. 134
  Adam's i. 76
  Age of, iii. 59, 76
  Ahriman, spirit of, iv. 86
  Animal an, i. 209
  Antiquity of man on, iv. 313
  Appearance of man on, i. 214, 238, 276; ii. 200
  Asiatic world our, iii. 119
  Astral envelope of, iv. 282
  Astral world, of, iii. 45
  Atmosphere of, i. 198; ii. 350
  Atom of the universe, v. 227
  Avitchi is, v. 496, 498, 501

Axis of, ii. 85; iii. 293, 315; iv. 104, 294
-Bound Spirits, v. 566
Brahmā personified in, v. 117
Brahmā upholder of, i. 125; ii. 138
Builders descend on, i. 309
Chain(s) of, i. 207, 224, 225; ii. 85, 166;
  iii. 236; iv. 72, 271, 328; v. 475
Colour of, v. 543
Cosmic dust new to, ii. 333
Cow and, ii. 113, 152
Creators of, ii. 391
Creators of beings on, iii. 88
Crust of, i. 304; iii. 22, 23, 254
Curse under, ii. 90
Desolate during one day, ii. 90
Development of, i. 297
Divisions of, iii. 365
Duality on, ii. 190, 328
Ecliptic and, iii. 332, 367
Egg becomes, ii. 81
Ego belongs to, ii. 48
Element an, ii. 152
Element of, i. 196, 326; iv. 154
Elohim creating, iii. 137; v. 202, 269
Esoteric kingdoms of, ii. 174
Ethereal condition of, iii. 253
Eve or, i. 285
Evolution of, i. 85, 206, 254; ii. 338
Fellow-globes of, i. 213
Fires, product of three, iii. 249
First round in, i. 302
Flames landed on, iii. 235
Flatness of, ii. 246
Formation of, iii. 254; iv. 167; v. 207
Formative period of, iv. 53
Fourth round and, i. 214, 238
Fourth world, the, i. 286
Gamma, symbol of (Gaia), iv. 163
Garuda in relation to, ii. 81
Generation, fallen into, iii. 42
Globe, a, i. 113
Globes which overshadow, i. 220
Globes which precede our, iv. 72
God of, ii. 74, 183
Gods forsake, iii. 357
Gods incarnated on, iv. 52
Great sea, or the, iv. 73
Gross body, moulded a, iii. 29, 113
Growth, has its, ii. 333
Habitable phase of, iii. 82
Haōma is on, iv. 86
Heaven and, i. 317, 332; ii. 135; iii. 106, 108,
  121, 376; iv. 54, 56
Hierarchy on, i. 256
Human stock and, iii. 313
Humanities of, iv. 103
Immortality on, iii. 278
Individuality on, iii. 244
Infernal applied to, ii. 123, 184; iii. 107
Isis, horns of, v. 165
Isis was, v. 234
Jehovah, spirit of, iv. 78
Jiva of, i. 271; iii. 58
Karshvares of, iii. 383; iv. 327
Kingdoms of, ii. 174; iii. 245
Lha, or spirit of, iii. 35
Lord of shining face, to the, iii. 40

EARTH (*Contd.*)

Lords of, i. 219; iii. 42, 284
Lotus, symbol of prolific, ii. 94
Lunar spirits connected with, iii. 87
Mahat and, i. 301
Malkuth or, i. 263, 284, 285, 286
Man, his body gives, i. 278
Manas and, iii. 106
Manūshi-Buddhas, govern, i. 169
Marriage of Heaven with, ii. 135
Material spirits of, iii. 349
Matter and, ii. 334; iii. 268
Measurements of, v. 91
Melha when on, iii. 74
Men constantly on, iii. 283
Mercury and, i. 210; iii. 41, 56
Meteoric showers and, ii. 397
Microcosm called, i. 326
Molecules composing, i. 179
Monad in relation to, i. 228
Monsters, creates, iii. 63
Moon and, i. 210, 225, 231, 232, 253; ii. 17, 102; iii. 56, 75, 124; iv. 42; v. 165, 535
Mother, iii. 28
Mout, queen of, i. 155
Mystery of creation repeated on, iii. 88
Mystery of Evil on, iv. 84
Nature, Moon and, v. 165
Nature of Logos on, iii. 234
North Pole of, iii. 359
Orbit of, iii. 152
Ormazd, father of, iii. 384
Oscillation of, iii. 325
Personifications of, i. 197
Phantom of the moon, iii. 124
Physical man, dwelling of, i. 289
Pit, or the, iv. 61
Planet and, i. 208
Plastic mass of, iii. 74
Poles of, i. 253; ii. 329; iii. 367
Position, changed, iii. 319
Prithvi the, i. 83; iv. 179
Rebirths on, i. 282
Regions of, seven, i. 171
Renovations of, iv. 353
Revolution of, iii. 160
Rheā, or, iii. 150, 151
Rishis and, ii. 113
Rivers of, i. 282; iv. 177
Rocky hard-crusted, i. 304; ii. 331
Rotation of, ii. 292
Rotundity of, iv. 277
Rūpa of, first, i. 303
Saparājni, called, i. 141
Seb, God of, ii. 74
Semi-astral, iii. 253
Sensuous existence on, iv. 82
Separation of heaven from, iv. 56
Septempartite, the, is, iv. 328
Serpent like the, i. 141
Shukra and, iii. 44
Shvēta-dvīpa and, sons of, iii. 319
Sidereal motions regulate events on, ii. 370
Smell, rudiments of, property of, ii. 88
Solid fire or, iii. 122
Solids synonym for, i. 198
Sons of, v. 111

Soul, and water make a human, iii. 133
Space and, ii. 219
Sphere, the fourth, i. 278
Spheres, and superior, iii. 270
Spirit, ii. 69, 181; iii. 40
Spirit of, i. 245, 264; ii. 135, 141, 177; iii. 29, 35, 110, 243, 275; iv. 45, 77
Spirit of moon, ruled by, iii. 324
Spirits of the, ii. 184; iii. 36, 118, 119, 250
Spiritual entities present on, i. 279
Stars connected with, iv. 353; v. 314
Stars contain elements unknown on, ii. 313
States of, iv. 272
Svastika and our, iii. 108
Sweat of, iii. 349
Teaching limited to, iv. 301
Toom, divider of, ii. 398
Transformations of, iv. 326
Twelve compartments of, v. 201
Universe in relation to, i. 114; iv. 272
Vāch the, ii. 152
Venus and, ii. 17, 317; iii. 42, 45
Vital soul of, ii. 326
Water and, ii. 44, 88; iv. 326
Wheel, called a, iii. 40, 324
Worship of spirit of, iii. 275
Zend Avesta on, iv. 327

EARTH-BORN CEMENT, Nitrogen an, ii. 351
EARTH-CHAIN, formation of, i. 225
EARTH-FORCE, ii. 233, 248, 255
EARTH-GLOBE, middle of, iii. 402
EARTH-LIFE, Desert of illusion called, i. 256
EARTH-MEN, in the Bundahish, iv. 206
EARTHQUAKES, Astronomers prophecy, ii. 371

Colossal, iv. 355
Late years, of, iii. 308
Lemuria destroyed by, iii. 268
Present day, iv. 269
Volcanoes and, iii. 312; iv. 294
Warning of modern, iv. 345

EARTHS, Companion, i. 219

Destruction of, ii. 157
Dhyan-chohans in charge of, ii. 160
Geographical faces of new, iii. 403
Mazdean view of the seven, iv. 328
Metals and, iii. 316
Rare, ii. 270; iii. 316
Seven, i. 231
Six, iv. 275
Universal ether, germinate in the, iii. 194
Vedic teaching of, i. 295

EASAM or ASAM, in Irish, to create, iii. 123
EASHOOR, in India, God called, iii. 123
EAST, Africa, iii. 199

Freemasonry derived from, v. 284
Frigid zone formerly in, iv. 104
Glory of God comes from, i. 181
Knowledge, land of, v. 41, 50
Maitreya Buddha, expected in, ii. 192
Miraculous births in, iv. 120
Mythology of, iii. 404
Occultists of, iii. 50
Philosophies and records of, iii. 53
Sacred Books of the, v. 407
Secret Books of, v. 103
Secret Doctrine of the, v. 44, 109
Secret Wisdom of, v. 74, 299

EAST (*Contd.*)
Seers of, ii. 355
Traditions of, ii. 15; iv. 35
Wise Men of, ii. 371
EASTER EGGS, ii. 83
EASTER ISLAND, Continent, proof of a sub-
merged, ii. 34; iii. 226, 227, 317; iv. 356
Cross on, statues, ii. 34; iv. 127
Cyclopean remains on, ii. 157
Decad, records combinations, of, ii. 34
Lemuria, remnant of, iii. 326; iv. 250
Statues of, ii. 34; iii. 317, 331, 336, 339;
iv. 127
Stone relics on, iii. 317
Symbols of evolution in, ii. 35
Third race, belongs to, iii. 327
Traditions of, iv. 356
EASTERN, Aryans, ii. 369
Astronomer, iii. 433
Axiom, ii. 379
Chelas, v. 74, 97, 228
Chronology of, iii. 83
Coast, iii. 266
Continent of Atlantis, portion of, iii. 405
Esotericism, v. 72, 185
Ethiopians, iii. 415, 427
Evolution, doctrine of, ii. 324
Greek Church, i. 272
Gupta Vidya, i. 249; v. 174 et seq.
Initiates, i. 53, 246, 303; ii. 371, 396; v. 274,
286, 407
Occultists, v. 47, 86, 104, 195, 226, 227, 229,
354, 483
Philosophy, v. 36, 208
Psychology, v. 380
Septenary teaching, v. 73
Symbology, v. 72, 286
EASTERN OCCULTISM, Earth, on our, i. 286;
v. 154, 227, 232, 249
Gross in, iii. 94
Kabalah and, ii. 343
Septenary in, i. 286
EBIONITES, Philosophical systems of, i. 247;
v. 160, 161
ECCENTRIC AND CENTRIC, ii. 370
ECHAD, the Eka, the Ahu, i. 172
Creation called, i. 187
Elohim called, i. 172
Hebrew name for Jehovah, i. 139
ECHATH or Achath, One, i. 188
ECLECTIC, Doctrines, v. 301, 307
School, v. 46, 145
System, v. 298
Theosophical System, v. 302, 303
ECLIPSE, Moon at Kali Yuga epoch, of, ii. 388
Moon of, ii. 388, 389; iii. 433
Spiritual sun of, iii. 252
Sun, of the, ii. 314, 387; iii. 85
ECLIPSES, Cauchy on, ii. 209
Dragon threatening sun in, ii. 123
Hindus calculated by, ii. 386
Lunar, iii. 379
Observation of Bel, in, iv. 263
Solar, iii. 379
ECLIPTIC, Circles, i. 253
Circuit of, iii. 330
Equator and, iv. 104

Inclination of, ii. 385, 390
Jupiter and, ii. 387
Mars, Lord of, iii. 391
Mercury and, ii. 387
Meridian, parallel with, iii. 356; iv. 354
Obliquity of, iii. 406; iv. 294
Plane of, iii. 356, 431
Poles of, iii. 332, 367, 429; iv. 120
ECPHANTUS, taught rotation of earth, i. 176.
ECPYROSIS or conflagration, iv. 353
ECSTATIC PHENOMENA, ii. 191
ECSTASY, v. 81, 299, 452
Defined by Plotinus, v. 76
Proclus, of, v. 76
St. John, of, v. 143
ECTENIC FORCE of Thury, ii. 52
ECUADOR, Giants in, iv. 323
EDDA, on serpent worship, the, iii. 214
EDDAS, Scandinavian, ii. 59; iii. 40, 385
EDDIN AHMED BEN YAHYA on tha Sabeans,.
iii. 361
EDEN, Adam in, iii. 381, 408; iv. 72
Adamic race, of our, ii. 123
Æden, or, iii. 54
Astrologers and, iii. 208
Cube and rivers of, ii. 83
Expulsion from, iii. 281, 284, 381, 408
Gan-Æden or, iii. 54
Garden of, i. 174, 185; ii. 98, 123, 132, 337;.
iii. 106, 121, 207, 208, 294, 316, 349;.
iv. 61, 64, 70, 72, 113; v. 67, 110, 202,.
308, 449
Genetic and Kabalistical, iii. 208
Illa-ah, iii. 208
Locality, a submerged, iv. 62; v. 110
Meaning of, iii. 207, 208; iv. 64
Meru to, i. 185
Races, of the first, iii. 206
Rivers of, ii. 83
Serpent of, iv. 97
Tree of, i. 174, iii. 106
Tree of life in, iii. 43
Typhon dragon of, ii. 114
EDENS, Eternal spring of, iii. 146
Serpents and dragons, iii. 207
EDENTATA, the, iv. 238
EDESSA, Henoch builds, iii. 366
EDITOR of *Revelation*, the, iv. 189
EDKINS, Rev. Joseph, see Book Index
EDOM, Kings of, iii. 16, 64, 93; iv. 24, 55, 274,.
275; v. 182
EDRIS, Enoch or, iii. 365
Koran of the, iv. 98
EDWARDS, Milne, investigations of, iv. 238.
EFFECT, Buddhi is an, ii. 294
Cause assigned to, iii. 250
Cause but, electricity not, ii. 241
Cause, of an eternal, ii. 170
Concatenation of cause and, i. 224; iv. 233.
Ego, of a previous cause, iv. 170
Eternal cause and, i. 118
Force an, ii. 242
Primal cause and, ii. 293
Seed-Manu the, i. 281
Spiritual dynamical, ii. 368
EFFECT-PRODUCING CAUSE, Karma an,.
ii. 359

EFFECTS, Borderland between causation and, iv. 56
  Causative, became, ii. 143
  Cometary matter of, ii. 332
  Energy known only by its, ii. 394
  Error for 1800 years, of an, iii. 73
  Forces of gravity are, ii. 213
  Kārmic law adjusts, iii. 306
  One cause and its numberless, ii. 158
  Plane of, ii. 239
  Re-become causes, will, ii. 366
  Souls causes of all, ii. 291
  Spiritual ii. 366
EFFICIENT CAUSE, First and, iv. 124
  Material and, ii. 86
EFFLORESCENCE of self-conscious egotism, iii. 89
EFFULGENCE, Ray of primordial light of, i. 277
EFFULGENT EGG, Hiranyagarbha means, i. 153
EGG, All-Being, of, v. 436
  Animal evolves from, iv. 223
  Auric, v. 472, 474, 486, 487, 508, 510, 511, 512, 519, 521, 534
  Bird and, ii. 69
  Brahmā of, i. 301; ii. 83, 88; iv. 203; v. 456, 476, 486
  Brahmā, split in two by, ii. 46
  Choas, i. 247
  Cosmogony in, ii. 161
  Creatures born from, iii. 189
  Darkness, of, ii. 81
  Divine, i. 136
  Emepht blows, ii. 82
  Erōs-Phanes evolves from spiritual, ii. 182
  Eternal, i. 133
  Germ, with central, ii. 79
  Glyphs, ii. 77
  Golden, i. 75, 134; ii. 49, 65; iv. 123; v. 472
  Great serpent swallowing, iv. 322
  IT, referred to as, ii. 47
  Kosmos an, i. 134
  Leda and, iii. 130
  Luminous, i. 134
  Matter of, i. 253
  Mundane, i. 69, 127, 133, 146, 154; ii. 69, 72, 74, 82, 83, 280; iv. 187; v. 424
  Mysterium of the, i. 325
  One from the, i. 152, 153
  Pentacle within, i. 187
  Primitive cell, or, iv. 229
  Ra remains in, ii. 80
  Radiant, i. 253
  Seb, of, ii. 80
  Serpent and, iv. 326
  Sibac means, iii. 188
  Space or mundane, infinite, ii. 69
  Spiritual, ii. 182
  Universal, ii. 59
  Virgin, i. 133
  World of, ii. 82, 127; v. 421
EGG-BEARING RACE, iii. 202, 313
EGG-BORN, Androgynes, the, iii. 125
  Creators will not incarnate in, iii. 168
  Dioscuri or, iii. 360
  Mānasa and, iii. 31, 178

  Race, iii. 141
  Second evolved, iii. 30, 139
  Sons of, iii. 198
  Sweat-born produced, iii. 179
  Third Race, iii. 131, 180, 203
  Twins and the, iii. 132
EGG-CELLS, Maturing outside the body, iv. 227
  Parthenogenesis, in, iv. 229
EGG-SHAPED, Aura, iii. 126
  Boxes, ii. 329
  Globe, i. 141
  Zero, i. 155
EGG-SYMBOL, Churches, in, ii. 83
  Origin of life, represents, ii. 82
  Savages, found among, ii. 82
  Secret teaching on, ii. 74
EGGS, Duck, of heavenly, iii. 26
  Man-bearing, iii. 141
  Pigeons and fowls, of, iv. 167
  Third Race, of the, iii. 202
EGO, Absolute neither, nor non-Ego, iv. 170
  Adept's, iii. 220; iv. 128, 186
  All-perceiving, ii. 43
  Alter, v. 315, 490
  Astral, v. 365
  Atomic, is, v. 550
  Awakenings, passes through progressive, ii. 113
  Birth of, v. 473
  Buddhi and, i. 43
  Consciousness of, ii. 43
  Deific state of, iv. 118
  Dhyān-Chohan, may become, i. 243
  Divine, v. 83, 486, 487, 488, 490-495, 499
  Eternal spiritual, i. 280
  Ferouer, v. 94
  Field of consciousness of, v. 549
  Fiery, v. 241
  Fravarshi, called the, iv. 48
  Higher, iii. 119; iv. 48; v. 362, 418, 452, 471, 490, 496, 498, 500-502, 517, 539, 551-553, 557, 563, 564
  Higher Manas, or human, iii. 89, 97; iv. 159; v. 108
  Human, v. 488, 495
  Ideas of time of, i. 116
  Immortal, ii. 97, 347; iv. 203
  Impersonal, v. 400; 473; v. 497, 498
  Individual i. 116; ii. 43; iii. 190; iv. 239; v. 354, 358
  Kārmic, iv. 176; v. 499, 500
  Kosmos, in, ii. 146
  Logos, reflected image of, iii. 170; iv. 164
  Monad or, i. 290; iv. 205
  Nirvāna, in, v. 397
  Non-dying, i. 293
  Organ through which, manifests, i. 111
  Parabrahman is not, i. 118; ii. 146
  Perfect, v. 400
  Periodical existences of, i. 274; v. 217-249
  Personal, i. 187, 290; iii. 243; iv. 181; v. 359, 495, 496
  Personalities of the, v. 247, 398
  Physical, v. 81
  Plato on, iii. 97
  Real, ii. 163
  Reincarnating, v. 247, 498, 499, 500
  Rings, in remote, iii. 290

EGO (*Contd.*)
  Sattva or Rajas, either, ii. 48
  Self, or, i. 273
  Separation from personality of, v. 499, 544
  Sixth plane, on, ii. 43
  Sleep, latent during, i. 111; ii. 147
  Soul is, i. 273, 288; iii. 120; iv. 224
  Spiritual, 280; iii. 118, 234; iv. 128; v. 249,
    298, 359, 421, 500
  Sum, i. 280
  Terrestrial, v. 364
  Universal, i. 189
EGOISM, Ahamkara and, v. 494
  Great, ii. 260
  Mahat called, i. 142
  Mind, created from, ii. 47
  Mortal man moved by, iii. 420
  Personality or, i. 318
  Self-consciousness becomes, iv. 201
EGO-MAN, Divine, iv. 131
EGO-SOUL, Butterfly, free as, iv. 131
  Conscious surviving, iii. 201
EGOS, Agnishvātta and human, iii. 89
  Apes, of, iii. 264
  Beads, likened to, iv. 82
  Bodies, freed from gross, ii. 21
  Conscious, ii. 356, 357
  Cycle of incarnations of, iv. 53
  Dhyānis become human, iii. 292
  Duty of, iii. 245
  Entities, of, iii. 174
  Esoteric philosophy and, iii. 171
  Future, i. 579; iii. 292
  Hierarchies of, ii. 354; v. 552
  Higher, v. 93
  Human, v. 493, 495
  Incarnating, tide-wave of, iv. 349
  Incarnations, of past, iii. 109
  Monads of, iii. 231
  Nirvāna, rest in, i. 291
  Protoplasmic forms of, i. 325
  Seventh round, in the, i. 232
  Souls, reincarnating, or, ii. 292
  Spiritual, i. 283, 309; ii. 357; iv. 129
EGOSHIP or I-am-ness, i. 247; ii. 260; iv. 185
EGOTISM, Ahamkāra or, i. 304; ii. 172; iv. 185
  Buddhi destroyer of, i. 43
  Jealous God, of a, iii. 417
EGOTISTICAL Principle, v. 361
EGOTISTICALLY, Effect of act produced,
    iii. 303
EGREGORES are spirits of energy and action,
    i. 303
EGYPT, Adepts in, i. 257; iv. 119, 128; v. 202
  Age of, iv. 319
  Ancient Monuments of, v. 58
  Ankh-tie of, iv. 118
  Apis Pacis of Hermontis in, ii. 383
  Assyrian dominion of, ii. 23
  Barbarism in, iv. 285
  Bunsen on, i. 50, 175, ii. 153; iii. 342
  Catacombs in, iii. 378
  Chemi is ancient, ii. 83
  Chemistry in, v. 63
  Chiun the God of Time in, iii. 389
  Civilization before that of, iv. 355
  Civilization of, ii. 334, 427, 429; iv. 285

Cross in, ii. 34, 383; iv. 117, 118, 127, 128,
    157, 159, 171; v. 161, 162, 318
Crypts of, iii. 379; v. 161
Delta of, iii. 21; iv. 315
Demon, fallen, of, iv. 54
Dragon of, v. 202, 489, 499, 502
Emblems in, ii. 100; iii. 385
Esoteric teachings in, ii. 397; iv. 130; v. 91
Ethiopian dominion of, ii. 23
Europe, older than, iv. 315
Fifth hierarchy in, i. 279
Fifth order in, i. 266
Fohat in, ii. 398
Genesis came from mysteries of, iii. 15
Giants of, iii. 335
Gods of, i. 186; ii. 154, 194; iii. 91, 101, 293, 378,
    381, 389; iv. 77, 151, 164, 202, 244, 247, 251
Great Bear in, ii. 125; v. 202
Grecian tenets from, i. 176; iv. 353
Greek colonization of, ii. 23
Henoch becomes king of, iii. 366
Hermes of, iv. 112; v. 162
Hermontis in, Apis Pacis of, ii. 383
Herodotus in, ii. 153
Heptanomis of, celestial, ii. 124
Hieratic symbols of, ii. 19; v. 248
Hierophants of, iii. 378, 379; iv. 127; v. 49,
    87, 248, 255, 257, 263, 271, 290, 297, 318, 382
India and, i. 155; iii. 415
Inscriptions of, iv. 361
IO or moon in, iv. 31
Isis in, iii. 373
Isis-Osiris in, iii. 365
Jews and, i. 175, 308; ii. 24, 28, 99
Kabirim, in, iii. 363
Kings of, divine, iii. 316, 367; iv. 54; v. 263
Lotus in, ii. 94, 100; iv. 40, 117
Measures of, ii. 25
Monstrous reptiles in, iv. 282
Moses in, i. 175; ii. 67; iv. 23, 33, 77
Mother of time in, ii. 125
Mysteries of, ii. 31; iii. 15, 394; v. 264, 271,
    275, 282, 286, 290
Nahbkoon, God in, ii. 194
Origin of, iv. 313
Persian conquest of, ii. 23
Political life of, ii. 23
Pyramids, ii. 34, 157; iii. 350, 428; v. 248, 272,
    296
Renouf on, ii. 117
Ruins in, iv. 175
Sacerdotal epoch of, v. 296
Sea formerly covered, iii. 367
Seats of learning in, v. 204
Secret observations of, v. 322
Septenary in, iii. 47; iv. 154, 184, 201, 202, 204
Sepulchres, of, iv. 159
Sesostris, King of, i. 52
Seth adored in, iii. 44, 91
Solon and priests of, iii. 268
Sorcerers of, iii. 216; v. 251
Stone age in, no, iv. 355
Sun-gods in, iii. 378
Temples of, i. 257; iii. 428; v. 279
Thot-Hermes of, ii. 179
Time-keeping in, ii. 153
Triple crocodile of, i. 267

EGYPT (*Contd.*)
Typhon adored in, iii. 44
Universal history and, v. 181
Works of Isis-Osiris in, iii. 365
Worship of Kabiri in, iii. 362
EGYPTIAN, Alphabet, ii. 19
Amenti, ii. 184; v. 247
Ammon, iii. 143
Angle of poles, representation of, iii. 359
Ankh, iii. 43
Anubis, iii. 384; v. 246
Artes, or Mars, iii. 151
Astrologers, v. 329, 332
Astronomical monument, v. 332
Atlantidae, iv. 360
Bas reliefs, iv. 128
Bible, and symbolism, ii. 33
Ceremony of judgment, v. 289
Christianity and symbols, ii. 99
Cosmogony, i. 267; ii. 60; iii. 36; iv. 188, 353
Cosmographies, iv. 175
Cosmology, v. 323
Crocodile, ii. 126; iii. 398; iv. 148; v. 202
Crocodile-headed God, iv. 151; v. 502
Cross, ii. 34; v. 161, 318
Crypt, iii. 379
Dancing girls, iv. 31
Dogma, ii. 24
Dynasties, i. 310; ii. 23; iii. 426
Egg, ii. 74, 79
Emblem of life, i. 72
Esotericism, i. 267, 274; ii. 99; iv. 203
Four, sacred number, i. 153
Fourth dynasty, ii. 23
Fragments, iii. 64, 188
Funeral ritual, v. 325
Glyph, i. 267; ii. 148; iv. 26
Gnostics, iii. 385; iv. 108; v. 128, 199
Heaven, sevenfold, iv. 185
Hieroglyphics, i. 56; iii. 139, 436; iv. 127
Hierophant(s), v. 49, 87, 248, 255, 257, 263, 290, 297, 318, 322, 382
Holy of holies, iv. 29, 34
Horus, iv. 41
Initiation, v. 233, 264, 270, 271, 290, 452
Khnūmū, v. 198
Khous, v. 244, 245, 248, 249, 250, 251
Knowledge, v. 264
Kosmos, symbol of, iii. 356
Labyrinth, iii. 433
Legend, iii. 272
Magi, iii. 426
Magic, v. 49, 243-247
Mars, iii. 133, 151; iv. 35
Menes, iii. 100
Metaphysical spirit, iv. 37
Monuments, iv. 75, 116
Mysteries, v. 264, 290
Neophyte, v. 290
Ophites, iii. 385
Osiris, see OSIRIS
Pantheon, iii. 385
Papyri, i. 273; ii. 17, 375, 398; iv. 122; v. 177, 241, 243, 246, 249, 251, 253, 257, 489
Priests, ii. 24; iii. 43, 268, 372, 392, 429; iv. 104, 319, 353; v. 262, 263, 264, 296
Principles in Man, v. 357

Principles in, metaphysics, iv. 204
Ptolemaic period, religion of, ii. 23
Pyramids, ii. 34, 157
Rebirth, religion and, i. 283, 284; v. 248
Religion, i. 45, 76, 284; ii. 24, 397, 399
Rites, i. 192, 310
Ritual, ii. 24, 74; iv. 206
Sacred books, v. 58
Sacred lake, v. 289
Sarcophagi, v. 176, 322
Serapis, v. 237
Seven earths, iv. 188
Soul, theory of, iii. 146
Sphinx, iii. 133
Symbolism, v. 51
Symbology, v. 129, 206, 246
Synchronistic tables, i. 50
System, i. 153; iii. 139
Tau, ii. 34, 79; iii. 43, 48; iv. 127, 152
Teaching, v. 357
Temples, curtain in, i. 183; iii. 361, 368
Texts, ii. 399; iv. 203
Theogony, i. 51, 142; iii. 69
Theory, ii. 54; iii. 146
Thoth, alphabet of, ii. 19
Thoth-Hermes, i. 64
Tombs, iv. 292
Traditions, iii. 312, 393, v. 58
Trinity, v. 188
Worlds, definition of, ii. 154
Year, iv. 192
Zodiacs, the, ii. 376; iii. 332, 352, 428, 430, 433, 436; iv. 319; v. 332, 340
EGYPTIANS, Ancestors of, iii. 328
Ancient, i. 273; ii. 398; iv. 122
Anubis-Syrius of, iv. 49
Astronomical records of, ii. 376; v. 332, 340
Astronomy of, ii. 384
Atlanteans and, iv. 319
Colonists, were, iii. 416
Descent of, iv. 337
Divine father and son of, ii. 114
Dragon symbol among, i. 141; ii. 126
Eggs, do not eat, ii. 81
Festival celebrated by, i. 275
Fragments of wisdom religion among, ii. 91
Great day of, i. 192
Hermes taught by, ii. 77
Hexagon, with, v. 120
Idolatry, among, iii. 145
Infernal region of, i. 274
Jews copied from, v. 176
Kabalah and the, iii. 242
Kabiri with, iii. 275
Logos with, i. 141
Lord God, smiting the, iv. 127
Manu Vina, led by, iv. 316
Mayas impart learning to, iii. 47
Mode of reckoning among, ii. 105
Moon, i. 274; ii. 102, 148
Nile of, iii. 415
Noot of, i. 275
Osiris, Eye of, iii. 38
Phallus added to Cross by, iv. 112
Reincarnation among, iv. 122
Scarabaeus of, iv. 122
Sons of God, had four, iii. 217

EGYPTIANS (*Contd.*)
Supreme Spirit of, ii. 82
Taurus sacred to, ii. 383
Teut of, iv. 173
Theogony of, iii. 417
Trinity of, iv. 30
Wheat sacred with, iii. 372
Vulcain God of, iii. 389
Zoolatry of, iii. 145
EGYPTOLOGISTS, v. 58, 94, 198, 245, 257
Astray, led, ii. 114
Errors of, iii. 373
Frog-symbol and, ii. 100
Funerary rites little understood, by, i. 52
Great Pyramid and, iii. 429, 430
Septenary doctrine and, iv. 204
Seven souls, iv. 175, 201
EGYPTOLOGY, v. 257
EHEJEH, " I am ", v. 191
EH'YEH, " I am ", iv. 19
EIDOLON, Astral, v. 237
EIGHTEENTH Degree of the Rosecroix, i. 146
EIGHTH Creation, v. 199
Sphere, v. 266, 486
EIKON, v. 210
EIS Zeus Sarapi, iv. 41
EKA, Achad, Ahu, i. 172
Chatur, is. i. 138
One, is, i. 138, 139, 172, 187
EKĀNEKA-Rūpa, Brahma addressed as iii. 58, 117
EKIMU, Spirits and Genii called, iii. 250
EKU gai no Kami, the female being, i. 264
EL, Chaldean, in, iv. 110
Divine Name; v. 212
Elion of Abraham, of, iii. 379
God or, iii. 375; iv. 110
Grace and mercy, of, iii. 51
Sun called, ii. 184; iv. 110
ELDORADO, Primeval, iii. 326
ELECT, v. 70, 103, 466
Angels, v. 109
Buddha, of, i. 45
Enoch, one of the, iv. 169
Ephraim, of Jacob, ii. 379
Foreheads of, iv. 127
Fourth Race, of the, iv. 169
Handful of those, iii. 349
Hierarchy of, iii. 319
Humanity, of our, i. 310
Initiates, v. 103
Jacob, of, ii. 379
Lemuria's, iii. 319
Messiah, ii. 379
One, v. 101
Pythagorean teaching to, ii. 343
Race, iii. 278
Root, v. 91
Saved, iii. 314
Third Race, of the, iii. 360
ELECTION, Vase of, iv. 97
ELECTRA a daughter of Atlas, iv. 337
ELECTRIA or Samothrace, Island of, iii. 17
ELECTRIC, Fire, ii. 245; iii. 68, 111, 122, 249
Fluid, v. 484, 553
Force, ii. 233, 398; v. 221
Kavyavāhana or, fire, iii. 110

Ocean, ii. 328
Pāvaka or, fire, iii. 67
Power of Fohat, i. 169
ELECTRICITY, ii. 222, 255, 263; v. 89, 221, 484
Atomic, ii. 396
Boehme and, ii. 217
Cause, an effect not, ii. 207, 241
Cosmic, i. 142, 150, 171, 201; ii. 278
Elements, and, ii. 273
Energy, a source of, ii. 273
Entity, is an, i. 142
Entity, not in itself an, i. 201
Flame correlation of, i. 147
Fluid, called a, ii. 216, 234, 240
Fohat is Cosmic, i. 142, 150, 171
Fohat the spirit of, i. 195; v. 484, 535, 553
Forces, at the head of, i. 338
God, called, ii. 397
Grove, Sir W., on, ii. 190, 220
Helmholtz on, ii. 308
Intelligence, is, v. 221
Kundalinī Shakti, manifested by, i. 333; v. 484
Laws of, iv. 193
Le Couturier's, ii. 226
Life, and, i. 143, 194; ii. 255, 303, 39
iii. 113, 122
Light and, i. 147; ii. 233, 303, 304
Materialism, and, i. 335; ii. 327
Maxwell on, i. 171
Mode of motion, not a, i. 203
Nature of, ii. 222
Negative, i. 201; ii. 275, 398
Noumenon of, ii. 255
One life, the, i. 147; iii. 122
Point, neutral, as to, ii. 274
Positive, i. 201; ii. 275, 398
Primordial substance, ii. 52
Sound and, ii. 279
Spirit of, i. 195
Storage of, ii. 304
Sun full of, ii. 326
Sun, stored in, v. 220
Terrestrial plane, on the, ii. 286
Understood, not, ii. 216, 222
Universal Force, v. 220
Vital, ii. 52, 254, 265, 315, 326
Zaliwsky's Theory of, v. 220
ELECTRO-magnetic Current, iii. 399
ELEMENT, Actual ultimate, ii. 350
Ahamkāra, i. 247
Angel-guided, v. 225
Aqueous, iii. 114
Bi-sexual, iii. 133
Boundary in defining an, ii. 270, 271, 307
Carbon as an, iv. 165
Causative, i. 335
Chemical, i. 230; ii. 349; iv. 165
Cosmic, i. 163, 192; ii. 190, 295
Creative, ii. 166
Dhyān of the first, iii. 114
Elementary group, or, ii. 271
Essence of, i. 272, 307
Eternal, the, v. 228, 230
Female, iii. 65, 74, 75
Fifth, i. 78, 301
Fire not an, v. 562
First, ii. 351; iii. 114

ELEMENT (Contd.)
First round, of the, i. 303
Form, iv. 203
Fravarshi spiritual counterpart of every, iv. 48
Generative, i. 335
Indiscrete, iii. 243
Irresolvable, ii. 266
Life, of, iv. 171
Male, i. 129; iii. 75
Many-faced, i. 78
Noumena of an, ii. 295; iii. 275
One, i. 77, 125, 142, 148, 170, 285; ii. 181, 272; v. 208, 228, 382, 562
Primordial, i. 114; ii. 56, 266, 350, 354; iv. 163
Progeny of the many-faced, i. 78
Rudiment, in Occultism means, ii. 290
Second, i. 303
Senses, of, iv. 185
Septenary, iv. 176
Thales, of, iv. 163
Water the symbol of female, ii. 74, 75
World-soul, called, i. 252
ELEMENT-BORN, Unborn cannot stand for, iv. 170
ELEMENTAL, atoms, i. 170; ii. 290
Creation, ii. 165, 171, 173
Deva kingdom, and, i. 230
Dissolution, i. 301; ii. 88; iii. 310
Evolution, ii. 276
Kingdoms, i. 230; ii. 173; iii. 312; iv. 187, 306
Man, iv. 212
Mechanical animal informed by an, iii. 425
Nebulæ, ii. 312
Occultist, so-called by an, ii. 190
Powers, i. 274; iv. 202
Prākritika or, iii. 79
Stages, i. 229
Vortices, i. 177; ii. 303, 348
World, v. 418
ELEMENTALS, v. 231, 239, 240, 424, 432, 452, 560, 564
Animals, of, v. 540
Air, of, v. 546
Astral light, in the, v. 544
Asuras and, i. 239
Bjerregaard on, ii. 355, 357
Centres of Forces, i. 229
Consciousness in, v. 562
Cosmic, iii. 276
Elements and, i. 334; v. 238, 239
Entities, are, v. 566
Evil spirits, are, iii. 385
Fire, iii. 425; v. 562
Form, without permanent, iii. 46
Genii or, i. 334
Gods of the elements are not, iii. 274
Higher, i. 236; iii. 111; v. 540
Human, v. 473, 560
Inferior, i. 320
Instincts of, v. 566
Jewish Kabalists, of, i. 280; ii. 357
Lives of, i. 332
Lokas of, 540
Matter and, i. 280; ii. 355
Metallic, v. 443

Nature-spirits or, i. 268, 320; ii. 181; v. 534
Order of, ii. 174
Physical body built by, i. 279
Rulers, guided by the, i. 202
Seven, iv. 203
Skandhas, and, v. 473, 560
South pole, of the, iii. 276
Space, in, ii. 345
Spiritual wickedness and, ii. 45
Spooks, and, v. 231, 473
Subjective existences, v. 559
Tānhic, v. 473
Theory of the existence of, i. 265
Worship of, 329
ELEMENTARIES, Spirits affecting mediums are often, i. 279
ELEMENTARY, Astral body, or, ii. 398
Atoms, substances composed of, i. 171
Daemons, ii. 290
Germs, i. 196
Man, ii. 290
Particles are vital forces, ii. 355
Spirits, ii. 355; iv. 204; v. 239
Spiritual atom, as opposed to, ii. 48
Spooks, ii. 345
Substance, i. 325; ii. 51; iii. 102
Units, i. 231
Water, iv. 112
World, v. 73
ELEMENTICITY, Degrees of, ii. 270
ELEMENTS, Aether, within, ii. 81
Air, of, i. 326
Ātmic, v. 528
Ancients' belief as to, i. 197; ii. 201, 264
Aristotle, of, ii. 182
Atomic, iv. 145
Beings in other, ii. 333
Bhūtādi means origin of the, ii. 172; iii. 116
Bhūtasarga creation of the, ii. 172
Bhūtesha, Lord of the, ii. 172
Birthplace of, ii. 291
Bright Gods of, iii. 274
Christian worship of, i. 182; ii. 188
Classification of, ii. 309
Combination of, ii. 66
Compound, i. 148, 295, 301; ii. 264
Comprehension, have, ii. 189
Concealed, nature of, ii. 245
Corporeal, ii. 184
Cosmic, i. 78, 147, 332; ii. 318, 328
Cosmic beings called, ii. 51
Cosmic matter forming itself into, i. 159
Cosmical system, of, iv. 130
Creation and, v. 234
Creation of, i. 265; ii. 145, 171; iii. 358
Cross and, iv. 116, 132
Curtain in the temples, symbol of, ii. 183
Development, i. 297
Dhyān Chohan in man, of, iii. 117
Differentiation of, i. 195
Discrete, iii. 245
Divinations, and, ii. 110
Divine life, a, i. 294
Divine substances, formed from, iii.123
Earth, of, i. 297, 326; ii. 313
Elementals attached to, i. 334
Equilibrium of, iv. 132

ELEMENTS (*Contd.*)
Ether and other, i. 338
Everchanging, iii. 67
Fire, air, water, earth, i. 297, 326
Fire, i. 179, 297, 326; ii. 192; iv. 120
First race, of, iii. 116, 122
Four, i. 78, 183, 184; ii. 56, 61, 81, 152, 166, 181, 183; iii. 144; iv. 159, 171
Humanities and, iii. 144
Hydrogen and, ii. 121
Ideograph of, iv. 154
Immaterial, iv. 147
Incorporeal, ii. 215
Intelligences and, ii. 259
Intelligent principle in, ii. 45, 295
Jupiter included in the four, ii. 183
Known, now, ii. 266
Krishna, lower form of, ii. 259
Leibnitz, of, ii. 355
Lives in, germs of, i. 302
Lives of, i. 332
Material, ii. 45, 186; iii. 122; iv. 147
Matter of, i. 201; ii. 175, 232
Meta-elements, and, ii. 270, 322
Molecules parading as, bastard, ii. 347
Mundane egg, of the, iv. 187
Mysteries of, v. 241
Nature of, i. 298, 338; ii. 272, 305, 307
Newly born, ii. 273
Nitrogen, saturated with, iii. 167
Notre Dame de Paris has figures of, ii. 110
Number of, i. 295; iv. 172
Opposition of, iv. 132
Order of, i. 297, 326; ii. 274
Past and future forms of the globe, i. 325
Paul on, ii. 51
Pillars raised to, i. 183
Plato, of, ii. 182
Pre-cosmic, ii. 171
Principles of, ii. 215
Procreation of, iv. 163
Protyle and, i. 188, 285
Race which controlled, iii. 224, 287
Range, beyond our, i. 78
Reynolds on, ii. 309
Rhizomata, called, iv. 171
Rudimentary, iii. 116
Rudra Shiva clothed with the, iv. 70
Seven, i. 78, 192, 196; ii. 181; iv. 176
Soul of, iv. 149
Sound as a generator of, ii. 279
Spirits of, ii. 110; iii. 355; v. 238
Spiritual, i. 269, 326; ii. 184, 186; v. 234
Symbols, as, v. 234
Symbols of, ii. 183; iv. 116; v. 234
Synthesis, are a veiled, ii. 53
Tāmasa, are, ii. 45
Terrestrial, ii. 318; iv. 175
Tetrad, and the, ii. 166
Triple unit produces, ii. 61
Universe, of, ii. 396
Vehicles, have their, ii. 191
Yazatas or spirits of, ii. 355
ELEPHANT, Behemoth, called, iv. 54
Infusoria compared with, i. 272
Invisible lives, composed of, i. 305
Man and, ii. 361

ELEPHANTA, Khnoom was adored at, ii. 82
Mahādeo of, iii. 94
Subterranean passages, built over, iii. 224
ELEPHANTS, Fossils of, iv. 343
Mastodons, and, iii. 223
Pigmy, iv. 291
Skeletons of men with, iv. 324
ELEPHAS antiquus, iv. 320
Meridionalis, iv. 320
Primigenius, iv. 257, 309, 315, 320
ELEUSINIAN Fields, v. 254, 255
Mysteries, v. 138, 161, 255, 279, 298, 412
ELEUSIS, submerged, iii. 272
ELEVEN years cycle of the sun, ii. 265
ELICIUS, Jupiter Fulgur, called, ii. 188
ELI, ELI, LAMA SABACHTHANI, v. 158, 159, 164, 167
ELIEZAR, R., quoted, iv. 102
ELIHU and Elijah, iv. 100
ELIJAH, Earthquake, and the, ii. 187
Josephus on, iv. 101
Small voice heard by, iii. 341; v. 145
Translation of, iv. 100
ELIMINATION, Calcareous matter, of, iii. 23
Unfit, of, iv. 218
ELION, Phoenician Elon or, iii. 379
FLIVAGAR, Streams of, ii. 83
ELIXIR of life, i. 200; ii. 193, 351; iv. 67; v. 364, 430
Knowledge of, v. 375
ELLENBOROUGH, Lady, v. 162
ELLIPSE and Cross, iv. 117
ELLIPTIC MOVEMENT, ii. 227
ELLIPTICAL, METEORS, Orbit of the, ii. 397
ELLORA, Gigantic ruins at, iii. 344
ELMES-FIRE, Ancient Germans, of, ii. 52
ELOÆUS, one of six stellar spirits, ii. 167; v. 201
ELOAH and Jehovah, iv. 78
ELOHA, the androgynous, iii. 70
ELOHI of Israel, iii. 51
ELOHIM, Abstraction, said to be a general, i. 276
Adam Kadmon and, i. 284; iii. 121
Adam and, iii. 381
Amshaspends are, v. 38
Androgynous Eloha and, iii. 70
Angels of Presence are, v. 386
Architects, the, v. 210
Barhishad became creative, iii. 87
Bible, in the, ii. 60
B'ne Alhim, sons of, iii. 36
B'ne Elohim, v. 299, 300
Chiim, identical with, i. 188; v. 211
Collective, iii. 311
Creative, ii. 168; iii. 15, 93, 134, 137, 293, 349; iv. 56, 167; v. 90, 209, 212
Deity in Nature, or, iv. 19
Demi-god robs, iii. 412
Demiurge and, iii. 246
Devas or Angels, v. 102
Dhyān-Chohans correspond to, i. 114; iii. 16; v. 386
Dhyāni-Buddhas or, i. 172
Double heaven, create, iv. 56
Duad, emerge from, ii. 344
Echad, were called, i. 172
Elu or, father, iii. 284
Emanu-el and, iv. 110

ELOHIM (Contd.)
Forces are, v. 187
Genesis in, iii. 15, 55, 91, 104, 113, 207, 246
Genii or, ii. 172
God called, v. 228
God of Christians is, i. 196; iv. 110; v. 234
God or, ii. 169; iii. 113
Host, a, v. 212
Ilda-baoth and, iii. 246, 388
Instructors or, iii. 349
Intelligence of, i. 292
Jehovah and, i. 140, 172, 247; ii. 156, 159
    215, 272; iii. 85; iv. 114, 167; v. 187
Jews of the, i. 111
Kabalistic, i. 174, 277; iii. 51; v. 202, 203, 209
Logoi, minor, iii. 49
Logos, aspects of, ii. 147
Lord God or, i. 298; iii. 15, 91, 143
Lower angels or inferior, iii. 72
Man, image of, v. 187
Meaning of, 208, 211
Mulaprakriti, developed, v. 90
Number for, i. 154
Outline shape of man, ii. 168
Pitris or, iii. 19, 145
Prajāpatis, identical with, v. 210
Primordial, i. 143
Rishis and, v. 191
Samael one of, ii. 135
Satan one of, iii. 387
Secret known to, iii. 133
Sephiroth, identical with, v. 191, 386
Septenary host of, iv. 169
Seven, v. 198, 201, 202, 203, 204, 325
Shadow-image of, iii. 145
Spirit of, v. 209
Spiritual perceptions real to, i. 276
Symbols, iv. 41
Synthesis of, iv. 179
Trimethius on, ii. 172
Tzelem shadow image of, iii. 145
" Word form " of, v. 207
ELOHIM-JAVEH, iii. 56
  -Jehovah, ii. 70; iii. 50
ELOHISTIC Creation, iii. 85, 254; v. 91
Figures, i. 276
Genesis, i. 298; iv. 196
Mosaic books, ii. 49; v. 186
Texts, iv. 41
Writers, iii. 264; iv. 41
ELOHISTS, v. 186, 187
ELOHITE CREATION, iii. 19
ELOI OF JUPITER, ii. 301; iv. 108
ELON or Elion, iii. 379
EL-SHADDAI, v. 375
ELYMAS, enemy of Paul, v. 146
ELYRUS, Council of, iii. 281
ELY STAR, quoted, i. 166
EMANATION, Adam Kadmon an, i. 263
Being, Supreme Source of every, v. 305
Buddhism, of Hinduism, ii. 392
Bythos from, iv. 139
Divine Essence of, i. 64
Energy, and, v. 213
Esoteric, iv. 139
Father-Mother, of, iii. 55
First, iv. 58; v. 187

Hydrogen, from a spiritual being, iii. 114
Iao-Jehovah, of Ilda-baoth, iii. 388
Jehovah an, i. 277
Logos of the, ii. 339
Macrocosmic, iii. 237
Manu, monad of, iii. 311
Matter, of, i. 332
Nature, from Absolute Consciousness, i. 320
Noumenon, from, iii. 114
Pairs of opposites, in esoteric, iv. 139
Point of, ii. 339
Sephiroth, of, v. 91, 191, 192, 210, 291, 299
Universal Mind, of, ii. 326
World of the, i. 69
EMANATIONS, Ain-Soph, of, iii. 52
Atomic, iv. 227
Auric, ii. 262
Centres of, ii. 360
Creative power of, iii. 87
Divine, iii. 71
Divine area, of, iv. 167
Doctrine of, v. 128, 210, 299, 383
Duality of, ii. 328
Dyooknah, from iv. 24
Immutable, of the one, ii. 53
Ovulary, iii. 173
Plane of, i. 188
Powerful, iii. 177
Primordial, v. 446
Principles of man, from, iii. 121
Procreation of, iii. 173
Secondary, v. 446
Secret, iv. 184
Seven, ii. 156; iv. 184
Sun, ii. 254
Supreme Being, from, v. 299, 305
Ten, v. 188
Unconscious, iii. 89
Universe, of, v. 91
World of, iii. 119
EMANCIPATION, Anger prevents, ii. 133
Cause of final, i. 151, 328
Causes of, ii. 259
Forms of, iv. 209
Self, of the, ii. 259
Seven senses, causes of, i. 151
Tree whose fruit is, iv. 210
EMANCIPATIONS, Maruts of, iv. 186, 187
EMANU-EL or El-ohim, iv. 110
EMANUEL Swedenborg, referred to, iv. 365
EMBLEM, Allegorically explained, ii. 18
Cyclic time of, iv. 135
Female, iii. 50
Female, generative power of, iv. 28
Fohat, activity of, iv. 159
Forces in Nature, of, iv. 153
Luni-solar, year, iii. 86
Male, iii. 76
Matter, iii. 137
Nature of, iv. 153, 163
Periodical time of, iv. 135
Pictures, series of, ii. 18
Sin, of, iii. 137
Society, of our, iv. 163
Solar cycle, iv. 135
Spiritual, i. 184
Stability of, iv. 127, 159

EMBLEM (*Contd.*)
Strait gate, iv. 119
Symbol and, ii. 17
Terrestrial life, of, iii. 102
Time, of, iv. 135
Wisdom, of, iii. 186, 385
Word, of the, iv. 112
EMBLEMS, Ancient archives recorded in, ii. 19
Bible written in, ii. 18
Esoteric societies of, ii. 18
Evil spirits, of chaos, iii. 385
Puranas are written, ii. 18
Sexual, iv. 155
Sovereignty of, iv. 181
EMBRYO, Adeptship of divine, iv. 186
Analogies of, iii. 259
Cosmic process, correspondence with, v. 422, 423, 424
Development of, i. 265; iii. 140, 194, 195
Diti, in the womb of, iv. 184
Eyes in the human, iii. 296
Germ cell in, iii. 125
Growth of, iii. 194
History of, racial epitome, iii. 193
Human, iii. 140
Physical, i. 235
Sex in, iv. 229
Sphere of, prenatal, iii. 195
Terrestrial, v. 422
EMBRYOGENESIS, iv. 238
EMBRYOLOGICAL, Argument, iv. 255
Cell, i. 270
Inference, iv. 239
Problem, iii. 294
Science, theories of, i. 269
EMBRYOLOGY, Mystery of, i. 265
Occult, i. 269, 270
Science of, i. 269; iii. 193, 257
Study of, iii. 179; iv. 229
Teaching of, iii. 261
EMBRYONIC, Evolution, iii. 193
Mammalia, iv. 254
EMBRYOS, Devaki of, iv. 96
Race of, iv. 29
EMBRYOTIC DEVELOPMENT, iii. 50
EMEPHT, supreme planetary principle, ii. 82
EMERGENCE of universe, ii. 319
EMERSON, Over-soul of, i. 119, 196; v. 298
EMIMS of Moab, iii. 335
EMOTION preceded motion, i. 318
EMOTIONALISM, Superstition under guise of, iii. 53
EMPEDOCLES, quoted, ii. 220, 222
Referred to, v. 61, 147, 255
EMPEROR, Constantine, ii. 190
Hia dynasty of, iii. 65
Julian, iii. 41, 47; iv. 158; v. 213, 218
Justinian, v. 307
Yu, i. 314
EMPIRE of Dead, iii. 233
EMPIRIC, Definition of an, iv. 234
Haeckel, the German, iv. 243
EMPTINESS or Baoth, i. 247
EMPUSES, v. 147
EMPYREAN, Centre of, ii. 338
Sphere, ii. 83
EN or Aiōr, i. 262; v. 391

ENCHANTER, Golcar the, iii. 344
ENCHANTMENT, seven arts of, iv. 212
ENCHANTMENTS, Hekate ruling over, ii. 102
Magic shield destroyed, iii. 393
ENCHANTRESS, Gultwerg the, iv. 89
ENCOMPASSER, universal, iii. 271
ENCYCLOPEDIAS, Ancient historians had no, iii. 416
Mesmer in, iii. 164
ENDEXOTERIC, Causes and effects are, iii. 84
ENERGEIA NATURÆ, ii. 327
ENERGIES, Cosmic, i. 170
Dhyānic, ii. 171
Divine, iii. 124
Divine workmen and, ii. 157
First triad of, ii. 391; v. 213
Great volcanic, iii. 362
Logos of, iii. 311
Nature of, ii. 395
Photogenic matter of, ii. 254
Physical, ii. 349
Reawakened, i. 152
ENERGY, Active, ii. 355
Æther quintessence of, ii. 233
Androgynous, i. 194
Aspects of evolving, ii. 345
Astral plane on, ii. 369
Atom, in an, ii. 275, 360; v. 558
Augmentation of, ii. 283
Caloric of, ii. 249
Ceaseless, iii. 241
Celestial, iii. 241
Central sun of, iii. 242
Centre of, i. 77, 170; ii. 308, 360
Chaos reflected in, ii. 51
Conception of, ii. 352
Conservation of, ii. 238, 242
Cosmic, ii. 360; iv. 168
Deity of, iv. 183
Dhyān Chohans of, i. 322; iv. 219
Emanation and, v. 213
Eros is, v. 557, 558
Eternal an, i. 324
Ether, matter, and, ii. 393, 394
Evolving, i. 229; ii. 345
First-born or Logos, an, v. 213
Fohat is, i. 81, 171; iv. 219
Force and, i. 121, 201; ii. 233, 278
Globe, transferred from a, i. 210, 213
Inherent, iii. 180
Kinetic, iv. 242
Leibnitz on, ii. 355
Light of, ii. 203
Logos centre of, ii. 146
Matter of, ii. 306
Monadic essence and evolving, i. 229
Motion of, iv. 242
Motion or, v. 558
Mulaprakriti is, v. 558
Parabrahman, of, ii. 148, v. 557
Planets, of, i. 213, 225
Quality, is a, ii. 233
Reservoirs of, ii. 264
St. Michael celestial, iii. 241
Satan as, iv. 76
Science, of, i. 77; ii. 306; v. 213
Shakti or, i. 193

ENERGY (*Contd.*)
Solar, i. 171; ii. 75, 264
Space, existing in, ii. 146
Spirits, of, i. 303
Spiritual plane, on, ii. 369
Stream of, iii. 241
Sun, of, ii. 203, 222
Supreme one, i. 86
Symbol, manifesting through, ii. 184
Transferred, i. 210, 213, 225
Transformable, iii. 37
Vishnu manifestation of, i. 171
Waves of ether, ii. 239
Word of the manifested, ii. 89
ENFIELD, quoted, iv. 166
ENGINEERS and ancient temples, iii. 379
ENGIS, Bone caves at, iv. 313
Man, iv. 314
Skull, iv. 257
ENGLAND, Catastrophe, and, ii . 371
Kings of, v. 264
Latitude of, iii. 401
Materialism in, iv. 221
Protestant, ii. 189
Shveta-dvīpa identified with, iii. 401
ENGLISH, *Bible*, ii. 375; iv. 108; v. 316
Jehovah in, iv. 35
ENGLISHMAN and African negro, iii. 441
ENGRAVING, Palaeolithic, iv. 289
ENGRAVINGS, Chipped-stone age, iv. 284
ENLIGHTENED, Buddhas or, iii. 421
Budh, ii. 194
Precursors of, iii. 206
ENLIGHTENMENT, Divine, iv. 84
Fire of knowledge or, iv. 136
Humanity will redeem, iv. 84
Ray of, iii. 234
Spiritual sun of, iii. 215
ENNEADS, angelic hierarchy, order of, i. 187
ENNEMOSER quoted, v. 297
ENNIS, Jacob, quoted, ii. 224
ENNOIA, Cycle representing, iii. 218
Divine mind or, iii. 218
Emanations of, v. 451
Gnostics of the, iv. 58
Logos, and Ophis the, iii. 219
ENOCH (see Enos, Hanoch) Angels of, ii. 247; iv. 156
Book of, see Book Index
Cain has a son, iii. 390; v. 106
Cataclysm of *Book of*, iii. 314
Chaldean Noah translated as, iii. 149
Christian Theology, and, iv. 65
Constellations seen by, v. 200
Disappearance of, iv. 101
Divine secrets and, iii. 285
Eliezer on, iv. 102
Enos or, iii. 360; iv. 98, 102
Esoterically, v. 106
Fallen angels on, iii. 232, 381
Fifth race, and, v. 106
Generic name, iii. 215, 270, 361; iv. 100, 101
Genesis of, iii. 270
Geology of, ii. 334
Hanoch or, iii. 361; iv. 98, 99; v. 106
Hermes and, iii. 361; iv. 102
Jared father of, iv. 169; v. 106

Jewish, iv. 99
Josephus on, iv. 99, 101
Libra or, iii. 138
Masonic legend of, iv. 100
Noah, and, v. 106
Opinions about, iv. 75
Patriarch, iv. 99
Plagiarism from, iv. 53
Present solar year, i, 23
Pymander on, iii. 270
Seer, means, v. 102
St. John borrows from, iv. 100
Seth father of, iii. 91, 360, 361, 365; v. 106
Six-pointed star in, iv. 102
Son of Man, v. 106, 190
Symbol a, iv. 102
Synonyms of, iv. 98
Tree, branch of the one, i. 256
Three Enochs, v. 106
Uriel tells, iv. 103
Visions of, iii. 232; iv. 105
Western mystics and, iii. 59
Wisdom of, iii. 143; iv. 51, 102
ENOCHIAN MSS. iv. 101
ENOÏCHION, or seer of open eye, iii. 215, 361; iv. 98, 99, 101; v. 102
ENOÏCHION-HENOCH, iv. 98
ENOS, Dhruva seen in, ii. 380
Henoch or, iv. 98, 283
Seers, generic name for, iii. 361
Seth, son of, iii. 134, 135, 390; v. 129
Son of man, iii. 136, 138; iv. 37, 99
ENOSH, v. 291
ENS, Absolute and Abstract, i. 43
ENTELECHIES, Emanated monads or, ii. 356
ENTIFIED ABSTRACTION, Atom an, ii. 237
ENTITIES, Amshaspends dual, i. 281
Androgynes becoming separate, iii. 37
Animal kingdom, i. 239
Apes in, iii. 264
Aristotle and, ii. 216
Astral statues of, iii. 103
Builders real, i. 167
Celestial, i. 276
Conscious, i. 268, 337; ii. 200
Cosmic, ii. 328
Devas called, i. 329
Dhyāni-Buddhas called, i. 76
Divine thought, moved by, iii. 166
Electricity and ruling, i. 171
Ethereal, i. 268, 273, 337
Forces and, i. 147; ii. 141, 215
Gandharva Devas are, iv. 157
Gods as, ii. 215, 243
Incorporeal, i. 265
Individuality of, i. 318
Inferior class of, i. 320
Kāmalokic, v. 566
Kāmarūpic, v. 566
Lipika real, i. 166
Manus are, i. 227
Mind-born, i. 186
Mystical, i. 253
Non-human, i. 318
Organisms are, iv. 224
Personality of, i. 318
Planetary period, of a pervious, iii. 235

ENTITIES (Contd.)
Progressed, i. 239; iii. 124
Rishi-Prajāpati called, i. 76
Ruling, i. 171
Self-conscious, iii. 174
Sephiroth, as separate, iii. 120
Septenary host as, i. 266
Spiritual, i. 201, 279, 320; ii. 200, 215
Substantial, i. 265
Sun and Moon personified, i. 275
Supersensuous, ii. 243
Thinking, i. 227
Trismegistus on, ii. 396
Worlds, from preceding, i. 293
Worlds, of higher, i. 190
ENTITY, Absolute, an, iv. 169, 170
Angelic, iii. 90; iv. 81
Astral, v. 473
Being, a, i. 157
Conscious, iii. 251
Devachanic, v. 472, 518
Divine, i. 167; iii. 114; iv. 223; v. 35
Electricity an, i. 142
Electricity an emanation from an, i. 171
Force and an, i. 201; ii. 231, 236
Force an emanation of an, i. 202, 334
Globe an, i. 20
Highest, in Kosmos, v. 550
Human, iii. 90; iv. 176
Immortal, iv. 122
Living, ii. 335, 340; iii. 353
Mahat the Highest, v. 528
Microscomic, i. 211
Monad not a separate, i. 230
Mythical, ii. 82
Nonentity, and, iii. 183; iv. 150
Number is an, i. 135
Personal, v. 502
Rasātala, in, v. 540
Ray as an, v. 77
Real, ii. 335, 354
Self as an, ii. 258
Space an, ii. 258, 340
Spook, of Personality, v. 473
Spiritual, iii. 363; iii. 167; v. 388
Star of an, ii. 296
Surviving, i. 276
ENTOMOLOGY, Septenary law in, iv. 194
ENVELOPE, Astral, iv. 282
Atoms, of ,ii. 287
Auric, v. 456, 457, 471,473, 475, 500, 516,
532, 533, 551, 552
Auric, Kosmic, v. 528
Matter of photogenic, ii. 254
ENVELOPES, Elements translated, i. 134
Monad-Ego of the, i. 283
ENVOÛTEMENTS, Magic and, v. 47, 48
EOCENE, Age, ii. 157; iii. 314, 431; iv. 247,
260, 285, 291, 347
Cataclysm, iv. 280
Civilization, iv. 314
Climate, iv. 283
Continents, iv. 263
Flora, iv. 350
Man, iii. 163, 164, 289; iv. 246
Period, iii. 22, 163, 256; iv. 249, 263, 265,
268, 283, 314, 350

Strata, iv. 260
Ungulates, iv. 304
EOZOÖN Canadense, a chambered shell,
iii. 256; iv. 281
EPHAPOS, Christ connected with, iii. 413
Dark, iii. 413, 414, 416
EPHEMERALS, Zeus and puny, iii. 410
EPHESUS, v. 144, 146, 157
Heraclitus of, i. 143
EPHIALTES, Anguipedal monster known as,
iii. 80
EPHOD, v. 239
EPHRAIM, Pisces and, ii. 379
EPICTETUS, v. 149, 266
EPICUREAN Indolentia, the, ii. 300
EPICUREANISM, v. 397, 414
EPICURUS, referred to, i. 70; ii. 214, 243, 291,
292, 303, 336, 354; iii. 287; v. 60, 78, 388
EPICYCLE and cycle, ii. 370
EPIDEMIC, disease of, i. 181
Spiritualism of, v. 94
Vice of, v. 526
EPIGENES, Chronology of, iv. 191
EPIMETHEUS, Pandora and, iii. 272
Prometheus, and, iii. 420; iv. 90
EPINOIA, First female manifestation of God,
v. 462
Simon Magus, of, v. 450, 451
Thought or, v. 447
EPIPHANIUS, quoted, i. 121; iv. 139;
v. 136, 161
EPOCH, Egyptian Sacerdotal v. 296
First root-race, of, iv. 254
Fourth race, of, ii. 371
Glacial period, of, iv. 248, 257
Great Pyramid, of, iii. 429, 430
Hindu, ii. 386, 389; iii. 433
Kali Yuga, iii. 433
Primordial, iv. 281
Universal renovation, of, ii. 384
EPOCHS, Hindu, ii. 387
Zodiacs, of the, iii. 433
EPOPTAI, EPOPTÆ, v. 137, 429
EPOPTEIA, v. 138, 280, 281
EQUATION, Sun's centre, of the, ii. 390
Velocity, of, ii. 281
EQUATOR, v. 345
Constellations, turning through the zodiacal,
iii. 330
Cor Leonis on, iii. 406
Ecliptic and, iv. 104
Fohat, a circle of, i. 253
Pole passed from, iii. 355
Poles agree with, iii. 324
Retrograde motion of, iv. 354
EQUATORIAL, Jupiter, rotation of, ii. 317
Plane of the Sun, iii. 242
Planets', diameter, iv. 113
Svastika, and belts, iii. 108
Velocity, Saturn, ii. 317
EQUILATERAL triangle, i. 28; ii. 339, 341;
iv. 163
EQUILIBRIUM, Atomic, ii. 288
Attraction and, ii. 227
Cosmos, in, ii. 134
First race of, iii. 16
Matter and Spirit, between, i. 167, 242

ÆQUILIBRIUM (*Contd.*)
  Nature of things in, ii. 129
  Static, ii. 220
ÆQUINOCTIAL, Points, ii. 388; iii. 330; iv. 354
  Shadow, iii. 400
ÆQUINOX, Apsis, and, iii. 330
  Autumnal, the, ii. 388
  Change in position of, iv. 263
  Chinese year, and, iv. 192
  Degrees behind, ii. 386
  Precession of, ii. 388
  Stars and, ii. 389
  Vernal, ii. 384, 389; iii. 434; iv. 354; v. 345
ÆQUINOXES, Cross of, iv. 117
  Enoch on, iv. 103
  Precession of, ii. 157; iii. 315; iv. 120, 263
  Solstices and, ii. 363
ÆRA, Dryopithecus of the, iv. 246
  Kali Yuga, ii. 85
ÉRARD-MOLLIEN, quoted, ii. 384
ERATAOTH the dog, iii. 124
ERATOSTHENES on the divine dynasties,
  iii. 366; v. 293
ERBIUM is an element, ii. 270
ERDMANN, quoted, ii. 355
ERASMUS, v. 181
EREB= evening twilight, iii. 254
EREBUS and Nux born out of Chaos, i. 170
ERECH, city of the Chaldean necropolis,
  iv. 30
ERIDANUS, Jordan, Hebrew, ii. 107
  Nile called, iv. 154
  Phaeton hurled into, iv. 340
ERIDU, the Babylonian city, iii. 148, 208, 229;
  iv, 263
EROS, iii. 183
  Aether produced under action of, i. 170
  Creation and, iii. 183
  Cupid and, i. 169; iii. 75, 237
  Divine love, i. 178
  Divine will, or, iii. 76
  Energy, v. 558
  Trinity, in the primeval, i. 169
  Venus, son of, iii. 75
EROS-PHANES, ii. 81, 182
EROSION of land, rate of, iv. 279
ERUPTIONS, Volcanic, iii. 356; iv. 93, 269
ERYTHRAIAN SEA, iii. 207
ESAR of the ancient Turks, iv. 173
ESAU, Jacob and, iii. 143
  Kings of Edom sons of, iv. 275
  Meaning and place, of, iv. 275
ESCULAPIUS, a serpent deity, iii. 39
ESDRAS, v. 178, 183, 198
  Pentateuch recomposed by, v. 195
ESIKEKAR, or Persepolis, iii. 397
ESKIMOS, dying out, iv. 349
ESMUN, serpent deity, iii. 39
ESNEH, engraved stones at, ii. 23
ESOTERIC, Alētheia, v. 462
  All Father, ii. 145
  Arhat school, i. 212
  Aryans, learning of, iii. 47
  Astrolatry, v. 319
  Astrology, v. 455
  Australians, view of, iv. 290
  Axioms, iv. 267

Bhagavad Gita, an, work, ii. 346
Brahmā, meaning of, iii. 135
Brāhmanism and Buddhism, iv. 208; v. 380, 403
Buddhism, v. 79, 403, 405
Cain, the, iii. 136
Calculations, i. 110; iv. 170
Chritos is sexless, i. 139
Chronology, iii. 22, 229, 394; iv. 278
Computation as to age of man, iv. 309
Continents, names of, iii. 19
Cosmogony, i. 169, 176, 215; ii. 321, 338;
  iii. 46, 154; v. 422, 476
Cycles, division into, iii. 80, 433
Deities, order of, iii. 117
Karmic cycles, ii. 362
Kingdoms of Kosmos, ii. 174
Knowledge, i. 336; ii. 371; iv. 111, 139
Language, ii. 22; iv. 39, 206
Lingam, significance of, iv. 39
Literature, inaccessible, v. 408
Masters of India, i. 151
Moses, Religion of, ii. 33
Mysteries of Samothrace, iii. 18
Nārada, facets of, iii. 92
Pneumatics, i. 288
Samael, aspect of, ii. 135
School(s) ancient, iv. 175; v. 336, 398, 409,
  439
Scriptures, iii. 110
Spiritual fire, actuality of, iii. 114
System, i. 60, 114, 218; ii. 28, 315; iii. 67, 80;
  iv. 29, 207
Teaching, i. 335
Trinities, i. 83
Vedāntin school, i. 273
Vidyā, i. 286
Volumes quoted, iv. 183
ESOTERIC BUDDHISTS, i. 121, 141; ii. 127;
  iv. 140, 157, 204
ESOTERIC DOCTRINE, v. 74
  Babylonians of, iv. 136
  Comets, on, ii. 323
  Devachan, of, ii. 80
  Dynasties and, iii. 368
  Essence, on the Infinite, i. 71
  Gnostic and, i. 190
  Hebdomad on, iv. 162
  One Life of, i. 170
  Origin of Life, on, iii. 172
  Pearl in every religion, the, v. 406
  Rig Veda, and, iv. 178, 179
  Sacred Islands of, iii. 326
  Septenary in, iv. 203
  Stanzas, based upon, i. 59
  Upanishads, i. 313
  Wars of the, ii. 137
  Yugas of, ii. 382
ESOTERIC MEANING, Adytum, of, iv. 27
  Ahamsa of, iv. 33
  Apāna, of, iv. 137
  Brahmā, of, iii. 135
  Crucifixion, of, iv. 130
  Enoch, of, iv. 102
  Hebrew scrolls, in, ii. 49
  Hermes, of, iv. 102
  Hindu cosmogony, of, ii. 348
  Iliad, of, iii. 382

ESOTERIC MEANING (*Contd.*)
Jehovah of, iii. 134
Logos, of, iii. 38
Makara, of, iv. 148
Manvantara of, i. 131
Maruts in their, iv. 184
Odyssey, of, iii. 382
Patriarchs, of, iii. 138
Prāna, of, iv. 137
Rig Veda, of the, iv. 17
Rule of proportion, of every, i. 257
Sānkhya philosophy, of the, iv. 141
Vedas, in the, i. 295; iii. 43
ESOTERIC PHILOSOPHY, v. 26, 336, 385,
　　439, 443
Asuras in, iii. 171
Atoms, of, i. 266; ii. 173
Attainment of consciousness, a fact in, i. 320
Buddhism and, iii. 164
Chaldean scriptures, in, iv. 23
Cis-Himālayan, iv. 145
Creators in, iii. 87
Deity according to, iii. 418; iv. 115
Demiurge in, ii. 95
Dhyānis, and, iii. 102
Gods in, i. 109
Pleiades and, ii. 374
Polygenesis, on, iii. 251
Problem of man solved by, ii. 361
Reality, and the invisible, ii. 339
Reconciles all religions, i. 43, 126
Reincarnation as taught by, v. 82, 83
Rudras in, iv. 156
Science, fills gaps of, iii. 201
Spontaneous generation, teaches, iii. 158
Time, according to, i. 116
Unity taught in, v. 127
Venus in, iii. 42
Virgil knew, iv. 166
Vishnu in, i. 172
ESOTERIC SCIENCE, v. 431
Mathematics or Gnosis is, v. 65
Divine Magic, v. 444
Manas and child, v. 483
ESOTERIC TRADITION, Buddhist, ii. 84
Himalayas, beyond the, i. 315
Vishvakarman, of, iv. 129
ESOTERICISM, v. 27, 36, 407
Androgyne of, iii. 414
Anu, in, iii. 72
Archaic, i. 125, 173
Arhats, of, iv. 207
Āryan, i. 174
Asiatic Religions, in, v. 72
Aspects of, two, ii. 149
Avalokiteshvara in, i. 139
Bhagavad Gītā, of the, i. 151; ii. 38
Bible, i. 308; iii. 255; v. 66, 67, 97, 449
Blinds of, iii. 309
Buddha, of, v. 405
Bull's eye called, light of, iii. 290
Cosmogony of, v. 422
Eastern, ii. 367, 397; iii. 122; iv. 15, 121;
　　v. 72, 185, 407
Egyptian, i. 267, 274; ii. 99; v. 91
Genesis, of, iii. 121, 208
Genii of, ii. 124

Geometrical, ii. 147
Hebrew, v. 186
Hindu, iii. 59
Jehovah, in, iii. 72
Jewish, ii. 52
Kabalah, of the, i. 187
Kabalistic, iii. 409
Kabalistic books, of, iv. 106
Lao-tse, of, iii. 49
Leo, in sign of, i. 261
Mysteries of, v. 77, 412
Nārada in, iii. 59
New Testament, ii. 99
No personal God in, v. 462
Numbers, chief doctrine in, ii. 151
Old Testament, of, v. 66
Origins of, iv. 24
Pagan, iv. 27
Pleiades and eastern, iv. 121
Purānas, in, iii. 182
Purāniç, iii. 254; v. 27, 258, 408
Pure, v. 78
Scriptures, Western, in, v. 407
Spirit of, ii. 397
Spiritual, v. 81
Symbolical man in, iv. 180
Tāntrika-Shastras, v. 185
Trans-Himālayan, i. 170; iii. 35
Yogis, in, iv. 149
Zoroastrian, iii. 355
ESQUIMAUX, Chinamen, and, iii. 185
Drawings, iv. 286
Palaeolithic ancestors of, iv. 286
ESSENCE, Absolute, i. 73, 317
Absolute light, of darkness, i. 137
Akāsha, of, ii. 240
Alaya, of, i. 120
Angels, i. 319
Atma, the, ii. 294
Atoms, of, i. 160
Brahmā, of, iii. 124
Chitkalā, of, i. 329
Cyclic rebirth of the same divine, iii. 249
Deity, of, ii. 181; iv. 49
Dhyān-Chohanic, i. 308; iii. 128
Dhyāni-Buddhas, of, i. 119
Divine, the, i. 64, 71, 126, 134; ii. 114, 339,
　　354; iii. 103, 194; v. 77, 188, 205, 227, 299,
　　426, 443
Element, of one, i. 303
Eternal, v. 208, 230
Existence, of, i. 81
Fire, of, i. 73
First Principle more occult than all, ii. 144
Force, of, ii. 235
Forty-nine fires, of the, iii. 67
Gods, of, iii. 101
Governors, of, iii. 112
Hebdomadic, iii. 100
Human, iii. 198
Impersonal, iv. 49
Innermost, v. 467
Lords of Wisdom, iii. 410
Mankind not of same, iii. 419
Material world, of, eternal, i. 323
Matter, of, i. 109, 203
Mind, of, iii. 90

ESSENCE (*Contd.*)
Monad, of, i. 193; iii. 118
Monadic, i. 229, 230; ii. 344; iv. 239
Noumenal, of, atoms, i. 160
One, i. 188
One in, three in aspect, iii. 122
One manifested eternal in, i. 157
Ozone, of, i. 200
Parabrahman, *i.e.*, i. 80
Particle, of every physical, i. 266
Personality not lost in Nirvāna, of, i. 309
Phenomena behind physical, ii. 244
Phenomena, of, ii. 365
Plastic, i. 118, 130
Prāna or life, iv. 168
Primal, of Nature, i. 176, 192; 261
Psychic, of man, iii. 40
Rebirth of the same, iii. 249
Sadaikarūpa, iii. 58
Self-existent, i. 118, 152
Seventh, the, i. 331
Spirit and the sun united in, iv. 123
Spiritual, of man, iii. 40
Substance, of, ii. 355
Suddhasattva or, i. 190
Sun, i. 192; iv. 123
Supersubstantial, or Akasha, ii. 240
Supreme, v. 304
Svabhāvat called, i. 71, 130, 161
Tetraktys, of the, iv. 172
Ultimate substance derived from, iv. 124
Universal Essence, v. 467
Universal sixth principle, of, i. 82
Vāsudeva, of, i. 328
Vishnu, of, ii. 46
Vishvakarman, of, iv. 129
Yoga, of Brahmā, iii. 124
ESSENCES, Angelic spiritual, iii. 244
Celestial hierarchies, of, i. 319
Dhyān-Chohanic, iii. 117
Divine, ii. 349
Ethereal, i. 286
Governors, of, iii. 269
Monads or, iii. 174
Noumenal, i. 317
Powers or, i. 244
Semi-divine beings, of, iii. 96
Seven, of the, iii. 269
Things, real, of, ii. 353
ESSENE, Jesus the, ii. 263
ESSENES, v. 65, 120, 271, 294, 302
Belief of the, iii. 120
ESUR, a God in India, iii. 123
ETERNITIES, Duration, constitute, i. 111
Ever-becoming, of the, ii. 257
Fohat acts during seven, i. 200
Hindus, of the, i. 110
Pralayic, i. 125
Seven, i. 109, 124, 200
ETERNITY, v. 300
Absolute, i. 268
Act not co-equal with, iii. 306
Aeon and, i. 132
Amenti, in, i. 282
Atma-Buddhi, in, i. 274
Circles in, ii. 362
Cycle of, iii. 60

Defunct in, i. 273
Duration of, i. 254; iii. 107
Forms existed as ideas in, i. 324
Fourth, i. 242
Future and past, i. 111
Heart of, i. 179
Karmic law is, iii. 306
Law from one, to another, iii. 97
Mahā-manvantaras and, iii. 89
Manas in, i. 274
Manvantaric, iv. 53
Nirvana, a limit in, i. 309
Osiris master in the, ii. 155
Parabrahman, meaning, ii. 68
Picture-gallery of, i. 165
Pilgrim, of the, i. 82
Pralaya, in, i. 69
Seraphim, v. 80
Serpent of, i. 134, 141; ii. 80, 123, 127; iii. 284, 376; iv. 73
Seventh, i. 131
Son of Immortality in, iii. 379
Sons of Manvantaric, iv. 53
Sparks of, i. 82
Spirit and matter wedded in, iii. 112
Spiritual lives in, ii. 360
Svastika and, ii. 127; iii. 108
Swan of, the, ii. 74; iv. 33
Third eye embraces, iii. 300
Thyan-kam in the, ii. 360
Time and, i. 173; ii. 145; iii. 236
Unconscious in, ii. 359
Universal life-giver in, ii. 318
Universe and, i. 82, 324; iv. 59
Vibration of the seventh, i. 131
Vishnu Purāna, in, ii. 50
Worlds in, iii. 54
ETHER, Aether, and, ii. 44, 45
Akāsha, and, i. 78, 130, 142, 159, 253, 299, 300, 301, 336; ii. 45, 88, 240
All-pervading, ii. 250
Ancients, of the, ii. 214
Astral Light and, i. 336; ii. 39
Bodies formed of, ii. 288
Body of, ii. 181
Chaldean oracles and, ii. 183
Concept of, ii. 208
Conditions in, new, ii. 212
Continuous, ii. 215
Corruptible, v. 388
Cosmic principle, a, ii. 45
Daughter of, iii. 26
Element, i. 78, 196, 301; iii. 101; iv. 187
Envelope, of, vibratory, ii. 287
Fire or, i. 155, 263; ii. 166
Human body, in, ii. 250
Instrument of nature, ii. 396
Interstellar, ii. 351; iii. 144
Keely's own, ii. 285
Kosmos, and, ii. 251
Lowest planes of, i. 298
Luminiferous, ii. 287, 308
Matter and, i. 127, 164, 171; ii. 318, 393, 394
Metcaff on, ii. 304
Molecular, ii. 210
Mystic Four and, ii. 51
Nārāyana present in, i. 277

ETHER (Contd.)
Nature of, ii. 44, 209, 310
Nervous, in, i. 327, 359; ii. 299
Newton and, i. 78; ii. 217
Nirvana, is, v. 388
Occultists, a reality to, ii. 39
Phenomenal positive, ii. 252
Planets bound together by, iii. 93
Primordiality of, v. 62
Principles of, ii. 45
Proteus, hypothetical, ii. 39
Ptomaine extracted by, i. 305
Purānas on, ii. 44
Recognition of, ii. 347
Resisting, ii. 225
Science and, i. 160, 336; ii. 39, 205, 208, 210
    231, 325
Soul atom dissolves in, ii. 292
Soul of, iv. 149
Sound and, ii. 88, 311; iii. 116
Space of, ii. 44, 126, 255, 257, 311; iv. 327;
    v. 423, 424, 475
Speech and, iii. 115
Spirit of, ii. 177
Sun, and the, ii. 251
Theogony, in, ii. 181
Universal, ii. 223; iii. 84
Unmodified, remains, ii. 88
Voltaire, of, iii. 97
Water-Mother, the, iii. 131
Wind or, iii. 113
ETHEREAL, Animals, i. 297
Astral man, iii. 159
Atlanteans, prototypes of, iii. 22
Being of a lower grade, iii. 74
Combination of Neshamah, iv. 24
Counterpart of man, i. 235
Creator of man, body of the, iii. 95
Dhyān Chohans, races of, i. 239
Dhyānis, iii. 111
Divine man, iii. 283
Doubles, iii. 18
Earth, iii. 252
First forms were, iii. 129
Flame, ii. 88
Fluid, ii. 251, 348, 351
Form, ii. 175, 367; iii. 67, 158, 159, 375; iv. 282
Forms, i. 227; iii. 78, 193, 300; iv. 301
Gods, form of, ii. 175
Hermaphrodites, iv. 250
Ischins, form of, iii. 375
Light of eternal spirit, iii. 49
Lilith and the, shadow, iii. 181
Lunar spirit, iii. 95
Man, i. 239; ii. 367; iii. 156, 165, 410
Mars more, men on, ii. 326
Men, i. 297; iii. 104, 189; iv. 301
Men and animals, i. 297
Models, iii. 193
Organism, i. 250
Physical state, and, iii. 413
Pitris, iii. 18, 111
Pre-human, race, iii. 172
Primal natures, i. 147
Primeval humanity, iii. 66, 159
Proto-organisms, iii. 190
Prototypes, i. 325; iii. 22; iv. 49

Races, iii. 165, 200, 235, 268, 291, 312;
    iv. 239, 309
Root race, i. 214; iii. 57
Seed, an, organism, i. 250
Shadows were, iii. 146
Shadowy, men, iii. 104, 165
Sheaths, iii. 193
Sons of the earth, iv. 19
Sons of Yoga, iii. 203
Transformation of matter, i. 254
Worlds, iii. 331
ETHEREO-SUBSTANTIAL or Astral envelope,
    i. 280
ETHERIC, Centres of J. W. Keely, i. 203-280
Flows, ii. 287
Force, ii. 279
Tremors, ii. 239
(= Astral), v. 521, 531, 561. See also Astral
    and Linga Sharira
ETHERODYNAMY (electricity, heat, etc.),
    ii. 263
ETH-H'OREBV, or Raven, ii. 161
ETHICS, Aryan codes of, iii. 255
Gautama, preached by, iii. 421
National, iv. 36
Races, of early, iii. 274
Universal, ii. 362
ETHIOPIAN, Africa, of, iv. 39
Egypt, dominion of, ii. 23
History of, affairs, iii. 407
ETHIOPIC MS. in Bodleian Library, iv. 50
ETHIOPS, river, iii. 415
ETHNOLOGICAL, Book of Enoch, events and,
    iv. 104
Classifications, iii. 235
ETHNOLOGY, Antediluvian, iii. 334
Antiquity on, iii. 435
Atlantis necessary to, iv. 351
Australian race, silent as to, iii. 202
Bible chronology disproved by, iii. 200
Esoteric, iii. 173; iv. 280
Modern systems of, ii. 31
Occult teaching in conflict with, iii. 441
Races named by, iii. 426
Scriptures, in, iv. 316
Turanians, Mongols and Chinese of, iii. 423
Varieties of the human race, ii. 36
ETRURIA, Mysteries of, v. 256
Raised stones in, iii. 345
ETRUSCAN, Aesar in old, iii. 123
Cities, iii. 224
Lares, origin of, iii. 360
ETRUSCANS, Aryan invasion, forerunners of,
    iv. 310
Etudes Egyptologiques, quoted, i. 275
ETYMOLOGIES, Iaho, of, iv. 33
Jehovah has variety of, iii. 138
ETYMOLOGY, Eden, of, iii. 208
Kwan, of, ii. 193
Lares, of, iii. 360
Man, of, ii. 330
Sacrament, of, iv. 35
Yin, of, ii. 193
EUA, EUE, EVA, or EVE, iii. 138
EUCHARIST, v. 156
EUCLID elements of, v. 113
Initiate, an, v. 524

EUDOXIA, Empress, v. 170
EUGIBINUS, quoted, iii. 142
EUHEMERIZATION, dual principle, of, iii. 156
Fictions, of old, iii. 273
Nature, of powers of, iv. 228
EUHEMERIZED, Evil spirits, iii. 385
Priapus, iv. 113
EULER and Occultists, ii. 214
EUPHRATES, country watered by, iii. 207
Eridue once seaport of, iv. 263
EURIPIDES, quoted, iv. 333
Referred to, v. 153, 266, 277, 310
EUROPE, Africa older than, iii. 367
America and, iii. 333, 405; iv. 295, 352
America, Miocene plants of, and, iv. 295, 352
Angels and spirits in, believers in, ii. 336
Australia one with, iii. 333; iv. 350
Cataclysm, on, eve of, ii. 371; iii. 442
Caucasian of, iv. 38
Civilization in, iv. 318
Colossal stones of, iv. 321
Continent of, iii. 21, 397, 423; iv. 177, 350
Continent preceding, iii. 404
Cradle of mankind, not a, iv. 309
Cross symbol in, iv. 126; v. 162
Cyclopean origin of towns in, i. 257
Egypt belonged to, delta of, iii. 21
Egypt older than, iv. 315
Elevation of, iv. 264
Fifth root race in, ii. 200
First settlers in, iii. 331
Fossil man in, iv. 293
Fully formed, iv. 310
Io has to quit, iii. 414
Miocene, iv. 295, 350, 352
Mystical learning in, i. 58
Occult sciences in, iv. 106
Palaeolithic men in, iv. 309
Planetary conjunctions in, ii. 382
Pythagoras in, teachings of, ii. 341
Quaternary epoch, of the, iv. 309
Sea-bottom, at the, iii. 324
Seas, emerging from, iv. 313
Sedimentation in, iv. 264
Seventh Atlantean sub-race in, iv. 312
Sinking of, iii. 268
Stones, raised, in north of, iii. 345
Waters, rising from, iv. 291
EUROPEANS, America was a myth for, i. 337
Atlanteans and, iii. 431
Buddhist canons lost to, i. 51
Chronology of, iii. 395
Grand Climacteric of, ii. 382
Hindus, confused with, iii. 324
History of, iii. 441
Mahābhāratan war, and, ii. 112
Sixth race and, iii. 443
Zodiacs of India, and, iii. 428
EURYDICE, v. 154
Pluto, carried off by, iv. 354
EURYMEDON, Giants the children of, iv. 335
EUSEBIUS, see Book Index
EUSTATHIUS, quoted, iii. 414; iv. 31
EUTERPE, quoted, ii. 77; iii. 334
EUTHANASIA of Adepts, iv. 100
EUTYCHES, v. 157
EUXINE, Ikshu sea, or, iii. 401

Kashmir, to, iii. 208
Samothrace overflowed by, iii. 18
EUXODUS, referred to, ii. 376
EVANGELISTS, Elements, and, ii. 78
Four, i. 185
Portraits of, ii. 78
Sacred animals and, ii. 159
EVANS, Sir John, on the Stone Age, iii. 439
EVE, Adam and, i. 187, 194; ii. 175, 331; iii. 73,
104, 109, 134, 155, 199, 387; iv. 216, 226,
231; v. 164, 165, 190, 206
Aditi and, iii. 55
Androgynous, iii. 272
Belita became, iv. 30
Cain-Jehovah, giving birth to, iv. 37
Disobedience of, iii. 408
Earth and, i. 285
Hava or, iii. 54; iv. 37
Hebel same as, iii. 143
Heva or, i. 285
Hovah means, iv. 35
Io and, iii. 413, 414
Isis, mother of, iii. 43
Kepha, and, v. 202
Kin (Cain), son of, iii. 387
Mother, ii. 70
Mother of all living, iv. 200; v. 164
Sarah and, iv. 40
Serpent and, i. 140; ii. 140; iii. 209, 281
Son of the terrestrial, i. 129
Tamtu became, iv. 30
Third and fourth races, of, iii. 409
Vāch and, iii. 55, 137; v. 164, 190
Yah-hovah is, ii. 109
EVEN numbers are terrestrial, iv. 146
EVENING TELEGRAPH of America, quoted,
iii. 439
EVENING twilight or Sandhyā, iii. 68, 70
EVENTS, Confused, intentionally, iii. 229
Ideographic records of, iii. 436
Impress, leave their, iv. 362
Karma more than succession of, ii. 370
Old Testament, of the, ii. 375
Pre-cosmic, ii. 85
Reappear, will, ii. 400
Shadows of coming, iv. 362; v. 301
Sidereal motions regulate, on earth, ii. 370
Succession of, in Asia, ii. 384
Symbolically, recorded, ii. 19
Time, a pitiless devourer of, iv. 312
Tradition, revealed through, iv. 344
Traditional, ii. 371
EVER-BECOMING, the, i. 295, 311; ii. 257,
293; iii. 444; iv. 116
EVER-DARKNESS, Ray of the, i. 127, 152
EVER-INCARNATING Logos, Active and,
iii. 59
EVER-PRESENT, Deity, v. 108
Manifestation of the, i. 70
Nature, iii. 444
Root Sat, the, iv. 16
Space, i. 70
EVER-UNMANIFESTED, Principle, iii. 236
Sat, i. 330
EVERARD, quoted, iii. 112
EVERLASTING, Cell, i. 270
King, iii. 51; iv. 51

EVERLASTING (*Contd.*)
　Mighty ones, monuments of, ii. 153
　Mother nature, iv. 167
　Nucleoles are, iii. 46
EVES, the animal, iii. 264
EVESTRUM or Ka, hieroglyphics, iv. 205
EVIL, Amrita, became mixed with, ii. 62
　Astral Light, effects of, ii. 57
　Binary the beginning of, iv. 146
　Cause of good or, iv. 81
　Conquest of, v. 374
　Demon, Seth an, iii. 91
　Dilemma of the existence of, iv. 78
　Dragon, iii. 64
　Dragons of, winged, iii. 407
　Duad the origin of, or matter, ii. 343; v. 116
　Earth, on, iv. 84
　Evolution, necessary for, iii. 387
　Experiences in dreams, v. 558
　Eye, iii. 425; v. 249
　Eyed Saturn, iii. 42
　Genius of, v. 94
　God cannot be divorced from, iii. 131
　Good and, i. 140; iii. 104, 133, 277, 304, 381;
　　iv. 45, 172; v. 116, 488
　Hall of misery, doers in, ii. 123
　Homogeneity contains essence of good and,
　　ii. 129
　Human nature, in, ii. 134
　Jehovah one with, iii. 388
　Karma and, i. 182; iii. 307; iv. 45
　Kin (Cain), iii. 387
　Knowledge of, iii. 17, 133, 381
　Matter and, i. 140; ii. 343
　Moon a symbol of, ii. 112
　Mysteries of, iii. 169; iv. 84
　One, iii. 80, 211, 385
　Ones, iii. 410
　Origin of, iii. 38, 276, 307; iv. 58
　Plato's idea of, iii. 371
　Powers of, iii. 112, 113
　Predominate, will, iv. 84
　Principles of, iv. 172
　Problem of, iii. 304; iv. 44
　Progress, necessary for, iii. 388
　Prometheus, brought by gift of, iii. 419
　Realm of, iii. 84
　Reversion, good, from, v. 557
　Serpent of, ii. 126; iii. 389; iv. 73, 159
　Shadow not, iii. 218
　Son of, mankind a, v. 289
　Spirit of, v. 48
　Tree of good and, i. 292; iii. 143
　War with, iii. 112, 113
　World's, ii. 368
EVIL SPIRIT, Dogma of, iv. 52
　Globe animating the, iv. 152
　Kakodaimōn, ii. 58
　Lightning and, ii. 188
　Who and what, iv. 43
EVIL SPIRITS, iii. 169, 180, 235
　Bhūtas called, iii. 110
　Devils and, iii. 169
　Emblems of chaos, iii. 385
　Gods fallen into generation and, iii. 235
　Karma and, ii. 133
　Nature of, iii. 180

Satan and, iii. 180
Seven, iii. 106
EVILS, Humanity, of, iii. 383
　Life of, ii. 369
　Nature in, ii. 135
EVOLUTION, Above, began from, iii. 177, 196
　Acme of physical development, has reached,
　　i. 278
　Almighty, iv. 222
　Ancients views of, ii. 46; iii. 116
　Angelic beings, of, ii. 134
　Animals, of, iii. 90, 176, 187, 255; iv. 264
　Anthropoid apes, of, iv. 250, 252
　Anthropological, iii. 215
　Ape into man, of, iv. 249
　Artificial, iii. 348
　Arvāksrotas, of, ii. 175
　Ascending, iii. 301
　Astral, iii. 259
　Atlantean, iii. 204, 371
　Atoms, of, i. 235, 265; ii. 246, 273, 347,
　　349, 350
　Basis of objective, iii. 37
　Chain of our, i. 301
　Climatic influence on, iv. 305
　Conscious spiritual, iii. 246
　Cosmic, i. 64, 80, 85, 130, 134, 147, 170;
　　ii. 145; iii. 78, 311; iv. 84, 207
　Cosmogonical, iii. 69
　Cosmos, of, i. 325
　Creation not, i. 263; iii. 53, 255
　Creation, of animal, iii. 255
　Creations mean stages of, ii. 173
　Cycles of, i. 310; ii. 362; iii. 194, 440
　Cyclic, i. 192, 278; ii. 134; iii. 46, 204, 301,
　　418, 420
　Darwinian, i. 237, 251; iii. 49, 160; iv. 256,
　　257, 280
　Darwinism and, iv. 219
　Definition by Webster of, iv. 223
　Descending, iii. 100, 301
　Dhyān-Chohans, of, iii. 117; iv. 270
　Dhyānis, of, i. 265
　Diagram of, ii. 349
　Dissolution and, i. 77, 78
　Divine man, of, ii. 134; iv. 316
　Doctrine of, ii. 324
　Downward, ii. 260, 274
　Earth, of, i. 206, 254; ii. 161, 333; iii. 74, 242
　Eastern doctrine of, ii. 324
　Element of senses, of, iv. 185
　Elemental, ii. 276
　Elements, of the, i. 196, 295; ii. 181, 309
　Embryonic, iii. 193
　Ethereal counterpart of man, of, i. 235
　Ever-becoming, v. 191, 231
　Eye, of the, iii. 301
　Fall a law of, iii. 303
　Final, iii. 196
　Fohat and, i. 203
　Forces of, ii. 271; iv. 192, 277
　Forms of, iii. 177
　Fourth race, of, iii. 23, 72, 295, 409, 443
　Fourth round, in our, i. 237
　Germ of the, i. 294
　Giants, of our race from, ii. 59
　Globe, of the, ii. 19; iii. 146; iv. 365

EVOLUTION (*Contd.*)
Globe, A., of, iii. 78
Globes of, i. 213, 224, 248, 278
Gods, ii. 106, 156, 273
Ground-plan of, iv. 306
Hierarchies of Egos, of, ii. 354
Human, iii. 72, 119, 125, 133, 174, 205, 235, 351, 364
Humanities, of seven, iii. 309
Humanity of, i. 226; ii. 161; iii. 431; iv. 341
Incognizable cause, and, iv. 55
Individual cycle of, iii. 194
Individuality and, iv. 46
Intellectual, i. 233; iii. 409
Involution and, i. 204; ii. 360; iii. 295
Isis Unveiled, in, iii. 262
Kapila on, i. 238; iii. 261
Karma and, i. 240; ii. 359, 362; iii. 285
Karmic, iii. 201, 251
Kosmos of, i. 79; ii. 158, 160; iv. 159
Kosmos, from, v. 166
Languages, of, iii. 204
Law of, i. 205, 258, 291; ii. 366; iii. 66, 73, 76, 93, 102, 179, 195, 203, 303; iv. 58, 103, 238, 301
Law of God, a, v. 69
Lemuria, traced to, iii. 178
Lemurians, of, iii. 57, 317
Life, of, i. 213; iii. 74, 242
Light, of, i. 198
Logos, and, i. 194
Mammals, iii. 186, 203; iv. 282, 303
Man, of, i. 168, 228, 239, 242; ii. 296, 362, 367; iii. 57, 90, 141, 160, 173, 184, 196, 197, 253, 260, 263, 276; iv. 44, 130, 216, 365
Manifestation, in its triple, ii. 54
Mankind, of, ii. 400; iii. 15, 95, 129
Manu on, i. 238; iii. 261
Manvantaric, iii. 175
Materials, out of pre-existing, i. 279
Matter, of, i. 203; iii. 349; iii. 275
Midway point of, iv. 305
Mind, of, i. 240
Mineral, of, i. 214
Monadic, i. 222, 223, 232, 292; ii. 345, 358
Monera, of, iii. 168, 172
Moon, of, v. 535
Moral, i. 214
Mystery of, i. 134, 244; v. 87
Mystic numbers in, iii. 48
Mythology, and, ii. 15
Nārada and, iii. 60, 92
Nations, of, iii. 413
Natural, iii. 192, 347; v. 291
Natural selection, without, iv. 218
Nature before, began, ii. 246
Nature in the light of, iii. 159
Occultism, and, i. 265
Order, of, ii. 203, 337, 337; iii. 21, 177, 180
Organic, iii. 128; iv. 218, 253, 300, 304
Periods, of, ii. 165, 166
Perpetual never-ceasing, iv. 116
Personality, and, iv. 46
Phenomena, by natural, iv. 287
Physical, i. 214, 233, 260, 271; ii. 134; iii. 66, 194, 259, 301

Planets, of, ii. 321
Populations, of Europeans, iv. 310
Potential force of, iv. 16
Pradhāna, from, i. 300, 326
Primeval divine races, of, iii. 164
Primitive men, of, iii. 328
Process of, i. 229, 320; iii. 51; iv. 267
Progressive, ii. 166, 367; iv. 216
Protoplasmic forms, of, i. 325
Psychic, iii. 408
Psychological and spiritual, iv. 107
Race, iii. 37, 117, 333; iv. 229, 267
Races, of, i. 63, 64; ii. 18, 367; iii. 83, 164, 203, 251, 257, 266, 301, 313, 409, 417, iv. 233, 278; v. 425, 518
Rephaim, from the, iv. 65
Root cool during, i. 78
Root races, of, iii. 59
Round, in first, ii. 174
Round, in fourth, ii. 174
Sephiroth, of, i. 263; v. 191
Septenary, i. 229, 310; iv. 194, 303
Sexes, of, i. 72; iv. 229
Sexual propagation, and, iv. 227
Shiva is, personified, iii. 189
Soul, of, i. 246; iii. 165
Soul-life, of, iv. 240
Spirit, of, ii. 348; iv. 224; v. 370
Spirit-matter, of, i. 319
Spirit-soul, of, ii. 166
Spiritual, ii. 366; iii. 96, 165, 194, 196, 245, 246, 408, 414, 419; iv. 220; v. 370
Stages of, i. 224; ii. 145, 173; iii. 125, 126, 235; iv. 114
Stanzas, in the, i. 85
Strata, of, iii. 251
Theories of, modern, iii. 423
Theory of, iii. 64, 196, 289; iv. 225
Theory of atomic, ii. 349
Third stage of, iv. 114
Transformation and, iii. 130
Tree of, iii. 262
Triple, i. 233
Uncoiling serpent compared to, an, iv. 73
Universal, i. 85; iii. 46, 60
Universe, of the, ii. 41, 309, 324; iii. 184; iv. 73, 114, 144
Vegetable, i. 214
Virgil and, iv. 166
Watermen, of, iii. 63; iv. 206
What is?, iv. 223
Wires of, i. 321
Words, by means of, iii. 53
World, iii. 128
EVOLUTIONAL gyrations, i. 223
EWALD on Chwolsohn, iv. 21
EXCAVATIONS, Dr. Schliemann, by, iv. 292
Layard, of, iii. 18
EXISTENCE, Absolute, i. 113, 116, 309
Bliss of sidereal, iii. 249
Breath of the One, i. 125
Causes of, i. 116, 328; iv. 81
Comets and cosmic, ii. 323
Conditioned, i. 80
Conditions of solar, iii. 144
Conscious, i. 80
Cosmic substance, periodic, of, ii. 292

EXISTENCE (Contd.)
Cycles of, i. 274; ii. 160, 296; iv. 82
Dasein or, i. 324
Elements, of, ii. 181, 346
Energy, of antecedent, ii. 350
Eocene period, of man in, iii. 163
Essence of, i. 81
God, of, ii. 361
Intellectual, ii. 203
Intercyclic phases of, ii. 291
Kāma rūpa inseparable from animal, iv. 165
Kārmic, v. 559
Manifested planes of, i. 129
Manifested universe, of, i. 81
Matter outside, ii. 181
Matter rising into intellectual, ii. 203
Māyā of phenomenal, i. 116
Non-being, as, i. 125
Non-existence, and, i. 112, 116
One, i. 70, 73, 109; iv. 170
One form of, i. 118, 120
One secondless, i. 124
Periods of, iii. 46
Physical, ii. 369
Planes of, i. 129, 205; ii. 293; iii. 111, 168; iv. 123; v. 513
Prehistoric times of Lemuria, of, iii. 20
Problem of, ii. 394
Purusha the One, iv. 170
Races, of ethereal, iv. 239
Sattā (sole), ii. 89
Secondary age, of man in, iii. 23
Self, i. 74, 82
Self-conscious, martyrdom of, i. 311
Sidereal, bliss of, iii. 249
Spirits, the, of, ii. 370
Spiritual, ii. 369
Struggle for, iii. 300; iv. 218, 232
Tertiary period, of man in, iv. 246
True, i. 73
Vishnu cause of, i. 328
Will, and, ii. 365
World of form and, ii. 328
EXISTENT One, ii. 157; iv. 197
Sat not in itself the, iv. 16
EXORCISMS, v. 245, 249, 250, 251, 449
EXOTERIC Allegories, iii. 18
Allegory of Visvakarman, iv. 129
Angelic Beings, texts on, ii. 177
Astrology, v. 455
Brāhmanism, iii. 42
Chronology of the Jews, iii. 395
Creeds, ii. 162; iii. 180; iv. 230
Cycles, ii. 369
Dogmas, ii. 24; iii. 414
Hindu philosophy, i. 216
Hinduism, i. 308; ii. 62
Judaism, iii. 52
Kumāras, ii. 177
Mythology, iv. 175
Purānic writings, i. 299
Philosophy, ii. 362; v. 476
Planets, ii. 298
Purānas, ii. 343
Records of the East, iii. 53
Religions, i. 307, 319; ii. 302; iii. 115, 283, 402; iv. 71, 159, 178; v. 88, 260, 266

Rites, iv. 41
Ritualism, iv. 137
Ritualistic form, iv. 139
Ritualistic worship, or, iii. 57
Scriptures, i. 218; ii. 18; iii. 110
Series of androgyne Gods, iv. 173
Symbology, esoteric and, v. 443
Triad, descriptions of first-born, ii. 348
Veil, iv. 228
Worship, lotus and, ii. 96
EXOTERICISM, Chaldean, iii. 102
Distortions produced by, ii. 132
Emanations in 10 and 7, ii. 151
Occultism and Greek, ii. 231
Purānas, of, i. 316
EXPEDITION, Argonauts, of, ii. 378
Bacchus into India, of, iv. 25
EXPERIENCE, Harvest of, Hindu, ii. 386
Monad, gained by, iii. 187
EX-POLE STAR, Dhruva, the, iv. 119
EX-PROTOPLASMIC moneron, iii. 161
EXSISTERE, from Esse into, iii. 37
EXTASIES due to interior phosphorus [?], iv. 80
EXTENSION, Atoms, of, ii. 353
Boundless, or unity, ii. 56
Descartes on, and Thought, ii. 353
Enlargement not admitted by infinite, i. 131
Leibnitz's ideas of, ii. 352, 353
Material points without, ii. 212
Motion not explainable by, ii. 352
Number, mass, weight, iii. 53
Property of, ii. 353
Substances without, ii. 356
EXTINCT, Animal men, race of, iii. 264
Apes will be, iii. 265
Bovey Tracey, lake of, iv. 295
Mankind, ii. 261
Races, physical side of, iii. 291
Satyrs, race of animal men, iii. 264
EXTINCTION, Karmic necessity, of races, iv. 349
Life, Nitya of, iii. 310
EXTINGUISHED THE SPARK, Those who, iii. 318
EXTRA-COSMIC God, an, i. 322; ii. 253, 293; iii. 53; iv. 69
EXTRA-TERRESTRIAL INTELLIGENCES, iv. 247
EXTREME of Confucius, the great, iv. 123
EYE, Atrophy of spiritual, iii. 307; iv. 339
Cat, of, ii. 103
Centres which, cannot penetrate, ii. 264
Dangma, of, i. 117
Divine, v. 483
Doctrine of, v. 387, 406, 407, 411
Eternal, of the, v. 117
Evil, iii. 425; v. 249
Inner Spiritual, i. 276; ii. 358; iii. 215
Light and, ii. 278
Loka-Chakshuh, of the world, i. 162
Mercury and right, v. 428
Mysteries of human, iii. 296
Odd, iii. 299
One, iii. 35
Ormuzd of, v. 314, 315
Osiris of, iii. 38; iv. 122
Seer of the open, iv. 99; v. 102

EYE (*Contd.*)
Seers of ancient, iii. 286
Self-existence of, i. 82
Shiva of, i. 118; iii. 186, 286, 297, 303; iv. 118, 150
Shiva-Rudra of, iv. 186
Single, v. 438
Soul, mirror of, iii. 300; v. 151
Spiritual, ii. 239; iii. 215, 307; iv. 339; v. 550
Spiritual Seer, of, ii. 358
Sun, the, of the, ii. 17, 118
Taurus of, ii. 388; iv. 354
Third, iii. 33, 230, 273, 290, 299, 302, 307, 349; iv. 186, 338; v. 438, 458, 479, 480, 554
Venus and left, v. 428
Wisdom, of, v. 438
World, of the, i. 162; iii. 27; v. 283
EYES, Ammon, of, iii. 217
Consciousness of, v. 557
Creatures with three, iii. 295
Cuttlefish, of, iii. 296
Embryo, in, iii. 296
Insects, of, iii. 296
Lord of the, iii. 35; v. 313
Most occult of sense organs, v. 550
Pineal gland and, iii. 299; v. 480, 483
Solar, ii. 398
Tears of their, ii. 301
Tetragrammaton of, iv. 196, 197
EZRA, Babylonian, iii. 151
Books of Moses restored by, iv. 29
Days of, v. 182, 185
Hindu figures, ignorant of, ii. 381
Mosaic books author of, ii. 31; iii. 151; iv. 20, 29, 228
Story of Moses, learned by, ii. 32
Story of Sargon, and the, ii. 32

F

FA, Note, v. 443, 454, 480
FABER, quoted, ii. 75; iii. 150, 151, 152, 266, 267, 343, 359, 392; iv. 39
FACE, Angels of the, ii. 152, 179; iv. 48; v. 314
Double, ii. 141
Enoch or man of, iv. 102
Father of the, ii. 66
Great, i. 129
Jehovah, of, iv. 109
Human, and Dragon's tail, iv. 69
Lesser, i. 129, 263, 285
Lord of the Shining, iii. 27, 40, 56
Macroprosopus, the great, i. 129
Microprosopus the lesser, i. 129, 263, 285
Mysterious, i. 267
Moon, of Moses in the, iv. 35
Seven spirits of the, i. 186; iii. 123
Spirits of the, i. 247
White, ii. 141
FACES, Brown-black, iii. 185
Creatures with two or four, iv. 72
Human beings with the, of ravens, iii. 16
Kabalistic, i. 246
Prakrit, of, iv. 207
Universe, of the, iv. 148
FAFNIR, the dragon slain by Sigurd, ii. 121
FA-HIAN, Cheta cave of, i. 44

FA-HWA-KING, quoted, ii. 192
FAILURES, Commentary, mentioned in the, iii. 198
Fate of, iii. 330
Nature of, iii. 444; iv. 43
Races in ethereal, iii. 235
Solar system borne ahead in a new, iii. 235
Spiritualized too far, iii. 235
FAIR FACED God, Ptah the, ii. 82
FAITH, mysteries of, v. 386
Buddhist, v. 385
FAIZI DIWAN, quoted, i. 63
FAKIRS, v. 282, 399
FALCONERI, E., a pigmy elephant, iii. 223
FALCONNET, M., quoted, iii. 341
FALL, Adam, of, iv. 23, 72; v. 203
Allegorical, iv. 100
Allegorical description of, iii. 16
Allegory of, ii. 134
Angelic, iii. 284
Angels, of the, i. 136, 244; iii. 169, 178, 231, 270, 284; iv. 55; v. 200
Atlanteans, of, iv. 208
Atonement, and, iv. 74
Celestial Virgin, of the, iv. 81
Cross into matter, of, iv. 123
Curse for, iii. 113, 284
Development after, iii. 231
Evolution, a law of, iii. 303
First, iii. 186
Full meaning of, iii. 231
Garden of Eden and, i. 185
Generation, into iii. 48, 112, 137, 387; iv. 79, 84, 180, v. 103
Goat the symbol of, iv. 79
Harmony of nature before, iii. 270
History of the third race after its, iii. 268
Incarnation or, iv. 52, 84
Knowledge, the result of, iv. 82
Lemurians, iii. 302
Logoi, of, iv. 84
Man, of, ii. 80; iii. 121, 180, 209; v. 291, 323
Matter, into, i. 307; ii. 260; iii. 48, 137, 191; iv. 37
Metaphorical, iv. 52
Mystery of, iii. 73
Natural, from the, i. 244
Origin of, ii. 136
Physical, iii. 302, 331
Physiological, i. 243; iii. 281
Primal pair, of the, v. 200
Procreative powers before, iii. 177
Prometheus before, iii. 420
Race, of the, iii. 277
Races at the time of, iii. 18
Samaël caused, iii. 121
Separation of the sexes, or, iv. 186
Serpent, of the, ii. 131
Seth the first result after, iii. 134
Seven Rectors', ii. 135
So-called, ii. 112; iii. 264, 353
Spirit into generation, of, i. 243
Spirit into matter, of, i. 307; iv. 37
Spiritual and physical events, refers to, iii. 147
Third root-race, of the, i. 72; iii. 268
War with evil followed, iii. 112

FALL (*Contd.*)
Wisdom, testified to by ancient, iii. 197
Zeus, of, iii. 413
FALLEN ANGEL, Dragon or Devil, the old, iii. 197
Man, a, ii. 169
Man taught wisdom by, iv. 82
Myth of, iii. 180
FALLEN ANGELS, i. 50, 244, 246, 248; ii. 44, 130, 178, 179; iii. 71, 102, 112, 123, 232, 233, 240, 244, 250, 276, 381, 388; iv. 43, 61, 65, 69, 78, 83, 95, 98, 105; v. 200, 315
FALLEN, Demon, iv. 54
Gods, iii. 44, 235
Light, iii. 212
Māra the, one, iv. 151
Matter, into, iii. 296
Race, iii. 281
Virginal and, iii. 238
Zohar, on the, iv. 59
FAMILIES, v. 545
Human race, of the, iii. 209
Speech, of, iv. 358
Stages in the linguistic, iv. 232
FAMILY, Man or grihasta, iii. 409
Priest or purohita, iii. 57
Race, iii. 203, 432
Races, iii. 154, 431, 432
Resemblances explained, i. 305
Sub-races, divisions of the, iii. 440
FAMINE, Sopatrus, and the, ii. 190
FANES, Arabians', iv. 175
Druids', iv. 325
India, of, iv. 25
Israelite, iv. 31
Proportions of the ancient, i. 257
FARADAY, Agnostic said to be, ii. 231
Aristotelian, an ii. 231
quoted, i. 171; ii. 231, 234, 304
FARGARD, quoted, iii. 41, 383; iv. 85
FARRAR on the Basque language, iv. 358
FARSIS or Parsis, iii. 397
FASHIONERS, Ancestors, or, iii. 103
Body of illusion, of, iii. 67
Cosmic substance, of, iii. 388
Divine, iii. 313
Elohim or, iii. 388
Inner man, of the, i. 151
Man, of, i. 272
Modeller of all things, or, ii. 192
World, of this, iv. 83
Worlds, of, iv. 85
FATALISM, Action of blind, ii. 368
Astrology not, ii. 364
FATALISTS, Believers in Karma not, iii. 306
FATE, Atlantis, of, iii. 370
Destiny, or, iii. 239
Iblis an agent of, iii. 393
Karma, or, iv. 89, 140
Karmic, of nations, ii. 400
Karmic Ego, or, iv. 176
Orlog, or, iv. 89
Strength of, iii. 419
FATES, Man need not accuse, ii. 369
Triform, iii. 367; iii. 412
FATHER, Ad is, iii. 54
Aether, ii. 181

Aether, Archaeus is, v. 32
Aether, Jupiter or, v. 499
Aether, True nature of, v. 562
Agni, of the three fires, iii. 67
Air, of, iii. 114
Ak-ad or, iii. 54
All, of, v. 210, 233
Boundless Time is, v. 235
Brain of, i. 201
Breath of fire, the, i. 148
Brihaspati, of the Gods, i. 179
Buddhi, generated by and generating the, v. 451
Buddhists recognize no, or Creator, ii. 360
Children of the yellow, iii. 30
Chokmah, the, v. 192, 214, 438
Christos, Son and, v. 499
Cold mist the, i. 147
Creator and, ii. 339, iii. 54
Dark hidden, i. 143
Deity, ii. 261
Deity having a mother cannot have a, i. 129
Deity neither, nor mother, i. 193
Divine, iii. 55
Ea, first father, v. 203
Earth and Sun, progeny of same, v. 293
Elu or Elohim, iii. 284
Emanation, First, v. 445
Fathers of, ii. 155, 298
Fire, i. 127; ii. 296; v. 446
Fire-seed of the hot, ii. 266
Genii, of, i. 245
God the, i. 335; ii. 66; iii. 239; v. 233
Gods, of the, i. 179; iii. 110, 131, 272, 362, 413; v. 324
Golden verses, of, iv. 175
Group belonging to same, ii. 298
Heaven, in, v. 203, 319, 358, 430, 532
Higher Self, or, v. 431
Highest of the aeons when emitted from the, iv. 58
Hokhmah, wisdom is, iii. 94
Hot breath the devouring, i. 78
Hydrogen is, iii. 114
Jod is, v. 190
Jupiter, iv. 112
Knowledge, space, of, iv. 70
Logos and, i. 262; ii. 66
Lord of the lotus, the, iii. 27, 56
Man, of, iii. 168, 412; v. 203
Mars born without a, iv. 120
Matter, ii. 340
Monad, ii. 339
Mortals, of, iv. 88
Mother, and, i. 78, 114, 137; iv. 25; v. 381
Mother of Nature, and, v. 209
Mysteries of the light of his, iv. 134
Nāgas or serpents, of the, iii. 141
Names of the, iv. 127
Noah, iv. 169
Non-creating, i. 264
One, iii. 122
One thing, the, of the, iii. 118
Osiris, of fathers, ii. 155
Pitā (Pitar) or, iii. 70; v. 282
Pneuma, of, iii. 121
Pole, the immutable, iii. 354

FATHER (*Contd.*)
Postdiluvian humanity, of, iv. 180
Sevekh, form of the first, v. 203
Shadow inferior to his, iii. 105
Son, and, i. 155, 267, 275, 300; iii. 234, 239; iv. 60; v. 351, 499
Son becoming his own, ii. 114
Son identical with his, ii. 194; v. 81
Son of the, ii. 96, 193; iii. 55; v. 368
Son of the unmanifested, iii. 311
Sound, of the, v. 442
Sun the, i. 275; iv. 30, 110; v. 310
Vishvakarman, of the Gods, iii. 110; v. 270
Voice of the, i. 327
Water, of, iii. 114
Wisdom, the, v. 438
World, of the, iii. 70
Yellow, iii. 30
Yarab, father of Arabians, v. 197
Yod-Heva, of, iii. 136
Zeus, the, of mankind, iii. 130, 412; iv. 154
FATHERHOOD, v. 204
FATHERLESS, Minerva the, iv. 174
FATHER-MOTHER, Aether the, i. 78, 142
Akāsha or, i. 83
Breath of, i. 200
Darkness is, i. 113, 130
Deep or, iii. 239
Dhyāni from the bright, iii. 28, 65
Emanation of, iii. 55
Germ furnished by, iii. 140
Gods, of, i. 136; ii. 24; v. 381
Gods sleep in the bosom of, i. 169
Mother became, before, i. 141
Noon called, ii. 24
Oeaohoo or, i. 136
Primordial æther, identical with, i. 142
Primordial, proceed from, i. 152
Seven, iv. 165
Soul, differentiated world's, i. 196
Space is called, i. 83
Svabhāvat identified with, i. 160
Web, spin a, i. 148
Yliaster is, i. 325
FATHER-MOTHER-ADITI, ii. 69
FATHER-MOTHER-ÆTHER, ii. 287
FATHER-MOTHER-SON, i. 83, 113, 114, 128, 129; ii. 154, 340; iv. 153
FATHER-RAY the Protogonos, iv. 164
FATHER-SON-HUSBAND, ii. 348
FATHER-SOUL of the Adepts, ii. 296
FATHER-SUN, Breath of the, ii. 118
FATHER-TREE in the Qu'rān, Mystical, iv. 188
FATHERS, Astral doubles of the, iii. 124
Australian savages descended from human, iii. 198
Barhishad, iii. 110
Beings, of various, iii. 261
Boneless, iii. 29, 99
Christian, i. 62, 140; iv. 120; v. 59, 266, 280, 304
Church, of the, i. 61, 65, 246; ii. 64, 65, 99, 183; iii. 105, 107; iv. 108, 140; v. 33, 71, 96, 149, 159, 167, 266, 307, 308, 313, 326, 327, 336, 566
Concrete forms of formless, ii. 296
Earth, of our, iii. 36

Elohim, seven, v. 203
Failure of, i. 245
Fire of, iii. 29, 110
Form to the Breath, gave, iii. 29, 110
Formless, ii. 296
Gods, of our, are our devils, iii. 44
Holy, iii. 31, 179, 180
Human monad, gave form to, iii. 113
Human race fashioned by, iv. 177
Kriyāshakti, born by the power of, iii. 180
Lunar, iii. 124
Manus, or, v. 201, 202
Messengers of the Sacred, i. 153
Mind-born progeny of, ii. 175
Model, of the, ii. 176
Mother (Earth) on, iii. 399
Partiarchs or, v. 201, 202
Pitris or, iii. 46, 56, 57, 97, 100, 183, 324, 357, 419; v. 201, 202
Prajāpatis are, v. 203
Progenitors or, iii. 97; v. 263
Rule of the, iii. 27
Sadik or Melchizedek, iii. 390
Self-born, were, iii. 129
Sweat-born, of second race, iii. 126
Three, from Three Mothers, v. 211
Wisdom, of, iii. 393
FAUNA, Ages, of bygone, ii. 67
Alternations of, iii. 325
Amphibian reptilian, iv. 254
Astral relics of, iv. 298
Atlantic island, iv. 351, 360
Australian archaic, iii. 202
Continent, of a former, iv. 357
Descendants of, iii. 192
Dwindling of, iv. 302
Europe, of, iv. 310
Flora and, iii. 278
Fossil mammalian, iv. 304
Fourth round mammalian, iv. 254
Globe, of the, iii. 64
Hermaphroditism of old, iii. 127
Intermediate types, iv. 237
Islands, of Atlantic, iv. 360
Migrations of, iv. 361
Pre-human, iv. 303
Similarity of living, iii. 177
FAYE, quoted, i. 219; ii. 219, 312, 323
FEAR; and Hatred, v. 514
FEATHRED tribe, Garuda king of the, iii. 256
Jatāyu king of the, iv. 141
FECUNDATION, Occult connection of moon with i. 307
FELIX, Father, quoted, ii. 395
FELLOW-GLOBES, Earth, of, i. 213; ii. 338
Moon, of, i. 210
Planets, of, i. 207
FEMALE, Abel symbol of first, iii. 275
Abel or Habel is, iii. 136
Adam-Kadmon male and, iii. 121
Aeons, iv. 139
Angle, iv. 167
Anu, and material, iii. 72
Anubis, busts at feet of, ii. 127
Ark and, generative principle, iii. 147
Axieros, aspect of, iii. 361
Beings in, form, iii. 286

FEMALE (*Contd.*)
  Binah is, v. 192, 214
  Binary or chaos, iv. 125
  Daksha converts half of himself into a, iii. 277
  Deity, Shakti personified as, v. 378
  Deities, i. 72
  Demons, iv. 185
  Double of, Gods, ii. 343
  Epinoia is, manifestation, v. 462
  Force, iii. 37
  Form, of Tetrad, ii. 66
  Form, of Deity, v. 211
  Generative principle, iii. 76, 147; iv. 28
  Genius, iv. 181
  Holy Ghost is, v. 189, 211, 470
  Jehovah, aspect of, ii. 343; iii. 72; iv. 31, 155
  Jupiter has, breasts, iii. 143
  Life and Jah-Hovah, iii. 134
  Logos, ii. 149; v. 291
  Male and, i. 114, 291, 292; iii. 43, 293; iv. 112, 134, 164, 193
  Noah, iv. 30
  Number, iv. 172
  One becomes male and, iii. 293; iv. 193
  Ovary, organ of, iv. 229
  Passive element, or, iii. 139
  Principles, iii. 361
  Procreative power, side of, iii. 54
  Providence, ii. 359
  Race, iii. 416
  Sea-dragon, iii. 71
  Seeds, iii. 48
  Sephira as, ii. 69
  Shekinah is, v. 189
  Symbol of, element, iv. 171
  Symbol of Mother of the Gods, iv. 31
  Trinity, v. 211
  Vertical line expresses male and, iii. 43
  Water gaseous, iii. 75
FEMALE PRINCIPLE, Abel, v. 291
  All things exist through male, and, iv. 97
  Ark or, iii. 147; iv. 283
  Deep or abyss, the, iii. 112
  Gross matter passive, ii. 249
  Holy Ghost a, ii. 67
  Matter or, iv. 127
  Root nature in, i. 114
  Sarcophagus symbol of, iv. 30
  Symbol of, iii. 43; iv. 30
FEMININE, Base number, iv. 131
  Divinity of the Waters, v. 212
  Earth is, v. 293
  Element, iii. 65
  Elohim is, plural, v. 211
  Generation, principle in, ii. 114
  Lotus, symbol, iv. 40
  Masculine of, form, the, iv. 172
  Number, iii. 220
  Number of generation, iv. 153
  Phenomena, ii. 105
  Principle, ii. 79, 178; iii. 313; iv. 37
  Sun as, ii. 112
  Symbol, iv. 40, 123
  Water principle, ii. 178
  YaH said to be, ii. 343
FERGUSSON, James, quoted, iii. 221; iv. 315
FERHO, Mano dwells with the greatest, i. 245

FERIDAN, one of the Persian heroes, iii. 397
FERMENTATION, Phenomena attending, i. 294
FERMENTS, Destruction caused by, i. 307
  Formation of, i. 294
FERN, Forests, iv. 282
  Period, iv. 166
FERNEY, Invalid of, iv. 311
FERNS, Gigantic, iii. 278; iv. 295
FEROUER, Ahura Mazda, of, iv. 46
  Christ, of, iv. 47, 49
  Fravashi, or, iv. 48
  Meaning of the word, i. 281
  Ormuzd of, v. 315
FEROUERS, Dual entities or, i. 281; v. 94, 314, 375
FERREL, referred to, iii. 74
FERRIER, referred to, i. 183
FESTIVAL, Dead, of the, v. 116
  Earth, day of the, ii. 124
  Egyptians', i. 275
  Fires, of the, i. 252
  Sabasia a sacred, iii. 417
FESTIVALS, Mother of God, of the one, ii. 115
  New moon, iv. 30
  Zodiac and Indian religions, ii. 384
FETAHIL, i. 245, 293; iii. 241
FETICHISM, Cosmolatry never a, ii. 181
FEUD between Initiates, iv. 62
FEVERS, Duration of, iv. 167
FIAT LUX, i. 263, 291, 303; ii. 203; iii. 241
FIAT LUX EX NILIHO, iv. 234
FICHTE, quoted, i. 122, 145, 323
FICIN, Marcellus, quoted, iv. 173
FIDELITY of the Hindu records, ii. 386
FIEND, Archangel and, i. 281
  Man has begotten the, iii. 276
FIENDS, Bhūtas or, iii. 170
  Catholics and Protestants, of, ii. 337
  Gods became, iii. 240
  Monkey-coloured, iii. 110
FIERCENESS of Rudra's progeny, iv. 185
FIFTH, Adam, iv. 25
  Book of the Commentaries, quoted, iii. 180
  Continent, iii. 47
  Element advocated by Science, i. 78
FIFTH PRINCIPLE, i. 334; ii. 47; iii. 97, 131, 244, 318; iv. 150, 186, 310, 329
FIFTH RACE, v. 91, 106, 261, 263, 268, 300, 418
  Apes and, iv. 258
  Aryan, i. 173; ii. 369; iii. 205, 268, 439; iv. 102; v. 261, 268
  Aryan adepts of the nascent, iii. 383
  Budha, under, iii. 42
  Buddhas of, iii. 421
  Chinese one of the oldest nations of, iii. 364
  Commentary twenty on, iii. 301
  Continents of, iii. 442
  Cosmogonies of, ii. 60
  Cradle of, iii. 422
  Creator of, iv. 23
  Deluges of barbarians in, iv. 312
  Destruction of, v. 267
  Divine instructors of, iii. 204, 349
  Earliest nations of, iii. 364; iv. 24
  Enoch, and, v. 106

FIFTH RACE (*Contd.*)
Fallen deeply into matter, v. 265
Flood, saved from, iii. 309
Forefathers of, ii. 333
Genealogical tree of, iii. 432
Genesis on birth of, iv. 275
Giant tribes of, iii. 295
History of, iii. 266, 435
Humanity, iv. 267, 293
Infancy of, iii. 349
Inheritors of Rishis, v. 91
Initiates of, iv. 177
Instructors, of, iii. 352, 358, 364
Isles of, iii. 441
Karma of, iii. 303
Kings of, v. 263
Krishna belongs to, iii. 148
Language of, iii. 205
Legends of, iii. 435
Mankinds before, iv. 278
Middle point of, iii. 191
Nascent, iii. 383
Nebo or Noah a creator of, iv. 23, 169
Noah belonged to, iv. 102; v. 106
Priests of, v. 261
Primitive types of, iv. 38
Progenitors of, iii. 393
Religious mysteries of, iii. 133
Rishis of, iv. 177
Rudra Shiva patron of, iv. 70
Rūpas for, iii. 67
Sages of, iii. 358
Seed race of, the, iv. 169
Serpent Instructors of the, iii. 354
Sorcery, of, iv. 71
Souls of, v. 300
Sub-races of, i. 72
Symbols during, ii. 99
Tenets of, v. 268
Types of, iv. 38
Unexplored regions of, ii. 122
White head or, iv. 275
Wise men of, i. 316
Worship of early, iv. 329
Yellow-faced nations of, iii. 426
FIFTH ROUND, v. 532
Apes in, iii. 265
Ether in, i. 301
Field of resurrection for, iii. 109
Human forms in, i. 236
Manas in, iii. 175, 302
Pitris, ourselves in, v. 532
FIFTH ROUNDERS, i. 215; iii. 175
FIGHTERS, the seven, i. 161
FIGURES, Arabic, iv. 124
Atlanteans gave us, for our cycles, iii. 61
Birth of the globes, relating to, i. 223
Brāhmanical, iii. 78, 80, 162
Confucius, of, ii. 158
Cycles of, the, i. 222; iii. 61; v. 336, 337 339, 340 to 348
Esoteric systems, key to, i. 218
Expression of thought, used as, ii. 33
Geometrical, ii. 148, 337, 353; iv. 146; v. 87, 111, 114, 116, 117, 162, 191, 453, 455
Glyphs, are, i. 134; v. 115
Hindu, iv. 191; v. 336, 340 to 348

India, accepted throughout, iii. 80
Kabalistic, v. 87, 114
Letters and, v. 114, 119
Logos, and, ii. 148
Magical, i. 161; v. 114, 118, 122
Mathematical point to solid, from, ii. 341
Occult calculations of, i. 224
Perfect, iii. 48; v. 117
Primitive, v. 109
Pythagorean, ii. 338; v. 113, 116
Quaternary, and, v. 117
Science, of, iii. 83
Secret, iii. 253
Six-pointed star, in, iv. 102
Triangle, first of, ii. 341; iv. 146; v. 116, 117
Vital, iv. 122
FIJI, Australia and, iii. 21
Viti or, iii. 227
FILAMENTOID, Infusoria, iii. 159
Primeval humanity, iii. 159
FILIA VOCIS, Bath Kol, the, ii. 149
FILIOQUE dogma, the, iv. 207
FILIPPI, Hypothesis of genesis evolved by, iv. 216
FINAL Cause, ii. 224, 293.
FINDS, Future, iii. 334
FINGERS, Idei Dactyli or Ideic, iii. 360
FINLAND, Epic poem of, iii. 39, 130
FINMARK, Ice age in the, iii. 81
FINNS offshoot of Chinamen, iii. 185
FIRE, Aerial, ii. 190
Æther, is, i. 151; v. 562
Agni, and, ii. 54; iii. 380, 412; iv. 135, 150, 184; v. 479
Air, and, ii. 88; iii. 122
Akashic, v. 482
Al-ait or Al-Orit God of, iii. 150, 360
Angels, iii. 245
Apāna and, iv. 139
Astral, i. 148
Atoms, i. 302
Aura of granite, is v. 562
Baptism by, v. 323
Black, of *Zohar*, iii. 169
Blood gives, v. 562
Breath of, i. 148, 149
Cause of manifestation, v. 445
Celestial Gods, of the, iii. 215
Circles, ii. 134; iii. 112, 235, 277
Cold, i. 294; ii. 323
Cosmic genius of, iv. 95
Creative, i. 250; iii. 110, 272, 412; iv. 95
Crocodile personified, iv. 149
Death gives, v. 562
Definition of, i. 179
Deity, an arcane, i. 70
Devas, iii. 248
Development of, i. 297
Dhyānis, iii. 100
Discovered, never, iv. 93
Divine, i. 228, 263; iii. 17; v. 451, 452, 562
Divinity, active side of, v. 445, 452, 462
Druids, of the, iv. 267
Dual, v. 445
Earth, in, iii. 110; iv. 88, 326
Element of, i. 303, 326; ii. 88, 152; iv. 120, 187
Elementals, iii. 425; v. 562

FIRE (*Contd.*)
Enchanter, iii. 123
Esoteric teaching as to, i. 180
Essence of, i. 73
Ether of, ii. 166
Ethereal, ii. 190
Fathers, of, iii. 29
First race had no, iii. 122
Flame and, i. 73; v. 445
Fluidic, iii. 122
Fohat makes balls of, i. 200
Formless, i. 151
Future, that gives knowledge of, ii. 52
Gandharva personifies, iv. 157
Genii of, iii. 362
God, Agni the, iii. 380, 412; iv. 135, 150, 184
God of, ii. 118, 183; iii. 150, 239, 282, 360; iv. 57, 118
Goddess, Mithra, iii. 139
Gods, ii. 184; iii. 46, 284; iv. 94
Great, iii. 30
Heat and, i. 137; v. 562
Human race sprung from, iv. 177
Ierna, of, v. 267
Incorporeal, iv. 173
Intelligence is, i. 143
Invention of, iii. 362
Inventors discovered, iii. 372
Invisible, i. 151
IT spirit of, i. 73
Kabalistic significance of, v. 166
Kabirim and, iii. 362
Kārtikeya, generated in, iv. 190
Kosmic, v. 446, 447, 462
Kriyāshakti of life, is, v. 562
Kundalini, of, v. 554
Land of, iii. 423, 425
Life, or, ii. 351
Light of the nature of, iv. 80
Light and, i. 228, 298; iv. 205
Light-giver, and, iii. 412; v. 562
Lives, i. 303
Living, i. 245; ii. 52
Lord of the Shining Face, from, iii. 27, 49, 56
Magnetic, iii. 311
Male principle, the, i. 127
Manas, of, v. 482, 517
Manifested cosmos, of, i. 151
Metal and, iii. 425
Mist, i. 141, 150, 196, 250, 255, 302, 314; ii. 172, 266, 308, 324; iii. 161, 319; v. 270
Monad a divine, i. 228
Moses's shining face is, v. 562
Motion and, i. 137
Mundane, iii. 139
Nature, and, iii. 269
Objective side of, v. 446
Old Testament, in, v. 562
One, alone is, i. 294
One element, the, i. 163; v. 562
One Life, the, v. 447
Osiris personified, iv. 154; v. 234
Passions, of the, iii. 107, 108; v. 543
Pervades all elements, v. 543
Philosophers, i. 146
Phoroneus, bringer of, iv. 88

Pillar of, v. 562
Pitris, of, iii. 68
Powers, iii. 123; v. 212
Prana, and, iv. 139
Priests, iv. 67
Primitive, iii. 123
Primordial, i. 298
Principle, iv. 163
Procreative properties of, v. 234
Producer, iii. 247
Production recombined a, i. 198
Prometheus of, i. 245; iii. 240, 410, 411; iv. 92; v. 203, 233
Pueblos adore, iii. 188
Pyramid, First Syllable means, v. 117
Pyramidal, is, iv. 166
Quaternary of matter, one of, iv. 171
Race that could live in, iii. 224
Radicals, head of the, iv. 139
Reflector, as, v. 562
River of, v. 212
Rotatory friction, by, iv. 93
Rudra God of, iii. 282; iv. 118
Sacred, ii. 52; iii. 87, 90, 179; v. 203, 323, 520
Sacred science, symbol of, iv. 63
Sacredness of, ii. 245
Science, and, ii. 245
Sea of, i. 138
Second round, in, i. 295
Second World born of, v. 447
Secret side of, v. 445
Self, means the, iv. 138, 209
Seven circles of, iii. 235, 277
Shiva, principle of, iv. 163
Solar, ii. 251; iii. 29, 113
Sons of, i. 150, 151; ii. 156; iii. 362; v. 445
Sound and, iv. 205
Spirit of, ii. 177, 216; iii. 239, 269; iv. 57, 136
Spirit of Deity represented by, i. 127
Spirit of God, latent in, iv. 163
Spirits, visible garb of, ii. 181
Sun or, of life, ii. 216, 315; iii. 115; iv. 157; v. 323
Symbol of Divine Nature, v. 446
Terrestrial, i. 332; ii. 190; iv. 90
Theft of creative, iii. 272
Third, iii. 68
Third Æons and, v. 450
Time, and, i. 151
Triangle, figure of, iv. 166
Universal, v. 562
Triangles, possession of, iii. 88
Vaishvānara, iii. 311; iv. 64, 138
Water, and, i. 137; ii. 24, 54, 94, 117, 192; iii. 75, 115, 118, 121; iv. 294, 345
Wisdom, of, iv. 137
FIRE, BORN, Agnibhū or, iii. 381; v. 213
FIRE-PHILOSOPHERS, v. 106, 543
FIRE-SEED of the Father, ii. 266
FIRE-SELF, name of the, iv. 140
FIRE-TEMPLE of Azareksh, iii. 19
FIRE-WORSHIP, i. 179; iii. 323, 360, 395
FIRE-WORSHIPPERS, Pārsis, i. 180
Persian, iii. 362
Titans said to be, iii. 150
FIRE-YAZATAS of the *Avesta*, iii. 399
FIRELESS Progenitors of man, iii. 89

FIRES, Ark saved in, iv. 181
  Celestial, iv. 90
  Commentary on, iv. 134
  Correlative forces and, iii. 115
  Dhyān Chohans, of, iii. 117
  Druids, of, iv. 329
  Festival of, i. 252
  Flames or, iii. 68, 74, 95
  Forty-nine, i. 332; iii. 361, 362; iv. 90, 134; v. 477, 517
  Four, v. 477
  Land destroyed by inner, iii. 33, 331
  Latent, iii. 269
  Lemuria destroyed by, iv. 332
  Lords of, iii. 425
  Mithra, of, iv. 175
  Occult teaching on, i. 151
  Philosophical, iv. 163
  Rudras and, ii. 179; iii. 95
  Sacred, iv. 329
  Secret of, iii. 114
  Seven, iv. 90, 134
  Sparks, with the, iii. 28, 74, 92
  Spirit, represent, iii. 74
  Submarine, iv. 332
  Three, iii. 249; iv. 134, 163
  Vital, iii. 269
  Yima's reign, during, iv. 181
FIRMAMENT, Air or, i. 298
  Elohim, decreed by, ii. 166
  God of the, i. 251
  Heaven, the, iii. 84
  Indra, the, iii. 381; iv. 185
  Stars of, ii. 380
  Stellar and nebular, ii. 323
  Waters, in the midst of, ii. 61; iii. 85
FIRMAMENTS, Deva-Loka, i. 189
  Millions of, ii. 329
FIRST CAUSE, Impersonal, v. 187, 455
FIRST KRISHNA, Mysteries of, v. 97
FIRST LOGOS, v. 476
FIRST RACE, Appearance of, iv. 345
  Astral figures of, iii. 304
  Chhāyās, formed from, iii. 145; iv. 102
  Colour, had no, iii. 251
  Continent of, iii. 19, 399; iv. 177
  Creation of, iii. 95, 181
  Cycle between, and the second, iii. 182
  Divine Pitris of, iii. 393
  Elements, had three, iii. 122
  Enos, the, iii. 134
  Esoteric text and, v. 102
  Eternal central land of, iii. 399
  Ethereal without, iii. 300
  Evolution of, iii. 103, 328
  First Round and, i. 239
  Form of, iii. 251
  Fourth Round of, i. 239
  Human, v. 291
  Images, were, iii. 124
  Imperfect, was, iii. 16
  Kandu stands for, iii. 182
  Man of, iii. 245
  Mind-born sons were, ii. 330
  Mindless, iii. 315
  Occult science on, iii. 300
  Old Book, in the, iii. 250

  Oozed out, iii. 181
  Prototypes of, ii. 175
  Second, and, iii. 94, 140
  Self-born, or, iii. 171
  Sense of Touch, v. 523
  Shells of, iii. 304
  Sons of the fifth Adam and, iv. 25
  Sons of Yoga were, iii. 117
  Speechless, was, iii. 203
  Spiritual within, iii. 300
  Sun, and, iii. 30, 37, 42
  Sweat-born from the, iii. 172
  Truths of God and, v. 69
  Type, had no, iii. 251
FIRST ROOT RACE, iv. 254, 283; v. 102, 523
FIRST ROUND, Earth in, i. 302
  Element in, i. 295
  Ethereal men during, i. 297
  Evolution in, iii. 78
  First race, and, i. 239
  Generally treated of, i. 214
  Globe A in, i. 225, 233; iii. 154
  Globe in, i. 303
  Lunar Pitris in, i. 227
  Mineral, vegetable and animal in, iii. 187
  Monad in, human, iv. 206
  Monads on Globe A of, i. 225
  Primordial men of, ii. 91
  Races of, iii. 308
  STANZA on, iii. 58
FISH, Avatāra, ii. 85, 100; iii. 308
  Branchiæ, iv. 254
  Ea the sublime, iv. 63
  Fiery, i. 160
  Giant, iii. 32, 206
  Horus, of the great, i. 267; iv. 148
  Intelligent, iii. 39
  Life, of, i. 160
  Man-, iii. 64; v. 163
  Meanings of, iii. 314
  Nun, in Chaldee is, ii. 109
  Pisces, the, ii. 379
  Sin and Soma, i. 283, 307
  Symbol of, v. 162, 163
  Southern, ii. 388
  Vaivasvata and, iii. 147
  Vishnu, and, iii. 308, 313
FISH-MAN or Oan of Nineveh, ii. 380
FISHES, Ages of, i. 297
  Androgynous forms still found in, iii. 127
  Bodies of, men with, iii. 28
  Christian symbol, v. 163
  Creatures in world of, iii. 369
  Dogs with tails of, iii. 65
  First trace of, iv. 281
  Lhas fought men with, bodies, iii. 74
  Physical man, preceded, iv. 166
  Septenary law, and the, iv. 193
  Two Zodiacal, v. 142
  Three, in triangle, v. 163
  Third Round, resultant of, iv. 254
FISKE, Prof. John, referred to, iv. 250
FISSIPAROUS act of reproduction, iii. 141
FITTEST, Survival of the, i. 320; iii. 300, 309, 329; iv. 43, 218
FITZEDWARD HALL, see Book Index

FIVE, sacred Pythagorean number, v. 163
  World represented by number, v. 117
FIVE BREATHS, v. 477, 479, 486
FIVE-FACED, Rudra Shiva, iv. 70
  Shiva, Panchānana or, iv. 150
FIVEFOLD, Chohans, iv. 149
  Lha, i. 283
  Nature, iv. 156
  World, iii. 170
FIVE-POINTED Star, the, i. 266; iv. 148
FIVE-SIDED sign or pentagon, iv. 149
FIVE WORDS of Brahmā, iv. 152
FIXED STARS, ii. 255; v. 222
FLAGÆ of Paracelsus, i. 268
FLAME, Brahmā, of the wrath of, iii. 114
  Dark, iii. 237
  Divine, v. 351, 447, 496
  Divine Entity or, v. 351
  Ego, Higher of the, v. 591
  Eternal Motion, is, v. 277
  Essence of fire, i. 73
  Fire and, i. 73, 150, 180; ii. 296
  Heat or, i. 73
  Light is cold, i. 146; ii. 323
  Lord of, iv. 55
  Lords of, iii. 31, 85, 86
  Lowest part of Æther, v. 562
  Monads, and the, v. 357
  One, the, v. 361, 362
  Pan, on altar of, ii. 52
  Phoroneus, on altar of, iv. 88
  Primordial, i. 152
  Primordial matter, and, i. 160
  Sacrificial, iv. 93
  Shiva, of, iv. 163
  Sons of, iii. 284; v. 260
  Sons of Fire and, v. 445
  Soul of things, the, i. 147
  Space one, ii. 88
  Spark and, i. 283, 284, 309
  Spirit of, i. 143; ii. 177, 351
  Subtle truth the, iv. 137
  Three tongued, i. 282
  Three-wicked, i. 282
  Time, of, ii. 86
  Universal divine, i. 318
  Uræus of, i. 274
  Wisdom, of, iii. 410; v. 300
FLAMES, Agnishvātta, or, iii. 89
  Aurora Borealis, of the, iv. 200
  Battle of, i. 251
  Black, ii. 161
  Celestial Hierarchy more brilliant than,
    v. 212
  Divine, i. 261, 318
  Evanescent, are, iii. 68
  Fires, and, iii. 92, 95
  Hierarchies of, i. 151
  Hierarchy of spirits, a, iii. 74
  Hot, i. 294
  Infernal regions, of the, iii. 107
  Lights and, i. 303
  Mahat, born of, iii. 235
  Man needs four, iii. 67
  Periodical, iii. 68
  Powers, and, ii. 158
  Prajāpatis, etc., or, iii. 250

Pure, iii. 318
Region of, i. 283
Rudras and, iii. 95
Sacred animals, and, ii. 160
Seven, v. 351
Solar, ii. 254
Spark projected by, iii. 318
Sparks and, ii. 160; iii. 92
Spirits or, iii. 74
STANZAS on, i. 152; iii. 28, 74; iv. 85
Surtur's, iii. 108
FLAMING fires, Monads called, ii. 357
  Messengers, Advent of, ii. 370
  Sword or animal passions, iii. 73
FLAMMA, iii. 122
  Durissima, iii. 123
  Virgo, Virgin oil or, iii. 123
FLAMMARION, Camille, see Book Index
FLASHES from the Monads, ii. 358
FLAT-HEADED Australian natives, iv. 231
FLAVIUS, Pope, v. 157
FLESH, Crucifixion of man of, iv. 131
  Dragon of, v. 491
  Flesh of, iv. 241
  Generation of, i. 172
  Our, is not there, iii. 28, 67
  Sixth Race and bonds of, iii. 443
  Sons of, iv. 38
  Spirit, conquers, iv. 186
  Word made, i. 171; v. 76, 230, 475
FLINT, Implements, iv. 308
  Psychic natures in, ii. 332, 333
  Relics, iv. 248, 257
  Sparks from, iii. 107
FLINTS, Abbé Bourgeois's, iv. 292
  Carved, iv. 320
  Jordan valley, in, iv. 324
  Magical properties of, iii. 341
  Miocene strata, in, iv. 245, 309
  Science on, iv. 321
  Thenay, of, iv. 309, 318
FLOCK of stars and solar rays, iii. 41
FLOOD, Allegorical, ii. 113
  Allegories, of, iii. 314
  Antediluvian giants and, ii. 54
  Asia, in, iii. 332
  Atlantis, of, iv. 179
  Belgium, which covered, iv. 313
  Cainites and, v. 62
  Cosmic, iii. 147, 310, 352
  Cross and circle earlier than, iv. 115
  Deucalion, of, iv. 88
  Duration of, ii. 105
  Dvīpas destroyed by, iii. 405
  Escape from, v. 109
  Esoteric meaning of, ii. 1 1
  Fourth race, of, ii. 162
  Great, ii. 54; iii. 147, 152, 330, 332; v. 91
  Great Atlantic, iii. 352
  Great Dragon, or, iv. 354
  Jews, of, ii. 113
  Legends, iii. 390
  Matter on earth, of, iii. 154
  Mazdean symbolism for, iv. 181
  M'bul water of, ii. 100
  Noah, of, ii. 85; iii. 149; iv. 34
  Old Dragon, and, iii. 351

FLOOD (*Contd.*)
Pralaya, called, v. 345
Pre-astronomical cosmic, iii. 352
Rota of Enoch and, v. 109
Slavonian mythology of, iii. 272
Stories of, iii. 226
Third race, of, iii. 330
Titans connected with, iii. 150
Universal, not, v. 109
Waters (matter), of, iii. 152
Waters of, ii. 179; iii. 153
FLOODS, Divining the coming, iii. 427
Records of, iii. 332
Successive, iii. 157
FLOORS, Ocean, iii. 314, 323
FLORA, Archaic, iii. 202
Atlantic islands', iii. 322
Australian, iii. 202; iv. 352, 357
Change in, iii. 64
Continent of a former, iv. 357
Dwindling of, iii. 278
Eastern Asia, of, iv. 350
Europe, of, iv. 352, 358
Fauna, and, iii. 278; iv. 302
Miocene, iv. 352
Pre-human, iv. 303
Rocky Mountains, east of, iv. 358
South America, of, iv. 351
Tertiary, iv. 295
United States, of, iv. 350, 352, 358
FLORENCE built on defunct Etruscan cities, iii. 224
FLORIDA Audubon's lily in, iii. 438
Forest trees of, iv. 358
FLOTILLAS, Third race built, iii. 398
FLOWER, Buddha, of, iv. 117
Evolution of a, iv. 223
Lotus, ii. 96; iv. 117
Power, of, iii. 422
Root and, i. 332
FLOWER, Prof. W. H., quoted, iii. 176, 201; iv. 38
FLUDD, Robert, quoted, i. 137; v. 164
FLUID, Ambient and all-penetrating, i. 299
Amniotic, v. 422, 423, 449
Astral, i. 147; ii. 248; iii. 194
Auric, v. 533
Cosmic Kundalini is Electric, v. 484
Electricity a, ii. 233
Ethereal, of Leibnitz, ii. 348, 351
Fohat electric vital, i. 171; ii. 216
Heat, theory of, ii. 240
Kant's primitive, ii. 348
Leibnitz's ethereal, ii. 348, 351
Magnetists, of the, ii. 52
Primitive, ii. 303, 348
Primordial, i. 298
Red blood cells are, v. 553
Solar atmospheric, ii. 226
Vital, i. 171; ii. 216
FLUIDIC fire or air, iii. 122
State, v. 477
FLUIDS, Gaseous, i. 304
Imponderable, ii. 253
Various kinds of, ii. 240
FLUORINE, ii. 274, 308
FLUTE, Pan's seven-piped, iv. 153

FLUTTER of renascent life, the first, ii. 359
FLYING, Camel, iii. 209
Dragon, iii. 210, 385; iv. 247
FOCUS, Cosmic, i. 77
Energy, of Creative, ii. 276
Light, of, iii. 283
Pleiades, of our universe, iv. 121
Powers, of, i. 331
Sun merely, ii. 304
FOETUS, Animal-like, iii. 104
Conception of, iii. 181
Correspondence to, v. 422, 449
Development of a, i. 269; v. 472
Digestion in, iii. 140
Embryo and, iii. 194; v. 422
Gill-clefts in human, iv. 254
Growth of, iii. 184; iv. 255
Matrix in, i. 304; v. 78
Period of the quickening of, ii. 105
Rudimentary tail in, iii. 193
Third race, in, iii. 140
Toe in, great, iv. 236
Transformations of human, i. 235
FOETUS-LIKE state of principles in animals, iii. 257
FOHAT, v. 528
Abodes of, i. 253
Action of, ii. 250; iv. 176
Activity of, iv. 159
Æther, son of, iii. 399
Akāsha and, i. 142, 170; iii. 399
Aliases of, ii. 398
Animal soul of nature, the, i. 171
Apām-Nāpat, named, iii. 399
Apāp, conquers serpent, ii. 399
Ares or, i. 326
Astronomers, unacceptable to, ii. 315
Atman, is. i. 170
Atoms acted on by, i. 170
Atoms, hardens, i. 150
Atoms, scatters, i. 150
Atoms, shaped by, i. 171
Avesta on, iii. 399
Balls of fire made by, i. 200
Brahmā, sprung from head of, i. 201
Brain of the father, sprung from, i. 201
Breath of their progeny, the, i. 193
Bridge, i. 81
Brothers of, i. 142, 201; ii. 278
Buddhist books, in, i. 194
Buddhist esotericist, of, i. 170
Builder of the builders, or, i. 195
Central sun and, i. 250
Centres of, ii. 281
Circle, crosses the, iv. 157
Cohesion and, v. 484
Collective, i. 199
Comet and, i. 250; iii. 329
Conscious force, is, i. 199
Constructive force, is, i. 201
Container of force, the, i. 171
Cosmic atoms set in motion by, ii. 397
Cosmic consciousness, acts on, ii. 41
Cosmic electricity, is, i. 142, 150, 201
Cosmic energy and, ii. 41
Cosmic evolution, and, i. 170
Cosmic force acted on by, i. 171

FOHAT (*Contd.*)
Cosmic ideation and, i. 81, 171
Cosmic matter, gathers, i. 149; ii. 397
Cosmic plane, on, i. 195
Cosmic substance and, i. 81
Cosmic world and, i. 169
Cosmogony, in, i. 169
Creative power of, i. 169
Crown of, i. 177
Curds turned by, ii. 397
Definition of, i. 195
Dhyān Chohanic energy, or, iv. 219
Dhyān Chohans, and, i. 81, 132
Divine Energy, v. 209
Divine light or, ii. 326
Divine love, as, i. 178
Divine son, and, i. 169
Divine thought and, i. 81
Dynamic energy, is, i. 81
Dzyu becomes, i. 168
Egypt, in, ii. 398
Electric power, or, i. 169
Electric vital power, or, i. 69
Electricity, is, i. 171, 201; v. 484
Elemental atoms acting on, i. 170
Emanation of, i. 195
Entity, an, i. 171
Eros, prototype of, i. 169, 178; iii. 76
Esoteric cosmogony, in, i. 169
Etheric centres of, ii. 281
Everywhere, v. 528
Fiery dust and, i. 200
Fiery sons of, i. 253
Fire-yazatas, and, iii. 399
Five strides of, i. 168, 180, 181
Force, is constructive, i. 201
Force of, propelling, i. 169
Force personifies, i. 195
Forces acted on by, i. 171; v. 528
Forces conscious and intelligent, i. 199
Fourth principle, the, i. 171
Functions of, i. 195
Great one of the seven magic forces, the,
     ii. 399
Great power, the, iii. 76
Guide, the, i. 81, 202; ii. 216
Guiding spirit, the, i. 81, 196
Heat and, v. 484
Hexagon, symbolized by, i. 263
Hisses as he glides, i. 143
Human ideation and, i. 171
Ideas in the divine thought and, i. 81
Ideation, messenger of, i. 171
Impulse of, i. 147
Indra, aspect of, ii. 398
Inert substance, action on, ii. 41
Intelligence, energizing and guiding, ii. 216
Intelligence of, i. 150; iii. 329
Intelligent force, is, i. 199
Ishvara, or, i. 194
Kama-Manas and, v. 528
Kosmic plane and, v. 528
Kundalini and, v. 484
Laya centres, produces seven, i. 203
Life, or, i. 283; ii. 250
Life-electricity, is, iii. 76
Life-giving, spirit of, iii. 95

Light of the Logos, is, iii. 399
Light or, i. 195; ii. 326; v. 484
Logos and, i. 170, 194; iii. 399
Magnetism and, v. 484
Manifestations of, i. 81, 195
Manufacturer, the, i. 171
Manus' errands, runs, i. 132
Matter and mind, link between, i. 81, 150
Matter, and primordial, i. 147, 150
Matter conquers, ii. 399
Matter moved by, i. 203; ii. 397
Matter to spirit, links, i. 81
Meanings of, several, i. 195
Messengers and, i. 196
Nature of, i. 150
Nebulae and, i. 149
Nerve force and, v. 484
Neutral centres of, i. 203
Occult power of, i. 169
Occultists and, i. 81, 170, 199; ii. 216, 281
One and seven, is, i. 195
One element, acts upon the, i. 170; iv. 176
ONE LIFE, related to, i. 170
Osiris, see OSIRIS
Personal God, not a, i. 196
Personification of, ii. 397
Personified elctric vital power, i. 170
Pervader, the, i. 171
Phenomenal world, in, i. 169
Power, electric, i. 169, 170
Power of, occult, i. 169
Power potential creative, i. 169
Power, the active, i. 169
Power vital, i. 170
Powers, an emanation of, i. 196
Powers of, i. 195
Pramatih son of, iii. 412
Primordial dust, collects, i. 250
Primordial matter and, i. 147, 150
Primordial seven, vehicle of, i. 168
Principles, guides transfer of, i. 202
Products of the breath, scatters, i. 199
Prototype of Eros, i. 178; iii. 76
Realm of fourth son of, ii. 286
Science and, i. 250
Seed turned by, ii. 397
Septenary chain and, i. 195
Septenary condition of, i. 195
Serpent symbol of, i. 143
Seven eternities, acts through, i. 200
Seven sons of, i. 201, 268; ii. 278
Seven strides of, i. 171
Shaktis, female aspect of, v. 484
Solar energy, is, i. 171
Son cosmically, i. 142
Son of, ii. 286; iii. 412
Son of aether, is, iii. 399
Son of the divine sons, is, i. 168
Son of the sons, is, i. 193, 194
Son of the waters, is, iii. 399
Son-brothers of, i. 201
Songs of, i. 253
Sons of, i. 201, 253; ii. 248, 278, 398; v. 484
Soul of nature, animal, i. 171
Sound and, v. 484
Space divided by, ii. 398
Spiral lines of, i. 177

FOHAT (*Contd.*)

Spirit, the guiding, i. 196
Spirit of electricity, is, i. 195
Spirit of life-giving and, iii. 95
Steed, the, i. 168
Substance, acts upon, i. 81, 170; ii. 41
Sun, central, and, i. 250
Sūrya and, i. 171
Svābhāvat and, i. 150
Symbol of force, a, i. 171
Thought divine, the, i. 81
Thought of the Gods, the, i. 171
Thread of, i. 283
Three and seven strides of, i. 171
Toom identical with, ii. 398
Transferrer, the, i. 81, 202
Twilight to another, acts from one, i. 200
Universal, i. 199
Universal electric fluid, and, i. 171; ii. 216
Universal mind and, i. 150
Universe to move, caused, i. 250
Unmanifested universe, in, i. 169
Vedic name of, iii. 399
Vehicle of primordial seven, the, i. 168
Vishnu and, i. 171; ii. 398
Vital fluid and, i. 171; ii. 216
Vital power or, i. 169
Wheels built by, i. 200
Winged wheel, builds a, i. 180
Word made flesh, the, i. 171
World has its, each, i. 199
World germs set in motion by, ii. 397
Worlds built by, i. 200
Zigzags, glides in, i. 143

FOHATIC, Divine thought, impress, of, i. 128
Forces, i. 253; v. 535
Principle, ii. 249; v. 553

FOH-MAËYU, temple of Buddha, iii. 219

FOH-TCHOU, or Buddha's lord, iii. 219

FOHI, Chinese, ii. 374; iii. 39
Men of, iii. 39
Trigrams of, iv. 124

FOIX, De, quoted, iii. 105

FO-KIEN, Province of, i. 314

FOLK-LORE, ii. 15; iii. 39, 392, 396; iv. 324

FONTENELLE, quoted, ii. 16

FOOTPRINTS, Fossil, iv. 324
Human, on rocks of the secondary age, iii. 23

FORAMINIFERA, iii. 260

FORBES, referred to, ii. 215

FORCE, Absolute, i. 203
Absolute will expands, ii. 69
Abstract ideas as to, ii. 342
Akāsha and, ii. 46
All-creative, i. 149
Anch or vital, iv. 205
Ancient religions based upon abstract, ii. 113
Angels a conscious, ii. 357
Astral light, or, i. 303
Atmospheric vibrations, and, ii. 358
Atom and, i. 147; ii. 231, 236, 353
Attack on scientific theory of, ii. 248
Attraction, of, ii. 213; iii. 112
Aura of a nascent world, in, iii. 235
Beings whose essence is spiritual, ii. 354
Brahmā creative, iii. 68

Bull the principle of life-giving, ii. 105
Ceased to act, ii. 233
Central informing, iv. 154
Centres of, i. 147, 176, 200; ii. 174, 231, 235, 353; iii. 312; iv. 242; v. 474, 475
Centrifugal, i. 324; ii. 223, 316
Centripetal, i. 324
Cohesive, ii. 232
Coming, ii. 278
Conscious, ii. 357
Cosmic electricity, of, i. 201
Creative, ii. 89, 274; iii. 68, 108; iv. 74, 79
Creator, iii. 38
Definition of, ii. 233
Deity, or, i. 156; ii. 57
Devil a creative, iv. 79
Divine man or, i. 152
Double stream of, iv. 300
Dual, ii. 306, 398; v. 205
Dynaspheric, ii. 283
Earth-force and sun, ii. 251
Electric, ii. 398; v. 221
Electricity called, i. 171, 338; v. 220
Elements, in cosmic, i. 332
Energy, and, i. 121, 201
Entity, an, ii. 236
Equilibrium, and, ii. 220
Etheric, ii. 279; v. 476
Forms of, iii. 41
First Logos of, v. 476
Generating power of every, ii. 190
Generation, presiding at physical, iv. 79
Generative, ii. 275; iv. 164
Gravity, or, ii. 253; iv. 193
Great breath, origin of, i. 80
Imponderable, ii. 311
Inertia and, ii. 235
Inherent, i. 202; ii. 226; iii. 118
Intelligence, and, ii. 226
Intelligent, i. 332
Keely's, ii. 287
Latent, i. 210
Life, ii. 253
Life-principle is a, iv. 242
Light called, i. 338; ii. 206
Living, i. 171
Logos guiding, iii. 38
Magic, of, v. 12
Matter, and, i. 76, 201; ii. 214, 232, 242, 283, 311, 340, 348, 364; iii. 112; iv. 218, 287; v. 476
Mass, without, ii. 235
Modifications of, ii. 332
Molecules, centres of, ii. 231
Monad, in, iii. 118, 312
Motion, and, ii. 226, 236, 242, 248, 352; iv. 287
Mūlaprakriti and, iii. 37
Newton calls inertia, ii. 235
Noumenon of, ii. 216, 241
Numbers, and, i. 135
Occult, iv. 183
Occult science on, ii. 348
Occultism on, ii. 236
Origin of, i. 80
Phenomena, behind, i. 324
Physical, ii. 327

FORCE (*Contd.*)
  Physical sciences, of, ii. 206
  Physics, nothing in world of, ii. 235
  Potential, iv. 16
  Primary quantity, not, ii. 352
  Primitive element, is, ii. 354
  Primordial, i. 324
  Primordial substance, and, iii. 37
  Purusha, v. 469
  Quality, a, ii. 233
  Real, only, iv. 160
  Science, of, i. 250
  Scientific theory of, ii. 248
  Seed in, iv. 16, 160
  Senseless, ii. 229
  Sound a stupendous, ii. 279
  Space, and, ii. 274, 340
  Spirit, and, ii. 61, 235; iii. 112; iv. 164
  Spiritual, ii. 354
  Storage of, ii. 233
  Substance, and, ii. 232, 235; v. 469
  Substantiality of, ii. 232
  Theories of, ii. 248, 311
  Unity as, iii. 37
  Universal, v. 220, 472
  Vis viva or moving, ii. 394
  Vital, i. 332; ii. 255, 359; iv. 205
  Vital electric, ii. 398
  Wheels are centres of, i. 176, 200
FORCES, Action, in, i. 220, 364
  Ah-hi or, i. 111
  Angels or intelligent, i. 181, 280
  Blind, iii. 265, 343; iv. 225, 234; v. 225
  Causation of, ii. 186
  Causes, effects of, ii. 244
  Central, ii. 317
  Centres of, i. 165, 229; iv. 301
  Conscious entity at its head, each has, i. 334
  Constructive, ii. 58
  Correlation of, i. 159; ii. 223, 304, 358, 398;
      iv. 25; v. 89
  Cosmic, i. 181; ii. 135; iii. 140, 420; iv. 184,
      324; v. 315, 428, 505
  Creative, i. 167; ii. 141, 157, 158, 204, 222,
      360; iii. 46; iv. 25, 60, 145, 222; v. 443
  Creators, or, iii. 166
  Deity, proceeding from, ii. 230
  Design in action of blindest, i. 320
  Divine, v. 171
  Divine honours, received, ii. 142
  Dynamical effect of, ii. 369
  Elemental, ii. 174
  Elementals, or, i. 201
  Elements, vehicles, of, ii. 191
  Elohim, are, v. 187
  Emanations are, ii. 315
  Entities are, ii. 141, 396
  Evolution and, i. 228; ii. 271; iii. 159; iv. 192,
      277
  Fohatic, i. 253; v. 484
  Force or, ii. 165, 215
  Gods, are, ii. 182, 215, 397; iv. 334
  Good and evil, of, iv. 65
  Gravity and, ii. 213
  Great ones of the seven magic, ii. 399
  Hierarchy of, ii. 142, 182
  Hosts of, i. 322

  Imponderable, iii. 275
  Inanimate, ii. 263
  Intellectual, ii. 200
  Intelligent, i. 111, 199, 280, 322; ii. 271;
      v. 220, 221
  Interdependence of, ii. 134
  Inter-etheric, ii. 279
  Interference of, iv. 287
  Interplay of, iv. 215
  Intra-cosmic intelligent, ii. 253
  Karma, of, iv. 192
  Knowledge of, ii. 310
  Kosmos, of, ii. 199; iii. 108
  Ladder, a, ii. 278
  Latent, iii. 87; v. 505
  Life governs inanimate, ii. 263
  Light, Spirit and Life, of, v. 299
  Living, ii. 199
  Logoi, Three, of, v. 476
  Maleficent, i. 276
  Manifested, v. 227
  Manvantaric, ii. 271
  Material, ii. 318
  Matter, and, ii. 226; iv. 53
  Mechanical, ii. 215, 253, 328, 365
  Modern learning, not understood by, ii. 241
  Modes of motion, are, ii. 325
  Molecular energy or, ii. 394
  Motion and, ii. 220, 325
  Mystery of physical, ii. 280
  Names of six, i. 334
  Natural, i. 325, 327; ii. 318; iii. 159, 265
  Nature, of, i. 111, 195, 203, 263, 333; ii. 60,
      90, 143, 360; iv. 153, 203, 340; v. 81, 382
  Noumena of, ii. 88
  Nucleus imagined as surrounded by, ii. 234
  Occult, ii. 235; v. 219
  Occultism, and, ii. 278
  Ocean, in the, iv. 352
  One force, of, ii. 51, 235
  Opposite, ii. 328
  Personified, v. 484
  Physical science and, ii. 230
  Physical, ii. 186, 191, 280, 365; iii. 347;
      iv. 219, 222
  Physicists, cannot see, ii. 330
  Physico-chemical, iv. 225
  Planes, on other, ii. 200
  Polar, iii. 93
  Powers, and, i. 192, 328; ii. 155
  Queen of night, of, ii. 111
  Rays, or, i. 331
  Realities, manifestations of, ii. 234
  Ruling, v. 220
  Sacred, i. 192
  Satanic, v. 94
  Science, of, ii. 56, 245, 317, 328
  Scientists, of, ii. 315
  Semi-intelligent, ii. 239
  Septenary, v. 484
  Seven, v. 472, 474, 484
  Six, i. 333
  Solar universe, in our, i. 331
  Solid gas or fluid, neither, ii. 241
  Space, iv. 55; v. 382
  Spirits or, ii. 207, 222
  Spiritual, ii. 357, 365

FORCES (Contd.)
Spiritual entities, or, ii. 215
Sound, and, v. 505
Subba Row on, i. 333
Substance matter and, i. 200
Supersensuous, ii. 239
Sympathetic, ii. 262
Tattvas, v. 475, 476, 505
Terrestrial, i. 228, 325
Three Mothers, symbols of all, v. 89
Titanic, iii. 420
Transitional, iii. 87
Unity of, ii. 341
Universe, of the, i. 196, 328; iv. 174
Upādhi of, ii. 240
Vital, iii. 41

FOREFATHERS, Arhats or Mahātmās, of, iii. 180
Aryan Brāhmans, of the, iii. 434
Creators, or, iii. 251
Fifth race, of our, ii. 333
High places, remains in, iv. 292
Men, of, ii. 162
Norwegians, of, iii. 422
Postdiluvian, iii. 428
Troy, of Greeks of age of, iv. 319
Yellow-hued nations, of, iii. 423

FOREHEAD, Neanderthal skull, iv. 257
Rudra springs from, of Brahmā, iv. 118

FORE-KNOWLEDGE, Prometheia means, iii. 411

FORE-MOTHERS of red-haired men, Giant, iii. 198

FORERUNNERS of the Aryan invasion, iv. 310

FOREST, Anugītā, in, the, iv. 209
Sounds of, v. 443
Symbol for man's life-time, a, iv. 209

FORESTS, Amercia, of, iv. 246
Land of the occult virgin, of, iv. 366
Man-ape in primeval, iv. 249
Spitzbergen, of, iv. 357
Virgin, ii. 400

FORGED pseudographs, iii. 439

FORGERIES of Purānic MSS., i. 53

FORGERY Book of Enoch not a, iv. 104

FORKS, vibratory, ii. 288

FORM, All that lives has a, ii. 86
Astral or shadow, i. 274, 278; v. 282, 471, 472
Bhūta without, iii. 29
Breath needed a, iii. 29
Centres of, ii. 352
Devas, origin of, ii. 172
Different Planes on, v. 534
Dissipation of, ii. 345
Divine ideation passing into, ii. 95
Divine, ii. 135
Energy, of, ii. 350
Fifth race, of, iv. 275
God, of, v. 188
Gods, of the, ii. 175
Greeks, among, ii. 39
Idea gives, ii. 347
Illusive, i. 193
Immaculate mother, gives birth to, i. 155
Implicit, ii. 365
Incarnation in, iii. 348
Individual Ego, of, v. 495

Life precedes, i. 269
Man's present gross, ii. 202
Matter, and, i. 128, 230; iii. 275
Model of man, or, iii. 110
One, of existence, i. 118, 120
Origin of, ii. 172
Permanency of, iv. 297
Physical man, latent in, ii. 290
Physiological, of man, ii. 290
Plastic, of the globe, i. 304
Principle of Limitation is, v. 534
Privation and, i. 128
Producers, of, i. 124
Rearrangement of, ii. 255
Retrogression of, iii. 290
Rudiment of, ii. 88
Rūpa or, i. 235
Sien-Chan, of, i. 193
Spirit, of, ii. 365
Substance, and, ii. 345; iii. 200
Symmetry of, i. 272
Unclean work of finite, ii. 216
Universal, iii. 38; iv. 274
Worlds of, i. 230; ii. 153, 328, 342
Worship of, iii. 275

FORMAL ATOMS, ii. 355, 356

FORMLESS, Arūpa or, i. 152, 249; iii. 79, 118
Deity is, i. 193
Fathers, ii. 296
Fiery breaths, i. 261
Fire, i. 151
Life, i. 260
One life, i. 294
Pitris, iii. 101
Plane, iii. 118
Radiations, ii. 357
Spirit, v. 408
Square, i. 160
Substance, ii. 269
Universe of thought, i. 178
World, i. 187, 249; ii. 296; iii. 79
Worlds, ii. 330

FORMS, Abstract, ii. 289
Ain Soph, in, iii. 291
Animals and men, of, iii. 313
Apes, of, iii. 264
Archetypal, ii. 95
Astral, i. 293
Atomic, i. 265
Atoms, of, ii. 349
Being, of, ii. 363
Bodhisattva in the world of, ii. 296
Cycle of being and, i. 192
Densest, i. 302
Divine, ii. 396
Divine man, emanated from, i. 153
Earliest, of organic life, iv. 165
Ether, in, ii. 183
Ethereal, iii. 129, 300
Force, of, iii. 41
Form that combines all, i. 155
Ideal, i. 324; ii. 91
Ideal world in the, ii. 95
Intermediate, iv. 266
Knowledge of past, iii. 299
Kosmos, of, ii. 150
Lords of being, of, iii. 46

FORMS (*Contd.*)
Man passes through all, i. 214
Man unites in himself all, iii. 291
Manvantara, in each, iv. 298
Materialized, v. 497
Matter, of, ii. 166, 332, 347
Monads and, iii. 89, 174
Nascent physical, iii. 188
Pitris, of, i. 293
Planetary powers as mystic, ii. 357
Plant whirls through seven, i. 283
Powers, of creative, ii. 141
Prakriti of, v. 469
Receptacle of, iv. 80
Round, in this, i. 302
Rūpa, the world of, i. 187
Rūpas, or, i. 243
Serpent, of the, ii. 123
Seven in perception of, iv. 193
Shadowy ethereal, iii. 129
Shiva destroyer of, iii. 251
Sons of Yoga, evolved by, iii. 168
Transitional, iv. 266
Two, one character, v. 165
Two and four-faced, iii. 28, 74
Universe of ever-changing, i. 317
Vile, of the first third, iii. 31
Wider apart, get fewer and, iii. 265
Within, iii. 29
World of, the, i. 187; iii. 296; iii. 36
FORMULA, Astronomical, an, iv. 130
Mystical, v. 395
Sacred Eastern, v. 418, 421
Symbolic, and intellect, ii. 195
FORMULAE, Mythical, iv. 178
FORTITUDE, Patience the parent of, iv. 97
FORTRESS of Cuzco, i. 257
FORTUNATE ISLANDS, iii. 397
FORTY-NINE, Earth elements divisible into,
    ii. 61
Fires, the, i. 332; ii. 157, 245; iii. 67, 361;
    iv. 90; v. 477, 517, 538, 541
Forces, v. 484
Impressions received, v. 547
Letters, v. 505
Powers of seven vowels, ii. 127
Stages of rest and activity, iv. 317
FOSSIL, Apes, iv. 245, 251, 260
Astral, forms, iv. 254
Europe, man in, iv. 293, 307
Europe, skulls in, iv. 309
Evidences of, flora, iv. 295
Fauna, mammalian, iv. 304
Idiom, iii. 205
Lower Dauphiné, remains at, iii. 279
Man, iii. 82, 279; iv. 237, 251, 293, 307
Missing link-like, iv. 230
Oxen, iii. 289
Pistis Sophia, a Gnostic, iv. 175
Plants, iii. 202
Primates, iv. 246
Relics of the anthropoid ape, iv. 245
Remains, iii. 199, 325
Series, iv. 244
Skulls, iv. 290, 309, 358
FOSSILIFEROUS ROCKS, iii. 196
FOSSILS, Animals, of, ii. 362

Anthropoid, iv. 249
Atlantis, and, iv. 352, 360
Devon, in, iv. 290
Domestic animals, of, iv. 343
Eocene strata, in, iv. 249
Europe, in, iv. 318
Evidence of, iv. 294, 353, 360
Giants, of, iii. 287
Human, iv. 318, 322
Kent's cavern, of, iv. 292
Man, of, ii. 362; iv. 256
Monsters, of, iii. 202
Orang, of the, iii. 265
Palæolithic men, of, iv. 256
Races, of our modern, i. 236
Relics which can never be found as, iii. 291
Rounds, of preceding, iii. 78; iv. 316
Science, reconstructed by, iii. 210
Smith's Sound, of, iv. 357
Strata, not present in oldest, iv. 266
FOSTER, Sir M., quoted, iii. 140
FOSTER-MOTHER of Jupiter, Amalthaea,
    iv. 150
FOULNESS, quality, iii. 70
FOUNDATION, Christianity, of, v. 99
Mysteries, of, v. 262
FOUNDER, Christianity, of, v. 136, 303
Religion, of, v. 155
FOUNTAIN, Divine, v. 76
Spirits, qualifying or, iv. 206
Spirits, seven, iv. 212
FOUR, Angels of Enoch, v. 104
Brahmā, bodies of, iii. 71
Circles of Fohat, i. 253
Decad contained in, v. 506
Divisions of Maha-Yuga, v. 345
Double one becomes, iii. 293
Fiery sons of Fohat, i. 253
Fires, v. 477
Forces, sacred, i. 192
Gospels, i. 115
Holy ones, i. 155, 180, 181; v. 439
Human Principles, v. 421, 472, 487
Images, ii. 158
Kinds, Vāch, of, ii. 150
Kingdoms, i. 230
Kumāras, i. 153; v. 78
Mahārajas or great kings, i. 181; v. 439
Mind-born Sons of Brahmā, v. 78
Modes of Birth, v. 559
Mystic, i. 159; ii. 166; v. 506
One, and the, iii. 284
Partitioned cross, iv. 171
Powers, sacred, i. 192
Pythagorean, v. 506
Quaternary and, v. 455, 507
Races, the, iv. 102
Sacred, i. 152, 192; iii. 283
Seats of Egyptian learning, v. 264
Shiva again becomes, iii. 251
Sons, i. 147
Tetraktys, or, v. 506
Three into, i. 128, 134
Truths, Nidānas based on, i. 112, 118; iv. 377
Truths of twenty-eight faculties, ii. 125
Vedas, i. 115
Wicks, i. 283

FOUR (*Contd.*)
Worlds, ii. 153; v. 73, 299
Youths of a yellow colour, ii. 36
FOUR ELEMENTS, Ancients, of the, ii. 19
Kabalistic, ii. 166
Svastika and the, iv. 159
FOUR-ARMED Cross, iv. 117
Human creatures, iii. 295
Men, iv. 314
Rudra Shiva, iv. 70
Shiva, ii. 118
FOUR-FACED, Brahmā, i. 125, 170; ii. 58, 184;
iv. 33; v. 519, 530
Forms, iii. 28, 74
FOURFOLD, Classification, iv. 207
Consciousness, v. 545
Division, ii. 124
Heavenly man, iv. 197
Knowledge, v. 519
Path, v. 545
Transformations of matter, i. 254
FOUR-FOOTED Cross or svastika, iv. 116
FOUR-LEAVED lotus flower of Buddhi, iv. 117
FOUR-LEGGED men, iv. 314
FOUR-LETTERED, Adam Kadmon or, symbol,
iii. 38
Deity, iii. 313; v. 163
Name, ineffable, iii. 283; v. 163
Tetragrammaton; iii. 37
FOURMONT, quoted, iii. 374
FOURTEEN, Lokas, v. 356, 421, 537, 539,
541, 542
Manus, iii. 308
Precious things, i. 135
Septenary is, v. 522
FOURTH, Centre in brain, v. 556
Continent, iii. 266
Dynasty, Egyptian Religion of, ii. 23; v. 59
Earth, ii. 45
Element, ii. 309
Evangelist, v. 96
Globe, ii. 234
Gospel, quoted, i. 272; iii. 232; v. 96
Hierarchy, v. 532
Initiation, i. 135
Life-cycle, i. 213
Matter, state of, ii. 286
Number, v. 189
Octave of Colour, v. 508
Path, v. 516, 522
Sense, v. 506
Solar Plane, v. 532
FOURTH PRINCIPLE, v. 154, 487
Fohat the preserving, i. 171
Helen personified, iv. 364
Kāma Rūpa, the, iii. 244
Moon is, v. 154
Vehicle, as a, iii. 169
FOURTH RACE, Abel and, iii. 143
Adam and Eve, iii. 409
Arts and sciences, ii. 185
Aryan overlapped by, iii. 443
Aryans' knowledge came from, iii. 424
Astronomy, iv. 42
Atlanteans, i. 242; ii. 334, 377; iii. 333, 439;
iv. 102, 156; v. 268
Atlantis, of, iv. 334

Atlas symbol of, iv. 62
AUM, lost, iii. 406
Begetting of, iii. 180
Beginning of, iv. 181
Birth of, iii. 230, 252; iv. 283
Black magic and, v. 91
Book of Enoch and, iv. 104; v. 103
Cain and, iii. 143
Cataclysm which befell, iii. 152
Civilization of, iii. 427; iv. 249
Curse not brought by, iii. 409
Cycle of, iii. 431
Daityas, iii. 190
Deluge of, i. 136; iii. 154; v. 103
Destruction of, iv. 103
Downfall of, iv. 220
Dvāpara Yuga of, iv. 186
Earliest pioneers of, iii. 323
Early ages of, ii. 40
Enoch is, iv. 169
Evolution of, iii. 295, 443
Eye of Shiva, iii. 303
Females of a semi-human race begot young
from, iii. 200
Fourth round, in, iii. 187
Fruit of the tree of Good and Evil, tasted of,
iii. 143
Giants of, iii. 44, 190, 228, 278, 282; v. 260
Hermaphrodite rod of, i. 174
Heroes of, iii. 144, 273; iv. 339
History of, iii. 230
Huge form of, man, iii. 159
Human period of the, iii. 286
Initiates of, iii. 339; v. 37
Instructors of, iii. 375
Land of bliss of, iii. 355
Language of, iii. 204
Lion, symbolized by the, iv. 102
Mankind, iv. 292
Manus, had four, iii. 149
Middle age of, iii. 296
Midway point of, i. 238
Miocene period and, iii. 163
Mysteries of, v. 258
Nebo a creator of, iv. 23
Noah and, v. 106
Origins of, iv. 282
Padmapāni, children of, iii. 185
Periods separating from fifth, iii. 435
Physical, iv. 258
Popul Vuh, mentioned in, iii. 225
Priapean monster, represented by a, iv. 25
Records since the beginning of, ii. 371; iv. 99
Remnants of, iv. 175
Ruta of, ii. 377
Schism between the sons of, iii. 216
Secret Doctrine of, v. 204
Semi-demons of, iii. 319
Senses of, v. 523
Serpent a phallic symbol of, iii. 72
Sinking of the continent of, iv. 263
Soma, born under, iii. 42
Sons of wisdom and, iii. 168; v. 204, 260
Speech, developed, iii. 32, 196, 203
Spirit of, earthly, i. 271
Spiritual condition lost by, ii. 259
Submerged, is, iv. 194

FOURTH RACE (*Contd.*)
  Sub-races of, iv. 169, 340; v. 121
  Suffering, i. 242
  Tenets of, v. 268
  Third eye in, iii. 307
  Third gave birth to, iii. 32
  Transmission of elements, by, ii. 56
  Two front eyes in, iv. 338
  Ulysses one of the heroes of, iv. 338
  Zeus deity of, iv. 345
  Root race, i. 167; iv. 253
FOURTH ROUND, Animal kingdom of, iii. 193
  Animal nature of man up to, iii. 169
  Beginning of, iii. 78
  Branch races of, iii. 88
  Cataclysms of, iii. 157
  Creation, iii. 289
  Elements in the, four, i. 297
  Ether and, i. 78, 196
  Fifth and sixth rounders in, i. 215
  Fifth root race, and, i. 237
  First half of, iii. 187
  First race of, i. 239
  Four paths of Nirvana in this, i. 255
  Four truths revealed in, i. 115
  Fourth root race of, i. 167; v. 103, 106, 259, 268
  Globe D. in, iii. 154
  Globe, on this, i. 232
  Herbs existed before, i. 298
  Human monad in, i. 227; iv. 206
  Humanity in, iv. 254
  Longest, is, v. 563
  Mammals in, iii. 289; iv. 166, 254, 258
  Man belongs to, i. 235, 238
  Mankind in, i. 234; iii. 193
  Monads in this, i. 227
  Planet, iii. 192
  Seven out of, iii. 58
  Seventh race in, iii. 175; v. 563
  Sons told to create in, i. 242
  Sphere, of, i. 304
  Spirit and matter in, equilibrium of, i. 242
  Stone in, i. 292
  Three rounds preceding our, iv. 274
  Tidal action in, iii. 74
  Vegetation in, iii. 121
FOURTH Sphere, Earth the, iii. 187
  Moon, born under, iii. 42
FOUTOUHA, or FOUTOUNA Pacific Islands, iii. 227
FRAGMENT, Atlantis known to Plato, of, iii. 21
  Babylonian, a, iii. 382
  Commentary, from, iii. 424
  Grecian wisdom, of, ii. 369
  Sanchuniathon, of, iii. 138
FRAMEWORK of all construction, Tau the, ii. 383
FRANCE, Academy of, v. 51, 57
  Continent from Newfoundland to, iv. 360
  Cycle, nearing a point of her, ii. 371
  Enormous bones found in, iii. 279
  Geologists of, iv. 255
  Grand Orient of, v. 69, 282, 296
  Great Britain by land to, iv. 320
  Institute of, ii. 384; iv. 321; v. 330
  Materialists of, ii. 310

  Orientalists of, v. 53
  Palaeolithic age in, iv. 91
  Rochas a man of science in, ii. 370
FRANCIS, King of France, v. 264
FRANCK, quoted, i. 64; ii. 65; iii. 16; iv. 14
FRANCOIS, Monsieur de Foix, quoted, iii. 105
FRANKENSTEIN, Animal, iii. 67
  Creation of, iii. 425
  Jehovah, iv. 77
  Monster of, ii. 319; iii. 348; iv. 222; v. 560
FRATERNITIES, Senza preserved in some, iii. 437
FRAVASHI, Ferouer or double, iv. 46, 48
FREEMASONRY, v. 273, 284
FREE-THINKERS, v. 37
FREE-THOUGHT, v. 50, 156
FREE WILL, Automaton without, ii. 131
  Prometheus preserved to passive slavery, iii. 419
  Responsibility of, iii. 410
FRENZY, David's dance a Bacchic, iv. 29
FREPPEL, Abbé, v. 146
FRESCOES on the Miaotse, iii. 339
FRESH-WATER strata, iv. 256
FRESNEL on polarization, ii. 205, 209
FRICTION, Causal substance in, effects of, ii. 247
  Electricity generated by, i. 201
  Fire by rotatory, iv. 93
  Fire produced by, ii. 245, 247; iii. 250, 372; iv. 89, 93
  Heat produced by, ii. 240
  Mechanical, ii. 261
  Nirmathya or, ii. 245
  Pavamāna, or fire produced by, ii. 245; iii. 67
  Vedas explain, ii. 247
FROG, Amphibious nature of, ii. 100
  Church lamps, on lotus, form of, ii. 101
  Moon, in, ii. 69
  Mummies, Goddesses on all the, ii. 101
  Symbol of, ii. 69, 100
FRONTAL LOBE, in the apes, iv. 216
FROST, snow and ice, iii. 329
FROST-GIANTS, Hrimthurses or, iii. 385
  Ymir, sons of, ii. 145
FRUIT, evil, of, v. 291
  Forbidden, v. 105
FUEL, Carbon, as, iv. 165
  Logs of, iv. 178
  Sun, of the, i. 164; ii. 309; iii. 144
FUERST, Mountain of the Moon, iii. 86
  Quoted, iii. 391; iv. 128; v. 164, 165
FULGUR, Jupiter, or Fulgurans, ii. 188
FUNERARY, Rites of Egyptians, i. 52, 192; v. 245, 250, 325
FUNGI, Venomous essence of certain, i. 305
FURIES, Ever-mindful, ii. 367
FURY, Lightning, a synonym in Hebrew, ii. 188
  Nemesis, ii. 367
FUSAIOLES, Terra cotta discs or, iii. 110
FUSION, Mass in igneous, ii. 229
FUTURE, is Present in Eternity, v. 301, 499
FUTURITY, a compound of chance and time, v. 116
  Mirror of, iii. 61
  Secrets of, v. 119
  Stars read in, iii. 287

FYLFOT, form of four-footed cross (Svastika), iv. 116

G

G, wanting in Arabic, v. 342
GABHASTIMAN, v. 270
GABRIEL, Angel, ii. 300; iv. 108; v. 310, 320
  Archangel, i. 114; iii. 248, 250; iv. 40; v. 117
  Churches, glorified in the, iii. 250
  Denouncer, as a, iii. 381
  Eagle corresponds to, i. 185; iii. 124
  Mercury, is, v. 325
  Moon, Substitute of, v. 439
  Virgin Mary, appears to, ii. 94
GADES at extremity of Atlantis, iii. 405
GADIR, Sacred coloumns of, iii. 344
GADOLINIUM not an element but a compound, ii. 350
GAEA, Aditi or, i. 169; iii. 271
  Kabalistic trinity, in, i. 169
  Tethys or, iii. 76
  Venus a variant of, iii. 75
GAGANESHVARA, lord of the sky, iv. 135
GAIA, the earth, Gamma symbol of, iv. 155, 163
  Gaea or, iii. 75
GALATIANS, quoted, v. 67
GALILEE, stone circles in, iv. 324
GALILEO, referred to, i. 177; ii. 291, 348; iv. 104; v. 71, 316
GALLERY, Mountains of Kaf, in the, iii. 395
  Pyramid, of, iv. 34, 37, 128
GALLI, Hebrew Kadeshim or, iv. 28
GALTON, Francis, referred to, v. 442, 485
GAMALIEL, quoted, v. 50
GAMBIERS and the lost continent, iii. 227
GAMMA, Tau and the Greek letter, iv. 163
GAMUT, Hindu, ii. 258
  Root race, of every, iv. 349
GAN-AEDEN, Eden or, iii. 54
GAN-EDEN, Position of, iii. 207
GANA or classes of being, i. 331
GANDER, Holy Ghost under the shape of, ii. 72
GANDHARA, a quality of sound, ii. 258
GANDHARVA, Loka, v. 537
  Pururavas and the celestial, ii. 247
  Rig Veda, of the, iv. 157
  Vedas, the occult, of the, ii. 247, 248
GANDHARVAS, Aspects of, ii. 247
  Creation of, ii. 295
  Four Maharajahs, and, i. 185
  Nārada, leader of, iv. 156
  Secret doctrine, in the, i. 155
  Spirits of heaven, or, iii. 369
  Vāch punishes, iii. 151
  Yakshas and, iii. 99
GANDHIC sense, v. 540
GANDUNIA (Gan-dunyas), Eden or, iii. 54, 207
GANESHA, v. 111
GANGA, Ganges or, ii. 100; iv. 142
GANGADVĀRA, gate of the Ganges, iv. 142
GANGAPUTRA, Kārtikeya called, iv. 120
GANGES, Bay of Bengal, and the, iv. 142
  Gandadvara or Hardwar gate of, iv. 142
  Heavenly, ii. 100; iii. 208

Kārtikeya and, iv. 120
  Jah-navi or, iii. 138
GANGGRIFTEN or tombs with corridors, iv. 321
GANOIDS and the primary age, iii. 167
GANOT, quoted, ii. 394
GANYMEDES or objects of lust personified, iv. 353, 354
GAOKERENA, tree of eternal life, iv. 86
GAOL of giants, iv. 345
GARD, Bones found in the department of the, iii. 280
GARDEN, Adam and Eve in the, ii. 121
  Delight, of, v. 305
  Eden, the, of, i. 65, 174, 185; ii. 123, 132, 337; iii. 121, 207, 316, 349; iv. 64, 113; v. 67, 110, 181, 202, 206, 308, 449
  Eden, of God, iv. 61
  Paradise, of, iv. 129
GARDENER of nature, Shiva the, ii. 178
GARDENER, Starkie, on distribution of life, iv. 351
GARGA taught astronomy by Shesha, iii. 60
GARLAND of seven lotuses, iii. 58
GARMENT, Anupadaka, of, i. 96, 178
  Doctrine, of the, iv. 14
  Earthly, of man, iii. 121
  Elements, of the Deity, ii. 181
  God, of, v. 187, 188
  Indivisible point, of the, ii. 70
  Jesus, of, iv. 152
  Neshamah, of, i. 290
  Seen and not seen, which is, iii. 316
  Soul's, i. 288
GARUDA, Aruna brother of, iv. 141
  Birth of, iv. 135
  Descendants of, iv. 141
  Great cycle, symbol of the, iii. 323
  Half-man and half-bird, iv. 134
  Hari riding on, ii. 139
  King of the feathered tribe, iii. 188, 256
  Magas, transports Samba to, iii. 323
  Mahā Kalpa, the, iv. 141
  Purāna, referred to, iv. 135
  Rāmāyana, in the, iv. 141
  Vishnu, vehicle of, ii. 81
GASSENDI, referred to, ii. 347, 354
GASTROPODA in Sahara, Shells of the, iii. 21
GASTRULA stage, the, iv. 254
GATES of Death, v. 290, 312
GATRA, Brahma, or limbs of, iii. 87
  Dhīmat or limbs of, iii. 183
GAUDAPADACHARYA, Commentary of, ii. 176; v. 320
GAUDRY, Albert, referred to, iv. 216, 246, 248
GAUL, Mysteries of, v. 206, 294, 295
GAURAMUKHA, Brahmans consult with, iii. 322
  White-face, or, iii. 323
GAURI, bridge of Shiva, iii. 86
GAUTAMA, see Buddha
GAUTIER, referred to, i. 305
GAVEL of the grand masters, iii. 108
GĀYATRĪ, Syllables in the, ii. 247
GAZZIM, Astrologers or, v. 333
GEBELIN, Count de, referred to, ii. 366; iv. 338
GEBERS, Hidden meaning of the, i. 174
GE'BOOR-AH, or Qai-yin, son of Adam, iii. 315

GEBURAH in the Chaldean Kabalah, i. 249
GEBURIM, Atlanteans were, ii. 133
    Giants or, iii. 281
    Hidden meaning of, i. 174
GEHENNA of the Bible, ii. 184
GEIGER, quoted, iv. 327, 328
GEIKIE, Reindeer picture after, iv. 289
GEIST, ghost or gas or spirit, ii. 186
GELUGPA, iv. 157
GELUGPAS, source, v. 398
GELUKPAS, Yellow caps, or, i. 169
GEMARA, The, v. 67
GEMARA Sanhedrim, referred to, iv. 41
GEMATRIA, v. 113
    Kabalistic, v. 115
    Science of, v. 212
GEMINI, Castor and Pollux, the bright, ii. 81
    Simeon and Levi, in sphere of, ii. 377
GEMMATION, Infusoria produced their kind
    by, iii. 159
    Polyp Stauridium, of, iii. 184
GEMS, Abraxas, iv. 135
    Basilidean, ii. 194
    Gnostic, ii. 194; iv. 41, 135, 140, 176
GENEALOGICAL, Table of Haeckel, iv. 239
    Tree, iii. 96, 431, 432; iv. 160, 234
GENEALOGIES, Archaic Bible, found in,
    iii. 424
    Cain, of, iii. 390
    Christian and Pagan Deities, v. 94
    Gods, of the, iii. 54
    Haeckel, of, iv. 238, 239
    Manus, of, iii. 250
    Patriarchal, iii. 321
    Prajāpatis, of, iii. 250
    Prehuman periods, of, iii. 321
    Rishis, of, iii. 250
    Series of, ii. 337
    Seth, of, iii. 390; v. 106, 190, 297
GENEALOGY, Ape-man, iv. 239
    Buddha, of, iv. 66
    Cain's, iii. 389
    Haeckel, by, iv. 237
    Hypothetical, of man, iv. 231
    Kings, of, iii. 320
    Man's from the ape, iv. 252
    Phoroneus, of, iv. 88
    Prometheus, of, iv. 88
    Rishis, of, ii. 154
GENERA of the seven kingdoms, ii. 360
GENERATING, Cycles, ii. 190; iv. 132
    Power, ii. 190; iii. 189
GENERATION, Angels fallen into, iii. 233
    Ansated cross, symbol of, iv. 171
    Astronomy and, ii. 25
    Atom, of an, ii. 395
    Being descended into, iii. 236
    Bodies, of, iv. 146
    Cosmical, iii. 139
    Cursed to fall into, iii. 99
    Devas who fell into, iii. 419
    Dhyānīs fall into, iii. 58
    Earth fallen into, iii. 42
    Equivocal, iii. 172
    Fall into, i. 243, 265; iii. 18, 37, 42, 43, 48,
    58, 99, 112, 138, 209, 233, 235, 252, 264,
    387; iv. 79, 84, 180, 335; v. 102, 103

    Feminine, number of, iv. 153
    Flesh, of the, i. 172
    Germ that will fall into, i. 265
    Goat the symbol of fall into, iv. 79
    God manifest in, i. 275
    God of, iii. 52, 236, 389, 391; iv. 35, 160
    Goddesses helping on, of species, ii. 115
    Gods of, ii. 114
    Gods fallen into, iii. 235
    Hexagon, symbol of, v. 120
    Humanity, of, i. 275; iii. 176
    Jehovah God of, iii. 52, 236
    Kumaras and, ii. 176; v. 203, 320
    Lotus symbolizing, iii. 186
    Man, a God fallen into, iii. 263
    Manu's descent into, iii. 321
    Mars the God of, iii. 389, 391; v. 161, 164
    Moon as the causative of, iv. 32
    Moon-Goddess of, iii. 414
    Moon's influence on, iii. 113
    Mystery of, i. 84; ii. 79, 177
    One, passeth away, iv. 273
    Race first falling into, iii. 18; v. 102, 430
    Regeneration, not, iv. 38
    Satan and, iii. 238
    Secret of, hidden, i. 244
    Sexes, of distinct, iii. 202; v. 102, 430
    Sexual, iv. 228
    Spirit gives, ii. 351
    Spontaneous, iii. 125, 158, 159, 165, 287;
    iv. 287, 288
    Sun source of, ii. 194
    Symbol of, iv. 38
    Tau the symbol of life in, ii. 80
    Third humanity fell into, iii. 37; v. 102, 430
    Universe in abstract space, of the, iii. 54
    Universe, of the, ii. 66
    Vehicle of, iii. 140
    World, of the, ii. 338
GENERATIVE, God, Jehovah a, iv. 34
    Influence of Khonsoo, iv. 32
    Logos, light of the, iii. 236
    Matrix, ii. 80
    Organs as symbols of measures, ii. 106
    Principle, female, iii. 76, 147
    Sun, capacity of the, iv. 129
    Symbol, iii. 134; iv. 28; v. 120
    GENERATIVE power, Cow a symbol of the
    passive, iii. 416
    Creation, of, iv. 123
    Female, iii. 313, 414; iv. 28
    Heavenly man, of the, ii. 70
    Manu, in, iii. 135
    Nature, in, iii. 416; iv. 29
    Primitive and initial, iii. 55
GENERATOR, Ammon-Ra the, ii. 82
    Elements, of, ii. 279
    Humanity of, iv. 88
    Hydrogen, of air and water, iii. 114
    Keely's, ii. 285
    Phoroneus the second, iv. 88
    Prometheus the, iv. 88
    Sound, the, of elements, i i.279
    Vishnu the, iii. 313
GENESIS and Genesis, Adam in, iii. 182; iv, 230
    v. 157, 208
    Akkad mentioned in, ii. 32

GENESIS (Contd.)
Akkadian, ii. 72; v. 202
Allegorical legends, a collection of, i. 77; v. 199, 308
Allegory of Adam in, iii. 182; v. 176, 199, 203
Androgyne ray, and, ii. 71
Anthropology, in, i. 291
Archaic, i. 255; iv. 15
Beliefs, and Assyrian, iv. 45; v. 199
Berosus knew source of, iii. 151
Book of, v. 74
Cain's genealogy in, iii. 389; v. 190
Captivity, a reminiscence of the Babylonian, iii. 207
Chronology of, v. 139
Cosmogony of, v. 92
Creations of, iii. 19, 91; v. 198, 203, 207, 208, 209
Darkness in, iv. 56
Date of primitive humanity not found in, iv. 260
Days of the week in, six, iv. 153
Dead letter of, ii. 98; iii. 96
Deluges of, iii. 307
Devil, of, iv. 45
Elohim of, iii. 207; v. 190, 198, 199, 201, 204, 208
Elohistic, iv. 196
Enoch of, iii. 270; v. 106
Esoteric meaning of, ii. 149; iii. 219, 387
Esotericism of, iii. 121, 187; v. 66, 67, 182, 449
Evolution in, order of, iii. 187
Exoteric, v. 228
Explanation of the third chapter of, iii. 409
Fallen angels, on, iii. 232
Fire-mist, of elements in the, ii. 266
First Four chapters of, v. 89, 187, 190, 198
Germinal cell, of, the, i. 270
Giants of, iii. 282, 285; iv. 344
Glyphs, v. 73, 165, 207
Gnostics, of man, iv. 182
Gods, of, ii. 271; iii. 37; v. 90
Grain of sand, of a, ii. 395
Heaven and earth, of, iii. 369
Hebrew, ii. 162, 399
Hypothesis of, iv. 216
Initial sentence of, v. 90
Jehovah in, i. 72
Kadesh in, v. 28
Key to, ii. 132; v. 200, 201, 203, 207
Kings of Edom, and, iv. 275; v. 182
Kosmos, of, ii. 342
Legend of, ii. 331
Light in, ii. 71
Literally, accepted, ii. 71
Lotus idea in, ii. 96
Mankind the serpent in, iv. 81
Manu compared with, i. 75; iii. 134
Melchizedek in, iii. 390
Mexican local, iii. 217
Moneron unknown to science, of the, iii. 107
Mosaic, iii. 424; v. 178
Moses in, iv. 20; v. 182
Myths in, iv. 17
Natural, of wisdom, iv. 201
Noah of, iii. 153, 268, 390; v. 190, 206

Number seven in, iii. 17
Oannes, of, iii. 64
Of man, by Dr. Carter Blake, iv. 293
Physical evolution, on, iii. 254
Pithecoid stocks, of, iv. 259
Planets, of, ii. 164
Primeval, of man, i. 276
Primordial substance, on, ii. 44
Revealed, ii. 337
Sadic in, iii. 390
Secret meaning of the first verse of, ii. 161; iii. 49; v. 90, 205, 206, 231
Sepher Yetzireh and, iv. 106
Serpent of, iii. 212, 236, 238, 246, 281, 357, 384; iv. 81
Seth of, iii. 91, 360
Sons of God of, iv. 71
Stars, of, ii. 164
Symbology of, v. 66, 206, 207
Synopsis of man's, iii. 434
Twin-births of, iii. 143
Vulcain in, iii. 391
Week of creation in, iv. 195
Wilder's definition of, iii. 37
GENERATRIX, Gods, of, ii. 178; iii. 137
Sāvitrī, iii. 137
GENETHLIACAL, influences, v. 250
Tables, v. 332
GENGHIS KHAN, destroyed Djooljool, iii. 338
GENII, Abraxas, antagonistic to, iv. 111
Celestial, iii. 373
Choirs of, i. 334
Classes of, iii. 250
Definitions of Asclepios, in, i. 329
Desert, of, i. 55
Development of, iii. 366
Divine nature, of, iii. 372
Father of, i. 245
Fire, of, iii. 362
Four cardinal points, or angels in, ii. 61
Heaven, of four quarters of, ii. 94
Hermes, of, i. 335
Instruction given by celestial, iii. 373
Jacob Boehme the nursling of, ii. 217
Lunar month, of, ii. 124
Men directed by, i. 335
Mountains, of the, v. 38
Names of, i. 329
Planetary, seven, iii. 35, 215
Planets, of, i. 247; ii. 374, 378
Rebels, and, i. 245
Seven planetary, iii. 35, 215
Several kinds of, ii. 120
Space and time, born to act in, ii. 136
Trismegistus, of, ii. 396
Trithemius on the, ii. 172
GENITRIX, Heptanomis, of first, ii. 125
Typhon and, iv. 117, 119
GENIUS, Abraxas the lunar, iv. 42
Atom a term for, ii. 292
Doubt, of, iii. 219
Emblem of the good, ii. 194
Embodied entity, of the, ii. 364
Evil, of, ii. 112, 364; v. 94
Flashes of, v. 466, 527
Frankenstein's monster plus, iv. 222
Higher Manas and, v. 547

GENIUS (*Contd.*)
Jehovah, of the lunar year, iv. 109
Jupiter, of the planet, iv. 66, 110
Karma, and, iii. 176
Loci, local God or, ii. 183
Lunar, iv. 42, 109
Mazdean Mithra, or God, iii. 41
Mechanical not spiritual, ii. 285
Mercury as a psychopompic, iv. 112; v. 159
Mercury, of, v. 369
Moon, of, iv. 108, 110
Personal, iv. 140
Saturn, of, iv. 108, 110
Serpent, of, ii. 120
Spenta Armaita or female, iv. 181
Sun, of, iv. 110
Tzyphon, of doubt, iii. 219
Water, of, ii. 193
GENOESE, adventurous, Columbus, iii. 427
GENTIL, M. C., on the Hindu zodiac, ii. 388
GENTILES, Adytum, placed in the, iv. 27
Apostle of, v. 130, 138, 215, 327
Gods of, iv. 79
Hebrews borrowed, from, iv. 130
Jews and Christians, iv. 39
Teachers of, v. 60
Temples of, iv. 102
Trinity, idea of the, iv. 110
GEOCENTRIC, System, v. 209, 437
GEOFFROY St. Hilaire, referred to, iv. 216
GEOGNOSY, Ancients' knowledge of, iv. 104
GEOGRAPHY, Kings, of dominions of, iii. 320
Mysteries, used to be part of, iii. 22
Planets, of three inner, iv. 276
GEOLOGICAL conflagration, v. 103
GEOLOGY, Ages in, iii. 23, 164
Ancient Aryan, iii. 255
Antediluvian, iii. 334
Antiquity of man, and, ii. 35
Archaic science, and, iii. 315
Bible chronology against, iii. 200
Calculations, and, iv. 335
Chronology, at sea as to, iii. 77
Creation, traces dawn of, iii. 256
Cycles, and evolutionary, iv. 302
Dates of, iv. 268
Deluge of, iii. 152
Egypt and, iii. 367
Esoteric antiquity on, iii. 435
Esoteric teachings confirmed by, iii. 202
Esotericism, of, ii. 38
Exact science and, iv. 226, 233
Flood first perceived by, iii. 153
Fourth race taught, iii. 424
Indian Ocean problem, and, iv. 180
Moon and earth according to, iii. 75
Occult, v. 227
Occultism, corroborates, iv. 348
Ocean, and universal, iv. 283
Periods of, iii. 23
Planets, and, iv. 271
Scriptures on, iv. 316
Tradition, confirms, iv. 54
Triangle, and, iv. 166
GEOMETRICAL Figures, v. 111, 114, 116, 453, 455
Form, Fifth sense, the, v. 509

Secrets in Pyramid, v. 91
GEOMETRICIANS, v. 110
GEOMETRIZES, Nature in all her manifestations, i. 159
GEOMETRIZING Deity, iv. 126; v. 87, 90
GEOMETRY, Architecture and, v. 420
Divine science of, iv. 39
Cross and, iii. 220
Elementary arithmetic, and, iii. 200
Great Pyramid, in the, ii. 25, 29; v. 43, 91
Isis-Osiris inventor of, iii. 365
Kabalah and, v. 186
Lunar worship based on, ii. 113
Man and woman, in terms, ii. 161
Mysteries and, v. 524
Occult cosmogony, and, v. 31
Plato, and, v. 87
Pythagorean, v. 87, 113, 120, 420, 459, 506
System of, used by Jews, v. 185
Transcendental application of, ii. 340
Triangle in, v. 116
GEORGE, St., referred to, iii. 241, 378, 381, 384, 396
GERLAND on Australian races, iv. 348
GERM, Active, i. 69, 292
Animal man, of, i. 292
Astrology and astrolatry, of, iii. 36
Atom of nature, in every, i. 127
Central eternal, i. 321
Consciousness, of awakening, ii. 174
Cosmic Gods, of, i. 332
Darkness, of unknown, i. 148
Darkness, that dwelleth in, i. 132
Egg, in the, ii. 79, 82
Evolution of, ii. 81
Female creator as a, ii. 81
Fiery, i. 78
Invisible, i. 69
Latent, i. 78
Life-cycle, of all things to the end of the, i. 138
Life flashes into, i. 127
Mahat, of Chit, i. 330
Meteor theory, on the, iv. 298
Mundane egg, in the, i. 69
Physical man, of, i. 292
Primal, of mind, iii. 183; iv. 150
Ray had not flashed into the, i. 127
Root, in the, i. 77
Sacr', carrier of, iv. 35
Solar systems, of, iii. 156
Son, of the, iii. 94
Sorrow, of, iii. 102
Terrestrial life, of all, i. 264
THAT, is, i. 143
Thought in, v. 534
Time in space, contained in infinite, i. 140
Toom a, of eternity, ii. 398
Two are the, and the, is one, i. 138
Universe, of, i. 86; ii. 95; iii. 94
Upādhi of seven principles, the, i. 332
GERM-BUDS reduced to spores, iv. 229
GERM-CELL, Development of a, iii. 125
Ovum, or, iii. 126
GERM-CELLS in yeast, i. 294
GERM-STAGE, Human, i. 233
GERMAIN, Count St., quoted or referred to, ii. 336; iii. 164, 242; iv. 154, 155

GERMAN, Mythologists, v. 54
Numerals, meaning of, v. 117
Orientalists, v. 53
Philologists, v. 385
GERMANIC races, the, ii. 142
GERMANY, Giant-tombs of, iv. 321
Leibnitz born in, ii. 353
GERMINAL, Cell, i. 270
Plasm, i. 265
Transformation of matter, ii. 254
GERMINATION, Process of, iii. 128
GERMS, Animals, for higher, iv. 286
Ark contained, of all living things, iv. 29
Elementary, i. 195, 196
Elements, of, i. 254; ii. 165
Ether the storehouse of, ii. 183
Golden egg, re-enter the, ii. 92
Life, of, i. 302; iv. 30
Lives, of other, i. 302
Living things, of all, iv. 35
New original, iv. 286
Night and day, of, iv. 76
Organic life of, iv. 287
Primordial, iv. 287
Ship of life, carried in, iv. 30
Sub-race, of sixth, iii. 442
Wheels, of, i. 175
GERSHOM, v. 166
GERYON, Tomb of, iii. 280
GESTATION, Cell, within the, iii. 126
Foetus, of, iii. 181; v. 488
Mammals, of, iv. 167
Moon's influence on human, i. 232; iii. 113
Periods of, ii. 105; iv. 155
Spiritual, v. 473
GESTURE preceded by internal feeling, i. 317
GHARMA-JA, born of Shiva's sweat, iii. 133
GHEBER, Heber or, v. 309
GHOST, Atoms, of the long vanished, iv. 243
Geist or spirit, ii. 186
Shadows of matter in motion, or, i. 202
GHOST-WORLD, Gods of the, iii. 365
GHOSTS, Elementary spooks or, ii. 345
Lares now signifies, iii. 360
Lord of, iii. 147
GHOULS, Moon like all, i. 211
Powers of, iv. 22
GIAMSCHID builds Esikekar or Persepolis, iii. 397
GIAN-BEN-GIAN, or wisdom son of wisdom, iii. 393
GIANT, Ancestors, iii. 351
Ape, i. 240
Argeak the, iii. 395
Asia, inhabitants of, iv. 346
Asuramaya the reputation of a, iii. 80
Atlantean, iii. 80; iv. 244; v. 260
Atlanteans, iii. 431, 443
Birds, iii. 206
Briareus, the, iv. 344
Cottus, the, iv. 344
Daitya or, iii. 380
Demon Dânava, iii. 289, 380, 381
Demrusch, the, iii. 397
Fish, iii. 206
Gyges, the, iv. 344

Henoch called the divine, iii. 365
Lemurians, iii. 443
Noah a, iii. 268
Pre-tertiary, iii. 22
Race, iii. 349
Races, iii. 394; iv. 329
Rahu, a, iii. 380
Red-haired men, iii. 198
Serpents, iii. 206
Temple, v. 340
Tombs, iv. 321
Typhæus, ii. 187
Virabhadra a terrible, iii. 78
Ymir the, iii. 106
GIANT-DEMONS or Râkshasas, iii. 289
GIANTS, Accursed race of, iii. 153
Age of, iv. 101
Antediluvian, ii. 135; iii. 273; iv. 331
Antiquity of, iii. 278, 339
Archaic past, in the, iii. 59
Atlantean, iii. 102, 267, 281, 287, 392, 422, 431; iv. 249
Atlantis, of, iii. 345; iv. 322, 346
Beauty and strength of, iii. 319
Bibles, in the, iv. 69
Bones of, iii. 280, 407
Central American history, of, iii. 278
Classical writers on, iii. 279
Coelus and Terra, sons of, iv. 338
Colossal stones, associated with, iii. 280
Cyclops or, iii. 337
Daityas or, iii. 44, 404, 406
Dânavas or, iii. 198, 380; iv. 69
Dance of, iii. 342
Deity, doomed by wrathful, iv. 103
Demons, signify, iii. 281
Devils, called, ii. 133
Dhyâni-Buddhas or, i. 174
Dwarfs and, iv. 323
Dynasties of, i. 310; iii. 368
Earth, on, iii. 161, 373; iv. 61
East, from the, iii. 422
First races, of, iv. 341
Fossils of, iv. 318
Fourth race, iii. 190, 228, 277, 278, 281, 282
Frost, iii. 385
Genesis, of, iii. 239, 285, 373; v. 309
Gibborim or, iii. 281
Godly strength, of, iii. 179
Gods, and, iii. 85; iv. 61
Hesiod, of, iv. 344
Historic, iii. 279
History, traced, in, iv. 310
Hundred-handed, i. 257
Huschenk made war against, iii. 395
Intellectual, iii. 176
Israel, foes of, iii. 200
Kronos, imprisoned by, iv. 344
Lanka, of, iii. 406
Legendary, iii. 347, 408
Lemuria, of, iii. 345
Metals concealed by, iii. 395
Modern, iii. 294
Monsters bred by, iv. 249
Mythology, in, iv. 323
Nephilim or, iii. 294; iv. 324, 344
Peris ill-treated by, iii. 396

GIANTS (Contd.)
　Pherecydes on, iv. 344
　Pigmies and, iii. 200, 330
　Polar, three, iv. 345
　Post-Adamic, iii. 291
　Post-diluvian, ii. 135
　Prehistoric, iii. 279
　Primeval, iii. 42, 228
　Primitive, iii. 235
　Progeny of, iii. 374
　Purānic, iii. 133
　Pyramids work of, ii. 153
　Quinane called, iii. 278
　Race of, iii. 295, 335
　Rock, cut in, iii. 337
　Rocks raised by, iii. 346
　Sarcophagus of, iii. 280
　Scientlsts and, iv. 314
　Self-produced princes of, iv. 55
　Sons of, iii. 227
　Sorcery, and, iv. 344
　Stature, not in knowledge but in, iii. 286
　Stories of, iii. 441
　Third race, of, i. 241
　Thor's hammer, and, iii. 107
　Titans and, iii. 347; iv. 69
　Tombs of Sardinia, iii. 351
　War between Gods and, iii. 85; iv. 61
　Witnesses to, iii. 340
　Yellow-faced, iii. 423
GIBBON, quoted, v. 362
GIBBONS or man-like apes, iv. 248, 251
GIBBORIM, Bible of the, iii. 80, 275, 339
GIBBS, Prof., quoted, iii. 138
GIBRALTAR, Connection of, with Africa,
　iv. 361
　Formation of Straits of, iii. 21
　Land across the Straits of, iv. 309, 319
GIGANTES translated Serpents, iii. 281
GIGANTIC Antediluvians, iii. 409
　Atlantean deluge, iii. 149
　Creature, ape-like, iii. 263
　Early men, stature of, iv. 296
　Forms, of first men, iv. 182
　Magicians, iii. 426
　Male, God not a, ii. 67
　Mathematical instruments, v. 341
　Men in Africa, iii. 423
　Monsters of the air, iii. 22
　Physical humanity, iv. 103
　Semi-human monsters, iii. 146
　Skeletons, iv. 322, 324
GIGNAT, De, quoted, iii. 120
GILGULAH a cyclic or revolving process, ii. 292
GILGULIM, or the revolution of souls, ii. 291,
　292
GILL-CLEFTS, Anthropologists, on, iv. 253
　Foetus, in human, iv. 254
　Hæckel on, iv. 255
　Presence of, iv. 253
GIMIL, Cave of, iii. 109
GIN-HOANG the King men, iii. 368
GINNUNGAGAP, Gulf, or yawning, ii. 145
　Illusion cup of, ii. 83
GINSBURG, quoted, v. 108, 176
GIRALDUS Cambrensis on rocking stones,
　iii. 345

GIRDLE, Death, of, iii. 237
　Isis, of, i. 299
　Stony, of the world, iii. 397
GIRONDE, Psammite found in the basin of the,
　iv. 313
GIVER of life, Idea of the, ii. 192
　Moon, ii. 102
GIZEH, Pyramid of, v. 186
GLACIAL, Epoch, iv. 257, 283, 319, 347
　Formations, iv. 256
　Period, ii. 377; iii. 149, 152, 155, 256, 276;
　　iv. 247, 248, 265, 309
　Sea, iii. 397; iv. 346
GLACIERS, Ancient, iv. 256
　Continental, iv. 265
　Extension of, iv. 320
GLADSTONE, W. E., quoted, iii. 254, 382;
　　iv. 17, 335, 336, 339
GLAND, Pineal, iii. 127, 296, 298, 299, 301, 302;
　　v. 478, 480, 481, 483, 521, 549, 550, 556
GLANVIL, and witches, v. 51
GLASS, Attraction of iron through, iv. 288
　Odorous particles confined in, ii. 288
GLASSES, Invention of, optical, ii. 306
GLAUCUS, v. 277
GLIDDON, Nott and, iv. 182
GLOBE, Age of, iii. 162, 163, 260; iv. 264, 281,
　364
　Architects of, i. 70
　Ascending arc, on, iii. 253
　Atmosphere of every, i. 200
　Beings in correlation with the state of each,
　　iv. 277
　Beings on our, i. 294
　Breathes, our, ii. 265
　Chain, and, ii. 382
　Chain of worlds, a septenary, iv. 269
　Changes on our, iii. 146, 329
　Comet passing our, ii. 331
　Conditions of life on this, i. 235
　Cooling of, iv. 264
　Cosmic dust reaches our, ii. 333
　Creation of, ii. 53
　Creation on seven portions of, iii. 86
　Creations of, ii. 364; iii. 170
　Cross, and, iii. 42, 43
　Cycles on, iv. 188
　Deluge and, iii. 149
　Development of, iii. 435
　Divine monads on, iv. 53
　Door of our, i. 229
　Dragon's head or, iv. 73
　Egg-shaped, i. 141
　Elements of forms on, i. 325
　Entity, an, i. 209
　Esoteric meaning of symbols identical all over
　　ii. 34
　Eternal spring all over, iii. 144
　Evolution of, ii. 19
　Evolution of races, of, iii. 238
　Evolution on, iii. 15
　Face of changed, iii. 329
　Fiery, i. 297
　Fire, changed by, iv. 294
　Fire, of, ii. 315
　First, i. 240, 285
　First round of, ii. 174

GLOBE (*Contd.*)
Formation of, iii. 64
Fourth, i. 242; v. 529
Fourth round of, iii. 157; iv. 283
Generally explained, i. 234; iii. 309
Geological life of, ii. 366
Geologists on age of, iv. 364
Gimil's heights, seventh, iii. 109
Hades our, iii. 237
Heat on our, iii. 40
Hell itself, our, iii. 107
Higher Ego, as, v. 552
History of, i. 206
Human religious thought developed all over, ii. 55
Jambu-dvīpa represents, iii. 320
Kamarūpic state, in, i. 304
Laboratory, its own special, ii. 307
Light on, iii. 40
Lost maps of, iv. 350
Man developed with, i. 272
Mankind not the only beings who dwell on a, iii. 157
Men evolving with, iii. 251
Men inhabited this, 18,000,000 years ago, ii. 333
Moon, fourth, i. 225
Moon the giver of life to, ii. 102
Moon's attraction on the liquid portion of, iii. 75
Motionless at the North Pole, iii. 399
Mystery of our, iii. 64
Nascent, our, i. 291
Nirmānakāyas reappearing on this, iii. 102, 103
Objective life on our, iii. 347
Occult relations of sun to our, ii. 298
Oviform shape of our, ii. 74
Periodical creations of our, ii. 364
Periodically convulsed, iv. 345
Phoenician vessels circumnavigated, iii. 427
Plastic form of, i. 304
Pralaya, during, iv. 230
Primeval form, tending to, i. 214
Races on our, iii. 105
Radiant, i. 297
Reawakens, convulsed each time it, iv. 298
Rebirths of our, iv. 273
Renewals of seven, iii. 396; iv. 134
Rock-bound, iii. 161
Round, i. 214
Round and our, ii. 337
Round IV of, i. 240
Rounds of, successive, i. 215
Self-luminous, iii. 161
Sidereal rulers of our, iv. 269
Six spheres above our, iv. 275
Sixth, i. 285
Spheres of seven planets on our, iii. 18
Spirit-guardian of our, iii. 35
Spirit of the earth, and, iii. 41
State of, ii. 200
Submersion which changed, iii. 314
Sun called, of fire, ii. 315
Sun not, a, in combustion, ii. 264
Surface of, iii. 146
Symbol of, iv. 152
Terrestrial, iv. 104

Terrestrial atmosphere of, iv. 186
Transitions of, iv. 273
Universe and our, i. 326
Vegetation of, iii. 121
Vishnu drinks up waters of, ii. 86
Water, changed by, iv. 294
Wheel symbolizes, i. 113
Winged, ii. 81
Wings, with two, iv. 122
Woman, likened to body of, iii. 399, 400
Yogis who take up their abode on our, iii. 249
Zones of our, seven, iii. 120, 402
GLOBE A, Evolution on, iii. 78
Human forms on, i. 227
Immetalization on, iii. 187
Lunar chain, of, i. 225
Monad from, to Globe G, i. 221
Monad on, iv. 206
Planetary chain, in a, i. 210
Root-Manu on, iii. 309
Round, in first, iii. 78, 154
GLOBE D, Earth, our, i. 239
Life-cycle on, i. 214
Seed of life on, iii. 154
Third round on, iii. 193
GLOBE G, Lunar chain, of, i. 226
Planetary round from Globe A to, i. 214
GLOBES, Birth of, i. 222
Chain of, iv. 317
Chain, of our, i. 124, 278; iii. 87, 109
Chains of, i. 218; ii. 299
Chains of worlds composed of seven, i. 207
Companion, i. 213
Consciousness, belonging to other states of, iv. 271
Creation of inhabited, iii. 104
Cyclic evolution, i. 278
Diagram of, i. 225
Earth chain, i. 224
Earth, which precede our, iv. 72
Earth, which overshadow our, i. 220
Earths or, three, i. 295
Evolution of, i. 224
Evolution on remaining, iii. 175
Explanation of, i. 223
Formation of, i. 213
Generally treated of, i. 210, 228, 232, 278
Inhabited, iv. 272, 278
Intelligences, rational, ii. 216
Invisible, i. 218; iii. 320
Lunar chain, i. 225
Man-bearing, ii. 360; iii. 87
Meteorites from other, iii. 165
Nebula formed of gaseous, ii. 323
Planetary chain, of our, i. 283; iv. 179
Planets or, iii. 308
Primordial matter ends by becoming, i. 176
Progress of organisms on, i. 237
Races, and seven, iv. 176
Rounds, during previous, i. 248
Sealed books which are, iv. 271
Six, i. 213, 286; iv. 179
Strings of, i. 220
Structure of, i. 303
Tales of life on other, iv. 272
Terrestrial chain, of the, i. 271; iv. 327
Transformations of, i. 254

GLOBES (*Contd.*)
  Upper, i. 218
  Venus and, iii. 42
  Winged, i. 185
GLOBULAR, Lightnings, shaped, iv. 352
  Mass, iii. 75
  Speck in infinity, iii. 167
GLORY, Divine essence, of, i. 64
  Excellent, of the fire, iv. 137
  Imperishable, iii. 117
  Jehovah, of, iv. 109
  Lord, of the, iii. 238; iv. 109
  Noon-day, i. 308
  Solomon of, v. 182
  Supreme, iii. 117
  Throne of his, i. 155
  Unparalleled refulgent, i. 138
GLOSS of Solomon, Zohar, iv. 123
GLOSSARIES, Ancient, iii. 434
  Kabalah, of the Mosaic books, iv. 196
  Keys to mysteries in later, iii. 36
  Modern, to Commentaries, i. 160
  Upanishads the esoteric, of the Vedas, iv. 52
  Voice of Silence, of, v. 497
  Zoharic system, of the, iv. 29
GLOSSES, Book of Dzyan, on the, i. 87
  Commentaries, of the, iii. 46
  Confused, v. 140
  Stanzas, of the, i. 87
GLYPH, Astral light, for, i. 140
  Astronomy, and, ii. 33
  Biblical, ii. 33
  Book of Dzyan, in, v. 206
  Cosmic, iii. 355
  Dog-headed ape, of, ii. 103
  Double, iv. 116, 117, 163
  Dragon, for astral light, i. 140
  Egg of, ii. 80
  Egyptian religions, i. 267
  Fabulous form of, ii. 187
  Female, ii. 34
  Generative matrix, for, ii. 80
  Hindu, i. 174
  Initiates, of the, iv. 116
  Kalahansa, of, i. 144
  Mummiform God, of a, i. 266
  Phallic significance, of, iv. 155
  Pharaoh's daughter, of, ii. 31
  Priapus not, for abstract creative power, iv. 25
  Tau, i. 72; iv. 163
  Tetragrammaton, of, i. 262
  Waves, for the, ii. 99
GLYPHS, Astronomical, v. 106
  Biblical, v. 73, 137, 196
  Complicated, of most, i. 135
  Cosmic, iii. 355
  Esoteric, ii. 160
  Figures, are conventional, i. 134
  Geometrical signs and, i. 316
  Hidden Deity, of, ii. 64
  Jews, of the, i. 174
  Male, ii. 34
  Numerical, v. 106
  Pyramids, of, v. 207
  Seven circles, of, iv. 57
  Sexual element in, v. 84
  Sidereal, iii. 355

  Spiritual, v. 84
  Symbols are but, ii. 113
  Symbols become, i. 110
  Temples, of primitive, iv. 149
  Tree of Knowledge, v. 85
  Vowelless, iii. 254
  Wrong interpretation of, ii. 122
GNOMES, Idea of, ii. 330
  Influence over men of, i. 334
  Lords of the fires or, iii. 425; v. 239
GNOSIS, v. 401, 489
  Archaic doctrine, an echo of, ii. 168
  Antithesis of, v. 138
  Christian, pre- and post-, v. 444
  Christos in esoteric, i. 139
  Divine wisdom, or, v. 74, 493
  Esoteric science, or, v. 65
  Jnāna, knowledge or, i. 131
  John the Baptist, of, iv. 136
  Knowledge, or hidden, i. 131, 321; v. 74, 168
  Master of, iv. 139
  Mysteries belonging to highest, ii. 121
  Paul, St. and, v. 215, 327
  Pythagoras, of, v. 74
  Science of Higher Self, v. 301
  Square, rested on a, iv. 144
  Still flourishes, v. 46
  True and false, v. 327
  Vidyā, divine, the, v. 305
GNOSTIC, Agathodaemon, ii. 159
  Aim of, schools, iii. 391
  Book of Enoch called a, work, iv. 101
  Celsus a, ii. 164
  Christ, ii. 35; iv. 110, 158
  Divine incarnation, Idea, v. 351
  Emanations, ii. 65
  Esoteric doctrine, compared with, i. 190
  Gems, ii. 194; iv. 41, 135
  Generative Deity, ii. 42
  God, held by the, view of, ii. 361
  Gospel, iv. 30, 140, 175
  Gospel of St. John written by, v. 138
  Ildabaoth, v. 204
  Indian origin of, wisdom, iv. 140
  Literature, iv. 133, 136
  Mystery, v. 129
  Number seven in, records, ii. 180
  Ophites, ii. 121
  Potency, v. 74, 447
  Priapus, iv. 112
  Priests, i. 257
  Satan, allegory of, iii. 246
  Saturnilus, an Asiatic, v. 129
  Saviour, v. 25
  Schools, ii. 391
  Sects, iii. 388; iv. 41; v. 204
  Serpent, i. 140
  Solar Chnouphis, iii. 376
  Sophia or wisdom, i. 139; v. 74
  Spirit of Mysticism, v. 27
  Stones, i. 274; iii. 214
  Symbol, iv. 25
  System, v. 446
  Systems given in Isis Unveiled, iii. 105
  Teachers, v. 449
  Teachings, iv. 202; v. 169, 204, 210
  Tenets, iii. 388

GNOSTIC (*Contd.*)
Vowels, iv. 135
Writing, v. 177
GNOSTICISM, Church fathers, explained by,
iv. 140
Ebionitic, v. 161
King, C. W., on, ii. 301
Plato, of, v. 36
Profanations, of, iv. 132
Western, founder of, v. 132
GNOSTICS, Adam of, second, iv. 25
Alexandrian, ii. 134
Anthropology of, iv. 182
Arts of enchantment of, iv. 212
Bardesanian, v. 368
Bythos of, i. 262
Chaldean, i. 261; v. 199
Christian, i. 261; iii. 354; iv. 29, 175
Christos of, iv. 110; v. 108
Creation, and, ii. 167
Dragon symbol of Logos among, i. 141
Egyptian, iii. 385; iv. 108; v. 199
Elohim, and, v. 201, 204
Evangel of, iv. 136
Five words of, iv. 152
God as viewed by, i. 248
Hermes-Christos of, iv. 49
Holy Ghost, and, v. 189
Iao of, iv. 111
Ideas, Essenean and, v. 271
Jehovah identified by, with evil, i. 247
Jewish God, on, iii. 237
Kabalistic, v. 161
Light and shadow, on, iii. 218
Logos, on, ii. 64, 79, 126
Mystery language understood by, iv. 145
Mystic, ii. 195
Naasenian, iii. 354
Nazarean, iii. 158
Occultists and, v. 327
Ophite, ii. 126
Pantheism of, iv. 78
Peratae, iv. 148, 149
Philosophical, iii. 104
Philosophical systems of, i. 247
Religious doctrines of, iii. 385
Saturnilus and, v. 93
Saviour of, iii. 380
Science of, iv. 144
Secret doctrine, and, ii. 168
Seven among, v. 203
Seven vowelled serpent of, iii. 282; iv. 135
Seventh Potency and, v. 447
Sophia and, ii. 344; iii. 54
Soul, on birth of, ii. 300
Spirit of earth was feminine according to, i. 245
Syrian, i. 261
Systems of, ii. 166
Tau and, v. 162
Teaching of, iv. 189; v. 210
Two lights of, iii. 213
Universal soul, on the, ii. 67
Visible world, and, iii. 72
Worship of, ii. 117
GOAL, Final, i. 311
Man, of animal life, iii. 63
Misery, of, ii. 364

GOAT, Androgyne, of Mendes, i. 297; v. 231
Azazel, the, ii. 159
Capricornus or, iv. 150
Generation, symbol of fall into, iv. 79
Gnostic meaning of, iii. 385
Headed Satan, Baphomet, iii. 388
Human beings with legs and horns of a, iii. 65
Men, iii. 65, 74
Symbol of, ii. 72
Victory, Azazel the God of, ii. 159
Witches' Sabbath, of, iv. 79
GOATS sacrificed to Amphitrite, iv. 150
GOBI, Desert of, iii. 18, 371, 404; iv. 71;
v. 39, 40
Island in the desert of, iii. 319
Oasis in, desert, iii. 224
Region, iii. 403
Statues, of, iii. 331
GOD, Abraham, Isaac, Jacob of, v. 84
Abrasax a supreme, ii. 64
Absolute, ii. 129
Abstract force now called, ii. 113
Adepts and, i. 135
Adonis, iv. 19
Agni, of fire, iv. 135
Air of, ii. 183
All, we call the, i. 135
Al-orit, of fire, iii. 360
Ammon, ii. 80
Angel or, ii. 358
Ani, Spiritual Sun, v. 462
Anthropomorphic, i. 20, 71, 319, 322;
ii. 139, 328
Apollo, iii. 20; iv. 343
Apostle-initiate, of, i. 75
Arch-deceiver, an, ii. 140
Aspects, of the three, ii. 58
Astral light created by, i. 303
Avenging, iv. 355
Azazel, ii. 159
Babylonian, i. 173
Beast, or, ii. 361
Being must pass human cycles to become,
iii. 322
Bes, ii. 100
Biblical, v. 110, 476
Black, v. 233
Body, needed a, iii. 236
Boreas, of winter, iii. 24
Brahmā, v. 476
Breath of, i. 135
Buddhists, ii. 360
Celestial being, i. 250
Chance, the pseudonym of, ii. 379
Chaos of, i. 264
Christian, v. 158, 476
Cosmic, v. 227
Creative, i. 84; iii. 242; v. 189, 195
Creator, v. 157, 212
Crocodile, i. 266
Cupid, iii. 416
Dead, of, ii. 68
Death, of, iii. 56; v. 161
Deity not, ii. 65
Demon inverse of, i. 281
Destinies, of, iv. 32
Devil, and, i. 147; ii. 133; iii. 232

GOD (*Contd.*)
Divine fully conscious, i. 167
Dyaus the unrevealed, ii. 92
Earth, of, ii. 183; iii. 372
Egyptian ram-headed, iii. 293
Electricity not, i. 171
Elohim called, iv. 56; v. 198, 234
Eternal, ii. 58; v. 195
Evil, of, ii. 129
Exile, in, ii. 169
Extra-cosmic, ii. 253, 293
Fancy, created by man's, iii. 305
Father, i. 141, 335; iii. 239; v. 127, 210
Female, double of, ii. 343
Female manifestation, v. 462
Finger of, v. 245
Finite, ii. 69, 257
Fire, a consuming, ii. 113
Fire, is a living, i. 180
Fire, of, ii. 183; iii. 282, 360; iv. 57, 118, 135
Fire referred to as, ii. 187
Firmament, of the, i. 251
First-born of, iii. 284
Fohat seems to exercise the powers of, i. 195
Footstool of, i. 209
Four races, of, iv. 343
Ganesha, of Wisdom, v. 111
Garment of, i. 148; v. 187, 188
Gautama of, i. 169
Generation, of, i. 275; iv. 35
Genuis or, iii. 41
Glory of, i. 18
Gods, ii. 139; v. 125, 214
Gods, amongst all, iv. 45, 160
Gods of pagans, of, i. 72
Good counsel of, v. 285
Handsome face, of the, ii. 68
Heavenly body temple of a, every, ii. 302
Hebrew Elohim called, iv. 56
Hebrews, of, iii. 276
Hidden mystery, iii. 217
Higher Self and, v. 78, 79, 452
Highest, v. 192, 219, 476
Himself, containing all things, within, ii. 105, 162
Holy Ghost, the, v. 127
Holy Spirit of, v. 52
Horse, of the, iii. 398
Horus, i. 274
Human dogma, of, i. 75
Hypothesis, called a, ii. 299
I am myself, ii. 361
Iao mystery, ii. 167
Image of, iii. 15; v. 326
Imperfect, ii. 257
Impersonal, v. 30, 380
Incarnation of, i. 334; v. 430
Indwelling, iii. 276; v. 431, 453, 512
Initiates and, i. 335
Intelligible, ii. 181
Intra-cosmic, i. 76
Israel, of, ii. 188; iii. 72
Jehovah, a fighting, iii. 55
Jehovah as one living, i. 277
Jews, of the, ii. 65; v. 128, 129, 190
Kabalah taught by, iii. 285
Kalpas, who lives in all, ii. 149

Kāma a supreme, iii. 183
Khem, v. 63
Kingdom of, is within us, i. 323
Khous, v. 251, 253
Kivan, v. 318
Knoom, ii. 100
Latin Church, of, v. 94
Law, and, i. 131; v. 70
Leibnitz, of, ii. 353, 356
Life, of, i. 274
Light, of, iii. 20
Limbus from the word of, i. 326
Local, ii. 183
LORD, as a designation of, iv. 78; v. 201
Lord thy, a consuming fire, the, i. 180
Love, of, iii. 416
Lunus, i. 275; iv. 32
Mahat is, ii. 327
Male, ii. 339; v. 190, 192, 228, 233
Man an immortal, iii. 248, v. 81, 419, 453
Man finally becomes, iii. 192
Man potential, iii. 247; v. 79, 431, 453
Man tends to become, i. 214
Man, temple of, v. 75, 82, 84, 463
Manifested, i. 333; ii. 147; v. 116, 555
Matter, manifest in, iii. 238
Matter, of, iii. 275
Meborach, Hebrew name of, ii. 100
Meru, mountain of, iv. 61
Messengers, of, i. 319; iii. 358
Michael called, iv. 46
Mind or spirit, not a, i. 327
Mono-theistic systems, of, ii. 399
Moon, i. 274
Moses, of, ii. 89
Multiform, ii. 155
Mystery, i. 162; ii. 100, 167; iii. 217; v. 216, 270
Mysteries of, v. 63
Nahbkoon, the, ii. 194
Nature, and, ii. 130; iii. 359
Nature, in, i. 75, 333; v. 87, 115, 421
Neiols, iii. 416
New Testament, v. 337
Noumenon, as, ii. 215
Number endowed with motion is, i. 135
One, v. 30, 351, 462
One life is, ii. 327
One living, i. 72; v. 70, 167, 189, 192
Osiris, i. 274, 275; ii. 398; v. 233
Pagans, of, i. 184
Pan, iii. 388; iv. 153; v. 117
Parabrahman not, i. 73
Path of darkness, giving light to, ii. 118
Paul, of, v. 382
Personal, i 69, 70, 195, 243; ii. 130, 135, 201, 269, 303, 338, 339, 360; iv. 43, 69; v. 76, 77, 81, 93, 187, 351, 358, 382, 425, 431, 462
Phallic, ii. 60; v. 63, 477
Philosophical symbol become a jealous, ii. 130
Plato, of, v. 382
Power of Simon Magus called, v. 126, 131
Poseidon, iii. 398
Prometheus must have been, iv. 94
Ptah the fiery, ii. 80
Pythagoras, of, v. 382

GOD (*Contd.*)
Rabbins, of the, ii. 111
Race of, v. 249
Radiant, i. 221
Ram-headed, iii. 293
Ray emanating as a finite, ii. 69
Rudra, of fire, iii. 282, 284; iv. 118
Sabbath, of, iii. 238
Satan, and, i. 246; iv. 346
Secondless, v. 209
Secret Wisdom of, v. 65, 287
Semite, of the, ii. 98
Seven-lettered, ii. 127
Seven-rayed, iii. 47
Shadow of, iv. 76
Shiva, ii. 179
Shoo, iv. 116
Solar, v. 206
Son, the, v. 127
Son of, v. 157, 159, 360
Sons of, i. 256, 257; iv. 57, 63, 68; v. 44, 152, 212, 289, 297, 300
Soul, and the, i. 334
Space, in, iv. 52
Spirit an agent of, i. 244
Spirit becomes a, i. 291
Spirit, of, ii. 60, 81, 166; iv. 57: v. 189
Storms and rain, of, iii. 352
Substance, of, ii. 257
Sun, v. 315
Sun and, v. 159
Sun the highest, iii. 360; v. 94, 315
Sun the hyperborean, iv. 339
Supreme, v. 212, 233, 240
Symbol of, ii. 95; iii. 359
Tabernacle designed to contain, iii. 303
Temple, of the, iv. 34
Theists, of, ii. 139
Theologians, of, iv. 44
Theologies, of, ii. 130
Thot, ii. 100
Thrones of, v. 122
Time, of, ii. 72; iii. 389
Tribal, iii. 276
Truths of, v. 69
Universal Spirit, the, i. 301
Union with, v. 78, 82, 419, 428, 453, 503
Universe, as synthesis of, ii. 131
Unknown, v. 408
Unrevealed, ii. 58, 92
Vayu, i. 241; ii. 189
Victory, of, ii. 159
Virtues of, v. 122
Vishnu not a high, in the Rig Veda, i. 171
Vishvakarman, v. 270
War, of, iii. 55, 381; iv. 119
Water, of, ii. 183
Wind and air, i. 241; ii. 189
Wine, of, iii. 362
Wisdom of, ii. 100; iii. 51, 229, 379; iv. 45, 128; v. 111, 180, 302, 369
Word of, i. 151; v. 180
World one with, ii. 138
Worship of, in ark, iv. 37
Yama, of death, iii. 56
Zeus not highest, ii. 144
GOD-HIEROPHANT, iv. 128

GOD-IDEA, Evolution of the, ii. 40
GOD-INFORMED, man, iii. 419
GOD-INHABITED continent, a, iii. 225
GOD-JAH or Jehovah, iv. 100
GOD-KINGS, Island of the, iv. 342
GOD-LIKE, Divine and men, ii. 366
Man, iii. 248
Symbols reveal the, ii. 15
GOD-MAN, Animal man becomes, iii. 131
Unity of, i. 123
GOD-MANIFESTED, iv. 123
GOD-NAME, Element of phallicism found in every, ii. 31
Jehovah, ii. 28; iv. 32, 114; v. 72
Jewish, iii. 138
Samael a, ii. 135
GOD-NAMES, Bible, in the, iv. 106
Elohim, of, ii. 28; iv. 114; v. 72
Phallicism, and, ii. 28
GOD-PRINCIPLE remains indivisible, ii. 186
GOD-SPIRIT, Substance called, i. 330
Universal principle or, i. 145
GODBOLE, Krishna Shastri, v. 341
GODDESS, Anouki, Egyptian, iii. 43
Ardhanari hermaphrodite, iii. 43
Aster't, iii. 54, 55
Basht or Pasht, ii. 17; iv. 122
Earth and water, the, iii. 139
Fate, Moira the, of, iv. 176
Fire, iii. 139
Fortune and prosperity, of, iii. 86
Great Bear, of the, ii. 125
Grecian, iii. 138
Hebe, iii. 138
Hermaphrodite, iii. 43
Hiquit, ii. 100
Ida or Ila, iii. 143, 155
Increase, of, iii. 86
Isis, iii. 39; iv. 225; v. 165, 253
Istar, lunar, iii. 153
Life, of, iii. 39, 43
Ma, iii. 367
Mercy, of, i. 139
Neith, iii. 143
Nemesis the dreaded, ii. 367
Primordial monsters, who gave birth to, iii. **75**
Rhea, iii. 151
Saga, iii. 284
Seven stars, of, ii. 125; iv. 117
Shri, iii. 86
Sovereign, iv. 30
Speech, of, iii. 155
Syrian, iii. 54, 55
Thalastha or Thalassa, iii. 75
Toad, ii. 100
Vesta, iii. 152
Wisdom of, v. 74, 165
Youth, of, iii. 138
GODDESS-MOTHER of the seven sons, iv. 96
GODDESS-QUEEN, Hel, the, iii. 108; iv. 343
GODDESSES, Diana-Luna, ii. 110
Dual aspect of, ii. 115
Dual-sexed images of, v. 292
Generative powers, of, iv. 29
Gods and, i. 52
Kanya-Durga, ii. 384
Lunar, ii. 115; iii. 36, 44

GODDESSES (*Contd.*)
Moon, i. 275; ii. 111
Mother, iv. 32
Norse, iii. 108
Owl- and ox-headed, iv. 292
Sati and Anouki are triadic, ii. 82
Virgin-mother, ii. 118
GODEFROY, quoted, ii. 223, 230
GODH, God in Saxon is, ii. 61
GODHEAD, Central sun, and, iii. 242
Persons in the, ii. 393
Triune, ii. 96
GODLING of the fields, Pan, iv. 153
GODS, Adepts enlightened by, iii. 215
Aditi, mother of, iv. 96
Adversaries of, iii. 171
Aerial, iii. 86
Aggregate, i. 84
Allegories of, ii. 134; iii. 235
Alphabet and language of, the, iii. 363
Ambhāmsi synonym of, ii. 178
Ancients, of the, i. 161; ii. 338; v. 309
Androgyne character of creative, ii. 146
Antiquity of, ii. 155
Arūpa, iii. 318
Asuras and, i. 251; ii. 136, 146; iii. 389;
    iv. 66, 68; v. 287
Assyrian, v. 202
Atoms, and, i. 206; ii. 273, 291
Attributes of, iii. 54
Auto-generation of, ii. 114, 115
Beneficent, iii. 363; v. 241
B'ne Alhim or sons of, iii. 36
Bodies of, ii. 212, 246
Body of the day, evolved from, iii. 170
Born or incarnated, iv. 335, 342
Bosom of, iii. 294
Brahma, and, i. 124; ii. 146
Brahma radiates the, ii. 165
Breath of, ii. 297
Builder of, iii. 344
Catholics, of, ii. 337
Celestial, ii. 195; iii. 215
Celestial fire belonged to, iv. 94
Chaldean, ii. 381
Chaldeo-Judean, ii. 381
Chastity of, ii. 193
Churning of the ocean by, i. 135
Circle of necessity, must pass through, iii. 304
City of, v. 337
Combats of, iv. 323
Conflict of, iii. 389
Corporeality invisible, iv. 83
Cosmic, i. 119, 332; ii. 68, 181, 183, 185
Create, desire to, iii. 237
Created, i. 268
Creation, of, ii. 295
Creative, ii. 142, 145; iii. 203; v. 199
Creatures, the, v. 212
Cycle, at beginning of every, ii. 152
Cycle of, v. 462
Cyrus, of, ii. 378
Daityas or, ii. 140
Daksha's sacrifice to, iii. 189
Darkness, of, iv. 52
Defeat of, ii. 137
Deified men, are, iii. 179

Deity, and, ii. 49, 139
Deluge, iii. 359
Demi-gods and, iii. 250
Demiourgoi or, v. 214, 218
Demons, and, ii. 137, 175, 178
Descent of, ii. 152; iv. 52
Development of, iii. 366
Devils, and, iv. 49, 81
Dhyāni-Buddhas or, i. 119
Dhyānis, or, i. 274, 334
Dragons, whom men call, iii. 354
Dual-sexed images of, v. 292
Dual state of, iv. 83
Dynasties of, iii. 366, 368; v. 181
Earth, exiles on the, iii. 270
Earth, of, i. 286; ii. 85; iii. 357; v. 110
Egos, or conscious spiritual, ii. 367
Egyptian, i. 166, 186; ii. 154; iii. 101; iv. 77;
    v. 164, 247, 251
Elementals issued from, ii. 356
Elements, of the, ii. 182; iii. 274
Elohim, v. 90
Emanation of Triad, v. 77
Entities of higher worlds, i. 190
Entities or supersensuous, ii. 243
Epicurus and Democritus believers in, ii. 336;
    v. 78
Evolution of, ii. 156, 273
Existence of, v. 78
Fall of, i. 185
Fallen, i. 267; iii. 235
False, ii. 337
Father-, v. 111, 463
Father-Mother of, i. 136, 169; v. 381
Father, of, i. 179; ii. 145; iii. 272, 362
Fathers are our devils, of our, iii. 44
Feed on man, v. 565
Fire, ii. 94; iii. 284
Fire of, ii. 245
First principle and, ii. 144
Fohat, thought of, i. 171
Forces are, ii. 183, 397
Form of, ii. 175
Four-armed Hindu, iii. 296
Fravarshi, endowed with a, iv. 48
Genealogies of, iii. 54
Genesis of, ii. 271; iii. 37
Genii, and, i. 329; ii. 292
Ghost-world, of the, iii. 365
Goddesses, and, i. 52
Great, iii. 360; v. 325, 333, 462
Greeks naturalized, iv. 339
Guardians, and, ii. 299
Heaven, ascended to, iv. 353
Hermes, of, i. 335
Herodotus on dynasties of, iii. 366
Heroes, and, iii. 367
Higher, v. 559
Hindu, i. 174; iii. 296; v. 111
Hindu Mythology, of, ii. 391
Hindu Pantheon, in, iii. 71
Hindu Scriptures, in, iii. 181
Holy youths or, i. 243
Hosts, instructors of, iv. 83
Human form, became princes in, iii. 365
Identity of various names for, ii. 359
Idols, and, ii. 189

GODS (*Contd.*)

Ignorant, of the, ii. 182
Ilda-Baoth, produced from, i. 247
Immoral stories of, iv. 333
Incarnations of, iv. 334
India in, iii. 99
Infernal, iii. 362
Informing, iii. 361
Intra-cosmic, iii. 258
Invisible, iii. 275
Jealousy of all, iii. 284, 354
Jews borrowed Chaldean, ii. 381
Jews robbed of, ii. 381
Kabirim were, iii. 359
Kama supreme among, iii. 183
Karma of, v. 376, 378
Karma, will of, i. 334
Land of, iii. 20, 266, 293
Language of, ii. 185; v. 114, 197, 264
Light of, iii. 284, 366; iv. 52
Limbs of Noon, created out of, ii. 24
Lower, v. 30
Lower region, of the, ii. 184
Lunar, i. 227; iii. 36
Male, v. 233
Malevolent, v. 241
Man, and, ii. 369; iv. 335
Manifesting, v. 253, 281
Manvantara, in another, ii. 113
Many, ii. 185
Masks over old, iv. 52
Men and, ii. 328, 330, 357; iv. 49
Men appealed to, iii. 206
Men had been as, iii. 258, 281
Men made, iii. 257
Meru the abode of, iii. 356
Metals, presiding over, iii. 362
Minor, ii. 219; iv. 273
Monads and atoms, ii. 335, 344, 348, 349, 357, 358; iv. 240, 241
Monads, and intelligent conscious, ii. 346
Monads, and living, ii. 277
Mortals, mixed freely with, iii. 275
Mortals, and, iii. 272
Moses forbids reviling, iv. 46
Mother of, i. 161; ii. 251, 399
Mysteries, of the, iv. 27
Mystery of, i. 239
National, ii. 381
Nature, and, iv. 334
Nature's lower powers worshipped as, i. 117
No-Gods, and, iii. 230, 240
Northern origin of, iv. 338, 343
Numbers and, v. 116
Odin, father of, ii. 145
Offspring of, i. 261
Olympus, of, v. 92
One, are, v. 430
Operating intelligent beings called, ii. 221
Opponents of, iii. 169
Orders of beings or, iii. 69
Pagans, of, v. 88, 245, 250, 325
Patriarchs, presented as, ii. 64
Personal, v. 233, 392
Planetary, ii. 106; iii. 215, 360; v. 310, 334
Planetary spirits or, ii. 345
Planets and, i. 207; ii. 299; iii. 36

Powers, or creative fashioning, ii. 215; v. 368
Prajāpatis are, v. 356
Prakriti and, i. 299
Priest-Initiates' belief in, iv. 87
Primitive, v. 333
Protestants, of, ii. 337
Prototypes of, v. 78
Ra creates, i. 277
Race of, iii. 18
Races evolved from, ii. 35
Races, of fourth and fifth, iii. 179
Racial, ii. 139
Raumas, and, iii. 189
Rebirths of, ii. 178
Regents or, i. 207
Reign of, iii. 371
Reigning over men, i. 310
Relation to our, ii. 176
Sanskrit, language of, i. 313
Second race, of, iv. 335
Secondary, v. 261
Selfish feeling among, i. 243
Seven, v. 202, 214, 356
Seven great, of Egypt, i. 186; iii. 101, 360; v. 333
Several, iii. 186
Sidereal, ii. 156, 379
Solar, ii. 382, 383; v. 314, 317
Sons of the, iii. 36
Soul which informs, divine, i. 267
Space, and, ii. 57
Speech of, v. 197
Spirits and, ii. 336, 393
Stars, of light from the, iii. 366
Stones poised in equilibrium compared to, iii. 344
Stories of, ii. 142
Substance of bodies of, ii. 246
Sun, iii. 36; v. 94
Sun, vehicle of host of, ii. 201
Supernal, ii. 325
Synonym of, ii. 178
Teraphim and, v. 238
Theogony of creative, ii. 142
Third race of, iii. 270, 433
Thou shalt not revile the, ii. 216
Tribal, ii. 139, 381
Tutelary, v. 238
Twelve Great, v. 462
Union with, v. 452
Vāch generated by, ii. 148
Vedas, and, ii. 136
Vishnu, and, ii. 139, 140
We are the, iii. 273
Will of, iii. 68
Wisdom, of secret, iv. 68; v. 74
World of, ii. 165
Ye shall be as, iii. 281
Zodiacal, iii. 356; v. 332

GODS-hierophants or sacrificers, iv. 17
GODWIN, W. quoted, v. 297
GOETHE, Archetype of, iv. 306
Garment of God, on the, i. 148
Plurality of worlds, on, iv. 275
GOGARD, the Hellenic tree of life, iii. 106
GOLCAR, Rocking-stones on the slopes of, iii. 344

GOLD, Basis of, ii. 126
  Coloured, Brihaspati the, iv. 66
  Manas thrice purified, iv. 89
  Masculine principle, or fiery being, ii. 79
  Race, signifies first, iii. 273
  Race yellow like, iii. 230
GOLDEN, Calf, the, iii. 302, 400; v. 71
  Candlestick, the, ii. 34; iv. 153
  City, the, iii. 381
  Cow of India, iv. 30, 37
  Eggs, birds that lay, iii. 131
  Eggs of the Heavenly Duck, iii. 26
  Light, luminous Sutra of, ii. 192
  Lotus, Padma the, iv. 149
  Mountain, guardian griffins of the, ii. 80
  Race, the, iii. 319
  Ray, Yellow or, v. 456
  Region of the Ural, iii. 414
  Ring, Yima's, iv. 181
  Star island, Asteria, iii. 382
  Stem, plant of the, iii. 422
  Tau, v. 318
  Thread, Continuous life, of, iii. 89; iv. 82
  Verses, father of the, iv. 175
  Womb, ii. 129
GOLDEN AGE, v. 302, 337, 339
  Aryans, of, ii. 369
  Ash tree of, iv. 89
  Astraea renews, iv. 353
  Fables of, iii. 371
  Gods walked the earth in, iii. 275
  Immortals and, iii. 272
  Iran of, ii. 375
  Kali Yuga called, iv. 119
  Last days of, iv. 89
  Period of, iii. 130
  Plato's, iii. 266
  Races, of seven, iii. 204
  Saturn, of, iii. 419; iv. 346
  Traditions of, iv. 290
GOLDEN EGG, ALL not created by the, i. 75
  Brahma, laid by, ii. 74
  Brahma, re-enters the, ii. 92; v. 472
  Brāhmanical, iv. 123
  Cosmogony preluded with, ii. 144
  Elements, surrounded by, i. 134
  Hiranyagarbha the, ii. 144
  Poles, with two, ii. 280
  Seed became a, ii. 46
  Sun, resplendent as the, i. 153
  Womb, or, v. 472
GOLDEN-Coloured, Men, iii. 204
  Mercury the, iv. 41; v. 428
GOLDEN-Winged cup the, iii. 382
GOLDSTUCKER'S Sanskrit Dictionary, iv. 93
GOLGOTHA of life, Path of the, i. 311
GOLIATH, iii. 336
GON-PA, Crypts in the, i. 47
  Lamasery, v. 393
GOOD, John Mason, quoted, ii. 293
GOOD, Astral light, effects of, ii. 57
  City, iii. 229
  Colours, v. 554
  Doctrine, v. 407
  Dragon of, iii. 39
  Evil essential to, ii. 131
  Evil servant of, iv. 45

Genius, iii. 214
God not derived from Anglo-Saxon, ii. 61
More evil than, in the world, ii. 131
Origin of, iii. 38
Satan allegorized as, iii. 240
Serpent, iii. 355
Shepherds, v. 289
Spirit Agathodaimōn, ii. 58
Spirits, islands of the, iii. 370
Sun, the Sovereign, v. 218
Supreme, of Plato, iv. 124
GOOD AND EVIL, Agathodaimōn had knowl-
    edge of, iii. 215
  Archaic philosophy, in, i. 140
  Battle between, iv. 63
  Cause of, iv. 81
  Cosmical elements are in their nature, ii. 61
  Eternal Principles, are, v. 129
  Forces of, iv. 65
  God and devil and, i. 147
  Homogeneity contains essence of, ii. 129
  Knowledge of, iii. 17, 133, 277, 281, 381;
    v. 493
  Nature, in, iii. 238
  One, iii. 218
  Principles, of, iv. 172; v. 129
  Problem of, iii. 304
  Relative are, v. 503
  Tree of, i. 292; iii. 143
  Tree of knowledge of, iii. 219; v. 28, 43, 85
  Triple deity said to be, ii. 61
  Twins are, iii. 104
  Two squares of, ii. 24
GOOD LAW, Adepts of, iv. 64
  Cheu of, v. 393
  Esoteric, v. 406
  Ethics of, v. 363
  Men of, iii. 424
  Propagation of, v. 374, 394
GOODNESS, First cause of all, iv. 124
  God not from the attribute of, ii. 61
  Gods endowed with, iii. 70
  Place of, iv. 134
  Providence, attributed to, ii. 367
  Satan, might be called, iii. 388
  Third creation abounding in, ii. 172
GOOSE, Eggs of the, iv. 167
  Hansa or, i. 145, 146
  Swan or, ii. 68; iii. 131
GOPIS, Mystic powers, v. 378
  Symbolize Planets, v. 311
GORDIAN KNOT, v. 217
GORGON'S head, Sparks on the, ii. 52
GORILLA, Bones of, iv. 251
  Brain of, iv. 246, 251
  Cranium of, iii. 199
  Dryopithecus and, iv. 249, 302
  Evolutionist, to, iv. 252
  Fierce appearance of, iv. 257
  Future fossils of, iii. 265
  Intelligence of, iv. 245
  Nergo separated from, iv. 248
  Special creation for, iv. 248
  Teeth of a male, iv. 236
GORILLAS, Dens of, iv. 246
GOSPEL, Enoch and, v. 100
  Fourth, i. 272; ii. 301; iv. 100; v. 81, 96, 97

GOSPEL (*Contd.*)
  Gnostic, iv. 30, 140, 175
  Hebrews, according to, v. 160
  Kabalistic reading of, v. 167
  Liberty, of light and, iv. 83
  Mysteries of the, v. 66
  Original, of Matthew, v. 143, 160
  St. John, of, i. 138; iii. 51
GOSPELS, Angels in, i. 185
  Central Figure of, v. 71, 72
  Doctrines of, v. 103
  Elements, and, iii. 123
  Irenaeus and four, i. 115
  Little ones in, iv. 73
  Miracles, magic, and, v. 125
  Platonic Element, in, v. 36
  Secret Meaning of, v. 66
  Synoptical, v. 336
  Revised version of, ii. 294
GOSSE, quoted, iii. 438
GOTHIC deities, iv. 175
GOTRAS of Brahmans or caste races, iv. 70
GOTT or God in German, ii. 61; iv. 173
GOULD, Charles quoted, iii. 21, 22, 23, 65, 427,
  438; iv. 257, 265
GOVERNMENT of Saturn, iii. 371
GOVERNORS, Builders, or, ii. 202
  Dhyān Chohans, or, ii. 325
  Essence of seven, iii. 112
  Fashioning of seven other, iii. 239
  Nature of the seven, iii. 16
  Rulers, or, iii. 105
  World, of the, ii. 157
GRADES, Consciousness, of, ii. 267
  Initiation, of, i. 255
  Invisible intelligences of various, ii. 336
GRADING, v. 483
GRAECO-Latin names, Haeckel's, iv. 244
GRAFTING of Divine on to material, v. 171
GRAHA-RAJA, v. 270
GRAIN, Lords of Wisdom produced, iii. 372
  Sand, contains an abyss, of, ii. 395
  Sand, essence of a, of, i. 205
GRĀMANĪS, Yakshas or minor Gods, iii. 215
GRAMMAR of Pānini, iii. 255, 437
GRAMMARIAN, greatest, Pānini, v. 27
GRAND, Agent magique, astral light the, i. 298
  Climacteric of Europeans, the, ii. 382
  Cycle, ii. 367
  Masters, mallet of the, iii. 108
  Symbol Kabbalistique, iii. 359
GRANDIDIER, Investigations of, iv. 238
GRANITE, Cannot burn, v. 562
  Enormous blocks of, iii. 343
GRAPHITE in meteorites, iv. 276
GRASS, Evolution of the blade of, ii. 361
GRASSES, Cereals developed from wild, iii. 372
GRASSHOPPERS called winged serpents by
  Greeks, iii. 210
GRATIOLET, quoted, iv. 251, 252
GRATTAN Guinness, see Book Index
GRAVITATION, Attraction and, ii. 220
  Axial motions and, ii. 229
  Bodies not subject to, ii. 308
  Combinations, owes its life to new, ii. 253
  Comets and, ii. 229
  Equatorial matter, of the, ii. 317

  Examined, must be carefully, i. 338
  Father Æther wedded to, ii. 218
  Hydro-dynamical theories of, ii. 209
  Intelligences, result of, ii. 325
  Jupiter, on, iii. 145
  King and ruler of matter, called, ii. 216
  Law of, ii. 213, 308, 328; v. 223
  Living beings subject to, ii. 263
  Peripatetic laws, and, ii. 227
  Phenomena unexplained by, ii. 221
  Prophet, is God and matter its, ii. 215
  Theories of, ii. 209, 215
GRAVITIES, atoms of different specific, ii. 237
GRAVITY, Abstract ideas as to, ii. 342
  Agent which causes, ii. 201
  Cause, an effect not a, ii. 207, 213
  Centrifugal tendency equal to, iii. 75
  Comets and, ii. 228
  Force of, the, ii. 228; iv. 193
  Keely and, ii. 283
  Law of, astronomers and, ii. 213
  Law of, ii. 228, 316
  Life, force or, ii. 253
  Lodge on, ii. 211
  Modern science, of, ii. 328
  Newton and, ii. 207
  Obsolete law, seems to be an, ii. 228
  Occultists' view, of, ii. 216, 238
  Solar system, and, ii. 226
  Spiritual, v. 300
  Transformation of, ii. 235
GRAY, Dr. Asa, referred to, iv. 352
GREAT, Adjuster, the, iii. 329
  Æther, Virgil called Jupiter, ii. 45
  All, Pan the, iv. 153
  Asura, Ahriman a, iv. 58
  Breath, the, i. 70, 77, 80, 116, 203, 273, 309;
    ii. 174, 219; iii. 20, 36; v. 479
  Britain, sinking of, iii. 268
  Cat of the basin of Persaea, iv. 116
  Causes of misery, i. 112
  Circle, the, ii. 147
  Deceiver, astral light the, i. 130
  Deity of the Zunis, sun the, iv. 200
  Deluge, the, i. 136; ii. 85; iv. 103
  Face, Macroprosopus the, i. 129
  Flood, the, iii. 147, 308
  Four, servants of the, iii. 425
  Illusion, the, i. 129, 138, 262
  Initiation, great, v. 296
  Jewel of Wisdom, v. 396
  Kabalah, v. 85
  King of the dazzling face, iii. 424
  Kings of the devas, i. 184
  Law, the, i. 203; ii. 365; iii. 89
  Men, Gebers, Kabeiri, etc., mean, i. 174
  Mysteries, Figurative death in the, iv. 30
  Night, Mahapralaya or, i. 192
  Personality, bodies of a, iii. 278
  Power, Fohat the, iii. 76
  Pralaya, i. 83
  Round or mahākalpa, iv. 186
  Sacrifice, the, i. 256; v. 270, 370
  Sages, the, iv. 210
  Saros, cyclic periods within the, ii. 366
  Stars, the seven, iv. 22
  Step in the pyramid, iv. 34

GREAT (*Contd.*)
  Thought, v. 447
  Tone, v. 463
  Unknown, iii. 116; v. 101
  Vehicle, v. 399
  War, Mahābhārata or the, iii. 389, 394
  Water, deep or chaos the, ii. 398
  Waters, i. 138; iii. 423
  Year, circuit, of the, ii. 376
GREAT AGE, Day of Brahma, or, i. 291
  Divisions of, ii. 380
  Liberation to end of, iii. 87
  Mahākalpa or, i. 110; v. 41
  Manifestation at beginning of, i. 252
GREAT AGES, Day of Brahma or a thousand, ii. 87
  Mahāyugas or, i. 132
GREAT ARCHITECT, Universe of, ii. 338
  World, of, iv. 129
GREAT BEAR, Constellation of, i. 260; iv. 119; v. 202
  Mother of time, and, ii. 125
  Seven Rishis of, ii. 72; iv. 57, 120
  Seven stars of, i. 274; ii. 124, 172; iv. 120, 202
  Typhon of, iv. 117
GREAT CYCLE, Garuda the, ii. 81; iii. 323
  Mahākalpa, or, i. 110; iv. 135, 141
  Mahāyuga or, ii. 366
  Messiah at end of, ii. 99
  Universe and, i. 301
GREAT DAY, Be with us, i. 187, 192, 195
  Manvantara or, i. 148
  Seventh round after, iv. 59
GREAT DEEP, Akkads, of the, iii. 64
  Brahma evolving out of, ii. 58
  Chaos or, ii. 149
  Nile called, ii. 31
  Soul of the world, or female, ii. 68; iii. 313
  Universal matrix or, iii. 75
  Water the, ii. 99, 179
GREAT DRAGON, Christians and, v. 325
  Ophis, or, ii. 179
  Rahu, v. 375
  Symbology of, ii. 123
  Venus identified with, iii. 44
GREAT EXTREME of Confucius, ii. 71, 158; iv. 123, 124
  Cosmogonies, the, the shortest of all, ii. 158
GREAT GODS, Bodies of birds, create men with, iii. 66
  Eight, iv. 152
  Jayas, or, iii. 99
  Religion, of every, iv. 178
  Reverence paid to, ii. 297
  Seven, iv. 30, 178
  Sun the chief of, iii. 36
  Twelve, iii. 36
GREAT GREEN, Chaos or, ii. 24
  One, ii. 152; iv. 151
  Primordial water or, ii. 24
GREAT KALPA, Age or, i. 150
  Duration of, i. 254
GREAT MOTHER, Abode of, iv. 71
  Aima, iii. 93, 383
  Existences, of all, iv. 30
  Great father and, iii. 93

Io is Eve, iii. 414
  Seven principles of, i. 332
  Signs of, ii. 152
  Universe absorbed by, i. 116
  Water of life in, i. 146
GREAT ONES, Evil thought, had an, iv. 58
  Names of, iii. 283
  Seven, ii. 399
GREAT PYRAMID, Creative principle, symbolized, ii. 30
  Date of, iii. 429, 430
  Egyptian Zodiac and, iii. 433
  Epoch, iii. 429
  Foundations of, iv. 32; v. 165
  Isis Unveiled, on, ii. 29
  King's chamber in, i. 308
  Meaning of, v. 91
  Measures, of, ii. 25; v. 166, 186, 196, 197
  Mysteries and Initiations in, ii. 30; v. 271, 296
  Parker on, ii. 27
  Period of, iii. 430
  Primordial Circle and, v. 207
  Proctor on, iii. 430
GREAT REVELATION, quoted, v. 446
GREAT SEA, Holy spirit or, ii. 108
  Kabalistic teachings on, ii. 56
  Mother-water, iii. 74
  Mystery of serpent of, iv. 72
GREAT SERPENT, Eternity of, ii. 58
  Garden of Eden, of, ii. 132
  Ruler of the night, was, iii. 44
GREAT WHEEL, Anupādaka, was, i. 119, 123
  Mahākalpa, a, i. 113
  Universe or, i. 123
GREAT YEAR, v. 341
GRECO-OLYMPIAN Don Juan, Zeus the, iii. 418
GREECE, Argos in, iii. 414
  Books of, v. 26
  Civilization before that of, iv. 355
  Classics of, iii. 439
  Cradle of Art and Science, v. 44
  Devas symbolized in, iii. 103
  Fables of, iv. 338
  Fallen demon of, iv. 54
  Giants of, iii. 335
  Homer and Hesiod and superstitions of, iv. 333
  India, and, iii. 416
  Initiates in, iv. 163; v. 265
  Literature of, iv. 16
  Magic in, iii. 366
  Origin of, iv. 313
  Orphic philosophy of, ii. 307
  Pelasgians and, iv. 343
  Philosophers of, v. 23, 74, 281, 303
  Philosophy of, 33, 35
  Prometheus in, mythos of, iii. 420
  Rishis handed on knowledge to, i. 257
  Sacred measures of, ii. 25
  Sages of, v. 33, 59, 218
  Seven sages of, iv. 312
  Superstitions of, iv. 333
  Temples of, i. 53, 257; v. 238
  Traditions of, iii. 392
GREEK(S), Alphabet, v. 118
  Adonis of, iii. 55
  Alexander, under, ii. 376

GREEKS (Contd.)
Alexandrian, ii. 384, 385
Amalthaea of, iv. 150
Aphrodite, v. 212
Argha of, iv. 30
Ash-tree of, iv. 89
Astronomy of, ii. 384
Asuramaya and, iii. 62
Atlanteans, and, iv. 312
Atlantis, notion of, iii. 394, 403
Atlanto-Aryans, remnants of, iii. 434
Caduceus modified by, ii. 273
Chemis, on the, ii. 83
Chronology of, iv. 191
Church, of, v. 41, 93, 117, 133, 483, 511
Ciphering among, ii. 76
Conception of deity of, iii. 166
Cross of the neophytes, iv. 132
Cycle of, v. 341
Decad and, iv. 152
Demiourgoi of, v. 325
Descent of, iv. 337
Diatessaron of, iv. 172
Dolphin with, iv. 148, 150
Egg-symbol among, ii. 75
Egyptians, taught by, i. 176
Ether among, ii. 44, 208
Geographical theories of, iii. 415
Helios of, iv. 110
Hercules of, v. 258, 259
Hermes of, iii. 41, 145; iv. 22; v. 74
Homer in days of, iii. 24, 437
Hyperborean continent known to, iii. 20, 24
To On, the One of, iii. 114
Jupiter chief daemon of, ii. 188
Land of the eternal sun, had a tradition as to, iii. 24
Logos of, i. 141
Luna, on, ii. 102
Lying, the, i. 174
Macedonian, iii. 62
Manes and mania appropriated by, iii. 151
Michael Mercury of, iv. 49
Moon-symbol of, ii. 102; iii. 132
Morning star, and the, iv. 329
Mysteries of, v. 137, 138
Mystery language understood by, iv. 145
Nabo of, iv. 22
Number five sacred to, iv. 152
Numeration of, v. 342
Older nation, a remnant of an, iv. 312
Olympus of, iii. 208
Pagan, Mysteries of, v. 66, 325
Pan of the, v. 117
Pater Æther of, i. 76
Polytheistic, ii. 187
Prometheus of, iii. 410
Ptolemaios of, iii. 61
Pureia of, v. 285
Records, iii. 408
Rings or circles of, ii. 362
Sabasius not property of, iii. 417
Scholars, v. 30, 158
Second monad of, ii. 146
Supreme being of, ii. 399
Teos of, iv. 173
Tetrad and, iv. 172

Tetraktys of, iv. 170
Titans of, iii. 275
Troy, of age, of, iv. 319
Wanderers of, v. 314
Writing unknown to, iii. 437
Zodiac, ii. 373, 374, 384; iii. 62; v. 241
GREELY, quoted, i. 46
GREEN, Colour of Lower Manas, v. 456, 516
GREENLAND, Bovey Tracey, and, iv. 295
Climate of, iii. 23; iv. 247
Perpetual snows in, iii. 24
Second continent, belonged to, iii. 146
Sinking, iv. 355
GREGOR, Dr. Henry, quoted, iii. 278
GREGORIE, quoted, iv. 35
GREGORY, the Great, Pope, iv. 158
GREGORY NAZIANZEN, St. v. 167, 170
GREY matter of the brain, iv. 225, 243
GREY WETHERS, Stones called, iii. 344
GRIFFINS, Persian winged, ii. 80
GRIHASTHA, Brahmans, iii. 87
Family man or, iii. 409
Laws of, i. 258
Married life or, i. 258
Soma never givern to, iv. 67
GRIMM'S law, Phonetic rules of, i. 52
GRIP of the lion's paw, Strong, iv. 152
GROSS, body, Breath needed a, iii. 113
Deep of wisdom becomes, iii. 64
Human principle, first, iv. 165
Matter, compound of, iv. 147
Ponderable, ii. 249
Realism in days of Moses, iv. 27
GROSS, the Heathen Religion, quoted, i. 127
GROTE, referred to, iii. 437; iv. 330
GROTTO of Zaratushta in Central Asia, ii. 185
GROTTOES of the Miaotse, iii. 338, 339
GROUP, Architects, of, i. 279
Beings of divine, i. 271
Builders, of, i. 186
Celestial beings, of, i. 268
Celestial men, of, i. 277
Creative planetary angels of, iii. 135
Creators, of, i. 279
Dhyān Chohans, of, i. 246
Element read elementary, for, ii. 271
Four and seven of, i. 187
Gods created a, of men, each seven, iii. 18
Hierarchies, of, i. 261, 279
Higher and more spiritual, i. 279
Human, iv. 237
Mammalia of, iv. 254
Rūpa angels, of, i. 265
Rūpas, among the, i. 265
Sixth, i. 268
GROUPINGS of primitive atoms, Fourteen, ii. 276
GROUPS, Bodies, furnished with, iii. 304
Builders, of, i. 186
Dhyān Chohans, of, ii. 297
Dhyāni-Buddhas of two higher, i. 310
Dhyānic, ii. 283
Divine and ethereal beings, of, i. 261
Elohim, of, iii. 387
Filiation of, iv. 236
Human, evolution of, iii. 15
Human progeny, of, iii. 17

GROUPS (*Contd.*)
  Humanity, seven, of, ii. 297
  Intermediate, four, iv. 237
  Lipika, of, i. 186
  Mammals, of, iv. 238
  Mankind, of, ii. 283
  Nations settling into distinct, ii. 142
  Paul, of disciples attracted to, ii. 298
  Planets, of, 221; ii. 297
  Primeval, of mankind, iv. 178
  Primitive, iii. 47
  Primordial human, iii. 41
  Progenitors, of divine, iv. 282
  Septenary, i. 265; iv. 165, 170
  Three descending, i. 262
GROVE, Sir William, see Book Index
GROWTH, Correlation of, iv. 307
  Law of birth, and decay, i. 200
  Phase of law of, ii. 295
  Plants affected by the moon, of, i. 232
  Secret meaning of Brahmā, iv. 230
  Septenary law of, iv. 193
  Suffering a stage of, iv. 43
GRYPES and Arimaspi, iii. 415
GUANCHES, Atlanteans, descendants of, iv. 359
  Basques and, iv. 358
  Canary Islands, of, iv. 248, 310, 360
GUARDIAN, Angel of the Jews, ii. 179; v. 76
  Angels of the Christians, i. 268; v. 357
  Kabalistic Angels, v. 439
  Men, of, iv. 45
  Nation, of each, ii. 300
  Protectors, of Manvantaric period, v. 88
  Scales, of the, i. 267
  Secret and Sacred Lore, of, v. 50, 75
  Spirit of the earth, iii. 44
  Spirit or angel, iv. 46
  Wall, v. 467
GUARDIANS, Corners of the world, of four, ii. 388
  Harmony, of, ii. 368
  Planets are, ii. 299
  Sadducees, of laws of Moses, iii. 71
  Watchers or, of the sky, i. 165; v. 356
  World, of the, i. 186; v. 88
GUATEMALA, Maya Indians of, iii. 62
GUATEMALAN, Medal, v. 43
GUBERNATIS a propounder of the solar mythos, ii. 16
GUEBRA, Derivation of the word, iii. 362
GUESTS in the forest, Seven, iv. 209
GUFF or body, iv. 24
GUHA the mysterious one, iv. 119
GUHYA Vidya, or the science of Mantras, i. 222
GUIDED forces, Genii or, i. 334
GUIENGOLA, Temple of, v. 283
GUJERAT, Flight of the Parsis to, iii. 323
GULF, Mexico, of, iii. 422
  Persia, of, iv. 180
  St. Vincent, of, iii. 201
GULL, Dr. referred to, ii. 264
GULLWEIG (Gold-ore) the enchantress, iv. 89
GUM, v. 483
GUNAS, see Attributes, v. 471
GUNAMS of Prakriti, Three, iv. 207
GUNPOWDER, Invention of, ii. 306

  Sun-force exerted on, ii. 249
GUPTA VIDYĀ, Eastern, i. 249; v. 123, **174**, 176, 188, 193, 482
  Science of, i. 60; iv. 67
GUPTA VIDYĀ SŪTRA, quoted, ii. 71
  Kabalah, and, v. 174-193
GURU, i. 20
  Daityas, of the, iii. 44
  Divine Instructor, or, iii. 122
  Draco symbol of, iii. 44
  Dravidian, v. 372
  Garga's, iii. 60
  Gods, of the, iii. 57; iv. 66, 67
  Instructor or, iii. 118, 122
  Pupil, and, iv. 25; v. 282, 353
  Shankara (Shiva), of, iv. 66
  Vision of the, v. 282
GURUDEVA, Initiates, of, iv. 177
  Lanoo and, i. 179
GURUS, Hindus have their, iv. 139
  Himalayan, v. 349, 390
  Pagodas, of the, ii. 91
  Pupils, and their, iii. 219
  Rishis are called, iv. 197
GUSHTASP, v. 61
GUSTAV SEIFFARTH on the Zodiac, iv. 71
GYAN, Gnan, Jnana, or occult wisdom, iii. 393
GYGES, Aspects and meanings of, iv. 344
GYMNOSOPHISTS, v. 41, 147
GYRATION, Eternities, through the, ii. 257
  Evolutional, i. 223
  Septenary, i. 192
  Sevenfold, i. 292
GYRATORY atoms, Movements of, i. 176
GYUT, Division of Kunjur, v. 375
  Tantrika Ritual and, v. 404

H

HABEL, Adam Rishoon, son of, iii. 396
  Feminine principle, the, iv. 37
HABIR-ON, Hebron or Kabeir-town, iv. 111
HABITABILITY of physical worlds, ii. 331
HABITABLENESS of other planets, iv. 268
HABITAT of angels and pure spirits, iii. 119
HABITATIONS called Sheba Hachaboth, seven, iii. 120
HACHOSER the reflected lights, ii. 230
H-ADAM-H, Adam under the form of, iii. 152; iv. 35
HADES, Father hurled into the, iii. 413
  Globe, our, iii. 237
  Gloom of, iii. 410; iv. 92
  Hyperborean, iii. 146
  Initiate descended, into, iv. 128; v. 286
  Kāma Loka or, i. 289; iii. 373
  Meaning of, v. 62
  Mercury guiding souls to, iii. 363; v. 159
  Satan angel of, iii. 238
  Seven mansions of, iii. 237
  Souls of the dead taken to, iv. 112
HÆCKEL, see Book Index
HÆCKELIAN, Moneron, ii. 266; iii. 161, 165
  Plastidular, iv 270
  View, iii. 296
HÆCKELII, Bathybius, iv. 240
HAGAR and Abraham, iii. 86

HAGGARD, Rider, quoted, iii. 317
HAILSTORM stopped by prayers, ii. 190
HAIMA or Hiranya, golden, ii. 75
HAIR, Microprosopus, of, iv. 196
  Samson's, v. 277
  Third eye under the, iii. 296
HAIR-Pores, Roma-Kupas or, iii. 78
HAIRY, Animal, human, iii. 288
  Animal, Lilith a female, iii. 265
  Arboreal ancestors, iv. 260
  Men, iv. 344
  Symbol, iv. 196
HAJASCHAR, the light forces, the, ii. 230
HALEVY, quoted, iii. 207
HALF-animal, iii. 201
  -Bird, Garuda half-man, iv. 134
  -Divine, Enoch, iii. 137
  -Initiated, Levites, iv. 36
  -Initiated Writers, iii. 54
HALIÆTUS Washingtonii of Audubon, iii. 438
HALIBURTON, quoted, iv. 362
HALL(S), Brahma and Vishnu, of, v. 518
  Five Hundred Lohans, of the, v. 394
  Hades of, v. 230
  Initiation of, v. 322
  Magic, of Stonehenge, v. 290
  Spirits, of, v. 290
HALL, A. Wilford, quoted, i. 201
HALLELUIAH, v. 100, 431
HALLEY, referred to, ii. 314
HALLUCINATION, Nature of, iii. 369; v. 244
HALO, v. 556
HAM, Accursed blood of, iii. 389
  Brazen columns of, iv. 184
  Biblical Name, v. 62, 63
  Cabiri and, iii. 392
  Cainites and sons of, iii. 153
  Cham, Kham or, v. 62
  Chaotic principle, symbolizes the, iv. 168
  Descendants of, iii. 379; iv. 20
  Jupiter, as, iii. 272
  Magic and, v. 62
  Mizraim, and, iii. 392
  Mythical, the, ii. 135; v. 297
  Son of Noah, v. 297
  Symbology of, iii. 396
  Pyramid measures and, v. 89
  Titan, iii. 343
  Treatise attributed to, v. 297
  Zu, Chaldean, iii. 285
HAMILTON, Sir W., quoted, iii. 166; iv. 235
HAMITIC races, iii. 154; iv. 20
HAMMER, Apes, using a, iv. 246
  Architect, of the great, i. 248
  Creation, of, iii. 107
  Light from the divine, iii. 108
  Svastika the worker's iii. 107
HAMSA (see also Hansa), Bird of wisdom, iii. 294
  Brahmā is, i. 85
  Caste named, i. 145
  Hansa or, i. 144
  Swan or, iii. 139
  Vehicle, used as, i. 144
HAMSA or Hansa-vāhana, Brahman as, i. 84, 144, 146
HANNEBERG, Dr., quoted, iv. 101
HANOCH or Enos, iii. 361, 390; iv. 98

HANOKH, Science of calculation, and the, iv. 102
  Yered son of, iv. 101
HANSA, Divine wisdom, represents, i. 145
  Swan of life, the, ii. 273
  Symbol of, i. 145
HANUMĀN, or Hanumāna, Lankā, in, iii. 171
  Monkey-God, the, iv. 250
  Pavana son of, i. 241
  Rāma, secretary of, ii. 104
HANUSCH, referred, to, iii. 273
HAOMA, Pippala or, iii. 106
  Tree of knowledge, fruit of, iii. 107
  White, iv. 86
HAOMAS, High and beautiful, iv. 86
HAROIRI, Khoom or, ii. 82
HARBINGER of light, iii. 246
HARDVAR the gate of the Ganges, iv. 142
HARDY, Spence, quoted, i. 50
HARE, Professor, referred to, ii. 244
HARE-rabbit, Leporine or, iii. 288
HARGRAVE JENNINGS, v. 292
HARI, Best of Gods, iii. 98
  Brahmā as, ii. 87
  Destroyer, the, ii. 86
  Hiranyagarbha, and Shankara, i. 83, 328; v. 188
  Hypostases, one of the three, i. 83
  Ideal cause the, ii. 87
  Ishvara, or, iii. 86
  Raivata manvantara, in the, iii. 98
  Preserver, 188
  Sambhūti born of, iii. 98
  Vishnu or, i. 328; ii. 139
HARI ASHVAS, sons of Daksha, iii. 277; v. 288
HARIKESA one of the seven rays, ii. 240
HARMONY, Adjustment is universal, iii. 306
  Agents of universal, iii. 107
  Divine, v. 459
  Eternal law which will produce final, iii. 418
  " Fall," before the, iii. 270
  Law of, iii. 303
  Logos source of, ii. 151
  Pythagoras on, iv. 172
  Science of, iv. 55
  Septenary, iv. 153; v. 556
  Tetraktys called, iv. 172
  Two contraries produce, ii. 134
  Universal will, of, ii. 357
HARP, Aeolian, v. 485
  Apollo, of, iv. 174
  Constellation of the, iii. 359
  Kronos, for, iii. 389
  Seven-stringed, iv. 174
HARPASA, Rocking stone, at, iii. 346
HARPOCRATES, Images of, iii. 395
  Isis suckling the babe, ii. 126
HARRIS, and Anastasi collections, v. 241, 243, 254, 332
  Papyrus, v. 241, 244, 249, 256
HAR-RU-BAH in book of the Dead, iv. 159
HARTMANN, Dr. F., quoted, i. 324, 325
HARTMANN, Von, see Book Index
HARVEY, of Life, v. 489
HARVEY, referred to, ii. 282; iii. 163
HASOTH, foundations, ii. 60

HATCHETS, Engravings, found with, iv. 286
  Mammoths with, iv. 308
  Palaeolithic, iii. 437; iv. 285, 291, 293
  Stone, iii. 222
HATE, and fear, v. 514
HATHA yoga, Discountenanced, i. 158; v. 468, 479
  Mysteries of, iv. 139, 211
  Planes used in, v. 399, 476, 480, 542
HATHO, quoted, iv. 169
HATHOR, an aspect of Isis, Moon becomes, i. 155; ii. 115; iv. 32
HATTERIA, Punctata, third eye of the, iii. 298
HAUG, Martin, quoted, i. 52, 163; iii. 163
HAÚTE, Garonne, Skeletons of, iv. 309
HAUVAH, HAVAH or, Eve, mother earth, iii. 43; iv. 37
HA-VA or, Eve, iii. 54
HAVYAVĀHANA, the fire of the Gods, ii. 245
HAWAIIANS, Dying out of the, iv. 349
HAWK, Abraxas gems, on, iv. 135
  Emblem of Sun, v. 181
  God hierophant with head of, iv. 128
  I am, iv. 206
  Seb issues from the egg-like, ii. 75
  Symbol, ii. 80; v. 247, 248
HAWK-Head, Hor, of, ii. 82
  Represented life, v. 159
  Serpent with, iii. 355
HAWKS, Serpents with heads of, iii. 359
  Wings, rods surmounted with, iii. 359
HAY on harmonious colouring, iv. 193
HĀYĀH, v. 190, 191
HÉ, Jod, Vau, i. 129, 154; v. 190
  Womb or opening, iv. 28, 41
HE of the four letters, i. 262
HEA, Ea or, iv. 45
  God, iv. 100
  Hoa or, the Chaldean triad, iii. 39
  Nebo great God of wisdom or, iv. 45
  Sa, or, iii. 19
  Silik-Muludag son of, iv. 45
  Universal soul, the, ii. 72
HEA-BANI raised heaven, Chaldean, iv. 100
HEAD, Adam Kadmon, of, i. 284
  Amesha Spentas, of, iv. 179
  Astræa falls on, iv. 353
  Cerebellum, Kāma of, v. 556
  Dragon, of the, ii. 118
  Earth of the, iii. 399
  Faces, and two, iii. 303
  Knowledge, of undying, iii. 283
  Numerical value of, ii. 162
  White, the fifth race, iv. 275
HEAD-dress of the hierophants, square, iv. 127
HEAD-Gear, Polar continent called, iii. 399
  Svastika on, of the Gods, iv. 157
HEAD-groups, four classes of, iii. 243
HEALER(S), Rudra the, iv. 118
  Jesus and Apollonius were, v. 263
HEALING, Priests and Kings, by, v. 263
HEALTH and disease, Cosmical elements both are, ii. 61
HEARING developed in fifth race, ii. 259
HEART, Ab Hati, iv. 205
  Ālaya of anima mundi, i. 128
  Ancestral, i. 267

Brahma of, iii. 183
Centre of all, v. 555
Divisions of the, v. 518
Doctrine of the, v. 387, 394, 405, 406, 407
Eternity, of, i. 179
Ever pulsating, iv. 160
Fishes, iv. 254
Hydra of the, ii. 388
Lion of the, ii. 388
Lotus, v. 483
Matrix of all forces, i. 331
Pineal gland and, v. 550
One Ray opened for the, i. 128
Represents the Triad, v. 555
Scorpion of the, ii. 388
Seat of Buddha, v. 527
Seven brains of, v. 550, 553
Solar world of the, ii. 264
Sun corresponds to, v. 441
HEAT, Air, proceeds from, ii. 44
  Age of, v. 348
  Breath or, i. 149, 165
  Causeless, i. 149
  Cold, and, ii. 328, 332
  Cosmic, energy generated by, i. 147
  Creative fire or, i. 250
  Cross, a branch of the sevenfold, iv. 132
  Elementals, results from, i. 201
  Fohat behind all manifestations of, i. 195
  Frictions produced by, ii. 240
  God, esoterically called, ii. 397
  Hydrogen gives off intense, iv. 165
  Lord of the Shining Face, from, iii. 27
  Mercury, given to, iii. 40
  Parāshakti includes powers of, i. 333
  Radiations, ii. 275
  Seven radicals, one of, i. 201
HEATHEN, Cross is, a symbol, iv. 158
  Deities, v. 94, 95
  Fire-worshippers, not the only, i. 180
  Gems, iv. 41
  Laws and institutions, iv. 39
  Our, ancestors, ii. 201
  Symbology of, i. 173
HEATHENS, Mythology of so-called, iv. 290
HEAVEN, Above, iv. 72
  Alhim created, ii. 56
  Allegory of war in, iii. 378
  Ana Chaldean for, i. 155
  Ash-boughs the sidereal, iv. 89
  Atmosphere the first, iii. 84
  Audlang, called, iii. 109
  Babylonian, v. 321
  Beings in, iii. 89
  Bird's nest, the, iii. 294
  Chinese, of the, ii. 71
  Cycles in, iv. 27
  Cyclic divisions applied to, iv. 193
  Divine monarch of the central, i. 261
  Earth, uniting with, iv. 54
  Earth, and, i. 298
  Ego belongs to, ii. 48
  Egyptian sevenfold, iv. 185
  Elohim create double, iv. 56
  Eternal rest in, i. 285
  Exile from, iii. 420
  Father in, v. 319, 358, 430, 532

HEAVEN (Contd.)
Genii of four quarters of, ii. 94
Gods, in, v. 430
Hebdomad in, ii. 167
Hindu war in, iii. 385
Indra the God of, iv. 69
Indra's, iii. 208
Mountain Kailāsa, iii. 415
Nature of the Logos in, iii. 234
North Pole, Lemurian, iii. 276
Perfect number in, iv. 144
Precise locality of, iv. 277
Progenitor in, v. 443
Prototype in, ii. 194, 364
Queen of, v. 319
Rulers of the sidereal, ii. 216
Secret things done in, iii. 381
Secrets of, iv. 156
Serpents of, i. 185
Sevenfold, iv. 202
Shell becomes the, ii. 81
Sidereal, ii. 370; iv. 89
Solid, iv. 85
Struggle in, iii. 376
Sung sages depict, iv. 124
Svah or, ii. 150
Time in highest, iv. 183
Vishnu, of, ii. 246
War in, i. 244, 248, 251; ii. 136; iii. 57, 112,
240, 270, 378, 379, 383, 385, 389; iv. 66,
67
HEAVENLY man, Adam Kadmon, i. 194;
ii. 148; iii. 57, 237; iv. 167, 274; v. 188, 215,
230, 419
Androgyne, v. 190
Celestial Logos or, i. 291
Crown, assumed form of, ii. 151
Dhyānis or, iii. 16
Divine phantom of, iv. 24
Elohim or, iii. 16
Father, v. 430
First cause, i. 262
Fourfold, iv. 197
Generative power of, ii. 70
Giant Ymir, ii. 83
Hierarchies, v. 128
Hermetic, i. 170, 332
Jupiter called, iii. 272
Kabalistic sense, in the, ii. 344; iv. 24
King, Osiris called, v. 276
Logos and, iii. 237, 239; iv. 170; v. 507
Manifested Logos, the, iv. 196
Manu-Svāyambhuva, iii. 137
Marriage, of, iii. 234
Men of Fohi or, iii. 39
Microprosopus, i. 285; iv. 197
Occultists believe in, iii. 199
Purusha, called, iv. 177, 178
Pymander, in, iv. 61
Rig Veda, of the, i. 245
Self-born, iii. 159
Sephiroth, ii. 51; iv. 114, 274
Six-fold, i. 271
Snails, i. 164
Tetragrammaton or, iii. 38
Titans or, i. 174
Total of the host of angels, the, iii. 239

Triangle, v. 507
Upper Adam or, iv. 25
Virgin and Astrology, v. 334
HEAVENS, the Ahriman seeks to conquer,
iv. 85
Ark typified in, by the moon, iii. 147
Aspect of, ii. 387
Belt of sacred animals, iii. 36
Dhyānis, of, iii. 275
Duplex, ii. 69
Earths corresponding with, i. 295
Immaculate virgin of, iv. 31
Karshvares and, iii. 383
Lord of the, v. 129
Pole of, iii. 355, 362
Seven, iii. 275, 383, 384; iv. 133, 135; v. 309,
437
Sidereal, i. 274; iii. 433
Three, i. 295
Toom crosses, ii. 398
Two, ii. 69
Upper and lower, i. 298
Virgin mother of, iv. 31
Yo or, i. 286
HEBDOMAD, Gnostic, ii. 167
Mysteries of, iv. 152, 161, 162
Second or inferior, ii. 167
Tetrad unfolded makes, iv. 171
HEBDOMADAL offerings, iv. 317
HEBDOMADIC essence, the, iii. 100
HEBE, the Grecian Goddess, iii. 138
HEBEL, Abel or, iii. 136
Eve, and, iii. 143
HEBREW, Allegories, v. 194
Alphabet, v. 114, 118, 178, 211, 212, 231
Bible, v. 178, 195, 196
Canon, v. 178, 197
Creation, v. 204
Esotericism, v. 186
Initiates, v. 197
Language, v. 178, 181, 184
Mosaic books, v. 26
Punctuation, v. 184
Scholars, v. 178, 184
Scribes, v. 196
Scrolls, v. 186, 198
Texts, v. 180, 182, 183, 231
Writing, v. 199
HEBREWS, the, Ankh taken from Egyptians by,
iii. 43
Astronomy of, iii. 85
Fourth race, Genesis begins at, ii. 162
Gospel according to, v. 160
Holy of Holies not originated by, iv. 36
Kabalah and, iii. 395; v. 174-193
Keys, never held the higher, ii. 23
Malachim of, ii. 183
Man, word for, iv. 130
Michael-Jehovah of, iv. 108
Mode of reckoning among, ii. 105
Nephesh Chiah of, i. 272
Nuchthemeron of, ii. 168
Onech or Phoenix of, iv. 188
Primal cause of, ii. 343
Ruach of, i. 273
Sacred number seven of, i. 174
Spirit of, iv. 37

HEBREWS (Contd.)
Supreme of, iv. 173
Targums handed down by, iv. 127
Tribal God of, iii. 276
T'sod Olaum of, iv. 154
Week of years of, iii. 394
HEBRON, Habir on or, Kabeir Town, iv. 111
Mysteries of Kabiri, v. 309, 310
Smaragdine Tablet found at, iv. 126
HECATE, Hekat or Moon, ii. 102
Orphic Deity, the triple, ii. 102
HECATE Luna counterpart of Jehovah, ii. 102
Rhombs of, v. 55
HEER, Prof., referred to, iv. 308
HEGEL, see Book Index
HEGEMONY of the Gods, iv. 77
HE-GOAT, Azazel said to be a, iii. 375
HELEN, Troy, of, v. 127, 450, 451
HELENUS foretold the ruin of Troy, iii. 341
HELHEIM, Hel queen of, iv. 343
HELIOCENTRIC, system, ii. 159; v. 218, 316
Galileo and, v. 71
Initiates taught, ii. 292
Latin church and, v. 71
Theory, i. 176
HELIOCENTRICISM in Vishnu Purāna, iii. 163
HELIOLATROUS religion, iii. 378
HELIOLATRY, ii. 108; v. 55, 313, 324-328
HELION, Jehovah and, iv. 78
Sun in his highest, iii. 356
HELIOPOLIS, An or, ii. 398
Book of the Dead at, ii. 23
City of the Sun, v. 266
Elementorum arcana of, ii. 110
Priests of, iii. 367; v. 266
Ra the one God at, ii. 399
Schools of, ii. 23
Twelve Stones of, v. 241
HELIOS, Apollo is, iii. 382
Father becoming, iii. 55
Greeks, of the, iv. 110
Most High, means, v. 277
Sun, the, iii. 55, 382
HELIUM, Ancestral cousin, to, ii. 320
Crookes on, ii. 307
Hypothetical, i. 266
HELIUS, Apollo or, iii. 115
HELL, Atala, a, iii. 403, 406; v. 544
Avitchi or, v. 501
Christians', ii. 88, 133; iv. 76; v. 486
Depths of, iii. 112; iv. 85
Devils of, iv. 76
Dogma of, iii. 249; iv. 52
Heaven and, i. 259; iii. 112, 356
Hindu, iii. 107
Inextinguishable, iii. 247
Initiates conquer, iii. 233; v. 153
Invention of, iv. 343
Kingdom of, iii. 233
Material, iii. 107
Paradise and, iv. 343
Satan and, iii. 388
South Pole, at the, iii. 402
HELLAS, Supreme Deity of, iii. 410
HELLENBACH, Baron, quoted, iv. 198, 199, 224
HELLENES, the, Æolus of, ii. 187
Greeks and, iii. 366

Pre-Homeric, ii. 16
Pelasgians and, v. 254
Prometheus older than, myth of, iii. 411
Unknown God, and the, ii. 40
Zodiac, and the, ii. 373
HELLS, Brāhmans, of, i. 253
Death and fire, withered up by, ii. 88
Globe divided into seven, iii. 402
Lokas or, i. 253
HELMHOLTZ, see Book Index
HELMONT, Van, referred to, ii. 336
HEMISPHERE, Inferior, i. 274
Obscuration of the, iii. 310
Population of one, perished, iii. 310
HEMISPHERES, Cerebral, iii. 298
HEMP is bi-sexual, iii. 142
HEN, Chickens, and, or Pleiades, ii. 388
Clucking, the great, ii. 75
HENOCH, iii. 365, 366; iv. 37, 283
HEPHÆSTUS, Legend of, iii. 389; iv. 88, 90
HEPHÆSTUS-Vulcan, ii. 184
HEPTACHORD, Apollo's, i. 220
HEPTAD of the Kabalist, iv. 171, 174
HEPTADS, Sub-groups of, i. 187
HEPTAGON, Number seven or, iv. 173
Tetraktys, in relation to, iv. 169
HEPTAKIS or Iao, Chaldean, i. 274
HEPTANOMIS, Stellar, ii. 124
HERACLES, Hebe bride of, iii. 138
HERACLIDES taught rotation of earth, i. 176
HERACLITUS, Ephesus, teaching at, i. 143
Homer, on, iv. 333
HERÆSCUS could distinguish animate stones, iii. 342
HERAKLES, deliverer of Prometheus, iii. 411
HERBELOT, quoted, iii. 393, 397
HERBERT, Lord, quoted, iv. 223
HERBS, Creation of, i. 298
Rain, needed the fall of, ii. 59
HERCULANEUM, iii. 239, 438; iv. 361
HERCULES, v. 153, 258, 260
Golden apples of, iv. 339
Greeks and, v. 259
Hades, in, iii. 240
Herodotus on, v. 258
Hillus, son of, iii. 280
Hiram's temple to, iv. 111
Indian origin of, v. 258, 260
Labours of, v. 152
Lord of the flames, v. 258
Palæmonius, the Tyrian, iii. 344
Pillars of, ii. 347; iii. 154, 226, 323, 393
Priests of, iii. 207
Ptah, identical with, ii. 68
Serpent, kills the, ii. 118
Solar myth, not a, iv. 338
Type, an earthly, iii. 55
Twelve Great Gods, one of, v. 258
HEREDITY, Atoms by, transmission of, iv. 242
Explained, i. 270
Karma, servant of, iii. 185
Kumaras and, ii. 176
Palingenesis and, iv. 229
Prāna and, iv. 241
Variations transmitted by, iv. 307
HERESIARCHS, of Christianity, v. 395

HERESIES, Gnostics, of the, ii. 121
Montanists, of the, iv. 53
HERMAPHRODITE, Androgynous or, iii. 127, 184; v. 438
Ardhanāri, the Goddess, iii. 43
Bi-sexual or, iii. 141
Condition, iv. 227
Divine, ii. 95; iii. 132, 135, 139; v. 291
Heavenly man and, iii. 16
Human, ii. 95; iii. 141; iv. 229; v. 438
Idols, ii. 107
Jesus in Revelation is, i. 139
Lotus a, type, ii. 95
Mammals, iii. 191
Mystery of, v. 104, 292
One, iv. 35
One-eyed and, iii. 300
Perfect or, iii. 134
Plato on, races, iii. 266
Races, iii. 112
Rod, i. 174
Separating, the, iii. 143
Solitary, man a, iii. 141
Species once, iii. 179
HERMAPHRODITES, Animal, iii. 179; iv. 229
Bible, in the, ii. 37
Double ones, or, iii. 43
Ethereal, iv. 250
Human, iii. 126
Independent sex and, iii. 148
Male-female, iii. 295
Plants are, iv. 229
HERMAPHRODITISM, iii. 127, 174, 179, 191
HERMAS, quoted, i. 137
HERMIAS (a fragment of), quoted, ii. 57
HEMERA, Æther and, i. 170
HERMES, quoted, i. 140, 143, 154, 322, 323, 329, 334; ii. 396
HERMES, Alexandrian Library and, v. 57
Anubis, iii. 41
Arcanum of, iii. 236
Bible and, iii. 382
Book of, iv. 57
Books of, iii. 38; iv. 99; v. 51, 58, 62, 68, 115, 331, 356
Büchner on, iv. 287
Budha or, iii. 57, 366; iv. 23
Chaldean tablets agree with, iii. 16
Cosmology and, v. 323
Cosmogony of, iii. 36; v. 107
Cubic, iv. 112
Cynocephalus and, ii. 104
Demi-God, a, iii. 363
Egyptian Sacred Books and, v. 58, 61
Egyptologists on, iii. 270
Enoch or, iii. 138, 361; iv. 98, 102
Esoteric wisdom, iv. 67
Father-Mother and son, on, ii. 154
Five, iii. 215, 366
Fragments of works, v. 57, 58
Freemasonry and, iii. 51
Generic nom de plume, a, i. 328; iii. 215
Greeks, of the, iii. 41, 145; iv. 22; v. 74
Gregory corroborates, iii. 270
Herodotus on, iii. 361
Heroes, one of the, iii. 363
Huxley or?, ii. 350

Ibis, in form of, ii. 77
Initiate, the, great, iii. 270
Isis and, ii. 103
Kabalistic Doctrines and, v. 107-112
Libra and, iii. 138
Longitudes ascribed to, ii. 389
Mercury, or, ii. 195; iii. 41; iv. 22, 110, 112; v. 438
Moist principle of, iv. 163
Mysteries of, iii. 236
Occultism and, i. 323
Ophites and, iii. 378
Parāshara, the Aryan, i. 328
Paul called, iv. 49
Pesh-Hun compared to, iii. 60
Pymander appears to, i. 141
Pyramid tomb of, iii. 361
Races, on destruction of, iv. 294
Satan, on, iii. 236; iv. 99
Sciences, and the, iii. 363, 366
Secret dogma of, v. 142
Serpent and, i. 140; iii. 39, 363
Seth, and, iii. 360, 379
Seven governors, of, ii. 202
Smaragdine Tablet of, iii. 108, 122; iv. 126
Sun and, v. 314, 321, 323
Thoth, ii. 301, 399; iii. 215; iv. 30, 75, 108, 153; v. 112
Thought divine of, iv. 59
Tree, one branch of, i. 256
Trismegistus, ii. 144, 396; iii. 16, 122, 215, 239, 378; iv. 102; v. 57, 61, 73, 218, 321, 329
Wisdom of, i. 140, 322; iii. 363
Word, emblem of, iv. 112
Worlds of, v. 73
HERMES-Christos of the Gnostics, iv. 49
HERMES-fire of the Germans, ii. 52
HERMES-Mercury, Greeks, of the, iv. 23
Symbols of, iv. 112
HERMESIANS, Symbol of truth with, iv. 171
HERMETIC, Axiom, iv. 122
Books, i. 329; ii. 399; iii. 143; v. 62
Cosmogony, ii. 57
Cross, i. 73; iv. 126
Doctrine, v. 226
Forces, ii. 182
Fragments, i. 323, 326, 327, 328; iii. 146
Literature, iii. 239
Matter, ii. 126
Narrative, iii. 112
Nature, i. 332
Philosophers, i. 170, 195; ii. 182; iv. 132; v. 297
Philosophy, i. 61, 143, 323; v. 57, 60, 120
Prayer, i. 328
Pymander, i. 132
Scales, iv. 159
Supreme All, i. 327
Symbol, ii. 103
Wisdom, iv. 126
Works, ii. 325, 399
Writings, ii. 127
HERMETICAL, operations, i. 143
HERMETICISM, i. 326; iii. 122
HERMITAGES, Seven, iv. 209
HERMITS, Early, i. 62
Initiate, iv. 70

HERMON or Mount Armon, iii. 407
HERMONE, Cassius, iii. 363
HERMONTIS, Apis Pacis of, ii. 383
HEROD, King, v. 153
HERODOTUS, Arimaspi of, iii. 414
  Atlantes, mentioned, iv. 331
  Atlas, on, iv. 332
  Cambyses, on, iii. 359
  Deluge, of, iii. 18
  Dynasties of Gods, on, iii. 366
  Eastern Ethiopians, iii. 427
  Egypt, and, ii. 153; v. 182, 255
  Egyptian empire and, iv. 319
  Egyptian mysteries and, iii. 394
  Egyptian priests and, iii. 332, 429; iv. 104;
    v. 257, 258
  Egyptian theogony, iii. 417
  Father of History, v. 53; v. 279
  Giants of, iii. 336
  Ibis, on, ii. 77
  Kabiri and, iii. 363
  Nemesis, from Homer to, iii. 306
  Oracle of Dodona and, v. 254
  Phoenicians of, ii. 25
  Polar night on, iv. 342
  Priests told, iii. 367
  Pyramid, on, ii. 29
  Scythia of, iii. 414
  Solomon not mentioned by, v. 182
  Statues in time of, iv. 319
  Thetis, on, ii. 188
  Zeus Belos of, iii. 215
HEROES, Dynasties of, i. 310; iii. 366, 368
  Fifth race of, iii. 433
  Fourth race, of, iii. 144, 273
  Pre-historic races, of, iii. 287
  Sciences revealed by, iii. 363
  Third root-race, of, iii. 103
  Traditions of, iii. 371
HERSCHEL, see Book Index
HESIOD, Bronze age, on, iii. 273; iv. 89, 341
  Constellations, on, iv. 175
  Existence denied, ii. 374
  Giants in, iii. 295; iv. 338, 344
  Job preceded, ii. 373
  Jupiter in, iii. 272
  Prometheus in, iii. 411, iv. 94
  Superstitions, ii. 187
  Theogony of, ii. 50, 136, 143; iii. 69, 270;
    iv. 16, 332, 334
  Theology of, iv. 99
  Titans and, i. 251; iii. 73
  Writing unknown to, iii. 437
  Zeus, on, iii. 188
HESIODIC, Æolus, Boreas, etc., ii. 187
  Ash tree, iii. 106
HESPERIDES, Apple-tree of, i. 187
  Garden of, iv. 359
HESPERORNIS, iii. 190
HETEROGENESIS, Science of, iii. 184
HE-VA, Adam and, iii. 223
  Eve or, i. 285
HEVAH, and Abel, iii. 133
HEVE or Eve, iii. 138
HEXAGON, Interpretations, of, v. 120 et seq.
  Seventh Key, v. 120-125
  Star, i. 271

Symbol of, i. 263
HEXAGONAL, Body, Property of, iv. 154
  System, iv. 166
HEXAGRAM, Symbol of, i. 144
HEZEKIAH, Brazen serpent, and, ii. 80
  David and, ii. 33
  Reforms of, iii. 386
HIA dynasty, ii. 65
HIARCHUS, King, v. 142
HICETAS, taught the rotation of earth, i. 176
HIDDEN Caves of Bactria, v. 65
  Deity, iv. 107
  God, ii. 155
  Hū, ii. 343
  Knowledge, iv. 82
  Lands, iii. 332
  One, ii. 68
  Science, i. 132
  Truths, i. 44; iv. 104
HIERAPOLIS, temple of, v. 253
HIERARCHIES, Angelic, ii. 168; iii. 36; v. 453
  Beings, v. 78, 442
  Buddhas, of, v. 539
  Celestial, 319; v. 111
  Chief, i. 261
  Colour and sound, of, v. 459
  Creative forces, of, iii. 46; v. 460 et seq.
  Creators, of, ii. 144
  Crime supposed, of, iii. 73
  Devas of, v. 539
  Divine, v. 77, 493
  Dhyāni Buddhas of, v. 539
  Dhyān Chohans, of, i. 156, 334; iii. 39;
    v. 453, 538
  Egos, of, ii. 354; v. 552
  Forces, of, ii. 182
  Heavenly, i. 151; iii. 35
  Higher, iv. 60
  Highest group of, i. 261
  Individuality of, i. 318
  Inferior, v. 448
  Japanese system, in, i. 261
  Jews ignored, ii. 106
  Kosmic, v. 538
  Lamas of, v. 105
  Logos of, iii. 36
  Lokas of, v. 539
  Monads, of, i. 224
  Noumena of, iii. 275
  Pitris, of, i. 214, 240
  Powers of, i. 140
  Rector of, iii. 36
  Rishis, of, ii. 154
  Rulers of Planets, of, v. 443
  Septenary division of, iv. 167; v. 522
  Series of, i. 318
  Seven, i. 140; v. 77, 459, 532, 553
  Spirits, of, i. 191
  Spiritual Rulers of, v. 443
  Subdivisions of, v. 461
  Two in heaven, v. 319
  Universe built on, i. 153
  Upper, i. 263
  Wise men, of, iv. 202
HIERARCHY, Adeptship, v. 371, 399
  Angelic, i. 187; iii. 71, 105
  Anupādaka, of, i. 123

HIERARCHY (Contd.)
  Archangels of, i. 114
  Being, of, i. 190, 331; ii. 175, 337
  Celestial, i. 190, 268; v. 212, 368
  Christian, i. 155
  Creative powers, of, i. 261
  Dhyān Chohans, of, i. 154; iv. 33; v. 539
  Died, which never, iii. 283
  Divine, i. 243
  Divine powers, of, i. 86
  Elect, of, iii. 319
  Fallen angels, of, ii. 44
  Fifth, i. 279
  Flames, of, i. 151; iii. 74
  Forces, of, ii. 142
  Fourth, v. 532
  Gods, of, ii. 106; iii. 104
  Group of the, i. 279
  Lāmas of, v. 105
  Logos a, iii. 36
  Man superior to any, i. 319
  Manus, of, ii. 172
  Monads, of, i. 226
  Rishis, of, v. 356
  Root-base of their, i. 255
  Sages, of, iii. 421
  Septenary, i. 86
  Spiritual beings, of, i. 111; v. 366, 539
  Trans-Himālayan, i. 193
  Venus ruling, v. 441
  Zuni Indians, of, iv. 199
HIERATIC, Alphabets, i. 310; v. 46
  Records of Egypt, ii. 22
  Sciences, ii. 19
  Writing, iii. 139
HIEROGLYPH, Book of the Dead, in the, ii. 398
  Water, iii. 75
HIEROGLYPHIC, Cake, iv. 116
  Cypher, iii. 437
  Documents, i. 52
  Inscriptions, i. 51
  Names of human principles, iv. 205
  Root of word, v. 264
  Ru, iv. 117
  Senary, iv. 163
  System, iii. 139
  Tau as a, iv. 127
  Thought, iii. 335
  Writing, iii. 429
HIEROGLYPHICS, Christian cross in, iv. 127
  Egyptian, iii. 436; iv. 26; v. 206, 264
  Ideographic, i. 46
  Kabeiric, v. 310
  Pillars, on, iv. 99
HIEROGRAM within a cirlce, ii. 144, 339
HIERONYMUS, St., quoted, v. 118, 143, 316
HIEROPHANT (S), v. 28, 271, 330
  Abodes of, iv. 71
  Adepts, or, iii. 366
  Ancients of, v. 322
  Aryan, iv. 39
  Astronomus, the highest, v. 318, 322
  Babylon, of, iii. 379
  Breast plate of, v. 240
  Categories of, two, iii. 225
  Chaldea, of, ii. 67; v. 173, 257, 262, 330
  Chief of Java-Aleim and, iii. 207

  Death of, ii. 24; v. 271, 272, 288
  Divine, v. 322
  Dogmas, and, ii. 78
  Egypt, of, iii. 378; iv. 127; v. 41, 49, 87, 197,
    240, 244, 255, 257, 262, 290, 294, 296, 318,
    382
  First, v. 102
  French Kabalists, of, iv. 119
  Great, v. 130
  Greek, v. 262
  Head of the, v. 104
  Heirs, no worthy, ii. 24
  Human Race, first of, v. 102
  Immortal, iv. 38
  Indian, i. 299; v. 262, 305
  Initiates or, iii. 217; iv. 128
  Interpreter, or, v. 140
  Java-Aleim or, iii. 207; iv. 102; v. 185
  Job, and, v. 290
  King, v. 244
  Land of libations of, iii. 416
  Language of, ii. 22
  Libraries of, iv. 98
  Mercury and, iii. 41
  Mexican, v. 43
  Moses, and, iii. 216
  Mystery God of, iii. 217
  Mystery tongue of, ii. 23
  Name, of, iv. 99; v. 145
  Neophytes and, v. 55, 180, 271
  Osiris, soul became, i. 192
  Priests or, iii. 366
  Sacerdotal colleges of, iii. 224
  Sacred books and, i. 57
  Sciences transmitted by, iii. 433
  Serpent's head of, iii. 217
  Skill of, ii. 112
  Symbols and, ii. 78; v. 272
  Tablets used by, v. 139, 140
  Tree, of one, i. 256
  Victim, v. 104
  Vishvakarman, the, v. 270
HIGGINS, G., quoted, iii. 114; v. 340
HIGH initiator, i. 169
HIGH priests, Jewish Tabernacle, of, iv. 22;
    v. 240
  Egypt, of, v. 240, 257
HIGH tides, Palaeozoic, iii. 74
HILAERIA, wife of Pollux, iii. 130
HILAIRE, Barthélemy St., quoted, v. 105
  Geoffroy St., quoted, iv. 221; v. 408
HILKIAH, the high priest, ii. 374; iv. 41; v. 333
HILLMEN, tribes of, iv. 246
HILLUS, son of Hercules, iii. 280
HIMĀLAYAN, Ashrams, v. 218, 390
  Chain, iii. 399
  Gurus, v. 349, 390
  Kailāsa, iv. 68
  Peaks, iv. 63
  Ranges, iii. 208; v. 389, 390
HIMĀLAYAS, Buddhist Arhats, i. 51
  Depositions of, iv. 355
  Esoteric schools of, i. 46, 181
  Giants in, iii. 295
  Hamsa, called, i. 145
  Hardwar at foot of, iv. 142
  Himavat or, ii. 113

HIMĀLAYAS (Contd.)
　Himmel and, v. 109
　Hindu tradition, of, iii. 153
　" Preservers " beyond, iii. 172
　Ranges of, i. 145, 314
　Secret Schools in, v. 400
　Secret recess of Buddha in, v. 363
　Sivatherium of, iii. 222
　Summits of, iv. 180
　Traditions, of, iv. 142
HIMALEH, the snowy range, v. 109
HIMAVĀN, Manu Vaivasvata lands on, iii. 154
HIMAVAT, Calf of, ii. 113
HINAYĀNA, Mahāyāna schools, and, i. 112;
　v. 399
HIND, Naphtali is a, ii. 377
HINDU, Adepts and Sādhus, v. 147, 231
　Ardhanārī, iv. 102
　Ark, legend of, iii. 292
　Aryan race, ii. 39; iii. 68, 229, 369, 405;
　　iv. 38, 175
　Astronomers, ii. 315; v. 344, 346
　Astronomical methods, ii. 389
　Astronomy, ii. 384; iii. 332; v. 344 et seq.
　Atlantis and the, iii. 268, 405
　Atomists, ii. 303
　Brahman and Brahmā of the, i. 83; iii. 418;
　　v. 190, 199
　Calculations, iii. 332
　Calender, iii. 77
　Choirs of Devas, v. 326
　Chronology, ii. 86; iii. 83, 394; iv. 191
　Cosmogony, ii. 33, 69, 348; iii. 56; iv. 196;
　　v. 199, 231, 347
　Cosmographies, iv. 175
　Cycles, v. 339, 340
　Eclipse, rite during, iii. 103
　Epochs, ii. 385
　Esotericism, ii. 374; iii. 59
　Gamut, ii. 258
　God of Wisdom, v. 74
　Gods, i. 162; iii. 181; v. 111
　Great Bear, view of, i. 274
　Helen, iv. 66
　Hell, iii. 107
　Hercules, v. 258, 260
　Kalpas, iii. 308
　Legends, iii. 292, 307, 404
　Lilith, iii. 182
　Mangala, iii. 133
　Manu Vaivasvata, v. 190
　Mathams, v. 49
　Meditation at dawn, ii. 52
　Music, v. 197
　Mystics, iv. 196; v. 145
　Mythology, iii. 150
　Naraka, iii. 107
　Pantheon, i. 138, 162, 185, 186; iii. 60, 71,
　　377; iv. 185; v. 286, 375
　Philosophy, i. 130, 216; ii. 165, 343, 374;
　　iii. 154, 311, 369; iv. 188; v. 475
　Prajāpati, v. 198, 210, 214, 386
　Purānas, ii. 327
　Religions, i. 45; ii. 84
　Religious systems, i. 174
　Scriptures, i. 172, 175, 328; iii. 181, 307, 357;
　　iv. 179, 188

　Sects, iv. 159
　Shastras and Pandits, v. 27
　Stanzas, view of, iii. 35
　Symbols, ii. 391; iii. 382, 430; iv. 146; v. 46,
　　436
　Systems, ii. 173, 384; v. 322
　Teachings, ii. 58
　Tradition, ii. 133; iii. 153, 312
　Trimūrti, v. 117
　Vāch, i. 194; v. 190
　Vithoba, ii. 34; iv. 130
　War, iii. 85, 385
　Year, v. 191, 192
　Yugas, iii. 308; iv. 195; v. 345 et seq.
　Zodiac, ii. 388; iii. 332; iv. 148; v. 345
　　et seq.
　Zones, v. 341
HINDU-Kush Chain, the, iii. 337
HINDUISM, Brāhmanism, or early, ii. 60
　Buddhism outcome of, ii. 392
　Demons in, ii. 62
　Exoteric, ii. 62; iii. 78, 81
　Hermeticism, and, i. 326
　Orientalists, as understood by, iv. 193
　Orthodox, ii. 173; v. 190
　Pantheism, ii. 269
HINDUS, Æther Aditi of, ii. 46
　" Ancient " of the, v. 189
　Apes' and monkeys' origin according to, i. 236
　Argha of, iv. 41
　Arts of, iii. 229
　Aryan, ii. 16, 390; iv. 177
　A-sexual reproduction and, iv. 228
　Astronomy and, ii. 376, 386
　Bhāshyas dead letter to, i. 315
　Division of day and night, with, v. 432, 433
　Dynasties, v. 346
　Hexagon, and, v. 120
　Lingam, of, v. 285
　Mathematics of, v. 343
　Planet of seventh, i. 162
　Primitive, v. 109
　Rishis of, i. 76, 161, 248; iii. 60, 423; iv. 202;
　　v. 382
　Rūdū of, iv. 192
　Science of, iii. 229
　Sun, and, v. 154
　Zodiac of, ii. 373-4, 383, 388; iii. 62, 433;
　　iv. 148
HINDUSTAN, Arab figures from, ii. 76
　Brāhmans' descent into, iv. 180
　Caves and Temples of, iii. 34
　High plateaux of, iii. 226
HIOUEN-THSANG, v. 40
HIPPARCHUS, referred to, ii. 376, 384, 385
HIPPARION ancestor of horse, iv. 285, 305, 360
HIPPOCENTAURS, bulls with men's heads,
　iii. 65
HIPPOCRATES, i. 270; iii. 140, 261, 312;
　iv. 257; v. 54
HIPPOLYTUS, quoted, ii. 111; v. 131-135
HIPPOPOTAMUS, iii. 223, 396, 398; iv. 305;
　v. 202
HIQUIT, the Goddess, ii. 100
HIRAM Abif, a solar myth, ii. 27; v. 194, 272,
　273, 274, 283
　Fabulous, v. 142

HIRAM (*Contd.*)
  Kabalah, in, iii. 122
  Osiris and, v. 272, 273
  Temples, built, iv. 111; v. 194
HIRANYA, resplendent or shining, ii. 75
HIRANYAGARBHA, Brahmā, is, i. 153, 328
  Devas, highest, ii. 123
  Egg of World, v. 421
  Golden egg, is, ii. 144; v. 472
  Hari and, i. 328; v. 188
  Hypostases, one of, i. 83
  Kosmic Auric Envelope, is, v. 528, 534
  Luminous egg, is, i. 134; v. 426
  Shankara and, i. 328; v. 188
  Temple, iv. 37
HIRANYAKASHIPU, Daityas, king of, iii. 229
  Satan, Purānic, ii. 138
HIRANYĀKSHA, Kashyapa, son of, iii. 381
  Posterity of, iv. 141
HIRANYAPURA, golden city of the air,
  iii. 381, 382
HIRN, G. A., quoted, ii. 205, 209
HISI, principle of evil, iii. 39
HISTORIOGRAPHER, Chung Ku, the, iii. 65
HISTORY, Adeptship, of, v. 155
  Berosus of, v. 180
  Church Councils, of, v. 156
  Diogenes of, v. 242
  Ecclesiastical, v. 155, 303
  France, of, v. 122
  Magic and, v. 257
  Mystery and, v. 110
  Occultism, of, v. 396
  Religions and, v. 155
  Vopiscus of, v. 148
HIUEN-Tsang, iii. 46; v. 39, 40
HIVIM, Chiefs of Votan call themselves, iii. 379
HOA, or Hea, member of the Chaldean Triad,
  iii. 39, 93
HOADLEY, West, iii. 342
HOANGTY, the Great Spirit, iv. 85
HOD in the Chaldean Kabalah, i. 249; ii. 69
HOKHMAN or wisdom, iii. 94
HOLY Bible, v. 239
  Church, v. 170, 176
  Ghost, i. 139, 146, 151, 169, 193, 247, 297;
    ii. 69, 72, 78, 118; iv. 81, 110, 136, 176;
    v. 33, 131, 184, 189, 196, 211, 447, 470, 476
  Holies, of, i. 174, 308; ii. 107, 182, 340;
    iii. 236; iv. 23, 27, 34, 35, 36, 37, 40, 87,
    109
  Light, v. 504
  Power, v. 504
  See, of Rome, v. 146
  Spirit, v. 152, 157
  Trinity, v. 156
  Word, v. 162
  Writ, v. 90
HOMER, Æther, silent on, ii. 144
  Allegories of, iii. 382
  Antiquity of, i. 52; ii. 373; v. 276
  Atlantis of, iii. 403
  Bible and, iii. 382
  Choas, silent on, ii. 144
  Constellations of, iv. 175
  Dragons, iii. 354
  Existence of, denied, iii. 239, 427

  Giants and, iii. 295, 336
  Greeks in days of, iii. 24, 437
  Job preceded, ii. 373
  Myths of, iv. 16
  Nemesis, and, iii. 306
  Night and, ii. 143
  Poseidon in, iii. 398
  Thought of, iv. 335
  Writing unknown to, iii. 437
HOMERIC, Heroes, iv. 226, 324
  Hymns, iii. 131
  Songs, iii. 390
HOMO diluvii, iii. 351
  Primigenius, iii. 195, 199, 289; iv. 260, 303
  Sapiens, iv. 245, 260
HOMŒOMERIAN system of philosophy, ii. 45
HOMOGENEITY, Absolute, i. 292; ii. 276
  Force and, ii. 242
  Human races, of, iv. 178
  Indivisible, is one and, ii. 129
  Man's nature, of, iii. 419
  Matter, of, ii. 313, 325, 365
  Region of, i. 318
  Universal unity or, i. 128
HOMOGENEOUS, Divine substance-principle,
  i. 316
  Elements, i. 199, 252; ii. 266, 272
  Heterogeneous, becomes, i. 188; iii. 419
  Matter, i. 229, 331; ii. 303, 319, 325, 397;
    iv. 223
HOMUNCULI of Paracelsus, ii. 59; iii. 129, 348,
  375
HONEY-combed with cells, Mountain, iii. 337
HÖNIR gives man Manas, iii. 106
HONOUR the Gods, We worship not but, ii. 216
HOOK, Vau a, iv. 28
HOOKE, Sir Robert, referred to, iv. 294
HOPPO a magician, ii. 190
HOR-AMMON, Ammon becomes, iv. 32
HOR-EB, Moses initiated at, iv. 111; v. 145
HOR-JARED or Ararat, iv. 169
HORCHIA, Titaea-Aretia worshipped as, iii. 152
HORIZON, Circular, i. 173
  Comet passing our, ii. 331
  Dusk rises at, ii. 91
  Lord of, ii. 398
  Neptune crossing, iv. 334
  Pole-stars in the, iii. 400
  Symbol, a, i. 173
  Zodiac and, iv. 354
HORIZONTAL, Line or matter, ii. 346; iv. 127,
  164, 172
  Squares, iv. 131
  Vertical and, i. 77; iv. 112
  Vishvānara, line in triangle, ii. 346
HORMING a name for Mercury, iii. 366
HORN implements, Early, iv. 284
HORNE, Rev. Mr., referred to, iv. 41; v. 195
HORNED moon and Virgin Mary, ii. 109
  Osiris, v. 247
HORNS, Dragon with ten, iv. 53
  Pan, of, iv. 79
  Satan with, iv. 76; v. 487
  Symbol of, iii. 416
HOROSCOPES, Astrology and, ii. 371; v. 325,
  340
  Stars of fixed, ii. 396

HOROSCOPY, Science of, i. 166
HORSE, Ass interbreeding with, iii. 288
  Derivation of one-toed, iv. 304
  Huschenk, of, iii. 396, 397, 398
  Origin of, iv. 360
  Pedigree of, iv. 266
  Twelve-legged, iii. 396, 389
  Types of, iv. 285
HORSES, Agni, of, iv. 177
  Fossils of, iv. 343
  Trace of, iv. 284
  Ungulate mammals, iv. 305
HORSESHOE continent, iii. 326, 333, 400
HORSUSI or Hor son of Osiris, ii. 82
HORUS, Ammon becomes, iv. 32
  Anubis and, v. 247
  Birth of, v. 440
  Brahmā classed with, iii. 236
  Christ, the, iv. 158, 206
  Christos or, i. 192
  Cross, raising dead with, iv. 127
  Dragon slain by, iii. 379
  Egyptian, iv. 41
  Elder, ii. 82
  Eye of, ii. 103
  Fish of, i. 267
  Freemason, v. 239
  Gem portraying, iv. 41
  God, i. 274
  Hathor and, ii. 115
  Isis as, ii. 96, 115; iii. 54
  Khem is, i. 267
  Logoi, one of the, i. 129
  Lotus and, ii. 96
  Male symbol, a, iv. 40
  Moon eye of, ii. 103
  Older, ii. 62
  Osiris and, i. 267; ii. 96, 148
  Reign of, iii. 367
  Servants of, iii. 373, 429
  Sevenfold myth of, v. 440
  Set and, iii. 285
  Sexes, of both, i. 139
  Threefold myth of, v. 440
  Typhon and, iii. 384
  Vehicle of, iv. 148
  Younger, ii. 62
HORUS-Apollo the Sun-God, ii. 83
HORUS-Osiris or father and son, i. 267
HORUS-Thot and the defunct, i. 267
HOSEA, v. 237
HOST, Ah-hi a, i. 111
  Angelic, i. 178; ii. 65; iii. 15, 38, 243; v. 319, 320, 325
  Arimaspian, iii. 414
  Azazel, of, iii. 375
  Builders, of, ii. 58
  Celestial, iii. 381; iv. 185
  Cosmic powers of, ii. 161
  Creator of humanity a, iii. 312; iv. 82; v. 129
  Demiurge, or, i. 322
  Elohim, of, i. 335; iii. 121; iv. 169; v. 325
  Heavenly, v. 170, 288, 319
  Indra, of, iii. 377
  Jehovah as, iii. 85; v. 192
  Logos, of, i. 157; ii. 152
  Lord of, v. 319

Manu or, iii. 148, 312
Mikael and, v. 320, 326
Monadic, i. 227
Operative beings, of, ii. 328
Pitris, i. 245
Planetary, v. 172
Primeval progenitors, of, iii. 419
Prometheus symbol of, iii. 411
Saba a, iii. 366
Satan, of, i. 244; ii. 129; iii. 180; v. 172
Sephiroth, of, iii. 15, 57; v. 234
Septenary, i. 265
Synthesis of, iii. 372
Tsabæan, v. 319
Uranus, representing, iv. 334
Ushanas or, iv. 69
Working, v. 213
HOSTS, Adityas the seven, iv. 57
  Archangels, v. 128
  Celestial, i. 187, 190; iii. 73; iv. 70, 119; v. 318
  Creative, i. 138, 170; iv. 55, 59, 177; v. 448
  Deities, of, ii. 129
  Devas, of, iii. 381
  Dhyān Chohans, of, i. 170; ii. 88
  Fallen angels, of, i. 246
  Heaven of, v. 318
  Lord of, v. 318; v. 522
  Planetary, v. 172
  Septenary, i. 265
  Seven, iii. 29, 95
  Seven creative, i. 139
  Sidereal, ii. 318
  Spirits of, i. 271; iv. 53
  Struggles between, i. 251
  Tridasha or, i. 138
  Tsabæan, v. 319
  World, of higher, i. 264
HOT breath of the father, i. 78
HOTRIS or priests, i. 151, 159
HOTTENTOTS descendants of Lemurians, iv. 348
HOUGHTON, Prof., quoted, iii. 23; iv. 264
HOUR, Origin of, v. 341
HOUR-glass of Rudra Shiva, iv. 70
HOURIS, Paradise full of, iii. 208
HOUSE, Earth, of the, iii. 27
  High, on, ii. 124
  Lord, of the, iv. 28
  Mars held, of Venus, iii. 391
  Planet palace or, iii. 41
  Tabernacle of the soul, of, i. 293
  Wisdom, of, ii. 124
  Zuni priests of, iv. 199
HOUSES, Logoi of seven, iv. 173
  Planets, called, i. 164
  Twelve, ii. 297
HOVAH or Eve, iii. 134, 387; iv. 35
HOVELACQUE, Abel, referred to, iii. 176
HOWARD on aerolites, iv. 352
HOWLER, Rudra the, iv. 118
H. P. B., Personal references to, i. 59; ii. 30, 210, 279
HRĀDA leader of Daityas, ii. 137
HRIMTHURSES or Frost giants, iii. 385
HROSZHARSGRANI the magician, iii. 346
HSÜEN Tsang, Chinese traveller, iii. 338, 339

HUA or He, i. 144
HUC, Abbé, quoted, iv. 71
HUELGOAT near Concarneau, Pond of, iii. 344
HUGGINS, referred to, ii. 322
HUGO, Victor, referred to, iii. 438
HUMAN-Spiritual to divine-spiritual, i. 269
HUMAN, Buddhas, v. 349, 365, 376, 425
Egos, v. 472, 493, 495
Elementals, v. 473, 560
Embryo, v. 430
Entity, v. 353
Incarnations, v. 350, 352
Mind, v. 499
Monad, v. 353
Mysteries, v. 167
Nature, v. 424
Self, v. 452
Septenary, v. 521
HUMAN PRINCIPLES, Ātma, the Cause of,
v. 487
Correspondences of, v. 433, 453, 454, 455,
461, 474, 478, 521, 542
Diagrams of, v. 533, 534
Hierarchies and, v. 461
Numbers and, v. 436, 440, 454, 461
Physical Body not one of, v. 521
Seven, v. 208, 361, 425, 426, 435, 471, 553
HUMAN RACE, Adam and, iii. 134; iv. 34
Ancestors of, iii. 217
Annihilation of, ii. 92
Antiquity of, ii. 371; iii. 212, 351; iv. 260
Appearance of, i. 286
Atlanteans first purely, iii. 268; iv. 283
Colour or complexion of each, iii. 105
Cradle of, iv. 357
First, i. 235; iii. 66, 168, 268, 328; v. 291
Origin of, iv. 216
Pair, not from one, iv. 287
Primitive families of, iii. 209
Rishis of, iii. 318
Sexual separation of, iv. 37; v. 291, 425
Spirits superior to, iii. 369
Third, iii. 179
Tree, compared to a, iii. 432
Varieties of, ii. 36
HUMAN RACES, Ancestors of, iii. 322
Animal and, ii. 19
Cast-off types of, iii. 265
Complete, iii. 224
Divine, from the, iii. 133
Divisions of, four, iii. 251
Evolution of, ii. 35; iii. 180; v. 425
Extinct, iii. 291
Homogeneity of, iv. 178
Millions of years claimed for, ii. 371
Sterility between, iii. 201
HUMAN SOUL, Animal and, i. 292
Conscious Ego or, iii. 97; v. 367
Divine and, iv. 240
Earth and Water, and, iii. 133
Immortality of, iii. 71
Intellectual, iii. 318
Manas the, i. 163, 209, 266; iv. 168; v. 488,
490
Mind or, i. 332; iii. 121
Plato on, iii. 97
Pneuma the, iii. 121

Spinal cord and, iv. 243
Zeus the, iii. 417
HUMAN SPECIES, iii. 66, 200, 205; iv. 178
HUMANITIES, Adam-Adami referred to, four,
iv. 24
Adaptation of, iv. 278
Appeared and disappeared, ii. 333
Atlanteans represented several, iii. 431
Evolution of, iii. 309
Far distant, ii. 333
Form, lacked the true, iv. 274
Future, past and present, i. 309
Series of, iv. 103
Worlds, of other, ii. 336; iv. 277
HUMANITY, Adam and, iii. 109, 142, 409
Adamic, i. 63
Age of, i. 205; iii. 253, 441; iv. 256, 263
Androgyne, iii. 177
Architects taught, i. 310
Aryan, iii. 408
Aspirations of divine, iv. 185
Astral, iii. 121
Axial point of, i. 240
Benefactors of, iii. 368
Bibles of, iv. 272; v. 232
Birthplace of, iii. 433
Child of cyclic destiny, iii. 444
Childhood of, i. 316
Climacteric year of, ii. 382
Collective i. 311; iii. 142, 310
Cradle of, iii. 207, 324
Creator of, ii. 61; iii. 312
Dhyān Chohans and, i. 156, 273, 322; iv. 239
Divine, iv. 178
Divisions, of, iii. 432
Drama of, ii. 337; iii. 147, 386
Earth round, of fourth, i. 213
Effects, can master, iv. 81
Elect of, i. 310
Enlightenment of, iv. 84
Eve and, iii. 109, 409
Evolution of, i. 226; iii. 431; iv. 341
Faculties of, i. 296; ii. 260
" Fallen angels " and, iii. 276
Father of post-diluvian, iv. 180
Fifth, iii. 147, 364, 408
Fifth race, i. 63, 64
Fifth Round, v. 518
First, iii. 121
Forms of, jelly like, iii. 159
Fourth round, iv. 254, 341
Generation of, i. 275
Gigantic, iv. 103
Gods and, ii. 189
Guides of, i. 256
Height of, iv. 319
Hierarchies and, i. 156
History of, i. 224
Idols and, ii. 190
Injustice to, apparent, ii. 369
Intellect of, iii. 362, 410
Io symbol of, iii. 414
Jah-Eve and, iii. 134
Karma of, iv. 82
Lipika and, i. 185
Manu creator of, iii. 310, 312
Manvantaras, of various, i. 226; iii. 154

HUMANITY (*Contd.*)
Noah saviour of, iv. 35
Origin of, one, iii. 251
Padmapāni and, v. 420, 421
Periods of, i. 64
Physical, ii. 61; iii. 157, 304; iv. 103; v. 291
Pioneers of, i. 234
Planetary chain, on our, iii. 79
Post-diluvian, iv. 180
Powers of early, iii. 319
Preceded by four races, i. 63
Primeval, i. 214; iii. 159, 308; iv. 365
Primitive, iii. 139; iv. 260
Principle (God) in, iv. 126
Progenitors of, i. 186; iii. 104
Race distinct from our, iv. 293
Races of, i. 63; ii. 261; iii. 364
Reason of, iii. 362
Religion and, v. 168
Root-races of, i. 72, 271; iii. 59, 192, 426; iv. 267
Round, in present, iv. 182
Second, i. 242; iii. 146
Senseless, i. 241; iii. 233
Senses of, ii. 260
Serpent, and the, ii. 120
Seven groups of, ii. 297
Seven sons, and, ii. 148
Seventh Round, v. 563
Sinless, v. 289
Spiritual, i. 167; iii. 88
Stars, bound together with, iii. 351
Triad and, v. 188
Vaishvānara and, iii. 311
Vaivasvata, i. 64; iii. 82, 253, 321, 329; iv. 263
Vishvakarman and, iv. 178
Third, iii. 37, 140
Total, i. 129
Twilight, of, iii. 70
Yugas of, i. 64
HUMANLY-born mortals, First, iii. 275
HUMBOLDT, quoted or referred to, i. 230, 254; ii. 35, 221; iii. 149; iv. 243
HUME, Nihilistic idealism of, iii. 164; v. 546
HUNDRED-formed, Shata-Rūpā, the, ii. 149; iii. 137
HUNGARIANS, i. 121; ii. 185, 279
HUNGARY Academy of Science, v. 221
Meteorites in, iv. 276
HUNT, Dr. James, quoted, iii. 176; iv. 309
Dr. T. S., quoted, ii. 218
E. B., referred to, ii. 209
R., referred to, ii. 222, 254, 255, 262, 304; iv. 265
HURRICANES, ii. 183; iii. 20, 24; iv. 269
HUSBAND, Mother's, i. 274; ii. 108, 111, 339; iv. 32
HUSCHENK, iii. 395, 396, 397
HUXLEY, Prof., see Book Index
HUXLEY-Haeckelian theories, iv. 229, 231, 235
HUYGENS, referred to, iii. 45
HVANIRATHA or Jambudvīpa, iv. 179, 328
HWERGELMIR, roaring cauldron of human passions, ii. 123
HYADES or rain constellation, iv. 353, 354
HYÆNA spelæa, Man co-existent with, iv. 315

HYBRID, Jews a, people, ii. 25
Races, iv. 283
HYBRIDITY, iv. 293
HYBRIDIZATION, iii. 206
HYBRIDS, Fourth race, of the, iii. 200
Idol-worship and, iv. 292
Sterility of, iii. 288
HYDRA, ii. 388; iii. 210
HYDROGEN, Air and, iii. 123
Chlorine and, ii. 308
Elements, and, ii. 308; iii. 121; iv. 164
First-born, one of the, ii. 348
Gas, ii. 287
Hypothetical element, ii. 307
Intelligence and, ii. 332
Kāma Rūpa and, iv. 165
Nebulæ, in, ii. 320
Oxygen and, i. 125
Platinum and, ii. 287
Protoplasm, in, ii. 362
Protyle and, ii. 351
Spiritual fire, is, iii. 114
Stars, of fixed, i. 199
HYGIEIA, Statue of, iii. 140
HYKSOS, ancestors of Phoenicians, i. 175; ii. 25
HYLE one of the quaternary, i. 147; iv. 171
HYLO-idealism, ii. 201, 202
HYLO-idealistic scheme, i. 337
HYLO-idealists, i. 159; iii. 164
HYLOZOISM, iii. 166, 167
HYMN, Agni, to, iv. 95
Budha, by, iv. 66
Jupiter, to, iv. 122
Minerva, to, ii. 116
Rig Veda, in, iv. 66
Sun, to the, ii. 263
Tomb, engraved on, ii. 155
Virgin, applied to, ii. 116
HYMNS, Accadian, v. 202
Egypt, of, ii. 154
Greek and Latin, iii. 49
Hindu, ii. 348
Homeric, iii. 131
Mantras, or, ii. 160
Orphic, iii. 143, 150; iv. 353; v. 59
Rig Veda, of, i. 314; ii. 160; iv. 16, 177; v. 270
Vedic, iv. 151
HYPATIA, murdered, v. 307
HYPERBOREAN, iii. 20, 24, 146, 276; iv. 177, 338, 339, 342, 344, 346
HYPERION, an Arkite Titan, iii. 151
HYPNOTIC state of Kandu, iii. 182
HYPNOTISM, Accepted by Science, v. 48
Artificial State produced by, v. 540
Arts of enchantment, iv. 212
Danger of, v. 511
Effects of, on the, Aura, v. 458
Experiments by, v. 47
Mesmerism, i. 337; iii. 164
Occult Sciences of, and Magnetism, v. 460
Use and Abuse of, v. 61
HYPNOTIZE the bird, Serpents, ii. 126
HYPOSTASES, Three, i. 83, 84
HYPOSTASIS, i. 328; ii. 147; v. 217
HYPOSTATICAL Trinity, the, ii. 393

I

I, Conception of, ii. 172; v. 546
  Personal, the, v. 490
I-Ah-O, Jehovah reads, iv. 33, 111
I-AM-NESS, Ahamkara or, iv. 185
  Egoship or, i. 247
  Egotism or, iii. 417
  Self-hood, outline of, ii. 172
I AM, Eh'yeh or, ii. 343; iv. 19
I AM HE, or Aham-sa, i. 144
I AM I, Kālaham-sa or, i. 81, 144; v. 475, 496
I AM THAT I AM, i. 144; ii. 240; iv. 36, 109, 173
I HI WEI in the Tao-te-King, ii. 194
IABÈ, or Yahva, iv. 33
IĀBESHAH, Earth, v. 166
IACCHUS IA IAO or Jehovah, iv. 28
IAH, or Jah and Jeho, iii. 138; iv. 111
  Mother in, v. 212
  Silent power of, v. 212
IAMBLICHUS, quoted, ii. 125, 194, 376; v. 277, 280, 301, 316, 321, 452
  Referred to, v. 58, 73, 279
IAO, v. 254, 277, 290
  Abrasax, iv. 41
  Chaldean Heptakis or, i. 274
  Genius of moon, the, iv. 108
  God, Mystery, ii. 167; iv. 32
  Iacchus or Jehovah, ii. 167; iv. 28
  Jehovah is, v. 277
  Moon of, iv. 108
  Mysteries, of, iii. 387; iv. 41
  Mystery-God, the, iv. 111
  Mystery-name, the, iv. 106
  Satan, is, iii. 387
  Triune, iv. 174
IAO-JEHOVAH, iii. 388
IAO-SABAOTH, Jod, full number of, iv. 174
IAPETOS, a son of Noah, iii. 151; iv. 332
IARDAN or Eridanus, iv. 154
IBERIANS and Aryan invasion, iv. 310
IBIS, ii. 68, 72, 77
IBIS-HEADED God-hierophant, iv. 128
IBLIS, the devil, iii. 393
IBN GEBIROL, quoted, ii. 91, 169, 343; iv. 19, 29
IBN WAHOHIJAH, referred to, iv. 22
IBRAHIM-ABRAHAM, iv. 21
ICARUS, Fall of an, v. 134
ICE, ages, iii. 81; iv. 308
  Ether and, ii. 251
  Desert of, iii. 326
  Frost and snow, iii. 329
  Increase of, cause of, iv. 294
  Period, iv. 251
ICELAND, iii. 421; iv. 350
ICHCHHĀSHAKTI or will-power, i. 333; iii. 180
ICHTHYOLOGY, Septenary law in, iv. 194
ICHTHYOSAURI, iii. 260; iv. 266, 282
ICHTHYS, Oannes or Jonas, ii. 380
ICONOGRAPHY, Catacombs, of, iv. 158
  Gnostic, iv. 135
  Pre-Christian, was, ii. 119
IDA, Ases in, iii. 107
  Field of, iii. 109
IDĀ or Ila, iii. 147, 148, 151, 155

IDĀ and Pingalā, v. 480, 510, 520, 524
IDAM or Idam, iii. 383; iv. 179
IDAS, Castor wounded by, iii. 131
IDAS-PATI, Hindu, iv. 334
IDEAN MYSTERIES, iii. 216
IDEAS, Eternity in, i. 324
  Greek Philosophers, of, v. 215, 327
  Numbers, of, v. 87
IDEATION(S), Absolute wisdom, of, ii. 41
  Activity, in, v. 534
  Astral, iv. 168
  Circuit of, iv. 207
  Cosmic, i. 81, 170, 171; iii. 37; iv. 131
  Darkness, of, ii. 95
  Divine, ii. 90, 95; iii. 300; v. 446, 475, 493
  Eternal, ii. 95
  Latent, iv. 168
  Lipika, amanuenses of eternal, i. 165
  Mind, of universal, i. 170, 322
  Physical plane, on, i. 111
  Pre-cosmic, i. 80, 81
  Spiritual, i. 309; iii. 245
  Things to be, of, ii. 90
  Universal, iv. 168; v. 382
IDEI identified with Kabiri, iii. 359
IDEI Dactyli or ideic fingers, iii. 360
IDENTITY, Ancient and Modern Initiations, of, v. 281
  Angels and Devas, of, 332
  Angels and Dhyān Chohans, of, 320, 332
  Eastern and Western Thought, of, v. 109
  Esoteric Teaching and Greek Philosophy, of, v. 281
  Zoroastrian and Christian Dogma, of, v. 316
IDEOGRAPH, Material elements, of, iv. 154
  Number of six, of, iv. 158
  Period of an, iv. 117
IDEOGRAPHIC, Hieroglyphs, i. 46; iii. 436
  Productions of tribes, iii. 436
  Records, iii. 436
IDEOGRAPHS, Symbolical, ii. 15; iv. 155
IDEOS, Chaos, or, i. 325
  Elements out of, i. 325
IDIOT, Ape not, iv. 248
  Congenital, i. 271; v. 564
  Consciousness of, on astral plane, v. 531
  Have only desire, v. 567
  What is an?, iii. 244
IDOL, Clay feet, with, ii. 302
  Moon, of, ii. 110; iv. 22; v. 237, 242
  Satan as an, ii. 131
  Vitoba, of, iv. 130
  Worship, ii. 113; iv. 292; v. 412
IDOLATRY, ii. 185; v. 77
  Bossuet on, iii. 281
  Egyptians, of old, iii. 145
  Exotericism, or, iv. 61
  Gentile world, of, iii. 267
  Judah, of, ii. 375
  Paganism, or, ii. 185
  Progress of, iv. 71
  Soma worship not, ii. 108
  Superstitions, full of, iii. 283
IDOLS, Bhons, of, iv. 157
  Clay feet, of matter with, ii. 283
  Devil, and, iii. 340

IDOLS (*Contd.*)
　Double number and, ii. 107
　Golden calf, ii. 400
　India, in, iv. 25
　Jews of the, iv. 160
　Moon, of, ii. 117
　Teraphim and, v. 237-242
　Tombs, in, iv. 292
　Vedas countenance no, iv. 292
　Worship of, iv. 60
IEOU four vowelled name, ii. 168
IERNA, Sacred fire of, v. 267
　Worship at the island of sacred, iv. 329
IEVO, Antagonistic to Abraxas, iv. 111
　Philo Byblus, iv. 33
IGIGI or Angels of Heaven, iii. 250
IGNIS, Fire or, iii. 122
　Latins, or agni, iii. 109
IGNITION, Fire state of, i. 198
IGUANA or lizard, iii. 161
IGUANODON, iii. 159, 161, 347; iv. 247
IHOH, Mysteries of, iii. 216
I. H. S., meaning of, iii. 314
I. H. V. H., iii. 51; iv. 28, 41
IKSHVĀKU or Euxine Sea, iii. 401
　Maru of family of, ii. 93
　Nimi son of, iv. 93
ILĀ, Goddess, iii. 143
　Idā, or, iii. 147, 148, 151
　Legends of, iii. 155
　Mania is, iii. 151
　Son of, ii. 247
　Vaivasvata Manu and, iii. 156
ILDA a child, i. 247
ILDABAOTH, v. 168, 201, 204
　Ambition of, iii. 246
　Astral Gods, sons of, ii. 167
　Gnostic jewels and, iv. 49
　God of Moses, iii. 388
　Jehovah or, v. 201, 204
　Material production of, iii. 219
　Ophites, by the, ii. 301
　Saturn, genius of, ii. 301; iv. 108
　Seven, one of, v. 201, 202, 204
　Spirit, not a, iii. 246
ÎLES FORTUNÉES, iii. 370
ILIAD, Apollo in, iv. 343
　Esoteric meaning of, iii. 382
　Quoted, iii. 130, 189
　Tartarus of, iv. 345
　Zodiacal signs in, ii. 374
ILIADOS or primordial matter, i. 325
ILITHYIA, the beauteous Goddess, ii. 110
ILLUMINATI, v. 89
ILLUMINATIST TEACHINGS, iv. 201
ILLUSION, Adi-Buddha an, i. 124
　All, except Absolute, ii. 247
　Angels are, i. 335
　Appearance is, i. 328
　Bhut are, i. 335
　Body of, iii. 67; v. 351, 378, 472
　Day of Brahmā of, ii. 360
　Domination of, iv. 25
　Eternal state beyond, ii. 306
　Ever-living and, ii. 273
　Form, v. 352
　Genii are, i. 335

Great, i. 138, 262; ii. 273
Life and death are, v. 488
Light an, i. 137
Limbo of, iii. 237
Mahāmāya or great, i. 321; iii. 97, 108, 383
Male Brahmā an, ii. 47
Man an, ii. 328
Mary, mare, sea an, i. 54
Matter the great, iii. 236
Māyā or, i. 112, 299; ii. 42, 83, 112, 356;
　iii. 117; v. 352, 388
Motion, of, iv. 161
Nature an, iv. 43
Nirmānakāyas beyond, iv. 186
Physical brain, of, i. 322
Plane of, i. 151, 187, 324; ii. 297; v. 352
Power of, v. 351
Pradhāna or, i. 131
Prakriti an, iv. 170
Regions of, iv. 209
Root of, iv. 171
Samvriti origin of, i. 120
Senses, of, ii. 290
Seven causes of, ii. 258
Spheres of, i. 318
Substance an, i. 316
Terrestrial, ii. 98
Time an, i. 110
Unconscious on plane of, ii. 172
Universal, v. 379
Universe an, i. 188, 201, 335; v. 488
World of, i. 320; ii. 329; v. 352
ILLUSIONISTS, v. 185
ILLUSIVE, Matter, v. 388
ILMATAR, Seven sons of, iii. 39
　Virgin daughter of air, iii. 39
ILUS, Berosus of, ii. 53
　Chaos, offspring of, ii. 54
　Lotus grows in, i. 128
　Mother or Hyle, i. 147
　Primeval, i. 196
　Spirit, i. 152
IMAGE, Adam an, iii. 182; iv. 34; v. 208
　Astral body, of man, i. 287, 290; iii. 110
　Boneless Gods, of, iii. 387
　Cell, of man in, i. 290
　Chhāya or, iii. 181
　Creators, of, i. 287; iv. 35
　Crucified, of, iv. 158
　Deity, of highest, iii. 132
　Divine Intelligence, of, v. 316
　Elohim, of, v. 187
　Evolution of own, iii. 181
　Fatal, astral, i. 290
　God, of, ii. 105, 162; iii. 15, 231; v. 326
　Logos, of, iv. 164
　Made in own, i. 311
　Pitris could not make, iii. 103
　Rind of, i. 288
　Shadow, of Elohim, iii. 145
　Spark, of flame, i. 309
　Sphinx, is, i. 290
　Triangle, of deity, iv. 153
　Tselem, or, iii. 377; iv. 24
IMAGES, Adoration of, iii. 281
　Allegorical, v. 301
　Atlantean, iii. 331

IMAGES (*Contd.*)
  Buddha, of, iv. 157
  Celestial hosts, of, iv. 69
  Cherubim, of, iv. 69
  Chhāyās, or, iii. 236
  Confucius, of, ii. 158
  Deified, of third race, iii. 179
  Dual-sexed, v. 292
  Easter Island, iii. 336
  Ether, ii. 183
  First race were, iii. 124
  Harpocrates, of, iii. 395
  Ladder of being, and, iii. 270
  Lemurian, iii. 316
  Sons create own, i. 105, 242
  Stars, of, iv. 17
  Svastika on, iv. 157
  Third and fourth race, of, iii. 33
IMAGINATION, Atoms and, ii. 395
  Materialistic, iv. 17
  Nature, of, i. 303
  Scientific, ii. 206; iii. 145
  Shape in prototype before, i. 324
  Use of, v. 535
IMBROGLIO of sidereal denominations, ii. 378
IMHOTEP, Logos creator becomes, ii. 68
IMMACULATE, Birth, ii. 114; v. 152
  Conception, i. 65, 128, 129; ii. 108
  Mothers, i. 155; ii. 115
  Parents, iv. 51
  Pilgrim, i. 311
  Principle, iv. 229
  Progeny, iii. 283
  Root, i. 134
  Virgin, son of, i. 129; iv. 31
IMMACULATELY-BORN son, ii. 115
IMMETALIZATION, Devas pass through, i. 239
  Gods pass through, i. 239
  Monads, of, iii. 158
IMMETALIZED, Light, iii. 177
  Monad, iii. 192
IMMIGRANT, sub-race, iv. 313
IMMIGRANTS, Aborigines or, iv. 309
IMMORTALITY, Bird of, iii. 48
  Chaos, of, ii. 62
  Conditional, v. 486, 491
  Conquest of, iv. 80
  Cross represents, iv. 126
  Destruction of Ashvattha Tree leads to, ii. 123
  Divine degree of, i. 272
  Dragon symbol of, iii. 378
  Earth, on, iii. 278
  Emblem of, i. 299
  Kalpa, to end of, i. 109
  Life in, ii. 80
  Lucifer giver of, iii. 387
  Man to conquer, iv. 80
  Personality, denied to, ii. 158
  Plant of, iii. 102
  Primordial chaos, in, ii. 62
  Quaternary symbol of, iv. 147
  Reincarnating ego, of, iii. 119
  Rudra's progeny, of, iv. 185
  Secret of, on earth, iii. 278
  Secured, v. 489, 493, 496
  Serpent symbol of, i. 140; ii. 121; v. 238

  Son of, iii. 379
  Spirit, of, iv. 122; v. 281, 290
  Spiritual, iii. 246
  Symbol of, i. 140, 299; iii. 378; iv. 126, 147; v. 238
  Time's axle is, iv. 183
  Waters of, i. 319; iii. 380
IMMORTALS, Communication with, ii. 185
  Creation of, ii. 173
  Daimones dwell near, i. 329
  Derived from, ii. 75
  Lipika, i. 165
  Mortals and, ii. 75
  Work of, iii. 272
IMPARTITE, Absolute unity is, iv. 154
  Spiritual monad is, i. 230
IMPEDIMENT, Spiritual, i. 319; iii. 297
IMPENETRABILITY of matter, ii. 212
IMPERCEPTIBLE spheres, ii. 200
IMPERFECTION, Cause of, v. 213, 214
  Geological records of, iv. 249
  World, of the, v. 224
IMPERFECTIONS, Badhas or, iii. 170
IMPERSONAL, Absorption into the, v. 380
  Divine Principle, v. 386
  Ego, v. 400, 498
  First Cause, v. 187
  God, v. 30, 380
IMPERSONALITY, Avatāras, of, iv. 46
  Substance, of, i. 317
IMPLEMENTS, Ancient stone, iv. 291
  Flint, iv. 308
  Neolithic, iv. 284, 293
  Rude, iv. 91, 293
IMPONDERABLES, King of, ii. 213
IMPRESS of past events, iv. 362
IMPERSSIONS, Brain, on the, v. 552
  Higher Ego, on the, v. 552
  Simultaneous, v. 547, 548
  Three sets of, v. 550, 551
IMPRISONED, Gods, iii. 18
  Soul, ii. 291
  Spirit, iv. 303
IMPRISONMENT, of Logoi, iii. 106
IMPULSE, Cyclic law, of, ii. 349
  Dhyān Chohanic, iv. 307
  Downward, cyclic, iv. 310
  Evolutionary, iii. 63, 245, 299; iv. 301
  Forces acting through inward, ii. 365
  Nemesis, to, ii. 367
  Orbs, to, ii. 318
  Outward motion and inward, i. 318
  Pesh-Hun gives, iii. 60
  Physical, iii. 159
  Primitive, of planets, ii. 326
  Protoplasm, producing, iii. 165
  Quasi-intelligent, iv. 218
  Unconscious, ii. 365
IMPULSES, Attractions or, ii. 214
  Cosmic energy, of, ii. 360
  Newton, on, ii. 214
  Physical senses, by, ii. 369
  Planetary, iv. 266
IN, Earth or, i. 286
  Material principle or, i. 264
INACHOS father of Phoroneus, iv. 88
INACHUS, Io daughter of, iii. 412

INACTIVE, Purusha, without Prakriti, iii. 53
    Svabhāvat, state of, ii. 360
INACTIVITY Spirit, of pure, iii. 111
    Unconscious, iii. 67
INAUDIBLE melody of planets, ii. 151
INCA, Ruins of, iv. 315
INCANDESCENCE, Particles in a state of, ii. 323
    Solar centre, of the, ii. 325
    Sun's supposed, ii. 315
INCANDESCENT MASSES, whirling, ii. 316
INCANTATIONS, Criminal, ii. 190
    Fables, now called, ii. 190
    Lahgash or, ii. 69
    Magic, v. 250
    Mantras and, ii. 185
    Mystical, i. 222
    Tantric works on, v. 185
    Zodiacal, v. 331, 332
INCARNATE, Being, i. 239
    Devas compelled to, iv. 85
    Dhyānis, iii. 231
    Image of the Elohim, v. 157
INCARNATED, Angel, iii. 285
    Gods, iii. 18; iv. 335
    Logos, iv. 96
INCARNATES, Chaste asceticism, iii. 283
    Divine, iii. 349
INCARNATING, Angels, iii. 235, 360
    Egos, iv. 349
    Gods, iii. 172, 235
    Powers, iii. 97, 98
    Satan, iii. 237
    Spirits of Mahat, iii. 233
INCARNATION, of Adepts, v. 352
    Astral Principles of Adepts, of, v. 359
    Divine and Human, v. 350
    Divine, v. 79, 350, 351
    Krishna of, v. 351
    Lamaic, v. 349
INCARNATIONS, Amitābha Buddha, of, ii. 193
    Angels, of, iii. 90, 234; iv. 55, 59
    Asuras, of, iii. 250, 318
    Avatāras or, ii. 84, 363; iii. 321; iv. 46, 52;
        v. 351
    Boar, ii. 84; iii. 321
    Bodhisattvas, of, ii. 295
    Buddha, of, ii. 295, 363; iii. 185; v. 407
    Buddhi after, i. 289
    Christians' divine, iv. 125; v. 211
    Curse of, iii. 248; iv. 84
    Cycle, i. 82, 234, 272; ii. 296; iii. 171, 187,
        192, 375; iv. 53, 85
    Dalai, iii. 185
    Dalai Lama, of, ii. 193; v. 105
    Deferred, iii. 231
    Demiourgoi, of, iv. 84
    Devas of, i. 239; iv. 63
    Dhyān Chohans, of, i. 239; iii. 360
    Dhyānis, of, iv. 55
    Divine on earth, i. 235; iv. 46, 125
    Divine kings, of, iv. 334
    Divine monad, of, iii. 376
    Divine ray, of, iii. 234
    Divine rebels, of, iii. 111
    Duration of, ii. 361
    Egos of past, iii. 109; iv. 53
    Elect in the, iii. 360

Empty forms, in, iii. 348
Empty shadows, in, iv. 55
Entity, of, ii. 296
Fall or, iii. 179; iv. 84
First-born, of, iii. 90
Flames, of, iii. 250
Gautama, of, ii. 193
Gods, of, i. 239; ii. 382; iii. 215, 234; iv. 52,
    63, 334
Heroes, of, iii. 229
Host, of, iii. 419; iv. 84
Human, iii. 185
Intermediate between, iv. 181
Instructors, of, iv. 83
Kabalah, in the, v. 176
Karma, in, iii. 185; iv. 84
Kepler and, ii. 380
Kings, of, iv. 83
Krishna, of, iii. 229, 318; v. 351
Kumāras, of, iii. 250, 251, 318; v. 472
Kwan-Shi-Yin, of, iii. 193
Lamas, of, iii. 185
Lilith, of, iii. 286
Logoi, of, iv. 84
Logos, of, iii. 318
Lower sidereal beings, of, iii. 286
Lower hosts, of, iv. 83
Lunar Devas, of, iv. 63
Manas after, i. 289
Manus, of, iii. 250
Manushi, of, ii. 295
Monad differes in its, i. 228
Monad, of, i. 234, 235; iii. 169, 187, 192,
    286, 376; iv. 222, 241
Mrira of, iii. 404
Mystery of evil and, iv. 84
Nether world in, iii. 215
Nirmānakāyas, of, iv. 222
Past, iii. 109
Pitris of, i. 239; iii. 250
Prajāpatis, of, iii. 250
Premature, iii. 419
Progenitors, of, iii. 348
Races in higher, iii. 169
Ray of, divine, iii. 234
Rishis, of, iii. 250
Rudras, of, iii. 318
Seat of God, of, iii. 90
Series of, iii. 229
Seven, ii. 363; iii. 358
Shiva, of, iii. 251
Shukra, of, iii. 45
Solar Gods, ii. 382; iv. 63
Sons of wisdom, of, iii. 231, 288, 318
Spheres, on other, iii. 286
Spirit, iii. 236
Successive, ii. 361
Suffering and, i. 244
Teshu Lamas, of, ii. 193; iii. 185; v. 105
Thot Hermes, of, ii. 400
Thrones, of, iii. 90
Trismegistus, in, ii. 400
Ushanas, of, iii. 45
Varāha, ii. 84
Vishnu, of, iii. 45, 229; v. 350
INCAS and the deluge, iii. 149
INCENSE burned unto Baal, ii. 375

INCEST, ii. 149

INCH, British measures, unit of, ii. 25, 26, 28
Cubits, and Egyptian, ii. 25; v. 111
Jehovah literally, iv. 35

INCHOATE matter, ii. 290

INCIDENTAL, Dissolution, ii. 86
Naimittika, iii. 79

INCIPIENT, Dhyān Chohans, or perfected men, i. 318
Evolution of fourth race, iii. 23
Human life, iii. 167
Human stage, i. 226
Incrustation, iii. 23
Monads, i. 318
Physicalization, iii. 167; iv. 306
Sketch of man, ii. 290

INCLINATION, Axial angle of, iii. 355
Axis, of earth's, iii. 63, 293, 329; iv. 294
Axis of Venus, iii. 45
Ecliptic, of, ii. 385, 390

INCOGNIZABILITY of the circle, ii. 338

INCOGNIZABLE, Bosom of, ii. 150
Brahma, iii. 117
Cause of Evolution, iv. 55
Creation and the, ii. 149
Deity, i. 173; ii. 151; iii. 64; iv. 40, 161
Element, the One, ii. 61
Principle, ii. 43

INCOMMUNICABLE axiom, the, iv. 127

INCONGRUITIES, Apparent, iv. 156

INCONSISTENCIES, Bible, iv. 103
Science, in, ii. 396

INCORPOREAL, Ābhūtarājasas are, iii. 98
Arūpa or, i. 247
Automata, ii. 356
Being, world of, ii. 295
Corporeal and, i. 327
Corporealities, ii. 289
Creator, iii. 244
Entities, i. 265
Fire, iv. 173
Garments of, man, iii. 316
Idea is a being, ii. 347
Intelligences, iv. 122
Laws, ii. 268
Man, i. 139; iii. 120, 200, 316
Pitris, iii. 98, 392
Principles, ii. 182
Races, iii. 200
Spirits, iv. 296
Stuff, ii. 232
Units, ii. 355

INCORPOREALITIES, Pure, ii. 357

INCORRUPTIBLE nature of man, iii. 387

INCREASE, Goddess of, iii. 86

INCRUSTATION, Beginning of, iii. 63
Earth, of, iii. 23, 75, 157, 325
Globe, of, iii. 251
Incipient, iii. 23

INCRUSTED world, iv. 264, 283, 289

INCUBATED, by the Divine Spirit, ii. 44

INCUBATES the waters, Serpent, ii. 68

INCUBUS, Ethnologists, of the, iv. 259
Karma, of Atlantean, iv. 310

INDECIDUATA group, Mammals of, iv. 220, 238

INDESTRUCTIBLE, Life-principle, iv. 242
Manvantara, of the, iii. 399

Primeval matter, ii. 333
Primordial matter, i. 125
Principle, iv. 138
Self, ii. 258
Units, i. 231; ii. 355

INDEX, Astral capacities, to, iii. 302
Skulls, of, iv. 92

INDIA, Birthplace of Mathematics, v. 341
Buddhism and, v. 411
Caste in, v. 354
Geometric Symbols in, v. 11
Home of occult knowledge, v. 256
Initiation in, v. 271, 275
Land of Knowledge, v. 41
Latin Cross from, v. 161
Pantheon of, v. 207
Priests of, v. 262
Secret observations of, v. 322
Temples of, v. 207, 322
Sages of, v. 59
Simon's journey to, v. 142

INDIAN, Aryans, v. 107, 109
Dialect, language of Moses was, v. 181
Esoterism, v. 115
Occult methods of calculation, v. 185
Orpheus, an, v. 304
Philosophy, v. 209
Rites, v. 104
Trinity, v. 189
Secret Doctrine, v. 146, 281
Yogis, v. 246, 468, 479, 480

INDIANISTS, Areus or Ares and the, iii. 391

INDIANS, Bull symbol, of, iii. 416
Druids akin to, iv. 325
Guatemala, of, iii. 62
Hercules, of, v. 258
Inferior race, said to be an, iii. 288
Jews borrowed from, i. 308
Logos of, iii. 416
Maya, iii. 61
Red, iii. 252
Seven Powers of, v. 203
Stature of, iii. 331
Symbols, iii. 416
Zuni, iv. 199

INDIGO, the Complement of Yellow, v. 441
Correspondences, v. 454, 458, 460, 461, 468, 507, 508
Not a shade of Blue, v. 543

INDISCRETE, Discrete lost in the, ii. 88
Fire, iii. 115
Principle, ii. 165, 246
Substance, iii. 135

INDISCRETION of Mnaseas, an, iii. 361

INDIUM, an element referred to by Crookes, ii. 276

INDIVIDUAL, Conscious spirits, or, iv. 208
Consciousness, iv. 239
Cycles, ii. 362; iii. 194
Ego, iii. 190; v. 354, 358
Elements of science, ii. 397
Evolution, iii. 46
History in, ii. 368
Intelligences, ii. 359
Karma, iii. 185
Liberty, iii. 306
Life, i. 304, 311

INDIVIDUAL (*Contd.*)
Monad, i. 230
Pralaya, i. 225; ii. 86
Souls, iv. 64, 138, 241
Sun Rays, and, v. 533
Svastika and, iv. 126
INDIVIDUALITIES, Rishis and Prajāpatis, of, i. 281
Sephiroth not, ii. 357
INDIVIDUALITY, v. 550
Atoms have no, ii. 355
Buddhi has to acquire, i. 82
Consciousness of, v. 498
Divine, v. 473
Earth, on, iii. 244
Existing in itself, i. 318
Immortal in, iii. 131, 420
Impersonal, iii. 249; v. 364
Jnānashakti generates, i. 333
Monad, of, i. 308; ii. 344
Nirvāna, not lost in, i. 309
Noumenon an, ii. 216
Personality and, iii. 307; iv. 46
Persons as to, three, ii. 393
Reincarnation of same, iii. 307; v. 487
Second death and, v. 498
Sense, of, ii. 257
Spiritual, i. 212, 308; ii. 344
INDIVIDUALIZED, Consciousness, iii. 243
Monad, ii. 345
Seven Powers of Logos, iii. 358
INDIVISIBLE, Circle, iv. 193
Entity of Spinoza, ii. 354
Homogeneity is one and, ii. 129
Omniscience, i. 320
Point, ii. 70
Substance, ii. 353
Unity, ii. 151
INDO-ĀRYAN, figures, iv. 195
Heaven and earth, v. 111
Occultists, iii. 21
INDO-CHINESE stature, iii. 331
INDO-EUROPEAN, Mongolo-Turanian and, ii. 31
Nations, iv. 361
INDO-GERMANIC race, the, iii. 173
INDO-IRANIAN, Asura, iii. 101; iv. 178
INDOLENTIA Epicurean, ii. 300
INDUVAMSHAS, Lunar kings or, ii. 108
Suryavamshas and, ii. 112
INDRA, Ahi-Vritra and, iii. 383
Air is, v. 111
Apollo answers to, iii. 381
Aryan philosophy, in, i. 76
Asura applied to, iii. 101; iv. 68
Calf, called, ii. 113
Divinity, a secondary, ii. 91
Elephant of, v. 111
Firmament, and, iii. 380
Flesh by spirit, conquers, iv. 186
Fohat, scientific aspect of, ii. 398
God of air, ii. 183
Heaven, God of, iv. 69
Heaven of, iii. 208
Highest God, v. 476
Jehovah and, v. 254
Kārtikeya, prototype of, iii. 381

King of the Gods, iii. 182
Loka, of, ii. 247
Maruts allies of, iv. 184, 185, 186
Michael, prototype of, iv. 66
Pramlocha sent by, iii. 183
Rudra and, iv. 66
Vedic powerful God, iv. 177
Vritra, and, iii. 383
Vul, the atmospheric, iii. 385
INDRĀNĪ, Aindu or, iv. 185
Lakshmi or Venus, iii. 86
INDRIYA or third creation, ii. 165, 172
INDRIYĀTMAN, spiritual or intellectual soul, iii. 117
INDU the physical moon, iii. 56
INDUCTIVE, Law, Haeckel on, iv. 234, 235
Logic, ii. 200
Method, i. 208; ii. 203; iv. 144
INDUS and NILE, iii. 415
INDWELLING GOD, iii. 276, 418
INEFFABLE, Ar (r) hetos, or, ii. 164
Mantrikāshakti, crown of, Name, i. 333
Name, iii. 283; iv. 127; v. 145, 162
Word, v. 309, 310
INELASTICITY of atoms, ii. 238
INERTIA, Body in motion tends to, ii. 225
Force, Newton calls, ii. 235
Occult force, greatest, ii. 235
Periods of, i. 209
Powers, subject to intelligent, ii. 244
Property of, ii. 351
Satan and, iv. 76
Spiritual, iii. 73
INERTNESS, Children of, v. 200
INFALLIBILITY, Dogma of, v. 133
Personal, author does not claim, iii. 35
Prestige, of, ii. 245
Revealed Scripture, of, ii. 37
INFANCY, Egypt, of, iii. 334
Fifth race, of, iii. 349
Frame in, iii. 194
Planet and moon, of our, iii. 75
INFANTS, Initiates called, iv. 72
Monads, separate, iii. 304
Soul, for, supposed new, iii. 304
INFERIOR, Avara or, iii. 170, 190
Eden, i. 289
Gods, iii. 71
Hosts, iv. 55
Lha, iii. 67
Mother, i. 285
Races, iii. 419, 423
Superior, iii. 122
INFERNAL, Deities, ii. 184; iv. 173
Gods, iii. 362
Hosts, iii. 73
Isis, ii. 115
Magic, iv. 151
Quaternary, iv. 172
Regions, i. 274; ii. 123; iii. 60, 74, 102, 107, 395, 405; iv. 353
INFINITE, the, All, v. 386
Circle, v. 438
Deity, v. 233
Light, v. 191
Potency, v. 445, 446, 447, 448

INFINITE (*Contd.*)
Potentiality, v. 445
Space, v. 387
INFINITES, Exoteric creeds, of, ii. 162
Two impossible, i. 74
INFINITESIMAL lives, i. 305
INFINITUDE, Beings of Leibnitz, of, ii. 353
Circle, of, ii. 338
Deific, iv. 111
Fields of, v. 482
Fiery dragon and, i. 141
Heaven and hell, of, i. 259
Monads, of, ii. 357, 358
One unity throughout, ii. 340
Serpent, and i. 134
Space, of, i. 279
Symbol of, i. 141; v. 233
Universal life given in, ii. 318
Visible, iv. 115
INFINITY, Absolute unity and, i. 75
Absoluteness of, i. 189
Bound and, ii. 144
Circle of, i. 172, 192; iv. 122; v. 206
Divine, v. 227
Divine breath through, i. 330
Emblem of, i. 299
Finiteness and, i. 126
Globular speck in, iii. 167
Manvantara of, v. 361
Mother stretched in, ii. 350
Plane of, i. 188
Presupposes extension, i. 75
Sphere emblem of, i. 133
Svastika points to, iv. 126
Vistas through, ii. 363
INFLAMED bough, iv. 89
INFLECTED stage of language, iii. 205; iv. 232
INFLUENCE, Angels, on, ii. 357
Conscious, on earth, iv. 270
Constellations, of, ii. 125
Cosmic divisions, of, iii. 83
Creation by, iii. 190
Luminaries, from two, iii. 113
Matter, on, ii. 248
Moon, of, iv. 34, 269; v. 330, 535
Omnipresent, ii. 190
Planetary powers as, ii. 357; v. 536
Pleiades, of, ii. 374
Potent, ii. 393
Quickening, i. 319
Stars of, ii. 372; v. 331, 335
INFOLIO of Johannes Magnus, iii. 346
INFORMING, Gods, iii. 132, 361
Principle, iii. 111
Vehicles, iii. 318
INFRA-ARCTIC masses, iii. 324
INFUSORIA, Elephant and, i.272
Filamentoid, iii. 159
Infinitesimal, i. 202
Polygastric, i. 230
INFUSORIUM, from Dhyān Chohan to, i. 179
INGENERABLE AEON, ii. 66
Potency, v. 448
INGERSOLL, Col., quoted, iv. 336
INGRESS of Osiris into moon, i. 275
INHABITANTS, Ethereal worlds, of, ii. 331
Globes, of other, iv. 278

Planets of, ii. 326, 329, 336; iv. 271, 276
Solar, ii. 264
Venus, of, iii. 45
INHALATION and exhalation, i. 78
INHALES, Eternal bosom, iii. 54
INHERBATION, Devas and Gods pass, i. 239
INHERITANCE of Jacob, iv. 108
INIQUITY, Land of, iii. 406
Physical, iii. 303
Spiritual, iii. 303
INITIAL, Existence, i. 330
Fourth evolution, period of, iii. 197
Generative powers, iii. 55
Letter M, ii. 99
Thot, of, iv. 153
Triad, i. 321
Version of Creation, v. 199
INITIATE, Dvīja or, v. 152
Kadesh means to, iv. 28
Mystic and, i. 113
INITIATED, Adepts, ii. 120; iii. 39; v. 238, 352
Ancient books intelligible only to, v. 145
Brāhmans, iii. 320; v. 520
Pagan, v. 386
Philosophers, ii. 40
Priest-architects, i. 257
Priests, iv. 98; v. 238
Writers, iii. 394
Yogi, ii. 241
INITIATES, Adepts, and, i. 335
Aeschylus and, iv. 92
Alexandrian, iv. 145
Allegories, and, ii. 245; iv. 354
Ancient kings were, iv. 62
Ape, and, i. 241
Apostle, i. 75
Arabian, v. 44
Arhat not highest, i. 255
Aristotle and, ii. 216
Arts and, iv. 143
Ascetics and, iii. 277
Asia Minor, of, iv. 128
Astral body of, v. 249
Astronomical knowledge of, iv. 57
Atlantis, of, v. 263
Atoms and souls, on, ii. 291
Babylonia, learning from, ii. 67; iv. 262
Biographies of, are mystic records, v. 152
Brāhman, iii. 61, 120; v. 395
Brāhmanical secret code, and, i. 315
Caste of, i. 259
Chaldea, of, iii. 216; v. 137, 242
China, of, i. 226; iii. 208, 303, 364
Christ one of, ii. 379; iv. 72
Christian, iii. 71
Christos, i. 245
Chronology of priests, iv. 191
Church, ii. 102
Code of Ethics of, v. 265
Colossal statues by, iii. 339
Commentaries exist for, i. 57
Common beliefs of, iv. 325
Cosmic knowledge of, iv. 68
Cross and, iv. 128
Crypts of, iv. 159
Dangers of, v. 305

INITIATES (*Contd.*)
  Details of narratives known to, iii. 147
  Devil, regard for, iv. 79
  Disappeared, v. 272
  Doctrines preserved by, v. 42
  Dragons called, ii. 125; iv. 72
  Duties of, 263, 294
  Dvija one of, iii. 80
  Early races, of, v. 265
  Eastern, i. 53, 246, 303; ii. 396; v. 274, 286, 407, 500
  Egyptian, i. 43; iii. 215, 216, 367
  Éliphas Lévi and, iv. 80
  Enemies of, v. 49, 64
  Esoteric emblems and, ii. 18
  European, i. 58
  Evolution of kosmos and, i. 79
  Fafnir one of, ii. 121
  Failure of, v. 402
  First human, v. 102
  Fourth root race, of, i. 257; v. 37
  Future, ii. 97
  Glyph and, iv. 116
  Gnostic sects and, iii. 388
  God principle, and, ii. 186
  Gods and, iv. 125, 334
  Great, iii. 352
  Greatest, i. 315
  Greece, in, iv. 163; v. 108
  Hebrew, ii. 67; v. 195, 196, 197
  Hermes, thrice great, iii. 270
  Hermits, iv. 70
  Hierophants, iii. 225; v. 490
  Hindu, i. 42; 229; iv. 68
  History known to, iii. 141
  Hungarian, i. 42
  Iao, and, iv. 111
  Imperial, v. 218
  Indian, v. 271, 275, 395, 396
  Intelligences and, iii. 46
  Japanese, i. 226
  Jewish, v. 333, 337, 431
  Jews, iv. 189
  Journeys of, iv. 320
  Kabalah, of, v. 212
  Keys in hands of, iv. 85, 155
  King, v. 43, 258, 263
  Language of, iv. 355; v. 118, 197
  Left Path, of, v. 284
  Leibnitz not one of, ii. 345
  Lived in every age, i. 66
  Magic, Black, v. 256, 329
  Massacre of, v. 296
  Maya and, i. 117
  Māyāvi Rūpa of, v. 354
  Memory of, v. 397
  Mexico, in, v. 43
  Miraculous creation and, ii. 246
  Monad, on, ii. 293
  Murder of, iv. 72
  Mysteries, of, i. 176; ii. 337; iii. 133, 205
  Nāgas, called, ii. 125; iii. 218
  Names given to, iv. 63
  Nazarenes were, iii. 105
  Northern, iv. 63
  Numerals, and, v. 87
  Olcott and, i. 42

  Orientalists and, iii. 401; iv. 79
  Pagan, v. 108, 174, 313, 337
  Paternoster, and, iv. 132
  Patron of, iii. 215
  Perfect, v. 154, 400
  Phenomenal powers of, v. 373
  Phraseology of, iv. 17
  Physical life and, iv. 73
  Physics, and, ii. 241
  Planes of consciousness explained to, i. 248
  Popes some, were, ii. 23
  Prayer of, v. 519
  Priests, iii. 346; iv. 62, 102
  Profane and, i. 57, 255; iv. 87
  Promised land of, ii. 291
  Prophets or, iv. 60
  Psychic faculties of, ii. 97
  Rakshasas are, iii. 172
  Records preserved by, ii. 371; iii. 434; iv 319.
  Resurrected, iv. 152
  Ring, and, i. 189
  Sacred books, on, i. 57
  Sacred Island, of, ii. 137
  Schools of, iv. 66
  Sciences, and, iv. 143
  Secrecy of, v. 64, 73, 75, 297, 395
  Seers, i. 316; v. 429
  Semi-, iv. 134
  Senzar known to, i. 64
  Serpents refer to, iii. 103
  Sidereal Gods, ii. 379
  Silence, pledged to, ii. 104
  Similarity of lives of, v. 151, 152
  Snakes, called, ii. 125
  Socrates on, v. 266
  Solon and, iii. 434
  Soma drunk by, iii. 67
  Sorcerers and, iv. 341
  Soul and body of, i. 280
  Souls, on, ii. 291
  Sufi, i. 329
  Suidas not an, iv. 191
  Svastika and, iv. 157, 158
  Symbolism of, iii. 436; v. 194
  Terrestrial form of, iii. 233
  Theophany, and, v. 281
  Third, fourth and fifth races, of, iv. 177
  Those who could learn the truth became, v. 265
  Tomb of, iii. 394
  Tree and, iv. 64
  Trials of, v. 282, 290
  Twice-born, v. 152, 279
  Universal symbolism and, iii. 436
  Verities, taught, i. 58
  Virtues of, v. 262, 290
  Vishvakarman of, iv. 187
  Voice speaking to, ii. 149
  Yaho and, iv. 111
  Yogis, v. 137
  Zodiac and, iv. 71
INITIATION, Archaic, v. 340
  Artufas or, caves, iii. 188
  Āryan, ii. 35
  Astrology and, iv. 68; v. 330
  Bhārata land of, iii. 368
  Boon of, v. 254
  Brāhman, of, v. 520

INITIATION (*Contd.*)
Buddha at last, ii. 298
Candidate for, ii. 127; iv. 34, 113, 129; v. 33, 284
Cave of, iii. 240
Ceremonies of, v. 271, 568
Chaldees ready for, two, iii. 354
Chelās preparing for, i. 314
Classical testimony to, v. 254, 255
Crucifixion, and, iv. 128
Cycle of, iv. 137; v. 154, 155
Degree in, iv. 70
Degrees of, 280, 281, 290, 313, 399
Egypt, in, v. 233, 264, 271, 290, 452
Enoch, a book of, iii. 232
Fall in, iii. 219
Fourth, i. 135
Grades of, i. 255
Great, v. 296
Great pyramid and, ii. 26
Halls of, iii. 216; iv. 26; v. 322
Higher Self and, iv. 134
Highest, i. 169
Holy mountains and, iv. 63
Inner man and, ii. 26
Inner vision and, iii. 296
Jnāna, of, v. 370
Keynote of, v. 154
King's chamber and, ii. 30
Knowledge acquired at, iv. 61; v. 297, 490
Last supreme, ii. 296
Limits outside, ii. 40
Lord Peacock, emblem of, iv. 83
Magic, into, ii. 195
Masonic rite of, v. 272, 282, 284
Mastery through, ii. 367
Moses, of, iv. 33, 111
Mysteries and, i. 276; iv. 30, 105, 128, 158; v. 108, 152, 154, 169, 172, 261, 271, 281, 284
Nature, of, i. 61
Neo-Platonic, v. 305
Occultists and, i. 134
Origin of, v. 260
Plato before, ii. 312
Poem of, v. 290
Powers acquired at, v. 240
Pre-Adamite nations, of, iv. 20
Questions pertaining to, i. 217
Rabbinical mysteries, into, iii. 395
Rites of, v. 104, 152, 159, 161, 168, 172, 282, 290, 291
Round Towers of, v. 284
Rules anciently taught at, i. 257
Russian mystics in search of, i. 58
Sabazius, of, v. 130
Sacred drama of, iii. 417
Science and Religion, was, v. 265
Secret teachings after, i. 218; v. 218
Secrets of, ii. 134; iii. 47, 63, 146, 377; iv. 188; v. 218, 251
Septenary constitution and, i. 222; v. 275
Seven forms of, iv. 99, 209
Sidereal year and, ii. 26
Sun of, v. 217, 269, 276
Supreme, iv. 16; v. 108, 140, 276
Symbols of events at, ii. 19; v. 194

Temples of, iii. 378; v. 175, 280
Third degree of, iii. 309; v. 282, 290
Trials of, iii. 379; v. 104, 152, 153, 159
Truths revealed during, ii. 24, 231; v. 73, 218
'Twelve Tortures' of, v. 290, 313
Veil of, iv. 127
Wand of, iv. 87
Wisdom, by, iii. 143
Work of Seven Planets, v. 108
INITIATOR, Ancient wisdom of, v. 98
Chaldean, v. 173
Death of, v. 272
Early, iv. 99
Enoch means, iv. 99
First, v. 68
High, i. 169
Initiates, of the, v. 81
Mysteries, into, iii. 270
Supreme, v. 104
Serpent, as an, iii. 354
Wondrous being, a, i. 255; iii. 344
INITIATORY mysteries, iv. 136
INLAND Chinamen, iii. 282
INMAN, quoted, iii. 50; iv. 116
INNOCENT Adam, iv. 24
INNOCENTS, Initiates called, iv. 72
INQUISITION, iii. 50, 241; v. 60, 73, 360
I. N. R. I. Kabalistic Interpretation of, v. 166
INSANE mother, Moon called, i. 204
INSANITY, Soul free in, i. 280
INSATIABILITY of lower passions, iii. 411
INSCRIPTIONS, Cuneiform, iii. 341
Characters, in, ii. 193
Egypt, of, iv. 361
Fragments of, iii. 18
Saïs, at, ii. 108
Stone, on temple and, ii. 116
Temple at Thebes, from, v. 252, 253
Tombs, on, ii. 154
Vessels found at Troy, on, iii. 438
Westminster stone, on, iii. 342
INSECTIVOROUS mammals, iv. 282
INSECTS, Creatures in world of, iii. 369
Eyes of, iii. 296
Gigantic, iii. 203
Lives, and small, iii. 63
Septenary law, under, iv. 193, 194
INSENSIBILITY, Tamas or, ii. 44
INSENTIENT forms of being, ii. 363
INSEPARABILITY of spirit and matter, ii. 365
INSEPARABLE from animal, Kama rūpa, iv. 165
INSPIRATION(S), Bible, of the, v. 200
Dionysius, of, ii. 186
Plane of, v. 527
Prophets of, iv. 202
Virgil, of, ii. 384
INSPIRER, *Esoteric Buddhism*, of, iii. 185
Pesh-Hun, iii. 60
INSTINCT, Consciousness or, i. 280; ii. 365; v. 546
Elementals of, v. 566
Experience is, iv. 351
Monad, of, i. 228
Necessities, of, ii. 332
Primordial blastema has, iii. 129
Sexless creative, iii. 277

INSTINCTUAL, Animal monad, faculty of, iii. 111
Beatitude, iii. 419
Breath of life, i. 287
Consciousness, v. 525, 531
Evolution of, nature, i. 310
Feelings, v. 567
Intellectual causes, not, i. 222
INSTRUCTOR, Brass and iron, in, iii. 389
Brihaspati or, iii. 57; iv. 66
Buddha the great, iii. 373
Gods, of, iii. 57; iv. 66
Guru or, iii. 118
Inner self or, iii. 121
INSTRUCTORS, Brāhmans, of, iv. 311
Divine, iii. 54, 122, 204, 364; v. 75, 103
Elect of, iii. 349
Fifth race, of, iii. 350, 353, 354, 358
Gandharvas, of men, iv. 156
Gods, iii. 357
Hosts, of lower, iv. 83
Man, of, i. 256, 310; iii. 392; iv. 156
Primeval races, of, iii. 392
Sons of earth, of, i. 150
Third race, of, iii. 200
Vaivasvata, of, iii. 147
INSULAR continents, iii. 320, 326
INSULATION of ether, ii. 283
INTELLECT, Adepts, of, v. 512
Brain and, v. 545
Kāma, and, v. 545
Mahat or, v. 423
Spiritual Perception, paralyses, v. 233
INTELLECTUAL giants, Ego of, v. 564
INTELLECTUALITY, Human, i. 243; iii. 166, 175
Rudras, of, iv. 156
INTELLIGENCE, Binah is, v. 192
Cosmic, v. 471
Divine, v. 277
Endless, v. 366
Guiding, v. 313, 533
Human, v. 488
Intuition or, v. 532
Second Power, v. 218
Stars, of the, v. 225
Solar, v. 218
Sons of, v. 204
Supreme, v. 336, 374
Wisdom and, v. 168
INTELLIGENCES, Chief of, v. 327
Living, v. 221
Pythagoras, of, v. 215, 327
INTELLIGENT, forces, v. 220, 221
INTELLIGIBLE, Plato of, v. 445
Triad, iv. 170, 171
World, v. 208
INTENTION, Karma heeds not, v. 361
Is everything, v. 511
INTER-ÆTHERIC, Forces, i. 280; ii. 279
Vacuum, ii. 280
Vibrations, ii. 286
INTER-BRAIN, the, iii. 299
INTER-MATERIAL space, ii. 251
INTER-MOLECULAR vibrations, ii. 286
INTER-ORGANIC space, ii. 251
INTER-PLANETARY space, ii. 251

INTERACTION, Matter, between, ii. 222
Molecules and atoms, of, ii. 327
Worlds, of, ii. 343
INTERCESSION of Mercury, iii. 41
INTERCYCLIC existence, ii. 291
INTERDEPENDENCE of animals and plants, iii. 291
INTERHUMAN intelligences, iii. 200
INTERIM between rounds, iv. 282
INTERLACED triangles, iii. 48, 359; iv. 163
INTERMARRIAGE in America, iii. 442
INTERMARRIAGES of Atlanteans, iv. 348
INTERMARRIED giants, pigmies and men, iii. 330
INTERMARRYING of hierophants, and Atlanteans, iii. 226
INTERMEDIATE, Aeon, iv. 56
Forms, iv. 266
Race, iii. 277
Spheres, iii. 67
State, iii. 249
Type, iv. 239
Unknown groups, iv. 237
Worlds, iii. 111
INTERNAL Organ, luminous, v. 78
INTERPENETRATED spheres, ii. 329
INTERPOLATORS, Christian Fathers as, iv. 120
INTERPRETATION, Key of, v. 27, 33
Esoteric, v. 97, 98, 246
Zohar, of, v. 175
INTERPRETER, Hierophant or, v. 140, 163
Mercury the, iv. 112
INTERREGNUMS of fourteen Manus, iii. 79
INTERRELATED in its units, Nature, ii. 379
INTERSTELLAR, Atoms, ii. 357
Ether, ii. 351; iii. 144
Shoals, motion of, ii. 358
Spaces, ii. 251; iii. 161
INTERVALS, Creations, between, iii. 308
Brahmā's days, of, ii. 86
Diastemes, corresponding to, ii. 151
Finite, ii. 209
Reincarnations, between, iii. 304
INTONATION or svara, i. 313
INTRA-COSMIC, Breath, i. 302
Deity, iii. 53
Forces, intelligent, ii. 253
Gods, iii. 258
Motion is eternal, i. 70
Soul had no beginning, i. 71
INTRICACIES, Knowledge of cyclic, iii. 60
INTROSPECTIVE summary, Book of Enoch, an, iv. 104
INTUITION, Ages, of, i. 322
Clear Vision, is, v. 532
Creuzer, of, iii. 369
Dimensions in space, as to, i. 295
Ignorance, unless equilibrated by, ii. 203
Knowledge expanded by, iv. 19
Leibnitz metaphysical, of, ii. 352
Materialism killed by, iv. 89
Mystics, of, ii. 219
Mysteries solved by, iii. 115
Orientalists' lack of, iv. 135, 140, 178
Ratiocinative thought, above, i. 69
Richardson, and Spiller, of, ii. 233

INTUITION (*Contd.*)
Science has no, ii. 395
Specific, ii. 280
Spiritual, true, i. 118; iii. 413
Student to use, i. 321; iii. 103
Truth, of, iv. 85
INTUITIONS, Men of, ii. 238
Pantheistic, iv. 115
Spiritual, ii. 369
Verities, of man, and divine, iv. 52
INTUITIVE perceptions, ii. 354
INUNDATIONS, Local, iii. 312
INVASION, Aryan, iv. 284, 310
India, of, i. 314; ii. 373
INVENTORS, Egyptian alphabet, of, iv. 153
Fire, wheat, wine, of, iii. 372
Gods, and demi-Gods were, iii. 372
System of crucifixion, of, iv. 130
Triangle, of, iii. 337
INVERSIONS of poles, iii. 352, 433
INVERTED stages of odd eye, iii. 300
INVOCATION, Angra Mainyu, against, iii. 384
Deities, in Egypt, of, v. 246
Earth to sun, of, iii. 35
Hermetic fragments, in, i. 328
Vishnu, to, i. 328
INVOLUTION, Evolution and, i. 235, 240; ii. 360
Septenary law controlling, iv. 194
Sex, of, iii. 290
Spirit of, into matter, ii. 134
Spiritual and psychic, iii. 295, 347
INVULNERABLE, Beings, iii. 370
Personality, iii. 420
INZOÖNIZATION, Gods pass through, i. 239
IO, Colony to be founded by, iii. 415
Descendant of, iii. 412
Moon and, iii. 413, 414; iv. 31
Moon-Goddess of generation, iii. 414
Mother and symbol of physical humanity, iii. 414
Mother of God, or, iii. 413
Pillar and circle of Pythagoras, iv. 31
Race of, iii. 416
IO-TEF, Diadem called, iv. 32
IOH, Coptic, iv. 31
IONIAN School, Anaximenes of the, ii. 314
IRAD, Mehujael the son of, iii. 390
IRAN, Angel Gabriel and, ii. 300
Folk-lore of, iii. 392
Golden age of, iii. 375
Legends of, iii. 392
Lord of, iv. 108
St. George of, iii. 396
IRANIAN, Atlanteans, referred to the, iv. 341
Belief, iv. 327
Tribes, iv. 328
IRANIANS, Aryan Brahmans, and, iii. 389
Dual systems of, iv. 144
IRELAND, Africa, and, iii. 344
Conquest of, by Henry II, iii. 345
Greeting morning star in, iv. 329; v. 267
Rocking stones of, iii. 346
Round Towers of, v. 284
Starkad went to, iii. 346
IRENÆUS, Four Gospels, on, i. 115
Heretics, and, ii. 168
Quoted, ii. 166, 168; iv. 182; v. 139, 199

IRISH, Easam or Asam in, create, iii. 123
Vivien in, tradition, iii. 182
IRON, Age, ii. 369; iii. 204, 272, 273; v. 337, 338, 339
Art of working, iii. 362
Beings invulnerable by, iii. 370
Bronze, unknown in age of, iii. 273
Correspondences of, v. 461
Duck is of, seventh egg of, iii. 26
Glass, attraction of, through, iv. 288
Kali Yuga the, age, ii. 369
Wooden, ii. 216
IRON-BOUND world, i. 192
IRONWORKERS or Rhodes, Telchines the, iii. 390
IRREGULARITY of orbits, ii. 227
IRRESOLVABLE nebulæ, ii. 320, 322, 323
IRRESPONSIBILITY, Period of a Nation's, ii. 369
Will-less men of, iii. 245
IRRUENTES, Nephilim or fallen ones, iii. 281
IS, Absolute, Mahāmāyā of the, iii. 444
Eternal, is, ii. 343
One ever-hidden, ii. 266
ISAAC, v. 165
Ikshvaku and, v. 110
Rebirth of, v. 84
ISAIAH and Isaiah, Phallic worship denounced by, iv. 160
Rebellious children on, iii. 216
Saraph of, iii. 74
Seraphim of, iii. 386
ISANAGI-ISANAMI, i. 264, (Tsanagi-Tsanami) i. 286
ISCARIOTES, Sect of the, iii. 388
ISCHINS, Angels, the lower, iii. 374
In the Zohar, iii. 375
ISHA, Lord from, iii. 123
ISHTAR, Eldest of heaven and earth, iii. 250
Venus, or, iii. 73
ĪSHVARA, Aesar, analogous to, iii. 123
Avalokiteshvara or, i. 170; ii. 146
Brahmā and, i. 194; ii. 152; iii. 117
Causal Soul, v. 351
Consciousness in nature, ii. 297
Created deity, a, iii. 117
Creator or, ii. 170
Deity, personal, iii. 44
God, is, ii. 297
Hari or, iii. 86
Hindus, of, v. 351
Iswarra or, iv. 41
Kenealy on, iii. 123
Logos or, i. 188, 193, 194, 301; ii. 64, 152, 296; iii. 86, 123; iv. 208
Lord, i. 190, 336; ii. 146, 296
Mahat called, i. 301
Manifested, i. 170
Māya, male aspect of, ii. 45
Parabrahman and, i. 126
Powers of, iii. 123
Purusha and, iii. 117
Sabda Brahman, called, i. 194
Sanskrit, in, iii. 123
Suddasattva forming body of, i. 190
Supreme Lord, iv. 41
Theogony starts from, ii. 152

ISHVARA (Contd.)
  Vedantins and, i. 74
  Verbum or, i. 194
ISIDORUS on Stones, iii. 341
ISIS, Aditi and Vāch of the Hindus, identical with iii. 55
  Agriculture, and, iii. 389
  Anouki a form of, iii. 43
  Cat sacred to, ii. 103
  Correspondences of, v. 439
  Cow's horns on head of, iii. 44; v. 165
  Defunct and, v. 246
  Earth or, v. 234
  Egg sacred to, ii. 81
  Egypt, in, i. 193; iii. 373
  Egyptian Goddess, v. 164, 265, 440
  Giants in days of, iii. 343
  Girdle of, i. 299
  Goddess, a demiurgical, ii. 115
  Goddess of life and healing, iii. 39
  Harpocrates, suckling the babe, ii. 126
  Hathor infernal, ii. 115
  Hindus, of, ii. 107
  Horus, emanates from Osiris and, iv. 40
  Horus, virgin mother of, iii. 54; v. 293
  Ibis sacred to, i. 77
  Io identical with, iii. 414, 416
  Kwan-Yin and, i. 194
  Lotus sacred to, v. 117
  Lunar goddess, a, ii. 111; iii. 36
  Mercury minister of, ii. 103
  Moon connected with, i. 275; iv. 155
  Moot aspect of, iv. 32
  Mother earth, ii. 96; v. 233, 293
  Mout shares titles of, i. 155
  Nile, bed of river, ii. 105; v. 239
  Osiris, and Thoth, iv. 30
  Osiris interchangeable with, i. 139
  Osiris, the daughter and mother of, i. 139; ii. 148
  Sigalions in the temples of, iii. 395
  Symbols of, iv. 154
  Tau and mundane circle attributes of, iv. 127
  Tetragrammaton is one with, iv. 173
  Vāch, identified with, i. 194; ii. 152
  Veil of, i. 338; iv. 225
  Venus or, iii. 43
  Worship of, iv. 29
ISIS-LATONA, Osiris and, iii. 139
  Water, Goddess of, ii. 54
ISIS-OSIRIS, iii. 365
  Allegories of, iii. 151; v. 140
  Ansated cross symbol of, iii. 220
  Antiquity of, iii. 373
  Egypt, prince in, iii. 365
  Kabiri, once living, iii. 363
ISLAM, i. 62-3
  Prophet of, v. 125
ISLAND, Atlantis, of, iii. 21, 393, 405, 431; iv. 334
  Atlantis, submerged, of, iii. 393
  Buddhists, sacred, of the, ii. 193
  Chinese holy, iii. 371
  Divine kings, of, iv. 342
  Electria or Samothrace, of, iii. 17
  Gobi desert, in great, iii. 224
  Initiates of the sacred, iv. 341
  Inland sea, of an, iv. 208
  Mahā Yogis, of, iv. 156

Ocean, sinks in, iii. 364
Plato and, of Atlantis, iii. 21
Rhodes, of, iii. 390
Sacred, i. 258; iii. 223, 319, 349; iv.341
Sidereal, of Asteria, iii. 382
Sons of God and sacred, i. 258; iii. 223
White, iii. 78, 322, 401, 402, 405, 406
White devil of the White, iii. 405
ISLAND-CONTINENTS, Ruta and Daitya, iii. 431
ISLANDER, South Sea, iii. 175
ISLANDERS, Atlantis, of, iii. 383
  South Sea, iii. 419
ISLANDS, Allegorical, iii. 321
  Baffin's Bay, near, iii. 400
  Blessed and the good spirits, of, iii. 370
  Classics, and continents in, iv. 330
  Continents became, iv. 313
  Fauna of Atlantic, iv. 175, 179, 328
  Pacific, one part of Lemuria, iii. 20
  Purānic, 404
  Seven, iii. 325, 349; iv. 175, 179, 328
  Zodiacal signs, representing, iv.71
ISLE of Candia, Mandrake on, iii. 40
ISLES, Fifth race of, iii. 441
  Seven, iv 188
-ISMS and no religion, Age of a hundred, ii. 400
ISOLATION, Differentiation due to, iv. 219
  Species, of, iv. 307
ISPAHAN, Huschenk built city of, iii. 395
ISRAEL, Adepts of, v. 185
  Azazel scapegoat of, iii. 386, 388, 407
  Bath-Kol and prophets of, ii. 115
  Children of, iv. 107, 109. 197
  Chosen people of, ii. 187; iv. 111; v. 237
  Elohi of, iii. 51
  Fanes of, iv. 31
  Giant foes of, iii. 200
  God of, iii. 72; v. 92, 239
  Jehovah and, ii. 132; iii. 418; iv. 37
  Lamp of, v. 108
  Master in, v. 83
  Satan tempts David to number, iii. 386
  Scapegoat of, iii. 386, 388, 407
  Sects of, iv. 40
  Seth reputed forefather of, iii. 379
  Seventy elders of, ii. 300
  Scriptures of, v. 81
  Spiritual rock that followed, iii. 341
  Tribal God of, iv. 108
  Tribes of, iii. 138
ISRAELITES, Adepts of, v. 185
  Afghans, and, iii. 205
  Baal of, ii. 113
  Carlyle on, iv. 38
  Chaldea and Egypt, in, ii. 25
  Candelabra of, v. 314
  Divination, and, v. 242
  Egypt, in, v. 251
  Ezra and, iii. 151
  Fire, sacrifice to, ii. 187
  Gentiles did not copy, iv. 39
  Heathen more sincere than the, iii. 135
  Initiated by Moses, v. 166
  Jehovah of, i. 308; iii. 418; iv. 77
  Legend, of, iii. 18

ISRAELITES (*Contd.*)
   Mystery Gods of, iii. 17
   Nebo adored by, iv. 23
   Priests of, v. 240
   Primeval faith of, ii. 33
   System of, ii. 382
   Tribal God of, iii. 418; iv. 77
   Tribes of, v. 182, 183
   Vaivasvata Manu, repeated story of, iii. 267
ISRAELITISH Jehovah, the, iii. 150
ISSACHAR, Taurus in sphere of, ii. 377
ISSRAEL, Origin of, iii. 205
ISTAR, Ashteroth or Venus, iii. 153
ISTER identical with Aditi and Vāch of Hindus,
   iii. 55
ISU no gai no Kami, i. 264
ISWUR a God in India, iii. 123
IT, anywhere, cannot be said to be, ii. 89
   Atom, is in every, i. 128
   Being, cannot be identified with, i. 317
   Causeless cause or, i. 302
   Desire first arose in, iii. 183
   Kālahansa, of the, called That, i. 144
   Magic term, a, iii. 404
   Man, steps into, i. 173
   Speech or words, would never be mentioned
   in, i. 331
   Spirit of the fire, is, i. 73
ITALIAN Zodiac in, Churches, v. 241
   School, Philosophers of, iii. 160
ITALY, Crosses on highways in, iv. 112
   Mandrake in, iii. 40
   Pliocene man traced in, iv. 309
   Temples of, i. 53
IURBO, a name of Iao-Jehovah, iii. 388
IURBO-ADONAI, ii. 184
IVI or bone, iii. 199
IZEDS or Peris, the, iii. 392; iv. 346

J

JABAL taken from Kabiri, iii. 389
JABLONSKI, quoted, iv. 31
JACK the Giant Killer, iii. 335
JACK O' LANTERN, i. 53
JACOB, Bargain of Jews through, iv. 38
   Dinah, daughter of, ii. 377
   Dream of, v. 357
   Ephraim elect of, ii. 379
   Esau and, iii. 143
   Inheritance of the Lord, iv. 107
   Jews and, iv. 38
   Ladder of, iii. 282, 357
   Lord God of, ii. 188; iv. 79, 107
   Pillar of, iv. 40
   Pillow of, v. 166
   Sons of, ii. 375, 377; iii. 205, 216; v. 41
JACOLLIOT, Louis, see Book Index
JADU, or sorcery, iii. 235
JAGAD--DHĀTRI, nurse of the world, iv. 96
JAGAD-YONI, womb of the world, i. 118;
   ii. 306; iii. 116
JAGANNATHA, Lord of the world, i. 63; iii. 138
JAGAT or universe, i. 73
JAH, Chokmah, or, ii. 70
   Divine name, ii. 70
   Iah or, iv. 111

Jaho or, iii. 138
Jehovah is, iv. 169
   Male, iii. 387
   Noah is, iv. 35
   Rod or, iv. 169
   Wisdom or, ii. 70; iii. 51
   Yah or, iii. 134, 138
JAH-EVE, hermaphrodite, iii. 134
JAH-HAVAH, male-female Jehovah, i. 83
JEH-HEVA, Adam becoming, iii. 137
JAH-HOVAH, Androgynous, iii. 134
   Jehovah or, iii. 134, 387; iv. 37
   Jehovah-Eve or, iii. 137
   Kabalistic, iv. 173
   Male and female, iii. 134
   Man or, i. 172; iii. 387
JAH-HOVIANS, Yahoudi, or, iii. 135
JĀH-NAVĪ, or Ganges, iii. 138
JAH-NOAH and cosmic quaternary, iv. 167
   Jaho or Jevo, iii. 138
JAH-VEH, male and female, iii. 387;
   v. 72, 110
JAHO is Jah, iii. 138
JAHO-JĀH or Yaho-Tah, iii. 138
JAHVĀ-ALHIM, in *Genesis*, ii. 60
JAIN and Hebrew characters, v. 184
   Settlement, colossal statue near, iii. 228
JAINA, Books quoted, v. 385
   Cross or Svastika, i. 72; ii. 383; iii. 107;
   v. 206
   Tradition, v. 409
JAKIN and Boaz, iv. 65; v. 120
JALA-RŪPA or water form, iv. 148
JAMAICA, Voodoos of, iii. 214
JAMBU and Pushkara, iii. 403
JAMBU-DVĪPA, iii. 188, 320, 326, 368, 402;
   iv. 327
JAMES, quoted, i. 247; ii. 132; iii. 143
JAMES, Sir Henry, quoted, iii. 315
JANA(R)-LOKA, place of animal rebirth, i. 175;
   ii. 87; iii. 321; v. 359, 537, 542
   Sanatkumara, abode of, v. 359
JANAKA, engendering of, iv. 93
JANARDANA, Rudra becomes, ii. 86
JANGAMA, Sthāvara and, ii. 173
JANITORS of the seven halls, ii. 398
JANNA, Dan or (Dhyāna), i. 44
JANUS, faced Agnosticism, ii. 252
JANUS-like character of serpent, ii. 120
JAPAN, Allegories in, Shinto, i. 286
   Cosmogony of, i. 264
   Esoteric schools of, i. 46
   Kaempfers, iii. 364
   Philosophy of, i. 44
   Sacred books, and lost, i. 56
JAPANESE, Artists, iii. 438
   Buddhist ascetics, i. 220
   Chinaman and, ii. 19; iii. 441
   Computations secret, iv. 136
   Cosmogony, i. 262
   Cuttlefishes, iii. 438
   Cyclopedia, iii. 208; v. 407
   Egg symbol, ii. 82
   Fables, i. 265
   Flora, iv. 295
   Hierarchy of system, i. 261
   Lao-Tse, folllowers of, i. 49

JAPANESE (*Contd.*)
  Narrative of Patriarchs, v. 409
  Secret Science, i. 135
  System, i. 261
  Yama-booshis of, i. 226
JAPHET and Titans, iii. 150; iv. 343
  Pyramid Measures and, v. 89
JAR, time contains a full, iv. 183
JARĀMARANA, v. 559
JARED or Irad, source or descent, iii. 366, 390;
    iv. 154; v. 348
JĀTA, one of seven Kumāras, iii. 319
JATĀYU, Garuda, son of, iv. 135
  King of feathered tribe, iv .141
JĀTI, Nāman, or rūpa, ii. 89
JĀTI, v. 559
JAUMES, Prof., referred to, ii. 230
JAVA and lost continent, iii. 226; iv. 357
JAVA-ALEIM, chief hierophant, iii. 207, 219,
    224; iv. 102
JAVE, JVE, or JUPITER, iv. 33
JAVELIN of Brahmā, Fiery, iv. 201
JAW, Apparatus of wild beast, iv. 252
  La Naulette, iv. 313
JAWS, Age in, iv. 252
  Ape-like, iv. 256
JAYAS, Great Gods, iii. 99, 188; iv. 156
JEALOUS GODS, i. 319; ii. 111, 130; iii. 181,
    417; iv. 168
  Hecate-Luna, counterpart of, ii. 111
JEBEL DJUDI, deluge mountains, iii. 153
JEHANGIR, reign of, i. 47
JEHO, JAH and IAH, iii. 138
JEHOSHUA or JOSHUA, ii. 301; iv. 110
JEHOVAH, Abraham and, v. 164
  Abraxas is the one, iv. 42
  Absolute Unity, not, v. 198
  Adam and, ii. 162; v. 72
  Adam Kadmon and, ii. 151; v. 72
  Adonai and, iv. 79
  Adversary, the, iii. 386
  Ancient views of, i. 247
  Androgyne, i. 129
  Angelic form of, iii. 381
  Anthropomorphic, ii. 187
  Arelim, or, v. 190, 192
  Automaton created by, iii. 246
  Azazel and, iii. 375
  Bacchus is, v. 277, 278
  Bible in, ii. 113; iv. 167
  Binah and, i. 277; v. 190, 192
  Bodyguard of, ii. 135
  Breath of, iii. 97
  Builder, a, v. 191
  Cain and, ii. 132; iii. 387; v. 72, 190
  Cainites destroyed by, iii. 390
  Christians and, iv. 83; v. 212
  Conception of, self-centred, iv. 278
  Crucify them before, iv. 128
  Cunning used by, ii. 139
  Deity not, unknown, iii. 411
  Demi-urge, the, iii. 143
  Devil older than, i. 138
  Double-sexed, iii. 134, 138
  Duad and, v. 211
  Dual, v. 291, 292
  Elements merge in, ii. 183

Elohim and, i. 140, 172; ii. 28, 215, 271;
    iii. 85, 121; iv. 114; v. 324
  Etymologies of, iii. 138
  Eve and, v. 190, 191
  Face of, iv. 109
  Father or, iii. 413; iv. 130
  Female, iv. 31
  Fighting God, a, iii. 55
  Function of, i. 308; iv. 34
  Generation, God of, ii. 107; iii. 236
  Genesis, in, ii. 60; iii. 136
  Glory of, iv. 109
  Gnostics and, iii. 388
  God-names of, ii. 28; iv. 114; v. 72
  Gods, a God among, iv. 77
  Heavenly Man, the, v. 215
  Hebrew esotericism, in, iv. 37
  Hebrew name for, i. 139
  Hebrew ten, or, iii. 414
  Hebrews of, v. 129
  Heirloom of, iv. 108
  Holy ones consecrated to, iv. 31
  IAO or, v. 254
  I Hi We said to mean, ii. 194
  Ideograph of, iii. 248; v. 190
  Ildabaoth and, v. 168
  Indra and, v. 254
  Israel of, ii. 300; iii. 148, 418; v. 241
  Jah or, iv. 169; v. 192
  Jacob, and, v. 165
  Jah-Havah or, i. 83; v. 190
  Jah-Hovah or, iv. 37
  Jave or, iv. 33
  "Jealous God", ii. 111
  Jesus and, ii. 300, 301; iv. 130; v. 164, 206,
    326
  Jewish Brahma, v. 191
  Jews and, ii. 54, 187; iv. 107; v. 168, 241, 277
  Jhoh or, v. 190
  Jod-Hevah, v. 431
  Jod-He-Vau-Hê or, i. 129
  Jve or Jupiter, iv. 33
  Kabalah and, i. 72; ii. 109; iii. 86
  Kabeiri and, v. 320, 325
  Later vowelled, ii. 184
  Letters of name of, ii. 49; iv. 28, 146, 174
  Light of, ii. 50
  Living God, the one, i. 262
  Lord, ii. 300; iii. 85
  Lunar, ii. 49, 106; iii. 396
  Malachim and, ii. 183
  Male, i. 71, 161; v. 190
  Male-female, i. 83; iv. 31, 35, 107; v. 190
  Man and, i. 129
  Meaning of, v. 190
  Measure, i. 129; iii. 50
  Metamorphosis of, iv. 30
  Michael and, ii. 135; iii. 73, 378, 381; iv. 48,
    78; v. 326
  Moon and, i. 247; ii. 102, 107; iii. 72, 85;
    iv. 42
  Moses and, iv. 109
  Mount Sinai of, v. 278
  Mystery-name, a, iv. 106
  Nach or, iii. 219
  Name of, i. 72; ii. 49, 159; iv. 28, 77
  Nārada and, iii. 60

JEHOVAH (*Contd.*)
Noah and, ii. 162; iv. 35, 169
Number of, iii. 50, 52, 414; v. 129, 151, 430
Numerical value of, i. 154; v. 129, 167
Osiris and, ii. 28
Parabrahman and, iii. 248
Passive potency of, ii. 70
Periphrasis of, ii. 156
Personal God, as a, ii. 144
Phallic Symbol, iv. 40
Portion of, ii. 300
Potency, a third rate, ii. 64, 70
Prayers unanswered by, ii. 187
Priapic deity, a, i. 72
Punishing, ever, ii. 204
Rabbis of, iv. 107
Rectors disobeying, ii. 135
Rivals of, iii. 282
Rod or, iv. 169
Sabaoth and, ii. 179; v. 107, 318
Samael and, ii. 135
Sarah and, iii. 181; v. 111
Satan and, ii. 108; iii. 388
Saturn and, ii. 135, 179, 301; v. 72, 129, 310, 318, 326
Schemal and, ii. 135
Seed of, iii. 148
Sephiroth and, i. 72; iii. 383
Sephiroth-Elohim and, i. 187
Seth and, v. 72, 190
Seventh Day, dedicated to, v. 129
Shaddai and, ii. 156
Spirit of the earth, iv. 77
Spirit personating, iii. 246; iv. 78
Spiritus Elementorum, v. 242
Substitute, a, iv. 40
Sun, the, ii. 113; v. 316
Symbols of, iii. 386; iv. 40, 110
Ten and, v. 129
Teraphim and, v. 239, 241
Terrestrial races led by, iii. 137
Tetragrammaton or, i. 139; iv. 173
'That which is', v. 214
Thundering, ii. 204
Tribal god, ii. 367; iii. 418; iv. 107
Tyrians, iv. 111
Unknown God, not the, ii. 40
Viraj and, v. 214
Vishnu and, ii. 139, 141
Yave or, iv. 32
Yehovah or, iv. 41
YHVH or, ii. 343; iv. 41
Yod first letter of, iv. 146
JEHOVAH-ADAM and Brahmā-Viraj, iii. 134
JEHOVAH-BINAH, or intelligence, iv .167
JEHOVAH-BINAH-ELOHIM, iv. 179
JEHOVAH-CAIN, male part of Adam, iii. 387
JEHOVAH-CAIN-ABEL, iii. 135
JEHOVAH-EVE and Cain-Jehovah, iii. 136, 137
JEHOVAH-ILDA-BAOTH, iii. 247
JEHOVAH-OPHIOMORPHOS, ii. 388
JEHOVAH-SATAN, iii. 108
JEHOVAH-SEPHIROTH and Brahmā-Prajā-pati, iii. 134
JEHOVISTIC, Creation, iii. 254
Deity, ii. 344
Genesis, version of, iv. 196

Jews, ii. 301
Schools, v. 186
Texts, iv. 41
Worship, v. 311
JEHOVISTS, i. 298; v. 187
JEHOVITE creation, the, iii. 19
JEHUDA-HA-LEVI, quoted, iii. 51
JEKYLL AND HYDE, DR., referred to, ii. 134; v. 500
JELLĀLABĀD, temples of, iii. 338
JELLY-SPECK, non-nucleated, iii. 161, 167
JEREMIAH, iii. 422; v. 449
JEREMIAH BEN ELIAZAR, quoted, iii. 143
JERICHO, Modern, i. 338
JERUSALEM, i. 64; iv. 326
New, v. 267
Temple of, v. 185
JERUSKOVEN, or frigid zone, iv. 104
JESU MARIA, i. 139
JESUIT *Kircher*, iii. 370
JESUITISM, Modern, ii. 141
JESUITS, v. 122, 145, 273, 274
De Mirville and, v. 95
Freemasonry, and, v. 273
Learning, ii. 23; iii. 50
JESUS, Abel, shown to be, v. 161
Aeon incarnated in, v. 351
Akashic garment of, iv. 152
Astral of, after death, v. 360
Astronomical figure, v. 151, 163
Baptism of, v. 168
Basilides' view of, v. 351
Bodhisattva, v. 369
Christ, the, v. 139
Christian and Occult views of, v. 163, 168
Christianity and, v. 136
Christos of Gnostics not, i. 190
Crucified, v. 168
Death of, v. 168
Descends into hell, v. 154
Disciples of, v. 369
Divine Nature of, v. 156, 289
Esoteric opinion of, v. 369
Essence, the, ii. 263
False Messiah, v. 368
Father on his, ii. 298; iv. 79
Fichte reveres, i. 145
Fish and, v. 163
Gnostic allegory of, v. 168
God incarnate, v. 337
Great character, v. 357
Great martyr, v. 84, 125, 158
Healer, v. 263
Hermaphrodite, i. 139
Human perfection, taught by, v. 82
Ideal of, v. 84
Initiate, ii. 30, 301; v. 158, 163, 286, 430
Inspired, Mercury, by, v. 369
Jehovah and, ii. 300; v. 164, 206
Jew, a, v. 137
King of the Jews, v. 166
Kingdom of Heaven, on, i. 323
Life of, allegorized, v. 163
Logos and, i. 139
Madonna and infant, ii. 126
Name of Sun, v. 161
Nazareth, ii. 379; v. 99, 125, 151, 155, 166

JESUS (*Contd.*)
Never called himself God, v. 72, 369
Only Saviour, v. 155, 167
Opinion of Mussulmans concerning, v. 125
Personality of, v. 151
Public life of, v. 167
Puja to, i. 139
Reincarnations of, v. 360
Revelation, in, i. 139
Sabbath day condemned by, i. 285
Saviour, v. 155
Secrecy enjoined by, v. 65
Secret Doctrine of, v. 160, 169, 304
Serpent, on wisdom of, i. 141; iii. 364
Son of God, v. 155, 156, 168, 289, 360
Strait Gate of, ii. 30
Teaching after Resurrection, v. 168
True nature of, v. 155
Type of, ii. 301
Vicarious atonement of, v. 499
Wind, rebuking, ii. 189
Wisdom, i. 141; iii. 364
JETHRO initiated Moses, iv. 33, 111; v. 180
JETZIRATIC world, iii. 120, 121
JEVE, (IEVE) *Old Testament* term, iii. 138;
    iv. 41
JEVO or Jaho, iii. 138
JEVONS, Dr. quoted, i. 166, 182
JEW, Aristobolus, forger, ii. 374
    Nabathean Agriculture, author of, iv. 21
    Noah cannot be monopolized by, iii. 389
    Practical measure known to, iv. 114
    Wandering, v. 49
JEWEL, Spiritual Ego, or, v. 421
    Lotus in, v. 418, 419, 420, 453
    Wisdom, of, i. 221
JEWELS, Seven, i. 226
JEWISH, *Bible*, v. 181, 195
    Biblical names are astronomical, v. 89
    Canonical books, v. 180
    Cosmogony and laws, v. 180
    Initiate, v. 167
    Kabalah, v. 174, 180
    Literature, antiquity of, v. 176
    Mysteries, v. 66
    Numerical system, v. 342
    Passover, v. 278
    Patriarchs, v. 263
    Priests, v. 186
    Rabbis v. 175, 192
    Sabbath, v. 179
    Scriptures, v. 32, 137
    Solar Theology, v. 313
    Teraphim, iii. 252
JEWS, Alphabet of, v. 178
    Black, v. 179
    Crimea and S. India, of, v. 179
    Generation and, v. 87
    Geometry and, v. 87
    Karaim, v. 179
    Mysteries of, v. 66
    Mystery God of, v. 278
    Numerations of, v. 342
    Occult Symbology of, v. 166
    Patriotic forgery of, ii. 374
    Sun-worshippers, v. 277
    Wilderness of, v. 277

JEZIRAH, Number, iii. 51
    Seat of passions, iv. 176
JIGTEN, Gonpo, protector and saviour, iii. 186
JIN, man or, i. 286
JISHNU, host, leader of, iv. 66, 185
    Indra surnamed, iii. 381
JĪVA, Chasm in shape of, iii. 192
    Functions of, i. 271
    Hindus of, ii. 291
    Identical in man and animal, iii. 90
    Imperishable, i. 265
    Life current of, v. 480
    Life principle, or, iv. 242; v. 471
    Man, complete in, i. 271
    Monad, or, i. 264, 291, 292; iii. 58 ,85, 168
    Prakriti contains, ii. 246
    Prana or, ii. 250; v. 208, 424, 440, 471, 480,
        511, 518, 523, 528
    Science and, ii. 327
    Sheath or, ii. 294
    Soul or, i. 190
    Spark is, i. 284
    Universal Deity, v. 528
    Vehicle of consciousness of, iii. 244
JIVANMUKTA, Adept, highest, i. 118
    Avatāra, difference between, v. 352, 353
    Mahātma, v. 498
    Nirvāna, reaching, ii. 86
    Perfect Intitiate, v. 402
    State, v. 79, 137, 542
JIVATMA, Lords of ,Being highest, iii. 46
    Mukta or, i. 190
    Occultism of, i. 196
    One life, or, i. 121
    Prana not, i. 273
    Universal life, v. 191
JNĀNA, Gnosis, i. 131; iii. 393; v. 370
JNANA SHAKTI, Manifestations, i. 333; v. 484
JNATA, ii. 146
JNYĀNENDRYAS, v. 538, 541
JOAN of Arc, v. 127
JOB and Job, Antiquity, ii. 373
    Arabian, ii. 373; v. 44
    Archaic Doctrine in, iv. 107
    Astronomical references in, ii. 374
    Behemoth on, iv. 51
    Initiate, an, v. 44, 290
    Leviathan of, iii. 210
    Quoted, ii. 44, 59, 130, 139; iii. 377; iv. 222
    Satan tempted, ii. 139; iii. 374
JOD, Ark, within, iv. 87
    Eva and, i. 129
    Hevah, v. 431
    Hé-Vau-Hé, or Jehovah, i. 129; iii. 137
    Iao-Sabaoth, full number of, iv. 174
    Jehovah and, iii. 248; iv. 78
    Jod-Hé or, iv. 78
    Male, iv. 37
    Number 10 is, ii. 61; iii. 51
    Sacred, iii. 49, 51
    Vau and twice Hé, i. 154
    Yod or, iii. 137; v. 117
JOD-HEVAH, iii. 143; v. 431
JODS, Ten, v. 420
JOGI or ZOGEE, ii. 194
JOHANNES Tritheim on Magic, iv. 81
JOHN of Constantinople, iii. 281

JOHN, St., Apocalypse of, iv. 106, 133; v. 131, 132, 133
Baptist, i. 245; iii. 123, 440; iv. 64; v. 83, 150
Church of, at Monza, iv. 158
Cycle of revelation, of, iv. 190
Eagle, air, iii. 123
Ecstasy of, v. 143
Enoch, Book of, iv. 65
Fourth Gospel, not author of, v. 138
Gospel of, iii. 51
Jesus, refers to, iv. 136
Jewish Kabalist, v. 138
Peter, and, v. 138
Revelation of, iii. 85, 382; iv. 65, 190; v. 138
Thunders of, iv. 135
Verbum of, ii. 383
Vision of, iii. 102
JOLY, Prof., iii. 110; iv. 231, 316, 318
JONAH, whole of, v. 67
JONAS, sign of, ii. 380
JONES, Sir William, quoted, i. 53, 127; ii. 94, 384; iii. 60, 440
JORDAN, Baptism in, v. 168
Nile and, iv. 154
Source of descent, ii. 107
Valley of, flints of, iv. 324
JOSEPH, dream of, ii. 375
Ephraim, son of, ii. 379
Initiate, an, v. 266
Sagittarius in sphere, ii. 377
Tvashtri, carpeneter or, iii. 110
JOSHUA and *Joshua*, Anakim of, iii. 340
Arabic, read in, iv. 128
Course of sun, stopping, iv. 104; v. 71
Debir of, iv. 98
Initiate, an, v. 282
Jehoshua or, iv. 110
Kirjath-Sepher, or, iv. 98
Nun, son of, i. 307; iii. 358; v. 163
JOSIAH, King, ii. 375
JOTUN, Mimir or, ii. 118
JOTUNS, war of Asathor with, iii. 385
JOVE, Aerial, ii. 184
God of Fire, ii. 183
JOVE-JUNO, Androgyne, iv. 173
JOVIANS, earth can perceive, our, i. 220
Eternal spring of, iii. 145
JUBILEE of planets, ii. 380
JUDAEAN TANAIM, iv. 37
JUDAEO-CHRISTIAN systems, iv. 40, 51
JUDAH, Cross on men of, iv. 127
Hindu Yadu, and, v. 110
Kings of, ii. 375
Leo in sphere of, ii. 377
Levi and tribes of, iii. 138
Tribe of, lion of, iv. 152
JUDAISM, Christianity, basis of, i. 308, iv. 40
Exoteric, iii. 52
Keys of, ii. 30
Phallic worship, built on, iv. 39
Symbols improvement on, ii. 99
Vāch before, iii. 115
JUDAS, Apostle, iii. 388
Roman Catholics and, ii. 375
JUDAS Maccabeus, v. 185

JUDEA, monstrous reptiles of, iv. 282
JUDEAN RELIGION, Angels of, i. 268
JUDEANS, Christians and, iv. 107
JUDGE, Dayanishi the, ii. 113
Mortals of, iii. 56
JUDGES of souls, Supreme, iv. 48
JUDGMENT, Calamity or, iv. 354
Day of, i. 192; iv. 188; v. 249
Nature of, iv. 18
Soul, of, v. 246, 247; v. 289
JUDICIARY Astrology, v. 330, 332, 334
JUICE, moon plant, of, iv. 162
JUKES, Prof. quoted, iii. 202, 223
JULIAN, Emperor, iii. 41, 47; iv. 158; v. 88, 218, 313
Apostate, v. 334
Initiate, an, iv. 158; v. 218, 315
Neo-Platonist, v. 307
Solar Priest, v. 218
JULIEN, Stanislas, quoted, i. 48
JULIUS CAESAR, Alexandrian library, destroyed, iv. 262
JUN or JUNO, Latin, iv. 33
JUNGLE, Sanjnā retired to, iii. 181
JUNO, Jun or, iv. 33
Latona pursued by, iv. 340
Mars, mother of, iv. 120
Matter or, iv. 173
Moon and, i. 275
Tree of, and Jupiter, i. 187
JUPITER, ii. 298; iv. 49
Adam and Ham, as, iii. 272
Aerius or Pan, iv. 184
Amalthaea and, iv. 150
Ammon, ii. 184
Ashwood, made men of, iv. 341
Astraea and, iv. 353
Atlantic Islands and, iii. 407
Atlantis, fought for, iv. 334
Bacchus and, iii. 362
Bel-Moloch, ii. 184
Brihaspati or, iii. 42, 57; iv. 23, 66; v. 340
Cain or, v. 320
Caster and Pollux and, iii. 130
Chain represents, i. 218
Correspondences of, v. 437, 441, 506
Cycles of, v. 340
Cyclic law, personifies, iv. 354
Daemon of pagan Greeks, a, ii. 188
Dodona and, v. 254
Dodonean, ii. 184
Dominions ruled by, ii. 153
Eloi of, ii. 301; iv. 108
Eternal spirng on, iii. 144
Eye of, v. 276
Fables of, iii. 203
Female breasts, has, iii. 143
Fourfold, ii. 184
God and planet, iii. 36
Great ether, Virgil calls, ii. 45
Heavenly man, called, iv. 272
Hymn to, iv. 122
Incandescent state in, iv. 276
Inclination of axis of, iv. 276
Io, passion for, iii. 416
Juno and, i. 187

JUPITER (Contd.)
  Kali-Yuga at, ii. 387
  Kronos and, iv. 52, 87
  Lapis, iii. 341
  Lucifer, Venus and, i. 251
  Mars and, ii. 317, 382
  Mercury and, iii. 41; iv. 112
  Minerva, from brain of, iv. 230
  Mnaseas, of, iii. 392
  Moon and, iii. 147; iv. 30
  Myths of, iii. 203
  Omnipotency of Deity, v. 325, 339
  Pater Æther and, v. 476
  Pluvius, ii. 188, 278
  Prometheus is, iii. 272
  Quench a race, wished to, iv. 92
  Romans, by, called, v. 305
  Sabasius called, iii. 417
  Satellites of, ii. 317
  Saturn and, i. 207; ii. 382
  Seasons of, iv. 276
  Semele, wife of, ii. 116
  Sun, guardian of, ii. 216
  Sun, Moon and, v. 339
  Swan, takes form of, ii. 72
  Throne of, iv. 354
  Titan, a, ii. 141
  Tonans, iv. 66
  Tree given to, i. 187
  World, re-entered bosom of, iv. 326
  Zeus or, i. 139
JURASSIC PERIOD, iii. 163, 202; iv. 282, 359
JUSTICE, Dharma or, iii. 183
  Divine, v. 503
  Eternal, iii. 305
  God and Satan, of, iii. 237
  Goddess of, iv. 353
  Hall of, i. 234
  Myths to, iv. 86
JUSTIN, St., v. 329, 445
JUSTIN MARTYR, Pythagoras rejected, ii. 151
  Referred to, i. 245; v. 104, 143, 160
  Religion, on, iv. 58
JUSTINIAN, Emperor, v. 307
JYOTIS, taught astronomy, iv. 335
JYOTISHA, Brahmā, name of, iv. 195, 335
JYOTSNA, (dawn) one of four bodies of Brahmā, iii. 68; iv. 97

K

KA, animal soul the, v. 357
  Astral body the, iv. 205
  God, v. 408
KA'BAH, Sins of the, i. 63
KABALA, Key of the, iv. 114
KABALAH, v. 42, 107, 138, 163, 187, 230
  Adam, in, iii. 133
  Adam Kadmon in, i. 160, 263; ii. 50; iv. 35
  Adams in, seven, iii. 17; iv. 24
  Anagrammatical method of, i. 154
  Auphanim of, i. 176
  Babylonian magism and, i. 77
  Bath-Kol in, iii. 115
  Bible and, i. 314; ii. 58; iii. 232; iv. 195
  Chaldean, i. 249, 286; ii. 65, 157, 344; iv. 29; v. 105, 189, 208, 271, 310, 390

  Christian mystics, of, i. 83, 84, 286; iv. 55
  Circle and, i. 72, 84
  Cosmogony of, ii. 106
  Definitions of, iv. 114
  Degradation of, iii. 236
  Deities in, i. 155, 156
  Divisions of, v. 200
  Doctrine of the, v. 210
  Egyptian Mysteries and, v. 386
  Elohim in, i. 276, 277
  Esoteric doctrine in, i. 291
  Esoteric study of, v. 355
  Exoteric, v. 192
  Fallen angels of, iii. 232
  Father-Mother-Son of, i. 83
  Fiat lux of, i. 263
  Figures of, i. 134
  Fohat and, i. 143
  Franck's, v. 85
  Genesis and, i. 77
  Germain's copy of, Count St., iii. 242
  Gnostics, iii. 242
  God of, i. 167
  He of the four letters in, i. 262
  Hebrew, ii. 67, 157
  Initiates, of, ii. 67; v. 212
  Interpretation of, i. 129; iii. 249
  Jehovah and, i. 72, 154, 247; iii. 248
  Kabalistic faces of, i. 246
  Key of, v. 118
  Kings of Edom of, iii. 16; iv. 24
  Later, iv. 25
  Light in, ii. 50, 150
  Limbs of microposopus in, i. 262
  Logos of, i. 161
  Luciferians and, iii. 242
  Macroposopus of, ii. 65
  Manifested universe in, i. 160
  Means " to receive ", v. 177
  Metaphysical, entirely, iv. 25
  Monotheists and, i. 187
  Moon and, i. 247
  Mosaic books and, ii. 49; iv. 196
  Mysteries of, iv. 114; v. 68
  Names in, v. 86
  No-thing and, ii. 67
  Number one of, iv. 146
  Occult teaching of, iv. 240
  Origin of, iii. 242
  Phallicism of, iv. 25, 37
  Philosophy of, ii. 162
  Pleiades and, iv. 121
  Pratt on, Dr. Henry, iii. 248
  Primitive men of, iii. 17
  Reuchlin and, iv. 171
  Rosenrath, of, ii. 106
  Sacred animals of, i. 155
  Samael or Satan in, iii. 238, 377
  Secret book, a, iv. 106
  Semi-exoteric, i. 246
  Sephira in, ii. 148, 150
  Sephiroth in, i. 160, 263, 277; iii. 387
  Septenary in, iii. 17, 105; iv. 195
  Seven in, number, i. 110; iii. 313; iv. 109
  Simeon Ben Jochai, of iv. 55, 274
  Teaching of, v. 209
  Tetrad in, iv. 170

KABALAH (*Contd.*)
 Tetragrammaton in, i. 161, 262
 Transcendental Methods, v. 113
 Triad or trinity of, i. 83, 160
 Universe, on, ii. 230
 Vatican MS. of, iii. 242
 Western, i. 82, 84
 Wisdom in, iv. 273
 World in, iv. 273
 Worlds compared to sparks in, i. 248
 Zohar, and, i. 84, 174
KABALAH, Adam Kadmon of, ii. 107; iii. 55
 Ain Soph of, v. 107
 Angels, taught to, iii. 285
 Archaic tradition or, v. 191
 Archetypal man of, ii. 107
 Balance of, iii. 93
 Blessed ones of, i. 271
 Christian, iii. 44; v. 231
 Circle in, ii. 107
 Conceptions of, iii. 53
 Creation and, iii. 64
 Doctrines of, v. 299
 Dual man of, iii. 49
 Eastern occultism and, ii. 343
 Eastern philosophy and, iii. 52
 Elohim of, iii. 95
 Emanations of, ii. 107
 Esoteric system of, v. 433
 Esoteric Vidya and, i. 286; v. 123
 Fallen angels of, iv. 76
 Foundation of, iii. 49
 Genesis and, iii. 49
 Guardian Angels of, v. 439
 Gupta Vidyā and, v. 174 *et seq.*
 Heads of, three, iii. 38
 Hebrew, iii. 72
 Hiram in, iii. 122
 Jehovah and, iii. 135, 138
 Jewish, iii. 44
 Jod in, iii. 134
 Lévi, of, v. 232
 Light in, iii. 49
 Moon in, iii. 72
 Moses, of, v. 198
 Original, iv. 76
 Primitive, iv. 94
 Raven of, ii. 161
 Samael in, iii. 120
 Scientific and symbolical, ii. 132; v. 116
 Secrets of, iii. 395
 Sephiroth in, ii. 107
 Septenary in, iv. 205
 Shekinah in, ii. 344; v. 107
 Tree of life of, iii. 220
 Universe and, ii. 230; iii. 38
 Western, i. 286
 Wisdom of, iv. 55
KABALISM, Western, i. 71, 153; v. 231
KABALIST(S), v. 46, 62, 71, 86, 111, 115, 129,
 131, 145, 162, 174, 175, 182, 186, 190, 234,
 305, 334, 384, 391
 American, i. 154; v. 46
 Astral light of, ii. 57, 81; v. 192
 Astrology of, v. 442
 Christian, v. 86, 310
 Daniel, and, iii. 85

 Doctrine, v. 107-112
 Éliphas Lévi the, i. 288, 303; v. 48
 Ether, on, iii. 57
 Europe, in, v. 46
 Figures and Signs, v. 122
 French, i. 290
 Geometrical figures of, v. 32
 God held by, view of, ii. 361
 Guardian Angels of, v. 439
 Holy of holies of, iv. 36
 Ibn Gebirol and, iv. 29
 Isis Unveiled, and, iv. 33
 Jewish, v. 86, 234, 305
 Jews, and, v. 194
 John and Jewish, v. 138
 Kabalah, on, i. 144, 174; ii. 56
 Language, and, v. 184
 Learned, quoted, iv. 110
 Marcus a, iv. 133
 Mathers a, i. 144
 Modern, v. 194, 220-225
 Numbers and, v. 32, 86
 Occultist and, disagree, i. 277
 Permutation of biblical names, on, iv. 35
 Peter, a Jewish, v. 141
 Physicists, on, ii. 340
 Pre-Christian, ii. 111
 Rabbin, a famous, iii. 136
 Rome in, v. 46
 Semite, iv. 38
 Seven among the, v. 203
 Space, on, ii. 56
 Sun of, v. 219
 Tau and, v. 162
 Teachings, v. 176, 355
 Tenets from Chaldeans, v. 178
 Vedantins compared, and, v. 107
 Western, i. 299; iii. 358; iv. 159; v. 193, 205,
 208, 230, 460
 Word of, iv. 114
 Zohar methods and, v. 113
KABARIM or KABEIRA, ii. 153
 Adamas, named, iii. 17
 Ehereal fire and, ii. 190
 Holy Lemnos, born of, iii. 17
 Noah was a, iii. 389
 Phtah the seventh, iii. 365
KABIRI, (KABEIRI) Agriculture, and, iii. 389
 Aletæ and, iii. 359
 Anactes and, iii. 359
 Arnobius on, iii. 151
 Axieros, etc., were, iii. 361
 Castor and Pollux were, iii. 362
 Celestial, iii. 363
 Chaldean, v. 230
 Cherubs and, iii. 123
 Confusion about, iii. 267
 Corybantes and, iii. 359
 Cosmic Gods, great, iii. 361
 Curetes and, iii. 359
 Cycles symbolized by, ii. 366
 Deities, most arcane, iii. 114
 Derivation of name, v. 309
 Dii Magni and, iii. 359
 Dioskouroi (Dioscuri) and, iii. 359, 362
 Divine dynasties, kings of, iii. 363
 Egyptian, iii. 275, 361

KABIRI, (KABEIRI) (Contd.)
  Faber on, iii. 150, 359
  Gabiri or, iii. 362
  Generic title, a, iii. 363
  Gods, v. 238, 309, 311, 318
  Guebra comes from, iii. 362
  Holy fires, named, iii. 17
  Idei and, iii. 359
  Isis-Osiris and, iii. 363
  Kadmos or Kasmilos was, iii. 361
  Lares and, iii. 359
  Lemnos-born, iii. 17
  Manes and, iii. 151, 359
  Meaning of, i. 174; iii. 362; v. 309, 310
  Mysteries of, v. 310
  Mysterious Gods, most, iii. 267; v. 310
  Mystery God, a, v. 277
  Penates, and, iii. 359
  Phoenicians, of, iii. 275
  Poles, personifying opposite, iii. 359
  Sacred fires and, iii. 361
  Samothrace, in, iii. 361, 390
  Seven, v. 202, 325
  Sidereal powers, rulers of, iii. 363
  Sons of Sydic or, iii. 391; v. 320
  Temple of, iii. 363
  Teraphim and, v. 238
  Titans and, iii. 151, 359
  Zedek, sons of, iii. 391
KABIRI (DIOSCURI), Dioskouroi, iii. 362
KABIRI-TITANS, the, iii. 360
KABIRIA or agriculture, iii. 389
KABIRIAN tradition, iii. 389
KABIRIM, v. 309
  Cambyses and, iii. 359
  Chthonian divinities, and, iii. 362
  Deluge Gods, and, iii. 359
  Fifth race, iii. 275
  Gibborim or, iii. 275
  Mighty ones or, iii. 392
  Planets, v. 320
  Sanctuaries of, iii. 363
  Worshipped universally, iii. 362
KABIRS and the devil, iii. 353
  Kabolitæ or Kabul tribes, iii. 205
KABUL, Arbas in, iii. 205
KADAMPA, Sects, v. 398
KADESH, Kadeshim, the holy ones, iv. 28, 31
KADMON, Adam, i. 129, 160, 263; ii. 107; iii. 16, 133; iv. 107; v. 86
  Sephira and, i. 291; iii. 15; v. 191
KADMOS AND KABIRI, iii. 361
KADRU, Kashyapa's Wife, iii. 141
  Many-headed serpent, iv. 143
KADUSH and EL-EL the Sun, ii. 184
KADUSHU of the Psalms, iv. 28
KADVAT, v. 408
KAF, Mountains of, iii. 395, 396, 397
KAFARISTAN, iii. 395
KAFFIRS a human race apart, iv. 293
KAIKOBAD, iii. 397
  Dynasty of, iii. 397
KAILAS, Buddhist monastery in, i. 51; v. 405
KAILASA or HEAVEN MOUNTAIN, Himalayan, iii. 414, 415; iv. 68; v. 109
KAIMURATH, Adam or, iii. 393, 395, 396
KAIN or CAIN, iii. 136

KAJBEE, Mount, iii. 55
KAKODAEMON the evil spirit, ii. 58, 126
KALA, KRONOS or TIME, i. 131, 139, 151; ii. 123, 145, 171, 179, 306; iii. 150, 236; iv. 119, 134, 325
  Chakra, v. 365
KALABAGH, Indus at, iii. 415
KALAGNI, the flame of time, ii. 86
KALAHAMSA or KALAHANSA Brahma called ii. 74
  Brahma-Prajāpati and, i. 145
  Brahman called, i. 84
  Goose, the, iii. 131
  I am I or, i. 144
  It of the, i. 144
  Kwan-Shi-Yin represnted as, ii. 193
  Swan or, i. 84; ii. 74, 77; iii. 130; iv. 33
  That called, i. 144
KALAKA daughter of Danava, iii. 380
KALANABHA, Taraka is called, iii. 381
KALAPA or KATAPA, Position of, ii. 93
KALAPANI, black waters of the ocean, i. 53; iii. 405
KALDHI, (KHALDI), v. 242, 329
KALEIDOSCOPIC transformations of world-symbols, iii. 335
KALI, Age, ii. 92; iv. 51, 120; v. 259, 339
  Agni, a tongue of, ii. 161
  Hamsa or black swan, i. 144
  Stars at the commencement of, ii. 388
  Waters of the, iii. 404
  Yuga, i. 64, 65, 73; ii. 85, 92, 192, 337, 369, 376, 387, 389; iii. 62, 79, 149, 154, 301, 309, 322, 394, 418, 433; iv. 96, 119, 120, 142, 185; v. 27, 229, 260, 337, 338, 344, 346, 347, 348, 396, 466
  Yuga, four ages of, ii. 92
KĀLĪ, Shiva's consort, iv. 118
  Vina of, v. 520
KALI-KARAKA or strife-maker, iii. 60
KĀLINĀGA, v. 289
KALIYA and KRISHNA, iii. 378
KALKI AVATARA, i. 151, 311; ii. 92, 99; iii. 414, 418; iv. 51; v. 337, 400
KALPA, Age or, i. 65, 150; v. 83
  Brahma in preceding, iii. 85, 183
  Brahma's creation at commencement of, ii. 176; iii. 75, 99
  Close of, i. 110; ii. 50, 160, 360; iii. 60, 324
  Commencement of, iii. 58, 68, 75, 99
  Creations of each, iii. 64
  Crores of, seven, iii. 312
  Cycles in one, v. 337
  Daksha born in every, iii. 249
  Day of Brahma or, iii. 80
  Descent and ascent during, i. 187
  Eternity and a, ii. 50
  Great, i. 151, 254; v. 353, 378
  Immortality and end of, i. 109
  Mahā, v. 41, 353, 367
  Manus for every, fourteen, iii. 308
  Meanings of, iii. 308, 320
  Minor, ii. 254
  Nandi in every, iii. 406
  Narada in this, iii. 92
  Padmapāni and, v. 420
  Sacrificial animals in first, iv. 196

KALPA (*Contd.*)
Shiva in every, iii. 283
Sons of Brahma reborn in every, iii. 91
Succeeding, ii. 87
Twenty-ninth, iii. 251
Vamadeva in every, iii. 283
Varāha, of, iii. 321
KALPAS, Beginning, after the, iv. 188
Events divided by, iii. 155
Evolution in many, ii. 173
Future, ii. 83, 154
God living in all, ii. 149
Great, ii. 84
Hindus, ii. 362
Life, of, i. 176
Manvantaras or, ii. 85; iv. 281
Mirror of Futurity records, iii. 61
Padmapani means supporter of, iii. 186
Reincarnation in previous, iii. 235
Rounds or, i. 235
Series of, iii. 320
Seven, ii. 38; iv. 183
Small, ii. 84
Vishnu and seven, iv. 183
Yugas and, iii. 59, 80
KALPIC MASKS, Elements called, ii. 397
KĀMA, Animal soul or, iii. 411; iv. 168, 240
Apsarases, king of, iii. 182
Body of desires, etc., 209; iv. 185
Colour of, v. 428, 461
Creator, a supreme, iii. 183
Daughter of, v. 165
Depends on Prāna, v. 523
Desire or, i. 290; iii. 168, 181, 257
Essence of blood, v. 551, 553
Evolution and, v. 543
Feeders of, v. 424
Fourth Principle, v. 487
God, a, iii. 181, 183
Head, of the, v. 556
Loka, i. 181, 289; ii. 48, 184, 398; iii. 373;
iv. 181; v. 208, 230, 253, 359, 491, 495, 499,
501, 512, 526, 559, 564, 566
Love, God of, iii. 181
Makara-ketu, the, iv. 150
Manas and, iii. 88, 257, 411, 417; iv. 185;
v. 494, 501, 508, 512, 513, 521, 525, 526,
531, 539, 553, 555
Mara or, iv. 151
Passions and, i. 209; iii. 257; iv. 185
Prāna and, v. 523, 528, 529, 531, 586
Principle, i. 212; iv. 185
Rūpa, i. 181, 199, 212, 245; ii. 48; iii. 31,
113, 120, 125, 243, 244; iv. 165, 168, 203,
205; v. 208, 353, 427, 454, 456, 457, 458,
472, 473, 496, 498, 512, 535, 553, 564
Samael or, i. 287
Temptations of, iii. 257; v. 532
World of, v. 365
KĀMA-DEVA, God of love and desire, iii. 182
KAMARINA or Uria, Abraham born in, v. 111
KĀMARUPIC Existences, v. 559
Entities, v. 566
Man, v. 489
State of our globe, i. 304
KĀMIC, Consciousness, v. 531
Hierarchy, v. 532

Impressions, v. 557
Impulses, v. 556
Plane Images on, v. 526
Principle, v. 493
Soul, v. 496
KAMSCHATKA, iii. 400; iv. 192
KAMU mi masubi no kami, i. 261
KAN COH, Sepulchre of, iii. 47
KANADA, Gods of old, ii. 219, 243, 303
KANDU a sage and yogi, iii. 178, 181, 182,
184, 410
KANGAROO, Men and the, iv. 237
KĀ'NITHI, Kain from, iii. 136
KANJUR of Northern Buddhists, i. 50, 123
KANOCH is, v. 106
KANSA, king, v. 153
Sons of Devaki killed by, iv. 176
KANSA and NĀRADA, iii. 59
KANT, see Book Index
KANTIAN theories, iii. 326, 328
KANYA or the virgin, i. 155, 333
KANYA-DURGA the virgin, ii. 384
KAP or Caucasus, iii. 398
KAP-KAZ or Caucasus, iii. 398
KAPH, Mountains of, iii. 361, 396
KAPI-VAKTRA or monkey faced, iii. 60
KAPILA, Antiquity of, iv. 141
Esoterically explained, ii. 324
Evolution taught by, i. 238; ii. 309; iii. 261;
iv. 222
Eye of, ii. 286
Hardwar, at, iv. 142
Infinite, on the, ii. 144
Intellect of, iv. 91
Kumara, a, ii. 176; v. 320
Pass of, iv. 142
Purushottama, the, iv. 141
Sagara's progeny slain by, iv. 141
Sānkhya philosophy of, i. 326; iii. 53; iv. 142;
v. 81, 469
KAPILAKSHA or Kapila's eye, ii. 286
KAPILASTHAN or Kapila's pass, iv. 142
KAPILAVASTHU, Gautama Prince of, i. 314;
v. 349, 381
KARA or hand, iv. 148, 149
KARABTANOS or Fetahil spirit of matter,
i. 245, 264, 293
KARAKORUM chain of Tibet, i. 55; iii. 356
KARAM or side, iv. 148
KARAMANIA, Mandrake in, iii. 40
KĀRANA, Ātmā, v. 351
Cause or, i. 114, 118, 156; iii. 58
Purānic Commentaries, of, 118
Sharīra, iii. 89; iv. 164; v. 77, 366
Unknowable, v. 323
KĀRANĀTMA Causal Soul, v. 77, 83, 351
KARANOPADHI or spiritual soul, i. 212
KARATALA, State of Consciousness, v. 538,
539, 542
KARENS of India, Seven souls of the, iv. 203
KARLI, Labyrinths under caves of, iii. 224
KARMA, Absolute eternal law, is, iii. 306
Absolute harmony, ii. 368
Abstract nature or, iv. 43
Adepts, and, v. 376, 467, 512
Adjuster of, iii. 60
African, iii. 175

KARMA (Contd.)
Agents of, i. 181, 185, 334; iii. 393; iv. 45
Amanasa, of, iii. 32, 197
America, of, iii. 443
Ancient science, and, v. 357
Angel incarnated prompted by, iii. 285
Apes, of, iii. 264, 265
Arūpa pitris and, iii. 102
Astral light and, i. 166; iv. 82
Astral light, of humanity, iv. 81
Asuras, and the fallen, i. 239
Atlanteans, of, iii. 304, 409; iv. 310
Atoms united by, ii. 360
Australians, of, iii. 175
Avatāras, and, v. 352
Book of Life and, ii. 259
Bréal on, iii. 271
Buddhi, and, i. 82
Cataclysms and, ii. 371
Cause and effect, as, iv. 82
Chance and, ii. 368
Christian Theology of, v. 315
Collective, v. 466
Compensation and, ii. 364
Create, does not, iii. 306
Creature subject to, every, ii. 361
Creatures of, ii. 360
Cruden knew nothing of, i. 185
Curse of, iii. 409
Cycle of racial, ii. 371
Cycles and, ii. 366
Cyclic evolution and, ii. 359
Death and life, and, iv. 82
Deity manifesting through, ii. 370
Deluge resulting from, iii. 349
Destiny and, ii. 364; iv. 176
Devas compelled by, to incarnate, iii. 372
Dharmakāyas are without, v. 370
Dhyān Chohans and, i. 181, 322; iii. 102
Divine soul and, i. 82
Divinity, the exacting, iv. 125
Ego, of the, v. 473, 474, 499, 500, 513, 552
Electricity and, i. 171
Elementals subject to, i. 268
Entity, a personal and impersonal, iv. 82
Eternal law of, iii. 306; iv. 46
Evil and, ii. 133
Evolution, and, i. 240, 359; iv. 192
Executor of, iii. 59
Ezekiel, addressed in, iv. 61
Ezra, of, iv. 20
Fatal destiny or, iv. 57
Fatalism and, ii. 368
Fate or, iii. 419; iv. 89, 140, 176
Fates or, triform, iii. 412
Fifth race, of, iii. 303
Forces of nature and, ii. 360; iv. 192
Fourth race, iii. 409
Fundamental law and, iv. 79
Generation of bad, i. 58; v. 513
Genesis, of author of, iv. 20
Genesis, of exoteric teachings of, i. 77
Genii, and, i. 334
God, iv. 61
God read, for, ii. 379
Gods, and, iii. 250; v. 376
Gods, will of the, i. 334

Great kings and, i. 181
Harmony and, ii. 368
Heredity and, iii. 185
Holy ones, Four, and, v. 439
Humanity, of, iv. 82
Iblis an agent of, iii. 393
Ignorance and, v. 502
Incarnation result of, iii. 372
Individual, v. 512
Indra's defeats due to, iv. 185
Intelligence guiding, i. 322
Inventors compelled by, to incarnate, iii. 372
Israel, of, i. 62
Jivatmas and, i. 190
Justice of, v. 378, 503
Laughter adjusts even human, ii. 371
Law of, i. 112, 171; iii. 304, 306, 307, 409;
    iv. 79, 249; v. 83, 247, 249, 371, 378, 560
Law of compensation, ii. 364
Law of retardation, iii. 262
Law of retribution, ii. 359; iii. 306
Liberty and, iii. 306
Life and death result of, iv. 82
Life and, law of, ii. 259
Lipika and, i. 165, 166, 187, 334
Lord of the sheep, v. 104
Mahārājahs and, four, i. 181, 285, 334
Manus, of, iii. 250
Meaning of, iii. 303
Minos or, i. 166
Moira is, iv. 176
Monads and, i. 190; iii. 251, 277, 303, 318
Moses, of, iv. 20
Muktas and, i. 190
Nārada executor of, iii. 59
Narrow-brained, of the, iii. 175
National, ii. 40; v. 195
Nature-spirits subject to, i. 263
Nemesis and, ii. 366, 367; iii. 306, 419
Nidānas, and, v. 560
Nineteenth century, of the, i. 63
One law, ii. 359
Orlog or fate, iv. 89
Osiris or, i. 166
Parentage, and, v. 545
Past Manvantaras, of, v. 552
Pesh-Hun adjuster of, iii. 60
Pessimists and, iii. 305
Physical proof of, iv. 349
Prajāpatis, of, iii. 250
Predestination and, ii. 366
Present state result of, iii. 371
Progress and, ii. 40
Prometheus and, iii. 247, 410, 419
Providence and, ii. 359, 368; iii. 307; v. 49,
    303, 370
Punishes not, ii. 368
Punishment, agent of, iv. 45
Pymander, referred to in, iv. 57
Racial, ii. 40, 371
Rebirth and, i. 224; iii. 304, 307; v. 247
Recorders of, i. 165
Reincarnation and, iii. 304; v. 512
Religions and, v. 247, 315
Respector of persons, no, iv. 249
Retribution and, ii. 359
Rewards not, ii. 368

KARMA (*Contd.*)
Rishis, of, iii. 250, 372
Satan and, iii. 237
Savages, and, iii. 318
Sexless principle, ii. 359
Sexual relation, of, iv. 25
Sin and, iv. 89
Sinful intercourse, and, iii. 198
Skandhas and, v. 473, 560
Sphere of, iv. 140
Sterility due to, iv. 349
Svabhavat and, ii. 360
Teachers and, v. 561
Third eye connected with, iii. 303
Third race, of, iii. 409
Triform fates, iii. 412
Unexhausted, v. 493
Universe, of, v. 528
Unknowable, one with, iii. 307
Vishnu Purāna on, ii. 133
Weapon of, iv. 46
Witnesses to, three, ii. 294
Working of, ii. 362; iv. 349, 247, 248
Yama or, i. 166
KARMA-LESS, shadows of bodies were sinless hence, iv. 181; v. 370, 513
KARMA-NEMESIS, ii. 367, 368, 370; iii. 304, 306
KARMASĀKSHIN, v. 270
KARMIC, Action, iii. 431
Cause, i. 243; v. 557
Compensation, i. 226
Conditions, iii. 217
Course incomprehensible, iii. 169
Curse, iii. 113
Cycles, ii. 362, 367
Deities, iii. 425
Development of monads, iii. 169
Disturbance of the axis, iii. 276
Duty, failure of, iii. 191
Effects, ii. 130; iii. 73, 174; v. 259, 473
Ego, iv. 176
Evolution, i. 227; iii. 201, 251
Exigencies, iii. 97
Existence, v. 559
Fate of nations, ii. 400
Gods, iii. 425
Justice, v. 511
Law, i. 82, 244, 318, 319; ii. 357, 367; iii. 87, 103, 203, 231, 263, 329, 444; iv. 84, 241, 337; v. 80, 144
Ledger, i. 187
Lipikas, i. 243
Necessity, iv. 349
Punishment of Dhyānis, iii. 231
Rebirth, iii. 174, 237
Record, v. 472, 511, 546
Retribution, iv. 83
Scales, world of, i. 234
Will, iii. 235
KARMENDRYAS, organs of action, v. 538, 541
KARNAC, Brittany, of, v. 47
Monolith from, ii. 115; iii. 80
KARNAK, Ruins of, iii. 428
KARNEIOS or sun-born applied to Apollo, iii. 55

KARSHIPTA the human mind-soul, iii. 294
KARSHVAR(E)S, seven divisions of the earth, iii. 383; iv. 178, 327
KARTA PURUSHA, v. 363
KARTTIKEYA, (or Kartikeya), Apollo and, iii. 381
Birth of, miraculous, iv. 120
Hindus, from, iii. 382
Kenealy on, iv. 190
Krittika, delivered to the, iv. 121
Kumara, a, iii. 114; iv. 190
Mars, and, iii. 55, 133
Pleiades and, iv. 190
War-God, a, iii. 55, 133; iv. 119
KASDIM, Astrologers, v. 12, 333
KASHI KHANDA of *Skanda Purāna*, iii. 189
KASHMIR, i. 51; ii. 92; iii. 326; v. 392, 404
KASHYAPA (or Kasyapa), Buddhism taught in China by, i. 51
Danavas, mother of, iii. 381
Disciple of Buddha, v. 407
Diti advised by, iv. 184
Father of reptiles, etc., iii. 262
Genealogy of, iii. 255
Kapila son of, iv. 143
Progeny of, iii. 59
Purānas, in, iv. 141
Sage, the, iii. 141, 380
Self-born, ii. 81
Tamra wife of, iii. 188
Ursa Minor, in, iv. 184
Vedas, in, iii. 141
KASHYAPA-ADITYA, Apollo answers to, iii. 381
KASMILOS or Kadmilos or Kadmos (Hermes), iii. 114, 361
KASPAR, one of the Magi, ii. 380
KATAPA or Kalapa, ii. 93
KATHARSIS, or trials, v. 279
KATIE KING referred to, iv. 306
KAUMARI and Kartikeya, iv. 190
KAURAVYA, king of the Nagas. iii. 218
KAV-KAZ or Caucasus, iii. 398
KĀVYAS or cyclic years, iii. 98
KAVYAVAHĀNA or electric fire of Pitris, ii. 245; iii. 110
KAYA, v. 408
KA-YIN, son of Adam Rishoon, iii. 396
KEBAR ZIVO, vine of food of life, i. 245
KEDARA, a dug-up place, a mine, ii. 133
KEDEM, Æolus called, ii. 187
KEDESHIM, Priests or initiated, iii. 216
KEELY, J. W., Centre, on a neutral, ii. 280
Explanations of, ii. 282
Failure of, partial, ii. 283
Limit, not allowed to pass, ii. 286
Motor Co., ii. 285
Motor phenomena of, ii. 279, 287
Occultism and, ii. 280, 289
Possible attainments of, ii. 283
Research of, ii. 284
Secrets of, ii. 280, 283
Sound, on, ii. 288
Vril, discoverer of, i. 57, 203, 299
KEFA, of Egypt, v. 199, 202
KELTO-Gaulic, civilization, v. 295
KEM-OOR, Horus of, iv. 148

KENEALY, DR., see Book Index
KENITE or Cainite, iv. 111
KENNEDY, Col. Vans, Quoted, i. 54; ii. 137; iii. 311
  Referred to, iii. 230
KENRICK, quoted, v. 63
KENT'S CAVERN, Arrowheads from, iv. 91
KEP, mother of time, ii. 124
KEPHA, the Mother of Revolutions, v. 202
  Signifies Mystery, v. 202
KEPHERN, builder of second Pyramid, iii. 230
KEPLER, see Book Index
KEPTI and SEBTI for two times, ii. 124
KERIYA, Buried cities in oasis of, i. 56
KERKES the Phoenix of the Turks, iv. 188
KERNEL, Powers of, i. 331
  Seers have seen, of matter, i. 316
  Tradition, of, iii. 238
KERSHVAR, Qaniratha, the, iv. 328
KESARI, Anjana wife of, i. 241
KESHIN slain by Avatar, iii. 59
KESIL or ORION, ii. 373, 374
KETHER, Crown, the, i. 284; ii. 67, 69, 70, 151; iv. 196; v. 211, 213, 438
  Principle, abstract, i. 263
  Sephiroth and, i. 154; ii. 156; iv. 167; v. 191
  Triad or, iv. 167; v. 438
  Yod symbolical letter of, ii. 109
KETHER MALCHUTH, quoted, ii. 157
KETU the dragon's tail, iii. 380
KEY, Anthropological and Physiological, v. 204
  Astrology lost to Europe, to, v. 335
  Indian and Buddhist Systems to, v. 407
  Master- of Nature, v. 455
  Measure, v. 69
  Seventh, of the sacred septenary, v. 120
  Universal Knowledge, to, v. 185
  Universal Symbology, to, v. 42, 121
KEY of Urania, the, quoted, ii. 381
KEYNOTE in nature, Radical, iv. 60
  Initiation, of, v. 154
  Secret Teaching, of, v. 65
KEYS, Initiate's headgear, on, v. 162
  Seven to all allegories, v. 201, 204
  Universal Mystery language, to, v. 195
KEYSTONE, v. 44
KHA or body, iv. 203; v. 357
KHABA, shadow, the, iv. 203; v. 357
KHADO, Female forms, beings in, iii. 286
  Minds, with little, iii. 273
  Third and fourth, from, iii. 33
KHAMISM or old Coptic, i. 175
KHANDAKALA, conditioned time, i. 131
KHANOCH or ENOCH, the Initiator, iv. 99
KHANOOM, Metropolis of, iii. 393
KHARGAKKURRA, v. 436
KHARTUMIM Asaphim, v. 121, 333
KHEEN or YANG, the membrum virile, ii. 193
KHEM, or HORUS-OSIRIS, i. 267; v. 63
KHEN, v. 252, 253
KHNOOM adored at Elephanta, ii. 82, 101, 194
KHNUMU, Egyptian, v. 198
KHODA, Persian for God, ii. 61
KHOEMNIS, v. 62
KHONS, God, v. 251, 253, 256
KHONSOO, the Lunar God, iv. 32
KHOOM, Water of space, ii. 80

KHOPIROO, Khopirron or Scarabaeus, ii. 81; iv. 122
KHOPRI or scarabaeus, iv. 122
KHOPROO or KHOPRON, to become, to be reborn, ii. 81; iv. 122
KHORASAN tribe from Afghanistan, i. 55
KHORLO used in Senzar version of Stanzas, i. 87
KHOU(S), v. 244, 246, 249, 250, 251, 253
KHUAN-KHE, river in Tibet, i. 54
KHUNRATH, Paracelsus, etc., ii. 336; iii. 129
KAI-YU, quoted, ii. 159
KIFFA, v. 139, 140
KIMAH, Pleiades and, ii. 373, 374
KIMMERIAN BOSPHORUS, iii. 414
KIMPURUSHAS, Dynasties of, iii. 369
KIN, CAIN, or evil, iii. 387
KINETIC, Energy, life atoms and, iv. 242
  Theories, in. 209
KING(S), Ai of, iv. 128
  Ashoka, v. 260, 271
  Chamber of, in great pyramid, i. 308; ii. 30, 107; iv. 29, 34, 38, 128
  Dynasties, of divine, iii. 282; iv. 70
  Herod, v. 153
  Initiates, iv. 113, 122, 273; v. 43, 263
  Kansa, v. 153
  Māra, v. 153
  Osiris, of duration, ii. 155
  Preacher, v. 234
  Race, iv. 318
  Raivata, v. 260
  Sagara, ii. 286
  Saturn, iii. 179
  Soma, of plants, i. 275; ii. 102, 110; iii. 383
  Stone, named by speaking, iii. 342
  Thevetat, iii. 225
  Worlds, of three, ii. 138
  Yima as, iv. 180
  Yudishtira a, ii. 85
KINGDOM, Animal, i. 310; iii. 15, 167, 291; iv. 206, 256, 266
  Darkness, of, v. 153
  Development from animal, iv. 256, 266
  Door into human, i. 226
  Elementals, of, i. 229; ii. 174; iii. 312; iv. 187
  God, v. 64, 83
  Heaven, of, v. 81, 169, 304
  Holy, v. 120
  Man a distinct, iii. 67, 291
  Mineral, i. 230; iii. 312; iv. 206
  Monad represents part of its, ii. 356
  Root-form of each, iii. 192
  Sparks of lower, i. 175
  Spirits, of, i. 244; iii. 244
  Vegetable, iii. 167, 312
  Vertebrate, iii. 127; iv. 166
  Violence, of heaven taken by, iv. 85
KINGDOMS, Elemental, i. 230; ii. 174; iii. 312; iv. 187, 306
  Evolution in all, iii. 192
  Lower, i. 310; ii. 330; iii. 177
  Man passes all, in first round, i. 214
  Monadic essence passes all, ii. 344
  Nature, of, iii. 168
  Objective, three, iii. 187

KINGDOMS (*Contd.*)
Rudimental, ii. 174
Series of numberless, iv. 21
Seven, four known, ii. 360; v. 460
Sons of lower, ii. 330
Three elemental, i. 230; ii. 174; iii. 312; iv. 187
Two sub-physical elemental, iv. 306
Universe, of, i. 317
Vehicles of lower, i. 310
KINGS, Divine, iii. 33, 198, 236, 316, 350, 352, 364, 392; iv. 333, 342; v. 258
Divine dynasty of, imparted astronomy, iii. 42
East, of, iii. 395
Edom, of, ii. 91, 157; iii. 64, 93; iv. 24, 55, 274, 275; v. 182
Egyptian human, iii. 433; v. 263
Fifth Race, of, v. 263
Healers, as, v. 263, 264
Pre-Adamite, iii. 93
Primordial seven, ii. 91
Races, of third and fourth, iii. 198
Real nature of, ii. 160
Seven, i. 286; ii. 377; iv. 135, 189, 317; v. 200
Shisthas or, iii. 308
Statues of, iii. 368; iv. 319
Superhuman, iii. 368
Third and fourth race claimed to be, iii. 33, 273
Third root race, of, iii. 103, 200
We are the, iii. 33, 273
KINNARAS, Inhabit the astral plane, iii. 99
KIOTO, Ascetic monks of, i. 226
KIPPŪR, Definition in prayers of, ii. 157
KIRANA or radiant applied to Krishna, iii. 55
KIRCHOFF, Achievements of, ii. 252
KIRJATH-SEPHER, city of letters, iv. 98
KISCHUPH, v. 121
KISMET, v. 539
KIUAY, Adepts, v. 38
KIU-TE, Books of, v. 389
KI-Y, Seven and ten, iii. 365
KIYUN, or Kivan, v. 238, 318
KLAPROTH, quoted, iii. 208; v. 178
KLEE, F., on the deluge, iv. 104
KLIPHOTH, world, iii. 119
KLIPPUTH, v. 299
KNEELING prohibited as idolatry, iii. 281
KNEPH, Concealed breath of, ii. 68
Egg issuing from mouth of, ii. 79
Eternity, and snake-emblem of, ii. 58, 68
Serpent, and, ii. 58; iii. 39
KNIGHT, discoveries of, v. 72
KNIGHTS of the Round Table, iii. 392
KNIVES, Azazyel taught men to make, iii. 375
KNOOPH, Symbol of, ii. 194
KNOWLEDGE, Absolute, ii. 294
Adepts cannot communicate, iv. 271
Adepts of, v. 465, 482
Ancients, of, i. 256; v. 42
Antiquity, and, iii. 127
Archaic, iv. 194
Aryans, of ancient, ii. 246
Astronomical, iii. 60; iv. 104
Atlantean nations, of, iii. 424, 434
Beginning of human, i. 314
Brāhman, i. 315; iv. 39

VI–17

Branches of, seven, i. 222
Cherubim, of, i. 185
Concealed, iv. 68
Cosmic energy, of guidance of, ii. 360
Cyclic intricacies, of, iii. 60
Dhyān Chohans, of, iv. 270
Divine, i. 184, 185; ii. 138, 183; iii. 70, 105, 368, 381; iv. 134, 138; v. 69, 240
Dragon symbol of secret, iii. 378
Dzyu real, i. 168
Egyptian Priests, of, v. 264
Elixir of, v. 375
Events, initiates, of, ii. 371
Eye of Dangma, through, i. 118
Fall result of, iv. 82
Fire of, i. 151; iv. 136
Forms, of past, iii. 299
Fourfold, v. 519
Fourth path of, i. 254
Fourth race, in, i. 240
Fruit of tree of, ii. 91; v. 493
Geological, in *Book of Enoch*, iv. 104
Gnosis or hidden, i. 321; v. 74
Good and evil, of, i. 292; iii. 90, 133, 219 281, 294, 381; v. 493
Gyan Gnan or true, iii. 393
Initiate into secret, iv. 67
Initiates, for highest, iii. 435
Initiation, acquired at, iv. 61
Intuition and, iv. 19
Jnāna, Gnosis or, i. 131
Keys to, v. 185
Kosmos of, v. 87
Lamp of, ii. 333
Land of, v. 41
Love and, Angels nature is, iii. 249
Mahā Vidyā, the great, i. 222
Metaphysical, v. 459
Mimir drew highest, ii. 118
Mind, and, v. 547
Mother of, i. 193; iv. 97
Non-separateness, of, i. 319
Ocean of, v. 52
Occult, i. 66, 275; ii. 148; iii. 39; iv. 190; v. 91, 256, 370, 432, 482
Paramārthasatya, through, i. 130
Parts and the whole, of, v. 31
Path of, i. 254
Paths of, right, and left, i. 243
Relics of ancient, ii. 336
Requisite for occultism, v. 418, 459, 467
Sacred and secret, i. 187, 315; iv. 102; v. 412
Science of occult, iii. 39
Secret, of self, iv. 139
Sense, differs from, i. 322
Serpent of, iii. 284
Shruti or revealed, i. 313
Siddhas, of, iv. 208
Soma fruit of tree of, iv. 67
Space called realm of divine, iv. 70
Spirit, is of the, v. 434
Spiritual, of Maha Yogi, iv. 184
Tree of, i. 187; ii. 91; iii. 17, 107, 182, 207, 208, 220, 384; iv. 159, 160, 197; v. 28, 43, 85
Wisdom hedged from, i. 219; v. 74

KNOWLEDGE (*Contd.*)
World one with divine, ii. 138
Zodiac, of, iii. 428
KOEPPEN, v. 394, 405, 408
Koios, and Arkite Titans, iii. 150
KOH-I-BABA, Bamian at foot of, iii. 337
KOH-KAF, Mountains of, iii. 396, 397
KOILON, the Greek Heaven, v. 109
KOKAB, or Mercury, iv. 22
KOLOË, An inscription of, ii. 111
KONCH-HOG, in Senzar version of stanzas, i. 87
KONIGSBERG, birthplace of Kant, ii. 325
KON-TON (Conton) or chaos, i. 261, 286
KOORGAN or tumuli in Russia, iv. 321
KOOTHOOMI, Moryas and, ii. 93
KOR, Rider Haggard's city of, iii. 317
KÖRÖS, Csoma de, v. 398, 402
KORSCHELDT, E., on eyes of reptiles, iii. 300
KORSHID, v. 315
KORYBANTES, Vulcan's progeny and the, iii. 114
KOSHAS, or sheath, i. 212; ii. 335; v. 361
KOSMIC, Auric Envelope, v. 473, 500, 528, 533
  Body, v. 519, 527
  Consciousness, v. 524
  Deity, shadowed, ii. 82
  Division, v. 542
  Eternal, v. 208
  Evolution, v. 479
  Fire, v. 446, 447, 562
  Hierarchies, v. 538
  Origin of Man, v. 152
  Planes, v. 527, 528
  Reflection of God, Satan, iii. 238
  Seed of Consciousness, v. 528
  Septenary, v. 521
  States, v. 541, 544
  Substance, v. 529 (See Cosmic)
KOSMOCRATORES, (See Cosmocratores)
KOSMO-GEOLOGICAL, iii. 396
KOSMOS, Active life of, iii. 236
  Aggregate of, i. 73
  All-inclusive, i. 73
  Atomic elements in, v. 528
  Atoms of, v. 382
  Awakening of, i. 176
  Being, manifested into, i. 251; ii. 158
  Birth in, law of, i. 200
  Birth of, v. 421
  Boundless, i. 69; ii. 107; v. 487
  Breathing of, iv. 152
  Builders of, ii. 53; v. 213
  Building of, i. 165; ii. 53, 318
  Causes of, i. 302; ii. 199, 365
  Chaos, Theos, iii. 56-63; v. 382
  Creation of, iii. 96
  Creator of, v. 213
  Cyclical processes in, iii. 84
  Day of, new, i. 176
  Death of, ii. 89
  Destiny of, ii. 319
  Differentiation in, iii. 239
  Divine thought, springs from, ii. 53
  Dual force acting beyond, ii. 220
  Egyptian symbol of, iii. 356

Emanates from cube, v. 189
Eternal, v. 208
Eternity in, i. 69, 206
Evolution of, ii. 62, 338; iii. 76; iv. 159
External, v. 363
Fohat in, v. 528, 535
Forces of, iii. 108; iv. 224
Genesis of, ii. 342
Geometry in, v. 453, 455
God the Father and, i. 141
Good and evil in, iii. 169
Gradations of colour and sound, in, v. 456
Growth in, law of, i. 200
Higher Decad, is, v. 436
Hiranyagarbha of, v. 534
Indiscrete principle, and, ii. 246
Infinitesimal point in, i. 320
Inhabitants of, ii. 336
Inorganic non-existent in, i. 293
Intra-cosmic soul or, i. 70
Invisible, ii. 339
Kingdoms, seven esoteric, of, ii. 174
Kwan-Shi-Yin and Kwan-Yin, and, ii. 195
Life and Will in, v. 533
Lives of, ii. 89
Logoi in, seven, iii. 41; v. 455, 507, 533
Lotus, Symbol of, v. 453
Manifestations of, i. 114, 200; ii. 257; iii. 37, 129; iv. 96; v. 453
Manifested, v. 189, 227, 447
Material, i. 299; ii. 199, 365
Mathematics, and, v. 87
Matter, totality of existences in, ii. 238
Metaphysical and physical, iii. 122
Monas applied to whole, i. 231
Mother's spawn and, i. 248
Mysteries of, ii. 33; iv. 197
Noumenon the, i. 70
Occultism and, i. 293
One soul, aspect of, ii. 257
Parabrahman and, i. 73
Philosophy, allegory, in every, ii. 62
Proportions of, v. 91
Pyramid and, v. 166
Pythagoras on, v. 440
Reabsorption of, i. 204
Reality pervading, i. 80
Re-awakenings of, iv. 27
Rebirth of, ii. 359
Reconstruction of, i. 165
Rests, ii. 220
Septenary division of, v. 521, 542
Seven Principles of, v. 208, 489
Son above is whole, i. 129
Space, in boundless, i. 133
Spirit and, i. 302; ii. 51, 168, 199, 251, 365
Spiritual, v. 166
Spiritual energy in, i. 170; iii. 36
Symbolism of, v. 291
Tetragrammaton in, iii. 37
Third plane of, v. 513
Triple one, emanated from, ii. 51, 166
Unity of parts of, ii. 202, 280
Universal, v. 436
Universe merging in, iii. 195
Vāch and, ii. 150
Visible, v. 363

KOUIN-LONG-SANG, Buddha's temple on, iii. 219
KOUYUNJIK, Mound of, iii. 18
  Sennacherib's palace of, ii. 32
KRANAN said to be a creative God, iii. 271
KRATU a mind-born son of Brahma, iii. 88
KRATU-DVISHAS enemies of the sacrifices, iv. 69
KRAUNCHA one of the seven Dvīpas, iii. 320, 403, 404
KRAUNCHA-DVĪPA, iii. 404
KRAUSE on plurality of worlds, iv. 275
KRISHĀSHVA, Sons of, iv. 201
KRISHNA, Arjuna and, iii. 218; v. 351
  Avataras, one of, iv. 120; v. 151
  Bala-deva, brother of, v. 258
  Bala-Rama brother of, iv. 185
  Bhagavad Gita on, i. 150; ii. 259; iii. 318; iv. 209
  Birth of, iv. 176
  Brothers of, six, iv. 96
  Buddhi, or, iii. 318
  Christ-state or, iv. 176
  Crucified, iv. 131; v. 288
  Date of, iii. 229
  Death of, i. 65; iii. 148; iv. 96
  Descends into Infernal Regions, v. 154
  Devaki mother of, iii. 59; iv. 96
  Dionysus one with, iii. 418
  Divine intellectual soul, iii. 318
  Div-Sefid slain by, iii. 405
  Fifth race, of, iii. 148
  Garuda and, iii. 323
  Hero, a, i. 65
  Incarnations of, v. 351
  Jivanmukta and, iv. 176
  Kali Yuga and, i. 64; iii. 148; iv. 96
  Kālināga and, v. 289
  Kaliya and, iii. 378
  Kansa and, iv. 176
  Keshin, slays, iii. 59
  Legend of, v. 503
  Logos or, ii. 123; iii. 79, 233, 318; iv. 96
  Man, as, iii. 233
  Manus of, iii. 148
  Mathura birthplace of, iv. 159; v. 260
  Mother of, iii. 59
  Mysteries of, v. 97
  Nārada, and, v. 287
  Nārāyana and, iii. 358
  Orientalists on, i. 54
  Purānic story of, i. 54
  Rāmāyana, in, iv. 185
  Reformer, a, i. 65
  Reincarnation, a, iii. 358
  Rishi Nārāyana, identified with, iii. 358
  Rishis and, seven, iii. 318
  Samba reputed son of, iii. 323
  Saviour, as, iii. 233
  Secret Wisdom, taught, ii. 263
  Seventh Principle, v. 154
  Shankhāsura killed by, iii. 403
  Shepherd, v. 289
  Shishupala slain by, iii. 229
  Splendour of Vishnu and, iv. 120
  Sun, incarnated, iii. 405
  Sun-God, Brighter, the, i. 65
  Supreme Self of, iv. 209
  Symbols of, ii. 49
  Unite oneself with, ii. 123
  Vaishnavas and, v. 292
  Vallabhacharya's, of, ii. 49
  Vishnu, last incarnation of, iii. 229; iv. 120; v. 311
  White devil slain by, iii. 405
KRISHNA-KIRANA, Apollo Karneios a transformation from, iii. 55
KRISHNA-VISHNU, Adept becomes, iv. 152
KRISTOPHOROS, neophyte made, v. 290
KRITA AGE, Devapi and Maru return at, ii. 93
  Race who follow laws of, ii. 92
  Wisdom imparted in, iv. 51
KRITA YUGA, Satya or, iii. 79, 154, 309, 322; v. 339
KRITTIKĀS, Pleiades or, ii. 153, 388; iii. 433; iv. 119, 121, 190; v. 343, 344
KRIYASHAKTI, Creation by, iii. 31, 179, 231; v. 430, 535
  Fruits of, i. 259
  Gift of, iv. 222; v. 446
  Meaning of, i. 333
  Plane, Creation on, iii. 284
  Power of, iii. 180, 188, 434; v. 449, 561
  Progenitors of, i. 258
  Progeny of, i. 255
  Third race powers of, iv. 208; v. 430
  Unconscious, v. 561
  Will or, iii. 148; v. 449
  Yoga-power or, iii. 70
KROENIG, referred to, ii. 238
KROIOS one of the Arkite Titans, iii. 151
KRONIDAE, Seven, v. 200
KRONOS, Adam and, ii. 366
  Arkite Titan, an, iii. 151
  Auxiliaries of, v. 202
  Creation of, ii. 171
  Curse of, iii. 413
  Dagon, and, ii. 366
  Duration, stands for endless, ii. 135
  Emblem of, i. 299
  Generation and, iii. 271
  Giants imprisoned by, iv. 344, 345
  Harp of, iii. 389
  Isis and, ii. 96
  Jupiter and, iv. 52, 84
  Kala or, ii. 179
  Lemurians governed by, iv. 334
  Meaning of, iii. 271
  Myth of, iii. 285
  Ormazd identical with, i. 173
  Orphic theogony, in, i. 84
  Osiris and, ii. 96
  Saturn, or, ii. 135, 179, 366; iii. 391; iv. 334; v. 334
  Sevekh or, ii. 124
  Sons of Saturn, iii. 150
  Sydic, iii. 391
  Symbolism of, iii. 271
  Time or, ii. 145; iii. 412, 414, 418; v. 202
  Titans, Sons of, iii. 150
  Uranus or, iii. 270, 272
  Zeus, and, iii. 271, 419; iv. 333

KRONOS-Saturn, Jupiter son of, i. 139
　Melchizedek and, iii. 390
KRONOS-Sydik and his sons, iii. 360
KRONOTYPES, Seven primary, ii. 124
KROTONA, sage of, v. 65
KRURA LOCHANA or evil-eyed, iii. 42
KRÜSS, Meta-elements of, ii. 270
KSHATRIYA, Buddha a, i. 44
　Military caste, or, i. 314
　Race of solar dynasty, ii. 93
KSHETRAJNA or embodied spirit, i. 326; ii. 294;
　iii. 117; iv. 209, 210; v. 533
KSHIRA OCEAN or Ocean of milk, iii. 402
KUCH-HA-GUF of the Kabalah, iv. 205
KUEN-LUN, Hiding places in passes of, i. 47
KUHN, Adalbert, quoted, iii. 109, 411; iv. 95
KUKLOS ANANKES, the unavoidable cycle,
　iii. 378
KULLŪKA on the Manava-Dharma Shastra, iii. 98
KULLŪKA BHATTA, referred to, ii. 48; iv. 63,
　316
KUMAON, Sculptured rocks of, iii. 345
KUMĀRA, God of War, v. 320
　Guha or virgin-youth, iii. 381
　Higher Ego, v. 563
　Kumāra creation, i. 142; ii. 176; iii. 115
　Sanat, v. 320
KUMĀRAS, Agnishvattas and, iii. 97
　Alter egos of four, iii. 114
　Apollo one of the, iii. 382
　Archangels, prototypes of, iv. 155
　Arūpa Gods or, iii. 318
　Asuras and iii. 98, 172
　Brahma, sons of, ii. 176; v. 203
　Celibate, iii. 204
　Chaste youths or, iii. 88
　Create, refuse to, ii. 179; iii. 183
　Deprived, called, iii. 248
　Devas, are real, iii. 99
　Dhyān Chohans called, iv. 151
　　iii. 204
　Dhyānis, are, ii. 176
　Eternal celibates, iii. 204
　Ever pure, ii. 177
　Five, ii. 177
　Flames, called, iii. 250
　Four youths, become, i. 153; ii. 36; v. 78
　Great concern of humanity with, ii. 178
　Hierarchies of, v. 539
　Hindu pantheon, of, iii. 180
　Incarnated in third race, v. 472
　Jata one of, iii. 319
　Kapila and, ii. 176; iv. 143
　Kartikeya one of, iv. 190
　Kūrma Purāna, in, iv. 149
　Lunar Pitris and, v. 565
　Makāra and, iii. 102; iv. 148
　Maker's sons, or, ii. 176
　Mars a, iii. 381
　Maruts as aspect of, iv. 185
　Mind-born sons, the, v. 78, 320
　Nahash or, iii. 248
　Nīlalohita and, ii. 176
　Ninth creation, so-called, ii. 176
　Panchashika one of the, ii. 176; iii. 319
　Planetary spirits, v. 465
　Prajāpatis and, ii. 176
　Pre-Adamic, v. 203

Purānas, in the, iv. 149
Rebels, divine, iii. 248
Reincarnation of, iii. 235
Ribhu one of, ii. 176
Rishis one of, iii. 91
Rudras and, ii. 176; iii. 114, 198; iv. 156, 185
Sanaka chief of, ii. 87; ii. 319; v. 320
Sananda, Sanātana, etc., were, ii. 176; iii. 319;
　v. 320
Sanatkumāra one of, ii. 176; v. 319
Seven, i. 282; ii. 176; v. 78, 320
Shiva, incarnations of, ii. 176; iii. 251, 283
Solar deities, are, i. 151
Sons of Brahmā, mind-born, ii. 176; v. 203,
　320
Tempting demons, called, iii. 181
Toyambudhi visited by, iii. 319
Vaidhatra name of, ii. 176
Virgin youth(s), iii. 245; iv. 119, 190; v. 359
Virgin-angels or, iii. 248
Virgin-Gods or, ii. 87; v. 320
Virgin-men or, iii. 283
Virginal estate of, iii. 238
Vodhu one of the, iii. 319
Yogis, were, ii. 177; iv. 149
KUMBHAKARNA, brother of Ravana, iii. 228
KUMUDA-PATI or moon, iii. 56
KUNDALINĪ, Cosmic and Human, v. 484
　Destroys as well as preserves, v. 510
　Fires of, v. 554
　Forty-nine Fires, of, v. 517
　Light of, v. 521
　Shakti, i. 333
　States of, v. 517
　Vital, v. 484
　Vital airs and, v. 510
KUNDZABCHIDENPA, illusion creating
　appearance, i. 120
KUNG, or the Great Tone, v. 443
KUNG CHIA, Compiler of Shan Hai King,
　iii. 303
KUNI To Ko Tatchino Mikoto, First man
　called, i. 286
KUNTĪ, Pandavas, mother of, iv. 96
KUNZA BCHI DEN PA, v. 400
KURILE ISLANDS, iii. 327
KURIOS, or Logos of the Greeks, ii. 68
KŪRMA, or tortoise, iii. 256
KŪRMA PURĀNA, iv. 149, 183
KURU, Devapi of the race, of, ii. 93
KURUKSHETRA, Rite, v. 97
KUSHA, one of seven Dvipas, iii. 320, 403
KUSHA DVĪPA, seven sons of King of, iii. 368
KUSHASTHALI, v. 259
KU-SUM, Septenary, v. 374
KUVERA, the deity of the North, i. 186
KWAN, Etymology of, ii. 194
KWAN SHI YIN, Avalokiteshwara, i. 96, 105,
　193; ii. 192, 193, 194, 195
　Female aspect of, ii. 149; v. 380, 391
　Golden Dragon in whom are, ii. 171
　Logos or, ii. 171, 194
　Oeaohoo, or, i. 138
　Triple of, i. 193
KWAN YIN, God of Chastity, i. 105, 139, 193,
　194, 329; ii. 149, 193, 195; v. 380, 391,
　392

KWAN YIN TIEN or melodious Heaven of Sound, i. 194
KWOH P'OH, commentator, iii. 65
KYRIEL of Gods, Ancients', ii. 157; iii. 35
KYRILETZA, alphabet, iv. 117

L

LA CAILLE'S Tables for the Sun, ii. 386
LA PLUCHE, quoted, ii. 338
LA VÉZÈRE, iv. 310
LABARUM, v. 104
LABYRINTHODON, Third eye of, iii. 300
LABYRINTHODONTS, Mivart on, iv. 267
LABYRINTHS, Egyptian temples, of, i. 51; iii. 433
  Explorers lost in, iii. 77
  Subterranean, iii. 224
  Tiers and passages of Egyptian, iii. 433
LACERTILIA, Lizard of order of later, iii. 298
LACHELIER, Henri, quoted, ii. 354
LACUSTRINE ANIMAL VARĀHA, an antediluvian, ii. 84
LAERTIUS, Plato, on, v. 151
  Zeno, on, v. 167
  Zodiacal signs, on, v. 241
LAHGASH, secret speech or incantation, ii. 69
LAIR Is Pleroma Satan's ?, iv. 75
LAKE, Bovey Tracey, of, iv. 295
  Dragons, of, iii. 208
  Dwellings, iv. 284
  Sons of Wisdom, abode of, iii. 209
  Temple, v. 168
  Villages, iv. 291, 308
LAKHANG in Mountains, i. 47
LAKSHMI, Agni son of, iv. 150
  Durga Kālī black side of, iv. 150
  Kāma a son of, iii. 183
  Venus and, iii. 86, 183; iv. 150
  Vishnu, female aspect of, ii. 95; iii. 43, 86
LĀMA, Jehovah of, v. 404
  Seat of the initiating, v. 140
  Succession of, v. 412
LĀMAISM, Apostles of, v. 39
  Buddhism and, ii. 263
  Reformed, v. 393
LĀMAIST, Chagpa Thogmed, v. 73
  Incarnations, v. 391
  Monks, v. 325
  Reincarnation, v. 349
  Secret Books of, v. 349
  Works, v. 73
LĀMAS, Dalai, v. 105, 325
  Gelugpa, v. 389
  Secret Rites of, v. 377
  Teschu, or Teshu, v. 105, 391, 393
  Tibet, of, v. 410
LĀMASARIES, (LĀMASERIES) of India, v. 390
  Subterranean crypts in, i. 47
  Tibet, of, v. 375, 390, 391
LAMB, a Christian emblem, v. 163, 246
  Sacrificial, v. 370
LAMBAKA, Co-latitude or, iii. 400
LAMBERT, Franz, referred to, iv. 204
LAMECH, Father of Noah, iii. 268, 390
LAMP(S), v. 108, 369
LAM RIN, books of, v. 389

LANCI Librarian at Vatican, quoted, iii. 375
LANGE, referred to, v. 243
LANGUAGE(S), of Abraham, v. 181, 197
  Agglutinative, iii. 204
  America, of, iv. 358
  Ancient, iii. 214; iv. 324
  Astronomy, the Sabaean, iii. 365
  Atlanteans, of, iii. 204
  Basques, of, iv. 358
  Centres of, i. 52
  Chaldean, v. 181
  Chinese, iii. 335
  Confusion of, v. 185
  Cyclic evolution of, iii. 204
  Divine, v. 197
  Dragon in ancient, iii. 214
  Esoteric, iv. 39
  Esoteric doctrine, of, iii. 368
  European, i. 227
  Fourth race, perfected from, i. 240
  Gods, of, iii. 363; iv. 114, 197
  Growth of, iv. 232
  Hebrew, v. 184, 198
  Hierophants, of, ii. 22
  Initiates, of, ii. 291; iii. 205; iv. 355; v. 118, 197
  Lolo, iii. 282
  Mystery, iii. 205; iv. 145; v. 195
  Occultism, of, iv. 187
  Origin of, iii. 203; iv. 232
  Phases of growth of, iv. 232
  Primitive symbolical, iv. 16
  Rabbinical, ii. 380
  Radical, iv. 232
  Reason coeval with, iii. 204
  Revelation, a, ii. 21
  Roots of, iv. 231
  Sanskrit, i. 313; v. 197, 530
  Semitic, iv. 324; v. 243
  Symbolical, ii. 21, 104; ii. 334; iv. 16, 189
  System, universal, v. 196
  Universal, iv. 37, 39; v. 175, 197
  Universal esoteric, v. 118
  Vedas, of, iv. 96
LANKĀ, Atlanteans of, iii. 239; iv. 63
  Giants of, iii. 406
  Hanuman, in, iii. 171
  Rākshasas of, iii. 278; iv. 321; v. 535
  Rāvana giant king of, iii. 228, 235
  Third race ended at, iii. 332
  Tombs of, iv. 321
  Zodiac taken to Egypt from, iii. 433
LANOO, Bhumi, child of, i. 260
  Calculations, O, make thy, i. 254; iii. 301
  Chela, a, i. 138; v. 412, 440
  Creation, to understand, iii. 122
  Disciple or, i. 77; iii. 30, 124
  Fear the undefiled, need not, iii. 296
  Lamp of the, i. 143
  Never speak, O, iii. 283
  Questions to, i. 179
  Second race, taught of, iii. 124
  Thou, I, he, O, i. 260
  Thread O, our, i. 277
LANOOS, of esoteric school, i. 181
LAO TZE, or LAO-TSE, Esotericism of, iii. 49
  Mystics of the sect, i. 226
  Predecessor of, Confucius, i. 48

LAOMEDON, Founder of archaic mysteries, iv. 364
LAOTSEU, v. 40
LAPIS Philosophorum or universal agent, iii. 122
LAPLANDERS call Corpses Manee, iv. 343
LAR, contraction of El-Ar, iii. 360
LARES, Etymology of, iii. 360
LARS conductor or leader, iii. 360
LARTET, Dr., quoted, iii. 280; iv. 260, 261, 315
LARYNGEAL Plexus, iv. 480
LASSEN, quoted, i. 51; v. 398, 405
LATENCY, Parabrahmanic, iii. 37
  Pre-cosmic, of primordial matter, i. 128
LATERES COCTILES or Babylonian Tiles, ii. 72
LATHE, Cruciform, iv. 113
  Vishvakarman, iv. 129
LATIN cross, v. 161, 162
  Deus and Greek Delta, v. 117
  Letters, numbers and colours, v. 505
LATIN CHURCH, v. 95
  Angels or, v. 94, 95, 386
  Astrology and, v. 332
  Devil of, v. 95
  Dogma and, v. 95
  Evil Eye and, v. 249
  Heliocentric System and, v. 71
  Idols and, v. 339
  Peter not founder of, v. 140
  Rites of, v. 95, 116
  Ritual of, v. 55
  Separation from Greek Church, v. 93
LATITUDE, Aksho or, iii. 400
LATONA, Diana and, iii. 417; iv. 340
  History of, iv. 339
  Lemuria, iv. 340, 341
  Leto or, iv. 339
  Niobe and, iv. 340
  Revelation, in, iv. 340
LAUGHING Philosopher, v. 44
LAURENS, quoted, v. 262, 264
LAURENTIAN, Fossil of the, iii. 256
  Life, iv. 281
  Period, iii. 158, 167
  Rocks, iv. 254
LAVA, iii. 316, 317
LAVANA, a sea of salt water, iii. 320
LAVOISIER, quoted, ii. 189
LAW, Absolute, iii. 96, 97, 171
  Absolute will, of, ii. 69
  Adepts, of celibate, iii. 92
  Ah-hi gives to nature her, i. 111
  Ahura Mazda, of, iii. 294; iv. 180
  Analogy, of, i. 206, 304; ii. 266, 309, 328; iii. 76, 161, 257; iv. 188
  Association, of, i. 116, 333
  Atavism, i. 305
  Atlantean race, of, iii. 409
  Biogenesis, of, iv. 241
  Birth, of, i. 200
  Buddha, of, i. 51; iii. 39; v. 387
  Catenated, stream of, i. 112
  Continuity, of, ii. 352
  Cosmological, ii. 199
  Cyclic, i. 82; ii. 310; iii. 84, 165, 299; iv. 292, 349
  Darwinian, iii. 178; iv. 232, 237

  Divine, v. 534
  Eternal, is, i. 207; ii. 379; iii. 235, 418
  Ethical causation, of, iii. 303
  Evolution, of, i. 299; ii. 345, 363, 366; iii. 66, 73, 76, 175, 179, 196, 203, 235, 263, 285, 303; iv. 58, 103, 222, 238, 300
  God, of, v. 69
  Good, the, v. 363, 393, 394, 406
  Gravitation, of, ii. 213, 316, 328; v. 223
  Great, i. 203; ii. 365; iii. 89
  Incarnation and karmic, iv. 84
  Intelligences behind, ii. 318
  Karma of, i. 82, 165, 171, 244, 318, 319; ii. 357, 359, 367; iii. 87, 102, 185, 285, 303, 306, 329, 409, 444; iv. 84, 249, 337; v. 64, 144, 180, 247, 249, 560
  Mahat and, ii. 170; v. 513
  Manu, of, iii. 100, 308, 409; iv. 144
  Manvantaric, ii. 60; iv. 57
  Matter, of, ii. 310; iii. 37
  Mechanical, ii. 319, 325; iv. 107
  Moses, of, ii. 33; iii. 105, 376; iv. 107; v. 179, 180, 185, 216
  Motion, of, ii. 221, 254, 360; v. 386
  Nature, of, i. 81, 86; ii. 41, 212, 309, 322, 336, 379, 396; iii. 90, 141, 158, 349; iv. 181, 300
  Non-intervention, of, v. 224
  Occult Science and, ii. 240
  Occultists and, i. 196
  One, and divine control, i. 86
  Periodicity, of, i. 198, 199
  Plato's, iii. 371
  Rebirths, of, iii. 235
  Repulsion, of, iii. 369
  Retardation, of, iii. 179, 202, 262
  Retribution, ii. 359; iv. 125
  Secret, v. 387
  Thorah or, iv. 29
  Universe, of, i. 82, 320; ii. 332; iv. 124
  Varuna's, iv. 177
  Zarathushtra, of, iv. 181
LAY-CHELAS, European, i. 217
  Master writes to two, i. 221
LAY FIGURES, iv. 336
LAYA, Atoms issue from, ii. 172, 292
  Central sun and, iii. 243
  Centres, i. 195, 200, 202, 203, 225, 232, 252; ii. 281; v. 512, 536
  Condition, ii. 211, 246, 313; iii. 243
  Divine breath from, i. 330
  Fohat and, centres, i. 203
  Ilus resting in, i. 196
  Imperishable, centres, i. 200
  Life in, i. 302
  Matter in, state, ii. 268
  Nature in condition of, ii. 246
  Neutral or, ii. 242
  Point, i. 189; ii. 280
  Prana, locked in, ii. 250
  Protyle into, ii. 246
  Radiant one and, i. 195
  Rod with serpents, ii. 273
  State of, i. 152, 251, 302; ii. 268, 274, 290, 292, 345
LAYAM, Protyle is our, iii. 114
LAYARD, referred to, i. 184; iii. 18

LAYCOCK, quoted, iv. 194
LAYERS, Auric envelope has seven, v. 429
 Globes of terrestrial chain, of, iv. 327
 Human skin, of, iii. 101
 Seven, of skin, v. 425
 Seven, of space, i. 75
 Skin, of, three strata or, iv. 327
LEAH, Mandrake of Rachel and, iii. 40
LEAP year, ii. 218; iv. 99
LEBANON, Cedars of, iv. 63; v. 64
 Nabatheans of Mount, iv. 22
 Talisman from, v. 162
LEBAS, Ph., v., 330, 331
LECTURES, Pythagoras of, v. 65
LEDA, Castor and Pollux, iii. 130
 Egg, and, iii. 130
 Fables and myths of, iii. 203
 Swan of, ii. 73
LEFT HAND, Adepts of, ii. 135; iv. 63
 Path of knowledge, i. 243; v. 60, 85, 122
 Science, v. 64
LEFT PATH, Adepts of, iii. 215, 330; v. 122
 Initiates in, iv. 62; v. 284
 Sodales of, iii. 215
LEGEND of Hiouen Thsang, v. 40
 of Raivata, v. 259
LEIBNITZ, see Book Index
LEMAITRE, Jules, quoted, iv. 22
LEMMING, Migrations of Norwegian, iv. 350
LEMMINKAINEN, the white magician,
 iii. 39
LEMNISCATE OR FIGURE of 8, ii. 274
LEMNOS, Kabir born of holy, iii. 17
 Volcanic formation of, iii. 390
 Worship of Kabirim in, iii. 363
LEMUR or MAKIS, iv. 237, 285
LEMURIA, Africa later than, iii. 367
 Atlantic portion of, iii. 333
 Atlantis and, iii. 21, 47, 268, 333; iv. 331, 345
 Atlas in days of, iv. 332
 Breaking up of, iii. 324
 Continent, of, ii. 157; iii. 20, 178, 314, 401;
  iv. 345, 351
 Dioscuri in days of, iii. 360
 Disappearance of, iii. 266
 Easter Island a relic of, iv. 250
 Elect of, iii. 319
 Evolution in, iii. 328
 Extent of, iii. 323, 327
 Fauna of, iv. 351
 Fire destroyed, iii. 316
 Flood did not destroy, iii. 149
 Fragments of, iii 266
 Giants of, iii. 345
 Haeckel and, iii. 199
 Human race, cradle of, iv. 357
 Indian Ocean, beneath, iv. 250
 Madagascar belonged to, iii. 184
 Modern science, and, iii. 266, 315
 Nations descended from, iv. 337
 New Zealand part of, iii. 298
 Origin of Gods in, iv. 338
 Pacific part of, iv. 356
 Periodical sinking of, iii. 325
 Position of, iv. 356
 Pythagoras and, iv. 173
 Relics of, iii. 404

Saturn, kingdom of, iv. 337
 Schmidt, Prof., on, iv. 357
 Stature of men after, iii. 331
 Submarine fires destroyed, iv. 332
 Symbol of, iv. 331
 Tertiary period, before, iii. 431
 Third root race, continent of, ii. 157; iii. 400
 Transformation of, iii. 332
 Widely accepted, iv. 358
 Witness to existence of, iii. 327
LEMURIAN, Atlantean, and, iii. 206
 Continent, iii. 225, 275, 278; iv. 177
 Earth, divisions of, iii. 356
 Forms, extinct, iv. 246
 Half animal tribes of, ancestry, iii. 201
 Late, iii. 343
 Physical men, first, iii. 57
 Race, iii. 350; iv. 305, 346
 Relics, iii. 201, 326
 River bed, iii. 333
 Sorcery, iii. 287
LEMURIANS, Battles between classes of, iv. 341
 Civilization of, iii. 318
 Descendants of, iv. 348
 Dogma had no, iii. 274
 Flood of, iii. 330
 Giant bodies of, iii. 443
 Greeks knew of the, what, iv. 319
 Highly intelligent, iii. 265
 History of progress of, iii. 266
 Kronos governed, iv. 334
 Kumāras and, iv. 156
 One-eyed giants or, iv. 338
 Physical fall of, iii. 302
 Semi-animal, iii. 201
 Survivors of, iii. 202
 Third race, iii. 333
 Unseparated, iv. 343
 Witnesses to, iii. 265
LEMURIDAE, Ancestors of men, iv. 220, 238
LEMURO-ATLANTEANS, Ancient writings of,
 iv. 341
 Cities of, iii. 316
 Continents of, iii. 23
 Divisions of, iii. 370
 Dynasty of spirit-kings, iii. 325
 Gigantic black and yellow, i. 236
 Half-animal tribes of, iii. 201
 Man, age of, iv. 320
 Origin of, races, iii. 204
 Peoples, iii. 201
 Race, i. 242; iii. 424
 Religion, iii. 274
 Remember, did not need to, iii. 286
 Wisdom, ii. 392
LENS, Sun a, ii. 304
LEO, Cyelon, vertical to, iii. 406
 Judah, in sphere of, ii. 377
 Libra and, iii. 367
 Sinha or, iii. 406
 Vanquished, iv. 354
 Virgo and, iii. 367; iv. 354
 Zodiac, and, i. 261; iii. 431
LEON, Moses de, referred to, i. 261; iii. 40;
 iv. 29; v. 177
LEONTOID Michael-Ophiomorphos, iv. 49
LEPORINE or HARE-RABBIT, iii. 288

LEPROSY, Surya cured Samba of, iii. 323
LÈSE-SCIENCE, ii. 335
LESSE, Caves on the banks of, iv. 313
LETHE, Cycles revolve in depths of, v. 219
   Millions of years sunk into, iv. 260
LETO, LATONA or, iv. 339
LETTERS, Chaldean, v. 114
   Colours and, v. 505
   Devanāgari, iv. 114, 118
   Ephesian, v. 121
   Figures and, v. 114
   Hebrew, v. 114, 178, 197, 206
   Latin, v. 505
   Milesian, v. 121
   Musical notes and, v. 197
   Numerical value of, v. 185
   Phoenician, v. 205
   Sanskrit, v. 197
   Senzar, v. 117, 118, 530
   Symbolism of, v. 118, 206
LEUCIPPUS, Atomist instructor of Democritus,
   i. 70
   Atomist, ii. 243,303
LEUCOMAINES Generated by men, i. 304, 305
LEVERRIER, Prediction of, iii. 439
LÉVI, Éliphas, Paradox, an incarnated, iv. 155
   See Book Index
LEVI, Gemini and, ii. 377
   Judah and, iii. 138
LEVIATHAN, iii. 210; iv. 148
LEVITES, Half initiated, iv. 36
   Left Path, Adepts, iii. 215
   Orthodox, iii. 216
   Text of, replaces Mosaic in Bible, v. 187
   Tomb and, iv. 27
   Tribe not a, iii. 138
LEWES, referred to, ii. 252
LHA, Ascetics in Tibet called, v. 38
   Fivefold, i. 283
   Melha an ancient, ii. 74
   Moon, of, iii. 110
   Spirits or, v. 38, 379
   Possessed of a dual body, iii. 67
   Servant to seven, turns fourth, iii. 27
   Spirit of earth, or, iii. 35; v. 38
LHA-CHOHAN used in Stanzas, i. 87
LHAMAYIN of below in Stanzas, iii. 28, 74
LHAS, High of the, iii. 28, 74
   Men, who had not built, iii. 32
   Solar, iii. 29, 113, 118, 119
   Spirits of high spheres, iii. 74, 197
   World, create, iii. 36
LIBERATION, Creators who have reached, iii. 87
   Desire for, iv. 141
   Maruta Jivas, of, iv. 187
   Way to final, iii. 322
LIBERIUS, Pope, v. 156
LIBRA, Asher, in the sphere of, ii. 377
   Degree of, first, ii. 384; iii. 434
   Egyptian Zodiac, in, iii. 367; v. 164
   Enoch or, iii. 137
   Greeks, invented by, iv. 71
   Zodiacs and, v. 430
LIBRARIES, Cave, i. 47
   Destruction of, iv. 262
   Imperial, in St. Petersburg, i. 58
   Mediæval, v. 121

Occult Fraternity, of, i. 56
   Temple, iv. 98; v. 59, 253
LIBRARY, Adyar, i 190
   Alexandrian, i. 46; v. 57, 295, 307
   Antium at, v. 148
   Bodleian, v. 99, 101
   Cæsarea, v. 143, 160
   Mazarine, iv. 101
   National, of Paris, v. 252
   Nineveh, of, iv. 262
   Occult, v. 253
   Sacred, of Fo Kien, i. 314
   Sargon, of, iv. 261
   Thebes of, v. 245
   Ulpian, v. 149
   Vatican, of, v. 307
LIBZU, Wise among Gods, iii. 19
LICE, Aphides of plant, iii. 142
LICHENS, Labrador, of, ii. 332
   Mineral or stone, from, i. 292
LICTORS, seven, v. 319
LIÈGE, bones found at, iii. 280
LIF, Descendants of, iii. 109
LIFE, Absolute, i. 293, 302, 319; iii. 47; v. 455
   All is, i. 293
   Antiquity believed in universality of, iv. 273
   Atoms, i. 106, 199, 272; ii. 353
   Auric Fluid and, v. 533
   Brahma, of, ii. 84, 86
   Breath of, i. 260, 272, 273, 287, 288; ii. 351;
      iii. 29, 36, 91; iv. 23, 160
   Cause of, i. 274
   Circle of, i. 268; iv. 126
   Crystalline, i. 120; ii. 356
   Dawn of, iv. 279
   Death and, i. 82, 275; ii. 62, 82, 87; iv. 29,
      43, 82; v. 44
   Death necessary for, iii. 388
   Divine, v. 387
   Divinity, is, v. 566
   Dragon of, v. 202
   Earliest forms of, iv. 165
   Electric fire of, iii. 122
   Electric ocean is, ii. 328
   Elixir of, v. 364, 430
   Elohim of, i. 271
   Eternal, v. 227, 511
   Eeternal bird, from, iii. 294
   Fiery spirit of, i. 264
   Fire is, i. 180; ii. 351
   First stage of cosmic, ii. 172
   Fish of, fiery, i. 160
   Fohat active force in, i. 171
   Forces of, v. 299
   Form, precedes, i. 269, 289
   Fountain of, ii. 71; iii. 397, 399; v. 280
   Globe, of our, ii. 366; iii. 41, 42, 347;
      iv. 281
   Golden thread of, iv. 82
   Graphite and organic, iv. 276
   Human, origin of, i. 72, 301
   Immortality, in, ii. 80; iii. 274
   Jiva, current of, v. 480
   Jivatma or one, i. 121
   Ledger, Chelā's, v. 468
   Light and, i. 73, 154, 195; ii. 192, 263, 303;
      iii. 382; iv. 134, 207; v. 492

LIFE (Contd.)
Linga Sharīra vehicle of, iv. 165; v. 566
Lives, and, i. 293
Logoi of, ii. 296
Logos is, second, i. 81, 173
Lunar magnetism and, ii. 109, 113
Matter, and, v. 384
Molecular action, and, ii. 327; iv. 299
Monads in space, of, ii. 345
Occultists and, i. 77, 196
Ocean of, i. 134
Odin endows man with, iii. 106
One, i. 70, 76, 121, 136, 178, 189, 273, 283, 294, 306, 311; ii. 359; iv. 242; v. 423, 447, 471, 479, 492, 523
Organic, i. 204; iv. 276
Origins of, i. 72, 155, 297
Parabrahman is, v. 566
Parallelism of, iv. 281
Pentacle of, v. 487
Planets, on, ii. 255; iv. 272
Prāna or, i. 212, 271; iv. 118, 165, 203
Primordial matter, and, i. 142; ii. 52, 261
Principle, v. 456, 457, 533, 565
River of, i. 319
Root of, i. 137
Rounds of, i. 242; iv. 135
Rule of, v. 290
Sentient, i. 196, 292, 304; iii. 35
Setting sun of, ii. 398
Ship of, iv. 31
Spirit and, i. 157, 188, 248, 264, 326; ii. 182, 349, 351; iii. 53, 113, 243; iv. 31, 97, 122, 151, 154, 155
Spiritual vision and, v. 515
Struggle for, i. 209, 250; iv. 229
Sun giver of, ii. 111; iv. 151, 167
Suns of, iii. 242
Tau symbol of, iv. 163
Thread of, iv. 82
Tree of, i. 128; iii. 142, 219, 220; iv. 64, 130, 159, 197, 209; v. 154, 163, 446, 493, 496
Universal, v. 191, 492, 528
Vegetable, i. 301; ii. 173, 304; iv. 246, 281
Virgins of, i. 262
Water of, i. 132, 135; ii. 71; iii. 364; iv. 128; v. 280, 375
Whence does, come?, ii. 395
Zodiac of, ii. 382
LIFE-ATOMS, Kinetic energy and, iv. 242
Prāna, of, iv. 241
LIFE-BRINGER, Lucifer the, iii. 120
LIFE-CENTRES, iii. 46, 243
LIFE-CURRENTS Thrill through space, ii. 255
LIFE-CYCLE, Atoms, of, ii. 338; iv. 224
Day of, last, i. 256
Day of Brahma or, i. 278
Earth, on our, iii. 193
End of this, iii. 61
Eternity and, iii. 107
Fourth, i. 213
Germ of all to end of, i. 138
Globe D, on, i. 214; ii. 21
Great, i. 283
Higher lives in, i. 302
Lunar chain, on, i. 231

Man lives through, and dies, i. 226; ii. 361
Manvantara or, iv. 162
Men of our, i. 310
Middle point of, iii. 157
Organism, of, iii. 125
Our, is middle point of fifth, i. 64
Planet, on this, i. 278; iii. 321
Present, i. 255
Rebirths throughout, iii. 304
Renewed, i. 215
Round or, i. 221
Septenary, iv. 119
Substances after a, i. 196
Support of man's entire, iii. 276
Terrestrial, iv. 192
World, of, iv. 181
LIFE-ELECTRICITY, Central sun and, iii. 243
Spirit of life-giving or, iii. 76
LIFE-ELEMENTS, Transfer of, i. 225
LIFE-ENERGY, Globes parting with, i. 232; iv. 242
LIFE-ESSENCE, Origin of, ii. 264
Prāna or, iv. 168
Wasting of, iii. 409
LIFE-FLUID, Our Nervous Ether, ii. 255, 262
LIFE-GERM, Comet, from a passing, ii. 211
Fire-atoms and, i. 302
Mother, from, iii. 147
Planets, from, iii. 165
LIFE-GIVER, Physical world, of, ii. 203
Universal, ii. 318
LIFE-IMPULSE, Globe A, reaches, i. 221
Mineral forms, giving birth to, i. 238
Planetary, iv. 267
Sweep of, i. 231
LIFE-ORIGINATION, Archebiosis or, ii. 174
LIFE-PRINCIPLE, Animal, and, i. 332
Archaeus and, iv. 224
Astral form and, iii. 126
Blood and, v. 565
Deity, and, i. 129
Fohat the, ii. 326
Fourth, i. 129, 299
Jiva or, iv. 242
Life-energy or, iv. 242
Living creature, of every, i. 246
Nature, in, v. 456
Noumenon, as, iv. 242
Prāna or, iv. 241; v. 457
Science and, iv. 299
Sun, evolved from, ii. 318
Universal soul, iv. 131
LIFE-Ray Divine, iii. 119
Effulgent light of, i. 127
Thread through beads, a, i. 269
LIFE-RENEWALS, Moon symbol of, i. 275
LIFE-THREAD or Sutratma, i. 269, 283, 284
LIFE-WINDS, Body, moving about, iv. 64
Lifthrasir the coming Adam and Eve, iii. 109
Nārada or, iv. 137
Senses or, iv. 138
Udāna translated, iv. 138
LIGHT, Absolute, i. 137, 250; iii. 49, 104, 169, 218; v. 227, 492
Abstract, iii. 50
Adam Kadmon, and, ii. 50
Air, from, i. 253

LIGHT (*Contd.*)

Alhim, of, iii. 50, 51, 52
Amun source of, ii. 54; iii. 139
Ancestors, essence of divine, i. 147
Angels of, iii. 102, 120, 241
Anima Mundi, in, i. 245; iii. 247
Apollo God of, iii. 20
Astral (see also under ASTRAL), ii. 248; iii. 122; v. 383, 424, 478, 521, 546, 560, 566
Atma a ray of, i. 289
Beams of, iii. 197
Birth of, ii. 57
Black, iii. 241
Body, a?, ii. 205, 206
Borrowed, i. 113
Brother of, v. 467
Buddhi, of, i. 290; v. 545
Cause of, ii. 88, 239
Chaos and, ii. 59
Chemical action of, ii. 321
Child of the widow and of, v. 275
Christos, of, iii. 50
Cold flame, is, i. 94, 146, 147; ii. 323
Cold ray of, ii. 83
Colour and, i. 253
Consciousness, of, ii. 148, 352
Cosmic, ii. 320; iii. 53, 122
Cosmogonies, from darkness in ancient, iv. 54
Creation and, i. 142, 298; ii. 72, 169
Creative, ii. 204; iii. 241
Cross, and, iv. 132
Currents of astral, iii. 84
Daiviprakriti, called, i. 334; iii. 50
Darkness and, i. 77, 113, 137, 148, 170, 192; ii. 95, 129, 157, 328; iii. 49, 104, 115; iv. 52, 54, 57, 60, 172; v. 208, 227, 489
Dawn of, iii. 372
Deity of, iii. 270; iv. 83, 340
Dhyān Chohans and, iii. 49
Divine, i. 196; ii. 64; iv. 176; v. 566
Divine hammer, from, iii. 108
Divine unity, of, iv. 173
Dragon of, ii. 129; iii. 206
Drama in sidereal, iv. 79
Ea God of, iii. 147
Effulgent dawn, of, iii. 372
Egg, fecundated by, divine, i. 136
Elementals and, i. 201
Essence of, i. 137
Eternal, iii. 24, 70; iv. 56, 96, 123; v. 233
Evil becomes, i. 140; ii. 131
Eye and, ii. 278
Face, from Lord of shining, iii. 27
Fathers Lords of, i. 245
Fetahil king of, i. 245
Fire and, i. 179, 198; iv. 80, 205
First-born, i. 137
Flames and, ii. 254
Focus of, iii. 283
Fohat and, i. 195; ii. 326
Forces, and so-called, i. 338; ii. 204, 230, 278; v. 299
Forms, condenses into, i. 140; iii. 46
Genii, of, ii. 120
God is, ii. 204
Gods and, i. 327; ii. 201, 397; iii. 20, 147, 362; iv. 52, 79

Harbinger of, iii. 246
Heat and, i. 70; ii. 146, 239, 291; v. 89
Higher Ego, of, v. 552
Holy, v. 504
Illusion or Maya, is, i. 137
Infinite, v. 191
Initiation, of, iv. 140
Īshvara, and, i. 193
Jehovah, of, iii. 50
Kabalists, of, i. 140; iii. 49, 51
Kings of, i. 245; iii. 422, 425
Laws of, iv. 193
Life and, i. 73, 142, 154; iii. 192, 351; iii. 382; iv. 57, 207; v. 115
Lights, of, ii. 127; iii. 270; iv. 134, 140
Living fire, of, i. 246
Logos, of, i. 194, 263, 334; ii. 147; iii. 50, 53, 236, 399; v. 189
Lord of Splendour and, v. 81
Lords of, i. 245
Lucifer, of, ii. 189
Manifested-unmanifested, of the, iii. 49
Matter, is, i. 137, 140; ii. 239
Māyāvic, i. 113
Mercury and, ii. 104; iii. 40; iv. 110, 112
Mineral kingdom and, iii. 177
Mode of motion, not a, i. 203
Mountain of, v. 40
Mulaprakriti, permutation of, ii. 148
Mysteries of, iv. 134, 136
Nature mirrored in, iii. 359
Numbers of, three sacred, iv. 162
Ocean of, ii. 204; v. 77
Od pure life-giving, i. 142
Oeaohoo, of, i. 136, 139
Osiris or, v. 273
Parāshakti and, i. 333
Particle of Divine, iv. 176
Pillar of, v. 511, 517
Planets, received by, ii. 299
Point of garment of, indivisible, ii. 70
Polarization of, ii. 209
Powers of, i. 333; ii. 303
Prakriti as, iv. 97
Primary creation of, ii. 169
Primeval, i. 179; v. 74, 91, 229
Primordial, i. 113, 263, 277; iii. 115, 139, 180, 408; v. 229, 233
Principle, iv. 111
Protogonos first-born, i. 137
Ra or, iv. 159
Race, Sarku the, iii. 18
Radiant, i. 137, 173; iv. 173; v. 503
Ray of, i. 127, 133, 136, 277; ii. 83
Reality, of one eternal, iv. 159
Rectors of, i. 182
Satan, might be called, iii. 388
Self-existent Lord, i. 150
Sephiroth and, iii. 51
Septenary, i. 179
Serpent first beam of, ii. 123
Seven, i. 179
Seven radicals, of, i. 201
Seven shades of, v. 550
Shadow, and, ii. 129, 131; iii. 218, 238; iv. 77, 79
Shekinah and, v. 191

LIGHT (*Contd.*)
  Shukra, through, iii. 42
  Sidereal, i. 298; iv. 79
  Solar, ii. 254, 315
  Solar flames and, ii. 254
  Son of darkness, i. 113
  Sons of, i. 64, 96, 164, 166, 177, 195, 246, 284; ii. 203, 296, 298; iii. 274; iv. 341; v. 91, 111, 270, 276, 289, 350, 370
  Sound and, ii. 257; iv. 205
  Sources of, i. 113, 262; ii. 54, 254, 257, 315, 346; iii. 139
  Substance cause of, ii. 239
  Svara and, i. 313
  Table of vibrations of, v. 458, 508
  Tenebrous, iii. 241
  Ultimate causes of, ii. 239
  Understood, not, ii. 46, 216
  Unknown, ii. 71; iv. 273
  Unmanifested, v. 78
  Veil of infinite, v. 191
  Web of, i. 130
  Wisdom, and, v. 109
LIGHT BEARER, Lucifer or, iv. 82
  One of, iii. 93
  Planets, iii. 93
  Venus, of Earth, iii. 45
LIGHT-BRINGER, Lucifer the, iii. 120, 241
LIGHT-FORCES, Hajaschar, ii. 230
LIGHT-GIVER, Zeus, iii. 412
LIGHT-MAKER, Bhāskara or, i. 161, 164
LIGHTNING, Cybele, of, ii. 52
  Earth, brought to, iv. 90
  Globular shaped, iv. 352
  Ideas concerning nature of, iv. 95
  Prometheus said to be, iv. 95
  Supposed incarnation of, iii. 294
LIGHTS, Body of those called, i. 303
  Crown, emanating from, ii. 151
  Hachoser reflected, ii. 230
  Name containing all, iv. 140
  Northern, ii. 358
  Phenomenon of polar, i. 254
  Primary seven, v. 78
  Rabbi Abba's six, iv. 199
  Seven, from one, i. 179, 180, 187
LIGNITE and bituminous coal, i. 297
LIGURIANS and Aryan invasion, iv. 310
LĪLA, amusement or, iii. 64, 135
LILITH or Lilatu, iii. 181, 182, 264, 286; iv. 249
LILLIPUTIANS possible, iii. 291; iv. 325
LIMBO, Illusion, of, iii. 237
  Kama Loka, Hades, i. 289
LIMBS, Brahmā Gātra, iii. 87
  Heavenly man, of, iv. 196
  Micropoposus, of, i. 262, 263; iv. 275
  Ra creates his own, i. 277
  Seven, or Sephiroth, i. 285
LIMBUS, Early Christians, of, ii. 68
  Earth, on this, ii. 184
  Great and little, i. 326
  Kāma Loka, or, ii. 48
  Major, or primordial matter, i. 325
  Of the Greeks, v, 230
LIME-SALT, Man evolving from, iii. 161
LIMESTONE, Formation of, i. 297

LINE, Adjustment, of, iii. 391
  Circle, issuing from, ii. 76
  Duality, corresponding with, ii. 341
  Neutral central, ii. 274
  One point fructifies, i. 155
  Rishi, of the, iv. 120
  Spiritual male, is vertical, iv. 164, 171
  Square and second, i. 154
  Vertical or male, iv. 164, 171
LINEAR measures, Origin of, ii. 20
LINES, Dots, circles, etc., Why?, i. 159
  Duad, representing, ii. 344
  Evidence of spectra and, ii. 313
  Map, in Confucian style of archaic, ii. 159
  Nidāna and, i. 156
  Points, from, ii. 152
  Purānas, between, of, iv. 97
  Seven paths or, iii. 197
  Sparks are called, i. 156
  Spectrum, of, ii. 267, 313
  Symbolic sets of, ii. 159
LINGA SHARĪRA, Astral Body and, i. 287; v. 168.
  After death, v. 208, 427, 473, 491, 563
  Corresponds with Spleen, v. 521
  Could not form in Vacuo, v. 566
  Emanation of the Auric Egg, v. 471
  Human Principle, third, iv. 165
  Passes through solids, v. 561
  Physical body, and, iii. 243; v. 440, 521
  Picture of the Man, v. 561
  Principle, second or sixth, i. 209
  Vehicle of Prāna, v. 208, 440, 566
  Vital, ii. 256
LINGAM, of the Hindus, iv. 39; v. 285
  Indecent form of, iv. 94
  Indian, ii. 61
  Jacob's pillar, iv. 39
  Jehovah and, iv. 41
  Jod and, iii. 134
  Sacr' means, iv. 35
  Shiva, and, iv. 159; v. 192
  Worshippers, iv. 40
  Yoni and, iv. 41; v. 292
LINGA-YONIC (see also Linyoni), Pāsha in hands of Shiva, is, iv. 118
LINGUISTIC case against ape ancestor theory, iv. 232
LINING of God or good, Evil is, ii. 131
LINK, Absence of, between ape and man, iii. 265
  Ancestry, between man and his real, iii. 196
  Angel and animal man, between, iii. 347
  Heaven and Earth, Man between, iii. 369
  Prosimia a, now disposed of, iv. 249
  Psychological, iii. 369
LINKS, Chain, in one and same, iii. 36
  Noumenoi and meta-elements, between, ii. 276
  Ungulates, between modern and Eocene, iv. 304
LINNÆUS, quoted, iii. 289
LINTELS and door-posts marked with blood, iv. 127
LIN TSI, aphorisms of, v. 412, 413
LINUS, referred to, ii. 374
LINYONI of ark of the covenant, iv. 41
LION, Crown of, seven rays of, iv. 135
  Egyptian Zodiacs, of, iii. 429

LION (*Contd.*)
Evangelical Zoolatry, of, ii. 78
Fourth race symbolized by, iv. 102
Gnostic jewels, on, iv. 49
God, who was the one, ii. 136
Heart of, ii. 388
Hydra, stands upon, iii. 430
Judah, of, ii. 377
Michael, corresponds to, i. 185; iii. 124
Paw of, strong grip of, iv. 152
Puma, and, iv. 360
Sacred animal, as a, ii. 159
Saint Mark, fire of, iii. 123
Scales, and three virgins, iii. 431
Six-pointed star, in, iv. 102
Solar, iv. 135
Virgin placed on a, ii. 384
LION-BIRD, Monstrous, iv. 189
LIONS, Fiery, i. 261
Life, of, i. 261
Toom luminous through two, ii. 398
LIP and word, Period of one, iv. 19
LIPI or writing, i. 166
LIPIKA, Assessors and, i. 166
Astral records, and, i. 165, 166; v. 546
Builders and, i. 165, 166, 168, 186
Circle guarded by, i. 189
Destiny, connected with, i. 166
Divine sons whose sons are, i. 104, 168
Errands, runs circular, i. 104, 168
Fohat, sons of, i. 104, 168
Groups of, three, i. 186
Humanity, and future of, i. 185
Karma, agents of, i. 165, 187, 214, 334
Lipi writing, derived from, i. 165
Mahārājahs and, four, i. 334
Middle wheel, in, i. 177
Occultists believe in, i. 166
Origin of, i. 168
Pass not guarded by, i. 189
Planetary spirits and, i. 168, 186
Recorders, or, i. 165, 187, 190; v. 546
Second seven who are, i. 165
Separate spirit and matter, i. 188
Spirits of universe, are, i. 186
Triangle, circumscribe, i. 104, 187
Wheel, in middle, i. 177
Writers or scribes, the, i. 165, 187
LIQUOR amnii in the womb, iii. 194
LIQUOR vitæ, ii. 256, 262
LITERA PYTHAGORAE as a symbol, v. 118
LITERATURE, Brāhmanical, v. 121
Classical, v. 121
Kabalistic, v. 176
LITHIUM, ii. 274
LITHOI, and combinations of Decad, ii. 34;
iii. 345
LITHOS our upright phallus, iii. 94
LITHUANIAN tribes, iii. 273
'LITTLE ALBERT', the, v. 122
LITURGY, Christian, v. 328
LIVER, work of, v. 544
LIVES, Alahim of, v. 116
Bodies built of, i. 272
Countless, in human tabernacle, i. 304
Crores of, numberless, i. 294
Dwellings for, no, iii. 28

Elements, of, i. 307, 332
Fiery, i. 306; iii. 125
Higher, i. 302
Immortal entity, of, iv. 122
Insects and small, iii. 63
Kosmos, of, ii. 89
Life and, i. 293
Life-germs produce other, i. 303
Manifested, i. 76, 189
Monads or, iii. 67
Myriads, of countless, i. 271, 305; ii. 332
Objective Consciousness and, v. 529
Periods, of first four, i. 295
Progress of countless, i. 311
Seven, and one, i. 283
Soul and body two, i. 280
Spiritual, ii. 360; iii. 171
Terrestrial, lowest, i. 271
Thriving without air, i. 294
Triangle and, i. 189
Universe of, i. 294
Unseen, surrounding us, ii. 333
LIVIA AUGUSTA and Delphic temple,
iv. 152
LIVING, Spirit of nature, ii. 61; iii. 117
Temple of God, v. 75
Tree of divine wisdom, i. 259
Word in Egypt, ii. 125
LIVING FIRE, ii. 58
First race had no, iii. 122
Light and, i. 246
Prometheus and, i. 245
Spirit of Light or, ii. 52
Thinking man needs, iii. 111
LIVING SOUL, Adam a, iii. 91; iv. 23
Bhūtāman or, iii. 117
Formation of a, i. 284
Man breathed into, iii. 158
Moses, and, i. 298
Serpent of evil has a, iii. 39
Vital or, i. 272
LIVY, referred to, v. 297
LIZARD, Evolution of, ii. 361
Megalosaurus and, iii. 200
Mesozoic times, and, iii. 161
New Zealand, with three eyes, iii. 298
Winged, iii. 66, 222, 260, 386
LOAF, Serpent round sacramental, iii. 218
LOB-NOR, Buried cities of, i. 56
LOBE, Middle, in ape, iv. 216
LOCALITY, Fall of third race, of, iv. 333
Garden of Eden, iii. 207
LOCALIZED PRAKRITI, iii. 76
LOCATION, Eden, of, iii. 207
World of illusion, only in this, ii. 329
LOCH-MARIA-KER in Morbihan, iv. 321
LOCI, Mystical, iii. 105
LOCKE, quoted, i. 75; ii. 340
LOCRIAN, Timaeus the, iv. 31
LODE-STAR, Draco ceased to be, iii. 44
Religion of Hindu-Aryan a, iv. 38
LODGES, Masonic, iii. 108; iv. 146; v. 273,
283
LODUR and creation of man, iii. 106
LOGAN or rocking-stones, iii. 342
LOGIC, Analogy of, iii. 161
Principles of inductive, ii. 200

LOGIC (*Contd.*)
Realm of probabilities and, ii. 336
Specialists ignore, ii. 208
Worlds, and invisible, ii. 331
LOGOGRAMS, Language by, iii. 335
Meaning of whole word in, ii. 19
LOGOGRAPHY, Occult, iii. 335
LOGOI, Antiquity of, i. 139
Builders, or, i. 146
Compound unit of, i. 291
Creative potencies, or, iv. 133
Deities and, male, i. 129
Dragon and, i. 140
Earth has seven, iv. 164
Elohim or collective, ii. 90
Evolution and, i. 233; iii. 311
First-born or, iii. 102
Fohat from, ii. 326
Hermetic philosophers, of, i. 195
Houses of, iv. 173
Incarnation of, iv. 84
Kosmos, in, iii. 41; v. 533
Life, of, ii. 296
Light, correlations of, ii. 150
Male-female, i. 139, 291
Minor, iii. 49
Nations, of all, ii. 192
Ophites, of, iii. 218
Pymander, of Western continent, i. 141
Religious systems, of, ii. 194
Self-born, ii. 79
Seven, i. 195; ii. 128; iii. 41; iv. 84, 133, 164, 173, 207
Sexual aspect of religions in, ii. 68
Spirit, endow men with, iii. 106
Sun, symbolized by, iii. 55
Three, ii. 168; v. 533, 534
Unmanifested, v. 214
World creative, in ideal, ii. 95
LOGOS, Absolute silent ALL, ii. 60
Adam Kadmon is, i. 161, 194, 231, 262, 291; ii. 147; iii. 49, 136, 137, 237; iv. 114
Ādi-Bhūta and, i. 193
Adversary, became, iii. 71
Agathodaemon or, ii. 126; iii. 71
Ahura Mazda and, iii. 236
Aja, is, iii. 79, 354; iv. 150, 174
Akasha mother-father of, iii. 399
ALL, of absolute silent, ii. 60
Amshaspends and, ii. 147; iv. 56
Androgynous, i. 139, 155; iii. 49, 219
Anima Mundi, or, i. 128; ii. 296
Anthropomorphized, iii. 414
Apex of Pythagorean triangle, iii. 37
Ar(r)hetos and sevenfold nature of, ii. 164
Atman is, i. 170
Avalokiteshvara or, i. 139, 169, 170, 188, 193; ii. 146, 147, 193; iii. 185; iv. 208
Basilides of, v. 462
Benevolent, iii. 71
Bhāva called, i. 301
Brahmā is, i. 75, 170, 194, 301; ii. 70, 96, 147, 152, 171; iii. 115, 137, 236, 249; iv. 196, 208; v. 476
Brāhmanical and Buddhist, i. 188; ii. 146; iv. 207, 208
B'raisheeth or, ii. 90

Buddha, supreme, i. 169; ii. 294
Buddhism, of, v. 374
Bull symbol of, iii. 416
Celestial, i. 291
Centre of unity, ii. 151
Christ, iii. 239; iv. 52
Christian, i. 188; iii. 239
Christos, is, i. 188, 192; iii. 233; iv. 46
Circle or, unifying, ii. 152
Conception, brought within range of our, ii. 147
Conception of one, i. 317
Conscious energy of, ii. 148
Cosmic, iii. 249; iv. 219
Cosmic, ideation called, i. 81; iii. 37
Cosmogony, of every, iv. 273
Create, desired to, iv. 59
Creation and being, in, iv. 46; v. 426
Creation, second, of, ii. 295
Creative, i. 169, 170, 264; ii. 171; iii. 237, 239
Creative deity, or, ii. 64
Creator, or, i. 301, 322; ii. 68, 70, 95, 146, 157; iii. 65
Crown, assumes form of, ii. 151
Daughter of, i. 194; ii. 145, 148
Deity, ii. 151
Demiurge, (Demiourgos) or, i. 170, 322; ii. 95; iii. 35, 38; iv. 46, 170; v. 270
Devas and, ii. 147
Devils subject to, iii. 233
Dhyān Chohans and, i. 322; ii. 147
Dianoia and, synonymous, iii. 38
Divine, iii. 48
Dorjechang, called, ii. 295
Dragon symbol of, ii. 139, 141; iii. 354
Duad or double-sexed, ii. 70
Dual, true, ii. 126; iii. 171
Dual man, or, iii. 49
Earth, self-active wisdom on, iii. 234
Eastern esotericism and, ii. 147
Ego reflected image of, iv. 164
Éliphas Lévi on, iv. 161
Elohim and, ii. 147
Emanation, first, ii. 90
Emanations not, by, iii. 65
Energies of, i. 195; iii. 311
Ennoia and Ophis are, iii. 219
Esoteric, ii. 339
Esoteric meaning of, iii. 38
Esoteric philosophy, in, ii. 95, 147
Ever-incarnating, iii. 59
Every creative, is host, iii. 239
Father and birth of first, ii. 66
Female, i. 139, 194; ii. 148; iii. 115; v. 291
Feminine word or, i. 125
Ferouer and, iv. 46
First, i. 81, 139; ii. 66, 96; iii. 136
First-born, i. 301; iii. 38; v. 213
First cause or, i. 80, 81, 262; ii. 123, 144; v. 187
Fohat and, i. 169, 194; iii. 399
Forms, has seven, iv. 207
Fravarshi, iv. 46
Generative light of, iii. 236
Genii presiding over, iii. 372
Gnostics, of, ii. 79, 126

LOGOS (Contd.)
Great unseen, iii. 311
Greek, i. 139, 141; iii. 46, 204
Gross matter and, v. 430
Heaven, in, iii. 234
Heaven-born, ii. 123
Heavenly man and, i. 285, 291; ii. 151; iii. 234, 237, 239, 411; iv. 114, 170, 196, 197
Higher Self, is, iii. 48, 234
Holy one or, iv. 59
Horus and, i. 192; ii. 62; iii. 236
Host of, i. 157; ii. 152; iii. 372, 411
Ideation of, ii. 150
Impersonal, i. 81
Incarnated, iv. 96
Individual consciousness as, iv. 239
Individualized, iii. 358
Intelligence, called, i. 82
Invisible, iii. 36
Invisible celibate, called, i. 264
Ishvara or, i. 188, 193, 194, 301; ii. 64, 146, 152, 296
Jesus and, i. 139
Jnāna or, i. 131
Jnāta or, ii. 146
Jupiter and, i. 139
Kabalistic, i. 231; ii. 147; iii. 49
Kakodaemon or, ii. 126
Kāma and, iv. 151
Krishna and, iii. 79, 233, 318
Kwan-Shi-Yin primordial, ii. 123, 171, 193, 195
Light and, i. 141, 193, 195, 263, 334; ii. 118, 147, 148, 150, 157; iii. 38, 49, 53, 233, 236, 399; iv. 273
Light of the, v. 189
Lord of all mysteries, ii. 295
Lucifer is, iii. 170
Mahā Buddhi, and, i. 82
Mahat and, i. 82; iv. 46
Male-female, i. 75
Manifestation of, i. 177
Manifested, i. 74, 81, 139, 140, 262, 263; ii. 118, 167; iii. 38, 49, 219, 311; iv. 164, 196, 197; v. 426, 445, 453, 459
Mercury as, iv. 112
Microprosopus and, i. 262, 263, 285; iv. 197
Mind, proceeded from, ii. 64
Mirror reflecting divine mind, iii. 38
Monad, or universal, ii. 339; iii. 311
Mother, i. 193; ii. 144, 148; iii. 399
Mūlaprakriti material to, ii. 146; iii. 37
Mystery of, iv. 58
Names of, iv. 58
Noumenon of matter, is, i. 82
Objective, iii. 36
Occultism on, i. 135; ii. 148, 297; iv. 219
Ogdoad as, ii. 166
One, i. 188, 317
One great unit, i. 145
Ophis manifested, iii. 219
Ophite Gnostics, of, ii. 126
Ormazd is, i. 173; ii. 147
Orphio-Christos or, ii. 79
Osiris, called, ii. 147
Padmapāni, called, iv. 208

Parabrahman and, i. 76; iii. 37
Pashyanti form of, i. 195; ii. 150
Paul called leader of, iv. 49
Personality, no, iii. 318
Pesh-Hun and, iii. 60
Planet, of each, iii. 38
Plato, of, i. 80, 262
Platonists, of, i. 170; iv. 114
Point within circle being, ii. 144, 340
Power of, ii. 148
Powers of seven, iii. 358
Prakriti and, i. 81
Pralaya, sleeps in, ii. 146, 147
Primeval divine thought, or, iv. 239
Prometheus symbol of, iii. 411
Purusha, called, i. 81; ii. 151
Pymander a, i. 141
Pythagorean, ii. 151, 338; iii. 37
Ray into spirit, a, i. 173
Rays, seven, of, v. 484
Reason, is, iii. 204
Revealed, ii. 339
Revealer of man, of God, iv. 161
Satan and, iii. 71, 170, 237
Second, i. 81, 139, 140, 262, 285; ii. 64, 66, 96, 167; iii. 35, 239; iv. 46, 114, 133, 139, 170; v. 455, 507
Second and third, v. 507
Self-born, iii. 354
Self-erected, v. 216
Self-existent Lord or, ii. 47
Serpent of wisdom and, iii. 414
Sevenfold, is, iii. 41; iv. 133, 208; v. 459
Seven rays of, v. 485
Sexless, iii. 49, 136
Shabda Brahman, ii. 146
Shakti, and its, ii. 195
Solar, ii. 168
Son or, ii. 261; iii. 239; iv. 193
Soul called Ptah, ii. 68
Sound and, i. 300; ii. 261, 263; iii. 399; iv. 133
Source of harmony, ii. 151
Speech, or, iii. 38, 204
Spirit, is, ii. 297
Spirit of the universe or, i. 81; iii. 37
Spirit-matter or, i. 81
Spiritual, i. 185
Spiritual angels and men collectively, iv. 56
Spiritual light radiating from, ii. 298
Subba Row on, i. 170, 188; ii. 64, 146, 147; iii. 311, 318
Sun and, i. 192; ii. 146; iii. 38; v. 332
Supra-conscious thought of, iii. 37
Supreme being or, ii. 123
Symbol of, i. 141, 262; iii. 354, 411, 416
Synthesis of the host, iii. 372
Synthesis of Seven Forces, v. 426
Tetragrammaton or, i. 139, 161, 285; iv. 170
That, and, ii. 144; iii. 311
Theologians, of, iv. 44
Third, i. 82; iii. 38; v. 476, 507, 519, 533, 558
Third man as, iii. 38
Unconscious, i. 81
Unconscious universal mind, the, iii. 37
Universal Buddhi, and, ii. 193

LOGOS (*Contd.*)
Universal monad, or, iii. 311
Universal principle, the, ii. 193; iii. 318
Universal world-soul, the, i. 82
Universe has its, every, iii. 38
Universe mirror of, iii. 38, 192
Unmanifested, i. 81, 140, 262, 263, 320; ii. 47; iii. 49; iv. 168; v. 214, 426, 430, 431, 455, 476
Unseen, iii. 311
Vāch, and, iii. 204
Vajradhāra or, ii. 295
Vedāntins of, iv. 174
Vedas and, iv. 151
Venus mother of, iii. 416
Verbum or, i. 139, 188, 193, 194, 300; ii. 146, 147, 261; iii. 38; iv. 112
Virgin of the world, and, iii. 234
Vishnu first, ii. 96
Visible, iii. 36; v. 322
Wisdom is, i. 131; iii. 233, 234
Word, or, i. 74, 145, 157, 161, 300; ii. 60, 64, 66, 125, 194, 339; iii. 38, 49, 170; iv. 49, 112; v. 229, 234, 327, 442, 475
World has its, every, iii. 38
Zeus and, i. 139
LOGOS-SOUL called Ptah, ii. 68
LOHANS, Adepts, v. 39, 393, 394
Hall of five hundred, v. 394
LOHITA is Kartikeya, the Red, iii. 55, 133
LOHITANGA, or Mars, iii. 42.
LOKA, Brahma, v. 353
Kāma, v. 353, 359, 501, 527, 559, 566, 567
LOKA CHAKSHUH, or eye of the world, i, 162; iii. 35; v. 283
LOKALOKA, in Mount Atlas, iii. 402
LOKANATHA, or Lokapati lord of the world, iii. 186
LOKAPALAS, or eight points of compass, i. 186; iv. 148
LOKAS, Atala and nether, iii. 401
Brāhmans, of, v. 356
Categories of, v. 537, 541
Devachans or, ii. 398
Divine and Terrestrial, v. 541
Elementals, of, v. 540
Fourteen, v. 356, 421, 539, 541
Hot and cold, i. 253
Inhabitants of, v. 542
Names of various, iii. 321
Rings and circles called, i. 253
Seven, iii. 237; v. 410, 421, 539, 541, 559
Spheres or, iii. 372
Stanza I, mentioned in, iii. 27, 56
Talas, v. 543, 545
Vedantic, v. 538, 539
Voice to other, raise thy, iii. 27, 56
LOKI, Moon hidden in, ii. 118
Odin, brother of, iii. 285
Scandinavia of, iii. 285; iv. 54
Water, fire god hidden in, ii. 118
LOLO Language, MSS. of the, iii. 282
LONGITUDE, Moon at time of Kali Yuga, of, ii. 388
Stars marked by Hindus, of, ii. 388
Sun and moon at Hindu epoch, of, ii.387, 389
LOOMS, Neolithic, iv. 284

LORD, Beings, of, v. 232, 233
God, v. 234, 239
Heaven, of, v. 129
Hosts of, v. 318
Īshvara, the, v. 350
Jehovah, v. 242
Kabalistic, v. 90
Lords, of, v. 314
Sheep, of, v. 104
Spirits of, v. 101
Splendour and Light, v. 81
LORDS, Beings, of, v. 356
Flame, of the, v. 258
Hierophants, v. 185
LORIS of HAECKEL, iv. 237
LOST ARTS, mementoes of, iii. 428
Post-diluvian forefathers of, iii. 428
LOST WORD, v. 395, 406
LOTUS, Astral light, and, i. 132
Brahma universe, containing, iv. 40
Bud of, i. 131, 132
Buddha and, v. 476
Christian Symbol, in, v. 117
Construction of seeds of, ii. 94
Cosmos, symbol for, i. 128
Flower of power, is, iii. 422
Generation, symbol of, ii. 96; iii. 186
Genesis, idea in, ii. 96
Glyphs, ii. 77
Holy of Holies, symbol of, iv. 40
Hor rising from, ii. 82
Isis holding a, ii. 81; v. 117
Jewel in the, v. 418, 419, 420, 421, 453
Lily replaces in Europe as symbol, v. 117
Lord of, iii. 27, 56
Man like, i. 235
Padma or golden, i. 127; ii. 84; iv. 149
Sacred, ii. 68; v. 117
Seeds of, i. 127; ii. 94, 96
Seven leaved, v. 550
Symbol, as a universal, ii. 94
Symbolizes Earth, Water and Fire, v. 117
Trimūrti, symbol of, v. 117
Vishnu growing from, iii. 43; v. 233, 476
Vishnu with, ii. 81; iii. 43
Water and heat, product of, i. 127; ii. 95
Womb, symbol of, ii. 96, 100
Worship and exoteric, ii. 96
LOTUS-BEARER, Padmapāni Chenresi, iii. 185, 186
LOTUS-BORN, Abjayoni or, ii. 87
LOTUS-FLOWER of Buddha, iv. 117
LOTUS-FLOWERS, Solar Gods, and, ii. 100
Symbols, as, ii. 72
LOTUS-LEAF, Brahma poised on, ii. 59
LOTUS-LEAVES, Seeds, concealed in the, ii. 95
Shveta-dvīpa, of, iii. 327
LOTUSES, Garland of seven, iii. 58
India and Egypt, of, iv. 40
LOVE, C. E., Theory of Forces of, v. 221
LOVE, Mother, v. 545
Wisdom of, v. 265
LOWER DECAD, v. 436
LOWER EGO, v. 490, 557, 563
Consciousness of, v. 519
Responsibility of, v. 551

LOWER MANAS, v. 436, 441, 457, 464, 485, 490, 492, 494, 496, 498, 514, 516, 517, 518, 532, 539, 547, 548, 549, 554, 555, 556, 558, 563, 564
Bhurloka begins with, v. 549
Degrees of, v. 517
Emanation of Higher, v. 551
Fall of, v. 449
Ray of, v. 553, 564
Triad reflected in, v. 516
LOWER SELF, v. 78, 410
LOYOLA, sons of, v. 95
LUCIAN, quoted, iii. 287; iv. 329; v. 44, 242, 253, 334
LUCIANISTS, iii. 242
LUCIFER, v. 309, 310, 312
Christ, as, iv. 110
Crescent-like horns of, ii. 44
Day-star, genius of, iv. 69
Devil and, i. 138
Earth, light-bearer, or, iii. 45
Hindu, iii. 240
Lightbearer or, iv. 82
Loki and, iii. 284
Mahāsura or Hindu, iv. 240
Power of, v. 309
Prometheus and, iii. 240
Satan or, iii. 120, 233
Sophia resides in, iv. 81
Star of, i. 138; ii. 154
Ushanas-Shukra is our, iii. 57
Venus or, iii. 44, 57; iv. 81
Venus said to be, iii. 42
Verbum, one with, iv. 84
Wheels of, v. 55
LUCIFERIANS, iii. 242
LUDOLPH, Father of Ethiopian literature, iv. 101
LUGRUB, Secret volume of, v. 399
LULLY, Raymond, v. 114, 282
LUMAZI, Seven, v. 202
LUMINOUS, Augoeides, v. 427
Egg, v. 426
LUNACY, proceeds from the Moon, v. 155
Study of, v. 531
LUNAR Disc, v. 334
Pitris, v. 472
LUNATICS, conscious on the Astral plane, v. 526
LUNG-SHU the Nāgārjuna of China, i. 130
LUNI-SOLAR YEAR, Emblem of, iii. 86
LUNUS, God, i. 275
Khonsoo God, iv. 32
LUN-YU, Chinesische Literatur, quoted by Max Muller, i. 59
LUTAUD, Dr. on Pasteur's theory, iii. 158
LUXOR, Unfading colours of, iii. 428
LUZ, Huschenk built city of, iii. 395
LY, a Dhyān Chohan, iii. 282
LYBIA, iv. 339
LYNCEUS killed by Pollux, iii. 131
LYRA NEBULA, ii. 322
LYRE, Seven Stringed of Apollo, v. 275, 276, 459

M

M. Derivation of letter, ii. 99, 100; iii. 75; v. 500, 506

MA., ii. 99; iv. 149
MACCABEUS, Judas, v. 185
MACE of Thor, v. 289
MACHAIRODUS latidens, the, iv. 320
MACRAUCHENIDÆ and ungulate mammals, iv. 305
MACROCOSM, v. 32, 78, 188, 322, 425, 459, 516
Decad applied to, iv. 144
Dual character of, i. 325
Egg of, v. 486
Hexagon star and, i. 271
Makaram and, iv. 148
Man a, iii. 184
Man and, v. 78
Microcosm and, i. 233, 311, 325; ii. 57, 318; iii. 177, 184; iv. 255; v. 300, 420, 510, 556
Miniature copy of, i. 317
Septenary constitution of, i. 222; v. 208, 477
MACROCOSMOS, Chaos and, i. 325
Deities of, iv. 210
MACROPROSOPUS, Abstraction, an, ii. 65
Ain, called, iv. 197
Ancient one, or, i. 129
Brow of, i. 284
Concealed, i. 144
Face, great, i. 129
Hua applied to, i. 144
Logos, the, ii. 65
Negatively existent, iv. 197
Square, perfect, iv. 197
Tetragrammaton, is, iv. 197
MADAGASCAR, iii. 20, 226, 266, 318, 324; iv. 357
MADDENA Nag, of Chaldeans, iv. 329; v. 267
MADEIRA and Atlantis, iv. 350, 359
MADHAVA and Madhavi, titles of Gods, ii. 100
MADHU, v. 345
MADHUSŪDHANA, quoted, ii. 123
MADHYA, Definition of, i. 195
MADHYAMĀ, i. 195; ii. 150, 258
MADHYAMIKAS, Paramārtha of, i. 116, 120
MĀDHYANTIKA, v. 394
MADURESE, Skull of the, iv. 92
MAGADHA, Cheta cave in, i. 44
Dynasty of, iii. 224
MAGAN, Diorite brought from, iii. 229
MAGAS, Caste of the, iii. 322
MĀGHA, v. 343, 344
Rishis in, iv. 120
MAGHĀYANTI one of the Pleiades, iv. 121
MAGI, v. 60, 232, 314
Ancient, v. 146
Aryan, iii. 355
Bactrian Caves, in, v. 65
Chaldean, i. 49; iii. 323, 393; v. 314, 333
Democritus pupil of, i. 176
Druids called, iv. 325
Egyptian, iii. 426
Fire worshippers and, i. 146
Occult literature of, i. 49
Orsi of, iv. 173
Persian, iv. 325
Sacred fires of, iv. 329; v. 267
Seven Devas of, ii. 301
Space and time and, v. 202
Star of, ii. 380

MAGI (*Contd.*)
Three, ii. 380
Xerxes, of, ii. 188
Yima and, iv. 180
MAGIANS, Babylon of, v. 279
Cologne cathedral and, ii. 380
Mazdeans and, iii. 97, 101; iv. 182
Origin of Evil on, iv. 58
Religion, iii. 101
Sacred books, i. 60
System, v. 302
MAGIC Agent, Astral light is, v. 120
Agneyastra, iii. 425; iv. 129
Ancient Alchemy and, ii. 305; v. 44, 170
Antiquity of, v. 42, 62
Arcanum, i. 299
Black, i. 298; ii. 188; iii. 143, 363; v. 37, 38, 47, 49, 62, 85, 91, 118, 123, 249, 256, 279, 329, 430, 450, 451, 458, 469, 470, 482, 485, 510
Blended with religion, v. 42
Book of, given to Charlemagne, v. 122
Cautious move towards, iv. 241
Ceremonial, i. 73, 280; iv. 241, 317; v. 48
Chaldean, ii. 378; iii. 148; v. 42
China, in, v. 38, 39
Church and, v. 132
Cyprian and, v. 173
Dangers of, v. 85-92
Democritus on, v. 44
Diabolic, v. 60
Divine, v. 48, 49, 60, 118, 125, 255, 279, 306, 344
Druids and, v. 306
Dual power of, v. 85
Egypt of, iii. 366; v. 42, 243-257, 332
Fifth race, during, i. 243
Great, agent, i. 299
Greece, of, iii. 366
History, and, v. 257
Incantations, iv. 331
India, in, v. 41
Infernal, iv. 151
Initiation into, ii. 195
Invention of, iii. 215
Jewish, v. 231
Mahā Vidyā or, i. 222
Mathematics meant, v. 65, 90, 114
Meaning of, v. 444
Mexican, v. 43
Mirrors, iii. 186, 375
Not Superstition, v. 44
Numbers and, v. 114
Occultism and, v. 447
Odin, and, v. 42
Offshoots of, v. 45
Old as man, v. 42
Origin of, v. 57-63
Papyri and Stelae full of, v. 244, 332
Passions personified by, iii. 379
Phenomena and, v. 244
Philosophy and, v. 59
Practical, v. 42, 50, 85, 217
Psychic, v. 80
Pythagoras and, v. 279
Roman Catholics and, v. 42, 45
Satan and, v. 51

Satanic, v. 125
School of, v. 253
Sound, agent, ii. 185
Spiritual, v. 80
Stonehenge and, v. 47
Syro-Chaldean, ii. 131
Tantrikas and, v. 185
Thot-Hermes, inventor of, iii. 215
Tibet, in, v. 39
Unconscious, v. 132
Use and abuse of, v. 61
What it is, v. 444-453
White, iii. 215, 363, 425; iv. 63, 211; v. 38, 49, 118, 123, 244, 249, 468, 487, 489
Work, seventh, of, v. 326
Works on, v. 185, 198
Zoroaster reformer of, v. 42
MAGICAL Texts, v. 198, 199
MAGICIAN (S), v. 327, 333
Black, v. 48, 170, 456, 479
Menander, a, v. 450
Natural, v. 81
Simon the, v. 79, 130
MAGIQUE, Grand agent, i. 298
MAGISM, Babylonian, i. 77
MAGNA GRECIA, v. 264
MAGNETIC influences, v. 49
MAGNETISM, Biune creative, ii. 122
Cosmic, i. 201; ii. 220
Elementals and, i. 201
Hypnotism and, v. 460
Key to, v. 460
Motion, not a mode of, i. 203; ii. 241
Origin of, iv. 225
Seven forms of, i. 201
Solar, v. 220
Substance, a, cause of, ii. 239
Terrestrial, iv. 132
MAGNETIZER, Nerve-aura and fluid of, ii. 52
MAGNOLIA in ancient Greenland, iii. 24; iv. 295
MAGNUM Mysterium, i. 326; iv. 80, 81
MAGNUS ÆTHER, Collective aggregate of, ii. 44
MAGNUS LIMBUS or Yliaster of Paracelsus, i. 326
MAGUS, Chaldean, v. 382
The, see SIMON
MAGUS AND MAGNES of Theurgists, ii. 52
MAHĀ Chohans, iii. 224, 368; v. 390
Great Ones, iii. 283
Pralaya, i. 192, 196, 206, 225, 262; ii. 86, 89, 275; iii. 154, 310; iv. 119
MAHĀ-ATMĀ (See also Mahātmā), ii. 81, 182
MAHĀ-DEVA, iii. 94; iv. 118, 163
MAHĀ-GURU, i. 256; v. 352
MAHĀ-KALPA, v. 41, 363, 365, 367
MAHĀ-LOKA, Progenitors reascend to, iii. 101
MAHĀ-MANVANTARA, i. 76, 77, 115; iii. 89; iv. 174; v. 493, 568
MAHADEO KUNTE, Prof., ii. 60
MAHALALEEL and CAINAN, iii. 390
MAHĀPURUSHA OR PARAMĀTMAN, Supreme spirit, iii. 117
MAHAR-LOKA, ii. 87; iii. 321; v. 537, 542
MAHĀRĀJAS, Four, i. 181, 184; ii. 95, 124; iii. 425; v. 439, 542

MAHĀ SHANKARA, v. 376, 377, 378
MAHASURA the Hindu Lucifer, iii. 240
MAHAT, Ahamkāra, progeny of, i. 304
    Aham-ship becomes, i. 142
    Ākāsha and, i. 301; v. 519
    Alaya and, v. 499, 528, 558
    Anima Mundi, is, ii. 296
    Bhāva, called, i. 301
    Brahmā-Creator, first product of, i. 263
    Buddhi and, i. 301; ii. 88, 173
    Cause of all things, i. 301
    Chit, root of, i. 330
    Cognition, universal, i. 142
    Collective, iii. 88
    Cosmic ideation, is, i. 82
    Cosmic Intelligence, v. 471
    Cosmic noumenon of matter, i. 82
    Cosmic principle of, iv. 185
    Creation and, i. 142; ii. 173, 174
    Creative power or, ii. 170
    Creator, is, i. 301
    Divine Ideation, v. 447, 493
    Divine intellect or, i. 330; v. 423
    Divine intelligence, is ii. 296
    Divine mind, the, i. 301; ii. 169; iii. 88; iv. 82
    Divine principle is, iv. 82
    Divine thought, i. 141
    Earth and, i. 301
    Egoism called, i. 142
    Egoism, progeny of, i. 304
    Emanation from, iv. 46
    Esoteric philosophy, in, i. 330
    First, was, ii. 170
    First-born, the, i. 131, 301
    Gnosis, first-born of, i. 131
    God, is, i. 131; ii. 327
    Great soul, or, ii. 138
    Highest entity, v. 528
    Hyle and, iv. 171
    Incarnating spirits of, iii. 233
    Indra and, iv. 185
    Intellectual, understanding or, iii. 377
    Intellectual, world of, iii. 377; iv. 171
    Intelligence, is, i. 82, 131, 268; ii. 44, 88, 169, 296; iv. 82
    Intelligent soul or, ii. 260
    Īshvara called, i. 301; ii. 170
    Jnāna, first-born of, i. 131
    Kosmos, or third plane of, v. 513
    Law, operating, ii. 170
    Logos and, i. 82, 131, 141, 301; ii. 64, 296; iv. 46
    Lord, called, i. 142
    Lower kingdoms, of, ii. 174
    Manas and, i. 142; ii. 173; iii. 302, 377, 412; v. 471, 519, 529, 531, 533
    Mānasaputra born of, iii. 174
    Manifested wisdom, is, i. 170
    Matih synonym for, iii. 412
    Matter and, i. 131; ii. 170
    Mens or, ii. 170
    Mind or, i. 122, 326; ii. 88; v. 513
    Mot or Mut and, ii. 170
    Mundane soul or, iii. 377
    Nature and, i. 301; ii. 88
    Nous and, ii. 64, 170; iv. 171
    Occultists and, i. 122

    Omniscience, is, iii. 69
    Outer boundary of universe, the, i. 301
    Parabrahman, reflection of, i. 131
    Parabrahmic Mind, v. 513
    Plane of, ii. 298
    Pradhāna and, i. 131, 263, 301; iii. 69
    Prakriti, i. 131, 301; ii. 49, 88
    Primordial evolution and, ii. 169
    Primordial matter and, iii. 69
    Principle of, i. 326; iii. 69
    Progeny of, i. 304
    Psyche and, iv. 171
    Rākshasas devour, iii. 171
    Reflection of, iii. 90
    Sat or, iii. 69
    Secondary creation of, i. 142
    Self-consciousness, develops, i. 142
    Seven females, one of, iv. 210
    Shiva, manifests as, i. 141
    Sons of, iii. 111
    Soul, universal intelligent, ii. 260
    Spirit of universal soul, ii. 169
    Spirit, vehicle of, ii. 138
    Spirits of, iii. 233
    Supreme, operating will of, ii. 170
    T'Agathon and, iv. 171
    Third Logos and, v. 519, 533, 558
    Thought, or, i. 141
    Tree trunk of, ii. 260
    Understanding or, i. 141
    Undifferentiated matter, i. 263
    Universal, iii. 97, 302
    Universal cognition or, i. 142
    Universal mind or Intellect, or, i. 122, 141, 263, 268, 326; ii. 88; iii. 69, 88, 171, 235
    Universal world-soul, i. 82
    Vaishnavas, with, ii. 170
    Vishnu appears as, i. 141
    Wisdom, is, i. 131
    World-soul or, i. 82
MAHĀTALA, v. 538, 540, 541
MAHĀTMĀ(S), v. 27, 282, 409
MAHAT-TATTVA, the universal soul, ii. 165, 169
MAHĀ VISHNU, v. 168, 350
MAHĀYĀNA School, i. 112, 120, 121, 213; iii. 46; iv. 208; v. 365, 366, 399; 401
MAHĀYOGI, or great ascetic, ii. 178; iv. 118, 156, 184
MAHĀ YUGA, v. 339, 346
MAHOMET, iii. 208; iv. 31
MAILLET, quoted, iv. 216
MAIMONIDES, Rabbi, quoted, ii. 110; iii. 142; iv. 22, 24; v. 66, 238, 252
MAITREYA, Brahma, body of, iii. 68
    Buddha, ii. 99, 192; v. 169, 337, 412
    Dvīpas, iii. 162
    Indian Asclepios, i. 328
    Parāshara and, ii. 88, 164, 186; iii. 322
MAKARA, Amphibious animal, iii. 353; iv. 147
    Tenth zodiacal sign, i. 266, 267, 279; ii. 91, 99, 149; iii. 102, 271, 353; iv. 147, 149, 150, 151
MAKARA-Ketu is Aja Kāma, the, iv. 150
MALABAR, Field of death, in, iii. 346
MALACCA and Polynesia, iii. 226

MALACHIM or messengers, ii. 60, 159, 183;
   iii. 374; iv. 83; v. 326
MALAY race, iii. 327, 331
MALAYAK, messengers, angels, etc., iv. 83
MALAYAN Archipelago and Lemuria, iii. 226;
   iv. 356
MALAYANS and Chinamen, iii. 185
MALAYS and Australians, iv. 348
MALE, Creator, v. 192
   God, v. 190, 191, 192, 228, 233
   Parent, v. 202
   Power, v. 165, 278
   Principle of Nature, v. 129
MALE-female Creator, v. 426
MALECH, Melech or Moloch, v. 326
MA-LI-GA-SI-MA, Chinese lost continent, iii. 364
MALKUTH, the earth, called bride of heavenly
   man, i. 249, 263, 284, 285, 286; iv. 167, 197;
   v. 418
MALLET, Grand-master's, iii. 108
   Masonic, and Svastika, iv. 126
MALTA, Cave deposits at, iii. 223; iv. 291
MAMMALIA, mode of birth, v. 559
MAN, Adamic, v. 204
   Age of, iii. 77
   Ancestors and, i. 232, 237; iii. 95
   Androgyne, v. 556
   Animal, v. 472
   Animal creation and, i. 238
   Ape and, gap between old, iv. 237
   Apes and, i. 237, 238, 241
   Archetypal, ii. 70; v. 233
   Awakening of consciousness in, i. 258
   Beginning of conscious life, at, iii. 292
   Canstadt, iv. 314
   Creative powers in, iii. 408
   Cross and, Origin of, v. 152
   Descent from, iv. 252
   Dhyān Chohans and, iii. 117
   Divine, v. 449, 487
   Dual nature of, iii. 40, 49
   Earth, and, iii. 252; v. 456
   Elementary, ii. 290
   Elohim, child of, i. 272
   Engis, iv. 314
   Ethereal, iii. 156
   Evolution of real, i. 228
   Evolution previous to, i. 86
   Exoteric religions regard woman as inferior to,
   i. 193
   Fall of, i. 243; iii. 180, 209, 231; v. 248, 272
   First round, i. 214, 239; iii. 192
   Fourth round form, i. 214
   Genesis of, iii. 136
   God created, iii. 18
   God in, v. 79, 131, 453
   Heavenly, i. 291, 293; ii. 51, 337; iii. 38, 112,
   239, 292; iv. 167, 170, 177, 197; v. 187
   215, 230, 322, 419, 426, 507
   Heavenly or Sephira, i. 194, 263
   Heir of highest Aeon, v. 449
   Hierarchies, and, i. 319
   Higher self in, iii. 111
   Incomplete, i. 293
   Incorporeal, i. 139
   Inner, iii. 119; iv. 48
   Jah-Hovah, and, i. 172

Jiva is complete in, i. 271
Kārmic ancestor, and, v. 350
Kumāras, and, ii. 178
Lion, iv. 135
Lower Decad is, v. 436
Lower principle of, i. 226
Macrocosm and Microcosm within, v. 419, 510
Madagascar tradition concerning, iii. 184
Mammals, and, iii. 15, 163, 176, 187, 190, 193;
   iv. 206, 238, 253, 258
Manifested Prism, v. 456
Microcosm of the universe, i. 230
Nature of consciousness in, iv. 220
Neanderthal, iv. 314
Origin of, i. 278; iv. 215, 236; v. 42
Outwardly an animal, i. 280
Palaeolithic, iv. 284
Physical, iii. 274
Physical body of, changes in, i. 306
Physical evolution of, ii. 361; iv. 229
Prajāpatis, progenitors of, v. 233
Pre-Natal, iii. 37
Primeval, iii. 89, 195; iv. 245
Primordial word, iv. 130
Principles of, v. 208, 361, 366, 426, 435, 528,
   533, 534
Product of nature, iv. 297
Progenitors of, iii. 97
Quaternary and Ternary, iv. 147
Real is invisible, i. 231
Ruled woman in alchemy, v. 430
" Satan ", i. 248
Saviour, iii. 418
Self consciousness in, i. 243
" Senseless " anthropoids the product of,
   i. 236
Septenary, iv. 211; v. 357
Seven senses in, i. 158; iii. 16
Seventh creation, ii. 164
Seventh principle in, v. 270
Shadow of silent watcher, i. 308
Sixth principle, in, i. 178
Son of, v. 131, 190, 291
Sons of, v. 103, 129
Sorrows, of, v. 360
Special creation for, iv. 248
Spirit and matter in, iii. 187
Spirit-soul body, i. 172
Spiritual, v. 426, 438, 457
Spiritual ancestors of, iii. 179
Spiritual evolution of, ii. 363
Storehouse of all seeds of life, iii. 291
Svastika applied to, iii. 108
Symbolism of crucified, iv. 131
Tabernacle or Temple of God, v. 76, 82,
   84
Tends to become God, i. 214
Third race, iii. 169
Tree is, symbolically, v. 510
Triple nature of, v. 361
Twofold, ii. 169
Ultimate form on earth, i. 235
Under karmic law, i. 244
Universe, and, v. 419
Upādhis in, v. 361
Vara, or, iii. 292
Will of, v. 428

MAN-animal, iii. 264
MAN-bearing, Eggs, iii. 141
  Worlds, i. 221; ii. 360; iv. 269
MAN-fish, v. 163
MAN-GOD, v. 270
MAN-swan, Hamsa or, iii. 139
  Third, of the later, iii. 30
MANAS, Affinities of, ii. 47; iii. 243
  Agent of transmission, iii. 68
  Akāsha, corresponds to and proceeds from, i. 78
  Akhu, and, iv. 203
  Aspects of, iii. 182
  Ātma, Buddhi and, v. 421, 503, 514, 515, 519, 558
  Brahman the Self, not the, iv. 210
  Buddhi and Kāma, connected with, iv. 185; v. 490, 491, 521
  Buddhi, light of, and, i. 290, 545
  Buddhi-, v. 438, 441, 451, 482, 493, 496, 497, 506, 508, 533, 555
  Buddhi, upādhi of, i. 163
  Castor and Pollux, and, iii. 131
  Chit quality of, i. 330
  Colour Correspondence, v. 441, 485
  Conscious soul or, i. 292; iv. 89
  Consciousness, necessary for, on earthly plane, iii. 131; v. 531
  Degrees of, v. 516
  Development of, iii. 169, 175, 257, 302
  Dhyānis endow third race with, iii. 58
  Divine aspect, of, iii. 417
  Divine swallow, called, i. 274
  Dragon of wisdom, i. 266
  Dual, ii. 47; iv. 64, 185, 210; v. 427, 441, 488, 489, 494
  Ego, the higher, iii. 89, 244; iv. 159, 203; v. 471, 486, 494
  Experiences accumulated by, i. 233
  Fallen angel, iv. 82
  Fifth principle, iii. 97, 131, 175, 244, 277; iv. 148, 165; v. 84, 300, 323
  Fifth round, full development in, iii. 302
  Fires of, v. 482, 517
  Function of, v. 494
  Higher, ii. 293; iii. 89, 120, 410; iv. 210; v. 441, 457, 458, 464, 488, 496, 511, 516, 518, 539, 543, 547, 549, 551, 555, 556, 557, 563, 574
  Higher Ego, or, v. 471
  Honir and, iii. 106
  Human plane, on, ii. 173
  Human soul, i. 163, 209, 266; iii. 277; iv. 168; v. 423, 472, 490
  Indra is, in its dual aspect, iii. 185
  Intellect, ii. 173; iii. 58, 106, 377
  Kāma and, iii. 88, 257, 411, 417; iv. 185; v. 501, 508, 512, 521, 539
  Kosmic Consciousness and, v. 524
  Lords of Wisdom and, iii. 410
  Lower, v. 441, 457, 458, 464, 471, 488, 494, 496, 497, 499, 500, 511, 514, 516, 518, 519, 529, 532, 535, 539, 542, 543, 547, 548, 549; 551, 555, 556, 557, 562, 564
  Mahat and, i. 142; ii. 173; iii. 302, 377, 412; v. 471, 493, 519, 528, 531, 533
  Mind or, i. 266, 287, 322; ii. 47, 48, 344; iii. 68, 106, 121, 235; iv. 168, 180; v. 77, 472

Mind-consciousness, as, ii. 43
Mind-Ego, v. 483
Mindless, given by Mānasaputras to, iv. 180
Monad conjoined with, i. 284, 290; iii. 250
Monad, conscious principle of, iii. 119
Moon and, iv. 64, 210
Nephesh and, i. 287, 288, 290
Nirmānakāya of Rudra-Kumāras, iii. 257
Passions, drawn into sphere of, i. 290
Pineal gland and, v. 521
Pivot, iii. 244
Plane of, iv. 306
Pralaya, withdrawn at, v. 558
Pranidhāna, lords of, endowers, of, iii. 97
Primeval man lacked, iii. 89
Ray of, v. 511, 512, 513, 539, 558, 564
Ray of World-Soul, v. 558
Seb, corresponds with, iv. 203
Septenary, v. 517
Sex and, i. 292
Solar angels endowers of, iii. 97
Solar portion of, iv. 64
Soma and, iv. 64
Sons of, v. 471
Sophia is, iii. 277
Soul, chief, iv. 64
Spirit and matter, link between, iii. 106
Spiritual mind upper portion of, i. 159; v. 489
Sun and, iv. 210
Sun, spirit of visible, endowed by, iii. 243
Sūtrātma, or, iv. 82
Taijasi, v. 427
Third soul, iv. 287
Triple, ii. 48; iii. 257
Understanding or, iii. 101
Unites with child at seventh year, v. 483, 488
Universal active intelligence, corresponds to, iv. 168
Vehicle of Monad or God, v. 84
MANAS-EGO, iii. 244
MANAS-LESS race, iii. 318
MĀNASA, Devas, iii. 107; iv. 94
  Sambhūti the divine, iii. 98
  Sons of wisdom, iii. 31, 178
MĀNASA-Dhyānis, intellectual evolution represented by, i. 233
MĀNASA-Pitris, iv. 94
MĀNASA-Putras, Hindu, iii. 373; v. 204, 438, 513, 532, 546
  Mahat or Brahma, born of, iii. 174; v. 513
  Mind-born sons or, ii. 267, 295; iv. 196
  Nārada as a, iii. 59
  Plane of, i. 232
  Reincarnating Ego called, v. 471
  Sons of wisdom, iv. 180; v. 204, 438, 471
MĀNASAS or Rājasas, iii. 98
MANASIC atoms, v. 513
  Body, v. 518
  Consciousness, v. 531
  Entity, v. 528
  Expansion, v. 511
  Perceptions, v. 548
  Plane, v. 554
  Principle, v. 511
  Ray, v. 513

MANASVIN the wise, iii. 99
MANAVAH, Chatvārah and, iii. 148
MANCHURIA, iii. 327
MANCO-Capac of Peru, iii. 365
MAND or Manth implies rotatory motion,
  iii. 411
MANDĀKINI the heavenly Ganges, ii. 100
MANDALA, ii. 100
MANDARA used by Gods to churn the ocean,
  ii. 100; v. 287
MANDEVILLE, Sir J., on giants, iv. 324
MANDRAGORA the mandrake of the *Bible*,
  iii. 40
MANEE, Lapland corpses called, iv. 343
MANES, v. 116, 132, 170, 251
  Annihilated, will be, i. 274
  Arnobius, of, iii. 152
  Dead men, or, iv. 343
  Deified shades of the dead, or, i. 282
  Development of, iii. 366
  Dynasties of, v. 257
  Exoteric dualism of, iv. 78
  Kabiri or Titans called, iii. 151, 359
  Religion of, iii. 373
  Reign over men, i. 309
  Third race, of, iii. 433
  Worship of, v. 148
MANES the Paraclete, v. 170
MANETHO, v. 257
  Dynasties, on the divine, iii. 366
  Magic and, v. 58
  Synchronistic tables of, i. 50; iii. 391; iv. 263
  Vindication of, iii. 366
MANIA, Kabiri, mother of, iii. 151
  Manes and, of Arnobius, iii. 152
MANICHEISM, iii. 241
MANI KAH-'BUM, v. 392
MANIPURA, King of, iii. 218
MANJUSHRĪ, Bodhisattvas or, iii. 46
MANKIND, Saviour of, v. 156
MANOJAVA, Indra as, iv. 186
MANOMAYAKOSHA of the Vedanta, i. 212
MANSAROVARA, Lake, Seven swans of, ii. 72;
  v. 399, 520
MANTEIA, v. 452
MANTRAS, Articulate Speech or, v. 189
  Hindu, ii. 348
  Incantations or, ii. 185
  Magical, i. 157; v. 394
  Rig Vedic, ii. 154, 160
  Vāch or, v. 189, 394
  Word made flesh, v. 230
MANU (as word) Analysis of word, i. 132
  Derivation of, ii. 171; iv. 343
  Initial letter of, ii. 100
  Nous, mind, or, i. 141
  Thinker, i. 106, 283; ii. 168; iii. 99
MANU (as a Being), v. 244, 291, 382
  Ark of, iii. 147
  Brahmā as, v. 190
  Chakshusa, of sixth period, iv. 186
  Cosmogenesis of, ii. 46
  Descent into generation of every, iii. 321
  Father of, iii. 256
  First Race and, v. 291
  Hindu, i. 245
  Ildabaoth, copy of, ii. 168

Illusion, of, iii. 68
Mania, female, iii. 151
Monad of, emanation of, iii. 311
Offspring of, iii. 155
Paternal grandfathers of, iii. 171
Progenitor of, iv. 239
Reign of, iii. 321
Seed of life, iii. 154
Son of first, iii. 369
Sub-race, in each, iv. 186
Svāyambhuva, calf called, ii. 113
Svāyambhuva, Dhyanic energies are, collect-
  ively, ii. 171
Svāyambhuva, heavenly, iii. 137
Svāyambhuva, son of, iii. 308
Svāyambhuva, synthesis of Prajāpatis, iv. 274
Svāyambhuva, Vāch-Shata-Rupa, daughter of,
  iii. 156
Thinking, v. 487
Thought divine, personified idea of, i. 132
Vaivasvata, iii. 48, 147, 149, 150, 153, 154, 155;
  iv. 169, 180, 181; v. 190
MANU-antara, Manvantara or, i. 132
MANUS, Appearance of, in different characters,
  iii. 366
  Crown, seven issues from, ii. 151
  Earlier times of, v. 201
  Fathers, Patriarchs, Pitris, v. 201, 202
  Flames called, iii. 250
  Forty-nine, iv. 188
  Four preceding, iii. 318
  Fourteen, i. 291; ii. 86; iii. 79; iv. 195
  Genealogies of, iii. 250
  Generations from, iii. 229
  Generic name of, iii. 311
  God or creator, each of, i. 132
  Hindus, of, iii. 423; v. 346
  Humanity, of primeval, iii. 308
  Individualities of, mixed, iii. 358
  Laws of, v. 354
  Krishna, of, iii. 148
  Manushyas, and, iii. 110
  Manvantaras, between two, i. 132
  Mothers of, iii. 152
  Periods personified by, ii. 90
  Potencies of Brahmā-Vishnu, i. 75
  Rishis, or, i. 281; ii. 160; 366; iii. 138,
    185, 255
  Second hierarchy of, ii. 172
  Seven, i. 281, 293; iv. 194
  Thinking entities or men, i. 227
  Vishnu and, iv. 183
MANUSCRIPT, Archaic, i. 69
MĀNUSHI, v. 68
  Bodhisattvas reappear as, ii. 295
  School of, v. 103
  Solar Gods, or, ii. 154
MĀNUSHI-Buddha, i. 123; v. 291, 368, 539
MĀNUSHI-Buddhas, Dhyāni-Buddhas and,
  i. 123
  Human, i. 123
  Liberated, i. 169
MĀNUSHIS, sages of the third race, i. 64
MĀNUSHYA, -Bodhisattvas, v. 366
  -Buddha, v. 364, 365, 539
  Human, first, iii. 148
  Pitris, first, on earth, iii. 100

MĀNUSHYA (*Contd.*)
  Second, iii. 173
  Sons of Mahat and, iii. 111
MANU(-SMRITI) or Institutes of Manu,
    referred to, i. 323; iv. 294
  Ape, according to, position of, i. 236
  Authority of, i. 74; iii. 98
  Brahma, days and nights of, in, i. 71
  Brahmā-Vāch, bi-sexual in, i. 75, 139
  Computations in, iii. 77
  Esoterically explained, ii. 324
  Evolution, and, i. 238; ii. 309; iii. 261
  Genesis compared with, iii. 135
  Hermes, Buchner, and, iv. 287
  Instructors of man, on, iii. 365
  Kapila, and, i. 238; ii. 324; iii. 261
  Legislator, ii. 52
  Sarīsripa of, iii. 192
MANVANTARA, v. 83, 189, 552
  Ananta during, ii. 124
  Buddhi during, i. 82; v. 374
  Celestial hierarchy of present, i. 268
  Commencement of great, iii. 37
  Creation, season of, iii. 170; iv. 168
  Cycle of activity, i. 132, 323
  Dawn of, i. 78, 125; ii. 349
  Deities change with every, iii. 98
  Dhyān Chohans, guide during, i. 178
  Dhyān Chohans, men of past or coming, i. 318
  Divine breath in, iv. 121
  Divisions of present, iv. 281
  End of, i. 304
  Esoteric meaning of, i. 132
  Evolution not confined to one, ii. 173
  Fire during, ii. 247
  First, iii. 321
  First-born of, iii. 90
  Five races of, v. 103
  Flutter of first, i. 77
  Great breath during, i. 203
  Great life-cycle or, i. 283
  Heavenly bodies and, v. 333
  Higher plane every, i. 71
  Humanity of future, i. 226
  Indestructible of, iii. 399
  Infinity of, v. 361
  Jyotis taught astronomy in second, iv. 335
  Man at new, iii. 67
  Manu during, i. 132
  Maruts born in every, iv. 184, 186
  Men during this, no more, i. 234
  Millions of worlds in, i. 199
  Minor, i. 255
  Monad during, i. 224, 308
  Monadic inflow in, i. 238
  Monads from previous, iii. 277
  Mystery known as, i. 321
  Nārāyana every, i. 146
  Nature during, i. 301
  Next, i. 236, 310
  Numbers and, v. 336
  Partial, i. 77
  Period of, i. 283
  Periodic agencies during, iii. 84
  Periods called, i. 70; ii. 84
  Planetary and human, i. 306; v. 465
  Pralaya and, i. 78, 285; ii. 84; v. 107

Primordial active during, i. 152
  Raivata, iii. 98
  Rebirth of globe after, iv. 273
  Reincarnations in every, iii. 235
  Root during, i. 78
  Rotatory motion during, ii. 229
  Round, our, in pre-septenary, iii. 309
  Rounds of, i. 295; iii. 431
  Seven periods of, i. 110
  Seventh round, at, i. 304
  Sixth creation in our, ii. 175
  Sun, new with new, ii. 382
  Suns, for next, seven new, i. 331
  Third, iii. 88, 103
  Turning point of, iv. 103
  Vaivasvata, i. 64; iii. 79, 154
  Vishnu at beginning of, iv. 142
  Vishnu during, ii. 124
  Wheels or, i. 114
  World's dissolution at end of, iii. 308
MANVANTARAS, Adepts of previous, iii. 103
  Agnishvatta in other, iii. 87
  Buddhas of previous, iii. 228
  Chhandajas will-born in different, iv. 156
  Fiery eggs of other, v. 543
  Karma and, v. 552
  Kings in future, i. 310
  Men of previous, i. 167, 320
  Munis from previous, i. 255
  Nirmānakāyas from other, iii. 103; iv. 222
  Periodical, iv. 27
  Pralayas and, ii. 89
  Rishis, from previous, i. 255
  Rishis, seven classes of, in all, iv. 183
  Seven, iv. 195
  Spaces between, v. 189
  Succession of, ii. 89
  Worlds of preceding, i. 200
MANVANTARIC year, v. 101
MAQOM or secret place, iv. 25
MĀRA, God of darkness, iv. 151
  King, Evil Power, v. 153
MARANGONE, quoted, iv. 47
MARCELLUS on seven dvīpas, iii. 407
MARCION, v. 93, 129
MARCO Polo, Travels of, iii. 438; v. 39
MARCOSIANS in second century, ii. 65, 166
MARCUS ANTONIUS, v. 334
MARCUS AURELIUS, v. 266
MARCUS, Dual Logos of, ii. 126
  Injunction given to, iv. 134
  Marcosians, chief of, ii. 65
  Pythagorean, iii. 168; iv. 133
MARĪCHI, Agnishvatta, sons of, iii. 98
  Brahmā, son of, iii. 98, 141
  Kashyapa, son of, iii. 141, 256, 381
  Mind-born son of Brahmā, a, iii. 141
  Sambhūti, wife of, iii. 98
MĀRISHĀ, Daksha born from, iii. 183
  Kandu, daughter of, ii. 184
  Prachetases, and, iii. 183
  Sweat-born from Pramlochā, iii. 182
MARIUS, iii. 279; iv. 342
MARQUESAS, iii. 227
MARS, Adam same as Madim or, iii. 152
  Adam-Jehovah Brahmā and, iii. 55
  Artes Egyptian, iii. 151

MARS (*Contd.*)
   Earth-chain, not in, i. 217, 218, 219
   Egyptian and Hebrew, iv. 35
   House of, i. 164
   Juno, and, iv. 120
   Jupiter and, ii. 317
   Length of day on, iv. 276
   Lohitanga fiery-bodied, iii. 42
   Luna, v. 164
   Mercury, earth, etc., on same plane, i. 207
   Mercury and septenary chains, i. 219
   Michael and, v. 325
   Music of spheres, and, iv. 172
   Ovid on, iv. 120
   Personification, as a, iii. 391; v. 325
   Races of, iv. 268
   Sabao or, iv. 108
   Sabaoth genius of, ii. 301
   Saturn, Jupiter, and, ii. 382
   Seasons of, iv. 276
   Selfish tendencies governed by, v. 442
   Septenary sacred to, iv. 174
   Sons of light, one of, ii. 298
   Symbol of generative power, iii. 133
   Venus, Mercury and, ii. 116; iv. 30, 443, 444
   Virtues, ruled by, ii. 153
   Warlike god, v. 161
   Water on planet, iii. 144
MARSH on monstrous animals, iii. 222
MARSUPIAL mammalia, iii. 21, 127, 202; iv. 166, 237, 282, 357
MARTIANS can perceive our earth, i. 220
MARTIANUS Capella, quoted, ii. 376
MARTIN, Sir Theodore, on Atlas, iv. 332
MARTINISTS, Astral light of, ii. 62
MĀRTTANDA or Mārtanda, Aditi, son of, ii. 167
   Dead breath given back by, i. 164
   Planets, watches seven, ii. 253
   Sun, our, i. 162; ii. 167, 251, 253, 350; iii. 215
MARTYR, Jesus, v. 84, 125
MARTYR, Justin, v. 160
MARTYROLOGY, v. 179
MARU (Moru) of family of Ikshvaku, ii. 93
MARUTA-Jivas or monads, iv. 187
MARUTS, Diti mother of, iv. 141, 185
   Indra deserted by, iv. 66
   Manvantara, emancipations in every, iv. 186
   Mysterious, seven, iv. 184
   Rudras and, iii. 282; iv. 118
   Shiva-Rudra, sons of, iv. 186
   Storm-gods, or, iii. 391; iv. 66
MĀRUTVAN or Lord of Maruts, iv. 186
MARY, Virgin, v. 95, 292
MASON Ragon, see RAGON
MASONIC Inch, v. 90
   Initiation, v. 272, 273, 282
MASONRY, v. 194, 261, 262, 274, 282, 284
   Cabbalah and, iii. 51; v. 90
   Degrees of, v. 282
   Foundation of true, iii. 344
   Hiram, hero of, v. 272
   Jesuits and, v. 274
   Kabalah and, v. 90
   Modern, v. 175, 282
   Numbers in speculative, i. 172

   Plumage of, borrowed, i. 174
   Roman Catholic Church and, i. 65; v. 274
   Solomon's temple and, iv. 363; v. 182
   Sun and, v. 272, 273, 284
MASONS, Builders or, iv. 301
   Clergymen who are, ii. 308
   English, v. 69
   French, v. 69, 282
   Geological time, and, iv. 265
   Hiram Abif of, ii. 27
   Jaina cross of, iii. 107
   Solomon and, v. 182
   Symbologists and, v. 194
   Systems of measurement of, v. 90, 111
   Three and seven are numbers honoured by, i. 172
MASORAH, scheme, v. 205
MASORETIC points, iii. 387; iv. 33; v. 184, 205
MASOUDI the Arabian historian, iv. 20
MASSEY, Gerald, quoted, i. 191, 266, 267; ii. 15, 17, 103, 108, 119, 121, 122, 153, 376; iii. 352; iv. 116, 122, 158, 174, 201, 203, 205, 206; v. 199, 200, 201, 203
MASSORA, point of the, iv. 32; v. 90
MASSORAH, Adonai by the, ii. 184
MASTER (S), Asiatic, v. 67
   Builder, v. 138
   Death of, v. 106
   Divine, v. 262, 263
   Ever present, v. 504
   Jesus, v. 82
   K. H., i. 30
   -Mason, v. 138
   Nicodemus, in Israel, v. 83
   Secrecy, and, v. 75
   Simon of, v. 131
   Teaching of, v. 67
   Western, v. 369
MĀTARISHVAN, Prototype of Promethues, iii. 412
MATAT, a sorcerer, v. 249
MATER Terra and Pater Sadic, iii. 391
MATERIALISATION, v. 566
MATERIALISM, v. 25, 88, 351, 434
MATERIALISTS, v. 385, 387
MATHAMS or monasteries, i. 315; v. 41, 339, 395, 409
MATHEMATICS, v. 89
   Abraham taught, v. 65
   Bible, in the, v. 89
   Divine, v. 90
   Jehovah and, v. 72
   Kosmos and, v. 87
   Magic is, v. 65, 90
   Occult cosmogony and, v. 31
   plato and, v. 87
   Truth and transcendental, v. 87
MATHER, quoted, i. 286; iii. 93
MATHERS, S. L., quoted, i. 144; ii. 67, 344; iii. 294, 313; iv. 196; v. 208, 211
MATHRA Spenta, iv. 48
MATHURA, Birthplace of Krishna, iv. 159; v. 260
   Ugrasena King of, iii. 323
MĀTRI-Padma, Mother-Lotus, i. 127
   Swollen, not yet, i. 127
MATRIX, Body, for soul, i. 273
   Cosmic, i. 161

MATRIX (*Contd.*)
Created things, of, i. 325
Eternal, darkness, i. 113
Foetus in, of space, i. 304
Glyph of generative, ii. 80
Heart and, of all forces, i. 331
Heavenly, iii. 94
Mother called universal, i. 131
Mother nature, of, iv. 28, 37
Soul's body the, i. 273
Space, of, i. 304
Suras, of, iv. 96
Universal, i. 146, 325; iii. 75; iv. 81
Virgin, of Kosmos, i. 155
World's, ii. 83
MATRONA, Malkuth called, i. 285
MATRONETHAH, i. 285; iii. 220
MATSYA, Avatara, allegory, iii. 79
Fish or, i. 307; ii. 85, 100; iii. 147
Vaivasvata Manu and, iii. 308
MATTER, Coeternal with Spirit, v. 62, 384
Cosmic, v. 166
Darkness and, v. 153
Dead, v. 384
Eternal, v. 227, 387, 449
Force, and, v. 383
Kāma-Rūpa corresponds to, v. 454
Kingdom of, v. 168
Kosmic, v. 354
Passive principle, v. 116
Pentacle symbol of, v. 487
Prakriti is, v. 469
Primordial, v. 227
Schopenhauer on, v. 383
Sons of, v. 168
Spirit and, i. 80, 81, 122, 134, 167, 177, 229,
233, 242, 247, 280, 292, 295, 302; ii. 39,
41, 94, 134, 135, 169, 170, 171, 269, 274,
275, 291, 304, 345, 348, 357, 365; iii. 53,
72, 73, 74, 93, 106, 108, 112, 117, 131, 143,
153, 187, 270, 275, 276, 376; iv. 29, 37,
96, 97, 111, 127, 164, 170, 197, 204, 302;
v. 129, 166, 384, 443, 469, 488, 489
States of, v. 454
Universe of, v. 154, 507
World of, v. 429, 454
MATTHEW and his original Gospel, v. 143,
160, 167
MATZEBAH, v. 237
MAUREYAS or ten Moryas, ii. 93
MAURICE, quoted, v. 341
MAURIGASIMA or Ma-li-ga-si-ma, iii. 364
MAURY, A. quoted, iii. 362; iv. 49; v. 54, 128,
222, 254
MAXIMUS of Tyre, quoted, iii. 123
MAXWELL, quoted, i. 171, 199; ii. 209, 238
MAYA Indians of Gautemala, iii. 62
MĀYĀ, Adi-Buddha an illusion or, i. 124
Advaita is, all but, i. 124
Akāsha and Nirvāna, when divided, ii. 360
Buddha, mother of, ii. 100
Cause of human, i. 76
Consciousness, until absolute, i. 113
Cycles of, iii. 154
Dhyān Chohans and, i. 318
Duad and, v. 116
Essence of things, on, i. 118
Eternal, ii. 297
Finite things, enter into, i. 112
Generic name, a, ii. 111
Great deep, and, ii. 99
Human, i. 76
Illusion or, i. 43, 77, 120, 124, 131, 137;
v. 387, 388, 402, 434, 478, 517, 541
Ishvara, male aspect of, ii. 45
Jesus, mother of, i. 54
Lap of, i. 128, 129
Light an illusion or, i. 137
Mary, or, iii. 110
Nidāna and, i. 112, 116
Noumena veiled by, i. 117
Objective in world of, ii. 148
Ocean of, v. 434
Phenomenal existence, of, i. 116
Pradhāna is called, illusion, i. 131
Prakriti is ever called, i. 299
Realities on this plane of, ii. 289
Reality nearer to, farther from, i. 201
Ring, one of centres of, i. 77
Samvriti origin of illusion or, i. 120
Sat is, manifestation of, i. 178
Sensation is, i. 69
Senses victims of, ii. 249
Serpent, tempting and deceitful, i. 140
Seven worlds of, i. 106
Shadow cast into lap of, i. 131
Snares of, v. 379
Sons of, ii. 99
Spirit and matter are, ii. 357
Spirit is no, v. 388
Spirit no hold on, v. 388
Tvashtri was, mother, iii. 109
Universe called, i. 317
Vedantin's use of term, i. 74
Veil of, i. 169; v. 434
Waves of, i. 283
Webs of, iv. 185
Worlds of, i. 106, 273, 283
MĀYĀMOHA, the deluder by illusion, ii. 136, 140
MAYAS, Hieratic alphabets of, i. 310
Quichés and, referred to, iii. 47
MAYASABHĀ, Sabhā and, iii. 424
MAYASURA, to Pandavas, Gift of, iii. 424
MĀYĀVI or astral body, iii. 244
MĀYĀVI-Rupa, v. 353, 354, 427, 472, 510, 518,
533, 555, 561, 564, 565
MAZARINE Library, iv. 101
MAZAROTH, Scorpio and, i. 373
MAZDA, Law of, iii. 294
Prayer to, iv. 86
Wise, means, iv. 180
MAZDAO, Ahura, iii. 101
MAZDEAN, Literature, iv. 44, 86
Mithra, iii. 41
Philosophy, iv. 46
Religion, i. 76; iii. 101
Scriptures, iii. 71, 105, 408; iv. 328
Seven earths, view of, iv. 328
Symbolism for flood, iv. 181
MAZDEANISM and Logos, iii. 357
MAZDEANS, Magi or, iv. 179
Sun and, v. 315, 316
Zoroana Akerne of, i. 172
MAZDEISM, Relics of, iv. 182

MAZDHA, Ahura and Asura, iii. 101
M'BO-Sha-arim, iii. 124
M'BUL, Name for flood, ii. 100
McCLATCHEY, ii. 193
McFARLAND, R. W., quoted, iii. 149
McMILLAN Lodge, i. 154
MEASURES, Man and woman, in terms,
    ii. 162
  Masonic, v. 90, 111
  Notions of early Christians on, ii. 28
  Jews and, v. 197
  Origin of, ii. 98
  Originator of, iii. 134
  Planetary times, of, iv. 113
  Pyramid and, v. 196, 197
  Religion of Aryans and, ii. 28
  Roman and British, v. 90
  Solomon's Temple and, v. 197
  Symbols, ii. 98
MEBORACH, holy or blessed, ii. 100
MEDEA, science of, v. 122
  Winged dragon of, i. 299
MEDES and Persians, ii. 111
MEDHA, an ascetic, iii. 369
MEDHĀ, Asura, iii. 101
MEDHĀTITHI, author of commentary, ii. 47,
    48; iii. 405
MEDIA and the Persian Magi, iv. 325
MEDIATOR, Buddhi plastic, i. 288
  Manas or plastic, i. 287
  Spirit and man, between, i. 288
  Spirit sole, i. 323
MEDIATORES, v. 172
MEDICINE Men in Mexico, iii. 189
  Septenary law and, iv. 194
MÉDICIS, Catherine de, iii. 80
MEDITATION, v. 402, 468, 555
  Abstract, v. 373
  Creation by, ii. 295
  Jayas lost in, iv. 156
  Maha Yogi, of, iv. 184
  Real knowledge through, ii. 152
  Tree of wisdom, on, iv. 86
  Visions during, v. 402
  Yoga or mystic, i. 119
MEDITERRANEAN Countries, v. 342
  Race, iv. 265
  Sea, iii. 21, 22; iv. 310, 321, 345
MEDIUM (S), v. 134, 526, 544
  Apollonius called, of Satan, v. 150
MEDULLA oblongata, iii. 397
  Pineal gland, and, iii. 297
MEDUSA, iii. 80
MEDUSAE, iii. 128
MEERUT, i. 53
MEGACEROS hibernicus, iv. 309
MEGALOSAURUS, iii. 159, 200; iv. 282
MEGANTHROPUS, iv. 303
MEGATHERIUM, iii. 222, 260
MEHUJAEL, Methusael son of, iii. 390
MELANOCHROICS, iii. 315
MELCHIOR, one of Magi, ii. 380
MELCHIZEDEK, Cain and, v. 166
  Father Sadik or, iii. 390
  Noah and, iii. 391
MELEK, messenger or angel, iv. 83
MELENITE, the Anarchists' baby-toy, ii. 286

MELHA, Lord of Flames, iii. 74
MELHAS, Fire-Gods or, iii. 46
MELIA, personification of Ash-tree, iv. 89
MELITA, queen of moon, iii. 143
MELITTA, lunar Goddess, ii. 111
MEL-KARTH, the Lord of Eden, iii. 207
MEM, water or chaos, v. 206, 212
MEMBRANE uniting placentæ, iv. 238
MEMBRUM virile, iii. 134; iv. 28, 35
MEMNON, ii. 114
MEMORY, Atlantean, of gigantic, iii. 273
  Brain, v. 547
  Eternal, v. 498
  Initiates, of, v. 397
  Jnānashakti, a manifestation of, i. 333
  Mind and, v. 347
  Organ of, iii. 303
  Physical, impressions on, i. 309; v. 547
  Plastidular soul, of, iv. 241
  Sleep, in abeyance during, i. 111
  Spiritual, v. 79
MEMPHIS, v. 68, 74, 171
  Fall of, ii. 23
  Menes built palace of, iii. 334
  Old Temple of, v. 217
  Orpheus in, v. 264
  Priest of, v. 253
  Sesostris, founder of, v. 296
  Stone Books at, v. 89
  Subterranean crypt at, iii. 378
  Temple of Kabirim at, iii. 363
  Thoth of, v. 74
MEMPHITE tomb, ii. 23
MEMRAB or word, ii. 60
MEN, Seven creations of, v. 203
MEN-spirits or Ischins, iii. 375
MENANDER, v. 93, 445, 450, 451
MENARD, Dr., quoted, i. 323
MENASSEH ben Israel, Rabbi, iii. 142
MENDELEEF, Prof., ii. 276, 309
MENDES, Androgyne goat of, i. 298; v. 231
  Sacred bull of, ii. 100
MENES, v. 244, 275, 296
  Dynasty of, iii. 429, 434
  Egypt before, iii. 334
  King, i. 310; iii. 368
  Osiris and, iii. 373
MENH, v. 252
MENOCERCA with tails, iv. 238
MENS, v. 131
MENTONE man, iv. 318
MENTUHEPT, queen, v. 139
MENUS, Wilford's seven, iii. 150
MERCABAH, chariot or vehicle, i. 262; ii. 69,
    78; v. 108
MERCATOR'S projection, iii. 400
MERCURIAL paradisiacal man, iv. 212
MERCURY, Alchemists, of, ii. 103
  Angels ruling over, v. 438
  Apollo-Python, son of, iii. 213
  Archangels, ruled by, ii. 153
  Argus, iii. 41
  Astaphai of, ii. 301; iv. 108
  Buddhi and, v. 428
  Budha or, iii. 40, 42, 56, 57, 373; iv. 22;
    v. 369, 391
  Cubic form, figured in, iv. 112

MERCURY (*Contd.*)
  Cynocephalus hieroglyph of, ii. 103
  Correspondences, v. 428, 433, 437, 439, 441, 442, 444
  Days of the week and, v. 438
  Earth chain, not in, i. 217, 218
  Eden or step-brother of earth, iii. 56
  God of death, v. 159, 161
  God of Secret Wisdom, v. 65
  Heat of planet, iii. 40
  Hermes called, v. 57, 438
  House of, i. 164
  Ibis, iv. 128, 159
  Intellectual, v. 442
  Jesus inspired by, v. 369
  Kali Yuga epoch, at, ii. 387
  Length of day on, iv. 276
  Lord of wisdom, or, iii. 40
  Mar-kurios, or, ii. 68
  Mars and, i. 207, 218, 219
  Messenger, the, ii. 104
  Michael, and, iv. 47, 49
  Moon, and, ii. 112
  Music of spheres, and, iv. 172
  Mythology, in, iv. 112
  Nebo deity of, iv. 22; v. 369
  Nuntius, called, iii. 41
  Omniscience of Deity, v. 325
  Order of Planets, in, v. 433, 444
  Pesh-Hun and, iii. 60
  Pillars of, iv. 99
  Principle, v. 460
  Rameses II (Sesostris) instructed by, v. 253
  Right eye corresponds with, v. 428, 438
  Satellites, has no, i. 210
  Sirius and, iii. 373
  Son in trinity, iv. 30, 110
  Son of Pythagoras called, v. 65
  Sun, and, ii. 68; iii. 40, 41; iv. 99; v. 441
  Thoth and, ii. 77; iv. 30
  Thread of Destiny and, v. 314
  Venus, and, iv. 30
  Wednesday or day of, ii. 378; v. 437
  Worlds, and our system of, i. 217
MERCURY-THOTH, son of Egyptian trinity, iv. 30
MERCURY-TRISMEGISTUS, Pascal borrowed from, iv. 115
MERGIANA the good peri, iii. 397
MERIAN, Madame, quoted, iii. 438
MERIDIAN, Ecliptic once parallel to, iii. 356
MERKABAH, v. 67, 74, 99
MERLINS, v. 122
MERODACH, Archangel Michael, iii. 383
  Dragon, slayer of, iii. 64
  Jupiter, became, iv. 23
  Sun-God, a, iv. 71
MEROPE, a daughter of Atlas, iv. 337
MEROPIS, iv. 333
MERU, Abode of Gods, i. 185; iii. 356
  Airyana Vaejo or, iii. 209
  Form of, iv. 117
  Hindus, mountain of, ii. 54
  Matrix of Universe, v. 432
  Milker, the, ii. 113
  Mode of, iv. 117
  Mount, iii. 361; iv. 336; v. 347, 422, 436

  Mountain of the Gods or, iv. 61
  North Pole, is, i. 253; v. 436
  Pushkara lies at the foot of, iii. 402
  Roots of, iii. 399
  Seat of Brahma, is, iv. 354
  Vegetation of, i. 187
MESHIA and Meshiane of old Persians, iii. 142
MESMER, Science and, v. 51
MESMERISM, v. 42, 57, 61, 148, 511
  Hypnotism and, i. 337; iii. 164; v. 42, 511
  Magnetism, and, i. 337
MESOMED, referred to, iii. 306
MESOPOTAMIA, Gandunia was, iii. 54
  Nebo of, iv. 23
MESOPOTAMIO-IRANIAN Mohammedan sects, iv. 83
MESOZOIC, Age, skeleton of, iii. 210
  Animals, iii. 300
  Batrachians of, iii. 256
  Fauna and flora, iv. 302
  Monsters, iii. 161, 295
  Secondary or, ages, iv. 166
  Times, iii. 161, 209; iv. 246
MESSECRATES of Stira, Skeleton found by, iii. 280
MESSIAH, Advent of, foretold by stars, ii. 380; v. 163
  Christos, iii. 36
  Date of, iii. 382
  Elect, iii. 379
  Enoch's ideal, v. 101
  Expected, v. 337
  Fishes, water and, ii. 100
  Kingdom of, v. 101
  Naaseni, of, iii. 355
  Pagan Deities and, v. 94
  Perfect, iii. 294
MESSIAHS, Pesh-Hun one of twelve, iii. 60
  Two, v. 286
MESSIANIC, Amulet, v. 163
  Kingdom, v. 101
  Mystery, v. 336
META-CHEMISTRY or new alchemy, ii. 348
META-ELEMENTS, Elements and, ii. 270, 275
  Noumenoi and, ii. 276
META-GEOMETRY, ii. 341
META-MATHEMATICS, ii. 341
METAL, Fire and, iii. 425
  Land of, iii. 423
  Stone, and, i. 283
METALLIC plates, attributed to Cain, v. 109
METALS, Adept-healers by, iii. 360
  Correspondences of, v. 432, 437, 441
  Dynasty of Huschenk and rediscovery of, iii. 395
  Formation of, ii. 320
  Gods presiding over, iii. 362
  Successive races named from, iii. 273
METAPHYSICS, v. 512
  Ancient knowledge of, iii. 115
  Atoms belong to domain of, ii. 237
  Builders of, ii. 53
  Contempt of scientists for, ii. 207
  Cosmic rebirths, of, iii. 90
  Descartes, of, ii. 353
  Dogmas of, ii. 346
  Esoteric teachings, in, iii. 73; iv. 203

METAPHYSICS (*Contd.*)
Fiction, said to be, ii. 393
Higher Manas domain of, v. 512
Indian, iii. 419
Modern western, ii. 40
Occult, i. 188; iii. 125; v. 381, 384
Occultism and scientific, ii. 212; iv. 220
Ontological, ii. 268
Physics and, i. 117; ii. 231, 267, 335
Prajna in Eastern, iv. 212
Prinicples of, ii. 200
Psychology, and, ii. 345; iv. 233
Science impossible without, ii. 312
Secret Doctrine deals chiefly with, iv. 219
Talmud, of, ii. 65
Theogony, of, ii. 358
Western and Eastern philosophy, i. 145, 204, 272
World of, iii. 37
METATOR, iv. 48
METATRON, or Mitatron, v. 315
Angel of Briatic world, iii. 119; v. 327, 375
Archangel called, iv. 48
Kabalistic, v. 215, 327, 375
Perfect man or, ii. 52
Rector of the Sun, v. 315
Shekinah, united with, iii. 219
METCALFE, quoted, ii. 222, 248, 250, 304; v. 220
METEMPSYCHOSIS, v. 247
Animal atoms and, ii. 174
Buddhists and, v. 410
Cycle of, i. 237
Definition of, v. 388
Pythagorean doctrine of, iii. 194
Reincarnation or, i. 83
Soul, of liberated, iv. 122
METEORITES, Constituents of, iv. 276
Globes, from other, iii. 165
Psychometrizing, i. 250
METEOROGRAPHY of early Aryans, iii. 424
METEOROLOGY of early Aryans, iii. 424
METEORS, Modern Science and, ii. 228
Movement of, ii. 370; v. 225
METHOREA or Mathura, v. 260
METHUSAEL, Lamech, son of, iii. 390
METHUSELAH or Methusael, Age of, iii. 390
METIS, Divine wisdom, or, ii. 99; v. 74
Water, or, ii. 54; iii. 139
METRE of *Vedas*, i. 313
METRODORUS, v. 77
Taught by Epicurus, v. 60
METROLOGICAL key of Hebrew symbolism, iv. 167
METROLOGY, v. 204
Bible in, v. 89
Figures and symbols of, ii. 113
Hebrew, ii. 179; iv. 130
Kabalah and, v. 90
Pyramid and, v. 89, 111
MEUNIER, S., quoted, iii. 167
MEXICO, Adept of, v. 43
Early man in, iv. 314
Fallen demon of, iv. 54
Gulf of, iii. 422
Initiates of, v. 43
Legends of, iii. 168, 189

Magic of, v. 43
Nagals of, iii. 214
Priest Hierophant of, v. 43
Records of, v. 283
Remains of, iv. 361
Sculptures, iii. 48
Temple-lake of, v. 168
Teocalli of, v. 285
Third race, of, iii. 106
Traditions, iii. 312
MIAOTSE, Grottoes of, iii. 339
Modern, iii. 337
Race, antidiluvian, iii. 282
MICHAEL, see also MIKAEL, Angel of the sun, iii. 380
Apollo and, iii. 381
Archangel, i. 114, 152; ii. 336; iii. 103, 232, 248; iv. 47; v. 288, 320, 325
Buddhist, a, iii. 74
Celestial host, generalissimo of, ii. 135; iv. 119
Christ, and, i. 245; iv. 47
Conqueror of dragon, iii. 383
Daniel, angel of, iv. 49
Dragon and, i. 244, 251; iii. 377, 383; iv. 119
Host against dragon, and his, i. 251
Hosts of, iii. 238
Indra Hindu, iii. 377; iv. 66
Jishnu Hindu, iv. 185
Kartikeya and, iv. 119
Lion, and, i. 185
Ophiomorphos and, ii. 179
Red dragon, and, iii. 378
Sanat Sujāta and, v. 320
Satan killed by, iii. 384
Substitute of sun, v. 439
Titan, a, ii. 135
Type, a, iii. 241
MICHAEL ANGELO, Moses of, iii. 217
MICHAEL-Jehovah, iv. 108; v. 325, 326
MICHAELS glorified in churches, iii. 250
MICHAL taunted King David, iv. 29
Teraphim and, v. 236, 237, 238, 239
MICHELET, quoted, ii. 400
MICROBES, Bacteria and, i. 294
Creators and destroyers, called, i. 306
Invasion of, i. 304
Invisibe, ii. 332
Poisons and, i. 306
MICROCOSM, Decad applied to, iv. 144
Human body, represented by, iv. 148
Liquor vitae, in, ii. 256
Macrocosm, and, i. 233, 311, 326; ii. 57; iii. 177, 184, 291; iv. 151; v. 208, 420, 425, 459, 556
Man is, i. 163, 230, 317; iv. 255; v. 208, 435, 459
Manas in, ii. 47
Microprosopus or, i. 262
Pentagon, represented as a, i. 271
Septenary constitution of, i. 222
Solar system is, ii. 318
Spirits or elements in, iv. 147
Spiritual, birth of, iv. 151
Svastika applied to, man, iii. 108
MICROCOSMIC forces, v. 485
Plane, v. 367

MICROPROSOPUS, Ateh applied to, i. 144
  Heavenly man, iv. 197
  Lesser face, i. 129, 263, 285, 286
  Limbs of, i. 262; iv. 275
  Lower face, ii. 65
  Macroprosopus, and, i. 144
  Microcosm, or, i. 262
  Tetrad is, iv. 197
  Tetragrammaton or, iv. 173
MID-MIOCENE age, iv. 255, 280
MID-TERTIARY period, Man in, iii. 163
MIDAS with Silenus, Dialogue of, iv. 329
MIDDLE AGES, Fanatics of, v. 30
  Horrors of, v. 388
  Rabbis of, v. 206
MIDDLE-circle of Kabalah, iv. 205
MIDDLE point, Atlanteans, of, iii. 304
  Evolution, of, iii. 187
  Life-cycle, of, iii. 157
MIDDLE Principle(s), i. 304; iii. 244
  Three, i. 272
  Two, i. 292
MIDDLE region or Bhuva-loka, ii. 87
MIDGARD snake encircles earth, ii. 123
MIDIAN, Giants at, iv. 325
MIDIANITE Priest initiator, Reuel-Jethro,
    iv. 33; v. 180
  Priest, seven daughters of, ii. 100; v. 180
MIDRASHIM, Hanokh, iv. 101
  Moses de Leon, used by, iv. 29
  Zohar and, iv. 105
MIGRATION, Fauna, of, iv. 361
  Flora, of, iv. 358
  Plants, of, iv. 295
  Species, of, iv. 352
MIGRATION of Abraham, quoted, ii. 58
MIGRATIONS of Norwegian Lemming,
    iv. 350
MIHR, or Mithras, ii. 99
MIKAEL, Angel of face and, ii. 179; v. 314,
    375
  Christ, Mithra and, v. 315
  Dragon, and, v. 324, 375
  Jehovah is, v. 326
  Lion, iii. 124
  Patron, seventh work of Magic, v. 326
  Prana or sun principle, i. 287
  Saturn and, v. 326
  Solar Gods and, v. 314
  Star Regent, v. 320
MIKAEL-JEHOVAH, ii. 300
MILAN, council of, v. 156
MILESIAN Letters, v. 121
MILETUS, Thales of, i. 143
MILK, Ocean of, iii. 402
  Sea of, iii. 320
MILKY OCEAN, Atlantic or, ii. 137
MILKY WAY, i. 135, 264; ii. 299; iii. 321, 355
  Central body in, iii. 242
  Cosmic matter and, i. 137
  Pleiades' relation to, iv. 121
  Stars of, iii. 426
  Tycho Brahé on, ii. 314
  Via Straminis or, ii. 154
MILLENNIUM, Christianity, of exoteric, ii. 91;
    v. 360
  Duration of a, iii. 394

Earth, above cursed, ii. 90
  Man created in sixth, ii. 54
  Nativity, divided by year of, i. 62
  Prelude to hoped-for, ii. 337
MILLENNIUMS, Allegory of Pymander ten,
    ago, ii. 134
  European history, of, iii. 441
  Kali Yuga, of, i. 65
  Thought, of, i. 257
  Week of, iv. 195
MILNE EDWARDS found cave deposits,
    iv. 291
MIMIR, thrice-wise Jotun, ii. 118
MIMRA, the word or Logos, ii. 99
MINARETS of Islam, iii. 94
MINAS, or Mina the Zodiacal sign, Pisces, ii. 91;
    iv. 151
MIND, Curers, v. 467
  Divine, v. 478, 534
  -Ego, v. 483
  Eternal, v. 127
  Higher, v. 497
  Lower, v. 497, 500
  Parabrahmic, v. 513
  Potentiality of, v. 534
  Rational element or, v. 456
  Reaction of, v. 565
  Universal, v. 30, 31, 447, 456, 519, 551,
    552
MIND-born, Adam-Kadmon, son of, iii. 134
  Boneless, iii. 164
  Deity, sons of, iii. 102
  Entities, first, i. 186
  First Races, v. 74
  Groups, i. 187
  Intelligences, seven, ii. 171
  Lord, sons of First, i. 260
  Men, ii. 267
  Nature, son of, ii. 115
  Prajāpati, sons of, iii. 148
  Primitive humanity, iii. 139
  Progeny, ii. 175
  Seventh Root Race, in, v. 277
  Sons of Brāhma, i. 152, 167, 259, 260; ii. 70,
    154, 295, 330; iii. 56, 88, 102, 141, 183,
    286, 373; iv. 150, 196; v. 78, 356
  Third Race, of, v. 209
  Will-born or, lords, iii. 95
MIND-Soul or Karshipta, iii. 294
MINDLESS, Ape from, man, iii. 193
  Creative Gods and, men, iii. 203
  Females, iii. 286
  First root-race, iii. 94, 265, 315
  Mānasaputras and, man, iv. 180
  Mankind, iii. 410
  Men, iii. 193, 203, 284; iv. 180
  Monster, iii. 201
  Primeval men, iii. 89, 195
  Races, iii. 94, 168, 265, 269, 288, 315, 396;
    iv. 259
  Sin of, iii. 195, 197
  Third race, iii. 168, 269
  Wives from, iii. 273
MINERVA, Sophia or, v. 128
  Temples of, v. 295
MING DYNASTY, Yang Sun, of, iii. 65
MING-TI and Kashyapa, i. 51

MIOCENE age or period, Anthropoid ape in, i. 236; iv. 246, 249, 250, 257, 259, 260, 263
  Atlantis and, iii. 21, 314, 431; iv. 308, 347, 350
  Civilizations in, iv. 355
  Climate in, iii. 23; iv. 247, 283, 295, 308
  Destruction in, iii. 314
  Europe and America in, iv. 350
  Flora of, iv. 352
  Geologists and, iii. 163, 314
  Insititutions of today in, iii. 269
  Mammalia in, iii. 256
  Man in, iii. 289; iv. 248, 260, 282, 314, 318, 358
  Monsters of, iv. 253
  Primeval man in, iv. 245, 248
  Sahara, a sea of, iv. 355
MIÖLNIR, Svastika is the, iii. 108, 109
MIRACLES, Adepts, of, v. 394
  Apollonius, of, v. 145, 146
  Divine, v. 132, 450
  Greek philosophers, of, v. 61
  Initiates, of, v. 431
  Jesus, of, v. 125, 168
  Moses, of, v. 61
  Occultists and, v. 125, 450
MIRANDOLA, Picus de, v. 216
MIRIAM or Mary, ii. 100
MIR-KU, God or noble crown, iii. 18
MIRROR, Astral fluid, of being, i. 156
  Azazyel introduced, iii. 375
  Breath needed a, of its body, iii. 113
  Eye, of soul, iii. 300
  Futurity, of, iii. 61
  Logos, reflecting divine, iii. 38
  Monads, of universe, ii. 348, 356, 357
  Mystery of creation in a, iii. 88
  Sun, is, v. 218
  Superior and lower, iii. 270
  Truth, of pure, iii. 270
  Wisdom, of eternal, iv. 52, 85
MIRVILLE, Marquis de, see Book Index
MISRA-ST'HAN, Wilford on, iii. 404
MISSIONARIES, v. 38, 157
MISSISSIPPI valley, Mounds of, iv. 322
MIST-PLACE, Niflheim or, ii. 83
MISTS, Cosmic, i. 168
MITFORD, Godolphin, known as Murad Ali Beg, iv. 83
MITHRA, Christ, Mikael and, v. 315
  Fire Goddess, ii. 54; iii. 139
  Fires of, seven, iv. 175
  Mazdean, iii. 41
  Temple of, v. 171
MITHRAIC mysteries, iii. 471; v. 313
MITHRAS, Abraxas and, iv. 42
  Persian, ii. 164
  Rock-born God, ii. 54; iii. 139
MITLA, " Place of Sadness ", v. 283
  Pyramids and Temples of, v. 283
MITRA, Secrets of, iii. 271
  Varuna, sacrifice to, and, iii. 155
MITRE of Jewish Rabbis, v. 138
MIVART, St. George, quoted, iv. 250, 266
MIZPETH, Hermon in, iii. 407
MIZRAIM and Ham races of Cabiri, iii. 392
MLECHCHHAS, outcastes, savages, i. 53, 57, 314, 315; ii. 92; iii. 60, 403

MNASEAS, referred to, iii. 361, 392
MOABITES, Nebo adored by, iv. 23
  Shemesh of, ii. 112
MOBED and PĀRSĪ, iv. 86
MODERN, Astronomy, v. 222
  Initiation, v. 286
  Kabalists and, Science, v. 26, 28, 31, 52, 58, 107, 351, 475, 477
MOHAMMEDANS, Azazel and, v. 180
  and Christians, i. 63
MOIGNO, Ed., quoted, ii. 212
MOIRA, Goddess of fate, iv. 176
MOKSHA, Attainment of, i. 190; v. 352
  Bliss, a state of, i. 189
  Nirvāna, called in India, i. 112; v. 83, 381, 384, 385
MOLECULE, Aggregation of atoms, ii. 349
  Life every, i. 272, 302
  Monad and, i. 230
  Principles in, higher, i. 266
  Science and, i. 197
  Unit a, ii. 344
  Universe, alive, every, in, i. 305
MOLECULES, Atmosphere, in our, ii. 278, 307
  Atoms and, i. 165, 205; ii. 42, 278, 357, 358
  Bastard, ii. 346
  Body of the, v. 557
  Brain, of, iv. 243
  Capabilities of, i. 205
  Chemist and, iv. 225
  Compound, ii. 278, 350
  Crookes on, ii. 271
  Eliminated, i. 199
  Exchange of, i. 198
  Force, centres of, ii. 231
  Jiva and, iv. 242
  Material, ii. 354
  Materialistic Philosophy, of, ii. 355
  Planetary ring, of, ii. 317
  Protista, of, iv. 220
  Repulsion among, i. 149
  Salt, of, iv. 166
  Soul of the, v. 537
  Specific gravity and, ii. 237
  Thomson, Sir W., on, ii. 238
  Transformation of, i. 203
  Tympanum, on, ii. 278
  Vibration of, ii. 239
  Weight of, ii. 237
MOLECULAR, separation of air, ii. 287
MOLESCHOTT, quoted, i. 182
MOLITOR, quoted, v. 118, 120
MOLOCH, ii. 113, 184; v. 194
MOMMSEN, historian, v. 256
MON or Ammon, concealed God of Egyptians, ii. 82
MONA, Stone which returned to its place in, iii. 345
MONAD(S), Absoluteness, a breath of the, ii. 292
  Activity of, iv. 232
  Adept, of, v. 80
  All-potential, iii. 118
  Ancients of, ii. 338
  Angel, ii. 298; iii. 269
  Animal, i. 231; iii. 53, 111, 201, 257; iv. 94
  Anthropoid apes, of, i. 236
  Astral body of progenitors, of, iv. 230

MONAD (S), (Contd.)
Astral doubles of, i. 232
Astral form clothing, iii. 126
Atomic souls, ii. 344
Beams, or, v. 357
Breath or human, i. 292; iii. 113; iv. 181
Buddhi or cosmic, i. 229
Central Point and, v. 188
Changelessness, v. 210
Classes of, i. 226
Conscious, iv. 222
Constitution of, i. 230
Corpuscles compared to, v. 565
Cosmic, i. 229; iii. 311
Creators of, ii. 295
Crown of all things, iv. 174
Cycle of evolution of, i. 232, 235
Cycle of incarnations of, iii. 187
Cycles round septenary chain, i. 224
Cyclic pilgrimage in, v. 357
Descent of, i. 292; ii. 391
Devachan, and, iii. 67, 201
Development of, i. 228, 233
Dhyān Chohan, and, i. 308; iii. 154, 304
Dhyāni Buddha and, ii. 296; v. 366
Differentiation of, i. 231
Disembodied, iii. 68
Divine, i. 228, 309; ii. 194; iii. 97, 376; iv. 53; v. 370, 493
Divine sparks or, i. 232
Double dragon, or, iii. 67
Duad and, ii. 343; iv. 146; v. 210, 498
Dual, i. 136, 230, 231
Dwelling of, first, i. 293
Dumb races, of, i. 234
Earth, and, i. 235; iii. 132
Ego or, i. 232; iv. 205; v. 83
Elemental, ii. 356
Emanators of, ii. 295
Entity, as separate, i. 230
Esoterism and, iv. 240
Eternal, iv. 170; v. 361
Evolution of, i. 215, 228
Experience acquired by, iii. 187
Fœtus and, i. 235; iii. 194
Form of transitional, i. 235
Forms of, iii. 169, 174, 259
Globe, A, on, i. 232, 233; iii. 187; iv. 206
God and, ii. 277, 335, 344, 349, 348; iv. 240; v. 84
Greeks, of, ii. 146
Higher self or, iii. 111, 171
Homogeneous, i. 292
Hornblende, of an atom of, i. 230
Human, i. 215, 230, 236, 237; ii. 172, 298, 356; iii. 58, 66, 103, 111, 113, 192, 311; iv. 206; v. 77, 366
Human kingdom, entering the, i. 234
Humboldt, of a, i. 230
Ideations of divine, i. 309
Identification man and animal, iii. 90
Immetallization of, iii. 187
Immortal, i. 179, 289; iii. 162; v. 357
Impersonal, i. 228
Imprisoned, i. 310
Incarnations of, i. 188, 228, 234, 310; iii. 187, 286; iv. 241

Individual, i. 230, 231, 308; ii. 345
Indivisible, ii. 293, 355
Infinitude of, ii. 357
Intiates on the, ii. 293
Inner being or, iii. 171
Jīva or, i. 264, 284, 291, 292; ii. 344; iii. 58, 85
Jīvātmas or, i. 190
Journeyings of, i. 235
Kabalists and the, iv. 171
Karma and, iii. 169, 217, 251, 277, 303
Kingdom of the, ii. 356
La Pluche on the, ii. 338
Later in Animal, v. 547
Leibnitz, see Book Index
Limited number of, iii. 304
Logos or universal, iii. 311
Lunar, i. 231, 232, 233
Man as a, iii. 259
Manas merging into, i. 284, 289; iii. 250
Manifested unity or, ii. 339
Manu on, iii. 311
Manvantaras of past, iv. 222
Maruta-Jīvas or, iv. 187
Masons and, ii. 338
Mathematical point or, ii. 338
Mentality of, plane of, ii. 228
Metaphysical bonds between, ii. 356
Mineral, i. 228, 229, 230, 231, 291; iii. 53
Muktas or, i. 190
Mundane, ii. 297
Nirmānakāyas and, iii. 103
Nirvāna, re-emergence from, i. 309
Occultism, and, ii. 272
Omniscient by nature, v. 498
Origin of, ii. 293
Origin of all things, iv. 174
Osirification of, i. 192
Paradigmatic man of, v. 507
Perfection of, iii. 118
Physical, human, not, i. 230
Pilgrim, a, i. 82
Pilgrimage of, ii. 293
Plane, not of this, i. 228
Plane of illusion, on, ii. 172
Plane of objectivity on, v. 211
Planetary chains, iii. 311
Planetary origin of, ii. 300
Planetary spirit, of, ii. 356; v. 233
Point, or, ii. 144, 341
Points, metaphysical points, ii. 355
Porphyry on, ii. 144, 343
Prakriti, manifesting in, i. 230
Pralaya, in, ii. 293
Principle of all things, ii. 152
Progress of, i. 227; iii. 290
Proper, ii. 294
Prototype, i. 292; v. 77
Pythagoras on, ii. 144, 338, 344; iv. 240
Races, of future, iii. 158
Rays or, v. 358
Reascent of, ii. 391
Reincarnations of, i. 308; iii. 154, 175, 251
Renewed, called the, iv. 205
Sattva, called, i. 136
Second Logos and, v. 507
Semiconscious, i. 310

MONAD (S) (*Contd.*)
Senseless, iii. 231
Seven lights or, i. 179
Seventh race and round, in, iii. 187
Shells, incarnating in empty, iii. 89, 304
Soul, and, i. 178; ii. 301, 344, 355; iii. 120, 158
Spark or, i. 283
Spirit in man, i. 178; v. 333
Spirits affecting mediums not, i. 279
Spiritual, i. 223, 230, 231; iii. 88, 162
Star, a, i. 228; iv. 55
Sub-planetary, ii. 344
Tabernacles for, iii. 124, 217
Ternary and, v. 507
Terrestrial, ii. 297
Third race, of, iv. 181
Third round, in, i. 232
Thoughts and, ii. 356
Totality of, absolute, i. 235
Transitory vehicles of, ii. 293
Tree of Life, v. 496
Triad and, ii. 145, 297; v. 498
Triangle, is a, v. 507
Trinitarian form of, v. 364, 471, 507
Triune, v. 493
Uncompounded things, i. 231
Unconsciousness of, i. 228; iii. 89
Undifferentiated human, iii. 311
Union with, 80
Unit or, ii. 172, 297
Unit-point, represents a, ii. 341
Universal, ii. 345; iii. 89, 311
Unprogressed men, of, iii. 265
Vegetable, i. 222, 231; iii. 53
Wisdom acquired by, iii. 187
World, not of this, i. 228
Zodiacal signs and, ii. 391
MONAD-EGO Envelopes of the immortal, i. 283
MONADLESS, ii. 357
Elements in Nature, ii. 357
MONADSHIP, Thread of immortal, impersonal, iv. 82
MONAS, Greek, ii. 339
Kosmos, applied to whole, i. 231
Peripatetics, of, i. 230
Pythagorean, i. 132; iii. 100
Super-cosmic, ii. 344
Unity, signifies, ii. 339
Universal, i. 230
MONASTERIES, Japan, of, i. 286
Mathams or, i. 315
MONATOMIC, Atoms, i. 265
Elements, ii. 275
Molecules, ii. 237
MONERA, Organisms of simplest kind, are, iii. 172
Protista, are, ii. 174; iii. 161
Stages of, iv. 255
MONERON, Darwinians, of, iv. 223
Exprotoplasmic, iii. 161
Haeckel, of, ii. 266; iii. 158, 161, 162, 165, 192; iv. 228, 243
Man and, iv. 283
Protoplasmic, speck called, iii. 173, 195
Sarcode, of, iii. 161
Science, of, iii. 107
Self-division of, iv. 228

MONERON-like procreation, iii. 173
MONGOLIA, Libraries of, i. 56
Statues of Buddha in, iv. 157
MONGOLIANS, Amilaka of, iii. 46
Asia, of, iv. 39
Burmese, iii. 338
Cherchen, destroy a city near, i. 56
Chinamen offshoot of, iii. 185
Europe, in prehistoric, iv. 313
Fourth race, and, iii. 252
Innovators, i. 44
Language older than Hebrew, v. 186
Scyths, perhaps, iii. 207
Svastika and, iv. 157
Tarim, visit remains at, i. 48
Wan of, iv. 126
MONGOLO-Turanian and Indo-European, ii. 31
MONGOLOIDS of Huxley, iii. 315
MONGOLS, Forefathers of, iii. 423
Negroes, Aryans and, iv. 178
MONIER WILLIAMS, Sir M., and Esoteric Buddhists, iv. 140; v. 27
MONISM, Materialism, and, i. 183; ii. 252
Psychologists, of, ii. 345
Single substance or, i. 183
Western, ii. 252
MONIST-Agnostic, ii. 305
MONISTIC nature, Primordial essence of, i. 325
MONKEY, Divine origin of, i. 236
Dryopitheus, iv. 318
God, of, iv. 44
Mammalian type, and, iv. 247
Miocene fossil, iv. 292
Primitive and present, iv. 285
Quadrumanous, iii. 260
MONKEY-coloured fiends, iii. 110, 171
MONKEY-faced, Kapi-Vaktra or, iii. 60
MONKEY-God, Hanumān the, iv. 250
MONKEY-kingdom of Rāmāyana, iii. 290
MONKS, Christian, iv. 101
Dark ages, of, iii. 439
Dwellings of, Buddhist, iii. 339
Kioto, of, i. 226
MONOGENESIS, De Quatrefages and, iii. 201
Theories of, iii. 126
MONOGENISM and Polygenism, iii. 176; iv. 182
MONOLITH from Karnac, ii. 115
MONOLITHS, Immense, iii. 342
MONOSYLLABIC speech, iii. 204
MONOTHEISM, Anthropomorphic, ii. 299
Deity degraded by, v. 387
Egyptian, geographical, ii. 399
Eighth God and, iv. 178
Jewish, iii. 52, 255; iv. 27; v. 176
Plato, of, v. 30
Polytheism, and, v. 351
Protestants, of, v. 78
Step towards, first, i. 172
MONOTHEISTS, Anthropomorphic God of, ii. 222
Blasphemies of, iii. 305
Creator of, iv. 124
Creators, blend totality of, i. 160
Deity of, ii. 257; iii. 110, 3o6
Interpretations of, iii. 382

MONOTHEISTS (*Contd.*)
Kabalah, and, i. 187
Mosaic Jewes, v. 206
MONSTERS, half-human, half-animal, iii. 63
MONTAIGNE, quoted, i. 67; iii. 340
MONTANISTS, Heresies of, iv. 53
MONTENEGRIN giant, Danilo, iii. 279
MONTESQUIEU, quoted, ii. 401
MONTFAUCON, quoted, ii. 116; iv. 112
MONTLOSIER, Count de, quoted, iv. 124
MONUMENTS, Egypt, of, v. 48
Phallic, v. 285
Pyramid, of Esoteric records, v. 190
Zodiacal, v. 332
MONZA, Church of St. John at, iv. 158
MOON, Abraxas and, iv. 42
Adam and, iv. 35
Adoration of, ii. 375
Age of, iii. 76
Airyana Vaējō, in, iii. 293
Ancient measurements of position of, ii. 390
Androgyne deity, an, iii. 76
Anu identical with, iii. 72
Arg and, iii. 414
Argha, is, ii. 75; iii. 72, 153; iv. 30, 35
Arjuna Mishra on, iv. 210
Ark and, ii. 75; iii. 147; iv. 35
Ārka and, iii. 414
Astral, symbol of the, v. 535
Artemis and, i. 275; ii. 102, 112
Astoreth and, ii. 113; iv. 30
Atlanteans and, v. 535
Asaradel taught motion of, iii. 375
Beams of, i. 282
Behaviour of, v. 224
Bel and, iii. 385
Bel-Shemesh, called, ii. 112
Beneficent emanations from, i. 211
Budha son of, iii. 57; iv. 23
Castor and, iii. 132
Cat and, ii. 16, 17, 103; iv. 122
Chain progeny of, i. 224
Childbirth and, i. 307
Christ-Judas and, ii. 108
Christians' deity, ii. 102
Clemens Alexandrinus, with, i. 102
Concealed side of, i. 274
Conception and, i. 307
Conjunction of sun and earth, iii. 85, 433
Correspondences, v. 433, 437, 441, 444, 506
Cosmic aspect of, female, iii. 76
Course of, calculated, iii. 368
Cowhorned, iii. 416
Crescent, iv. 31
Darwin on, i. 210; iii. 74
Dead, i. 204
Dead yet living body, a, i. 211
Death, as Goddess of, ii. 102
Deity, iv. 340.
Deity of mind, ii. 241; iv. 64
Demeter and, iii. 413
Determination of place of, by Brāhmans, ii. 390
Deus Lunus and, ii. 102, 112; iv. 34
Diana and, i. 275; ii. 102; iii. 132; iv. 30, 340
Diana-Hecate-Luna, personified, ii. 102
Dissolution of, i. 211
Divine soul and, iii. 121

Dog-headed ape a, Glyph, ii. 103
Dracontia and, iii. 346
Dual aspect of, ii. 112
Dual purpose of, ii. 112
Earth and, i. 209, 210, 211, 232, 253; ii. 17, 113; iv. 45, 56, 75, 172, 269; v. 442, 535
Earth, becomes, v. 532
Earth, parent of our, iv. 42
Earth's axis, and, iv. 340
Eclipse of, ii. 386, 387
Egypt, in, i. 274; ii. 104; iv. 32
Eve and, iii. 413, 414
Evolution of, v. 535
Fellow-globes of, i. 210
Female generative power and, iii. 414
Female generative principle and, iii. 147
Female Goddess, a, ii. 112
Feminine principle, or, iii. 153
Feminine with Greeks, iii. 132
Festival at new, iv. 30
Fish, sin, and, i. 283, 307
Fourth globe, was, i. 217, 225
Fourth Principle, v. 154
Full, female, iv. 31
Generation, and, i. 275
Genius of, ii. 301; iv. 42, 108, 110
Genius of evil, standing for, ii. 112
Giver of death, ii. 102
Globe, fourth, i. 225
Globe, gives life to our, ii. 102
Glyph of, ii. 148
God, i. 274, 275; ii. 112; iii. 73, 86, 148; iv. 204
Goddess, i. 307; ii. 115; iii. 414
Greeks, with, iii. 132
Growth of, ii. 333
Hathor and, v. 32
Hindu measurements of, ii. 389
Horned, ii. 109
Horus, eye of, ii. 103
Human being came from, i. 274
Iaō and, ii. 167; iv. 108
Ibis and, ii. 77
Idol of, iv. 21
Indu and, iii. 56
Influence of, iv. 269; v. 330, 535
Inner principles of, i. 204
Insane mother, i. 204
Instincts and, v. 442
Invisible, real, i. 231
Io and, iii. 413, 416; iv. 31
Isis and, i. 275; ii. 77, 103; iii. 44, 416; iv. 30, 155
Jehovah and, i. 247; iii. 72, 85, 148; iv. 154; v. 30, 42, 155
Jehovah-Satan and, ii. 108
Jehovah's living symbol, ii. 102; iii. 72
Jewish religion and, i. 232
Jews and, iii. 148
Juno and, i. 275
Kabalah, in, i. 247; iii. 72
Kali-Yuga, and, iii. 433
Kārtikeya beautiful as, iv. 120
Khonsoo and, iv. 32
King of plants, iii. 383
Kumuda-Pati is, iii. 56

MOON (*Contd.*)

Latin church, in, ii. 117
Lha of, iii. 110
Life microbes and, i. 307
Life renewals, symbol of, i. 275
Lord of the sun called, ii. 112
Lords of, iii. 85
Lower Manas, Symbol of, v. 535
Luminous ring round, ii. 314
Lunar genius, or, iv. 42
Magna mater and, ii. 108
Maier's tables for, ii. 387
Male, is, i. 275; iii. 76
Maleficent emanations from, i. 211; v. 535
Man came from, i. 274
Man in, ii. 108
Manas and, iv. 64, 210
Mary and, ii. 118; iv. 31
Master of, iv. 172
Matter, dark with, i. 247
Melita and, iii. 143
Metaphysical nature of, i. 211
Mind and, ii. 241; iv. 64, 210
Moot and, iv. 32
Moses in, ii. 321; iv. 35
Mother, iii. 113, 147
Mother, great, iii. 414; iv. 30
Mother of earth, i. 211, 253
Mother-water disappeared in, iii. 74
Mountain of, iii. 86, 236
Mysteries of, seven, i. 226
Mysteries of our globe and, ii. 17
Mysterious power in, iii. 113
Mystery of eigth sphere, and, i. 217
Mystery plant and, v. 536
Nature, Earth and, v. 165
Nature of, i. 211
Nebo son of, iv. 23
New, festivals, iv. 30
New, in Seventh Round, v. 535
Newton's idea of, v. 224
Night, and, ii. 129
Nodes of, ii. 118
Number seven and, iv. 167
Occult force in, ii. 247
Occult potencies of, ii. 112
Occult properties of, i. 275
Occultism on, i. 204
Occultist understands nature, etc., of, i. 211
Odin, eye of, ii. 118
Older than earth, i. 210; iii. 75
Omorōka or, iii. 124
Origen, with, ii. 102
Osiris and, i. 275
Osiris, eye of, ii. 103
Osiris inhabits, i. 274, 275
Osiris-Lunus and, ii. 112
Osiris-Sut and, ii. 108
Parent of earth, i. 232; iii. 56
Paul on, iii. 85
Phoebe or, ii. 102
Phosphorescent, is, v. 535
Physical, iii. 56
Physiology ignorant as to, i. 307
Pitris and, i. 232, 307; iii. 85, 324
Planet, a dead, i. 204; iii. 253; v. 439
Plant, i. 258; iv. 162

Plants and, v. 535
Potency, a sexless, ii. 112
Power of calling down, iv. 331
Primitive physical man and, iii. 113
Principles, gave to Earth, v. 535
Progeny of, i. 224
Properties of, occult, i. 275
Prophet of, iv. 34, 35
Psychic nature of, i. 211
Pueblos adore, iii. 188
Rāhu and, iii. 380
Regent of, ii. 167; iii. 56, 324
Reincarnations, symbol of, i. 275
Religion, ancient, and, i. 232
Sapphire and, v. 536
Science and, i. 232
Semitic races and, iii. 112
Septenary, and, iv. 167
Serpent and, iii. 346
Seventh round, in the, v. 536
Shell of, all-potential, iii. 124
Shelley, on, ii. 102
Sidereal influence of, v. 330, 332, 536
Sin and, i. 283, 293, 307; ii. 112; iii. 36, 72, 236
Sinai, mountain of, iii. 236
Soma and, i. 275, 283; ii. 102, 112, 113, 247; iii. 36, 56, 57, 147, 183, 383, 385; iv. 23, 34, 63, 64, 67
Son of, iii. 118, 385; iv. 23
Sorcerers and, i. 211; iv. 331
Soteira and, ii. 112
Sparks of, i. 282
Spirit of, iii. 324, 369
Sri, and, iii. 86
Substitute for a Secret Planet, v. 433, 536
Sun, reflects light of, iv. 122
Sushumnā (Sun) ray and, ii. 240, 261
Sweat, cooled the, iii. 139
Symbol, as, i. 275; v. 535
Tantrikas and, i. 211
Tārā carried away by, iii. 57
Telita and, iii. 143
Thalassa is, iii. 124
Thot (-Hermes) and, ii. 118
Tides and, iii. 324
Time-measurer, as, iv. 192
Trinity and, iii. 103
Twofold in sex, ii. 108
Unseen Gods of, iv. 30
Valley in, v. 73
Venus and, iii. 44
Virgin Mary and, ii. 108; iv. 31
Vitalizing power of, iii. 85
War in heaven and, iii. 385
Water, in clear tranquil, i. 120
Water, progeny of, iii. 76
Waters of, iv. 154
Weather, influences, iv. 269
White swan from, iii. 139
Wife of, iii. 86
Witches and, i. 211
Woman and, iv. 29
Worship of, ii. 117
Zarpanitu, the, iv. 23
MOON-coloured, Faces, iii. 185
Race, iii. 230, 231, 350

MOON-like complexion, Celestial kings of,
iii. 423
MOOR, referred to, iii. 43; iv. 118, 130, 131
MOORS and Egyptian-Atlantidae, iv. 360
MOOT, Daughter, wife and mother of Ammon,
ii. 148
  Moon, name of, iv. 32
  Mooth, or, iv. 32
  Mother, the, ii. 99, 170
MOOT(H), Isis, iv. 32
MOR-ISAAC, quoted, ii. 153
MORBIHAN, Initiates at Carnac or, iv. 319
  Menhirs of, iii. 351
MORE, Henry, v. 51
MORERI, quoted, v. 355
MORGANA, sister of King Arthur, iii. 397
MORNING STAR *Bible*, of, ii. 357; v. 314
  Bright and, iv. 110
  Christian belief in, ii. 328
  Greeting of, iv. 329
  Hathor, ii. 115
  Lucifer, iii. 57; v. 267
  Mikael, v. 314
  Son, and, iii. 71, 241
  Virgin addressed as, iv. 97
MORTILLET, G. de, quoted, iv. 248, 255, 289,
318
MORYA dynasty, ii. 93; iv. 120
MORYA-nāgara, ii. 93
MOSAIC Bible, v. 192, 195
  Books, iv. 29; v. 27, 33, 131, 179, 181, 183,
    184, 185, 187, 195, 198, 232, 234, 333
  Commandments, v. 206
  Cosmogony, v. 216
  Hebrew, v. 505
  Jews, and, v. 206
  Law, iii. 71, 105, 376; v. 162, 178, 179, 180,
    216
  Period, v. 245
  Records, v. 178
  Scrolls, v. 186
  System, v. 107
  Texts, v. 187, 198
MOSASAURUS and flying camel, iii. 210
MOSES, Age of, v. 245, 311
  Alchemy and, v. 297
  Ancient philosophers before, ii. 46
  Angels and, v. 320
  Ankh introduced by, iii. 43
  Anonymous authors, and, iv. 21
  Ark of rushes, and, ii. 31
  Biography of, iii. 426
  Brazen serpent and, i. 299; ii. 79, 80
  Burning bush, and, ii. 52; v. 191
  Cain-Adam Pyramid, in, v. 167
  Chaldean tablets prior to, iii. 16
  Chronology of, iv. 261
  Chroub or cherubs of, iii. 123
  Creation ideas from, iii. 17; v. 199
  Death of, v. 182, 282
  Disappearance of, v. 272
  Egyptians, and, i. 175; ii. 67; iv. 77, 130
  Elements, and, four, ii. 182
  Esoteric wisdom of Egypt, and, iv. 130
  Exodus, did not write, ii. 32
  Fire on Mount Sinai, and, iv. 137
  First book of, iii. 424

Genesis of Enoch, and, iii. 270; iv. 20
Giants in time of, iii. 273, 336; iv. 325
Glory of the Lord, and the, iv. 109
Gods, forbids to revile, iv. 46
Hebrew of, v. 179
Hermes and, i. 140; v. 112
Human soul of, iii. 55, 133
Iao, of, iv. 33, 111
Ilda-baoth God of, iii. 388
Initiate, an, ii. 24, 28; iv. 33; v. 91, 180, 197,
  234, 278
Jehovah and, iv. 35, 109; v. 206
Jews date from David not, iv. 41
Job prior to, ii. 373
Kabalists, cited by, iii. 194
Kings before, v. 58
Language of Initiates and, v. 178, 197
Living soul of, i. 298; ii. 59, 69
Mathematics (Magic) taught, v. 65
Michael Angelo's statue of, iii. 217
Moon, and, ii. 321; iv. 35
Mount Sinai, and, ii. 89; iv. 137, v. 92, 114
Mystery instructions, and, v. 66, 92
Nebo, dies on, iv. 23
Noah, on, iii. 149
Numbers in name of, iv. 109
Pelican and swan forbidden as food by,
  i. 146
Principle, and first, ii. 144
Promised Land, and, v. 195
Prophets before and after, iv. 37
Rabbi, iv. 29
Ram's horns on head of, iii. 217
Sabbath of, iv. 175
Saraph of, iii. 386
Sargon and, ii. 31, 32
Saturn prevailed according to, iii. 73
Seventy Elders of, v. 71
Shining Face of, v. 92, 562
Sodales, chief of, iii. 216
Story of version of an Atlantean legend,
  iii. 424
Symbolical consonant in name of, ii. 100
Symbolical teaching of, v. 92
Tabernacle of, i. 184; ii. 27, 61, 107
Tables of stone, and, iv. 99
Tau, orders people to mark doorposts with,
  iv. 127
Teachings of, v. 133, 234
Temple of, v. 320
Thoth equivalent to, v. 112
Tribes, and twelve, ii. 375
Wife of, v. 180
Wilderness, and fiery serpents in, ii. 79
Wisdom of Hermes, and, i. 140
Yaho told to, iv. 111
MOSES Cherenensis, quoted, iv. 169
MOSES de Leon, iv. 29; v. 117
MOSHEIM, quoted, v. 126, 128, 303
MOSSES, Bacteria and, iii. 174
MOST HOLY PLACE, No, 10 in, ii. 107
MŌT, Ilus, mud or, ii. 54
  Phoenician Mut or, ii. 170
MOTHER, Aditi, of Mārtānda, i. 124; ii. 70,
  350; iv. 96; 233, 381
  Aima, great, iii. 93, 383
  Ākāsha is, iii. 46

MOTHER (Contd.)
Bal-i-lu, of, i. 162
Binah, ii. 108; iii. 94; v. 191
Book of Dzyan and, ii. 152
Bosom of, i. 148, 149, 201
Brahmā is, father and son, i. 114
Breath of, i. 148, 149
Bud of lotus, swells as, i. 131
Chaos or, ii. 323
Chaste, v. 270
Cold, comely, but stone, ii. 130, 266; iv. 43
Cometary matter, i. 163
Cosmos, of, i. 83, 159
Creative nature, i. 157
Crystalline abode of, iv. 45
Deep, i. 133; v. 235
Deity neither, nor father, i. 193
Depths of, i. 134
Diti, of Maruts, iv. 185
Divine, of seven, i. 156
Duad, ii. 339
Eight houses built by, i. 162
Eternal, i. 199
Ether is, i. 127
Eve, iii. 414; v. 190
Existences, of all, iv. 30
Father, and, i. 75, 77, 114, 128, 137; iii. 399; v. 209, 335
Fifth principle of cosmic matter or, i. 334
Fire and, v. 446
Fish of life, is fiery, i. 160
Formation of, v. 212
Fourth spoke is our, i. 254
God of, ii. 115; iii. 413
Goddesses, iv. 32
Gods, of, i. 124, 161; ii. 70, 152, 251, 399; iv. 30, 81, 96; v. 165, 381
Great, i. 94, 116, 263; ii. 152; iii. 93, 383, 413, 414; iv. 30, 43, 45; v. 211
Greek derivation of Maia, ii. 111; iii. 205
Holy Spirit, i. 141; v. 131
Hovah, of all living, iii. 134
Husband of his, i. 155, 274
Jah, in, v. 212
Ilus, or Hyle, i. 147
Immaculate, i. 155, 300; ii. 115; v. 152
Inferior, i. 285
Invisible robes of, i. 116
Isis, iii. 43, 54; iv. 225; v. 164, 233, 293
Jehovah, and, v. 190
Juno, of Mars, iv. 120
Kwan-Yin merciful, ii. 149
Logos, and daughter of, i. 193; ii. 145
Lotus, Mātripadma or, i. 127
Love, v. 545, 546
Male element in nature, and, i. 129
Manifested, ii. 348
Mary, v. 293
Matter, or abstract ideal, i. 193; ii. 340
Matronitha, i. 285
Māyā, ii. 99
Mercury, of, i. 54; iv. 110
Mercy and knowledge, of, i. 193
Moon, iii. 113, 147
Mout (or Moot) signifies, i. 155; ii. 170; iv. 32
Moves, of all that, i. 141
Nārā, becomes, v. 235

Nature, v. 209, 233, 293
Nature, in, iv. 205
Parent, v. 204
Pneuma, of, iii. 121
Primeval, iv. 152
Quaternary of father, son, and life, i. 129
Ray of first, ii. 304
Refuse and sweat of, i. 164, 200
Revelations, of, ii. 383
Revolutions, of, iv. 117; v. 202
Rudimentary objective, being first, i. 264
Saïtic, iv. 225
Sanskrit, of Greek, iii. 205
Saviour, of, iv. 140; v. 293
Scatters and ingathers, i. 78
Seven proceed from, i. 152, 156; ii. 276; v. 200
Son, and, i. 114, 128, 148, 155; ii. 114
Sons of, i. 139, 141
Soul of, i. 154; iv. 81; v. 115
Source, one with, i. 283
Space called, i. 83; v. 235
Space, in, v. 202
Spawn of, i. 248
Spirit and matter, Moot or first product of, ii. 170
Spiritus, i. 245, 264, 293
Spoke is our, fourth, i. 254
States of, i. 202
Substance, seventh principle of, i. 331
Substantial, only, ii. 144
Time of, i. 274; ii. 125; iv. 202
Universal soul called, ii. 67; v. 499
Vāch, of Vedas, ii. 148, 152; iii. 115, 137; v. 164
Virgin, Venus great, iii. 75
Waters mean, i. 131; ii. 88, 179; v. 233, 235
Wisdom of Ogdoad, i. 139
World of, i. 118
MOTHER-EARTH, i. 209; iii. 17
Man born in head of, iii. 399
Woman, likened to a, iii. 400
MOTHER-NATURE, i. 72, 194; iv. 37, 167
MOTHER-NIGHT, Athtor or, ii. 60
MOTHER-of-pearl, Photosphere compared to, ii. 254
MOTHER-Space, i. 161, 164; iii. 124
MOTHER-Spirit, i. 260
MOTHER-Water, the Great Sea, iii. 74
MOTHERLESS, Minerva, iv. 174
MOTHERS, Three of Air, Water, Fire, v. 107
Three of Hermes, v. 88, 89, 107
Three of Kabalists, v. 211
Shaktis of three great Gods, v. 89
MOTION, Absolute, i. 80, 125, 126; v. 557
Abstract Deity, v. 515
Abysses of, i. 135
Atoms are, ii. 358
Beginnings of, i. 254
Breath or, i. 115, 124, 125, 160, 176, 324; v. 229
Circular, i. 176
Cosmic, i. 70
Deity, v. 515
Electricity and, i. 171
Elements of, i. 303
Eternal, i. 70, 115, 324; iii. 90; iv. 116, 152; v. 387

MOTION (*Contd.*)
 Eternal Law, is, v. 387
 Ether and, ii. 251
 Fire is, i. 137, 179, 198
 Focus of, iv. 121
 Force or, ii. 233, 236, 242, 248, 278; iv. 287
 Ghosts of matter in, i. 202
 Hindus knew exact, ii. 390
 Hypothesis of, ii. 219
 Illusion of, iv. 161
 Inertia and, ii. 225, 244
 Jivatma, or, i. 121
 Kosmos, of invisible, iii. 108
 Laws of, ii. 254, 360; v. 387
 Life and, i. 70; v. 227
 Light and, i. 137, 179, 198; ii. 239
 Logos, begets, i. 135
 Mand or manth implies rotatory, iii. 411
 Manifested Force is, v. 227
 Manvantaric, ii. 254
 Matter and, i. 78; ii. 326
 Mechanical, ii. 219, 240
 Modes of, i. 201, 202; ii. 203, 215, 240, 241, 325, 328, 330, 393; iii. 275; iv. 287
 Molecular, i. 191, 296; ii. 240
 Monad is circular, of, ii. 358
 Nature, from indivisible, ii. 341
 Perpetual, i. 70, 203; ii. 220, 280; v. 229, 387
 Powers, subservient to intelligent, ii. 244
 Psychic, v. 575
 Ruler, sovereign, iii. 240
 Shadow of matter in, ii. 239
 Source of, iii. 242
 Thought is molecular, i. 191
 True nature of, ii. 221
 Universal, i. 70, 203
 Unmanifested in, i. 160
 Vortex of, i. 302
 Vortical, i. 177
MOTOR, Keely, i. 203; ii. 279, 287
MOULD, Astral, iv. 296
 Basic, human upadhi or, i. 325
 Developing for use of man, iii. 263
 Nephesh, of, i. 290
 Physical Man of, iv. 296
MOUNDS, Mississippi valley, of, iv. 322
 United States and Norway, of, iii. 421
MOUNT, Ararat, iv. 169
 Armon, Ardis top of, iii. 375
 Ashburj, iii. 401, 405
 Atlas, Meru in, iii. 402; iv. 332
 Caucasus, Prometheus chained on, iii. 412
 Cyllene, iv. 112
 Descent, of, iv. 169
 Fire on, iv. 36
 God, of, v. 145
 Jared, iv. 169
 Kajbee, crucified of, iii. 55
 Lebanon, Nabatheans of, iv. 22; v. 162
 Meru, i. 145, 185, 187, 253; ii. 94; iii. 19, 208, 402; v. 347, 422, 436
 Nissa, v. 278
 Olympus, v. 171
 Ossa, giants under, iv. 324
 Parnassus, v. 110, 278
 Patmos, of, v. 143
 Pisgah, v. 272

 Rhipaeus, iii. 20
 Sermon on the, v. 363
 Serpent's, Carnac or, iii. 379
 Sinai, iii. 86; iv. 137; v. 67, 92, 114, 186, 278
 Sumeru, v. 110
 Transfiguration on the, v. 167
MOUNTAIN, Azazel a, iii. 375
 God, of, iv. 61
 Golden, ii. 80
 Ischins chained to a, iii. 375
 Kailasa, iii. 414
 Light of, v. 40
 Moon, of, iii. 236
 Peaks, of hundred, ii. 85
 Pit, and, iii. 356
 Snowy, v. 389, 390
MOUNTAINS, Allegorical, iii. 321
 Atala, of, iii. 403
 Caucasus, of, iii. 414
 Damavend, of, iii. 396, 397
 Holy, iv. 63
 Kaf, of, iii. 395, 396
 Seven, iv. 175, 188, 189, 317; v. 200
 Tree of life and three, iii. 220
 World, or great men of, iii. 316
MOUSSEAUX, Des, quoted, iii. 345, 413; v. 225
MOUT signifies mother, i. 155
MOVER, Nārāyana, on waters, i. 132
 One life, of all, iv. 242
 Unknowable, i. 126
 Waters, of the, ii. 59; iv. 335
MOVERS, quoted ii. 60, 254
MOYST principle, Radical, iii. 239; iv. 112
MRIDA or Mrira a form of Rudra, iii. 404
MRIGASHĪRSHA, v. 343, 344
MUD, Ilus or, ii. 54
MUESIS, v. 280
MUGHEIR or Ur of the Chaldees, iii. 230
MUHAMMADANS, Max Muller on religious doctrines of, i. 63
 Mystics, i. 298
MUIR, Dr., quoted, ii. 140; iv. 183
MUKHYA, ii. 165, 173
MUKTA, Unconditioned, i. 74
MUKTAS, Jīvātmās or, i. 190
MUKTI, Enoch reached, iv. 101
 Maya, freedom from, i. 43
 Nirvāna or, i. 43; iv. 101
MŪLĀDHĀRA chakra, v. 480
MŪLAPRAKRITI, Absolute, aspect of, i. 80; v. 494
 Absolute point, conceals, ii. 60
 Adam's earth called, i. 76
 Adi-Shakti emanation of, i. 76
 Akasha radiates from, i. 76, 109; v. 519
 Anupādaka, is, i. 131
 Asat or, iv. 168
 Bhagavad Gīta on, i. 76
 Brahma, female aspect of, i. 76
 Brahman as one with, i. 131
 Buddhi corresponds to, i. 136
 Chaos, primary aspect of, ii. 260
 Cosmic matter, and, i. 109; ii. 147
 Cosmic veil, ii. 147, 148
 Creative cause, female aspect of, i. 76
 Derivation of word, i. 76
 Differentiations of, i. 229; ii. 346

MŪLAPRAKRITI (*Contd.*)
  Duad, ii. 144
  Eternal Root, v. 227
  Ever-invisible robes, i. 109
  Evolution and, i. 193
  Force and, iii. 38
  Head-source, v. 90
  Īshvara and, i. 188
  Light of Logos, and, iii. 148
  Logos and, i. 188; ii. 144, 146, 148, 151
  Manvantara, at commencement of great, iii. 37
  Matter abstract ideal, i. 193
  Matter, unmanifested primordial, i. 76
  Mother, i. 193
  One principle, aspect of, i. 83
  One symbol of, i. 136
  Parabrahman and, i. 76, 83, 118, 136, 188,
    231, 317; ii. 51, 60, 144, 146, 151, 164,
    246, 260; iii. 37; v. 107, 475, 530
  Phenomenon, basis of upādhi of every, i. 109
  Pradhāna, i. 131, 229, 300
  Prakriti, becomes, iii. 76; v. 423
  Precosmic root-substance, i. 80
  Presence, invisible yet comprehensible, ii. 354
  Primordial cosmic substance, iii. 37
  Primordial homogeneous matter, i. 229
  Primordial substance, i. 109; ii. 306; v. 558
  Pythagorean triangle and, ii. 346
  Root, i. 142
  Root of all, i. 203, 300
  Root of all matter, i. 109
  Root of nature, i. 131, 193
  Root of That, i. 76
  Root-matter, ii. 260
  Root-nature, i. 109
  Root-principle of world stuff, ii. 246
  Sea of fire first radiation from, i. 142
  Shekinah, or, ii. 354; v. 107
  Soul of the one infinite spirit, i. 109
  Subba Row on, i. 76, 194, 317; ii. 147, 346
  Super-astral light first radiation from, i. 142
  Svabhāvat Buddhistic aspect of, i. 130
  Undifferentiated cosmic substance, i. 142
  Undifferentiated matter, i. 76; iv. 168
  Unevolved, i. 84
  Vedanitc, i. 300; v. 107, 227, 475
  Veil of Parabrahman, i. 76, 317; ii. 60, 144,
    146, 148
  Zero-line, beyond, ii. 246
MULE symbolizes Uriel or Thantabaoth, iii. 124
MULIL, Sin the son of, iii. 147
MUL-LIL, Gods of the ghost world, iii. 365
MULLER George, v. 132
MÜLLER, Max, see Book Index
MULUK-TAOOS, Lord Peacock, iv. 83
MUMIA in hieroglyphics, iv. 205
MUMMERIES of Brāhmans, iv. 56
MUMMIED dead, Sacred cross carried by,
  iv. 117
MUMMIFORM, Glyph of a, God, i. 266
MUMMY, Crocodile's head, with, i. 267
  Egg floating above, ii. 80
  Egyptian, i. 52
  Egyptian cross laid on, iv. 127
  Frog Goddesses on all, ii. 101
  Ptah unveils face of dead, ii. 68
  Sensaos, v. 332

  Symbolism, v. 248
  Wheat placed in Egyptian, iii. 372
MUMMY-form God with crocodile's head,
  iv. 148
MUMMY-God, Theban Triad represented as,
  iv. 32
MUNCK, quoted, iv. 29; v. 177, 213
MUNDANE, Circle, Isis, attribute of, iv. 127
  Cross, disc crossed by two diameters form, i. 72
  Cycle, interval after every, iv. 28
  Dissolution, *Book of God* on, iv. 326
  Intelligence or nous of Plato, i. 121
  Plane, universal life on, ii. 296
  Satan, home and source of, iii. 247
  Snake, matter, i. 147
  Soul is Mahat on earth, iii. 377
MUNDANE Egg, Ain Soph penetrates, i. 146
  Brahmā emerges from, i. 146; v. 188, 422
  Brahmā or universe contained in, iv. 187
  Chemis evolved out of, ii. 82
  Circle or, i. 154
  Dionysus sprang from, ii. 75
  Elements of, seven, iv. 187
  Finite God, and, ii. 69
  Germ in, i. 69, 127, 133; ii. 82
  Golden womb, i. 153
  Hiranyagarbha, i. 153
  Horus-Apollo, Sun-God and, ii. 82
  Infinite space, ii. 69
  Khnoom modeller of men out of, ii. 82
  Khoom placed in, ii. 80
  Mysteries, during, ii. 75
  Nārāyana penetrating, i. 146
  Phantom-germ of universe, ii. 83
  Point in, i. 69, 127
  Prajāpati emerges from, i. 146
  Ptah, the fiery God carries, ii. 80
  Ray emanating from, ii. 69
  Seven zones of, v. 199
  Shell of, v. 424
  Sphere of our universe, i. 153
  Swan and goose symbols of, ii. 72
  Svāyambhuva, self-existent, i. 146
  Symbolism of, ii. 74, 83, 280
  Ulom, born out of, ii. 81
  Universe of matter born out of, ii. 81
  Water of space, placed in, ii. 80
  Wöluspa, in, ii. 83
  Womb, as, ii. 69
  Zones, of, v. 199
MUNDANE God, Deus mundus or, ii. 183
  Chaldean Oracles, of, ii. 62
MUNDANE tree, Norse legends of, i. 259
  Serpent in, iii. 106
  Tree of evolution, iii. 262
MUNDI Domini, or world dominators, ii. 44
MUNDI Tenentes, or world holders, ii. 44
MUNDUS, Jupiter, ii. 183
MUNTE, Bones of giants near, iii. 337
MŪRTTIMAT=embodied, ii. 88
MURUDUG, or Silik-Muludag, iv. 45
MUSES of Sicily, v. 337
MUSEUM, British, Babylonian cylinders in,
  v. 123
  Papyrus in, v. 243
  Tantrika works in, v. 245, 329
MUSEUM, Boulaq, ii. 101; iv. 32; v. 243, 329

MUSEUM, Louvre, v. 246
MUSIC, Hindu, v. 197
  Inventor of, iii. 365; iv. 98
  Isis-Osiris and, iii. 365
  Manas and, v. 513
  Mathematics, one of four divisions of, ii. 151
  Nature, Man and, v. 514
  Pythagorean school in, v. 459
  Septenary law confirmed by, iv. 199
  Septenary scale in, v. 474, 509
  Spheres, of, i. 220; ii. 150; iv. 172; v. 479
MUSICAL, Notation, ancient, iv. 172
  Notes, v. 197
  Proportion, world constructed on principles of, ii. 151
  Scale, notes of, iv. 174, 199; v. 454, 484, 485, 508, 509
MUSICIANS, Celestial, iv. 156
  Indra's loka, of, ii. 247
MUSPEL, Sons of, i. 251
MUSSALMĀNS, v. 82, 125
  Temple, v. 171
MUT, Muth or Mout, Goddess, i. 155; v. 164
MYALBA, v. 501, 540, 559
MYCENAE, Creuzer writes of, iii. 344
MYLITTA identical with Aditi and Vach of Hindus, iii. 55
  Moon is, v. 332
MYORICA, Swans of, iv. 341
MYRRHA, mother of the Christian Logos, ii. 100
MYSORE, Western Ghats of, i. 315
MYSTAE, v. 130, 161, 281, 301, 429
MYSTAGOGY, Esoteric, iii. 100
MYSTERIA of the Sabasia, iii. 417
MYSTERIES, Adonis of, iii. 216
  Æschylus had profaned the, iii. 417
  Allegorical plays of, v. 301
  Amazons' circle-dance of the, iv. 28
  Ammianus Marcellinus on, iii. 427
  Ancient, iv. 163; v. 54, 138, 295
  Anthropography, of, i. 276
  Anthropological, iii. 92
  Antiquity of, v. 258, 275, 276, 279, 289, 293
  Arcane doctrine allegorically enacted in, i. 61
  Archaic, i. 222; iii. 232; iv. 364; v. 274
  Argha, of the, iii. 414; iv. 28
  Aristophanes, v. 255
  Ark of the, iv. 28
  Art of agriculture, of, ii. 366
  Aryan, v. 165
  Astrology and the, iv. 68
  Astronomical knowledge, based upon, ii. 26
  Astronomy, of, ii. 25, 121, 320
  Atlantean race, of, iv. 175; v. 261, 262, 269, 283
  Baal, of, iii. 216
  Baal-Adonis of, ii. 184
  Babylonians, iv. 136
  Bacchus, of, iii. 216; v. 161, 255, 278
  Being, of, ii. 314; iv. 157
  Bible, of the, v. 69, 87
  Candidates in, iv. 30
  Chaldea, of, v. 271, 293
  Christian, iv. 130; v. 274
  Chronological, iii. 92
  Church fathers and the, i. 61

Cicero on Sabasian, iii. 417
Circle-Dance and, v. 311
Clemens Alexandrinus and, i. 65; v. 266, 279
Cosmic and Sidereal, v. 70
Cosmogonical, v. 165, 201
Creation of, v.196
Cross-symbolism, of, iv. 118
Crucifixion of regenerated Man in, iv. 131
Curses, may become, ii. 281
Custodians of, iii. 283
Cyclic transformations, of, iii. 413
Dark Epaphos in Sabasian, iii. 413
Death in the great, iv. 30
Death penalty and, v. 218
Demeter, of, v. 171
Desecration of, v. 277
Dionysiac, ii. 75
Dionysus-Sabasius in Sabasian, iii. 413
Disappearance of, v. 294
Discipline and stimulus to virtue, a, i. 57
Divine, i. 61, 110; iii. 381
Downfall of, i. 61
Dragon-slayers and, iii. 216
Druids and, v. 295, 306
Egg of the land of, ii. 75
Egyptian, i. 51; iii. 394; v. 254, 264, 271, 282, 286, 290, 293, 295
Elements, of the, v. 241
Eleusinian, v. 66, 138, 161, 255, 276, 279, 298, 412
Emblem of mystery in the, ii. 121; iv. 130
Esotericism of, v. 77, 378, 412
Essences of, v. 271
Euclid and, v. 524
Europe, in, v. 293, 294-297
Explorer of ancient, iii. 47
Expressions used in, iv. 134
Faith, of the, iv. 14; v. 66
Fathers of the church initiated into, i. 65
Fires, secret of, taught in, iii. 114
Fourth Root Race and, v. 258
Freemasonry, and, iv. 363; v. 138, 272, 282, 284
Gaul and, v. 299
Gautama Buddha, of, v. 287
Genesis came from Egypt, of, iii. 15
Geography formerly part of, iii. 22
Gnosis, of the highest, ii. 121
Gnostic vowels, of the seven, iv. 135
Gods of, iv. 27
Gospels of, v. 66
Gradations of, v. 280
Great, v. 275, 279, 280, 295, 429
Great, death of candidate in the, iv. 30
Great pyramid and, ii. 26, 29
Grecian, v. 66, 138, 271, 275
Hebdomad, of, iii. 221; iv. 152, 162
Hermes, of, iii. 236
Hierophants of, iii. 379; v. 140, 159, 185, 271, 272, 290, 296
Higher, iv. 137
Human, v. 167
Idæan, iii. 216
Incarnation, of, v. 79
Indian, v. 140, 264, 275, 293
Initiates, inherited by, iii. 133
Initiates of, i. 176; iii. 270; v. 277, 304

MYSTERIES (Contd.)

Initiation, of, i. 276; iv. 61, 105, 128; v. 104, 152, 154, 169, 172, 175, 218, 261, 264, 271
Inner, v. 33
Intuition, to be solved, by, iii. 115
Java-Aleim, of, v. 185
Jesus initiate of the higher, iv. 136
Jews, of, v. 66
John could initiate, into which, iv. 136
Kabalah, of, iv. 114
Kabalistic, ii. 341
Kabiri of the, v. 310
Kingdom of Heaven, of, v. 169, 304
Krishna, of, v. 97
Lesser, v. 280, 429
Lord of all, v. 374
Magic and, v. 255, 257
Magic of, v. 254
Meaning of, v. 28
Mediaeval, iv. 201
Mercury, of, v. 159, 161
Mithraic, v. 314
Moon-God in, death of, ii. 112
Moses hierophant of, iii. 216
Name only used in, ii. 60
Nature of, v. 42, 295, 374
Number six in, iv. 163
Number ten, based upon, iv. 175
Objects of, v. 279 to 283
Occult, ii. 281; iii. 132; v. 45, 59, 109, 121
Occult Science, v. 121, 217
Olympic Zeus in, iii. 417
Origen initiated into, i. 65
Origin of, v. 258-268, 272
Orpheus and, v. 293, 304
Orphic egg part of, ii. 75
Orphic hymns sung during, iii. 143
Osiris, of, ii. 30; v. 159, 161, 283
Pagan, v. 35, 138
Paul and, v. 130
Penance connected with, iv. 211
Persian Mithras, of, ii. 164
Phoenician, v. 279
Pre-Adamite nations, of, iv. 20
Pre-archaic period, of, i. 61
Pre-Babylonian Jews of, ii. 184
Pre-Christian, v. 124
Primeval men taught, ii. 121
Primordial, the seven, iv. 184
Prometheus in, iii. 417, 418
Pyramids and ancient, iii. 427
Pythagoras of, v. 147, 279
Rabbinical, iii. 395
Ragon on, iv. 363
Real, iii. 36
Reincarnation taught in Egyptian, iv. 122
Religions, fifth race and, iii. 133; v. 138
Revelation of, v. 105, 218, 304
Sabasian, iii. 413, 414, 417
Sacred, iv. 17; v. 266, 294
Samothracian, iii. 17, 18, 114, 361; v. 279
Satan Iao of, iii. 387
Satya Yuga, no, in, v. 260
Secrecy of, v. 30, 66 et seq., 296
Secret in, great, iii. 142
Secret school, and, i. 65
Serpent as a symbol in, i. 143; ii. 121

Seven, i. 226
Seven planets and Sun Initiate, v. 108
Seven Sabbaths of, iv. 317
Socrates on, v. 266
Sōd name for, ii. 184; iii. 216
Sodalian, iv. 204
Solar God, in, iv. 29
Sons of the dragon, of, iii. 379
Sun's initiation, of, iii. 380
Svastika of, meaning of, iii. 107; iv. 159
Synesius initiated into, i. 65
Tāntriks of, v. 140
Testimony to, v. 254, 255, 261, 265, 266, 279
Theogony as taught in, iii. 385
Thorah of, v. 67
Time, and, iii. 433
Traces of, v. 284-293
True, v. 270, 276
Truths were perpetuated in, i. 58; v. 301
Victim of the, v. 291
Vikartana's initiation, of, iii. 380
Voltaire on, v. 261
Wheat and corn, of, iii. 373
Zohar of, v. 219
Zunis, religious, of, iv. 200

MYSTERIES of life of Nazarenes, iii. 105
Kosmos, of, ii. 33
Zodiac of, v. 429

MYSTERIUM, meaning explained, i. 325
MYSTERIUM MAGNUM, Elements are sprung from i. 326
Paracelsus, of, i. 130; ii. 308
Primordial matter or, i. 325
Synonyms of, iv. 80

MYSTERY, Buddha of, v. 349, 361
Final, v. 139, 140
Gnostic, v. 129
Hermaphrodite, of, v. 292
Initiation, of, v. 152
Mysteries, of, v. 91, 291
Name, v. 277, 408, 520
Names, iv. 106, 111; v. 290, 305, 408
Natural Primeval, v. 155
Nature, of, v. 154
Planet, v. 310, 332, 536
Prometheus, of, v. 323
Sacred, v. 408
Separated Man, of, v. 430
Stone, of the, v. 217
Sun of Initiation, of, v. 277
The One and the All, of, v. 305
Tongue, ii. 23
Word, v. 140, 309

MYSTERY-GOD, Iao, iv. 111, 174; v. 63, 270, 277, 286, 310
Logos or, v. 270
Name unpronounceable, ii. 82
Soma is, iii. 57
Sun and, v. 276
Uranus, i. 162
Vishvakarman is, v. 216, 286

MYSTERY-GODS, Kabeiri are, v. 310
Seven chief, iii. 36; v. 325

MYSTERY-LANGUAGE, v. 174, 175, 176, 185, 195
Bible and, ii. 30
Christian Church, origin of dogmas of, ii. 23

MYSTERY-LANGUAGE (*Contd.*)
  Church rituals, in, ii. 23
  Cycle of, ii. 30
  Facets of, ii. 23
  Kabbalists, discoveries made by, ii. 22
  Keys, of, ii. 22-38
  Mathematicians and, ii. 22
  Prehistoric races, of, iv. 145
  Scientists will adopt, ii. 38
  Seven sacraments and, ii. 23
  Strange records embedded in, ii. 21
  Theology sprung from, ii. 22
  Words of, ii. 22
MYSTERY-meaning of cross, iv. 158
MYSTERY-names, iv. 106, 111; v. 251
MYSTERY-tongue, ii. 23
MYSTIC, Christian, v. 214
  Four, Arbor-al or, ii. 51
  Idea, Astronomical value in, iv. 130
  Mirror, v. 412
  Nature, v. 293
  Permutation, v. 203
  Sign, v. 161, 356
  Speech, v. 394
  Tau, v. 162
  Western, v. 226
MYSTICAL meaning, Crucifixion, of, iv. 131
  Lotus, of, ii. 94
  Noe-Platonic, Philosophy, v. 34
  Number five, of, iv. 147
  Primordial chaos, of, ii. 45
  Quaternary, of, iv. 153
  Root-principle, of, ii. 45
  Sacred four, of, iv. 159
MYSTICISM, Bath-Kol in Jewish, iii. 115
  Circle, of, iv. 122
  Criticism, is not, v. 34
  Earliest, v. 293
  Hindu religions, of, i. 260
  Kabalistic, iv. 130
  Literature of, v. 404
  Northern, v. 208
  Oriental, v. 30, 35, 249
  Plato of, v. 29, 30, 35
  Pythagoras, of, v. 35
  Religions, ii. 245
  Rig Veda, in, iv. 17
  Roman Catholic church against heterodox, i. 65
  Speculative, v. 350
  Spirit of, iv. 140
  Swedenborg's, iii. 54; v. 406
  Tibetan, v. 404
MYSTICS, Antiquity of, iv. 99; v. 29
  Astral body, on, iii. 157; v. 359
  Authority of, ii. 336
  Buddhist, i. 135
  Chinese view of Svabhāvat, i. 130
  Christian, i. 83, 84, 262, 286; ii. 65, 379; iii. 106; iv. 24; v. 175
  Climacteric year of, ii. 382
  Double sign of Venus and Earth explained by, iii. 42
  Dreams of, ii. 239
  Empirics, are, iv. 234
  European, ii. 348; v. 104
  Fire defined by, i. 180

Generations of, i. 328
  Greek, iii. 145
  Hindu, iv. 196; v. 145
  Japan, of, i. 135
  Kabalah preferred by, ii. 230
  Lao-tze sects, of, i. 226
  Medieval, v. 174
  Modern, v. 175
  Muhammadan, i. 298
  Occultism among, i. 62
  Planetary conjunctions significant for all, ii. 382
  Rosicrucian symbols not understood by modern, i. 84
  Russian, i. 58
  Shiva patron of, ii. 178
  Spirits, believers in, ii. 336
  Svastika placed on defunct, iv. 157
  Tibet, in, i. 58
  Triad of, i. 83
  Western, iv. 114
  World of, ii. 396
MYTH, Apollo of, ii. 311, 382
  Astronomical, iv. 202
  Atlas, of, iv. 331
  Bordj, of, ii. 54
  Egyptian, i. 251
  Fallen angels of, ii. 180; iv. 43
  Fiske, on, iv. 355
  Greek, of evolution, iii. 130
  Jiva, a, is? ii. 327
  Leda, of, ii. 73; iii. 130
  Meaning of, ii. 143
  Osiris and Typhon in Egyptian, i. 251
  Prometheus of, iii. 109, 411, 413, 417
  Satanic, iii. 377; iv. 98
  Serpent of, iii. 380
  Solar, Hiram Abif as, v. 194
MYTHICAL Buddha, v. 476
  Dragon v. 202
MYTHOI of Peak of Teneriffe, iv. 359
MYTHOLATORS, iv. 158
MYTHOLOGISTS, Ancient, v. 201
  German, v. 56
MYTHOLOGY, Ancient, includes astronomy and astrology, ii. 104
  Ancient history, is, iv. 323
  Ancient science, and, ii. 16
  Aryan, ii. 16; iv. 89
  Atlantides of, iv. 330
  Australians, of, iv. 348
  Babylon, of, iii. 138
  Comparative, i. 53
  Disease of language, said to be, ii. 16
  Early thought, and, ii. 16
  Egyptian, v. 440
  Exoteric, ii. 175; iii. 132
  German, iii. 421
  Greek, i. 170, 307; iii. 41, 132, 183, 273
  Hindu, i. 86; ii. 16, 391; iii. 150; v. 289
  How to read, ii. 114
  Norse, iv. 323
  Northern, i. 251; iv. 104
  Origin and meaning of, ii. 16
  Phoenician, v. 202
  Pre-Homeric Hellenes, of, ii. 16
  Renouf on, ii. 16

MYTHOLOGY (*Contd.*)
Scandinavian, iii. 421
Slavonian, iii. 272
Vaidic Aryans, of, iv. 66
MYTHOPOEIC age, i. 310
MYTHOS, Bird, of enormous, iv. 189
Egpytian, iv. 154
Moon, of, ii. 102
Prometheus, of, iii. 402
Solar, ii. 16
MYTHS, Chaldean pantheon, of, iii. 238
Definition of, v. 53
Dual meaning of, ii. 54
Explanations of, ingenious, iv. 356
Facts and truth, built on, iii. 238
Genesis, in, iv. 17
Greek, iii. 238; iv. 16, 163
Hindu pantheon, of, iii. 238
Homer of, iv. 16
How to read, iv. 86
Jewish pantheon, of, iii. 238
Leda and Jupiter, or, iii. 203
Max Müller on Vedic, iv. 16
North, come from iv. 343
Origin of, iii. 295
Pococke on, ii. 53
Universal, v. 233
Veda of, iv. 16

N

NAASENI, Messiah of the, iii. 355
NAAŚENIAN GNOSTICS, iii. 354
NABATHEANS, Busrah to Syria, came from, iv.22
Lebanon, v. 54
Midan, came from iv. 325
Revelations, v. 89
Sabaeans and, iv. 20, 22; v. 54
Star-worshippers and, iv. 22
NABHAS-TALA, Space or, ii. 87
NĀBHI son of Agnīdhra, iii. 320
Bharata, son of, iii. 321
Prophets, or, v. 187
NABIN, a seer and prophet, iv. 23
NABO of the Greeks, iv. 22
NABONIDUS, the Babylonian king, iv. 261
NACH, the tempter, iii. 219
NACHANIDES, v. 90
NACHASH, Hebrew for serpent or brass, ii. 79
NĀCHNIS in India, iv. 31
NADEYLAC, M. de, on Colossi, iii. 338
NADIR and number six, iv. 158, 163
NADIR SHAH, Vandal warriors of, iv. 357
NĀDIS, v. 480, 520
NĀGA, or Nāgi, iii. 218
Meanings of, iii. 213
Reasons for calling an initiate a, ii. 125
Sarpa and, iii. 188
Serpent of wisdom, a, iv. 143; v. 286
Ulūpī, daughter of, iv. 200
NĀGA(S), Adepts, or, ii. 120; v. 287, 400
Allegorical nature of, i. 185
Astronomically, attend the sun, iii. 215
Asuras and, ii. 62
Buddhist (exoteric) and, iii. 39, 215
Celestial, iii. 125

Cosmic, or dragons, iii. 381
Ethnologically, iii. 215
Father of, iii. 141, 188
Incarnation of, iii. 215
India and, ii. 79; iii. 217
Indra, conqueror of, iii. 377
Initiates or, iv. 70
King-snakes or, iii. 380
Nāgārjuna, initiated by, v. 287
Nether world incarnations of, iii. 215
Nirmānakāyas, of, iii. 206
Orientalists describe, iv. 69
Primitive, iii. 188
Pulastya, father of, iii. 188
Secret books, of the, ii. 125
Serpents, or, iii. 141; v. 399, 400
Shesha, couch of Vishnu, v. 287
Sons of will and yoga, iii. 188
Vāsuki, the great, v. 286
NĀGA DVĪPA, a division of Bharatavarsha, iii. 141; iv. 69
NAGAL, chief sorcerer of the Mexicans, iii. 217
NAGALISM called devil worship, iii. 189
NAGALS, American, iii. 217
Mexican, iii. 214
Nargals and, iii. 189
NĀGĀRJUNA, Allegory of, v. 287
Aryasanga rival of, i. 121
Lung-shu of China, the, i. 130
Referred to, v. 287, 399, 410
School of, v. 399, 410
NĀGELI'S Principle of Perfectibility, iv. 219
NĀGPUR, iii. 345; iv. 69
NĀGASENA, the Arhat, v. 352, 385
NAGY, referred to, v. 220
NAHASH or deprived, iii. 248
NAHUATLS, Ancestors of the, iii. 47
NAIL, Vau a, iv. 28
NAILS of the cross a Pyramid, iv. 131
NAIMITTIKA, occasional or incidental, ii. 86; iii. 79, 310
NAJA and Nāga, ii. 155
NAKSHATRAS, or lunar asterisms, iv. 121
NALJORNGONSUM, meditation by self-perception, v. 402
NALTOR-CHOD-PA Yoga teaching, v. 411, 412
NAMĀN, ii. 89
NĀMARŪPA, v. 559
NAME, Avatāra, of, v. 337
Being defined by, i. 157
Deity, of, v. 108
Fire self, of, iv. 140
Ineffable, i. 245; iii. 283; iv. 127; v. 145, 162, 254
Jehovah, of, iv. 78; v. 192
Logos, of, ii. 66
Mystery, v. 277, 408, 502, 520
Potency of secret, iv. 105
Pronunciation of the ineffable, iii. 283
Secret, v. 108, 227, 337
Unpronounceable, ii. 156; iv. 77
Unutterable, ii. 60
NAMELESS DEITY, i. 178; iv. 110
NAMELESS ONE, i. 256; iv. 78
NAMES, Astronomical, v. 86, 89
Attributes or mystic, ii. 67
Geometrical relations of, v. 86,

NAMES (Contd.)
Hebrew, v. 134
Jehovah, ii. 156
Logograms composed of, iii. 335
Mentioned, not to be, iii. 283
Mystic, v. 251
Mythological, v. 433
Occult, v. 461
Power of, i. 157; iv. 336
Records in, iii. 335
Symbolic, v. 86, 87
NAMKHA, universe of, v. 379
NANAK, Nannar, or moon, iii. 147
NANDA, Buddhist Sovereign, iv. 120
NANDI, the sacred bull, iii. 406
NAN-SHAN, or eastern Tibet, i. 55
NAPHTALI, Capricornus in the sphere of, ii. 377; v. 184
NAPLES, Eclipse observed at, ii. 314
NAPOLEON, v. 250, 357
NARA, Spirit of God or, iv. 63
Universe, or, iii. 43
Water, body of, ii. 177; iv. 63
NĀRĀ, Waters or, iv. 163; v. 235
NARA-SIMHA (man-lion) the Avatāra, iii. 229
NĀRADA, All knowledge of, iv. 138
Asuramaya and, iii. 59
Brahmā and, iii. 91; v. 288
Brāhmana, iv. 138
Brahmans advised by, iii. 323
Brahmaputra, ii. 130
Calculations of, iii. 80
Daksha curses, iii. 91, 277; v. 288
Deva Rishi of occultism, the, iii. 92
Devamata and , iv. 137
Devarishi, a, iv. 70
Founder of Mysteries, v. 288
Immediate rebirth of, iii. 277
Initiate, v. 287, 288
Interpretations of statements of, iv. 139
Kumāras and, iv. 156
Michael, and, v. 288
National destinies in charge of, iii. 60
Nature of, iii. 60
Rishis, one of the greatest, ii. 130; iv. 70; v. 288
Sacrifice, on, iv. 137
Secret meaning of, v. 287
Seven senses, on, i. 151
Son of Brahmā, v. 287
Strife-making ascetic, the, iii. 178
Symbolism of, v. 287
Virgin-ascetic, the, iii. 148
NARAKA, Hindu hell or, iii. 107
NARAM-Sin, son of Sargon, iv. 261
NARĀS, or Centaurs, iii. 75
NĀRĀYANA, Brahmā, a permutation of, ii. 149
Brāhmanical, i. 132
Krishna identifies himself with, iii. 358
Meanings of, ii. 50, 149; iv. 63, 163
Mover on the Waters, v. 189, 233, 311
Neptune identical with, iv. 334
Prāchetasas worshippers of, iv. 149
Purusha, i. 277
Self-born spirit, ii. 177
Self-created Logos, v. 215

Self-existent Lord, ii. 46; v. 215
Shrī, wife of, iii. 86
Svāyambhuva or, i. 146
Vishnu or, ii. 59; v. 447
Waters of space, moving over, i. 74; ii. 351; v. 189, 233
NARGAL, Assyrian and Chaldean, iii. 217
Ulūpī, daughter of the, king, iv. 200
NARJOL, v. 498
NAROS, Cycle of the, iv. 190; v. 341
NARRATIVES the cloak of doctrine, iv. 14
Separation of sexes, of, v. 182
Three aspects of, v. 110
NARROW GATE of the King's Chamber, ii. 30
NARROW-HEADED, Spark absent from the, iii. 190
Third race, iii. 169
Wives from, iii. 273
NARTHEX, the wand of candidate for initiation, iv. 87, 94
NASIREDDIN, Tables of, ii. 384
NASMYTH, Discoveries of, ii. 254
Willow leaves of, ii. 264, 315
NĀSTIKA, a rejection of idols, i. 322
NATAR KHARI, Hieratic Alphabet, v. 114
NĀTH or LORODS, iii. 97
NATIONAL Deity of Israel, iv. 111
Ethics, iv. 36
Faith, exoteric, iv. 40
Features, Jewish, iv. 38
Gods and heroes, ii. 381
Idea, evolution of the, ii. 142
Library of Paris, iv. 129; v. 252
Polity of the Jews, iv. 27
Progress, karma and, ii. 40
Religion, v. 121
Symbols, iv. 22
NATIONAL REFORMER, quoted, i. 337
NATIONALITIES, Admixture of, iii. 442
NATIVITY, Creation and, iv. 195
Lunar year of the, ii. 381
Millennium divided by year One of the, i. 62
NATURA Naturans, ii. 130
NATURA non facit Saltum, iii. 288; iv. 266
NATURAL PHILOSOPHY, Magic or, v. 43
NATURAL SCIENCE, Prof. Pfaff on, iii. 96
Testimonium paupertatis of, iv. 233
NATURAL SELECTION, i. 168, 251; ii. 324; iii. 192, 300, 423; iv. 217, 224, 225, 227, 232, 247, 249, 251, 253, 296
NATURE, Absolute, underlying, i. 80
Abstract, v. 187
Actuality of, ii. 342
Adam Kadmon as, iv. 167
Aggregate of forces, an, i. 298
Alchemical transmutations and, iii. 177
Ancient creeds and, iv. 228
Animal soul of, is, Fohat, i. 171
Animate, i. 268
Astoreth a symbol of, iv. 30
Author of, ii. 212
Binah or intelligent, iii. 94
Body of the whole or, iii. 195
Breathing of, v. 107
Boundless, v. 52
Cessation of motion not in, i. 160

NATURE (*Contd.*)

Chance, no, in, ii. 379
Circulatory work, a, i. 78
Colour, Sound and, v. 485
Conscious, i. 156
Contrasts, in, v. 116
Corporeal, of Brahma, iii. 183
Cosmos as receptive, i. 134
Coverings built by, iii. 85
Co-worker with, i. 322; iii. 444; v. 501, 514
Cow's horns a symbol of mystic, iii. 44; v. 165
Creative, i. 72
Creative forces of, seven, ii. 360; v. 421
Creative power, the dual, i. 127
Creative principle of, i. 70; ii. 29; iii. 38; v. 43
Cult of, v. 263, 367
Cycles in, iii. 440
Decree of, iv. 103
Definition of, v. 487
Deity in Cosmic, i. 144; ii. 344; iv. 19
Diameter stands for, i. 155
Divine, iii. 55, 84; v. 117, 442, 445
Divine form, love of, for, ii. 135
Divine omniscience in, v. 265
Dual, i. 301; ii. 190; iii. 40; iv. 102; v. 38, 49, 116
Earth, Moon and, v. 165
Economy of, i. 224; iv. 253, 270; v. 212, 367
Efforts of, early, iii. 66
Element in, male, i. 129
Elementals, v. 534
Emblem of physical, iv. 163
Essence of, primal, i. 176
Eve and, v. 191
Ever becoming, is the, i. 295; v. 191
Ever eternal, i. 72
Evolutionary scheme in, i. 233
Fa, and, v. 443, 454, 514
Factor element in, iv. 169
Failure of, to create alone, iii. 313
Failures of, iii. 444
Father-Mother, v. 209
Feminine, is, i. 72; v. 164
First, i. 240
Fivefold, iv. 156
Fohat carries out the plan in the mind of, i. 171
Forces of, i. 195, 199, 263; ii. 60, 184, 396; iv. 153, 203, 234; v. 81, 469, 470
Freaks of, iii. 66
Gaea or, iii. 76
Generative powers in, iv. 29
Geometrical working of laws of, ii. 310
Germs of all, iv. 28
God as related to, i. 301, 333; ii. 130, 184; v. 87, 115
Goddess of active forces in, i. 194
Gross, v. 436
Grossest physical transformation of, ii. 122
Ground plan of, iv. 307
Harmony of numbers in all, iv. 193
Heavenly man, mingled with, iii. 16
Hermetic, i. 332
Hidden truths of, i. 183
Highest consciousness in, ii. 297
Homogeneous element in, ii. 114
Illusions, a bundle of, iv. 43

Imagination of, i. 303
Immutable (laws of), ii. 322; iii. 58, 90, 117
Inorganic in, nothing is, ii. 232, 351; iv. 241
Intelligences and, i. 168
Intelligent, iii. 94
Intelligent Powers of, i. 156; ii. 142
Isis or, iv. 173; v. 165
Judgment of, iv. 18
Jumps and starts not in, iii. 200, 443
Karma-Nemesis whose bondmaid is, iii. 304; iv. 43
Key keeper of, iv. 172
Kingdoms of, iii. 168, 193; iv. 300; v. 460
Laws of, i. 81, 86, 159, 244; ii. 310; iii. 158; iv. 181, 300; v. 266, 321, 323
Life principle in, v. 456
Living spirit of, iii. 117
Lotus sacred to, ii. 94
Male principle in, v. 129, 292
Man and, v. 331, 456, 487
Man mingled with, iii. 269
Man the product of, iv. 297
Manifestation of creative, i. 72
Manifested, i. 207; iv. 106, 166, 224; v. 455
Mankinds, with its many, iv. 60
Man's place in, iv. 226
Manvantara, never stationary during, i. 301
Material, man not the product of, iii. 90
Material soul of, v. 456
Matrix of, iv. 28, 37
Mechanical processes of, iii. 299
Men evolving from, iii. 16
Men not created by, iii. 271
Metaphysical, iv. 155, 185; v. 187
Middle note of, v. 454, 514
Mind in, ii. 328
Miracle of, iv. 223
Mother, v. 233
Mother and, v. 165, 293
Mūlaprakriti root of, i. 131
Mysteries of, i. 210; ii. 336, 397; iii. 156, 243, 372; iv. 151, 192, 197; v. 42, 154, 174, 264, 295, 374
Mysteries of occult, iv. 119; v. 154, 174, 194, 293, 295
Mystic, ii. 152; iii. 44; v. 293
Necessity of, to run down, i. 204, 206
Newton and, v. 54
Numbers in, iv. 134; v. 418, 420, 421, 456, 461
Occult, i. 205, 326; ii. 268; iii. 360; iv. 119; v. 45, 91, 431, 456, 461
Occultism and, i. 209; iii. 114, 200; iv. 43
One element in, ii. 181
One God in, i. 75
Order of, i. 320; iv. 103
Pan, is God, iii. 388; iv. 79, 150, 153
Perennial, iv. 175
Personal God outside, iv. 40
Phenomena of, iv. 233; v. 261
Physical, ii. 393; iii. 46, 63, 66, 78, 111; iv. 163, 165
Plan uniform in, iii. 263
Plane, does not act on a flat, ii. 273
Prakriti or, iii. 76; v. 469
Pralayas and, iv. 230
Primary forces in, six, i. 333
Primitive models of, iv. 165

NATURE (*Contd.*)
  Principle in, third, iii. 177
  Principles of, i. 83, 178; iii. 42; iv. 165
  Procreative power in, iii. 54; v. 265, 456
  Productive and generative power in, symbols of, i. 135
  Properties of, iv. 201, 205
  Prototype in, ii. 194
  Protyles in, iv. 306
  Pymander on, iii. 234, 239; iv. 59
  Qualities of the elements in, ii. 250, 260
  Radiations of primordial, ii. 357
  Radical keynote in, iv. 60
  Repeats herself, never, i. 236; iv. 270
  Root number of, ii. 180
  Root principles of, i. 114, 161, 193
  Rose, symbol of, v. 293
  Ruler of, ii. 98
  Rulers of various departments in, i. 186
  Secret operations of, v. 255, 263, 264
  Secrets of, v. 121, 142, 174, 263, 407
  Seminal principles in, iii. 167
  Septenary division of, iv. 145; v. 477
  Sevenfold, i. 310; ii. 88; iv. 198, 341; v. 469
  Shatarūpa or, i. 157
  Sounding board, a, v. 522, 523
  Space and, are one, ii. 279
  Spirit and, iii. 49
  Spirit and soul in, i. 178
  Spirit beyond manifested, iii. 122
  Spirit of, iii. 122, 275
  Spirit, male, or female, iv. 31
  Spirit-soul pervading all, i. 123
  Spirits which guide, ii. 202; iv. 54
  Spiritual, i. 272; ii. 312; iii. 46, 118; v. 87
  Stability of the laws of, ii. 396
  Stars, and, v. 222
  Structural energies of, ii. 395
  Subjective and Objective, v. 558
  Substance of, v. 485
  Submission of, to law, ii. 41
  Supreme sacredness of the religion of, iv. 365
  Symbol language taught by, ii. 33
  Symbols of, iii. 359; iv. 39; v. 293
  Temple of, ii. 193
  Tentative efforts of, iii. 197
  Transformation of, ii. 122
  Triune co-equal, ii. 339
  Truths in, v. 283
  Two agencies in, ii. 248
  Unaided, failures of, iii. 63, 66
  Unconscious, cannot be, i. 320
  Uncovered face of, iv. 225
  Uniformity in laws of, ii. 336
  Unity in, i. 179, 319; ii. 183; v. 86
  Universal and abstract, iv. 37
  Universal cause in, v. 261
  Universal deity in, iii. 258
  Universal plane of productive, ii. 339
  Vāch a synthesis of all forces in, i. 194
  Vacuum abhorred by, i. 133; ii. 57, 218, 243, 393
  Vitality in, dormant, iii. 166
  Voice of, ii. 247; iv. 172; v. 443
  Woman and, v. 442
  Womb of abstract, ii. 88; iii. 236; iv. 29

  World Virgins and, v. 293
  Worship based upon profound knowledge of, ii. 113; iii. 275
  Zi or spirit in, iii. 64
NATURE-FORCE or elemental, i. 202
NATURE-POWERS, SEVEN, i. 274; iv. 204
NATURE SPIRITS, Elementals or, i. 202, 268; ii. 181; v. 239, 540
  Lower angels are, iii. 111
  Model for, i. 272
  Phenomena and, i. 203
  Psychic, i. 202
NAUDIN, referred to, iii. 128, 188; iv. 216
NAUMACHY, (Bibractis), v. 295
NAUTCH-GIRLS, Kedeshim of Bible and Indian, iv. 28
NAVE, Christian symbol of, iv. 31
NAVEL, Ark corresponds with, iv. 29
  Centre in Man, v. 555
  Correspondences, v. 478
  Earth, of, iii. 399
  Lotus flower growing out of Vishnu's, ii. 95; iii. 43; iv. 40; v. 233, 476
NAVES, Time's wheels and, iv. 183
NAVI-FORMED ARGHA, iii. 414; iv. 28
NAVIGATION, Aerial, ii. 284
NAVIS, Ship, ark or, iii. 147
  Ship-like form of crescent or, iv. 31
  Sidereal vessel or, iv. 31
  Vehicle, boat-shaped, or, iv. 30
NAYA-harmony, iv. 97
NAZAR, Moses, a, iv. 33
NAZARA OR NAZARETH, iii. 105
NAZARAEAN, GNOSTICS, iii. 158
NAZARENES, Belief of, v. 160
  Demiurge of, iii. 246
  Disciples called, v. 136
  Jesus and, v. 104, 160
  " Heretics ", v. 168
  Kabalistic Gnostics were, v. 161
  Mano of, i. 245
  Mystery tongue and, ii. 23
  Philosophical systems of, i. 247
  Pupils of, v. 161
  Religion of, i. 58
  Sage, v. 369
  Scripture of, i. 245; iii. 105
  Spirit a female power among, i. 245, 246
NAZARETH, Jesus of, ii. 379; iii. 385; iv. 77; v. 99, 125, 151, 155, 166, 175
NAZARITE, Chela, v. 277
NAZARS, v. 137, 193, 369
N'CABVAH, i. 72; iv. 35
NEANDERTHAL SKULL, iii. 199; iv. 256, 257, 293, 298, 314
NÉANT, non-being, ii. 370
NEAPOLITAN Sailor's Prayer, ii. 189
NEBAT LAVAR BAR LUFIN, the third life or Mano, i. 245
NEBO, Babylonian, iv. 45; v. 74
  Generic name, a, iii. 215
  Moses dies on, iv. 23
  Mystic name of the caste devoted to, iv. 22
  Son of, the moon, iv. 23
  Wisdom, God of, iv. 22, 45; v. 369
NEBU, False Messiah, v. 368
NEBUCHADNEZZAR, iv. 20; v. 102

NEBULA, Bright lines of, ii. 320
  Primeval, ii. 316
  Specturm of, ii. 322
  World's system reborn through a, ii. 325
NEBULAE, Annulation of, i. 163
  Astronomy of, i. 189
  Condensation of, iii. 255
  Congeries of, iii. 321
  Cosmic matter of, i. 149
  Existence of, ii. 312
  Fohat and, ii. 397
  Gaseous, ii. 322
  Irresolvable, i. 294; ii. 266
  Mill explains, ii. 312
  Nature of, ii. 318
  Planetary, ii. 322
  Starry clusters mistaken for, ii. 267
  Stars and, ii. 314
  What are?, ii. 319
  World-stuff or, ii. 303, 319
NEBULAR, Astral light, in the, ii. 83
  Firmament, ii. 323
  Hypothesis, ii. 324
NEBULAR THEORY, the, i. 160, 163, 338;
  ii. 221, 230, 252, 268, 311, 312, 313, 314, 315,
  318, 319, 320, 321, 322, 323; v. 107
NEBULOSITY of cosmic matter, ii. 316
NEBULOUS, Almighty, the, ii. 52
  Matter, ii. 71, 229
  Primeval matter, ii. 314
  Rings, i. 205; ii. 221
  Substance, i. 164
NECEPSO, Astrologer, v. 329
NECESSARIANISM, i. 321
NECESSITY, Circle of, iii. 304, 378
  Cycle of incarnation or, i. 82, 274; v. 213,
    300
  Matter, force and, iv. 218
  Sons of, i. 115
  Universe son of, i. 114
NECK, Earth, of, iii. 400
  Three heads on one, ii. 103
NECROMANCER, Serpents in tombs of each,
  iii. 214; v. 124
NECROMANCY, v. 40, 298
NECROPOLIS, the Chaldean, iv. 30
  Christian, v. 328
NEGATION, Absolute, i. 80
  Ain Soph a term of, ii. 147
  Asat not merely, of Sat, iv. 16
  Cecity of, ii. 336
  Deity, Satan, of, iv. 79
  Spirit of paradoxical, iv. 59
NEGATIVE, Dual Nature positive and, i. 301
  Electricity positive and, i. 201
  Elements, ii. 308
  Forces, i. 324; iii. 37
  Life is positive and, ii. 328
  Perfection of first humanity, iii. 104
  Pole, ii. 280; iii. 93
  Positive and, mutally attracted, i. 292
  Positive awakening, i. 332
  Sexes, iii. 269
  Svastika implies positive and, iii. 42
NEGATIVELY EXISTENT ONE, iv. 197
NEGATIVENESS, Realm of, i. 196
NEGRITOS and Lemuro-Atlanteans, iii. 201

NEGRO, African, iii. 441; iv. 349
  Central American, traces of, iv. 358
  Europe, types in, iv. 331
  Methodists, v. 50
  Papuan, iii. 199
  Race, iv. 293, 349
  Simian type, of, iv. 248
  Skulls, iv. 308
  Turanian and, iv. 313
  Type, bones of, iii. 280
NEGROES, Aryans and Mongols, iv. 178
NEGROIDS, Huxley on, iii. 315
NEHHASCHIM, or serpents' works, iii. 408
NEHUSHTAN, Brazen serpent or, iii. 386
NEIBBAN, Burmese for Nirvana, i. 112
NEILOS, Indus or, iii. 416
  Nile or, iii. 415; iv. 154
  Sacred water of, iii. 415
  Value of the word, ii. 105
NEÏTH, Aditi is, v. 214
  Ammon was, iii. 143
  Goddess, a demiurgical, ii. 115
  Mother of Ra, v. 334
  Nephtys or, ii. 111
  Queen of heaven or, ii. 108
  Saïs Goddess of, ii. 114
NEITHA, Female Divinity, v. 74
NEMESIS, Greek, the, ii. 367
  Karma, iii. 306, 419
  Pantheists, of Western, ii. 366
NEO-ARYANS, Post-diluvian, iii. 355
NEO-PLATONIC, Inspirations, v. 305
  Schools, v. 138, 298, 303, 304, 306, 307
NEO-PLATONIC PHILOSOPHY, v. 34, 451
NEO-PLATONIC WORKS, v. 444
NEO-PLATONISM, Christian veil over, i. 65;
  v. 302, 306
  Mysteries of, v. 333
  Period of early, iii. 399; v. 306
NEO-PLATONISTS, Alexandrian, ii. 125;
  v. 116, 299, 305
  Archetypal ideas of, i. 324
  Buddha, and, i. 66
  Chaldeans and, iv. 111
  Clement of Alexandria and, iii. 281; v. 59
  Fragments by, iv. 174
  Iamblichus and, v. 58
  Interpretations of, v. 27, 33, 34, 299, 307
  Jowett and, v. 28, 32, 35
  Microcosm applied to man by, i. 326
  Plato's works, and, v. 29, 30, 33
NEO-PYTHAGOREANS, ii. 76
NEODYMIUM, i. 197; ii. 270
NEOLITHIC, Caves, iii. 351
  Celts, iv. 291
  Civilization, iv. 284
  Era, date of, iv. 268
  Flints, iv. 324
  Lake villages, iv. 284, 308
  Man, iv. 246, 255, 284, 291, 293
  Palestine, men in, iv. 344
  Remains, iv. 293
NEOPHYTE, ii. 29, 62; v. 104, 106
  Trials of, v. 290
  Twelve labours of, v. 62
NEOPHYTES used the Sign of the Cross, iv. 132;
  v. 159

NEPĀL, Old school of Buddhism in, i. 71
  Temple in, v. 97
NEPHESH, Aptitudes of, i. 290
  Breath of life or, i. 260, 288; iii. 169, 377;
    iv. 23; v. 518
  Chaiah, i. 272
  Garment of, iii. 316
  Immortality of, i. 289
  Living soul or, i. 243, 272
  Lower, iv. 24
  Manas or, i. 287
  Mould of Ruach, i. 290
  Seat of the physical appetites, or, iv. 176
  Tzelem of, iv. 205
  Vital soul, i. 272
NEPHILIM, the Fallen Angels, iii. 71, 232, 281,
    294; iv. 324, 344
NEPHTYS OR NEĪTH, ii. 111; v. 246
NEPTUNE, Astronomical places, v. 536
  Atlantic islands sacred to, iii. 407
  Atlantis divided by, iii. 405; iv. 334
  Chozzar or, iv. 148
  Dragon or, iii. 355
  Emblem of, v. 117
  God of water, ii. 183
  Happy new year to Noah from, ii. 161
  House of, i. 164
  Laomedon after, iv. 364
  Leviathan, riding on, iii. 271
  Light received by, ii. 299
  Nārāyana identical with, iv. 334
  Nereus an aspect of, iv. 149, 336
  Occult theory about, v. 222
  Orbit of, ii. 397
  Phlegyan isle and, iii. 152
  Problem about, v. 222
  Satellites of, i. 163; ii. 317
  Uranus and, i. 204; ii. 299
  Varuna or, iii. 75
NEREIDS, Goats sacrificed to, iv. 150
  Patronymic of, iv. 336
NEREUS an Aspect of Neptune, iv. 149, 336
NERGAL-SEREZER the Assyrian God, iii. 217
NERGAS the death God, iii. 16
NERO, v. 120
NEROSES and SAROSES, ii. 381
NERVE, Apperception, i. 231
  Auditory, ii. 358
  Aura, ii. 52; iii. 299
  Cells, iv. 240, 243; v. 523
  Currents, i. 333
  Diseases, iii. 369
  Excitation, ii. 262
  Fibrils of brain, i. 337
  Force, ii. 174, 190, 233; iv. 224; v. 484
  Optic, v. 521
  Plane, v. 531
  Plexuses, iii. 101
  Sensation, i. 231
  Sushumnā, i. 190
  System, ii. 249
  Vibrations, v. 485
NERVES, Animal sensations, of, ii. 289
  Infusoria without, iii. 159
NERVOUS Centres, i. 303; ii. 264; v. 531
  Ether, ii. 233, 255, 257, 261, 262, 327, 359;
    iii. 299

Fluid, ii. 256; iii. 370
NERYOSANGH, translator of the Yasna, iv. 327
NESCIENCE, Agnosticism and, i. 74
NESHAMAH, Bundle of life and, iii. 316
  Ethereal combination of, iv. 24
  Garment of, i. 290
  Inspirations of, i. 290
  Progressive, i. 289
  Reason or, iv. 176
  Soul or, iii. 377
  Spirit or, i. 288
  Tzelem of, iv. 205
NEST, Bird, or eternal, iv. 294
  Solar God, of, ii. 75
NETEROO, Egyptian, v. 214
NETHER Abyss, Lady of the, iv. 30
  Lords, iii. 426
  Region, iii. 107, 356
  World, ii. 79, 198; iii. 443
NETWORK of Destiny, the, ii. 364
NETZACH in Chaldean Kabalah, i. 249
NEUMANN referred to, iii. 422
NEUROPATHIC persons, iii. 369
NEUTRAL CENTRE(S), Being, of, iv. 300
  Fohat produces seven, i. 203
  Keely on a, ii. 280, 281
  Latest force, of, i. 210
  Laya or, ii. 242, 281
  Life, of, iii. 263
  Line, ii. 274
NEUTRAL POINT, Curve must pass through a,
    ii. 274
NEVER-CEASING Evolution, iv. 116
NEVER-DYING BREATH OF LIFE, iv. 160
NEVER-ERRING KARMA, iv. 43
NEVER-RESTING PRINCIPLE, iii. 311
NEVOLEN, or Nevo-loo v. 246
NEW DISPENSATION, i. 62; iii. 376
NEW GUINEA, Australia and, iii. 21, 328
NEW LIFE, Oeaohoo the younger, the, i. 138
NEW MOON, Astoreth, and, iv. 30
  Paul on, iii. 85
  Seventh Round, in, v. 536
NEW ORLEANS, Skeleton found at, iii. 351
NEW WORLD, America the old, i. 337
  Fourth race, and, iii. 218
  Mankind of, iii. 443
  Norwegians and Scandinavians settled in, i. 337
  Secret Doctrine in, iii. 422
  Svastika in the catacombs of, iv. 158
NEW YORK, Aryan Theosophical Society of,
    ii. 355
  Statue of Liberty at, iii. 337
  Wilder, Prof., of, iii. 142
NEW ZEALAND, iii. 227
  Lemuria and, iii. 298
  Lizard with atrophied third eye in, iii. 298
  Traditions of, iv. 356
NEW-BIRTH, Water, of, iv. 128
NEW-BORN, Miracle of the, ii. 97
NEWCOMB, Prof., quoted, i. 149; iii. 157
  Cooling of the globe, on the, iv. 264
  Nebulae, on, ii. 267
NEWFOUNDLAND, Continent, from France to,
    iv. 360
  Cuttle fish in, iii. 438
NEWMAN, Prof., quoted, iii. 414

NEWTON, Sir Isaac, Agent of, ii. 201
  Alleged blasphemy to the memory of, ii. 213
  Corpuscular theory of, ii. 39, 207
  Ether of, i. 78; ii. 217, 225
  Force, on, ii. 213, 235
  Gravitation and, ii. 213, 214, 216
  Great mathematical knowledge of, ii. 207
  Hebrew Scriptures and, v. 182
  Kant and, ii. 326
  Letter to Bentley of, ii. 201
  Moon, the, and, v. 224
  Nature and, v. 52
  Neglect of, ii. 218
  Philosophy of, ii. 331
  Plurality of worlds, on, iv. 275
  Principia of, iv. 243
  Quoted, i. 78, 164; ii. 318, 319, 331; iv. 91, 243
  Scientists since, ii. 268
  Speculations of, iv. 53
  Spiritual monad of a, iii. 244
  Teachings and inner convictions of, ii. 217
  Zodiac, on the, ii. 378
NICÆA, Council of, iii. 282; v. 156
NICKEL, ii. 270
NICODEMUS, mentioned, v. 83
NICOLAÏTANS, v. 133
NIDĀNA, Eternal, i. 156
  Māyā and, i. 112, 116
NIDĀNAS, Causes, i. 112; v. 249, 513, 517, 523, 558, 561
  Dual meaning of, v. 558
  Karma and, v. 560
  Sound, and, v. 523
  Four truths, and, i. 118
  Occultist, verified by, ii. 234
  Twelve, i. 112; v. 379, 397, 558, 559
NIDHOGG, Dragon, i. 259
  Great serpent, ii. 123
NIFFER OR NIPUR, iii. 147
NIFL-HEIM mist place, ii. 83; iii. 248; iv. 343
NIGHT, Asuras and body of, iii. 100
  Body of, iii. 170, 172
  Brahmā, of, i. 79, 114, 165, 266, 285; ii. 86, 91, 173; iii. 80, 308
  Brahmā's body turned into, i. 266; iii. 168
  Dawn after that, ii. 86
  Dawn to, manvantaric, i. 132
  Dawn, until the future, ii. 92
  Day and, i. 82; iii. 69; iv. 76, 137
  Day of Brahmā equals, iv. 73
  Fires, iii. 74
  Globe, sevenfold, for each, iv. 326
  Great, duration of, i. 192
  Homer ascends no higher than, ii. 143
  Latona as, iv. 339
  Planet, of a, iv. 230
  Planets though dead remain intact during, i. 83
  Polar, iv. 342
  Pralaya or, i. 111; ii. 166
  Queen of, i. 283
  Rātri or, iii. 68
  Sandhyā interval between day and, iii. 70
  Set, darkness of, iii. 384
  Sons of, iii. 168; iv. 341
  Sun, iv. 151
  Symbol of, iii. 130
  System after, i. 186

  Time, of, ii. 136
  Unborn, ii. 87
NIGHTMARES, ii. 16, 293
NIGHTS, Brahmā, of, i. 110, 114, 125, 131; iii. 90
  Deity of, iv. 115
  Planetary chain, of, i. 209
  Rest of Brahmā, iii. 247
NIGIDIUS FIGULUS, v. 334
NIHIL, Creating out of, ii. 297
  Divine principle, v. 387
  Infinite, v. 387
  Meaning of, v. 384, 387
NIHILISM, attributed to Buddha, v. 385
NIHILISTS, Buddhists called, v. 380
NĪL, Ethiops, iii. 415
  Indus called, iii. 415
NĪLĀ, Blue river or, iii. 415
  Contests on the banks of, iii. 404
  Mountain, blue, iii. 402, 404, 405
NĪLAKANTHA, i. 158; iii. 98; iv. 64, 138, 209
NĪLALOHITA, Red and blue or, ii. 176; iii. 115, 198
NILE, Banks of, iii. 404
  Celestial, iv. 151; v. 331
  Crocodile of sacred, iv. 148
  Floods of, iii. 352
  Great deep or, ii. 31
  Indus, Neilos or, iii. 416
  Io to follow Ethiops to, iii. 415
  Isis-Osiris and, iii. 365
  Isis personified, iv. 154
  Lotus of, ii. 96; iv. 40
  Moses rescued from, iii. 426
  Naming of, iii. 416
  Osiris or river, ii. 105; iv. 155
  Present, iii. 316
  Relics of history along, i. 51
  Ruins on the banks of, iii. 428
  Soundings in the valley of, iv. 319
  Sources of, i. 60
  Thebes, at, iii. 378
  Tropical year and, ii. 105
  Valley of, iii. 429; v. 43
NILGIRI HILLS, Mula Kurumba of, iii. 443; v. 47, 122
NILSON, referred to, ii. 270; iv. 318
NIMITTA, the efficient cause, i. 126; ii. 86
NIMROD, Akkad capital of, ii. 32
  Bible, and, iii. 281
  Cush, son of, iv. 20
  Epic of, iii. 352
  Izdubars or, iii. 335
  Mighty hunter, iii. 374; v. 309
NIMRODS, Prototypes of, iii. 274
NINE Chambers, Qabalah of the, i. 144
  Divinites, v. 270
  Letters only of Max Müller, ii. 76
  Lives of a cat, iv. 122
  One he is and, i. 160
  Male number, iii. 220
NINEFOLD Divisions of the World, iv. 193
NINETEEN Years of the Lunar Cycle, iv. 339
NINETEEN Years of the Lunar Cycle, iv. 339
NINEVEH, Library of, iv. 262
  Oan or Fishman of, ii. 380
  Relics of, v. 431
  Tahmurath said to have founded, iii. 396
NINTH KUMĀRA in *Vishnu Purāna*, i. 142

NIOBE, Allegory of, iv. 340
NIPPANG, the Chinese Nirvana, i. 112
NIPUR or NIFFER, iii. 147
NIRAKSHA, the abode of the Gods, iii. 400
NIRGUNA, Negative, iii. 104
    Parabrahman the absolute, i. 131; v. 350
    Vishnu, as, v. 350, 359
NIRMĀNAKĀYĀS, Adepts, v. 351, 353, 427, 453, 543
    Astral Ego of, v. 168
    Birth, and, v. 559
    Body, v. 402
    Boehme, guided by, ii. 217
    Buddhas, Bodhisattvas and, v. 364, 366, 401
    Divine Incarnation, v. 76, 370
    Egos of, iv. 186
    Manvantaras, from other, iii. 102, 222
    Monads and, iii. 103
    Nāgas, of, iii. 206
    Nirvāna and, v. 351, 354, 360
    Nirvānakāya, or, v. 402
    Rudra-Kumāras, of, iii. 257
    Sacrificial, v. 370
    Siddhas are, iv. 208
    Spirits affecting mediums are often, i. 279
    Spiritual principles of men and, i. 190
    State of, v. 427
    Two kinds of, v. 354
    Watchers, invisible, v. 466
    Watchers or, v. 466
NIRMATHYA, Fire produced by friction or, ii. 245
NIRUKTA and the Sushumnā Ray, ii. 240; v. 275
NIRUPADHI, Prakriti and Prusha are, ii. 306
NIRVĀNA, i. 45
    Adept can renounce, v. 80
    Akasha and, ii. 360
    Ālaya not, i. 119
    Annihilation, no, v. 384
    Attainment of, iii. 90
    Buddha, of, v. 105, 350, 362, 364, 366, 373, 378, 407, 410
    Buddhist, ii. 300; v. 367
    Devachan and, i. 226; v. 497
    Dhyāni-Chohans are all in, i. 176
    Divine Peace and, iii. 248
    Doctrine of, v. 384, 410
    Dogma of, i. 45
    Earth, reached on, iv. 101; v. 401
    Egos in, i. 291; v. 397
    Eternal, v. 388
    Ever-present Is, v. 352
    Fourth path leads to, i. 254, 255
    Genetic Eden and, iii. 208
    Globes, of, i. 226
    Individual pralaya, ii. 86
    Inner man of the first knows not, iii. 283
    Jīvanmukta, and, v. 402
    Krishna, Vishnu merged in, iv. 152
    Ku-sum, triple form of, v. 374
    Laya or, i. 196
    Liberation, final, iii. 245
    Māyā and, i. 43
    Meaning of, i. 309; ii. 89, 291; v. 385, 386, 387, 388
    Moksha, or, v. 83, 381, 384

    Monads who have not reached, iii. 67
    Mukti or, i. 43; v. 381
    Mysteries of, v. 352, 353
    Nirmānakāyās who have renounced, iv. 186; v. 80, 351, 354, 360
    Opinion of, iii. 248
    Parabrahman, is, v. 353
    Paradise of bliss, a, iii. 208
    Path to, v. 366, 402
    Pitris and, v. 532
    Post-manvantaric, iv. 59
    Promised land or, ii. 291
    Sabbath or, i. 285
    Shankara on, ii. 294
    Shekinah a state like, ii. 344
    State of, v. 386, 388
    Third race, no, before the, iv. 181
    Thread of radiance in, iii. 89
    Two kinds of, v. 401
    Vanishing point of differentiated matter or, i. 229
    World, called, v. 83
NIRVĀNIC, Body, v. 366
    Condition of the seventh principle, i. 330
    Dissociation of all substances, i. 196
NIRVĀNIC STATE, Lower, v. 360
    Monad and, iii. 192
    Negation of, ii. 43
    Purely, i. 243
NIRVĀNIS, v. 353, 354, 362, 401
    Highest and earliest, iii. 235
    Jīvanmukti or, v. 359
    Mahāmanvantaras, from preceding, iii. 89
    Spirits of men becoming, i. 285
NIS, Nissa, Sinai, v. 278
NISAN, Jewish month, v. 150, 278
NISHĀDA, a quality of sound, ii. 258
NISSI, the God, iii. 19
NITATUĪ, one of the Pleiades, iv. 121
NĪTI, parent of harmony (Naya), iv. 97
NITROGEN, Air or, i. 179
    Crookes on, ii. 274
    Elements, one of the four, iv. 164
    Elements saturated with, iii. 167
    Linga Sharīra and, iv. 165
    Molecules of, iii. 165
    Noumenon of, iii. 351
    Paracelsus and, i. 337
    Protoplasm contains, ii. 362
    Terrestrial manifestation of, ii. 348
NITROZONIC Gases, i. 147
NITYA, Constant dissolution or, ii. 87
    Eternal, i. 136
    Perpetual, iii. 79, 310
    Pralaya, iii. 310
    Sarga, iii. 310
NIZA, referred to, iii. 47
NIZIR, Mountain of, iii. 153
NO-BRĀHMAN, A-Bram, iii. 205
NO-FORM from form, i. 124
NO-GODS, Gods became, iii. 250; iv. 68
NO-NUMBER, Non-being or, i. 152
    Oi-Ha-Hou or, i. 160
    One number issued from, i. 150, 152, 157
NO-THING, Absolute, iv. 123
    Ain Soph or, ii. 57, 342; iii. 137
    Boundless and endless, iii. 134

NOACHIAN records, v. 104
NOACHIDAE, History of, iii. 150
NOAH, Adam and, ii. 162; iii. 424
  Allegory of, iii. 225, 314
  American, iii. 149
  Ancient tradition about, iii. 267
  Androgyne man symbolized by, ii. 162
  Ark of, ii. 75; iii. 48, 79, 293, 309; iv. 29, 31,
    35, 113, 181, 184; v. 197
  Atlantean, iii. 268
  Black raven of, ii. 161
  Chaldean, iii. 149
  Chinese, iii. 364
  Cubical structure of, iv. 169
  Cush descendant of, iv. 20
  Deluge of, i. 136; ii. 85; iii. 17, 18, 45, 149,
    352, 391, 398; iv. 34, 103, 343; v. 73
  Egg and the ark of, ii. 75
  Enoch and, iv. 102, 294
  Female, iv. 30
  Fifth race, belonged to, iv. 102
  Grandfather of, iv. 294
  Greek, iv. 338
  Ham, son of, v. 297
  Hanokh and, iv. 102
  Hind, iv. 168
  Iapetos, one of the sons of, iii. 151
  Indian, iii. 308
  Jehovah and, ii. 162
  Jewish, iii. 152
  Kabir, was, iii. 389
  Melchizedek identical with, iii. 390, 391
  Pagan Gods and, iii. 390
  Patriarch, iii. 359; iv. 167
  Peiruun, the Chinese, iii. 364
  Period of, v. 89
  Pithecoid, the, iv. 225
  Prithu said to be, ii. 380
  Purānic MSS., and, i. 53
  Root Manu, Seed Manu, and, iv. 169
  Shista, identical with Hindu, iv. 168
  Son of, v. 297
  Spirit, the, iii. 153
  Stories of, iii. 18
  World deluges and, iii. 335
NOAH-XISUTHRUS, iii. 396
NOAHS, Deluges and their, iii. 146, 307
NOBLE CROWN, God Mir-Ku or, iii. 19
NOBLE LIFE, God Zi-ku or, iii. 18
NOD, Land of, iii. 288, 393
NODE, Ascending, of moon, iii. 85
  Determination of moon's, ii. 388
  Moon approached her, fourteen days after
    epoch of 1491, ii. 387
NODES, Botanical term, ii. 33
  Moon, of, ii. 118
  Motions of, ii. 385
NODUS in study of Symbology, i. 178
NOËTIC, Dianoia, iii. 38
  Family, the, iii. 150
NOFIRHOTPOO, he who is in absolute repose,
  iv. 32
NOFRE, meaning of, v. 285
NOMADIC, Life, iii. 318
  Tribes and Zodiac, ii. 373
NOME, God of the town or, ii. 399
NOMINALISM, Conceptionalists and, i. 70

NOMINALISTS, Mediaeval, i. 317
  Question signed by, i. 70
NON-BEING, Absolute, i. 119; ii. 204
  Absolute being and, of Hegel, i. 81, 124
  Atman passes into, i. 243
  Being born from, ii. 58
  Be-ness and, iv. 16, 197
  Bliss of, i. 124
  Chaos and, ii. 365
  Intellectual life starting from, ii. 370
  Mystery of, i. 70
  No number or, i. 152
  One being eternal, i. 116, 117
  Pralaya and, i. 137; ii. 382
  Real being or, i. 117
  Secret of being and, i. 220
NON-EGO, Absolute, neither Ego nor,
  iv. 170
  Divine, v. 367
  Parabrahman is not, i. 188; ii. 146
  Parikalpitā causes a belief in, i. 120
  Perfect, v. 400
NON-ENTITY, i. 199; iii. 183; iv. 150
NON-EVOLUTIONISTS, Mythology and,
  ii. 16
NON-EXISTENCE, Bliss of, i. 112, 116
NON-EXISTING or latent Principles, iii. 269
NON-INITIATED, Christians, iii. 72
  Commentator, a, iv. 209
NON-INTELLIGENT, Elementals, i. 320
  Lunar Dhvāni, are, i. 239
NON-INTERVENTION, Law of, v. 224
NON-KABALISTS, Explanation for, iv. 36
NON-LUMINOUS Fire-mist, ii. 324
NON-MANIFESTED Logos, v. 430
NON-NUCLEATED Jelly Speck, iii. 161
NON-OCCULTIST, Disadvantage of the,
  iii. 330
NON-PANTHEISTIC Evolutionists, iv. 232
NON-RATIONAL Stage, Man has passed the,
  iii. 300
NON-SEPARATENESS, All that lives, of, i. 136,
  319
  Self in the sense of, iv. 138
  Universe, of, iii. 383
NONNUS, quoted, ii. 116; iii. 152
NOO, the Goddess, primordial water, ii. 155
NOOM, the heavenly artist, iii. 272
NOON, Androgyne unity, the, ii. 68
  Celestial river, ii. 24
NOOR ILLAHEE, the light of the Elohim,
  iv. 83
NOOSE, cruciform, or Pasha, iv. 118
NOOT, Celestial abyss, the, i. 274
  Expanse of heaven called, i. 275; ii. 68
  Fohat issued from, ii. 398
NORDENSKÏOLD, Islands discovered by,
  iv. 343
NORNS sprinkle Yggdrasil, iv. 89
NORSE, Ask, iii. 106
  Cosmogony, ii. 145
  Goddesses, iii. 108
  Legends of Asgard, iii. 105
  Legends of Loki, iii. 284
  Legends of mundane tree, i. 259
  Mythology, iv. 323
  Yggdrasil or, iv. 89

NORTH, Cradle of physical man in, iv. 344
    Cross of, iv. 117
    Eastern occultists of, i. 156
    Evil comes from, i. 181
    Gods and religious beliefs from, iv. 344
    Positive electricity on, ii. 275
    Prayer turning to, iii. 361
NORTH AMERICA, Colossal ruins of, iii. 337
    Geometry of the Semites and, ii. 20
NORTH CORNWALL, iii. 326
NORTH PACIFIC, iii. 404
NORTH POLAR REGION, iii. 326
NORTH POLE, Cap of, iii. 371
    Capricorn at, iii. 429
    Continent, at first, iii. 400; iv. 353
    Dragon is, iv. 340
    Hyperborean continent and, iii. 20
    Lemurians gravitated towards, iii. 276
    Mount Meru is, i. 253; iii. 402; v. 436
    Separation of, iii. 146
    Serpent and, iii. 355
    South and, i. 253; ii. 329
    Zodiac horizon and, iv. 353
NORTH WIND, Apollo and, iv. 340
    Boreas or, iv. 340
    Cursing, i. 181
    Toom, ii. 398
NORTHERN Buddhism, v. 370
    Europe, v. 148
    Lights, ii. 358
    Stocks, origin of, iv. 313
NORWAY, iii. 333, 421; iv. 344, 355
    Arctic circle or, iii. 332
    Atlantis, and, iii. 421
    Lemuria and, iii. 332, 333, 401
    Pre-Lemurian continent, and, iv. 344
    Rise of land in, iv. 355
    Runic writing in, iii. 346
    Scandinavia or, iii. 24
    Severed parts, one of the, iii. 398
    Tumuli in, iii. 422
NORWEGIAN, America settled by, i. 337
    Lemming, migrations of, iv. 350
    Mariners, iii. 421
NORWICH, Orthodox of, iii. 434
    Philosopher of, ii. 381
    Self-made adept of, iii. 361
NOSTRIL, Breath from Toom's right, ii. 398
NOSTRILS, Lord God with smoke coming from
    his, ii. 187
NOT-GODS, Asuras or, iii. 101
NOT-SPIRIT, Shánkaráchárya on, ii. 297
    Unknown, ii. 302
NOTARICON, Method of calculation, v. 113
NOTATION, Ancient musical, iv. 172
    Decimal, ii. 76; v. 342
    Planets' movements, of, iv. 114
    Vedas of, v. 197
NOTES Archaic stanzas, on the, iii. 15
    Keynote which gives birth to the seven,
        iv. 60
    Peoples, of history of, iii. 331
    Scale of Seven, ii. 258; iv. 174
NOTHING, Nothing can come out of, ii. 293
    Something which is, ii. 74, 146
NOTHINGNESS, Abyss of, i. 204
NOTRE DAME DE PARIS, ii. 110; v. 241

NOUGHT, Absolute no-thing or, iv. 123
    Circle or the, iv. 145
    Nothing or, ii. 65
    Was, ii. 137
NOUMENA, Cosmic element, of a, ii. 295
    Elements, of, iii. 275; v 164
    Forces of, ii. 364
    Gods as, iv. 334
    Mánasic plane, on, v. 554
    Nature, of the powers of, iv. 334
    Occultism treats of, ii. 200
    Phenomena, of all, i. 203; iv. 87
    Realm of, i. 178
    Region of, iii. 114
    Substance and, ii. 42
    World of, ii. 165
NOUMENAL, Absolute independent of, power,
        iv. 170
    Barriers of, matter, ii. 341
    Basis of the second triangle, ii. 339
    Cause, i. 202
    Cosmos phenomenal and, separated by a rope,
        i. 154
    Creative force as, ii. 89
    Elements, homogeneous, i. 265
    Essences, i. 317
    Existence, iv. 170
    Nature, ii. 97
    Nature, aspect of the female power in,
        ii. 149
    Phenomenal expression of, ii. 355
    Phenomenal plane and, i. 132, 324
    Super-astral or, light, i. 142
    Super-spiritual or, iv. 192
    Universe of thought, ii. 342
    Universe phenomenal and, i. 201
    World, plane of the, iv. 153
NOUMENOI, Meta-elements and, ii. 276
    Sravah, of Amshaspends, iii. 384
NOUMENON, Aether, of ether, ii. 232
    Akásha, of ether, i. 298
    Akásha, of Prakriti, i. 300
    Conscious cause, ii. 241
    Conscious guiding, of forces, ii. 358
    Cosmolatry concerned itself with the, ii. 181
    Cosmic matter, of, i. 109
    Cosmic, of matter, the third Logos, i. 82
    Cosmic phenomena, of, ii. 247
    Ego, of personal, i. 187
    Electricity, of, ii. 255
    Elements, of, ii. 88
    Ether, of, ii. 181, 232, 395
    Fohat the power dividing the, i. 169
    Forces, of, ii. 358
    Hydrogen, of, iii. 121
    Individuality and intelligence of, ii. 216
    Kosmos and i. 70; iii. 37
    Life principle as, iv. 242
    Light, of, ii. 203
    Matter, of, i. 127, 149; ii. 234, 325, 335;
        iii. 269
    Múlaprakriti, i. 131; iii. 76
    Nebulae, of, irresolvable, i. 164
    Newton on God as, of all, ii. 215
    One being is, i. 117
    One reality of, ii. 40
    Osiris of, v. 233

NOUMENON (*Contd.*)
Oxygen, hydrogen and nitrogen, of, ii. 351
Parabrahman beyond the, of all noumena, ii. 150
Powers of cognition influence appearance of, i. 112
Phenomenon and, i. 111, 117; ii. 215
Physical particles of, i. 266
Seventh state, of, i. 203
Spiritual fire, of, iii. 114
Thought of, i. 80
Three in one, of, iii. 121
Time, of infinite, i. 131
NOUR, Fire, v. 166
NOUS, Dianoia, and, iii. 38
Divine wisdom or, iii. 375
Greeks, of the, v. 94, 447, 451
Logos, and, iii. 38
Mahat, and, ii. 170
Manu or, i. 141
Matter moving, i. 123
Mens or, ii. 170
Mind or, ii. 66, 170; iii. 119; iv. 124, 144
Mundane intelligence of Plato or, i. 121
Potency, v. 447
Psyche and, iii. 143; iv. 171
Quaternary, one of a, iv. 171
Spiritual soul or, iv. 144
Wisdom, the higher divine, i. 247
NOUTI OR NOUTIR, ii. 399
NOVA ZEMBLA NORTH OF PERSIA, iii. 397
NOVALIS, referred to, i. 260
NOVEMBER, Extinguishing of fires on the first of, iv. 329
Meteoric showers of, ii. 397
NUAH, Chaldean, the, iii. 153
Noah and, iii. 153
Universal mother or, iv. 30
NUBIA, Egypt reached through, iv. 316
NUCHTHEMERON of Apollonius of Tyana, ii. 169
NUCLEATED CELL, iv. 228
NUCLEI, Centres of life are isolated, iii. 46
NUMA, POMPILIUS, v. 194
Books, of, v. 297
Tomb of, v. 122
NUMBER, Colour, Form, Sound, and, v. 418, 420
Manifested Universe and, v. 418
NUMBER 1, v. 116, 189
NUMBER 2, v. 116, 189
NUMBER 3, v. 189
NUMBER 4, Creative God, v. 189
NUMBER 9, Ancient language, and, ii. 20
Cosmogony, place of, in, ii. 33
Triple ternary, iv. 152
NUMBER 10, Perfection of, iii. 414
Pythagorean Decad and, iv. 123, 144
Reproductive organs and, ii. 107
Sephiroth and, iii. 237
Total of, ii. 151
NUMBER 30, Deity as the, ii. 66
NUMBER 318, Civil calendar and, ii. 35
Gnostic value of Christ is, ii. 35
NUMBER 365, iv. 99
NUMBER 700, iv. 87
NUMBER 888, iv. 87

NUMBER VALUES, iv. 129
NUMBERS, Aristotle on, ii. 77
Astrological, v. 151
Birth of the globes of, i. 223
Celestial Chinese, iii. 48
Celestial deities revealed, ii. 151
Creation of, iii. 52
Divine mysteries expressed, by, ii. 66
Every being has, v. 116
Expression of thought by, ii. 33
Figures, and, ii. 185
Figures key to esoteric, i. 218
Force which organizes, i. 135
Fourth is manifested Cosmos, v. 189
German, v. 117
Gods and, iv. 147; v. 116
Great Pyramid, in, ii. 25
Identical symbolic, ii. 35
Infinite correlations of, v. 456
Jehovah measure, of the, iii. 50
Jesus, put in the mouth of, iv. 189
Lucky and unlucky, v. 116
Masonry and, i. 172
Mathematical, iv. 122
Moses's name, of, iv. 109
Mountains, of, iv. 36
Mystic nature of all, ii 99
One beginning of all, ii. 157
One, gathered into, i. 291
Perfect, v. 423, 507
Perpetual recurrence of, 4, 3, 2, iii. 83
Phallic interpretation of, v. 85
Points or, and the duad, ii. 343
Powers of, ii. 148; iv. 171; v. 115
Pyramid, v. 151
Pythagorean, ii. 62, 76, 151, 179
Rounds and their, i. 223
Rudra's progeny, of, iv. 185
Sacred, iv. 170
Self-moving, iv. 122
Septenary groups of, iv. 165
Sounds and, ii. 185
Stanza IV, referred to in, i. 152
Syllabic signs possessing the meaning of, ii. 20
Symbolism of, v. 113, 114, 115, 117, 118, 235
System defined by, iv. 130
Tetrad is sacred, iv. 170
Ten of scale, v. 210
THAT was before all, ii. 343
NUMERAL SYSTEM, Origin of the, ii. 144
NUMERALS, Antiquity of, iv. 155
Cosmological theory of, v. 87, 115
Hebrew alphabet and, v. 212
Hindu symbolism of, iv. 146
Kabalistic, i. 284; v. 86
Occult, ii. 158
Pythagoras, of, v. 87, 113
Sacred Science of, i. 153
31415, the famous, i. 174
Various systems of, v. 341
NUMERATION, Geometry and, v. 185
NUMERICAL, Abraxas, value of, iv. 42
Bible symbols, v. 206
Coincidences, ii. 364
Divisions, iv. 169
Harmony of Moses and Jehovah, iv. 109
Hebrew letters, value of, v. 206

NUMERICAL (*Contd.*)
    Kabalistic methods, iv. 169
    Keys of *Bible*, ii. 30
    Meanings in, iv. 110
    Method, *Bible* read by the, iv. 113
    Mysteries of the Persian Simorgh, iv. 134
    Pythagoras, evolution of, ii. 158
    Symbols, patriarchs are, iii. 390
    System, Europe, in, v. 342
    System, Greece, of, v. 342
    System, Language of Initiates of, v. 178
    System, Universal Knowledge and, v. 185
    System of Egypt, iv. 130
    System of science in the Mosaic books, ii. 25
    System of the universe, i. 178
    Value of relation between diameter and cir-
        cumference, iv. 114
NUMERICALLY, Hebrew scrolls read, iii. 213
    Jehovah, Adam and Noah one, ii. 162
NUN THE FISH, i. 307
NUNTIUS, Mercury called, iii. 41
NURAGHI of Sardinia, iii. 351
NURSE, Earth a kind, i. 209
    Egypt, of Isis, iii. 373
    Ether as agent referred to as, iii. 114
    Ma, the root, ii. 111
    One Thing (man), of, iii. 118
    World, of, iv. 96
NURSERY, Adepts, for, i. 255
    Monads, of all mundane, ii. 297
    Souls, of human, i. 265
NURSES, of Kārtikeya, iv. 119
NURSLING, Ether or wind, of, iii. 118
    Gods-revealers, of the, ii. 287
    Kārtikeya, of, Pleiades, iv. 190
NUTATION, Dr. Croll on, iii. 315
NUX, Birth of Erebus and, i. 170
NYAM-NYAM, dying out, iii. 443
NYSSA, tradition of, v. 278
NYĀYA, Atoms of the, ii. 49
    Vedānta and, i. 126
NYINGPO or Ālaya, i. 120
NYMPHAEA LUTEA of Audubon, iii. 438
NYMPHAL STATE of Animals, iii. 128
NYMPHS seduced by Indra, iv. 185

O

OAKS, Druids and, v. 49
OAN the Fish Man, ii. 380
OANNES, Babylonian Dag, iv. 150
    Berosus, of, iii. 229
    Chaldæan, i. 307
    Dagon, iii. 18, 64, 147, 365; iv. 63
    Ichthys, Jonas or, ii. 380
    Man-fish, the, ii. 59; iii. 196; iv. 63, 71
OASES, Tibetan, i. 55
OASIS in the Gobi desert, iv. 71
OATH, Sodalian, v. 29
OB, Aub or, a serpent, ii. 80
    Od, and Aour, i. 142
    Sorcerers, messenger of death used by,
        i. 142
OBELISKS, British Columbia, of, iii. 428
    Egyptian inscribed, i. 62
    Meaning of, i. 184
    Saïs, at temple of, iii. 394

OBJECTIVE, Astral, v. 526
    Consciousness, v. 525, 530
    Plane, v. 529
    Terrestrial, v. 526
    Universe, v. 488
OBJECTS, of Mysteries, v. 279-283
OBLATE, Spheroid unaccounted for, ii. 317
OBLIQUITY of the ecliptic, iii. 406; iv. 294
O'BRIEN, quoted, ii. 194
OBSCURATION, Manvantara and, iv. 273
    Mars at present in a state of, i. 219
    Period, i. 234; iii. 58
    Pralaya of, iii. 79, 308; iv. 230
    Spirit, of, i. 228; iv. 302
    Worlds under, iv. 274
OBSCURATIONS, Cyclic, i. 213, 215; iv. 230
OBSERVATION, secret scientific, v. 323
OBSESSION, v. 250, 500
OCCULT Arts, v. 62, 271
    Astronomy, Kabalists, and, v. 220-225
    Astrology, v. 333
    Books, v. 469, 470
    Calculations, v. 116
    Centre in Brain, v. 438
    Correspondences, v. 464
    Cosmogony, i. 204, 320; ii. 313; v. 31,
        180, 227
    Doctrine, ii. 353; v. 226, 247, 258, 266, 501
    Geology, v. 227
    Hexagon, v. 120
    Interaction, v. 428
    Knowledge, i. 66, 275; ii. 148; iii. 39; iv. 190;
        v. 256, 370, 432, 482
    Knowledge of priests, v. 58, 91
    Law, v. 106, 180, 394, 492
    Learning, v. 271
    Literature, destruction of, v. 295
    Lore, v. 49, 194
    Masonry, v. 175
    Metaphysics, i. 188; iii. 125; v. 381, 384
    Mysteries, ii. 281; iii. 132; iv. 68; v. 45, 424,
        444
    Nature, i. 205, 206, 326; ii. 268; iii. 360;
        iv. 119; v. 91, 456, 461
    Numbers, v. 264
    Phenomena, v. 257
    Philosopher, v. 282
    Philosophy, i. 143, 206; ii. 260, 324, 343, 353,
        365; iii. 96, 195, 203, 442; iv. 121, 140,
        211; v. 226, 228, 232, 287, 331, 362, 462, 488
    Powers, v. 180, 240, 354, 458, 469, 479
    Principles, division of, v. 470
    Properties, v. 443
    Records, i. 205; iv. 200; v. 178
    Rites, v. 242
    Science(s), i. 135, 206, 315; iii. 77, 103;
        v. 41, 51, 60, 61, 75, 80, 86, 88, 121, 165,
        242, 245, 287, 295, 331, 389, 406, 423, 429,
        460, 463, 474, 479, 484
    Symbolic reading, v. 205, 246
    Symbology, v. 135, 316; iii. 376; v. 115, 166,
        206, 207, 537
    Teaching, i. 65; ii. 380; iii. 19, 96, 234, 376;
        iv. 176, 177; v. 97, 220, 350, 355, 356, 485
    Theogony, v. 190
    Training, v. 474
    Truths, v. 295, 355, 368, 445, 531

OCCULT (*Contd.*)
Universe, v. 275
Volume, Bible is, v. 91, 105
Weapons, v. 121
Wisdom, i. 168; iii. 376; v. 289, 382
OCCULTISM, Advance in, v. 514
Ākāsha of, i. 196
Anthropology, and, iv. 258
Antiquity of man, on, iii. 156
Apollonius and, v. 142
Archaic, i. 173; ii. 391
Archaic Aryan works on, ii. 348
Archaic cosmogony and, i. 200
Astronomy and, v. 222
Atoms called vibrations in, ii. 358
Atoms, on the selective power of, ii. 272
Bacteria as viewed in, i. 272
Cavities of brain and, v. 556
Cis-Himālayan, iii. 59; iv. 174
Colour and, v. 442
Consciousness and, v. 547
Corroborated by science, v. 449
Cosmic Logos of, iv. 219
Christian era, in early days of, i. 57
Christian Trinity and, i. 173
Creators, on, iii. 87
Crucifixion of Christos and, v. 552
Darwinism and, i. 238, 265; iii. 201
Defence of, iv. 219
Deity abstract triangle in, i. 84
Dogma in, oldest, i. 76
Double sign and, iii. 42
Double radiation and, v. 424
Dweller on Threshold and, v. 500, 501, 512, 567
Eastern, i. 80, 137, 286; iii. 94; iv. 212; v. 154, 229, 232, 249
Eastern and Western, v. 226-236
Eastern schools of, i. 157
Eastern student of, iii. 59; v. 154
Electricity is matter according to, i. 171
Elementals of, i. 201
Elements of, i. 265
Errors examined in defence of, ii. 229
Etheric tremors, on, ii. 239
Evolution, and, iii. 192
Fiery lives, and, iii. 125
Flashes of Genius and, v. 466
Fohat, key in, ii. 397
Form on, i. 324
Fundamental law in, i. 160
Genesis, in, v. 449
Geology and Anthropology, iii. 81
Haeckel, answers, iv. 222
Heart, and, v. 518
Hebrew, i. 187
Hermaphroditism and, iii. 127
Himālayan chain, and, iii. 399
Hinduism, and, iii. 78
History of, v. 326, 396
Inorganic accepted by, nothing, i. 293
Jesuits, of the, v. 274
Kabalah and, ii. 343
Kant, and, ii. 326
Kārmic effects of, iii. 73
Keely and, ii. 289
Kismet, contrary to, v. 539

Knowledge of, v. 226
Language of, iv. 187
Law of, v. 417
Leibnitz and, ii. 351, 352
Light in, three kinds of, iii. 49
Maelstrom of, i. 182
Magic and, v. 112, 447
Masonry and, v. 112
Materialistic science and, ii. 358
Metaphysics of, iv. 220
Minor teaching of, iv. 211
Monad in, third, ii. 343
Monads or Jivas of, ii. 354
Moon's influence, on, iv. 34
Motion and force, on, ii. 236
Mysteries of, v. 217
Mysteries revealed by, ii. 122; v. 293
Mystic tenets of, i. 192
Mystics before our era knew, i. 62
Nārada in, iii. 59, 92
Nature in, v. 477
Nature recognizes nothing outside, iii. 199
Nebular theory and, ii. 320
Neptune and, v. 222
North Pole, and, iii. 399
Number 7 in, ii. 382
One existence and, i. 70
Opponents of, iv. 234
Orientalists and, v. 287
Origin of the universe according to, ii. 318
Panorama of, in *Isis*, i. 63
Paramātma and, v. 486, 487
Personal God and devil, on a, iv. 43
Phantasies of, ii. 206
Phantom made apprehensible by, ii. 212
Phraseology of, ii. 329
Pineal gland, on, iii. 299; v. 483
Planets of seven, i. 145
Pleroma of, v. 462, 463
Practical, i. 201; ii. 148; v. 112, 510
Primeval, of Aryāvarta, iv. 135
Primordial races, seven and, iv. 182
Principles of, iv. 205; v. 125
Proofs of, iii. 195
Real divine, i. 276
Reasons for belief in, iv. 17
Ritualism and Symbolism of, v. 273
Roman Catholic Church and, i. 65
Root of ungulate mammals according to, iv. 305
Rudimentary organs, and, iv. 253
Sat as viewed by, iii. 69
Science, and, i. 323; ii. 205, 219, 275, 313; iv. 221; v. 382, 444
Science of, ii. 244
Science of numerals important in study of, i. 153
Secrecy and, v. 142, 465, 468
Secret Books of, data from, iii. 62
Secret Doctrine wirtten for students of, i. 87
Seers of, ii. 328
Senzar of, iii. 437
Seven Stars of, v. 202
Sexual intercourse forbidden in, v. 510
Solar flames, on, ii. 254
Spheroidal form, on, i. 133

OCCULTISM (*Contd.*)
Spiritual, v. 464
Stanzas emanate from, i. 59
Students of, i. 46; ii. 399; iv. 157; v. 110, 170, 174, 218, 243, 256, 295, 333, 410, 443
Study of, v. 464
Superstition, and, i. 59; iv. 363
Tattvas and, v. 469, 475
Teaching of, iii. 57; iv. 241
Terminology of practical, i. 148; v. 389, 537, 538
Ternary and, v. 116
Theory and Practice in, v. 465
Theoretical, v. 85
Theurgy or, v. 78, 170
Treatises on, v. 59
Triangle and, iv. 166
Tyro in, iii. 159
Universal unity, on, i. 128
Untrained mind in, i. 216
Visible, makes the Logos, ii. 148
Water and, v. 233
Western, v. 115, 227
Western students of, iv. 139
Wisdom of, v. 449
Zohar on, v. 112
OCCULTIST(S), Adam-Adami, and, iv. 19
Adept, i. 201; ii. 207; v. 78
Adi-Shakti as viewed by, i. 76
Advaitin, i. 73, 74
Akāsha, not ether of, i. 336; iv. 256
Ancestors or Pitris of, i. 268
Anthropology of, iv. 245
Antiquity of man as estimated by, iv. 256
Antiquity of writing claimed by, iii. 437
Ape and, i. 238
Appeal, right of, iv. 249
Asia, in, v. 381
Astral form, and, iv. 230
Astral light of, i. 300; ii. 81; iii. 408; v. 383
Astral shadows spoken of by, iii. 193
Astrologers, and astronomers, ii. 371
Astrology and, v. 329, 331
Astronomy of the, i. 164
Asuramaya and, iii. 62
Asuras the highest breath for the, iii. 101
Ātmā, view of, i. 273
Axiom of, ii. 364
Balzac an, i. 235
Basis of, iv. 126
Bible, on, v. 91, 105
Boehme an, iv. 167
Book of Dzyan, and, iv. 167
Brahman, and, iii. 82
Brāhmans differ from, iii. 308
Cause with effect, never confuse, ii. 141
Causeless cause of, i. 80
Christians and, i. 83; ii. 379; iii. 80; v. 127, 163, 217
Chronology of, iii. 164
Church and, v. 167, 327
Climacteric year of, ii. 382
Colour, vibration, and, v. 485
Consciousness, and, v. 547
Continental, v. 174
Cosmic evolution, and, i. 147
Cosmolatores, not, iii. 199

Count d'Ourches and early, iv. 45
Creation of man and, iii. 57
Crookes and, ii. 346, 351
Cross, on the, iv. 111
Cycle merging into cycle traced by, iii. 195
Cyclic re-incarnation, and, v. 357
Cyprian and, v. 170
Czolbe and, iii. 162
Dark sayings in sacred books understood by, iv. 104
Darwinism and, i. 239; iv. 266
Devils, and, v. 60, 62
Diagrams made by, i. 265
Duty to religion of, v. 124, 125
Eastern, i. 132, 147, 156, 160, 164, 276, 326; ii. 341, 346; iii. 95; iv. 25, 115, 151, 159, 164; v. 195, 226, 227, 229, 354, 483
Egyptian zodiac, and, iii. 433
Elementals, and, i. 320; ii. 190
Empirics and, iv. 234
Entities of, i. 147
Esoteric Vedāntin school of, i. 273
Ether, a reality to, ii. 39
Evidences which satisfy, i. 67
Evolution, on, ii. 361
Evolutionists and, i. 196; iv. 222
Father-mother as viewed by, i. 160
Fearlessness of, v. 106
Fire, and, iii. 115
Fire of wisdom on, iv. 137
Five-pointed star, and, i. 73
Foetus, on growth of, iv. 255
Fohat, on, i. 81, 171
Followers of Cain, v. 71
Forces, and, i. 77; ii. 315; v. 383
French literature, of, i. 135
Geologist and, iii. 23
Gnostics, and, v. 168, 327
God, and, ii. 67; v. 127
Hæckel and, iv. 240
Heart, knowledge of, v. 518
Hierarchy of sages, believe in a, iii. 421
Hindu, v. 115, 117, 191
Hindu Mahābhāratan war historical to, ii. 112; iv. 24
Hindu symbology, and, ii. 391
History and, v. 254
Ignoramuses, will be thought, ii. 201
Indo-Aryan, iii. 21
Inner man, in the, iii. 166
Interpretation, modes of, ii. 80
Jehovah, and, v. 190, 277
Julian an, v. 218
Kabalists and, i. 142, 280, 290, 308, 319, 329
Kant as viewed by, ii. 326
Keely, an unconscious, ii. 281
Laws, do not modify, ii. 212
Legends among, i. 256
Leibnitz, agree with, ii. 352
Lévi and, i. 298
Life of an atom, on, i. 199
Light of, iii. 50
Light to, ii. 203
Living fire of, ii. 52
Magic and, iii. 186
Mahat of, i. 122
Man, on double nature of, iv. 203

OCCULTIST(S) (*Contd.*)

Manas, view of, i. 231; v. 77
Man's principles and, v. 361
Materialism and, iv. 15, 216, 286
Matter, and, i. 203; v. 384
Mediæval, i. 64
Mesmerism, and, v. 511
Miracles, and, v. 450
Modern theory of development and, iii. 194
Moon, and, i. 211
Mother philosophy, and, iii. 157
Mystery of cross, and, iv. 126
Nāstika, a, i. 322
Naturalist, and, iii. 23
Nature, view of forces of, i. 199
Nidānas, and, iii. 23
Noumenon, and, ii. 216
One Law, believe in, iv. 124
One life of, ii. 267
One Unity, and, iv. 241
Orientalists and, iii. 155
Origin of Man, on, iii. 178
Paracelsus an, i. 307
Perceptive senses, estimate of our, ii. 353
Phenomena of, iv. 222
Philosophy of, ii. 324; iii. 147
Pithecoid ancestry, and, iii. 160
Powers, called Dhyān Chohans by, i. 276
Practical, i. 280
Proposition, i. 206
Providence, and, ii. 367
Pure air as life-giving known to, i. 303
Religion, and, v. 70
Sabbath of, ii. 203
Sacred books of the east and, i. 57
Sacred numbers known to, i. 134
Sage known only to a few, iii. 444
Satan, and, v. 312
Science and, i. 336; ii. 53, 199, 200, 239, 361;
iv. 232; v. 51, 52, 467
Scientists, and, i. 362; iv. 224
Second death, and, v. 491
Semi-initiated, i. 189
Semite's God rejected by, iv. 444
Septenary law and. iv. 194
Sidereal beings, and, i. 182
Soul, and, ii. 313
Space, on, i. 204
Species, and differentiation of, iv. 303
Spirit and soul, on, iv. 241
Spirits, and, iii. 369
Spontaneous generation and, iii. 158
Stanzas understood only by a few, i. 87
Substance, use of the word, ii. 235
Sun, and, v. 219
Supernatural powers and, v. 459
Tables of correspondences of, v. 433
Tasmanian women's sterility understood by,
iii. 201
Theosophists and, i. 338; ii. 327
Traditions known to be correct by, iii. 17
Trans-Himālayan, iii. 97
Unbelief, prepared for, iii. 436
Unconscious All of, i. 132
Unity of human species, and, iv. 178
Universe, view of, iv. 114
Vedāntins, view of monad differs from, i. 82, 194

Vishishtādvaita philosophy, and, i. 128
Water a term used by, i. 133
Western, v. 226, 460
Willow-leaf theory and, ii. 315
World Philosophy, and, v. 265
Worlds, of Metaphysicians, ii. 324
OCEAN, Abysses of, ii. 332
Ākāshic, ii. 177
Atlas and Proteus, and depths of, iv. 331
Black waters of, iii. 405
Celestial, i. 141
Churning of, i. 135, 136; ii. 62, 113; iii. 380
Cosmic matter, iii. 167
Curds in, of space, i. 160
Daughter of, iii. 405
Devs, iii. 398
Electric, ii. 328
Existence, of, iv. 141
Floors, disturbance of, iii. 314, 323, 327;
iv. 269
Gods emerging from, iv. 63
Gods father of, ii. 59
Gods fled to shore of milky, ii. 137
Himālayas, flowed to, iv. 142
Immortality, of, i. 137
Indian, and Lemuria, iii. 20, 404; iv. 180, 249
Infinite and shoreless, i. 149; ii. 204
Infinite, of the, ii. 154
Island sinks in, iii. 364
Karshvars, which flows between the, iv. 327
Kshīra, of milk, iii. 402
Life, of, i. 134
Matter, of, i. 230; iv. 254
Monad, a drop out of shoreless, iii. 192
Mysteries beyond and within radiant, ii. 358
Prachetasas and, iv. 149
Primordial, of space, ii. 177
Radiant light, was, i. 137
-Shell, palace an, iii. 402
Sidereal, iv. 30
Slime, protoplastic dweller in, iv. 220
Solar system one, ii. 87
Space called, i. 160; ii. 177; iv. 327
Talk across, ii. 284
Tethys, wife of, iii. 76
Universal, of space, iv. 188, 283
Varuna, God. iv. 148
Venus from, foam. ii. 95
OCEANIC, Earth expanse on, iii. 75
Tribes, inferiority of some, iii. 169
OCEANID Clymene, Prometheus son of, iv. 89
OCEANS, Black, water or, ii. 134
Carbonic acid of, i. 297; iii. 167
Continents make way for, iv. 273
Displacement of, iii. 359
Giants of old buried beneath, iii. 279
Indian, Atlantic and Pacific, iii. 327
Seven, i. 301; ii. 88; iv. 188, 273
Shifting of, iii. 325
OCEANUS, or Okeanos, Arkite Titans, one of,
iii. 151
Daughters of, iii. 412
ŌD, Light, pure life-giving, i. 142
Ob, Aour and, i. 142
Reinchenbach, of, ii. 52
ODIC or magnetic chord, ii. 279
Fluid, v. 427

ODIN, Ases, father of Gods and, ii. 145
　Buddha and, i. 52
　Buddhas, one of the, iii. 421
　Eye of, ii. 118
　Life of soul, endows man with, iii. 106
　Loki brother of, iii. 284
　Magic, and, v. 42
　Max Müller on worship of, i. 52
　Mimir, at feet of, ii. 118
　Ravens of, ii. 161; iii. 108
　Spirit, or, ii. 145
ODOUR, Keely on, ii. 288
　Substance, a, ii. 288
OD PAG MED, v. 392
OEAOHOO, Archaic doctrine, of, i. 140
　Father-mother of Gods or, i. 136
　Light of, i. 139
　Mystic name, i. 136
　Oi-Ha-Hou, permutation of, i. 156
　One, is, i. 136
　Rootless root of all, i. 156
　Son of the Sun, i. 139
　Younger, i. 138
ŒDIPUS, Astronomy, of, i. 211
　Riddle of signs of Egyptian Zodiac, to read,
　　iii. 367
　Sphinx, and riddle of, iv. 85
　Students of occultism, and, i. 215
　Truth, dishonoured great, iv. 85
ŒDIPUSES, Imagination of would-be, ii. 86
　Series of, iv. 110
OERSTED, referred to, ii. 207, 313
OG Moses speaks of, iii. 336
OGDOAD, Ancients, of the, v. 221
　Earth-born horses, of, iii. 44
　Eight or, iii. 357; iv. 152
　First begotten, ii. 167
　Gnostics of, v. 199
　Kabiri and Sun, a powerful, v. 310
　Likeness of the, ii. 167
　Materialized religions, of, iii. 357
　Seven powers, v. 199
　Wisdom mother of, i. 139
OGENOS, or Hades, v. 62
OGHAM wirting, iii. 346
OGYGIA, the island of Calypso, iv. 339
OKEN, Urschleim of, iii. 165
OKHEE Math, Secret cave of, i. 53
OLCOTT, Col., referred to, i. 42, 171; ii. 360
OLD TESTAMENT, see Book Index
　Allegorical teaching of, v. 163, 198
　Authenticity of, v. 196
　Babylonian captivity and, iv. 41; v. 43
　Canon, v. 179
　Compilers of, v. 196
　Contradictions in, v. 182
　Crucifixion in, iv. 131
　Exodus, in story of, iii. 424
　Ieve in, iii. 138
　Origin of, v. 192
　Phallicism and, iv. 115
　Relations between, and New, v. 150
　Symbology of, v 66, 69, 72
　Teachings of, v. 198
　Writers of, v. 71
OLIFACTORY property, ii. 289
OLIPHANT, Laurence, referred to, ii. 202, 284

OLIVE branch, Dove and, ii. 162
OLIVER, Rev. G., quoted, i. 173; ii. 338, 341;
　iv. 171, 172, 173, 174, 211, 352
OLLAS, Sacred MSS., v. 197
OLYMPIAN bride of Heracles, Hebe, iii. 138
OLYMPIC Zeus, iii. 417, 420
OLYMPUS, Castor and Pollux in, iii. 131
　Gladstone on Gods of, iv. 335
　Gods of, iv. 334; v. 92
　Greeks, of, iii. 208
　Indian, ii. 384; iii. 57, 402
　Lay figures on, iv. 336
　Mount, v. 92, 171
　Prayers directed to, iii. 361
　Seat of immortal Gods, iv. 173; v. 171
OM ii. 150; iii. 55; v. 418 et seq., 505, 506
OM MANI PADME HUM, v. 418, 419, 420,
　421, 453, 459, 506
OMEGA and Alpha, Being and Non-Being, of,
　v. 384
　Creative force, of, iii. 108, 177
　Eastern esotericism, of, iv. 15
　Manifested nature, of, ii. 192
　Mystical conception, of, ii. 340
　Road between, i. 311
　Secret Doctrine contains, of Universal Science,
　　v. 44
　Spirit and matter, of, iv. 127
　Tau, of secret divine wisdom, iv. 153
　Theogonies, of, iii. 54
OMNIFICENT, The, v. 270
OMNIPRESENCE, v. 227, 387
OMNIPRESENT mind, i. 196
OMOIE, quoted, i. 264
OMOROKA, Chaldean Thlavatth, iii. 124
　Lady of Urka, iii. 143
ON, or Heliopolis, v. 266
ONE Absolute, i. 300; ii. 305; iii. 383; v. 421,
　430
　Absolute Be-ness, i. 80
　　,,　　Homogeneous, and, ii. 129
　　,,　　reality, i. 79, 124
　　,,　　truth, i. 124
　　,,　　wisdom, iii. 383
　Abstract Unity, v. 206
　Adi, first or, i. 43
　Ain Soph is, i. 172; iii. 291
　Aja first manifestation of, iv. 150
　All, i. 75, 85; ii. 170; iv. 113; v. 305
　Atom-souls and the, ii. 291
　Becomes two, i. 277
　Being, eternal non-being, i. 116, 117; v. 215
　　,,　noumenon of all phenomena, i. 117
　Be-ness, That is, i. 74
　Blessed, v. 371
　Breaths, of breath, iv. 181
　Cause, causeless, i. 80, 125; v. 227
　Cause of all causes, v. 261
　　,,　　impersonal, v. 91
　　,,　　Kosmos merging in, iii. 195
　　,,　　Occult philosophy, of, ii. 343;
　　　　　v. 227
　　,,　　Universal, v. 261
　Circle or ring and, i. 77, 173; ii. 107; iv. 193;
　　v. 438
　Conception, original, ii. 142
　Cosmic element, i. 163

ONE (*Contd.*)
Creator, ii. 158
Darkness, spirit the light of, i. 148
Deity, ii. 215; iv. 155, 209; v. 108, 120, 189, 210, 383, 462
Dimensional quality of triangle, iv. 171
    ,,   space, i. 295
Divine, region of the, i. 318
Divinity, v. 462
Dragon used to denote, i. 140
Echad, i. 139
Egg, from the, i. 152, 153
Element, Absolute Pralaya, and, i. 77
    ,,   Akasha, i. 170
    ,,   Conditional modifications of, i. 78
    ,,   Eternal, i. 125; v. 208, 228, 382
    ,,   Fire, i. 163; v. 562
    ,,   Fohat, iv. 176
    ,,   Primeval, i. 148
    ,,   Space is, v. 382
    ,,   Universal, i. 142
Essence, ii. 70, 114; v. 208, 369
Eternal, i. 277; v. 209
    ,,   God, ii. 215
    ,,   monad, v. 361
Existence, Asiatics apply idea of Eternity only to, i. 109
    ,,   Occultism sums up, i. 70
    ,,   Purusha, iv. 170
    ,,   Solar world, in our, i. 332
    ,,   True, i. 73
Eye of the world, iii. 35
Father, To On or, iii. 122
Fire made threefold, ii. 247
First movement, or, iii. 183
First-born of, ii. 261
Flame, v. 361
Fohat is, i. 180
Force, i. 195; ii. 51
Form of Existence, i. 118, 120
Four sons who are, i. 147
God, iii. 386; iv. 78, 179; v. 167, 189, 192, 214, 240, 311, 351, 462
God in nature, i. 75
Great Waters and, i. 138
Harmony is, iv. 146
Higher self or breath of, i. 159
    ,,   than the four is only, ii. 284
Immutable, emanations of, ii. 53
Indivisible Flame, v. 361
Infinite absolute wisdom, iii. 383
    ,,   circle, v. 438
    ,,   God, iv. 40; v. 209
    ,,   spirit, the soul of, i. 109
    ,,   unconditioned, the, v. 213
Kosmos, from the triple, ii. 51
Law, i. 186; iv. 425
Life, Absolute, ii. 263
    ,,   Absolute deity or, i. 293
    ,,   Atma, Jiva or, v. 471
    ,,   Electricity, i. 147
    ,,   Eternal, i. 70
    ,,   Fohat as, i. 170, 196
    ,,   Formless and uncreate, i. 294
    ,,   Invisible, i. 70, 272
    ,,   Is very God, ii. 327
    ,,   Many into, from, i. 311

Life,   Motion, Jīvatma, or, i. 121
    ,,   Occultists, of, ii. 267
    ,,   Oeaohoo a name for, i. 136
    ,,   Omnipresent, i. 70, 272
    ,,   On this earth, iii. 305
    ,,   One law related to, ii. 359
    ,,   Out-breathings of, i. 311
    ,,   Parabrahman, or, i. 273
    ,,   Sat co-eval with, i. 178
    ,,   Solar system, of, ii. 315
    ,,   Source and mover of all, iv. 242
    ,,   Spiritual, iv. 242
    ,,   Svara and, v. 479
    ,,   That we call, i. 302
    ,,   Universal, v. 423, 492
    ,,   Universe of, i. 306
    ,,   Unmanifestable, i. 76
    ,,   Vital principle or, iii. 311
Light, Reflex of, ii. 360
    ,,   Seven lights from, i. 180, 187
Logos, i. 317; iii. 147; 164; v. 189
Man, separator, of, iii. 276
Manifested, i. 138, 157, 170; ii. 152
    ,,   Consciousness of, i. 263
Many, in, i. 172; ii. 64; iv. 301; v. 213
Māyā, v. 381
Monads emerge from, i. 86
Nameless, i. 256
Nine, and, i. 160
Number, i. 150, 152, 157; v. 333
Omnipotent, v. 377
Only, and, v. 351
Pan was once, iv. 153
Parabrahman, the, v. 213, 233
Perfect, v. 400
Primordial, ii. 267; v. 446
Principle, Creator and, ii. 143
    ,,   Eternal, i. 157
    ,,   Nations lost sight of, ii. 143
    ,,   Parabrahman and Mūlaprakriti, two aspects, i. 83
    ,,   Seventh and, i. 83
    ,,   Sexless, unconditioned and eternal, i. 83; v. 214
    ,,   Unity of, i. 72
    ,,   Universal, iv. 169
Ray, i. 128, 146; ii. 69, 149
Real entity of Leibnitz and Spinoza, ii. 354
Reality, v. 214, 411
    ,,   Absoluteness, i. 81
    ,,   Conditionless, v. 400
    ,,   Cosmic ideation and, ii. 40
    ,,   Eternal and living, v. 488
    ,,   Gautama and, v. 411
    ,,   Great breath a term for, i. 80
    ,,   Illusive reflection of, ii. 235
    ,,   Nameless deity, i. 178
    ,,   Only, v. 388
    ,,   Parabrahman or, i. 80, 131
    ,,   Personality, and, ii. 354
    ,,   Plane of, i. 294; v. 361
    ,,   Potential latency in, iii. 37
    ,,   Regions of the, v. 400
    ,,   Sat, i. 81
    ,,   Seventh principle or, i. 83
    ,,   Universe the dual aspect of, i. 82
    ,,   Unknown yet existing, v. 208

ONE (*Contd.*)
Reality, Veil of, i. 317
Rejected sun, is the, i. 161
Ring is the, i. 77
Sacrifice, iv. 177
Saka or Eka, i. 139
Secondless, i. 122; iv. 125; v. 209, 210, 216, 233
  ,,   existence, i. 124
  ,,   principle, iv. 125
Self, ii. 293; iv. 145; v. 269, 418
Self-existent, eternally, i. 152
Septenary, triad, decad, and, i. 284
Soul, Kosmos an aspect of the, ii. 257
Spirit of the Alahim of Lives, v. 116
States of, two, i. 302
Substance for Spinoza, ii. 353
  ,,   the extreme poles of, i. 134
Sun of our system, i. 161
Supreme and eternal, i. 170; v. 305, 462
  ,,   energy, i. 86
  ,,   essence, i. 187
  ,,   spirit, or, iii. 154
Swift and radiant, i. 195
Tetraktys and, v. 77
Things in *Tabula Smaragdina*, iii. 118
Three in, i. 115; ii. 298; v. 426, 498
Threefold appears and three are, i. 277
Triple and, i. 169
Two, becomes, ii. 41; iii. 206, 257
Unity, i. 81; ii. 340; iii. 37, 321; iv. 241; v. 227
Universal Deity, v. 70, 306
Universe, manifested, i. 152
Unknown space, and, ii. 58, 147
Unknowable, iv. 297
  ,,   causality, i. 196
Without beginning or end, v. 374
ONE-eyed, Cyclopes, iv. 338
Hermaphrodite and, iii. 300
ONE-faced, Double-faced became, iii. 296
ONE-legged men in the Bundahish, iv. 206
ONE-toed horse, iv. 304
ONECH and Kerkes stand for race cycle, iv. 188
ONES, Living, i. 319
Seven great, ii. 399
ONKELOS, quoted, iv. 128
ONLY one, iv. 169
ONLY-begotten son is Brahma, ii. 64
ONOKORO, the newly created island world, i. 264
ONTOGENESIS, Fundamental law of, iv. 229
OOLITIC, Australian fauna and flora, iii. 202
Period, iii. 202, 260
OPHIDEAN symbols, iii. 354
OPHIOMORPHOS, Demiurge and, iii. 246
Michael identified with, ii. 179
Serpent, Satan or evil, ii. 388
Zodiac, Ophis and, ii. 131
OPHIOMORPHOS-Chrestos, ii. 131
OPHIR, gold of, v. 143
OPHIS, Cycle representing, iii. 218
Gnostic, i. 140
Logos and Ennoia are, iii. 219
Zodiac, and, ii. 131
OPHIS-Christos, ii. 131

OPHITE, Adamas, iv. 25
Cherubim, i. 185
Gems, iv. 111
Priest of religion, iii. 378
Spirits, i. 185
OPHITES, i. 185
Christ with the, ii. 194; v. 168
Creator, call the serpent, iii. 214
Diagramma of, iv. 108
Egyptian Gnostics, iii. 385
Genii, on various, ii. 120
Greek, ii. 179
Iao and, iv. 111
Ildabaoth of, ii. 301
Orpheus, and stones of, iii. 341
Serpent of, ii. 194; iii. 214
Symbology of, iii. 124
OPTIC, Nerve, v. 521
Thalami, iii. 302; v. 481
Vesicles, iii. 298
ORACLE, Delphi, at, ii. 187; v. 82, 417
Persian, iv. 189
ORACLES, Ancient and Modern, v. 147, 244
Chaldean, v. 55
Claros, of, v. 316
Mercury of, iv. 112
Pagan, v. 276
ORACULAR stones, iii. 340, 341, 346
ORAI or Venus, ii. 301
ORAL, Teachings, i. 46; iv. 178
Tradition, ii. 143
ORANG OUTANG, iii. 198, 263, 265; iv. 236, 248, 253
ORANGE, colour, occult significance of, v. 461, 507, 508
ORATORY, Power of, is Magic, v. 49
ORBITAL, Motions, axial, and, ii. 229
Planes of the planets, iii. 326
Venus, path of, iii. 45
ORBITS, Angels outside, ii. 227
Moon, of, and Newton, v. 224
Plane, conformity of planetary, to one, ii. 221
Planets, of, v. 224
Uranus and Neptune, of satellites of, i. 204
ORBS, Three secret, iii. 299
ORCUS, ignorant of, i. 245
Living fire of, ii. 267
Mercury evokes souls from, iii. 41
ORDEAL, Stone of the, iii. 342
ORDER, Masonic and Jesuits, v. 274
Spirits, of, v. 318
OREUS, one of the stellar spirits, ii. 167
ORGAN, M.D., Mrs. M.S., quoted, ii. 289
ORGANIC Evolution, ii. 173; iv. 218, 253, 304
ORGANIC life tries to beget psychic life, iv. 224
ORGANS, Action of, v. 538
Correspondences of, v. 539
Human principles and, v. 521
Perception of, v. 549
Sensation of, v. 538
OERGELMIR, Ymir, seething clay; ii. 145
ORIENTAL, Church, v. 139
Doctrines of Pythagoras, v. 36
Element in Gospels, v. 36
Gnosticism, v. 36

ORIENTAL (*Contd.*)
Mysticism in Plato, v. 27, 30, 35
Wisdom, secrets of, v. 29
ORIFICES, Correspondences of, v. 429, 430, 435, 484
ORIGEN, *Book of Enoch*, and, iv. 105
Celsus, on, ii. 164
Chart of, ii. 167
Cruciform couches, knew meaning of, iv. 129
Egyptian gnostics, and, iv. 108
Garden of Eden, and, v. 308
Kabalah and the Bible on, iv. 106; v. 66, 67
Mysteries, initiated into, i. 65
Quoted, v. 308, 439
Seven names given by, ii. 301
ORIGIN, Anthropoid, of, and man, iii. 787
Bible, divine, of, v. 201
Chronology and, of man, iv. 260
Darwinism and, of man, iii. 165; iv. 237
Dogma of atonement, of, v. 272
Egg symbol and, of life, ii. 82
Esoteric philosophy and, of man, ii. 361
Information on, of man, ii. 18
Life, of, Blanchard on, i. 297
Magic, of, v. 59
Mammals and man, of, iv. 233, 235
Man and Cross, of, v. 152
Mysteries of, v. 258-268
Mystery and, of man, i. 277
Polygenetic, of man, iii. 176
Problem of, of life, iii. 159
Round, in this, i. 278
Science and, iv. 215, 216, 260
Septenary group of celestial men, from a, i. 277
Shinto accounts of, i. 286
Universe, and, iii. 369; v. 558
ORIGINAL, of seven worlds, v. 208
ORIGINAL SIN, ii. 98; iii. 264, 281, 305, 411; iv. 52, 83, 269; v. 450
ORION, Atlas, or, iii. 279
Briareus and, not myths, iii. 80
Ephialtes, brother of, iii. 280
Kesil Hebrew for, ii. 374
Making of, ii. 373
Nebula of, ii. 322
ORISSA, Nila in, iii. 402
ORLOG, Karma or fate, iv. 89
ORMAZD (ORMUZD) Ahriman, ii. 130
Ahriman and the bull of, iii. 102; v. 315
Ahura Mazda or, iii. 357, 418; iv. 179; v. 214
Amshaspends, chief of, i. 186; iii. 365
Christianity and, v. 315
Eternal light, formed from, iv. 56
Eye of, v. 314
Face of, v. 315
Father of our earth, iii. 384
King of life, iv. 56
Logos, is the, i. 173; ii. 147, 155
Lord, or, iii. 270
Twig off, tree of, iv. 86
Types of, earthly, iii. 55
Universal sun or, i. 173
ORNITHOLOGY, Septenary law in, iv. 194
ORNITHORHYNCHUSES, aquatic animals, iii. 210

ORNITHOSCELIDAE of Vogt, iii. 190
ORPHEANS and the moon, ii. 111
ORPHEUS, v. 255, 264, 412
Adept, an, iv. 99; v. 64
Æther and chaos, on, ii. 144
Astrology taught by, v. 334
Demi-god, a, iii. 363
Doctrines of, v. 304, 321
Edris called in Greece, iv. 98
Eurydice, and, v. 154
Existence of denied, ii. 374
" False ", v. 51
Generic name, a, iii. 270
Glacial sea, on a, iv. 346
" God of Good Counsel " of, v. 285
Gods of, v. 309
Hero, a, iii. 363; v. 293
India and, v. 288, 293, 334, 412
Memphis in, v. 264
Mysteries, and, v. 255, 275, 276, 278, 288, 293
Mystic, great, iv. 99
Nature, on, v. 89
Phorminx, possessor of the, iv. 99; v. 275
Soter or Saviour, v. 153
Trinity and, v. 188
Widowhood and murder of, v. 282
ORPHIC, Cosmogony, ii. 57
Deity, ii. 111; v. 276
Egg, Aristophanes and, ii. 75; v. 423
Greece, philosophy of, ii. 307
Hymns, ii. 81, 182; iii. 143, 150; iv. 75, 353, 354; v. 59, 293
Protologos, Vishnu, iii. 116
Theogony, i. 84; iv. 228
Thrace, priesthood of, iv. 325
Titan, iii. 80
Triad on creation, ii. 171
Verses, v. 59, 316
Zodiacal signs in, poems, ii. 374
ORPHIO-Christos of the Alexandrian mystic, ii. 79
ORSI, one of the Magi, iv. 173
OSERICTA, Asteria called, iv. 342
OSH, Kesil and Kimah, ii. 373
OSHOI, Rabbi, the thaumaturgist, i. 64
OSIRIAN, the quoted, iv. 159
OSIRIFICATION of every monad, i. 192
OSIRIFIED, i. 192
Defunct, i. 266, 267
OSIRIS, Aanroo in domain of, ii. 398
Abraxas gems, on, iv. 135
Abydos, one God at, ii. 399
Aerial demons, conqueror of, v. 249
Æther, representing, ii. 54
Aish and Asr, compounded of, iii. 123
Amenti, in, ii. 24; iv. 49
Ark or Solar Boat, enters, iii. 150
Assimilation to, i. 274
Black God, is, v. 233
Brahma, born from an egg like, ii. 81
Builders, synthesis of, ii. 155
Candidate initiated by, iv. 128
Church and, v. 313
Creative God, a, iv. 39
Defunct became, i. 192; v. 357
Defunct receives judgment of, i. 274; v. 246, 247, 250

OSIRIS (*Contd.*)
　Defunct sun, iv. 151
　Demons, conquered, v. 249, 251
　Dionysus is one with, iii. 418; v. 278
　Egyptians, of, i. 170, 186
　Eye of, iii. 38; iv. 122; v. 314
　Father of Horus, v. 440
　Fire is, v. 234
　God whose name is unknown, i. 142
　Great God, a, iii. 358
　Hawk symbol of, ii. 80
　Horned, v. 247
　Horus, i. 267; ii. 62, 94
　Initiate of Atlantis, v. 263
　Jehovah, a not very flattering copy of,
　　ii. 28
　Khou and, v. 246, 250
　Life, represented, v. 159, 161
　Logoi, one of, i. 129; ii. 147; iv. 273
　Lotus associated with, and Horus, ii. 95
　Lunus, i. 275; ii. 112
　Mamuram-Kahab, v. 251
　Menes not identical with, iii. 373
　Minos, or karma, i. 166
　Moon and, ii. 103, 108
　Mother of, ii. 148
　Mount Sinai, born on, v. 278
　Murderer of, iii. 384; v. 283
　Noumenon, v. 233
　Onnofre, a title of, v. 285
　Phoenician worship of, iv. 338
　Primordial God, as, ii. 398
　Prince on earth, as, iii. 358
　Ra or, -Ptah, i. 277
　Reign of, iii. 367
　Sarcophagus of, v. 283, 290
　Septenary sacred to, iv. 174
　Seven luminous ones who follow, ii. 24
　Sevenfold application of myth, v. 440
　Seventh principle is, v. 357
　Solar myth, not a, iv. 338
　Solomon, and, v. 272
　Soul before, accusers of, i. 166
　Soul of each became an, in Egyptian rites,
　　i. 192; v. 257
　Spirit of the earth, ii. 184
　Sun, ii. 80, 103; iv. 128, 155; v. 159, 161,
　　272, 273, 276, 312, 313, 317
　Symbol of, iv. 154
　Taurus and, ii. 383
　Thoth, and, iv. 128
　Tiaou and, iv. 275
　Toom, says he is, ii. 24
　Types of, iii. 55
　Typhon, and, i. 251; ii. 130; iii. 102, 378,
　　379; v. 283, 285
　Word, the, iv. 273
　Workshop of, iv. 154
OSIRIS and ISIS, Androgyne Gods, iv. 173
　Bull and cow sacred to, ii. 105
　Crocodile sacred to, ii. 126
　Hor, son of, ii. 82
　Horus and, ii. 62, 148; iv. 40; v. 440
　Interchangeable, i. 139
　Kronos, father of, ii. 96
　Mercury, minister of, ii. 103
　Thoth, iv. 30

OTOLITHS, Atmospheric vibrations trans-
　mitted to the, ii. 358
OTUS, brother of Ephialtes, iii. 280
OU, a minister of Poseidon, iv. 149
OUEEHA, or Ouvea, iii. 227
OULOM, Jewish meaning of, ii. 68
　Wisdom proceeded from, iv. 58
OUO, Ou or Ouoab, one of Poseidon's minis-
　ters, iv. 149
OURANOS, or Varuna, the chief Aditya, iii. 76
OVER-soul, the, Emerson on, i. 119, 196
　Guardian Angel of Church, v. 75
　Ideation of, ii. 90
　Universal, i. 82
　Universal sixth principle or, i. 82
　Unknown root or, i. 82
OVER-spirit, ii. 298
OVERLAPPING of races, iii. 431, 442, 443
OVERSEER, Every angelic virtue has an, i. 182
　Nebo the, of seven Gods of planets, iv. 23
OVID, exile of, v. 218
　Metamorphoses of, v. 230
OVIFORM, Ball formed by vital fluid, iii. 140
　Curve, iv. 116
　Globe, shape of our, ii. 74
OVIPAROUS, Humanity, iii. 140, 173
　Procreation, iii. 188
　Sons of passive yoga became, iii. 173
　Stage, iv. 229
　Third race produced by, method, iii. 140
　Vetebrates, iv. 304
　Wisdom symbolized by serpent, it being, ii. 79
OVOID, Bodies from perspiration, iii. 184
　Figure, iv. 117
OVULES, Cosmic children become, iii. 194
OVUM, or Egg, v. 436
　Future man in, iii. 194
　Germ cell or, iii. 126
　Human, ii. 82
　Protoplasm of, iii. 140
　Segmentation of an, i. 269
　Septenary law in, of an insect, iv. 194
OWEN, Prof., quoted, iii. 334; iv. 216, 219, 251,
　　257, 282; v. 481
OWL and Ox-headed Goddesses, iv. 292
OX, Aleph, symbol of, ii. 159; iv. 121, 146
OXEN, Temple, driven from, ii. 160
　Ungulate mammals, place among, iv. 305
OXFORD, Philologists of, v. 197
OXFORDSHIRE, Stonefield slates of, iii. 202
OXHYDROGENIC, i. 147
OXUS, the, ii. 183; iii. 205, 208
OXYGEN, Air, in, i. 179
　Crookes on, ii. 270, 274
　Current of, i. 294
　Elements one of four, iv. 164, 165
　First born, one of, ii. 348
　Hydrogen and, i. 125; ii. 351
　Intelligence and, ii. 332
　Microbes derive, i. 294
　Molecules of, iii. 165
　Nitrogen mixed with, iv. 165
　Ozone and, i. 200
　Phosphorus and, ii. 308
　Prāna, and, iv. 165
　Protoplasm contains, ii. 362
　Ptomaine free from, i. 305

OXYGEN (*Contd.*)
Substances, absorbed from, i. 307
OZIMANDYAS (Osymandias), Catacombs of, ii. 34; v. 58
OZONE, Allotropize oxygen into, i. 200
Chemistry, not to be made by, ii. 279
Chemists, of modern, i. 303
OZONIC gases, i. 147

P

PA, the men-serpents of China, iii. 214
PACCHAM, fifteen solar days, iv. 191
PACHACAMAC, Temple of, iii. 317
PACHYDERMATA, the, iv. 238
PACIFIC Ocean, Blue the colour of, iv. 200
Discovery of the, iv. 357
Great waters, and, iv. 345
Indian and, iii. 332
Large former continent in, iv. 356
Lemuria disappeared beneath, iii. 20; iv. 351
North and south, iii. 404
PACIFICUS of Dr. Carter Blake, iv. 351
PADMA, Chakras or, v. 483
Indian water lily or, i. 127
Kalpa, golden lotus or, ii. 84
Lakshmi called, ii. 95
Lotus or, iv. 149
Sambhava, v. 39
Symbolism of lotus or, i. 127
PADMAPĀNI, Avalokiteshvara or, iii. 185; v. 420, 421
Brahmā or, iv. 208
Daksha or, iii. 185
Fourth race children, of, iii. 180, 185
Kwan-yin in China is, iii. 186
Lotus-bearer, or, iii. 185, 186; v. 420, 421
PADMA'S Creation, ii. 145; iii. 64
Kalpa, ii. 173; ii. 186
PADMAYONI or lotus-born, ii. 87
PAGAN, Cross of, v. 161
Gods, v. 88, 245, 250, 271, 325
Historians, v. 149
Initiates, v. 108, 174
Latin church, v. 93
Mysteries, v. 35, 138
Nations, v. 176
Oracles, v. 276
Philosophers, v. 71, 278
Philosophy, v. 163
Planets and, v. 321
Pope as, v. 152
Religions, v. 201
Rituals, v. 95
Sidereal Worship, v. 318-323
Symbols, v. 175
Teraphim, v. 240
PAGANISM, and modern Christianity, v. 164, 217, 338
PAGODA of Mathura, iv. 159
Pi-yün-sï, v. 394
PAGODAS, Dragons on, iii. 210
Gurus of, ii. 91
Nautch girls of Hindu, iv. 28
Phallic stones in, iii. 94
Seven, of China, v. 325

PAHLAVI translation of the Parsi scriptures, iv. 327
PAIRS of opposites, Æons of, iv. 64, 139; v. 543
PALACE, Ocean shell, a, iii. 403
Planet or house, iii. 41
Seventh, ii. 71
Solomon, of, iii. 395
Truth, of, v. 246
PALACES, Seven of the sun, iii. 44
Tree of knowledge, of, iii. 17
PALÆOCOSMIC men in European caves, iv. 297
PALÆOGRAPHER, Cryptographic characters defying, i. 47
PALÆOGRAPHY, v. 93
PALÆOLITHIC, Age, iv. 91, 293
Ancestor, iii. 260
Cave men, i. 256; iv. 309
Cro-Magnon, type, iv. 257
Engraving, iv. 289
Hatchets, iii. 437; iv. 285, 291, 293
Neanderthal skull, iii. 199
Races in Europe, iv. 307
Savages, iii. 317, 345; iv. 257, 314, 319
Skeleton, iii. 260
Sketches, iv. 286
Tools, iv. 285
PALÆOLITHIC man, Age of first, iii. 211
Ancestor of, iv. 245
Arboreal, iv. 225
Atlantean, an, iv. 358
Certainty, a, iv. 246
Dolmens remains of, iv. 322
Engravings by, iv. 284, 289
European, iv. 290
Neolithic and, iv. 255, 284, 291, 293
Palestine, of, iv. 344
Quaternary epoch, of, iv. 284, 309
PALÆOMONIUS the Tyrian Hercules, iii. 344
PALÆONTOGRAPHY, iii. 210
PALÆONTOLOGICAL record, iii. 176
PALÆONTOLOGIST, Ideographic productions, iii. 437
Lartet the, iv. 260
Researches of the, iv. 245
PALÆONTOLOGISTS, Age of man, on, iii. 222; iv. 314
Inscriptions in characters unknown to, iii. 438
Third eye, on, iii. 298
PALÆONTOLOGY, iii. 210; iv. 254
PALÆOTHERIDÆ among ungulate mammals, iv. 305
PALÆOZOIC, Ages, iv. 166
Fishes, iii. 177
Rocks, iii. 253
Speculations on high tides, iii. 74
PALENQUE, Cross, ii. 106
Egyptian crosses in the remains of, iv. 127
Nachan identified by some with, iii. 47
Palace of, iv. 127, 320
Ruins of, ii. 34, 428; v. 283
PALESTINE, Abraham coming to, ii. 91
Crusaders and, ii. 72
Dolmens in, iv. 321
Jewish burial in, iii. 292
Nations remote from, iv. 39
Nebo adored throughout, iv. 23
Palæolithic man in, iv. 344

PALESTINE (*Contd.*)
Promised land not only, ii. 291
Set primitive God of, iii. 91
Teaching penetrated into, ii. 382
PALGRAVE, Jews and, shepherds, ii. 25
quoted, iii. 361
PALINGENESIS, iv. 229
Helm of, ii. 52
Pallas, Cybele or, ii. 115
PALINGENIUS, Marcel, v. 73
PALLAS ATHENE, v. 144, 171
PALMYRA, Gigantic race at, iv. 324
PALMYRENE characters, Line of, ii. 127
PAMIR, Garden of Wisdom on the Plateau of,
iii. 208
PAMPAS of America, Symbols in, ii. 183
PAMPHILIUS, v. 160
PAMPHOS, quoted, ii. 111
PAN, Aerius or, ii. 184
All or, v. 108
Flame on altar of, ii. 52
Khem and, v. 62
Meaning of God, iv. 79
Nature God, ii. 73; iii. 388; iv. 150, 153
PANCHA-ANANA, Rudra Shiva as, iv. 70
PANCHADASHA or Vedic hymns, iv. 151
PANCHAKARAM or pentagon, iv. 148
PANCHAKRISHTAYAH or five races, iv. 177
PANCHAMA, a quality of sound, ii. 258
PANCHĀNANA, Shiva, or five-faced, iv. 150
PANCHAPRADISHAH, the five regions, iv. 177
PANCHĀSHIKHA, one of the Kumaras, i. 282;
ii. 176; iii. 319
PANCHĀSYA, Brahmā and the, i. 261
PANDAVARANI in the *Mahabharata*, iv. 96
PĀNDAVAS, v. 378
Kunti mother of, iv. 96
Mayasura, and, iii. 424
PANDORA, Gift of, iii. 272, 410
Hephaestus moulding, iv. 88
PĀNDUS or PANDAVA, Five, iii. 346; v. 275
PĀNINI, Grammar of, iii. 255; v. 27, 408
Modern thinkers, and, iv. 91
Writing in India in days of, iii. 229, 275, 437
Yaska and, v. 275
PANNONIAN, Language, v. 148
PĀNODORUS, quoted, iii. 368
PANOPOLIS, v. 62
PANSOPHIA or wisdom, iii. 141
PANSPERMIC, Occult teachings are, iii. 141
PANTÆNUS, v. 36, 303, 304
PANTHEISM, Buddhism and, v. 410
Cosmolatry and, ii. 63
Erroneous ideas of, i. 73
Hinduism of, ii. 269
Hylozoism and, iii. 166
Indian, long unknown to Europe, i. 51
Pagan philosophy, and, ii. 132
Philosophical, ii. 130
Polymorphic, iv. 78
Polytheism or, iii. 115
Rediscovered, may be, ii. 257
Symbol of, cross within a circle, i. 72
Vedantin philosophers, of, iv. 40
PANTHEIST, Unknown of the, ii. 41
PANTHEISTIC, Avatāras, conception of, i. 123
Conceptions, i. 172; ii. 97

German schools, i. 183
Ideas, abstract, iv. 40
Intuitions of old world, iv. 115
Occultism answers on, grounds, ii. 272
Occultist on the divine revealer, ii. 29
Sense of, word, Monas, i. 231
Spirit-soul, idea of a general, i. 123
PANTHEISTICAL PERIPATETICS, ii. 344
PANTHEISTS, Advaitins, and, i. 74
Adytum venerated by, iv. 27
Atheists, and, i. 74; v. 384
Atlanteans, and, iii. 275
Atomists were, ii. 292
Creator not denied by, i. 74
European, i. 81, 122
Fichte and German, i. 145
First cause nameless to early, ii. 98
Leibnitz and Spinoza both, ii. 354
Manu supports, i. 74
Nemesis of Western, ii. 366
Personal God, and a, iv. 43
Triad of, i. 83
Upanishads and, i. 74
Western, i. 83; ii. 366; iii. 37
PANTHEON, Ancient, v. 110
Buddhist, v. 375
Heathen Deities of, v. 95
Hindu, v. 375
India, of, v. 111, 207, 270
PANTHEONS, Hindu and Buddhist, v. 375
Symbolical, v. 409
PANTOMORPHOS, giver of divine forms,
ii. 396
PAOPHS, month of, v. 243
PAPANTLA, Pyramid of, ii. 35
PAPUAN(S), Civilization of, iv. 231
Dying out, are, iv. 349
Hæckel on, iii. 327
Lemurians and, iv. 348
Negro, iii. 199
Skulls of, iii. 175; iv. 92
PARA, Meanings of, i. 147, 195
Vāch as, ii. 149, 150
Vaikharī Vāch as, i. 195; ii. 152
PARA-ĀTMĀ or Para-Purusha, v. 382
PARABLE, Good shepherd, of the, v. 96
History deduced from, ii. 19
Life realities represented by, ii. 19
Religious mysteries and, iii. 132
Spoken symbol, ii. 19
PARABLES of both Testaments, ii. 27
PARABOLICAL mode of thought, iii. 335
PARABRAHMAN, Absolute all or, ii. 353;
v. 210
Absolute cause or, i. 74
Absolute consciousness and, i. 80
Absolute motion, v. 557
Absolute Nirgūna or, i. 131
Abstraction called, i. 124
Ādi-Buddha and, ii. 294
Advaitis and, iv. 170
Ain Soph synonym for, i. 172, ii. 106; iii. 236;
v. 198
Anthropomorphized, even, i. 279
Ātmā-Buddhi and, i. 136
Brahmā and, i. 85, 262
Central point, v. 233

PARABRAHMAN (*Contd.*)
  Centres of energy in, i. 192
  Changeless, v. 210
  Chinmātra or, iv. 168
  Concealed unity or, iv. 123
  Cosmic aspect of, iii. 69
  Create, does not will or, ii. 170
  Ever-manifested principle or, iii. 236
  First cause not, iii. 116
  Four forms of, ii. 150
  God, not a, i. 73
  Hindus, i. 73
  Indivisible unknown, iii. 107
  Īshvara and, i. 126
  Jehovah not a synonym of, iii. 248
  Jīva pervaded by, ii. 246
  Kosmos and, i. 73
  Life is, v. 566
  Logos and, ii. 37
  Lower Manas of, v. 558
  Manvantaric aspect of, v. 530
  Mūlaprakriti and, i. 83, 136, 188, 317; ii. 51,
    53, 60, 146, 164, 246, 260; iii. 37; v. 475,
    530
  Nirvāna identical with, v. 354
  Oeaohoo one with, i. 136
  One Absolute Nature, v. 402
  One everchangeless, iii. 49
  One life or, i. 273
  One reality or, i. 80, 131
  One unknown, ii. 294
  Para aspect of Vāch or, i. 195; ii. 150
  Point, only known through luminous, ii. 150
  Pradhāna aspect of, i. 300
  Prādhānika, Brahma spirit is, ii. 164
  Prakriti is, v. 367
  Purusha and, ii. 306; v. 367
  Reality, unconditioned, i. 76, 128
  Row, T. Subba, on, ii. 146
  Secondless, ii. 247; v. 233
  Seed, the, ii. 260
  Semitic, v. 187
  Soul of whole, iii. 195
  Sound of names answering to, ii. 168
  Spirit and matter aspects of, i. 80
  Spirit of earth not, ii. 141
  Spirit of European Pantheists and, i. 122
  Substance or, i. 128
  Supreme All, i. 74
  Supreme as cause, i. 73
  Trinity of, i. 128
  Universe contained within, ii. 105
  Vedāntins, and, i. 76, 81, 118, 324; ii. 43, 68,
    72, 157; v. 107, 127, 386
  Veil of, ii. 144
  Verbum of, i. 193
  World, and manifested, ii. 170
  Zeruana Akerne or, iii. 236
PARABRAHMIC ĀTMĀ, Latency, iii. 37; v. 528
  Mind, v. 513
  State of, ii. 297
PARACELSUS, Archaeus and, i. 123; ii. 256
  Cause and phenomenon, on, ii. 215
  Father of modern chemistry, iv. 226
  Hæckel must have read, iv. 242
  Homunculi of, ii. 59; iii. 129, 348
  Isis Unveiled said to be a plagiarism from, i. 67

  Liquor vitæ of, ii. 256, 262
  Mysterium magnum of, i. 130; ii. 308
  Nitrogen discovered by, i. 337
  Referred to, i. 268, 307, 323, 324, 325, 334;
    ii. 239, 336; iii. 129; iv. 81; v. 28, 78, 174,
    175
  Sidereal light of, i. 298
  Teachings of, iv. 226
  Trials of, v. 282
PARACLETE, Manes called, v. 170
PARADESHA of Sanskrit-speaking people,
  iii. 209
PARADHA or half the existence of Brahmā, ii. 84
PARADIGM, Violet of all forms, v. 507
PARADIGMATIC, Adam Kadmon, iv. 23
  Man, v. 507
  Universe, ii. 91
PARADISE, Arctic circle, beyond, iii. 397;
    iv. 343
  Bliss, of, iii. 208
  Eden or, iii. 207
  Garden of, iv. 129
  Heart, of man's own, iv. 159
  Mahomet, of, iii. 208
  Northern regions of, iv. 343
  Theosophic school in, iii. 285
  Unphilosophical, i. 309
  Western, v. 393, 410
  Womb, as, iv. 449
PARADISES, Lokas called, iii. 321
PARADISIACAL man, Mercurial, iv. 212
PARAHYDROGENIC, i. 147
PARAMA=above everything, i. 120, 153
PARAMAPADA, Bliss in, ii. 189
  Immaterial worlds or, i. 190
PARAMAPADĀTMAVAT, above the condi-
    tions of spirit, ii. 137
PARAMARISHIS, greatest Rishis, ii. 137
PARAMĀRTHA, Absolute being or, i. 119
  Ālaya and, i. 92, 119
  Madhyamikas' View of, i. 116, 120
  Possession of, i. 124
  Self-consciousness or true, i. 116, 124
  Svasamvedanā or, i. 116
  Yogacharya's view of, i. 116, 120
PARAMĀRTHASATYA, Absolute truth, or,
    i. 120, 124; v. 400
  Knowledge through, i. 130
  Self-consciousness or, i. 120
PARAMĀRTHIKA, one true existence, i. 73;
    ii. 71
PARAMĀTMĀ, Jīvātma and, iii. 46
  Perfect Yogi or, v. 354
  Spiritual Sun, v. 487
  Universal Spirit or, i. 308; v. 487, 488
PARAMĀTMAN, Mahapurusha or, iii. 117
  Paramitās, v. 468
  Paranirvāna, v. 374, 403
  Six, v. 366, 401
  Supreme soul or, iv. 63
PARANIRVĀNA, Absolute perfection or,
    i. 114
  Arhat must reach absolute knowledge before
    he can attain, i. 120
  Bliss of, i. 311
  Explanation of, i. 309
  Paranishpanna or, i. 124

PARANIRVĀNA (*Contd.*)
Past, present and future humanities in, i. 309
Perfection, not absolute, i. 115
Taught, formerly openly, i. 115
Threshold of, i. 192, 193; iv. 16
PARANIRVĀNIC state, i. 309
PARANISHPANNA, Absolute perfection and, i. 114, 115; v. 400
Ah-hi in their, i. 92
Paramārtha and, i. 120; v. 400
Parinirvāna or, i. 124
Seeming existence and, i. 124
Senzar version of Stanzas used in, i. 87
Son of necessity and, i. 91
Unknown darkness, i. 123
PARAOXYGENIC gases, i. 147
PARAS, Pars, Pers, Persia, iii. 393
PARASAMĀDHI, v. 539
PARASHAKTI, supreme force or power, i. 333
PARASHARA, Aryan Hermes, i. 328
Asuras, on, iii. 235
Daksha, on, iii. 249
Dhruva, on, iv. 57
Dissolutions, on, iii. 310
Divinities of, iv. 157
Earth described by, iii. 322, 400
Explanation of, iii. 69
Fallen Gods alluded to by, iii. 235
Institutes of, iv. 195
Kumāras, on, iii. 235
Magic arts of, ii. 133
Maitreya and, ii. 88, 164
Manu, on creation of, iii. 321
Munis, on, iii. 235
Nārada referred to by, iii. 59
Planets, on chariots of nine, iv. 57
Pralaya described by, iv. 326; v. 267
Rishis on, iv. 120
Rudras, on, iii. 188, 235
Sacred islands and, iii. 326
Sorcery, of, iii. 235
Time, on, iii. 308
Vedic Rishi, ii. 176
Vishnu, on, iv. 183
Vishnu Purāna in, iii. 86, 170
War recounted by, ii. 137
PARASHURĀMA of race of Bhargavas, iii. 45
PARATANTRA, Parikalpita and, i. 120
PARAVARA=supreme, i. 73
PARCHA, Rabbi, referred to, iii. 374, 396
PARCHMENTS from the Alexandrian library, i. 56
PAREDOI or Solar assessors, v. 310
PARENT, Being, v. 447
Doctrine, i. 66
Earth, of, iii. 42
Ego, source of, i. 187; v. 500
Eternal, i. 91, 109
Flame, v. 358
Luminary, v. 430
Planet, ii. 298
Race, iii. 396
Sound, iv. 133
Space, i. 109
Stars, world and, iii. 45
Stock, variation from, iv. 301
Supreme, v. 303

World, v. 447
PARENTAGE and Karma, v. 545
PARENTLESS, Anupādakas or, v. 202
Second Logos, ii. 295
Space, i. 77
PARENTS, man of, Psychic and spiritual, iii. 179
Mercury and Venus, of, i. 210
Our heavenly, ii. 299
Sons of God born of immaculate, iv. 51
PARICSHIT, v. 347
PARIKALPITA, Paratantra and, i. 120
PARINĀMIN, the expanding, ii. 306
PARIS, National Library of, v. 252
Notre Dame de, v. 241
PARISIAN, Cranial capacity of, iii. 175
PARIVATSARA, v. 339, 340
PARKER, J.A., quoted, ii. 25, 27, 28; iv. 114; v. 197
PARKHURST, quoted, iii. 138; iv. 28
PARMENIDES, referred to, v. 231 252
PARNASSUS, the holy mountain, iv. 63; v. 110, 278
PAROPAMIRIAN CHAIN, iii. 337; v. 110
PARS, Pers or Persia, iii. 393
PARSIS, Few, ii. 104
Fire worshipper or, i. 180
Forefathers of, iii. 323
Guebra or, iii. 362
Heliolatry, and, v. 55
Jews, Armenians and, iv. 38
Masons and, i. 172
Mobed and, iv. 86
Mythology of, iv. 179
Peris ancestors of, iii. 397
Proof for, iv. 327
Sacred fire of, ii. 52
Sun, and, ii. 201; v. 154, 277
Uninitiated, iv. 179
Vendīdād of, iv. 178
PARTHENOGENESIS, Heterogenesis and, iii. 184
Virginal reproduction or, iv. 227, 229
PARTHIAN, coronet, v. 289
PARTICULARS, Human fancy, and, i. 317
Universals and, i. 208; ii. 341; iv. 155; v. 464
PARVATI PAMIR or Paropamisus, v. 110
PARZUPHIM, ii. 91
PASCAL referred to, v. 355
Circle of, i. 133
Nature and God, on, ii. 130
Plagiarism by, iv. 115
PASHA, a cord used by Shiva, iv. 118
PASHAI or Udyana, v. 39
PASHAVAH or sacrificial animals, iv. 196
PASHT, Cat form of, ii. 17
Goddess Basht or, iv. 122
Serpent bruised by, ii. 17
Sun watched for by, ii. 17
PASHUT or literal interpretation, ii. 89
PASHYANTI, Vāch as, ii. 150
Vaikhari Vāch as, i. 194, 195
PASS not, Circle of, i. 154, 188
Ring called, i. 187, 189
PASSOVER month of Jewish, v. 278
PASTEUR, Experiments of, i. 307; iii. 158
Referred to, i. 294, 306, 307
PASTOPHORIS, degree of, v. 290

PĀTĀLA, America is, iii. 141, 401
  Antipodes or, iii. 188, 405, 443; iv. 200; v. 286, 538, 540
  Arjuna descended to, iii. 218
  Hell or, ii. 88
  Hiranyaksha a ruler in, iii. 381
  Infernal regions or, iii. 60; v. 286, 288, 538, 540, 541
  Initiate descended into, iv. 128
  Mahāsura hurled down to, iii. 240
  Nether regions or, iii. 356
  Svastika in depths of, iii. 107
  Vāsuki, ruling deity of, v. 286
PĀTĀLAS or hells, ii. 88
PATANJALI, Adept of the school of, i. 213
PATER AETHER, i. 76; ii. 211; v. 172, 476,
  Mars and, iii. 391
  Omnipotent aether, ii. 44, 45
  Zeus not sexual or phallic, iv. 145
PATERNOSTER, Real, iv. 132
PATER SADIC, v. 320
PATH(S) Adepts of right and left, iv. 70; v. 378, 419
  Antahkarana is, v. 497
  Buddha of, v. 401
  Christos helping Sophia on right, i. 190
  Deliverance, of, v. 374
  Dzyan, of, v. 373
  Fourfold, v. 545
  Fourth, of knowledge, i. 254; v. 522
  Golgotha of life, of, i. 311
  Initiates of right and left, iv. 62
  Left, iii. 330; v. 60, 85, 122, 284
  Lunar, i. 151, 308
  Nirvāna, to, i. 255; v. 363, 402, 403
  Perfection, of, v. 371
  Persecution of prophets of right, iv. 71
  Rebirths, of, ii. 292
  Right and left, ii. 360
  Seeing, of, v. 405
  Seven, iii. 197; v. 519
  Seven portals on, v. 519
  Two, i. 150; v. 403
  Wisdom of thirty-two, iii. 51
PATMOS, Drama of the seer of, iv. 79
PATRIARCH(S), the, ii. 70
  Abraham, i. 64
  Adam, ii. 36
  Babylonian and Egyptian Gods transformed into, ii. 381
  Biblical, ii. 374; v. 387
  Biblical chronology and, iii. 389
  Biblical legends of, iv. 21
  Bodhidharma, v. 409
  Book of Enoch, work of a, iv. 51
  Daksha, iii. 183
  Destiny of, ii. 377
  Enoch, iv. 99
  Fables of, iii. 390
  Gods presented as, ii. 64
  Hebrew alphabet and, v. 114
  Hosts led by Rishis as, ii. 60
  Jewish and Christian, v. 263
  Jews robbed of their, ii. 380
  Names in Bible, iv. 406
  Noah, iii. 307, 350, 390; iv. 103
  Numerical value of, v. 206

  Periods and, iii. 424
  Pitris, Manus, Fathers, and, v. 201, 202
  Prediluvian, iii. 137
  Progenitors or, iii. 139
  Reign over men, i. 309
  Rishis and, v. 263
  Seven angels or, iii. 365; v. 203
  Sons of Earth, v. 111
  Verses concerning, ii. 171
  Zodiac, and, ii. 106, 377
PATRIARCHAL, Genealogies, iii. 321
  Life, iii. 318
PATRIOTISM, v. 552
PATRISTIC, Creation of, fancy, iii. 377
  Fathers, ii. 383
PAUL, Bishop of Samosata, v. 156
PAUL, ST., Archaic mystery of cross and, iv. 126
  Cautious hints of, iv. 84
  Christ and, v. 137
  Cosmic Gods and, ii. 185
  Cosmocratores and, v. 315
  Creation of man, on, iv. 82
  Elements of, ii. 51, 88
  Founder of Christianity, v. 136-138
  Gnosis and, v. 215, 301, 327
  Initiate, an, i. 285; iii. 270; iv. 273; v. 71, 137, 386, 488
  Jehovah and, v. 241
  Little one, iv. 73
  Lystra, at, iv. 49
  Master builder, v. 138
  Monads referred to by, ii. 357
  Mystagogue, as a, iii. 86
  Peter, John, James and, v. 138
  Pleroma and, v. 170
  Prince of air of, iv. 53
  Princes of Principalities of, v. 331, 332
  References to, i. 281; ii. 298; iii. 85, 91, 120; v. 133, 146, 301, 327, 382
  Secrecy and, v. 76, 80, 370
  Simon Magus and, v. 129, 131, 138
  Teachings of, v. 215, 301, 332
  Triple man and, v. 81
  Unknown God of, ii. 40; iv. 146; v. 382
  Wisdom and, v. 130
  Worlds, on other, iv. 273
PAUSANIUS, Apollonius and, v. 148
  Hyperboreans, on, iv. 338
  Prometheus, on, iii. 362
  Referred to, ii. 111; iii. 18, 41, 131, 152, 363, 417; iv. 88; v. 254, 293
  Speaking stones, on, iii. 341
  Testimony of, ii. 190; v. 254
  Tombs of giants, on, iii. 280
  Zeus of, ii. 52
PAUSHA, is December-February, v. 344
PĀVAKA, Electric Fire or, ii. 245
  Progeny of, iii. 111
  Three fires, one of, iii. 67, 68, 250
PAVAMĀNA, one of the three fires, ii. 245; iii. 67, 250
PAVANA, Hanumana son of, i. 241
PAYNE Knight, Richard, quoted, ii. 122
PEACE offerings and wave offerings, iv. 317
PEACOCK, Wisdom, bird of, iv. 190
  Worship of the Lord, iv. 83
PEDIGREE, Apes, of, iv. 258

PEDIGREE (*Contd.*)
  Scientists denying, iv. 224
  Ungulates, of, iv. 304
PEDIGREES, Homeric heroes, of, iv. 226
  Modern man, of, iii. 172
PÈGUES, Abbé, iii. 280
PEIRUN or Peiruun, Chinese, iii. 364; iv. 343
PELAGUS or the great sea, iv. 343
PELASGIAN, Genius loci of the, ii. 183
PELASGIANS, Aryan invasion, and, iv. 310
  Cyclopean remains of, iv. 315
  Future Greece and, iv. 343
  Mysterious, iii. 17
PELASGIC, Mounds said to be, iv. 322
PELICAN, Feeding its young, i. 146
  Rosecroix, symbol of, i. 146
  Rosicrucian symbol, a, i. 84; ii. 72
PELION, Mount, ii. 188
PELOPONNESUS, v. 65
PENANCE, Demons, of, ii. 137
  Mysteries connected with, iv. 211
  Perfection of austere, iv. 184
PENANCES of the Yogis, iv. 185
PENATES identified with Kabiri, iii. 359; v. 310
PENDULATES with mighty energies, ii. 254
PENETRALIA, ii. 97
PENGELLY, W., Geological time, on, ii. 290;
    iv. 265
  Referred to, iii. 76, 82, 322; iv. 347
PENHAKAHAKAHERHER, invocations to,
    v. 251
PENINSULA, Atlantis, iii. 23, 149
  Florida, of, iii. 142
PENINSULAS, Formation of new, iii. 403
  Secret Doctrine and, iii. 21
  Seven, iv. 175
PENTACLE, Chakra inscribed with a, i. 173
  Egg contains, i. 187
  Five root races symbolized by, i. 183
  Life, of, v. 487
  Ring pass not, and, i. 189
PENTAGON, Five-sided sign or, ii. 33; iv. 148
  Makaram, Panchakaram or, iv. 148
  Microcosm represented as a, i. 266, 271
  Monogram, a divine, ii. 99
  Triangle becomes a, iii. 88
PENTAGRAM, Line, triangle and, i. 154
  Symbol of, i. 144, 266; v. 232
PENTAMENOPH, v. 246
PENTATEUCH, Adversary, on, iv. 46
  Allegorical legends, a collection of, i. 77
  Angels in, v. 319
  Dark-cloaked Mosaic, iv. 55
  Dead letter of, ii. 50
  Diodorus and, iv. 344
  Ezra and, ii. 31; iv. 228
  Five books or, iv. 29; v. 178
  Gladstone and, iii. 382
  Moses puts veil on, v. 92
  Not original Mosaic records, v. 178, 181, 187
  Origin of birth and, iv. 115
  Primitive documents, origin of, iv. 41
  Rabbis knew inner meaning of, i. 77
  Samaritan, v. 74, 179
  Symbology of, i. 174; v. 182
PENTATEUCHAL garb, Jewish property in,
    ii. 381

PENTE, origin of, v. 117
PENTECOST, Jewish liturgy for, ii. 343
  Tongues of fire at, i. 180; ii. 52
PENTEGLOTT of Schindler, quoted, iii. 216
PER SALTUM, Nature never proceeds, ii. 310
PERATAE GNOSTICS, iii. 355; iv. 148, 149
PERCEPTION, Clairvoyant, v. 481, 557
  Organ of, v. 549
  Stage of, v. 548, 549, 554
PERDITION, Eternal, iv. 52
  Prometheus saves race from, iii. 410
PERFECT, Circle, circumference value of a,
    iv. 144
  Cube, ii. 58; iv. 33
  Devotee enjoined to approach form of, circle,
    iv. 122
  Ego, v. 400
  Figure, triangle first, iv. 146
  Figures, 1, 3, 5, 7, are, iii. 48
  Finite cannot be, iv. 55
  Holy Adam, iv. 24
  Number, v. 507
  Spiritual evolution impossible to, iii. 245
PERFECT MAN, Divine, i. 307
  Formation of, i. 293
  God-like and, iii. 248
  Heavenly man and, i. 294
  Initiate, v. 154, 400, 402
  Man-God or a, i. 290
  Metatron, ii. 52
  One, iv. 35; v. 400
  Physically, iv. 181
  Quaternary and ternary a, iv. 147
  Spiritual, iii. 122
  Square, iv. 126
PERFECT NUMBER, Heptagon a, iv. 173
  Odd said to be, iv. 173
  Quaternary, iv. 153, 173
  Ten, iv. 121, 134, 144, 146; v. 423
  Tetrad, iv. 170
  Tetraktys contained, iv. 31
PERFECTED MEN, Dhyān Chohans incipient
    or, i. 318, 319
PERFECTIBILITY, Ever-growing, iv. 43
PERFECTION, Absolute, i. 115, 120; iv. 125;
    v. 213
  Absolute all, or, i. 140; v. 213
  Austere penance, of, iv. 184
  Ceaseless striving towards, iv. 305
  Corruptible, grows out of, iii. 104
  Evolutionary, i. 237
  First, v. 117
  Intellectual, iii. 414
  Motionless, iii. 245
  Paranishpanna or absolute, i. 115, 120
  Path of, v. 373
  Physical, iii. 414
  Quiescence natural state of, iv. 58
  Reformation and evolutionary, i. 237
  Secondary, iv. 153
  Serpent symbolizes, iv. 140
  Tau called, iv. 153
  Unit, of, iv. 154
  Wisdom and, symbolized by the serpent, i. 140
  Work of, everlasting, i. 200
  Worshipper of absolute, iii. 411
PERI, Tahmurath liberates the, iii. 396

PERIGENESIS, Plastids, of, iv. 233, 243
  Plastidule, of, iv. 241
PERIGORD, Reindeer hunters of, iv. 318
PERIOD, Cambrian, iii. 23
  Carboniferous, i. 297
  Eocene, ii. 22; iv. 249, 314
  Fern, iv. 166
  Fire mist, ii. 172
  Fourth race, iv. 186
  Geological, iii. 167
  Glacial, iii. 149, 152, 155, 276; iv. 71, 247, 248
  Jurassic, iii. 202
  Laurentian, iii. 158
  Mid-tertiary, iii. 163
  Miocene, i. 236; iii. 21, 24, 431; iv. 245, 248
  Oolitic, iii. 202
  Palaeolithic, iii. 437
  Post-tertiary, iii. 67
  Pre-diluvian, iv. 168
  Quaternary, iv. 256
  Saïtic, iv. 32
  Secondary, ii. 173; iv. 254, 255
  Silurian, iii. 81
  Tertiary, i. 241; iii. 96, 431; iv. 246, 250
  Time-, War in Heaven and, v. 201
  Two, symbolized by Enoch, v. 106
PERIODICITY, Chakra denotes, iv. 116
  Law of, iv. 192, 198, 199
  Phenomena of life, of, iv. 198
  Secret Doctrine and law of, i. 82
  Septiform, iv. 194
  Sun, moon and planets, of, iv. 192
PERIPATETIC laws, ii. 227
PERIPATETICS, the, i. 133, 230, 231; ii. 57, 344
PERIPHRASIS, Jehovah, of, ii. 156
  Shlokas and a, iii. 15
PERIS, Ancestors of Parsis, iii. 397
  Devs made raids on, iii. 396; iv. 346
  Izeds or, iii. 392; iv. 346
  King of, iii. 393
  Persian, iii. 368
PERISPRIT, Fluidic, i. 246
PERMANENCY, Divine, v. 119
PERMANENT Atoms, iv. 241
PERMEABILITY of matter, i. 296, 302
PERMIAN, Geological period, iv. 282
PERONNE, Rev. Father, quoted, iii. 374
PERPETUAL motion, i. 125, 203, 324; ii. 220, 249, 280; iv. 16, 116; v. 227, 229, 322
PERSAEA in An, Basin of, iv. 116
PERSEPHONE, iii. 361; v. 267
  Worship of, v. 267
PERSEPOLIS, Esikekar or, iii. 397
PERSEUS, Cyclops indentified with, iii. 344
PERSIA, Christian legends come from India through, i. 248
  Druids akin to Magi of, iv. 325
  Legendary history of, iii. 397
  Magi of, iii. 394; iv. 325; v. 299
  Nova Zembla, north of, iii. 397
  Pers, Pars, or, iii. 393
  Seven worlds in, iv. 178, 188
  Songsters of, iii. 398
  Sovereigns of election of, iii. 346
  Tahmurath, king of, iii. 396
  Temples of, v. 322
  Traditions of, iii. 50, 392, 395; iv. 182

PERSIAN, Atlantean traditions, iii. 404
  Borean wrecked, fleet, iii. 188
  Dev, iv. 108; v. 94
  Egypt, conquest of, ii. 23
  Fireworshippers, iii. 362
  Folklore, iii. 396
  God, name of, iii. 353
  Gulf, iii. 147; iv. 180
  Heroes, Feridan one of, iii. 397
  Hieratic texts, v. 57
  Invasions, v. 271
  Legends, iii. 393
  Mithras, mysteries of, ii. 164
  Otizoe, iii. 346
  Peris, iii. 368, 397
  Phoenix, iii. 396
  Primal cause of, philosophy, ii. 343
  Romances, iii. 401
  Simorgh, iv. 134
  Symbology, iv. 189
  Winged griffins, ii. 80
  Yezidi, iv. 22
PERSIANS, Ancestors of, iii. 328
  Astronomical elements of, ii. 385
  Egg symbol among, ii. 74
  Fire among treatment of, iii. 123
  India and, v. 316
  Meshia and Meshiane among, iii. 142
  Mithras of, ii. 54
  Nassireddin, tables of, ii. 384
  Religion of, iv. 177
  Sire of, iv. 173
  Stars of, ii. 388
PERSONAE of churches, three distinct, ii. 153
PERSONAL, Action impersonal and, iii. 306
  Appearance, false, iv. 49
  Creative Elohim, iii. 134
  Creator, theory of a, iii. 165
  Deity, ii. 363; v. 81
    ,,   Creative of orthodox Christians, i. 84
    ,,   Definition of, ii. 359
    ,,   Demiurge no, ii. 322
    ,,   Leibnitz on, ii. 354
    ,,   Seventh principle or, ii. 363
    ,,   Worshippers of, i. 309
    ,,   Zeus a, iii. 412
Devil, iii. 376
Divinity in man, v. 137
Ego, Adept, of, v. 353
  ,, Experience on every plane of, ii. 43
  ,, Immortality and, v. 495, 496
  ,, Individual consciousness or, iii. 243
  ,, Soul of, iv. 181
  ,, Substance and, ii. 43
Entities or Creative Gods, ii. 145; v. 502
Genius, iv. 140
God, Advaitist view of a, iv. 170
  ,, Anthropomorphic, ii. 269
  ,, Argument regarding a, i. 70
  ,, Believers in a, ii. 131
  ,, Buddhist recognizes no, ii. 360
  ,, Chinese Buddhists and a, ii. 158
  ,, Christian's, ii. 144, 338; iv. 40
  ,, Extra-cosmic and, iv. 69
  ,, Finite or, iv. 114
  ,, Fohat not a, i. 195, 196
  ,, Inner God, or, iv. 125

PERSONAL (*Contd.*)
    God, Jehovah, a, ii. 144
    ,, Kabalists, of, ii. 135
    ,, Male, ii. 339
    ,, Man created a, ii. 130
    ,, Plato did not believe in a, iv. 124
    ,, Self-created, ii. 337
    ,, Superior spirit, i. 243
    ,, Theism, of orthodox, i. 69; v. 233
    ,, Theology, of, ii. 57
    Gods, Kronos devours, iii. 414
    ,, Third stage of manifestation is, ii. 155
    Qualities, angels have no, i. 319
    Self, iii. 118; v. 361
    ,, Divine, v. 92
    Soul, v. 496, 500
    Will, body of, iii. 244
PERSONALITY, the, Absolute, and oneness with, i. 124
    Angels have no elements of, i. 319; ii. 357
    Aroma which remains from each, i. 284
    Avatāras, of, iv. 46
    Correlation of individuality and, iv. 46
    Dhyān Chohans, no feeling of, i. 318
    Dual, iii. 244
    Ego within, i. 189
    Egoism, or sense of, i. 318
    Essence of, in Nirvāna, i. 309
    Garment is perfect, endures when, i. 290
    Gross ideas attached to, ii. 97
    Higher Ego and, v. 491, 492
    Immortality of, v. 489, 490, 491, 493
    Intervention of a creative, iv. 222
    Invulnerable in his, man will become, iii. 420
    Jesus, of, iii. 234; v. 151
    Kapilas, of, iv. 142
    Logos, no, iii. 318
    Man concealed under, i. 267
    Man not immortal in his, ii. 158
    Manas on plane of, iii. 69
    Melha assumes, of a Buddha, iii. 74
    Mortal, ii. 364
    Multiple, i. 75
    One reality weeded of, ii. 354
    Paralyzing, i. 319
    Selfishness of, iii. 118
    Star of, ii. 296
    Terrestrial false, iii. 244
    Third race and, iv. 181
    Unreality of, iii. 307
    Yogi destroys passions within his, iv. 185
PERSONATOR, Demon or, iv. 78
    Jehovah as a, iii. 246
    Spirits as, iv. 78
PERSONIFICATION, Aindriyaka, of, iv. 185
    Allegory and, ii. 302
    Cross symbol, of, iv. 129
    Cyclic law, of, iv. 354
    Devil, of, iv. 45
    Eighth God, becoming, iv. 178
    Fohat, of, ii. 397
    Force behind phenomena, of a, i. 324
    God of Theists a, ii. 139
    Human passions, of, iii. 379; iv. 141
    Nebo, of the secret wisdom, iv. 23
    Ra, of, iv. 116
    Symbolical, of creative power, iii. 135

Twelve tribes of great Gods, ii. 115
    Uranus a, iii. 271
    Virtues, of, ii. 156
    Yama, of shadows of Pitris, iv. 180
PERSONIFICATIONS, Abstract attributes of, ii. 156
    Bible astronomical, ii. 377
    Mystical, iii. 105
    Poles, of terrestrial, iii. 362
    Powers, of, iii. 116
    Purānas, in, ii. 132
    Sons of wisdom, of, iii. 272
    Symbolical personages and, iii. 137
    Three fires, of, iii. 249
PERSONIFIED, Attributes of God, iii. 240
    Moon, ii. 102
    Primordial light, iii. 139
    Symbols, iv. 25
PERSONS of the Trinity, ii. 194; v. 337
PERSPIRATION, Evolution through drops of, iii. 181
    Marisha born from Pramlocha's, iii. 182
    Ovoid bodies produced from, iii. 184
    Pramlocha, of, iii. 182
PERU, Ancient buildings in, i. 257
    Chulaps of, iv. 321
    Cyclopean erections in, iv. 315
    Early man in, traditions of, iv. 314
    Manco-Capac of, iii. 365
    Remains of, iii. 361
    Ruins in, iii. 317, 336
PERUVIAN, Records destroyed, v. 283
PERUVIANS, Fairy tales of, i. 310
    Svastika found with, iv. 158
    Tradition of, iii. 149
PERVADER, Fohat called, i. 171
PESH HUN, Hindu possession, not only a, iii. 60
    Nārada or, iii. 59, 60
    Stanzas on, iii. 60
PESHAWAR, Cave of, v. 39
PESSIMISM, Schopenhauer, of, iii. 164
    Von Hartmann, of, iv. 219
PESSIMISTS, Karma only reply to, iii. 305
    Nature on, iv. 43
PETALS of the lotus in the seeds, ii. 94
PETALOON, of the Rabbis, v. 138
PETER, St., Church of Rome and, iii. 341; v. 124, 125
    Epistle of, i. 267
    Last days, on, iv. 326
    Kabalist, not Initiate, v. 139-141
    Not founder of Latin Church, v. 190
    Paul and, v. 133, 138
    Pope personifies, iv. 34
    Quoted, iv. 198, 332
    Simon Magus and, v. 126, 129, 131, 132, 134, 135, 146
    Transfiguration at, v. 167
    Trustee of, iii. 376
PETER the Hermit referred to, ii. 72
PETERMANN, referred to, iv. 136
PETITION, Red Indian, iii. 437
PETOSIRIS, Egyptian astrologer, v. 329
PETRA, Keffa, or, v. 139, 140
PETRARCH, Story told of, iii. 212
PETRIE, Flinders, Piazzi Smyth and, ii. 26
    Referred to, iii. 230, 344

PETRIFIED third eye, iii. 296
PETROMA, Initiation stones, v. 139, 140
PETRONIUS, referred to, ii. 73
PEUVRET, Theosophic degrees of, iv. 172
PFAFF, Prof., quoted, iii. 96, 199; iv. 231, 251, 256
PFOUNDES, Capt. C., referred to, i. 286
PHAETON, Death of, iv. 340
  Sun, and, iv. 104
PHALANX of active stellar systems, i. 204
PHĀLGUNI, Pūrva and Uttara, v. 343, 344
PHALLI, oil-anointed, iv. 40
PHALLIC, Brazen serpent is, ii. 80
  Chaldeans, notions of, iii. 18
  Conception which is not, ii. 149
  Cross when, i. 72; ii. 34; iii. 43; iv. 113, 117, 132
  Crucifixion nails, iv. 131
  Crucifixion when, iv. 131
  Deities, ii. 73
  Element in old scriptures, iv. 228
  Emblems, ii. 106
  Fish, meaning of, iii. 314
  Form and use, iii. 134; iv. 35
  Functions, symbols of, iii. 390
  God, ii. 60; iv. 28, 40; v. 63
  Hebrew letters are, symbols, i. 174
  Hebrew records and, worship, i. 175
  Holy of Holies as, iv. 27
  Jehovah, becomes, i. 72; iv. 37, 40, 41; v. 233
  Jupiter, symbols of, iii. 363
  Lingam and Yoni, iv. 33
  Monuments, v. 285
  Nails of cross, iv. 131
  Number, ii. 107; iv. 31
  Pan a, deity, iii. 73
  Pater, Zeus not, iv. 145
  Physiological meaning of cross, ii. 383
  Profound science, become, ii. 78
  Prometheus, idea of, iv. 95
  Ram's head and horns, iii. 189
  Religion, element in, iv. 153
  Rites became, iii. 361; v. 292
  Rose as, v. 292, 293
  Sacr' is of, derivation, i. 72
  Serpent, a fourth race, symbol, iii. 72
  Shiva worship not simply, iv. 159
  Signification, iv. 118
  Stone, iii. 94
  Svastika separated from its circle becomes, i. 73
  Symbol, ii. 194
  Tetragrammaton as a quaternary, ii. 156
  Theology, element of, ii. 25
  Venus, significance of sign of, iii. 43
  Worship, i. 45, 308; ii. 193; iv. 39
PHALLIC symbols, Ancient deities becoming, iii. 55
  Antiquity, of later, iv. 154
  Meaning of, ii. 31; iv. 155
  Natural in beginning, were, ii. 31
  Uses of, ii. 162
PHALLICISM, ii. 80; iii. 110, 275, 281, 286; v. 86, 196
  Anthropomorphists led to, iii. 275
  Architect of the universe and, iii. 110
  Bible and, v. 206
  Body worship or, iii. 281

  Divine, iv. 115
  God names and, ii. 28, 31
  Humanity led to, ii. 80, 171
  Idea of, iii. 56
  Jewish, iii. 213
  Pentateuch, in, v. 182
  Rabbis, of, iii. 94
  Semites introduced, iii. 65
  Sexual worship and, iii. 286
PHALLICIZED, Arcanum has been, iii. 236
PHALLUS, Ark, in the, iv. 35
  Cross, often added to, iv. 112
  Lingam or, iv. 34
  Lithos upright, iii. 94
  Male principle or, iii. 112
  Natural symbol, a, ii. 106
  Yod, or, iv. 41
PHANEROGAMOUS plants, i. 127
PHANES, Chaos, Chronos and, ii. 171
PHANTOM (S), Astral, iii. 98; v. 257
  Bhūta, or, iii. 99, 110
  Dyooknah or divine, iv. 24
  Fathers of, iii. 217
  Germ of u iverse, ii. 83
  Inapprehensible, ii. 211
  Mind, of, ii. 342
  Nebular theory of, ii. 312
  Protoplasmic, i. 242
  Races, iii. 281, 291
PHARAOH (S), Abraham's wife and, ii. 139; iii. 181
  Ansated cross of, iv. 113
  Eden, compared to fairest tree in, iv. 62
  Glyph of daughter of, iii. 31
  Lord God tempts, ii. 98
  Moses and, ii. 100; iii. 426; iv. 33
  Mummy of, Sesotris, i. 52; v. 329
  Obduracy, of, iii. 424
  Sacred cross carried by, iv. 117
  Seven souls of, iv. 203
  Sinaitic peninsula ruled by, iii. 229
  Spiritism and, v. 257
  Sun Gods in land of, iii. 378
  Thotmes worships Hathor, ii. 115
PHARAONIC Egypt, Rites and dogmas of, i. 51
  Source of Measures, v. 111
PHARISEES, Christian angelology from the, iii. 71
  Jehovah, father of, ii. 302
  Jesus and, ii. 301; iii. 377
  Pentateuch and, v. 186
  Sign from heaven, ii. 380
PHASES of the moon, Eye of cat and, ii. 103
  Marital relations and, i. 275
  Seven esoteric, ii. 112
  Time periods marked by, ii. 105
P'HELINGS, or foreigners, v. 396
PHENOCH, symbol of secret cycle and initiation, iv. 188
PHENOMENA, of levitation, v. 225
  Spiritualistic, v. 556
PHERECYDES, Cosmogony of, i. 246
  Giants, on, iv. 344
  Hymn to Jupiter of, iv. 122
  quoted, v. 57, 60, 61, 62
PHIDIAS, Model in the mind of, iv. 230

PHILADELPHIA, Centennial exhibition in, ii. 282
  J. W. Keely of, i. 57, 299
PHILADELPHUS, Hellenic teachers under, v. 302
PHILAE, Bas-reliefs from, iv. 128
  Egg in temple of, ii. 79
  Khnoom was adored at, ii. 82
  Ruins of, iv. 127
PHILALETHEIANS, v. 34, 46, 303, 308
PHILALETHES, quoted, i. 304; ii. 239; v. 174
PHILIP the apostle, *Pistis Sophia* of, iv. 136
PHILISTINES, David with the, iv. 111; v. 311
PHILLIPS, Sir R., Theory of, iv. 294
PHILO BYBLUS, quoted, iii. 138, 341; iv. 33
PHILO JUDAEUS, quoted, i. 139; ii. 58, 375; iii. 120, 205; iv. 39; v. 68
  Adam Kadmon, on, iv. 58
  Adversary, on cursing, iv. 45, 46
  Book of the Law, on, v. 198
  Creator on, ii. 65
  Inconceivable, on, ii. 66
  Number seven, on, ii. 124
  Number six, on, ii. 124
  Origin of Evil, on, v. 213
  Pentateuch and, v. 302
  Wisdom, on, iv. 58
PHILOLAUS, v. 32, 218, 219
PHILOLOGICAL disquistions, iii. 54
PHILOLOGIST, Max Müller, i. 51, 52
PHILOLOGISTS, Antiquity of writing, on, iii. 437
  Ares and, iii. 391
  Dzyan, unknown to, book of, i. 46
  German, v. 385
  Problem for, i. 139, 140
  Riddle for, i. 142
  Secret Doctrine not written for benefit of, i. 87
  Vedas, on, i. 52
PHILOLOGY, Comparative, i. 48
  Discoveries of, iii. 428
  Science in its department of, ii. 29
PHILOSOPHER (S), Antiquity, of, v. 77, 257, 329
  Greek, v. 29
  Hebrew, v. 66, 198
  Pagan, v. 71
  Priest-, v. 265
  Primitive; v. 315
  Sumian, v. 36
  Stone of, v. 467
  Thales, a, v. 234
PHILOSOPHY Age of mankind, and, iii. 163
  Antahkarana and, v. 497
  Atoms of, i. 266; ii. 173
  Attainment of consciousness a fact in, i. 320
  Brahmanical, i. 237; v. 358
  Buddha's Esoteric, v. 363, 385, 387
  Buddhist, v. 387
  Chaldean scriptures and, iv. 23, 24
  Christian mysteries, and, iv. 130
  Cis-Himālayan, iv. 145
  Consciousness of, i. 120, 320
  Cosmology connected with, ii. 338
  Creation in, iii. 96

Creators in, iii. 87
Correspondences, v. 439, 441
Cycles and, iv. 140
Deity and, iii. 50
Egyptians and, iii. 373
Essential Truth of, i. 143
Etymology of, v. 265
Evolution and, iii. 195
Extension, on, ii. 338
First cause and, ii. 324
First lesson of, iv. 55
Greek, v. 33
Hermetic, i. 329; v. 57, 60, 120, 142, 226
Immortality of Gods and, i. 109
Isis and, i. 63
Jesus, of, v. 155
Kabalah and, iii. 52
Law of analogy and, i. 206
Leibnitz and, ii. 353
Life and consciousness and, i. 120
Life periods and, iv. 281
Matter, on, ii. 356
Māyā and, i. 77
Minor details of, iv. 211
Mysteries of nature, and, ii. 260
Number four and, iv. 171
Occult, i. 143, 206; ii. 260, 324, 343, 353, 365; iii. 96, 195, 203, 442; iv. 121, 140, 211; v. 226, 228, 232, 287, 331, 362, 462, 488
One and primal cause of, ii. 243
Origin of language and, iii. 203
Pagan, v. 163, 164
Planets and, iv. 110
Platonic, v. 30, 36, 303
Primeval evolution and, ii. 346
Primitive and Modern, v. 265
Problems of evolution, on, ii. 361
Pure esotericism of, v. 78
Pythagorean, v. 387
Races, on new, iii. 442
Reconcilement of all systems in, i. 126
Rudras in, iv. 156
Sanskrit, v. 470
Science and, iii. 77; iv. 201
Seven sons of, i. 162
Seventh eternity of, i. 131
Sidereal symbols of, iv. 121
Solar system and, ii. 85
Special privileges not admitted by, i. 83
Spirit of, ii. 345
Spontaneous generation and, iii. 158
Three strides of Vishnu and, i. 172
Time according to, i. 116
Traditions of, iii. 17
Universal wisdom of, i. 139
Universe in, i. 321
Virgil knew, iv. 166
Western, v. 466
PHILOSTRATUS, Life of Apollonius by, v. 142, 146, 151
  Revealed scripture, and, iii. 336
  Serpent legend of, ii. 120
  Skeleton, spoken of by, giant, iii. 280
PHILO-THEO-SOPHIA, ii. 257
PHINEATAE, Hermes worshipped by the, iii. 366

PHLEGYAN island, iii. 152
PHLOGISTON, derided name of. ii. 236
PHO, Buddha Sang-gyas, or v. 381
PHOBOS, Mars and, i. 219
    Periodic time of, i. 219
PHOCIS, Slime of the deluge in, iv. 88
PHOEBE, Castor, wife of, iii. 130
    Moon, ii. 102
PHOEBUS, iii. 237
PHOENICIA, Worship of the Kabirim in,
    iii. 362; v. 310
PHOENICIAN, Agruerus the, God, iii. 150
    Ancestors of, iii. 328
    Animated Stone of, iii. 342
    Astarte, prayer to, ii. 189
    Ball of, iv. 110
    Coin, cross and circle on, iv. 116
    Colonies of, v. 333
    Coptic kinsman of, i. 175
    Cosmogony, i. 170; ii. 171; iv. 188
    Descent of, iv. 337
    Divinities, v. 202
    Eldon or Elion, iii. 379
    Empire, iii. 268
    Globe, vessels circumnavigated, iii. 427
    Herodotus, of, ii. 25
    Hieratic texts, v. 57
    Hindus said to have learnt Astrology from,
        iv. 121
    Iao of, v. 277
    Kabiri with, iii. 275
    Letters, v. 205
    Mot, Mahat and, ii. 170
    Mysteries of, v. 279
    Mysterious voyages of, iv. 333
    Mystery Gods of, iii. 17
    Mythology, v. 202
    Numerical system of, iv. 130
    Origin of, iv. 313
    Record of, religion, iii. 437
    Samothrace colonized by, iii. 17
    Sanchuniathon the, v. 279
    Southern Gaul, settlements in, iv. 319
    Supreme God of, iv. 111
    Writing, and, iii. 437
PHOENIX, Bennoo or, ii. 24
    Garuda, Indian, iv. 134, 135; iv. 190
    Onech, Hebrew, iv. 188
    Persian, iii. 396
    Primordial man like, iv. 181
    Resurrection of, iv. 188
PHOIBOS APOLLO, Light of life and the
    world, iii. 382
PHONOGRAPH, Edison's, iv. 352
PHORCUS, one of the Arkite Titans, iii. 151
PHOREG, seventh of the Uranides, ii. 136
PHORMINX, the seven-stringed lyre, iv. 99;
    v. 275
PHORONEIDAE, an ancient poem, iv. 88
PHORONEUS, Hero, a, iv. 88
    Melia, son of, iv. 90
    Plato on, iv. 88
    Prometheus and, iv. 88
PHOSPHATES, ii. 307
PHOSPHOROS, Satan lord of, iv. 82
PHOSPHORUS, ii. 274, 307, 308; iii. 82, 257;
    iv. 80

PHOTIUS on stones, iii. 341; v. 170
PHOTOGENIC matter, Envelope of, ii. 254
PHOTOGRAPHED, Divine ideation of things to
    be, ii. 90
PHOTOGRAPHS, Akashic or astral, i. 83
PHOTOGRAPHY, Spiritual, v. 298
PHOTOMETERS, ii. 304
PHOTOSPHERE, envelope of sun, ii. 254, 255
PHRENIC LOGOS, iii. 38
PHRYGIA, Priests of, iii. 370
    Worship of Kabirim in, iii. 362
PHTA, Action is life of, v. 89
PHTAH, Deity concealed by, iv. 123
    Kabir, seventh, iii. 365
    Khonsoo confounded with, iv. 32
    Unity of, ii. 399
PHURBU, Magical figures of, v. 398
PHYLOGENESIS Hæckel's, iv. 226
PHYLOGENETIC speculations, iv. 233
PHYLOGENY, iv. 229, 233, 234, 303
PHYSICAL Body, v. 473
    Man, Age of, iii. 253
    ,,   Animal and, i. 304, 305
    ,,   Auric envelope and, v. 429
    ,,   Beginnings of, iii. 200
    ,,   Consolidation of, iii. 300
    ,,   Cradle of, iii. 422; iv. 343
    ,,   Cretaceous rocks and, iv. 249
    ,,   Daksha creator of, iii. 189
    ,,   Esoteric philosophy on, ii. 163
    ,,   Evolution of, iv. 229, 239
    ,,   Fashioners of, iii. 67
    ,,   First truly, iii. 273; iv. 334
    ,,   Form of, ii. 53
    ,,   Formation of, ii. 361
    ,,   Nascent, iii. 229
    ,,   Originally a giant, iii. 22
    ,,   Period of, ii. 91; iii. 113
    ,,   Rounds, and, i. 239, 240
    ,,   Science only recognizes, iii. 315
    ,,   Shadow of, i. 283
    ,,   Simply, iii. 269
    ,,   Spiritual and, iv. 102
    ,,   Third race, of, iv. 231
    Mind, v. 487
    Nature, i. 326; ii. 312
    ,,   Construction of perfect animal impossible
            to, iii. 111
    ,,   Double, iii. 46
    ,,   God of science is, ii. 393
    ,,   Left to herself, iii. 66
    ,,   Matter emanation of, ii. 169
    ,,   Principles of, iv. 165
    ,,   Spiritual extinguished by, iii. 297
    ,,   Transformation in, iii. 441
    Plane, Appearance of nature on, ii. 335
    ,,   Astral and, ii. 369; v. 516
    ,,   Dhyān Chohan and, iv. 239
    ,,   Nidānas and, v. 517
    ,,   Psychic action and, v. 515, 516
    ,,   Root of all things on, iv. 153; v. 517
    ,,   Sleep and, i. 111
    ,,   Sound and colour on, ii. 258; v. 522,
            523
    Science, Absolute darkness, on, i. 250
    ,,   Arbitrary divisions of, ii. 260
    ,,   Atoms of, ii. 53

PHYSICAL (*Contd.*)
Science Chemistry and, ii. 345
,, Colour and, v. 457
,, Domain of, iv. 233
,, Ether and, i. 78, 300
,, Evidence supplied by, i. 218
,, Fire and, i. 137, 179
,, Hindu of, v. 475
,, Hypothetical speculations of, i. 209
,, Ignorance of, i. 238
,, Kama Manas and, v. 512
,, Last word of, ii. 325
,, Master key to, iv. 126
,, Materials now unknown to, iii. 168
,, Metaphysics and, ii. 207, 208
,, Microscopic cells and, iii. 125
,, Modern, ii. 352
,, Natural progress in, i. 177
,, Occult teaching and, i. 150, 191; ii. 313
,, Periodicity as observed by, i. 82
,, Phraseology of, i. 230
,, Problems of, iii. 436
,, Pymander and, iii. 115
,, Riddle of the past and, ii. 361
Senses, Consciousness through, iv. 240; v. 530
,, Correlation of seven, ii. 258
,, Deities of, iv. 139
,, Development of, v. 547
,, First plane, on, v. 525
,, Five, v. 525, 530
,, Impulses produced by our, ii. 369
,, Mental feeling precedes, v. 547, 550
,, Origin of, iii. 116
,, Plane of our, iii. 422
,, Psychic counterpart of, v. 557
,, Seven, v. 429
World(s) Material or, i. 249
,, Metaphysical and, iii. 402
,, Revolution of, ii. 366
,, Space of, ii. 353
,, Sun life of, ii. 203
,, Unity in, i. 179
PHYSICALIZATION, Astral, out of the, iv. 219
Incipient, iv. 306
PHYSICIST(S), Abyss of nothingness of, i. 204
Ancients' belief as to the elements, i. 197
Atoms and, i. 198
Azoic ages, and, iii. 167
Cometary matter and, ii. 321
Esoteric teaching and, i. 335
First cause, and, ii. 324
Hindu allegories and, iii. 57
Hindu chronology and, i. 209
Illogical, ii. 203
Kabalist remarks on, ii. 340
Kepler and other, ii. 313
Light, flame and electricity according to, i. 147
Matter and, ii. 311, 353
Mechanical theories of, v. 28
Modern, ii. 205
Monads and, ii. 345
Moon a closed book for, i. 211
Nebulae and, i. 189
Origin of things according to, ii. 340
Our planet's age unknown to, i. 205
Primeval matter and, i. 165

Primordial substance and, i. 202
Protyle, searching for, ii. 342
Psychometer, should be a, i. 250
Rocks and rivers real to, ii. 42
Rotation theory rejected by, ii. 223
Substance of occultist and, ii. 239
Theosophists and, ii. 395
Two distinct schools of, ii. 236
Unknowable of, i. 45
Worlds which are invisible denied by, ii. 330
PHYSICO-astral, Man, iii. 290
Root types, iv. 305
PHYSICO-chemical, Forces, iv. 222
PHYSICS, Ancients and, ii. 218, 291; iii. 115
Archaic, ii. 303
Brain, of, iv. 243
Chemistry and, ii. 324
Colour, Sound and Number in, v. 456
Domain of Kama-Manas, v. 512
Elements of, ii. 181
Ether and, ii. 57, 208
Fifth element and, iii. 144
Fourth race taught, iii. 424
Inductive science and, ii. 310
Law of analogy the key to cosmic, i. 205, 206
Material universe and, ii. 394
Metaphysics and, i. 117; ii. 231, 335; v. 435, 512
Modern science and, ii. 206
Mysteries of, v. 73
Nature, as a science of, ii. 241
Occult, i. 306; ii. 214; iv. 242
Pure force nothing in, ii. 235
States of matter known to modern, ii. 210
Unity in sphere of, iii. 37
World germ of occult, i. 250
PHYSIOLOGICAL, Age of mankind, iii. 164
Anthropologists, proofs of, iii. 193
Change, cause of, i. 306
Conjectures in, works, iii. 140
Creation, secrets of, iv. 114
Cross, meaning of, ii. 383
Dhyān Chohans and humanity, relationship between, i. 273
Differentiations, iii. 129
Dual, potency, ii. 194
Equipment, iv. 306
Evolution, i. 271
Fall, i. 243; iii. 281
Fourth race, nature of, iii. 409
Hebrews, spirit of, iv. 37
Jewish allegory of deluge is, ii. 162
Law, iii. 201
Lemurians, transformation of, iii. 317
Magic, i. 307
Man and apes, differences between, iv. 235
Man, form of, i. 290
Manasas' refusal on, grounds, iii. 178
Moon, mystery of, i. 274; ii. 106; iv. 125, 202
Mysteries, iii. 255
Phenomena, ii. 191
Pre-eminence given to the, iv. 38
Process, iii. 188
Procreation, spiritual and, iii. 413
Psychic and, element, iii. 183
Psychic discoveries, and, i. 191
Purity of third race, iii. 179

PHYSIOLOGICAL (Contd.)
 Racial, transformations, iii. 185
 Secret key, iii. 78
 Seer, purity of, iii. 297
 Selection, iv. 217, 307
 Senses, iii. 299
 Sexes, transformation of, iii. 155
 Structure of the brain, iv. 220
 Sun and moon, deities, i. 275
 Symbols, iii. 109, 390; iv. 108, 119, 155
 Theories of science, i. 269
 Titans founded on a fact, iii. 161
 Union, iv. 37
 Variation, iv. 219
PHYSIOLOGIST (S), Astronomers and, ii. 203
 Hæckel on, iv. 234
 Optic Thalami and, v. 481
 Pineal gland and, v. 483
 Soul's working, and, iv. 219, 220
 Teratological Phenomena and, iii. 194
PHYSIOLOGY, Celestial bodies and, ii. 31
 Charcot's patients and, iii. 370
 Curse, from standpoint of, iii. 409
 Esoteric doctrine and, iv. 203
 Foster on, iii. 140
 Lunar worship and, ii. 112
 Magician of future, i. 304
 Man as known to, ii. 361
 Materialistic view on, ii. 31
 Mind and brain and, ii. 327
 Mistakes of modern, i. 241
 Moon's connection with fecundation unknown, to, i. 307
 Mysteries of, v. 73
 Nature of female and, i. 275
 Nervous centres and, v. 531
 Organisms, iii. 120
 Phallicism or, v. 86
 Physics and, iv. 192
 Psychology and, v. 151
 Science, ancient, of, v. 292
 Septenate in, iv. 194; v. 483, 484
 Soul-functions, of, iv. 240
 Spiritual senses rejected by, ii. 258
 Vital principle denied by, ii. 327
PHYTOPHAGOUS MAMMALS, iv. 282
PI, Astronomical, i. 174
 Value of, i. 154, 189
 Variations of, iii. 51
PICARDY, Britain joined to, iv. 320
 Hatchets and mammoths in, iv. 308
PICTURE, Gallery of eternity, i. 165
 Writing of the Egyptians, iii. 139
PIERIUS, quoted, iv. 122
PIERRET, Paul, quoted, i. 192, 275
PIGMIES, Age of, iv. 283
 Ancient giants and modern, iii. 80
 Giants and, iii. 200, 330
 Science and, iv. 291
PIGMY animals, iii. 223; iv. 291
PIGS among the ungulate mammals, iv. 305
PIKERMI, Monkey fossils at, iv. 292
PILE villages of Borneo, iv. 284
PILGRIM, Divine, iii. 257
 Eternal, i. 82; ii. 293; iv. 297
 Humanity and, i. 311
 Monad, called, i. 82; ii. 293

 Soul, journey of, i. 228
PILGRIMAGE, Cyclic, iii. 111, 444
 Individual, ii. 344
 Soul, of every, i. 82
 Wheel of the son, on new, i. 113
PILGRIMS, Comets or, i. 294
PILLALOO-KODI, Pleiades called, ii. 388
PILLAR(S), Adam Kadmon, as, v. 116
 Attributes of, ii. 146; v. 285
 Christianity, of, iv. 84; v. 62
 Circle, and, iv. 31
 Curtain in temples drawn over five, i. 183; ii. 182
 Deity, form of, iv. 41
 Earth, of Atlas sustainers of, iv. 331
 Egyptian, iv. 100
 Fire, of, ii. 52, 155; v. 562
 Heaven, Mount Atlas called, of, iv. 332
 Hercules, of, ii. 347; iii. 154, 226, 323, 393
 House of wisdom, ii. 71, 124
 Jacob's, iv. 39, 40
 Light, of, v. 472, 511, 517
 Matzebah, Statue or, v. 237
 Mercury or Seth, of, iv. 99
 Pyramids became, ii. 61
 Solomon's temple, of, iv. 29
 Stone, of, iv. 99
 Symbol for a book, v. 180
 Wisdom, of, iv. 212
 World, iii. 105
PILLOW of Jacob, as Symbol, v. 166
PILOT, Sun in a ship as its, ii. 126
PINDAR, Immorality of pantheons, on, iv. 333
 Magic, on, v. 254
 Referred to, ii. 116; iii. 17, 131, 272; v. 254, 266
PINEAL GLAND, iii. 127, 296, 301, 302; v. 480, 481, 483, 521, 549, 556
PINES, Pyramidal shape of, iv. 166
PINGALĀ, Idā, and, v. 480, 510, 520, 523, 524
PINO, Don Baptista, iii. 188
PIPPALA, Haoma or, ii. 106, 107
PISCES, iii. 172; iv. 227, 263
 Christ and, ii. 379; v. 163
 Haeckel on, iii. 172; iv. 227
 Mina, or, iv. 151
 Vernal equinox in, iv. 263
 Zabulon, in sphere of, ii. 377
 Zodiacal sign of, i. 307; ii. 91
PISCINE ancestors, iv. 255
PISGAH, Mount, v. 272
PISHACHA, a female demon, iii. 132, 295
PISHUNA the spy, iii. 60
PISTIS SOPHIA, Bhagavad Gita in light of, iv. 140
 Book of Enoch quoted in, iv. 105
 Brahmans recognize Upanishads in, iv. 136
 Date of, ii. 126
 Gnostics and, ii. 301; iv. 30, 175, 189
 Ieou in, ii. 168
 Knowledge-wisdom, or, i. 190
 Quoted, iv. 140
 Rabbi Jesus in, iv. 134, 189
 Revelation of St. John and, ii. 127
 Valentinian gospel, iv. 81
 Vowels of, iv. 133
PIT, Earth bottomless, iii. 240; iv. 61
 Leo in, iv. 354

PIT (*Contd.*)
  Mountain and, iii. 365
  Mysteries in, v. 153, 154, 286
  Pātāla, v. 286, 288
  South pole is, iv. 354
PITĀ, Father or, iii. 70
PITAR, Human, v. 282
PITARA DEVATA, Pitris or, *q.v.*
PITARAS, Pitris or, *q.v.*
PĪTHA STHĀNA, or seal, v. 140
PITHECANTHROPUS of Haeckel, iv. 231, 247, 249
PITHECOID, Ancestry, supposed, i. 237; iii. 22; iv. 206, 220, 251, 252, 260, 285
  Ape in, family, i. 241
  Apes, iv. 285
  Creation an accidental, iii. 263
  Extinct, iii. 287
  Fossil, iv. 244, 245
  Genesis of, stocks, iv. 259
  Man, i. 280; iii. 201; iv. 239, 296
  Man not, iii. 198
  Neanderthal skull, iv. 257
  Noah, iv. 225
  Origin of man, iv. 256
  Theoretical, man, iv. 237
PITIR LOKAS, v. 537
PITRI-PATI, the Lord or king, ii. 56
PITRIS, Agnishvatta, i. 233
  Arūpa, three classes of, iii. 102
  Astral and Ātmā-Buddhi and, v. 532
  Asuras and, iv. 55, 56
  Barhishad, iii. 103
  Brahmā stands esoterically for, iii. 70
  Brāhmanical system, of, iii. 129
  Brāhmans count, sacred, iii. 100
  Celestial men or, iii. 57, 150
  Chhāyās of, i. 233; iii. 128, 145; iv. 55; v. 335
  Chitkalā and, i. 329
  Classes, seven, i. 231, 264; iii. 87, 100
  Corporeal and incorporeal, iii. 392
  Daksha synthesis of, iii. 170
  Dhyān Chohans and, i. 239; iii. 89, 217, 236
  Divine sparks or, i. 232
  Doctrines of, v. 281
  Doubles, have evolved their, i. 235
  Elohim or, i. 292; v. 201
  Ethereal doubles of, iii. 19
  Evolution from, iii. 328
  Fathers or, iii. 56, 324, 357; v. 201
  Fetahil is one with host of, i. 245
  Fire of, ii. 245
  Fires, and, iii. 110
  First race oozed out from bodies of, iii. 181, 304
  Flames or, iii. 250
  Forefathers of men, ii. 162, 163
  Formation of animal man by, i. 293
  Gods and demons, of, iii. 98
  Governors or, iii. 269
  Heavenly man or, iv. 252, 253
  Hierarchies of, i. 240; v. 532
  Hosts of, seven, iii. 16
  Humanity in future, v. 532
  India, of, iii. 106, 365
  Intelligences, informing, iii. 46
  Kāma and, iii. 183

  Kandu son of, iii. 182
  Kumāras confounded with, iii. 115
  Ladder, at lower end of, ii. 263
  Lha or, iii. 67
  Lords of moon called, iii. 85
  Lunar, iv. 226; v. 472
  Lunar ancestors or, i. 214, 274, 307
  Lunar Gods or, i. 151, 227
  Lunar monads or, i. 232
  Lunar spirits or, iii. 396
  Mahar-loka, in, ii. 87
  Mankind offspring of, i. 271; v. 532
  Messengers of Sacred fathers are, i. 153
  Occultists, of, i. 268, 269
  Peris may be derived from, iii. 393
  Pitara Devatas or, iii. 150; iv. 177, 191
  Pitri Devatas or, iii. 179
  Planetary, v. 281
  Prajāpatis, and, ii. 176; iii. 171
  Progenitors or, iii. 175, 330; iii. 69, 70, 97, 119
  Rishis and, i. 161
  Rulers and, iii. 98
  Science declares, are fictions, ii. 336
  Secret Doctrine synonym for, i. 155
  Seven, v. 201
  Shadows of, iv. 180
  Shista or, iii. 171
  Solar and lunar, ii. 160
  Solar deities or, i. 151
  Somapa, iv. 162
  Sons of God, v. 26
PITUITARY BODY, v. 480, 481, 482, 521, 556
PIVOT, Manas the, iii. 244
PIYADASI, Inscription, iii. 61
PI-YÜN-SÏ, pagoda of, v. 394
PLACENTA, iv. 29, 220, 237, 238; v. 422, 449
PLACENTAL, Animals before man, iv. 306
  Mammal, i. 241; iv. 283
  Man, v. 425
PLACENTALIA, Divisions of, iv. 283
PLAGIARISM, Demon accused of, ii. 116
  Evangelical, iv. 50
  Legendary, iv. 49
  New Testament, of, v. 99
  Pascal, by, iv. 115
  Sepp, Dr., by, ii. 381; iv. 191
  Systematic, iv. 50
PLAKSHA, one of the seven dvipas, iii. 320, 403
PLANE (S), Absolute consciousness, of, i. 320
  Absoluteness, of, i. 188
  Abstraction of, i. 110
  Action of lower host, of, iii. 420
  Ākāsha, of circle, i. 83
  Arūpa or formless, ii. 118
  Astral, *q.v.*
  Atoms on, of matter, ii. 360
  Atoms, of existence of, i. 205
  Being; occult principles on every, of, ii. 178; v. 560
  Being, Invisible, i. 298
    ,,   of each atom has seven, i.205
    ,,   Seven, iii. 243; iv. 204
    ,,   Various, i. 152
  Beings from higher, iii. 97
  Budhic, v. 532
  Circle, of boundless, i. 77; ii. 339

PLANE(S) (*Contd.*)

Consciousness of, i. 181, 248; iv. 57, 271; v. 530, 566
Consciousness, of our, i. 330; ii. 42, 266, 315, 327; iv. 57, 242; v. 529
Consecutive matter, of, i. 203
Correlation of each, i. 57
Cosmic, i. 195, 201; iii. 116
Creative, cube on, iii. 48
Creators active on intellectual, iii. 87
Death on terrestrial, iv. 101
Devachanic, v. 551, 566
Devalokic, i. 189
Descending, iv. 60
Dhyānis and Elohim, of, i. 319
Diagrams of, v. 524-530
Differentiation, of, i. 292
Differentiation on, v. 513
Divine instructors on various, iii. 357
Divine, mystery on, i. 129
Dual idea carried through every, ii. 107
Earth, of, i. 284
Effects, of, ii. 239
Elements and gases on objective, iii. 121
Eternity of universe as a boundless, i. 82
Ether, of, i. 298
Evolution, of, i. 216
Evolution of ethereal races, of, iii. 165
Evolution on cosmic, iii. 116
Existence, of, iii. 168, 247; v. 361
Existence of phenomenal world, of, iv. 123
Experience of any, an actuality for percipient, i. 335
Fall of angels repeated on every, iii. 270
First, of perception, i. 240
First race mindless on our, iii. 203
Fohat acts on all, i. 171
Fourth Kosmic, v. 532
Fourth or lowest, of material life, i. 242
Globes overshadowing earth on superior, i. 220; iv. 328
Globes two by two on each, iv. 327
Good and evil on manifested, ii. 131
Higher, of being, ii. 330; iii. 90
Hydrogen is gas only on this, iii. 114
Illusion, of, i. 151, 187, 324; ii. 306
Intermediate, of lower consciousness, iii. 277
Kāmalokic, v. 567
Kosmic, *q.v.*
Kosmic, v. 429, 527, 528
Leibnitz, not risen above first, ii. 351
Life, of conscious, ii. 296
Light waves on lower, ii. 141
Lower manifested, i. 301
Macrocosmos divided into seven, v. 477
Mahat, seven of, v. 535
Mānasic (Mental) *q.v.*
Manifestation, of, i. 199, 285, 294, 295
Manifestation of light on our, i. 303
Material and terrestrial, iii. 68
Material, of evolution, a, iii. 72
Materialist, inaccessible to, ii. 258
Matter, of, i. 110, 306; ii. 212, 340
Matter on next higher, ii. 266
Matter on objective, iii. 46
Māyāvic, i. 291
Mentality, of, i. 228

Metaphysical, i. 171
Midway halt between two, iv. 306
Mind on sensuous, i. 159
Modes of thought on different, iii. 334
Monad not of this, i. 227, 228
Monads on higher, ii. 345, 357
Moon on same, of perception as earth, i. 225
Mortals, of, i. 289
Mystic, i. 159
Nature, of differentiated, iii. 89
Nature on physical, ii. 335
Nirvāna, a higher, after, i. 309
Noumenal world, iv. 153
Number on ideal, ii. 65
Objective, ii. 174, 258; iv. 164
Objective and subjective, of nature, i. 204
Objective globe and chain, of our, ii. 382
One unconditioned all, of, i. 311
Orbital, of planets, ii. 326
Oxygen, etc., on a deeper, ii. 351
Perception, matter on another, of, ii. 210
Perception, of, i. 240, 317; ii. 42; iii. 369
Perceptions, of deceptive, iv. 43
Personality, Manas on, of, iii. 69
Phenomenal, i. 160
Phraseology, beyond ordinary, iii. 335
Physical, *q. v.*
Physical senses, of our, iii. 422
Pilgrimage through all, of existence, iii. 111
Pleroma, of, iii. 123
Polarity on our, ii. 238
Prakritic, v. 524, 525, 538
Presence, of abstract, i. 69
Primeval differentiation, of, iii. 192
Principle of life on our, ii. 263
Protyles corresponding to various, iv. 306
Psychic, *q. v.*
Rays on, of spirit, ii. 360
Reality, of, v. 361
Reality, of only eternal, ii. 342
Reflection, of, v. 454
Revolution, iii. 242
Senses, known by our, iii. 72
Septenary kosmos, i. 249
Seven circles are seven, iv. 57
Sevenfold, each, v. 516, 524
Seventh, i. 330; iv. 187
Sexual, iii. 93
Shapes from one, all, ii. 107
Six-pointed star and, i. 263
Sound and colour on physical, ii. 258
Spheres, light on our, is darkness in the higher, ii. 169
Spirit, of, v. 477
Spiritual, *q.v.*
Spiritual or astral, energy on, ii. 369
Spiritual repeats itself on cosmic, i. 230
Square, iv. 197
States of matter have only a relative existence on our, ii. 42
Subjective, i. 324
Subjectivity and objectivity, of, ii. 396
Surface of circle, of, iv. 125
Surface, study by inductive method limited to, iv. 144
Sūtrātmā, of, iii. 89
Terrene, our, i. 220

PLANE(S) (*Contd.*)
　Terrestrial, i. 200; ii. 61; iii. 100; iv. 57
　Terrestrial, sidereal, and moral, iv. 192
　Third, v. 558
　Third, of kosmos, v. 513
　Thought, of, i. 296; iv. 108
　Thought on astral, i. 183
　Triangle on lower, ii. 344
　Triangular, ii. 34
　Two, iii. 282
　Universal consciousness, iv. 168
　Universal manifestation, of, iii. 50
　Universal, of productive nature, ii. 339
　Universe, of, i. 243, 316; ii. 357
　Upper and lower, ii. 343
　World of formation, of, i. 207
　Worlds, or, iv. 179
　Zones and, ii. 127; iv. 327
PLANET(S), Aditi mother of seven, ii. 167
　Age of our, i. 205
　Allegories about, iv. 157
　Ancient view of, ii. 297; iii. 369
　Angels identified with, iii. 98, 318
　Angels on this, of dense matter, iv. 52
　Angels or regents of a, ii. 135, 300; iii. 93
　Astronomer's theories about, ii. 321
　Astronomy, unknown to, i. 217
　Aura of, i. 280
　Ball of fire-mist becoming a, iii. 161
　Battles of, i. 163
　Becoming Moon, v. 535
　Biographies of all, iii. 57
　Blessed ones, on, iv. 157
　Brihaspati, Jupiter, iii. 57
　Calculation, predicted by a, iii. 439
　Chain of our, iv. 328
　Chariots of, iii. 44
　Choir of, ii. 380
　Combustible matter of, ii. 325
　Comets and, i. 251
　Configuration of, Venus, iii. 45
　Conjunction of all, at Kali Yuga, ii. 387
　Conjunction of, in Pisces, ii. 380
　Correspondences of, v. 432, 437, 438, 441
　Course of, iv. 183
　Creation of our, ii. 37
　Creator of our, iii. 38
　Days of week and, v. 433
　Dead, v. 439
　Density of, ii. 317
　Difference of volume in, ii. 281
　Direction of revolution of, i. 205
　Discovered, ii. 299
　Duality of, v. 315
　Earth as, iii. 82; v. 75
　Earth, as seen on, ii. 215, 216
　Earth, influence of, on our, iv. 269
　Earth one of a group of seven, i. 221
　Earth or any visible, i. 208
　Elements, constellation and, iii. 124
　Elements, of our, i. 199
　Evolution of chain of, i. 85
　Freaks of, ii. 226
　Garga knew about, iii. 60
　Generally treated of, i. 207
　Genesis of, ii. 164
　Genii of, ii. 375, 378

Globes at pralaya have their energy transferred
　to, i. 213
　Globes or, iii. 309
　Gods or, i. 70; iv. 49, 179
　Great architect over each, ii. 160
　Growth of, ii. 333
　Guardian of, iv. 47
　Habitability of, iv. 268, 271
　Harmonious motion, of, ii. 151
　How an astral earth could affect, iii. 253
　Human groups and chief, ii. 297
　Human races in connection with, iii. 428
　Human stock adapted to, i. 220
　Identity of motion in, ii. 321
　Importation into area of, iv. 254
　Incense burned to, ii. 375
　Inhabitants of every, iii. 56
　Inter-Mercurial, v. 439
　Intra-cosmic, regarded as Māyā, i. 77
　Jupiter a critical, iii. 145, 147
　Jupiter and Mars between, ii. 317
　Jupiter and other, ii. 387; iii. 144
　Karshvares and seven, iii. 383
　Lares, or regents of seven, iii. 360
　Length of day on four inner, iv. 276
　Life cycle on this, i. 278
　Life-germs from other, iii. 165
　Life on other, ii. 255; iii. 45; iv. 272, 276
　Lord is one of seven, iv. 108
　Lucid stars and, i. 255
　Man born under a, v. 460
　Mankind, connection between, and, iv. 68; v. 460
　Mars, iii. 55, 133, 381; iv. 190
　Mars, Mercury and other, are septenary units,
　　i. 218
　Mārtānda, sun watches, ii. 253
　Matter composing, ii. 201, 326
　Measures of size of, iv. 113
　Mercury, ii. 103; iii. 40, 366; iv. 22, 110
　Mercury and Venus, iv. 110
　Misconceptions as to, i. 207
　Moon and, Jupiter, iii. 147
　Moon, becoming, v. 535
　Moon said to be a dead, i. 204
　Moons of other, i. 211
　Motions of, ii. 385; iii. 85; v. 536
　Mutation, orbits of, subject to, ii. 227
　Mystery, v. 536
　Mystery Gods of seven, iii. 35
　Names of, ii. 374
　Nascent, ii. 316
　Nativity, v. 331
　Nature's adjustment of, iv. 114
　Nebo deity of Mercury, iv. 22
　Nebula formed from a, i. 86
　Neptune as a, v. 222, 536
　Night, remain intact during, i. 83
　Obscuration of resting, iv. 230
　Occultism, of, i. 145
　One by one, extinguished, ii. 92
　Orbits of, v. 224
　Organic evolution on, iv. 253
　Origin of the, i. 164; ii. 224, 319
　Palace, house, or, iii. 41
　Periodical conjunction of, ii. 376
　Plurality of chains of, iv. 269
　Primitive impulse of, ii. 326

PLANET(S) (*Contd.*)
  Principle animating, i. 176
  Principles of, transferred, i. 202
  Pulse, of, iv. 194
  Radiation round, v. 424
  Rector, moved by an intrinsic, ii. 216
  Regent of every, v. 333
  Regents of, ii. 109, 300; iii. 36; v. 320
  Religion of every, iii. 357
  Resurrection of, after a minor pralaya, i. 77
  Revolution of our, ii. 366
  Rotation of, ii. 227
  Rulers of, v. 443
  Sacred, iv. 173; v. 429, 460
  Satan God of our, iii. 237
  Saturn, sun and moon opposed to, iii. 73
  Science, known to ordinary, i. 216
  Self moving, ii. 395
  Seven, i. 261; ii. 297; iii. 35; iv. 173; v. 108,
      129, 155, 309, 320, 429, 460, 536
  Seven Aletae, the, iii. 360
  Seven circles are the seven, iv. 57
  Seven days, alters its appearance every, iv. 172
  Seven principles of man, correlated to, i. 57
  Seven sons of light called after their, ii. 298
  Seventy, ii. 380
  Shani, ii. 179
  Signs of Zodiac and, v. 332
  Solar, i. 205
  Solar world, limbs and pulses of, ii. 264
  Spheres, and, ii. 302, 396
  Spheres of seven, iii. 17, 18, 294
  Spirits from another, iv. 182
  Spirits of, i. 186, 280; v. 314, 317, 319, 324
  Spirits of this, iii. 19
  Star or inhabited, iii. 56
  Stars and, iii. 92
  Stellar chemical action not identical with that
      on this, ii. 321
  Stellars of seven, i. 245
  Strings or chains of, i. 220
  Sub-planes of all, v. 524-530
  Sun and, i. 255; iii. 36; v. 437
  Sun, detached from, ii. 313
  Sun, motion of, round, iv. 29
  Sun near, ii. 224
  Suns, comets and, i. 164
  Symbols, as, v. 241, 444
  System, of our, iv. 164, 271
  System of progress of, iv. 98
  Temperature differs on every, i. 198
  Theologians' view of mankind on this, iii. 157
  Tidal action on our, iii. 74
  Time measurers, as, iv. 192
  Tower of Nebo, iv. 23
  Undiscovered, ii. 300
  Varied nature of, iv. 272
  Venus, iii. 42, 43, 45
  Vital soul of, ii. 326
  Well known, i. 217
  World, sister, of every, iii. 45
PLANETARY, Angels, v. 208, 253, 309, 329,
      460, 462
  ,,   Flocks of stars and, iii. 384
  ,,   Forces or, i. 280
  ,,   Group of creative, iii. 135
  ,,   Incarnating, iii. 360

Archangels, v. 325
Atmosphere, i. 199
Babylon, temple of, iv. 23
Beings, v. 421, 466
Chain, Antiquity of, iv. 267
  ,,   Architect of, i. 186
  ,,   Bibles and, iv. 272
  ,,   Brahma and, i. 114
  ,,   Days and nights of, i. 209
  ,,   Development of, i. 226
  ,,   Dhyān Chohans of, iii. 154
  ,,   Dvīpas and, iii. 320
  ,,   Earth and, iv. 188
  ,,   Evolution of, i. 57
  ,,   Formation of, i. 207, 224
  ,,   Globes of, i. 283; iv. 179
  ,,   Last round of, i. 210
  ,,   Life cycle of, iii. 321
  ,,   Major manvantara and, iii. 309
  ,,   Monads of, iii. 311
  ,,   Mysteries of, i. 221
  ,,   Nebula condenses forming, i. 86
  ,,   Noah and, iv. 169
  ,,   Obscuration of, iii. 310
  ,,   Rebirth of, i. 213
  ,,   Root-races of, i. 114
  ,,   Seven spheres of, i. 172; iii. 383
  ,,   Seven wheels are, i. 200
  ,,   Stanzas on, i. 130, 206
  ,,   *Vedas* on, i. 295
  ,,   Wheel or, i. 278
  ,,   Worlds of, seven, iv. 178;
              v. 222
Chambers, ii. 292
Combinations, ii. 297
Composition of, bodies, ii. 321
Conjunctions, ii. 382
Creators, i. 170
Dhyānis, iii. 41
Division, i. 208
Elohim, iii. 135
Evolution, i. 63
Forces, i. 280; iii. 344
Genii, i. 35
Gods, v. 310, 334
  ,,   Adepts taught by, ii. 215
  ,,   Aditya of, iii. 76
  ,,   Patriarchs and, ii. 106
  ,,   Qualities of, ii. 259
  ,,   Sun worshipped by, iii. 360
  ,,   System, of our, ii. 154
Humanity on our, chain, iii. 79
Impulses, iv. 266, 267
Influence, v. 536
Inhabitants, ii. 336
Macrocosmos, iv. 210
Manvantara, i. 77, 236, 306
Motion, ii. 207, 208, 253; iv. 193
Nebula, ii. 320, 322
Period, entities of previous, iii. 235
Powers, ii. 357
Pralaya, i. 225
Principle, Emepht supreme, ii. 82
Races of men, iv. 206
Regents, iii. 215; v. 329, 333
Round, i. 214
Spheres, i. 247; iv. 187

PLANETARY (*Contd.*)
　Spirits, v. 109, 220, 221, 309, 460, 465
　　,,　Angels or, ii. 366; iii. 318
　　,,　Brahmā and, i. 114
　　,,　Builders and, i. 168
　　,　Christians recognized, i. 165
　　,,　Creative powers or, iv. 122
　　,,　Dhyān Chohans and, ii. 193, 360
　　,,　Gods and, i. 76; ii. 345; iii. 65; v. 281, 309
　　,,　High, i. 320; v. 309
　　,,　Host of, v. 109
　　,,　Karma of, iv. 140
　　,,　Kumāras or, v. 465
　　,,　Lipika and, i. 168
　　,,　Man and, v. 298
　　,,　Monad of, ii. 356
　　,,　Primary or, iii. 42
　　,,　Radiation of, ii. 298
　　,,　Seven, iii. 35,106; v. 220, 221, 460
　　,,　Stars, informing spirits of, i. 186
　　,,　Three groups of the, i. 186
　　,,　Vital soul or, ii. 326
　　,,　Watchers and, ii. 300
　Suspension, ii. 281
　System, v. 129, 154
　　,,　Formation of, ii. 319
　　,,　Higher plane on a, i. 124
　　,,　Kingdom or, i. 162
　　,,　Mysteries beyond, i. 176
　Pregenetic day of, ii. 113
　Pyramids and, iii. 361
　Rotatory motion of, ii. 160
　Stanzas treat only of, i. 79
　Sun as seventh Principle of, v. 154
　Temple of Babylon, iv. 23
　Times, measures of, iv. 113
　Venus, sign of, iii. 43
　World, i. 310, 330; ii. 323
PLANETATION of rings, ii. 316
PLANETOIDS, ii. 299
PLANISPHERE, iii. 226, 342
　Dendera of, iii. 344, 367
PLANT (S) Alkaloids generated by, i. 305
　Animal becomes a, i. 167; iv. 287
　Animals, and, ii. 174; iii. 168
　Aphides or lice, iii. 142
　Apperception developed in, ii. 174
　Astral shadows of present, iii. 193
　Atoms composing, living, i. 305
　Beast, becomes a, i. 291; iii. 261
　Coloured juices of, ii. 304
　Creation of, i. 298
　Die, to live as a, seed must, ii. 178
　Forms of, iv. 193
　Gigantic, iv. 329
　Golden stem and azure blossom, of, iii. 422
　Greenland, iii. 24
　Hard, that softened, iii. 28; iv. 165
　Hermaphroditism of, iii. 179; iv. 229
　Human, quickeners of, iii. 111
　Immortality, of, iii. 102
　Jīvas of, iv. 162
　Lake villages, of, iv. 308
　Life, ii. 307
　Man a, iii. 192
　Medical use of, iii. 363

Migration of, iv. 295
Miocene, iv. 295
Monad's life, iii. 158
Moon's influence on, i. 232; iii. 113
Occult powers of, iii. 84
Old and new world, of, iv. 360
Physical embryo a, i. 235
Protoplasm animal and, iii. 159
Sacred aquatic, ii. 68
Sapta-Parna, iv. 145, 162
Senses of, ii. 331
Sensitive, ii. 174
Soma, iii. 383; iv. 67
Spark becomes a, i. 283
Sunlight, would perish in eternal, ii. 131
Three ages before Gods, came, iii. 63
Vital and intelligent force in, i. 332
PLASM, Immortal part of our bodies or, i. 270
　Spiritual and germinal, i. 265
PLASTIC, Form of the globe, i. 304; iii. 74
　Mediator, Buddhi the, i. 288
　Mediator, Manas or, i. 287
　Minds of first races, i. 313
　Modellers, iii. 158
　Svabhavat, essence, i. 130
PLASTIDS of Hæckel, iv. 233, 240
PLASTIDULAR souls, iv. 220-244
PLASTIDULE, Perigenesis of, iv. 241, 243
PLATEAUX of Central Asia, iii. 226; iv. 180, 313
PLANTINUM, Decomposition of, ii. 242
　Hydrogen gas and, ii 287
　Psychic natures in, ii. 332, 333
PLATO, Adept, an, i. 57
　Androgyne of, ii. 146
　Anima Mundi, i. 121
　Atlantis of, iii. 21, 149, 154, 266, 314, 323, 401, 403, 404, 406, 427; iv. 312, 334, 337, 359; v. 73
　Chaos soul of world of, ii. 58
　Christian dogmas reminiscences of, iii. 270
　Decussated circle of, iv. 160
　　,,　cross in space of, iv. 131
　　.,　man of, ii. 34
　Deductive, method of, iv. 144
　Deity of, iv. 124; v. 31, 382
　Divine idea of, ii. 81
　Dual soul of, v. 387
　Dynasties, on, divine, iii. 366
　East and, v. 36
　Ethics of, v. 145
　Four elements of, ii. 181, 182, 290
　Gnosticism of, v. 36
　God of, v. 363
　Greeks, on descent of, iv. 337
　Heraclides a pupil of, i. 176
　Highest God of, ii. 143, 144
　Highest principle of, ii. 185
　History of, v. 151
　Human soul, on, iii. 97
　Idea of evil of, iii. 371
　Infinite and finite of, ii. 144
　Initiate, an, i. 70, iii. 393; v. 29, 30, 254, 281, 304, 464, 524
　Island of, iii. 252, 351; iv. 263, 347
　Knowledge of, iv. 330
　Koros or Kurios, on, ii. 68

PLATO (*Contd.*)
  Kosmos, on formation of, ii. 62
  Light, on, ii. 304
  Logos as first cause of, i. 80, 262
  Māyās coeval with Atlantis of, iii. 47
  Method of, iii. 160; iv. 155
  Motto of, v. 87, 90
  Mysteries and, v. 30, 257, 266, 275, 279, 281, 304
  Origin of Man, on, v. 92
  Pantheons, on immortality of, iv. 333
  Pelasgians, on, iv. 343
  Persian tales, and, iii. 393
  Philosophy of, iii. 145; v. 28, 30, 36, 53, 68, 303
  Phoroneus, on, iv. 88
  Planets and, v. 318, 319
  Protagoras of, iii. 411
  Rectors of planets of, ii. 216
  Saïs, on words of priests of, iv. 312
  Second God of, v. 289
  Secrecy, and oath of, iv. 333
  Socrates and, v. 60, 308
  Solomon not mentioned by, v. 182
  Solon, respecting story of, iii. 268
  Soul of world, of, ii. 52
  Sun, on, v. 266, 277, 316
  Supreme good of, iv. 124
  Theology of, iv. 170
  Theos defined by, iv. 115
  Trinity and, v. 188
  Universal soul of, ii. 68
  Winged races of, iii. 66, 105, 266
PLATO PANODORUS, iii. 365
PLATONIC, Method, v. 387
  Teachings, ii. 343
  Theory, adaptation of, iv. 176
PLATONIST (S) Archetypal world of, i. 249
  Gospel of John written by a, v. 138
  Logos of, i. 170; iv. 114
PLATYRRHINE apes, iii. 178
PLATYRRHINI of Hæckel, iii. 198
PLEIAD, Disappearance of the seventh, iv. 121
PLEIADES, Alcyone in, ii. 225
  Atlantides and, iv. 337
  Central group, iv. 121
  Colure passed through, iii. 406
  Giants watched by, ii. 153
  Hyades, and. iv. 353
  Influences of, ii. 374
  Krittika or, iii. 433
  Making of, ii. 373
  Niobe daughter of one of, iv. 341
  Occult meaning of, iv. 190
  Rishis, wives of seven, iv. 119, 121
  Rising of, at beginning of Kali Yuga, ii. 388
  Symbols, and astronomical, iv. 190
PLEISTOCENE formations, iv. 256
PLENUM, Boundless space of divine, i. 204
  Connection of all matter in, ii. 341
  Container of all that is, i. 75
  Everywhere, ii. 218
  Gods and Genii within, ii. 292
  Matter, of, ii. 348
  Philosophies not insane enough to deny a, ii. 395

PLEROMA, i. 246
  Occultism of, v. 463
  Ogdoad of, ii. 167
  Paul and, v. 170
  Powers, of, v. 462
  Satan's lair, iv. 75-87
  States of, iii. 88
  Stellar Spirits of, v. 170
  Trunk of tree crossing planes of, ii. 123
  Universe of, iii. 38
  Valentinus of, v. 462
  Vehicle of light and, iv. 80
PLESIOSAURUS, iii. 210, 211, 260; iv. 247, 282
PLEXUSES, Seven nervous, iii. 101; v. 480, 483, 484, 556
PLINY, Ancient science and, iv. 257
  Argonauts, on, iii. 345
  Astrology and, v. 334
  Druids, on, iv. 325
  Egyptian year, on, iv. 192
  Giant, speaks of a, iii. 280
  Glacial sea, on a, iv. 346
  Northern seas, places Asteria in, iv. 342
  Persian Otizoe, on, iii. 346
  Polar night, on, iv. 342
  Rocking stones, on, iii. 342
  Sphericity of earth taught by, i. 176
PLIOCENE, Atlantis, portions of, iii. 394
  Chartres, sands near, iv. 321
  Giants, remains of, iv. 324
  Man, iii. 289; iv. 245, 260, 309, 315, 358
  Period, iii. 256, 314; iv. 246, 250, 257, 283, 308
PLONGEON, A. Le, quoted, i. 310; iii. 47
PLOTINUS, Ecstasy, on, v. 76
  Referred to, v. 33, 308, 451
  Thaumaturgist, a, v. 301
  Triple hypostasis on, v. 188
PLUTARCH, Annus Magnus spoken of by, iv. 354
  Antæus the giant, on, iii 280
  Cimmerians, on, iv. 342
  Egyptian year, on, iv 192
  Initiate, v. 254
  May, on month of, ii. 111
PLUTO, v. 153, 295
  Atlantic islands sacred to, iii. 407
  Eurydice carried off by, iv. 354
  Fire-flame of helm of, ii. 52
  God of earth, ii. 183
  Gold-abounding flood of, iii. 414
  Hades, or, iii. 361
  Month dedicated to, vi 116
  Spirits of the earth and, ii. 184
  Temples of, v. 295
PLUTO-AIDONEUS, the aerial Jove, ii. 184
PNEUMA, Anemos and, ii. 56
  Breath, voice, synthesis of senses, i. 159
  Collective Deity or, v. 309
  Father and mother of, iii. 121
  Holy Ghost and, v. 476
  Simon Magus and, v. 131
  Wind or, i. 273
PNEUMATICS, Occult and kabalistic, i. 288
POCOCKE, quoted, ii. 53
POEM of Initiation, Book of Job is, v. 290

POINT, Central, Atoms emanated from, ii. 360
    ,,   Circle with, i. 84; ii. 79, 144;
    ,,   iv. 123; v. 455
    ,,   Disk with, denotes dawn of dif-
    ,,   ferentiation, i. 69
    ,,   Hexagon with, v. 120-123
    ,,   Monad as, v. 188
    ,,   Navel means, v. 233
    ,,   No number to circle with,
    ,,   i. 154
    ,,   Parabrahman is, v. 233
    ,,   Triangle in, v. 455, 507
    ,,   Waters of infinite space,
    ,,   in, iv. 40
Compounds and their dissociation, ii. 308
Concealed and unknowable, ii. 171
Cycle, meridian, of, iii. 301
Eastern esotericism, a symbol in, ii. 33
Evolution, midway, of, iv. 305
Foundations of universe said to rest on an
    inter-etheric, ii. 280
Genesis of Gods and men from same, iii. 37
Indivisible, ii. 60, 70
Kosmos a single, ii. 58
Line generated from, i. 155
Logos or, ii. 339
Luminous, ii. 150
Mathematical, ii. 339, 353; v. 422
Metaphysical and physical, ii. 355
Milky way, unseen in, iii. 242
Mundane egg, in, i. 69, 127
Neutral, ii. 274
Pluche, La, on mathematical, ii. 338
Primordial, ii. 304; v. 191
Sephira and later Sephiroth, iii. 119
Triangle, in, ii. 144; v. 455
Universe evolving from a, ii. 95
Veil over circle and, ii. 341
Vernal equinoctial, iv. 354
Zero, ii. 274
Zodiac, sun at the first, ii. 386
POISON (S), Effects of various, v. 467
Medici and Borgia, of, v. 467
Nervous ether and, ii. 262
Occultists and, v. 467
Ptomaine alkaloid, i. 305
Visha or death, evil or, ii. 62
POITOU, Colossal stones of, iv. 321
POLAR, Antitheses, two, i. 228
Axes, iii. 429
Cells, iii. 125, 126
Centre, v. 202
Circles seven, i. 253
Continent, iii. 392
Day and night, iii. 293; iv. 342
Dragon, ii. 123; v. 202
Jupiter and Mercury, compression of, ii. 317
Lands, iv. 344
Lands, submersion of, iii. 359
Lands, three giants are three, iv. 345
Latona as, region, iv. 339
Lights, i. 254
Planets, diameters, iv. 113
Regions, iii. 293, 326; iv. 342
Satan represents, opposite, iii. 388
Seas, land beyond, iii. 24
Serpent, Eurydice bitten by, iv. 354

Sun, iii. 243
Sun revolving on, plane, iii. 242
POLARITY, is Evil, of matter and spirit, ii. 134
Latent and active, iv. 238
Like and unlike, i. 201
Physical, ii. 238
Spirit substance, of, iv. 96
POLARIZATION, Light, of, ii. 209
Sexual, ii. 122
POLE (S), Africa, southern, shall crush, iv. 326
Changes at, iii. 319, 332; iv. 345
Continent, north, first, iv. 353
Dragons and serpents, called, iii. 276
Dwarf races at, iii. 330
Earth and ecliptic, of, iv. 120
Earth has two fixed points in, ii. 329
Ecliptic, with plane of, iii. 356
Elevation of, iii. 400
Fourth movement of, iii. 349
Ganymedes or Aquarius raised above north,
    iv. 354
Generators, as, iii. 361
Golden egg, of, ii. 280
Great dragon or, iv. 354
Heavenly measure, iii. 362
Heavens, of, iii. 356
Immutable father or, iii. 354
Inversions of, iii. 352, 433; v. 346
Inverted, Kabirim and, iii. 359
Loss of sun at, iv. 338
Mahat, of, i. 268
Meru or, v. 347, 436
North, iv. 354; v. 436
Passage of, iii. 359
Personifications of, iii. 362
Pit is south, iv. 353, 354
Red dragon of, v. 202
Right angles, at, iii. 429
Southern, iii. 399; iv. 326
Sphere of, v 543
Star(s), Continent, has its watchful eye upon
    first, iii. 20
    ,,   Dhruva now Alpha, iv. 57, 183, 184
    ,,   Draco once, iii. 44
    ,,   Prajāpatis all connected with, iv. 338
    ,,   Pyramid builders and, ii. 153; iii. 430
    ,,   Svarloka between sun and, v. 541
    ,,   Two Dhruvatārā or, iii. 400
Storehouses, said to be, i. 253
Terrestrial and ecliptic, once coincided, iii. 294
Tropical, iv. 295
Ursa Minor's tail, of earth, iv. 338
POLLUX, Castor and, iii. 130, 131, 132, 362
POLYBIUS, referred to, v. 53
POLYGASTRIC infusoria, i. 230
POLYGENESIS, Modified, iii. 251
POLYGENETIC origin of man, iii. 176
POLYGENISM, iii. 176; iv. 182
POLYGENISTS and the Darwinian theory,
    iii. 176
POLYHISTOR, Alex., quoted, iii. 63, 65, 75
POLYMORPHIC pantheism, iv. 78
POLYNESIA, aborigines of, iii. 327
Continent of, iii. 227, 327
Lemuria and, iii. 226; iv. 356
Malacca and, iii. 226
POLYNESIANS, iii. 175, 331; iv. 92, 349

POLYPHEMUS, iv. 335, 338
POLYPS, Primordial epoch, at, iv. 281
Procreation of, iii. 184
POLYTHEISM, Belief in creators no, iv. 164
Hindu, v. 89
Monotheism and, v. 78, 351
Pantheism and, iii 115
Philosophical, ii. 299
POLYTHEISTS, Greek, ii . 187
Occultists are not, iii. 199
POMATOU or Poumoutou, iii. 227
POMPEII, iii. 239, 438; iv. 361
PONIARD, Yima's, iv. 181
PONTIFF-name, Lucifer a, iii. 45
PONTIFFS-PIROMIS of Egypt, iii. 368
POPE (S), Authority, as, iii. 317
Cardinal de Cusa and, v. 355
Gregory the great and the cross, iv. 158
Heliocentric system and, ii. 159; v. 71
Infallibility of, iii. 240; v. 155, 187
Initiates, some of early, were, ii. 23
Literature branded by, ii. 103
Lucifer one of, iii. 45
Masonry and, v. 112, 274
Peter and Jesus Christ personified by, iv. 34
Roman Pontiffs or, v. 147
POPLARS in ancient Greenland, iii. 24
POPULATION of earth, iv. 167
PORCH, Solomon's, iii. 236
PORES, Parents, men born from the, of their, iii. 78
Roma-Kūpas hair or skin, iii. 78, 189
Vīrabhadra created from, of skin, iii. 189
PORK, symbolizes Occult Knowledge, v. 105, 246
PORPHYRION, the scarlet Titan, iii. 382
PORPHYRY, Chaldean oracle and, v. 333
Christianity, renounced, v. 34
Demons of, v. 240
Ecstasy of, v. 76, 306
Mundane egg, on, ii. 75
Numerals on, v. 113
One principle, on, ii. 143
Pythagorean monad and duad, on, ii. 144, 343
Pythagorean numerals, and symbols, on, ii. 76; v. 113
Referred to, 73
Speech of Hermes, and, iv. 112
Theurgy and, v. 451
Tree of Planets of, v. 439
Was Malek the Jew, v. 298, 301
Writings destroyed, v. 307
PORPOISE, Shishumara or, Heavenly, iv. 119, 183
PORTAL(S) of Temples open to East, v. 217
Seventh, v. 543
PORTENTS, Akibeel taught meaning of, iii. 375
PORTUGAL, Trigonocephalus of, i. 305
POSEIDON, Amours of, iv. 344
Dragon, iii. 355
Fourth root-race symbolized by, iv. 335
Giants, personation of vices of, iv. 344
Homer, in, iii. 398
Ministers of, iv. 149
Neptune or, ii. 184; iv. 148, 334
Nereus and, iv. 335
POSEIDONIS, Atlantis or, iii. 314, 323, 406
Confusion between great continent and, iv. 337

Inhabitants of, iii. 407
Third step of Vishnu and, iv. 334
POSITIVE, Electricity, ii. 398
Ether, phenomenal, ii. 232
Matter, pole acts in world of, ii. 280
Negative, awakening, i. 332
Philosophy, i. 244
Polarity, iv. 238
Pole of creation, iii. 69
POSITIVE and NEGATIVE, Electricity, i. 201; ii. 275
Forces, i. 324; iii. 37
Mutually attracted, i. 292
Polar forces, iii. 93
Poles of dual matter, i. 301
Sexes, iii. 269
Svastika implies, iii. 42
Triple deity said to be, ii. 61
POSITIVISM, i. 76
POSITIVIST(S), Buddhists of old school called, i. 71
Materialistis and, ii. 345
Paul d'Assier a, iii. 156
School of Spencer is, iii. 164
Stellar systems, asked to explain, i. 204
POST-CHRISTIAN, Successors to the Mysteries, v. 298-308
POST-DILUVIAN, Age, iii. 355
Father of, humanity, iv. 180
Forefathers, iii. 428
Jews, language of, i. 276
Navigators, iii. 404
Neo-Aryans, iii. 355
POST-GLACIAL, Drift, iii. 81; iv. 256
Relics of Somme valley, iv. 308
POST-HUMAN, Mammalia are, iv. 254, 258
POST-MAHĀBHĀRATAN period, India of, i. 87
POST-MANVANTARIC Nirvāna, iv. 59
POST-MORTEM, Separation of animal and divine man, iv. 64
Zones of, ascent, ii. 127
POST-PLANETARY, Ethereal fluid of Leibnitz, ii. 351
POST-SECONDARY man, iv. 257
POST-TERTIARY period, the, iii. 67; iv. 280
POST-TYPES of Aditi and the spirit, iv. 25
POST-VAIDIC works, v. 344
POSTEL, Guillaume, iii. 270
POSTULANT, Sun at mysteries represented by, iv. 30
POT Amun, v. 302
POTASSIUM, ii. 274, 309
POTENCIES, Divine, v. 211
Motion and, v. 231
Planetary spaces, in, v. 431
POTENCY, Aristotle on, v. 445
Chaos, in, v. 192
Deity, of, v. 449
Dual, v. 189
Extraneous, v. 431
God within, of, v. 431
Gnostic, v. 74
Infinite, v. 445, 446, 447, 448
Seventh, v. 447
Sound is a, v. 431
Spiritual, v. 272

POTENCY (*Contd:*)
Third, v. 192
Thought and, v. 447
POTENTIALITIES, Concealed, v. 445
Infinite, v. 445
World Stuff, of, v. 424
POTHOS, the union of spirit and chaos, ii. 54
POTIPHAR (Petephre) priest of the Sun, v. 226
POTTER and the clay, iii. 292
POTTER, ED., referred to, iii. 417
POTTER'S wheel, Ammon making men on a, iii. 217, 293
Khnoom, fashioner of men on, ii. 82
POTTERY, Ancient art of, iv. 291
Fragments of, iv. 293
Neolithic, iv. 284
POUMOUTOU (POMATOU?), iii. 227
POUSSINÈRE, or PLEIADES, ii. 388
POWER(S), Adepts of, v. 354, 419
Air, of the, v. 432
Creative, i. 71, 127, 261; ii. 141, 143, 155, 170, 204, 215; iii. 52, 87, 135 188, 199, 249, 271, 385, 408, 409; iv. 107; v. 213, 460
Divine, v. 198, 270, 272, 309, 320, 459, 462
Evil, v. 124, 153
Gods or, v. 368
Highest of the, v. 211
Holy, v. 544
Jehovah, a female, v. 214
Magic, actual, v. 85
Man, of, v. 472
Manifested, v. 270
Occult, v. 61, 65, 240, 459
Pleroma, of, v. 462
Rays, seven primeval, or, v. 356
Sacerdotal, of Brāhmans, v. 394
Seven primordial, v. 199, 201
Space, of, v. 200
Wisdom and, begot heavenly hierarchy, v. 128
Wisdom, knowledge and, v. 449
Yoga, v. 270
PRABHAVĀPYAYA, the place of origination, i. 118; iii. 116
PRACHETĀS, the Sanskrit of Varuna, iv. 149
PRĀCHETASAS, Deep, come forth from, iv. 63
Devotions, absorbed in their, iv. 63
Nārāyana, worship, iv. 149
Personified soul or, iv. 64
PRACHETASES, Mārishā, and, iii. 183, 184
PRACHIDAS, buildings for offerings, v. 162
PRADHĀNA, Ālaya in one sense is, i. 121
Beginningless and endless cause, ii. 269
Brahmā, a cause superior to, i. 86
Chaos or, ii. 171
First product of, iii. 69
Matter, unmodified, ii. 164, 306
Māyā, called, i. 131
Mūlaprakriti, is, i. 300; v. 519
Prakriti, an aspect of, i. 121
Primeval matter or, i. 300
Primordial homogeneous matter or, i. 229
Primordial substance or, i. 326
Sānkhya teaching as to, i. 126
Substance undifferentiated or, i. 131, 263
PRĀDHĀNIKA Brahma spirit, One, i. 300; ii. 164
PRADYUMNA, Son of Krishna, v. 359

PRAHLĀDA, son of HIRANYAKASHIPU, ii. 138
PRAJANĀTHA yuga, v. 347
PRAJĀPATI, Ākāsha, derived from, iv. 139
Arjuna Mishra refers to, i. 158
Athivāhikas or, i. 190
Brahmā or, i. 146, 158; ii. 144; iv. 196; v. 233
Bhrigu one of, iii. 42, 45, 86
Creative forces, iv. 145
Creators or, iii. 88
Dhruva and, iv. 119
Elohim and, v. 210, 386
First, v. 233
God Ka is, v. 408
Hindus, of, v. 198, 210
Intelligences, as informing, iii. 46
Jehovah is, v. 214
Lord, ii. 295
Male, called first procreating, i. 155
Mindborn sons of, iii. 148
Osiris, chief, ii. 155
Purānas, and, v. 210
Rishis, ii. 160
Seed of life and, iii. 158
Seven i. 153; ii. 177; v. 198, 203, 356, 460
Universe, or, ii. 149
Vāch of Vedas, i. 194; ii. 146, 149; v. 189
PRAJĀPATIS, Brahmā, mind born sons of, iii. 183; iv. 196
Brahmādicas were, iii. 150
B'raisheeth, synthesized by, ii. 90
Chief and Lord, of, iii. 170
Half human, v. 213
Higher, ii. 176
Hindu, v. 386
Individualities of, i. 281
Jyotis, one of, iv. 335
Lords of being or, iii. 170
Manu produced the, iii. 309
Manu Svayambhuva synthesis of, iv. 274
Manus or, i. 293
Pitris, and, iii. 171
Pole star connected with, iv. 338
Progenitors and, iv. 182; v. 460
Rishis and, ii. 295
Sephiroth, are, ii. 70; iii. 137; v. 107
Seven and ten, iii. 255, 365
Seven builders or, ii. 154; v. 203
Ten semi-divine, ii. 64
PRAJAS or creatures, Lords, the, iii. 150
PRAJNĀ, Perception, or capacity of, iv. 168
Potentiality of, i. 195
Seven states of consciousness or, iii. 41; iv. 207, 212
PRAJNĀ PĀRAMITĀ, or "Knowledge across the River", v. 400
PRĀKRITA, Creations, ii. 145, 172, 174
Primary or, creation, ii. 172, 175
PRAKRITI, Ākāsha and, i. 300
Arani as, iv. 96
Atom and, v. 537
Brahma in its totality has aspect of, i. 84; ii 266
Buddhi spiritual modification of, ii. 294
Essence, or, iv. 96

INDEX

PRAKRITI (*Contd.*)
Ether and, ii. 232
First form of, ii. 306
Gæa, earth as, i. 76
Jīva in every particle of, i. 246
Light as, iv. 96
Lower, v. 418, 537
Male of, ii. 171
Malkuth or, v. 418
Material kosmos or, i. 299
Matter or, i. 131, 146, 148, 292; ii. 170; iv. 170; v. 469
Mineral kingdom and, i. 230
Mūlaprakriti and, i. 131; v. 423
Nature and, i. 76; ii. 269
Plane of, v. 524, 525, 527
Pradhāna is subtile, i. 121
Prism of, v. 207
Purusha and, i. 81, 122, 293, 326, 330; ii. 275; iii 53, 131
Septenary, v. 469
Seven forms of, v. 469
Spirit and, one Brahman, ii. 138
Time aspect of, i. 84
Womb, which bore Brahma in its, iv 96
PRAKRITIC or Terrestrial Plane and Sub-Planes, v. 524, 525, 526, 527, 528
PRĀKRITIKA, Brahmā, occurs at end of age of, ii. 86
Elemental dissolution or, ii. 88; iii 79, 310
PRAKRITIS, Seven, ii. 41, 49
PRALAYA Absolute, i. 77
Atoms during, ii. 349
Atyantika third, ii. 86
Beginning of, i. 331
Builders reconstruct kosmos after every, i. 165
Chain after, i. 234
Cosmic deluge or, iii. 79
Cosmic idealism ceases during, iv. 170
Darkness symbolical of universe during, i. 137
Day of judgment means minor, iv. 188
Deity latent in, ii 61
Dissolution or, ii. 84, 275
Divine Beings and, v. 493
Duration of, ii. 382
Eternal Absolute and, v. 425
Evolution after, iv. 73
Final, ii. 89; iv. 183
Geological race, iii. 403
Great, v. 267
Great age and, i. 291
Great and minor, i. 83, 220
Hour of, i. 299
Kinds of, many, i. 124
Kosmos will run down to appear after, i. 204
Latency in, v. 189
Logos in time of, ii. 146
Mahā, ii. 85, 86
Manvantara and, i. 78, 285
Meaning of, iii. 310
Minor, i. 77, 83, 220
Monad, in, ii. 293
Mother during, ii. 350
Motion finds intervals in, ii. 220
Night of Brahma or, i. 114; ii. 166
Noah's raven symbol of cosmic, ii. 161
ONE ALL during, i. 85

Passivity of being or, i. 323
Periodical, of globes, i. 248
Planetary dissolution or, i. 213, 225
Prākritika second, ii. 86
Primordial latent during, i. 152
Process or creation after, ii. 90
Purānic account of great, iv. 326; v. 267
Purusha and Prakriti one during, ii. 306
Races of, v. 336
Races, of, third, iii. 329
Reabsorption or, ii. 192
Reawakening of universe after, i. 86
Ring not passable till next, i. 190
Round, after seventh, iv. 136
Round preceded and followed by long, i. 215
Seventh period, after, ii. 91
Solar, i. 79, 124; ii. 255
Soul slumbers during, i. 69
Spiritual energy during, i. 188
Uniformity in, i. 309
Universal, ii. 41
Vāch disappears during, ii. 149
Worlds after manifestation going into, i. 200
Yudhister and, v. 345
Zodiac foretold, ii. 375
PRALAYAS, Allegory of two, iv. 340
Cosmic and solar, i. 83
Interval between minor, iii. 308
Obscurations, or, iv. 230
Poles, at, iii. 324
Round, during this, iii. 329
Seven sabbaths are, iv. 317
Times of, iv. 338
Universal unity during, ii. 338
PRALAYIC, Darkness of chaos and non-being, ii. 382
Eternities, i. 125
Inactivity, iii. 107
Non-existence of cosmic ideation during, periods, ii. 42
Sleep, i. 291
PRALINA, or withdrawn, i. 88
PRAMANTHA, God armed with, iv. 95
Prometheus and, iv. 90
Sanskrit word, ii. 411
Stick, or, iv. 94
PRAMATHA signifies theft, iii 411
PRAMATIH, son of Fohat, iii. 412
PRAMLOCHA, Kāma sent, iii. 183
Kandu and, iii. 182
Nymph, iii. 178
Pious, ii. 410
PRAM'ZIMAS, the master of all, iii. 272
PRĀNA, v. 511, 514, 566
Apāna and, i. 158; iv. 139
Astral Plane, not on, v. 518
Ātmā and, i. 273
Auric Egg and, v. 508
  ,, Envelope and, v. 528
Breath of life or, iv. 203
Heart and, v. 521
Human principle, second, i. 288; iv. 165
Jīva and, ii. 249; v. 424, 440, 471, 479, 511, 518, 523
Kāma and, v. 551
Life or, i. 212, 271, 287; ii. 250; iv. 168, 241; v. 191, 523, 563

PRĀNA (*Contd.*)
  Linga Sharīra and, v. 566
  Material, or life, i. 306
  Offering, portion of the, iv. 137
  Pentagram contained, in, v. 487
  Principle, fifth or third, i. 208, 209
  Universal Life Principle, v. 423, 454, 457
  Vitality, v. 485
PRĀNAMAYAKOSHA, Astral body and Prāna,
  or, i. 212
PRANAVA, Most sacred term is, ii. 150; v. 479
  Vāch, called, i. 195; ii 150
PRĀNĀYĀMA, Vital winds or breath, i. 158
  Yoga practices, in, i. 158; iv. 139; v. 479,
  486
PRANIDHĀNA of the Yogis, iii. 97
PRASANGA Madhyamika teaching, i. 116
  School, v. 402, 403
PRASENAJIT, king, v. 39
PRASEODYMIUM mentioned by Crookes,
  i. 197
PRASHRAYA explained by vinaya, iv. 97
PRATISANCHARA, the incidental dissolution,
  ii. 87
PRATISARGA, or secondary creation, iii. 115
PRATT, Henry, M. D., quoted, i. 76, 272; ii. 56,
  340; iii. 248
PRATYAGĀTMĀ, Jīvatmā or, iii. 46
PRATYĀHĀRA, Dissolution or, i. 158, 301
PRATYAYASARGA, or intellectual creation,
  ii. 175
PRATYEKA, Buddhas, v. 390, 399
PRAYĀGA or Allahabād, ii. 108
PRAYER, Action should go with, v. 431
  Mantra-chanting not a, v. 394
  Right, v. 70, 71
  Selfish and Unselfish, v. 70
  Unconscious Magic, v. 132
PRE-Adamic First root-race, ii. 91
  Men, iii. 311
PRE-Adamite, Deluge, iii. 396
  Kings, iii. 93
  Man, ii. 37
  Nations, iii. 393; iv. 20
  Period, iii. 285
  Races, ii. 37; iii. 179, 254, 291; iv. 274
  Races, Atlantean not Satanic, were, ii. 37
PRE-animal human races, iv. 220
PRE-archaic periods, mysteries of, i. 61
PRE-astronomical cosmic flood, iii. 352
PRE-atlantean Titans, iii. 389
PRE-Brahmanical Asuras, etc., iii. 171
PRE-Christian, Cross is, iv. 158
  Europe, v. 75
  Gnostic gems are, iv. 135
  Kabalist, ii. 111
  Scandinavia, iv. 127
PRE-cosmic, Darkness, ii. 169
  Deluge, iii. 153
  Ideation, i. 80
  Latency of primordial matter, i. 128
  Periods, iii. 254
  Root substance, i. 81
PRE-diluvian, Ages, iv. 168
  Patriarchs, iii. 137
PRE-existence, Consciousness, of a universal,
  iv. 59

Creature, of each renewed, iv. 189
Universe, of, i. 320
PRE-genetic, Ages, ii. 351; iii. 254
  Appearance of manifested point, ii. 338
  Battles, i. 163
  Day, ii. 113
  Glory of unit, ii. 343
  Kosmos, i. 84; ii. 342
  Matter electrified into life, i. 142
  Primordial atom, i. 204
  Primordial matter, ii. 314
  Pūrvaja, or, iii. 116
PRE-geological ages, ii. 351
PRE-glacial man, iii. 81; iv. 284
PRE-Homeric Greeks, iii. 24
PRE-human, Ethereal race, iii. 172
  Evolution of, water-men, iv. 206
  Fauna and flora, iv. 303
  Monsters, iii. 124
  Period, iii. 285, 321
  Type, iv. 248
PRE-Lemurian continent, iv. 344
PRE-matter or protyle of Crookes, iii. 42
PRE-natal, Man, iv. 37
  Shells of third race, iii. 203
  Sphere of embryo, iii. 195
PRE-physical, Races, iv. 287
PRE-planetary forms of Saturn, ii. 125
PRE-protyle, World stuff and, ii. 322
PRE-septenary manvantara, our round in a,
  iii. 309
PRE-tertiary man, originally a colossal giant,
  iii. 22
  Science and, iv. 257
PRECEPTOR of the Daityas, iii. 44
PRECEPTORS of mankind, first, iii. 357
PRECESSION, Cycles of, ii. 153, 376
  Cyclic, of all the lives, iii. 265
  Equinoxes, of, ii. 388; iii. 315; iv. 120, 263;
  v. 344, 346
PRECINCT of Minerva, sacred, iii. 394
PRECIOUS Gifts, seven, v. 373
  Stones, ii. 375; iii. 395, 424; v. 240, 536
  Sun, Moon and, v. 536
PREDESTINARIAN, iii. 305
PREDESTINATION, Dogma of, v. 64
  Geological life of our globe in, ii. 366
PREDETERMINATION of events, ii. 370
PREHISTORIC Ages, Atlanteans and, iii. 275
  Atlantis, events, of, iii. 392
  „ Figure of Satan in, ii. 130
  „ Lyell on, iv. 294
  „ Mystery language of, ii. 21
  „ Negro type in Europe in, iv. 313
  Brussels, Congress at, iv. 321
  Cities, iv. 292
  Civilization in Central Asia, i. 54
  Civilization in, times, iii. 429
  Continents, iii. 15, 307
  Giants, iii. 279
  Hierophants, ii. 78
  India, iii. 326
  Knowledge, v. 89
  Lemuria, existence of, iii. 20
  Man, antiquity of, iv. 289
  „ Continents, in submerged, iv. 294
  „ Lubbock's, iv. 291

PREHISTORIC (*Contd.*)
Man, Mementoes of, iii. 427
,, Remains of, iii. 223
Nations, iii. 398; iv. 311
Races, Anthropogenesis of, iii. 91
,, Heroes of, iii. 287
,, , Mystery language of, iv. 145
,, Philosophy of, iv. 362
,, Symbolism of, ii. 74
Ranges of mountains, iv. 54
Science, iv. 289
Truths, landmarks of, iv. 346
World, Secret Doctrine religion of, i. 56
PRESENCE, Abstract ever-incognizable, i. 69
All, iv. 160
Angels of, v. 386
Deity an unseen, witnessed to by, light, i. 70
Ever-invisible, i. 284
Invisible, ii. 354; v. 431
Planetary powers may become a, ii. 357
Sacrificial victims to, i. 323
Shekinah an absolute, ii. 344
Spirits of, ii. 156; v. 309, 320
Universal, i. 330; iv. 126
Unknown, v. 282
PRESENT, Past, Future, and Eternity, v. 301, 482, 499
PRESERVER (S), Fire the, i. 147; iii. 122
Noah, of animal life, iv. 169
Rakshasas called, iii. 172
Vishnu the, i. 328; ii. 178, 250
World, of this, iv. 83
PRETAS, devouring demons, v. 559
PRETEXTATUS, quoted, v. 266
PREVISION, Astrology not, ii. 371
Holy ones, of, iii. 349
PRIAPUS, Celestial, iv. 25
Euhemerized, iv. 113
PRIDE, Demon of, iii. 276
First physical men, of, iii. 273
Flying dragon, of, iv. 54
Third and fourth became tall with, iii. 273
PRIDEAUX, quoted, v. 195
PRIEST(S), Ahura Mazda, of, iv. 180
Aleim a college of, iii. 207
Angirasas said to be, iv. 177
Apollo, of, iii. 20
Architects, initiated, i. 257
Argha of high, iv. 29
Armenian, iv. 127
Assyrian, iii. 379
Babylonian, v. 264
Bath Kol and Jewish, iii. 115
Chaldean, v. 27
Chronology of, iv. 191
Colleges, iii. 216
Daitya Guru a, instructor, iii. 42
Egypt, of, v. 262, 264
,, Alexandria, before, v. 297
,, Astronomy, and, iii. 429; iv. 104
,, Atlantis and, iii. 403
,, Breast plate of, v. 240
,, Cosmogony and, iv. 353
,, Eggs not eaten by, ii. 81
,, Egyptian dynasties and, i. 310
,, Great nation mentioned by, iv. 319
,, History of, iii. 334

Egypt, Initiated, v. 296
,, Knowledge of, ii. 24; iv. 333; v. 264
,, Occult Science and, v. 41
,, Ragon on, v. 262, 264
,, Resources, of, iv. 356
,, Rulership of, v. 262, 263, 296
,, Sacred Books and, v. 58
,, Sages were, v. 263
,, Septenary and, ii. 125
,, Solon and, iii. 268, 394; v. 264
,, Universal language known by, v. 178
,, Wheat sacred to, iii. 372
,, Wisdom of, iii. 43
,, Zodiacs of, iii. 434
Every man a, to himself, ii. 55
Good actions only, i. 323
Hercules, of, iii. 207
Hierophants, iii. 366; iv. 122; v. 244
High, personified God, iv. 34
Hilkiah the high, ii. 374
Hortis or, i. 151
Hyperboreans, of sun, iv. 339
Initiated, iv. 102; v. 238, 296
Initiates, iv. 86
Jethro, of Midian, iv. 111
Jewish, iv. 40; v. 240
Kabiri, of, iii. 360
King-Initiates and, iv. 113
Libraries under care of, iv. 98
Magas as, iii. 322
Marriage rite, at the, ii. 340
Meaning of word, v. 263
Mexican, iii. 189
Midian, initiator, iv. 33
Moses a, iv. 23; v. 91, 272
Most High God, of, iv. 35
Odin, Scandinavian, v. 42
Ophite religion, of, iii. 378
Paternoster and, iv. 132
Philosophers, v. 265
Phrygia and Asia Minor, of, iii. 370
Roman Catholic, v. 98
Saïs, of, iii. 370
Sanctum Sanctorum and, ii. 182
Seven, i. 159; iv. 138, 139, 201
Solar, Julian last of, v. 218
Sun, of, iii. 322; iv. 339
Termini of Hermes-Mercury anointed by, iv. 112
Troy, iv. 158
Ugrasena, of, iii. 323
Vibratory motion of astral light known to ancient, ii. 62
Zunis, of, iv. 200
PRIESTESS-mother of the Zuni Indians, iv. 200
Aztec, v. 43
PRIESTHOOD, Babylonian, iv. 261
Materialism, responsible for, ii. 302
Orphic, iv. 325
Phraseology of ancient, iii. 139
Tenets disfigured by, iii. 103
Thrace, of, iv. 325
PRIESTLY caste of the Levites, iii. 139
PRIESTLEY, referred to, ii. 348
PRIMA Materia, Cosmic matter, ii. 54
Kant, of, ii. 322
Mother or, i. 332

PRIMA Materia (*Contd.*)
  Protyle and, ii. 350
  Solar system, of our, ii. 264
  Universal mind, emanation of, ii. 326
  Water and earth as, v. 234
  Water as, ii. 59
PRIMAL, Pair, v. 200
  Principles, v. 55
  Thought, v. 211
PRIMARIES Cosmical elements, of, ii. 61
  Matter, of, iv. 164
  Reflections of their, i. 331
PRIMARY CREATION, iv. 56; v. 210
  Brahmā and, iii. 64
  Elemental kingdoms and, iii. 312
  Elements of, i. 265
  Eternal light of, iii. 70
  Law of, iv. 300
  Light, ii. 169
  Mahat in, i. 142
  Meaning of animals in, ii. 174
  Prākrita or, ii. 175
  Secondary and, iii. 64, 116
PRIMATE, Man in the uterus becomes a, iii. 193; iv. 236
PRIMATES, Fossil, iv. 246
PRIME cause, Root-Manu the, i. 281
PRIMEVAL chaos, Deluge and, iii. 63
  Evolution of life from, i. 164
  Female space or, iii. 94
  Gods, v. 356
  Light, v. 74, 229
  Man, Astral, iv. 258
  ,, Ethereal, iii. 156
  ,, External form of, iii. 195
  ,, Mindless, iii. 89
  ,, Ophite Adamas, iv. 25
  ,, Pitris and, iii. 97
  ,, Progenitors, iii. 139
  ,, Pygmalions of, iii. 111
  ,, Scientific research as to, iv. 245
  Matter, i. 300; ii. 303, 313, 314, 325, 326, 333
  Races, iv. 226
  ,, Culmination of four, iii. 185
  ,, Divine, iii. 164
  ,, Double-sexed, iii. 141
  ,, Esoteric classification of, iii. 251
  ,, Hæckel and, iv. 226
  ,, Mindless, iv. 259
  ,, Rebirths, iv. 203
  ,, Records, v. 89
  ,, Sacrifice, v. 370
  ,, Sages, v. 42
  ,, Seven, i. 293; iv. 177
  ,, Soul, v. 391
  Waters or, ii. 52
  Wisdom, Adi Buddha, i. 124
  ,, Fountain of, i. 256
  ,, Proof of existence of, i. 65
PRIMITVE Astrology, v. 332
  Forces, v. 299
  Gods, v. 333
  Man (men), Apes and, iv. 246
  ,, Bhūta, a senseless, iii. 110
  ,, Consciousness in, i. 258
  ,, First or, i. 308
  ,, Instructors of, iii. 349

Man, Lower, iii. 191
  ,, Physical, iii. 113
  ,, Seven, iii. 17, 105
  ,, Shape of future, iii. 194
  ,, Streams of, iv. 309
PRIMOGENEITY of the primordial atom, i. 204
PRIMOGENITAL forms of cereals, iii. 372
PRIMORDIAL, Circle, v. 207
  Germ (s), v. 230, 233
  Light, Angels of, iii. 241
  ,, Breath, from, v. 229
  ,, Divine, iii. 180
  ,, Personified, ii. 54; iii. 139
  ,, Ray of, i. 277
  ,, Reawakening germs, v. 233
  ,, Shekinah or, iii. 115
  ,, Source unknown of, i. 113
  ,, Unity of, i. 263
  ,, Word or Logos is, v. 229
  Matter, Atoms, or, i. 150; ii. 42
  ,, Chaos and, v. 227
  ,, Coexistent with space, i. 125
  ,, Cosmic, i. 176
  ,, Evolutionary impulse to, iii. 245
  ,, First form of, i. 135
  ,, Flame descends into, i. 160
  ,, Homogeneous, i. 229
  ,, Inherent law in, i. 159
  ,, Latent spirit in, i. 132
  ,, Life infused into, i. 143
  ,, Limbus major, i. 325
  ,, Mūlaprakriti or, v. 227
  ,, Physical, ii. 319
  ,, Pradhāna or, i. 300; iii. 69
  ,, Pregenetic, iii. 314
  ,, Protyle and, ii. 322
  ,, Shadow and, i. 250
  ,, Space, and, i. 147
  ,, Tethys is, iii. 76
  ,, Unmanifested or, i. 76
  ,, Vortical movement in, i. 176
  Occultism, v. 447
  Plane, v. 455, 539
  Point, Active power called, ii. 69
  ,, Light, of, ii. 309
  ,, Sephira and, ii. 51
  ,, Powers, v. 199, 201
  Principle, v. 446
  Seven, i. 152, 166, 168; v. 191, 448
  Substance, Ākāsha or, ii. 39
  ,, Alchemy and, ii. 43
  ,, All of manifested nature and, ii. 43
  ,, Arani and, iv. 96
  ,, Astral light or, i. 303
  ,, Chaos and, iv. 96
  ,, Cosmic, iii. 37
  ,, Divine thought and, ii. 39; v. 145
  ,, Dream, regarded as a, i. 202
  ,, Kant on, ii. 326
  ,, Nucleus of, i. 251
  ,, Occultists and, ii. 39
  ,, Phenomena and, ii. 43
  ,, Plane of, v. 455
  ,, Pradhāna or, i. 326
  ,, Pre-cosmic latency of, i. 128
  ,, Real, ii. 325
  ,, Separation of, i. 298

PRIMORDIAL (*Contd.*)
  Substance, Space, and boundless, ii. 318
    ,,   Triangle, v. 507
    ,,   Unity as, iii. 37
  Water(s), Abyss of, iv. 151
    ,,   Cosmic matter, i. 141
    ,,   Deep, of, i. 146
    ,,   Great green or, ii. 24
    ,,   Goddess Noo, ii. 155
    ,,   Ra-shoo or, ii. 24
    ,,   Space, of, ii. 179
    ,,   Vahana of Vishnu on, i. 140
  World stuff, v. 424
PRINCIPALITIES, Christian dogma, of, i. 155
  St. Paul, of, ii. 64, 357
  Venus ruled by, ii. 153
PRINCIPLES or genii, i. 246
PRINCIPIUM, Parable in work in, iv. 72
  Viarum Domini Behemoth, iv. 54
PRINCIPLE Astral is second, v. 522
  Creative, v. 43, 69, 145, 234, 272
  Evil, v. 116, 129
  Feminine, v. 234
  Fifth, Ākāsha or, i. 78
    ,,   Human soul or lower, i. 84
    ,,   Individuality and, iii. 131
    ,,   Kosmos of, v. 233
    ,,   Latent, i. 258
    ,,   Manas, i. 266; iii. 97
  Fohat, i. 171; v. 553
  Fourth, v. 487
    ,,   Helen personified, iv. 364
    ,,   Mind has affinity with, i. 212
    ,,   Nephesh, i. 288
    ,,   Vehicle for fifth, iii. 169
  Great or Mahat, v. 471
  Intellectual, v. 78
  Life, Auric fluid and, v. 532
    ,,   Blood as, v. 565
    ,,   Nature, in, v. 456
    ,,   Prāna or, v. 457
  Mānasic, v. 511
  Middle, i. 304; iii. 88, 244
  One and unconditioned, v. 214
  Parātma, not a, v. 487
  Paternal and meaning Patriarch, v. 213
  Physical body, not a, v. 521
  Prana is Life-, v. 423, 454, 457
  Seven degrees of every, v. 512, 517
  Seventh overshadowing, v. 83
    ,,   Daimon is, v. 133
  Spiritual, v. 78, 94
  Universal, v. 445
  Wisdom, v. 364
PRINCIPLES, Active and passive, iv. 97
  Ākāsha's lower, iv. 186
  Allegory of Orpheus and, v. 154
  Animal kingdom, of, i. 310
  Animals, latent in, iii. 269
  Apotelesmetic, v. 330
  Aspects and, v. 471
  Astrology of, v. 325
  Atom of, v. 537
  Barhishad on a level with lower, iii. 88
  Brahmā unites in himself male and female, ii. 49
  Chaos, in, iii. 384

Chitkalā furnished man with his fourth and fifth, i. 329
Conquest of lower, iii. 274
Correspondences of, v. 433, 440, 454, 455, 456, 457, 470, 478, 521, 542
Cosmic and human, i. 180, 195, 260; iv. 168, 211
Cosmic great body, of, ii. 351
Cosmic space, of, iv. 183
Creation by spirit mixing with, ii. 170
Dhyān Chohans, of, i. 318
Divine essences, of, ii. 349
Earth, of, iv. 213
Eastern initiates, of, i. 246
Esoteric division of man's, iii. 373
Ether one of, of Ākāsha, i. 336
Faculties and senses, of, iv. 138
Five inner, i. 274
Fohatic, v. 581
Four, v. 477
God, of unknown, ii. 393
Gods as first, v. 78
Heavenly man, of, iv. 167
Higher, of man, i. 226
Human, i. 208, 224, 273; iv. 165; v. 208, 426, 455, 529, 533, 534
Inner and lower, of third race men, iii. 130
Latent in man, iii. 175
Lower, of man, i. 226, 282; iii. 88; v. 512
Male and female, lower aspect of one principle, i. 83; iii. 94
Man, of, i. 272; ii. 90; v. 435
Matter, enclosed, in, iii. 286
Metaphysics, in Egyptian, iv. 203
Middle two, i. 292
Middle, three, i. 272
Monad a combination of last two, in man, i. 230
Moon of, and earth, v. 535, 536
Mūlaprakriti, of, ii. 346
Mystic, in nature, ii. 374
Nature, in, i. 83
Number of, six not seven, iv. 187
Objective, i. 128
Occult, division of, v. 470
Occultism, of, iv. 205
Passive, v. 386
Philosophical order of our, ii. 47
Physical body Upādhi of all, i. 208
Planets transfer their, i. 202, 225
Primal, of Chaldeans, v. 55
Primordial, i. 133; v. 446
Rishis stand for seven, iii. 147
Root, three, v. 208
Rudimental, or Tanmātras, ii. 171
Science cannot discover six higher, in man, i. 191
Septenary, i. 181; ii. 57; iv. 187, 198; v. 203 357, 522
Seven, Adept cannot separate, i. 213
  ,,   Antiquity of belief in, iv. 201
  ,,   Aryan scriptures and, iv. 184
  ,,   Classification of, v. 361
  ,,   Cosmical and human, i. 83
  ,,   Hierarchies and our, v. 453
  ,,   Human, i. 180, 208; iv. 60, 175, 283; v. 361, 425, 428, 435, 454, 471, 533, 534
  ,,   Kosmos, of, v. 208
  ,,   Letters represent, iii. 67

PRINCIPLES (*Contd.*)
  Seven, Macrocosmos of, v. 208
    ,,   Man's, in *Isis*, i. 278
    ,,   Matter or, seven forms of, ii. 166
    ,,   Metaphysical sense, in, iii. 197
    ,,   Mystery of Buddha and, v. 361, 362
    ,,   Planes of, i. 284
    ,,   Saptaparna refers to, i. 282
    ,,   Sevenfold occult forces and, i. 57
    ,,   Shankarāchārya and, v. 367
    ,,   Solar system, i. 170
    ,,   States of matter and, iv. 207
    ,,   Vehicles and, v. 208
  Seventh, v. 77, 154, 290, 365, 375
  Six, ii. 48
  Sixth and Seventh, v. 208, 474
  Souls or, iv. 139
  Spiritual, i. 190; v. 427
  Spiritualism and higher, i. 279
  Sthūla sharīra grossest of our, i. 304
  Subtle bodies or, ii. 335
  Tanmātras or rudimental, ii. 171
  Tattvas, and, v. 470, 476
  Two eternal, v. 129
  Unconscious, v. 386
  Uncreated lights within man's, iii. 293
  Union of three, depends upon a fourth, i. 129
  Universal, v. 445, 487
  Upper triad, of, iii. 220
  Vāch, and four forms of, i. 195
  Vehicles, and, v. 208
PRISM, Divine, v. 438
  Seven colours of, v. 420, 442
PRISMATIC aspects of colour, Seven, iv. 60;
  v. 555
  Colours called Father of sound, v. 442
  Spectrum, v. 442
PRITHIVĪ, Earth or, i. 83, 282; iii. 383
  Rajamsi above, iv. 179
  Solar system or, iv. 187
  Tattva, v. 476, 477, 479
  World, iv. 188
PRITHU, Earth, father of, iii. 262
  Earth fleeing before, ii. 113
  Noah, said to be, ii. 380
PRIVATION, Anima mundi lowest plane of,
  i. 129
  Form and matter, i. 128
PRIYAVRATA, Division made by, iii. 405
  Heirloom left by, ii. 326
  King, iii. 369
  Seven sons of, iii. 320
PRJEVALSKY, the Russian traveller, i. 56
PROCLUS, Doctrine of Hermes and, v. 321
  Doctrines of Orpheus and, v. 304
  Ecstasies of, v. 76
  Goddess Rhea, on the, ii. 164
  Mysteries and, v. 280, 281
  Second death and, v. 360
  Thaumaturgist, v. 301
  Referred to, ii. 144, 376; iv. 122, 170, 175
PROCREATION, Act of, iv. 115
  Adam Kadmon and organs of, iv. 34
  Adam of dust and, iv. 25
  Allegory of, by Brahma, ii. 149
  Animals, of, iii. 264
  Cross a symbol of human, iv. 116

  Elements, of, iv. 163
  First race, of, iii. 181
  Forms, of, iii. 290
  Generative powers for human, iii. 55
  Man and species, of, iv. 159
  Modes, of, iii. 95, 125, 176, 179, 189
  Mystery of, iii. 409
  Nārada enemy of physical, iii. 59
  Planes, on earthly, iii. 284
  Powers of, iv. 67
  Primitive stages of, iv. 230
  Reproduction and, iv. 164
  Seasons of, iii. 411
  Semites and, of species, iv. 113
  Sexual intercourse and, iii. 189
  Sin, called, iv. 83
  Sons of Brahmā and human, iii. 91
  Species, of, iv. 227
  Spiritual to physiological, iii. 413
  Superhuman and human, iii. 284
  Sweat-born, of, iii. 183
  Water female element of, ii. 69
  Will, sight, touch and Yoga, of men by, iii. 183
  Yodh, organ of, v. 206
PROCTOR, quoted, ii. 26; iii. 351, 430
PRODUCTRIX and Tetraktys, iv. 172
PROGENITORS, iv. 182; v. 263, 443, 460
PROMETHEANS or spiritual men, iii. 419
PROMETHEIA, Meaning of, iii. 411
PROMETHEUS, v. 92, 105
  Allegory of, iii. 112, 240, 246
  Altruism of, iii. 420
  Asia, son of, iv. 338
  Baptism of Fire, of, v. 323
  Chorus to, ii. 367
  Chrestos or, iii. 418
  Consolation of, iii. 420
  Deucalion son of, iv. 338
  Devas symbolized by, iii. 103
  Divine soul, was, iii. 417
  Fable of, v. 92
  Fetahil is, i. 245
  Fire and light-giver, a, iii. 413
  Fire brought by, iii. 410, 411; v. 203
  Gift of, iii. 419
  Greeks, in, iii. 410; iv. 94
  Heavenly host, iii. 419
  Hebrew, iii. 375
  Hindu views of, iv. 94
  Human body, modelling a, iv. 88
  Humanity, as suffering, iii. 412
  Ideas of, iv. 94
  Indian origin of, iv. 93
  Jupiter is, iii. 272
  Kabiric deity, a, iii. 362
  Logos, symbol of collective, iii. 411
  Loki and, iii. 285
  Meanings of name, iv. 90
  Moses understood, v. 92
  Mystery of, v. 323
  Myth of, iv. 92
  Orientalists on, iv. 90
  Pausanias on, iii. 362
  Pramantha and, iv. 90
  Race of men called forth by Athena and, iv .88
  Separation of Sexes and, v. 203
  Soul spark from, iv. 88

PROMETHEUS (*Contd.*)
Spiritual creators, stands for, iii. 419
Symbolism of, iii. 103, 420; v. 323
Titan, the, iii. 420; iv. 88
Type, an earthly, iii. 55
Zeus and, iii. 282, 413, 417
PROPATOR, Gnostics, of, i. 262
Only begotten son, only known to, ii. 64
PROPHECIES, Ancestors, of, iii. 109
Ancient and modern, ii. 370
Natural, ii. 380
Prometheus fixed modes of, iii. 412
Shankarāchārya, i. 65
Sidereal, ii. 379
Tibet in, v. 396
PROPHECY, Astrology not, ii. 371
Christ, of, iii. 413
Earthquakes, of, ii. 371
Gift of, iii. 366
Gravitation about, ii. 219
Hindu figures and Christian, ii. 381
Joseph's dream called a, of Christ, ii. 375
Kali Yuga, concerning end of first period of, i. 65
Kepler and a, of Saviour, ii. 379
Mysteries of, iii. 407
Promethean myth is a, iii. 413, 415, 417
Roman Catholic, iii. 412
Secret books, of, iii. 442
Seventh race, about, iii. 109
Sibylline, v. 338
Stones, by, iii. 345, 346
PROPHET(S), Abominations of, iii. 216
Adam as, of moon, iv. 34, 35
Ancient World of, v. 43
Baal, of, iv. 28
Balaam, iii. 407
Breath, and mystery of, i. 176
Chosen people, of, iv. 37
Cross and, iv. 130
Dag-on, ii. 380
Enoichion, can be called, v. 102
Ezekiel, iv. 123
Generations of, i. 316
Hebrew, ii. 111
Holy, ii. 375
Initiate attacked by a, iv. 70
Initiates or, iv. 60
Inspiration of, iv. 202
Israel, of, iii. 115
Jealous God of Hebrew, ii. 111
Jewish phallic worship and, iv. 160
Jewish realism and, iv. 27
Mahomet, iv. 31
Martyrdom, v. 282
Moses, iv. 130
Nabin, iv. 23
Nazarene, iv. 189
Nebo, God of wisdom, iv. 23
Right path, of, iii. 215; iv. 71
Samaritans do not recognize, Books of, v. 181
School of, v. 118
Secret colleges of, iv. 102
Seers, and, i. 276
Spiritual eye of, iii. 77
True and false, v. 300
Word, supreme reason of, or, i. 135
PROPHETESS, Scandinavian song of, ii. 83

Sibylline, v. 338
PROPOSITION, forty-seventh of Euclid, v. 113
PROSERPINE, ii. 111; iii. 407
Temples of, v. 295
PROSIMIÆ, Haeckel's, iv. 237, 249
Loris allied to, iv. 237
Mammals, or indeciduate, iv. 220, 238
PROSPERITY, Goddess of, iii. 86
PROTAMŒBA, one of the Monera, iii. 172
PROTEAN, Evolution, ii. 365
Light, ii. 303
Mother, i. 199
Substance, ii. 394
Toom, God, ii. 398
Unknowable, differentiation of, iv. 297
PROTECTOR(S), Asia, of, iii. 185
Atman, the Lord and, v. 75
Chosen peoples of Israel, iv. 111
Excellent land, of, iii. 423
Gods the, iii. 357
Law of Buddha, of, iii. 39
Tibet, of, iii. 186
PROTEIN the base of protoplasm, ii. 362
PROTESTANT(S), Angels and, v. 318
Bible, v. 313
Biblical society, iv. 108
Catholics, and, ii. 222; iv. 317; v. 315
Church, iii. 376; iv. 108; v. 313
Deity and, v. 117
England, ii. 189
Garden of Eden, and, ii. 337
Providence of Christians, ii. 359
Spirits and, v. 315
Theologians, i. 272; iii. 374; v. 312
PROTEUS, hypothetical, ii. 39
India, Logos a, in, ii. 64
Ocean, Atlas and, and depths of, iv. 331
Primordial substance or, ii. 43
Venus, wife of, v. 310
PROTISTA, Animals not, iv. 166
Molecular souls of, iv. 220
Molecules of lively, iv. 220
PROTISTIC Monera, ii. 174; iii. 161
PROTO-Chaldeans or Akkadians, iii. 208
PROTO-organisms, Creation from, iii. 129
Ethereal, iii. 190
PROTOGENES, one of the Monera, iii. 172
PROTOGONOI, the first-born, iii. 55
PROTOGONOS, First-born, iv. 58, 273
Heavenly man, iii. 38
Light, or first-born, i. 137; ii. 57
Manifested Logos or, iv. 164
PROTOLOGOI, all the creative, Brahma, ii. 49
PROTOLOGOS, Archetypal man or, ii. 70
Pūrvaja or, iii. 117
Vishnu Orphic, iii. 116
PROTOMATERIA, Primordial, i. 325
PROTOMYXA, one of the Monera, iii. 172
PROTOPLASMIC, Body and cell soul, iv. 243
Egos, i. 325
Molecules of Protista, iv. 220
Moneron, speck called, iii. 195
Phantom of earth, i. 242
Plastidules or, molecules, iv. 241
Primordial, form of man, iii. 82, 196
PROTOPLASTIC, Androgyne Adam, iv. 24
Body of man, iii. 121

PROTOPLASTIC (*Contd.*)
  Ocean slime, dweller in, iv. 220
PROTOPLASTS furnished with means of return-
  ing to their pristine nobility, iii. 285
PROTOTYPAL form of mankind, i. 271
PROTOTYPE (S) Act of procreation, of, iv. 115
  Adam, of second, iv. 24
  Animals, of, iii. 187
  Archangels, of, ii. 336; iv. 155
  Aryan, of Jehovah, iii. 133
  Astral, iii. 78, 193, 259, 297; iv. 196, 306
  Astral envelope of earth, out of, iv. 282
  Astral regions, of man from, i. 228
  Atlanteans, of, iii. 22
  Buddhas, of, i. 168
  Dhyān Chohans, are, v. 78
  Divine, i. 168, 308; v. 79, 358
  Elohim, of man, iii. 93
  Fohat, of Eros, iii. 76
  Forms and shapes, of all, i. 324
  Fourth round, of, iii. 193
  Heaven, in, ii. 194, 363
  Human being in spiritual sphere, of every, i. 281
  Ideal, caused by Fohat to expand, i. 132
  Incarnating Jivas, of, i. 263
  Indra, of Kārtikeya, iii. 381
  Kronos, of Jehovah, iii. 150
  Macrocosmic, of microcosm, i. 186
  Mammal, iv. 258
  Man, of, i. 263; v. 358
  Man shadow of his, i. 308
  Monera, of, iii. 165
  Patristic fancy, of, iii. 377
  Physical from Astral, iv. 306, 307
  Prometheus, of, iii. 412, 418
  Roman Catholics and ethereal, iv. 49
  Saraph of Moses, of, iii. 386
  Sargon 1, of Moses, iv. 261
  Serpent, of Azazel, iii. 386
  Spiritual, i. 292
  Tzure or, iv. 24
  Types and, of our present race, i. 237
  Venus spiritual, of earth, iii. 44
PROTOTYPIC causes of the heavenly orbs,
  iv. 122
PROTOZOA, No change in the, iii. 260
PROTYLE, i. 118, 128, 129, 188, 285, 325; ii. 42,
  53, 246, 273, 276, 305, 306, 308, 342, 346,
  347, 350; iii. 114; iv. 306
PROVIDENCE, Active, ii. 138
  Divine light or, ii. 64
  Karma and, ii. 359; v. 303, 330, 370
  Man need not accuse, ii. 369
  Synonym of, ii. 367
  Ways of, ii. 368
PRUNER BEY, referred to, iv. 251
PRYTANEUM, stone which ran from the, iii. 345
PSALMISTS, King, i. 167
PSALMS of David, Samaritans and, v. 179
PSAMMITE, Amulets made of, iv. 313
PSELLUS on ether, ii. 45
  Magic, on, v. 255
PSEUDO-BEROSUS, iii. 151
PSEUDOGRAPHS, Forged, iii. 439
PSEUDOLOGY and chemistry, ii. 346
PSEUDONYM of God, Chance the, ii. 379
PSUCHE, the reflection of Nous, iii. 375

PSYCHE, Caterpillar, emblem of, i. 141
  Greek emblem of soul, i. 141
  Nous and, iii. 143
  Quaternary, one of a, iv. 171; v. 515
  Wisdom, lower terrestrial, i. 247
PSYCHIC action, v. 515
  Animal, guided by, iii. 411
  Apperception, v. 548
  Cell, iii. 243
  Consciousness, i. 220; v. 429
  Counterparts of senses, v. 557
  Craze, iii. 349
  Cycles, iv. 362
  Dhyān Chohans and humanity, relationship
    between, i. 273
  Elements, aspect of, iii. 358
  Energy of God or Adept is Shakti, v. 373
  Evolution, i. 265; ii. 337, 345; iii. 73, 96,
    118, 245, 364, 408
  Faculties, ii. 245
  Force, ii. 52
  Function, prototype of every, iii. 100
  Gandharva Devas of a, character, iv. 157
  Hallucination, powers, of, iii. 369
  Intellect, i. 258
  Intuition, spirit and idea of, ii. 266
  Involution, iii. 295
  Man, characteristics of, ii. 300
  Monads, principles of, ii. 357
  Moon, phases of, ii. 112
  Mysteries, v. 96
  Nature, i. 202, 211, 271; ii. 312, 333; iii. 198,
    318, 319; iv. 186, 203
  Organizations of adepts, i. 316
  Parents of men, iii. 179
  Physiological and, discoveries, i. 191
  Plane, iii. 119; v. 513, 515, 521, 525
  Powers, iii. 297
  Primitive man, form of, iii. 162
  Principles, ii. 177
  Realms, ii. 203
  Relations, man in his, i. 273
  Rounds, changes in man in every, i. 216
  Satan and Deity, aspect of, i. 247
  Seer and, i. 246
  Semi-divine, i. 310
  Shadow, i. 274
  Spheres of action, iv. 192
  Spiritual and, teachings, i. 219
  Spiritual life, and, iii. 157
  States, v. 155
  Stones, powers of, iii. 341
  Struggle between spiritual and, iii. 274
  Struggle on physical and, plane, iii. 74
  Sun and moon, deities, i. 275
  Symbol, meaning to each, iv. 108
  System, ii. 78
  Universe from a, standpoint, ii. 314
  Vibrations of atmosphere seen by a, ii. 358
  Vision, v. 515, 521
  World, ii. 233; v. 418
PSYCHICAL, Ether, cause of sound, i. 336
  Mankind, groups of, ii. 283
  Moon on earth, influence of, i. 232
  Mystery of moon, i. 274
  Phenomena, spiritual and, i. 231
  Principle, iv. 220

PSYCHICAL (*Contd.*)
 Regeneration and immortality, i. 140
PSYCHICALLY, Man, considered, ii. 181;
 iii. 418
 Moon, dead, i. 204
PSYCHICS in European armies, ii. 287
PSYCHISM Eastern book and, v. 73
 Not Psychology, iii. 164
PSYCHO-chemical principle, ii. 54
PSYCHO-mental evolves from the spiritual, i. 266
PSYCHO-physicist, Evolution of the, ii. 345
PSYCHO-physiological Man, v. 545
 Phenomenon, iii. 156
 Symbol, ii. 18
PSYCHO-spiritual faculty, iii. 369
PSYCHO-theistic thought, Ancient, ii. 122
PSYCHOD of Thury, ii. 52
PSYCHOLOGICAL, Aspect, a, iii. 35
 Creation, secrets of, iv. 114
 Evolution, iv. 107
 Hindu and Egyptian, spirit, iv. 37
 Kandu's, state, iii. 182
 Link, a, iii. 369
 Manifestations, iii. 164
 Mystery, i. 308
 Physiological and, iv. 37
 Plane, iv. 212
 Problems, i. 191
 Prometheus taught, insight, iii. 412
 Soul of man, iv. 202
 Vagaries of modern, sciences, iii. 90
PSYCHOLOGISTS, Allegory of Jesus, and,
 v. 168
 Eternity of universe rejected by, iv. 59
 Law of periodicity and, iv. 192
 Materialists and, iv. 223
 Matter and, v. 515
 Modern, ii. 345; iv. 17
 Soul, and, iii. 91
PSYCHOLOGY, Ancient's knowledge of, iii. 115
 Āryan and Egyptian, i. 273
 Eastern, i. 125; v. 380
 Fifth element more to do with, than physics,
 iii. 144
 Lunar worship based on, ii. 113
 Man as known to, ii. 361
 Materialism, now crass, iii. 164
 Metaphysics and, ii. 345
 Modern, ii. 201
 Negative, i. 183
 Physiology, and, v. 151
 Science a trespasser on grounds of, iv. 233
 Septenary division in Egyptian, iv. 204
 Sevening and, iv. 203
 Spiritual science, claimed as a, v. 240
 Transcendental, iii. 255
PSYCHOMETER, Every astronomer should be
 a, i. 250; v. 522
PSYCHOMETRY, Jnānashakti and, i. 333
 Stomach and, v. 557
PSYCHOPATHIC persons, Spirits and, iii. 369
PSYCHOPOMPIC genius, Mercury as a, iv. 112
PSYCHOSTASY, or Judgment of the Soul,
 v. 247
PTAH, ÆSCULAPIUS or, ii. 68
 Egyptian, ii. 52
 Fiery God, ii. 80

He who opens, means, ii. 66, 82
 Logos soul or, ii. 68
 Sons, of, v. 202
PTAH-RA, the Egyptian, ii. 52
PTERODACTYL, iii. 159, 210, 211, 222, 386;
 iv. 247, 266
PTOLEMAIC, period, Egyptian religion of, ii. 23
 System, v. 437
PTOLEMAIOS of the Greeks, iii. 61
PTOLEMIES, dynasty of, v. 302
PTOLEMY, Astronomer, as, ii. 384
 Calendars of, ii. 388
 Geocentric system and, v. 437
 Hindu epochs not derived from, ii. 385
 Hypothesis of, iii. 157
 Kabolitæ, on, iii. 205
 Positions determined by, ii. 388
 "Reincarnated", iii. 325
 Vindication of, iii. 367
PTOLEMY PHILADELPHUS Founder of
 Alexandrian Library, v. 57
 Septuagint and, v. 183
PTOMAINE of modern science, i. 305
PTR, Mystery of, v. 140
"PUDDING BAGS", v. 518, 532
PUEBLOS, Artufas of the, iii. 188
PUENTE, NACIONAL, ruins of Lodges at,
 v. 283
PŪJA made to a statue of Jesus in Southern
 India, i. 139
PULAHA, a mind-born son of Brahma, iii. 88
PULASTYA, Brahma, son of, iii. 88, 235
 Progeny, one of first, ii. 133
 Serpents and Nāgas, father of, iii. 188
 Vishnu Purāna received from, ii. 176
PULOMĀ, daughter of Dānava, iii. 380
PULSE, Desire, of, iii. 236, 237
 Septenary law and human, iv. 194
 Universe, of, i. 263
PUMA to lion, Similarity of, iv. 360
PUMS, Brahma and, i. 300; ii. 164
 Supreme spirit, a portion of, ii. 88
PUNARJANMAM or rebirth, i. 333
PUNDARIKASHA, iii. 117
PUNJAB, Buddhism in, v. 394, 405
 Finest men in the, iii. 409
PURĀNA, Allegory of calf in, ii. 113
 Seven creations found in almost every, ii. 165
 Taraka war described in every, iv. 66
PURĀNAS, Āgneyāstra of, iv. 200
 Allegories of, ii. 245; iii. 68, 172, 178, 181; v. 72
 Arctic continent referred to in, iii. 24
 Atala of, iii. 401
 Atlantis, and, iii. 404, 405
 Bhūtas in, iii. 110
 Brahmā in, i. 170; iii. 64; iv. 144, 188
 Brahmā Vāch bisexual in, i. 139
 Brahmans and, iii. 156; iv. 136; v. 408
 Branches of knowledge in, i. 222
 Calf allegory in, ii. 113
 Chronology of, ii. 28; iii. 228
 Computations in, iii. 77
 Contradiction in, iii. 320
 Cosmogony of, ii. 62, 348; iii. 64
 Creation in, i. 264; v. 199
 Creation, on first, ii. 170; iii. 85, 91
 Creators, on, ii. 96

PURĀNAS (Contd.)
Criticism of, ii. 137
Cube in, perfect, ii. 58
Dark sayings in, iv. 104
Date of, v. 343
Dead letter of, i. 300; iii. 319
Demons and, iii. 69
Departed lands in, iii. 266
Diti in, iv. 184
Doctrines of, said to be incompatible, ii. 138
Emblems, written, ii. 18
Esoteric, blinds in, v. 27
Esoteric lining to, i. 218
Esoteric works, once, ii. 141
Esotericism of, v. 27, 258, 408
Ether, on, ii. 44, 311
Evolution, on, iii. 188, 254; iv. 227
Fables of, ii. 50
Fall in, iii. 285
Fallen Gods, on, iii. 235
Geology of, iii. 256
Geometrical figures in, i. 134
Golden egg, on, ii. 75
Hindu, i. 64, 174, 327; iii. 62, 404; iv. 22
Historical, iii. 322
Initiated Brāhmans, written for, iii. 320
Jewish liturgy and, ii. 343
Kāma-deva in, iii. 182
Kapila in, iv. 141, 143
Kumāras in, ii. 177; iii. 180; iv. 149
Legends of giants in, iii. 295
Magical bow mentioned in, v. 121
Manus and Rishis in, iv. 186
Mārishā in, iii. 183
Mind-born sons, on, iii. 277
Mosaic books and, v. 232
Mythical language in, iii. 36
Nārada in, iii. 60
Nirmānakāyas in all, iii. 103
Noah and, iv. 168
North of Meru referred to in, iii. 326
Number seven in, iii. 47
Origin of, iii. 408
Personifications in, ii. 132
Personnel of, iii. 286
Pitris, on, iii. 100, 129
Pradhāna in, i. 300
Prakriti of, ii. 327
Pratisarga in, iii. 115
Pre-human period, on, iii. 286
Primordial substance, on, ii. 44
Progenitors in, account of our, iii. 146
Proofs of old teachings in, ii. 19
Pushkara in, iii. 402
Radiant matter in, ii. 348
Religion in, i. 174, 175
Rishi Yogis in, iii. 88
Rudra in, iv. 185
Rulers of, iii. 105
Sacrifice of Daksha in, iii. 189
Sankhya philosophy and, iv. 141
Secondary creation of, iii. 115
Secret Doctrine and, v. 258
Septenary in, iv. 182, 183, 187, 203
Serpent symbolism in, iii. 380
Seven continents, on, iv. 328
Seven creations of, i. 85

Seven prakritis of, ii. 49
Shaiva, iv. 147
Shākadvipa in, iii. 403
Shistas, on, iii. 308
Shukra in, iii. 43
Sibylline Prophecy and, v. 339
Sound and speech in, iv. 133
Spirit in, iii. 49
Sweat-born in, iii. 182, 183
Symbolic religion of Aryans, on, ii. 28
Tāra-daitya of, iii. 401
Veiled language of, iii. 153
Vishnu's Shveta-dvīpa in, iii. 365
Vishvakarman and, v. 270
Wars in heaven in, i. 251
Wilford, Col., and, i. 53; ii. 381
World, on great architect of, ii. 160
Year of, iv. 192
Yugas, on, iii. 80
PURĀNIC, Adversary in, literautre, ii. 130
Allegories, iii. 145
Allegory of birth of Brahmā, v. 421
Allegory of Raivata, v. 259
Aryan idea of creation, iii. 135
Astronomy, iii. 255
Atlantis, accounts of, iii. 405, 407
Characters, iv. 149
Chronology, iv. 141
Cosmogony, iv. 195
Cross symbol in India, version of, iv. 117
Deva-loka, accounts of, i. 189
Devas in, legend, iii. 73
Dualistic system, a, i. 300
Exoteric writings, i. 299
Fancy of, authors, iii. 184
Flood, versions of, iii. 148
Great Pralaya account of, v. 267
Islands, iii. 403
Kārana of, commentators, i. 118
Later, narratives, iv. 66
Legends, iii. 18, 56, 73
Manus, account of, iii. 149
Monads, histories of our, iii. 286
MSS., iv. 120
Phrase, oft recurring, i. 167
Pralaya, account of great, iv. 326
Shveta-dvīpa in literature, iii. 19, 365
Tradition, iii. 401, 404
Writers referred to, i. 251
PURGATIONS of matter, i. 271
PURGATORY, ii. 292; v. 230, 359
PURIFICATION, Effort of will towards, ii. 363
PURITY, Air would secure continuous life, of,
    i. 303
Corruption of physical, a temporary curse,
    iii. 285
Director of, iii. 18
Krita age of, ii. 93
Mind and body, of, v. 543
Mysteries, of, v. 280
Nirvāna a state of, iii. 90
Satya age of, ii. 369
Seer, of, iii. 297
Spirit is inherent, of, i. 243
Spiritual, destruction of, i. 267
State of, iv. 142
Third race, i. 241; iii. 179

PUROHITA or family priest, iii. 57, 323
PURPLE Tyrian, iii. 428
PURŪRAVAS and the celestial Gandharva, ii. 247
PURUSHA, iv. 273; 426
 Aja, v. 370
 Being or born from non-being, ii. 58
 Brahmā and, v. 165
 Created deity, a, iii. 117
 Force, v. 469
 Heavenly man called, iv. 177
 Logos, and, iv. 273
 Matter and, union of, ii. 81, 182
 Parabrahman distinct from, ii. 306
 Phanes, Eros or, ii. 171
 Pradhāna and, are one, ii. 306
 Prakriti and, i. 81, 122, 293, 326; ii. 275; iii. 53, 131; v. 209; v. 469
 Pralaya, during, v. 189
 Principle or, seventh, iv. 145
 Principles, or, seven, ii. 48
 Spirit or, i. 146, 148, 246, 292; ii. 170, 306; iv. 170; v. 426
 Sūkta, iv. 178; v. 370
 Supreme spirit, and, resolve into, ii. 89
 Thousand-headed, v. 370
 Waters created by, ii. 177
PURUSHOTTAMA, ii. 266; iv. 141; v. 215, 233
PŪRVAJA, Living spirit of nature or, iii. 116, 117
PŪRVARDHI, quoted, iii. 235
PŪRVĀSHĀDHĀ in the *Bhagavata Purāna*, iv. 120
PUSHKARA, Dvīpa or, iii. 319
 Jambu-dvīpa and, iii. 320, 403
 Pātāla of India, iii. 405
 Seas, surrounded by, iii. 320
 Varshas of, iii. 405
 Zone, seventh, iii. 402
PUTAH, the first intellectual father, iv. 203
P'UTO in China, Island of, ii. 193; v. 394
PUTRA, Priyavrata son, of, iii. 369
 Progeny or, iii. 190
PUTREFACTION, Son of, iv. 146
PU-TSI-K'IUN-LING, ii. 193
PUZZLES Biblical, v. 201
 Sacerdotal, v. 390
PYGMALION in the Greek allegory, iii. 158
PYGMALIONS of primeval man, iii. 111
PYMANDER, DIVINE, Celestial man, on, i. 277
 Darkness, on light from, iv. 54
 Deluge, on, iii. 63
 Descent into materiality, on, ii. 134
 Divine thought, on, iv. 57
 Duality of sex, on, iii. 105
 Esoteric, truly, iv. 59
 Heavenly man, on, iii. 112, 272; iv. 61
 Hermetic, i. 132; iii. 239
 Jupiter, on, iii. 272
 Kabalists disfigured, Christian, iii. 123
 Logoi, one of, i. 141
 Mouth of mystery, or the, iii. 123
 Nature, of, iii. 239
 Pitris, on, iii. 269
 Seven circles of fire in, iii. 235, 277
 Seven regents of, iv. 56
 Seven sons of God of, iii. 217

Texts found in Egypt, v. 58
Thought divine, ii. 325
Traces of the real, iv. 59
Trinity, on, iii. 115
Verbum of, iv. 112
Virgin of world, on, iii. 234
Workmen or rectors of, iii. 106
PYRAMID(S), Alpha Draconis of, ii. 123
 America, of, ii. 34; v. 283
 Architecture of, v. 248
 Aztecs', ii. 35
 Black, ii. 141
 Builders, ii. 26; iv. 262
 Cement of, is indestructible, iii. 428
 Cheops, of, i. 174; ii. 77; iv. 29, 128; v. 89, 296
 Dates of, iii. 429, 430; iv. 262
 Deluge associated with, iii. 351
 Dodecagonal, iv. 148
 Egypt, of, i. 51; ii. 61, 157; iii. 428; v. 43
 First syllable of, means fire, v. 117
 Gallery of, iv. 37
 Gizeh of, ii. 29
 Gods, built under supervision of, ii. 153
 Great, iii. 429, 430; iv. 319
 ,, Architecture of, v. 248
 ,, Biblical pyramidalists and measures of, ii. 27
 ,, Cheops, of, v. 89, 296
 ,, Cholula, of, iii. 278
 ,, Cosmogonical Mysteries of, v. 92
 ,, Egyptian Zodiac and, iii. 433
 ,, Esoteric foundations of, iv. 32
 ,, Exact science in, ii. 25
 ,, Geometrical secrets in, v. 91
 ,, Hebrew text of *Bible* and, ii. 25
 ,, Initiatory rites in, v. 271
 ,, King's chamber of, ii. 107
 ,, Kosmos and, v. 166
 ,, Mysteries, indestructible symbol of, ii. 26
 ,, Mystery of Mysteries, v. 91
 ,, Solomon's Temple and, v. 80
 ,, Symbology of, v. 248
 ,, Units of measurement and, iii. 230; v. 166, 186, 206
 Initiates and, iii. 352; v. 283
 Inverted, ii. 141
 Kephren builder of second, iii. 230
 Mackey on, iii. 434
 Meaning of, i. 184
 Mexico and Peru, of, v. 43, 283
 Molecules of salt form, iv. 166
 Nails of cross a solid, iv. 131
 Notation, of Cheops built on measures of decimal, ii. 77
 Number, a, iv. 36
 Numbers, v. 151
 Old and New World of, v. 217
 Passages in, iii. 427
 Perfection of proportion in, i. 257
 Points, of, ii. 341
 Pythagorean triangle and, ii. 342
 Quaternary and, v. 117
 Seth and Idrus, burial place of, iii. 361
 Seven chambers of, v. 248
 Solomon's temple and, ii. 28
 Sound, could be lifted by, ii. 279
 Symbol, iii. 366

PYRAMID(S) (*Contd.*)
  Symbology of, i. 184; v. 91
  Ten points inscribed, like, ii. 341
  Theodosius and king builders of, ii. 24
  Triad or, is from, iv. 171
  Triangular base of, iv. 147
  Triangular stones or, iii. 351
  Various, iii. 351
PYRAMIDAL, Fire is, iv. 166
PYRAMIDALISTS and the solar system, ii. 26
PYRAMIS, Cube, and, iv. 171
  Tetrad, with base of a, iv. 173
  Triangle figure of fire, whence word, iv. 166
PYROLITHIC age, iii. 167
PYRRHA, Deucalion and, iii. 272
PYRRHUS, a healer, v. 263
PYTHAGORAS, Adept, an, i. 57; iv. 99;
  v. 75
  Aristotle and, ii. 340
  Astronomer, v. 322, 331
  Biography of, v. 151
  Buddhism and, v. 387, 388
  Copernican System and, v. 331
  Cosmogony of, ii. 158; v. 440
  Date of, ii. 76
  Decad of, v. 382
  Disappeared, v. 148
  Doctrines of, v. 302, 321, 388
  Duad of, ii. 144, 344; v. 116
  Dual system introduced by, iv. 144
  Earth's rotation taught by, i. 176
  Egypt and Babylon, in, v. 255, 264, 279
  Gnosis, and, v. 74
  Gods of, ii. 143, 215, 219, 338; v. 382
  Harmony and music of the Spheres, on, ii. 150;
    iv. 172
  Hexagon, and, v. 120
  India, brought allegory from, ii. 62, 76;
    iv. 153; v. 87
  Initiate, v. 279, 304, 321, 524
  Instructions of, iv. 122
  Kosmos of, iv. 171; v. 440
  Macrocosm of, v. 299
  Mathematics of, v. 87
  Method of, iii. 160
  Monad of, ii. 144, 338
  Mysteries of, v. 147
  Neo-Platonists and, i. 66
  Number seven, and, iii. 47
  Number six, and, iv. 164
  Numbers, studied, v. 264
  Numerals of, v. 87, 113, 264
  Philosophy of, v. 68, 387
  Physical knowledge of, iv. 91
  Pillar and cirlce (10) perfect number with,
    iv. 31
  Plato and, v. 35, 68
  Point of, ii. 341, v. 188
  Referred to, iv. 174; v. 60, 116
  Sacred number of, v. 163
  Sacred planets of, iv. 173
  Sage, v. 65, 265
  School of, v. 459
  Scientist, v. 28, 524
  Secrecy of, v. 34
  Secret wisdom of, iv. 104
  Separation of sexes, and, iii. 221

  Shukra-Venus and, iii. 44
  Spirits, believer in, ii. 336
  Sun, on, v. 217
  Symbolism of, v. 113, 120
  Symbols of, ii. 337; v. 113
  Teaching of, v. 65
  Tetrad, esteemed by, iv. 170; v. 420
  Tetraktys of, v. 113, 420, 506, 516
  Theban Sanctuary, in, v. 264
  Twelve sacred to, number, ii. 375
PYTHAGOREAN(S), v. 387
  Apollonius of Tyana, a, v. 116
  Binary hated by, iv. 146
  Cipher, v. 116
  Decad, i. 110; ii. 33; iv. 123, 144
  Dogmas, v. 382
  First and Final figures of, ii. 76
  Formula of cosmogony, ii. 57
  Fragments, iv. 211
  Heptagon, and iv. 173
  Hicetas, i. 176
  Ideas, ii. 151
  Initiates, were, iii. 161
  Key, iv. 155
  Key-keeper of nature, and, iv. 172
  Logos, idea of, ii. 151
  Marcus whose philosophy was, ii. 168;
    iv. 133
  Metempsychosis, doctrine of, iii. 194
  Monad, ii. 338, 344; iv. 240
  Monas, i. 132; iii. 100
  Number seven and, iv. 154
  Numbers, ii. 179; v. 87
  Numbers, and Gods, and connection between,
    iv. 147
  Philolaus, a, v. 218
  Plato best of, iv. 170
  Sacred books, knowledge of existence of, i. 57
  School, v. 146
  Soul of world of, ii. 52
  Sun and, v. 219
  Svastika and, scales, iv. 159
  Symbol, iv. 123
  System of Numbers and Geometry, v. 87
  Teachings, ii. 343
  Tetrad, v. 420
  Tetraktys, i. 129; iv. 172, 174; v. 506
  Theory, corpuscular, ii. 207, 231
  Triangle, i. 47, 337, 341, 342, 346; iii. 37, 120;
    v. 188
  Vow of Silence, v. 45
  Writings, v. 304
PYTHIUS, Helius and, iii. 115
PYTHON, Apollo and, iii. 378
  Demon dragon or, iii. 382
  Dragon-serpent oracle, iii. 380
  Egyptian, iv. 85
  Sun conqueror of, iii. 213
  Universal symbol, a, iv. 54

Q

QABBALISTS, Balance of the, iv. 25. *See also*
  Kabalah
QAI-YIN, Ge'boor'ah or, iii. 315
QANIRATHA, or Hvaniratha, iv. 328
Q'LIPPOTH, or shells, iv. 72

QUADRATURE, Parker's, of circle, ii. 28
Perfect, of infinite circle, ii. 58
QUADRUMANIC Ancestors, supposed, iii. 199
QUADRUMANOUS Order, iii. 257, 260, 347; iv. 236, 247
QUADRUPEDS and bipeds, ii. 332; iii. 170, 190
QUAIN on pineal gland, iii. 298
QUALITIES, Determine properties of Selfhood, v. 551
QUARTERS, Cords of four, iv. 159
Cross symbol of four, iv. 116, 117
QUARTILES and signs of Zodiac, ii. 33
QUATERNARY, Ages, iii. 164, 211; iv. 237, 248, 256, 280, 308
Correspondences, v. 455, 507, 556
Cube, Mystic, v. 189
Dhyān Chohans of, iii. 242
Double, iv. 171
Eyes and nostrils and, v. 439
Extinct species of, iv. 320
Father, mother, son and life, i. 129
Figure is, first, iv. 147
Four Mahārājahs and, v. 439
Four wicks are, i. 282
God, a, ii. 66
Group of rūpa angels, i. 265
Hierarchies of, i. 261
Higher or lower, iv. 175
Interlaced triangles in, iv. 164
Jah-Noah at head of lower cosmic, iv. 167
Kabalistic, v. 189
Key keeper of nature, iv. 172
Logos and light of, ii. 147
Lower, i. 287; v. 498, 534, 563, 564
Macrocosm, of the, v. 516
Magical and scientific, iv. 126
Man may disappear with, i. 289
Manifested, i. 152
Men of epoch, iv. 309
Microprosopus and, iv. 196
Middle nature of, iv. 165
Perfect number, iv. 153
Planets and Angels, v. 439
Principles of lower, i. 268; v. 458, 498
Pyramid, in, v. 117
Races of, period, iv. 307
Rocks, iv. 279
Sacred Tetraktys, v. 426
Savage of, iv. 318
Science and occult science on, iv. 284
Sephiroth and, v. 191
Strata, iv. 245
Symbol, iv. 168
Syrian ten worlds our, ii. 154
Tetragrammaton or, triangle concerting into, i. 140
Tetraktys or, v. 426
Triad and, i. 287, 288; v. 191
Triangle and, iv. 183; v. 507, 512, 514, 516
Triangle and, became Tetraktys, ii. 340
Triangle and, symbol of septenary man, iv. 163; v. 507
Wisdom and intellect, of, iii. 47
YHVH, ii. 343
QUATERNITY, the superficies of Olympus, iv. 173

QUATREMÉRE, quoted, iv. 20
QUEEN, of Heaven, v. 319
Mentuhept, Coffin of, v. 139
Navarre, of, referred to, iii. 105
QUETZO COHUATL, or serpent deity, iii. 379
QUICHE Manuscript, Ancient, iii. 105
QUICHES referred to, iii. 47
QUIESCENCE, First aspect of eternal, iv. 56
Perfection, natural state of, iv. 58
QUIETISTS, v. 401
QUINANES, Giants called, iii. 278
QUINARY, Man when bad a, iv. 147
Interlaced triangles, in, iv. 164
QUINQUEPARTITE Division, Vedantic, i. 273
QUINTESSENCE, Philosophies of, iv. 109; v.109
Universal, iv. 155
Voltaire, of, iii. 97
QUINTUS CURTIUS referred to, iv. 191
QUIS UT DEUS, Michael the, iv. 47
QŪ-TĀMY, Bible of, iv. 23
Chaldean Adept, v. 89, 237, 242
Chaldean doctrines of, iv. 24
Idol of the moon, and, ii. 110, 117; v. 237, 242
Saturn, and, iv. 20

R

RA, Assimilation to, i. 274
Egg, in his, ii. 75, 80
Hymn to, v. 463
One God, ii. 399
Osiris favourite of, ii. 155
Osiris-Ptah, or, i. 277
Seven Spirits of, v. 202
Shu and, ii. 82; iv. 116
Toom is, ii. 398
RAB-MAG or Magi, iii. 217
RABBI (S), Abahu, iii. 64; iv. 274
Al-Chazari and, iii. 51, 53
Archaic doctrine, and key to, iv. 107
Bible and, v. 192
Christianity, on, i. 77
Companion, entered, iv. 197
Companions, iv. 197
Heathen more sincere than, iii. 135
Initiated, v. 175
Jesus, iv. 134, 136
Jochai, Simeon ben, q. v.
Kabalah and Bible, on, iv. 106
Measure known to, iv. 114
Moses, iv. 29
Numbers 10, 6 and 5 sacred to, i. 154
Phallicism of, iii. 94
Scriptures, and, Jewish, iv. 27
Sepher Yetzireh and, v. 205
Solomon ben Yehudah, ii. 157; iii. 316
Yogel, ii. 154
Zohar as interpreted by, iv. 29
RABBINICAL, Caprice, iii. 138
Commentators on Enoch, iv. 169
Fallen angels, teaching on, iii. 249
Hebrew letters, value of, ii. 28
Holy of Holies, iv. 36
Language, ii. 380
Lilith, iii. 286
Literature, iv. 188

RABBINICAL (*Contd.*)
    Methods, and pagan, iv. 115
    Mysteries, iii. 395
    Symbol for God, iv. 183
    Workmanship, iv. 110
RABBIN-KABALIST, iii. 134, 135, 136
RABBINS, Ain-Soph, and, iii. 385
    Bird of, iv. 189
    Chaldea, brought calculations from, iv. 136
    Fathers of Church, and, ii. 183
    Globe, and, iii. 396
    Gnostics and, iii. 388
    God of, ii. 111
    Jehovah, and, i. 139; iii. 387
    Kabalists, and pre-Christian, ii. 111
    Kin, and Cain or, iii. 387
    Purānic expressions and, iii. 135
    Seven souls, and, iv. 203
RACA or fool, ii. 302
RACE (S), Abraham, father of our, iii. 52
    Adam, before, iii. 37
    Adamic, iii. 19, 100
    Adam's sons represent, iii. 396
    Adi first speaking, called, iv. 19
    African, iii. 198, 423
    Age of our, iii. 432
    Ages of each of seven, iii. 204
    Allegory of Raivata and, v. 259
    America, of, iv. 359
    Americans as a, iii. 442
    Androgynous, iii. 105; iv. 102
    Animal, ii. 19; iii. 330
    Animal and human, iii. 93
    Antiquity of human, ii. 371; iii. 351; iv. 340
    Arhatship in sixth, i. 255
    Aryan, i. 173; iii. 23, 114, 130, 394, 431, 439; iv. 38, 102, 283; v. 261, 268
    Aryan Hindu belongs to oldest existing, iv. 38
    Asia, which took refuge in plateaux of, iv. 313
    Astral or phantom, iii. 281
    Astronomical cycles and, iii. 330
    Atlantean, i. 243; ii. 133, 334; iii. 275, 370, 371, 421, 422, 424, 442; iv. 102, 175; v. 256, 260, 268
    Atlanto-Aryan, iii. 423
    Australian, iii. 201, 327
    Beginnings of this, i. 258
    Birth and death of each, v. 249
    Birth to animal and man, giving, i. 286
    Black, iii. 422; iv. 265
    Blue, iii. 198
    Book of Enoch, and, v. 104
    Boneless, iii. 199
    Branch or family, iii. 432
    Brown, iv. 265
    Cabiri, or, iii. 392
    Canaries, of, iv. 359
    Cast-off types of human, iii. 265
    Catacylsm at end of each, v. 163
    Chhāyā, iii. 29, 99
    Colossal statues, represented by, iii. 339
    Coloured, iii. 198, 230, 350, 422; iv. 265, 313
    Commentary on four, iii. 283
    Complete human, iii. 224
    Conception during previous, i. 275
    Confusion of, for blind, iii. 322
    Consolidated, less, iv. 357

    Continents, and, three, iv. 181
    Cradle of human, iv. 249
    Création of first, iii. 95
    Creators of, iii. 435
    Cycles, and, iii. 301, 302, 439; iv. 188, 260, 303
    Daksha synthesis of preceding, iii. 185
    Days stand for side-, v. 102
    Deluge, before, iii. 149
    Details of four preceding, iii. 408
    Deucalion ancestor of human, iv. 88
    Development of human, iii. 411, 435; iv. 192
    Dhyān Chohans, i. 239; ii. 185; iii. 277
    Diagram showing evolution of, iii. 301
    Dies, that never, iii. 78
    Differences in, i. 265; iii. 441
    Divine, iii. 133, 368
    Divine leaders of, i. 309
    Divine progenitors produced each a different, iii. 86
    Dragon, of, iii. 379
    Dumb, iii. 32, 190
    Dwarfish, iii. 423
    Dying out, iv. 349
    Dynasties are, iii. 368
    Earth changing, its, iv. 103
    Earth, on, i. 215; iii. 45
    Egg of future, iii. 30
    Egg-born, iii. 131, 141
    Eighth, iii. 376
    Embryos of, iv. 29, 299
    Enoch and, iv. 102; v. 102, 104, 106
    Esoteric classification of, iii. 251; iv. 290
    Ethereal, iii. 235; iv. 206, 239
    Evolution of, i. 63; ii. 19; iii. 21, 203, 238, 251, 256, 266, 301, 313, 408, 417; iv. 233, 257, 278, 289; v. 249, 425, 518
    Extinct, iii. 291
    Faculties of humanity of earlier, ii. 260
    Failures in ethereal, iii. 235
    Fall, two, at, iii. 18
    Family, iii. 431, 432
    Fifth, i. 63, 64, 72, 173, 235, 255, 256, 271; ii. 251, 333, 369; iii. 42, 144, 179, 191, 209, 252, 295, 301, 316, 393, 421, 426, 431, 439, 442; iv. 24, 38, 102, 177, 186, 194, 255, 283, 310, 312; v. 91, 106, 109, 256, 261, 263, 265, 267, 268, 300, 337, 376, 474
    First, i. 64, 235, 239; ii. 175, 203, 330; iii. 16, 19, 42, 65, 94, 95, 103, 116, 122, 124, 125, 134, 145, 158, 164, 171, 181, 182, 203, 245, 250, 251, 272, 291, 300, 328, 393, 399; iv. 25, 102, 255; v. 67, 69, 102, 291, 300, 523
    Five, i. 286; v. 101
    Formative powers of, iii. 119
    Forty-nine, iv. 189
    Fourth, i. 72, 167, 174, 242, 243, 271; ii. 112, 334, 371; iii. 32, 33, 42, 43, 44, 72, 143, 152, 159, 163, 179, 180, 185, 187, 196, 198, 200, 203, 230, 252, 282, 286, 295, 296, 303, 316, 319, 349, 360, 375, 406, 409, 424, 427, 431, 439, 443; iv. 25, 102, 103, 156, 175, 181, 186, 194, 220, 249, 255, 282, 312; v. 37, 91, 103, 106, 121, 204, 258, 260, 268, 523
    Fourth round, of, iii. 187
    Garments of, iii. 316
    Genealogical tree of our, iii. 432

RACE (S) (Contd.)
  Generally treated, i. 240, 241
  Generation, and, iv. 221
  Generation falling into, iii. 18
  Giants, of, iii. 295, 394
  Gigantic fourth, iii. 152
  Globe and, development of our, iii. 435
  Gods, from, ii. 35
  Gods, of, iii. 18, 270
  Great, seven, iii. 42
  Greek poets mention, iii. 273
  Haeckel on distribution of, iii. 327
  Head of dragon for each, ii. 124
  Hindu Deva, allotted to each, iv. 108
  History of first five, i. 64; iv. 102
  History of our, iii. 435
  Human, ii. 371; iii. 133, 138, 200, 224, 251,
    265, 291, 322, 441; iv. 88, 192, 340; v. 69
  Human, first, v. 102, 291
  Humanity of future, will differ from our, ii. 333
  Instructors of primeval, iii. 392
  Kalki Avatāra issues, from which, iii. 414
  Knowledge, destitute of, iii. 288
  Lemuria and third root, ii. 157
  Lords of third and fourth, iii. 198
  Mammals and, of men, iii. 283
  Manasa period of our, iii. 302
  Manas-less, iii. 318
  Manu representative of, iii. 308
  Mars and Venus, of, iv. 268
  Meridian of, iii. 301
  Metals, named from, iii. 273
  Mind-born, v. 74
  Mindless, iii. 265, 284; iv. 253
  Monsters, of, iii. 197, 374
  Mystery language of prehistoric, iv. 145
  Nebo creator of fourth and fifth, iv. 23
  Noah Androgyne of first three, ii. 162
  Origin of human, iv. 216, 222
  Overlapping, iii. 431, 432
  Palaeolithic, iv. 307
  Panoramic view of early, iii. 265
  Parallel evolution of, and strata, iii. 251
  Pentacle symbol of five root, i. 183
  Period of various, iii. 228
  Periods, iv. 253, 350
  Persian traditions of, iii. 395
  Physical, iii. 197; iv. 341
  Pitris of third, iii. 98
  Planets, and, iii. 428
  Plastic minds of first, i. 313
  Position of, ii. 367
  Post-tertiary period, during, iii. 67
  Pralaya of, iii. 329, 403
  Pre-Adamite, iii. 177; iv. 274
  Predestination in history of, ii. 366
  Prehistoric, iv. 145, 362
  Pre-physical, iv. 287
  Primeval, i. 293; iv. 226, 259, 260
  Primitive, iii. 141, 197
  Primordial, and occultism, iv. 182
  Principles more material in every, i. 272
  Procreation of third, iii. 188
  Production of second, iii. 30
  Prometheus and, early, iii. 412
  Records of ancient, iii. 105, 345
  Red, iii. 198, 422

  Religious ethics of early, iii. 274
  Representative of first three, iv. 180
  Return of adepts in seventh, iv. 100
  Revealer for each new, i. 115
  Rishis stand for seven, iii. 147
  Root, i. 114; ii. 90; iv. 267; v. 102, 300
  Rounds, and, i. 214, 221, 234; ii. 398;
    iv. 135, 187, 316
  Rudimentary elements of first, iii. 116
  Science, and, iii. 427
  Second, i. 64, 255; ii. 20, 42, 94, 111, 116,
    117, 124, 125, 143, 158, 168, 172, 182, 183,
    203, 250, 272, 304, 399, 400; iv. 180, 254;
    v. 339
  Second continent, of, ii. 85
  Seeds of, iii. 441; iv. 200
  Semi-divine, iii. 168
  Semi-human, iv. 309
  Senzar handed down from third, i. 64
  Septenary law, and, iv. 178, 194
  Serpent symbol of fourth, iii. 72
  Seth progenitor of, earth, iii. 134
  Seven, i. 57, 286, 293; ii. 376; iii. 42, 147,
    204, 371, 440; iv. 135, 176, 177, 206, 275,
    317; v. 101, 165, 249
  Seventh, i. 78, 236, 285; ii. 192, 240; iii. 61,
    109, 175, 187, 398; iv. 51; v. 83, 300, 518, 563
  Sexless, iii. 112, 143; v. 83
  Sixth, i. 78, 236; iv. 51; v. 267, 518
  Size of men of early, iv. 296
  Spiritual, purely, iii. 137
  Stars influence, ii. 372
  Sterility between two human, iii. 201
  Structure of, lowest, iv. 248
  Sub-races of, iv. 189; v. 102
  Superior and inferior, iii. 423
  Svastika and ancient, iv. 126
  Symbolical history of, v. 104
  Symbology of, i. 72; iii. 292; iv. 27
  Third, i. 64, 236, 255, 259; ii. 157, 376; iii. 22,
    31, 32, 42, 43, 78, 98, 100, 113, 125, 131,
    134, 143, 144, 148, 163, 164, 168, 171, 178,
    179, 180, 183, 184, 187, 188, 190, 193, 197,
    200, 202, 203, 250, 290, 360, 374, 396, 398,
    399, 400, 409, 427; iv. 37, 102, 156, 208,
    222, 231, 249, 282, 309; v. 91, 102, 106,
    165, 190, 204, 260, 291, 299, 339, 341, 425,
    429, 430, 472, 546
  Two and a half, first, i. 293
  Two, last, v. 101
  Undying, iii. 277
  Venus, of, iv. 268
  Vishnu protects three, iv. 51
  Weeks stand for sub-, v. 102
  White, yellow and negro, iv. 349
  Winged, iii. 105
  Wise, iii. 423
  Written records of oldest, iii. 345
  Yima symbolizes three, iii. 292
  Zeus, of, iii. 188
  Zohar on, v. 300
RACHEL and Leah, Mandrake, of, iii. 40
RADIANCE, Chaos a cool, ii. 323
  Divine light, of, i. 303
  Elohim, of, iii. 387
  Mutable, ii. 359

RADIANCE (*Contd.*)
Solar selenic, i. 253
Thread of, iii. 89
RADIANT, Buddhi and Mercury are, v. 428, 456
Central sun, energy of, iii. 242
Child of two, i. 138
Discoverer of, matter, ii. 348
Dwellings or gaseous clouds, i. 175
Egg, iv. 37
God, Lyre of, i. 221
Heat, ii. 275
Light, Ocean was, i. 98; iv. 173
Luminous Augoeides of, v. 427
Matter, ii. 239, 267, 286, 346, 348, 350
Monads like, snow, ii. 358
One swift and, i. 195
Ptah, God, ii. 82
Second of seven transformations, i. 253
RADIATION from cosmic seed, v. 424
RADICALS, Seven, i. 201
RADIOMETER, Crookes, ii. 239
RAGON, referred to, see Book Index
RAHASYA, Brāhmanical wisdom in the, i. 314
RAH'MIN, or Seth, iii. 315
RĀHU is mythologically a Daitya, iii. 380
Great Dragon and Eclipses, v. 375
RAIVATA, Legend of, v. 259
Manvantara, iii. 98
RĀJA YOGA, India, of, i. 158, 211, 213; v. 403, 451, 452, 476, 477, 479, 480, 515, 520, 542
RĀJAGRIHA, Cave in, i. 44
RAJAMSI, Prithivi, above, iv. 179
Vishnu, and, iv. 193
Worlds, or, iii. 383; iv. 193
RAJARISHIS or royal, iv. 70
Damaghosha, iii. 229
RAJAS, Active, ii. 48, 62, 259
RĀJASAS, Deities called, iii. 98
Manasas and, iii. 98
RĀKSHASA(S), Bharateans, war with, iv. 345
Cainites, and, ii. 133
Ceylon, of, iii. 335
Creation of, ii. 295
Demons, ii. 132; iii. 235, 289
Devours father of Parāshara, ii. 133
Dwellings of, iii. 346
Evil spirits, or, iii. 171
Indian races, of, iii. 275
Lanka, of, iii. 80, 278; iv. 321, 345; v. 535
Loka, v. 537
Pioneers became human, iii. 323
Preservers or, iii. 172
Pulastya progenitor of, iii. 235
Rāmāyana of, iii. 392
Sinhalese heirs of, iii. 406
Sons of will and Yoga, and, iii. 230
RĀKSHASI Bhāshā, Language of, iii. 204
RAM, Discus and horns of, iii. 217
Phoenician coin, on, iv. 116
Rams, not in authority over a flock, iii. 372
Symbol of generating power, iii. 189
RAM-headed, God of Egypt, iii. 293
Khnoom and Ammon are, ii. 82
RĀMA, Hanuman, adviser of, ii. 104
Lanka conquered by, iii. 228
Opponents conquered by, iii. 278
Parashu, iii. 45

Rāvana, and, iv. 63
RĀMANUJĀCHĀRYA, ii. 246
RAMSES, Fifth, v. 243
Records going to time of, iii. 367
Second, v. 243, 253, 329
Third, v. 243, 251
Twelfth, of Lepsius, v. 252
RAPA-NUI or Easter Island iii. 336
RAPHAEL, Archangel, ii. 347; v. 320, 325
Denouncer, iii. 381
Dragon, i. 185
Mercury and, v. 310, 439
RASA, Devas, v. 540
Mandala, v. 311, 322
Tala, v. 538, 540, 541, 546
RĀSHICHAKRAM, Zodiac, ii. 91
RA-SHOO or solar fire, ii. 24
RASIT or Wisdom, iv. 28
RĀTA or sacrificial offering, iv. 86
RATIO, Diameter to circumference of, i. 154
Modified form of, ii. 25
Musical Notes, of, v. 105, 509
Rational Refutation, A, quoted, i. 336
RĀTRI, night, one of four bodies of, Brahma, iii. 68
RAUMAS, Gods and, strife between, iii. 189
Roma-kupas, created from, iii. 78, 189
Vīrabhadra, created from, iii. 78
RĀVANA, Atlantean race, personification of, iv. 63
Lanka, king of, iii. 228, 235
Sita, carries off, iv. 141
RAVEN, Dove and, iv. 34
Source, number and value of word, ii. 161
RAVENS, Black, ii. 161
Human beings with, faces, iii. 16
Odin, of, iii. 108
RAWLINSON, quoted, i. 54; iii. 18, 39, 138' 429; iv. 290
RAY, Ain Soph, of, i. 262; ii. 64
Androgyne, or double, iv. 58
Ātmā, of absolute, i. 277, 289; v. 427
Ātmic, vehicle of, i. 229; v. 427
Boundless Unity of, v. 233
Central, from, i. 299; ii. 298
Cold light, of, ii. 83
Constellation of certain, iii. 186
Cosmic depths, dropped in, i. 138
Creative, i. 169
Divine, i. 137, 269; iii. 119, 197; v. 44, 128, 456
Energizing, iv. 29
Eternal egg to thrill, causes, i. 133
Ever-darkness, of, i. 127, 152
First mother, of, ii. 304
Flame of the, v. 362
Germ, had not flashed into, i. 127
Hansa-vāhana, is, i. 146
Higher Ego and, v. 553, 563, 564
Higher self and, v. 76, 128
Immaculate root, fructifies, i. 134
Incarnation of divine, iii. 234; v. 564
Life, of, iii. 119
Light drops one solitary, i. 133
Logos one, i. 146, 173
Male, iv. 127
Man, of unseen spirit, in, iii. 275
Mānasic, v. 511, 513, 533, 539, 564

RAY (*Contd.*)
Manifested, first, i. 167
Mundane egg, penetrated into, ii. 69
Noumenon of spiritual fire, from, iii. 114
Omnipresent spiritual, i. 136
One, i. 128, 178, 269; ii. 149; iv. 60
Paramārthika, from, ii. 71
Personal Deity and, v. 76
Primordial, i. 152
Radical triple, iii. 37
Ray, from, to, ii. 363
Reason, of, iii. 197, 234
Reincarnating, v. 552
Sanat Kumāra, of, v. 359
Septenary, iv. 175
Sevenfold, iii. 38
Severed, v. 564
Sunlight, of, ii. 332
Sun of, and Intiation, v. 270
Supreme, of, in all, v. 305
Uncreated, ii. 294
Universal Mahat, from, iii. 302
Universal mind, of, i. 81
Vehicle of, by Jīvas, i. 264
Water, of space, and, i. 277
Waters, of darkness moving on, ii. 68
White, one, iv. 60; v. 455
World soul, of the, v. 558
RAYS, Atoms become, ii. 360
Brightness, from home of, ii. 145
Chaldean Heptakis, of, i. 274
Creative forces, are, ii. 204
Dark flame, of, iii. 237
Dhyān Chohans, or, i. 181, v. 209
Essence, of, i. 181
Father-ray, of one, iv. 164
Hierarchies or, v. 459
Intercepted, ii. 321
Lion's crown, of, iv. 135
Logos of, v. 484
Monads are, i. 292; iii. 174; v. 358
Osiris, seven, of, iii. 150
Plexuses, seven, of seven nervous, iii. 101
Prakriti, seven, of, iv. 207
Procreation, i. 146
Religion, in every, ii. 297
Self-God and lower, ii. 363
Seven, i. 146, 179, 188, 274, 331; ii. 86, 240, 248, 249, 294, 297, 298; iii. 79, 101, 150; iv. 176, 179, 182, 184, 207, 341; v. 207, 356, 365, 423, 426, 459, 484
Soil shed on uncongenial, iii. 283
Solar, iii. 166; v. 423
Spiritual, i. 230; v. 456
Sun, of, i. 331; ii. 86, 240, 248; iii. 79,118; iv. 179, 182, 341; v. 423
Sūrya, of, iv. 176
Tetragrammaton, of, i. 140
Thought, direct, of, ii. 147
Time's seven, iv. 183
Velocity of chromatic, ii. 209
Vishnu enters, of sun, ii. 86
Wisdom, of, iii. 197
REABSORPTION, Dreamless sleep, not a, i. 309
Kosmos, of, i. 204
Laya state, into, ii. 274
Renovation and, ii. 192

READE, T. Mellard, quoted, iii. 23
READE on sedimentation in Europe, iv. 264
REAL life and death, v. 488, 491
REALITY, Conditionless, v. 400
One, v. 208, 214, 361, 388, 400, 411, 488
World of, v. 154, 456
REASON, Creation of, ii. 203
First race endowed with, iii. 251
Humanity endowed with, iii. 362
Intelligence and, v. 532
Logos, and speech, iii. 204
Number seven, and, ii. 124
Radicals, one of six, iv. 139
Ray of, iii. 234
Seat of, i. 288
REBEKAH, iv. 275; v. 239
REBELLION, Angels, of, i. 245, 246; ii. 301; iii. 72, 240, 249, 384
Archangels, and fall of, iii. 73
Children of, ii. 24; iii. 216
Demon of, iii. 276
Intellectual life, of, iii. 111
Kronos, of angels and Devas against, ii. 136
Nārada against Brahmā, of, iv. 156
Rudra, of, iv. 185
Satan, of, iii. 376; iv. 60
Sons of, iii. 385
REBELLIOUS, Divine law, to, iii. 89
Gods. iii. 71
Spirits, iii. 180
REBELS, Kronos destroys mightiest, ii. 136
Divine, iii. 111, 248
Genii separated from, i. 245
Kārmic law, under, iii. 103
Self-sacrifice, of, iii. 245
REBIRTH, Bhārata, of, iii. 321
Brāhmans, of, ii. 295
Cosmic, iii. 90
Cyclic law of, iii. 235, 248, 307
Devotees not exempt from, i. 150
Divine essence, of, iii. 249
Doctrine of, i. 224, 284; v. 83
Doom of continual, iv. 187
Druid belief in, iv. 329
Duration of successive, ii. 361
Ego or monad, of, iv. 205
Essenes believed in, iii. 120
Globe, of our, iv. 273
Gods and Demi-gods of, ii. 178; iii. 372
Individuality, of same, iii. 304
Isaac and Jacob, of, v. 84
Karma and, v. 247
Kārmic and cyclic, iii. 237, 304
Kosmos, of, ii. 359
Mahā Pralaya, after, ii. 86
Man, of, ii. 81
Monad, of, ii. 296
Nārada and, iii. 277, 323
Period between, v. 566
Planetary chains, of, i. 213
Primitive Gods, of, iii. 365
Punarjanman or, i. 333
Purification, after 3,000 years of, ii. 101
Religions and doctrine of, i. 284
Spiritual, iv. 37, 113; v. 83
Symbol of reclothing and, ii. 121
Theory of, v. 356

REBIRTH (Contd.)
Three kinds of, v. 351
World-saviours, of, ii. 383
Worlds, of, iii. 171
REBORN, Dhyāni, a, iii. 259
Gods and demi-Gods, iii. 250
Gods, in every age, iii. 235
Initiate, iv. 67, 72, 130
Kārmic effects, by reason of, iii. 174
Kumāras cursed to be, iv. 156
Nārada, in every cycle, iii. 323
Phoenix, from itself, iv. 188
Rishis, as men, iii. 318
Sages sacrificed themselves to be, iii. 358
RECKONING among all nations, Mode of,
  ii. 105
RECOALESCENCE, Brahma's contingent,
  iii. 79, 310
RECORDERS, Ancient wisdom, of, iv. 98
Archaic teaching, of, iv. 219
Lipika, of Karma, i. 165, 187, 190
RECORDS, Alpha and Omega of, iii. 54
Ancient, ii. 335; iii. 105
Antediluvian, iv. 105
Antiquity, of, iii. 436, 437
Archaic, iii. 15, 16, 36, 72, 162, 421, 434
Astral, i. 166
Astronomical, iii. 352
Atlantis, of, iii. 422
Babylonian, iv. 261
Belus, in temple of, i. 49
Buddhas of confession, of thirty-five, iii. 421
Chinese, i. 314; ii. 71
Christian wars, ii. 188
Church, destroyed by, i. 65
Cycles, of, v. 339, 340
Egyptian, i. 56; ii. 100
Floods, of, iii. 332
Fourth race, of, iv. 99
Hermaphrodite, of primeval divine, iii. 139
Hindu, ii. 386
History, symbolical of, iv. 323
Initiates, and, iii. 434; iv. 319
Jewish, iii. 408; iv. 41, 130
Kabalistic, iv. 24
Lemurians, of, iii. 265
Lipika and, of our world, i. 186
Matter, of every act in world of gross, i. 165
Mexican and Peruvian, v. 283
Mosaic, v. 178
Names, in, iii. 335
Nations, of, iv. 362
Number seven in, of peoples, iii. 47
Occult, i. 205; iv. 200; v. 178
Oldest races, of, iii. 345
Past and future of, iii. 428
Pesh-Hun, of, iii. 60
Philosophers, of early, ii. 395
Pre-Christian history, of, i. 62
Prehistoric periods, of, iii. 77; v. 89
Preservation of, iii. 254, 331
Racial development, of, iii. 371
Rig Veda oldest known, iv. 177
Sealed, of past, ii. 363
Secret, v. 144
Secret Doctrine, of, i. 56, 60; iii. 62, 72, 441
Serpents of wisdom, of, iii. 351

Tanned skins, on, iv. 262
Temples, of, iii. 436
Zodiac, and, ii. 371; iii. 61, 332, 367
Zuni, Indians, of, iv. 199
RECTOR (S), Ahriman of this world, v. 215
Egyptian Temples, in, v. 321
Hierarchies, of, iii. 36
Light of, i. 182
Mahārājah or, i. 182
Planets, of, ii. 216; v. 321, 332
Powerful, iv. 47
Pymander, seven, of, iii. 106
Regents, or, ii. 299
Seven, v. 287, 321
Spirits of the Sun, or, v. 216
World, of, ii. 125, 134; v. 331
RECTORES, Kepler's, ii. 222; iii. 239
Progenitors or, iii. 294
Tenebrarum, i. 182
RED, Atlanteans, iii. 431
Colour of Animal form, v. 454
Dragon, iii. 378, 382, 384
Green absorbs, v. 456, 457
Earth, iii. 199; iv. 21
Kāma Rūpa and, v. 456
Mars and, v. 437, 441
Quaternary and, v. 507
Races, iii. 198, 230, 251, 350, 422, 437;
  iv. 313, 349
Sandstone, Stonehenge built of, iii. 344
Sea, ii. 127
Spectrum in, v. 461, 508
Spiritual, v. 461
Zone was, third on every, iii. 313
RED-brown faces, iii. 185
RED-haired, Men going on all fours, iii. 191
Monsters, iii. 191
REDEEMER, Crucified, iv. 158
Good serpent, and, ii. 114
Satan our, iv. 82
REDEMPTION, Man, of, ii. 367; iii. 248; iv. 84
Sin, and, iii. 418
Theological dogma of, iv. 83
REES, A., referred to, iii. 390
REFLECTOR, Fire as, v. 562
REFORMATION, Father of, v. 165
REFORMER Tsong-Kha-Pa, the Tibetan,
  v. 391
REFULGENT face, iii. 423
REFUSAL to create, ii. 178; iii. 241, 245; iv. 57
REFUSE of human matter, iii. 177
REGENERATION, Destruction before, ii. 131
Generation, not, iv. 38
Life and, from old truths, i. 339
Sabbath, on, i. 285
Serpent symbol, of, i. 134, 140
Spiritual, ii. 81
REGENERATOR, Shiva, is, iii. 189
REGENT (S), Angel or, i. 181; iii. 93
Elohim are seven, iv. 56
Four Mahārājahs or, i. 181, 184
God of specific element, ii. 185
Gods, or, i. 207; iv. 56
Great Bear, of stars of, iii. 318
Group of Saturn, iii. 135
Iao, of Moon, ii. 167
Jupiter, of, iv. 66

REGENT (S) (Contd.)
Kabiri, over seasons, ii. 366
Kalpa, of each, iii. 186
Lokas of, v. 356
Mercury, of, v. 369
Moon, of, ii. 167; iii. 56, 324
Planets, of, ii. 110, 299, 300; iii. 35, 215, 360; v. 329, 333
Rulers or, of worlds, i. 161
Seven, ii. 139; iii. 215; iv. 57; v. 333, 356
Shukra, of, iii. 45
Soma, of visible moon, iii. 56
Star, iii. 361
Star of salvation, of, iii. 193
Supervisors, of, iii. 36
Theogony, moon one of seven, ii. 109
Zodiacal signs, of, iii. 357
REGIMEN IGNIS, i. 246
REGIONS, Earth of, v. 356
Seven, of Planetary System, v. 129
REGISTER, of Sacred Accounts of Pharaohs, v. 243
REINCARNATION (S), After sudden death, v. 564
Belief in, v. 82
Buddhas and Christs, of, ii. 364; v. 373
Chemistry as new alchemy, ii. 348
Cycle of, iv. 27
Cyclic and evolutionary, v. 357
Dreaded to be, i. 112
Druid belief in, iv. 329; v. 267
Ego of, v. 498, 499, 512, 552
Ego passes repeated, i. 83
Egyptians and, i. 273
Great men, of, v. 358
Immediate, v. 498
Individuality of same, v. 358
Jesus, of, v. 360
Kant and, ii. 326
Karma and, v. 247, 552
Krishna and Buddha, of, iii. 358
Lamaistic, v. 349
Manvantara, in every, iii. 235
Monad of, i. 308
Moon a symbol of, i. 275
Necessity for, i. 234
Process of, v. 473, 563
Ray of, v. 552
Skandhas, the, and, v. 560
Soul, of, iv. 122
Tibet, in, v. 393
Time between, iii. 304
Zarathushtra, of, iii. 19
REINCARNATIONISTS perceive mystery of life, i. 283
Allan Kardec school of, v. 82
REINDEER, Perigord, hunters of, iv. 318
Period, iv. 291
Pictures of, iv. 286, 289, 290, 291
Retreat of, iv. 310
REJECTED Son, i. 161, 162
REK, or Ark, Noose is a, iv. 117
RELATION, of Heavenly bodies to Man, v. 333
R-EL-AZAR, ii. 109; iii. 316
RELIGION, Age of no, ii. 400
Ancients of, ii. 113; iii. 115
Angels of western, i. 268

Anthropomorphic, Jewish is, v. 409
Apostles of western, iv. 126
Aryan Hindus and Persians, of, iv. 177
Astronomy, and, iii. 276
Australians, of, iv. 348
Babylonian, iv. 261
Brāhmanical, v. 41
Brihaspati and, iv. 69
Centres of, i. 52
Chaldean, iv. 111
Chemistry, and, i. 265
Christian, ii. 160; iii. 35, 388; v. 124
Christ's, and theology, ii. 160
Comparative, v. 55, 407
Concealed deity in every, ii. 155
Cyclic rise and fall of, iv. 292
Degraded, iv. 39
Dogmatic, iii. 113
Druids, of, iv. 325; v. 147
Dualism in Mazdean, iv. 86
Earlier copied by later, ii. 114
Egyptian, v. 298
Esotericism in, iv. 24
Evidence alien, estimated on external, ii. 138
Fiction, no, based on, iv. 365
Founders of, i. 58
Great Gods of every, iv. 178
Heliolatrous, iii. 378
Hindu Āryan, iv. 38, 177
Humanity, one ennobling, of, ii. 97
Indian, iv. 97
Jews, of, ii. 107
Lemurians, of, iii. 274
Magic and, v. 42
Mazdean or Magian, iii. 19, 101; iv. 86
Metaphor in every, iii. 107
Modern, v. 70
Monotheistic Jewish is, v. 185
Moon in, i. 231; ii. 102
Nabatheans, of, iv. 22
Nature, of, iv. 365
Occultist, and, v. 70, 123, 124
Ophite, iii. 378
Phallic element in, iii. 275; iv. 153
Phoenician, iii. 437
Primeval, iv. 189
Primitive, ii. 184
Race which never originated a, iv. 293
Roman Catholic, iii. 94; v. 128, 231
Science and, i. 117; ii. 22, 331, 393; v. 350
Scripture of a prehistoric, iv. 51
Seven in, ii. 297; iii. 357; iv. 162, 169
Sexual element in, ii. 96; iii. 230
State or National, v. 121
Supernatural, v. 168
Svastika and Christian, iv. 158
Symbols of, i. 286; v. 291, 407
Theosophy not a, i. 58
Thinkers produce a, i. 337
Third and fourth, races, of, iii. 274
Trojan, iv. 364
True definition of, iii. 274
Truth, no higher than, i. 63; iv. 366
Western, i. 268; iv. 126, 145
Wisdom, iii. 377; v. 68, 181, 302, 364
Xenophantes, of, iv. 104

RELIGIONS, Analysis of, ii. 142
  Ancient, and philosophies, iv. 227
  Dogmatic, i. 246; iii. 376, 413
  Eastern, iv. 240; v. 436
  Esotericism in Asiatic, v. 406
  Exoteric, i. 307, 319; iii. 115, 283, 402;
    iv. 71, 151, 159
  Founders of, v. 155
  Hindu sects, of, iv. 159
  Justin Martyr on identity of, iv. 58
  Karma of, v. 247, 315
  Modern, iv. 228
  Mysteries of, v. 138
  Old, i. 76; iv. 178
  One conception in all, ii. 142; iv. 329; v. 267
  Origin of modern, iii. 276
  Past, never to return, i. 62
  Seeds of old, iv. 51
  Sexual emblems of, iv. 155
  Source of, i. 60
  Systems of, iv. 163
RELIGIOUS, emblems, v. 248
  Reformers, v. 128
REMUSAT, Abel, referred to, ii. 194; v. 408
RENAN, referred to, i. 67; v. 53
RENEWALS, of globe Seven, iii. 109, 134, 189
RENOUF, referred to, ii. 16, 114, 117
RENUNCIATION, of Adepts, v. 80
  Nirvāna, of, v. 351, 354
REPENTANCE, Deathbed, v. 560
  Ego and, v. 502
REPHAIM or primitive men, ii. 59; iii. 281; iv.65
REPRODUCTION, Animal, iii. 220
  Budding, by, iii. 125
  Chasm between systems of, iv. 304
  Engravings, of, ii. 233
  Fissiparous act of, iii. 141
  Modes of, iii. 173, 179; iv. 228, 229
  Powers of, iv. 24
  Processes of, ii. 332
  Ram's head symbol of, iii. 189
  Season of, iii. 126
  Sexual, iii. 109, 141
  Tendency to, iv. 164
  World, of, iv. 188, 273
REPRODUCTIVE system, Sensitiveness of,
    iv. 217
REPTILES, Ages of, iii. 66, 163, 206, 209, 260
  Amphibious, iii. 194, 206
  Avarice, iv. 209
  Birds and, ii. 120; iii. 190, 347; iv. 303
  Eyes of, iii. 300
  First trace of, iv. 282
  Foetus like, a, iii. 194
  Garuda's descent from, iii. 256
  Physical embryo, i. 235
  Physical man, preceded, iv. 166
  Saliva of, poisonous, i. 305
  Septenary law and, iv. 193
  Third round, resultant of, iv. 254
REPTILIA to the Aves, iv. 227
REPTILIAN, Fauna, iv. 254
  Gigantic, monster, iii. 161; iv. 166
  Secondary age or, iii. 164
RESHA, Hiv Rah, the white head, iii. 93
RESPONSIBILITY, Beginning of wisdom,
    the, v. 552, 553

of Ego, v. 499, 551, 552, 564
  Physical or Karma, v. 503
REST, Activity, and, i. 131
  Brahma, of, ii. 92
  Centre of, iii. 242
  Ccsmic, iii. 311
  Creative force, of, ii. 89
  Cycles of, iv. 115
  Eternal, i. 285
  Forty-nine stages of, iv. 317
  Land and water need, iv. 294
  Motion and, i. 176
  Nirvāna and, iii. 283
  Paranirvāna, of, i. 192
  Sabbath means, i. 285
  Worlds at, iv. 274
RESURRECTION, Adytum symbol of, iv. 27
  Church lamps, I am the, on, ii. 101
  Dogma, v. 83
  Emblem of, of nature, ii. 194
  Field of, iii. 109
  Frog symbol and, ii. 100
  Jesus, of, iv. 112; v. 150
  Life, of, iv. 29
  Many into one life, of, i. 311
  Mystery language, and, ii. 23
  Phoenix bird of, ii. 24; iv. 188
  Sadducees deny, v. 83
  Sarcophagus symbol of, iv. 28
  Son of, v. 360
  Sound, by, ii. 279
  Spiritual, v. 451
  Witnesses, of old, iv. 308
RETARDATION, Law of, iii. 179, 262
  Planet, of a, ii. 227
  Tidal, iii. 74
RETRAHENS muscle, iv. 251
RETRIBUTION, Bitter cup of, i. 239
  Karma law of, i. 165; ii. 359; iii. 306; iv. 125
RETZIUS, Professor, quoted, iv. 360
REUBEN, Aquarius, in sphere of, ii. 377
REUCHLIN John, referred to, v. 216
REUEL Jethro, the Midian Priest Initiator,
    iv. 33
REUVENS, quoted, v. 254
REVEALER, Fifth, in next round, i. 115
  Logos of God, of man, iv. 161
  Mystery, of the, v. 163
REVELATION (S), Bible and other, iv. 230
  Christ in, iv. 204
  Christian, v. 176
  Conditions of new, iii. 291
  Cosmogony, of system of, i. 222
  Cycle of, iv. 190
  Damaged has been, iii. 390
  Divine and Jewish derivations, i. 49; ii. 16;
    v. 95, 167
  Enoch, and, iv. 53, 65, 80
  Eternal, v. 364
  Genesis not a, iv. 17
  Haeckel's, iv. 240
  John, of Saint, ii. 127; iii. 355; iv. 51, 75;
    v. 100; v. 202, 313
  Marcus, of, ii. 66
  Meaning of, ii. 21
  Mother of, ii. 383
  Occult, v. 73

REVELATION (S) (*Contd.*)
Pentateuch a, iii. 16
Primeval, i. 53; ii. 71, 347
Prometheus, of myth of, iii. 417
Races and rounds in, iv. 135
Religion and, iv. 365
Sciences, of, iii. 363
Secret spiritual knowledge, of, i. 313
Semitic, from Aryans, ii. 381
Seven, four out of, i. 115
Shruti or, i. 313
Spiritistic, iv. 270
Thought inspired by, ii. 55
Universal language, and, ii. 29
Vāch to Rishis, of, iii. 115
Veiled, are misleading, iv. 80
World, to each, iv. 278
REVERSION, Ancestral features, to, iv. 255
Science, of, iii. 66
Tree, of growth of, ii. 123
Type, to, iv. 294
REVISED Version of Gospels, ii. 294
REVOLUTION of Poles of the Earth, v. 347
REYMOND, Du Bois, referred to, ii. 243
REYNOLDS, Prof., Emerson, referred to, ii. 274
RHEA, Goddess, ii. 164; Kronos and, iii. 271
Titans, sons of, and Kronos, iii. 150, 151
RHINOCEROS, iv. 305, 320, 343
RHIPAEUS, Mount, iii. 20
RHIZOMATA, Four elements called, iv. 171
R'HIZ'QEE-YAH, a Kabalist, ii. 109
RHODES, Ironworkers of, iii. 390
Telchines, birthplace of the, iii. 390
RHOMBOID, Egyptian egg of world, ii. 127
RHOMBS, Chaldean, v. 55, 123
RIBHUS, Planetary spirits or, ii. 176; iii. 65
RICCIOLI, Mean motions of, ii. 390, 391
RICCIUS, Augustinus, quoted, ii. 388
RICE, Symbolic Meaning of, v. 105
RICHARDSON, and Barth, quoted, iii. 345
RICHARDSON, Dr. B. W., quoted, ii. 222, 248, 249, 251, 255, 256, 261, 304, 327, 359; iv. 224
RICHET, C., quoted, ii. 365; iii. 164
RICHTER, quoted, ii. 201
RIDDLE, Ages, of, iii. 358
Apollonius of, v. 143
Biblical, iii. 374
Birth, of, i. 290
Chinese, iv. 33
Comprehension of, ii. 369
Cross, of, iv. 126
Eighth sphere, of, i. 211
Past, of, ii. 361
Science, of, iii. 76
Sphinx, of, i. 215; iii. 133, 401; iv. 85, 110
RIDER, Thought is the, i. 168
RIGHT One, or Pater Sadic, iii. 391
RIGHT-hand, Adepts, ii. 135; v. 123, 419
Jupiter, of, ii. 116
Paths of knowledge, i. 243
RIGHT path, Initiates of, iv. 62; v. 85
Prophets, adepts of, iii. 215
Sodales of, iii. 215
RIGHTEOUSNESS, Sons of, v. 153, 276
RIKSHA and Great Bear, i. 274; iv. 202; v. 324
RIKSHAS, Bright-crested, ii. 172
RIMMON, God of storms, iii. 352

RING(S), Body in, during worship, iv. 122
Dvīpas form concentric, iv. 328
Lokas called, i. 253
Luminous, round moon, ii. 314
Nebulous, i. 189, 205; ii. 221, 224, 316
One is, i. 77
Pass not, called, i. 187, 189; v. 517
Planetary chains or, i. 213
Pralaya, not till next, i. 190
Rounds, used for, i. 221
Saturn, of, iii. 237
Septenary our, i. 200; ii. 297
Servants small, iii. 15, 40
Wheels watch, i. 187
Yugas called, ii. 362
Zodiacal, relic of, iv. 71
RISHA Havurah, White hidden fire in the, ii. 52
RISHABHA, a quality of sound, ii. 258, iii. 406
RISHAYAH, Deva-putra, iv. 177
RISHI AGASTYA. i, 24
RISHI BRIHASPATI, v. 165
RISHI Kapila, branch of one tree, i. 256
RISHI-Manus, Seven and ten, iii. 365
RISHI- Prajāpati, Primeval, i. 76, 186
RISHI-Yogis more powerful than Gods, iii. 88
RISHIS, Agni, and, iv. 120
Allegory of, iv. 283
Ancient, iv. 177
Anupādaka and, ii. 295
Ark, in, iii. 314
Aryan scriptures, of, iv. 184
Asuras and, ii. 301
Brahmā and, iv. 196; v. 291, 325
Brahmā-Prajāpati and, iii. 56
Brahmā-Vishnu and, i. 75
Bhrigu one of, iii. 45, 86
Buddhas or, iii. 421
Cabiri Titans, resemble, iii. 150
Caves of, iii. 380
Classes of, iv. 183
Cosmogony of, iv. 16
Creative, i. 260
Creators or, ii. 70
Crown, issue from, ii. 151
Cyclic return of Virgin, and, v. 337
Daksha's daughters and, ii. 245
Deep, come forth from, iv. 63
Deity is, i. 173
Descendants of, iii. 228
Devas and, iii. 95
Earth, walking, ii. 113
Fathers, iii. 261, 292
Fifth race, of, iv. 177
Falmes and, iii. 250
Genealogies of, iii. 250
Generic name of, iii. 311
God of, i. 75
Great, iii. 148
Great Bear, of, ii. 72; iv. 57, 120, 202, 338
Gurus, called, iv. 197
Hindus, of, i. 75; iii. 423
Hierarchy of, v. 356
Indian, iii. 106, 138, 365
Individualities of, i. 281; iii. 358
Intelligences, iii. 46
Inventors were, iii. 372
Kabiri and, iii. 360

RISHIS (Contd.)
Kāshyapa one of, iii. 381
Krishna, from mind of, iii. 318
Lords of being, are, ii. 60
Mantras, authors of, ii. 160
Manu saved with, iii. 147
Manus and, ii. 366; iii. 185, 255, 286, 360, 366
Manvantaras, from past, i. 255; iii. 88
Meanings of, historical and ethical, i. 174
Messengers or angels to, i. 248
Mortals, reborn as, iv. 345
Mysterious, iv. 119
Nārada one of, ii. 130; iii. 59, 91, 277 iv. 156; v. 287
Nine, instead of seven, ii. 154
Paramarishis or, ii. 137
Parāshara on, ii. 176; iii. 235
Past and present, iv. 139
Period, created and perish at one, ii. 91
Pesh-Hun one of, iii. 60
Pitris, and, i. 161; iii. 56
Pleiades, and, iv. 119, 121
Pramlocha's child by, iii. 182
Progeny of, iii. 188
Purānas, in, iii. 286; iv. 186
Ruler, would not leave earth without, iv. 93
Saptarishis, become, iii. 98
Satya Yuga, appeared during, v. 324
Second race, of, iv. 335
Secret wisdom of, iv. 104
Seven, i. 274; ii. 64, 87; iii. 79; iv. 196; v. 41, 202, 203, 207, 333
Soma, and, iv. 67
Stars, and, i. 248; ii. 172
Third root-race, of, i. 257; iii. 103
Three classes of, iv. 70
Transformations of, ii. 160
Ursa Major, and, iv. 338
Vāch and, ii. 148; iii. 115
Vaivasvata Manu and, iii. 48, 150, 154, 215
Vedas, wrote down, v. 371
Vishnu and, iii. 313
Year of seven, iii. 308
RISHOON is lunar spirit, Adam, iii. 396
RITE(S) Funeral, v. 245, 250
Initiation, of, v. 152, 159, 161, 168, 282, 290 291, 313, 377
Kurukshetra, of, v. 94
Latin Church, in, v. 95
Occult, v. 248
Sun, of the, v. 272
RITUAL, Aryasanga, of, v. 168
Egyptian, ii. 24, 74; iv. 206
Exoteric, iii. 275
Initiation, of, v. 96
Judaism, of, v. 200
Latin Church, of v. 53
Magic, founded on, ii. 192
Spirits of stars, for, i. 182
RITUALISM, Biblical, iv. 113
Church, iii. 382; v. 463
Hindu, iii. 87
Masonry, in, v. 463
Orthodox and sectarian, iv. 137
Yogis, opposed by great, ii. 133
RITUALISTIC, Astrology, v. 335
Dogma of John the Baptist, iv. 136

Exoteric, form, iii. 57; iv. 139
Pomp, iv. 71
Worship, iii. 57; iv. 317
RIVER-Gods of Greeks, ii. 59
RIVERS, Animals in, ii. 332
Genius loci of, ii. 183
India, of, iv. 175
Life, shores of, i. 319
Past, of, iv. 45
Running waves of, i. 282
Seven, of heaven and earth, ii. 60; iii. 322; iv. 176, 188
Sky, of, iv. 177
RIVETT-CARNAC, referred to, iii. 345
ROARER, Passions of Rudra make him, iv. 118
ROBE of my strength, Glorious, iv. 152
ROBES, Ever invisible, i. 109, 116
Noumenon, stand for, i. 109
Sun's outward, ii. 252, 307
ROCH or seers, v. 186, 187
ROCHAS, A. de, quoted, ii. 370
ROCHESTER Cathedral, iii. 94
ROCHETTE, Raoul, quoted, ii. 115; iii. 344; iv. 116
ROCK-born God, Mithras, ii. 54; iii. 139
ROCK-temples of Hindustan, ii. 34
ROCKET, Āgneyāstra a, iv. 200
ROCKING stones, iii. 342, 346
ROD, Caduceus, of, ii. 273
Four kārmic deities, of, iii. 425
Two serpents twined round, iii. 363
RODS, Bunch of metallic, iv. 86
Hawk's wings, with, iii. 359
ROGER Bacon, an adept, ii. 276
Knowledge of, ii. 305
ROHANEE, Ātmā-Vidyā called, i. 249
ROHINI, Krishna and Logos, iv. 96
ROLLESTON, Prof., quoted, iv. 296
ROMA-kūpas, Raumas created from, iii. 189
Sanskrit for hair-pores, iii. 78
ROMAKA-pura, Asuramaya lived in, iii. 78
Atlantis, part of, iii. 62
Māyā assigned to, iii. 62
ROMAN, Civilization, iii. 427
Colonization, era of, iv. 293
Foot, inch is base of, ii. 25
Gallows cross, iv. 158
Lustrum, v. 340
Numeral system, v. 342
Sacred records, iii. 408
Sacr-factum of, priest, iv. 35
Septenary in, thought, iv. 184
Week, v. 433
ROMAN CATHOLICISM, Christian Kabalah and, v. 231
Proofs of inspiration of, ii. 117
Religion of sensualism, iii. 94
Symbolism, in, ii. 263
ROMAN CATHOLICS, Angelology of, v. 320, 326
Angels recognized by, i. 185, 280, 281; iii. 98; v. 76, 128, 319, 320, 327, 386
Ardent, ii. 188
Belief, i. 280
Bible, version of, i. 186
Borrowings of, iv. 49

ROMAN CATHOLICS (*Contd.*)
Christians, i. 328
Colossal stones, and, iii. 345
Count de Maistre and, ii. 328
Creation, on, ii. 185
Deduction from a dogma of, ii. 135
Esoterism, and, v. 78
Ethereal prototype, and, iv. 49
Fathers, v. 46
Genii of seven planets of, i. 247
Gnostics and, v. 93
Greek Church and, iv. 207; v. 93, 139
Heavenly hosts of, i. 163
Interpretation of, ii. 203
Intolerance of, ii. 121
Kabalists and, iv. 47
Luther and, iii. 136
Magic and, v. 45, 48
Magicians, legends of, iii. 240
Marriage with, is a sacrament, iv. 35
Mazdean literature, and, iv. 44
Missionaries, v. 38, 390
Moon, and, Virgin Mary and, ii. 108
Mussulmans, and, iii. 44
New Testament, ii. 78
Occultists, and, i. 65, 181
Priests, v. 48
Prometheus, and drama of, iii. 411
Prophecy by, iii. 412
Providence female with, ii. 359
Purgatory of, v. 359
Ritual of, i. 182
Satan and, ii. 337; iv. 79
Scholiasts, iii. 407
Stars, believe in seven great, iv. 22
Sun worship and, v. 219, 317
Supernatural and, v. 54
Theologians of, iii. 374
Vase of election of, iv. 97
Virgin Mary, and, i. 155; ii. 108
Writers, v. 216, 240, 302
Zodiac, and, ii. 375, 377
ROMAN (or ROMISH) Church
Bible and, v. 313
Bishops of, v. 93
Conversions of, v. 37
Gnostics and, v. 93, 327
Idolatry and, v. 219
Magic and, v. 48, 257
Monotheists and, v. 216
Occultists and, v. 121
Pagan origin of rites, personages and symbols
of, v. 95
Pentateuch and Vulgate of, v. 179
Peter did not found, v. 139
Spiritualism and, v. 45
Sun and, v. 317
ROMAN EMPIRE, Referred to, v. 165
Scholars of, v. 33, 34
ROMANES, G. J., F. R. S., quoted, iii. 423;
iv. 217, 251
ROMANS, Ævum of, v. 108
Atlanto-Aryans, remnants of, iii. 434; iv. 312
Atma and wind identical, thought, i. 273
Chronology of, from India, iv. 191
Ciphering among, ii. 76
Cross used by, for torture, iv. 130

Cycle of five years, v. 340
Hindus gave, astronomy, ii. 384
Races, used vowels to denote five, iv. 26
ROME, Civilization before that of, iv. 355
Classics of, by monks, iii. 439
Éliphas Lévi and, iv. 132; v. 231
Pope of, styled Lucifer, iii. 45
Simon Magus visited, v. 126
Spirits of stars honoured at, i. 182
Svastika found at, iv. 158
ROMULUS, disappearance of, v. 148
Regarded as a myth, ii. 64
RONORORAKA, Images at, iii. 337
ROOT(S), All, of, Ākāsha is, v. 381
Color and sound, of, v. 459, 460
Elect, v. 91
Eternal, v. 227, 233
Sigē, as, v. 446
Trinity, of, v. 519
ROOT-abstraction, iv. 116
ROOT-base of hierarchy of Arhats, i. 255
ROOT-essence, Creative force radiating from,
ii. 360; v. 488, 494
ROOT-form of each kingdom, iii. 192
ROOT-Kumāra, Shvetalohita, iii. 251
ROOT-manu, every round a, iii. 321
Globe A, on, iii. 154
Noah and, iv. 169
Prime cause, i. 281
Seed-manu, and, i. 281; iii. 309
ROOT-Principle, One Element of, v. 208
Primordial chaos, and, ii. 45
Universe, of, i. 293
World stuff, of, ii. 246
ROOT-Race (s), America and Europe, in, ii. 200
Ancient people of fifth, iv. 175
Apes descend from fourth, iv. 253
Arhatship at end of this, i. 255
Aryan, our, iii. 21; iv. 268, 349
Atlantean of fourth, i. 240
Avatāras and, v. 336
Bible chronology and, v. 102
Bi-sexual unity of third, iii. 144
Changes with every, i. 235
Course run by every, iv. 349
Dawn of a new, iv. 349, 353
Dhyānis and, i. 114; iii. 58
Distinct, iii. 136, 440
Divine dynasties in every, iii. 426
Divisions of, iii. 431
Downward tendency of each, iv. 354
Earliest, iii. 164
Enoch and Noah and, iv. 102
Equatorial line, our, has crossed, iii. 302
Ethereal, first, iii. 57
Eruopean humanity, of, iv. 267
Evolution, of, iii. 23, 59
Evolvers of first, ii. 175
Fifth, i. 87, 173, 236, 237; ii. 183, 200, 334,
376; iii. 21, 431, 432; iv. 175, 208, 267,
349; v. 106, 109
First, i. 214, 242; ii. 91, 175; iii. 47, 57, 94,
146, 154, 256, 269; iv. 254, 275, 283, 331,
370; v. 102
Fourth, i. 167, 240, 257; iii. 133, 148, 153,
175, 185; iv. 239, 253, 283; v. 37, 103, 106,
121, 260

ROOT-Race(s) (*Contd.*)
  Genealogical tree of fifth, iii. 432
  Globe D, on, i. 214
  Greek temples, recorded in, iv. 29
  Hermaphrodites of third, iii. 43
  Human, iv. 24
  Incarnation of third, iii. 250
  Last sub-races of third, iv. 334
  Mankind of first, iii. 154, 256
  Men at close of third, iii. 204
  Mind, v. 472
  Nārada in each, iii. 92
  Origin of Āryan, iv. 268
  Pentacle symbolized five, i. 183
  Period of a, iii. 403
  Pole-star and founders of, iv. 338
  Pre-Adamic, ii. 91
  Present or fifth, ii. 376
  Primitive, iii. 43
  Production of life in next, ii. 122
  Races, applies to one of seven, iii. 203;
    iv. 267
  Raivata and, v. 259
  Religion of third, iii. 274
  Revealer necessary for each, i. 115
  Rishis and Devas of third, i. 257; iii. 88
  Round, of each, iii. 396; iv. 135
  Rudra Shiva and, iv. 70
  Sacred tree typifies, iii. 112
  Sages of fifth, iv. 208
  Second, iii. 18, 78, 126, 146, 153, 172, 174;
    iv. 254; v. 102, 103, 165
  Seed of fifth, i. 173
  Seed of man at beginning of, iii. 154
  Senses of each, iii. 116
  Seven, v. 249
  Seven keys open mysteries of seven, ii. 38
  Seventh, i. 168; iii. 277, 441; iv. 189
  Shells in first two, ii. 176
  Sixth, i. 168, 236, 338; iii. 441, 442; iv. 349
  Sons of wisdom and third, i. 255
  Species change with every, iv. 267
  Sub-races of, iii. 331, 431; iv. 186
  Tau glyph of third, i. 72
  Third, i. 72, 173, 232, 239, 240, 255, 257, 271,
    309; iii. 43, 58, 78, 88, 103, 106, 133, 144,
    155, 174, 179, 184, 204, 250, 274, 307, 368,
    424, 433; iv. 100, 239, 334; v. 102, 260,
    291, 300, 429, 430
  Three and a half, iii. 119
  Yuga may mean, a, iii. 155
ROOT-types, Astral, iv. 306, 307
  Mammalian, iv. 258, 298, 305
  Primeval animal, iv. 219
ROOTLESS, Root, i. 79, 80, 136; ii. 123;
    v. 90, 425
  Tree, iv. 55
ROPE of angels, i. 154
ROSARY, Blessed Virgin, of, iii. 50
  Serpent, on neck of a, iii. 186
ROSCELINI, referred to, i. 70
ROSE, Crucified, v. 292
ROSE and cross, Union of, i. 84
ROSECROIX, Symbol of, i. 146
ROSENKRANZ, Fludd on, i. 137
ROSENROTH, quoted, i. 262; ii. 106
ROSETTA stone, ii. 400; iv. 31

ROSICRUCIAN (S), Adepts and, v. 105
  Alchemist, and, ii. 336; v. 85, 174, 175
  Fire, definition of, i. 180
  Jehovah screen for, ii. 156
  Magi, idea of fire from, i. 146
  Manuscript, cypher, iii. 207
  Masons and, v. 274, 284
  Paracelsus a great, i. 325
  Philosophy, i. 73
  Rosy cross, origin of name, i. 84
  Sidereal light of, ii. 52
  Symbol of, v. 292, 293
  Tenets of, i. 137; iii. 240
ROSSMASSLER, quoted, ii. 365
ROSY CROSS, Brothers of, i. 84; iv. 172;
    v. 292
ROTA or Taro, v. 109
ROTAE, Wheels called, i. 176
ROTATION, Axis of, displacement of, iv. 104
  Caused by collision of nebular masses, ii. 224
  Collision produced, i. 294
  Contradictory hypotheses as to, ii. 229
  Disturbances in axial, iii. 314
  Earth of, ii. 292; iii 74, 324
  Etheric centres, of, ii. 281
  Force of, ii. 223
  Generation of, ii. 291
  Incipient, ii. 229
  Intelligences, result of, ii. 325
  Magnet, of molecules of a, iv. 288
  Mand or manth implies, iii. 411
  Motion of, ii. 253
  Nebula, of a, ii. 316
  Planet's, on its axis, ii. 316
  Satellites, inverse, of, ii. 299
  Science, theories of, in, ii. 224
  Svastika and, of time, iii. 108
  Theory of, ii. 223
ROTATIONAL evolution of our solar system,
    ii. 225
ROTH, Professor, quoted, iv. 177
ROUGÉ, Viscount de, referred to, i. 192; ii. 114;
    iii. 357; v. 140, 243, 245, 247, 249, 252,
    253, 256
ROUGEMONT, De, quoted, iii. 370; iv. 21;
    v. 329
ROUND, Antiquity of man in this, iv. 267
  Astral man, began with, iii. 177
  Awakening at beginning of, iii. 308
  Cast-off materials of, iii. 78
  Cataclysms in every, iii. 332
  Continent lasts through each, iii. 19
  Culmination of a, ii. 367
  Cycle of our special, iii. 366
  Deluge in this, ii. 85
  Development, brings a new, i. 216
  Duration of, iv. 134
  Earth, in this, governors of, i. 169
  Evolutionary work of preceding, i. 238
  Fifth, i. 215, 216, 236, 301; iii. 264; v. 532, 563
  First, i. 214, 227, 295, 297, 302, 303; iii. 58.
    78, 154; iv. 206
  Fourth, i. 78, 115, 167, 196, 216, 229, 237
    238, 242, 255, 292, 297, 304; ii. 161; v. 563
  Geological cataclysm which put end to, iii. 265,
  Globe and, our, ii. 337
  Humanity, our, and, iv. 182

ROUND (*Contd.*)
  Island at North Pole prevails during this, iii. 399
  Kalpa or, iii. 58
  Lunar chain, of, i. 224
  Mammalians in this, iii. 163, 187
  Man in this, i. 87, 239; iii. 15; iv. 23
  Manu, of every, i. 132
  Manus in every, fourteen, iv. 186
  Manvantara or, iv. 184
  Midway, present, is, iii. 169
  New, compound elements in every, i. 295
  New type at beginning of each, iii. 291
  Planetary chain in last, i. 210
  Pralaya and, i. 215; iii. 329
  Race and, this, i. 331
  Relics of preceding, iv. 282
  Renewal or, iv. 134
  Root-races in each, seven, iv. 135
  Second, i. 226, 295, 296, 297, 303
  Sedimentation in this, iii. 283
  Seven, Races of each, ii. 398
  Seventh, i. 78, 210, 285; ii. 240; iii. 175; iv. 59, 136; v. 536, 563
  Seventh race of our, iii. 109
  Sixth, i. 78, 215; v. 563
  Speaking race in this, first, iv. 19
  Spirit and matter in this, i. 233
  Terrestrial, i. 214; iv. 255
  Third, i. 280, 292, 297, 304; iii. 67, 88, 124, 193, 196; iv. 253, 254, 300
  Third root-race in fourth, i. 240
  Transition point of this, iii. 263
  Vaivasvata manvantara, or, i. 64
  Yuga may mean a, iii. 155
ROUND TABLE, iii. 392, 397
ROUND TOWER (S), Bhagulpore of, iii. 94
  Ireland of, v. 217, 284, 285
ROUNDS, Actuality of seven, iv. 267
  Cycle, in preceding, i. 310
  Destruction of fossils of, iv. 298
  Ego in remote, iii. 290
  Esoteric Buddhism, in, i. 228, 237
  Evolution, as arena of, iii. 259; iv. 135
  First four, i. 295
  Generally explained, i. 227, 229, 233, 234, 235, 239, 277, 278
  Globes, and, i. 213, 215, 248
  Interim between, iv. 282
  Life and evolution, of, iv. 135
  Man, cycles and, i. 221
  Man in previous, iii. 257; iv. 303
  Manvantaras and, iii. 187, 431; iv. 317
  Material evolution through, i. 296
  Monads and, iii. 67, 175
  Numbers concerning, i. 223
  Pralaya makes gulf between, i. 215
  Races preceding our, iv. 187
  Root-races, and, i. 114
  Scriptures, and races in, iv. 316
  Seven, i. 213, 283; iii. 396; iv. 189; v. 374
  Three, to come, i. 214, 286; iii. 187, 308
  Types from preceding, iv. 230
  Wheels, small, or, i. 113
  Zodiac, of, v. 347
ROUTERS or rocking stones, iii. 344, 345
ROW, P. Sreenivas, Computations by, iii. 79

ROYAL ACADEMY (of France), referred to, v. 51
ROYAL ASIATIC SOCIETY, ii. 85
ROYAL INSTITUTION, referred to, ii. 15
ROYAL SOCIETY Bacon to, from, iii. 437
  Fellow of, ii. 351
  Geological periods, on, iii. 22
  Mellard Read before, iii. 23
  Nebular theory and, ii. 319
RU, Hieroglyphic, iv. 117
  Third eye is, set upright, iv. 118
RUACH, Evolution of ideas and, i. 289
  Hayum, Boreas called, ii. 187
  Image, able to substitute, i. 290
  Nephesh, united to, i. 243
  Seat of passions or, iv. 176
  Spirit or, i. 272, 287; iii. 93, 377; v. 166, 209
  Spiritual soul or, i. 287
  Tzelem of, iv. 205
  Wind, equals, i. 273
RUA'H or spirit, iii. 316
RUBIDIUM, Crookes on, ii. 276
RUDBECK, a Swedish scientist, iii. 401; iv. 342
RUDIMENT, Element, ii. 290
RUDIMENTARY, Elements, iii. 116
  Man, i. 293; iii. 121
  Organs, iii. 179, 191; iv. 251, 253
  Principles, ii. 174
  Tail, iii. 328; iv. 251
RUDIMENTS First and second races, of, iii. 116
  Senses, of future, ii. 165
RUDRA, Brahma, from head of, i. 201
  Creates beings, ii. 177
  Getting married, after, iii. 284
  God of fire, iv. 118
  Indra and, led Gods, iv. 66
  Janardana, becoming, ii. 86
  Kārtikeya, son of, iv. 190
  Kumāra, a, iii. 251; iv. 147
  Mahadeva, as, iv. 118
  Mrida form of, iii. 404
  Nilalohita or, ii. 176; iii. 115, 198
  Principle, immediate production of first, ii. 174
  Saints, birth of, and, ii. 175
  Shiva, a form of, ii. 86, 176, 179; iii. 381; iv. 184
  Vishnu as, ii. 86
RUDRA-Kumāras, iii. 114, 257; iv. 185
RUDRA-Shiva, destroying God, iii. 171
  Names of, iv. 70
  Seed of, iv. 120
  Vishnu becomes, ii. 250
  Yogi, great, iv. 70
RUDRAS, Apsarasas and other, iv. 157
  Arūpa Gods, are, iii. 318
  Aryas, of ancient, iii. 95
  Classes of, iii. 188
  Dhyān Chohans and, iii. 282
  Grandfathers, called, iii. 250
  Incarnation of, iii. 248
  Maruts, or, iv. 118, 187
  Parāshara on, iii. 235
  Pre-Brahmanical, iii. 171
  Tempting demons, called, iii. 181
  Vedic deities, eleven, were, i. 138
RUDU is two months of mortals, a, iv. 191, 192

RUINS, Archaic town of, Tibet, of, i. 55
  Atlantis, of, iii. 407
  Babian, of, iv. 175
  Colossal, iii. 338
  Cyclopean, iii. 265, 340
  Palenque, of, iii. 428
  Peru, in, iv. 315
  Primitive system, of, iv. 29
  Uxmal, of, iii. 428
RULER, Dayanisi, of men, ii. 113
  Ego, not the, ii. 48
  Hiranyaksha, of Patala, iii. 381
  Invisible, ii. 326
  Mithras, of year, iv. 42
  Nature, God of Semite, of, ii. 98
  Sphere, of, iv. 140
  Universe, of, iii. 48
  Vara, of, iii. 19
  Zarathushtra, iii. 19; iv. 181
RULES, Appearance, with man's, iii. 328
  Atoms, of these groups of, ii. 276
  Divine, iii. 317, 365
  Elementals guided by, i. 201
  Four high, i. 183
  Globe, sidereal, of our, iv. 269
  Governors, or, iii. 105
  Heaven, of sidereal, ii. 216
  Pitris, and, iii. 98
  Planet, of this, iv. 82
  Planetary Gods and, iii. 57; v. 443, 460, 536
  Primeval races, of, iii. 392
  Regents or, of world, i. 161
  Seven, ii. 126
  Sidereal powers, Kabiri, of, iii. 363
  Spheres, astral, of, ii. 301
  Stars, of, ii. 127
  System, of our, iv. 192
  Third race men, of, iv. 351
  World, of, ii. 376; iii. 105; iv. 83
RUMBLING stone of Irish, iii. 342
RUNES, Fragments of, v. 121
  Sigurd learned in, ii. 121
RUNIC writing, iii. 346
RUNNERS or Theoi, ii. 60
RŪPA, Arūpa, and, i. 177, 187
  Chhāyā, a, iii. 29, 110
  Corporeal, i. 247
  Devas, v. 540
  Earth in her first, i. 303
  Form of, i. 124, 235, 243
  Group of angels, i. 265
  Hierarchies, iii. 318
  Kāma, iv. 427, 454, 473, 498, 553, 564, 565
  -Loka, v. 380
  Lords, of, iii. 31, 168
  Manas, plus, ii. 49
  Māyāvi, v. 354, 427, 510, 518, 535, 555, 561, 564, 565
  Orgin of, ii. 172
  Pitris and, iii. 110
  Species, ii. 89
  Stanza IV, in, i. 152
  Vishnu, of, ii. 137
  World of, v. 365
  Worlds, equals, i. 180
RŪPAS, Brothers, for our, iii. 28

Destroyed, iii. 75
Fifth race, no, for, iii. 67
Forms or, i. 243
Group among, highest, i. 265
Wheel constructed, iii. 28, 63
RŪPIC, State of Consciousness, v. 540
RUSSIAN, Alphabet, iv. 117
  Archives of freemasonry, i. 58
  Giant-lore, iv. 324
  Koorgan, iv. 321
  Persian legends in, iii. 393
  Pigeon not eaten by, i. 146
RUTA, Atlanteans, iii. 434
  Daitya, and, iii. 149; iv. 280
  Island of, iii. 314, 431; iv. 309
  Magicians of, iii. 426
  Sanskrit from, iii. 226
  White Island, was, iii. 154
RUTILIUS, quoted, iii. 357
RUTIMEYER, Professor, quoted, iv. 357

S

SA, Hea or, the snythesis of Gods, iii. 19
SABA, host, iii. 366
SABAEAN, Language, astronomy, iii. 365
  Origin of Henoch, iii. 366
  Worship, iv. 29; v. 311, 318
SABAEANISM and astrolatry, ii. 117; v. 56, 98, 313, 317
  Chaldean, v. 318
SABAEANS, iii. 360, 361; v. 54, 180, 207, 219, 312
  Jews were, v. 277, 316
  Maimonides and, iv. 22
  Moses and, iv. 23
  Nabatheans thought to be, iv. 20
  Star-worshippers, or, iv. 20, 22; v. 329, 330
SABAEORUM foetum, iv. 23
SABAISM, Seth the founder of, iii. 361
SABAO, the genius of Mars, iv. 108
SABAOTH, Jehovah is, v. 107, 201, 212, 318
  Mars, Genius of, ii. 301
  Meaning of, v. 318
  Saturn or, ii. 300
  Stellar, spirit, ii. 167
SABASIA, Mysteria of the, iii. 417
SABASIAN mysteries, iii. 413, 414, 417
SABASIUS, Dionysus, iii. 413
  Mithras called, iii. 417
SABBAOTH, Jehovah, ii. 156, 179
SABBATH, ii. 103; v. 115
  Bible, of, iv. 195
  Creation of Brahma, and, v. 199
  Duration of Hebrew, i. 285; iii. 394
  Eastern philosophy, of, ii. 165
  Excellence of, i. 285
  Goat of witches', iv. 79
  God, of, ii. 203; iii. 238
  Greek text, in, i. 285
  Jewish, ii. 107; v. 179, 326, 433
  Meaning of, i. 285; ii. 124; iv. 317
  Morrow after, iv. 317
  Moses, of, iv. 175
  Mystic, of, iv. 285; ii. 203
  Saturn, day of, ii. 179; v. 62, 129, 326

SABBATH (*Contd.*)
  Seventh, iv. 59, 317
  Witches of, v. 172
SABBATHIEL, mystery name of Mikael, v. 326
SABBATHS, *Leviticus*, of, iv. 135, 317
  Mysteries, of, iv. 317
  Pralayas, are, iv. 317
SABBATICAL week and years, iii. 394
SABEAN Bedouins, iv. 83
  Type of Samael, ii. 135
SABEANISM, Chaldean religion and, i. 77;
  v. 56, 98, 313
SABEANS, v. 54, 312
SABEKH to Seti I, i. 275
SABHĀ and Māyāsabhā, iii. 424
SABINE, Col., v. 335
SABINES, Rapes before that of, iii. 278
SACAS, v. 347
SACERDOTAL, Castes, iv. 71
  College, Java-Aleim of, iii. 219
  Dominion in Egypt, iii. 433
  Epoch of Egypt, v. 296
  Powers, v. 395
  Puzzles, v. 390
  Science, v. 255, 287
  Speech, Egyptian, v. 115
  Theban, class, ii. 23
  Tongue, Senzar, i. 64
  Years, ii. 381
  Zuni Indians, hierarchy of, iv. 199
SACERDOTALISM, Christian, iv. 130
SACR', Chakra, or circle of Vishnu, iv. 33
  First-formed races of our fifth race, of, i. 72
  Hebrew words, means lingam (phallus),
    iv. 34, 35
  Sacred, sacrament, derived from, i. 72
SACRAL Plexus, v. 480
SACRAMENT, Etymology of, iv. 35
  Marriage, of, ii. 340
  Sacr' derivation of word, i. 72
SACRAMENTAL words of initiation, iv. 129
SACRED, Accounts, v. 243
  Adytum of occult mysteries, ii. 351; v. 265
  Aged, or Sephira, i. 291; v. 214
  Alphabet of Phoenicians and Egyptians,
    v. 114, 115
  Anagram, v. 115
  Animal, i. 283
  Animals, Bible, of, i. 155; ii. 159
  ,, Divine man, emanated from, i. 153
  ,, Evangelist, grouped around, ii. 159
  ,, Glyphs of, ii. 77
  ,, Zodiac, and, i. 156; ii. 165; iii. 36,
    187
  Ark of the covenant, iv. 27
  Auric Body is, v. 427
  Books, Brāhmans, of, ii. 81
  ,, Buddhist, i. 60; v. 408
  ,, Canon of Tibetans, v. 390
  ,, Commentaries on, i. 56
  ,, Cryptographic characters, in, i. 47
  ,, East, of the, v. 407
  ,, Egyptians, of, v. 58
  ,, Enoch of, v. 109
  ,, Jerusalem, of, v. 185
  ,, Magians, i. 60
  ,, Root-race, called manvantara in, iv. 186

Books, Temple, of, v. 185
Birds, v. 246
Brāhmanical books, i. 314
Brāhmans, caste of, i. 314
Bull, Nandi, iii. 406
  ,, Thot, of Mendes, a form of, ii. 100
Cats, ii. 103
Ceremonies, of Egyptians, iii. 427
Circular Dance of Planets, v. 310, 311
College of Druids at Bibractis, v. 295
Crocodiles, iv. 148, 151
Cross of Egypt, iv. 117
Cycles and computations, with the ancients,
  iii. 395
Decad, Pythagorean, iv. 123
Device, Vesica Piscis, v. 162
Divine symbol, cross a, iv. 153
Doctrine of Buddhism, iii. 422
Dragons and serpents, iii. 354
Drama of Initiation, iii. 417
Drink, Soma, v. 280
Fathers, messengers of, i. 153
Figures of the cycles, i. 222
Fire, v. 267, 323, 520
  ,, Angels robbed seven circles of, iii. 90
  ,, Barhishad and Agnishvatta Pitris classed
    in relation to, iii. 87
  ,, Higher beings, from spark of, iii. 179
  ,, Prometheus of, v. 203
  ,, Psellus on, ii. 45
  , Purānas in, v. 517
  ,, Side of, v. 446
  ,, Svastika, instrument for kindling,
    iii. 109, 411
Fires, Kabiri, or Kumāras, personified, iii. 114
Formula, v. 418, 421, 506
Formulary, v. 140
Four, iii. 283
  ,, Circle enclosed within, i. 161
  ,, Primordial flame and, i. 152
  ,, Svastika, an emblem of, iv. 159
  ,, Tetraktys or, i. 152, 161; iv. 193
History, v. 46
Ierna, v. 267
Immutability of primitive truths, ii. 24
Institution, Inner Mysteries were, v. 33
Island, iii. 319; iv. 341
  ,, Central Asia, in, i. 258
  ,, Initiates of, ii. 137
  ,, P'u-to, v. 394
  ,, Sons of God and, iii. 223
Islands, iii. 325
Knowledge, iv. 102; v. 294, 412
Land, imperishahble, iii. 19
Land of Āryavarta, iv. 155
Letters, M the most, of all, ii. 99
  ,, Two, iii. 67
Literature' Babylon, of, i. 56
  ,, Kumāras in, iv. 149
Lore, Guardians of, v. 50
Lore, life-giving, i. 57; v. 118
Magian religion, iii. 19
Measures, Jewish and other, ii. 25
Militia, v. 325
Mysteries, iv. 17
  ,, Egypt in, v. 294
  ,, Great pyramid of, ii. 29, 30

SACRED (Contd.)
Mysteries, Greeks of, v. 266
,, Kuklos Anankēs, of, iii. 378
,, Science and, iv. 17
,, Seven, number of numbers for those initiated into, iii. 47
Mythoi, v. 440
Name, Jah-Hovah, a, iii. 134
,, Mystery, of Absolute, v. 408
,, Sanskrit and Hebrew conceal, i. 144
,, Tetragrammaton, of Deity, iii. 313
Names, and letter M, ii. 99
Nile, crocodile of the, iv. 148
Number five with Greeks, iv. 152
,, Four, with all mystics, i. 153
,, Nature, in, iii. 408
,, Pythagorean, i. 129
,, Seven, i. 174; ii. 103; iii. 47; iv. 175; v. 201
,, Tetrad, most, iv. 170
,, Twelve held to be, ii. 375
Numbers, Book of Dzyan and the Kabalah, in, i. 136
,, Metaphysical, are purely, i. 136
,, Ten, six and five, i. 154
Numerations, v. 341
Ollas of Sanskrit, v. 197
Place of Initiation, v. 285
Planets, antiquity, of, 221
,, Hierarchies rulers, of, v. 460
,, Seven, iii. 93; v. 429, 460
,, Spheres ruled by, iv. 173
Plants and animals, ii. 68
Precinct of Minerva, iii. 394
Rites, v. 452
River, sacred crocodiles re-emerge from, iv. 151
Sacr', root of word, i. 72
Sanctuaries, v. 59
Scarabaeus, winged globe became, iv. 122
Science, ii. 258; v. 75, 242, 253, 294, 329, 502
,, Birth and evolution of, iv. 362
,, Death and, v. 105, 106
,, Legends of Initiator among students of, i. 256
,, Nature of, i. 61
,, Numerals, of, i. 153
,, Sciences of, v. 253
,, Self of, v. 75
,, Vidya, or, iii. 436
Scribe of Amenti, ii. 100
Scribes of Nile, v. 244, 294
Scriptures of West, v. 407
Secret knowledge, and, i. 187
Septenary, v. 120
Serpents and Phoenician alphabet, v. 114
Seventh Nadi, v. 520
Shamballah, iii. 399
Sibylline book, iii. 395
Sign, pentagon, a, ii. 99
Signs on Babylonian Cylinders, v. 123
Spark, Human reason, expands into, iii. 103
,, Savages missing in, iii. 419
Square buildings of antiquity, i. 184
Sun temples, iii. 378
Symbol, É Delphicum, iv. 152

Symbol, Serpent, of immortality, v. 238
,, Svastika, iii. 110
,, Tetraktys, v. 426, 516
Syllable, v. 195, 418
Symbologies, iii. 115
Text, v. 141
Tortoise, ii. 159
Tree, on Babylonian cylinder, iii. 112
Water, Neilos, of, iii. 415
Wheat, with the Egyptians, iii. 372
Wisdom, withheld from all but Brāhmans, i. 315
Word, v. 108, 109, 273, 395
Works of esoteric schools, i. 46
Writings of Judaism, iv. 39
SACREDNESS of pledges, v. 466
SACR-FACTUM and sacr-fice, iv. 35
SACRIFICE, Abel, of, iii. 275; v. 291
Artemis, of human victims to, ii. 111
Ashvamedha, iv. 141
Black magic and, ii. 133; iii. 235
Bright spirits, of, iii. 275
Buddha, of, v. 370
Butter purified by, iii. 109
Cain, Abel and, v. 291
Ceremonial of, reviled by Asuras, ii. 140
Daksha, of, iii. 78, 189
Fiery angels, of, iii. 249
Fruit proceeds, whence all, iv. 96
God pleased with, i. 319
Great, i. 256; v. 270, 370
Higher Manas, of the, v. 556
Initiates, of the, v. 154
Lamb, of, v. 370
Let thy, cease, ii. 133
Objective, an evidence of piety, iv. 137
Prometheus, a, iv. 131
Purusha, of, v. 370
Queen of heaven, to, iv. 30
Self, i. 311; iii. 103, 245, 420; iv. 177; v. 154, 270, 289, 291
Senses offered in, iv. 138, 139
Son, of the, v. 142
Triform, iv. 96
Victim of the Gods', man as, iv. 178
Vishvakarman, of, i. 311; iv. 177; v. 154, 270
Winds, to, ii. 187
Yajna or, v. 542
SACRIFICED themselves, Four, iii. 283
SACRIFICER, Cain, as, iii. 275; v. 291
Yima his own, iv. 180
SACRIFICERS, Adityas or, iv. 177
Atlanteans first, to God of nature, iii. 275
Gods-Hierophants, divine ancient, iv. 17
SACRIFICES, Brāhmans, and, iv. 56
Fire produced by attrition at, iv. 93
Kratu-dvishas enemies of, iv. 69
Nemesis, to, ii. 367
Special prayers are, ii. 187
Thetis, to, ii. 188
SACRIFICIAL, Animal, man, a, ii. 165
Animals, Pashavah or, iv. 196
Ceremony, iii. 109
Fires, iii. 87
Flame, iv. 93

SACRIFICIAL (*Contd.*)
Lamb, v. 370
Mysteries, v. 275
Nirmānakāya, v. 370
Ritualism, iv. 211
Victim, i. 323; v. 291, 376, 530, 563
Victim, Azazel, iii. 375
SACR-MENT, iv. 35
SACROVIR, v. 295
SACTI, Yoginī adored as, ii. 194
SACY, M. de, quoted, iv. 103
SADAIKA-RŪPA, Changeless, or, iii. 117
Essence, or, iii. 58
SADDUCEE, i. 45, 67; v. 54, 105
SADDUCEES, Guardians of the laws of Moses,
iii. 71; v. 83, 179, 185, 186, 195, 198, 257
Israelite sects, most refined of, iv. 40
Laws of Moses, held to, ii. 33
SĀDHUS, (SĀDDHUS) Hindu, v. 147, 396
Third age, of, iii. 319
Rākshasas shown to be, iii. 172
SĀDHYAS, Divine sacrificers, iv. 177
Great Gods called, iii. 99
SADIC, Cain or Vulcan or Pater, iii. 391
Sadik or, Sydic or, iii. 390; v. 202
SADOC, founder of Sadducees, v. 185
SADU, Spirits and genii called, iii. 250
SAGARA, Kapila slew progeny of, iv. 141
Rāmāyana, in, iv. 141
Weapon bestowed by Aurva upon his Chela,
iv. 200
SĀGARA or Bay of Bengal, iv. 142
SAGE, Actualities visible only to real, i. 58
Agastya, iii. 235
Apollonius, v. 148
Āryāsanga, v. 412
Bhrigu a Vedic, iii. 42
Confucius, i. 59
Devamata, iv. 137
Greek, v. 218
Kandu, iii. 181
Kapila, ii. 286; iv. 142
Kashyapa, iii. 380; iv. 184
Krotona, of, v. 65
Nārada, iii. 91; iv. 137
Nazarene, v. 369
Pānini, iii. 437
Parāshara, ii. 133, 176
Plato, iv. 124
Quality of darkness cannot exist in a, iv. 141
Quoted, iii. 444; iv. 210
Reverence of, for unknowable, iv. 161
Samian, v. 113
Shankarāchārya, v. 367
Tyana, of, v. 130, 133, 136, 143, 145
Ulysses, iv. 339
Vaivasvata, iii. 148
Western plains of, iii. 332
Zoroaster, aphorism of, iii. 440
SAGES, Aja on, iv. 150
Ancient, i. 251; iv. 17; v. 28, 31, 43, 77
Antiquity of, v. 59, 77
Anugītā, in, iv. 137, 209
Archaic, iv. 124
Arhats, or, iii. 174
Authority of legions of, ii. 336
,, Āryan, v. 382

Authority, East of, v. 68
Brahmā, Kumāras, live as long as, ii. 176
Chaldea and Babylonia, of, v. 59
Deep, come forth from, iv. 63
East, of the, v. 68
Egypt of, iv. 312; v. 59
Fifth race, taught, iii. 358
Fifth root-race of, iv. 208
God in nature, of ancient, i. 333
Great, iv. 210
Greece of, iv. 312; v. 33, 59
Hindus, of, ii. 140
Historical, thirty-five Buddhas are, iii. 421
India, of, v. 59, 74, 400
Inner vision of, iii. 296
Intellect, searching with their, iii. 183
Lives, v. 375
Mānushis, or third race, i. 64
Modern, ii. 19
Modern theory and ancient, iii. 194
Mystic, i. 151
Philosopher-teachers of antiquity, iii. 142
Power (Kriyāshakti) of holy, iii. 188
Primitive, ii. 132
Purānic, ii. 133
Religious austerities of, iii. 190
Rishis do not only represent living, iv. 183
Rishis of the Aryan race, iv. 63
Rishis, or, iv. 41, 186
Satya Yuga, during, v. 324
Senary applied by, to physical man, iv. 163
Seven perfect, abide in Brahman, iv. 210
Seven primordial, iii. 270
Siddhas, on earth, iv. 119
Sung, iv. 124
Superstition, accused of, ii. 187
Tree, branches of one, i. 256
Trees, destroy the iniquitous, iv. 63
Wise men, or, iii. 198
Wrath, shun, ii. 133
SAGITTARIUS, Joseph in sphere of, ii. 377
SAGUNA and Nirguna, v. 350
SAH, He, iv. 33
SAHAGUN, quoted, iii. 47
SAHARA, Desert of, iii. 345, 404, 422
Elevation of, iii. 21; iv. 361
Miocene sea, basin of, a, iv. 355
Sea, a, iv. 309, 350
SAHARAKSHA fire of the Asuras, ii. 245
ST. AMBROSE, v. 312
ST. ANTHONY, v. 162
ST. AUGUSTINE, ii. 159; iii. 314; v. 207,
209
ST. BERNARD and Virgin Mary, ii. 116
ST. CHRYSOSTOM, v. 217
ST. CYPRIAN, v. 170 *et seq.*
ST. DENYS, v. 207, 209, 312, 321, 386
ST. DIONYSIUS the Areopagite, ii. 186
ST. GABRIEL, the archangel, i. 114
ST. GEORGE and the dragon, ii. 178; iii. 378
ST. GERMAIN, v. 46
ST. GREGORY of Nazianzen, quoted, iii. 270;
v. 167, 170
ST. HILAIRE, Brathélemy, v. 105
Geoffroy, iii. 210; v. 408
ST. JEROME, (HIERONYMUS), v. 33, 34,
118, 143, 149, 160, 167, 316, 321

ST. JOHN, Dragon, did not originate the allegory of, iii. 355
,, Synoptics and, ii. 99
,, Vision of in *Revelation*, i. 39; v. 100
ST. JÚLIEN, v. 408
ST. JUSTIN, v. 329, 337, 445
ST. MARTIN, v. 282
ST. MICHAEL, Archangel, i. 114; ii. 336
Conquers Solar Gods, v. 314
Conquers the Devil, v. 325, 375
Kumāra a prototype of, ii. 87
Mars as, v. 325
Ormuzd and, v. 315
St. George, and, ii. 178
ST. PAUL, Christ and, v. 137
Cosmic Gods, refers to, ii. 185
Cosmocratores and, v. 315
Disciples and, v. 138
Elementals, refers to, ii. 45
Elements, ii. 51, 88
Founder of Christianity, v. 136-138
Gnosis and, v. 215, 301, 327
Gods and, v. 382
Initiate, an, iii. 270; v. 71, 137, 387, 488
Jehovah and, v. 241
Lystra at, iv. 49
Master Builder, v. 138
Pillars of World, of, v. 331
Pleroma and, v. 76, 80, 370
Principalities and Rectors of, v. 332
St. Denys and, v. 209
St. Peter and, v. 130
Secrecy and, v. 76, 80, 370
Simon Magus and, v. 129
Unknown God, on, ii. 40
Wisdom and, v. 130
Worlds, on other, iv. 273
ST. PETER, v. 126, 129, 131, 134, 138, 139, 140, 141, 146, 241, 267, 312
Key of, iv. 87
ST. PETERSBURG, Imperial libraries in, i. 58
Professors Bulterof and Wagner of, i. 295
ST. PREST, Fossils in Pliocene sands of, iv. 320
ST. REINE, v. 294
ST. ROMANS, Gigantic bones found near, iii. 279
ST. THOMAS AQUINAS, v. 207, 311, 321
SAINTS, Adepts and, iii. 421
Blood of, iv. 317
Buddhist, v. 40
Coming of the Lord with ten thousand, iv. 51
Glory to thee who art one with, ii. 137
Jāna-loka, of, ii. 87
Leaders of, iii. 381
Rudra and, birth, ii. 175
Theosophist and, v. 124
Time accuseth even, iii. 237
SAÏS, Initiate's tomb at, iii. 394
Legislation of, v. 26
Neïth of, Goddess, ii. 114
Priests of, iii. 370; iv. 312
SAÏTIC, Isis, mother, iv. 225
Period, statuette of, iv. 32
Priests of, iii. 370
SAKA or Eka and dragon of wisdom, i. 139
SAKKARAH, Inscriptions at, ii. 153
SAKRIDĀGĀMIN, degree of Initiation, i. 255; v. 399

SAKYA doctrines of, v. 39
SAKYAPA, v. 398
SALAMANDER, Gigantic, iii. 351
Venomous alkaloid in saliva of, i. 305
SALAMANDERS, ii. 330; v. 239, 562
SALEM, Melchizedek king of, iii. 391
SALISBURY plain, Stones on, iii. 342
SALIVA, Venomous alkaloid in human, i. 305
SALPETRIÈRE, v. 27
SALT, Alchemical, iii. 122
Seas, for, ii. 307
Solution, iv. 166
SALTS of nature, Spirits of the, iii. 123
SALVATION, Ark of, iii. 313
Dogmas of, ii. 338
Mankind, of, iii. 220, 283
Spiritual humanity, of, iii. 88
Star of, ii. 193; iv. 97
Sun of, ii. 382
Thoth Lunus, he who operates, iv. 32
Waters of, v. 234
SALVATIONISTS, v. 50
SALVERTE on winged serpents, iii. 210
SAMĀDHI, i. 43; v. 80, 543
Adept and, v. 532
Bodhi or, i. 43
Bodhisattva in, v. 403
Buddha in posture of, iii. 338
Buddhic consciousness in man, v. 539
Ecstasy v. 306
Jayas lost in, iii. 99
Jīvanmukta in, v. 402
Mystic trance or, iv. 140; v. 452
Nirvāna of Buddha differs from, v. 350
Septenary, v. 539
Turīya state of, ii. 294
Vitala and, v. 539
SAMAËL, Angel of death, iii. 120
Cain generated by, iii. 388
Chief of the demons in *Talmud*, ii. 135
Devil, iii. 387
Dragons of evil, chief of, iii. 407
Elohim, one of, ii. 135
Fall of man, caused, iii. 121
Kabalah, in, iii. 238
Kāma, kabalistic name for, i. 287
Lucifer-Venus abode of, iii. 44
Mars is, v. 310
St. Michael shown to be, iii. 377
Satan is, iii. 377, 384, 387
Saturn and Schemal a symbolical form of, ii. 135
Serpent of *Genesis*, is, iii. 384
Simoom, is identical with, iii. 384
SAMAEL-LILITH, iii. 265
SAMAEL-SATAN, iii. 377
SAMAELS must be dethroned, All the, iii. 418
SAMĀNA, Prāna, subject to, iv. 139
Principle offering to Udāna, iv. 137
Speech finally dwells in, i. 158
Vyāna, and, iv. 137, 139
SAMANO, ascetic, v. 387
SAMARIA, Giants probably existed in, iv. 324
Simon Magus in, v. 126
SAMARITANS, v. 179
Alphabet of, v. 178, 179
Iabé (Yahva) of, iv. 333

SAMARITANS (*Contd.*)
Pentateuch, v. 74, 179, 185
Tau closed alphabet of, iv. 153
Yahva, pronounced Jev, iii. 138
SAMARIUM, a so-called element, ii. 270
SĀMBA, reputed son of Krishna, iii. 322
SAMBHOGAKĀYA Buddhas, v. 366
SAMBHŪTI, Hari born of, iii. 98
SAMIAN Philosopher, v. 36
SAMMA Sambuddha, v. 412
SAMOA, Aborigines of, iii. 227
SAMOANS, Stature of the, iii. 331
SAMOS, Aristarchus of, i. 176
SAMOTHRACE, Island of Electria, or,
iii. 17
Kabiri in, iii. 361
Mysteries of, iii. 18, 114; v. 267
Phoenicians, colonized by, iii. 17
Titanic tradition in, iii. 389
Volcanic formation, of, iii. 390
SAMOTHRACIAN mysteries, iii. 17, 18, 360,
361
SAM-SAM, v. 181
SAMSĀRA, world of, v. 271
SAMSKARA, v. 559
SAMSON, Allegory of, v. 278
Initiate an, v. 277
Modern, ii. 310
SAMUEL, Rabbi, quoted, iii. 142
SAMVĀRTA, the wind, iii. 308
SAMVATSARA, v. 339, 340, 343, 345
SAMVRITI, origin of illusion or delusion,
i. 116, 120
SAMVRITSATYA, only relative truth, i. 120;
v. 400
SAN GIULIO, Catacombs of, iv. 158
SAN MARCO, Campanile of, iii. 94
SANA and the Kumāras, ii. 177, 179; v. 320
SANADDHA, one of the seven rays, in. 240
SANAKA and Kumāras, i. 153; ii. 87, 177;
iii. 114, 148, 319; v. 320
SANAKADIKAS, Kumāras who visited Vishnu,
iv. 156
SANANDA, Create progeny, refused to, iv. 156
Kabir, may be the alter ego of a, iii. 114
Kumāras, one of four, i. 153; v. 320
Kumāras, one of the exoteric seven, iii. 319
SANANDANA, ii. 177; iii. 148
Brahmā, son of, iii. 87; iv. 150
Kumāra, a, ii. 177
Vedhas, son of, iii. 180, 183
SANAT, Ancient, v. 189
Brahmā called, i. 161; iv. 196
Kumāra, and, ii. 179; v. 320, 359
Sujāta, v. 320
SANĀTANA, Kabir, may be alter ego of a,
iii. 114
Kumāra, one of, i. 153; ii. 177; iii. 319;
v. 320
SANATKUMĀRA, iii. 148; v. 320, 359
Create progeny, refused to, iv. 156
Kabi may be alter ego of a, iii. 114
Kumāra, a, i. 153; iii. 319
Meaning of name, ii. 177
SANATSUJĀTA, Kumāra, a, ii. 177, 179;
iii. 148; v. 320, 359
SANCHONIATHO, Cabiri of, iii. 392

VI—24

SANCHUNIATHON, (SANCHONIATHON),
Aletae on, iii. 150, 360
Atlantides, has preserved the history of, iv. 330
Cosmogony of, i. 170; ii. 54, 57
Eusebius, in, iii. 379, 391
Kabiri, on, iii. 391; v. 202
Mysteries and, v. 279
Philo Byblus and, iii. 138
Phoenicians, and. iii. 437; iv. 337; v. 202
Stones, on animated, iii. 341
Synchronistic tables of, iv. 263
Time, and, iv. 58
SANCTUARIES, Arts and sciences preserved in,
iv. 143; v. 261
Celestial Spheres in, v. 322
Chaldea of, v. 59, 176
Egypt of, iii. 429; v. 176
Heart of, v. 75
Hellenic, of sun, iii. 20
Himālayas in, v. 96
Memphis of, v. 171
Sacred, v. 59, 96
Secret Doctrine, of, iii. 441
Secret Teaching in, v. 73
Seven, v. 322
SANCTUARY, Egyptian Gods and, ii. 82
God of heaven, of, iii. 285
Holy of holies, has become, iii. 236
Keys to the, iii. 236; v. 109
Pope entering inner, iv. 34
Theban, v. 264
Veiled language of, iii. 393
SANCTUM REGNUM, v. 232
SANCTUM SANCTORUM, Adytum, or, iv. 27
Asectics of, v. 380
Egyptian and Hebrew temples, of, ii. 182
Occult, ii. 309
Pagans, of, iv. 28
Stooping man at entrance of, iv. 37
"SAND", Pituitary Body and, v. 482, 483
SANDHIS, intervals between each Manu, iii. 79
SANDHYĀ, Dawn or, ii. 254
Evening twilight or, iii. 70
Four bodies of Brahmā, one of the, iii. 68
Length of, ii. 309
Period of, iv. 159
Vāch called, ii. 149
SANDHYĀMSHA and Sandhyā, iii. 309
SANDHYĀS, Central sun during, iii. 241
Twilights or, i. 254
SANDS, Gobi, of, v. 41
Spirits of the, i. 264
SANDWICH ISLANDS, Lemurian origin of,
iii. 227; iv. 356
SANGBAI DAG-PO, Concealed Lord or, i. 123
SANG-GYAS, v. 381, 391, 393, 411
SANGUIS in alchemy, iii. 122
SANGYE KHADO, chief of the Liliths, iii. 286
SANJNĀ, Spiritual consciousness, or, iii. 110
Vishvakarman, daughter of, iii. 181
SĀNKHYA(S), Evolution elaborated in philo-
sophy, i. 326
Intellectual creation of the, i. 175, 176
Kapila, founder of philosophy, iv. 141, 142;
v. 81
Lokas, category, v. 537
Philosophy, pure, ii. 49

SĀNKHYA(S) (Contd.)
Pradhāna in, philosophy, i. 126; ii. 86
Purusha and Prakriti in, philosophy, i. 292; iii. 53; v. 469
Sankhya Bhasya, v. 320
Seven Prakritis in philosophy, i. 300
System, iii. 255
SĀNKHYAN more than a Purānic idea, ii. 167
SAN-KIAN-YI-SU, v. 409
SANNATI, daughter of Daksha, iv. 97
SANSKRIT, Abra, Abram and, v. 111
Ahura is in, Asura, iv. 180
Alphabet, i. 157; v. 114, 197, 505
Antiquity of, v. 184
Ares, scholars on etymology of, iii. 391
Atlanteans did not speak, i. 87
Babylonia seat of, learning, i. 54
Commentary in, iii. 426
Commentators, i. 143; iii. 320
Creation, words used in describing, ii. 170, 171, 173
Derivation of, iii. 226
Devanāgari characters and, v. 114, 197
Difference between Shastra and Astra in, iv. 201
Disappearance of, works in India, i. 56
Divine language, v. 197
Forgery in correct and archaic, i. 53
Greek, said to be progeny of, i. 60
Hebrew, not derived from, i. 140
Jah and Yah, in, iii. 138
Language of the Gods, i. 313; v. 114, 197
Musical notes and, v. 197
Nomenclature, iv. 147; v. 185
Numerals, ii. 76; v. 197
Occult significance of sound and, v. 114
Prometheus derived from, word, iii. 411
Root of, mystery tongue, iii. 205
Sarsvatī, inventress of, v. 114
Scriptures, i. 161
Senzar commentaries, translations of, i. 87
Shlokas, ii. 348
Sounds, v. 394
Stanzas, i. 87
Texts, iv. 182
Words, hidden meaning of, v. 117, 185
Works, i. 46
SANSKRIT LITERATURE, Imposition, said to be an, iii. 440
Seat of, v. 111
Testimony of, iv. 144
Weber, on, iii. 61
SANSKRIT MSS., Astronomy, on, iv. 122
Secret doctrine scattered through thousands of, i. 46
SANSKRIT-speaking, Agni with, races, iii. 109
People, iii. 209
SANSKRITIST, Dayānand Sarasvati, i. 53
Fitzedward Hall, iii. 98
Max Müller, great Oxford, iv. 138
Pandit and, iii. 228
Rāma Prasad, v. 469
Romaka-pura and the, iii. 62
Western, iv. 157
Wilson, iv. 200, 201

SANSKRITISTS, Agneyāstra and modern, iv. 201; v. 248
Chronology of, ii. 176
English and American, ii. 373
Researches of, i. 45
Rig Veda, and, iv. 16, 17
Trojan inscriptions in characters unknown to, iii. 438
SANTATI of a particular Manu, Each root race, iii. 149
SAPHAR, one of the three seraphim, i. 156
SAPTA, Chatur and Tri produce, i. 138
Hapta, same as, v. 238
Samudra, or seven oceans, ii. 62; iv. 273
SAPTALOKAS, Seven lokas or, iii. 237; v. 537, 542
SAPTAPARNA, Ātmā-Vidyā and, i. 249
Cave, i. 44; v. 368, 550
Heart of the man-plant called, i. 277
Man became a, iv. 162; v. 368
Man-plant, i. 282
Plant, a seven-leaved, iv. 145, 162
SAPTARISHI, Great Bear, abode of, iv. 202
Planetary spirits, and, iii. 318
SAPTARISHIS, Brahmā, mind-born sons of, ii. 154
Great Bear, stars in, ii. 124
Hindus, of, ii. 155
Krittikā, and, iv. 119
Present age, closely connected with our, iv. 119
Rishis become, ii. 160; iii. 98
Stellar and lunar spirits connected with, i. 248
SAR, Saros, cycle or circle, i. 173; v. 181
SARAGOSSA, Council of, v. 157
SARAH, Abraham's wife, iii. 181
Human womb, Eve or, iv. 40
Saraī, name changed to, iii. 86; v. 111
SARAĪ, Pharaoh and, i. 139
SARAMĀ, Hermes and Hindu, iii. 41
SĀRAMEYA, Hermes and Hindu, iii. 41
SARAPH, Fiery, of Isaiah, iii. 74; v. 309
Fiery or flaming venom, iii. 211, 216
Mehophep, iii. 211
Seraphim, singular of, iv. 69
Serpent, or, iii. 386
SARASVATI, Brahmā and, iii. 86; v. 271
Devanāgari Script, Sanskrit and, v. 114
Devasenā aspect of, iii. 204
Goddess of Wisdom, v. 165
Vāch, later form of, i. 158; ii. 67
Watery, iii. 86
SARCODE, Moneron, of, iii. 161
Protoplasm, generally known as, iii. 161
SARCOPHAGUS Adytum, placed in, iv. 27
Ark and, iv. 28
Candidate for initiation entered, iv. 29
Corn in, v. 45
Egyptian, v. 176, 332
Female principle, symbolic of, iv. 30
Giants, of, iii. 280
King's chamber, in, iv. 38, 128
Zodiacs in, v. 332
SARDINIA, Giant tombs of, iv. 321; v. 285
SARGINA, king of Akkad, ii. 32
SARGON, Accad, of, iv. 261
Agadi, or Akkad, capital of, ii. 32

SARGON (*Contd.*)
Babylonian Moses, was, ii. 32
Kouyunjik, and history of, ii. 31, 32
Moses, and, ii. 32; iii. 426
Naram-Sin, son of, iv. 261
Reign of, iv. 261
SARISRIPA, Svapada, insects and small lives, iii. 63
SARKU, Light race or, iii. 18
SARMATIAN Bouh, iv. 173
SAROS, Great, ii. 366
Sar, and, or cycle, i. 173; v. 181
Synodial months composed of, ii. 381
SAROSES, Berosus and the, ii. 381
SARPA, Nāga, serpent, iii. 188; iv. 69; v. 238
SARPARĀJNI, Book of, quoted, i. 141
Earth called, i. 141
Queen of the serpents, iii. 58
SARPAS, Flying, iii. 190
SARVA-MANDALA, the egg of Brahmā, i. 301; ii. 88
SARVA-MEDHA ceremony, iv. 177
SARVAGA, All-permanent, ii. 306
World, substance of, ii. 170, 306
SARVĀTMAN, Lords of being concealed in, i. 153
SARVĀVASU, one of the seven rays, ii. 240
SARVESHA, Spirit or, ii. 89
SAT, Asat and, iv. 16
Be-ness, absolute, i. 79, 178, 199; iii. 311; v. 191, 231, 475
Ever-unmanifested, i. 330
Existent nor being, in itself is neither, iv. 16
Hermes (the later Sat-an) or, iv. 99
Is or, ii. 266
One reality, Absoluteness, the, i. 81
Satya or, i. 136
Universal soul or, iii. 69
Unknowable absoluteness of, ii. 280
Untranslatable term, an, i. 130
World of truth, or, i. 178
SATAN, iii. 357; iv. 76, 78
Adversary or, iii. 71, 374
Ambition of, iii. 285
Angel of death, same as, iii. 384
Angel of the manifest worlds, is. iii. 237
Anointed, identified with, iii. 237
Apollo, Dragon, and, v. 289
Archangel, and, v. 468
Athenaeus on name of, iii. 44
Belief in existence of, iv. 346
Chaldeans never worshipped, v. 55
Christ and, iv. 65
Christian church and, iv. 78
Christianity, not first conceived by, ii. 129
Conqueror of, Michael regarded as the, iv. 73, 325, 375
Creator, the real, iii. 246
Deity, in relation to, i. 247
Dethroned, will be, iii. 418
Devil, or, ii. 132
Dogma of redemption, cornerstone of, iv. 83
Doorkeeper is, iii. 236
Dragon of wisdom, miscalled, iii. 103
Dragon, or, i. 244
Eliphas Levi describes, iv. 76
Enemy of God, or, iii. 57

Energy, ever active, iv. 76
Energy of universe, represents centrifugal, iii. 247
Esoteric view about, iii. 235
Evil, personification of abstract, iv. 46
Fiends, and, ii. 337
Followers of, v. 121
Gnostic allegory of, iii. 246
God and, two supremes, i. 246
God, kosmic reflection of, iii. 238
God of Secret Wisdom, degraded to, v. 287
Gods become, iii. 240
Hades, angel of, iii. 237, 238
Hermes called, iii. 379; iv. 99
Holy Ghost and, iv. 82
Host of, i. 244; iii. 180; v. 170
Ideals, grandest of, iv. 76
Idol, as an, ii. 131
Immortal in, v. 501
Initiator, v. 171
Innocence of, ii. 37
Jehovah, identical with, iii. 386
Jewish, Samaël, iii. 407
Justice of God, magistrate of, iii. 237
Kabalah, in, iii. 120, 238
Lair of, iv. 75
Legions of, iii. 238
Lightning, seen to fall as, iii. 233, 234; iv. 54
Logoi of non-Christian religions, masquerading as, iii. 239
Logos, one with, iii. 233; iv. 84
Logos, the first-born brother of, iii. 170
Lower Self or, v. 503
Lucifer or, i. 138; iii. 73, 233, 285; v. 310
Madonna and, ii. 118
Magic and, v. 55
Man inextricably interwoven with, iv. 46
Many names hath God given, iii. 237
Materialism, of, ii. 327
Matter, or, iii. 238
Meaning of, iii. 241
Medium of, Apollonius called, v. 150
Merodach or, iii. 64
Messenger, ever-loving, iii. 246
Mind in man, iv. 82
Much-slandered, ii. 130
Ophiomorphos, or, iii. 246
Orthodox, types of, Nimrods, etc., iii. 274
Pember, on, iii. 232
Philosophical view of, i. 248
Phōsphoros, lord of, iv. 82
Polar opposite or reverse of everything, is metaphysically, iii. 388
Reality of, iii. 213; iv. 79
Rebellion, and his, iii. 376; iv. 60
Roman Catholics and, ii. 337; iv. 79
Root-idea of orthodox, iv. 45
Samael and, the *Talmud*, iii. 387
Samael, or, serpent of *Genesis*, iii. 384
Saturn and, v. 326
Sea dragon Tiamat, female, iii. 71
Secret of, quoted, iii. 236
Serpent-formed, iii. 246
Serpent is not, iii. 386, 387
Serpent, seducing, iii. 120; v. 287
Shamaël or, iii. 209
Simulacra, of, v. 148

SATAN (*Contd.*)
  Slayer of, iii. 384
  Son of God, ii. 129, 130; iii. 377; iv. 57
  Svastika and, iii. 107
  Talmud on, iv. 46
  Tempter, v. 171, 311
  Theologians of, iv. 44
  Theology, iii. 71
  Transformation of divine alter ego into, iv. 44
  Transformation of universal soul into, iv. 80
  Tsaba, or army of, iv. 69
  Typhon, or, iv. 159
  Venus-Lucifer and, iii. 42, 44
  War between the angels of God and, iv. 346
  Western theology, holds copyright of, iii. 234
  Worship, v. 55
SA'TAN, in Hebrew Sātān, an adversary, iii. 386
SATANIANS, Sect of, iii. 388
SATANIC, Agency, v. 38
  Blushing bride, ii. 37
  Character of Gods of Egypt, v. 247
  Eternal injustice quite, i. 268
  Forces, v. 94
  Kriyāshakti power regarded as, iii. 231
  Legions of the church, ii. 44
  Magic, v. 125
  Myth, iii. 377; iv. 98
  Power, v. 38
  Pride amongst the seven rectors, ii. 135
  Science said to be, iii. 57
  Will-effort called, iii. 248
SATANISM, Hypnotism will soon become, iv. 212
  Idols of, iii. 341
SATELLITE(S), Earth, moon, only physically, of, i. 232
  Gross body of its invisible principles, i. 231
  Jupiter of, ii. 317; iii. 145
  Mother, of child, i. 232
  Occult connection of our, with fecundation, i. 307
  Origin of, ii. 319
  Our, only, i. 232
  Planets and their, i. 163; ii. 316, 321
  Rarefied spirits in earth's, i. 280
  Uranus and Neptune, of, i. 204; ii. 299, 317
  Venus and Mercury have no, i. 210, 219; iii. 45
SATI and Anouki, triadic Goddesses, ii. 82
  Osiris, as, v. 140
SATIETY, Kāma Rūpa results in, iv. 165
SATTĀ or sole existence, ii. 89
SATTAPANNI of Mahāvansa, i. 44
SATTVA, ii. 62, 259
  Ātma-Buddhi, name given in Aryāsanga school to, i. 136
  Buddhi, rendered by Shankara to mean, i. 136
  Understanding, is original for, i. 136
SATURDAY or day of Saturn, ii. 378; v. 62, 129, 326
SATURN, ii. 298, 299; v. 242, 433
  Abraham and, ii. 301
  Agruerus and Sydyk same personage, iii. 150
  Angel presiding over, ii. 179; v. 129
  Chaldean, v. 242
  Chiun, or, iii. 389
  Dagon, and, ii. 366

Doctrines of *Nabathaean Agriculture* taught by, iv. 20, 21
  Dragon and, v. 202
  Elements, Faculties and, v. 442, 444,
  Emblem of prudence and infinity, i. 299
  Father of Gods, v. 324
  Genius of, iv. 108, 110
  God and planet, iii. 36; v. 324
  Golden age of, iii. 266, 419
  Government of, iii. 371, 372
  House of, i. 164
  Ildabaoth, ii. 167, 301; iv. 108
  Jehovah identical with, ii. 136, 301, 302; iii. 135; v. 129, 310, 318
  Jupiter and Mars, conjunction of, ii. 382
  Jupiter, and our earth on same plane, i. 207
  Kali Yuga, at commencement of, ii. 387
  Kivan, and, v. 318
  Kronos or, i. 299; ii. 135; iii. 150, 366; v. 202
  Kronos-Sydyk, or, iii. 360
  Krūra-Lochana, Shani or, iii. 42
  Lemuria, kingdom of, iv. 337
  Lemurians ruled, iv. 334
  Mass huge as, ii. 226
  Michael (Mikael) is, v. 326
  Moon and, fourth race born under, iii. 42
  Moon-God or Jewish, iii. 73; v. 242
  Music of spheres, and, iv. 172
  Mystery Name of, v. 310
  Nations born under, ii. 301
  Period, transformed from eternal duration into a limited, ii. 136
  Planets, and rarefied, iii. 145
  Planets, sun and moon opposed to, iii. 73
  Pre-planetary form of, ii. 125
  Progeny, devoured his, ii. 398
  Regent group of, iii. 135
  Reign of, iv. 346; v. 337
  Reviled by worshippers of other Gods, ii. 301
  Rings of, iii. 237; v. 324
  Sabaoth, or, ii. 300; v. 318
  Sabbath, Egyptian, Jewish and, v. 326
  Satan, or, iii. 237; v. 326
  Saturday, or day of, ii. 378; v. 62, 129, 326
  Septenary of, v. 45
  Seth Jehovah and, v. 72
  Sevekh or, v. 202
  Shani or, iii. 42
  Stone, Jupiter swallowed by, under form of a, iii. 341
  Sydic, Kronos, or, iii. 391
  Thrones, ruled by, ii. 153
  Times, is Kronos or, iii. 341
  Uranus denser than, ii. 317
  Velocity, equatorial, of, ii. 317
  Vul-cain, Chiun, Kivan, or, iii. 389
SATURN-JEHOVAH, ii. 301
SATURN-KRONOS, Rudra-Shiva, or, iv. 70
  Titans of third race personified by, iv. 335
SATURNILUS of Antioch, v. 93, 129, 207
SATURNINE LAND, Hyperborean or, iv. 346
SATYA, Absolute true being, or esse, means, i. 120
  Age, ii. 93; iii. 154
  Krita Yuga, or, ii. 93; iii. 154
  Loka, iii. 321; v. 537, 542

SATYA (*Contd.*)
Purity, age of, ii. 369
Sat, or, i. 136
State, v. 545
SATYA-YUGA, iv. 61, 89; v. 332, 339
Age after deluge, first, i. 136
Ages always first in series of four, ii. 92
End of, iii. 206
Golden Age, v. 260
Great flood at end of, iii. 153
Kapila of, iv. 142
Manvantaras, plus period of one, make a day of Brahmā, fourteen, iii. 79
Rishis of, i. 281; v. 324
Sages, in, v. 324
Watchers reign during, i. 309
SATYAS lost Samādhi, iii. 99
SATYĀT NĀSTI PARO DHARMAH, i. 63
SATYAVRATA, Noah seen in, ii. 380
SATYRS, iii. 288
Fables, not, iii. 264
Nephilim of the *Bible*, of tradition, iv. 324, 344
SAUL who became Paul, v. 137
SAUL, Armies of, discomfited, ii. 188
Divination practised by, iv. 22; v. 239, 242
King, ii. 188; iv. 22; v. 237
SAURIAN, Flying, iii. 210
Scale-bound gigantic, iii. 159
SAURIANS, Aquatic animals, and, iii. 210
Mesozoic, iii. 300
SAVAGE(S), American, ideographs of the, iv. 437
Anthropoid, and, iv. 249
Apes not imitated by, iv. 246, 247
Atlanteans, condition of later, iv. 313
Chiefs, white, iv. 313
Crossing of Europeans with certain, tribes produces sterility, iii. 201
Discerns good from bad, ii. 140
Haeckel's speechless, iv. 247
Immigration of, into Somme Valley, iv. 308
Inferiority of, accounted for, iii. 251
Neolithic man more of, than Palaeolithic, iv. 291
Palaeolithic, iii. 317, 347; iv. 255, 289
Primeval, iii. 178; iv. 248, 290
Proof that there have been, iv. 90, 91, 284
Quaternary ages, of, iv. 318
Races, Max Müller's remarks upon, iv. 290
South Sea Islands, in, iii. 419
Spirits, inferior to lowest, iii. 369
Stone hatchets used by, iv. 285
Trees, tribes builds abodes on, iv. 246
SAVAGERY, Golden age has no features of, iv. 290
Relapse, a, iv. 290
State of relative, Europeans might fall back into a, iii. 423
SAVAHI in chain of our planet, iv. 328
SAVARNĀ, mother of Prachetasas, iv. 150
SAVIOUR, Animalism from, iv. 82
Apollonius of Tyāna and, v. 146
Christ as, iv. 65; v. 315
Christian, ii. 383; iii. 233, 413; v. 65, 97, 312
Civilized nations, of present, ii. 192
Cross of, v. 282
Dhyān Chohans transformed by church into, iv. 155

Divine mother of, iv. 140
Divinely begotten, v. 153
Earth, Christ the Logos, on, iv. 52
Epithets applied to Christian, ii. 383
Gnostic, Agathodaemon, iv. 25
Gods imprisoned, from death of, iii. 19
Hierophant, first of Human Race, v. 102, 103
Humanity, of, iii. 186; iv. 35
Jehovah, Saturn, Jupiter and, v. 326
Jesus, v. 155
Kali Yuga, of humanity cannot appear in, ii. 192
Kepler finds prophecy of, ii. 379
Kwan-shi-yin, of all living beings, ii. 193
Man his own, ii. 369
Mother of, v. 293
Mystically is man-woman, v. 164
Oracles that related to birth of, ii. 383
Sacred Island, will come from, iii. 349
Sacred name of, in connection with brazen serpent, ii. 80
Satan in light of a, iii. 246
Theological picture of, v. 84
Vaivasvata, of our race, iii. 149
Worlds put into mouth of, ii. 131
World, v. 345, 362
SAVIOURS, Agnishvātta our, iii. 410
Avatāras, and, ii. 363
Creators of divine man, and, i. 244
Cyclic, iii. 413
Eastern and Western, v. 368
Humanity, or, iii. 180
Humanity, or of Brahmā, of, iii. 171
Rebels are our, iii. 111
Satanic origin, said to be of, iv. 50
Serpent crushed, v. 289
Sōters or, v. 94, 153
Spiritual, Pisces a symbol of all, ii. 379
World-, v. 350
SĀVITRĪ, Vāch named, iii. 137
SAXON derivation of God, ii. 61
SĀYANA and Idā or Ilā, iii. 147, 151
SAYANĀCHĀRYA, v. 365
SAYCE, Prof. A. H., quoted, iii. 64, 208, 229; iv. 23, 27, 29, 261, 262, 263; v. 27, 29, 199, 200
SAYINGS, Dark, in Sacred books, iv. 104; v. 71, 84, 182, 192
SCALE, Angelic beings, of, i. 265
Causes, of, v. 443
Chemical elements and colour of, iv. 198, 199
Colours, Sounds, Numbers, v. 453, 454
Cosmic, ii. 349
Creative forces, of, iv. 60
Evolution, of, iv. 236
Existence, of, Beings on Highest, i. 152
Hierarchic degrees, of, ii. 263
Manifestation, of, i. 196
Matter, of, iii. 141
Musical, v. 420, 453, 454, 457, 484, 485, 505, 508, 509, 547
Nature, of, ii. 382
Seven notes of, ii. 164, 258; v. 475, 508, 509, 547
Spirit and matter, of, i. 247
Spirituality, of, i. 279
Temperature in universe, of, i. 198

SCALED dragons, Winged and, iii. 353
SCALES, Consciousness of, seven, v. 548, 549
　Evolution, of, i. 296
　Guardian of, i. 267
　Karmic, i. 234
　Lion and, iii. 431
　Pythagorean and Hermetic, iv. 159
SCALY, one, iii. 353
SCANDINAVIA, Ases of, iii. 105
　Cross in pre-Christian, iv. 127
　Falling demon of, iv. 54
　Kings of, iii. 346
　Norway, and, iii. 24
　Runic inscriptions in, iii. 346
SCANDINAVIAN, Cosmogony, ii. 83
　Creation, ii. 145
　Eddas, ii. 59; iii. 40, 385
　Hel, iv. 343
　Legends of war in heaven, i. 251
　Odin or Woden in, mythology, iii. 421
　Priest and Monarch, Odin, v. 42
SCANDINAVIANS, America reached and
　　settled by, i. 337
　Fair faced, iv. 323
　Fire and water, beliefs as to, ii. 118
SCANDIUM, an element, ii. 270
SCAPEGOAT, Azazel, of Israel, iii. 388
　Fall into generation, symbol of, iv. 79
　Israel, of, iii. 386, 407
　Satan needed as a, ii. 130
SCARABAEUS, Egyptians, of, iv. 122
　Khopiroo, or, ii. 81
　Soul represented by, iv. 122; v. 246
SCARLET Lady, v. 200, 202
　Woman in purple and, iv. 317
SCENE of initiation, Bas-relief at Philae repre-
　　senting a, iv. 128
SCEPTIC, All-denying, ii. 336
　Beliefs, i. 310
SCEPTICISM, v. 129
　British Bacon's advice to representatives of,
　　iii. 440
　Fever, malignant, of, iii. 84
　Greeks were moderns in their, iii. 287
　Inadequacy of, ii. 203
　Jungles of modern, ii. 400
　Mad, makes a man, ii. 202
SCEPTICS, Astrology, laugh at, ii. 370
　Handful of modern, ii. 336
SCEPTRE, Osiris of, origin of bishop's crosier,
　　v. 247
SCHELLING, Avatāras, accepted the idea of,
　　i. 123
　Fichte, and, i. 122
　Force, on, ii. 235
　Plurality of worlds, on, iv. 275, 276
　References to, iii. 123; iv. 29
　Religion, on primitive, ii. 184
　Serpent, on, iii. 214
SCHEMAL, Alter ego of Samaël, ii. 135
SCHERER, Christopher, quoted, iii. 211
SCHESOO-HOR or servants of Horus, iii. 429
SCHILLER, on the veil of Isis, iv. 225
SCHILLER'S skull, Measurement of, iv. 92
SCHINDLER'S Penteglott, iii. 216
SCHISM between sons of Fourth race, iii. 216
　Crept into early Buddhism, v. 399

SCHLAGINTWEIT, E., quoted, i. 50; iii. 39,
　　186; v. 287, 373, 376, 377, 398, 402, 403
SCHLEGEL, Dr., on the zodiac, ii. 384
SCHLIEMANN, Dr., iii. 110, 239, 437; iv. 158,
　　292; v. 40, 54
SCHMIDT, quoted, iv. 236; v. 40, 373
SCHOLARS, Ancient world, of, v. 43
　Greek and Sanskrit, v. 29, 33, 158
　Hebrew, v. 158, 184
　Mediaeval, v. 28
　Modern, v. 29
　Orient, v. 408
　Roman Empire, of the, v. 33
SCHOLIASTS, Ambitious, iv. 346
SCHOOL, Astrology, of, v. 334
　Black Magic, of, v. 256
　Eclectic, v. 46, 145, 303
　Esoteric, v. 366, 405, 408, 439
　Esoteric Buddhism in China, of, v. 408, 439
　Life, of, v. 532
　Magic, of, v. 118, 253
　Māhāyana, v. 401
　Neo-Platonic, v. 34, 59, 298, 302, 304, 306, 307
　Prasanga, v. 366, 402, 403
　Prophets, of the, v. 118
　Pythagoras, of, v. 459
　Vedāntic, v. 494
SCHOOLS, Brāhmanical, v. 400
　Buddhism, of, v. 399, 400, 401, 408, 409,
　　410, 411
　Catechism of inner, iii. 283
　Drashanas or, i. 119
　Esoteric, i. 46, 181; iv. 175; v. 409, 411
　Heliopolis, of, ii. 23
　Hīnayāna and Mahāyāna, i. 112; v. 366
　India, of, i. 313, 321; iii. 53; v. 402
　Materialistic, atoms of the, ii. 338
　Occultism, of, i. 157
　Philosophy, of, i. 119
　Secret, v. 262, 400, 403
　Secret doctrines of, preserved in the Vatican,
　　i. 65
　Struggle between Initiates of two, iv. 66;
　　iv. 400
SCHOPENHAUER, referred to, i. 159; iii. 164,
　　305; v. 383
SCHOPENHAUERIAN idea, iv. 97
SCHOTT, quoted, i. 59; v. 401
SCHWARTZE, Pistis Sophia, Latin translation
　　of, by, iv. 136
　Quoted, iv. 30, 136
SCHWEGLER, quoted, i. 122
SCHWEINFURTH, Dr. quoted, iv. 235, 323
SCIENCE(S)
　Note: For specific Sciences and Scientists see
　　under appropriate alphabetical letters
　Alchemy, a, v. 297
　Amniotic Fluid and, v. 449
　Ancient, iv. 257; v. 357
　Animals unknown to, iii. 256
　Antiquity of man, and, ii. 80, 81, 221, 222;
　　iv. 247, 255-259, 260, 264-269, 288, 309;
　　v. 92
　Applied, v. 524
　Archaic, i. 63; v. 45, 98, 357
　Aryans inherited, from Fourth Race, iii. 424;
　　iv. 100

SCIENCE(S) (*Contd.*)
Astrology of, v. 329, 330, 335, 460
Astronomy, of, v. 223
Atlantean Race, of, iii. 32, 157
Breaths, of, v. 476, 477, 479
Church and, v. 25, 37
Circe and Medea, of, v. 122
Corner stone of, v. 287
Correspondences of, v. 86, 87
Corroborates wisdom of ancient Occultism, v. 449
Divine, iv. 39; v. 80, 106, 121, 255, 256, 257, 444, 451
Divine Theogony, of, v. 331
Egyptian priests' knowledge of, v. 264
Elements and, iv. 164
Esoteric, i. 339; ii. 312; iii. 289; iv. 281, 300, 303; v. 65, 421, 431, 444
Ether of, i. 336; ii. 39, 53, 210, 215, 217; iv. 166
European, v. 47
Evolution of man, and, iii. 158-168, 176, 194, 259, 262, 263, 287, 299, 347; iv. 215-244, 255-259, 264-269, 284-298, 305; v. 92
Exact, ii. 103, 186, 199, 276, 337, 342, 393; iii. 290, 347; iv. 232, 239, 255, 361; v. 419
Force(s) and, ii. 201, 248-263; v. 474
Good and evil of, v. 85
Gupta Vidya, of, i. 60
Hidden, v. 507
Higher Self, of the, v. 301
History of our Globe and, iv. 281 *et seq.*, 311-330
Hungarian Academy of, v. 215
Indian, v. 41, 334
Kabbalists and, v. 220 *et seq.*
Laws known to, v. 125
Magic and, v. 255, 256, 306, 307, 450, 451
Materialism and, i. 331; ii. 395
Materialistic, ii. 29, 340; iii. 66; iv. 202, 216, 288
Mathematics of, v. 419, 420
Matter and, i. 171; ii. 394, 395
Missing link and, iv. 288
Modern, i. 144, 163, 283, 288; ii. 206, 218, 262, 338, 371; iii. 255, 274, 289, 441; iv. 194, 195, 232, 235, 257, 287, 303; v. 26, 28, 52, 88, 107, 351, 421, 475, 477
Nature, of, ii. 398; iv. 221
Nature, problems of, and, v. 32
Occult, i. 78, 163, 191, 198, 338; ii. 54, 199, 210, 239, 241, 338; iii. 265, 282, 322, 347; iv. 274, 278; v. 41, 51, 59, 60, 61, 75, 80, 86, 88, 121, 165, 242, 254, 263, 287, 389, 405, 429, 460, 463, 474, 479
Occult Numbers, of, v. 264
Occult Teachings and, i. 165, 182, 304, 337; iii. 258, 273; iv. 278; v. 125, 382
Occultism, of, v. 441
One Divine, at dawn of Mankind, v. 121
Orientalists and, v. 27
Origin of Man, and, ii. 35; iii. 21; iv. 215-244, 247, 249, 258, 259, 260, 267-269, 289, 309
Orthodox, iii. 77

Past civilizations, and, iv. 307-309, 311-330
Periodicity of Seven, and, iv. 192, 194
Physical, i. 238; ii. 202, 226, 236, 244, 247, 281, 313, 361; v. 28, 396, 457, 512
Primitive man and, ii. 285
Progress of, v. 55
Psychic and physiological secrets unknown to, v. 274
Psychic, of the, v. 515
Raja Yoga of, v. 451, 479
Religion and, ii. 393; v. 292
Religion, of, i. 48
Sacerdotal, v. 255, 287
Sacred, i. 61; ii. 258; iv. 71; v. 75, 106, 242, 253, 329, 502
Sacred Numerals of, i. 153
Science of (Initiation), i. 61; v. 43, 265
Secret, ii. 303; iv. 71, 255, 363; v. 44, 91, 107, 109, 192, 213, 242, 296, 302, 411, 412, 443
Senses, five and, v. 474
Senses, seven, i. 151; v. 429
Senses, two unknown to, v. 429
Septenary doctrine and, ii. 276
Seven, iii. 334; v. 429
Seven Liberal and Seven Accursed, iv. 212
Solar theory, and, ii. 264, 277
Submerged Continents and, iv. 347-381
Substance and, ii. 327
Suggestion, magic and, v. 47, 48
Symbolism and, ii. 35; v. 55, 407
Third Eye, and, iii. 295, 296, 297; v. 480
Three Kingdoms of, v. 467
Truth and, ii. 200
Universal Science and, v. 44, 287, 464
Vital Principle and, iii. 327
Works from Particular to Universal, v. 464
Zodiac, of the, ii. 378
SCIENCE-PHILOSOPHY of Initiates, iv. 355
SCIENTIFIC basis of Astrology, v. 460
Observation, v. 261
SCIENTIFICO-MATERIALISTIC theory, Naudin's, iii. 128
SCIENTISTS (*see note above at SCIENCE*)
Christian or Mental, v. 428, 468
Modern, v. 52
Occult, v. 384
Philosopher, synonymous term, v. 234
Pythagoras, first in Europe, v. 75
SCINDE, Jews refugees in, iii. 205
SCINTILLAS, Elohim issue from, ii. 344
Upper and lower worlds, of, ii. 343
Worlds called, iv. 274
SCINTILLATING POINTS, Monads as, ii. 358
SCIOLISTS and, Scientists, i. 321
SCLATER, P.L., referred to, iii. 20, 178
SCORPIO, Chrestos and, v. 164
Constellation, eighth, ii. 374
Dan-, v. 161, 166
Dan, in sphere of, ii. 377
Job, mentioned in, ii. 373
Libra and, v. 430
Mars and, iii. 391; v. 164
Pātāla, synonym of, v. 286
Separation of sexes and, v. 430
Virgo becomes, iii. 137; v. 430

SCORPION, Heart of, ii. 388
   Mars held house of, iii. 391
   Worm that never dies, is, iv. 159
SCOTLAND, Director, Royal Observatory of, v. 110
   Raised beaches in, iv. 355
SCREEN, Eternity of, v. 517
   Illusion, of, i. 319
   Objects placed behind a, Kosmos is like, i. 321
   Seven colours on a, ii. 252
   Silhouettes on external, iv. 362
SCRIBE of Amenti, Thot the, ii. 100
SCRIBES, Christian, v. 177
   Lipika literally, iv. 165, 187
   Nile of, v. 244, 257
SCRIPTURAL Japhet, iii. 150
SCRIPTURE, Archaic, Kalpa in, iii. 58
   Archaic teaching and, ii. 38
   Christian, i. 308
   Chronological system in Hebrew occult, iv. 195
   Double origin of Hebrew, iii. 207
   Elohists, of, i. 298
   Giants, references to, iii. 278
   Hebdomad in every, iv. 162
   Nazarenes, Codex Nazaraeus, of, iii. 105
   Nazarenes, of, i. 245; iii. 105
   Prehistoric religion, of, iv. 51
   Record, tree symbol of a, i. 187
   Rig-Vedic, compiled by Initiates, iv. 17
   Theology not warranted by any ancient, iii. 71
SCRIPTURES, Ancient, i. 321; iii. 86, 207
   Androgynes in revealed, iii. 133
   Anthropogenesis, and, iii. 176
   Archaic, i. 293
      ,,   Brāhmanical distortions of, iii. 101
   Aryan, v. 195
   Astrological, v. 331
   Chaldea of, i. 49
   Chaldean, resemblance between Jewish and, i. 49
   Christian, v. 32, 36
   Deva-loka, accounts in exoteric, of, i. 189
   Eastern, Genesis and, iii. 161
   Evolution and ancient, iii. 120
   Exoteric and esoteric, iii. 110
      ,,   Avyaya in, iii. 79
      ,,   World religions, of, i. 218
   Fires, sparks and flames in ancient, iii. 92
   Geometrical figures used in all ancient, i. 134
   Gods and ascetics, in Hindu, iii. 181
   Hebrew, v. 181, 182, 183, 186
   Hermaphrodite, in, of almost all nations, iii. 132, 133
   Hindu, i. 172, 175, 328; iv. 140, 179
   India, of, i. 326
   Israelitist, v. 181
   Jewish, iv. 27; v. 32, 36, 137, 195
   Mazdean, Vendīdād and other, iii. 105, 408; iv. 328
   Metaphysical in, iv. 316
   Nations, of all ancient, iii. 19
   Phallic element in old, iv. 228
   Renan on the Chaldean, iv. 23
   Sacred, of the West, v. 407
   Sanskrit, i. 161
   Satan in Pagan, iii. 71
   Secret, iii. 156

Septenary in ancient, iv. 182
Septenary in Āryan, iv. 184
Symbols of national, i. 276
Time referred to in, i. 116
Translators of Bibles and, iv. 108
Vedas and other, are chanted by the Brāhmans, i. 157
Vishnu in exoteric, iii. 116
Woman made from man in all, v. 199
Worlds spoken of in all ancient, iv. 270
Zoroastrian and Hindu, iii. 357
Zoroastrian, antiquity of, iii. 355
SCROFULOUS, Fifth Race, iii. 409
SCROLL, Anubis holding out a, ii. 127
SCROLLS, Mosaic, remodelled, iv. 41
   Mysteries were never recorded in, i. 276
   Numerically, read, iii. 213
   Porta Pia, discovered at, ii. 126
SCROLLS of Wisdom, referred to, iv. 108
SCULPTOR, Model in mind of, iv. 230
   Model of molten brass poured into, iii. 120
SCULPTURE, Mars the lord of, iii. 391
SCULPTURED Implements, bone, iv. 284
SCULPTURES, Mexican, old, iii. 48
   Temples, in most ancient, ii. 76
SCULPTURING on rocks, ancient, iii. 345
SCYLLA, and Charybdis, Church between, v. 146
SCYTHE, Deucalion called a northern, iv. 338
   Kronos with his, ii. 136
   Old time with its, ii. 79
SCYTHIA, Herodotus, of, iii. 414
   Hyperborean land not near, iii. 20
   Hyperborean land said to be beyond, iii. 24
SCYTHIAN people, Arimaspes a, iii. 414
SCYTHOPOLIS, in Palestine, v. 278
SCYTHS, Origin of the, iii. 207; iv. 343
SEA, Abyss of learning, called, iv. 70
   Aral, of, iii. 414
   Caspian, iv. 180
   Consecrated inland, iv. 70
   Culture-god comes from, iii, 229
   Curds, of, milky way, iii. 320, 321
   Deity compared to a shoreless, ii. 71
   Ethereal fluid, of, ii. 251
   Extermination of first product of, iii. 410
   Fire, of, is noumenal, i. 142
   Great, of, space, iv. 73
   Great, waters of, iv. 73
   Hathor, light of the, ii. 115
   Jambu-dvīpa surrounded by, iii. 320
   Knowledge, of, iv. 71
   Mare or, ii. 100, 178
   Milk, of, Lakshmī springing from, ii. 95
   Milky way, iii. 321
   Monsters, iii. 22
   Mother-water great, iii. 74
   Pelagus, great, iv. 343
   Sahara, a, iv. 309
   Salt water, of, iii. 320
   Shoreless, of fire, i. 138
   Sorrow, of, iv. 73
   Space, of, iv. 45, 73
   Thalassa, iii. 75, 124
   Thallatth, iii. 65, 124
   Venus Aphrodité, personified, ii. 178
   Virgin Mary, Mare the, ii. 178

SEA (*Contd.*)
  Visible Waters became, iv. 55
  Zohar on secrets of land and, iii. 22
SEA-ANEMONE, iii. 174
SEA-BOTTOM, upraising of, iii. 325
SEA-DRAGON, iii. 71; iv. 71, 148
SEA-GODS and Greek Word for three, v. 117
SEAL, Apocalypse seventh, iv. 85
  Solomon's, double triangle, i. 177; iv. 190;
    v. 120, 163
  Svastika, on living initiates, iv. 157
SÉANCES, v. 48
SEANG of Wei, king, iii. 303
SEAS, Allegorical, iii. 321
  Carbonic acid, of, liquid, i. 297
  Metaphorical names of, iii. 320
  Midgard snake coiled at bottom of, ii. 123
  Neptune ruler over, iii. 75
  Salt for, ii. 307
  Seven, iv. 175, 188
  Silurian period, iv. 254
SEA-SERPENT, iii. 212; iv. 45
SEA-SLIME, our ancestors were, iii. 266
SEASONS, Beginning of change of, iii. 206
Book of Enoch on, ii. 334
  Cause of, ii. 334; iii. 355
  Confucius on, ii. 158
  Corresondences of, v. 444
  Cosmic divisions of, iii. 83
  Hanokh computed, iv. 102
  Jupiter, of, iv. 276
  Kabiri regents over, ii. 366
  Mars, Mercury, Venus, of, iv. 276
  Points of compass, meaning, ii. 158
  Procreation, of, iii. 411
  Periodical return of, ii. 370
  Shifting of, iv. 269
  Titan-Kabirim regulators of, iii. 362
  Vicissitudes of, ii. 366
SEAT of Peter, v. 139, 140
  Brothers, of the, v. 390
  Buddha, of, v. 527
  Gods of, v. 171
  Life, of, v. 555
  Pitah, v. 139
  Sanskrit Literature, of, v. 111
  Three Secrets, of the, v. 377
SEATS of Blessed, iii. 422
  Knowledge, of, iii. 422
  Learning of, Famous Four, v. 264
  Mercy, of, iii. 422
SEAWEEDS, algae, iv. 281
SEB, Ancestral soul of, iv. 203
  Egg of, ii. 75, 80
  Egypt of, v. 326
  God of time and earth, ii. 74
  Goose, carries a, ii. 72
  Hawk, issues from egg like a, ii. 75
  Osiris, son of, ii. 155
  Tefnoot and, iii. 373
SEBEKH, Crocodile called, i. 267
  Sevekh, or, i. 266
SEBTI, Kepti and, ii. 124
SECCHI, Father, quoted, ii. 265; v. 220
SECOND
  Adam, Androgyne formed from, iv. 25
  ,, Gnostics, of, iv. 25

Adam Protoplastic androgyne Adam called,
    iv. 24
  ,, Septenary, iii. 15
Birth for the dead, ii. 80
Causes, Naudin does not consider, iii. 128
  ,, Science, of, iii. 128
Continent, Greenland belonged to, iii. 146
  ,, Primeval races, of, ii. 85
  ,, Remnants of, iii. 23, 24
Creation, v. 203, 204
Death, v. 250, 360, 489, 491, 496, 498
Division of ancestral series of man, iv. 237
Dogmas of Hermes, v. 142
Earth, no earth, is, ii. 90
  ,, Vapour, disappeared as, ii. 157
Flood, Universal or, iii. 153
God, Creator, Philo called, ii. 65
  ,, Logos, or, ii. 66; v. 455, 476
  ,, One who has no, v. 462
  ,, Plato, of, v. 289
Line, Chakra inscribed in, i. 173
Logos, Adam Kadmon, i. 262; iii. 38
Logos, Ampsiu-Ouraan, iv. 139
  ,, Demiurge, or, iii. 35
  ,, Manifested, i. 140; ii. 167
  ,, Platonists, of, iv. 114
  ,, Sound, or, iv. 133
  ,, Tetragrammaton, iv. 170
Manifestation, stage of, ii. 155
One and pentacle, in the egg, i. 187
Person, the Son, v. 210
Primal cause becoming, ii. 343
Race, Adam-Eve or, iii. 143
  ,, Androgyne, iii. 143
  ,, Appearance of, iii. 156
  ,, A-sexual, iii. 124, 125
  ,, Astral, iii. 250; iv. 258
  ,, Belt of earth during, iii. 399
  ,, Brihaspati (Jupiter) born under, iii. 42
  ,, Chhāyās evolved, iii. 125
  ,, Continent of, iii. 314
  ,, Cycle between first and, iii. 182
  ,, Ethereo-physical, iii. 300
  ,, Evolution of, iii. 117
  ,, Fathers of sweat-born, iii. 125, 126
  ,, First created, by budding, iii. 140
  ,, First, emanated from, iii. 172
  ,, First, how formed from, iii. 125
  ,, Forms of, iii. 129, 130
  ,, Fourth round humanity, of, iv. 255
  ,, Groups of, iii. 304
  ,, Hyperborean continent, on, iii. 20
  ,, Jod-Heva, or, iii. 143
  ,, Kāma Rūpa, devoid of, iii. 125
  ,, Land during, iii. 399, 400
  ,, Mammalia contemporary with, iv. 254
  ,, Mārishā symbol for, iii. 182
  ,, Mentally, psycho-spiritual, iii. 300
  ,, Mexican primitive ancestor and, iii. 168
  ,, Northern Asia and, iii. 400
  ,, Preservers and incarnating Gods, en-
    dowed by, iii. 172
  ,, Primitive race, merged in, ii. 129
  ,, Sons of Mahat and, iii. 111
  ,, Sound-language, had, iii. 203
  ,, Spiritual State of, v. 239
  ,, Sub-races of, iii. 126

SECOND (*Contd.*)
  Race, Sweat-born, called, iii. 126, 156, 172, 182, 183
  ,, Third, evolved, iii. 139
  ,, Third, gives birth to, iii. 140
  ,, Third produced unconsciously by, i. 255
  ,, Uranus a Dhyān Chohan of, iv. 335
  ,, Yima progenitor of, iv. 180
  Round, Element of, i. 303
  ,, Elements, developed two, i. 295
  ,, Explanation of, i. 214
  ,, Globe luminous during, i. 287
  ,, Human element in, i. 227
  ,, Matter in, i. 296
  Sight, astral light cause of, i. 303
  Sun, v. 270
  Universal soul, principle of, ii. 261
  World, i. 283; v. 374, 447
SECONDARIES, Trithemius on the seven, ii. 172
SECONDARY
  Age, iii. 164
  Age, Cataclysms of, iv. 283
  ,, Homo Primogenius of, iv. 303
  ,, Man in, iii. 23, 290; iv. 282
  ,, Northern Lemuria in, iii. 333
  ,, Primary and, iii. 164
  ,, Tertiary, twice length of, iv. 283
  ,, Third race and, iv. 280
  ,, Third race Titan of, iii. 22
  Angels, ii. 50
  Causes, Intelligence beyond, iv. 124
  ,, Variations, and, iv. 218
  Cosmic evolution, stage of, ii. 145
  Creation, Beginning of, ii. 168
  ,, Eleventh crore, or, iii. 312
  ,, Every cosmogony begins by, iii. 70
  ,, Mahat of, i. 142
  ,, Ninth and, i. 142; ii. 176
  ,, Pratisarga or, iii. 115
  ,, Primary and, iii. 116, 122
  ,, Vārāha or, iii. 64
  Creations, ii. 165
  Deity, iv. 197
  Evolution, stage of, ii. 324
  Formations, iii. 256
  Gods, iii. 88; v. 261
  ,, Maruts, iv. 184
  Laws, of Darwinism, iv. 232
  Man of de Quatrefages, iv. 257
  Mesozoic ages, or, iv. 166
  Period, Australia during, iii. 21
  ,, Fourth creation and, ii. 173
  ,, Mammalia in, first traces of, iv. 254
  ,, Man in, iii. 263, 269; iv. 255, 315
  ,, Modern and esoteric science on, iv. 282
  ,, Triassic rocks of, iv. 254
  Rocks, iv. 279
  Spirit, Spiritus representing the, iv. 147
  Strata twice the thickness of the Tertiary, iv. 283.
  Suns, iii. 242
  Transmutations, iv. 236
SECONDLESS,
  Existence, one, i. 124
  ,, Parabrahman, ii. 246; v. 233
  ,, Sat, i. 178
  Gods, v. 209

ONE, v. 210, 216
  Principle, God, iv. 125
  Reality, Parabrahman, i. 73
  ,, Unknowable cause of all, iv. 77
SECRECY, Chelas of, v. 97, 305
  Divine truths, with regard to, iv. 141
  Initiates of, v. 64-74
  Maimonides enjoins, iv. 24
  Mysteries of life and death preserved in, v. 17
  Mysteries, of the, v. 29, 34, 68, 297, 304
  Occult and religious mysteries of, iii. 132
  Occult truth, regarding, iv. 157; v. 465-468
  Reasons for, v. 65, 75-84, 185, 465
  Symbology, of, ii. 78
  Tattvas of doctrine of, v. 470
  Theology, less dangerous than, iv. 87
  Tower of Babel, and, v. 185
SECRET, Ages of, iv. 85
  Ancient thought, of, ii. 18
  Annals, iii. 334; iv. 362
  Archangel whose name was, ii. 155
  Being and non-being, of, i. 220
  Birth or social position, of, iii. 169
  Book, Apocryphon, iv. 98
  ,, *Bible* is, according to Origen, Clemens and Rabbis, iv. 106; v. 66
  ,, *Kabalah* is, iv. 106
  ,, Posture during contemplation, on, iv. 122
  Books, Astronomy, on, i. 252
  ,, Atlantis, on, iii. 403
  ,, Buddhism of, v. 408
  ,, Celestial Nāgas of, ii. 125
  ,, Data of, iv. 269
  ,, East, of, v. 101
  ,, Four hidden dragons of wisdom of, ii. 125
  ,, LAM-RIN and DZYAN considered, v. 389, 390
  ,, *Mirror of Futurity* among, iii. 61
  ,, Occultism, of, iii. 62
  ,, Planets enumerated in, i. 207
  ,, Procreation, explained in, iii. 95
  Brotherhoods, v. 46
  Catechism of Druses of Syria, iii. 40
  Colleges of prophets with Jews, iv. 102
  Computations of Japanese, iv. 136
  Cycle Babylonian, v. 341
  ,, Naros as, v. 341
  ,, Phoenix symbol of a, iv. 188
  ,, Van of Tartar, v. 341
  Cycles, v. 340-348
  ,, Ancients of, kept, iii. 395
  ,, Nārada closely connected with, iii. 92
  Death, which gives, i. 338
  DOCTRINE, see Book Index
  Doctrine of Āryans, iii. 242; v. 412
  Dragon, of, iii. 379
  Elements, three, iv. 187
  Elohim, of, iii. 412
  Embryology explained of, i. 270
  Figures of man's age, iii. 253
  Fires, of, iii. 114, 115
  Folios of Kiu-te, v. 389-391
  Formation of a body, of, ii. 395
  Fragments of Asuramaya's data, iii. 62, 80
  Generation of a single atom, of, ii. 395

SECRET (*Contd.*)
  Great, ii. 276
  Heliocentric system of, v. 316
  Idea attached to scarabaeus, iv. 122
  Inequalities of intellect, of, iii. 169
  Initiations and Satanic myth, iii. 377
  ,,   Dogma of Hermes, v. 142
  Knowledge, Disappearance of, iv. 102
  ,,   Dragon guarded entrance to, i. 185
  ,,   Dragon symbol of, iii. 378
  ,,   Gupta Vidyā or, iv. 67; v. 188
  ,,   Self, of, iv. 139
  ,,   *Upanishads* and, i. 313
  Kumāras, three of, ii. 176
  Language, ii. 76; v. 115, 184, 185
  Law, v. 412
  Law, of the, v. 188
  Learning, Thoth God of, iv. 128
  Libraries in Temples of Antiquity, v. 59, 253
  Malleable glass, of, iii. 428
  Meaning, Adytum, of, iv. 27
  ,,   Bible of, v. 66
  ,,   Book of Thoth of, v. 68
  ,,   Brahmā, of, v. 230
  ,,   Daityas, of allegory of, ii. 140
  ,,   Eastern glyphs of, v. 73
  ,,   *Exodus*, of, ii. 100
  ,,   Gospel, of, v. 66
  ,,   Nārada, of, v. 287
  ,,   Purusha Sukta, of, iv. 178
  ,,   Statement of Hierophants, of, v. 356
  Mysteries, Avatara, of, v. 337
  ,,   Deity, of, v. 108
  ,,   Hermaphrodite, of, v. 242
  ,,   Initiation into, iii. 47; v. 275
  ,,   Mystery God of, v. 277
  ,,   State religion of, v. 297
  Name, Phoenician God, of, iv. 111
  ,,   Potency of, iv. 105
  ,,   Unpronounceable, ii. 156
  Observations, of India and Egypt, v. 264
  Occult sciences, in, iv. 274
  Orbs, three, ii. 299
  Philosophy, i. 292; iv. 207
  Place or the shrine, iii. 94
  Planet(s), v. 433, 536
  Potency of sacred formula, v. 418
  Power of Satan, iv. 104
  Priests have kept things, iii. 367
  Reading of first verse of *Genesis*, ii. 161
  Reincarnation kept, iv. 122
  Records, v. 144
  ,,   Calculations of, iii. 62
  ,,   Exoteric texts and, iii. 334
  ,,   Hebrews', iv. 130
  ,,   Mystery of genesis of man and, ii. 35
  Satan, of, iii. 236
  Schools, v. 262, 403, 407
  Science, Alexandrian library, and, i. 46
  ,,   Ammonius Saccas and, v. 302
  ,,   Asiatic nations have, iv. 363
  ,,   Astrology and, v. 443
  ,,   Concealed for ages, i. 57
  ,,   Creative Powers and, v. 213
  ,,   East and West in, v. 109

Science, Eastern, v. 192
  ,,   Kabalistic Astrology and, v. 443
  Sciences, Buddha and, 411
  ,,   Creation of man and, iv. 255
  ,,   Deity, emanate from, i. 135
  ,,   Doctrines of, v. 107
  ,,   Gandharvas instruct man in, iv. 156
  ,,   History of, iv. 71
  ,,   Japanese, i. 135
  ,,   Mysteries and, v. 296
  ,,   Student of, v. 44, 175, 411
  Scientists and occultists, ii. 391
  Secrets, of, ii. 69; iii. 283
  Sense in *Bhagavad Gītā*, iii. 147
  Septenary system kept, iv. 175
  Side of Fire, v. 445
  Signs in Zohar, v. 112
  Societies, v. 294
  Symbol, Kārtikeya a, iv. 190
  Symbology, v. 46
  Systems, Hindū and Kabalistic, ii. 70; v. 322
  ,,   Septenary constitution of man in, i. 286; iv. 175
  ,,   Teaching on the egg symbol, ii. 74
  Teachings, Ahura, respecting, iv. 180
  ,,   Aryan, v. 357
  ,,   Atlantis and Lemuria, about, iii. 401
  ,,   Bible and, v. 110, 208
  ,,   Christian Saviour and, iii. 233
  ,,   Cis-Himālayan, iii. 309
  ,,   Earth of, v. 299
  ,,   Elements, on, order of, ii. 297
  ,,   Evolution of universe, on, ii. 309
  ,,   Heliocentric theory, on, iii. 163
  ,,   Necessity for, v. 65, 70
  ,,   Planets and, v. 324
  ,,   Sanctuaries of, v. 73
  ,,   Universal kosmos, as to, i. 79
  ,,   Vairājas, on, iii. 98
  Texts, Kabalistic, iii. 137
  Theogony of Chaldeo-Hebrews, iv. 110
  Things done in heaven, iii. 381
  Vedas, of, i. 258
  Volumes, Anthropology of, iv. 259
  ,,   Doctrine of Avātaras in, v. 349
  ,,   Kabalistic books, of, iv. 106, 107
  ,,   Tibet of, v. 375, 389, 390
  Wisdom, v. 72, 108, 246, 443
  ,,   Adept in, iv. 101
  ,,   Astrology and, v. 264
  ,,   *Bible*, of, ii. 28; v. 66
  ,,   Chaldean hierophants, of, ii. 67
  ,,   Dual power of, iii. 363
  ,,   East, of the, v. 74, 108, 109
  ,,   Enoch represents, iv. 101, 102
  ,,   Female form symbolizes, ii. 66
  ,,   God of, v. 65, 287
  ,,   Hebrew initiates got, ii. 67
  ,,   Jonas and, ii. 380
  ,,   Mercury, God of, v. 65
  ,,   Moses and, ii. 67
  ,,   Nebo God of, iv. 22, 23
  ,,   Patrons of, iii. 215
  ,,   Purānas and, iv. 156
  ,,   Pythagoras, of, iv. 104
  ,,   Rishis and, iv. 104
  ,,   Tau and, iv. 152, 153

SECRET (*Contd.*)
  Wisdom, Thot-Hermes representative of, ii. 118
  ,, *Upanishads*, in, iv. 162
  Work of Chiram, iii. 122
  Works, Figures of, iii. 80
  ,, King Initiates, of, v. 258
  ,, Number of, inexhaustible, iii. 436
  ,, Paracelsus, of, ii. 256
  Worship of Jews, iv. 40
  Year of World, v. 200
SECRET DOCTRINE, Abrahma and, v. 110
  Ancient races, on, iii. 105
  Androgynes and first three races of, iii. 132
  Antiquity of, v. 275
  Archaic ages, of, i. 45
  Archaic, echo of, i. 141
  Aryan, v. 91, 180
  Atheism, teaches no, i. 322
  Atlantis, date of, iii. 293
  Axiom in, i. 80; iii. 144
  Basic conceptions on which rests, i. 85
  Be-ness, symbolized, i. 79
  Books of, iii. 320
  Brāhmans, of initiated, i. 44
  Buddhism upreared on tenets of, i. 118
  Cataclysms, on, iii. 157
  Century, all of, that can be given out this, i. 60
  Chaldeans, of, v. 180
  Christian fathers endeavour to obliterate, i. 62
  Chronology of, iii. 22, 23, 61, 81, 83; iv. 16
  Collection of facts, a, i. 67
  Corroboration of, ii. 154, 155; v. 258
  Cosmogony of, i. 316; ii. 398; iii. 70
  Cosmos and man, elements of, i. 128; v. 208
  Cradle of physical man, iii. 422
  Creation, on, iv. 121
  Crookes's near approach to, ii. 346
  Curse of incarnation, on, iii. 248
  Daksha's sacrifice and, iii. 189
  Darwinian accounts of origin of man, and, iii. 165
  Defenders of, ii. 400
  Deluge of geology and, iii. 152
  Derision expected for, iii. 438, 439
  Dhyān Chohans, on groups of, i. 86
  Divine essence explained by, i. 71
  Divine Pymander and, iii. 16
  Dogma, not, iii. 263, 264
  Dragon, meaning of, in, iii. 378
  Earlier men, common property of, iv. 362
  East, of, i. 41; iii. 165; v. 44, 51, 108
  Egyptian papyri and, ii. 398
  Egyptians believed in, iii. 145
  Esoteric Buddhism and, i. 42, 214
  Esoteric cosmogony of, ii. 321
  Esotericism of Jews and, iii. 52
  Evolution in, corroborated, iii. 188
  Evolution of man according to, iii. 161
  Father, evolution of life and, i. 141
  Father and mother, Aditi, iii. 69
  Few fundamental truths from, i. 45
  Figures symbolical in, i. 110
  First book of, man's appearance and, i. 86
  Full consciousness, teaching as to, i. 167
  Fundamental principle of, iv. 106
  Garuda, furnishes key to, iv. 134

  Gautama, of, i. 44
  Genesis and, iii. 132, 373
  Gerald Massey and, iv. 206
  Gnostics and, ii. 168; iii. 72
  Great flood, records, ii. 54
  Hebrew *Bible* and, iii. 281
  Heptad, on, iv. 174
  Hermetic fragments and, i. 328
  History, authentic, i. 56
  History teaches, i. 310
  Illusion, on, ii. 329
  Indian philosophy, religion and, iii. 97
  Initiation of Egyptians, taught at, iii. 145, 146
  Isis Unveiled not, i. 63
  Islands, takes no account of, iii. 21
  Japanese fables and, i. 265
  Kabalah and, accord, iii. 136
  Karma, and, v. 370
  Logos or collective creator, admits, i. 322
  Mānasa in, iii. 178
  Metaphysics dealt with, iv. 219
  Minds, first beings called in, i. 151
  Modern science and, iii. 441
  Nāgas of, iii. 188
  Natural genesis and, ii. 376
  Nazarenes, echoed by, iii. 105
  Nebular theory, on, ii. 321
  Norse legends and, iii. 105
  Once open to all, iv. 179
  One absolute beness first axiom of, i. 80
  One form of existence, postulates, i. 118
  One number issued from no-number, i. 157
  Order of nature, on, iv. 103
  Orientalists and, iv. 16
  Origin of man, on, iii. 176
  Partial sketch of, attempted, i. 118
  Periodicity, asserts law of, i. 82
  Philosophies, on antiquity of, ii. 103
  Planet, v. 433
  Planetary chain, especially occupied with, i. 130
  Plato's teaching and, iii. 372
  Preached by Jesus, v. 169
  Primeval matter, on, ii. 310
  Pristine bi-sexual unity in, iii. 144
  Progressive development, taught, i. 115
  Propositions of, i. 82
  Records of archaic, iii. 72
  Rejected Stone, v. 287
  Religion of prehistoric world, i. 56
  Renovation and reabsorption, on, ii. 192
  Rishis, genealogy of, ii. 154
  Root-and Seed-Manus on, i. 281
  Rosicrucian creed outcome of, i. 84
  Scholars will recognize, in twentieth century, i. 59
  Schools, of oldest, iv. 174
  Science, and, iii. 167; iv. 215
  Sciences, esoteric key to all, iv. 296, 336
  Sepher Yetzireh and, i. 151
  Small portion of, imparted, i. 42
  Solar systems and, i. 130
  Sons of fire, on, i. 151
  Sons of God and wisdom, on, iv. 231
  Specific unity of mankind taught by, iii. 201
  Speech, v. 115
  St. Paul's Epistles, in, v. 215

SECRET DOCTRINE (*Contd.*)
  Sun, teaching as to, i. 162
  Synonyms in, i. 155
  Teachings on, v. 108
  Theogonies, esoteric key to all, iv. 336
  Third race built boats before houses, iii. 398
  " This " cannot create, teaches, i. 74
  Tibetans, traditions, and, i. 55
  Traditions of, iv. 125
  Two lost continents, on, iii. 227
  Unity conceded by, iv. 123; v. 290
  Universal, v. 50
  Universal cosmogony of, ii. 54
  Universe, on, i. 328; iv. 121; v. 229, 231
  Upanishads rest on, i. 118; v. 27
  Vedas, antedates, i. 59
Voltaire knew nothing of, iv. 312
  Wisdom of ages, accumulated, i. 316
SECRETARY, Isis of Hermes, ii. 104
  King Saturn, of, ii. 179
SECRETS, Alphabetical, v. 115
  Angels, of, iv. 104
  Astral light, of, i. 336
  Creation, of, iv. 114
  Dangerous in ignorant hands, ii. 18
  Esoteric doctrine, of, i. 313
  Generation one of the most hidden, i. 244
  Geometrical, in Pyramid, v. 91
  Gods, of, iii. 395
  Heaven, of, ii. 247
  Hermes, of, iii. 236
  Important to humanity, ii. 18
  Initiation, of, ii. 134; iii. 63; iv. 218; v. 169, 172
  Keely at threshold of great, ii. 280
  Kouyunjik, of, iii. 18
  Land and sea of, iii. 22
  Nature's, i. 244; iii. 83, 224, 319, 371; v. 91, 121, 263, 407
  Primeval, loss of, iv. 179
  Race, only in our, iii. 319
  Satan uncovering heavenly, iii. 238
  Seat of Three, v. 378
  Svara and, light profound, i. 313
  Terrestrial plane, on, ii. 310
  Unknown, of, ii. 351
  Unrevealable, i. 57
SECT(S), laughter at the mutual expense of, ii. 371
  Tananim, of, v. 67
SED et Serpens, iii. 212
SEDIMENTATION, Commencement of, iii. 165
  Europe, in, iv. 264
  Huxley on period of, iii. 82
  Round, in this, iv. 283
SEDIMENTS, Primary epoch of, iii. 159
SEE, Rome, of, v. 146
SEED, Abraham's, ii. 301
  Action, of, i. 282
  Adulterer, of, iv. 160
  Animal man, of the, of the, i. 271
  Appearing and reappearing, i. 248, 250
  Ark, of all things in an, iii. 308; iv. 181
  Avatarism, of, v. 168, 350
  Cosmic, v. 422, 424
  Die to live as plant, must, ii. 178
  Divine knowledge, of, i. 259

Dust of earth, shall be as, iv. 38
  Ethereal organism, is an, i. 250
  Evolution from, i. 326
  Fifth root-race, of, i. 173
  Fohat turns, ii. 397
  Force that makes, germinate, iv. 160
  Force which informs, i. 332
  Fruit whose, is in itself, ii. 96
  Genesis, in, ii. 96
  Golden egg, became, ii. 46, 65
  Humanity, of futre, iii. 20
  Incomprehensible drops, ii. 65
  Jacob's, iv. 38
  Karma and divine wisdom, of, iii. 409
  Kārtikeya born out of, iv. 120
  Knowledge, of, iii. 283
  Kriyāshakti, i. 259
  Life, of, iii. 149, 154, 158
  Lotus bears its own, iv. 40
  Maha-Vishnu the One, v. 168
  Material life, of all, iii. 72
  Men, of, iii. 154
  Mysterium of plant, is, i. 325
  Permanent, Chhāyā is, v. 565
  Potential force in, iv. 16
  Pothos, sprung from, ii. 54
  Rudra-Shiva, of, iv. 120, 190
  Self-existent Lord cast, it, 46
  Serpent's and woman's, iii. 409
  Terrestrial, or Sperm, i. 326
  Theogony, in, i. 250
  Tree of Life and being, of, iv. 160; v. 154
  Triple aspect of, iv. 160
  Universe, of, iv. 112, 163
  World-germ, or, i. 250
SEED-HUMANITY or Shista, i. 234
SEED-MANU, Noah and, iv. 169
  Prime cause, is effect of, i. 281
  Round, in every, iii. 321
SEED-MANUS, i. 281; iii. 171, 309, 310
SEED-RACE Fifth, iv. 169
SEEDS, Ark, brought into, iii. 292
  Atlanteans, of future, iii. 274
  Civilization, of, iii. 203
  Human beings, of, ii. 92; iv. 51
  Life of, iii. 147, 291
  Lotus, of, ii. 94
  Male and female, iii. 48
  Primitive atoms or, ii. 274
  Races, for new, iii. 441
  Races, of past, present and future, iv. 200
  Religions, of existing, iv. 51
  Wisdom, of trinity of, iii. 278
SEEMANN, Prof., quoted, iii. 289, 333; iv. 350
SEER, Actualities visible to real, i. 58
  Allegorical language, and, v. 127
  Beings of higher plane, can commune with, iii. 282
  Böhme, mediaeval, iv. 205
  Divine breath seen by, i. 330
  Enoch means, iv. 101, 102; v. 102
  Enoïchion, Book of, iv. 98
  Enoïchion means, iii. 215, 361; iv. 99, 100, 102; v. 102
  Mau denotes, ii. 16
  Moon was, by night, ii. 16

SEER (Contd.)
   Nabin a, iv. 23
   Natural, born, v. 429
   Open eye, of, iv. 99
   Opened eye of, i. 118
   Patoms, of, iv. 79
   Physiological purity of, iii. 297
   Planetary powers seen by, ii. 357
   Primary creation only realizable to a great,
      iii. 312
   Revelation, of, iv. 135
   Sound visible to Spiritual, ii. 358
   Spiritual eye of, iii. 77
   States of Consciousness, and, v. 79
   Supersensuous states of matter, visible to,
      ii. 239
   Swedish, v. 407
   Theurgy and, v. 79
   Trained, v. 554, 557
   Trance, during, ii. 240
   Unit followed by eye of, ii. 343
   Unseen, i. 267
SEERS, Apollo God of, iv. 339
   Atoms according to, ii. 358
   Beings of other spheres seen by, ii. 329
   Bible of, v. 324
   Breath, perceive mystery of, i. 176
   Christianity, of, v. 277
   Commune on higher planes, v. 282
   Cosmic Space, and, v. 382
   Cycles and, v. 338
   Daniel and Ezekiel, like, i. 276
   Dhyān Chohans, on, ii. 152
   East, of, ii. 355
   Elohists were, v. 186
   Enos generic name for, iii. 361
   Every age of, v. 324
   Generations of, i. 318
   Greek, iii. 380
   Initiated, i. 316; v. 429
   Knowledge acquired by, iv. 269
   Mistakes of untrained, iv. 272
   Monads according to, i. 318
   Mystery on divine plane referred to by, i. 129
   Mystics and, v. 359
   Natural, iv. 272
   Prophets and, i. 276
   Shiva eye of ancient, iii. 286
   Sun and moon known to, iv. 167
   Svastika used by, iv. 158
SEERSHIP, Abnormal or spiritual, iii. 297
   Apollo personified, iv. 340
   Böhme's inspired, iv. 201
   Traditions of, confirmed, ii. 371
SEFEKH ABU builds his house on high, ii. 124
SEGMENTATION, Cell, of, i. 270
   Embryo develops from, in cell, iii. 125
   Fire atoms, of, i. 302
   Ovum, of an infinitely small, i. 269
SEIR ANPIN, v. 111
SEISMIC activity, Early, iv. 93
SEKHEM, Khem, residence of God, i. 267
   Merged in, i. 267
SELDENUS quoted, ii. 110; v. 238, 240, 318
SELECTION, Natural, ii. 324; iii. 192, 300, 347,
      423; iv. 217, 266, 296, 303, 305, 307
SELENE (Moon), v. 65

SELENIC mysteries, Ancients learned, ii. 111
SELENOGNOSIS, ii. 17
SELENOGRAPHY, Division of lunar symbology,
      i. 17
SELEUCUS of Seleucia, i. 176
SELF, Adept, of progressed, i. 121
   Ākāsha, and, iv. 139
   Ālaya, i. 121
   All, v. 269
   Animals, of, v. 546
   Ātmā spiritual, ii. 48, 335
   Ātman or, iv. 210; v. 75, 269
   Ātmanah or, ii. 47
   Brahmā, one with, iv. 209
   Brahman, the, iv. 210, 211
   Breath, or, i. 159
   Buddhi becomes higher, iii. 234
   Consciousness, v. 546, 552
   Control, v. 81
   Cosmic, ii. 48
   Daiviprakriti, or one root of, ii. 148
   Divine, ii. 193; iv. 138, 139, 145; v. 77, 79,
      92, 269, 420, 452
   Divine voice of, v. 380
   Ego or, i. 187, 273
   Elements of, ii. 48
   Essence of, ii. 258
   Evolution, v. 223
   Fire means, iv. 137, 138, 139, 209, 210
   Forms in numerous, i. 159
   Generation, v. 225
   Higher, i. 155, 159, 309, 319; iii. 234; iv. 139,
      209, 210; v. 76, 77, 79, 80, 128, 301, 354,
      359, 370, 431, 452, 466, 502, 503, 504, 511
   Highest, symbolized by sun, v. 269, 270, 362
   Human, ii. 193; iv. 138; v. 452
   I or, iv. 138
   Illusion, emancipating itself from, ii. 258
   Impersonal, i. 187; iv. 210
   Inner, iii. 121; v. 407
   Knowledge of, v. 380
   Kshetrajna, iv. 209, 210
   Life should humanize, iii. 248
   Life-winds attached to, iv. 64
   Lower, v. 78, 503
   Manifestation of, ii. 258; iv. 64
   Matter, in, v. 557
   Mental, ii. 148
   Mind created from, ii. 47
   Nirmānakāya, of, v. 402
   One absolute, i. 319; v. 269
   One or higher, i. 159
   Outer terrestrial, iii. 270
   Personal, Adepts of, v. 361
   Personification of divine, iv. 138
   Physical, ii. 148
   Principle, seventh, ii. 48; iv. 145
   Progenitors of true, ii. 176
   Purity, represents highest state of, iv. 142
   Purusha the divine, iv. 145
   Qualities devoid of, i. 151
   Root of, ii. 148
   Seat abiding in, iv. 64, 138
   Secret knowledge possessed by, iv. 139
   Self within, iv. 211
   Senses and, i. 151, 159; ii. 48, 259
   Soul or, i. 273

SELF (*Contd.*)
Soul's spiritual sun, iv. 210
Spiritual, ii. 335; iii. 234
Spiritual fire within, iii. 121
Sun, iv. 209, 210
Supreme, iv. 209
Unit, v. 269
Universal, iv. 210; v. 374, 418
Universe of, v. 379
Vaishvānara often denotes, iv. 64, 138
Voice or, i. 159
Wind or, i. 159
Wisdom of divine, iv. 139
Worship, v. 77
SELF-BORN, Chhāyās, iii. 129, 146
Daksha, power, iii. 249
Dragon symbol means, iii. 354
Fathers were, iii. 129
First race was, iii. 171, 203
Gods, i. 252; ii. 169; iii. 129
Heavenly man, iii. 159
Hindu Aja, iii. 354
Kashyapa, ii. 81; iii. 381
Logoi, or, ii. 79
Logos, iii. 354
Mānasa rejected, iii. 178
Pitris and, iii. 129
Progenitors, iii. 129, 171
Serpent emblem of, ii. 79
Sons of, iii. 129, 146
Sons of Yoga, astral, iii. 203
Svāyambhuva or, iii. 311, 312
Time, sprang from, ii. 81; iii. 381
SELF-CONSCIOUS, Beings, iii. 99
Divinity through, efforts, iii. 102
Egotism, iii. 89
Entities, iii. 174
Evolution, ii. 134
Existence, i. 311
Host preferred, pain, iii. 419
Inner subject, and, iv. 224
Intelligent men, iii. 56
Man made, iii. 88
Men, new race of, ii. 176
Mind, iii. 235
Senses, use of, ii. 259
Spirit, i. 243
Thinking men, iii. 111
SELF-CONSCIOUSNESS, Absolute attained by, i. 122
Abyss of, iii. 90
Active and passive, iii. 318
Ahamkāra or, ii. 47
Atoms have potentiality of, i. 167
Brahmā called them forth to, iv. 145
Buddhi in union with, iii. 234
Consciousness and, v. 546, 552
Cross, and, iv. 132
Ego must attain full, i. 243
Ego sum necessitates, i. 280
Egoism or, ii. 47
Fallen angels and man's, iii. 276
Hegel's theory of, i. 122, 167
Idiot, absence of, makes an, iii. 171
Intelligence or, iv. 132
Leibnitz on, ii. 351
Living fire, due to, iii. 111

Mahat develops, i. 142; iv. 210
Mind and, ii. 47; iv. 82; v. 546
Monads may reach a higher plane of, i. 232
One Self, consciousness, or, iv. 145
Origin of delusion necessary to, i. 116
Paramārthasatya or, i. 120
Pilgrim soul passes through, i. 228
Pitris endow man with, ii. 263
Plane of, i. 232
Sat at root of, iii. 69
Spark expands into, iii. 103
Speck, seed or germ have no, iv. 223
Spirit, in pure, iii. 89
Tortures of, iii. 419
Universal, ii. 47
Universal soul at root of, iii. 69
Wisdom, of, iii. 121
SELF-DEVELOPMENT of Rudras, iv. 156
SELF-DIVISION, Procreation by, iii. 173; iv. 22
SELF-EVOLUTION of Mahat, ii. 169
SELF-EVOLVING forces, ii. 165
SELF-EXERTION, Divine powers through, iii. 88
SELF-EXISTENCE, Created personally, i. 74
Eye of, i. 82
SELF-EXISTENT, Angelic or, iii. 244
Ātma-bhū or, iii. 183; iv. 150
Concealed Lord is, i. 123
Creations, called, iii. 244, 245
Earth, on, iii. 171
Heavenly man or self-born, iii. 159
Kāma is, iii. 183
Lord, i. 150; ii. 46
One, i. 152
Spirit, iii. 49
Svayambhū-Nārāyana, iii. 137
Svāyambhuva, i. 146
Theory of, iii. 159
Three in one, i. 115
Tsi-tsai, ii. 71
SELF-EXISTING, Basis, matter, ii. 41
Reality, i. 70
Unknowable mover or, i. 126
SELF-GENERATED, Being, ii. 74
Rotation, ii. 225
SELF-GENERATION, Mystery, of, i. 134; v. 223
SELF-GOD, Unity with, ii. 363
SELF-HOOD, first outline of, ii. 172; v. 551
SELF-INITIATED higher Gods, iii. 133
SELFISHNESS, cause of sin, v. 434
Personal, v. 69
SELF-LUMINOUS, Globe, iii. 161
Matter, ii. 314
Nebula, ii. 312
SELF-MANIFESTED Kwan-Shi-Yin, ii. 193
SELF-MOVING, Atoms, ii. 395
Numbers, iv. 122
SELF-PERCEPTION, living fire, due to, iii. 111
Pilgrim-soul, of, i. 228
SELF-PRODUCED Giants, princes, iv. 55
Kosmos consists of, beings, ii. 360
SELF-REDEEMED MAN, iii. 418
SELF-SACRIFICE, Christos is, v. 556
Divine Hermaphrodite of, iv. 291
Dragon of wisdom and of, iii. 103
Krishna, of, v. 289

SELF-SACRIFICE (Contd.)
 Prometheus, of, iii. 420
 Rebels, of, iii. 245
 Vishvakarman, of, i. 311; iv. 177; v. 154, 270
SELF-WORSHIP and Atlanteans, iii. 275; v. 77
SELI-ALLAH, v. 180
SELVES, Celestial, ii. 295
 Personal, iii. 118
SEMELE and Jupiter, ii. 116; iii. 362
SEMI-ASTRAL, Earth, iii. 253
 Forms, iv. 259
 Race, iv. 253, 258
SEMI-DEMON of Babylonia, iii. 196
SEMI-DEMONS of fourth race, iii. 319
SEMI-ETHEREAL, Conditions, iii. 157
 Earth, iii. 312
 Evolution from ethereal to, ii. 367
 Monad and, being, iv. 206
SEMI-INTELLIGENT, Elementals, i. 320
 Forces, i. 328; ii. 200, 239
SEMI-SPIRITS and androgynes, iii. 133
SEMI-TERRESTRIAL mixed natures, i. 311
SEMINAL principles, iii. 167; iv. 112
SEMITE, Kabalist, iv. 38
 Man stopping with, iv. 37
 Mind, iv. 114
 Temptation invented by, ii. 98
SEMITES, Adam, descendants of red, iii. 423,
   424
 Adami taken by, iv. 19; v. 203
 Āryans and, iii. 150, 205
 Deep of wisdom and, iii. 64
 Divine hermaphrodite and, iii. 135
 Ea changed into Tiamat by, iii. 64, 71
 Holy of holies of, iv. 25
 Procreating highest purpose of, iv. 113
 Proto-Chaldeans, borrow from, iii. 208
 Savages and, iii. 419
 Seth primitive God of, iii. 91
 Teraphim and, v. 237
 Triadic deities of, iii. 65
SEMITIC, Alphabet, v. 178
 Āryans, iii. 268
 Cosmogony, iii. 243
 Deity, iv. 108
 Dialect, v. 181
 Empire, iv. 271
 Genius Loci, ii. 183
 Khamism contains germ of, i. 175
 Language(s), iii. 205; iv. 324; v. 243
 Milton, Enoch is, iv. 51; v. 100
 Mind, ii. 98
 Nations, crucifix unknown to, v. 162
 Parabrahman, v. 187
 Races, iii. 154
 Religion, i. 49, 52, 58; ii. 98
 Revelation, ii. 381
 Systems, ii. 162
 Theo-anthropographies, iii. 137
 Traditions of Satan, iii. 389
 Tribe, Jews, a little, ii. 31
SEMOTHEES, Druids, v. 306
SEMPA, Tibetan for soul, ii. 123
SEMPITERNAL depth and silence, iv. 139
SEMPITERNITY, i. 109
SENĀ, Kārtikeya, female aspect, iv. 190
 Yoginī equivalent with, ii. 194

SENARY, Hieroglyphical, iv. 163
 Interlaced triangles, in, iv. 164
 Man, applied by sages to, iv. 163
 Six or, iv. 152
 Unity, and, iv. 154
SENECA, quoted, ii. 375; iv. 326; v. 266
SENILE representative, iv. 349
SENNACHERIB'S PALACE, ii. 31
SENSAOS, Mummy, v. 332
SENSATION, Animal life of, iv. 94
 Animals have, iv. 240
 Atom, in every, iv. 242
 Consciousness, resting on states of, i. 69
 Māyā, is, i. 69
 Occultists on, iv. 241
 Plane of, ii. 266
 Sound, of, ii. 358
 Space outside any act of, ii. 279
 Sun, radiated from, ii. 264
SENSATIONS, Animals, ii. 289
 Jnānashakti, power of mind in interpreting,
   i. 333
 Objective consciousness and, ii. 327
SENSE, All that lies beyond threshold of, ii. 239
 Buddhi seventh, iv. 210
 Chaos obtaining, ii. 57
 Creation of, ii. 203
 Explorer of nature's secrets must transcend
   limitation of, ii. 200
 Hæckel on organs of, iii. 298
 Individuality of every, ii. 257
 Knowledge differs from, i. 322
 Manas merged in sixth, iv. 210
 Mental feeling precedes development of,
   v. 547
 Mind serving for both, and action, ii. 47
 Personality, of, i. 318
 Self and five organs of, ii. 48
 Seventh, v. 508
 Six organs of, v. 368
 Sixth, i. 302; iii. 259; iv. 210; v. 508
 Solidarity, i. 258
SENSE-BORN phenomena, ii. 278
SENSELESS, Anthropoid apes direct product of,
   man, i. 236
 Astral man, i. 235
 Chaos called, ii. 54, 57
 Forms, first men were, iv. 182
 Humanity, iii. 233
 Life, desire to live, a, iii. 119
 Mankind, physiologically, iii. 410
 Motion, i. 196
 Pitris created, iii. 419
 Primordial men, ii. 9 1
SENSES, Aindriyaka or creation of, ii. 172, 174;
   iv. 185
 Anugītā on, ii. 258, 259
 Consciousness through physical, iv. 270; v. 557
 Correspondences of, v. 543
 Creation of, ii. 172, 174
 Deities of physical, iv. 139
 Development of higher, i. 302
 Division into five of, ii. 259
 Double set of, ii. 258
 Elements and, iii. 115, 116
 Emancipation, are causes of, ii. 259
 Evolution of, iii. 116

SENSES (*Contd.*)
Existence, five not necessity for, ii. 332
Eyes most occult of, v. 550
Fatal destiny or world of, iv. 57
First Race, v. 523
Five, v. 474, 508
Growth of outer, iii. 295
Higher, iv. 210
Higher self and, iv. 210
Impulses produced by our physical, ii. 369
Inner, atrophied during racial development, iii. 295
Insufficiency of our, ii. 329
Kāma-Rupa and, v. 493
Kosmic, v. 541
Lost, replaced by others, ii. 257
Material plane of evolution not known to our, iii. 72
Matter, and, i. 296
Matter attenuated to our, ii. 331
Matter of science at lowest extreme of our, ii. 353
Mental plane, on, ii. 258
Mind and understanding two higher, iv. 210
Physical plane, on, ii. 258; v. 429, 474
Planets outside our terrestrial, i. 207
Prabhavāpyaya, from, iii. 116
Primary colours, v. 508
Primeval matter beyond five, ii. 325
Primeval physical matter beyond our normal, ii. 319
Principles and their, iv. 138
Protean substance that eludes, ii. 394
Rudiments of future, ii. 165
Sacrificial priests, are seven, i. 159; iv. 200
Scientist, of, ii. 342
Secondary creation, pertain to, iii. 115
Seven functions of seven, iv. 209
Seven, in man, i. 158, 311; iii. 334; iv. 200; v. 429, 508
Seven principles and seven, iv. 201
Sight, all included in, v. 562
Sixth and seventh, v. 482, 508, 523
Spiritual, ii. 258; iii. 116; v. 429
Spiritual or intellectual soul one with, iii. 117
Substance, transitory illusion of, ii. 290
Symbolized by five temple pillars, ii. 183
Synthesis of seven, i. 159
Tattvas and, v. 474
Third race, physiological of, iii. 300
Touch, v. 523
Vaikharī Vāch objective to our physical, ii. 150
War result of opening of men's, iii. 278
SENSIBLE and INTELLIGIBLE, The, of Plato, v. 445
SENSITIVE, Fire that develops eloquence in, ii, 52
Plants, ii. 174
SENSITIVES, Beings of outer spheres seen by, ii. 329
Inner vision of, iii. 296
SENSUOUS, Existence, cycles of, iv. 82
Life, matter or, iii. 39
Perception, Induction method depended on, iv. 144
  ,,   Thraldom of, iv. 159
Plane, mind on, i. 159; v. 525
  VI–25

SENTIENT beings, Formless Life, beginnings of, i. 260
Individual, Life microcosm of its higher macrocosm, i. 311
Kosmos is guided by, i. 318
Second round developed individual, i. 304
SENZAR, Alphabet, v. 115, 117, 505, 506
Atlantis in, i. 64
Catechism, i. 75
Commentaries, i. 87
Occultism, of, iii. 437
Sacerdotal secret tongue, i. 64
Stanzas, version of, i. 87
SEPARATION OF THE SEXES, Adam and Eve, and, iii. 199; v. 291
Animals, among, iii. 186, 190; iv. 306
Binary symbol of, ii. 99
Bronze age of third race, during, iv. 89
Daksha, and, iii. 277
Death known after, iv. 180
Dhyānīs, incarnate after, iii. 231
Evolution and, i. 72; iv. 227
Fall of man or, ii. 112; iii. 180; iv. 186
Fifth sub-race of third race, during, iv. 283
First manifested beings, of, i. 193
Fourth Adam after, iv. 72
Genesis, in, ii. 60; v. 291
History of races begins at, iii. 313
Holy of holies, Hebraic, pointed to, iv. 37
" How " of, iii. 202
Human crossing and, iii. 201
Human orifices and, v. 429, 430
Monosyllabic speech after, iii. 204
Naudin on, iii. 128, 188
Noah and, ii. 161
Occurred slowly, iii. 206
Placental animal-man after, v. 425
Polar cells and, iii. 126
Pre-Adamic period before, v. 203, 204
Programme of nature, in, iii. 221
Races mindless even after, iii. 288
Schmidt on, iii. 179, 191
Shatapatha, in, iii. 155
Signs of zodiac and, iv. 71; v. 425, 429, 430
Symbolical narrative of, in Pentateuch, v. 182
Third eye began to lose power after, iii. 295, 296
Third race mindless at period of, iii. 269
Third root-race in, i. 146; iii. 141, 250, 269, 295; iv. 89, 208, 258
SEPARATED MAN, Mystery of, v. 430
SEPARATENESS, Sense of, v. 553, 557
SEPARATOR of the one, Man is the, iii. 276
SEPHER, Cipher, means to, iii. 51
M'bo sha-arim, iii. 124
Seraphim, one of three, i. 156
SEPHIR, Aditi or Space, v. 386
SEPHIRA, Active power emerges as, ii. 69
Adam Kadmon, and, i. 161, 194, 263, 291; ii. 50, 146, 148
Aditi is, i. 124; ii. 69; iii. 54; v. 107, 191
Ain Soph on left hand of, ii. 339
Androgyne, as, ii. 69
Binah female, i. 262, 277; ii. 109; v. 72, 214
Brahmā identical with, i. 161
Chokmah, Binah, and, i. 160; v. 191

SEPHIRA (Contd.)
Creator, assumes office of, ii. 69
Crown, i. 160, 263; v. 191
Descent, fourth in, ii. 339
Devamātri in Zohar called, i. 124
-Eve, ii. 70
Father and mother Aditi of Hindu cosmogony, ii. 69
Globe, or sixth, i. 285
Heavenly man and, ii. 151
Holy Ghost, air or, ii. 51
Jehovah, a, i. 277
Kabalistic tree of life, in, ii. 339
Kadmon, and, i. 291; v. 191
Kether, Chokmah and Binah, v. 191, 438
Kether, in abstract only, i. 263
Kwan Yin, and, ii. 149
Latent deity emerges from within, ii. 69
Logos, female, ii. 149
Male, becomes, ii. 69
Malkuth generated by, i. 285
Mother of, i. 124
Numbers of, ii. 67
Osiris chief, ii. 155
Permutation of Eve, v. 190
Point, iii. 119; v. 191
Potency, third, v. 191, 192
Primeval waters, creates, ii. 69
Primordial point, or, ii. 51
Sacred aged, i. 291; v. 191
Sephiroth, androgyne synthesis of four and ten, i. 160; ii. 69; iii. 120; v. 191
Sephirothal triangle and upper, i. 160
Septenary, v. 191
Seven Names of, v. 191
Shekinah or first, ii. 70, 148
Spiritual light, ii. 50, 70
Triad, of, i. 153
Triad—Quaternary, v. 191
Triangle, emerging from dotted side of, ii. 69; v. 438
Triple, v. 191
Universal soul, of Jews, ii. 67
SEPHIRA-EVE, ii. 70; v. 164
SEPHIRAH, Binah third, iii. 383
Chokmah male, iii. 93
SEPHIROTH, Abba, father and Amona, mother are two, ii. 70
Adam Kadmon, and, ii. 107; iii. 15, 237, 294; iv. 274
Ain Soph, manifestation of, iii. 51
Alhim created six, ii. 56
Amshaspends are, v. 386
Androgyne synthesis of ten, i. 161
Angels, or, iii. 15, 120
Archetypal man, composing, ii. 107
Architect generic name for, ii. 303
Ases of Scandinavia identical with, iii. 105, 106
Binah and, i. 72
Builders are representatives of, ii. 186
Builders of universe, ii. 90, 303; v. 192, 208
Chokmah and Binah, ii. 70; iv. 197; v. 191, 192, 211
Circle with diameter picture of ten, ii. 107
Construction, of, ii. 90
Creation, in their work of, ii. 148
Creators, become, ii. 70; v. 214

Dabarim, called, ii. 150
Deity manifests itself through ten, i. 284
Dhyān Chohans are, ii. 90; iii. 365; v. 214, 386
Divine attributes, called, ii. 156
Divisions of ten, ii. 67
Doctrine of, v. 210
Duad or double sexed Logos, and, ii. 70
Egyptian Tau, and, iii. 48
Emanation from Adam Kadmon, v. 291
Emanation of First Cause, v. 91
Elements are veiled synthesis standing for, ii. 53
Elohim in, hidden wisdom of, iii. 51
Elohim, or, i. 277; iii. 387
Elohim-Javeh, iii. 56
Elohim-Jehovah and, ii. 70
Emanations, ii. 107; v. 91, 191, 299
Emanations of heavenly light, iii. 49
Forces, or, ii. 15
Forces of nature, or, ii. 90
Heavenly Adam created by ten, iii. 121
Heavenly man, iii. 237; iv. 114, 274
Host of, iii. 15; v. 234
Individualities or abstractions, as, ii. 357
Jehovah one of, i. 72, 247
Jetziratic world, of, iii. 121
Kabalah rests on ten, iii. 49
Kabalistic, iii. 48; v. 210
Kabalistic meaning of male and female, iv. 132
Kether, Chokmah and Binah are, of upper triad, i. 284; v. 191, 213
Light, described as, iii. 51
Limbs of body, and, i. 284; ii. 67
Logos, or, iii. 237
Lower, v. 439
Lower creation, are applied to, ii. 67
Man was created by, iii. 56
Manus, or, ii. 90
Material world, create manifested, iii. 15
Men and, connection between, i. 277
Metaphysical, ii. 156
Nine, v. 191
Numbers, or, iii. 49, 51
Oeaohoo contains in himself, i. 139
Patriarchs, become, ii. 70
Periphrasis of Jehovah or metaphysical, ii. 156
Physical man emanates from, v. 439
Physical or sidereal, ii. 156; v. 439
Prajāpatis, or, ii. 70, 90; v. 214, 386
Prajāpatis and, the, iii. 137; v. 107
Pythagorean triangle, and, iii. 120
Rays or Dhyān Chohans, or, i. 188
Root-races, and, ii. 90, 91
Second Adam, seven lower, iii. 15
Second and Third, v. 211
Sephira and, ii. 148; iii. 119
    ,,   Esoterically contains but two, ii. 70
    ,,   Exoterically contains all the other nine, ii. 70
    ,,   Mother of, i. 124
Sephirothal triad emanates lower, i. 188
Sephrim, or, iii. 51
Seven, i. 153, 186; v. 191, 213
    ,,   Angels of Presence, or, ii. 90; v. 207, 208, 333, 386, 439
    ,,   Centres of energy, or, iv. 176
    ,,   Creative hosts, i. 139

SEPHIROTH (Contd.)
  Seven, Physical planets are lower, v. 442
    ,, Spirits of presence, i. 114; ii. 24, 156; v. 74, 198, 209, 309
    ,, Splendours, iv. 175
    ,, Ten, and, v. 91, 116, 191
  Sidereal, ii. 156; v. 191
  Sixth and seventh principles in man, or, ii. 90
  Smaller face is formed of six, i. 286
  Sounds of Eastern philosophy, are, v. 439
  Spirito-psycho-physical spheres of septenary chain, or, ii. 90
  Spiritual man, are applied to, ii. 67
  Ten exoterically, i. 153
    ,, limbs of heavenly man are, i. 262
    ,, word called in Kabalah, ii. 150
  Tetragrammaton and, ii. 58; iv. 196
  Theory of, v. 177
  Three groups of, ii. 156; v. 191
  Totality of subordinate creative powers called, iv. 114
  Tree of, iii. 294
  Triad, of upper, i. 284; ii. 67; iii. 15
    ,, synthesized by upper, iii. 106
  Uni-triad and, ii. 69
  Universe, symbol of manifested, i. 160
  Weight, measure and number attributes of, iii. 237
  Wheels of Circles, represented as, v. 116
  Words, ten, iii. 49
  Zohar, in, v. 205 et seq., 439
SEPHIROTH-ELOHIM, Jehovah called, i. 187
SEPHIROTHAL Crown, v. 439
  Host, Adam is, iii. 57
  Number, Ten, i. 229
  Tree, iii. 17; v. 227
    ,, Binaries, of, i. 283
    ,, Crown, of, i. 229
    ,, Logos and, iii. 38
    ,, Mexican MS. represented in, iii. 48
    ,, Porphyry's Tree or, v. 439
    ,, Ten number of, iv. 167
    ,, Tetragrammaton and, iv. 196
    ,, Triangle, of, ii. 344
    ,, Unities, of, i. 283
  Triad, Archetypal world, in, i. 261
    ,, Binah, Chokmah and first, iii. 272; v. 191
    ,, Formless fiery breaths identical with upper, i. 261
    ,, Jehovah-Binah left angle of, iv. 167
    ,, Sephiroth, emanates from lower, i. 188
  Triangle, i. 160
SEPHIROTHIC ASPECTS of Ain Soph, ii. 65
SEPHIROTHIC TREE, Religions, in other, iii. 106
  Universe, is, ii. 67
SEPHRIM, Sephiroth, or, iii. 51, 237
  Wisdom of Alhim in, iii. 51
  Words in ciphers or figures, or, iii. 52, 237
SEPP, Dr., quoted, ii. 380, 381; iv. 50, 191
SEPTEMPARTITE, Earth, iv. 327, 328
SEPTENARY, Ākāsha is, ii. 251, 261
  Ancient esoteric school teaches man is, iv. 175
  Ansated cross is ensouled living man, iv. 171
  Anugītā, symbology in, iv. 209
  Army of the voice, and, i. 159

Atoms, aggregation of, ii. 344
Being, man is seventh race and round, iii. 175
Biblical chronology is, iv. 195; v. 201
    ,, creative God is, iv. 167
Brāhmanical, v. 199
Celsus's system, ii. 164
Chain, Earth lowest sphere of our, i. 248
    ,, Fohat formed our, i. 195
    ,, Genii of seven spheres of our, i. 247
    ,, Globe, is, iv. 269
    ,, Manu and doctrine of, iii. 309
    ,, Manvantara, of, ii. 382
    ,, Many more besides our, ii. 380
    ,, Monads cycling round any, i. 224
    ,, Purānas, and, ii. 175
    ,, Sephiroth and spheres of, ii. 90
    ,, Seven wheels are our, i. 200
Chains, Mars and Mercury are, i. 219
    ,, Worlds, of, i. 213
Consciousness, v. 547, 548
Constitution, Ātmā and physical body in, iv. 96
    ,, Chain, of our, i. 278; iv. 327
    ,, Egyptians, of, iv. 204; v. 357
    ,, Macrocosm, of, i. 222
    ,, Scriptures, in, iv. 316
    ,, Secret system, pre-eminent in all, i. 286
    ,, Sidereal bodies, of, i. 222
Cosmic substance, basis of evolution of, ii. 42
Creation of man, iii. 116
Creative Elohim lowest, iv. 167
    ,, Forces, scale of, iv. 60
Creators, seven hierarchies of, i. 140
Cycle law in nature, iv. 194
Cycles, iv. 193, 194
Divine consciousness, ladder of, ii. 49
Division, Āryan psychology and, i. 273
    ,, Brāhmans and, iv. 164
    ,, Cosmic and human constitutions, iv. 167, 187
    ,, Egypt, used by priests of, ii. 125
    ,, Egyptian psychology, in, i. 273; iv. 204
    ,, Esoteric, until now, i. 221
    ,, Fourfold, preceded, iii. 124
    ,, Heart, of, iii. 100
    ,, Hierarchies, in divine, iv. 167
    ,, Human principles, of, iii. 100; v. 353
    ,, Indian systems, in, i. 212
    ,, Kabalah following, i. 286
    ,, Microcosm, of, i. 222
    ,, Nature and man, of, iv. 145; v. 353
    ,, Practical occult teaching, iv. 164
    ,, Time, of, v. 433
Doctrine, Antiquity of, iv. 211
    ,, Book of the Dead, in, i. 282
    ,, Chemistry, and, ii. 276
Dogma, various forms of, iv. 207
Dragon, meaning of, iii. 213, 354
Each really fourteen, v. 522
Element, qualities of every, ii. 258
    ,, Second principle of, ii. 249
Ether is, ii. 44, 251
Evolution, cycles of, ii. 310
    ,, Forms of, iv. 303
    ,, Ladder of, i. 229

SEPTENARY (*Contd.*)
 Exoteric works, in, iv. 182
 Fire of manifested Kosmos is, i. 151
 Forces, v. 484
 Gods, sacred to several, iv. 174
 Group, celestial men or angels, of, i. 277
  ,, Man emanates from, i. 277
 Groups, Earliest forms of life appear in, iv. 165
  ,, Hosts, or, i. 265
  ,, Numbers, of, iv. 165
  ,, Physiology and, v. 483, 484
  ,, Universe composed of, iv. 70
 Harmony, iv. 153
 Hebdomad or, iv. 171
 Heptad our, iv. 174
 Hierarchies, ii. 182; v. 522
 Hierarchy, conscious divine powers, of, i. 86
  ,, Differentiation of germ of universe into, i. 86
 Host, Elohim of, iv. 169
  ,, Imperishable Jīvas group of first, i. 265
  ,, Noah represents, of Elohim, iv. 169
  ,, Number seven as applied to, i. 266
 Human, v. 521
 Interlaced triangles produce, iv. 163
 Jehovah lowest, iv. 167
 Kabalistic numerals based on, i. 284
 Kosmos, i. 249; v. 521
 Law of periodicity, iv. 199
 ,, Universal, ii. 309, 310
 Leibnitz, system of, ii. 355
 Life-cycle, iv. 119
 Light, i. 179
 Lunar months, fevers and gestations in, v. 522
 Man, Completion of, iii. 88
  ,, Heavenly man is resolved into, iv. 197
  ,, Triangle and quaternary symbol of, iv. 163
  ,, Virtuous, when, iv. 147
 Manifestation, scale of, i. 196
 Matter, manvantaric differentiation of, ii. 41
  ,, or Substance is, i. 330
 Monad, gyration of, i. 192
 Mysteries of Hebdomad and, iv. 152, 162 *et seq.*
 Nāga, meaning of, iii. 214
 Nature of the, v. 477
 Nature of Psychic and Spiritual Worlds, v. 438
 Number of virgin because unborn, iv. 174
 Object, every, v. 522
 Oeaohoo or, root, i. 131
 Periods and moon, iv. 167
 Phenomenal world, in, iv. 154
 Physical man plus immortal soul, iv. 163
 Plane, on each, v. 516
 Planetary creators, or, i. 140
 Prakriti, v. 469
 Pre-Adamic first root-race, ii. 91
 Principle, v. 203, 357, 521
  ,, Eastern Books in, v. 73
  ,, Esotericism, in, iii. 308
  ,, *Five Years of Theosophy*, in, ii. 335
  ,, Glyphs of Eastern books, v. 73
  ,, Man and nature, ii. 49
  ,, Medhātithi and, ii. 47
  ,, Zuni Indians, and, iv. 199
 Races, primeval, iv. 178

Ray from the one, human entity is, iv. 176
Ring, i. 200; ii. 297
Root, or Oeaohoo, i. 131
Rudras, ii. 179
Sacred, v. 120
Samādhi is, v. 539
Scale, v. 474
Second Adam is esoterically, iii. 15
Sense, iii. 258
Sephira, v. 191
Serpent, meaning of, iii. 214
Shani's triple, v. 45
Souls, i. 274
Spectrum, v. 456, 474
Substance, gradation of, ii. 349
Substances are, v. 522
Sun, nature of, i. 331
Symbolism, in ancient religions, iv. 167
System, v. 374
Tattvas, v. 469
Ten Sephiroth, of, ii. 67
Triad, hanging from, i. 284
Units, Mars and Mercury are, i. 218
Universal septenate, of, iv. 168
 ,, Soul was, iv. 131, 132
Vedas, of, iv. 176
Week of India, v. 433
Worlds, Nature of, v. 438
SEPTENATE, Absolute is, iv. 169, 170
 Alchemists and, iv. 164
 Correspondences of, v. 429
 Heavenly man becomes, iv. 167
 Man is, iii. 42
 Physical realm, for, iv. 175
 Physiology, in, iv. 194; v. 483, 484
 Pleiades sidereal, iv. 121
 Purānas, in, iv. 182, 183
 Second Adam, of seven Sephiroth, iii. 15
 Universal, iv. 168
SEPTIFORM periodicity, law of, iv. 194
SEPTIFORMITY of Biblical chronology, iv 195; v. 201
SEPTUAGINT Origin of, v. 184
SERAPEUM, v. 161, 217
SERAPH or fiery-winged serpent, ii. 78, 159
SERAPHIM, Avengers, called, i. 185
 Cherubim, and, iv. 69; v. 212
 Fiery serpents of heaven, or, i. 185
  ,, ,, of Moses were, iii. 386
  ,, ,, Winged, or, ii. 80
 Flames parallel to, iii. 74
 Four Mahārājahs and, i. 185
 Jehovah, symbols of, iii. 386
 Michael and, iv. 47
 Ministering angels, as, i. 155
 Nāgas are, iv. 69
 Sepher, Saphar, and Sipur, i. 156
 Sepher Yetzireh, in, i. 155, 156
 Serpent of eternity God, and, ii. 80
 Solomon's Temple in, v. 237
 Spiritual immortality, conferred on us, iii. 246
 Teraphim and, v. 237, 238
 Throne of the Almighty, attend, iii. 74; v. 309
 Winged wheels, called, i. 185
 World, made, i. 156
SERAPHS, Christian belief in, ii. 328
 Cosmic elements, rule, ii. 328

SERAPHS (Contd.)
Dhyān Chohans called, i. 81
Michael, called, iv. 47
Nāgas, or, iv. 69
Ninth world of Syrians has, ii. 153
Synonyms of, in our secret doctrine, i. 153
SERAPIS, Agriculture and, v. 237
Sarpa, serpent, and, iv. 69; v. 238
Serpent, with attributes of, iii. 39
Sigalions in temples of, iii. 395
Statue of, v. 237
SERMON on the Mount, v. 363
SERPENT, Absolute wisdom, of, ii. 127
Adept, symbol of, iii. 363, 379
Adepts and initiates, refers to, iii. 103
Adoration of, iii. 213
Adversary not applicable to, iii. 386
Agathodaemon, good, ii. 126
Aker, Set's, iii. 217
Akkadian seven-headed, ii. 124
All-knowledge, of, iii. 284
All-wisdom, symbol of, ii. 79
Ananta, ii. 124; iii. 107, 108
Androgyne, creator of man, iii. 387
Apap, ii. 399; iii. 217
Apophis, iv. 159
Aschmogh, iii. 209
Astral light and, i. 140, 299
Azazel, prototype of, iii. 386
Brazen, ii. 79, 80, 194; iii. 212, 364; iv. 40;
v. 278
Brotherhood of, iii. 385
Caduceus, of, i. 299
Catacombs of, at Thebes, iii. 378
Central spiritual sun, iii. 218
Chateaubriand, de, on the, ii. 120
Cherub meant, ii. 78, 80
Chnouphis and, iii. 214
Chozzar, good and perfect, iii. 355
Christ with templars, emblem of, ii. 194
Circle, in, ii. 80
Cosmic, iv. 73
Cosmic-dust like, i. 141
Creative God as winged, ii. 79
Cross, and, iii. 220
Dan described as, ii. 377
Darkness, and idea of, iii. 44
Devil, regarded as symbol of, ii. 160
Divine symbol, always, iv. 73
Dracontia, sacred to, iii. 346
Dragon and, iii. 39; v. 171
   ,,   Head and tail of, with, iii. 384
   ,,   Seven headed, v. 202
   ,,   Tiamat sea, iv. 45
   ,,   Wisdom and, of, iii. 236
Dual androgyne, iii. 218
Earth casts off old skins as does, iii. 58
Eden, of, iv, 97, 269
Egg and, ii. 79; iv. 322, 326
Eight coils of, iii. 356
Elohim, one of, iii. 384
Eternal sun Abrasax, iii. 218
Eternity, ii. 80, 123, 124; iii. 218, 284
Eternity, Infinitude, and, emblem of, i. 134
Evil, of, iii. 39; iv. 159
   ,,   Devil, and, symbol of, ii. 126
   ,,   Never regarded as ,iv. 73

Evolution of universe like uncoiling of, iv. 73
Fall of man, and, iii. 209
Fallen from on high, iii. 233
Fohat represented by, i. 143
Fourth race, phallic symbol of, iii. 72
Garden of Eden, of, ii. 132, 139
Genesis, Celestial pole, and, of, iii. 357
   ,,   Churches anathematize, iii. 376
   ,,   Dragon of wisdom, iii. 236
   ,,   Evil, and, iii. 389
   ,,   Father of spiritual mankind, iii. 246
   ,,   Mankind has become, iv. 81
   ,,   Meaning of, iii. 239
   ,,   Satan, iii. 384; iv. 171
   ,,   Ye shall be as Gods, says, iii. 281
Globular shape of all bodies, symbolizes, i. 141
Gnostic, i. 140; iii. 282
   ,,   Meaning of, iii. 385
   ,,   Ophites and, ii. 121
God Nahbkoon represented as, ii. 194
Gods of Atlanteans, symbols, of, iv. 325
Good and bad, i. 140; ii. 126
Hawk's head, with, iii. 356
Heathen wand and Jewish, iii. 213
Hermes called most spiritual by, i. 140
Hevah and Abel feminine, iii. 133
Humanity, service of, to, ii. 120
Iao of mysteries, iii. 387
Immortality and time, type of, ii. 121; v. 238
India, symbol translated from, iii. 219
Initiated adept, name given to, ii. 121
Initiator, symbolizing, iii. 354; v. 171
Janus-like character of, ii. 120
Jehovah and, i. 140; ii. 132, 139, 194;
iii. 388; v. 190
Jesus and wisdom of, i. 141; iii. 364
Kakodaemon bad, ii. 126
Kalevala, in, iii. 39
Kālināga, Krishna slew, v. 289
Kapila, many headed, iv. 143
Knooph represented by, ii. 194
Legends, iii. 213
Legs, on two, iii. 217
Lion with head of, on his tail, iii. 430
Loaf, coiled round sacramental, iii. 218
Logoi, or self-born, emblem of, ii. 79
Lord God, was, iii. 219, 272
Macrocosmic tree is, iii. 106
Manas is, in tree, iii. 106
Manvantaric, ii. 367
Mighty, iv. 325
Mound in Ohio, iv. 322, 325
Mundane trees, in, iii. 106
Mysteries taught to primeval men by, ii. 121;
v. 171
Mystery of, great sea, iv. 72
Mystical interpretation of, iii. 212
North pole and pole of heavens, is, iii. 355
Occult knowledge, symbol of, iii. 39
Ophiomorphos, iii. 388
Ophiomorphos-Chrestos after its fall, ii. 131
Ophis-Christos before its fall, ii. 131
Ophites, of, iii. 214
Osiris, on head of, ii. 155
Phallic, without egg, ii. 79
Polar, iv. 354
Primordial, iii. 408

SERPENT (*Contd.*)
Rāhu had tail of, iii. 380
Regeneration, emblem of, i. 134
Rejuvenation, emblem of, i. 134; ii. 121
Runs with 370 leaps, ii. 52
Sacred tree, on, iii. 112
Sarpa or, v. 238
Satan and, i. 244; iii. 120, 387; iv. 76; v. 171, 287
Saviour, as, iii. 218
Sea of fire called fiery, i. 142
Seed of, iii. 409
Septenary meaning, has, iii. 213
Seraph, ii. 78, 159; iv. 69; v. 171, 238
Seven-headed, ii. 56, 124; iii. 107
Seven thunders, of, ii. 127
Seven-vowelled, iii. 282
Shadow of light, iii. 218
Shamaël, used by, iii. 209
Shesha, iii. 60
Son of snakes or, iii. 378
Space, of, ii. 56
Spirit of God symbolized by fiery, i. 141
,, represents, iii. 376
Svastika and, iii. 107, 108
Symbol found everywhere, i. 134
Tail, swallowing its, i. 113; iv. 122
Tau, and, iii. 218
Theosophical, of eternity, iii. 376
Tree, and, ii. 120, 121, 123; iii. 106, 107, 220
,, Life and, of, ii. 121
True and perfect, ii. 127
Two mystic eyes of Ammon over, iii. 217
Vāsuki, ruling Deity of Pātāla, v. 286
Vendīdād, in, iii. 365
Vishnu, of, iii. 107
Votan, Mexican Demi-God, iii. 378
Wisdom, Emblem or Symbol of, i. 134, 140; ii. 79, 160, 383; iii. 39, 186, 218
,, of, iii. 107, 414; iv. 143; v. 43
Woman, and, glyph of, v. 85
,, Matter, or, and, iii. 207
,, Seduces, iii. 113
World-egg and, i. 133, 134
Worship, ii. 121
Zeus and, iii. 413, 417
SERPENT-DEMON, Vritra or Ahi, iii. 381
SERPENT-EMBLEM of Cosmic fire, Uraeus is, ii. 155
SERPENT-FIRE, Kundalini, v. 554
SERPENT-GOD, ii. 155; iii. 379; iv. 99; v. 171, 238
SERPENT-GODS, iii. 377
SERPENT-HOLES, Adepts came from, iv. 317
SERPENT-QUEEN, or Sarparājni, i. 141
SERPENT-RACE, ii. 137
SERPENT-STONE, iii. 341
SERPENT-WALL, iii. 39.
SERPENTES, Gigantes translated, iii. 281
SERPENT'S MOUNT, Carnac means, iii. 379
SERPENTS, Adepts are, v. 287
Angels fallen into generation, iii. 233
Arabia, came every spring from, ii. 77
Astronomical, iii. 355, 356
Balaam said to be inspired by, iii. 407
Be ye wise as, iii. 364
Birds or, iii. 407

Caduceus, of, ii. 273
Cherubim, and, i. 185
Cobra most deadly of, i. 305
Dolmens connected with, iv. 322
Dragons and, iii. 207, 354; iv. 321
,, Light, and, of, iii. 206
,, Wisdom, and, of, iii. 233
Edens, and, iii. 207
Emperors of Chinese, emblems of, iii. 364
Fifth race, and, iii. 350, 354
Good and bad, iii. 276
Grasshoppers called winged, iii. 210
Hawks, with heads of, iii. 359
Heads of, on animal bodies, iii. 66
Heaven of, i. 185
Hercules kills, ii. 118
Hierophants styled themselves, iii. 378
Hindu, i. 185
Ibis killing winged, ii. 77
Initiates, or, iii. 364
Jupiter and other Gods, symbols of, iii. 363
Kabalists explain fiery, iii. 216
Levites called fiery, iii. 216
Logoi symbolized by, ii. 194
Mount Meru guarded by, i. 185, 187
Nāgas, and, iii. 188, 377; iv. 69; v. 286, 287, 399
Nodes of moon symbolized by, ii. 118
Poles, symbols of, iii. 276, 359
Pulastya father of all, iii. 188
Rod, entwined round, iii. 363
Sacred Phoenician alphabet from sacred, v. 114
Sarpas or, iii. 188; iv. 69; v. 238
Seraphim are fiery, i. 185
Seraphs, or, iv. 69; v. 237, 238
Shell-heads, with, iii. 206
Spirit and matter represented by, ii. 273
Sun-Gods symbolized by, iii. 215, 380
Symbolisms under different, iii. 353
Trees guarded by, i. 187
Triangular stones, under, iii. 350
Wisdom, of, iii. 188, 350, 351
,, Ever emblems of, iii. 363
Winged, iii. 210
Woman and, dual meaing of, v. 85
SERPENTS' works or Nehhaschim, iii. 408
SERVANTS, Apollo, of, iii. 20
Great four, of, iii. 425
Horus, of, iii. 373, 429
Sparks are, i. 156
SERVETUS, v. 60
SESOSTRIS (Ramses II), Mummy of, i. 52; v. 337
Sacred Sciences and, v. 253, 296, 337
SESQUIALTERA and **SESQUITERTIA**, iv. 172
SET, Hermes called, iii. 379
Reign of, iii. 367
Typhon, Egyptian, iii. 365, 384
,, Sank into, iii. 217
SETH, Adam, third son, of, iv. 37; v. 297
Agathodaemon none other than, iii. 361
,, Begat, in his own likeness, iii. 133
,, Rishoon, son of, iii. 396
Ancestor of Semites, semi-divine, iii. 91
Arab beliefs about, iii. 365, 366
Astronomy established by, iii. 365
Biblical patriarchs and, ii. 374

SETH (Contd.)
Bunsen on, iii. 91
Cain, and, iii. 390; v. 106, 190
Cain and Abel, progeny of, iii. 136
Dhyān Chohan, iii. 360, 361
Edris, and, iii. 365
Enoch (Enos) and, iii. 91, 134, 135, 360, 361, 365
Enos son of, iii. 134; v. 129, 190
Genealogy of, iii. 390
Henoch (Kanoch) son of, iv. 283; v. 106
Hermes called, iii. 379
Israel reputed father of, iii. 379
Jehovah, Saturn and, v. 72, 190
Man, first, iii. 134
Man, Son, of, v. 291
Pillars of, Mercury or, iv. 99
Planetary God, iii. 360
Primitive God of Semites, iii. 91
Qabbalah on, iii. 315
Races of earth, progenitor of, iii. 135, 360
Sabaeans, borrowed by Jews, from, iii. 360
Sabaism, founder of, iii. 361
Serpent, symbol of, iii. 39
Third race, represents, i. 22; iii. 134, 396; iv. 37; v. 190
Typhon, and, iii. 44, 365
Vulcan or, iii. 389
SETH-ENOS, Fourth race, iii. 143
SETI, I, i. 275
SETTLERS in Europe, First, iii. 351
SEVEKH or SEBEKH (seventh), i. 266; ii. 124; v. 202
Adam one with, v. 202
God of Number Seven, v. 203
Solar Dragon, v. 202
SEVEKH-KRONOS, ii. 124
SEVEN, Activities of brain, v. 556
Adam, Chief of The, v. 203
Aditi, sons of, ii. 152, 167; v. 199
Aeons and Basilides, v. 128
Agents contain material worlds, ii. 154
Ages of man, iii. 312
Amshaspends, i. 186; ii. 155; iv. 179; v. 198
Angelic planes, iii. 243
Angels, creative, v. 129
,, of the Face, ii. 64; v. 314
,, Planetary, v. 129, 208, 326
,, Presence, of the, i. 165; ii. 49, 90; v. 207, 208, 320, 333, 356, 386, 439
,, Rebels, v. 200
Apollo, patron of number, iv. 341
Arhats, i. 162
Beings in sun are, i. 331
Book of the Dead, in, ii. 398, 399
Brains of heart, v. 550, 553
Breath gave life to the, iii. 35, 36
,, of all the, i. 164; v. 357
Breaths, v. 357
,, of Dragon of Wisdom, i. 166
Brothers, i. 142; v. 200
Buddhas, v. 368, 409
Builders, ii. 154, 202; v. 171, 208, 375
Burning lamps, v. 309
Capital sins and virtues, ii. 23
Cavities of brain, v. 556
Celestial Principles, v. 366

Celestial Spheres, v. 322
Centres of Energy, iv. 176
,, ,, Force, v. 474, 475
,, ,, Spiritual, psychic and physical worlds, v. 435
Chakras, v. 481, 483
Chambers of Pyramid, v. 248
Churches, seven, v. 316
,, ,, keys of, iv. 204
Circles, Cosmos contained in, v. 321
,, Fire, of, iii. 235; v. 198
,, Heaven, of, v. 191, 198, 199, 309, 321
,, Hierarchies symbolized as concentric, v. 459
,, Robbed of sacred fire, iii. 90
,, Super-spiritual planes, of, ii. 136
Colours, v. 420, 442, 454, 457, 459
Companions, v. 202
Continents, v. 199
Constellations, v. 200, 203
Cosmic forces, v. 315
Cosmic planes, v. 429
Cosmocratores of world, i. 281; v. 315, 562
Creators called Elohim, i. 196; v. 198
,, Progeny, of, iii. 57
Creations, i. 85; ii. 164; iii. 64; v. 199
Creative Forces, v. 507, 532
Creative Gods, Assyria of, v. 198, 199
,, Hierarchies, v. 208
,, Hosts or Sephiroth, i. 139
,, Spirits, i. 114; ii. 156; v. 74, 198
Cycles and cosmic planes, ii. 107
Cyclops, v. 325
Daimons of Origen, v. 439
Dark and light Gods, ii. 24
,, Evil spirits, ii. 24
Dawns and twilights, iii. 308
Demiourgoi, v. 325
Deities, v. 233
Dhyāni-Buddhas, i. 168; v. 539
Dhyān Chohans, v. 74, 375
Dialects referring to mysteries of nature, ii. 22
Divine dynasties, iii. 365
,, Lokas, v. 541
,, Mother of, i. 156
,, States of consciousness, v. 542
Divisions of astral, v. 522
,, of earth, v. 542
,, of Fohat, v. 528
Eastern occultism alone has, keys, ii. 30
Egg, coverings of, ii. 81
Eight, became, iii. 357
Element ruled by one of, each, iii. 358
Elements, i. 192; ii. 61; iv. 176; v. 204
Elohim, v. 198, 201, 202, 203, 204, 325
Eternities, Æons or periods are meant by, i. 109
,, Eternal parent slumbered once again for, i. 109
,, Fohat acts during, i. 200
,, Mahākalpa as well as solar Pralaya, i. 124
,, Manvantara, seven periods of, i. 110
,, Paranishpanna without Paramārtha is extinction for, i. 124
Evolution of life proceeds in, rounds, i. 213
Eyes of the Lord, iii. 35; iv. 197; v. 313
Father-Mother, iv. 165

SEVEN (*Contd.*)
Fathers, ii. 298; iv. 134; v. 203
Fiery tongues, iv. 179
Fighters, i. 161
Fires, ii. 127; iv. 134
First, born of, ii. 168
Flames, v. 351
Fohat is one and, i. 195
Forces and occult powers, typical of, ii. 107
,, Nature are, of, i. 195; v. 474
,, Universal, v. 472
Forms of cranium, ii. 56, 90
,, Principles, of prakriti, or, ii. 88
Gates of ladder of creation, ii. 164
Gateways of Brain, v. 556
Globes of planetary chain, iv. 179
Gnostic vowels, i. 140; iv. 135
Golden dragon in whom are, ii. 171
Governors, ii. 202; iii. 269
Great gods at beginning of every cycle, ii. 152; v. 333, 356
Great gods of Egypt, i. 166, 186; ii. 154; iii. 101, 361, 362; iv. 77; v. 164, 165, 214
Great ones of great mother, ii. 399
Gunas or conditioned qualities, ii. 62
Harmonies, v. 556
Headed Serpent or Dragon, v. 202
Heavens, ii. 167; iv. 133
Heptagon religious perfect number, or, iv. 173
,, and correspondences, v. 461
Hierarchies of Egos, v. 552
,, of planetary creators, i. 140; v. 77, 361, 442, 459, 553
Higher angels had broken through seven circles, iii. 90
Higher make seven Lhas create world, iii. 36
Hippocrates on number, iii. 312
Hosts, will-born lords, iii. 95
Ildabaoth, chief of, v. 204
In one, v. 428
Inferior, v. 204
Infernal Lokas, v. 541
Invisible logos, hierarchies, with, iii. 36
Islands, v. 199
Kabalah and number, i. 110
Kabiri, i. 166, 167; iii. 360, 361; v. 202, 309, 325
Keys allegories, to, v. 201, 204
,, Knowledge, to, v. 186
,, Mystery tongue, to, ii. 23
,, Not yet delivered to science, ii. 35
,, Open mysteries of seven races, to, ii. 37, 38
,, Universal esoteric language, to, iv. 39
Khnūmū of Egypt, v. 198
Kingdoms of Nature, v. 460
Kings of Edom, ii. 91; v. 200
Kings of *Revelation*, iv. 135; v. 200
Kronidae, v. 200
Kumāras, i. 282; v. 78, 320
Language of hierophants having, dialects, ii. 22
Laya centres produced by Fohat, i. 195, 203
,, Zero points, are, i. 195
Layers of man's skin, v. 425, 429
Lemurian and Atlantean divisions of earth, iii. 365
Letters of name of Jehovah, ii. 49

Lictors, v. 310, 318, 319
Lights Arūpa World, of the, v. 363
,, from one light, i. 187; v. 78, 320
,, whose reflections are human immortal monads, i. 179
Lives and one life, i. 283
Logoi of hermetic philosophers, i. 195
Logos, mother of, planetary powers, i. 139
Lokas, v. 421, 537, 539, 541
Lords created seven men, iii. 217
Lords of the Flame, v. 258
Lower Sephiroth, ii. 58
Lumazi of Assyria, v. 202
Luminous ones who follow Osiris, ii. 24
Magic forces, great ones of, ii. 399
Manifested proceed from mother alone, i. 152
Mansions of Assyrian cosmology, v. 199
Manus, i. 281; 293; iii. 309; iv. 194
Matter, states of, ii. 283
Meanings and results in sacred formula, v. 418
Meanings in every symbol, iv. 108
Meanings in Kabalah, iv. 109
Mind-born, the, v. 90
Minor pralayas in each round, i. 225
Monads divided into hierarchies, i. 224
Mystery-Gods of planets, iii. 35, 36
Mystic sages or Kumāras, i. 151
Notes of scale, ii. 164; v. 509, 542
Number, holy feminine, i. 124; iii. 220
Oceans or Sapta Samudra, ii. 62
Oeaohoo and, vowels of Gnostic Ophis, i. 140
Organs at base of brains, iv. 482
Origin of sacred number, ii. 103
Original Stars, v. 202
Pagodas, v. 325
Pātālas, iii. 60
Paths, i. 112; iii. 197; v. 363, 542
Planes, astral, v. 526
,, cosmic consciousness, of, ii. 41; v. 429, 524
,, of being, iii. 243; v. 422, 521
,, Skandhas on, v. 560
,, sub-divisions, seven of, v. 524
Planetary genii or spirits, iii. 35
,, Gods, v. 309, 310, 333
,, Pralaya after, rounds, i. 225
,, Spirits, i. 165; v. 215
Planets, iv. 179; v. 108, 129, 155, 221, 310, 320, 324, 429, 439, 460, 536
Portals to Dhyāni, v. 542
Powers of logos, iii. 358; v. 203
Powers of Ogdoad, v. 199
Powers of Space, v. 177, 200, 202, 303
Prajāpatis, ii. 154; v. 198, 202, 351, 460
Prajnā exists in different aspects, i. 195
Prakritic Planes, v. 525, 527
Prakritis, ii. 49
Precious gifts of a Buddha, v. 373
Priests of *Anugītā*, iv. 139
Primary and secondary creations, ii. 165
Primeval, v. 91
Primeval sages, v. 42
Primitive and dual Gods, iii. 365
Primordial, i. 152, 166, 168; v. 448
,, Adams, iii. 57
,, Powers, v. 201

SEVEN (*Contd.*)
  Principles, Ain Soph, of, ii. 49
    ,,   Celestial, v. 366
    ,,   Different systems, in, i. 213
    ,,   Ego and, v. 553
    ,,   Esoteric system in, v. 361, 362
    ,,   Four basic, and their three aspects, v. 471
    ,,   Great mother and man, i. 332
    ,,   Kosmos, of, ii. 168; v. 208, 361, 366
    ,,   Man of, v. 361, 425, 426, 435
    ,,   Man-plant Saptaparana refers to, i. 282
    ,,   Prakriti has, ii. 88
    ,,   Seven-headed dragons, typified by, ii. 124
    ,,   Seven rays which fall from Macro-cosmic centre, iii. 197
    ,,   Solar system consists of, i. 170
    ,,   Space container and body of uni-verse in its, ii. 56
    ,,   Universal Life, of, v. 435, 528
  Procreative rays of Powers, i. 146
  Protyles or seven prakritis, ii. 41
  Races, First continent will remain to end of, iii. 371
  ,, Guardian of each of, v. 249
  ,, Men, of, ii. 376; v. 165
  ,, *Revelation*, doctrine of, may be found in, iv. 135
  ,, Round, of each, ii. 398
  ,, Seven minor Manus preside over, iii. 310
  ,, Thunders, sounds or vowels and, iv. 135
  Radiant essence becomes, inside, outside i. 134
  Radicals, i. 201
  Rays, Brahma's head, from, v. 325
  ,, Fall from Macrocosmic centre, which, iii. 197
  ,, Forces or, v. 426
  ,, Hang from, seven worlds of being, i. 179
  ,, Logos of, v. 484
  ,, Manifested Logos of, v. 459
  ,, Powers or, v. 233, 356
  ,, Primordial, v. 365
  ,, Rishis or, v. 207
  ,, Sun of, iv. 179; v. 423
  Rectors breaking through seven circles of fire, ii. 134
  ,, Christian Church of, v. 287
  ,, World of, ii. 125; v. 321, 327
  Regents, ii. 139; iii. 35; v. 333
  Regions above and below, i. 168; v. 129
  Religions in all, iii. 47
  Rishis, v. 191, 203, 207, 333
  ,, Agni on line with, iv. 119
  ,, Great Bear, of, ii. 72; iv. 119, 202; v. 202
  ,, Lead host, on rivers, ii. 60
  ,, Manvantara, of third, iii. 88
  ,, Pleiades, and, iv. 110
  ,, Prajāpatis identical with, v. 203
  ,, Rays or, v. 207
  ,, Svargas in, v. 325
  ,, Vaivasvata Manu, with, iii. 292
  Root number of nature, ii. 179, 180
  Rounds, iii. 187, 308; iv. 135, 267; v. 374
  Rulers, of seven planets, v. 309, 460

Sabbaths, iv. 135
Sacraments, ii. 23
Sacred number is, v. 201
Sanctuaries, v. 322
Sapta in whom are, i. 138
Scales and shades of light, v. 550
Scales of Consciousness, v. 548
Seals, v. 313
Seas, v. 199
Second, who are Lipika, i. 165
Secondaries or spiritual intelligences, ii. 171
Senses, Breath, voice, self is synthesis of, i. 159
  ,, Emancipation, cause of, i. 151
  ,, Hotris or priests symbolized as, i. 151
  ,, Mental and physical correlations of, ii. 258
  ,, Physical, v. 429
  ,, Self to be emancipated from, i. 151
  ,, Spiritual, v. 429
  ,, Synthesis of, i. 151
  ,, Two unknown of, v. 508
  ,, Upanishads, according to, i. 311
  ,, *Vedas* and *Anugītā* on, ii. 258
Sephiroth separated from first triad, i. 186; v. 191
Septenaries, of alphabet, v. 505
Servant to Lhas of, iii. 35
Seventh of, i. 156
Shadows of future men, seven times, iii. 99
Shaktis, v. 484
Shining, mind-born sons, i. 260
Skins of earth, iii. 56, 58, 59
Solar colours of prism, v. 443
Solar rays become seven suns, ii. 86
Son-brothers, i. 201
Sons, Aditi, of, ii. 152, 167; v. 199
  ,, Creators of planetary chain, i. 130
  ,, Divine Sophia, of, ii. 148
  ,, Fohat, of, i. 201
  ,, God of, v. 320
  ,, Light and Life, of, i. 195; v. 350
  ,, Ptah of, v. 202
  ,, Sydik, of, v. 202
Souls of Egyptologists, iv. 201-212
Sounds, v. 547
Spark radiating from primeval, ii. 294
Sparks of, i. 156
Spheres of our chain, v. 248, 249
  ,, Souls of, v. 73
  ,, watchers of, i. 124; v. 73
Spirit of the, v. 375
Spirits, Church of, v. 303, 313, 321
  ,, Face, of, i. 186; iii. 123
  ,, Ildabaoth, of, v. 198
  ,, Mikael chief of, ii. 179
  ,, Planetary, v. 109, 220, 221, 298, 320, 425, 465
  ,, Presence, of, i. 114; ii. 24, 156; v. 74, 191, 198, 209, 309
  ,, Ra of, v. 202
  ,, St. Paul of, v. 215, 327
  ,, Stars, of, ii. 164
Spiritus conceives, figures and, stellars, i. 245
Stages, Divine Essence circles through, v. 443
  ,, Perception of, v. 554
Star-Angels of Church, v. 37, 320
Stars, Goddess of, iv. 117

SEVEN (*Contd.*)
  Stars, Great Bear, of, i. 124, 125; ii. 172; v. 202
    ,,   Original seven not planetary, v. 202
    ,,   Revelation, of, v. 313
  States of Consciousness, v. 429, 542, 545
  Steps of Antahkarana, v. 543
  Steps of Rāja Yoga, v. 515
  Strides of Fohat, i. 168
  Stringed Lyre, v. 275
  Sublime Lords has ceased to be, i. 114
  Sun has, rays, i. 331; v. 423
  Suns, iii. 243
  Svargas, v. 325
  Swans which descend on Lake Mansarovara, ii. 72
  Syllabled-formula, v. 418, 419, 505
  Tattvas, v. 469, 470, 474, 475, 538
  Ten, iv. 144
  Theogonic evolution, typical of, ii. 107
  Third Logos becomes, v. 532
  Three-tongued flame shot out by, i. 282
  Thunders, ii. 127
  Timekeepers, v. 200
  Titanidae, who are, ii. 165
  Triad, emanated from, ii. 145
  Trials of Initiation, v. 152
  Truths had ceased to be, i. 115
    ,,   only four revealed out of, i. 152
  Twice, sum total, i. 152
  Universal, v. 203
  Uranides discovered to be, ii. 136
  Valentinus on power of great, ii. 164
  Vasishtha-Daksha, sons of, iii. 88
  Virtues, v. 357
  Vowels with their forty-nine powers, ii. 127; iv. 134
  Watchers, v. 200, 356
  Waters stop at region of, Rishis, ii. 87
  Ways to bliss were not, i. 112
  Web of light, were not yet born from, i. 129
  Wheels are our planetary chain, i. 200; v. 322
    ,,   Small, revolving, i. 196
  Wicked Gods or spirits, iii. 72
  Winds of *Anugītā*, iv. 139
  Wise Ones fashion seven paths, iii. 197
  World Powers, v. 469
  World reformer essential incarnation of one of, iii. 358
  Worlds, v. 208, 297, 418, 489
    ,,   Māyā, of, i. 283
    ,,   Upper and seven lower, ii. 81
  Zohar, in, i. 186; ii. 67; v. 191, 439
  Zones Mundane Egg of, v. 199, 421
    ,,   Post-mortem ascent, of, ii. 127
    ,,   Two by two on, iii. 230
SEVEN-BRANCHED CANDLESTICK, v. 313, 314, 316, 320, 321
SEVENFOLD, Agneyāstra, iv. 201
  Application, psycho-physical, of Osiris myth, v. 440
  Asura, iv. 178
  Brāhmans, classification of, iv. 212
  Constitution of man, archaic belief in, i. 281
  Correspondences, v. 422-426
  Cross, universal soul, represented as, iv. 131, 132
  Cube, iv. 197

Divine spirit who is, iii. 358
Ea, v. 202
Each plane is, v. 516
Elohim, v. 204
Esoteric, classification, iv. 207
First Logos, ii. 167
Glyph, v. 202
Heaven was, primary, iv. 202
Image, v. 204
Kosmos, iii. 322
Light, Christos and Hermes called, iv. 110
Logos, differentiated into seven Logoi, iv. 133
Mystery of Initiation, v. 275
Nature, septenary evolution in, i. 310; v. 202, 203
Number, ever-recurring, iv. 179
Prakriti, v. 469, 470
Sevekh, v. 202
Sign, interlaced triangles, iv. 163, 164
World, divisions of, iv. 193
SEVEN-HEADED, Ananta, serpent, iii. 107
  Dragon, iv. 53; v. 202
  Dragon-Logos, ii. 125
  Dragons and serpents are all, ii, 124
  Serpent, ii. 127, 128
SEVEN-KNOTTED Wand of Initiate, v. 282
SEVEN-LEAVED Lotus, v. 550
  Plant, Saptaparna, i. 282; iv. 162
SEVEN-POINTED crown, iv. 190
SEVEN-RAYED, God, iii. 47
  Hymn to, iv. 174
  One, ii. 167
SEVEN-SKINNED eternal mother-father, i. 75
SEVEN-STRINGED harp of Apollo, iv. 174; v. 275, 459
SEVEN-SYLLABLED phrase, v. 421
SEVEN-VOWELLED Serpent of Gnostics, iii. 282
  Sounds, ii. 168
SEVENING, Astronomy and process of, ii. 124, 125
  Cis-Himālayan occultism, of, iv. 174
  Genesis, in, iv. 169
  Principle of, ii. 124, 125; v. 203
SEVENTH, all things depend from, iii. 313
  Atlantean sub-race, iv. 312
  Bridges from one plane to another, v. 522
  Creation, Adam Kadmon is, v. 199
  Crown, i. 177
  Day of Creation, iv. 56; v. 129, 198
  Eternity, last vibration of, i. 131
  Globe, Gimil's heights, iii. 109
  Key, v. 120, 121
  Manu, Vaivasvata, iii. 309
  Member, ii. 309
  One principle and, i. 83
  Osiris, over six primary Gods, ii. 155
  Period of creation, ii. 91
  Plane, spirit is matter on, ii. 357
  Planet, v. 322
  Portal, v. 543
  Potency of Simon Magus, v. 447
  Principle, v. 76, 101, 290, 303, 365
    ,,   Anthropomorphic number, became, iii. 357
    ,,   Ātmā-Buddhi-Manas, or, i. 83
    ,,   Ātman, or, ii. 193; v. 375

SEVENTH (*Contd.*)

Principle, Buddhi, perceived by, ii. 193
,, Central spiritual and polar sun, passes through, iii. 243
,, Christos is, iii. 234
,, Daimon, on, v. 303
,, Father in secret, is our, i. 323
,, Father-mother-son, or, i. 83
,, First Emanation, v. 101
,, God in man besides his own, i. 334
,, Krishna as, v. 154
,, Kwan-shi-yin, ii. 193
,, Manifested universe, i. 83
,, Non-entity, iv. 150
,, Of the Seven, v. 375
,, One reality, or, i. 83
,, Personal deity, ii. 363
,, Planetary system of, v. 154
,, Prototype of man is highest essence of, i. 281
,, Root of every atom is, i. 83
,, Sacred is, v. 520
,, Seven elements, of, iv. 176
,, Seventh thousand and, ii. 91
,, Six principles in nature outcome of, i. 83
,, Sixth and, in man, ii. 91; v. 208
,, Substance, of kosmos, ii. 318, 319
,, Sūrya sun, of great body of matter, ii. 251
,, Universal, ii. 193
,, Universal, merged in, ii. 193
,, Universal spirit, identical with, ii. 294

Principles, merging of sixth and, i. 123; v. 208

Race, v. 300, 518
,, Adepts will produce mind-born sons in, iii. 277
,, Arctic continent and, iii. 398
,, Buddhas in, ii. 192
,, Dhyāni-Buddha to come in, i. 168
,, Element corresponding to, i. 78
,, Fourth Round, of, v. 563
,, Great Adepts will return in, iv. 100
,, Life cycle or, iii. 61
,, Prophecy about, iii. 109
,, Race of Buddhas, iv. 51
,, Seventh round, in, iii. 175, 187; v. 83, 563

Round, v. 83
,, Animals will reach verge of humanity at close of, i. 234
,, Buddhas in, v. 563
,, Earth will reach ultimate form after, i. 304
,, Element corresponding to, i. 78
,, Great day after, iv. 59
,, Lunar chain, of, i. 225
,, Monads or egos of men of, i. 232
,, Moon will have dissolved in, i. 210; v. 536
,, Reproduction in, v. 563
,, Seventh race in, iii. 175, 187; v. 83
,, Time will cease after, iv. 136

Sabbath, iv. 59

Sense, ii. 259; iv. 474, 508

Seven, of, i. 156

Sixth whose essence is, ii. 90
Son of seventh son, iii. 217
State of force, noumenon, of, i. 203
Thousand, ii. 91
Work of Magic, v. 326
World, v. 353

SEVERUS, EMPEROR Alexander, v. 147

SEWALIK range, iv. 142

SEX, Derivation of word, iii. 361
Distinction of, fundamental, iv. 227
Human species, in, iv. 229
Involution of, iii. 290
Moon twofold in, ii. 108, 110
Problem of, iii. 413
Spiritual man disconnected from, v. 438
Symbols, of, iv. 25

SEXES, Adam Kadmon name of two, iv. 34
Animals neutralized in, iii. 411
Beards common to both, iv. 236
Esotericism ignores both, i. 193
Evolution of both, iv. 229
First race was born before, existed, iii. 16
God possessing double fecundity of two, iii. 143
Jehovah, and humanity of two, v. 190
Kabalah had no concern with terrestrial, iv. 25
Kabiri of both, iii. 363
Men having potentially two, iv. 60
No differences in 7th Race of 7th Round, v. 83
Separation of, i. 72, 193; ii. 60, 99, 112, 161; iii. 112, 126, 128, 141, 155, 156, 179, 180, 186, 188, 191, 199, 201, 202, 204, 206, 221, 231, 250, 269, 277, 288, 295, 313; iv. 37, 71, 72, 89, 180, 186, 208, 227, 258, 283, 306; v. 203, 425, 429, 430
Seven men of opposite, iii. 269
Union of two, iv. 164

SEXLESS, Absolute spirit, v. 408
Abstract deity is, i. 129
Adam-Kadmon (first) Logos is, iii. 136
Adam of *Genesis*, iii. 187
A-sexual from, iii. 124
Chhāyā birth or, procreation, iii. 181
Deity, v. 408
Dhyān Chohans incarnate in race evolved by, creative instinct, iii. 277
Elohim first produce, race, iii. 143
Eternal matter or substance is, ii. 269
First race was, iii. 16, 94
First round man was, i. 239
Highest deity of esotericism is, i. 193
Infusoria, iii. 159
Karma, principle, ii. 359
Light of *Genesis* is, angels, iii. 49
Man was first, iii. 141
Narāyani, v. 189
Primary humanity like kings of Edom, iii. 66
Races were, three earliest, iii. 112
Second race, iii. 117, 172
Semi-spirits of first race, iii. 133
Shekinah in *Book of Numbers* is, ii. 344
Spirits, v. 408
Third race were, iii. 141, 202
Three in one ever, iv. 170
Unknown deity is, ii. 41

SEXTILES and signs of Zodiac, ii. 33

SEXUAL, Age of, mankind, iii. 164
  A-sexual organisms, and, iii. 125
  Astral light and, passion, iv. 80
  Brain, action and, iii. 297
  Cain God of first, bloodshed, iii. 389
  Cross, element of, iv. 159, 191, 192
  Crucifixion nails, meaning of, iv. 131
  Cupid, Eros became, iii. 183
  Daksha established, intercourse, iii. 189, 190, 277, 374; iv. 228
  Dogmatic religion, element in, ii. 96
  Duration of, man, iii. 164
  Eastern occultists view of, relation, iv. 25
  Element in religious symbols, v. 291, 292
  Emblems, orginal purity of, ii. 73; v. 49
  Evolution and, propagation, iv. 227
  Form of man on, plane, iii. 93
  Globe under Cross and, reproduction, iii. 42
  Lemurians evolved from hermaphrodite parent-age, iii. 184
  Logoi, aspects of, ii. 68
  Lunar mysteries and, generation, i. 275
  Pater Zeus, nothing, about, iv. 145
  Physical, creature from ethereal hermaphrodite, iv. 250
  Polarization, creative magnetism in, ii. 122
  Process of kindling fire and reproduction, iii. 109
  Propagation not general, iv. 228
  Religion, iii. 230, 276
  Reproduction through, union, iv. 229
  Rose-Croix, sexual symbolism of, v. 292
  Rudimentary, organs, iii. 191
  Selection, iv. 219, 307
  Separation of human race, iv. 37
  Sons of God inaugurated, connection, iii. 374
  Speechless animal first began, connection, iii. 264
  Spirit and matter, union of, iv. 96
  Symbols, iv. 155; v. 292
  Talmudic Jews, mysteries of, iv. 39
  Third race, iii. 16, 174
  Worship, i. 45; iii. 335; iv. 159
SEYFFARTH, (SEIFFARTH), quoted, iii. 151; iv. 31, 71; v. 72, 150, 181
SHABALĀSHVAS, sons of Daksha, iii. 277
SHABDA BRAHMAN, Ishvara called, i. 194
  Logos of the Hindus, ii. 146; v. 539
  Sound is, v. 539
SHABDIC, v. 540
SHADDAI the omnipotent, ii. 156, 343; iv. 78
SHADE, Khaba the, iv. 203
SHADES, realm of, iv. 343
SHADJA a quality of sound, ii. 258
SHADOW, Ahriman manifested, of Ahura-Mazda, iv. 56
  Astral body, of, iii. 130
  ,,   Form, or, i. 274
  ,,   Light, of cosmic matter, ii. 54
  ,,   Man, or, iii. 117
  Breath, astral, of, iii. 113
  Brother(s) of, v. 466, 467, 502
  Buddha, of, v. 39, 40
  Chhāyā or, iii. 99, 110, 181; v. 454, 472, 477, 565, 566
  Creator, of light on earth, iii. 218
  Deity, of passive, iii. 38

Deity, of Unknown and, iv. 81
Divine Ego, of, v. 490
Divine thought, ideal prototype in, i. 131
Dragon of wisdom, of, iv. 76
Elohim, of, iii. 145
Eternal light, the, of the, iii. 270
Events past and to come, of, iii. 422
Everything on earth, of something in space, ii. 219
Evil, of light, ii. 131
Five inner principles or psychic, i. 274
Glory of Satan, of lord, iii. 238
Gnostics, immutable principle of, iii. 218
God, man pale, of, iii. 245
Ladder of being, at lower rung of, i. 108
Light makes brighter, ii. 129
  ,,   to manifest, enables, iii. 218
  ,,   without, would be absolute, i. 250
Perfect holy Adam, that disappeared, iv. 24
Personal God gigantic, ii. 360; iv. 124
Phenomenal, of pre-existing, i. 320
Psychic, i. 274
Sacred animal first, of physical man, i. 283
Sanjna leaving to her husband her, iii. 110, 181
Serpent of light, iii. 218
Sexless or, iii. 124
Shadow, of, iv. 55
Silent watcher, of, i. 308
Sons of, iv. 68
Spark, of flame, i. 309
Spheres, of something in superior, iii. 270
Spirit of creative fire, appears as, i. 250
Substance, cast by ever invisible, i. 131
Sun, of central sun, i. 299; ii. 363
Sun and moon Gods of light and, iv. 77
Things visible are, of things invisible, iii. 270
Third race bright, of Gods, iii. 270
Tzelem-Adam, iv. 72
Uraeus devoured by, i. 274
Wing became new, iii. 129
Wisdom revealing itself as light and, iii. 238
Woman-light of, ii. 118
SHADOW-SUN, iii. 244
SHADOWS, Amānasa called, iii. 100
  Astral bodies, or, iii. 95
  Atoms, of primaries in astral realms, ii. 202
  Bodies of sons of twilight, from, iii. 146
  Chhāyās, or, i. 243; ii. 296; iii. 129, 146
  Creative progenitors, astral, of, iii. 130
  Creators, inferior to, iii. 105
  Deities, of all, iii. 418
  Devas cast no, iii. 121
  Dhyāni-Buddhas, emanate from, ii. 296
  Dhyānīs incarnating in empty, iv. 55
  ,,   Throw off their first, i. 272
  Early races had, of bodies, iv. 181
  Falling stars enshrined in, iv. 55
  First race were, ii. 91; iii. 130, 146, 171; iv. 275
  Fourth race, left over for perfecting till, iii. 288
  Future men, of, iii. 99
  Ghosts or, of matter in motion, i. 202
  Holy youths refuse to enter, of inferiors, i. 243
  Kosmos, thrown by, i. 321
  Lords, of, iii. 121

SHADOWS (*Contd.*)
Lunar spirits, of, iii. 95
Men were shadows of, iii. 95
Past, of, iv. 206
Progenitors, of, ii. 91; iii. 57, 101, 130, 146, 171, 269
Realities and, i. 113
Self-existent projected their, iii. 245
Seven times seven, iii. 99
Solar Lhas warm, iii. 119
Sons of self-born, called, iii. 129
Spirits of earth clothed, iii. 119
Stones, plants and animals, of, iii. 193
Watcher, of, i. 308
Yima personification of, Pitris, iv. 180
SHADOWY, Astral light, side of, iv. 81
First forms were, iii. 129
First men were, iv. 182
Men created by Gods, iii. 104
Pitris, Chhāyā of, iv. 55
Prototype of astral body of progenitors, iv. 230
World of primal form, i. 178
SHAITAN is illusion, i. 335
SHAIVA PURĀNAS, quoted, ii. 177; iv. 147
SHAIVAS, ii. 122, 175, 399
SHAIVITIC Mysteries, v. 412
SHĀKA one of the seven Dvīpas, iii. 320, 403
SHĀKA-DVĪPA, iii. 322, 323, 403; iv. 156
SHAKAS, Sacae or, ii. 85
SHAKERS, v. 50, 311
SHAKESPEARE, quoted, i. 49; ii. 102; iii. 40, 126, 312, 417; iv. 243, 330
SHAKRA or Indra, ii. 91
SHAKTI, Durgā Kāli white side of, iv. 150
Energy or, i. 193; v. 213
Generative power, or, ii. 70
Heavenly man, of, ii. 70, 71
Helena, of Simon Magus, v. 450, 451
Kanyā represents, i. 333
Logos and its, ii. 195
Mahāmāyā, or, i. 333
Mother of mercy and knowledge, i. 193
Shekinah is, ii. 343
Soul power, v. 373, 378
Untranslatable word, v. 213
Yoga power, v. 378
Yoni or, ii. 194
SHAKTI-DHARAS or spear-holders, iii. 381; iv. 190
SHAKTIS, Classification of, i. 333
Female Potency, v. 451
Represented by cow, ii. 105
Seven, v. 484
Soul-power, is, v. 373, 378
Three, v. 89, 378
SHĀKYAMUNI or Gautama, i. 168; iii. 421; v. 287, 368, 377, 378, 391, 393, 400, 409, 410
SHAKYA-THUB-PA, or Gautama Buddha, iii. 421; v. 391
SHĀLAGRĀMA in the *Vishnu Purāna*, iii. 321
SHĀLMALI or Shālmalia one of the seven continents, iii. 403
SHAMAEL, the supposed Satan, iii. 209, 219
SHAMANS, v. 398, 403
SHAMBALAH or SHAMBALLA the Sacred Island in Gobi desert, iii. 319, 339; v. 337, 339, 404, 409, 412

SHAMBALAH, Brotherhood, of, v. 372
SHAME of Atlantean giants, iv. 249
SHAMO (or Schamo), desert of, iii. 326, 404, 414; iv. 71
SHĀNĀH or lunar year, iv. 130
SHANAISHCHARA is Saturn, ii. 179
SHANI or Saturn, iii. 42; v. 62
Triple septenary of, v. 45
SHANKARA, Avatāra, v. 351, 365
Brihaspati helps, iv. 66
Buddha and, v. 364
Hiranygarbha, Hari and, i. 83, 328; v. 188
Hypostasis of spirit of supreme spirit, i. 83
Mahā, v. 376, 377
Quoted, i. 119, 136; ii. 294
Shiva, or, iv. 66; v. 365
SHANKARĀCHĀRYA, Abode of, v. 365
Associated with Shankara, v. 365
Avatāra, v. 359, 367
Buddha's successor, i. 65; v. 364
Disappearance of, v. 148, 371, 377
Gautama Buddha and, iv. 208; v. 364-368, 371
Generic name, v. 376
Gospel of St. John, compared with teaching of, ii. 294
Incarnation of, v. 80
Initiate, greatest, i. 315
Living, still, v. 371, 372
Paraguru of, ii. 176
Philosophy of, v. 364, 401
Quoted, i. 73, 151; ii. 293, 294, 297; iv. 210
Rāja, took body of, v. 80
Secret wisdom taught by, ii. 263
Sixth-rounder, i. 216
Smārtava Brahmans and, i. 315
Upanishads, wrote Commentaries on, i. 315
SHANKHA-DVĪPA, iii. 403, 404, 406
SHANKHĀSURA, a king, iii. 403, 406
SHARĪRA, Faculties of, v. 541
One, form of, ii. 48
Subtile elements, of, i. 129
SHASTRA connected with Agneyāstra, iv. 200, 201
SHASTRA-DEVATĀS, Gods of the divine weapons, iv. 201
SHĀSTRAS of Hindū system, i. 174; v. 185, 347, 352
SHATA (of Veda), iv. 51
SHATANA to be adverse, iii. 386
SHATARŪPĀ hundred forms, of, ii. 149; v. 190
Nature, or, i. 157
Vāch named, iii. 137
SHE of Rider Haggard, iii. 319
SHE-ANIMALS and narrow-headed men, iii. 190, 191
SHEATH, Anandamaya, ii. 294
Kosha or, i. 212
SHEATHS, ii. 294; iv. 222
SHEBA Hachaloth, iii. 120
Is oath, iv. 174
SHEEP, Lord of, v. 104
SHE-HE or Yah-hovah, ii. 109
SHE'KEENAH the hidden Hū, ii. 243; iii. 294
SHEKINAH, Adam Kadmon knew only, ii. 151
Aditi, iii. 218; iv. 96
Ain-Soph, ii. 344; v. 107

SHEKINAH (*Contd.*)
  Chokmah and Binah, synthesizing spirit of, ii. 343
  Devamātri called, in *Zohar*, i. 124
  Divine grace, is, iii. 220
  Eternal light in world of spirit, or, iv. 96
  First radiation, v. 189
  First Sephira, or, ii. 70
  Jewish, Feminine, v. 189
  Kabalistic trinity, one of, i. 169
  Light of the Logos one with, v. 189
  Metatron, wife of, iii. 220
  Mūlaprakriti, ii. 354; v. 107
  Music of spheres or, ii. 150
  Primordial light or, iii. 115
  Sephira or, ii. 148
  Sexless is, ii. 344; v. 189
  Shakti, no more than, ii. 343, 344
  Spiritual substance sent forth by infinite light, ii. 70
  Vāch or, ii. 150
  Veil of Infinite Light, v. 191
SHELL, Antediluvian monsters appeared without, iii. 159
  Astronomy, of, iii. 370
  Cosmic space, of, ii. 313
  Earth, of, i. 304
  Egg of Brahmā, of, iv. 187
  Fire-mist, outskirts of, ii. 308
  Free atomic matter, outside, ii. 309
  Germ in, development of, ii. 74
  Kāma Loka for, of man, i. 289
  Kosmos, of, i. 221
  Man, of, iii. 258; iv. 303
  Man's body, of principle, iv. 187
  Moon, is, iii. 124
  Mundane Egg of, v. 424
SHELL-HEADS of birds and serpents, iii. 206
SHELLEY quoted, ii. 102
SHELLS, Contraires called, iii. 120
  Creatures in, iv. 72
  Demons or, iii. 120
  First races of third race were, iii. 172
  Human kingdom of, iii. 197
  Kumāras incarnating in senseless, ii. 176
  Mānasaputras endow senseless, with mind, i. 232
  Monads incarnating in empty, iii. 89, 304
  Pitris create and inform senseless, i. 232; iii. 263
  Sahara, sea-, in, ii. 21
SHEM, Biblical name, v. 89
  Pyramid measures and, v. 89
  Titan, a, iii. 343
SHEMITES, iii. 207
SHEPHERD, Logos became first, of men, iii. 372
  One of early Christian emblems, v. 163
  Parable of good, iv. 50; v. 96
  Zodiac, of, v. 315
SHEPHERDS, Invasion of, i. 140; ii. 23
SHESHA, Ananta, or, i. 140; iii. 60
  Astronomy teacher of, iii. 60
  Couch of Vishnu, or, i. 140; v. 287
  Cycle of eternity, or, iii. 60
  Nāga, God of Secret Wisdom, v. 287
  Serpent of infinity, ii. 87

Serpent, Thousand-headed, iii. 380
  ,, Who bears Pātālas on his head, iii. 60
  Seven heads of, ii. 124
  Time or infinite, i. 140; iii. 61, 107
  Vishnu (the lord) rests on, ii. 87; iii. 107, 380
SHESHA-ANANTA, iii. 107
SHEU, -Adept, v. 38, 39
SHEW-BREAD and signs of zodiac, ii. 375
SHIBBOLETH (SHIBB∴) vegetable kingdom symbolised, iv. 146
SHIELD, of David, v. 120
SHIELDS, Azazyei taught men to make, iii. 375
SHIFTING of continents, iii. 333; iv. 269
SHILOH, Dance of daughtes of, iv. 28; v. 311
SHIN, v. 206
SHINING, Ākāshic, garment of Jesus, iv. 152
  Amesha spentas, iii. 357
  Face, Lord of, iii. 27, 40, 56
  Face of Moses, v. 92, 562
  Likenesses, Teraphim considered, v. 238
  Ones, i. 138
  Seven or builders, i. 260
  Taijasa or the, v. 78
SHINTO sects, Cosmogenesis of, i. 261, 286
SHIP, ark, Navis, iii. 147; iv. 31
  Astoreth, of life, iv. 30
  Crocodile, carried along by, ii. 126
SHIPS, canoes and arks, iv. 343
SHISHUMĀRA, or Porpoise, iv. 119, 183
SHISHUPĀLA, son of a King Rishi, iii. 229
SHISTA, Celestial ancestors or, i. 293
  Imperishable sacred land, iii. 19, 20
  Initiators, the, v. 81
  Noah identical with, iv. 168
  Seed-humanity or, i. 234
  Seed-manus or, iii. 171
  Seed of life on earth, throws, iii. 158
  Sons of light or holy, iv. 100
  Spiritual lives, divine, iii. 171
SHISTAS or the surviving fittest, iii. 308, 309
  Preceding cycles of, v. 81
SHITTIM wood, iii. 416
SHIVA, v. 89
  Anaitia, wife of, i. 155
  Avatāra and, v. 352
  Brahmā, four-faced, v. 192, 530
  Brahmā thrown by, into abyss of darkness, iv. 84
  Brahmā, Vishnu and, i. 328; ii. 262; iii. 124, 313; v. 89, 117, 190, 530
  Bull of, ii. 105
  Central eye of, iv. 150
  Complexions of, ii. 36
  Consort, and his, iii. 155
  Creator and saviour of spiritual man, ii. 178
  Cyclic character of, ii. 155
  Daksha's sacrifice, and, iii. 189
  Destroyer, or, iii. 123, 251
  Devī-Durgā wife of, i. 155
  Evolution and progress personified, iii. 189
  Eye of, i. 118; ii. 267; iii. 286, 297, 303; iv. 150
  Ganesha's head and, v. 111
  Gaurī bride of, iii. 86
  God of death or destruction, ii. 82
  Hindu Trimūrti and, v. 117
  Isha primary name of, iii. 123

SHIVA (Contd.)
Kivan or, v. 238, 318
Kumāra reborn in each kalpa, iii. 283
Kumāras incarnations of, iii. 251
,,   mind-born sons of, ii. 178
Lingam, v. 192
Logos, v. 365
Mahat manifests itself as, i. 141
Mahāyogī, ii. 178
Mars born of sweat of, iii. 55, 133
,, generated in fire from seed of, iii. 381; iv. 190
Maruts children of, iv. 184
Meru, personated by, ii. 54
Nāgās, crowned with, ii. 155
Nīlalohita is, ii. 176
Panchānana five-faced, iv. 150
Principle of fire, iv. 163
Regenerator, v. 192
Repeated births of, ii. 36
Rig-Veda, not in, iv. 184
Rudra or, ii. 174, 176, 179; iii. 115, 284; iv. 147
Saturn or, ii. 179; v. 238
Shankara or, iv. 66
Shvetalohita as, iii. 251
Shukra and, iii. 45
Tattvas and, v. 469
Triangle with apex upward is, iv. 163
Vaivasvata, preceded, iii. 152
Vāmadeva, called, ii. 36; iii. 251, 283
Vina of, v. 518, 520
Yogīs and adepts, patron of all, iii. 283
Worship, iv. 159
" SHIVAGAMA," v. 469, 475, 477
SHIVA-GHARMAJA, Mars and, iii. 55
SHIVA-KUMĀRA, ii. 36
SHIVA-RUDRA See above
Destroyer, ii. 178
Maruts sons of, iv. 186, 190
Regenerator of spiritual and physical nature, ii. 178
Third eye of, iv. 186
Virabhadra, creates, iii. 189
SHOALS, Motion of interstellar, ii. 358
SHRADDHĀ or faith, Kāma son of, iii. 183
SHRAMANA, Gautama, v. 377, 378
SHRAMANAS, i. 47; v. 398
SHRAVAKAS, v. 398
SHRĪ, ii. 95; iii. 86
SHRĪ-ĀNTARA, Double triangle, i. 177
SHRĪDHARA SVĀMIN quoted, ii. 123
SHRINGA-GIRI of Mysore, i. 315
SHRUTI or revealed knowledge, i. 313; v. 364, 371
SHU or SHOO, books of Confucius, four, i. 49
Children or rebellion and, ii. 80
City of Eight, on the stairway in the, ii. 24
Devachan, in, iii. 373
Egyptian God of creation, i. 142
Horus the elder contemporary with, ii. 82
Personification of Ra, iv. 116
Ra awakens, ii. 75
Solar energy, ii. 75, 80
Solar force, the, ii. 24
SHUCHI, iii. 113, 250
Drainer of waters, iii. 113
Pārvaka and, iii. 111

Saura, or, ii. 245
Solar fire, iii. 68, 110, 111
SHUCKFORD, Dr., quoted, iii. 267
SHUDDASHATTVA, or SUDDASATTVA, i. 190; ii. 246
SHŪDRA, v. 378
SHU-KING (SHOO-KING), China's primitive Bible, i. 64
SHUKRA Bhrigu, son of, iii. 42, 45
Car of, iii. 44
Daitya-guru of primeval giants, iii. 42, 44
Earth, and, iii. 44
Light comes through, iii. 42
Male deity in Brāhmanism, iii. 42
Purānas, in, iii. 43
Regent of, iii. 45
Shiva, and, iii. 45
Spirit of earth subservient to Lord of, iii. 42
Ushanas, iii. 57
Venus or, iii. 42, 57
SHUKRA-VENUS, iii. 44
SHUNAMITE, Husband of, iii. 85
SHŪNYAM, Sanskrit for nought, ii. 76
SHVETA-DVIPA, Atlantis not, iii. 406
Celestial abode or, iii. 365
Lemuria, during early days of, iii. 266
Lotus leaves of, iii. 327
Mount Meru, or, iii. 19
Panchāshikha goes to, i. 280
Siddhapura or, iii. 406
Sons of, iii. 319
Vishnu, abode of, iii. 401
White Island or, iii. 319, 322, 401, 402, 406; iv. 156
SIAM, Philosophical teaching when transferred to, i. 44
SIAMEK, son of Kaimurath, iii. 395
SIAMESE, astronomical tables, ii. 390
Ears of, iii. 338
Egg symbol, and, ii. 82
SIBAC means egg, iii. 188
SIBERIA, iii. 327, 343, 400, 401
,,   Shamanism of, v. 404
SIBREE quoted, i. 123; ii. 365, 366
SIBYL, Cycles and, v. 337, 338, 339
False, v. 51
SIBYLLINE books, Secrecy of, iii. 395; v. 61, 312
Prophecy, v. 338, 339
Virgin's return announced in all, ii. 384
SICANIANS, Āryan invasion, forerunners of the, iv. 310
SICILY, Africa joined to, iv. 320
Muses of, v. 337
Worship of Kabirim in, iii. 362, 363
SIDDARTHA BUDDHA, v. 357
SIDDHA-SENA Kārtikeya called, iii. 381; iv. 119
SIDDHAS, fourth root-race, of, iv. 208
Kārtikeya commander of, iv. 119
Nirmānakāyas, are, iv. 208
Purānas, of the, v. 462
Saints or, ii. 87
Shvetāshvatara-Upanishad on, iv. 208
Siddha-sena leader of, iii. 381; iv. 119
Vidyādharas, kind of, ii. 263
SIDDHIS or phenomena of an Arhat, i. 160
SIDEREAL, Apollo born on, Island called Asteria, iii. 382

SIDEREAL (*Contd.*)
 Army or angelic hosts, v. 319
 Beings, i. 182
 Bodies, Anaximenes on formation of, ii. 314
 ,, Animals of *Genesis*, iii. 121
 ,, Co-essential with terrene plane, i. 220
 ,, Cosmic substance forms, from itself, ii. 292
 ,, Formed from one another, i. 252
 ,, Intermediate space between, ii. 214
 ,, Personages transmuted, into, v. 112
 ,, Septenary constitution of, i. 222
 Body, deceased, i. 251
 ,, Globes of, 213
 ,, Outer crust of every, v. 424
 ,, Planet forming itself into new, i. 202
 Contents of Ether, v. 423
 Cycle symbolized by tabernacle, ii. 26
 Despots, our, iv. 269
 Don Juan, a, i. 275
 Draco guiding, divinity, iii. 44
 Dvīpas, position of, iii. 320
 Earth's lords, i. 219
 Existence, bliss of, iii. 249
 Flocks of stars and constellations, iii. 384
 Flood, iii. 154, 308
 Forces or angels, i. 280; ii. 222
 Glyphs, iii. 355
 Gods, reflection of Deity, ii. 156
 Great dragon in, fields, ii. 123
 Heavens birth-place of humanity, iii. 433
 Horus circling round, heavens, i. 274
 Hosts, motion of, ii. 318
 Influence, v. 330
 Initiates of, Gods, ii. 379
 Intelligent forces or angels, i. 280; v. 320
 Isis, moon, symbol of, ii. 77
 Jelly-speck, iii. 167
 Ka or, man, iv. 205
 Kabiri rulers of, powers, iii. 363
 Kalpa, iii. 308
 Light, drama enacted in, iv. 79
 ,, Paracelsus, of, i. 298
 ,, Rosicrucians, of, ii. 52
 Localities Solar gods and, v. 317
 Manu, of, flood, iii. 308
 Maruts, representation of, iv. 186
 Moon, great lunatic, i. 204
 ,, Symbol of Isis, ii. 77
 Motions affect cycles, ii. 369
 ,, regulate some events on earth, ii. 370
 Mysteries, v. 176
 Ocean-beds, i. 218
 Patriarchs are, symbols, iii. 390
 Phenomena model for earth, iv. 70
 Planes, laws on, iv. 192
 Pleiades and, symbology, iv. 121
 Powers in, world awakened, i. 182
 Principles, ii. 177, 178
 Prophecies of zodiac, ii. 379
 Rulers of, heaven, ii. 216
 Science and giants, iii. 279
 Sephiroth, iii. 156; v. 191
 Septenate, Pleiades, iv. 121
 Serpent as spirit, iii. 212
 Ship of life and, Ocean, iv. 30
 Sisters, seven, iv. 190

Souls in planets, v. 313
Sovereignty and Primitive Astrology, v. 332
Space according to materialists, ii. 311
 ,, Ether and, v. 424
Substance in, space, ii. 249
Sun, king of, orbs, iii. 132
Symbols of Occult Philosophy, iv. 121
Terrestrial and, substance, ii. 321
Tetragrammaton, sum total, ii. 156
Theologians and, facts, ii. 379
Vessel, Navis, iv. 31
Virgin great magic agent, iv. 80
West, or, i. 181
Wheels in Temples, v. 321, 322
World, denizens of, i. 155
Worlds and our globe, iv. 269
Worship, or Astrology, v. 318-323
Year, Catastrophe comes at renewal of, ii. 375
 ,, Circles of, called serpents, iii. 355
 ,, Cyclic year is, ii. 157
 ,, Family race and, iii. 433
 ,, Great pyramid and, iii. 430
 ,, History of nations and, iii. 330
 ,, Initiation and cycle of, ii. 26
 ,, Length of, ii. 26, 153, 157, 375; iii. 330, 430; iv. 339
 ,, Mighty ones appear at beginning of every, ii. 153
 ,, Tropics and, iii. 330
Years, Dendera zodiac shows passage of three, ii. 430
Years, Egyptian and Hindu, iii. 332
 ,, Eight coils of serpent or, iii. 356
SIDEREO-COSMICAL Gods, iv. 110
SIDEREO-TERRESTRIAL imagery or cat symbol, ii. 17
SIDERITES, or star-stones, iii. 341
SIDON, navigators of, iv. 320
SI-DZANG in Tibet, seat of occult learning, i. 314
SIEMENS, Dr. C. William, quoted, i. 164
SIEN-CHAN, Elementary germs surrounding, i. 196
 Fohat fills, with elementary germs, i. 196
 Phenomenal World, or, v. 379
 Illusive form of, iv. 193
 Universe or, i. 193, 194, 196
 Voice calls forth, i. 194
SIGAEUM, giant skeleton of, iii. 280
SIGALIONS or images of Harpocrates, iii. 395
SIGĒ silence, or thought, iv. 144, 145, 146; v. 446, 447
SIGHT, Cause of, ii. 257, 258
 Fire or light and sense of, iii. 116
 Fourth race of unlimited, iii. 225
 Initial existence is substance to our spiritual, i. 330
 Monads (Atoms) is marvellous, the, of the, ii. 358
 Procreation of men by, iii. 183
 Spiritual, of mankind blinded, iii. 84
 Third eye organ of spiritual, iii. 300
 Third race organ of, iii. 300
SIGILLARIA or primary age, iv. 282
SIGN, Ankh, of life, ii. 127; iv. 117
 Anubis holding out cross, of life, ii. 127
 Circumference, of, iv. 152

SIGN (*Contd.*)

Cross or double, iii. 42

Cross used by adepts and neophytes, iv. 132

Egg is, in every cosmogony, ii. 74

Globe over cross, of Venus, iii. 43

Heaven, from, ii. 380

Jonas, of, ii. 380

Language, ii. 16

Makara, of, i. 266, 268, 279; ii. 91, 99, 149; iii. 102, 271, 353; iv. 147-151

Minam, ii. 91; iv. 151

Svastika universal, iii. 108

Thought, i. 156

Venus, of, iii. 43

Vishnu, of, iv. 163; v. 120, 163

Zodiac, of, Capricornus tenth, iv. 147, 151

,,   Libra, v. 430

,,   Pisces, i. 309; ii. 91, 379, 380; iv. 151

,,   Scorpio, v. 164, 286, 430

,,   Secret, iv. 71

,,   Taurus, v. 267

,,   Virgo, ii. 377; v. 430

See also Makara *and* Minam *above*

SIGNS, Akibeel taught meaning of, iii. 375

Ideographic, on hatchets of palaeolithic period, iii. 437

Lunar zodiac of twenty-eight, ii. 124

Mystery, iv. 71

Patriarchs are sidereal, iii. 390

Sacred, on Babylonian Cylinders, v. 123

Secret Doctrine expressed in few pages of geometrical, i. 316

,,   Zohar, in, v. 112

Zodiac, of, v. 152, 164, 241

,,   Akkadian month named after, ii. 375

,,   Animals in *Genesis*, i. are, iii. 15, 121

,,   Antiquity of, ii. 33

,,   Cherubs wings and, v. 316

,,   Creative powers, twelve orders of, i. 261

,,   Dendera, iii. 430

,,   Ecliptic and twelve, iii. 368

,,   Egyptian, iii. 367; v. 332

,,   Gods, who ascended and descended, iii. 357

,,   Great Bear and, v. 202

,,   Great dragon spread over seven, iii. 44

,,   Heaven's belt or, iii. 36

,,   Humanity intimately connected with, iii. 428

,,   *Iliad* and *Odyssey*, in, ii. 374

,,   Indian, ii. 384

,,   Jewish patriarchs and, ii. 377

,,   *Job*, in, ii. 373

,,   Kārtikeya, hidden on body of, iv. 190

,,   Makara and, iv. 149

,,   Monads descent and reascent, and, ii. 391

,,   Mystery of, iv. 151

,,   Mystical epithets and, ii. 383

,,   *Old Testament*, in, ii. 375

,,   Regents of, iii. 357

,,   Sacred animals or, i. 156; ii. 165; iii. 36, 187

,,   Sacrificial animals or, iv. 196

,,   Symbolic Dance of, iv. 28; v. 310, 311

,,   Theogonies, in, ii. 378

VI-26

Zodiac, Twelve, v. 429, 430

,,   Twelve small islands representing, iv. 71

,,   Two secret, v. 429

,,   Worshipped, were, ii. 375

SIGNUM TAY in Church of St. Denis, France, v. 162

SIGNUM THAU in *Ezekiel*, iv. 127

SIGURD and Fafnir, the Scandinavian, ii. 120, 121

SIKKIM (Sikhim), Dugpas, v. 47, 48, 122, 403

SILENCE, Eternal from Bythos, iv. 139

Evolution of universe out of, iv. 144

First Cause passed over in reverential, ii. 143

First Principle more ineffable than, ii. 144

God the, ii. 66

Law of, imposed on chelas, v. 29, 61, 74, 75

Maimonides enjoins, upon true meaning of Mosaic sayings, iv. 24

Matter born in, iv. 146

Monad that dwelleth, in, ii. 151

Mysteries, as to, iv. 17

Pythagorean vow of, v. 45

Sigé or, iv. 144, 145, 146; v. 446, 447

Sound, nor, there was neither, i. 124

That, concerning, ii. 144

SILENT, All absolute, ii. 60

Power of Iah, v. 212

Sanctuary of Heart, v. 75

Unknown Universal soul, depths of, iv. 145

Watcher, i. 308; v. 532

SILENUS and Midas, iv. 329

SILICATES, ii. 307

SILICON, ii. 274, 276, 309

SILIK-MULUDAG, Akkadian God of wisdom, iv. 45

SILO from Lake of the Dragons, river, iii. 208

SILOAM, sleep of, iv. 128

SILURIAN age or period, Chronology of, iii. 81

First and second races during, iii. 158

Fossil life of, iii. 256

Geology has traced primordial life down to, iii. 82

Life, iv. 281

Molluscs before, i. 297

Oceans of, iii. 167

Primordial matter in, iii. 258

Seas, iv. 254

SILVER, ii. 276

Age, iii. 204, 272, 273; iv. 89

SIMEON, Gemini and, ii. 377

Levi, and, ii. 377; iii. 216

SIMEON, Ben Jochai (Shimeon Ben Yochai)

Rabbi, quoted, i. 263; ii. 71, 168; iv. 72, 175, 176, 177

Doctrine of, v. 67, 108, 109

Kabalah, of, ii. 106; iv. 55, 274; v. 211

Zohar and, v. 67, 108, 175, 176, 211

SIMEON BEN SHETAH, v. 116

SIMIAN, Ancestry, iv. 249

Earlier, creatures, iii. 172

Human and, brains, iv. 216

Man not descendant of, type, iv. 216

Stirps, iv. 247

SIMON de SIENNE, Picture by, iii. 212

SIMON MAGUS, v. 131-135

Adept, v. 129

SIMON MAGUS (*Contd.*)
Baptised Christian, a, v. 126, 132
Claims of, v. 79, 128
Disciples of, v. 449
Helena, and, v. 450, 451
Infinite potency of, v. 446
Invocation of Demons by, v. 133, 134
Kabalist and Mystic, v. 127, 129
Magic and, v. 450, 451
One with Paul, v. 129, 131, 138
Philosophy of, v. 449
Reformer and Adept, v. 129
Six radicals of, iv. 139
System of, near to Occult truth, v. 445
Teaching of, v. 444-451, 462
Traditions of, v. 126, 127, 132, 134
Versed in Magic Arts, iv. 133, 134
Writings of, v. 245
SIMON of Cyrene, v. 351
SIMONIUM, in Rome, v. 134
SIMORGH, Numerical mysteries of Persian,
iv. 134
Phoenix same as, iii. 396; iv. 188
Romance of, quoted, iii. 396
Tahmurath winged, of, iii. 398
SIMORGH-ANKE, ii. 396, 398
SIMPLICIUS, quoted, ii. 376
SIMPSON, Sir J., quoted, iii. 345; iv. 117
SIN, Animals, committed with, iii. 197
Anu identical with moon, iii. 72
Atala or land of, iii. 322
Atlanteans fall into, iii. 230; iv. 249
Atlantis, land of, iii. 322
Babylonian God, ii. 104
Body and mind defiled by, iv. 221
Celestial virgin, of, iv. 81
Creative powers not result of, iii. 408
Deus Lunus, called by Greeks, ii. 104
Fall and original, iii. 264
Fall of spirit into matter, or, i. 307
First physiologically complete couples accused
of, iii. 219
Fish, and Soma, i. 283, 307
Fourth race black with, iii. 319, 349
Inhabitants of White Island became black with,
iii. 406
Kali age of, iv. 120
Karma or, iii. 303
Lunar God, iii. 36
Man will be born from woman without, iii.418
Meaning of, iii. 303
Messengers of Anu overpowered by, iii. 72
Mindless, of, iii. 186, 191, 197, 269; iv. 253,
259
Misuse of powers, iii. 303
Moon and, i. 293
Mountain of moon or, iii. 86
Mulil, son of, iii. 147
Origin of, iii. 206
Original, iii. 281, 305, 386, 411; iv. 52, 83
Satan makes man free from, of ignorance,
i. 248
Scorpio emblem of, iii. 137
Seven holy rivers of Atlantis which washed
away, iii. 322
SINAI, Agar is, v. 67
Deity, descending on ii. 162

Geometrical figures given to Moses on, v. 114
Green diorite from Peninsula of, iv. 262
Hagar is mount, iii. 86
Holy mountain, iv. 62, 63
Jehovah of, v. 278
Moon, mountain of, iii. 236; iv. 262
Moses on mount, iv. 137; v. 92, 114, 186
Mount, as monument of exact time, iii. 86
Nis, Nissa, from, v. 278
Osiris born on, v. 263
Secret Doctrine infuses life into figures on,
iv. 336
Sni, or, iv. 33
Womb, symbol of, ii. 62
SINAITIC peninsula, iii. 229
SIND and the Ethiops river, ii. 415
SINDHU or Hindu, iii. 230
SINFUL, Adam-Eve son of, thought, iii. 136
Matter, ii. 311
Prohibition of, intercourse, iii. 198
Substance, iii. 64
SINGERS, celestial, ii. 247; iv. 156
Sweet, v. 394
SINGH of Hindus, winged, iv. 189
SINGHALESE priest and sacred Buddhist books,
i. 53
SINGING stones, iii. 340
SINGLE eye of spirit, v. 438
,,　　substance doctrine, i. 183
SINHA the lion, iii. 406, 430; iv. 135
SINHALESE, Buddhist, ii. 361
Rākshasas, heirs of, iii. 406
Veddhas, iii. 288
SINKING of continent, ii. 31; iii. 308
SINLESS, Shadows of bodies, iv. 181
Shākadvīpa, iii. 323
Sons of third race, iii. 374
SINNERS, days of, ii. 334
SINNETT, Mr. A.P., Initiates permit, to publish
books, i. 43
Lay Chela, a, v. 440
Philosophy expounded by, taught in America,
i. 42
Quoted, i. 41, 168, 181, 218, 223, 239;
iii. 431, 434
Teacher of, i. 217, 218, 239
SINOLOGUES, western, i. 49
SINS, Black-faced, of, iii. 424
Earth quivers because of, of men, iii. 422
SIPH-O-R, one of three seraphim, iii. 51
SIPPARA, City of the Sun, v. 180
SIPPOR or S'phor, iii. 53
SIPUR, one of three seraphim, i. 156
SIRE of Persians, iv. 173
SIRES, spoiled dumb man's, iii. 289
SIRIUS, iii. 373; iv. 277
SIRMIUM, Council of, v. 156
SIROCCO, materialistic thought like deadly,
ii. 40
SISTER Planet, every world has, iii. 45
SISTERS, Bhūmi appears with six, i. 295
Seven sidereal, iv. 190
SISTRA used in circle-dance, iv. 29
SISTRUM, cat in hand of Isis on, ii. 103
SĪTĀ, Rāvana carries off, iv. 141
SIVAITIC magic, v. 39
SIVATHERIUM of Himālayas, iii. 222

SIX Brothers of Krishna, v. 154
Days of creation, iii. 254; iv. 56, 273
Dhyān Chohans or Sephiroth of construction, ii. 90
Directions of space, i. 175, 177
Double triangle or, directions of space, i. 177
Limbs of Microprosopus, i. 262, 263
Oeaohoo, in one, i. 136
Organs of sense, v. 368
Principles of nature outcome of seventh and one, i. 83
Sephiroth, ii. 56
Seventh, whose essence is, ii. 90
Shall continue, ii. 91
Spiritual elements, i. 269
Thousand years, ii. 91
SIX-FACED planet Mars, iii. 381
SIX-FOLD Dhyān-Chohans, i. 269
Dhyānīs or spirits of earth, i. 271
Division of world, iv. 193
Heavenly man, i. 271
SIX-POINTED crown, iv. 190
Star, Adonai, iv. 102
,,   Forces of nature, refers to six, i. 263
,,   Logos, symbol of, i. 262
,,   Snow crystal, iv. 166
,,   Symbol of, ii. 90
SIX-PRINCIPLED DHYĀNĪ, i. 270
SIX-RAYED STAR of double triangle, i. 177; iv. 190; v. 163
SIXTH, Continent, iii. 443
Plane, faculties of ego on, ii. 43
Principle, Alaya is Kosmic, v. 528
,,   Brahmā or, i. 83
,,   Buddhi, in, man, i. 178
,,   Māyāvic, is, i. 83
,,   Sun of solar system, ii. 251
,,   Universal, pure essence of, i. 82
Principles, merging of, and seventh, i. 123
Race, v. 267, 518, 523
,,   Advanced thinkers of, i. 338
,,   Dawn of, iv. 349
,,   Dhyāni-Buddha of, i. 168
,,   Element corresponding to, i. 78
,,   Ether, its gross sub-division developed in, ii. 56
,,   Fifth race will overlap, iii. 443
,,   Mankind going towards, ii. 281
,,   New continents for the, iv. 326
,,   Preparation of, iii. 443
,,   Seventh race, and, iv. 51
Round, element corresponding to, i. 70; v. 563
Rounders, meaning of, i. 215, 216
Sense, i. 158; ii. 259, 269; iv. 210; v. 474
Seventh principle in man, and, ii. 90
Sub-race of fifth race, iii. 442
SKANDA, Collective body and, ii. 83
God of war, iii. 381
Rudra, son of, ii. 177
SKANDHAS, v. 473, 518, 559, 560, 561
SKELETON(S), Age and size of, iii. 280
Ape, of man and, iv. 236
Atlantean, of, iv. 244
Early man, of, iii. 260; iv. 288
Eocene strata, of, iv. 260

Giants, of, iii. 279, 280, 294, 336; iv. 322, 324
Guanches, of, iv. 359
Haute Garonne, of, iv. 309
Human, iv. 248, 292
Neolithic age, of, iv. 318
New Orleans, at, iii. 351
Specialization of, iv. 288
Stanzas form, iii. 24
Unspecialized, iv. 288, 303
SKIN(S), Atlantean records on tanned, iv. 262
Coats of, ii. 331, 367; iii. 82, 207, 283; iv. 306, 317
Earth changes its, iv. 278
Eye beneath, iii. 300
Pores, Roma-kūpas or, iii. 189
Seven, iii. 56, 58, 59
Seven layers of man's, v. 425, 429
Thermal sensibility of, iii. 300
Three, of earth, iii. 58
SKINNER, J. Ralston quoted, i. 154; ii. 20, 28; iii. 51, 387; v. 72, 110, 111, 166, 206, 235, 286
SKRYMIR and his brethren, iv. 323
SKULL(S) Austria, exhumed in, iv. 308
Capacity of, iv. 91
Comparison of, iii. 175
Cross bones and, v. 161, 164, 166
Engis, iv. 257
Enormous, iii. 280
European and Carib, iv. 358
European and Hottentot, iv. 92
Forms of, iv. 360
Fossil, iv. 309
Human, iv. 248
Index, iv. 92
Macroprosopus, of, iv. 196
Neanderthal, iv. 256, 257, 293, 298
Negro, iv. 248, 308
Pithecoid, iv. 251
Quaternary, iv. 318
SLACK, H.J., quoted, ii. 312, 324
SLAUGHTER, Rev. W.B., quoted, i. 160
SLAVONIAN alphabet, iv. 117
Giant tombs, iv. 321
God, derivation of, ii. 61
Leibnitz of, descent, ii. 353
Mythology of flood, iii. 272
Peasant, Easter-egg of, ii. 83
SLAYER, Dragon, iii. 377, 383, 384; iv. 75
Vitra, iii. 383
SLEEP, Adam, of, iii. 187, 188
Antahkarana in, v. 497
Aura in, v. 457
Dreamless, i. 118, 119
Dreams and, iv. 331; v. 497, 558
Ego latent during, ii. 147
Extinction in, iii. 310
Ideation ceases in, i. 111
Mental, long ages of, iv. 44
Mental of third race, iii. 199
Nervous centres act during, iv. 331
Nirvāna compared to, i. 309
Profound, iv. 270
Siloam, or, iv. 128
Spiritual man free during, v. 457
Universe, of, i. 137

SLEEPING and waking states, i. 82, 323; v. 457, 497
SLEEPING-ATOMS, iv. 242
SLIME, Protoplasm, and, iii. 165
    Rounds, of former, iii. 65
SLOTHS, iv. 357
SMARAGDINE TABLETS, of Hermes, iii. 108, 111, 118; iv. 126; v. 114
SMĀRTA, caste of Brāhmans, i. 315
SMELL, Animals without, ii. 332
    Rudiment of, ii. 88
    Sense of, iii. 116
SMITH, George, Discoveries of Assyrian, Babylonian and Chaldean antiquity, i. 49; ii. 31, 32, 72; iii. 16, 18, 72, 112, 250, 284, 353, 382, 385; iv. 261; v. 94, 199
SMITH'S Sound, forests of, iv. 357
SMOKE, Baptism, of, iv. 136
    Clouds of, iv. 53
    Fire, of, iv. 137, 139
    Sacrifice, of, iv. 139
SMRITI, word Kabalah identical with, v. 177
SMYTH, Prof. Piazzi, Astronomer Royal of Scotland, v. 43
    Divine language on, ii. 29
    Mosaic books and measures, ii. 25
    Opponents of, ii. 26
    Pyramids, on, i. 174; ii. 29; iv. 34; v. 43, 110, 186
SNAILS, Heavenly, i. 164
    Parthenogenesis, and, iv. 229
SNAKE, Brazen, of Moses, i. 299
    Creative power and, iii. 188
    Emblem, ii. 58
    God, Vasūki, v. 286
    Initiate called, ii. 125
    Mundane, matter, i. 147
    Passage-like hole of, iii. 378, 379
    Tortuous, iii. 233
SNAKE-GODS, Daksha and, iii. 190
    Hiranyāksha, iii. 381
SNAKES, City of, iii. 345
    Son of, iii. 378, 379
SNI or Sinai, iv. 33
SNOWY, Mountain, Teachers of, v. 390
    Range, v. 109, 390
SOCIETIES, Secret, v. 58, 294
SOCIETY, Antiquaries of London, of, quoted, iii. 379
    Psychical Research, of, i. 22
    Masonic, of Trinosophists, iv. 146
    Theosophical, iii. 413; iv. 163; v. 53, 304
SOCRATES, Daimon of, iii. 417; v. 65, 333
    Death of, v. 65, 218, 333, 380
    Gods, believed in, ii. 336
    Historian of fifth century, i. 50
    Initiated, not, v. 218, 524
    Injunction of, v. 75
    Intellectual capacity of, iv. 91
    Mysteries, on the, v. 266
    Plato, Master of, v. 60
    Prayer, on, v. 71
    Saluting the Sun, v. 277
SOCRATIC sense, Daimones in, i. 329
    Mysteries of Baal Adonis and Bacchus, iii. 216
    Mysterious assembly, or, iv. 197
    Secret or, iii. 216
SODALES of right and left path, iii. 215, 216

SODALIAN mysteries, iv. 204
    Oath, v. 29
SODIUM, ii. 270, 274, 309
SŌDS (Sod Ihoh), Mysteries of Pre-Babylonian Jews, or, ii. 184; iii. 216
    Sabbath in secret calculations of, iii. 394
    Secret of Law or, v. 188
SOGDIANA, Āryan Magi emigrate to, iii. 355
SO-HAM, He (is) I, i. 144
    Sah and Aham, equal to, iv. 33
SOHAR or light, iii. 50, 51
SOIL, Abel life-bearing, iii. 275
    Animals in, ii. 332
    Mystery, and Saptaparna plant, iv. 145
    Promised Land, of, ii. 292
SOKHIT, Cat sacred to, iv. 122
SOL, Alter, iii. 44
    Mercury is, ii. 68
    Souls became, iv. 146; v. 116, 277
SOLAR
    Angels, iii. 97
    ,,   Agnishvattas or, iii. 97
    ,,   Barhishads or, iii. 97
    ,,   Endow man with ego, iii. 97
    ,,   Kumaras or, i. 151
    ,,   Lords of persevering ceaseless devotion, or, iii. 97
    Bacchus, Dionysos or, iii. 413, 418
    Birds, eagle and hawk are, iv. 135
    Boat, i. 274; iii. 150; iv. 99
    ,,   Osiris of, or Ark, iii. 150
    ,,   Thoth travels in, iv. 99
    ,,   365 degrees or, iv. 99
    Body, Substance in sun and, ii. 249
    Car, Kanya Durga on lion dragging, ii. 384
    Centre, nebula result of incandescence of, ii. 238
    Chnouphis, gnostic, iii. 376
    Colours of prism, v. 442
    Cosmos, man microcosm of, ii. 318
    Cosmic veil, ii. 252
    Course, periods of, ii. 363
    Cycle, iv. 27, 135
    ,,   Garuda emblem of, iv. 135
    ,,   Naros, of, iv. 190
    ,,   Phoenix and, iv. 188
    Day, value of, iv. 169
    Days make Paccham, fifteen, iv. 191
    Deities, Angnishvattas are, i. 151, 233
    ,,   Cow and bull symbols connected with i. 135
    ,,   Hosts of, ii. 129
    ,,   Kumaras are, i. 151
    ,,   Lares are, iii. 360
    ,,   Seven mystic sages are, i. 151
    Devas or Mānasa-dhyānis, i. 128, 129
    Discus, Thoth with the, iv. 99
    Disk on hawk-head of Hor, ii. 82
    ,,   Thoth wears, ii. 100
    Dragon, v. 202
    Dynasties, Hindus call themselves of, ii. 104
    Dynasty, Maru restorer of Kshattriya race of, ii. 93
    Eclipses, iii. 379
    Electricity, v. 220
    Energy, i. 171; ii. 80
    ,,   Fohat is, i. 171

SOLAR (*Contd.*)

Energy, Vishnu, manifestation of, i. 171
Existence, conditioned of, iii. 144
Fields, lotus which comes from, ii. 96
Fire, ii. 24, 245, 247, 251; iii. 68, 110, 113, 249
,, Æther, Aithur, or, ii. 251
,, Demiurge became, ii. 24
,, Gandharvas are aggregate powers of, ii. 247
,, Rashoo or, ii. 244
,, Saura, or, ii. 245
,, Shuchi, or, ii. 245; iii. 111, 250
,, Space filled with, ii. 251
,, Spirit of each called to his help, iii. 110
,, Sushumnā Ray, or, ii. 247
Fires, i. 149; ii. 275; iii. 110; iv. 112
,, Extinction of, ii. 275
,, Seed of universe fecundated by, iv. 112
Flames, are reflections, ii. 254
Fourth Plane of, v. 532
God, i. 82; iii. 405; iv. 27, 29, 34
,, Adytum of Temple, in, iv. 27
God, Bull, whole, symbolized in Egypt, v. 206
,, Candidate at initiation represented, iv. 29
,, Elder Horus, aspect of, ii. 82
,, Jehovah as, iv. 34
,, Krishna as, iii. 405
,, Ptah as, ii. 82
,, Satan and, v. 314
,, Vishnu as, iii. 405
Gods, ii. 100, 153, 154; iii. 215, 425; iv. 63, 215, 425
,, Adepts taught by, iii. 215
,, Births and rebirths of, ii. 383
,, Every man true to, iii. 425
,, Fourth group of, ii. 154
,, Fourth world, of, iii. 153
,, Incarnation, Divine dynasty of early Aryans, iv. 63
,, Lotus flowers and water and, ii. 100
,, Mikael conquers, v. 314
,, Pagans of, v. 317
Heart, contraction of, ii. 265
Heat, crocodile personified, i. 267
Kosmos, septenary chain of worlds in, i. 213
Lhas, iii. 113, 118, 119
Light, ii. 17; iv. 122
,, Cat's eye reflected, ii. 16, 17
,, Moon mirrors, iv. 122
Light and heat, sources of, ii. 315
Lion, iv. 135
Logos, one of three logoi, ii. 168
Man, iv. 212
Manvantara, i. 77
Matrix, v. 422
Myth, ii. 26; iii. 131, 335
,, Castor and Pollux not interpreted as, iii. 131
,, Hiram Abif of masons is, ii. 26, 27; v. 194
,, King Solomon is, ii. 26
,, Orthodox symbolism of, iii. 335
Mythos, propounders of, ii. 16
Orb, Constitution of, i. 338; iii. 37, 166
,, Creators like rays of, ii. 166

Planets, trans-solar systems and, i. 205
Plexus, v. 556
Pralaya, i. 79, 83, 87, 124; ii. 87
Priests, v. 218
Rays, iii. 41, 79
Resurrection, Adytum symbol of, iv. 27
Spectrum, v. 432
Sphinx, v. 226
Spirit, v. 216, 217
Spots, ii. 265
Substance is immaterial, ii. 222
Symbols, mystic sense of, i. 151
,, Venus, stores light in, iii. 37
System, v. 332, 424, 535, 536
,, Adepts thoroughly acquainted with, iv. 271
,, Anima Mndi of, iv. 241
,, Astronomy and age of, iii. 82
,, Attraction and repulsion in, ii. 221
,, Central sun and three secondary suns of, iii. 242
,, Chains of globes in, i. 218
,, Cosmic evolution refers only to, iii. 79
,, Crust of, v. 424
,, Dhyān Chohans and, ii. 322
,, Dhyān Chohans and worlds beyond, iv. 270
,, Differentiated matter in, iv. 168
,, Differentiation of elements of, i. 195
,, Earths and moons not of same order of matter beyond, ii. 221
,, Elements of planets differ in, i. 198
,, Events before reappearance of, ii. 85
,, Evolution of, ii. 316, 323
,, Failures pass into new, iii. 235
,, Fire septenary throughout, i. 151
,, Forces have origin in one life of, ii. 315
,, Formation of, v. 535
,, Great pyramid and, ii. 26
,, Great serpent that draws down, ii. 135
,, Intelligences besides men in, i. 190
,, Kosmos often means only, i. 248
,, Laplace on evolution of, ii. 316
,, Law of cosmic evolution and, i. 170
,, Laws ruling, fully developed, i. 198
,, Limits of, iv. 270
,, Matter in, ii. 321
,, Matter outside, ii. 325
,, Microcosm of the one macrocosm, iii. 318
,, Monad term applying to vastest, i. 86
,, Motion of bodies outside, ii. 397
,, Nebular hypothesis as to formation of, i. 205
,, Ocean, one, ii. 87
,, Origin of, iv. 301
,, Planets of, v. 438
,, Pralaya, falls into, ii. 255
,, Primeval matter homogeneous not far from limits of, ii. 313
,, Prithivī, iv. 187
,, Radiations round, v. 424
,, Rays of Primordial light concentrated upon, ii. 304
,, Rotational evolution of, ii. 225
,, Secret Doctrine in stanzas chiefly deals with, i. 130

SOLAR (*Contd.*)
System, Septenary chains of world planets in, ii. 380
,, Seven Planetary Angels, built by, v. 208, 438
,, Seven principles, consists of, i. 170
,, Sphere of, v. 424
,, pheres as invisible as if millions of miles beyond, ii. 329
,, Stanzas deal with, i. 206
,, Stanzas treat of cosmogony after Pralaya of, i. 79
,, Sūkshma form, in its, i. 192
,, Sun and stars in, 309-317
,, Sun is heart of, ii. 264
,, Sun universal life-giver of, ii. 318
,, Theories on revolution of, ii. 225, 226
,, Titans or, ii. 135
,, Unique phenomenon of our, ii. 221
,, Vaishvānara living magnetic fire that pervades, iii. 311
,, War before building of, ii. 137
,, Worlds of, i. 217
Systems, i. 79, 163, 330; iii. 156, 311; v. 529
,, Cosmic monads progenitors of, iii. 311
,, Germ of all, iv. 156
,, Initial existence in, i. 330
,, Matter homogeneous beyond, i. 163
,, Millards of, i. 79
,, Nebular theory and orgin of, ii. 319
Trinity, v. 217
Universe, Nebula forms, i. 86
,, Real substance of, ii. 331
,, Stanzas can be applied to evolution of, i. 85
Vortex, Kepler's, ii. 348
World, one existence in, i. 332
,, Sun, is heart of, ii. 264
Year, Number of, iv. 154; v. 101, 112, 129, 433
,, Period of, ii. 105, 107; iii. 154, 192
,, Purānas, of, iv. 192
,, 3102 epoch of, ii. 387
Years, ii. 382; iii. 390; iv. 190, 335
Zodiac, Egyptian, v. 332
,, Indian, ii. 384
SOLAR-FIRE devotee, crocodile personified, iv. 149
SOLAR-LUNAR Dynasty, Budha starts, iv. 23 Regions, iii. 65
SOLAR-SELENIC radiance of Fohat, i. 253
SOLARITES and weather mongers, ii. 16
SOLI-LUNAR cycle, v. 336
SOLIMĀN'S ring, iii. 397
SOLINUS Polyhistor on Hyperboreans, iv. 342
SOLITARY watcher, i. 256
SOLOMON, v. 142, 143, 176, 182
Moses not recognized by, iv. 111
Quoted, on, i. 123
Seal of, double triangle, i. 177; v. 120, 163
,, Interlaced triangle wrongly called seal of, iv. 163
Temple of, ii. 26, 107; iv. 29, 32, 113, 363; v. 89, 162, 186, 196, 237, 241, 272, 320
,, Boaz left pillar of, v. 29
,, Masonry and, iv. 363; v. 182
,, Porch of, Satan standeth in, iii. 236

Temple of, Pyramid and, i. 174
,, Triple Tau and, v. 162
SOLOMON BEN YEHUDAH IBN GEBIROL, see Book Index
SOLOMON ISLANDS, Australia and, iii. 21
SOLOMONS or Sulimāns, iii. 395
SOLON, v. 264
Atlantis, on, iv. 354
Egyptian dynasties enumerated by, i. 310
Initiates and, iii. 434
Legend of separation of sexes vouched for by, iii. 221
Names, knew power of, iv. 336
Priests of Sais, and, iii. 370; iv. 312
Priests' statements to, iii. 268, 394; iv. 354
SOLSTICE, sun at winter, iv. 147
SOLSTICES, ii. 363; iv. 103, 117
SOLSTITIAL points, ii. 388
SOLUS in relation to only God, iv. 146; v. 116
SOLVE, on smaragdine tablet, iii. 108
SOLVENT, Alchemical, of life, i. 302
Occult, soul of world, iii. 122
Universal, i. 304
SOMA, Adepts of right path, makes alliance with, iv. 63
Asuras headed by, iii. 383; iv. 69
Budha son of, iii. 147; iv. 23, 66, 67
Churning of ocean of life, produced by, ii. 113
Esoteric wisdom, parent of, iv. 69
Fish, Sin and, i. 283, 307
Fourth race under, iii. 42
Fruit or tree of knowledge, iv. 67
Gandharvas mystically Occult Force in, ii. 247
Hindus, with the, i. 275
Initiate, to make new man of, iv. 67
Jehovah connected with king, iv. 34
King, i. 275; ii. 102, 110; iv. 34, 66, 67
Lunar Gods, iii. 36
Manas, and solar portion of, iv. 54
Mārishā and, iii. 182, 183; iv. 63
Moon, i. 283, 307; ii. 113, 247; iii. 42, 56, 57, 147, 182, 183, 383; iv. 23, 34, 63, 64, 66, 67
Moon as king, ii. 102
Moon-plant or, i. 258
Mystery God, iii. 57
Occult nature in man and universe, presides over, iii. 57
Plant is Asclepias Acida, iv. 67
Plants, king of, iii. 383
Powers of, iv. 67
Prachētasas, and, iv. 64
Rishis milking earth whose calf was, ii. 113
Sacred beverage of Brāhmans and initiates, iv. 67
Sacred drink, v. 138, 280
Shukra bosom friend of, iii. 57
Sons of, iii. 56
Tārā carried off by, iv. 66, 67
Trimūrti, embodies triple power of, ii. 113
Tvashtri, poured on, iii. 109
Ushanas, finds allies in, iv. 66
Vegetable world, sovereign of, iv. 63
War in heaven between, and Gods, iii. 385
Wisdom, giver of, iv. 67
Worship of, ii. 108

SOMA-DRINKING of Indra is allegorical, iii. 377
SOMA-JUICE, Indra drunkard on, iii. 377
SOMĀKARA, v. 343
SOMAPA, Pitris, iv. 162
SOME Things the Āryans Knew, iii. 425
SOMME Valley, the, iv. 308, 309, 320
SON, Consubstantiality of the, v. 156
  Divine, v. 499, 501
  Evil, of, v. 289
  God, Every Adept is a, of, v. 276
  ,, of, Jesus the, v. 66, 155, 156, 168, 360, 369
  ,, the, of, v. 76, 253
  Light, of, v. 276
  Man, of, v. 99, 101, 103, 106, 129, 131, 190, 204, 291
  Mercury, of, v. 65
  Resurrection of, v. 360
  Second Emanation, the, v. 128
  Second Person, the, v. 210
  Seth, of, v. 106, 291
  Sun from the, v. 312
  Thunder, of, v. 144
  Widow, of the, Freemason, v. 273
  ,, ,, ,, Hiram, v. 272, 283
  ,, ,, ,, Ragon, v. 193
  Woman, of the, v. 131
SON-BROTHERS, of Fohat, i. 201
SON-SUNS, i. 162, 165
SONS, Ad, of, i. 255
  Adam, of, iv. 107
  Adepts will once more produce mind-born, iii. 277
  Aditi, of, v. 199
  Agni, of, iii. 150
  Atri, of, Barhishad pitris reborn as, iii. 98
  Bhūmi, of, ii. 330
  Brahmā of, i. 175, 282; ii. 70; iii. 56, 87, 91, 100, 124, 180, 373; iv. 150; iv. 111, 291, 320, 356
  Cycles, of, Cyclopes, i. 257
  Daksha, of, iii. 148, 277; v. 288
  Dark wisdom, of, iii. 250
  Darkness, of, Asuras, iii. 274; iv. 56
  Deity of, First mind-born, iii. 102
  Deva-lokas, of, ii. 330
  Devakī, of, iv. 176
  Devas of, First race were mind-born, ii. 330
  Dhyāna, or Yoga, of, iii. 124
  Dissociate and scatter, i. 148
  Divine, Fohat swift, of, i. 168
  ,, Immaculate mother, from, i. 155
  ,, Sophia, seven, of, ii. 148
  Dragon of, Hierophants called, iii. 378, 379; iv. 99
  Earth, of, v. 111
  Egg-born, iii. 198
  Elohim, of, v. 89, 201
  Evil, of, v. 289
  Expand and contract through own selves, i. 148
  Father, of, i. 139
  Fifth Adam, of, iv. 25
  Fire, of, i. 150
  ,, Seven emanations, or, ii. 56
  Fire-mist, of, i. 150; iii. 216; v. 270
  Flame and Fire, of, v. 445

Flame of wisdom, of, iii. 410; v. 260
Fohat, of, i. 168, 193, 200, 201, 253, 263; ii. 278, 398; v. 484
God, of, iv. 63; v. 26, 44, 73, 106, 152, 253, 258, 289
  ,, Angels in Bible spoken of as, iii. 71
  ,, Arts and sciences, taught man, iv. 142, 143
  ,, Beni-Elohim or, iii. 389; v. 299, 300
  ,, B'ne Aleim, or, ii. 158; iii. 232, 373
  ,, B'ne Alhim, or, iii. 36
  ,, Born of immaculate parents, i. 131; iv. 51
  ,, Builders, or, i. 257; v. 44
  ,, Creation of men by, iii. 40
  ,, Daughters of men and, ii. 247; iii. 232, 285, 373; iv. 69, 344; v. 106, 297
  ,, Devaputra Rishayah or, iv. 177
  ,, Dragons and serpents, names given to, iii. 276
  ,, Elohim, or, iii. 36, 224; v. 73, 82, 201
  ,, Forces of creation, or, ii. 157, 158
  ,, Four, Egyptians had only, iii. 217
  ,, Genesis in, v. 297
  ,, Hierophants instructed by, iii. 225
  ,, Humanity, teach, i. 256
  ,, Jesus one of, v. 289
  ,, King's chamber, and, iv. 38
  ,, Male Parent of, v. 202
  ,, Manas of, v. 471
  ,, Mind-born astral children of Brahma, iii. 286
  ,, Nephilim, fallen angels or, iii. 71
  ,, Physical frames have developed around, iii. 286
  , Pitaras or Pitris, iii. 150; v. 26
  ,, Pymander gives seven, iii. 217
  ,, Revelation accepted by occultists from, i. 76
  ,, Sacred island and, iii. 223
  ,, Satan one of, iii. 377, 389
  ,, Seventh race, iv. 51
  ,, Sons of shadow and, iv. 68
  ,, Virgins, born of immaculate, i. 131
  ,, Wisdom, and, iv. 231; v. 73
  ,, Wrath of, iv. 340
Gods, Enoch's angels are, ii. 247
  ,, of, iii. 100
Ham, of, Fourth race are, iii. 153
Heaven, of, Earth, and of, iv. 184
  ,, Mother (Earth) would call no, iii. 6
Hoang-ty, of, iv. 85
Husbands of their mothers, and, ii. 111
Images are told to create their own, i. 242
Intelligence, of, iv. 204
Jacob, of, ii. 377; v. 41
Krishāshva, of, iv. 201
Kriyashakti, of, i. 259
Kronos, of, Titans said to be, iii. 150
Life and light, of, i. 195, 196, 284
Light of, iv. 341
  ,, Absolute darkness, evolved from, ii. 204
  ,, Allegorical mystery and, v. 270
  ,, Army of, i. 177
  ,, Darkness, clothed in fabric of, i. 164

SONS (*Contd.*)
 Light, of, Dhyāni Buddhas, v. 370
  ,, Dhyāni Pitris are, v. 111
  ,, Genii are, i. 246
  ,, Jesus one of, v. 289
  ,, Joined by those who conquered lower principle, iii. 274
  ,, Logoi of Life, are, ii. 296
  ,, Noumena of all phenomena, or, ii. 203
  ,, Occultists believe in existence of, i. 166
  ,, Planets, called after, ii. 298
  ,, Seven, ii. 296, 298; v. 91, 350
  ,, Stars also called, ii. 296
  ,, Very root of spiritual man, i. 167
  ,, Wisdom and, iii. 274
  ,, Words of Divine Beings received by, i. 164
 Lord of Shining Face, of, iii. 40, 56
 Lower kingdoms, of, ii. 330
 Mahat, of, iii. 111
 Male Parent of, v. 202
 Manifested Ray, of, i. 167
 Manvantaric dawn, of, i. 124
 Manvantaric eternity, of, iv. 53
 Marīchi, of, Agnishvatta pitris reborn as, iii. 98
 Maruts, of heaven and earth, iv. 184
 Matter, v. 168
 Men, of, iii. 426
 Mind-born, i. 167, 259, 260; ii. 70, 330; iii. 56, 102, 209, 277; iv. 150; v. 78, 320
 Mother, of, i. 139, 162
 Nārada, Brahmā, of, iii. 91
 Night, of, iii. 168, 341
 Noah, of, iv. 20
 Passive Yoga, of, i. 225; iii. 173, 277
 Primeval creative Breath, of, iv. 69
 Primordial matter, of, i. 147
 Ptah of, v. 202, 310
 Rebellion, of, iii. 385
 Root matter, Elements with power and intelligence, i. 148
 Rudra, of, iv. 147
 Saturn, of, iii. 150
 Serpent-God, of, Hierophants styled, iii. 379; iv. 99
 Seven, i. 130, 195; ii. 148
  ,, Fathers, and forty-nine, iv. 134
  ,, Fighters, i. 161
 Shadow, of, iv. 68
 Shveta-dvipa, of, iii. 319
 Soma, of, iii. 56
 Sorcerers, of, iv. 160
 Sun, iii. 341
 Sun and moon, of, iii. 118
 Sydic, of, iii. 391; v. 202
 Third race, of, ii. 259
 Thor, of, iii. 108
 Three fires, of, iii. 67
 Twilight of, iii. 117, 129, 146
 Viraja, of, Mānasa are, iii. 98
 Will and Yoga, of, v. 262
  ,, Ancestors of Arhats, or, iii. 180
  ,, Androgynous third race progeny are, iii. 283
  ,, Answer of, to brethren of same race, iii. 277
  ,, Asura and Rakshasas and, iii. 230
  ,, Brahmaputras descended from, i. 258
  ,, Daksha and, iii. 170
  ,, Fathers of Wisdom, or, iii. 393
  ,, Nāgas are, iii. 188
  ,, Sacred Island, inhabited, iii. 224
  ,, Separation of sexes of, i. 258
  ,, Sons of fire-mist are, iii. 319
  ,, Sons of Wisdom had incarnated in, iii. 204
  ,, Third race, created, iii. 179, 180
  ,, Wrath, of, are, iv. 340
 Wisdom, of, Angels from higher spheres, or, iii. 238
  ,, Dhyān Chohans, or, iii. 269
  ,, Fall and, iii. 269
  ,, 'Four-mouthed Dragon', abode of, iii. 209
  ,, Incarnated in Adepts, iii. 421
  ,, Incarnated in more spiritual races of Lemurians, iii. 318
  ,, Incarnation of, iii. 288
  ,, Lhas, or, iii. 197
  ,, Mānasa, or, iii. 178
  ,, Mānasaputras, or, iv. 180; v. 204, 438
  ,, Mind-born, iii. 209
  ,, Mindless man, inform, iv. 180
  ,, Mother (Earth) would ask no, iii. 63
  ,, Rebirth, ready for, iii. 168
  ,, Seed of divine knowledge among, i. 259
  ,, Serpent of *Genesis* and, iii. 238
  ,, Sons of men led by, iii. 426
  ,, Sons of Will and Yoga incarnated in, iii. 204
  ,, Spark those who received, iii. 175
  ,, Teachers of Life, or, i. 314
  ,, Third race, spurned early, iii. 191
 Yoga, of, iii. 117, 124, 126, 168, 434; v. 262
  ,, First race were, iii. 117
  ,, Forms created by lunar fathers, called, iii. 124
  ,, Forms evolved by, iii. 168
  ,, Kriyashakti, born by power of, iii. 434
  ,, Passive, i. 255; iii. 173, 277
SOOTHSAYERS and astronomers, ii. 371
SOOTHSAYING by cyclic calculations, iv. 194
SOPATRUS, the philosopher, iv. 190
SOPHIA, Achamōth, daughter of, i. 247; ii. 167
 Achamōth, or, i. 190; v. 204
 Aditi is, iii. 54; v. 199, 215
 Aditi or divine, with Gnostics, ii. 152
 Ākāsha or, i. 247
 Chaos, lost in waters of, i. 190
 Divine wisdom, or, i. 247; v. 168
 Feminine with Gnostics, ii. 343, 344
 Holy Ghost and Creator of all, i. 139

SOPHIA (*Contd.*)
  Holy Ghost of early Christians, i. 247
  Holy Ghost with Gnostics, iv. 81
  Manas, is. iii. 277
  Mother of Ogdoad, i. 139
  Power of, resides in planet Venus, iv. 81
  Seven sons of, ii. 148; iii. 215; v. 199, 204
  Simon Magus and, v. 127, 128
  Spirit of Wisdom, iv. 110; v. 128, 168, 271
  Universal soul called, by Gnostics, ii. 67
  Virgin called, v. 168
  Wisdom, or, i. 139; ii. 67, 167; iii. 215, 385;
    v. 74, 215, 271
  Word, Living is, v. 199
SOPHIA-ACHAMŌTH, Barbelo and, iv. 140;
    v. 74
  Ildabaoth son of, i. 247; ii. 167; v. 204
  Sophia, daughter of, i. 247; ii. 167
  Spiritual principle of first human couple,
    iii. 219
SOPHOCLES, referred to, iv. 243
SORCERER(S), Amazarak taught, iii. 375
  Asuramaya, iii. 78, 80
  Atlantean, iii. 102, 228, 274; iv. 61, 208;
    v. 256, 299
  Atlantis, ii. 137; iii. 383
  Bhons, Dugpas or, iv. 157
  Christian, v. 252
  Conscious and Unconscious, v. 47, 48, 129
  Cyprian of Antioch, a, v. 171, 173
  Destruction of Atlantean, iii. 102
  Dvāpara Yuga, during, iii. 154
  Earth unprotected and, iv. 63
  Easter Island statues represent, iii. 228
  Egyptian, v. 251
  Enoch called, iv. 101
  Fourth race, bulk of, iii. 370
  Giants or, iii. 349
  Hoppo and Stadlein, ii. 190
  Initiates destroy, among Atlanteans, iv. 341
  Lords of dark face, iii. 425
  Magnetic Potency, and, v. 48, 49
  Moon is friend of, i. 211
  Races of previous, ii. 275
  Roman Catholic legends of, iii. 273, 274
  Rome, in, v. 256
  Satan at head of, iii. 388
  Serpent or, iii. 39
  Sons of, iv. 160
  Sons of God victorious over Atlantean,
    iii. 228
  Stones brought to Ireland by, iii. 343
  Struggle between Adepts and, iii. 383
  Thessaly, of, iv. 331
  Trees, called, iv. 65
  War between Initiates and, ii. 137
SORCERY, Antediluvian giants and, iv. 344
  Astrological knowledge and, iii. 186
  Atlantean, iv. 71; v. 91
  Black Magic or, v. 47, 85
  Book of, given to Charlemagne, v. 122
  Cain and Ham associated with, iii. 389;
    v. 62
  Christianity, followed, i. 62
  Danger of, i. 57; v. 85
  Deus Lunus for purpose of, ii. 112
  Devs, of, iii. 393

Divine Magic and, v. 132, 249
Divine Science of Third Race became,
  v. 106, 242
Egyptian, v. 245, 251, 252
Fable, now regarded as, ii. 190
Five-pointed star reversed, is sign of human,
  i. 73
Fourth Race and, v. 91
Giant Races of, iii. 287
Indian population, among, v. 405
Jesuits, of, ii. 23
Jews were acquainted with, i. 276
Lemurian and Atlantean, iii. 287
Modern, v. 47, 122
Nabathean Agriculture, in, iv. 21
-Names, v. 251
Occultists charged with, v. 97
Pherecydes and, v. 61, 62
Tibet and, v. 37
Tsong-Kha-Pa burnt books of, v. 404
SOSHIOS, Kalki Avatāra or, iii. 418; v. 337,
  400
White Horse, will descend on, i. 131
SŌTERS, v. 94, 153
SOTHIAC Cycles, ii. 153
SOUL Adam made a living, iii. 91, 96
  ,,   no living, till after Fall, iv. 23
  ,,   of dust requires a, ii. 292
  ,,   slumber of, iii. 187, 188
Æther, breath of Universal, i. 163
Ākāsha or Universal, iv. 81
Ākāsha or World, i. 119
Ālāya, Universal, i. 121; ii. 80
Amenti, in, ii. 80
Anatomy does not explain, i. 123
Ancient of Days and, i. 284
Anima Mundi or Spiritual, v. 144
  ,,   ,,   Universal, i. 121; ii. 182; iv. 131
  ,,   ,,   Universe, of, i. 119
Animal, Death of, v. 491, 492
  ,,   Nature, of, i. 171
  ,,   Not immortal, iii. 242
  ,,   Man, of, i. 208, 289, 292; iii. 244;
             iv. 168, 203, 205
  ,,   Manas, and, iv. 64; v. 471
  ,,   Severed Ray and, v. 499, 564
Animals, have only latent germ of, i. 246
Ank signified, iv. 171
Astral, i. 245
  ,,   Body, vehicle of, i. 280
  ,,   Light furnishes, i. 246
Astrology, of Astronomy, ii. 370; v. 151
Atma, informing Spirit of divine, ii. 291
  ,,   Spiritual, and, i. 230
  ,,   Within every man's, i. 190
Atma-Buddhi, dual, i. 230
Atmu or Eternal, iv. 203
Atom immanent in every, i. 123; ii. 292;
  iv. 241
Atom, of molecule, v. 537
Atom ready to receive transmigrating, i. 305
Ba or, of breath, iv. 203
Bai or intellectual, iv. 205
Beast has, every, iii. 201
Belief in, iii. 439
Bhūtāman living or life, iii. 117
Bird symbol, iii. 294

SOUL (Contd.)
  Blood of, iv. 204
  Body, and, i. 280
    ,, Builds, iv. 296
    ,, Informing, ii. 335
    ,, Matrix for development of, i. 273
    ,, Numbing weight on, i. 318
    ,, Relations to, iii. 299
  Book of The Dead and reward of, i. 282
  Boundless light, born in and from, ii. 300
  Brahmā is spirit, and body, i. 114
  Breath, of, iii. 203, 204
  Buddhi or divine, i. 82, 163, 178, 264, 332;
    ii. 193, 291; iii. 234, 318
  Buddhi or spiritual, i. 43, 209, 212, 287, 322;
    iv. 152, 168, 203, 204, 205; v. 438, 496
  Causal, v. 77, 83, 351
  Celestial spark, and, iv. 95
  Cheybi or spiritual, iv. 205
  Child, of a, v. 563
  Chit and, i. 330
  Chitragupta reads account of life every,
    i. 166
  Christos Ātmā in, i. 190
  Circle of necessity of, iii. 378
  Composition of, according to Epicurus, ii. 292
  Conscious ego or human, iii. 97
  Cosmic, ii. 254; iii. 122
  Cosmic consciousness or intelligent, of Dhyān
    Chohans, i. 322
  Cosmic space, of, ii. 313
  Crocodile, personified highest, with Egyptians,
    iv. 148, 149
  Crocodile whose, comes from men, iv. 206
  Death, after, iii. 363, 364; v. 289, 290
  Death of, v. 486-492, 496, 499, 500, 563
  Defunct, of, i. 192, 273
  Demiourgos is, iii. 38
  Depravity and, i. 280
  Descartes on, iii. 299
  Descent and reascent of, ii. 391
  Dhyān Chohan, of, i. 322
  Dhyāni-Buddhas one with Ālaya in, i. 119
  Differentiated world's, i. 196
  Disembodied, i. 267, 282
  Diti made to represent divine, in ascetic, iv. 185
  Divine, i. 82, 163, 178, 245, 264, 267, 322;
    ii. 193, 291, 362; iii. 84, 121, 182, 417, 422;
    iv. 185; v. 77, 208, 306, 362, 496, 564
  Divine voice of, ii. 149
  Doctrine, iii. 84
  Dragon Apophis and, ii. 179; v. 489, 491
  Dragon of wisdom or human, i. 266
  Dream produced by, ii. 356
  Dual, i. 230; v. 387, 489
  Dwellings has three, i. 289
  Earth and water to create human, ii. 59;
    iii. 55, 133
  Earth dwelling of animal, i. 289
  Eclipse, v. 495
  Egg of Immortality, gestating in, ii. 80
  Ego or, i. 272, 288; iii. 97, 120; iv. 224
  Egyptian rites, and, i. 192
  Egyptian theory of, iii. 146
  Electricity of flame, of things, i. 147
  Elemental atom, ii. 290, 291
  Elements, of, iv. 149

  Epicurus on, ii. 292
  Eternal, is, v. 221
  Ether corresponding to, i. 263
  Ether, of, i. 83
  Ether, of Universe, ii. 57
  Evolution of, iv. 220
  Existence of, ii. 370
  Existences, same through myriads of, iii. 422
  Eye mirror of, iii. 300
  Father-mother differentiated world's, i. 196
  Ferouer and, iv. 47, 48
  Fires, one of three, iii. 249
  Fohat animal, of nature, i. 171
  Fohat brings spirit, into union with, i. 178
  Formation of, i. 286
  Gautama spoken of as great, i. 169
  Genesis, of, i. 280
  Genii, not subject to, i. 334
  Gods, of, i. 267; iv. 148, 206
  Gold, thrice purified or conscious, iv. 89
  Great, ii. 138
  Great mother, second principle of, i. 332
  Hæckel and, iv. 238, 242, 243
  Heavenly Father, of, v. 431
  Higher, i. 278; v. 452
  Holiness of, v. 452
  Holy ones, alienated from, iii. 120
  Human, i. 84, 163, 209, 266, 299, 332; ii. 355;
    iii. 55, 71, 91, 97, 121, 133, 277, 417;
    iv. 95, 168; v. 208, 423, 472, 490, 496
  Human Monad applies only to dual, i. 230
    ,, Monad or, ii. 356
  Illusive conception of human, i. 84
  Immortal, v. 32
  Independent, i. 183
  Individual, v. 402
  Indriyātman spiritual or intellectual, iii. 117
  Inferior natures and divine, of man, iii. 84
  Insanity and, i. 280
  Intellect, making room for physical, i. 272
  Intellectual, iv. 204, 205
  Intellegent, v. 493
  Intra-cosmic, i. 70
  Intuitive omniscience, of spiritual divine, i. 322
  Jīva or, i. 190
  Judgment of the, v. 246, 247, 257
  Jupiter Fulgur, of lightning, ii. 188
  Kabalists made of, and body two lives, i. 280
  Kāma Rūpa or animal, iv. 168, 203
  Kāmic, v. 496
  Khem punishes disembodied, i. 267
  Kosmos, of, i. 221; ii. 202
  Kshetrajna or embodied, iii. 117; iv. 210, 211
  Kumāras having, of five elements, iv. 149
  Kwan-Yin divine voice of, ii. 149
  Leibnitz on, iv. 242
  Life, of, i. 292; v. 397, 407
  Light, clothed in, i. 288
  Light, or, i. 290; ii. 291
  Lightning, of, ii. 188
  Living, i. 243, 272, 284, 298; ii. 59; iii. 39,
    91, 96, 117, 158, 169; iv. 23
  Living fire necessary for formation of divine,
    ii. 246
  Logos falling as ray into, i. 173
  Logos perceived by universal, ii. 193
  Lost, Orpheus seeks his, v. 154

SOUL (*Contd.*)

Lower fifth principle or human, i. 84
Mahābhārata and tribulations of, iii. 64
Mahābuddhi or great, ii. 138
Mahat or mundane, iii. 377
,, Spirit of universal, ii. 138, 260
,, Universal, or, ii. 169
Mahat-tattva universal, ii. 165
Man not merely union of, and body, i. 278
Man, of, v. 298
Man or living, i. 284
Man, Spirit and, v. 208
Manas and its animal, iv. 64
,, Conscious, iv. 89
,, Human, or, i. 154, 163, 209, 266; iv. 168
,, Individual or, i. 292
,, Third is, i. 288
Mānasa Devas endowed man with consciousness of immortal, iv. 94
Materialism denies, ii. 202
Matter, vehicle for manifestation of, i. 120
Meru region of pure, iii. 402
Mind of demiurgic creator or universal, ii. 67
Mind, or, i. 156, 332; v. 500
Modern science believes not in, of things, i. 316
Molecule, of, Atom is, v. 537
Monad, Human, or, ii. 355
,, Latent in, iii. 158
,, Man, in, spirit and, i. 178
,, or, ii. 300, 391
Mother basis of universal, i. 163
Movers, Intelligences within Cosmic, ii. 254
Mummy donning head of crocodile, and, i. 267
Mundane, iii. 377
Mysterious nature of, in man, iv. 220
Naturalist and working of, iv. 219
Nephesh Chiah or living, i. 272
,, Living, or, i. 243
,, or animal, iv. 205
,, Vital, or, i. 272
Neshamah highest, iv. 24
Neshamah or, iii. 377
Newly created at birth impossible dogma, i. 167, 224, 234; iii. 304
Nothing motionless within universal, i. 70
Nous animating, i. 123
Nous or spiritual, iv. 144
Number, is, iv. 147
Objective rendered, iv. 81
Occultism, of materialistic science, ii. 358
Occultists on spirit and, iv. 241
Odin endows man with, iii. 106
One infinite spirit, of, i. 109
One life or universal, i. 121
Osiris and, i. 166; v. 246, 257
Over-, i. 82, 119
Panoramic visions, i. 309
Parabrahm, of whole, iii. 195
Parabrahm, spirit and, of nature, i. 74
Paralyzed and atrophied, becomes, i. 45
Paramātman or supreme, iv. 63
Perfectly purified, v. 381
Personal, v. 496, 500
Personifies in clothing, itself, i. 290

Physical body house of tabernacle of, i. 293
Physical cell, of, i. 265
Physiology and, iv. 203
Pilgrimage of, obligatory, i. 82
Pineal gland seat of, iii. 299
Plane of circle is universal, i. 69
Plane of surface of circle, or World, iv. 125
Planes, lives on three, i. 289
Planetary origin of, ii. 300
Planets and faculties of, iv. 176
Plato on, iii. 97; v. 387
Pneuma human, iii. 121
Powers of, iv. 81
Pralaya, slumbering during, i. 69
Primeval, v. 391
Primordial substance is, ii. 318
Prometheus divine, iii. 417
Psuche or, iii. 375
Psyche, or, i. 141, 245
Psycho-animal, v. 499
Pubescence, of, iv. 204
Purified, v. 489
Ra is divine universal, i. 277
Ray furnished with future vehicle divine, i. 264
Reasoning or Manas, i. 287
Recollection of past incarnations in divine, iii. 422
Reincarnations of, iv. 122
Rejuvenates every 14,000 years, i. 291
Reward of, i. 282
Rind of image is garment of, i. 288
Root-nature of one infinite spirit, i. 109
Ruach or spiritual, i. 287, 288; iv. 205
Ruach united to living, i. 243
Sadducees, and, iii. 71
Samael and Michael emanate from mundane, iii. 377
Same and other, or, iii. 97
Same individual, through various incarnations, iv. 241
Sarvātman super-, i. 153
Satan, Lucifer, is, iv. 120
Satan, transformation of universal, into, iv. 80
Scarabaeus symbol of reincarnation of, iv. 122; v. 246
Seat of, iii. 299
Seb or ancestral, iv. 203
Self or, i. 273
Self-consciousness, and, iii. 69
Separation of sexes and incoming of, i. 292
Septenary symbol for man plus immortal, iv. 163
Septenary universal, iv. 131, 132
Serpent of evil endowed with living, iii. 39
Shade or covering, iv. 204
Shankarāchārya on, ii. 293
Silent depths of unknown universal, iv. 145
Sixth principle in man or divine, i. 178; ii. 193
Sixth principle of intellectual kosmos, or universal, ii. 138
Sleeping man, of, i. 222
Soma and solar portion of, iv. 64
Son refers to, iii. 234
Sophia is manas, or, iii. 277
Souls, of all, ii. 157
Spirit and, i. 263, 273

SOUL (*Contd.*)

Spirit, Body, and, i. 181, 272; iv. 174
,,   Intellect, and, i. 265
,,   Matter in man, and, i. 120
,,   Mind, and, iii. 121
,,   Union with, brought into, i. 178
,,   United too loosely to, ii. 179
,,   Vehicle for manifestation of, i. 120
Spiritual, i. 43, 208, 212, 230, 287, 288;
       iii. 117; iv. 144, 152, 168, 203,
       204; v. 438
,,   Ālaya or, v. 471
,,   Divine or, v. 496
,,   Ego or, i. 280; v. 500
,,   Plasm, of physical cell, i. 265
,,   Severed, v. 501
,,   Sun of, iv. 210
,,   Universe of, Central Sun is, ii. 53
,,   Wisdom or, iii. 277
Struggle between spirit and, iii. 375
Substance, of, ii. 244
Sūkshma Sharīra and, i. 190
Sun and stars, of, ii. 326
,,   Evolves, of planets and comets, ii. 318
,,   Gods, of, iv. 148
Suns, moons and planets, vital, of, ii. 326
Super-, 153
Supreme, ii. 92, 170; iv. 63; v. 298, 390
Survival of, v. 281
Sūtrātmā or thread, i. 82
Svabhāvat body of, i. 130
Symbols of spirit, and body, i. 172
Ten is mother of, i. 154; v. 115
Thought evolved by, i. 156
Thread, i. 82
Thy, and my, i. 179
Tiaou, emerges from, i. 274
Transformation, v. 301
Universal, i. 69, 70, 76, 121, 163; ii. 67, 138,
   165, 169, 182, 193; iii. 69, 234; iv. 80, 81,
   131; v. 391, 452, 471, 483, 493, 494, 497,
   499
Universal Sixth principle or over, i. 182
Universe evolved out of unknown depths of
   spiritual, iv. 144
Universe, of, i. 119; ii. 57; iv. 241; v. 558
Unknown universal iv. 145
Unseen worlds dwelling in, i. 280
Upādhi of spirit, i. 208
Upanishads on, i. 314
Upper Triad or, i. 289
Vishnu as universal substance or, ii. 172
Vital, i. 272; ii. 326
Water and moon symbols of divine, iii. 121
Water production of supreme, iv. 63
Water required to make living, i. 298
Whirling of, ii. 292
Wind or air symbol of human, iii. 121
Wisdom guiding, after death, iii. 363, 364
World, i. 76; iv. 125; v. 558
World, of, v. 558
,,   Ākāsha is, i. 78, 196
,,   Ālaya is, i. 119
,,   Anima Mundi, or, i. 119
,,   Brahmā evolves from, ii. 95
,,   Brahman or, ii. 182
,,   Chaos became, ii. 58

World, of, Circle and, i. 172
,,   Divine astral light, i. 196
,,   Great deep, or, ii. 68
,,   Jīvātmā, i. 196
,,   Knooph, ii. 194
,,   Logoi correlative with female, ii. 68
,,   Mahā-Ātmā or, ii. 182; v. 423
,,   Primordial substance or, ii. 52
,,   SELF and, v. 428
,,   Serpent of, iii. 214
,,   Spirit of life or, ii. 182
,,   Substance or, ii. 306
,,   Symbol of, ii. 194
,,   Union of three elements is occult
      solvent in, iii. 122
Zeus as human, iii. 417
Zodiacal signs and, 391
Zohar on, iii. 120
SOUL-ATOM, ii. 292
SOUL-BIRD divine swallow, i. 274
SOUL-DOCTRINE, i. 35; iii. 84
SOUL-ECLIPSE, v. 495
SOUL-LESS, Animal, iv. 175
Man, iii. 243
Men, many are, i. 280; v. 486, 489, 492, 496,
   498, 499, 500, 501
Pre-physical races, astral form of the, iv. 287
Primeval man was, iii. 195
SOUL-LIFE, iv. 240; v. 397
SOUL-LIKE MAN, iv. 212
SOUL-ORGANS, Morphology of, iv. 240
SOUL-PERCEPTION, i. 323
SOUL-PRINCIPLE of universe, iii. 54
SOUL-SPARK, Prometheus endows man with,
   iv. 88
SOUL-SPIRIT, v. 281
SOUL-SUBSTANCE, body vehicle of, i. 205
SOUL-VOICE and tradition, iii. 422
SOULS, Angels, and, iii. 294
Animal, v. 565
Archis are pure, i. 190
Astral light which, must conquer, i. 299
Astral rulers of spheres create, ii. 301
Atomic, ii. 344
Atoms, being, ii. 292
,,   of, ii. 344
,,   Shape of, in, ii. 291
Auphanim informing, of spheres and stars,
   i. 176
Buddhis or formless divine, i. 179
Compound, ii. 291
Cosmic Gods informing, of four elements,
   ii. 181
Development of, iii. 366
Divine, i. 179
Egos, of men who had no personal, iv. 181
Egregores chiefs of, i. 303
Elements, of, i. 326
Eternal, that which is part of, is, iii. 422
Four elements symbols of informing, ii. 181
Gilgulim or whirling, ii. 291, 292
Heavenly Bodies, of, v. 324, 333
Initiate ministered to, of men, iv. 128
Intelligent existence of compound, ii. 291
Kingdom of, i. 244
Manifestations of self as individual, iv. 64
Mathematical points or real, ii. 354

SOULS (*Contd.*)

Mercury conducted, of dead to Hades, iii. 363; iv. 112

,, Leader and evocator of, iii. 41

,, Raising, in Hades to life, iii. 363

Molecular, of Protista, iv. 220

Monads are, of atoms, ii. 344

Monads, or, ii. 301; iii. 120

Moon-God, of, i. 274

Mortal leaves one of his on each zone of post-mortem ascent, ii. 127

Nirvāna, rest in, i. 291

Occultists believe in, ii. 222

Planetary spirits, of heavenly orbs, iv. 122

Plastidular, iv. 220, 240, 242

Powers of God, of, iii. 54

Powers, of manifested, iii. 384

Principles, or, ii. 127; iv. 139

Revolution of, ii. 292

Scintillas, are, ii. 344

Self's manifestations as individual, iv. 138

Septenary of, i. 274

Seven, of Egyptologists, iv. 201 *et seq.*

Seven, of man, i. 273

Seven Spheres, v. 73

Sidereal, v. 313

Space full of, v. 382, 388, 387, 404

Spheres and stars, of, i. 176

Spirits or, of Planets, v. 319

Sravah or, iii. 384

Stars, of, v. 324-328

Supreme judges of, iv. 48

Triads and twin, ii. 298

Universal over-soul and identity of all, i. 82

Whirling, ii. 290

Worlds of emanations pre-existent in, iii. 120

SOUND, Absolute life and, ii. 263; v. 455

Æther and, ii. 260

Air medium of motion of, ii. 257

Ākāsha, Attribute of, v. 475, 522

,, Characteristic of, i. 253

,, Material cause of, is, i. 336

,, Mother-Father of, iii. 399

,, One quality of, ii. 261

Ākāshic, v. 505, 522, 523

Ancients, to, iii. 115

Army of voice and mystery of, i. 156

Atoms called, ii. 358

Audible and colour, v. 484

Bhagavad Gītā on, ii. 259

Bhūtādi devours, ii. 88

Cause of, ii. 239

Colour and, roots of, v. 418, 421, 443, 456, 457, 459, 460, 484, 485

Colour, Number and, v. 420, 421, 443

Colours, Forms and, v. 455-459

Correlation of Ākāsha, v. 475

Creation in Kabalah, factor of, ii. 150

Dhyān Chohanic Hierarchy and, v. 453

Elements, closely related to four, ii. 19

Eternal, v. 114, 523

Ether and, i. 300, 336; ii. 88, 258, 311; iii. 115

Father of the, each prismatic colour called, v. 442

Feminine logoi correlations of, ii. 150

Fire light and, iv. 205

Fohat and, 195; ii. 278

Fohatic forces at north and south poles and, i. 253

Force, and, v. 431, 505

Gandharvas noumenal causes of, ii. 247

Genesis of, ii. 164

Harmony, or, ii. 151

Inaudible and colour, v. 484

Keely and, ii. 279, 287

Kwan-yin-tien or melodious heaven of, i. 194

Logoi, Colour, form and, v. 455

Logos or, i. 300; ii. 261, 263; iii. 399; v. 442

Loka of, v. 539

Magic agent, most potent, ii. 185

Manifested Logos and, v. 453

Materialists, has no objective being for, i. 335

Melodious heaven of, i. 194

Mystery Word is a, v. 502

Nature and Æther, in, i. 194; v. 443

Nervous ether conductor of vibrations of, ii. 261

Number guides, v. 419, 453

Numbers, and, v. 418, 421, 443, 456

Occult, i. 194

Occult powers of, ii. 279

Ozone, will produce, ii. 279

Parā form of Vāch latent light and, ii. 150

Physical science on, ii. 278

Pleiades connected with, ii. 374

Potency of, v. 418-421

Prismatic colour, father of the, v. 442

Properties of, ii. 246

Purānas on, ii. 311; iv. 133

Qualities of, ii. 258

Repercussion, ii. 249

Resurrect man, may, ii. 279

Sacred formula and, v. 418-420, 454, 459, 506

Scale of causes and, v. 443

Science and, v. 484

Second Logos or, iv. 133

Septenary nature of, ii. 261

Seven in world of, iv. 199; v. 428

Seven notes of scale or principles of, ii. 258; v. 420, 454, 509

Seven planes on, v. 522

Seven radicals, and, i. 201

Seventh sense is spiritual, v. 508

Shabda is, v. 539

Silence nor, there was neither, i. 124

Son of Deity, iii. 115

Son or, ii. 261

Space, one quality of, ii. 258

Substance, real, ii. 288

Svara, Ākāsha and, v. 479

Upanishads, in, iv. 133

Vāch and Kwan-yin are magic potency of occult, i. 194

Vāch or, ii. 150; v. 189, 394

Verbum or, i. 300; v. 234

Verbum vibrates through Shekinah, of, ii. 354

Vibrations of, v. 457, 508

Waves of equal length, iv. 57

Word of God or, iii. 115

Word or, i. 300; ii. 88; v. 402, 442, 502

World called out of chaos by, ii. 151

SOUND-LANGUAGE of second race, iii. 203

SOUNDING-BOARD of kosmos, i. 220
　Nature, of, v. 522, 523
SOUNDS, Colours and the Formless, v. 453
　Colours, Numbers and, v. 421, 456
　Colours with Hiearchies, v. 453
　Communication through, and colours,
　　ii. 239
　Language composed of, not words, ii. 185
　Mantras and, v. 394
　Pythagorean, ii. 168
　Sanskrit, and Mantras, v. 394
　Seven, iv. 184; v. 420
　Seven in perception of, iv. 193; v. 508, 547
　Spiritual, are, v. 523
　Tattvas and, v. 477, 478
　Vāch and, v. 394
SOURCE of all that breathes, Divine Powers
　　are, v. 462
　of Measures, cubit and inch, v. 69, 111
SOUTH AFRICA, Bushman of, iv. 91
　Lemuria and, iii. 332, 333
SOUTH AMERICA, Bird-eating spider in,
　　iii. 438
　Esoteric schools in, i. 46
　Iguana lizard of, iii. 161
　Lemuria and, iii. 332, 333
　Mountains, carving on, ii. 34
　Mysteries of Central and, v. 283
SOUTH ASIA, Haeckel on, iii. 199
SOUTH PACIFIC and Atlantis, iii. 404
SOUTH POLE, Abode of demons, iii. 402
　Cancer represented at, iii. 429
　Cosmic Elementals of, iii. 276
　Pit, or, iii. 276
SOUTH-SEA Islanders, iii. 175, 419
SOUTH-WEST Greenland and Lemuria,
　　iii. 400
SOUTHALL, Dr., quoted, iv. 309
SOUTHERN Buddhists, v. 363, 406
SOUTHERN INDIA, Brāhmans of, iii. 77
　Catechism of, iii. 43
　Egyptian zodiac brought from, iii. 433
　Fragments of old work in, iii. 62
　Initiates in, iii. 181; v. 395
　Smārta Brāhmans in, i. 315
SOUTHERN POLE, Atala at, iii. 403
SOYUTI, Arabic writer, iii. 361
SOZOMEN, Historian, v. 161
SOZURA of Haeckel, mythical, iv. 222, 226,
　　239, 314
SPACE(S), Ab Soo, of Chaldees, iv. 70
　Absolute, abstract symbol of, i. 79, 115
　Absolute All, i. 75
　Abstraction to Scientist, v. 381
　Aditi or infinite, i. 72, 161; v. 192, 379, 381,
　　386, 478
　Æther of, ii. 260
　Air, etheric medium in, ii. 311
　Ākāsha or, 258, 261; iv. 81; v. 379, 381,
　　475
　All things developed in, iii. 366
　Anupādaka, eternal, i. 77
　Ashtadisha or eight faces bounding, iv. 148
　Astral prototypes in, iv. 230
　Atom takes flight into, i. 199
　Atoms, eternally filled with, i. 70; ii. 358
　Atoms in world of, ii. 353

Ball of fire-mist in interstellar, iii. 161
Battles fought for, i. 248
Be-ness, absolute abstract aspect of, i. 79
Bell-sounds in, ii. 280
Bodies dead and dissolved, ii. 325
Brahmā-Vishnu being infinite, i. 75
Breath, filled with invisible, iv. 82
Breath of Father-mother cools in eternal bosom
　of inner, i. 200
Bright, son of dark, i. 138
Caloric flowing from sun through, ii. 248
Cause of all, is eternal, i. 109
Centre, circumference, and, ii. 341
Chaos is, i. 169; ii. 50, 52; iii. 94, 271;
　v. 234
　,,　Primordial waters of, or, ii. 149, 179;
　　v. 235
　,,　Theos: Kosmos are containment of,
　　ii. 56
Christ, God in, iv. 52
Churning of Ocean of, ii. 95
Circle symbol of unknown boundless, i. 173
Circles of time in, i. 362
Collective mind finite, when contrasted with,
　iv. 55
Conditioned or limited, has no real existence,
　ii. 329
Container and body of universe, ii. 56;
　v. 234
Cosmic, i. 73; v. 382, 420, 429
Couch of Vishnu symbol of infinite time in,
　i. 140
Creations born in, iv. 119
Creator Hari sleeps on ocean of, ii. 87
Curds and, i. 137, 160, 294
Darkness reigned throughout, ii. 145
Deep or primeval, iv. 45
Deity abstract presence of, v. 227
　,,　Manifesting in, and time, iii. 166
　,,　Pervades, that, ii. 52
　,,　Unseen and unknown, is ever, ii. 50
Differentiation in, and time, iv. 297
Dimensional, Two, three and four, i. 295;
　iv. 171
Divine, v. 475
Divine Plenum, of, i. 204
Division into Heaven and earth, v. 198
Double Triangle and six directions, in, i. 177
Ea wisdom, birthplace of, iii. 64
Earth floats on universal ocean of that, iv. 188
　,,　Foetus in matrix of, i. 304; iii. 109
　,,　Rose out of waters of, iii. 109
Earth, unknown to, iii. 167
Eastern occultist on, ii. 340, 341
Energies in, reawakened, i. 152
Energy of sun existing unknown condition
　in, ii. 146
Entity, first, ii. 258
Eternal and limitless, v. 476
Eternity, and, in Pralaya, i. 69; v. 189
Ether occupying all, ii. 88
Ether of, ii. 257, 311; iii. 115; v. 423, 442,
　475, 484
Ethereal waves of, ii. 213
Everything on earth shadow of something in,
　ii. 219
Everything generated in abstract, i. 84

SPACE(S) (*Contd.*)
Factor, as third, ii. 273
Father-Mother, is called at first stage of re-awakening, i. 83
Fiery waters of, iii. 399
Fire which formed curds in, i. 294
Flame, is, ii. 88
Fohat divides, ii. 398
Fohat places wheels in six directions of, i. 175
Force existing in open, ii. 236
Force, Matter, spirit and, i. 76; ii. 340; v. 382
Forces discovered in, v. 215, 382
Forces, ten, spread in, v. 423
Four dimensions of, i. 295
Gods and atoms swept out of, at Mahāpralaya, i. 206
Gods, Rishis and Manus potencies of, i. 75
Good and evil progeny of, iii. 104
Great breath digs through, i. 203
Great deep or, ii. 398; iv. 45
Great sea or seven-headed serpent of, ii. 56
Great waters of, ii. 145
Hamsa bird of wisdom in, iii. 294
Heavenly matrix or female, iii. 94
Holy one created and destroyed worlds in, iii. 64
Ideal nature or abstract, iii. 54
Immeasurable, is, i. 295
Impossibility of there being, ii. 396
Incognizable deity, garb of, i. 173
Infinite and eternal, iii. 162; v. 235, 387
Intelligent rulers, dwelling in, iv. 70
Inter-stellar, v. 381
Invisible, v. 484
Invisible beings in, ii. 395, 396
Invisible worlds in, ii. 330
Kabalist, defined by learned, ii. 56
Kalpas divided in, and time, iii. 186
Khoom or water of, ii. 80
Knowledge, realm of divine, called, iv. 70
Kosmos emerging from boundless, i. 113
Kosmos in, ii. 107
Kronos stands for duration beyond, ii. 136
Leucippus on, i. 70
Life and behaviour of monads, ii. 344
,, Containing, iv. 168
,, Pulsated unconscious in universal, i. 118
Limitless void and conditioned fulness, is both, i. 75
Manvantaras, between, v. 180, 189
Maqom or, iv. 183
Mārtānda and mother, i. 164
Materialists consider, void, ii. 311
Matrix of, v. 291
Matter and, i. 110; ii. 326
Matter in heavenly, ii. 326
Monad re-emerging from matrix of, iii. 58
Moon being ark on watery abyss of, iii. 150
Mother, i. 161, 164; v. 202, 235
,, Before cosmic activity called, i. 83
,, Called waters of, i. 131
,, Dry waters of, ii. 350
,, or, i. 135
Mūlaprakriti one with, in its abstract senses, i. 109
Mundane egg or infinite, ii. 69
Mundane egg placed in water of, ii. 80

Mystic, v. 386
Nārāyana moves on primordial ocean of, ii. 177
Nārāyana moving on waters of, i. 74
Nature and, are one, ii. 279
No beneath or above in, ii. 227
No-number has application in, i. 152
No void, in universe, i. 330
Noot or, i. 275; ii. 68
Nucleus of cosmic matter born in unfathomable depths, i. 252
Occult catechism, defined in, i. 77
Occult Philosophy, of, v. 462
Occultists and soul and spirit of, ii. 313
Ocean or, iii. 76; iv. 327
Oeaohoo turns upper, into shoreless sea of fire, i. 138
One-dimensional, i. 295
One eternal element, i. 125; v. 382
One eternal thing, is, i. 109; v. 381
One incognizable deity, form of, iii. 381
Parabrahman is infinite cosmic, i. 73
Parent or, i. 109
Parentless, i. 77
Period of cyclic evolution in time and, iv. 300
Physicist on, ii. 340
Pilgirm having connected himself with every atom in, i. 311
Pralaya, during, i. 114
Primeval, iv. 45
Primordial matter eternal and co-eval with, i. 147
,, Matter in, ii. 314
,, Ocean of, ii. 177
,, Substance diffused through, ii. 318
,, Waters of, ii. 149, 179
Pure, ii. 219
Radiant essence spreads throughout depths of, i. 135
Ray differentiates water of, i. 277
Ray penetrating infinite, ii. 69
Rays awaken life in waters of, ii. 145
Root of all, v. 382
Self-Existent beyond, and time, iii. 245
Senzar catechism on, i. 75
Sephir is mystic, v. 386
Sephirothic aspects of Ain Soph in, and time, ii. 65
Septenary nature of, ii. 56
Serpent in, i. 141
Serepnt of, seven-headed, ii. 56
Seven layers of, i. 75
Seven Powers of, v. 172, 200, 303
Seven-skinned eternal Mother-father, called, i. 75
Sidereal, ii. 249
Six directions of, i. 175, 177
Sixth and seventh principles of, iv. 81
Souls, is full of, v. 382, 388, 397, 404
Sound connected with ether of, iii. 115
Sound one quality of, ii. 261
Spaces of, ii. 345
Sparks from flint or, iii. 107
Spirit first differentiation of, i. 302
,, God, of, lived in sea of, iv. 45
,, God, of moves on dark waters of, iv. 163
,, Sun, of, and moon, concealed, i. 275

SPACE(S) (*Contd.*)
Spirit, Ultimate substratum of, ii. 305
Spiritual entities in infinitudes of, i. 279
Storehouse of Creation, v. 234
Substance or boundless, iii. 242; v. 422
Substance principle in, i. 317
Sun evolved from cosmic, i. 163
Sun-force, supposed to be filled only with, ii. 249
THAT, form of, iii. 166
Tho-og or Tibetan, v. 379, 381
Three eternal things, one of, v. 381
Time and, are one, iv. 183; v. 428
Time in, i. 140
Tohu Bohu or primeval, iv. 45
Trans-solar, ii. 221
Unborn and undecaying, iv. 55
Undifferentiated, v. 447
Universal matrix or waters of, i. 131
Universe and, v. 91, 107, 381
Universe held in solution in, during Pralaya, i. 114
Universe in sense of limitless ever present, i. 70
Universes in, iii. 38; v. 107
Unknown first cause, i. 76; ii. 56
Unmanifested deity or, iii. 271
Unrevealed, one, i. 76
Uranus personification of creative powers in, iii. 271.
Vacuum, not, ii. 251
Vishnu deity in, and time, ii. 139
,,   One with time and, iv. 183
,,   Represents eternal and limitless, v. 476
,,   Rests in waters of, ii. 95
Vishnu's navel central point in waters of infinite, iv. 40
Void of, ii. 360
Waters deluge or, containing life, iv. 168
,,   great deep of infinite, ii. 50
,,   of, i. 74, 131, 277; ii. 80, 95, 350; iii. 75, 109; iv. 40, 163, 327; v. 192, 199, 230, 233, 235, 238, 447, 448
Watery abyss of, iii. 150
,,   ,,   or, iii. 64
World-germs scattered in, i. 251
SPAGYRIZATION of matter, iv. 164
SPAIN, Africa extension of present, iv. 309
Atlantis joined to, iv. 361
Barbary joined to, iv. 320
Dolmen near Malaga in, iv. 321
Gades which included, iii. 405
Kings of, v. 264
Mandrake in, iii. 40
North Africa peninsula of, iii. 21
SPANIARDS, in America, v. 43, 283
Pueblos refused, admission to Artufas, iii. 188
White savage chiefs, met in Cibola, iv. 313
SPANISH Escurial, v. 122
SPARK, Agni carrier of divine, iv. 90
Ain Soph, from head of, ii. 71
Assimilation of soul to celestial, iv. 95
Astral rulers of spheres endowing monads with, ii. 301
Barhishad pitris could not give to man sacred, iii. 103
Beings, of higher, iii. 179
Consciousness, of, i. 258

Destitute of knowledge, those who received, but, iii. 168
Divine, v. 450, 475
Divine Egos and, v. 452
Divine Fire and, v. 452
Divine man, enters into and informs, i. 291
Emanating, from uncreated ray, ii. 294
Fifth principle quickened by, iii. 111
Fire by friction relates to creative, iii. 250
Flame and, i. 282, 283, 309
Flames projected by, iii. 318
Homogeneous, from primeval seven, ii. 294
Human animal, that vivifies, iii. 111
Jīva of, i. 284
Kingdoms, animates all, i. 291
Lords of wisdom into man, of consciousness, i. 258
Lords projected, iii. 168
Manas and, or, i. 284
Metempsychosis of psychic, ii. 292
Mineral, lying latent in, i. 332
Monad or, i. 283
Monads endowed with, ii. 301
Narrow-headed men without, iii. 190
Nephesh or vital, i. 287
Psychic, ii. 292
Sacred fire from, of higher beings, iii. 179
Second race endowed with weak, iii. 172
Seven worlds of Māyā, and, i. 283
Sons of mahat are, iii. 111
Sons of wisdom projected only, iii. 288
Third race, endowed with, iii. 179
Those which had no, iii. 190
Those who extinguished, iii. 318
Vital, i. 287
Wisdom, of divine, iii. 283
SPARKS, Atoms, or, i. 165, 168
Centres of force at first, i. 165
Divine man emanated, from, i. 153
Division of, iii. 322
Elohim, and cherubs, iii. 95
Eternity, of, i. 82
Fires and flames, iii. 92
Fires with, iii. 74
Flames or, ii. 160
Fohat calls, and joins them together, i. 168
Hammer, worlds like, under smith's, iv. 274
Holy four, within, ii. 160
Invisible, i. 165
Lower kingdom, of, i. 175
Lunar ancestors or divine, i. 232
Manifesting stars and, of eternity, i. 82
Mineral atoms or, of lower kingdom, i. 175
Molecules, differentiate into, i. 165
Monads or divine, i. 232
Moon, beams and, of one, i. 282
One unity, first manifested, of, iii. 321
Personalities of monad-ego compared to, i. 283
Scintillae or, i. 161
Seven, of, i. 156
Spheres, triangles, cubes, lines and modellers, called, i. 156
Suns, become, i. 165
Universal divine flame, reflecting, i. 318
Wicks are, i. 282

SPARKS (*Contd.*)
Worlds compared to, in Kabalah, i. 248; iii. 92, 107
Worlds, or, i. 161
Worlds, primordial, are, i. 291; iii. 292·
SPARSHA, cohesion, touch, ii. 88; v. 539, 540, 559
SPARTA, Castor's tomb in, iii. 131
SPAWN, Fish of life, of, i. 160
Mother's, i. 248
SPEAKING, Beasts or magic watchers, iii. 425
Race called Adi, iv. 19
Stones, iii. 340, 341, 345
SPEAR-HOLDER or Shakti-dhara, iii. 381; iv. 190
SPECKLED corn of Zuni priestess-mother, iv. 200
SPECTRA of constellations, ii. 322
SPECTRES or phantoms, iii. 281
SPECTROSCOPE, Colour, and world of, iv. 198
Irresolvable nebulae, and, ii. 322
Magic power of, ii. 320
Revelations of, ii. 321, 322
Terrestrial and sidereal substance as shown by, i. 198, 199
SPECTROSCOPIC peculiarities of elements, iv. 199
SPECTRUM, Analysis, ii. 319, 320; v. 453, 458
Eye of Shiva, modern, ii. 267
Line, of three or four bright, ii. 320, 323
Nebula, of, ii. 322, 323
Observations, ii. 270, 271
Rays of, iv. 207
Rays of Hierarchies and, v. 459
Reactions, ii. 271
Sun, of, i. 199; v. 432, 459
SPEECH, Agglutinative, iii. 204
Ancients on, iii. 115
Animal sounds, arose from, iv. 231
Anugītā on, i. 157, 158
Apāna and, i. 157
Army of voice and, i. 156
Articulate, Vāch is, v. 189
Atlanteans, of most civilized, iii. 204
Brain necessary for, iv. 231
Creation, Light and, v. 230
Ether of space, associated with, iii. 115
Existence of ready-made materials of, iv. 232
Fourth race developed, iii. 203
Fourth round, acquired in, i. 240
Gods, of the, Devanāgarī, Sanskrit, v. 197
Idā personified as goddess of, iii. 155
Inflexional, iii. 205
Kabalistic and other characters, and, v. 115
Kwan-Yin or, i. 194
Logos and, iii. 38, 204
Lords, of men of earth cannot reach, ii. 185
Magnetic potency of human, i. 157
Mantras and, v. 189, 394
Mantrikā-shakti, power of, is, i. 333
Mercury and power of, iv. 112
Mind and, i. 157
Monosyllabic, iii. 204
Mystery of sound and, i. 156
Mystic, ii. 148; v. 394
Occult properties of, i. 157
Origin of, i. 157

VI–27

Power of, ii. 148
Prāna and, i. 158
Sacerdotal, v. 115
Samāna and, i. 158
Sarasvatī goddess of, i. 158
Secret Doctrine, v. 115
Seminal principle or creative, iv. 112
Third root-race, of, iii. 204
Thought, as expression of, i. 194
Udāna and, i. 158
Unknown darkness, not to be addressed in, ii. 143
Upanishads and *Purānas*, in, iv. 133
Vāch Goddess of, i. 194; ii. 152; v. 189
Vāch or mystic, ii. 148; v. 394
Vaikharī Vāch is, ii. 150
Verbum or creative, iv. 112; v. 189
Word or, i. 194; v. 230
SPEECHLESS, Animal first began sexual connection, iii. 264
Apes are, men, iii. 262
Fires race was, iii. 203
Savage of Haeckel, 247
SPENCER, Herbert, See Book Index
SPENTA ĀRMAITI, Spirit of earth, iii. 384; iv. 86, 181
SPENTAS, Amesha, iii. 357, 383; iv. 86, 179
SPERM or terrestrial seed, i. 326
SPERMATOZOON, i. 269
SPEUSIPPUS followed Plato, iv. 125; v. 383
SPHERE, Action of, iv. 192
Activity, terrestrial, of, ii. 344
Ain Soph, ii. 147
Aquarius in, of Reuben, ii. 377
Atom, ii. 205
Aura, egg-shaped, of, iii. 126
Being of one step higher than terrestrial, iii. 74
Chinese astronomical, ii. 384
Dodecagonal pyramid converted into, iv. 148
Dominion of outermost, iii. 236
Dry land on right end of, iii. 399
Each individuality an oval, v. 421
Earth or fourth, i. 278; iii. 187; v. 80
Egg and earth, ii. 74
Eighth, i. 211, 217; v. 266
Eternity and infinity, emblem of, i. 133
Existence, our objective, of, ii. 329
Fathers of first race, entities from preceding though lower, iii. 124
Fire-mist, ii. 308
Fourth, ii. 42
Fourth globe, of final evolutionary adjustments, i. 234
Globe formed into, i. 303
Host, earth, of lower, iii. 420
Invisible magnetic, of man, v. 426, 427
Laws of unseen worlds no relation to our, ii. 329
Manas drawn down into, of material passions, i. 290
Monad, of, ii. 355
Moon, iii. 42
Moon-God as eighth, i. 274
Occultist, of, iv. 235
One absolute unity in, of objectivity, iii. 37
Parabrahman greater than greatest, ii. 72
Passions and desires, of material, i. 290

SPHERE (*Contd.*)
Primal causes, of, ii. 200
Ruler of, of fate, iv. 140
Seven hosts born within, of operation, iv. 57
Sublunary, v. 172
Sun glowing, ii. 264
Svar-loka upper, ii. 87
Vital-force luminous, ii. 262
World an infinite, v. 356
SPHERES, Action of combined forces of evolution and Karma, iv. 192
All on earth shadow of something in superior, iii. 270
Angel , from higher, iii. 238; v. 429
  ,,   in, of seven planets, iii. 294
  ,,   of, i. 176
Astral rulers of, create monads, ii. 301
Astronomical, v. 321, 322
Auphanim, angels, of, i. 156, 176
Being, of, iii. 45; iv. 187
Beings of imperceptible, ii. 200, 201
Celestial, v. 321
Centres of force meant by, i. 200
Centres of life or, of being, iii. 46
Chain, of, i. 113, 124, 254; iv. 73, 178, 328; v. 248
Chain of, on three plains beyond earth, iv. 271
Creative angels operating in, of seven planets, iii. 17
Dhyān Chohans men who lived on, in previous Manvantaras, i. 320
Dhyān Chohans of supra-mundane, ii. 378
Divine dynasties, beings from higher, iii. 328
Dots, cubes finally, i. 159
Earth is septempartite because of seven, of chain, iv. 328
Egg of Brahmā refers to, of being, iv. 187
Elect of multitudes passing on to other, ii. 21
Elements of, eternally in perfect harmony, iii. 84
Expectation, of, iii. 67
First-born first to fall into lower, of materiality, iii. 90
Fruits and grains brought from other, iii. 372
Globe, above our, iv. 275
Gods of will who deserted superior, iii. 68
Gyratory movement of, i. 176
Illusion, of, i. 318
Inner man and rebellious Æons of, iv. 176
Intermediate, of monads which have not reached Nirvāna, iii. 67
Invisible, ii. 329
Kabalists, of, ii. 235
Karshvaras refer to, of planetary chain, iii. 383
Kliphoth contains six other, iii. 119
Light on our plane is darkness in higher, ii. 169
Lords of, ii. 301
Lower, of materiality, iii. 90
Mineral wave in its progress round, i. 229
Music of, i. 220; ii. 150; iv. 172; v. 453
Nirmānakāyas sages of, on higher plane, iv. 208
Planetary, i. 247
Planetary chain of, i. 172; iii. 383
Planets, of, iii. 294
  ,,   on our Globe, iii. 17, 18
  ,,   or wandering, ii. 396
Primordial matter ends by becoming, i. 176

Prototype of every human being spiritual, i. 281
Rāhu placed in, stellar, iii. 380
Rebellious Æons of, iv. 176
Rebellious angels and lords of, ii. 301
Sacred Planets, ruled by, iv. 173
Septenary ring of, ii. 297
Seven, i. 113, 124, 172; v. 172, 248, 249
Seven orders of pitris in eternal, iii. 98
Seven rounds of terrestrial chain of, iv. 135
Shekinah or music of, ii. 150
Six limbs of Microprosopus or, above our globe, iv. 275
Six not seven, iv. 187
Small wheel is our chain of, i. 254
Sons of wisdom or angels from higher, iii. 238
Soul's downward progress through, iv. 176
Souls of, v. 73
Sparks are called, i. 156
Spiritual, i. 281
Terrestrial chain of, iv. 135
Third race vehicle for denizens of higher, i. 259
Transformations of heavenly, seven fundamental, i. 254
Triangles, cubes, lines and modellers, i. 156
Two letters descend from, of expectation, iii. 67
Vāch or music of, ii. 150
Watchers of seven, i. 124
Within, ii. 396
World, our and, i. 155, 176; ii. 329
World-wheels or, in Egypt, Babylon, Persia and Tibet, v. 321, 322
SPHERICITY of earth, Aristotle and Pliny, taught by, i. 176
Confucius, taught by, ii. 159
SPHEROID, Atom oblate, ii. 205
Centrifugal theory cannot account for oblate, ii. 317
Kosmos can be only represented by, i. 134
SPHEROIDAL, Nebulae, bodies formed from, ii. 316
Reason why drop of liquid assumes, form, i. 160
SPHINX, Egyptian, iv. 189
Image (man) that offers riddle of birth, i. 290
Narthex has to be wrenched from, iv. 87
Riddle of, i. 215; iii. 133, 401; iv. 85, 110; v. 110
Shakespeare, like Æschylus, iii. 417
Solar, v. 226
We accuse great, of devouring us, ii. 368
S'PHOR or Sippor, iii. 53
SPILLER, Prof., quoted, ii. 216, 232
SPINAL cord, and human soul, iv. 243
Brain, and, v. 550
Plexuses and, v. 517, 518, 520, 524
Second, v. 517, 518, 524
SPINOZA quoted, ii. 353, 354, 355; iii. 15
SPIRAL, Creative force, lines of, iv. 74
Cycles, motion of, iv. 152
Cyclic law, course of, iii. 165
Eternal motion which is, iii. 90
Evolution downward of spirit, ii. 274; iv. 302
Evolution, lines of, i. 178
Fohat, lines of, i. 177
Progress of four kingdoms, i. 230
SPIRIT, Absolute, ii. 65; v. 408
Absolute Divine, and absolute divine substance, ii. 51

SPIRIT (*Contd.*)

Absolute existence, facet of one, ii. 39
Absolute, knowledge of, i. 73
Absolute, neither matter nor, iv. 169, 170
Absolute, One, symbol of, i. 80
Absolute, only faintly realized by Liberated, i. 122
Absolute Unity becomes, of universe, iii. 37
Absolute Unity worshipped in, iv. 160
Abstraction, unconscious negative, i. 243
Action in, v. 452
Adam Rishoon is lunar, iii. 396
Ahura Mazda addressed as most blissful, iv. 180
Air or, ii. 56
Ākāsha, and soul of ether, i. 83
Ākāsha, is, ii. 39; v. 493
Alahim of Lives, of, v. 116
All things, which is, ii. 89
Alpha and Omega or, and matter, iv. 127
Amenti, one becomes pure, in, ii. 398
Ammon or Mon supreme, ii. 82
Ancients never dissociated, from matter, ii. 291
Anima mundi or, of life, ii. 81
Animals have no, v. 515
Antagonistic principles of, and matter, iii. 72
Aquatic bird moving on waters like, i. 146
Ark represents supremacy of, over matter, iv. 29
Ascending arc centripetal for, iii. 264
Ascent into, i. 295; iv. 302
Astral, i. 245
Astral light is, i. 246
Astrology, of astronomy, ii. 370
Asura synonym for supreme, iii. 69, 101
Atlantean worshippers of one unseen, of nature, iii. 275
Ātmā, Irradiating, i. 179
  ,,   or, i. 178, 273, 287, 332; ii. 294, 335; iii. 48, 121; iv. 152, 168, 203
  ,,   Universal, ii. 294; iv. 168
Ātmā-Buddhi or, and soul, i. 263
Ātmā-Buddhi-Manas or, soul-intelligence, i. 83
Ātman, i. 308
Ātman or Pūrvaja, living, of nature, iii. 117
Atom becomes seven rays on plane of, ii. 360
Avalokiteshvara-Kwan-Shi-Yin is omnipresent universal, ii. 193
Awakening of, iv. 296
Bacchus post-type of, iv. 25
Baptism of, iv. 136
Basic ideas upon, i. 326
Basis of Magic, v. 450
Before its Time, never sleeps, ii. 89
Bel, of God, ii. 72
Bird of immortality of divine, iii. 48
Blending of, and matter, i. 292
Blind without help of matter in material spheres, iii. 131
Body with informing soul and, ii. 335
Brahmā has aspect of, and time, i. 84
  ,,   Leading aspect of, ii. 266
  ,,   Soul and body at once, is, i. 114
Brahma, or, i. 300
Brahman is Prakriti and, ii. 138
Breath needed, of life, i 272, 273
Breath of life, and, iii. 113

Buddha, of, i. 169; ii. 193; v. 366
Buddhi and its informing, ii. 291
  ,,   Carries Manas to realm of eternal, i. 290
  ,,   Manas is, v. 497
  ,,   Material when compared with divine, i. 178
  ,,   Not Supreme, ii: 294
  ,,   Vehicle of, i. 308
Celestial beings composed of fiery, of life, i. 263
Central spiritual sun, in manifested universe, iii. 122
Central sun illumines intellectual world of, i. 299
Chaos, in, iii. 76
  ,,   Incubated by, ii. 44
  ,,   Matter and, i. 132
  ,,   of, iii. 112, 383
  ,,   of God, moving on, (brooding over), i. 141; ii. 812; iv. 227
  ,,   of Light, called, ii. 58
  ,,   Primeval, in, iii. 94
  ,,   Union of, with, i. 137
Chaotic matter requires, to permeate it, iv. 171
Christ, of teaching of, iv. 126
Christos, of, v. 169
Chu or divine, iv. 205
Church, dogmatic, independent, iii. 377
Circle, symbol of, of life and immortality, iv. 122
Circle transformed into, i. 172
Co-eternal with matter, v. 62
Concealed lord, one with, i. 123
Conqueror of, iii. 73
Conscious immortal, reflected in mind alone, iii. 106
Consciousness or, i. 80, 81; ii. 41
Consubstantiality of, matter and universe, ii. 339
Correlation of, force and matter, ii. 54
Cosmic ideation or, i. 81; ii. 39, 52; iii. 37
  ,,   solar body, of, i. 332
  ,,   space, of, ii. 313
  ,,   substance and, are one, ii. 52
  ,,   terrestrial, iii. 116
Counterfeit of, iv. 176
Creation, mixing with principles, ii. 171
  ,,   Light of, ii. 169
Creative emanation of, of God, ii. 60
  ,,   Fire or heat, of, i. 250
  ,,   Force evolving from, iii. 108
  ,,   Nature, of, iii. 416
Creator or, of earth, iv. 45
Crescent moon symbol of male aspect of, iv. 31
Curse not pronounced by superior, i. 243
Cycle of being, must pass through every, i. 243
Daimon is, v. 303
Darkness pure, i. 137
Degrees of, iv. 196
Deity, i. 127
Deity or, in chaos, iii. 76
Delphic and Kabalistic commandments, of, ii. 361
Demon, or, ii. 358
Demon or guardian, iv. 46

SPIRIT (*Contd.*)
  Depths, of rayless, i. 264
  Descending arc centrifugal for, iii. 264
  Descent and re-ascent of, v. 534
  Descent of, into matter, i. 173, 229, 306; ii. 345; v. 356
  Disembodied, or future man, is either, i. 320
  Divine, i. 178, 236, 272; ii. 81; iii. 48, 121; iv. 152, 166; v. 143, 310
    ,,   Daimon, or seventh principle is, v. 303
    ,,   Fiat, collectively of father-mother and son, ii. 154
    ,,   Formless world of, and, i. 249
    ,,   Personal God or, v. 351
    ,,   Purushottama or, v. 233
    ,,   Soul and its informing, ii. 291
    ,,   Stars and, v. 309
    ,,   Substance emitted from itself manifested, ii. 51, 166
    ,,   Unknowable, v. 128
    ,,   Wisdom, or, iii. 39
  Divorce of, from matter, iv. 37
  Dogma of Evil, distinct from, of all Good, iv. 52
  Double stream of, and matter, iv. 300
  Double triangle blending together of, and matter, i. 177
  Dragon or, iii. 39, 376
  Each power and object of nature has its, iii. 65
  Earth, Animated by, of life, iv. 154, 155
    ,,   Impotent on, alone is, i. 292
    ,,   Informed by evil, iv. 152
    ,,   Man, equilibrized compound of, and matter, iii. 93
    ,,   Matter, and, cemented together on, iii. 112
    ,,   Matter, containing potentially as much as, i. 295
    ,,   of, i. 245, 264; ii. 135, 141, 183; iii. 35, 40, 41, 42, 110, 113, 243, 292; iv. 45, 168, 181
  Earthquakes, of earth who appeared in, ii. 183
  Eastern esotericism, of, ii. 397
  Egg of darkness or, of life, ii. 81
  Ego compound unit of matter and, iv. 204
  Electricity, of, i. 195
  Element master principle of Atlanteans, iii. 303
  Elements and, ii. 246
  Elohim, of, ii. 90; v. 209, 211
  Embodied, ii. 89; v. 380
  Equilibrium of, and matter in man, iii. 187
  Esoteric philosophy, of, ii. 345, 354
  Eternal, v. 370, 494
  Eternal history of, i. 123
  Every differentiated unit one in essence with supreme, iii. 154
  Evil, iii. 387; iv. 43, 52
  Evil denotes polarity of matter and, ii. 134
  Evil of, v. 48
  Evolution from, to matter, ii. 274, 348; iii. 275
  Evolution of, iv. 224; v. 370
  Fall of, into generation, i. 243
  Fall of, into matter, i. 292; iii. 153; iv. 37, 96
  Father and mother, and substance, i. 114
  Father-mother and son, of, ii. 154
  Father-mother-son or, soul and body, i. 114
  Father or, ii. 169

Female and evil power by Nazarenes, regarded as, i .245
Feminine with Nazarenes and Gnostics, i. 245; v. 211
Fiery breath, beyond manifested nature, is, iii. 122
Fiery, of life, i. 264
Fifth race, of fourth strong in, i. 271
Fire and, iv. 57
  ,,   corresponding to, i. 263
  ,,   Nature, and, iii. 269
  ,,   of, i. 73; ii. 95, 177; iv. 136
  ,,   of Deity, stands representing, i. 127
  ,,   or, ii. 73
  ,,   Water and, products of electrifying, ii. 54
Fires, one of three, iii. 249
First-born, Creation that of, of universal soul, ii. 169
    ,,   Ideal world self-impregnated by, of life, iii. 43
    ,,   Near to confines of, iv. 57
Five, or, of life, iv. 155
  ,,   Symbolizes, of life and love terrestrial, iv. 151
  ,,   Symbolizes, of life eternal, iv. 151
Flame that burns in thy lamp, i. 143
Flame, which is invisible, ii. 351
Flames or fires represent, iii. 74
Flesh conquers, iv. 186
Fohat, Guiding, of laws and forces, i. 196
  ,,   of electricity, i. 195
  ,,   or, of life-giving, iii. 76
  ,,   Trying to bring, into union with soul, i. 178
Force, guiding noumenon of, ii. 358
Force, or, iv. 264, 300
Formless, v. 408
Fourth race, alone worshipped in early ages of, ii. 40
  ,,   Race, of, i. 271
  ,,   Round, equilibrium between, and matter, i. 242
Full moon symbol, female aspect of, iv. 31
Ghost, or, ii. 186
Globe propelled by, of earth, iii. 41
  ,,   Ready to be animated by, iv. 152
  ,,   Vital forces, gets, from, of sun, iii. 41
Globes of planetary chain ascending to, i. 208
God, becomes, i. 167, 246, 291
  ,,   Corresponds to, in man, ii. 344
  ,,   of, i. 149, 156; ii. 50, 59, 72, 81, 182; iii. 137, 153, 276; iv. 147, 163, 227; v. 189
  ,,   of, and Fire, iv. 57
  ,,   of Moses held to be impure, iii. 388
  ,,   or, i. 264
Goddess Moot first product of mixture of, and matter, ii. 170
Goeth where it willeth, i. 272
Good and bad magicians sons of, and matter, iii. 276
Grace, or, ii. 343
Gravity supposed to be due to a, ii. 214
Great mother breath of her first principle is man's, i. 332
Great soul of world or, of life, ii. 81
Group four, of visible sun, iii. 243

SPIRIT (*Contd.*)

Guardian, Demon is, iv. 46
Guardian, of earth and men, iii. 44
Haeckel and, iv. 238
Harmony in world of, ii. 368
Heat, of, ii. 95
Heat or flame and, i. 73
Heavenly man is unmanifested, of universe, i. 263
Heavenly man or pure, iv. 197
Heavens, of, iv. 45
Hegel and, i. 122; ii. 365
Hidden voice of Mantras, or, ii. 59
Hierarchy, conditions on which, can belong to divine, i. 243
Highest, in Man, v. 421
History of creation opens with, of God, ii. 60
Hoa, from, iii. 93
Holy, iii. 416; iv. 31, 123, 190
,, Conception by, v. 152
,, Early Christians, of, was feminine, ii. 343
,, Holies, of, and infinite, iv. 40
,, Light, of, iv. 136
,, Simon Magus and, v. 127
Human, v. 306
Human frame begins with body and ends with, ii. 338
Humanity, of, iii. 311, 380
Hydrogen and, iii. 121
Idea of, ii. 365
Identity between, and its material double, i. 281
Immortality of, v. 281, 290
Indiscrete principle or absolute, ii. 165
Infinite, iv. 40
Innumerable incarnations of, iii. 236
Inseparable from matter, ii. 365; iii. 53
Intelligence endowed with, i. 320
Intuition, idea of psychic, ii. 266
Involution of, into matter, ii. 134
It, causeless cause of, and matter, i. 302
,, is, of fire, i. 73
,, is no body, v. 380
,, Matter, and, ii. 269
,, Neither, nor matter but both, i. 317
Jehovah, of earth, iv. 168
Kabalistic teaching as to, and matter, i. 244, 280
Knwoledge of absolute, i. 73
Kosmos, moving over face of, ii. 58
Kosmos, of, i. 221
Kshetrajna or universe of, and matter, iii. 117
Kwan Yin, Divine voice or, v. 380
Language cannot express what, perceives, iii. 196
Latent in matter, iii. 53
Lha ancient term for, iii. 35
Lha or, of earth, iii. 35
Life, Eternal, in, iv. 164
,, Eternal, of, iv. 151
,, Immortality, and, iv. 122
,, Is, i. 326
,, Light, and, v. 299
,, Love terrestrial, of, and, iv. 151
,, of, i. 157, 248; ii. 81, 351; iii. 43, 113; iv. 31, 97, 154, 155

Light, of, ii. 52, 58, 203
,, or, ii. 169
,, Pure ethereal emanated by, iii. 49
Line remains triadic, iv. 172
Linked with impure demon of matter, iii. 276
Lipika produced by word, voice and, i. 165
Lipika separate world of, from matter, i. 188
Living creature is, i. 326
,, Soul, united to, i. 243
Logoi strive to endow man with conscious immortal, iii. 106
Logos Falling as ray into, i. 173
,, is, iii. 38
,, Universal, and, iv. 46
Lunar, iii. 95, 396
Mahā-Atmā, Brahmā, of life, i. 81
Mahāpurusha or Paramātman supreme, iii. 117
Mahat or Mahābuddhi vehicle of, ii. 138
Male god or, of life, iv. 31
,, or, ii. 171
Man becomes, i. 246, 291; iii. 192; iv. 287
,, Creature of, and matter, i. 114
,, Son of unknown deity and planetary, i. 114
,, Tabernacle for divine, i. 236
Manas, and, of Lords of wisdom, iii. 409, 410
,, connected with, iii. 182
,, Link between, and matter, iii. 106
,, Visible sun endows man with, iii. 243
Mānasic, iii. 284
Manifested nature beyond, iii. 122
Manifested universe, in, iii. 122
Manifesting deity, space, matter and, iv. 183
Mankind, of, iii. 311
Man's thought born from, v. 449
Materialism which denies, ii. 202
Materiality, plunging into, iii. 97
Matter, and, i. 80, 81, 122, 134, 167, 177, 229, 233, 242, 247, 280, 292, 295, 302; ii. 39, 41, 94, 134, 135, 169, 170, 171, 269, 274, 275, 291, 304, 345, 348, 357, 365; iii. 53, 72, 73, 74, 93, 106, 108, 112, 117, 131, 143, 153, 187, 270, 275, 276, 376; iv. 29, 37, 96, 97, 111, 127, 164, 170, 197, 204, 302; v. 129, 166, 234, 370, 384, 387, 443, 469, 488, 489, 501
,, Becomes pure, ii. 268
,, First differentiation of, i. 302
,, Is, at lowest point of its cyclic activity, ii. 357
,, of Life ever coalescing with, iv. 97
,, of sensuous life, transformed into, iii. 39
,, on seventh plane is, ii. 357
Māyā, matter and, ii. 357; v. 380, 388
Mediator between men and universal, i. 323
Mental unfolding differentiated from, iv. 58
Mercury offspring of, iii. 56
Metaphysical, psychological, with Hindus and Egyptians, iv. 37
Mind, Link between, and, matter, i. 233
,, Mediator between, and man, i. 288
,, of earth never had, iii. 113
,, or, ii. 166
Molecular aggregation can only act through some, ii. 42

SPIRIT—(Contd.)
  Monad, and planetary, ii. 356
    ,,   cannot be called, i. 292
    ,,   Indivisible part of, i. 82; v. 135
  Moses and Jewish tutelary, iv. 111
  Mother's seventh, last emanated, i. 264
  Mūlaprakriti soul of one infinite, i. 109
  Myriads of existences, is same through, iii. 422
  Mysterious nature of, in man, iv. 220
  Mysterious Word, v. 218
  Nārāyana is, i. 146
    ,,   or, of God, ii. 50
    ,,   Self-born, ii. 177
  Nature, and, ii. 89; iii. 49
    ,,   and, both resolve into supreme spirit,
           ii. 89
    ,,   In man compound of, and matter, iii. 53
    ,,   of, iii. 122, 275
  Navis is fructified by, of life, iv. 31
  Neither weighed nor measured, v. 91
  Neshamah or, i. 287; iv. 24
  Newton on subtle, ii. 214
  Nine symbolized earth informed by evil, iv. 152
  Nirvānic state of, i. 243
  Nitrogen separated alchemically would yield,
    of life, ii. 351
  No, nor matter in reality, ii. 266
  Noah is, falling into matter, iii. 153
  Non-being, lost in absoluteness of, ii. 204
  Nous or, iii. 143, 375
  Number one is born of, i. 154; v. 115
  Obscuration of, iv. 302
  Obscuration of, of monad, i. 228
  Ocean of light whose one pole is, ii. 204
  Occult doctrine, of, ii. 353
  Occult wisdom on earth or, iii. 376
  Occultist deals with soul and, of cosmic space,
    ii. 313
  Occultists on, iv. 241
  One and indiscrete, is, i. 274
    ,, and matter being, ii. 357
    ,, Becomes two referred to as, and matter,
       ii. 41
    ,, Eternal, v. 494
    ,, Infinite, i. 109
    ,, Is, of living God, ii. 166
    ,, Is the, of Elohim of life, i. 188
    ,, Monad emanates from, i. 82
    ,, Neither, nor matter, i. 302
    ,, of living God, i. 157
    ,, or, of life, i. 157
    ,, Prādhānika Brahmā, i. 300
    ,, Primeval aspect of, i. 122
    ,, Substance, opposite pole of, i. 134
    ,, Unity, aspect of, i. 81
    ,, Universal, i. 308
  Only witness, is, ii. 294
  Ophiomorphos rebellious, ii. 179
  Organic form, endeavoured to manifest in,
    iv. 222
  Origin of all things in, iii. 177, 196
  Origin of, same as that of matter, i. 292
  Parabrahman, Of earth not confused with,
           ii. 141
           or, i. 122
    ,,   Soul of nature, and, i. 74
  Physical body of earth builds, iii. 243

  Plane of, v. 477
  Planetary, i. 114; ii. 300, 356; iii. 42; iv. 140;
    v. 277
  Pneuma or, ii. 56
  Polarity of matter and, ii. 134
  Prādhānika Brahmā, i. 300; ii. 164
  Prakriti, Mounts on shoulders of, i. 292
    ,,   Not, i. 299
    ,,   of, ii. 171
  Primeval waters, that broods over, ii. 52
  Primordial matter with latent, i. 132
    ,,   Ocean of space on which self-born,
           moves, ii. 177
    ,,   Substance, impregnated by, ii. 52
    ,,   Substance of soul and, of mani-
           fested kosmos, ii. 318
    ,,   Substance or, of light, ii. 52
  Principle fructifies nature, i. 72
  Protogonos from union of, and Chaos, i. 137
  Pums or, ii. 88, 164
  Pure force all in dominion of, ii. 235
  Purity of, i. 243
  Purusha or, i. 122, 146, 292; ii. 81, 89, 170,
    275; iii. 131; v. 170; v. 426
  Purushottama or infinite, iv. 141
  Queen fabricating, of universe, iii. 48
  Ray inseparable from one absolute, or, i. 178
  Realistic and physiological with Hebrews,
    iv. 37
  Reality, v. 388
  Rebellion of, against matter, iii. 73
  Rebellion of intellectual life against inactivity
    of, iii. 111
  Reincarnation of, v. 567
  Ruach or, i. 243, 272, 288; iii. 93, 377;
    iv. 205
  Rules the Sun's Course, v. 313
  Sage identified with supreme, iv. 141
  Sands, of, i. 264
  Sarvesha, or, ii. 89
  Satan adversary because matter opposeth,
    iii. 237
    ,, Gives man law of, of life, i. 248
    ,, Highest divine, iii. 376
    ,, Samael, and, evil, iii. 387
  Schemal and Samael are, of earth, ii. 135
  Second Logos or of universe, i. 81
  Second order of celestial beings corresponding
    to, i. 263
  Seed of Shiva or holy, iv. 190
  Self separates itself no longer from universal,
    iv. 209
  Self-born, ii. 177
  Self-conscious, to become, i. 243
  Septenary man, is resolved into, iv. 197
  Serpent of eternity and all knowledge that
    Mānasic, iii. 284
  Serpent or, iii. 376
  Seven creations preceded absolute, ii. 165
    ,, Hosts propelled by, of life-giving, iii. 95
    ,, Planetary genii, of, iii. 35
    ,, Principles of Kosmos, permeated, ii. 168
    ,, Was, of everything, iv. 154
  Seventh, i. 264
    ,,   or central informing force, of life,
           iv. 154
         Principle, or, v., 72,

SPIRITS (*Contd.*)
 Sexless, v. 408
 Shadow not cast by good holy, iii. 121
 Shadow of deity permeated egg with vivifying, ii. 82
 Shankarāchārya, of, v. 367
 Sheaths, remains after substraction of, ii. 294
 Shekinah or synthesizing, ii. 343
 Single Eye of, v. 438
 Six, symbol of globe ready to be animated by divine, iv. 152
 Solar Lhas breathed, of life into its form, iii. 113
 Solidarity, of, i. 319
 Solidification of, which will produce earth, ii. 69
 Son, fecundates germ of, iii. 94
 Sons of, and matter, iii. 276
 Soul as distinct from, ii. 292
 ,, Auric Envelope and, v. 436
 ,, Body, and, i. 172, 181, 272; iv. 174
 ,, Intellect, and, i. 265
 ,, -Life, v. 397
 ,, Matter, and, i. 120
 ,, Mind, and, iii. 121
 ,, Upādhi of, i. 208
 ,, Vehicle for manifestation of, i. 120
 Space, First differentiation of, i. 302
 ,, Matter and, iv. 183
 ,, or, ii. 58
 ,, Ultimate substratum of, ii. 305
 Spirit within, v. 479
 Spiritualist, of, ii. 242
 Steps symbols of, soul and body, i. 172
 Strangled in coils of matter, iii. 376
 Struggle between, and matter, iii. 74
 Struggle between, and soul, iii. 375
 Sun, Earth, and, iii. 40
 ,, in, v. 218
 ,, is, ii. 201
 ,, Jupiter, Venus, Saturn and, v. 326
 ,, Nature, of in our system, iii. 122
 ,, of, iii. 41
 ,, or fire symbol of divine, iii. 121
 ,, Under, iv. 123; v. 216
 Substance and, v. 476
 Super-Spirit and, v. 438
 Supremacy of, over matter, iv. 29
 Supreme, i. 83, 122; ii. 82, 89, 171, 294; iii. 69, 101, 117, 154; iv. 141
 ,, Brahma, is leading aspect of, i. 84
 ,, Soul drawn into matter and, ii. 170
 ,, Spirit, of, i. 84
 Sūtrātmā or, ii. 335
 Svara beyond, v. 479
 Svastika meaning, and matter, iii. 108
 Svayambhū or universal, i. 123
 Terrestrial, iii. 35
 ,, God, iii. 122
 That, first differentiation from, i. 109
 Third order of celestial beings correspond to, soul and intellect, i. 265
 Third race child of pure, i. 259
 Thought and, one basis of magic, v. 450
 Three is, iv. 164
 Three strides relate to descent of, into matter, i. 173

Three, water out of, i. 156
 Tiamat, of chaos, iii. 112, 383
 Toom is north wind and, of west, ii. 398
 True knowledge is of, v. 434
 Truth, of, v. 261
 Truths of, iii. 376
 Twelve great transformations of, into matter, ii. 169
 Two, air out of, i. 156
 Unconscious designated by European Pantheists as, i. 122
 Union of, and matter, iv. 96, 111
 Union with great, of universe, iv. 184
 Unknowable deity, aspect of, ii. 275
 Unknown darkness, of, ii. 81
 Universal, i. 82, 123, 323; ii. 87, 193, 294; iv. 31, 46, 168, 209
 ,, Father Son and, v. 49
 ,, Kosmos and, v. 487
 ,, Soul, of, ii. 169
 ,, Soul or, of life, ii. 81
 ,, Soul, vehicle of, ii. 138
 ,, Svayambhū, i. 123
 ,, Enveloping, i. 327
 Universe, of, i. 81, 263; iii. 37, 49; iv. 184; v. 558
 ,, of father, mother and son shapes, ii. 154
 ,, Resultant of, and substance, i. 114
 Upanishads on, ii. 314
 Vegetable kingdom, of, i. 264
 Vehicle of, ii. 138; iv. 152
 Virgil on, iv. 166
 Vishnu, aspect of, ii. 269
 Vishnu or, of God, ii. 50
 Voice and, i. 161
 Voice, and word, i. 156; ii. 51, 166; v. 380
 Volition, iii. 244
 Wakes, when universal, ii. 87
 War between, and matter, iii. 270
 Water and blood, and, ii. 294
 Waters, brooding over, v. 447
 Waters, of God moved on face of, ii. 50, 72; iii. 137, 153
 ,, of life, latent in, i. 132
 ,, of Space, of God moves on dark, iv. 163; v. 212
 Web whose upper end is fastened to, i. 148
 West of, ii. 398
 Whirleth about continually, iv. 123
 Wind being, of God, ii. 81, 182
 Wind or, ii. 56
 Wisdom, love and truth, of, iv. 110
 Word or Logos in union with voice and, i. 161
 Word, voice and, i. 165
 World, of, v. 154
 Y. H. V. H., synthesizing, of, ii. 343
 Yima and, of earth, iii. 292; iv. 181
SPIRIT-FIRE, iii. 75
SPIRIT-GUARDIAN of our globe, iii. 35
SPIRIT-HYLE or father-mother, i. 152
SPIRITISTIC revelations, so-called, iv. 270
SPIRIT-KINGS, Dynasty, of, iii. 225
SPIRIT-KNOWLEDGE, Ātma-Vidyā or, i. 249
SPIRIT-LIFE, Invisible subjective, iii. 347
SPIRIT-MATTER, boundless darkness symbolizing co-eval and co-eternal, ii. 41

SPIRIT-MATTER (*Contd.*)
 Matter-Spirit, and, ii. 353
 Phenomenal world, and, ii. 41
 Primeval evolution of, i. 320
 Second Logos, i. 81
SPIRIT-RAY, self-existent appeared in, iii. 245
SPIRIT-RAYS on flood of waters, iii. 152
SPIRITS, Ancestors of man's forms or lunar, iii. 110
 Ancestors or, of earth, i. 271
 Ancestral, iii. 17
 Androgynous, who were, i. 264
 Angels, or, iii. 96
 Ascend and descend, of those who, i. 192
 Ases of Scandinavia identical with planetary, of Christians, iii. 106
 Astral light, body of, i. 303
 Astral, superhuman, i. 334
 Asuras fallen into, of earth, iii. 250
 Asuras, of evil, iii. 169
 Atoms, of, i. 268
 Barhishad or lunar, iii. 87
 Belief in, ii. 393
 Believers in, ii. 336
 Brahmā, embodied produced from limbs of, iii. 87
 Briatic world called throne abode of pure, iii. 119
 Builders, representatives of seven, of face, i. 186
 Celestial, ii. 87; iii. 368
 Chaldean, seven, iv. 175
 Christians, of, i. 181
 Confucianists and, v. 39
 Conscious, iii. 174
 Constellations of, v. 203
 Cosmic, ii. 356
  ,, Gods or, of earth, ii. 183, 184
  ,, Gods or, of elements, ii. 181
 Creative, iii. 16
 Daimons, daimones or dæmons, i. 329; v. 171, 303, 310
 Darkness, of, iii. 73, 102, 169, 235
 Dead, of, i. 319, 329, 335
 Demons more material, iii. 69
 Departed, of, i. 319; v. 497
 Destinies of men, planetary, rule, i. 186
 Dhyān Chohans or creative, i. 114
  ,, Planetary, or, i. 320; ii. 193, 360
  ,, Pure, are not, i. 318
 Dhyānī or planetary, iii. 65
 Dhyānīs who were material, iii. 225
 Disembodied, v. 401
 Disobedient, iv. 84
 Divinations and, of elements, ii. 110
 Dynasties of, lower, iii. 349
 Earth created by terrestrial, iii. 36
 Earth, of, i. 271; ii. 184; iii. 36, 118, 119, 250, 349
 Egregores, of energy and action, i. 303
 Elemental, i. 280; iv. 128
 Elementals, Issued from Cosmic, ii. 356
  ,, or, of atoms, i. 268
  ,, Terrestrial, or, i. 279
 Elementary, ii. 355; iv. 204; v. 172
 Elements of, i. 265; ii. 110; iii. 355, 356; v. 238
  ,, or, iv. 147
  ,, Symbols of informing, ii. 181

Elohim, lunar, became creative, iii. 87
Elohim or seven creative, i. 247
Evil, ii. 118; iii. 169, 171, 180; v. 375
Exile of seven choirs of celestial, upon earth, iv. 54
Existence of, ii. 370; iii. 96
Face, seven of, i. 186, 247; iii. 123
Flames are hierarchy of, iii. 74
Fountain, iv. 201, 206
Four Mahārājahs called, i. 181
Gods for men, planetary, who have become, i. 76
Guardian, i. 329
Hall of, v. 290
Heaven, of, iii. 250
Hosts of Celestial beings, or, i. 190
Human astral selves or, of earth, iii. 119
Ilda-Baoth produces from himself seven stellar, i. 247
Immortal, v. 281
Incorporeal Intelligences or Planetary, iv. 122
Ischins or, iii. 375
Islands of good, iii. 370
Jehovah one of creative, i. 247
Jehovah personating, iv. 78
Kabalistic teaching as to, i. 280
Kabiri as planetary, ii. 366
Kimpurushas or celestial, iii. 368
Kwan-Shi-Yin synthetic aggregation of all planetary, ii. 193
Lha, of moon or lunar, iii. 110
 ,, or, iii. 67; v. 38
Lhamayin or, iii. 74
Lhas are, of highest spheres, iii. 74
Lhas or, iii. 74, 197; v. 38
Light of, iii. 169
Lipika and seven planetary, i. 165
Lipika are, of universe, i. 186
Logos compound unity of living, ii. 297
Lord of, and Trinity, v. 101
Lords of Wisdom degraded to evil, iii. 180
Lower orders of, v. 449
Lunar, i. 233, 247; iii. 87, 110
 ,, Ancestors or stellar, i. 247
 ,, Gods or, i. 227
Mahar-loka, in, ii. 87
Mahat, of, iii. 233
Mankind in physical aspect progeny of, of earth, i. 271
Mankind partly ruled by, of earth, iii. 349
Material worlds fashioned by inferior, iii. 67
Men are handiwork of hosts of various, i. 271
 ,, become, then Gods, iii. 146
 ,, Lunar, have to become, i. 232
Monads and cosmic, ii. 354
Moon, evil, war against, ii. 118
Mount Hermon, chained on, iii. 407
Mundane and Supermundane, v. 452
Nabathean Agriculture on powers of, iv. 22
Nats or, v. 380
Nature, i. 272; ii. 181
 ,, Guided by high planetary, i. 320; ii. 202
 ,, Terrestrial, of, iv. 302
Nirvānīs, of men becoming, i. 285
Occultists know themselves surrounded by, iii. 369

SPIRITS (*Contd.*)
Ophite, i. 185
Paracelsus, of, v. 78
Pitris or lunar, i. 227
Planet, of this, iii. 19
Planetary, i. 76, 165, 168, 186, 320; ii. 193,
    326, 345, 360, 366; iii. 65, 106, 318; iv. 122;
    v. 109, 220, 221, 240, 277, 281, 291, 298,
    309, 460, 462, 465
Planetary angels, connected with, i. 248
Planets, of, i. 280; ii. 156
Presence, of, ii. 156; v. 74, 170, 209, 309, 320
Progenitors are advanced from another planet,
    iv. 182
Pyramid symbol of hierarchy of, iii. 366
Rākshasas or evil, iii. 171
Rishis or seven great planetary, iii. 318
Ritual for, of stars, i. 182
Sacrifice of bright, iii. 275
Salts of nature, of, iii. 123
Saturn placed, to rule over men, iii. 372
Science objects to, ii. 336; iii. 66
Séance room, of, i. 279; iv. 306
Seven builders, which guide operations of
        nature, ii. 202
    ,,   Church, of the, v. 303, 313, 315
    ,,   Circles or seven invisible, in angelic
           spheres, iv. 57
    ,,   Constellations, of, v. 203
    ,,   Creative, i. 114, 247; v. 215
    ,,   Divine, i. 264
    ,,   Evil, iii. 106
    ,,   Orders of purely divine, i. 191
    ,,   Presence, of the, v. 209
    ,,   Primeval men evolving from creative,
           iii. 16
    ,,   Ra of, v. 202
    ,,   Sexless, v. 408
    ,,   Sublime lords are seven creative, i. 114
    ,,   Wicked, iii. 72
Shadows clothed by, of earth, iii. 118, 119
Shadows warmed by solar, iii. 118, 119
Signs of zodiac prior to, of earth, iii. 36
Sixfold Dhyānīs or, of earth, i. 271
Sons of Will and Yoga now regarded as evil,
    iii. 180
Soul of earth emanation of planetary, ii. 326
Spheres of, ii. 297
Spiritualism, of, i. 279
Spiritualists believe in, i. 329; ii. 393
Sravah or, of manifested powers, iii. 384
Stars of, i. 165, 182; ii. 164; v. 225, 238
Stellar, i. 247; v. 170
Subdivisions of noumenal elements informed
    by nature, ii. 181
Sun, of, iii. 369
Supernatural beings, regarded as, ii. 400
Sūtrātmā thread on which all, of man are
    strung, i. 282
Swedenborg of, v. 406
Ternary or three, in number five, iv. 147
Terrestrial, i. 279; iii. 36
Three chief groups of planetary, i. 186
Third race animated by, of Mahat, iii. 233
Toom creates, ii. 398
Unclean, iii. 407
Universe, of, i. 186

War on Gods, credited with making, iv. 83
Wickedness, v. 204
Wisdom in shape of incarnating, of Mahat,
    iii. 233
Yama, Pluto, Osiris, of earth, ii. 184
Yazatas, or celestial, of elements, iii. 355
SPIRIT-SOUL, Aspirations of, lie buried, i. 45
Ātmā-Buddhi or, i. 260
Evolution of, ii. 166
Nature, pervading, i. 123
Universal, i. 123
SPIRIT-SUBSTANCE, Kosmic polarity of,
    iv. 55
SPIRIT-SUN, Hierophants address, iv. 129
SPIRITUAL Beings, v. 77, 321, 365
Conqueror, v. 396
Consciousness, v. 488, 494, 555, 567
Current, Sushumna, v. 520
Development, v. 81
Ego, v. 249, 298, 359, 421, 487, 500
Element in *Bible*, v. 194
Entities, v. 329
Essence, v. 488
Evil, for, v. 501
Gestation, Devachan is, v. 473
Gravitation, v. 534
Life, v. 397, 434
Man, v. 426, 427, 438, 453, 457, 460, 545, 560
Memory, v. 79
Mysteries, v. 76
Natures, v. 488
Perception, v. 397, 549
Photography, v. 303
Plane, iii. 119; v. 567
Purification, v. 79
Rulers of Plants, v. 443
Self, v. 380
Self-consciousness, v. 494, 552
Senses, v. 429
Soul, v. 438, 471, 498
Sound, v. 508
States, three higher lokas are, v. 545
Sun, v. 219, 277, 462, 486
Universe, v. 275
Vision, v. 515
Vitality, v. 456
Wisdom, v. 497
World v. 73, 365, 418, 438
SPIRITUALISM, i. 279, 280, 329; v. 42, 43, 45,
    48, 94, 251
Spiritism or, v. 251
SPIRITUALISTIC, Facts, iii. 95
Materializations, iv. 306
Phenomena, iii. 164; v. 566
SPIRITUALISTS, v. 40, 121, 135, 497
Angels, as believers in, ii. 336
Armies, in European, ii. 287
Astral body, and, iii. 156, 157
Dimensions of space as viewed by, i. 295
Dogma, deny, ii. 393
Empirics are, iv. 234
Materializations of, ii. 244
Phenomena of, i. 337; iv. 222
Projection of ethereal body familiar to, iii. 95
Scientists and phenomena of, i. 337
Spirits of dead, believe in, i. 319, 329
Summerland of, v. 359

SPIRITUALITY, v. 512
  Angel-man, primordial, of, i. 240
  Bible, of the, v. 195
  Character, of most refined, i. 309
  Cross after loss of, iv. 131
  Cycles of, iii. 444
  Degrees of, iii. 96
  Different meanings of term, i. 240
  Generating power of, ultimate, ii. 186
  Jewish Symbols, of, iv. 27
  Law of re-ascent into, ii. 134
  Lunar Pitris, of, i. 225
  Meru region of, iii. 402
  Monad descends into realms of mental, i. 228
  Perfection of physical form with loss of, iii. 119
  Quiescence natural state of, iv. 58
  Semites degenerated in, iii. 205
  Sixth Hierarchy on downward scale of, i. 279
  Sons of light, of, iv. 57
  Spirits of darkness fought for, on earth, iii. 73
  Third eye and, gradual disappearance of,
      iii. 297
  Third root race, of, i. 271
SPIRITUS, Alchemy, in, iii. 122
  Greek signs, of, iv. 147, 152
  Mother, i. 245
  Mother of matter, i. 293
  Mundi, ii. 256
  Nazarenes, female portion of astral light, i. 246
  Ventus and, ii. 56
  Vitae, ii. 256
  Wind or, i. 273
SPIRIT-VOLITION, i. 244
SPIRIT-WORLD, Kant and, i. 191
  Matter, and world of, i. 280
SPITTLE, Serpent of evil born from, of Suoyatar,
    iii. 39
SPITZBERGEN, Climate of, iii. 23, 24; iv. 247
  Continent line from, to Straits of Dover,
      iii. 324, 326
  Fossil remains of forests of, iv. 357
  Hyperborean continent and, iv. 344
  Nova Zembla and, iii. 397
  Second continent and, iii. 400
SPLEEN, iii. 297; v. 518, 544, 553, 561, 565, 566
SPLENDOUR and Light, Lord of, v. 81
SPOOKS, Elementary, ii. 345; v. 231, 251, 453,
    472, 473, 500, 566
SPORE, iv. 229
SPORES, Germ-buds reduced to, iv. 229
  Increase by, iii. 174
  Science, of, iii. 178
SPORT of creative God, Creation, iii. 64
SPOTS, Moon, in, iv. 35
  Solar, ii. 265
SPOUSE of Son, Christian Magna Mater, ii. 108
  Zeus of, iii. 412
SPRENGER quoted, ii. 190
SPRING, correspondences of, v. 444
  Equinox, origin of, iii. 433
  Eternal, iii. 144, 206, 355, 399; iv. 308
  Seven Symbol of earth in, iv. 154
SQUARE, Attributes of, v. 166
  Chakra, inscribed in, i. 173
  Circle, and, i. 161; ii. 337; iv. 114, 167
  Eastern Esotericism and, ii. 33
  Forces and, four sacred, i. 192

Gnosis rested on, iv. 144
Head-dress of Hierophants, iv. 127
Hebrew letters, v. 178, 179
Hindus could, circle, iv. 114
INRI, of, v. 166
Mathematical Science, of, ii. 27, 28
Nature, in, iv. 166
Perfect, i. 129, 153; iv. 126
Pyramid, and, ii. 342; v. 165
Quaternary or, ii. 66
Triangle and, ii. 337; iii. 37, 48, 120; iv. 197
SQUARES, Cross composed of seven, iv. 131
  Distances, of, ii. 213
  Four interior, of Israelite encampment, v. 166
SQUARING the cirlce, v. 207
SRAVAH, the seven bright, iii. 384; iv. 85
SRI = the wife of Abram, iii. 86
SRI, wife of the moon, iii. 86
SRIP to creep, root of Sarpa, serpent, iii. 188
SROTÂPANNA, one of four paths to Nirvâna,
    i. 255; v. 271
SROTÂPATTI, v. 399, 498
STABILITY, Eternal of law of nature, ii. 396
  Tat, (That) emblem of, iv. 127, 159
  Tau, emblem of, iv. 127, 159
STAG, four-horned, iii. 222
STAIRWAY in city of the eight, ii. 24
STALLO, quoted, ii. 205, 206, 208, 209, 210,
    211, 232, 235, 268, 280
STANLEY JEVONS, quoted, ii. 148
STANZAS, Abastract formulae in, i. 85
  Allegorical, iii. 335
  Archaic, ii. 200; iii. 15; iv. 206
  Builders of, ii. 90
  Commentaries on, i. 109-311; iii. 35-434
  Cosmogony of our planetary system, treat only
      of, i. 79
  Cross in, ii. 34
  Defence of, iii. 200
  Dzyan, of, i. 91-107; iii. 27-33
  Eleven, omitted, i. 207
  Esoteric doctrine based upon, i. 59
  European library contains source of, no, i. 46
  European museums, in, iii. 92
  Evolution and, i. 85, 237
  Explanations in, iii. 65
  Exposition, are skeleton of, iii. 24
  Faculties, appeal to inner, i. 86
  Fohat on, ii. 278
  Forbidden passages of, i. 87
  Idea of, ii. 159
  Intermediate race, on, iii. 277
  Kwan-Shi-Yin, in, ii. 193
  Language of, unknown to philology, i. 59
  Lipika, on, i. 334
  Mahârâjahs of, i. 334; ii. 95, 124
  Mindless, on sin of, iv. 253
  Minerals, on, iv. 165
  Pesh-Hun in, iii. 60
  Pitris in, iii. 46
  Portions only of seven, given, i. 87
  Post-Mahâbhâratan period, and, i. 87
  Preliminary, i. 46
  Racial divisions on, iii. 251
  Records of a people unknown to ethnology in,
      i. 59
  Relation of moon to earth as shown in, ii. 17

STANZAS (*Contd.*)
Science, vindicated by a man of, iii. 289
Solar system and, i. 206
Sons of dark wisdom, on, iii. 250
Subject matter of, i. 85
Summary of, iii. 37
Symbolism of, ii. 179
Synonyms in original, i. 87
Terms, of, iii. 35
Third eye of, iii. 286
Version of, modern, i. 87
STAR, Asteria, golden island, iii. 382
Atom to, i. 179
Bethlehem, of, v. 232
Born, under which an entity is, ii. 296
Bright and morning, iv. 110
Cassiopeia in, ii. 314
Central, v. 219, 277, 439, 441
Centre of energy, as, ii. 308
Five-pointed, i. 73, 266; iv. 148
Genii and, i. 334
Groups belonging to same, ii. 298
Hexagon, i. 271
Longitude of, a, ii. 385
Magi, of, ii. 380
Monad like and indestructible, i. 228
Morning, iii. 241; iv. 7, 329; v. 267
Morning and Evening, Venus is, v. 441
Planet or, inhabited, iii. 56
Pyramids consecrated to a, iii. 361
Regents, v. 320
Rites, v. 313
Rush-light linked to, ii. 328
Salvation, of, ii. 193; iv. 97
Sea, of the, v. 212
Seven, of, ii. 124
Six-pointed, i. 262, 263; iv. 102, 166
Six-rayed, iv. 190
Snow-crystal or six-pointed, iv. 166
Son of morning, and, iii. 71
Sun central, ii. 167, 298
Venus, of sea, ii. 108
Virgin addressed as Morning, iv. 97
World has its parent, iii. 45
STAR, ELY, a French astrologer quoted, i. 145
STAR-ANGELS, ii. 297, 299; v. 238
STARCHATERUS or Starkad the giant, iii. 346
STAR-GOD, Lucifer the, iii. 241
STARS, Actions of, ii. 256
Ancients' views of, iii. 369
Angels if, i. 176, iii. 357; v. 320
Apparition of certain, ii. 371
Archangels and, vi. 22
Army of, v. 320
Atmosphere of, iii. 320
Black faces, on lands of, iii. 425
Centres of vortices, becomes, i. 255
Chaldeans found letters by, v. 114
Christ, in hand of, iv. 204
Comets, become first, i. 251
Constellation of dragon, in, iii. 354
Constellations, and, i. 251
Constitution of, ii. 307
Course of, iv. 183
Courses, in their, ii. 44
Destiny is written in, ii. 364
Disappeared, that have, iv. 54

Division of, iv. 119
Dragon's head, called, iv. 73
Eye of Taurus, called, ii. 388
Fallen cherub from, iv. 70
Falling upon earth, iv. 55
Filiation of, ii. 320
Firmament, of, ii. 380
Fixed, v. 222, 340
Flocks of, iii. 384
Futurity read in, iii. 287
Genesis of, ii. 164
Genius Loci of, ii. 183
Goddess of, iv. 117
Gods of light, wherein dwell the, iii. 366
God's powers, are, iv. 206
Golden flock of, iii. 41
Great Bear, of, i. 279; ii. 172; iii. 318; iv. 119, 120, 202
Habitability of distant, ii. 331
Harmony of, ii. 326
Heaven, of, ii. 334
Heaven of, *Book of Enoch*, alluded to in, iv. 103
Heaven of, Dragon and, iii. 102
Heaven emptied of one-third of its, iii. 240
Hindus, observed by, iii. 389
History written in, iii. 436
Humanity bound together with, iii. 351
Hydrogen of fixed, i. 199
Inhabited, iv. 271, 272
Intelligences that rule, iii. 351; v. 313
Joseph's dream of, ii. 375
Kepler and Tycho Brahé, of, iv. 54
Keys, represent, iii. 436
King of, iv. 47
Lucifer, of, ii. 154
Manifesting, i. 82
Masses not inanimate, ii. 216
Materials differ in constituent, ii. 313
Matter of, ii. 322, 323
Mind and soul of, ii. 326
Monads, or, iv. 55
Motion, in, ii. 225
Movements and position of, iii. 85
Nebulae to, bond uniting, ii. 322
Nebulous, iii. 255
Occult influence on individuals, have, ii. 371, 373
Physical constitution of, ii. 318
Planets, and, iii. 92
Principle, animating, i. 176; v. 241
Religious house, a, ii. 302
Renovations of earth, connected, iv. 353
Revelation in, iii. 354; v. 313
Rishis of, i. 248
Rites, v. 313
Ritual for spirits of, i. 182
Rulers of, ii. 127
Self-moving, ii. 395
Seven, v. 202
,, Angels of, v. 320
,, Original were not planetary, v. 202
,, Sons of Light are called, ii. 296
Shadows, enshrined in, iv. 55
Souls of, v. 324-328
Spirits, abode of, v. 225, 238
Spirits, of, i. 165, 186; v. 225, 238, 333
Sun and, ii. 323

STARS (*Contd.*)
Sun-God and knowledge of, iii. 61
Symbolism, of, v. 309—317
Telescopes, within range of, iv. 277
Twenty-four, judges of the World, v. 332
Universe, of, i. 330
Variable, iv. 54
Walking and numberless, ii. 153
Wisdom descends from, iii. 366
Worlds, not known as, iv. 273
Worship of, v. 219, 309, 325
STAR-STONE, the, iii. 341
STAR-STUFF, seen from the earth, i. 137
STAR-TRANSFORMATION, ii. 321
STAR-WORSHIPPERS, Chaldean, iv. 20; v. 219
Sabaeans, iv. 20
STAR-YAZATAS of Zoroastrians, iii. 357
STATE Religion, v. 121
STATES of Consciousness, v. 362, 429, 538, 539, 540, 542, 544, 548
Matter, of, v. 453, 454
STATUE, Buddha of, at Dardu, v. 394
Exhumed in Pacific States, v. 43
Gilding of colossal, iii. 339
Hygeia, of, iii. 140
Idol or Pillar, v. 237
Liberty, of, iii. 337
Shiva, of, iv. 163
STATUES, Archaic, iii. 296; iv. 262
Astral, iii. 103
Bamian, iii. 228, 336, 337, 338
Easter island, iii. 227, 228, 317, 327, 331, 336, 337, 339; iv. 127
Egyptian kings, of, iii. 368; iv. 319
Esoteric teaching, an imperishable record of, iii. 339
Gigantic, iii. 331
Gods, to, iii. 390
Initiates, work of, iii. 339
Lemuro-Atlanteans, of the, iii. 316
Lord Tathāgata, made to represent, iii. 339
Mountains of Kaf, in, iii. 395
Svastika on, of Buddha, iv. 157
Tel-loh, at, iii. 230; iv. 262
STAURIDIUM, Medusa and, iii. 184
STAUROS or cross as a type of Horus, iv. 158
STELLAR, Firmament, phenomena in, ii. 323
Heptanomis, ii. 125
Spheres, iii. 380
Spirits, i. 247
Systems, phalanx of active, i. 204
Temples, iii. 351
STELLARS or planets, seven, i. 245
STELLATE crystals of snow, iv. 166
STEM, Root Race or, iii. 432
STENOPS, Loris or, iv. 237
STERILITY, Bestiality, only present result of, iii. 200
Hybrids, of, iii. 288
Karmic, iv. 349
Races, of worn-out, iv. 349
Sinful intercourse, resulted from, iii. 198
Species, in wild, iv. 217
Tasmanian tribe, of a, iii. 201
STEVENSON, R. L., referred to, v. 500

STEWART, Prof., Balfour, quoted, ii. 208; iv. 221
Dugald, Max Müller and Co., on, iii. 440
STHĀVARA and Jangama, ii. 173
STHŪLA *Sharīra*, iv. 168; v. 208
Ākāsha's, iv. 186
Annamayakosha, or, i. 212
Differentiated condition, or, ii. 246
Physical body, or, i. 209, 269, 287, 304; ii. 344
Universe, of sevenfold Kosmos, ii. 322
Upādhi, or basis of the principle, i. 212
STIGMATA, wounds or, iv. 131
STIRLING, Dr. J. H., referred to, ii. 359, 362
STOCKHOLM, Great fire at, v. 147
STOCKWELL, quoted, iii. 149, 152
STOICS, Catastrophes, belief of, in, iv. 353
Interpretation of, ii. 111
Zeno, founded of, i. 143
STONE(S) Animated, iii. 341, 342
Books of, v. 89
Corner-, v. 44, 287
Cup-like markings on, iii. 345
Guardian Wall of, v. 467
Key-, v. 44
Monuments, v. 341
Oracular, iii. 340, 341
Peter, of, at Simonium, v. 134
Philosophers v. 467
Poem on, attributed to Orpheus, iii. 341
Precious, iii. 395, 424; v. 240, 530
Rejected, v. 44, 217, 237
Rocking, iii. 343, 344, 345, 346, 347
Sun-, v. 217
Tablets, v. 140, 245
Walking and talking, iii. 340, 342
Zodiac and twelve, v. 241
STONE-AGE, Engravings of, the, iv. 284, 288, 289
Men in, iv. 251
Writing in, iii. 439
STONE-ATOM, Human Monad in the, iii. 192
STONE-FIELD Slates, the Oxfordshire, iii. 202
STONEHENGE, iii. 80, 341, 342, 344, 378; iv. 321, 323; v. 47, 48, 340
STORM, lords of the, iii. 425
STORM-DRAGONS, black, iii. 423
STORM-GODS, Indra deserted by, iv. 66
Maruts or, iii. 391; iv. 184
STORM-HAMMER, Svastika is Miölnir or, iii. 107
STORMS, the God of, iii. 352
STOTRA, prayers or, ii. 139
STRABO, quoted, iii. 18, 367, 389; iv. 329, 350; v. 58, 254, 267, 290, 391
STRACHOF, N. N., quoted, iv. 224
STRAIGHT-EYE, Men of the, iii. 426
STRAIGHT-HAIRED, races, iii. 328
STRAIT-GATE, Jesus, alluded to by, ii. 30
Kingdom of Heaven, of, iv. 119
King's chamber, to, ii. 30
STRANGULATION, urea increased in blood during, i. 294
STRATTON, Dr., quoted, iv. 194
STRAUSS, quoted, v. 53
STRAWS, the divining, ii. 159
STREAMERS, Northern, the, ii. 346

STRIDES, Fohat, of, i. 180
  Three and seven, i. 171
  Vishnu, of, iv. 193
STRIFE-MAKER, Kali-Kāraka or, iii. 60
  Nārada surnamed, ii. 130
STRING, terrestrial chain or, i. 217
STRINGS, globes, of, i. 220
  Heptachord of the, i. 221
STROBIC circles, iv. 161
STRONGEST, survival of the, iv. 43
STRONTIUM, ii. 276
STRUGGLE, Existence, for, iii. 300; iv. 218, 232
  Life, for, i. 209, 252; ii. 134; iii. 256; iv. 229
STUDY of Man, v. 181
STUFF, Force or incorporeal, ii. 232
  Protyle not primary, ii. 322
STYGIAN Lakes, v. 154
STYLI on Fourth Dynasty monuments, v. 58
SUB-ASTRAL, Miniature of itself, iii. 126
  Sphere of action, iv. 192
SUB-ATOMS, particles or, ii. 244
SUBBA ROW, quoted, i. 188, 194, 211, 333;
  ii. 64; iii. 311, 318; iv. 147; v. 185
SUB-CONSCIOUS intelligence pervading
  matter, iv. 219
SUB-COSMIC mysteries, i. 221
SUB-ELEMENTS, Chemistry, of, ii. 181
  Divine essences, from, ii. 349
  Earth, unknown to our, ii. 397
  Materialism, of, ii. 346
SUBHĀVA from which is Svabhāvat, i. 130
SUB-HUMAN Entities, iii. 290
SUBJUGATION, Body, of, v. 543, 544, 545
SUBMERSION, Atlantis, of, iii. 132, 148, 149,
  268, 307, 314, 351; iv. 208, 322
  Continents, of, iii. 252, 421
  Plato's Atlantic island, of, iii. 21, 252, 314
  Polar lands, of, iii. 359
SUBMERSIONS, Destructions, and, iii. 443
  Foretelling, ii. 376
  North Polar, iii. 327
SUBMERGED continents, ii. 34; iii. 307, 316,
  332, 336, 392; iv. 177, 294, 347 et seq.
SUB-MOLECULES, ii. 349
SUBMUNDANE Gods, the, ii. 154
SUBNATURAL evolution, the, i. 229
SUBNUCLEI, two, iii. 173
SUB-PHYSICAL, Kingdoms, elemental, iv. 306
  Stages, i. 229
SUB-PLANETARY Monads, ii. 344
SUB-RACE(S), Aryan of, iv. 312
  Atlanteans, of, iii. 154; iv. 312
  Australians low, of Lemurians, iii. 202
  Books of Enoch and, v. 102
  Branches, and, iii. 203
  Cleansing process for all, iii. 330
  Continent, which perished with the Lemurian,
    iii. 278
  Cycles of every, iii. 302
  Descending arc, still on the, iii. 302
  Fifth, our race has reached, iv. 39
  Fifth root race, of, ii. 183, 334; iii. 431, 433;
    v. 106
  Fourth Humanity, of the, iii. 185, 230; iv. 169
  Fourth Race, of, v. 121
  Germs of sixth, iii. 442
  Hebrew Semite, a small, iv. 38

  History of, preserved, iii. 421
  Intermediate race, evolved an, iii. 277
  Kings of, Atlanto-Aryan, iv. 319
  Lemurians, of, iii. 317
  Lemurians, one-eyed giants were last, of,
    iv. 338
  Mother-races, and, iv. 337
  Nascent simplicity of first, iv. 353
  Nations, and, iii. 441
  Preceding, of our race, iii. 432
  Race, of present, iv. 189
  Races and, overlap, iii. 432
  Root-race and, iii. 331, 396, 431, 440; iv. 186;
    v. 102
  Second race, of, iii. 126
  Seventh, iii. 443
  Sixth, iii. 154, 443
  Special, our own, ii. 134
  Third humanity, of, iii. 140
  Third race, of, iii. 179, 203
  Tropical year, for each, iii. 444
  Yuga may mean, iii. 155
SUB-ROOT, Ākāsha called the, i. 78
SUBSTANCE, Deity's own, v. 91, 187
  Divine Essence, v. 227
  Eternal one, v. 208
  Ether differntiated, v. 475
  Evolving, v. 423
  Matter as, v. 449
  Undifferentiated, v. 448
  Universe of, v. 425
  Septenary, v. 522
  Spirit, and, v. 477
  Tattvas, Force and, v. 469
SUBSTANTIALISTS, American, i. 201; ii. 289
SUBTERRANEAN, Cave of initiation, iv. 128
  Convulsions, iii. 314
  Crypts, iii. 378; v. 253
  Fires, iii. 268, 316
  India, cities in, iii. 224
  Passages, iii. 427
  Stores of Tibet, i. 55
  World, king of, ii. 184
SUBTILE, Vāsudeva corporeal and, i. 328
SUBTLE BODIES, Five, ii. 335
  Kalpa, at beginning of, ii. 87
  Man, of, v. 561
  Progenitors, projected by, iii. 101
SU-DYUMNA, Idā or Ilā becomes, iii. 143, 151,
  155
SUETONIUS quoted, v. 134
SŪFI (S), Arabic word, iii. 428; v. 180
  Ātma-Vidyā called by, Rohanee, i. 249
  Initiates, i. 329
  Mystics, iii. 247
  Persian, v. 180
SUHHAB, the God, iii. 19
SUIDAS, quoted, i. 327; ii. 381; iii. 342; iv. 190
SŪKSHMA, Latent or undifferentiated, ii. 246
  Sharīra, i. 190
  Solar system, form of, i. 195
  Subtle matter, v. 480
SŪKSHMOPĀDHI, Manas and Kāma Rūpa,
  ii. 212
SULIMANS or Solomons, iii. 395
SULPHUR, ii. 274; iii. 122, 312
SUM of forces, v. 49

SUMATI, son of Bhārata, iii. 321
SUMATRA, iii. 20, 226
SUMERU Mount, v. 110
SUMMER, correspondences of, v. 444
SUMMIT of Manifestation, Fire is, v. 445
SUM TOTAL, Aum called, i. 204
  Buddhis, the, i. 179
  Energies, of, i. 152
  Eternity, that exist from, i. 111
  Stanza on, i. 179
  Tetragrammaton sidereal, ii. 156
  Twice seven, the, i. 152
SUN, Abraxas, iv. 42; v. 129
  Adonaï, genius of, ii. 301; iv. 108; v. 314
  Adoration of, ii. 375; v. 314
  Affrighted, iv. 326
  Age of, ii. 225; iii. 22, 76, 157
  Agni, son of, iv. 138
  Aldebaran in conjunction with, iv. 354
  All-Seeing God, v. 276
  Angel of, iii. 381; v. 314
  Apollo is, iii. 20, 130, 184, 382
  Atman of the, v. 421
  Atmosphere of, ii. 320
  Atoms become, i. 165
  Axis of, movement of, ii. 225
  Bel, or, iii. 73; v. 312
  Bel-Jupiter and Baal, v. 285
  Birth of new, i. 126
  Birthplace of, iv. 117
  Born daily, iii. 79
  Breath of, i. 254
  Brothers of, i. 314
  Caloric energy of, ii. 242
  Caloric flowing from, ii. 248
  Candidate awakened by, iv. 128
  Capricornus enters, iv 147
  Castor and Pollux nothing but, and moon, iii. 132
  Central, i. 79, 151, 162, 250, 277, 299, 319; ii. 251, 298, 363, 397; iii. 122, 218, 241, 243; v. 218, 219, 277
  Central Star, is, v. 219, 277, 439, 441
  Changes in course of, iii. 371
  Chemical composition of, ii. 252
  Children of, iv. 75
  Christ, is, v. 211, 276
  Chromosphere of, ii. 307
  Colour of, v. 441, 456
  Colour of plants and, ii. 304
  Conjunction of, and moon, iii. 433
  Conjunction of moon, earth and, iii. 85
  Constitution of, ii. 307
  Correspondences of, v. 437, 439, 441
  Cosmic space, evolved from, i. 163
  Course of, calculated, iii. 368
  Creation of, iii. 153
  Creation of life by, i. 334
  Cross, and, iv. 128
  Crucifixion before, iv. 131
  Cruciform lathe, crucified on a, ii. 35
  Dayanisi or, ii. 113
  Day-star, and, i. 299
  Deity-symbol of, iv. 155; v. 116
  Disk of, iv. 129
  Divine, iii. 360
  Divine spirit symbolized by, iii. 121
  Dragon and, ii. 123; iii. 377, 379
  Dual aspect of, v. 285
  Eclipse of spiritual, iii. 252
  Effect on Humanity, of, v. 536
  Eight brilliant, i. 162
  Elect of the, v. 159
  El-El or, ii. 184
  Emblem of Deity, v. 154
  Emblem of Soul, v. 269
  Eternal, land of, iii. 24
  Ether from, ii. 251
  Ether of space and, v. 423
  Evil spirits and, iii. 385
  Evil under, i. 181
  Explosion of, ii. 224
  Eye of Jupiter, v. 276
  Eye of Ormuzd, v. 276, 314
  Eye of Osiris, is, iii. 38; v. 314
  Father, iv. 110
  Feminine with Semitic races, ii. 112
  Fire we call, ii. 250
  Fohat set in operation by, i. 250
  Freemasonry, in, v. 284
  Fuel of, ii. 309
  Gandharva of *Rig Veda* personified, iv. 157
  Garuda, emblem of, iv. 135
  Gauls, was Bel with, iv. 110
  Genius between, and moon, iii. 41
  Genius, of, iv. 110
  Globe, occult relations of, to our, ii. 298, 299
  Globe of fire, ii. 315
  Globe's position in relation to, iv. 104
  Glowworm and, law same for, i. 200
  Gnostics, an emblem of, iii. 213
  God, highest, iii. 360
  -God, the, v. 94, 311, 315
  God, vehicle of, ii. 201
  Golden egg resplendent, i. 153
  Growth of, ii. 333
  Hawk represented, iv. 128
  Heat of, ii. 207
  Heaven, in, v. 153
  Helios, or, iii. 55
  Heliopolis or On, City of, v. 266
  Hermes, description of, i. 334
  Hindu Trimūrti and, v. 117
  Hiram Abif is, v. 272, 273
  Holy island, beyond, iii. 371
  Hor, rising, ii. 82
  Hyperborean, God, iv. 339
  Hyperborean land, and, iii. 24
  Iamblichus and, v. 277
  Immobility of, i. 176
  Incandescent, fallacious conception of an, i. 204
  Initiate, v. 108, 269-274
  Initiation, and, iv. 127; v. 272
  Initiation of, iii. 380; v. 217, 275-278
  Invisible, i. 331
  Invocation to, iii. 35
  Jatāyu turns his back on, iv. 141
  Jews worshipping, ii. 113
  Judge, called, ii. 113
  Jupiter, guardian of, ii. 216
  Kabbalistic, v. 219
  Kadush or, ii. 184
  Kārtikeya bright as, iv. 120
  Krishna, incarnated, iii. 405

SUN (*Contd.*)
La Cailles, tables for, ii. 386
Latona giving birth to, iv. 339
Life, and death, giving, v. 285
  ,, and light, dependence on, for, i. 254
  ,, fire of, or, iii. 115
  ,, -Giver, ii. 111, 203; v. 161
  ,, of, iv. 151
  ,, Source of, ii. 255
Light created before, i. 298
  ,, Supreme being of, ii. 396
  ,, Wisdom, of, iii. 237
Logos, stands for, i. 173, 192; ii. 146; v. 322
Lord of the Heavens, v. 129
Magnet, a, ii. 220, 222
Mahārajās, one of the Four, v. 439
Makara, and, ii. 91; iv. 151
Male emblem, iii. 76
Male-female deity, ii. 115
Manvantara, a new, with a new, ii. 382
Mārtānda, the, ii. 167, 350
Masonic Symbol, v. 284
Material Sun, manifested symbol of true, v. 218
Matter composing, ii. 326
Māyā, is, i. 317
Mercury and, iii. 40, 41; iv. 49, 112, 276
Michael angel of, iii. 380
Mind and soul of, ii. 326
Mirror of fire, is, v. 218
Mithra, and, iv. 175
Moon, and, i. 275; ii. 93; iii. 73, 76, 132, 329; iv. 122; v. 339, 442
Most High, is, iv. 108; v. 313
Music of Spheres, and, iv. 172
Mystery Gods, chief of, iii. 35
Mystery of, v. 217, 218
Mystic rays of, ii. 240
No new thing under, iv. 273
Neïth, first-born of, ii. 114
Nucleus, said to have no, iii. 144
Occult philosophy and, ii. 264
Oeaohoo shines forth as, i. 138
One circle, was, i. 173
One existence and, i. 332
One rejected, of our system, i. 161
Organisms in, ii. 253
Origin of, ii. 319
Ormuzd-Ahriman is, v. 285
Ormuzd is, i. 173
Osiris is, ii. 103, 105; iii. 384; iv. 151, 154, 155; v. 159, 161, 238, 273, 276, 312
Osiris-Typhon is, v. 285
Our Lord the, v. 328
Palaces of, iii. 44
Path of, iii. 355
People who cursed, iv. 331
Perfect Number, v. 423
Phaeton and, iv. 104
Philosophical, ii. 126
Phta, Emepth or, v. 310
Pilot, in a ship as its, ii. 126
Pisces, entering, ii. 379
Planets, and, i. 162, 255; ii. 201, 313, 321; iii. 36; iv. 29, 174; v. 324, 535
Planetary system, gives life to, ii. 102
Plato on, v. 277
Poetical symbol as, iv. 27

Pole, loss of, at, iv. 338
Postulant in mysteries represented, iv. 30
Priests of, iii. 322
Principle or Prāna, i. 287
Pueblos, said to adore, iii. 188
Ra, and, i. 274; ii. 75
Rāhu and, iii. 380
Rays of, iii. 118; iv. 182
Real, hidden, ii. 264
Realm of, iv. 159
Reflection, v. 535
Regulator and factor of manifested life, iv. 166
Rejected Son our, i. 162
Revolution of our planet round, ii. 366
Righteousness of, ii. 113, 382; v. 153, 247, 276, 312
Robes, of, outward, ii. 252
Ruler of men, called, ii. 113
Sāmba built a temple to, iii. 322, 323
Sanjnā married to, iii. 181
Saturn and, iii. 73
Sea of fire, iii. 247
Second, v. 270
Sentient life shown in atom and, desire for a, i. 116
Sephirothal Crown and, v. 439
Set, twice risen where it then, ii. 153
Setting, of life,.ii. 398
Seven-branched candelabra and, v. 313, 314, 316
Seven rays of, iv. 341; v. 423
Seven Principle, v. 154
Shuchi, spirit in, iii. 110
Sirius, and, iv. 278
Sky, and, i. 138
Socrates saluted rising, v. 277
Solar Gods, the, ruled by highest, ii. 153
Solar world, is heart of, ii. 264
Solomon refers to, iv. 123
Solus became Sol, or, iv. 146
Sons of, i. 138; iii. 118; v. 312
Soul of Gods, iv. 148
Soul's spiritual, iv. 210
Source of generation, ii. 194
Spectrum of, i. 199
Spirit of, ii. 201, 222; iii. 41, 369; v. 216, 313
Spiritual, ii. 203; iii. 36; iv. 179, 210; v. 219, 277, 462, 486
Star, a central, i. 162
Stars, and, ii. 323
Statue of God, v. 312
Stomach of, insatiable, i. 252
Storehouse of Electricity, v. 220
Substitute for secret planet, v. 433
Sūrya or, ii. 251; iii. 110, 149; iv. 129, 176; v. 111, 270, 322
Sūryamandala region of, i. 190
Sweat warmed by, iii. 139
Symbol of, dragon, iii. 379
Symbol of God, v. 312
Symbolism, in ancient, ii. 363
Symbolism of, v. 269, 270, 289, 309-317
System, centre of our, iii. 161
Taurus, in, v. 267
Temple of, iii. 323; iv. 175
Temples, and, iii. 378; v. 217
Ten numbers of, v. 423

SUN (*Contd.*)
Theban triad, in, iv. 32
Thompson on age of, iii. 157
Three in one, v. 218
Time measurer, as, iv. 192
Trinity, v. 217
Triple, v. 217, 315
True, v. 535
Type, as, ii. 129; v. 272
Understanding, is, iv. 210
Underworld, at night in, ii. 16
Universal, i. 271
Universal, or Ormazd, the, i. 173
Universe, of, i. 164
Venus and, ii. 317
Vessel of the Most High, v. 313
Vikartana or, iii. 380
Vishnu and, ii. 86; iii. 50, 147
Vishnu Purāna on, iii. 162
Visible, v. 218, 277, 535
Vital electric principle in, iii. 113
Vital heat and, ii. 328
Vital principle of, ii. 252
Winter with, in Cancer, iii. 429
Wisdom, of, iii. 41; v. 277
Word of central, i. 277
" Word " or, v. 277
Worship, i. 179; ii. 104, 117; iv. 341; v. 316, 317
Year, meant a, iii. 293
Zuni, priest of, iv. 200
SUN-BORN, Apollo Karneios, iii. 55
SUN-CHAN, term used in Stanzas, i. 87
SUN-CHRIST, iii. 104, 116
SUNDA, Island and Straits of, iii. 226; iv. 355, 357
SUNDAY, v. 151, 433, 435, 436
Ought to be called Uranus-day, i. 162
Religion confined to, v. 70
SUN-FLUIDS, ii. 254
SUN-FORCE, Caloric, or, ii. 249
Earth-force, and, ii. 248, 251, 255
Life and motion, primal cause of, ii. 253
Material nature of, ii. 250
Matter, received by different kinds, of, ii. 250
Richardson, on, ii. 233, 255
Vital-force connected with, ii. 261, 262
SUN-GOD(S), Æsculapius, iv. 31
Apollo, ii. 83; iii. 215, 381
Comparison of, iii. 380
Creative power, of, iii. 385
Evil dragon conquered by, iii. 64
Honover or, Eternal, v. 315
Horus, ii. 82, 83
India to Egypt, came from, iii. 378
Knowledge of stars and, iii. 61
Krishna, i. 65; v. 311
Later, and seven souls, iv. 204
Male Gods first became, iii. 55
Merodach was, iv. 23, 71
Osiris, ii. 94, 383
Ptah classed as, ii. 68
Serpent symbol of, iii. 216
Sōters or, v. 94
Supreme deity everywhere, iii. 148
Sūrya, iii. 78
Systems, in exoteric, iii. 380
Universes had nothing to do with, iii. 38

SUN-INITIATE, iv. 113; v. 270-274
SUN-OSIRIS, iv. 128
SUNS, Forty, expiration of, iii. 293
Life, of, iii. 242
Nebulous, iii. 255
Planet and, v. 535
Physical, i. 330
Righteousness, of, iii. 55; v. 153
Secondary, iii. 242
Self-moving, ii. 395
Seven, iv. 183
Vital soul of, ii. 326
SUN-SPOT Phenomena, ii. 265
SUN-VISHNU, Seven rays of, ii. 248
SUN-WOLF, Mercury called, iii. 41
SUN-WORSHIPPERS, Parsīs, regular, ii. 104
SUNG Sages of China, iv. 124
SUNG-MING-SHŪ, or Tree of Knowledge, iii. 219
SUNKEN continents, iii. 268
SUNLIGHT, Pressure of, ii. 239
SUOYATAR and serpent of evil, iii. 39
SUPER-ASTRAL Light, i. 142
SUPER-COSMIC, Monas, ii. 344
Mysteries, i. 221
SUPER-ETHEREAL link, i. 247
SUPER-HUMAN, Atlantis, powers of inhabitants of, iv. 333
Beings, not supernatural, iii. 200
Creator, iv. 182
Kings, iii. 368
Lha, any, being, iii. 35
SUPERNATURAL, Beings, ii. 400; iii. 199; iv. 182
Nature, implies above or outside, ii. 279
Phenomenon, iv. 202, 222
Pretensions to, iv. 202
Super-human, not, iii. 200
SUPERNATURALISM, Christian theology and, iii. 53
Seeming, iii. 16
Wise men, rejected by, iv. 202
SUPERSENSIBLE, Essence of, Ākāsha, ii. 240
SUPERSENSUAL world, ii. 235; v. 436
SUPERSENSUOUS Beings, ii. 349
Effects, i. 201
Energy, forms of, ii. 306
Entitites, Gods or, ii. 243
Essence, sublimated, i. 325
Forces, ii. 239
Matter, i. 250
Regions, i. 279
Spiritual eye, ii. 239
States, matter existing in, ii. 239
States of matter, i. 199, 202; ii. 239
Substances, yet atomic, i. 148
World, ii. 340
SUPER-SPIRIT, Atma is, v. 438
SUPER-SPIRITUAL, Lunar Dhyāni, i. 239
Noumenal, or, iv. 192
Planes, ii. 136
Worlds, i. 230
SUPERSTITION, Ancient sages accused of, ii. 187; v. 88, 97, 250
Christians and, v. 97
Devils of, iii. 233
Dogmatic religion, of, iii. 113

SVASTIKA (*Contd.*)
  Serpent of eternity, on, ii. 127
  Sūrya bound on, iv. 129
  Symbol in India, most sacred, iii. 107; iv. 157
  Tau and, iv. 127
  Wan, now, iv. 126
  Water, pouring through, iii. 44
  World-symbol, as, iv. 158
SVAYAMBHŪ, or universal spirit, i. 123
SVAYAMBHŪ-NĀRĀYANA, the self-existent, iii. 137
SVĀYAMBHUVĀ, Manu and self-manifest, i. 293; ii. 90; iii. 137, 156, 311, 312, 321, 326, 369
SWĀMĪ DAYĀNAND SARASVATĪ, i. 53; ii. 75
SWAN, Darkness, in, ii. 275
  Double, ii. 72
  Eternal, or Kālahamsa, i. 84
  Eternity, of, ii. 74, 77; iv. 33
  Hansa, i. 145
  Leda assumes shape of a white, iii. 130
  Life, of, ii. 273
  Priapic, of Leda not, ii. 73
  Rosecroix, symbol of, i. 146
  Space name of Brahmā, in, ii. 75
  Vehicle used by Brahman, i. 85
SWANS of Myorica, iii. 341
SWANWICK, Mrs. Annie, quoted, iii. 410, 417
SWEAT, Animals first produced from, iii. 187
  Drops of, grew, iii. 139
  Earth, animals produced from, of, iii. 349
  Shiva, of, iii. 55, 133
  Third race formed from, iii. 184
  Torments, of their, ii. 301; iv. 176
SWEAT-BORN, Androgynes and, iii. 184
  Astral bodies, progenitors of, 146
  Chhāyā of, v. 553
  Commentary on, iii. 329
  Egg-born, produced, iii. 179
  Evolution of, iii. 139
  Evolvers of, ii. 175
  Fathers of, iii. 125, 126
  Hermaphrodites descended from, iii. 43, 184
  Mānasa spurned, iii. 178
  Mārishā, iii. 182
  Progeny of first race, iii. 130
  Purānas, in, iii. 181
  Second or, race, iii. 153, 172, 180, 339
  Secret doctrine and, iii. 189
  Third race, of, iii. 78, 202, 203
SWEDEN, Atlantis of Plato, said to be, iii. 401
  Pre-Lemurian continent, part of, iv. 344
  Runic writings in, iii. 346
  Shores of, have risen, iv. 355
SWEDENBORG, Element vortices and theory of, i. 177; v. 282, 528
  Fire of Stockholm and, v. 147
  Mercury and, iv. 272
  Mysticism of, iii. 54
  Quoted, ii. 347, 348; iii. 45; iv. 270
  Seer, v. 407, 429
  Spirits of, v. 406
SWEDISH scientist, iii. 401
SWIFT and radiant one, i. 195
SWISS cattle, Descent of modern, iii. 289
SWORD of Damocles, and Church, v. 94

SYDIC, Sadic, Kronos or Saturn, iii. 390, 391, 392
  Seven sons of, v. 202
SYENE, Well of, i. 257
SYLLA, Augurs, in days of, iv. 87
SYLLABLE, sacred, v. 395, 418
SYLPHS, ii. 330; v. 239, 540, 566
SYMBOL(S), Abstractions, represents, ii. 340
  Active side of Nature, Fire is, v. 445
  Adam-Adami a manifold, iii. 54
  Adam of dust, of, iv. 25
  Adami manifold, iv. 19
  Allegorical, of pentacle and curtain, i. 183
  Ancient, iii. 48
  Ankh or life, for, iii. 43
  Ante-Christian, Gnostic, iv. 25
  Anthropomorphized, generative, iv. 77
  Aquatic, of elements, iv. 149
  Archaic, ii. 339; iii. 105
  Ark, of the female generative principle, iii. 147
  Arkite, iii. 150, 151
  Āryan religion did not rest on physiological, i. 175
  Astoreth, of nature, iv. 30
  Astronomical, ii. 377; iii. 130; iv. 118, 190
  Atlas, of the fourth race, iv. 62
  Bible astronomical, ii. 377
  Bible, of, v. 206
  Bird, of an enormous, iv. 189
  Bi-sexual man, of, iii. 139
  Borrowed, iv. 49
  Candlesticks, of, v. 313, 316, 320, 321
  Castor and Pollux, of brotherly devotion, iii. 132
  Cat, of moon, iv. 122
  Chaldean form of, iv. 22
  Chinese characters, of, v. 118
  Christian, iv. 31; v. 94, 95, 117, 162, 163, 164, 288
  Church fathers disfigure, iii. 107
  Circle and its diameter, of, iv. 107, 123, 124
  Confucius, of, ii. 158
  Conventional, ii. 340
  Convertible, v. 72
  Cosmic Gods, of, ii. 183
  Cosmical significance, ii. 18
  Cosmo-Astronomical, of Abram, v. 111
  Cosmogonical, iii. 54
  Cow as, iii. 416
  Creation, of, v. 210
  Creative God, Jehovistic, ii. 69
  Creative triad, of, i. 321
  Cross, of, iv. 111, 113, 116, 117, 127, 131, 152, 153, 157, 158; v. 152, 159, 161
  Cube a, of angelic beings, iii. 88
  Cycle, of racial, ii. 135
  Deity, of, ii. 173; ii. 60
  Diamond, many faced, ii. 17
  Divine, iii. 398
    ,,   Cross, a, iv. 153
    ,,   Earthly wisdom, of, and, iii. 375
  Double-sexed organ, iv. 41
  Dove and Lamb, of, v. 246
  Draco, of guide and director, iii. 44
  Dragons of, iii. 214, 378, 379
  Eastern Books of, v. 73
  E Delphicum, iv. 152

SYMBOL(S) (*Contd.*)
Egyptian cross and circle, of, iv. 117
Egyptian in *New Testament*, ii. 99
Elements, of spirit, ii. 181
Emblem, and, ii. 17
Esoteric, in every national religion, ii. 160
  ,,   Teaching needs, iii. 90
  ,,   Truth expressed in identical, iv. 151
Eternal law, of an, ii. 379
Eternal Monad does not stand as a, iv. 170
Evolution of universe, of, iii. 337
Explanation of chief, ii. 20
Facts, are, ii. 113
Female principle, of the, iv. 30
Fohat, i. 171; iii. 397
Forest for man's lifetime, iv. 209
Four-lettered, iii. 38
Generation and, v. 85
Generation, of, i. 276; iv. 38; v. 210
Generative and creative power, iii. 133; v. 238
Geometrical, ii. 337
Globe, number six, of our, iv. 152, 155
Glyphs, become, i. 110
God and nature, of, iii. 359
Hair, of, iv. 196
Hermes-Mercury, of, iv. 112
Hexagon, creation and generation of, v. 210
Hidden deity, of, ii. 64
Hieroglyphic, v. 113
Hindu and Chaldean religions, iii. 382
Holy of Holies, of, iv. 36, 37
Human existence, of, iv. 126
  ,,   Monad cannot be rendered by
        chemical, constitution of, i. 230
  ,,   Races, of, iv. 52
Hydrogen, iii. 114
Idea-language and, ii. 20
Identical meaning of, ii. 99
Ideographs, iv. 155
Imaginary and feminine, iv. 123
Immortality of, v. 238
India, transplanted from, iii. 219
Initiates, for, iv. 64
Injustice, of eternal, i. 268
International, iv. 36, 125
Interpretation to, iii. 35
Jehovah, of, iii. 386; iv. 110
Jewish exoteric, v. 165
Jod, forefinger and Lingam, of, iii. 134
Kārtikeya, of, iv. 190
Kosmos, of evolution, of, ii. 158
Latin Church and, v. 55
Life and power, of, iii. 44
Life, Ashvattha tree, of, iv. 210
Lingam, of, iii. 134; iv. 118
Logos, of, i. 262
Lotus, of, ii. 94; iv. 40; v. 117, 421, 453
Lunar, ii. 110
Male and female principles, of, iii. 42
Male, figure four is, i. 110
Marriage formerly a, ii. 340
Master, examined by, ii. 19
Mathematical, v. 233, 292
Matter, of, ii. 344
Meaning, more than one, v. 85
Mercury in Grecian Mythology, of, iii. 41
Misconceived, iv. 364

Moon as, i. 275; iii. 414; iv. 32
Mundane egg, of, ii. 74
Mundane fire, Mithras, of, iii. 139
Mystic nature, cow's horns, of, iii. 44
Names are, v. 86, 87
Nature, Language taught by, ii. 33
  ,,   of, v. 293
  ,,   Profaned, of, iv. 39
Nucleus of truth concealed by, ii. 187
Number seven, of life eternal, iv. 154
Numerals of Pythagoras, were, ii. 76
Occult have spiritual meaning, v. 443
Occult sciences, used in, iv. 106
Ogdoad, of, iv. 152
One principle, of, ii. 144
Ophidian, iii. 354, 385
Orientalists misunderstand, iv. 140
Origin of measures, of cross, iv. 129
P, of paternity, iv. 145
Paganism, classical, of, iii. 267
Pagans, of, i. 140; v. 175, 293
Past, present and future, of, ii. 343
Patriarchs are, iii. 390
Pentacle, of our five root races, i. 183
Pentagon, of man, iv. 148
Perfect man, a, i. 292
Personification of, iv. 129; v. 462
Phallic, i. 174; ii. 194; iii. 55, 72, 94, 189,
        363; iv. 33, 131, 155; v. 187, 233, 292
Physical generation of, v. 234
Physiological, ii. 109; iv. 155
Pillow of Jacob, v. 166
Pisces, a, ii. 379
Pork, Apple, Rice, Geese, Eggs, of, v. 105, 246
Powers, of, iii. 385
Presence, of abstract, i. 69
Primary signification of, iv. 202
Psycho-physiological, significance of, ii. 18
Pyramid, of, ii. 242; iii. 366; v. 92, 117
Pythagorean, iv. 123; v. 113
Quaternary, of, iv. 147, 168
Ram's head and horns of, iii. 189
Religious, i. 139, 286; iv. 108, 190; v. 291, 407
Ritualistic worship, of, iii. 57
Rose, of, v. 292, 293
Sacr' marks on, iv. 33
Sacred, v. 238
Sacred and secret knowledge of, i. 187
Sarcophagus as, iv. 28, 30
Sarpa, v. 238
Scarabaeus, of human life, iv. 122
Second race of mankind, for, iii. 182
Secret cycle and initiation, of, iv. 188
Semi-savage tribes, used by, iii. 436
Serpent, of immortality, v. 238
Sexual significance of, iv. 96; v. 292
Sidereal, iv. 121
Similarity of Pagan and Christian, ii. 126
Solar and lunar years, of, iii. 390; v. 129
Space, chaos, theos, kosmos, of, ii. 58
Spirit, of, ii. 72
Spores of science, of, iii. 178
Square, of four sacred forces, i. 192
Svastika, of, iii. 107, 108, 109; v. 206
Steps are, i. 172
Sun, of, iii. 50, 121; v. 284
Superstition, of, iv. 317

SYMBOL(S) (*Contd.*)
  Survival or, iv. 118
  Swan as, ii. 72
  Tau of, iv. 160, 163
  Temporary aids only, in spiritual Occultism, v. 464
  Tetraktys dual, iii. 37
    ,,   Ten Jods of, v. 420
  Threefold meaning of occult, v. 443
  Three Mothers, of, v. 87
  Titan, of finite reason, iii. 410
  Tree, for man, v. 510
  Trees, of, v. 510
  Triadic and tetradic, iv. 174
  Triangle, of, i. 172, 263; iv. 145
  Tribes of Jacob and Zodiac, of, ii. 377
  Trinity, of, i. 267
  Triple flame, of Shiva, iv. 163
  Truth, of, iv. 171
  Truths, land marks of prehistoric, iv. 346
  Universal, ii. 49, 74; iv. 24; v. 117
  Universal abstract nature, of, iv. 37
  Universal presence, of, iv. 126
  Universality of, ii. 183
  Virāj and Horus, male, iv. 40
  Vowles, five and seven, iv. 26
  Water, of, ii. 177; iii. 75; iv. 136
  Wheat as, iii. 373
  Womb, of, i. 308
  Yoni, of exoteric Hinduism, i. 308
  Zeus, of, iii. 414
SYMBOLICAL, Animals in Taro and Teraphim, v. 111
  Apex of Pyramid, v. 248
  Attributes, iv. 116
  Caduceus, ii. 273
  Consonant, ii. 100
  Creation, accounts of, iii. 91
  Creed, Pagan, iii. 390
  Dance of Planets and signs, v. 310, 311
  Genesis, is, iii. 424; v. 205
  Hieroglyphs, of Kabiri, v. 310
  Holy of Holies, meaning of, ii. 340
  Imagery, iv. 275
  Jewish, v. 91, 201, 212, 318
  Key to allegory of Enoch, iv. 102
  Language, ii. 96, 104, 114; iii. 36; iv. 16, 37, 189
  Light in, sense, iii. 50
  Literature, v. 89
  Lotus, v. 117
  Man, Yima, iv. 180
  Meaning of Bible, v. 97
  Meaning of Pork, Rice, etc., v. 105
  Meaning of Pyramid, v. 91
  Mysteries in nature, figures of greatest, iii. 83
  Mystery language, iv. 145
  Numbers, i. 110
  Personages, iii. 137
  Place, Adytum, iv. 27
  Purānas are, v. 27
  Record of human races, iii. 433
  Records of science, iii. 54
  Sayings of Christianity, v. 136
  Thought, iii. 335
  Upanishads are, v. 4, 27
  White island, name, iii. 78

SYMBOLISM, Antiquity of, iii. 354
  Archaic, iv. 15, 174; v. 293
  Astronomy, and, iii. 428
  Bible of, v. 71
  Buddhist Discipline of, v. 413
  Bull's head of, v. 206
  Chapters on, i. 88
  Circle, of, iv. 120, 123; v. 206
  Colours, Sounds, Numbers, of, v. 421
  Concrete, of egg becomes, ii. 80
  Corner and keystone of all knowledge, v. 44
  Cosmic, iii. 156
  Cross, of, iv. 120, 160
  Dual, v. 85
  East, of, iii. 103; v. 286
  Egyptian, v. 46, 51, 57
  Esoteric, i. 175; ii. 20; iii. 435; v. 26, 111, 443
  Genesis, contained in, iii. 386
  Gnostic, Ophis of, i. 140
  Gnostics, tenets of, based on, iii. 388
  Hebrew letters of, v. 206
  Hexagon, of the, v. 120-123
  Hidden, iv. 36; v. 287
  Hindu, iv. 146; v. 46
  Hindu deities, in names of, i. 155
  Iao and Jehovah, of mystery names, iv. 106 *et seq.*
  Identity of, iv. 200
  Ideographs, and, ii. 15
  Initiates, knowledge, of, iii. 436
  Initiation, of, v. 194
  Inner sense of, iv. 37
  Key to, v. 292
  Keystone of modern knowledge, v. 44
  Language, now called, ii. 21
  Large-eared statues, of, iii. 338
  Magic and, v. 114
  Mahābhārata, of, iv. 64
  Manus and Kabiris, of, ii. 366
  Max Müller's view of, ii. 16
  Mazdean, for Flood, iv. 181
  Measurement and, v. 90
  Mosaic allegories and, iii. 132
  Mother and Nature, v. 293
  Mothers, Three, v. 89
  Mummy, of, v. 248
  Mystery names, of, iv. 36
  Nārada, of, v. 287, 291
  Numbers, of, v. 113, 114, 116, 117, 118, 235, 236
  Occult, i. 134, 135, 316; iii. 376; v. 115, 165, 537
  Ocean of popular, iv. 72
  Œdipuses of, iv. 110
  Old world, of, iv. 115
  Origin of Pagan, iv. 24
  Pātāla, of, v. 286
  Prehistoric races, of, ii. 74
  Primitive, of Kabalistic books, iv. 107
  Progress of, v. 55
  Prometheus, of, iii. 420
  Psycho-metaphysical, iv. 138
  Pyramids, finding expression in, ii. 342
  Pythagoras, of, v. 113, 116, 120
  Recent work, in, ii. 263
  Religious, iii. 354

SYMBOLISM (*Contd.*)
Rishis and Pleiades, of, iv. 121
Rules of, iii. 423
Sacred books veiled in, i. 47; v. 89
Sacred, of reawakening universe, i. 84
Science of Physiology and, v. 292
Septenary in religions, iv. 167
Serpent, dual, v. 85
Serpents and dragons under different,
   iii. 353-355
Seven keys of, iii. 35, 334; iv. 39
Seven-Stringed lyre of, v. 275
Sexual, v. 292
Solar deities, of lunar and, ii. 77
Stages of, i. 110
Stanzas attached to, ii. 179
Sun and Stars, v. 309-317
Sun in, ii. 363
Svastika, of, iii. 107, 108, 109, 110
Theological, v. 326
Traditions that have outgrown, iii. 199
Tree of Life, v. 85
Trees as, v. 510
Triangle, of, ii. 341, 342
Trimurti, v. 101
Trinity, v. 117
Truths revealed to different nations under
   special, i. 58
Universal, iii. 436
Water, deluge, etc., iii. 313
SYMBOLOGICAL, Fallen angels, legend of,
   iii. 276
SYMBOLOGISTS, v. 110, 140, 198
Adam Kadmon and, iv. 34
Āryan, iv. 121
Christian, ii. 379; iii. 123
Church Dogmas, and, v. 95, 128
Contradict each other, v. 42
Cross and Biblical, ii. 383
Eastern, v. 441
Generation and, v. 85
Gerald Massey, ii. 122
H. P. B. disagrees with, ii. 15
Jehovah and, iv. 110
Magic and, v. 42
Masons and, v. 194
Modern, iii. 421; v. 49, 54
Mysteries, ignorant of, ii. 122
Mythopoeic age, and, i. 310
Norwich, iii. 429
Numbers and, v. 85
Our day, of, ii. 44
Phallicism and, v. 49, 85, 194
Pre-Christian, iv. 158
Purānas, may study with profit, i. 251
Scoff of, iii. 351
Serpent and, iii. 44
Sun with, iii. 131, 132; v. 276
Superficial, iv. 159
SYMBOLOGY, Adytum, of, iv. 27
Ancient Hebrew, ii. 20
Ancient scripture and, ii. 17
Anugītā, in, iv. 209
Āryan, v. 194
Aspects, of, ii. 17
Astrology and, v. 325, 326
Biblical names and, v. 90

Chaldean scriptures, of, iv. 23, 24
Colours of temple curtain, of, ii. 182, 183
Eastern, v. 72, 287, 436
Egg in, v. 436
Egyptian, ii. 79; v. 128, 129, 206, 246, 247
Esoteric, v. 72, 182, 234
Exoteric, and esoteric, v. 443
Heathen, of, i. 173
Hindu, ii. 391
Kabalistical, iv. 106
Kings of Edom, iv. 24, 75
Knowledge hidden from profanation by, iv. 19
Kosmos, of, v. 453
Letters, of, v. 115, 117, 118, 119, 206
Lunar, i. 307
Men of research in department of, ii. 35
Nodus, in study of, i. 178
Numerical, v. 115, 118, 200
Occult, v. 166, 206, 207, 208, 537
Old Testament, v. 66, 68, 69, 72, 111
Pentateuch, of, i. 174
Persian, iv. 188, 189
Pyramids, of, v. 166, 207, 248
Pythagoras, of, v. 113
Races, First three, of, iii. 132
Religious, iv. 31, 182, 234, 436; v. 395, 407
Sacr' of, i. 72
Sacred, iii. 115
Scriptures and, v. 195, 197
Secret, v. 46
Seven departments of, ii. 17
Seven keys to, iii. 35, 334; iv. 39
System of sidereal, iv. 121
Tarot, of, v. 123
Tree of Knowledge, of, v. 85
Universal, v. 42
Writers of Epistles well versed in, iv. 326
SYMPATHETIC Cords, v. 520, 524
Nerve, v. 518
System, v. 520
SYNAGOGUE, Pentateuch of, v. 179
Zohar in the rendering of, iv. 29
SYNCELLUS, i. 50; v. 257
SYNCHRONISTIC
Tables of Abydos, iii. 397
  ,,   of Manetho, iii. 366, 367, 391
  ,,   of Sanchuniathon, iv. 263
SYNEDRION, v. 99
SYNESIUS initiated into the Mysteries, i. 65;
   v. 89, 307
SYNODIAL month, ii. 381
SYNOPTICAL Gospels, v. 336
SYNOPTICS, Egyptian symbols and Pagan doc-
   trines, incorporated into, ii. 99
SYNTHESIS of Occult Nature or Egg of
   Brahmā, v. 456
SYRIA, Ad-on, or Lord of, iii. 54, 55
Druses of, iii. 40
Esoteric schools of, i. 46
Gnostics of, iv. 29
Initiates of, iv. 128
Kabalists of, iv. 23
Mandrake in, iii. 40
Nabatheans came to, iv. 22
SYRIANS, Egg symbol among, ii. 74
Gnostics, Christian, i. 261
Goddess Aster't, of the, iii. 54, 55

SYRIANS (*Contd.*)
  Indian figures, knew, ii. 76
  Rulers, world of, ii. 153
  Sacred operations of, v. 279
  Worlds, ten, of, ii. 154
SYRIANUS quoted, iv. 170
SYRO-CHALDEAN, Magic, ii. 131; v. 100
SYROS, Pherecydes of, v. 57
SYSTEM(S), Astrology of, v. 455
  Christian Chronological, v. 101
  Copernican, v. 331
  Electric, v. 298
  Measurement, English, of, v. 111
  Numerical, v. 342
  Occult Interpretations of Alphabets and
    Numerals, of, v. 113-119
  Planetary, v. 129, 154
  Pythagorean, v. 87
  Solar, *q. v.*
SYSTEMIC Vortices of Kepler, ii. 348
SYZYGIES, v. 446, 447

                          T

TAAROA, the creative power, iii. 199
TABERNACLE, Archaic Telephone, v. 240
  Curtain of, i. 183
  God, designed to contain, iii. 303
  High Priests of, iv. 22
  Host, prepared for, iii. 419
  Jehovah, for, iv. 107
  Maker of, iii. 119
  Man is, of God, v. 84
  Measurements of, iv. 113
  Moses, of, ii. 61, 107
  Sidereal cycle and form of, ii. 26
  Square, i. 184
TABLE-LANDS of Tibet, iv. 180
TABLES, Astronomical, iii. 42
  Conjunction of 1491 in western, ii. 386
  Geological periods, of, iv. 279
  Hindus, of, ii. 386, 389
  Manetho's, iii. 391
  Mystical, v. 509
  Nassireddin, of, ii. 384
  Siamese astronomical, ii. 390
  Stone, in ark, iii. 52; iv. 41, 99; v. 245
  Synchronistic, iv. 263, 281
  Vibration, of, v. 509
TABLETS, Assyrian, iii. 72
  Brick-clay, iv. 262
  Buddha, of, iii. 421
  Chaldean, iii. 16, 63, 72
  Cosmogonical, iii. 64
  Cutha, iii. 63, 65
  Richardson and Gest, ii. 106
  Smaragdine, iii. 118; iv. 126; v. 114
  Smith quotes from, iii. 153
  Stone, of, at Initiation, v. 140
TACHYGRAPHY, v. 243
TACITUS and Astrology, v. 333
TAD in Sanskrit is that, i. 144; iii. 269
T'AGATHON, one of a quaternary, iv. 171
TAHITI and Polynesian continent, iii. 227
TAHITIAN, Ivi, iii. 199
  Stature of, iii. 331
  Tradition, iii. 199

TAHMURATH, or Taimruaz, king of Persia,
    iii. 396, 398
TAHT-ESMUM, moon-god of Egyptians, iv. 204
TAIJAS(A), Manas, v. 427
  Shining, v. 87
  Tattva, v. 476
TAIL, Catarrhine, of, iv. 238
  Comet, of, ii. 228, 330, 331
  Dragon, of, ii. 118; iii. 350
  Foetus, in human, iv. 255
  Problem, iv. 253
  Rudimentary, iii. 328; iv. 251
  Serpent and its, ii. 273, 367; iv. 74
  Stars of heaven, whose, drew a third part of
    the, iv. 53
TAILLESS APE, iv. 225, 238
TAILS in Bundahish, men with, iv. 206
TAIMURAZ, or Tahmurath, iii. 396, 398
TAINE, H. A. quoted, iii. 334
TAIRYAGYONYA creation, ii. 165
TAIT, Professor, quoted, ii. 208
TAKA mi onosubi no Kami, i. 261
TALAS, States of consciousness, v. 538, 539, 543,
    544, 545
TALĀTALA or Karatala, v. 538, 542, 546
TALIESIN, quoted, iii. 379
TALISMAN, Charles the Great, of, v. 122
  Cross, of, iv. 127, 159
  Knowledge of, v. 121
  Lady Ellenborough, of, v. 162
  Ophite, creed, from, ii. 127
  Porcelain, of, iii. 434
  Preparation of, iv. 22
  Tau was Mystic, v. 161
TALK across ocean, ii. 284
TALLIES found with bones of men, iv. 297
TALMUDIC, Axiom, iii. 127
  Jews, iv. 39
  Scheme, iv. 27
  Sectarianism, iv. 29
  System, v. 384
TALMUDISTS, ii. 33, 134; iv. 101; v. 369
  Jews, successors to the initiated, iv. 189
TAM, Adam in Tamil, iii. 143
TAMAS, Insensibility or, ii. 44, 48, 62, 259
TAMASA, Elements are, ii. 45
  Intellect unenlightened by, ii. 45
  Spiritual darkness, ii. 88
TAMAZ, Adam Kadmon, iii. 55
TAMIEL taught astronomy, iii. 375
TAMIL, *Bagavadam*, edition of, iv. 191
  Calendar, iii. 77
  Continents, references to sunken, iii. 325
TĀMRA, wife of Kashyapa, iii. 188
TAMTU, or Belita sea, iv. 30
TANAIM (TANANIM), Jewish Initiates, v. 431
  Judaean, i. 251; iv. 37
  Kabalists, v. 67, 131
  Pre-christian, v. 176
  Simon Magus pupil of, v. 131
  Talmud and, v. 305
TANAIS, Plutarch on the, iv. 342
TANHĀ, Desire to live, iii. 118; v. 473, 511,
    512, 560
  Senseless life, iii. 119
TANJUR and Kanjur of Northern Buddhists,
    i. 50

TANMĀTRAS, Esoterically, ii. 295
  Five, ii. 49, 260; v. 538, 541
  Lower, v. 494
  Rudimental principles, or, ii. 171, 174
  Second or elemental creation, ii. 165
  Seven, v. 538
  Subtile elements, or, ii. 48
TANTALUS in infernal regions, iii. 395; v. 270
TANTRA, Pre-christian, v. 404
  Read esoterically, v. 470
  Tables, v. 477
TANTRIC, Five Ma-karas, iv. 151
TĀNTRIKA, Mysteries of, v. 140
  Ritual, v. 404
  Sutras, v. 122
  Works, v. 120, 185, 197, 485
TĀNTRIKAS, v. 479, 518
  India, of, v. 140
TĀNTRIST, personality of, v. 480
TAO, genius of moon, ii. 301
TAO-ISTS of China, iv. 124
TAPA-LOKA (TAPAR-LOKA), iii. 321; v. 537, 542
TAPAS, or religious devotions, iii. 181
TAPHOS, or tomb, iv. 27
TAPIRS, Ungulate mammals and, iv. 305
TĀRĀ, Jupiter's wife, iii. 147
  Priest's wife, iii. 57
  Secret knowledge, personification of initiate into, iv. 67
  Tārakā, wife of Brihaspati, or, iii. 57; iv. 66
TĀRADAITYA, Abode of, iii. 405
  Demon, a, iii. 402
  Purānas, of, iii. 401
TĀRAKA, Dānava demon, iii. 381
  Kārtikeya, conqueror of, iv. 190
  Rāja classification, i. 213
  Rāja Yoga of India, iv. 174; v. 361, 520
  Tāra or, iii. 57
  Titan, iv. 119
  Vanquisher of, iii. 381
  War, iv. 66
  Yoga system, iv. 164
TĀRAKA-JIT, Kārtikeya called, iii. 381; iv. 190
TĀRAKA-MAYA, Age of, ii. 136
  Indian allegory of, iii. 383
  War in heaven, or, iii. 57, 73
TARANA, Hindu Year, iii. 78
TARATAKAMALA, VENKATA KRISHNA RAO, referred to, iii. 62
TARCHON, the disciples of Targes, v. 121
TARGES, the Chaldean, v. 121
TARGUMS handed down by Hebrews, iv. 127
TARIJA, giants of, iv. 323
TARIM, Basin of, i. 55
  Tiles and cylinders in, i. 48
TARO, v. 109, 111, 112
TAROT, v. 63, 123
TARTARS, Astronomical elements of, ii. 385
  Cycle, v. 341
  Ulug-beg, and tables of, ii. 384
TARTARUS, Atlas and Japetus in, iv. 332
  Iliad, of, iv. 345
TARTARY, iii. 327; v. 39, 40, 406
TASK, Cyclic, i. 322
TASMANIA, Continent from India to, iii. 225
  Darwin on tribe in, iii. 201

  Extinct tribes of, iii. 331
  Geological survey of, iii. 22
  Half-animal tribes of, iii. 201
  Race of men in, iv. 293
TASTE, Animals without, ii. 332
  Sense of, iii. 116; v. 540, 543
TAT, Egyptian God of wisdom, iv. 99
  Emblem of stability, iv. 127
  Hermes called, iii. 379
  Tau or, iv. 127, 159
  That or, v. 425
TATHĀGATAS, v. 371, 373, 374, 394, 409, 411
TATIAN, Disciple of Justin Martyr, v. 160
TATOO, Tat, in, iv. 159
TATTVAS, Colours and, v. 485
  Correspond to Human Principles, v. 474, 476
  Esoteric and Tantric Tables of, v. 478
  Forces, v. 475, 476, 477, 505
  Lokas and, v. 538
  Modifications of Svara, and, v. 479
  Plexuses, and, v. 480
  Principles and, v. 514
  Seven, v. 460, 470, 474, 475, 538
  Tantrika and, 479
  Twenty-five, v. 393
  Universe built form, v. 505
TAU, Apophis bound on, iv. 159
  Astronomical cross, iv. 113
  Christianity borrowed, i. 62; v. 162
  Circle, and, i. 72; iv. 171, 193
  Cross or, iv. 113, 117, 118
  Cube unfolded is, ii. 34
  Egg and, ii. 79
  Egyptian Cross or, ii. 383; iii. 43, 48; iv. 127, 152; v. 161; 162, 163, 318
  Form of, i. 72; ii. 122
  Gnostics revealed, iv. 144; v. 162
  Greek gamma and figure seven, iv. 163
  Initiated adept bound to, iv. 128
  Israelites' doorposts, marked on, iv. 127
  Mysteries and, v. 161
  Mystery, a, iv. 160
  Mystic, v. 162
  Perfect, iv. 127
  Snake encircling, i. 299; iii. 218
  Son of Gaia, called, iv. 163
  Tree of Life is, v. 163
  Triple, v. 162
TAURI sacrificed human beings to Artemis, ii. 111
TAURUS, Asterisk a, with, ii. 383
  Atlantis, vertical to island of, iii. 406
  Constellation of, ii. 383; iv. 121
  Druids and Sun in, v. 267
  Eve, v. 164
  Eye of, ii. 388, 389; iv. 354
  Issachar, in sphere of, ii. 377
  Scorpio and, v. 164
  Sun in, iv. 263, 329
TAURUS Draconem gemuit et Taurum Draco, iii. 142
TAUT, or Thoth, serpent symbol of, iii. 39
TAYGETA, daughter of Atlas, iv. 337
TAYLOR, Thomas, quoted, ii. 143, 172; iv. 170; v. 281
TCHAN-GY, Chinese demi-Gods, iii. 365
TCHEOU, Sun, iii. 371

TCHONG, A Dhyān Chohan, iii. 282
TCHY-YEOO, beguilements of, iii. 282
TEACHERS, of the Snowy Mountain, v. 390
TEACHINGS, Archaic, ii. 143; iii 108; iv 257
  Belief in old, iii. 439
  Buddha, of, v. 371
  Esoteric, i. 60, 329; ii. 325, 366, 397; iv. 15, 175; v. 363, 365, 492, 497
  Gnostics, of the, iv. 189
  Kabalah, of, iv. 240
  Occult, i. 65; ii. 366, 380; iv. 19, 77, 96, 234; iv. 176; v. 277, 234, 472
  Paracelsus, of, iv. 226
  Pre-Christian, i. 61
  Protest, imparted under, i. 241
  Pythagorean and Platonic, ii. 343
  Regents of planets, of, ii. 110
  Secret, i. 297; v. 70, 259
  Secret Doctrine, of, i. 59; ii. 376; iii. 167
  Vedic, iv. 177
TEAK found at Mugheir, iii. 230
TEAPI, or Easter island, iii. 336
TEARS, Niobe, of, iv. 340
  Rulers create Monads from, ii. 301
TECTUM, a roof, iv. 153
TEFNOOT in Devachan, iii. 373
TEIRESIAS, Abodes of, iii. 380
TEJAS, v. 475, 486
TELANG, K. T., quoted, i. 142, 151, 163; ii. 258, 295
TELCHINES, of Rhodes, iii. 390
TELEPATHIC impacts, iii. 164
TELEPHONE, ii. 284
TELESCOPE, Limits of, ii. 201, 315
  Nebulæ, and, ii. 322
  Stars in range of, iv. 277
  Worlds and firmaments seen by, ii. 329
TELESPHORUS, Heptagon called, iv. 173
TELETE, v. 280
TELITA, queen of moon, iii. 143
TEL-LOH, Statues at, iv. 261, 262
TELL, William, iv. 330
TELLURIAN spirit, Serpent as a, iii. 212
TELLURIUM, ii. 274
TEMPERATURE, Earth, of, iii. 22, 162
  Existence and, ii. 332
  Sun, of, ii. 206
  Universe, of, i. 198; ii. 273
  Venus, of, iv. 276
TEMPLAR degree in masonry, i. 194
TEMPLE, Amun, of, v. 302
  Bishop, iii. 37; iv. 215
  Crypt, iv. 128
  Delphic, iv. 152
  Dendera, of, iii. 373, 430
  Earth, a mystic, i. 259
  Egyptian, planisphere in an, iii. 367
  God, of, ii. 97, 198, 302; iv. 34; v. 76, 82, 463
  Golden candlestick of, iv. 153
  Hiranya-garbha, of, iv. 37
  Holy of Holies in, i. 308
  Initiates, i. 45; v. 280
  Japan, Secret Subterranean, of, v. 320
  Jerusalem, of, v. 185

Kabirim, of, iii. 359
Khous, of, v. 252
Kosmos, of, ii. 193
Libraries, iv. 98
Lord, of, iv. 28
Memphis of, v. 89, 217, 253
Naram-Sin, built by, iv. 261
Nebo at Borsippa, of, iv. 23
Northern India, in, iii. 430
Pachacamac, of, iii. 317
Philae, of, iv. 128
Planetary, of Babylon, iv. 23
Sāmba, built by, iii. 322
Satan, door-keeper of, iii. 236
Science, of, ii. 310
Sigalions in every, iii. 395
Solar God, of, iv. 27
Solomon, of, i. 174; ii. 26, 107, 110; iv. 29, 32, 113, 363; v. 89, 182, 237, 241, 272
Stonehenge, a giant, v. 340
Sun, seven vases in, of, iv. 175
Thebes, at, v. 252
Universe, of, i. 260
Veil of, ii. 149
West end of, iv. 27
TEMPLE-BRĀHMANS, Vedas kept by, i. 314
  Vishnu Purāna, passed into hands of, ii. 141
TEMPLES, Ancient archives of, ii. 19
  Ancient college, i. 222
  Antiquity of, v. 217
  Archaic Masonry, of, v. 194
  Babylonian, v. 321
  Cave, iii. 224
  Chaldean, v. 238
  Construction of, ii. 28
  Dragon, sacred to, iii. 379
  East, sacred imagery in, of, ii. 76
  Egypt, of, i. 51, 183; iii. 428; iv. 129; v. 279, 322
  Facing the sun, v. 217
  Gentiles, of, iv. 102
  Glyphs of primitive, iv. 149
  Grecian, iv. 26
  Hierophants of, i. 57; v. 263
  Hiram built, iv. 111
  Human body, for, iii. 273
  India, of, v. 322
  Initiation, of, iii. 378
  Kabiri, of, iii. 360
  Kadeshim of Jewish, iv. 31
  Made with hands, ii. 41
  Mysteries of inner, iii. 232
  Persia, of, v. 322
  Priest-architects of Indian, i. 257
  Pueblos, impenetrable, of, iii. 188
  Records of, iii. 436
  Rockcut, of, India, i. 184; iii. 224, 338
  Secret libraries of, v. 59, 253
  Serpents at, v. 171
  Stellar, iii. 351
  Sun, sacred to, iii. 378
  Teachings of, inner, ii. 53
  Tibet, of, v. 322
  Volcanic localities, iii. 362
TEMPORO-sphenoidal convolutions, iv. 216
TEMPTATION, Kingdom of, v. 153

TEMPTER, *Genesis* of, i. 299
 God of Semite, ii. 98
 Intellectual, of man, iii. 417
 Lower Manas, v. 532
 Man, of, iii. 353
 Satan our, and redeemer, iv. 82
 Woman, of man, iii. 386
TEMURA, anagrammatical method of Kabalah,
  i. 144, 154
 Zohar method of calculation, iv. 113, 115
TEN, Creator, perfect number of, i. 160
 Decad or sign of, ii. 47
 Dual numeral, iv. 123
 Emanations, v. 188
 Enos and, v. 129
 Lettered God, iv. 174
 Lights in their totality made, ii. 151
 Lost tribes, v. 183
 Man, and, v. 426, 429, 430, 435
 Mother of the Soul, is, v. 115
 Number, iii. 237
 Numbers and Deity, v. 210
 Perfect number, v. 129, 426, 430, 507
 Points of Pythagorean triangle, ii. 341
 Sacred, ii. 114
 Svastika means, thousand truths, iv. 157
 Universe, numbers of, ii. 76, 145; v. 129
 Universe, Symbol of, v. 129, 139
 Words or, Sephiroth, ii. 150
 Zodiac, signs of, ii. 71
TENBREL, Chugnyi not, i. 87, 112
TENERIFFE, iii. 406; iv. 296, 332, 359
TENETS, Brahmanism of, v. 371
 Esoteric, i. 308; iv. 15
 Mysterious, iii. 303
 Occult sciences, of, ii. 359
 Pharisees, of, iii. 71
 Philosophical, iv. 156
 Religious mysteries, of, iii. 132
 Satanians, of, iii. 388
 Secret doctrine, of, iv. 22
TEOS of Greeks, iv. 173
TEOTIHUACAN, ruins at, v. 283
TERAH, Abraham's Father, v. 112, 237, 238, 318
TERAPHIM, Chaldean, v. 242
 Divination by, iv. 22
 Idols, and, v. 237-242
 Instruments of Revelation, v. 239
 Jewish, v. 111, 252, 318
 Pagan, v. 240
 Seraphim or, v. 237, 238
TERATOLOGICAL, Phenomena, ii. 198;
  iii. 194
TEREBINTHUS, v. 170
TERMINI, of Hermes-Mercury, cruciform,
  iv. 112
TERMINUS, a symbol of shelter, iv. 153
TERMITES, or white ants, ii. 400
TERNARIES, Animals only, iv. 147
TERNARY, Divine figure, v. 116
 Monad, and, v. 507
 Nine triple, iv. 152
 Odd numbers, first of, iv. 146
 Pythagoreans, of, iv. 147
 Tetragram, at beginning of, iii. 137
 Tetraktys and, v. 516
 Third life, symbol of, ii. 99

Triangle included in a, ii. 341
TERRA, Giants sons of Coelus and, iv. 338
TERRA-cotta discs or fusaioles, iii. 110
TERRENE, Ancestors, i. 233
 Chain, i. 210
 Element, iii. 358
 Plane, i. 220
 Products, creation called, iii. 245
TERRESTRIAL, Adam, iv. 24
 Animal human being, ii. 361
 Beings evolution of, ii. 158
 Branches of tree reach, plane, ii. 123
 Bull emblem of, life, iii. 102
 Casket, physical, i. 236
 Centres of, forces, i. 253
 Chain, i. 210, 217; iv. 275, 327
 Conflagration, iv. 54
 Continents, ii. 137
 Cosmic man, iii. 116
 Creators, iii. 170
 Deluge, iii. 148
 Diti, forms of, iv. 185
 Divine natures, and, iii. 420
 Dust of, origin, ii. 370
 Earths, three, iv. 187
 Elements, ii. 318; iv. 175
 Even numbers are, iv. 146
 Evolution, ii. 344
 Fire, ii. 190; iv. 90
 Floods, iii. 352
 Forces, i. 171; ii. 200
 Globe, the atmosphere of the, iv. 186
 Globes of, chain, i. 217; iv. 104
 God, iii. 122
 Heavenly, to, man, ii. 337
 Hebdomad, ii. 167
 Humanity, i. 167, 318, 325
 Illusion, a mere, ii. 98
 Infernal deities, and, iv. 173
 Initiates, form of, iii. 233
 Life, iii. 159, 249; iv. 73
 Life-cycle, iv. 192
 Light, ii. 201, 321
 Lokas, v. 542
 Love, iv. 151
 Lunar and, chain, i. 231
 Messengers, iii. 311
 Mortals, ii. 330
 Mysteries, iv. 39
 Nature, ii. 149; iii. 83
 Objective consciousness, v. 526
 Occult side of, nature, iv. 167
 Organisms, ii. 332
 Period of fourth round, iv. 254
 Personality, false, iii. 244
 Phases of, life, ii. 378
 Phenomena, i. 201
 Physical nature, iv. 167
 Physiological union, iv. 38
 Plane, i. 181, 200; ii. 61, 238, 278, 396;
  iii. 68, 100; v. 524, 525
 Poles, iii. 362, 429
 Races, iii. 136
 Regions, Varshas and Dvipas regarded as,
  iii. 320
 Round, i. 214; iii. 329
 Seed or sperm, i. 326

TERRESTRIAL (*Contd.*)
  Self, iii. 270
  Senses, i. 207
  Septenary, law in, life, iv. 194
  Sphere, our, ii. 344; iii. 74
  Spirits, i. 279; iii. 36
  Sublime and, iii. 94
  Substance terrestrial and sidereal, ii. 321
  Vitality cosmic and, i. 253
  Wisdom, iv. 210
  Workshops, ii. 350
TERROR, Demon of, iii. 401
  Thou shalt be a, iv. 62
TERTIARIES, Development in newest, iv. 257
TERTIARY period, The age of, iv. 246, 255
  Ancestor of ape in, i. 241; iv. 250, 251
  Australia of, iii. 21
  Civilization during, iv. 249
  Climate of, iv. 283, 308
  Croll on, iii. 22; iv. 255, 257, 265
  Date of, iv. 246, 320
  Disturbances in, iii. 314
  Duration of, iii. 164; iv. 263
  Flora in Europe in, iv. 358
  Glacial, iv. 283
  Immigration in Europe in, iv. 309
  Lemuria and, iii. 314, 431
  Mammals of, iii. 260
  Man in, iii. 211, 289; iv. 246, 316, 320, 351
  Rocks of, iv. 279
  Science and, iv. 282, 283
  Transmutations of, iv. 236
TERTULLIAN, Fallen angels, on, ii. 44; v. 99
  Fish, on name of, iii. 314
  Giants found at Carthage, on, iii. 280
TERUPH, Sacred anagram, v. 115
TESHU LĀMA an incarnation of Amitābha
    Buddha, ii. 193
TESHU LĀMAS, iii. 185; v. 389, 391, 393
TESTIMONIUM PAUPERTATIS of natural
    science, iv. 221, 233
TESTIMONY, Ages, of, iii. 156, 199
  Ancient wisdom, as to, i. 59; iii. 197
  Bible, of, for plurality of worlds, ii. 331
  Discoveries, of modern, iii. 428
  Giants, as to, iii. 279
  History of, i. 67; ii. 336
  Tradition and scientific, iii. 145
  Unseen intelligences, for, iii. 373
TETH, Hebrew letter used symbolically, i. 143;
    iv. 99
TETRACHORD, iv. 172
TETRAD, Duad and, iv. 170, 172
  Four elements and, ii. 166
  Kabalah, in, iv. 170
  Microprosopus, iv. 197
  Pyramis, base of, iv. 173
  Pythagorean, v. 382, 420
  Truths, shows, to Marcus, ii. 67
TETRADIC symbols, iv. 174
TETRAGON, Form and matter from, iv. 171
TETRAGRAMMATON, v. 102, 162
  Adam Kadmon or, i. 129, 161; iv. 167
  Androgynous deity, an, i. 139
  Brahmā-Prajāpati, is, iv. 196
  Eyes of seven, iv. 196
  Four lettered, iii. 37, 67, 313; iv. 127

  Generation, symbol of, ii. 156
  Glyph of, i. 262
  Heavenly man, or, iii. 38
  Jehovah, or, i. 139
  Jews of, iv. 171
  Light, seventh, iv. 199
  Microprosopus, Macroprosopus and, iv. 173,
    197
  Mystery, of four-lettered, i. 285
  Profane, to mislead, ii. 156
  Quaternary or, i. 140; iv. 196
  Sacredness of, iv. 153
  Sephiroth and, ii. 58; iv. 196
  Synthesis, holy in its abstract, ii. 156
  Ternary of, iii. 137
  Tetraktys or, iv. 170, 193, 197
  Western Kabalists, of, iii. 360; iv. 31
TETRAKTYS, (TETRACTYS), Brahmā and,
    v. 519
  Celestial and terrestrial, iv. 175
  Chatur Vidyā or, v. 519
  Circle, within, iv. 197
  Concealed, iii. 313
  Dhyān Chohans, and, i. 247
  Emanates from the One, v. 77
  Essence of, iv. 172
  Four-faced Brahma, is, v. 519
  Four represented by, i. 152
  Harmony, called, iv. 172
  Hetagon, and, iv. 169
  Lower, iv. 171
  Mystery of, ii. 58
  Mystic square of, iii. 48
  Perfect Cube, v. 116
  Pythagorean, ii. 158; iv. 174; v. 113, 420,
    421, 506, 516
  Quaternary or, v. 426
  Sacredness of, iv. 153; v. 426, 516
  Symbol of Kosmos, v. 506
  Tetragrammaton, or, iv. 170, 193, 197
  Triad forms, i. 161; v. 76
  Triangle became, ii. 340; iii. 37; v. 507
TETRATOMIC in chemical phraseology, i. 265
TEUFEL, D'Evil, Diavolo, i. 143
TEUT of Egyptians, iv. 173
TEUTOBODUS, bones attributed to, iii. 279
TEUTONIC, Giants, iv. 323
  Names of Magi, ii. 380
TEXTS, Babylonian, iv. 262; v. 198, 199
  Eastern doctrine, of, iii. 239
  Egyptian, ii. 399
  Elohistic and Jehovistic, iv. 41
  Exoteric, and secret records, iii. 334
  Hermetic literature, of, iii. 239
  Religious, no mythical element in, iii. 335
  Stanzas, and glosses of, i. 87
THACKERAY quoted, iii. 422
THALAMENCEPHALON or inter-brain,
    iii. 299
THALASSA or Thalatth, Sea, iii. 75, 124
THALATTH, Binah is, of Berosus, ii. 109; iii. 71
  Omoroka or, iii. 143
  Sea or water, iii. 65
  Thalassa, or, iii. 75
  Thavatth or, iii. 124
THALES, referred to, i. 143; ii. 44, 59, 100;
    iv. 163; v. 27, 60, 234, 255

THALLIUM, ii. 276
THAMMUZ a lunar God, ii. 111
THANGO-PA-CHHE-GO-MO, v. 390
THANTABAOTH, Uriel or, iii. 124
THAT, Absolute all, iii. 166
  Aditi in, i. 72
  Brahman and Pums and Pradhāna which is, ii. 164
  Duad and, ii. 343
  Expression of, is point, ii. 144
  Immutable, ii. 89
  Lord of all beings, one, i. 153
  Manifestation, ii. 170
  Manvantaric manifestations of, iii. 46
  Non-being is, i. 74
  One life, called, i. 302
  Prādhānika Brahma spirit, one, i. 300
  Root eternal of, i. 76
  Sleepeth not, iii. 311
  Space and time are, iv. 183
  Spirit is first differentiation from, i. 109
  Subject of cognition not possible to, i. 73
  Tad in Sanskrit, is, i. 144
  This and, i. 73
  Vedas, of, ii. 107; iii. 90
THAUMATURGISTS, Rabbis Chanina and Oshoi, i. 69
THAUMATURGY, v. 254, 298
THAVATTH, Chaldean word for sea, iii. 124
THAYNGIN Grotto, iv. 286
THEAGENES, v. 334
THEBAN, Sacerdotal class, ii. 23
  Sanctuary, v. 264
  Triad, iv. 32
  Trinity, v. 253
THEBEIAN Egyptian and Ptah, ii. 399
THEBES, Age of, iv. 319
  Ammon adored at, ii. 82
  City, v. 260
  God of destinies in, iv. 32
  Heroes who fell at, or Troy, iii. 273
  Library at, v. 245
  Menes, founder of, v. 296
  Rivals of, v. 295
  Subterranean crypts of, iii. 378
  Temple of Kabirim at, iii. 363
  Trials at, v. 290
THEBITH, Arabian Astronomer referrred to, ii. 388
THE-EIN to move, Theos from, iv. 115
THEIST, Theology to a, iii. 178
THEISTIC KABBALIST on divine revealer, ii. 29
THEISTS, Anthropomorphic God of, ii. 139
  God, make Satan shadow of, ii. 131
  Great law called God by, i. 203
  Providence with, ii. 359
THEMIS, Nemesis, Adrasteia and, iii. 306
THENAY, Miocene flints of, iv. 309, 318
THEO-anthropographics, Semitic, iii. 137
THEO-anthropological meaning of primitive human race, iii. 234
THEO-cosmological symbols in Bible, ii. 377
THEOCRACY, perished, v. 297
  Persecution of, v. 296
THEOCRITUS, referred to, iii. 131
THEODICE, Fallen angels, of, iii. 102

THEODICY, Roman Catholic, v. 326
THEODIDAKTOS, Title of Ammonius, v. 33
THEODOLINDE, Queen of Lombardy, iv. 158
THEODORET, quoted, iii. 138; iv. 33; v. 138,
THEODOSIUS, iv. 53
  King-builders of pyramids, and, ii. 24
THEOGONIC, Astronomical and, struggles, i. 251
  Evolution, ii. 107
  Jehovah, aspect of, iv. 167
  Leda a, myth, iii. 130
  Moon, characters of, iii. 76
THEOGONIES, Astral light in ancient, i. 299
  Brāhmanical and Biblical, iii. 54
  Meaning of great, iii. 270
  Pythagorean triangle and, ii. 337
  Religious calendars and, ii. 378
  Secret Doctrine and, Grecian, iv. 336
  World Religions, of, v. 213
  Zodiac and, ii. 378
THEOGONY, Allegorical, i. 193
  Ancient, iii. 69
  Asuras legitimate place in, iii. 71
  Budha, of, iv. 66
  Celsus, of, ii. 164
  Chaldean, iii. 250; v. 326
  Christian, i. 114; v. 94
  Comparative, iii. 114
  Creative Gods or, ii. 78, 142
  Deluge in, iii. 152
  Divine, v. 331
  Divine thought conceals every future, i. 339
  Egyptian, i. 51, 142; iii. 417
  Esoteric, i. 157; ii. 135
  Evolution of gods in every, i. 277; ii. 156
  Fallen angels of every, i. 267
  Geometry and, ii. 340
  Greek, iii. 76
  Hebrew, iii. 74
  Hesiod's, ii. 136; iv. 16, 94, 334, 344, 346
  Intelligences in every, independent, iii. 89
  Jews, of, iv. 33
  Key which opens mystery of, ii. 106
  Metaphysics of, iii. 358
  Mochus, of, ii. 81, 181
  Mysteries of, iii. 36, 385
  Nāgas in, iii. 215
  Occult, v. 190
  Oldest permutations of, ii. 114
  Orphic, i. 47, 50; iv. 228
  Phallic worship and sexual, i. 175
  Pre-cosmic, iii. 102, 155
  Primeval, best definition of, ii. 146
  Primitive, iii. 250
  Primordial, mysteries of, iv. 157
  Prometheus in every ancient, iii. 418
  Pythagorean, Gods were numbered in, ii. 151
  Races, and, v. 104
  Real manifested, ii. 152
  Secret, iv. 110
  Septiform, v. 201
  Seven regents of, ii. 109
  Shveta-Dvipa of, iii. 322
  Titan-Kabirim in every, iii. 362
  Valentinian, iv. 146
  Vedic, iv. 16, 157

THEOI, Gods of Hermetic Philosophers, i. 329;
ii. 60; v. 318
THEOLOGIANS, Adaptation of, ii. 379
Antiquity of man, and, iv. 245
Brazen Serpent and, ii. 79
Christian, ii. 381; v. 103, 109, 327
Clerical classes of, ii. 141
God and Satan of, iv. 44
Hindu mystics, and, iv. 196
Jehovah, a tribal God, and, iv. 107
Law of periodicity, and, iv. 192
Mercury and sun, on, iii. 41
Nebular theory and, ii. 324
Occultists and, ii. 329
Pithecoid ancestor of Adam, and, iii. 22
Protestant, i. 272; iii. 374; v. 132
Suns of righteousness male Gods of, iii. 55
War before creation, on, iv. 60
THEOLOGICAL, Astronomy, v. 220
Chronology, iv. 364
Creation, legend of, iv. 259
Delusion, iv. 140
Dogmas, iii. 73, 102, 408
Ether and atoms, associations of, ii. 395
Fall of angels, idea of, iii. 178
Flights, ii. 339
Generation and, dogmas, i. 276
Infernal religions, iii. 102
Magic, v. 223
Personal deity, idea of, ii. 359
Prejudice, iii. 69, 169
Shadow, ii. 344
Sleight of hand, ii. 183
Sophistry, iii. 166
Sources, enumeration from, iv. 212
Symbolism, iii. 376; v. 326
Theogonies from, brain, ii. 337
Typhon in, teaching, iii. 102
Western, dogma of newly created souls, i. 224
THEOLOGIES, Exoteric, iv. 171
Faith, evolve blind, ii. 337
Mythology and false, ii. 16
THEOLOGY, Abstract beliefs, from common
source of, iii. 22
Adversary or Satan of, iii. 71
Anthropomorphism of, i. 70, 120
Antiquity of man, and, iii. 200
Approval of dogmatic, iii. 66
Archangel of, i. 81, 281
Astronomy and, ii. 33
Asuras and, iii. 69
Beaten paths of, ii. 35
Biblical, iii. 22
Brihaspatis of, iii. 57
Cain of, ii. 132
Cainite races of, iii. 179
Calvinists, of, iii. 305
Christian, ii. 98; iii. 53, 80, 103, 104; iv. 53
Christos in Exoteric, i. 139
Christ's religion and Christian, ii. 160
Chronology of, iii. 200
Church and, v. 125
Churchianism and, v. 54
Creation, and, ii. 35
Dead letter, iv. 83
Devil of, ii. 58; iv. 77
Distortions produced by, ii. 132

Ether personal God of, ii. 57
Exoteric, Septenary in, iv. 184
Falls in, iii. 73
First-born, and, iii. 102
Fourth root-race, and, iii. 153
Genesis of man, and, ii. 36
Godhead, and, ii. 393
Gods of antiquity, and, iv. 18
Hell of Christian, ii. 88
Helping hand gives, ii. 36
Jehovah, a tribal God, and, iv. 107
Latin dogmatic, i. 114
Materialistic, iii. 157
Mystery language, from one, ii. 22
Occultists and, iv. 15
Orthodox, v. 25
Paganism, and, iv. 76
Pan a devil, makes, iv. 153
Phallic element of, ii. 25
Philosophy and, ii. 338
Plato, of, iv. 170; v. 280
Popes, under guidance of, ii. 103
Quarrel with, iv. 43
Roman Catholic, ii. 300; iii. 374
Satan in Christian, iii. 71, 234
Science and, i. 84; ii. 331, 393, 394; iii. 213,
347, 349; iv. 363
Sectarian, ii. 110
Self-consciousness and, v. 546
Semites, of, iii. 208
Serpent legends, on, iii. 213
Seth in Egyptian, iii. 91
Solar and lunar worship in Christian, ii. 110
Standards of, iii. 420
Thrones of, iii. 90
Virgin and, v. 293
War in heaven, and, iv. 65
THEOMANTIC, consulations, v. 254
THEO-MYTHOLOGY, Brāhmanical, iii. 101
THEON, referred to, iv. 172; v. 280
THEOPATHY, v. 76
THEOPHANE and Poseidon, iv. 344
THEOPHANIA, v. 76, 79, 240, 358
THEOPHANIST, v. 78
THEOPHANY, v. 76, 281
THEO-PHILOSOPHY, lines of, ii. 337
THEOPHILUS and cruciform couches,
iv. 129
THEOPHRASTUS referred to, iii. 132; iv. 329;
v. 60
THEOPNEUSTY, v. 76, 79
THEOPOMPUS, quoted, iii. 370; iv. 333
THEOS, Amrita latent in, ii. 62
Brahmā is, ii. 58
Chaos, kosmos, ii. 56; v. 234
Collective, ii. 60
Cosmic circle, and, iv. 115
THEOSOPHIA, v. 449
THEOSOPHICAL, School, v. 303
Society, v. 302, 304, 417
System, v. 302
Writers, v. 25
THEOSOPHIST(S), Alexandrian, v. 299
Astrology and, v. 331
Chinese Buddhism and, v. 409
Clergy and, v. 167
Miracles and, v. 124
Persecution and, v. 144

THEOSOPHIST(S) (*Contd.*)
Religion and, v. 70, 109, 110
Swedish, v. 406
THEOSOPHY, Ancient Texts and, v. 59
Avowed origin, of, iii. 232
Böhme, of, iv. 201
Buddhism, and, ii. 391
Eastern school of, iv. 212
Exoteric, v. 55
Religion, and, i. 58
Student of, i. 206; v. 77
Weapon against, i. 41
Western students of, iv. 139
THERA, giants of isle of, iii. 280
THERAPEUTAE, of Egpyt, v. 302
THERMO-DYNAMICS, ii. 209
THERMUTHIS, Crown formed of an asp, iii. 39
THESAURUS of Vedānta, *Upanishads*, i. 313
THESIS, Kānt's, ii. 339
THESMOPHORIA, Symbolism of, v. 412
THESODOSIUS, v. 161
THESSALY, Deluge of, iv. 345
Sorcerers of, iv. 331
Symbols in mountains of, ii. 183
Witches of, i. 211
THETIS, Sacrifices to, ii. 188
THEURGISTS, Blessed, iii. 47
Chaldean, v. 137
Disciplne to become, v. 132
Living fire of, ii. 52, 58
Revelation and, v. 76, 78
Rosicrucians and, i. 146
Tyanean, v. 143
THEURGY, v. 78, 132, 279, 280, 298, 301, 304, 451, 452
THEVETAT, King, iii. 225
THIBAUT referred to, v. 367
THIERRY, A., referred to, ii. 400; iii. 189
THIGH of Brahma, iii. 69
Constellation, v. 202
THINKER, Divine thought does not imply a, i. 130
THIRD, Age, Sādhus and ascetics of, iii. 319
Creation, of Brahmā, iv. 114
Earth was consumed, ii. 157
Eye, i. 118; iii. 186, 230, 273, 290, 295, 300, 303, 307, 349; iv. 118, 251, 338; v. 438, 458, 479, 480, 517, 554
Group or hierarchy of being, ii. 175
Humanity who fell into generation, iii. 37
Logos, iii. 38; v. 476, 533, 558
Monad, ii. 343
Plane, v. 513, 558
Pride, became tall with, iii. 273
Round, i. 227, 292, 297, 304; iii. 67, 88, 124, 193, 196
Sephiroth, v. 211
Soul, i. 287
Stage of creation, v. 207
Stage of evolution, iv. 114
Step of Vishnu, iv. 334
World of Simon Magus, v. 447
THIRD RACE, Adam and Eve types of, iii. 275, 409
Agnishvāttas incarnated in, iii. 100
Ancient worship of, ii. 112
Androgyne, iii. 179; iv. 102

Animal man from, ii. 376
Animals in, iii. 193
Animation of, iii. 233
Appearance of, iii. 163
Astronomy in, v. 341
Atlanteans and, iii. 443
Bisexual, iii. 143, 202
Boats, built, iii. 398
Boneless animals of, iii. 190
Bones of men of, iii. 113
Books of Enoch, and, v. 102
Celestial teachers of, iii. 283
Civilisation of, iii. 427
Cradle of, iii. 332
Daksha and, iii. 190, 197
Death and, iv. 181
Demi-gods of, iii. 319
Development of, iii. 183
Disappearance of, iv. 283
Divine dynasties began with, iii. 426
Early, iv. 309
Earth of, iii. 399
Easter island and, iii. 327
Egg-born, iii. 125, 131
Egos at end of, v. 472
Elect of, iii. 360
Esoterism of, v. 91
Fall, after its, iii. 268
Females of, iii. 277
First man of, v. 180
Flood of, iii. 330
Fourth Race and, v. 106
Fourth round, in, iii. 169
Gods, bright shadow of, iii. 270
Hermaphrodite or, iii. 143
History of, iii. 282; iv. 104
Human seed at end of, iii. 148
Humanity in, iv. 222, 283
Incarnation in men of, iii. 231
Initiates and, v. 103
Intellectual, iii. 215
Jared is, iv. 169
Kings and instructors of, iii. 200
Kriyāshaktic powers of, iv. 208; v. 430
Kumāras in, v. 472
Language in, iii. 203
Lankā, ended at, iii. 332
Last branches of, v. 165
Lemuria of, iii. 323, 332, 400; iv. 156
Lohitānga, born under, iii. 42
Magic in, v. 430
Mammals, before, iv. 282
Men of, i. 236; iv. 357; v. 341
Mental torpor of, iii. 187
Mind-born sons of, i. 259; iii. 209
Noah-Xisuthrus represents, iii. 396
Period, middle, iv. 253
Physical man of, iv. 94, 231
Pitris of, iii. 98
Plesiosauri and, iii. 211
Powers of Deva-man of, iii. 303
Pre-sexual state of, iii. 43; v. 429
Primeval, iii. 208
Procreation in, iii. 184, 188; iv. 37
Pterodactyls and, iii. 211
Religion of, iii. 274
Sages of, iii. 188

THIRD RACE (*Contd.*)
Second creates, iii. 140
Second portion of, iii. 328
Secondary age, and, iv. 280
Secret Doctrine and, v. 204
Self-consciousness and, v. 546
Semi-astral, iv. 258
Senseless, iii. 168
Seth represents later, iii. 134
Sexes in, i. 255; iii. 16; v. 204, 425, 429
Sinless, iii. 374, 409
Sons of the Flame and, v. 260
Sons of Will and Yoga of, iii. 180, 224
Sons of wisdom and, iii. 191
Spiritual state of, v. 339
Sub-races of, iii. 179
Survivors of, iii. 224
Sweat-born of, iii. 78, 183
Symbol of, iii. 131
Three Yugas during, iv. 89
Titans of, iii. 22
Transformation of, iii. 329
Vāhan of Lords of Wisdom, became, iii. 179
Vile forms of first, iii. 168
Will-born of, iii. 164
THIRTEEN depend on thirteen forms, ii. 90, 91
THIS, Cannot create, i. 74
That and, collective aggregate of kosmos, i. 73
Universe (Jagat) refers to, i. 73
THLINKITHIANS, Father of, iii. 226
THOLUCK, quoted, v. 177
THOMAS, Adam identical with, iii. 143
THOMAS AQUINAS, v. 212, 309, 331
THOMPSON, Professor S., quoted, iv. 161
THOMSON and Tait, referred to, iii. 22
THOMSON, Sir, W., referred to, i. 177; ii. 82,
    200, 205, 208, 211, 215, 225, 229, 238, 276,
    303; iii. 22, 74, 157, 162, 165, 260; iv. 264,
    287, 364
THONGLAM-PA, a Seer, v. 374
THO-OG, Yinsin, a term used in Tibetan version
    of Stanzas, i. 87; v. 379
THOR, Fylfot of, iv. 117
Reptile and, v. 289
Sons of, iii. 108
Svastika is hammer of, i. 72, 73; iii. 107
THORAH, or Law, iv. 29; v. 67, 68
THORNS, Valley of, v. 300
THOTH, or Thot, Alphabet of, v. 123
Arts and sciences invented by, iv. 98
Biblical patriarchs and, ii. 374
Egypt civilised by, ii. 366, 379
Egyptian Gnostics, of, ii. 301
God of wisdom, ii. 100; iv. 128
Hermes or, iv. 30, 99, 153
Horus and Set, regulates fight between, iii. 285
Ibis sacred to, ii. 77
Khonsoo and, iv. 32
Meaning of name, v. 68
Memphis, of, iv. 98; v. 74
Mercury or, iv. 110
Moon, retreats to, ii. 118
Moses, Hermes and, v. 112
Osiris-Isis and, iii. 365; iv. 30
Pymander, an abridgment of one of books of,
    iii. 270
Self-created, v. 215

Solar-boat, in, iv. 99
Taut or, serpent symbol of, iii. 39
Wednesday sacred to, iii. 366
Wisdom, God of, iii. 363
THOT-HAPI, the lord of the horizon, ii. 398
THOT-HERMES, i. 54, 64; ii. 68, 118, 179, 399;
    iii. 215, 358, 365, 367
THOTHORI-NYANG-TSAN, v. 404
THOT-LUNUS, ii. 112; v. 32, 99
THOT-SABAOTH, or Bear, iii. 124
THOU ART THAT, ii. 296
THOU ART THYSELF, ii. 157
THOUGHT(S) Abstract absolute, i. 111, 161;
    v. 534
Action and, i. 332; v. 543, 546
Active Idea and Passive, iv. 60
Ah-hi vehicle of, i. 111
Archaic mode of, iii. 335
Astral tablets, impressed on, iii. 204
Bodies not necessary for, ii. 332
Bound of, a great circle, ii. 147
Brahma, of, ii. 147
Brain and, v. 554
Circle, as radii of a, ii. 147
Descartes on, ii. 353
Designing, v. 451
Desire and, v. 456
Dhyān Chohanic, i. 322
Divine, i. 69, 71, 81, 116, 128, 130, 132, 133,
    139, 141, 142, 156, 170, 171; iii. 270; iv. 54,
    57, 61; v. 207, 450, 451, 521
Dress, ancient, in a modern, ii. 303
Eternal, v. 229
Fohat, of Gods, iv. 168, 171
Germ in, v. 534
God the Father, which is, i. 141
Gradation of, infinite, ii. 352
Great one had an evil, iv. 58
Identical, and language are, iii. 204
Leaders of, ii. 336
Light and Life, which is, iv. 57
Mahat understanding, i. 141
Matter, is, i. 182; ii. 53
Millenniums of, i. 257
Modern, i. 118; v. 53
Molecular motion, called, i. 191
Motion, precedes, i. 318
Nascent physical man, in, iii. 204
Not evil, iv. 58
Objective aspect on astral plane, exhibits, i. 183
Phosphorus and, iii. 247
Plane of, concerning Nirvāna, i. 309
Planes on different, iii. 334
Plato, divine, of, i. 165
Potency of, v. 446, 447
Power of, iii. 180
Primal, v. 211
Prototype in divine, i. 132
Psycho-theistic stage of ancient ii. 122
Quiescence, opposed to pure, iv. 58
Radicals, one of, iv. 139
Ratiocinative, below intuition, i. 69
Results produced by, i. 333
Revelations, inspired by same, ii. 55
Soul, evolved by, i. 156
Speech and, i. 194
Spirit and, v. 450

THOUGHT(S) (Contd.)
Transference, ii. 260; iii. 204
Unity in, and action, ii. 369
Universal, iv. 59
Universe existing only in divine, i. 112
Universe of, ii. 342
Upanishads, in, i. 314
Visible made, ii. 96
Will and feeling, i. 111
World of, ii. 341
THOUSAND-headed monster, iii. 107, 189, 380
THOUTMES, mentioned, v. 243
THRACE, Orphic priesthood in, iv. 325
Worship of Kabirim in, iii. 362
THRASYMEDES, Art of, v. 133
THREAD, Ariadne, of, iii. 161
Beads, through many, i. 269
Being of, i. 282, 284
Destiny woven, by, ii. 364
Esoteric or, doctrine, ii. 335
Fohat, of, i. 283
Golden, on which personalities are strung,
iii. 89
Koshas or, Soul, ii. 335
Pearls upon a, ii. 259
Radiance, of, iii. 89
Silent watcher and his shadow, between, i. 308
-Soul, v. 78
Sūtrātmā or, i. 82, 283
THREE, Basic Principles, v. 471
Biographies to every Divine hero, v. 110
Compound Spirits of man, v. 78
Eternal things, v. 379
Fires, earth and man, product of, iii. 249
Four, fall into, i. 134
Maries, ii. 100
Mothers, v. 88, 89, 107
Murderers of Hiram, v. 272
Races symbology of, iii. 132
Unit becomes, v. 499
Vital Airs, v. 510, 517, 520
Wisdom of, ii. 72
THREE-dimensional, Space, iv. 171
World, ii. 43
THREE-divisioned line of matter, iv. 172
THREE-eyed, Animals, iii. 298
Colossus, iii. 296
Men, iii. 296, 297; iv. 239, 314
Mortals, iii. 295
Rudra-Shiva, iv.70
THREEFOLD, Being, i. 277
Buddha, manifestation of, ii. 296
Divisions of world, iv. 193
Manvantara, fire in our, ii. 247
Moon, character of, ii. 108
Units, i. 264
THREE-headed, Mercury, iv. 112
THREE-in-One, i. 115; ii. 102, 298; iii. 121;
iv. 160, 170
THREE-toed Anchitherium, iv. 304
THREE-tongued flame, i. 282, 283
THREE-vowelled sound, names of, ii. 168
THREE-wicked flame, i. 282
THRESHOLD, Dweller on the, v. 500, 501, 512,
567
Light, of, i. 256
Limitless and unutterable, of, iii. 196

Secrets, Keely at, of some great, ii. 280
Sense, of, ii. 239
Svastika on, of Eternity, iii. 108
THRĒTAONA and Ashi-dahaka, War between,
iii. 389
THRICE Great Hermes, i. 323
THRONE, Almighty, of, iii. 74
Briatic World, called, iii. 119
Chinese, is dragon's seat, iii. 364
Glory, of his, i. 155
Hathor, legend on, of, ii. 115
Jupiter, of, iv. 354
Monad degraded into a, ii. 339
Omnipotent Deity, of, ii. 338
Satan, of, iii. 238
THRONES, B'ne Aleim belonged to subdivision
of, iii. 374
Celestial, iii. 422; v. 212
Christian hierarchy, of, i. 155
Empires, and, iii. 236
God, of, v. 122
Saturn ruled by, ii. 153
Theology, of, iii. 90
THUCYDIDES, referred to, v. 53
THUMMIM, Urim, and, ii. 377; v. 239, 240,
310, 335
THUNDER, Son of, v. 144
THUNDERBOLTS, ii. 188; iv. 352
THUNDERS of St. John, iv. 135
Serpent of seven, ii. 127
THURSDAY, or day of Jupiter, ii. 378
THURY, Psychod of, ii. 52
THY name, meaning of, iii. 234
THYAN-KAM, Power or knowledge, ii. 360
Term used in Tibetan version of stanzas, i. 87
TI, Proud spirit who rebels against, iv. 54
TIA-HUANACO, in Peru, ruins of, iii. 317, 336
TIAMAT, Animal of, iii. 383
Creature of, dragon, iii. 112
Dragon, iv. 45
Ea changed into, iii. 64, 71
Female power, Chaldean, ii. 109
Sea, or, iv. 71
War with evil, and, iii. 113
TIANI-TSANG, v. 376, 377
TIAOU, Egyptology, in, i. 274
Noot to, crossing, i. 274
Osiris N. and, i. 275
Realm of Cause of Life, i. 274
Spirit not in, i. 274
TIBERIAS, v. 205
TIBERIUS, and Astrology, v. 334
TIBET, Ascertics of, v. 39
Borderland of, alone known, i. 55
Buddha in, statues of, iv. 157
Buddhism in, i. 44; v. 39, 40, 392, 397, 398,
410
Civilization of, hods secrets for mankind, i. 55
Deity of, patron, i. 139
Esoteric records of, v. 406
  ,,   schools of, i. 46
Kalāpa in, ii. 93
Lhassa capital of, iii. 74
Little, iii. 414
Mountains hem in tableland of, i. 54
Nāgārjuna in, v. 287
Protector of, iii. 185, 186

TIBET (*Contd.*)
" Red Caps " of, v. 122, 398
Russian mystics in, i. 58
Schlagintweit and, v. 287
Si-dzang, i. 314
Symbolism of rice, in, v. 105
Tablelands of, iv. 180
Yogīs of, ii. 193
TIBETAN, Ālaya in, i. 120
Bhons of, borderlands, iv. 157
Buddhism, v. 405
Chenresi in, iii. 185; v. 420
Chinamen, offshoot, iii. 185
Exclusiveness, v. 39, 396
Exoteric Worship, i. 184
Jigten Gonpo, name for Padmapāni, iii. 186
Lāmas, iii. 185; v. 389, 393
Lāmaseries, v. 375
Magic, v. 39, 40
Mysticism, v. 403, 404
Nidānas in, i. 112
Occultists, v. 381
Od, a Thibetan word, i. 142
Parikalpita in, i. 120
Region, iii. 46
Sacred canon of, v. 390
Samvriti in, i. 120
Sects, v. 402
Stanzas, version, i. 87
Temple literature, i. 46
Tradition, iii. 406
Tsong-kha-pa, reformer, i. 169; v. 391
Yoga and Dhyāna same in, iii. 124
Young-Grub, i. 87
Zampun, iii. 106
TICHORRHINUS, an extinct species, iv. 315
TIDAL, Action, iii. 74
Cycle of, changes, iv. 166
Elevation, iii. 75
Evolutionary wave, ii. 281
Retardation, iii. 74
TIDES, Effect of, iii. 324; iv. 166
First great, iii. 63
Moon and, i. 232; iii. 75
TIEN, Heaven, and Amitābha, ii. 71
Waters, dropped an egg into, ii. 82
TIEN-HOANG, Fohi or twelve, iii. 39
Kings of heaven or, iii. 368
TIENT-T'-AI, Monastery of, v. 394, 411
TIGRIS, Seleucia on, i. 176
TI-HOANG, or Kings on Earth, iii. 368
TIKKOUN, First-born from Passive Deity, iii. 38
TIKKUN, Form of Protogonus or, iv. 274
TILES, Assyrian, i. 313; iii. 47, 426, 436; v. 193
Babylonian, iii. 210; v. 176
Chaldeo-Assyrian, iii. 17; iv. 45; v. 177
Fragments, of, iii. 284
TILLER OF SOIL, Cain, iii. 275
TIMAUS, Region of, iii. 209
TIME, Action of, ii. 273
Aiōn, iv. 58
Aspect of, i. 84; ii. 269
Aspects of Ain Soph in, ii. 65
Astronomical measure of, i. 232
Auxiliaries of, v. 202
Beginning of, i. 284
Births and deaths every second of, iii. 304

Boundless, ii. 69; iii. 236; iv. 56; v. 235
Brahma aspect of, i. 84; ii. 266
Chiun God of, iii. 389
Circle representing, i. 173; iv. 119
Collective mind in manifested, the, iv. 55
Consciousness and, v. 536
Cosmos and, iii. 37
Creations born in, iv. 119
Cycles, in space proceeds in, iv. 56
Deity manifesting in, iii. 166
Delusion of, v. 403
Differentiation in space and, iv. 297
Duration divided into universal and conditioned, i. 131; ii. 136
Egyptian Zodiac, from, iii. 430
Emblem of Kronos, i. 299
Eternal deity, iv. 325
Finite Absolute, made, ii. 136
Fire, presides over, i. 151
Greek circles of, ii. 362
Heaven, beginning of, ii. 124; iv. 202
Illusion, only an, i. 110
Kāla or, i. 145; iv. 134
Kalpas, divided in, iii. 186
Kashyapa, sprung from, ii. 81
Kep mother of, ii. 124
Kronos is, ii. 96, 145; iii. 150, 412, 414, 418
Measure of, iv. 192
Mother of, i. 274; iv. 202
No-number in, i. 152
Pagan's abstraction of Deity, ii. 370
Past, present, and future, i. 110, 116
Prakriti and, i. 84
Progeny of space and, iii. 104
River of, Nile, iv. 154
Roaring loom of, i. 148
Saints accuseth even, iii. 237
Saturn or, iii. 341
Scandinavian, legend of, ii. 145
Seb, God of, ii. 74
Serpent a type of, ii. 121, 123
Shesha or infinite, iii. 61
Signs of, ii. 370
Son of, ii. 179
Soul of world and, ii. 306
Space and, i. 140, 296; ii. 107; iii. 381; v. 428, 482
Spirit ray beyond, iii. 245
Symbols of, iv. 119
Triumphs of, iii. 236
Truth daughter of, iv. 141
Vishnu a form of, iii. 308
Wheels of, v. 365
Work, swallows its own fruitless, iii. 271
TIMEKEEPERS, Seven, v. 200, 202
TIME-PERIODS, Early perception of, ii. 104
TIME-SPACES between Hierarchies, i. 225
TIMOTHY, Paul writes to, v. 301
TIMUR, Hordes of, iii. 337
TIN, ii. 276; v. 437, 441
TIPHERETH, in Chaldean Kabalah, a, i. 249; iii. 218
TĪRTHANKARAS of Jainas, iii. 421; v. 97
TĪRTHIKAS, v. 385, 399
TIRVALOOR, Brahmans of, ii. 386, 387, 390

TIRYAKSROTAS, or creation of sacred animals ii. 165; iii. 170
TIRYNS, structures of, iii. 344
TISALAT, Tiamat or Thalatth, iii. 71
TIT, the Deluge, iii. 360
TITAEA, wife of Noah, iii. 151, 271
TITAEA-Aretia, or Horchia, iii. 152
TITAEA-Magna, Berosus speaks of, iii. 151
TIT-Ain, or Titan, iii. 150
TITAN, Crucified, iii. 411
    Divine, iii. 410, 419
    Noah a, iii. 389
    Orphic, iii. 80
    Perphyrion scarlet, iii. 382
    Prometheus, iii. 410, 412, 414, 415, 416, 420; iv. 94
    Secondary age, of, iii. 22
    Tāraka, iv. 119
TITANIC, Age, iii. 410
    Forces, Host masters of, iii. 420
    Passions, iii. 411
    Remains, iii. 222
    Struggle, iii. 271
    Tradition, iii. 389
TITANIDAE, Goddess Rhea comprehends seven, ii. 165
TITANIUM, ii. 276
TITAN-Kabirim, Energies, great volcanic, iii. 362
    Manus or, iii. 152
    Regulation of seasons, iii. 362
TITANOSAURUS Montanus, iii. 222
TITANS, Allegory of, iii. 44
    Anthropological fact, founded on an, iii. 161
    Architects or fashioners, iv. 85
    Arkite, iii. 343
    Atlantean, iii. 295, 360
    Atlas and, iv. 61
    Bailly and Faber on, iii. 267
    Daityas and, iii. 289; iv. 69
    Dānavas or, iii. 190, 380
    Deities and, iii. 114
    Devil, and, iii. 353
    Diodorus on, iv. 344
    Diluvians, or, iii. 151
    Divine, iii. 150
    Dynasties of Giants or, iii. 368
    Gebers, signify, i. 174
    Generation of, iii. 271
    Giants, beliefs of, and, ii. 134; iii. 239, 278
    Greek, iii. 239, 275, 335
    Hesiodic, ii. 136
    Hyperboreans of race of, iv. 344
    Japhet on list of, iii. 150
    Kabiri and, iii. 150, 275, 359
    Men, were, iv. 324
    Northeners, iv. 346
    Purānic Giants and, ii. 133
    Rebellion of, iv. 345
    Solar system or, ii. 135
    Symbols, not mere, iv. 324
    Third race, of, iv. 335
    Titæa mother of, iii. 151
    Uranides or Divine, ii. 135
    War of, i. 251; iii. 73; iv. 66, 68; v. 201
    Works of, iii. 347
TITLES, Archangel, the same given to God and the, iv. 48

TIT-THEUS or Tityus, iii. 150
TITUS LIVIUS, v. 148, 256
TITYOS in Odyssey, iv. 163
TITYUS or Tit-Theus Divine Deluge, iii. 150
TJI-GAD-JE, v. 391
TMEI, v. 247
T'MURA, iii. 52
T'PHILLIN, Cross and, v. 195
TO ON, Hydrogen identified with, iii. 144
    One father or, iii. 122
TOAD, Goddess, ii. 100
    Venomous alkaloid of, i. 305
TOD, Col., v. 258
TOGA, Colossus draped in, iii. 338
TOHU-VAN-BOHU, Deep or primeval chaos, iv. 45; v. 189, 227, 228, 230-235
TOLTEC, forefathers of, i. 64
TONE, Great, v. 443
TONGA, Lemuria and, iii. 227, 331
TONGUES, Blaze of Vaishvānara, of, iv. 138
    Fiery, ii. 54, 94; iv. 179
TONKIN, War in, v. 38
TONSURE-KNIFE of Buddhists, v. 412
TOOM, creative force in Nature, ii. 24
    Fohat known as, ii. 398
    Noon, issued from, ii. 24
    Osiris saying he is, ii. 24
    Primordial Deity, iv. 151
TOPINARD, Anthropology of, iii. 252
TOPOGRAPHY, Christian, iii. 398, 415
TOPSY, immortal, i. 270
TORAH, v. 179
TORMENTS, Sweat of their, ii. 301
TORQUAY, Fossils of Kent's cavern at, iv. 292
TORQUEMADA, referred to, iii. 80
TORRICELLI, referred to, iii. 348
TORS in West England, iii. 343
TORTOISE, Brahmā in shape of a, iii. 85
    Divining straws and, ii. 158
    Kashyapa means, iii. 256
    Prajāpati in form of, iii. 256
    Sacred, ii. 159
TORTUOUS SNAKE, iii. 233
TORTURES, Apollonius of, v. 282
    Twelve of Egyptian Mysteries, v. 161, 209, 313
TOTAL, Host of Angels, of great, iii. 239
    Unity, in, iv. 167
    Universal, iii. 90
TOTALITY, Infinite, i. 170
    Nature, of kingdoms of, iii. 261
    Rays, of seven, ii. 240
    Subordinate creative powers, of, iv. 114
TOUCH, Air, property of, i. 253; iii. 116
    First Race and, v. 523
    Procreation by, iii. 183
    Sense of, v. 550
    Sparsha, or cohesion, ii. 88; v. 539, 540
TOURS, F. de, referred to, iii. 123
TOWER(S), Babel, of, iii. 16, 274; v. 185
    Bhagulpore, of, iii. 94
    Built by priest-architects, i. 257
    Round, of Ireland, v. 217, 284
TOYĀMBHUDI visited by Kumāras, iii. 319, 401
TRACK, change in form of, ii. 274
TRADITION(S), Gnostic, v. 203
    Myth means, v. 53
    Persian, v. 199

TRAGEDIES OF Æschylus, Sophocles and, Shakespeare, iv. 243
TRAGOS, scapegoat of Israel, iii. 386
TRAGULIDAE, one of the Ungulate Mammals, iv. 305
TRANCES, ii. 240; iii. 296; iv. 129; v. 458, 555
TRANSCENDENTALISM, ii. 208
TRANSFORMATION, Adams, of four, iv. 24
  America in, iii. 442
  Anthropoid mammal, of, iii. 178
  Climate, of, iii. 146
  Date of last, iii. 252
  Evolution and, iii. 129
  Gravity, of, iii. 235
  Human fœtus, of, i. 235
  Inspiration, by, v. 212
  Man has escaped, iii. 67
  Nature's grossest physical, ii. 122
  Nebulae into stars, of, ii. 314
  Nothing dead if capable of, ii. 232
  Organic, iii. 23
  Physiological, of sexes, iii. 155
  Races, of, iii. 83, 94
  Realm of, i. 270
  Species, of, i. 251; iii. 347; iv. 232
  Star, of a, ii. 320
  Theory, iv. 303
  Third race, of, iv. 181
TRANSFORMATIONS, Animals, of, iii. 159
  Apes, of, iii. 264
  Cycle of, i. 270
  Defunct, of every, i. 273
  Descending arc, on, iii. 264
  Ethnological, i. 237
  Fundamental, i. 254
  Future human, iii. 299
  Incessant, iv. 300
  Logos, of, ii. 64
  Man, of, ii. 158
  Mysteries of Cyclic, iii. 413
  Pre-cosmic, iii. 152
  Pymander, of, iv. 59
  Racial physiological, iii. 185
  Series of, ii. 361; iii. 66
TRANS-HIMĀLAYAN, Adept, i. 213
  Arhat Esoteric School, i. 212
  Chakra, i. 173
  Esotericism, i. 170; iv. 207, 208
  Occultists, iii. 97
  Region, iii. 46
  School, v. 480
  Teachings, i. 193
TRANSLUCID earth, iii. 312
TRANSMIGRATION, Cycle of, i. 235
  Life Atoms, of, v. 384
  Souls, of, i. 305, 333
TRANSPACIFIC migration, iv. 358
TRANS-SOLAR systems, i. 205
TRAVELS of Marco Polo, iii. 438
TREATISES of Shri Shankarācharya, i. 315
  Astronomical, v. 341
  Magical and Occult, v. 59
TREE(S), Ababel, the mystical, iv. 188
  Adept sorcerers called, iv. 63
  Āryan mythology, of, iv. 89
  Astrology and astrolatry, iii. 36
  Avataras are, of salvation, v. 350

  Being, of, ii. 129; iv. 160
  Bodhi, of, iv. 160
  Buddhi transformed into a, iv. 210
  Divine Planets, of, v. 430
  Dragon on a, ii. 384
  Evolution of, iii. 262
  Fruit, known by its, ii. 139, 188
  Garden of Eden, in, i. 174; iii. 106
  Genealogical, iii. 431, 432
  Genius loci, of, ii. 183
  Growth of, reversed, ii. 123
  Infamy, of, v. 162
  Initiates, symbol for, iv. 64
  Knowledge, of, i. 187, 292; ii. 55, 91, 120; iii. 17, 107, 133, 143, 182, 208, 219, 294, 384, 395; iv. 67, 83, 159, 160, 197; v. 28, 43, 85
  Life, of, i. 128; ii. 121, 122, 260, 272, 273, 339; iii. 43, 106, 142, 219; iv. 25, 86, 130, 159, 197; v. 85, 154, 163, 375, 446, 493, 496
  Living, of divine wisdom, i. 259
  Man is a, v. 510
  Mountains, ascending above three, iii. 220
  Norse legends of, i. 259
  Occult nature of, ii. 260
  Ormazd's, iv. 86
  Pine most primitive, iv. 166
  Pole of Heaven or, v. 202
  Prophyry, of, v. 439
  Sacred, iii. 112
  Sephirothal, i. 229, 283; ii. 344; iii. 17, 38, 48, 294; iv. 167, 196; v. 227, 439
  Serpent, and, ii. 120, 121; iii. 220, 354
  Symbol of, i. 187; v. 180, 510
  Truth, of, v. 49
  Tzité, iii. 106
  Waters of Life, sprinkled with, ii. 123
  Wisdom, of, iii. 274; iv. 51, 86
  Yggdrasil, of universe, ii. 145
TRENT, council of, iii. 213
TRES MATRES, v. 88
TRETĀ YUGA, iii. 79, 309, 322; v. 347, 348
TRETĀGNI or sacred triad of fires, ii. 247
TRI, Chatur takes to itself, i. 138
  Three, is, i. 138
TRIAD(S), Adam Kadmon, of, i. 284
  Aima, the Mother, v. 211
  Akkadians formed their deities into, iii. 65
  Ana Belita and Davkina female, iv. 30
  Aristotle, of, ii. 340
  Arūpa, i. 261
  Ātmā-Buddhi-Manas human, i. 267
  Celestial planets, and, v. 444
  Chaldean, iii. 39
  Christian, or Trinity, i. 83
  Circle comprises a, ii. 341
  Cosmical and human principles, branches into seven, i. 83
  Death, disappears at, i. 181
  Double, v. 211
  Duad made a, ii. 343; iv. 172
  Energies of, ii. 391
  First, i. 186
  Great Gods, iv. 30
  Grecian philosophers, of, ii. 307
  Higher, v. 502, 515, 516

TRIAD(S) (*Contd.*)
  Immortal, i. 287
  Initial manifested and creative, i. 321
  Intelligible, iv. 170
  Interlaced triangles and, iv. 164
  Jewish, ii. 70
  Metaphysical, i. 80
  Microprosopus and, iv. 196
  Monad(s) and, ii. 145, 297; v. 498
  Parent Planet, born under, ii. 298
  Pre-cosmical, v. 188
  Pyramid and, iv. 147
  Quaternary, and, i. 287; iv. 147; v. 191
  Sephira of, i. 153
  Sephirothal, i. 188, 261; iii. 272; iv. 167; v. 191
  Septenary and, i. 284
  Spiritual, ii. 67
  Tetraktys, and, i. 129, 161; v. 77
  Theban, iv. 32
  Three-tongued flame, i. 282
  Three vital airs and, v. 517
  Transformed, iv. 32
  Triangle, and, i. 161; ii. 66; iv. 165
  Tri-mūrti, or, iv. 163
  Trinity an astronomical, iv. 110
  Unseen Gods higher, iv. 30
  Upper, i. 230, 289; iii. 15, 106, 220; v. 421
TRIADIC, Goddesses, ii. 82
  Hypostasis, ii. 147
  Phenomena of moon, ii. 102
  Semites, deities of, iii. 65
  Shaddai, ii. 343
  Spirit line, iv. 172
  Symbols, iv. 174
TRIAL(S) Paracelsus of, v. 282
  Sun-Initiate of, v. 269-274
  Thebes, at, v. 290
  Twelve of Initiation, v. 152
TRIANGLE(S), Apex of four, ii. 342
  Atma-Buddhi-Manas as, v. 514
  Base of, ii. 341, 344
  Chakra, inscribed in, i. 73
  Circle, and, iv. 167
  Colours and, v. 507
  Cross, formed by nails of, iv. 131
  Deity, symbol of, i. 84, 172; iv. 153
  Development of third, iii. 38
  Double, i. 177, 263; v. 120, 356
  Eastern Esotericism, in, ii. 33
  Equilateral, ii. 339, 340
  Fire possession of, iii. 88
  First, v. 455
  Geometrical figures, first of, iv. 146
  Greek Delta, Deity and, v. 117
  Higher, iv. 175
  Image of, v. 514, 515, 516
  Importance of, v. 116, 117
  Interlaced, iii. 48, 359; v. 356
  Kether of, i. 161
  Line, and Pentagram, i. 154
  Lipika and, i. 62, 187
  Lower, v. 426
  Lower line of, iii. 89
  Manifest, iii. 313
  Monad and, v. 507
  Point in equilateral, i. 144

  Primordial, v. 426
  Primordial abstract, iv. 171; v. 426
  Primordial light and, i. 263
  Pyramids, and, ii. 342
  Pythagorean, ii. 337, 341, 342, 346; iii. 37, 120; iv. 174; v. 180
  Quternary, and, iv. 163, 164; v. 426, 507, 513, 514, 516
  Radius of, ii. 28
  Ring round, i. 189
  Sephirothal, i. 160
  Shiva, apex upward is, iv. 163
  Side-lines of, iii. 68
  Six-pointed star and, iv. 102, 190
  Sparks called, i. 156
  Square, and, ii. 34; iii. 48; iv. 197
  Symbol of blending of Rūpa and Arūpa, i. 177
  Ternary and, v. 116
  Three, symbol of, i. 134
  Triad, or, i. 129; ii. 58, 66, 340
  Tribhujam a, iv. 148
  Upper, ii. 69, 107, 344; iv. 121, 145; v. 426, 507
  Vaishvānara of, ii. 346
  Visible, v. 188
  White head and face in black, ii. 141
TRIANGULAR stones, Serpents whose holes are under, iii. 350
TRIASSIC rocks, Marsupials of, iv. 254, 282
TRIATOMIC, i. 265
TRIBAL Cycles, ii. 367
  Deities, iv. 38, 77
  God of Jews, iii. 276, 418; iv. 107, 108
  Gods, ii. 139, 215, 381
TRIBES, Twelve, of Israel, v. 183
TRICEPHALUS, Mercury called, iv. 112
TRIDANDINS, v. 520
TRIDASHA, Hosts and multitudes, i. 138
  Thirty alludes to Vedic deities, i. 138
TRIDENT of Poseidon, iii. 389; v. 117
TRIFORM Fates, Karma, ii. 367; iii. 412
TRIGONIAS, iii. 202
TRIGONOCEPHALUS of Portugal, i. 305
TRIGRAMS of Fo-hi, iv. 124
TRIGUNAS and Gunas, ii. 62
TRILITHIC stones, iii. 345
TRILOBITES, iii. 167; iv. 267
TRI-LOCHANA, Rudra Shiva as, iii. 297; iv. 70
TRILOGY of Æschylus, iii. 412, 417
TRILOKA, v. 560
TRIMETRIC system, iv. 166
TRIMŪRTI, Enoch, in, v. 101
  Hindu, ii. 70, 96; v. 117
  Triad or, iv. 163
  Trinity and, v. 101
  Vedic, i. 153
TRIMŪRTIAN hypostases, ii. 295
TRINITARIAN, Alexandrian School, v. 101
  Chinmātra, aspect of, iv. 168
  God, i. 252
  Hydrogen, nature of, iii. 121
  Personages and Heathen Deities, v. 95
TRINITIES, Esoteric and Christian, i. 83
  Three, i. 321
TRINITY, Action and matter or a, iii. 47
  Adam Kadmon a, ii. 151
  Astronomical, iii. 357

TRINITY, (*Contd.*)
  Books of Enoch and, v. 101
  Cabbalah and, iii. 50
  Chaldean, iii. 72
  Chemical and alchemical, iii. 114
  Christian, i. 84, 173; ii. 111, 298; iii. 239; v. 33, 157, 211
  Cosmic, iii. 115
  Creative, ii. 229
  Deity and, i. 184; v. 188, 210, 219
  Egyptians, of, iv. 30; v. 189
  Ever-living, iii. 444
  Feminine, v. 211
  Fire, air and water, of, ii. 60
  Gnostic, iii. 354
  Holy, v. 156
  Hypostatical, ii. 393
  Immaculate conception, and, i. 128
  India, v. 189
  Jewish, ii. 70
  Kabalistic, i. 169; ii. 51, 166; v. 176
  Lunar, ii. 104
  Male, not entirely, ii. 103
  Man a, i. 278; v. 357
  Masculine, v. 211
  Material universe, of, i. 120; ii. 394
  Mystery language and, ii. 23
  Olympus, wall of, is, iv. 173
  Pagan dogma, ii. 99
  Parabrahman is inseparable from his, i. 128
  Persons of, three, ii. 194, 294
  Root of, v. 519
  Solar, v. 217
  Sun and, v. 219
  Symbol of, i. 80, 267
  Ternary and, v. 117
  Theban, v. 253
  Triad or, i. 83; iii. 15; v. 421
  Triangle and, v. 117, 519
  Unity in, ii. 108, 306; v. 210
  Universal, ii. 57
  Wisdom seeds, iii. 278
TRINOSOPHISTS, iv. 146
TRIPARTITE earth, iv. 327, 328
TRIPITAKA, Buddhist, no one could translate in A. D. 1820, i. 60
TRIPLE, Aspect of deity, ii. 61; iv. 160, 168
  Crocodile of Egypt, i. 267
  Fire spoken of as, i. 151
  Flame of Shiva, iv. 163
  Hecate, ii. 111
  Kingdom of the elementals, the, iv. 187
  Man, ii. 40, 276; iv. 174
  Nemesis, character of, iii. 306
  One whole Kosmos form, ii. 166
  Powers, ii. 113; iv. 30, 81
  Sephira, v. 91
  Septenary of Shani, v. 45
  Sun, v. 217, 315
  Ternary, iv. 152
  Unit is producer of four primary elements, ii. 61
  Unity of eternal fires, iii. 68
TRIPLEX, Mercury called, iv. 112
TRIPURĀNTAKA SHIVA, iv. 163
TRIPURĀSURA, Mahādeva destroying, iv. 119, 163
TRISHNĀ, v. 559

TRISHULA, Shiva's, iv. 118
TRISMEGISTUS, quoted, v. 107
TRISTAN D'ACUNHA, iii. 333
TRISUPARNA, Brāhman is, i. 258; iv. 162
TRITHEMIUS, ii. 172; v. 174, 207
TRITON, Poseidon's ministers symbolized in, iv. 150
TRITONS, Sea-gods, v. 117
TRITTENHEIM, v. 274
TRIUNE, Almighty, ii. 343
  Brahmā in form, ii. 179
  Iao, iv. 174
  Idea, v. 211
  Man, i. 272
  Monad, v. 493
  Seven emanate from, i. 153
TRIYUGAM, Three ages or, iii. 63
TRIVENI Sacred spot, v. 520
TROAD, worship of Kabirim in, iii. 362
TROGLODYTE, Gap between man and, iv. 237
TROJANS, iii. 110, 435; iv. 364
TROPHONIUS, Den of, iv. 148
TROPICAL, Colure, summer, iii. 406
  Crocodile and, regions, iii. 161
  Cycle of 19, years, iii. 86
  Greenland once, iii. 24
  Scandinavia, iii. 421
  Year, ii. 26, 105; iii. 355, 444; iv. 73
TROPICS, Cancer and Capricorn, of, iii. 355, 401
  Circles of, i. 253
  Pole, at, iii. 24, 330
TROY, Ancient, iii. 239, 437; iv. 364
  Giants and size of, iii. 280
  Greeks of age of, iv. 319
  Heroes who fell at, iii. 273
  Myth, regarded as a, iii. 438; v. 54
  Svastika found under ruins of, iii. 110; iv. 158
TRUE, Existence or Paramarthika, ii. 71
  Serpent, leader of souls, ii. 127
TRUTH, Absolute, i. 120; v. 400, 420
  Acceptance of, iii. 439
  Advent of, iv. 100
  Alethiea or, iv. 144
  Angelic entity presiding over light of, iv. 81
  Central Sun of, i. 299
  Champions of, i. 337
  Demonstrated, a, which cannot be, ii. 122
  Enigmatical mirror of pure, iii. 270
  Error and, mixed, ii. 336
  Esoteric, iv. 24, 228
  Eternal, v. 363
  Facts, rests on, iv. 280
  God, ii. 66
  Goodness and, iv. 134
  Highway of, i. 308
  Historians, suppressed by modern, iii. 366
  Ignorance of, iii. 410
  Intuition, known by, iv. 85
  Keynote of, v. 465
  Laboriously climbs hill, i. 41
  Light of, iv. 81
  Lines between, iii. 229
  Mathematics of, v. 37
  Nucleus of, ii. 187
  Occult, v. 445, 531
  Occultism and, v. 462, 463

TRUTH (*Contd.*)
  One absolute, i. 124
  One dark, v. 462
  One Spirit of, v. 261
  Palace of, v. 246
  Poetized fiction now as, once, iii. 20
  Primitive, v. 466
  Satya Yuga or, age, iii. 153
  Science, and, ii. 200, 234, 271
  Scripture, unveiled, iii. 267
  Sole custodians of, ii. 336
  Standpoints, from two different, i. 59
  Stones of, iii. 345
  Symbol of, iv. 171
  Time, Daughter of, iv. 141
  Tradition based on approximate, iii. 227
  Wisdom and, iii. 94
  Woman, as a naked, ii. 67
  World of, or Sat, i. 178
TRUTHS, Adepts concealed, i. 41
  Adumbration of great, i. 222
  Dzyu deals with, i. 168
  Esoteric, v. 466
  Falsehoods and errors of yesterday are, today,
    iii. 439
  Four, v. 377
  God, of, v. 69
  Hidden, reserved for Arhats, i. 44
  Initiation, revealed during, ii. 24, 231
  Life and regeneration brought by, i. 339
  Nidānas based on four, i. 112
  Primeval esoteric, iv. 151
  Races, inheritance of future, i. 220
  Secrecy with regard to divine, iv. 141
  Seven, i. 115
  Spirit of, iii. 376
  Spiritual, i. 310
  Vedic, in Purānas, iv. 97
  Vital, i. 45
TSABA Archangels or, v. 128
  Army of Satan or, iv. 69
  Meaning of, v. 320
TSAN or fraction, i. 196
TSANG and Nyingpo in Tibetan equal Ālaya,
  i. 120
TSAYDAM, in Kuen Lun Range, i. 47
TSELEM, Image, iii. 377
TSIN Dynasty, destruction of books by founder,
  of, iv. 262
TSI-TSAI, the Self-Existent, ii. 71
T'SOD-OLAUM of Hebrews, iv. 154
TSONDA and Buddha, allegory, v. 105
TSONG-KHA-PA, Reincarnation of Buddha,
  v. 148, 377, 378, 391, 393, 396, 403,
  404
TSOVO, or chief of Dhyāni Buddhas, v. 374
TSUNG-MEN, v. 409
TUARICKS, iv. 360
TUBALC', or Tubal Cain, iv. 146
TUBAL-CAIN, Kabir, is a, iii. 389
  Mineral kingdom, and, iv. 146
  Vulcan or, iii. 383
TÜBINGEN, Authorities of, v. 133
TUISCO, Tiu or, v. 305
TULPA, Incarnation in living body, v. 374
TUMULI, iii. 351, 421; iv. 321; v. 340
TURAMAYA, Asura Maya from, iii. 61

TURANIAN, Adami, iv. 19
  Adept, v. 418
  Assyrians, iii. 207
  Class, i. 52; iii. 419
  Dwarfs, iv. 323
  Esotericism, i. 173
  Forefathers, iii. 423
  Founders of religion, i. 58
  Language, iii. 205
  Nergo and, iv. 313
  Religion, i. 52
TURBID, Drops became, iii. 129
  Waters not, iii. 67
TURIN PAPYRUS, iii. 367
TURIYA state, ii. 294; v. 513, 515, 516
TURKESTAN, i. 48
TURKS, Esar of ancient, iv. 173
  Phoenix called by the, Kerkes, iv. 188
TURNING-POINT, Cycle of, i, 237
  Evolution of races, of, iii. 203
  Fourth round, of, i. 234
  Manvantara of, iv. 103
TUSCAN SAGES, ii. 376
TUSHITA or Devachan, v. 392, 412
TUSHITAS, Rudras who had been, iii. 99, 188
TUTELARY Genius, Jehovah as, v. 241
  Gods, ii. 110; v. 238
TVASHTRI divine artist and carpenter, iii. 110
  Vishvakarman, a synonym of, iv. 187
TWELVE, Apostles, ii. 115
  Great Gods, ii. 115
  Hours of day, ii. 168
  Labours of Hercules, v. 152
  Nidānas, v. 379, 397, 558, 559
  Orders, i. 261
  Signs of Zodiac, v. 241
  Tortures, v. 161, 290, 313
  Transformations, ii. 169
  Trials of Initiation, v. 152
  Tribes of Jews, iii. 205; v. 183
TWELVE-eyed Dvādashāksha, iv. 190
TWELVE-handed Dvādasha-kara, iv. 190
TWELVE-legged horse of Huschenk, iii. 396, 398
TWELVE-oared ship, iii. 398
TWENTIETH CENTURY, Secret Doctrine in,
  i. 59; iii. 439
TWENTY-four hours, our globe breathes every,
  ii. 265
TWICE-born, Brahmans, i. 44; iii. 80, 120
  Initiates, ii. 258, 266; v. 152, 276, 279,
  291
  Invasion of India by, i. 314
TWILIGHT, Action, Demiurge born in, of, ii. 95
  Body of, iii. 100, 129
  Day of great breath, of, iii. 20
  Fohat acts from one, to another, i. 200
  Hilaeira personified, iii. 130
  Humanity of, iii. 70
  Mahāmanvantara, of, i. 330
  Past and shadows of, iii. 330
  Pitris issue from, iii. 170
  Precursor of, iii. 42
  Sandhyā or, i. 254; iii. 68, 70
  Seven, iii. 308
  Sons, of, iii. 117, 129, 146
  Vāch called, ii. 140
TWIN-BIRTHS of *Genesis*, iii. 143

TWIN-BROTHERS, ii. 129; iii. 418
TWINS, Castor and Pollux, iii. 131
   Primal, ii. 130
   Two, i. 274
TWIN-SISTERS, Earth and Venus, iii. 42
TWIN-SOULS, ii. 296, 298
TWO, Brothers, legend of, iii. 272
   Dual Potency, v. 189
   Figures make four images, ii. 158
   Heads from one, ii. 273
   Keys, ii. 30
   Letters descend from spheres of, expectation,
      iii. 67
   Natures in Christ, v. 157
   .One becomes, iii. 206, 257
   Squares of good and evil, ii. 24
   Substances, i. 148
   Truths, i. 120
   Worlds, iii. 282
TWO-dimensional space, i. 295, 296
TWO-faced forms, iii. 74
TWOFOLD, Androgynes, iii. 172
   Man, i. 263; ii. 169; iii. 190
   Race or third, iii. 179
   Units, i. 264
   World, divisions of, iv. 193
TWO-HEADED children, iii. 66
TWO-HORNED Dulkarnayn, iii. 397
TYCHO BRAHÉ mean motions of, ii. 390
   Stars, on, ii. 216, 314; v. 324
TYMPANUM, Sensation produced on, ii. 278,
     358
TYNDALL, referred to, i. 293; ii. 206, 234, 252,
     358, 362, 393, 395; iii. 158; iv. 243;
     v. 28, 32
TYNDARIDAE, the twin-brothers, iii. 130
TYNDARUS, Leda spouse of, iii. 130
TYPE, Animal, iv. 252
   Argha, of Queen of Heaven, iv. 30
   Caduceus, of, ii. 274
   Catarrhines, of, iv. 236
   Cross was a, of Horus, iv. 158
   Enoch, of dual man, iv. 102
   Heavenly man, of, iv. 252
   Humanity of, i. 239
   Ideal, for every form, i. 324
   Intelligence, of, i. 266
   Intermediate, iv. 239
   Man's, iii. 17, 290
   Repertory, human, is, iv. 253
   Reversion to, iii. 294
   Species, and, iii. 256
   Unity of, iv. 307
TYPES, Ancestral, iv. 219, 267, 306
   Astral, during Pralaya, iv. 230
   Atlantean, affinities of three, iv. 360
   Cast-off, iii. 265
   Correspondences of, ii. 309
   Divine forms to divers, ii. 396
   Heterogeneous, iii. 423
   Horse, of, iv. 285
   Ideal, iv. 57
   Innumerable, iii. 258
   Jews, of twelve vicious, ii. 391
   Manvantara, new, each, iv. 298
   Marsupial, of Australia, iii. 21
   Phenomena chosen from cosmic, ii. 129

Pre-physical, iv. 254
Primitive, of fifth race, iv. 38
Race, of our present, i. 237
Rounds, from preceding, iv. 230
Satan, of, iii. 274
Species of animals, ii. 332
Spiritual, ii. 230
Store of, in microcosm, iii. 193
Sun and moon as, ii. 129
Third round man, of, iv. 255
Unknown, iii. 195
TYPHÆUS, Giant, ii. 187
TYPHON, iv. 54
   Constellation of, v. 202
   Diana hiding from, ii. 103
   Dragon Apophis or, iii. 379, 384
   Genetrix, iv. 117, 119
   God of Darkness, v. 312
   Hermes also, iii. 379
   Osiris and, i. 251; iii. 102, 378; iv. 85; v. 312
   Pan and, iv. 150
   Satan or, iv. 159
   Seth, Egyptian, iii. 44, 91, 365
   Seven stars of, ii. 125
   Thoth escaping from, ii. 77
TYPHONS will be dethroned, iii. 418
TYPOLOGY of Cross, iv. 116
TYRANT, Olympic, iii. 420
TYRE, Cherub, king of, called, iv. 70
   David stayed at, iv. 111; v. 311
   King of, reproved, iv. 60
   Maximus of, referred to, iii. 123
   Mysteries of, v. 279
   Navigators of, iv. 320
   Purple of, iii. 428
   Pyramids of, ii. 61
   Tabernacle pillars in, i. 184
TYRRHENIAN COSMOGONY, iii. 54
TYRUS, origin of prince of, iv. 61
TZABAOTH, Elohi of Israel, iii. 51
TZALA, a Hebrew word, iii. 143
TZELEM, Elohim, image of, iii. 145
   Image, iv. 24
   Nephesh, of, iv. 205
   Neshama, of, iv. 205
   Ruach, of, iv. 205
   Shadow-Adam, or, iv. 72
TZEPHUM, Boreas called, ii. 187
TZITÉ, Third race from, iii. 188
   Tree of Popol Vuh, iii. 106
TSONG-KHA PA, or Amitabha, a Tibetan re-
     former, i. 169
TZURE, prototype of Second Adam, iv. 24
TZYPHON, Science of, iii. 219

U

UDANA, Excellent seat of, iv. 138
   Life-winds subject to, iv. 139
   Physical organs of speech or, i. 158
UGRASENA, King of Mathura, iii. 323
UHLEMANN, Rosetta stone of, iv. 31
ULOM, Intelligible Deity or, ii. 81, 181
ULPIAN Library, v. 149
ULTIMA Thule of the Universe, ii. 313
ULTIMATES, Cosmic, iii. 37
   Matter of, iv. 164

ULTRA-MONTANES, and Zodiac, ii. 377
ULUG-BEG, tables of, ii. 384, 385
ULŪPI, Arjuna marries, iii. 218; iv. 200
ULYSSES, Calypso, Circe, and Polyphemus, iv. 338
UMA-Kanya, Esoteric name of Virgin, i. 155
UMBILICAL cord, iii. 140; iv. 29; v. 499, 518
   Vesicle, v. 422, 423, 449
UNBORN, Aja the, iii. 183; iv. 150
   Baby, analogy of seven months, iii. 259
   Element born not, iv. 170
   Nature of spirit ray, iii. 245
   Space, iv. 55
   Universe created by, ii. 87
UNCONDITIONED, Absolute Deity, iii. 166
   All, one, i. 311
   Consciousness and abstract motion, i. 80
   One reality is, i. 317
   Unity, i. 309
UNCONSCIOUS, All, i. 132
   Blind or, law, i. 317
   Conscious and, beings, ii. 173
   Creative plan of, i. 69
   Creator, man and, iii. 292
   Esoteric school rejects idea of anything being, ii. 172
   Eternity, in, ii. 359
   European philosophy, of, i. 79
   Evolution guided by, iv. 219
   Experience, appeals to, ii. 210
   Hartmann's philosophy of, i. 122
   Hegel's theory of, i. 122
   Inactivity of monad, iii. 67
   Latent and, life, i. 302
   Life, iii. 247
   Magic, v. 132
   Magicians, v. 50
   Manifestation of, iv. 232, 239
   Mission of units of humanity, iii. 444
   Occultist, ii. 281
   Personality, mortal or, in the, iii. 131
   Primeval men were, ii. 91
   Principle, v. 386
   Purposiveness, ii. 41
   Self-consciousness, to attain, i. 122
   Sorcerers, v. 47
   Spirit referred to as, i. 122
   Universal mind, iii. 37
   Universe evolved by, i. 167
UNCONSCIOUSNESS, Absolute non-being, and, i. 119
   Phase of, iii. 128
   Races, of first two, iii. 187
   Semi-perception, to, i. 229
   Spiritual, of monad, i. 228
   State of perfect, iv. 170
   Vedantins and, i. 324
UNCREATE, God foreseeing and, i. 323
   One Life formless and, i. 294
UNCREATED, Absolute unity is, iv. 154
   Beam, i. 319
   Lights, iii. 293
   Ray, ii. 294
UNDERSTANDING, Binah or, iii. 94; v. 211
   Buddhi, or, iv. 209
   Mahat or, i. 141
   Men endowed with, iii. 269

   Mental eye opened to, iii. 274
   Past, the, iv. 361
   Proverbs of Solomon and, iii. 143
   Sattva or, i. 136
   Subtle bodies remain without, iii. 101
UNDERWORLD, Sun saw at night the, ii. 16
UNDEVELOPED man, Relic of an, iv. 230
UNDIFFERENTIATED, Asat or, matter, iv. 168
   Cosmic Protyle, i. 129
   Cosmic substance, i. 142, 203
   Essence, i. 247
   Matter, i. 263
   Monads, iii. 311
   Protyle or, substance, i. 285
   Space, v. 447
   Substance, a nucleus of, i. 210; v. 448
UNDINES, ii. 330; v. 239, 540
UNDULATORY, theory, ii. 39, 218, 252, 303, 304
UNGULATE mammals, iv. 304
UNICELLULAR classes, the, iv. 227
UNICORN called a lunar myth, iii. 222
UNIFORM laws, of evolution works by, iv. 300
UNION, of Man with God, v. 210, 419, 428, 453, 494
   Man and Universe, of, v. 419, 453
   Self with All-Self, of, v. 269
   With THAT, v. 387
UNISEXUAL creature, iii. 202
UNIT(S), All, merged in, ii. 43
   Androgynous, iii. 196
   Aspects of universal, ii. 328
   Atoms only a compound, ii. 338
   Complex visible, ii. 344
   Differentiation of, iii. 419; iv. 85
   Divided *ad infinitum*, ii. 342
   Divine, v. 291
   Divine mind or, iv. 172
   Ego a compound, on incarnation, iv. 204
   Humanity of, ii. 363; iii. 444
   Indestructible and elementary, i. 231
   Indivisible, ii. 341
   Interlaced triangle, in, iv. 164
   Karma and, ii. 400
   Logoi of, i. 291
   Logos one great, i. 145
   Male, iv. 125
   Male God or First, ii. 47
   Man, a, v. 421
   Man living, iii. 292
   Mass and primordial, ii. 237
   Measure of, ii. 29; iv. 113
   Monad universal, iii. 339
   Nature and inter-related, ii. 379
   Perfection of, iv. 154
   Point, a, ii. 341
   Possible, ii. 342
   Ray, v. 421
   Self, v. 269
   Septenary, in chains of our system, i. 218
   Tel-loh, of measurement, iii. 230
   Tetrad issued from, iv. 170
   Third race, of, iii. 202
   Twofold and threefold, i. 264
   Unity of, ii. 354

UNITED STATES, Americans of, iii. 442
   Flora of Asia and, iv. 350
   Mounds in, iii. 421
   President of, iii. 437
UNITIES, Binaries and, in decad, i. 284
   Four, i. 283
UNI-triad, Invisible dew falling from, ii. 69
UNITY Absolute, i. 75, 128; iii. 122, 242; iv. 116,
   160; v. 86, 198
   Ain Soph infinite, ii. 64
   All potential, ii. 307
   Aspects or facets of same, i. 281
   Basis of Occult Science, v. 86
   Boundless and infinite, iii. 54
   Boundless extension or, ii. 56
   Cause of all, ii. 144
   Deity as an absolute, i. 128; iv. 116; v. 462,
   463
   Digits brought back to, iv. 152
   Diversity, in, iii. 311
   Divine, i. 309; ii. 399; iv. 173; v. 77
   Divine, and circle, i. 69
   Divine essence, of, ii. 339
   Divine names, of, iii. 51
   Ever-to-be-unknown, ii. 61
   Father-mother-son as, i. 129
   Fires of, iii. 68
   First manifested sparks of one, iii. 321
   First principle of, of unities, ii. 144
   Fohat transcendental binding, i. 170
   Forces combined as, ii. 246, 341
   God-man, of, i. 123
   Graduated, ii. 338
   History of, ii. 363
   Homogeneous, ii. 249
   Human species, of, iv. 178
   Immutable eternal and absolute, iii. 37
   Impersonal, an, iii. 243
   Infinite, v. 189, 227
   Kosmos, of all parts of, ii. 202, 280
   Local God expressed, in nature, ii. 183
   Logos as, ii. 151, 297; iii. 219
   Manifested, ii. 339
   Monad cause of all, ii. 343
   Monas, or, ii. 339
   Multiplication opposed to, i. 72; ii. 157
   Multiplicity, in, v. 383
   Name of, in the, ii. 343
   Nature, of all in, i. 179, 319
   No number, is, ii. 151
   Numbers begin with God as, i. 135
   Occult science and, i. 179
   One, i. 75, 81; ii. 340; iv. 241; v. 206, 210,
   227
   One life eternal living, i. 136
   Parent of all numbers, v. 210
   Phtah, of, ii. 399
   Plan, of structural, iv. 253, 307
   Platonic and Oriental Philosophy, v. 36
   Plurality and, iv. 144; v. 86
   Potencies of an interacting, ii. 340
   Primordial light, of, i. 263
   Secret doctrine and, iv. 123; v. 290
   Self-God, with, ii. 363
   Senary and, iv. 154
   Space a substantial, i. 76
   Specific, of humanity, iii. 201

Spirit and matter two facets of unknowable,
   ii. 267
Spirit of Nature is a, iv. 81
Spiritual and physical, of, iii. 414
Substance, of, i. 161
Supreme, i. 321
Synthesized, ii. 294
Ten and, v. 115
Thought and action, in, ii. 369
Total in, or universe, iv. 167
Trinity in, v. 211
Unconditioned, i. 309
Units of, ii. 354
Universal, a, ii. 338, 353; v. 127
Universal life, of, i. 327
Verbum a duality in full, iv. 84
Yang the, iv. 124
Zohar on, v. 115
UNIVERSAL Cause, v. 261
   Code of Ethics, v. 265
   Deity, v. 70, 206, 528
   Essence, v. 188
   Fire, v. 562
   Flood, v. 109
   Force, v. 229, 385, 475
   Generation, v. 192
   Ideation, v. 382
   Illusion, v. 379
   Intelligence, Mahat or, i. 122, 141, 263; ii. 332
   Knowledge, Egyptian Priests of, v. 264
   Knowledge, Keys to, v. 185
   Kosmos, v. 436
   Language, ii. 22; v. 175
   ,,   Direct Revelation and, ii. 29
   ,,   Egyptian Hierophants and, v. 197
   ,,   Initiates of, v. 178
   ,,   Kabbala and, ii. 30
   ,,   Ragon suspected, ii. 22
   ,,   Science Scholar, Tries to learn,
        ii. 30
   ,,   Seven dialects of, ii. 22
   ,,   Wisdom Religion and, iv. 37
   ,,   Wisdom science has, ii. 22
   Law, Man witnesses to, i. 317
   ,,   Mankind under, ii. 334
   ,,   Occult science and, ii. 240
   ,,   Physical evolution and, iii. 126
   Life, seven-principled, v. 528
   Magic, is, v. 43
   Matrix, v. 422
   Mind, Ahamkara and, iv. 187
   ,,   Ah-hi and, i. 91
   ,,   Alaya is, v. 519
   ,,   Being, God and, i. 327
   ,,   Builders and, ii. 303
   ,,   Christians and, iii. 239
   ,,   Collective or, iv. 55
   ,,   Cosmic ideation, ii. 41
   ,,   Creative logos or, i. 170
   ,,   Divine ideation or, v. 449, 456
   ,,   Divine thought and, i. 69
   ,,   Elemental vortices and, ii. 348
   ,,   Emanation of, ii. 326
   ,,   Flames born of, iii. 235
   ,,   Fohat and, i. 150
   ,,   Ideation of, i. 170, 322; v. 382
   ,,   Infinite, i. 323

UNIVERSAL (*Contd.*)

Mind, Light of, v. 31
,,   Mahat, i. 122, 141, 263; iii. 69, 88, 97, 171
,,   Man and, v. 551, 552
,,   Omniscience of, v. 552
,,   Plan of universe in, i. 165
,,   Pralaya, during, i. 111
Myths, v. 232, 233
Pralaya, Age of Brahma and, i. 225
,,   Cosmic or, iii. 79
,,   Cosmic substance and, ii. 41
,,   Maha—or, ii. 275
Principle, v. 455, 543
Ray of the, v. 402
Science, v. 44
Self, v. 374, 418
Secret Doctrine, v. 50
Seven Forces, v. 472
,,   Powers, v. 203
Soul, Adi Buddhi the, v. 391
,,   Akasha or, v. 483
,,   Alaya the, i. 121; v. 471, 494, 499
,,   Anima Mundi, i. 121; ii. 81; iv. 131
,,   Atma and, iii. 234; v. 497
,,   Conduct governed by, ii. 138
,,   Creation and, ii. 138
,,   Creator, Mind of Demiurgic, ii. 67
,,   Divine, i. 277
,,   Hea or, ii. 72
,,   Intelligent, v. 493
,,   Nothing motionless within, i. 70
,,   Philosophically a Māyā, i. 76
,,   Plane of abstract presence, i. 69
,,   Sat, iii. 69
,,   Spirit of, ii. 169
,,   Union of Higher with, v. 452
,,   Unknown, v. 145
,,   Upādhi or basis of, i. 163
Spirit, Ātmā, iv. 168
,,   Christos, iv. 46
,,   Divine Ray and, v. 128
,,   God, i. 301
,,   Monad emanates from, i. 82
,,   Omnipresent, ii. 193
,,   Svayambhu or, i. 123
,,   The, i. 323; iv. 209; v. 487
Symbol, Pyramid is, v. 117
Symbology, v. 42
The, Plato on, v. 31
Unit, v. 129
Unity, v. 127
Whole, v. 419
Wisdom, v. 374
UNIVERSALITY, Archaic teachings, of, i. 261
Births, of periodical, ii. 383
Duality, of doctrine of, i. 281
Life, of, iv. 273
Zodiac, of, ii. 378
UNIVERSALS, Particulars from, i. 208; iv. 155; v. 464
Plato and Pythagoras proceeded from, iii. 160
UNIVERSE, the actual, ii. 322
Ain Soph and, v. 386
Ākāsha, Ether and, v. 475
Ālaya of, i. 102, 119, 120
All-being is Brahmā, or, i. 125

Analogy in, i. 230
Angels or spirits in, iii. 96
Archetypal, i. 207
Architect of, iii. 110
Arupa, i. 161
Astral fluid womb of, iii. 194
Astral light recorder of, i. 165
Ātmā-Buddhi-Manas and, v. 558
Ātman of, Christos, i. 190
Atom in, self-consciousness possible to every, i. 167
Atom in, tends to become God, i. 214
Atom in, trace, every, iv. 241
Basic ideas upon, i. 326
Basis of the object, iv. 306
Boundaries of, i. 301, 330; ii. 88
Brahmā or, i. 75; iii. 43, 310; iv. 187; v. 379, 476
Brahmā progenitor of, i. 74, 146, 148; ii. 173
Brahmā, Vishnu, Shiva, Supreme Triad in, v. 444
Brahman and Brahmā or, i. 75
Breath of Fire and expansion of the, i. 148
Breathes, ii. 265
Builders of, i. 123; ii. 90; v. 74
Building of, ii. 70; v. 505, 539
Celestial bridge of, i. 264
Central sun, evolving from, ii. 95
Chaos seven elements and, i. 194
Composition of material, ii. 394
Conceived homogeneous, ii. 242
Consciousness of Ego, of, v. 552
Contradictory exposition of, ii. 229
Correspondence to Amnion, v. 423
Cosmogony of, i. 206
Created by accelerated motion, iv. 121
Creation of, i. 261; iii. 388
Creative force of, iii. 68
Creative nature, proceeds from, i. 157
Creators of, i. 187; iii. 70; iv. 111
Culmination of, iv. 173
Death of physical, iv. 151
Decad in, i. 161
Deity considered as, i. 156
Deity geometrizes in forming, iii. 51
Deity in, i. 173, 231; iii. 117
Description of creation of, i. 319
Desire of life abstract cause of, i. 117
Diagram of planets in, v. 437
Dissolution of, iii. 154
Divine manifesting in, iii. 53
Divine powers frame, i. 86
Divine Ray manifested in, i. 146
Divine thought determines existence of, i. 112, 116, 130
Dodecahedron of, iii. 48
Dragon seeking to devour, iii. 383
Dreamless sleep applied to, i. 119
Dual, v. 466
Duration of, iv. 189
Earth in relation to, iii. 157; iv. 272; v. 227, 437
Egg became, ii. 74
Egg-shaped globe and, i. 141
Electricity life of, i. 195; v. 229
Emanation of, ii. 165; v. 91
Emergence out of chaos of, ii. 319

UNIVERSE (*Contd.*)
Eternal, arises from, ii. 48
Eternal becoming, an, iv. 16
Eternal foundations of, i. 195
Eternity of, i. 82; iv. 59, 114
Ether female principle and, i. 127
Ether recipient of heat radiations of, i. 164
Evolution of, i. 122; ii. 309, 323, 337; iii. 76;
    iv. 73, 114
Extent of, iii. 277
Faces of, iv. 148
Facts relating to, i. 318
Falls into matter, iv. 114
Flame filled with ethereal, ii. 88
Fohat caused, to move, i. 250
Forces of, i. 196, 328; iv. 174
Formation of, ii. 319
Formless condition of, i. 123
Foundations of, i. 195
Finite condition of, i. 224
Fire septenary throughout, i. 151; v. 562
Fulness of, ii. 395
Garment of God, v. 187
Generation of, ii. 66
Genesis of, iii. 369
Germ in mundane egg which will become, i. 69
Germ of son or visible, iii. 94
Globe, and our, i. 326
Globular shape of all bodies in, i. 141
God as synthesis of, ii. 131
Great, ii. 57
Great architect of, ii. 338
Great breath and, i. 70, 116
Great cycle and, i. 301
Great mother absorbs, i. 115
Guiding action of higher intelligences in,
    i. 318; ii. 53; iv. 70
Has neither centre nor periphery, v. 439
He who is beginning of, ii. 87
Heterogeneity in evolution of, ii. 41
Hindu cosmogony and evolution of, ii. 145
Human principles and, v. 453, 470
Ideal and visible, ii. 342
Ideal plan of, i. 165, 324
Ideas, of, iii. 49; iv. 170
Ideation of, i. 322
Illusion, of, i. 188, 201, 335; iii. 49; v. 488
Incipient stage of, ii. 293
Intellectual progress of, iii. 84
Jagat or, i. 73
Kabalah and, iii. 38; iv. 134
Karma of, v. 528
Kosmos and infinite, i. 248
Lawgiver of, iv. 124
Laws of, i. 82; ii. 332, 370; iv. 248
Life and light of, i. 73
Life and motion of, i. 70
Life everywhere in, i. 294
Life, heart, and pulse of, i. 263
Light on objective, iii. 49
Lipika spirits of, i. 186
Lives, of, i. 294
Living and sentient, i. 124
Logos and, i. 177; iii. 38, 192
Lotus and, ii. 94; iv. 40; v. 476
Macrocosm, iii. 184; v. 322
Man, and, v. 419, 453

Manifested, i. 76, 81, 83, 140, 203, 298;
    iii. 70, 122, 388; iv. 161; v. 453
Manifested God known through, ii. 147
Manifested, number root of, v. 418
Manifesting, iv. 57; v. 528
Manifold, i. 75
Matrix of, iv. 81
Material, ii. 395
Material of, iv. 183
Matter and, i. 303; ii. 183, 339, 351, 400;
    iv. 164; v. 154, 507
Matter force, and necessity of, iv. 218
Mechanical, ii. 216
Metaphysical illusion, ii. 42
Mind of, i. 320
Mind to embrace, iii. 29, 30, 113
Mirror of the Logos, iii. 38
Modeller of, ii. 69
Molecules of, i. 179
Monads expression of, ii. 348, 355, 356
Mundane egg and, i. 133
Myriads of systems in, iii. 54
Mystery of, i. 153; iv. 157
Nam-Kha, of, v. 379
Nativity of, v. 331
Nature, a mind-born son of, ii. 115
New, ii. 51
No annihilation in, v. 387
Nothing profane in, ii. 302
Noumenal and phenomenal, i. 201
Numerical system of, i. 178
Objective, i. 109, 218, 262; ii. 356; iv. 230;
    v. 488
Occult or Spiritual, v. 275
One absolute omniscience in, i. 320
One and secondless principle in, iv. 125
One causeless cause and, i. 125
One law of, iv. 124
One life of, i. 306
One manifested, i. 152
One reality its dual aspect in, i. 82
Organisms, full of, ii. 315
Origin of, i. 314; ii. 318
Our, one of many, i. 115
Parabrahman, itself, ii. 105
Periodicity in, i. 311; ii. 362; iv. 60
Phantom germ of, ii. 83
Phenomenal, i. 71, 201
Phenomenalization of, i. 117
Philosophical conceptions of, ii. 159
Plane of our, i. 194, 243, 316
Plane of subjective, ii. 357
Planes of, v. 524-529
Planetary chain in relation to, i. 114
Pleroma, of, iii. 38
Point, and single, ii. 212
Prajāpati was this, ii. 149
Pralaya, during, i. 137
Primal Cause of objective, i. 114; ii. 343
Privileged beings in, no, i. 268
Production of, iv. 178
Prototype is present of all things in this, i. 132
Pythagorean decad contained, of Gnostics,
    iv. 144
Reality in, i. 83
Re-awakening of, i. 84, 86
Recoalescence of, iii. 79, 310

UNIVERSE (*Contd.*)
Reconstruction of, v. 229, 230
Regions of, i. 171
Representations of, i. 320
Rest and activity of, ii. 84
Rhythm in all changes in, i. 78
Root of, mystic, i. 109
Root-principle of, i. 293
Rudimental, ii. 59
Ruler of, iii. 48
Scale of temperature throughout, i. 198
Science and, ii. 200; iv. 234
Seed of, iv. 112, 163
Self of the, v. 379
Seminal principle of, iv. 112
Sephirothal tree is, ii. 67
Septenary, i. 76, 213
Series, one of an infinite, i. 71
Serpent, cast off its old skins, like, i. 141
Seven and, ii. 164
Seven regions of, i. 171
Shoreless in magnitude, i. 133
Sien Chan our, i. 193
Single substance, of a, ii. 267
Sleep of, i. 114, 125, 137
Solar, evolution of, i. 85, 86, 331
Soma and, occult nature of, iii. 57
Son of necessity or, i. 114
Son, or, i. 130
Space and, i. 75, 114; v. 107, 382
Speech produced, ii. 148
Spencer and Von Hartmann and, i. 84
Spirit and matter, of, i. 114; ii. 53; v. 558
Spirit enveloping, i. 327
Spirit of, Logos, i. 81, 263; iii. 37; iv. 184
Spiritual and physical aspects of, i. 268
Spiritual beings in, i. 279
Stars of, i. 330; iv. 121
Substance, of, i. 264
Symbol of, i. 114; iv. 152, 171
System merging in central, iii. 195
Tattvas, built from, v. 470, 505, 539
Temple in, but one, i. 260; iv. 221
Ten and the, v. 435
Ten principles of, v. 129, 425, 435
Ten points symbolize, ii. 341
Ten sacred numbers of, ii. 76
This refers to, i. 73
Thought, of, ii. 342
Three Eternal Things in, v. 381
Transcendental conceptions of, ii. 348
Tree of being or, iv. 160
Trinity of material, ii. 394
Two infinites impossible in, i. 74
Type and prototype in, iii. 129
Ultima Thule of, ii. 313
Unconscious evolved, i. 167
Unmanifested, i. 169; iv. 197
Unseen, v. 322
Vast body of, iv. 166
Virgin mother of, ii. 179
Vishnu and, iii. 50; v. 188, 233, 250
Visible, i. 248; iv. 109; v. 188
Water, built by, v. 234
Wear and tear of body of, ii. 275
Web is, i. 148, 150
Wing, touching, with its swift, i. 102, 132

Wisdom, of, nature of, ii. 138; iv. 212
Worlds of the, v. 209
Zeno and evolving, i. 143
UNIVERSES, Formation of, i. 291
Infinite number of, i. 115
Invisible, iii. 38
Leibnitz and, ii. 354
Manifesting and disappearing, i. 82
Phenomenal, ii. 340
Playground of numberless, i. 82
Three, i. 321
UNKNOWABLE, Absolute cause is, ii. 399
Accepted, ii. 138
Ain Soph as synonym for any, i. 172; iii. 52
All, iv. 58
Causality, one, i. 196
Creator and architect, behind, iii. 55
Crookes, Prof., very close to, ii. 307
Deity, ii. 275; v. 471
Differentiation of the, iv. 297
Eternal or causeless cause, i. 80
European philosophy, of, i. 79
Karma one with, iii. 307
Mover, i. 126
Point, concealed and, ii. 171
Principle, iv. 71
Reflection of, iii. 50
Rig Vedic verse, in, iii. 137
Spencer, of, i. 124, 324; ii. 40
Theology attempts to unveil, i. 84
Unity, spirit and matter two facets of, ii. 267
UNKNOWN, All, v. 321
Cause, v. 218, 227, 229
Essence, v. 188
God, v. 408
Great, v. 101
Supreme, the, v. 129
UNLUCKY numbers, iv. 146, 152
UNMANIFEST, the, iii. 238
UNMANIFESTED, Absolute or, i. 152
Light, v. 78
Logos, i. 81, 140, 262, 263, 320; ii. 47; iv. 168;
v. 214, 426, 430, 455, 476
Manifested begotten by, ii. 114
Motion eternal in, i. 160
Ray in, iii. 37
Son of, father, iii. 311
Spirit of the Universe, the, i. 263
Universe, i. 169; iv. 197
UNMANIFESTING Principle, v. 129
UNNAMEABLE, Absolute cause to Egyptians
was, ii. 399
Ain Soph, iii. 52
UNPOINTED Hebrew, Jehovah in, iv. 41
UNPRONOUNCEABLE, Absolute cause, ii. 399
Names of three highest worlds are, ii. 153
Word, v. 310
UNPUBLISHED MS. referred to, ii. 162
UNREACHABLE, Land, iii. 400
Life which radiates from the summits of, i. 129
UNSEEN UNIVERSE referred to, ii. 183, 208
UNSPOKEN Word, v. 455
UNTIED, the animal creation, iii. 277
UNTRANSLATABLE Names, ii. 200
UNUTTERABLE, the, Name, ii. 60
Threshold of, iii. 196
UPĀDĀNA the material cause, i. 126; v. 559

UPĀDHI(S), Basic mould or human, i. 325
  Basic Principles or, iii. 99
  Basis (Bases), i. 163, 208, 213, 323; iii. 46; iv. 164; v. 361, 367, 558
  Basis or, of air and water, iii. 114
  Body an, v. 521
  Buddhi, of Eternal Essence, v. 493
  Degree of, ii. 43
  Divine thought Ākāsha, ii. 39
  Ether, of, ii. 240
  Every cause, of, v. 558
  Foundation or, of world, i. 330
  Germ which becomes, of seven principles, i. 332
  Hierarchies, v. 553
  Man of, v. 361
  Material, iv. 170
  Mind as, v. 543
  Nidānas and, v. 558
  Objective universe, of, ii. 90
  One Absolute, iii. 46
  Organism as an, iv. 239
  Pātāla means, v. 538
  Periodical, i. 233
  Primordial substance, of every phenomenon, ii. 44
  Shankarāchārya's spirit, of, v. 367
  Soul, of spirit, i. 208
  Spiritual, ii. 319
  Substance of, of ethereal man, iii. 165
  Three periodical, i. 233
  Vehicle(s) or, i. 109; ii. 191
UPADVIPAS or Root Island, iii. 403
UPANISHAD KATHA, ii. 149
  Shvetashvatara, i. 76
UPANISHADS referred to, i. 194, 218, 311, 313, 314, 315; iii. 39; v. 27
  Advaita Vedantins, of the, ii. 247
  Anugita one of the oldest, i. 157
  Bhashya on, i. 315
  Gnostic literature in, iv. 133, 136
  Meaning of, v. 27
  Pantheists echo, i. 74
  Philosophy of, v. 232
  Science in, ii. 258
  Scope of, i. 314
  Secret Doctrine, and, i. 118
  Teachings of, v. 353
UPASALA, Configurations of, iii. 401
UPHEAVAL, Alps of, iv. 320
  Americas, of two, iii. 405
  Continent, of, iii. 21
  Continents, of new, iii. 359
  Oceans, of, iv. 269
UPPALA VARNA, (UTTALA) a mystic power, v. 378
UPPER, Adam, iv. 25
  Circle, iv. 124, 205
  Egypt, ii. 79, 183; iv. 175
  Region, iv. 200
  Sea of fire turned into, i. 103, 138
  Triad, i. 230, 287
  Worlds, and lower, ii. 343; iii. 129
UR, Abraham came from, ii. 91; iii. 230
  Moon God at, worship of, iii. 148
URAEUS, Cosmic fire and, ii. 155
  Devoured by, i. 274

Osiris and, ii. 155
  Serpent, ii. 398
URAL, Mountains, i. 58
URANIDES or Titans, ii. 135, 136
URANIUM a chemical atom, i. 266
URANUS, ii. 299
  Ākāsha, and, v. 476
  Ancients and, v. 310, 322
  Astronomical Teacher, iv. 335
  Atlantean King, first, iv. 331, 334, 335
  Discovery of date of, i. 162, 164
  Gaea, destroyed his children by, iii. 271
  Hindus, known to, i. 162
  Kronos mutilating, ii. 136; iii. 270, 285
  Mystery Planet or, v. 316, 322
  Neptune and, i. 204
  Satellites of, i. 163, 204; ii. 317
  Saturn, denser than, ii. 317
  Second race, a Dhyān Chohan of, iv. 335
URANUS-day and Sun-day, i. 162
URD, foundation of, iv. 89
URDHVASROTAS, the, ii. 165, 173, 175; iii. 170
UREA, i. 294, 306
URIEL, Atlanteans, and, ii. 334
  Bull, i. 185; iii. 124
  Denouncer, iii. 381
  Enoch and, ii. 334; iv. 51, 103
  Venus is, v. 439
URIM and Thummim, ii. 377; v. 240, 242, 310, 335
URJA, Progeny of, iii. 154
URKA, Omoroka or Lady of, iii. 143
URNS, Engravings of, by the Emperor, Yu, iii. 303
URSA Major, iii. 360; iv. 338
  Minor, iii. 360; iv. 184, 338
URSCHLEIM of Oken, iii. 165
URSUS SPELÆUS, iv. 309, 315
USES, Gravity and cohesion, of, ii. 283
  Life, of, iii. 248
USH, Fire or heat, iii. 123
USHANAS, Danavas and, iv. 66
  Demon Deity, degraded into a, iii. 57
USHANAS-SHUKRA, Venus or, iii. 44, 45, 57; iv. 66, 69
USURPATION of divine rights, iii. 231
USURPER, Zohac the, iii. 397
UTERUS, condition of man in, iii. 193
  Solar matrix and female, v. 422-425
UTTARA KHANDA of the Padma Purāna, iii. 319
UTTARA MIMANSA, Buddhists and the, i. 118
UXMAL, iii. 428; iv. 320

V

VĀCH, Aditi, form of, i. 194; v. 164, 165
  Articulate speech, on, v. 189
  Brahmā and, i. 75, 153, 194; ii. 149, 150; iii. 137, 155; iv. 40
  Brahmā-Prajāpati and, ii. 151; v. 439
  Daksha and, ii. 149
  Female Logos, v. 291
  Female power, v. 165
  Four kinds of, i. 195; ii. 150
  Goddesses, most mysterious of Brahmanical, ii. 152

VĀCH (*Contd.*)
Hindu, i. 194; iii. 55
Ila or, ii. 247
Kwan-Yin and, i. 193, 194
Logos, daughter and mother of, i. 194; ii. 148; iii. 204
Madhyamā, ii. 150
Mantras, hidden power of, ii. 69; v. 189
Melodious cow or, i. 144; ii. 145; iii. 416; v. 165, 291
Mystic speech, v. 394
Para, ii. 150
Pashyanti, i. 195; ii. 150
Prajāpati or, ii. 148, 151
Pranava called, i. 195; ii. 150
Rhea repetition of, iii. 151
Rishis and, ii. 148
Sarasvati later form of, i. 158
Shatarupa, is, ii. 149
Twilight, Sandhya or, ii. 149
Universal soul, or, ii. 67
Vaikhāri, i. 194; ii. 150, 151; v. 165, 199
Vaivasvata, daughter of, v. 190
Viraj and, i. 194; iii. 151
Voice feminine, i. 157; iii. 115
VĀCH-SHATA-RUPA, iii. 156
VĀCH-VIRAJ, iii. 137
VĀCHASPATTYA, Sanskrit encyclopedia, ii. 93
VĀCHĪSHWARA, the voice deity, v. 380
VACUITY, Ākāsha is, for Rationalists, i. 336
Plenum and, ii. 218
VACUUM, Absolute, of Newton, ii. 217
Force, is latent, ii. 57
Gravity acting through, ii. 214
Inter etheric, ii. 280
Nature abhors a, i. 133; ii. 57, 243, 393
Newton on, ii. 218
Radiation through, ii. 244
Sidereal bodies and, ii. 214
Space not, ii. 251
VADUKKU, Genii called, iii. 250
VĀHAN, or Vehicle, Atman, of, i. 308
Brahmā-Prajāpati, of, i. 145
Buddhi, iii. 244; v. 493
Flame, of, i. 309
Matter, of spirit, iii. 69
Spark, of flame, i. 309
VĀHANA, Conventional existence used as, ii. 71
Garuda, of Vishnu, iv. 134
Primordial seven, of, i. 168
Sun, of solar system, ii. 251
Varuna, of, iv. 148
Vehicle or, i. 140, 262; ii. 191, 251
VAIDHATRA, Fourfold mystery and, i. 153
Kumāras and, ii. 176
VAIDIC, or VEDIC, Aditi, v. 192
Āryans, Mythology of, iv. 66
Deity, v. 87, 98, 188
Indra, v. 254
Literature, v. 91
Poets, v. 28
Structures, v. 87
Works, v. 344
VAIDYUTA, Electric fire of, ii. 245
VAIKHĀRI, Para becomes, ii. 152
VAIKHĀRI VĀCH, Forms of, ii. 150
Madhyamā of, i. 194

VAIKUNTHALOKA, the heaven of Vishnu, ii. 246
VAIKUNTHAS refused to create, iii. 99
VAIRĀJAS, Devas, Gods or, iii. 98, 99
Fiery Egos, v. 543
VAISHĀKHA, v. 344
VAISHNAVA system, the, ii. 176
VAISHANAVAS, India, in, ii. 399
Maha-Buddhi, on, ii. 170
Speculations of, i. 126
Vishnu God of, ii. 139; v. 233
VAISHVĀNARA, Agni or, iii. 380
Fire, iii. 311; iv. 64, 138
Humanity, spirit of, iii. 311
Vaivarta, Brahmā, ii. 84
VAIVASVATA, Adityas in, period, iii. 99
Brahmā, Vishnu and Shiva precede, iii. 152
Deluge of, i. 136; ii. 85
Hindu Noah, iii. 226; iv. 343
Humanity, iii. 329
Humanity saved by the racial, iii. 310
Legends and allegories of, iii. 314
VAIVASVATA, Manu, ii. 162, 176, 247; iii. 48, 147, 149, 150, 153, 154, 155; iv. 169, 180, 181
Manvantara or round, i. 64; iii. 79
Sixth creation or, ii. 176
World-deluges, and, iii. 335
VAJRADHARA the diamond-holder, i. 123; v. 366, 374, 375
VAJRAPANI the diamond-holder, i. 123; v. 375
VAJRASATTVAS, Diamond-souled, i. 123; ii. 295; v. 374, 375
VALAS, anterior to Odin, v. 42
VALCKENAER, referred to, v. 33
VALE of Mexico, Aztecs in the, ii. 35
VALENTINIAN, Pairs of male and female Æons, iv. 139
Theogony, iv. 146
VALENTINIAN, table in Ephiphanius referred to, iv. 25
VALENTINUS, referred to, ii. 23, 126, 164; iv. 136, 139; v. 128, 462
Gnosis; the profoundest doctor of the, ii. 63
VALLABĀCHĀRYAS of Bombay, ii. 49; iv. 159
VALLANCEY, Col., referred to, ii. 366; iii. 267; v. 267
VALLEY of Thorns, v. 300
VĀMADEVA, Rebirths of, ii. 36; iii. 283
Shiva called, iii. 251
VĀMADEVA MUDALIAR describes coming night, ii. 91
VAMPIRES, Moon like all, is friend of sorcerers, i. 211
Preconceptions like, iv. 296
VAMPYRELLA one of the Monera, iii. 172
VAN, the Tartar Cycle, v. 341
VANANIN-LAMERTADE, iv. 25
VANCHUG, Chenresi, iii. 185
VANDAL warriors of Nadir Shah, iii. 337
VAPOUR, Creatures born from, iii. 189
Ether, and, ii. 251
Heat Genenerates, i. 294
Incandescent, ii. 266
Nebulae formed of, ii. 320
Second earth disappeared as, ii. 157
VAPOURS, Ring of, ii. 316

VAPOURY, one of the seven transformation, of
    matter, i. 254
VARA, Lord and ruler of the, iii. 19
    Man, meant, iii. 293
    Superior or, iii. 170, 190
    Yima, or ark of, iii. 292, 293; iv. 181
VARAHA, Avatara, ii. 85; iii. 64
    Boar, ii. 84
    Creation, iii. 64
    Padma Kalpa, or, ii. 176
VARANASI, see Benares
VARIATION, Nature end, iv. 266
    Physiological, iv. 219
    Species, in, iv. 249
    Stature, in, iii. 441
VARIATIONS, cause of, in organisms, iii. 300;
    iv. 218
    Cross-symbolism, of, iii. 117
    Elements, of, ii. 272
    Mammalian type, of, iv. 247
    Man and climatic, iii. 265
VARIETIES, Genus homo, of, ii. 36, 297
    Modes of procreation, of, iii. 176
VARNAS, Orders, ii. 137
VARRO, referred to, v. 309
VARSHAS, Dvipas and, iii. 266
    Portions or, iii. 368
    Pushkara with its, iii. 402, 405
    Terrestrial regions as, iii. 320
VARSHAYANTI one of the Pleiades, iv. 121
VARUNA, Asura applied to, iii. 101; iv. 68
    God of water, ii. 183; iv. 149
    Indra punishes breaker of laws of, iv. 177
    Mitra and, iii. 155
    Neptune and, iii. 271
    Ouranos or, iii. 76
    Space, dragged down from, iii. 75
    Sublime position of, iv. 177
    Uranus a modified, iii. 271
    Vāhana of, iv. 148
    Vehicle of, i. 267; iv. 148
    West, deity of, i. 186
VASISHTHA, Curse of, iii. 250
    Evil, on, ii. 133
    Mind born son of Brahma, iii. 88
    Mysteries imparted by Varuna to, iii. 271
    Rākshasas saved by, iii. 235
    Seven sons of, iii. 154
VASTUBHŪTA or substance, iv. 183
VĀSUDEVA, Liberator, i. 328
    Lord of all, ii. 137
    Nature of, iii. 60
VĀSUKI, v. 286
VASUS the eight Vedic Deities, i. 138; iii. 250
VATES, v. 452
VATICAN, Claim to be seat of Peter, v. 139
    Doctrines of secret schools preserved in, i. 65;
        iv. 75
    Lanci librarian to, iii. 375
    Library of, v. 307
    MS. of Kabalah in, iii. 242
VATSARA, Cycle, v. 339
VAU, crook, hook or, iv. 28
    Jod and Hē in Jehovah, i. 154
VĀYU, Indra, iii. 377
    Loka, v. 80
    Tattva, v. 475, 476, 477, 478, 479, 485

Vedic Trimurti, one of, i. 153; iii. 123
    Wind, God of, i. 241
VEDA-VYĀSA, Bricklayers mentioned by, ii. 25
    Jews may be referred to by, ii. 25
    Vishnu as, iii. 154; iv. 51
VEDANĀ, One of twelve Nidānas, v. 559
VEDĀNGAS, v. 341
VEDĀNTA, Aspect of Basic idea of, i. 122
    Books of, i. 313
    Buddhists and, i. 118
    Esoteric Philosophy and, i. 126
    Esotericism in, iv. 52
    Nyāya and, i. 126
    Philosophy, iii. 255; iv. 16
    School, v. 494
    Septenary in, i. 212
VEDANTIC, Advaita Philosophy, iv. 168
    Brahman, i. 145
    Doctrines, i. 323; v. 127
    Doctrines distorted, i. 145
    Features in eclectic system, v. 304
    Idealism, ii. 328; v. 187
    Koshas, five in, classification, v. 361
    Lokas, v. 538, 539
    Lucretius endroses a, conception, i. 74
    Mulaprakriti, i. 300
    Philosophy, ii. 72, 308
    Principles of man in division, i. 212
    Quinquepartite division of human principles,
        ii. 273
    Row, T. Subba, a, scholar, i. 211; ii. 346
    School, v. 494
    Septenary dogma, scholar on, iv. 207
    Teaching, i. 328; iii. 164
    Wisdom, i. 69; iv. 97
VEDĀNTIN, Advaita, philosophers, i. 74; v. 383
    Affirmation of, v. 127
    Creation, tenet of, i. 74
    Creed of, v. 380
    Dreamless sleep according to a, i. 119
    Faith of true, ii. 293
    Hegelian Unconscious, on, i. 122
    Hindu, v. 231
    Maya in esoteric and, teaching, i. 131
    Metaphysical mind of Hindu, iii. 166
    Nirvāna, and, v. 352
    Occultist, on Vāch, i. 194
    Pantheism of, philosophers, iv. 40
    Parabrahman of, v. 107, 386
    Principles taught by, v. 427
    School in Tibet, v. 402
    Sects, apple of discord between three, ii. 170
    Visishthadvaita philosophy and the Advaiti,
        i. 128
    Visishthadvaita, sect, of, i. 189
VEDĀNTINS, the, Advaita, ii. 247
    Aja, of, iv. 174
    Atheists, called, ii. 247
    Ātman of, i. 170
    Belief of, v.299
    Catechism of, ii. 246
    Consciousness, identity of universal and indi-
        vidual, on, i. 123
    Definition in spirit of, ii. 146
    Disguise in, iv. 208
    Esotericism of, and Daiviprakriti, i. 193
    Goal of, v. 380

VEDĀNTINS (*Contd.*)
  Ishvara on, ii. 297
  Kabalists and, v. 107
  Koshas divided by, iv. 174
  Mahat as Prakriti for some, i. 131
  Moksha of, v. 384
  Mystical tenets of, iii. 241
  Nirvāni of, iii. 89
  Parabrahman of, i. 76, 81, 118, 324; ii. 44, 68, 157
  Principles of, v. 427
  Quaternary of, v. 530
  Seven higher worlds of, v. 380
  System of, v. 299
  Tibet, of, v. 402
VEDANTISTS, Philosophy of the Advaita, i. 126, 335
VEDAS, the Ad-iti in, iii. 54
  Ahi-Vritra in, iii. 383
  Ākāsha and, i. 336
  Antiquity of, iv. 177; v. 176, 342, 343, 345
  Aryan literature oldest, i. 50
  Aryans, of Indian, iv. 284
  Asura of, iii. 123
  Bhumi in, i. 295
  Brahmā, a word not in, i. 43
  Brāhmana portion of, i. 313
  Brahmans' chant, i. 157
  Buddha and, v. 371
  Chhandajas of, iv. 156
  Commentaries explain, i. 56
  Cosmogony of, iii. 70
  Crookes will vindicate, ii. 348
  Cross from standpoint of, ii. 180
  Cycle of, iv. 195; v. 341
  Daityas led astray from path of, ii. 140
  Date of, ii. 83
  Division of, iv. 51
  Dual meaning of, i. 313
  Early humanity of, iii. 105
  Elements, conceal real nature of, ii. 245
  Esoteric lining of, i. 218
  Ether and, i. 336; ii. 44
  Fire and Deities, on, iv. 137
  First God in, iv. 151
  Forgeries, called, i. 60
  Four truths and four, i. 115
  Gautama and, v. 371
  God, on immortality of, i. 109
  Idols not countenanced by, iv. 292
  Incongruities in, ii. 138
  Initiates wrote, iv. 17
  Interpretation of, v. 154
  Key needed for, iv. 187
  Logograms in, iii. 335
  Loka-Chakshuh of, i. 162
  Max Müller and, i. 52
  Metres of, i. 331
  Milked out from fire, air, and sun, v. 111
  Musical notations in, v. 197
  Mystic speech, Brahmā revealed by, ii. 148
  Myth of, iv. 16
  Occult Ghandharva of, ii. 248; iv. 156
  Odin, Max Müller and, i. 52
  One Deity, one caste, one, i. 145
  Pitris, on, iii. 87
  Planetary chain in, allusions to, i. 295

  Preservation of, i. 60
  Purānas and, iv. 96
  Radiant matter and, ii. 348
  Scientific explanation of friction in, ii. 247
  Secrecy enjoined by, v. 68
  Secret doctrine, and, i. 59
  Secret of, i. 258
  Senses explained in, ii. 258
  Septenary element in, iv. 176
  Serpent worship and, iii. 214
  Seven Rishis visit locality where, were written, ii. 72
  Shiva's name unknown in, iv. 118
  Surya in, i. 162
  Symbolism in, v. 73, 87, 91
  Synonym of Gods in, ii. 178
  Text of, could not be obtained by Akbar from Brahmans, i. 47
  That in, ii. 107; iii. 90
  Translation of, could not be made in 1820, i. 60
  Tree of Being, the leaves of the, ii. 123
  Tvashtri in, iii. 109, 110
  Universal, once, iv. 51
  Universal language and, ii. 30
  Upanishads are esoteric glossaries of, iv. 52
  Vāch mother of, iii. 115
  Vishnu and, iii. 154; iv. 183
  Vishvakarman in, iii. 109, 110
VEDDHAS, Ceylon, of, iii. 201, 419; iv. 291
  Jungles, of, iii. 288
VEDHAS, Mind-born sons of Brahma, i. 152; iii. 183
  Sanandana one of, iii. 87, 180
VEDIC, Babylonian mythology and, influence, i. 54; iii. 136
  Bhrigu a, sage, iii. 42
  Calendar, iv. 121
  Cosmogony, iii. 54
  Deities, i. 138; iii. 271
  Deity, v. 188
  Demon of drought, iii. 384
  Devas of, nations, iii. 378
  Earths, of teaching, i. 295
  Fohat, Apam Napat, name for, iii. 399
  Hymns, iv. 16, 151
  Indra powerful God, iv. 177
  Influence on Mythology of, v. 110
  Kāma, character of in, iii. 183
  Kashyapa, sage, iii. 141
  Nārada, Rishi, iii. 59, 92
  Parāshara, Rishi, ii. 176
  Period, v. 41
  Poet, v. 75
  Rebirth, teaching of, i. 259
  Secret meaning of, texts, i. 314
  Teachings, iv. 178
  Trimurti, i. 153
  Truths, sublime, iv. 97
  Vishnu of later times unlike, god, i. 171
  Vishvakarman, ii. 192
  Women in, period, ii. 97
VEGA, Arctic voyage of the, iv. 343
VEGA, de la, referred to, iii. 344
VEGETABLE, Bodies, Life, ii. 173
  Cloth, iii. 230
  Development, iii. 157
  Element, iii. 358

VEGETABLE (*Contd.*)
First round, in, iii. 187
Forms, iii. 195; iv. 298
Fourth round, impulse stops at, i. 229
Jiva in, particle, i. 271
Kingdom, i. 214, 227, 237, 239, 264, 278;
ii. 344; iii. 167, 312
Leaflets, with, iv. 255
Life, i. 301, 311; ii. 304; iii. 291; iv. 246,
281
Monad, i. 231; iii. 53, 192
Progenitors after, life, iv. 281
Remains, iii. 65
Tissues, i. 294
World, i. 310
World, Soma sovereign of, iv. 63
VEGETABLES, Creation, of, iii. 170
VEGETARIAN(S), Atlantes were, iv. 331
Buddha was, v. 105
VEGETATION, Abundant, i. 264
Astral relics of previous, iv. 298
Bosom of stone, born from, iv. 165
Consciousness of, i. 320
Creatures born from, iii. 189
Ethereal, iii. 291; iv. 282
Moon feeds, ii. 261
VEHICLE(S), Ah-hi, of divine will, i. 111
Ain Soph, of, ii. 151; iv. 298
Argha or, iii. 292
Atmic Ray, of, i. 229
Brahmā, of Brahman, i. 83
Brahma-Prajāpati, of, i. 145
Being, of Spirit, ii. 138
Buddhi, of Ātmā, i. 178, 243, 290; iii. 69;
iv. 152, 176
Cosmic substance, of, i. 81
Crocodile, of Horus, iv. 148
Desires and passions, Kāma Rūpa, of, i. 209
Dhyānis, of incarnation of highest, iii. 278
Divine, i. 261
Divine man, human form, of, iii. 291
Divine ray, for, i. 264
Dolphin, of Poseidon, iv. 148
Egotism, of, v. 354
Ephemeral, i. 305
Fifth principle, for, iii. 169
Forces, for manifestation of, ii. 216
Generation, of, iii. 140
Gods, of a hosi of, ii. 201
Hamsa-Vāhana uses swan as its, i. 84
Hīnayāna school of little, i. 112
Horus, of, iv. 148
Intellectual, for moral forces, ii. 191
Jīva, of personal consciousness of, iii. 244
Kāma Rūpa, of desire, iii. 125, 168
Kingdoms, of lower, i. 310
Light, of, iv. 80
Linga Sharīra an inert, iv. 165
Mahāyāna school of great, i. 112
Matter, of becoming, i. 323
Matter, of, consciousness requires, i. 81
Matter, for soul on this plane, i. 120
Men occasionally, of hosts of, spirits, i. 271
Monad degraded into a, iii. 339
Monads, of, i. 235; ii. 293; iii. 89
Navis or boat-shaped, iv. 31
Number seven, of life, iii. 47

Prāna, of, i. 212
Primordial seven, Fohat, of, i. 168
Principles and, v. 493
Ray, Buddhi, for, i. 264
Schools of little and great, i. 112
Soul substance differs from, body, i. 205
Space a, i. 125
Substance of, ii. 319
Sun, of Higher Deity, v. 314
Three, ii. 349
Unknown deity, of, iv. 153
Upādhi or, i. 109
Vāhan (Vāhana or), i. 140, 208, 309, 309;
iv. 134
Varuna, of, crocodile, i. 267
Wisdom and rebirth in great and little, i. 112
Wisdom, of divine, iii. 143
Yāna or, i. 112
VEIL, Allegory of, v. 105
Circle and point, over, ii. 341
Creation, between incognizable and logos of,
ii. 149
Cosmic, ii. 147
Darkness of, ii. 348
Deity of, iv. 115
,,   Elements are, ii. 181
,,   Universe is, v. 91
,,   Unseen space, ii. 57
Fourteenth Manu an additional, ii. 90
Indivisible point forms a, ii. 60, 70
Infinite Light, of, v. 191
Initiation, of, iv. 127
Intelligence behind, i. 322; ii. 244
Isis, of, i. 338; iv. 225
Manifested, ii. 318
Matter, of, ii. 244, 335, 358; iii. 283
Mystery, of, round Apollonius, v. 143
Nature, of, ii. 337
Nucleus of truth, over, ii. 187
One reality, of, i. 317
Parabrahman, of, ii. 144, 146
Principles hidden under a, ii. 184
Secrecy, of, iii. 132
Secret Doctrine, of, v. 216
Solar cosmic, ii. 252
Temple, of, ii. 149
Unknown, of, iii. 218
VEILING of esoteric meaning, ii. 166; v. 260
V'ELCAIN or V'ulcain, iii. 391
VELOCITY, Earth's rotation, of, iii. 324
Monad, of, ii. 358
Nascent planet, ii. 316
Sound, of, ii. 288
VENDĪDĀD, the Ahura Mazda of, iv. 180
Airyana Vaejō, in, iii. 19
Bestower of weal of, iv. 86
Celestial militia of, iii. 41
Chain of worlds, on, iv. 328
Daevas in, iv. 85
Fravarshi in, iv. 48
Geographical changes pointed to in, iii. 356
Michael in, iii. 383
Origin of, iii. 408
Roman Catholics and, iv. 44
Serpent in, iii. 355
Yima in, iv. 180
VENERABLE, of the Age, v. 40

VENEZUELA and ATLANTIS, iv. 360
VENTRICLES of Heart, v. 556
VENTUS and SPIRITUS, ii. 56
VENUS, Aditi and Vāch identical with,
     iii. 55
   Anael, Regent of, v. 310
   Asphujit or, iii. 45
   Astoreth or, iv. 30
   Axis of, iii. 45
   Bearded, i. 139; iii. 143
   Celestial Priapus born from, iv. 25
   Correspondences of, v. 437, 441, 444
   Cow's horns on head of, iii. 44
   Cupid son of, iii. 416
   Earth, light bearer to, iii. 42, 45
   Earth more dense than, ii. 317
   Earth twin sister to, iii. 42
   Eve or, v. 164
   Evil spirits and, iii. 385
   Friday or day of, ii. 378
   Governs tenacious faculties, v. 442
   Holy Ghost, iv. 110
   House of, i. 164
   Influence of, iii. 37
   Informing Spirit of, v. 326
   Ishtar or, iii. 73
   Isis or, v. 246
   Istar Ashteroth or, iii. 153
   Jupiter and Lucifer-, i. 251
   Kabar, called, v. 309
   Kali Yuga epoch, at, ii. 387
   Lakshmi or, iii. 86, 183; iv. 150
   Left eye, and, v. 438
   Length of day on, iv. 276
   Less adapted for human life, iv. 276
   Lucifer and, iii. 42, 44; v. 310, 428
   Lunar goddess, ii. 111
   Manas and, v. 438, 441
   Mars and, iii. 391; iv. 30; v. 433, 442
   Men on, more gross than we, ii. 326
   Mercury one with sun and, iv. 112
   Morning and evening Star, v. 441
   Mother Virgin, iii. 75
   Music of spheres, and, iv. 172
   Muth is, v. 164
   Number six sacred to, iv. 164
   Orai genius of, ii. 301; iv. 108
   Principalities rule, ii. 153
   Races of, iv. 268
   Roman Catholics and, iv. 49
   Satellites of, not known, i. 210, 219
   Seasons of, iv. 276
   Semele presides between Mars and, ii. 116
   Sign of, i. 72
   Sons of Light and, ii. 298
   Sophia resides in, iv. 81
   Star of sea, ii. 108
   Taurus, house of, v. 164
   Temple of Hiram to, iv. 111
   Temples of, v. 267, 295
   Uriel and, v. 439
   Ushanas or, iv. 66, 69
   Worship, iv. 28
VENUS-APHRODITE, Foam of ocean, from,
     ii. 95
   Sea personified, ii. 178
   Westerns, of, iii. 86

   Worship of, iv. 29
VENUS-ASTRATE, Bust of, iv. 29
VENUS-LUCIFER, Astraea, Virgo or, iv. 354
   Earth, alter ego of, ii. 17
   Morning star, iv. 329; v. 267
   Titans connected with, iii. 44
VERA CAUSA, ii. 211
VERBUM, Christ or, v. 277
   Creative, princeps, iii. 240
   Creative speech or, iv. 112
   Dual aspect of, iv. 84
   Esoteric meaning of Christian, ii. 146
   Face, and his, iv. 47
   Ishvara or Brahma called, i. 194
   Logos, Word, or, i. 157, 188, 300; ii. 147;
     iii. 38, 354
   Lucifer, one with, iv. 84
   Manifested, i. 320
   Master, of the, i. 141
   Mercury, iv. 112
   National versions of, v. 84
   Parabrahman, of, i. 193
   Son or, ii. 261
   Sound of, ii. 354
   St. John, of, ii. 383
   Sun, and, of, iv. 49
   Taurus and, or Christ, ii. 383
   Thought divine, of, i. 139
   Word, Sound, or, v. 234
VERITIES in Bible, v. 97
VERMES of naturalists, iv. 227
VERMIFORM, appendix, iv. 251
VERMILION, Bird, ii. 125
   Luxor at, iii. 428
VERTEBRATA, First, iii. 256
   Lower, iv. 254
   Man highest, iv. 194
   Third eye atrophied in, iii. 297
VERTEBRATE(S), Blind, iii. 300
   Descendants of, first, iv. 236
   Kingdom, iv. 166
   Life, lower, iv. 254
   Life, primitive germ of, iv. 300
   Lowest, the, iv. 233
   Oviparous, iv. 304
   Structural plan of all, iv. 253
   Third race, in, iii. 190
VESICA PISCIS, v. 162
VESICLE, Blastodermic, v. 424
   Umbilical, v. 423
VESPASIAN, Emperor, v. 147, 264, 334
VESTA, Fire in temple of, ii. 52
   Goddess of earth, iii. 152
VIA STRAMINIS the Milky Way, ii. 154
VIBHAVASU, or fire, ii. 88
VIBHUTAYAH or Potencies, i. 75; iv. 183
VIBRATION(S), approximate rate of various,
     ii. 286
   Atoms, of, ii. 358
   Brain, and of sound, ii. 278
   Causes that produce ethereal, ii. 239
   Colours and sounds of, v. 421, 453, 454, 456,
     457, 508, 509, 550
   Correlation of, ii. 239; v. 457
   Eternal, i. 177
   Eye and too rapid, ii. 232; v. 457
   Factor other than, ii. 289

VIBRATION(S) *(Contd.)*
  Heat, of, ii. 261
  Joy and Sorrow, v. 550
  Keely works by sympathetic, ii. 284
  Last of the Seventh Eternity, i. 131
  Light called a, ii. 206
  Molecular, ii. 284
  Molecules of air broken up by, ii. 287
  Motion, is eternal, ii. 174
  Muscial Instruments, of, v. 485
  Nerve, v. 485
  Notes of musical scale, of, iv. 198, 508, 509
  Phenomena produced by, ii. 310
  Powers and, in air corresponding, ii. 19
  Senses, and, ii. 257
  Skandhas, are, v. 560
  Sound and colour, of, v. 457, 508
  Sweeps along, i. 132
  Thought, of, v. 549
  Wing of, touches the germ, i. 132
VIBRATORY, Astral light, motion of, ii. 62
  Cause, waves proximate, ii. 239
  Keely's engine, ii. 280
  Metcalfe against, theory, ii. 248
  Occultists and, theory, ii. 239
  Range of perceptible, v. 457
  Scale of, v. 508, 509
VICARIOUS, Atonement, v. 499
VICEGERENT of God, v. 126
VICRAMĀDITYA, v. 346
VICTIM,
  Mysteries, of the, v. 291
    ,,   Christ as, v. 84
    ,,   Hierophant-, v. 104
    ,,   Sacrificial, v. 530
    ,,   Vishvakarman, as, v. 270
    ,,   Vithoba, Vishnu, as, v. 288
VIDADHAFSHA or South, iv. 328
VIDYĀ, Ātmā, i. 249
  Bīja, v. 396
  Chatur, v. 519
  Divine, v. 305
  Esoteric, i. 286
  Gupta, v. 174-193, 482
  Highest Magical knowledge, iii. 425
  Paths of, i. 243
  Sacred Science or, iii. 436
VIDYADHARSA, Inferior Pitris, ii. 263
VIDYAS, The four, i. 222
VIHĀRAS, or caves of Buddhist monks, iii. 338
VIJNĀNAM, i. 212; v. 559
VIJNĀNAMAYA, one of the sheaths, ii. 294
VIJĀNAMAYAKOSHA or higher mind,
  i. 212
VIKARTANA, Rites, v. 284
  Sun, or, iii. 380; v. 154, 270, 272
  Surya, v. 274
VIKRAMĀDITYA, v. 244
VILLAPANDUS referred to, ii. 375
VILLIERS French savant referred to, i. 305
VILLIPLACENTALIA, iv. 283
VIMĀNA VIDYA or aeronautics, iii. 424
VIMĀNAS, air-vehicles or, iii. 424, 425
VINA, Shiva's or Kali's v. 518, 520
VINATA daughter of Daksha, ii. 81
VINE, Food of life, of, i. 245
  Isis-Osiris showed use of, iii. 365

VIOLET, Colour of the Astral, v. 555
  Correspondences of, v. 454, 455, 461, 507, 508, 516
  Esoteric colour of Moon, v. 442
  Hierarchy, v. 461
  Ray, v. 442
  Vibrations, v. 456, 457, 458
VIPASHYA, religious meditation, v. 373
VĪRABHADRA, Raumas created from pores of, iii. 78
  Shiva-Rudra creates, iii. 189
VIRAJ, Brahma as, i. 153, 194; iii. 55
  Daughter of Kāma, v. 165
  Heavenly man born from, iv. 177
  Male deity, i. 129
  Male symbol, iv. 40
  Manu created by, iii. 309, 311
  That male, ii. 168
  Vāch and, i. 75; iii. 151; v. 165, 190, 191
VIRĀJA, Mānasa sons of, iii. 98
VIRĀJA-loka inhabited by the Agnishvatta, iii. 98
VIRAJ-MANU, v. 190
VIRASVANIM, ii. 47
VIRCHOW, Prof., referred to, iii. 438; iv. 220, 221, 288, 310, 321, 360
VIRGIL, Christ and, v. 337
  Evolution, on, iv. 166
  Geography of, erroneous, iii. 415
  Great Æther, called Jupiter, ii. 45
  Indus or Nile of, iii. 415
  Inspiration of, ii. 384
  Mercury on, iii. 41
  Quoted, v. 154, 312
  Virgin, and, ii. 116; v. 312, 337, 338
VIRGIN, Alm or, iv. 31
  Angels, iii. 248
  Apollo and, v. 312
  Archangel Michael and, v. 320
  Blood, Jehovah-Cain sheds, iii. 387
  Celestial, " son " of immaculate, i. 129
  Chinese celestial, iv. 55
  Christian, v. 94
  Cold, Hyle is, i. 147
  Combatant, iii. 241; v. 320
  Cyclic return of, v. 337
  Dragon, and, ii. 383
  Forests, ii. 400
  God or Dhyān Chohan who refuses to create, ii. 87
  Goddesses, ii. 111
  Gods, v. 320
  Heavenly and celestial, i. 263; v. 334
  Immaculate of heavens, iv. 31; v. 293
  Isis, v. 293
  Kanya, i. 155
  Kanya Durga, ii. 384
  Kumāra, iv. 119
  Light, of, i. 155
  Magi and Chaldean, v. 293
  Matrix of Kosmos, i. 155
  Moot called, iv. 32
  Number of seven, iv. 174
  Pagans, of ancient, ii. 115
  Personated, v. 94
  Prayer to, ii. 189
  Rosary of Blessed, Mary, iii. 50

VIRGIN (*Contd.*)
Sea, of, ii. 189
Sin of celestial, iv. 81
Synonyms of sidereal, iv. 80
World, of, iii. 234; v. 293
Zeus said to be beautiful, i. 139
Zodiac, in, iii. 213, 429, 431
VIRGIN-ASCETIC, Nārada the, iii. 148
VIRGIN-ASCETICS, Kumāras or, ii. 178
VIRGIN-EGG, Eternal, is, i. 133
Ray shoots through, i. 133
Virgin mother and, i. 134
VIRGIN Mary, Anna mother of, i. 155
Archangel gives a lily to, ii. 99
Crescent moon and, iv. 31
Human, v. 293
Mare sea is, ii. 178
Moon connected with, ii. 108
Saviour, mother of, v. 293
Spiritual ideal of, ii. 115
Sun, arrayed with the, ii. 109
VIRGIN-MEN, Seven, iii. 283
VIRGIN-MOTHER, Celestial, ii. 179
Goddesses, and moon, ii. 118
Heavens, of, iv. 31
Horus of, iii. 54
Immaculate, i. 152
Virgin egg symbol of, i. 134
VIRGIN-OIL or Flamma-Virgo, iii. 123
VIRGIN-SNOW in radiant sunlight, Monads
like, ii. 358
VIRGIN-WARRIOR, v. 320
VIRGIN WORLDS, v. 293
VIRGIN-YOUTH, Chaste, iii. 251
Kārtikeya a, iv. 190
Kumāra or, iii. 381
Mysterious, iii. 381
VIRGINAL, Estate, iii. 238
Reproduction, iv. 227
VIRGINIA, Forests of, iv. 358
Seedless apple in, v. 563
VIRGINS, Fifty, iii. 416
Kumāras celestial, iv. 142
Life, of, i. 262
Michael and Kārtikeya both, iii. 381
Sons of God born of immaculate, i. 131
World, v. 293
Zodiac, in Denon's, iii. 431
VIRGO, Astraea is, iv. 353
Cyclic return of, v. 337
Dan, in sphere of, ii. 377
Inverted, iv. 354
Kanya, or, i. 333
Leo inseparable from, iv. 353
Quintessence and, iii. 123
Scorpio, Libra, and, v. 430
Separation of pure, iii. 137
Three Virgins and, iii. 433
Wheat ear of, ii. 388, 389; iii. 433
Zodiac, in circular, iii. 430, 431
VIRGOS, Zodiac with three, iii. 367
VIRGO-SCORPIO, Androgyne, ii. 131
Separation of, iv. 71
VIRTUES, Angelic, i. 181
Archangels are, of God, iii. 240
Cardinal, i. 246
Celestial beings or, v. 327

Christian hierarchy, of, i. 155
God, of, ii. 156
Heavenly man, of, i. 271
Initiates, of, v. 290
Mars, rulers of, ii. 153
Occultists, of, v. 106
Plants, of, v. 263
Precious stones, of, iii. 424
Seven, iv. 212; v. 357
Theological, v. 223
Thrones of God, or, v. 122
VIS, energeia naturae, or, ii. 327
Formativa, iii. 184, 290
Generatrix, ii. 274
Viva, ii. 394
VISCID earth, a, iii. 253
VISH, Vishnu from, i. 75, 171; iv. 183
VISHA or poison, Death, ii. 62
VISHISHTADVAITA sect, the, ii. 170
VISHISHTADVAITA Vedantins, i. 126, 128,
131, 189, 279; ii. 246
Tibet of, v. 402
VISHNA, Internal knowledge, v. 402
VISHNU, Abhūtarājasas incarnations of, iii. 98
Abode of, iii. 19
Achyuta a name of, i. 84
Ananta Sesha a form of, ii. 58; iv. 73
Ark of salvation towed by, iii. 313
Avataras of, i. 83, 307; iii. 45, 147, 406;
v. 105, 349, 352
Banyan tree, teaching under a, iii. 219
Bhagavan or, iii. 59
Bhutesha or, ii. 172
Boar, in the form of a, ii. 84
Brahma and, i. 75; ii. 138
Brahma, Shiva and, v. 117, 444
Breath of, ii. 87
Breath of the ABSOLUTENESS, i. 331
Buddha an Avatara of, iv. 149; v. 349, 368
Chakra or circle of, i. 173; iv. 34, 116
Christian Trinity, and, i. 53
Cyclic character of, ii. 155
Daitya and, parallel evolution of, iii. 229
Derivation of, i. 75
Destroyer, as Shiva, ii. 86
Divine spirit is, iii. 313
Double sexed, iii. 43
Double triangle, sign of, i. 177
Eternal Law, personification of, ii. 62
Eternal life symbolized by, iii. 79
Fish, as a, ii. 109; iii. 313
Fish Avatāra of, iii. 308
Fohat, Surya and, i. 171; ii. 389
Form emitted from body of, illusory, ii. 140
Garuda vehicle of, ii. 139; iii. 323; iv. 134
Hall of, v. 518
Hypostasis, in his triple, i. 328
Incarnation, seventh of, v. 259
Jehovah and, ii. 141
Kāla one of names of, ii. 145
Kali-age, at end of, iv. 51
Kalki, will return on, i. 151
Kapila shown as a portion of, iv. 142
Krishna incarnation of, v. 259, 311
Krita age, imparts wisdom in, iv. 51
Kumāras who worship, i. 282
Lakshmi, wife of, ii. 95; iii. 86

VISHNU (*Contd.*)
Lord of elements, ii. 172
Lotous and, ii. 81, 95, 96; iii. 43; iv. 40; v. 233, 476
Mahā Kalpa co-eternal with, iv. 135
Mahat as, iv. 210
Manufacturer, called, i. 171
Manvantara, Ananta carries through, ii. 124
Mayamoha, as, ii. 136
Moist principle, God of, iv. 163
Nāgas, crowned with, ii. 155
Names of, iii. 116; v. 236
Nārāyana, form of, v. 311, 447
Pervader, i. 171
Prakriti, entered into, ii. 171
Prayers of Gods to, ii. 137
Preservation, holy spirit of, iv. 73
Purāna, described in, ii. 63
Rahu denounced to, iii. 380
Regenerators, and Shiva, ii. 178; v. 192
Re-unites all, his creatures to, ii. 86
Rig Veda, in, ii. 162
Rudra, or, ii. 86
Rudra Shiva or, ii. 250
Saguna and Nirguna, v. 350, 359
Self-existent Lord, ii. 46
Serpent of, iii. 107
Serpent on which rests, iii. 380
Serpent race, one with, ii. 137
Shesha or Ananta name of, i. 140; v. 287
Shveta-dvipa abode of, iii. 401
Shiva and, ii. 179
Sign of, v. 120
Six pointed star sign of, i. 262
Solar energy and, i. 171
Solar God, iii. 405
Space and, v. 476
Sun or, iii. 50; v. 288
Svar-loka, abode of, iii. 402
Symbology of, iv. 119
Three steps of, ii. 151
Time a form of, iii. 308
Two aspects of, ii. 138, 269; iii. 313
Universe reposed in bosom of, ii. 59; v. 188
Vaikunthaloka, heaven of, ii. 246
Vaivasvata and, iii. 152
Vedas, and, iv. 183
Vish, from root, i. 171
Vishvarupa and, ii. 172
Vithoba, a form of, iv. 130; v. 288
White Island, on, iv. 156
Wicked restrained by, iv. 51
VISHNUYASHAS, v. 339
VISHVAKARMAN, All-seeing God or, iv. 129
Architect of Universe, v. 270
Artificer of Gods, iii. 383
Creative God, iii. 271; iv. 129
Divine humanity, is, iv. 178
Father Principle, v. 154
Great architect of world, iv. 129
Mystery God, v. 270, 286
Omnificent, v. 270
Purusha or, iv. 178
Rays, one of seven, ii. 240
Redeems all creatures, by sacrifice, i. 311
Rites, v. 284
Sacrifice of, i. 311; v. 154, 270

Sanjnā, daughter of, iii. 181
Sarva-medha ceremony, performed by, iv. 177
Sun crucifying, ii. 35; v. 272
Symbolism, v. 274
Temple of, iii. 344
Tvashtri or, iii. 110; iv. 187
Type of the Sun, v. 272
Vedic, ii. 192
Vithoba, called, v. 270
Yogasiddha, son of, iv. 129
VISHVAMITRA, in the day of, iv. 316
VISHVANARA, the cosmic duad, ii. 346
VISHVARUPA, Vishnu as, ii. 172
VISHVATRAYARCHAS, one of the seven rays, ii. 240
VISHVAVEDAS, Lord Asura, iii. 101
VISIBLE Logos, v. 322
Sun, v. 217, 218, 277
Triangle, v. 158
Universe, v. 188
VISION, Adept's mental, i. 220
Animals have psychic, v. 515
Cosmogonic, of St. Paul, ii. 357
Dimness of spiritual, iii. 296
Psychic, v. 515
Sceptics unopened spiritual, ii. 370
Spiritual, v. 515
VISIONS, Adepts, of great, i. 316
Astral light cause of, i. 303
Enoch, of, v. 100, 101
Excitation, form of, iv. 80
Panoramic, i. 309
Physical hallucinations, and, iii. 369
Spiritual, iii. 296; v. 515
VITAL airs, v. 510, 517
Force(s), Anch or, iv. 205
,, Elementary particles are, ii. 355
,, Globe, of, iii. 41
,, Materialists and, i. 335
,, Seed germinates through, iv. 160
Fluid, Circulation of, iv. 122
,, Exudation of, iii. 140
,, Fohat guiding, ii. 216
,, Life or, iv. 147
Perception, v. 548
Principle, ii. 41, 252, 315, 327, 362; iii. 311; iv. 166, 242, 288; v. 456
Sound, v. 549
VITALA, v. 538, 539, 544
VITALIS VITALIA, iv. 158
VITALITY, Animal, v. 565
Cells, in, i. 307
Cosmic, i. 163
Manifestations of, ii. 365
Occult theory, of, ii. 264
Potential, ii. 291
Spiritual, v. 456
VITATHA, Kapila son, iv. 142
VITELLIUS and Astrology, v. 334
VITHOBA, iv. 130, 131; v. 270, 288
VITI or FIJI, iii. 227
VITRUVIUS POLLIO, referred to, i. 256, 257
VĪVANGHAT, the symbolical man, iv. 180
VIVASHAT, the sun or Surya, iii. 215, 256
VIVEKA CHUDAMANI, ii. 293
VIVIEN AND MERLIN, iii. 182
VODHU, one of the seven Kumāras, iii. 319

VOGT, Carl, referred to, i. 191; ii. 263, 362; iii. 178, 190, 199; iv. 216, 221, 222, 231, 235, 236, 251
VOHU-MANO, or good thoughts, iv. 86
VOICE, Angel, of seventh, iv. 136
  Army of, i. 156, 157, 159
  Breath and, synthesis of the senses, i. 159
  Concrete, i. 161
  Daughter of Divine, v. 240
  Divine, iii. 115
  Father, of the, i. 327
  Heavenly, of our prototype, ii. 364
  Holy spirit or, ii. 51
  Initiates hear audible, ii. 149
  Interpreter of divine, ii. 383
  Kwan Yin, or divine, i. 194
  Nature, of, ii. 247; v. 443
  Secret wisdom, of, ii. 380
  Soul, of, ii. 149
  Spirit, Word and, ii. 166; v. 211
  Still small, i. 326
  Vāch, i. 157
  Will, of, ii. 60
  Word, of, i. 161
  Word or logos in union with, i. 161, 165
VOID, Great, spatial, v. 475
VOLCANIC, Adam Galatea from, dust, iii. 158
  Conflagration, iii. 308
  Easter island destroyed by, fire, iii. 326
  Energies, iii. 362
  Sentient beings may be in a, ii. 332
  Titan Kabirim, and, iii. 362
VOLCANO (ES), Asburj was a, iii. 406
  Colossal stones and, iii. 280
  Sun force in, ii. 249
  There, in isle of, iii. 280
  Worlds destroyed by, iv. 294
VOLCKER, quoted, iii. 20
VOLGA, Io crosses the, iii. 414
VOLGER, Calculations of, iii. 162
VOLITION, Result of, i. 318; ii. 365
VOLITIONAL Perception, v. 548
VOLITIONS and feelings, i. 212
VOLNEY, referred to, ii. 384; iii. 434
VOLTAIRE, iii. 440; iv. 272, 311, 312, 346; v. 51, 94, 261, 341
VOLUMES, Secret, v. 349, 399
VOLUPTUOUSNESS, Bower of, iii. 209
  Eden means, iii. 208
VON HALLER, referred to, v. 225
VON HARTMANN, Philosophy of, v. 383
VOODOOS, of Jamaica, iii. 214
  Negro, v. 252
VOPISCUS, the Historian, v. 148, 149, 150
VORMIUS on rocking-stones, iii. 346
VORTEX, Kepler's solar, ii. 348
  Motion, of, i. 302
  Movements, ii. 211
VORTEX-ATOM theory, ii. 210, 211
VORTICAL, atoms, ii. 303
  Motion, i. 177; ii. 211
  Movement in primordial matter, i. 176
  Swedenborg's theory, i. 177
VORTICES, Atomic, ii. 292
  Elemental, i. 177; ii. 215, 303, 348
  Kepler's systemic, ii. 348
  Stars become centres of, i. 255

VORUBARSHTI and VORUZARSHTI, iv. 328
VOSSIUS, quoted, i. 182; ii. 216; iii. 41
VOTAN, the Mexican demi-God, iii. 47, 378
VOW, Pythagorean, of Silence, v. 45
VOWEL, Seven heavens sounding each one, ii. 168
VOWEL-PARENT, iii. 204
VOWELS, Brahma at creation uttered five mystic, iv. 151
  Gnostic, iv. 133
  Greek alphabet, of, iv. 135
  Mystery of seven, iv. 134
  Svastika, and, ii. 127
VOX POPULI, Vox Dei, iii. 300
VRATA, Law or power, iv. 177
VRATANI, or active laws, iv. 177
VRIDDHAGARGA, v. 339
VRIL, i. 57; ii. 286; v. 122
VRITRA, Ahi or, iii. 381
  Demon of drought, iii. 384
  Indra and, i. 251; iii. 381, 383
VRITRA-HAN, Indra called, iii. 381, 383
V-S'PH-R and V-SIPH-O-R, iii. 51
VUL, Atmospheric God, iii. 385
VULCAN (VUL-CAIN), Hephaestus or, iii. 389
  Island sacred to, iii. 17
  Jehovah identical with, ii. 302
  Lord of the Ecliptic, iii. 391
  Suidas on, iv. 191
  Tubal-Cain or, iii. 383
VULGATE, Jehovah, on, ii. 300; v. 317
  Reuben in, ii. 377
  Signum Thau in, iv. 127
VU-VEI-TCHEN-JEN, v. 411
VYAKRITIS, Aum or, ii. 150
VYAKTA, differentiated matter, i. 76; iii. 58
VYANA, subject to the Apana, iv. 137, 139
VYĀSAS, Vishnu the twenty-eight, iii. 154
VYĀVAHĀRIKA, conventional existence, ii. 71
VYAYA, a Māyāvic period, ii. 306

W

WAGNER, Prof., referred to, i. 295; iii. 108
WAITE, A.E., referred to, i. 299
WAKE, C., Staniland, referred to, ii. 26, 27, 30; iii. 39, 44, 91, 351, 361, 365, 429, 430
WAKING and sleeping states, i. 82, 323, 330
WALHALLA, or hall of heroes, ii. 145
WALL, Guardian, v. 467
WALLACE, A.R., referred to, i. 168; ii. 53, 244, 309; iii. 21, 199; iv. 216, 221, 231, 266, 347, 351, 357
WALTON, Bishop, referred to, v. 179
WAN, or swastika, iv. 126
WAND, Devil's, iii. 213
  Initiate's, iv. 87
WANDERERS, Advents of, ii. 370
  Comets called, i. 250, 255, 294
WANDERING JEW, the, iii. 246
  Legend of, v. 49
WAR, Adepts, between two classes of, iv. 70
  Asuras and Gods, of, iv. 68
  Atlantis, which ended in submersion of, iii. 225
  Dragon, of, iii. 383; iv. 71
  Gods and giants, between, iii. 85; iv. 61
  Gods, spirits credited with making, on, iv. 83

WAR (*Contd.*)
  Heaven in, ii. 36, 248; iii. 57, 73, 112, 240, 270, 378, 379, 383, 385; iv. 65, 74; v. 201, 300, 375
  Himālayan Kailasa, in, iv. 68
  Kārtikeya, God of, iii. 133; iv. 119, 190; v. 320
  Mahābhārata, or great, ii. 112; iii. 389, 394
  Race, at close of fourth, ii. 137
  Record of, iv. 66
  Skanda, God of, iii. 381
  Tāraka, iv. 66
  Titans, of, iii. 73; iv. 68, 345
  Trojan, v. 121
  Yellow and black men, between, iii. 227
WARBURTON, Dr., quoted, v. 280
WARD, Robert, ii. 207
WARREN, Col. quoted, v. 340
WARRIORS, Planets called, the, i. 163
WARS, Cosmogony, in every, ii. 136
  Heaven of *Purānas* in, i. 251
  New Testament, i. 244
  Struggles of Adjustment or, i. 244
WASHINGTONII, HALIETUS, bird discover-ed by Audubon, iii. 438
WATCHER(S), i. 124, 165, 178, 279, 309; iii. 357; v. 466
  Each nation has its, ii. 300
  Guardian Angel, or, v. 357
  Seven, v. 200, 356
  Silent, and his shadow, i. 308; v. 532
  Solitary, i. 256
WATCHMAN, Sarameya, the Divine, iii. 41
WATER, Air, proceeded from, ii. 51, 166
  Ākāsha symbolized by, ii. 177
  Amrita, of life, i. 135
  Black, ii. 134
  Buddha and, v. 454
  Cataclysms by, iii. 310
  Chemical constituents of, i. 179
  Cosmogonies, in all, i. 133
  Creation of, i. 298
  Critical condition, in, iii. 144
  Development of, i. 298
  Divine soul symbolized by, iii. 121
  Elements of, i. 326; ii. 278
  Fire, and Air—Cosmic Trinity, iii. 115
  Fire and, born of, ii. 192
  Fire or, no, iii. 121
  Fluid, primordial, i. 298
  Form, Jalarupa or, iv. 148
  God of, ii. 183, 184
  Goddess Noo primordial, ii. 155
  Golden Lotus on, iv. 149
  Human race sprung from, iv. 177
  Immortality of, i. 135
  Infant world created out of, ii. 59
  Isis personified, iv. 154
  Letter M symbol of, ii. 99
  Life, of, iii. 375, 399
  Mercury, on planet, iii. 144
  Meteorites, in, iv. 276
  Metis or, iii. 139
  Nara, body of, iv. 63
  Occultism, of, i. 265
  Origin of, iii. 75
  Personifications of, i. 197
  Plane, on a higher, ii. 266
  Prince of, ii. 179

Principle, symbol of fifth, i. 267; v. 233, 234
Principle, the Third, i. 304
Progeny of moon, iii. 76
Quaternary of matter, one of, iv. 171
Soul of, iv. 149
Space of, i. 74, 277; v. 192
Spirit, visible garb of, ii. 181
St. Mathew and, iii. 123
Symbol of one plane of matter, iv. 136
Three and, v. 117
Universe submerged in, ii. 59
Varuna, God, iv. 149
World born of, ii. 118
Worlds destroyed by, iv. 294
WATER LILY, annunciation, and, ii. 94; v. 117
  Archangel holds, ii. 99
  Audubon of, yellow, iii. 438
  Christian symbol, v. 117
  Padma, of India, i. 127
  Symbol, as a, v. 117
WATERMAN (MEN), Aquarius or, iii. 352
  Bundahish of, iv. 206
  Evolution of, iii. 63
  Terrible and bad, iii. 28, 63, 65
WATER-MOTHER, Ether, iii. 131
  Kalevala, of, iii. 26
WATERS, Abyss of, iii. 64; iv. 151
  Ambhamsi or, ii. 179
  Black, ii. 161
  Body, separated from, iii. 29
  Brahma as mover of, ii. 59
  Breath above, v. 228, 230
  Chaos of, v. 228, 233, 234
  Creation of, v. 230
  Concrete substance of, created by Narayana, i. 74
  Deluge, iv. 168
  Drainer of, iii. 29, 113
  Earth raised from, ii. 85
  ,, sea became visible, on face of, iv. 45
  ,, synonym for, v. 234
  Eliwagar, called steams of, ii. 83
  Ends, flow to, iii. 324
  Family saved from, iv. 169
  Feminine divinity of, v. 212
  Fire and, v. 234
  Firmament in midst of, ii. 61
  Flood of, iii. 152
  Fresher mixed with old, iii. 129
  Grace, of, ii. 178
  Great, iii. 349, 423
  Great Deep or, ii. 58
  Heads of dragons broken in, iv. 73
  Infinite Space, of, iv. 40
  Life, of, ii. 123; iv. 154; v. 233, 234
  Light drops solitary ray into, i. 133
  Michael prince of, iv. 73
  Nārāyana mover on, i. 132; iv. 334; v. 189, 233, 447
  Philosophical three, iv. 163
  Primordial, i. 140, 141, 146
  Pure, not turbid, iii. 28
  Race and, iii. 30
  Saura drinker of, ii. 245
  Sons of Mahat are, iii. 111
  Space, of, i. 74, 131; ii. 84, 145, 350; iii. 75, 109; iv. 327; v. 105, 230, 235, 447

WATERS (*Contd.*)
  Spirit of Elohim brooding over, ii. 90; iii. 137
  Tohu-vah-Bohu and, v. 228
  Universe, of, iii. 79
  Vishnu drinks up all, ii. 86
  Wisdom symbolized by, iv. 63
WATER-URN, snake encircling, ii. 58
WATERY, Abyss, iii. 64; iv. 283
  Abysses, atom of, iv. 223
  Earth a, globe, iii. 243
  Primal natures, one of, i. 147
WATER-YAZATAS, Fohat and, iii. 399
WATSON, Dr. J., on moving rocks, iii. 344
WATTS, Dr., referred to, i. 209
WAYS of Wisdom, of the Sepher Yetzireh, v. 107
  Seven, of Buddha, v. 377
WE son of Ymir, ii. 145
WEALDEN, Iguanodon of, iii. 347
  Lemurian river, bed of, iii. 333
WEB, atoms each part of, i. 150
  Breath of fire expands, i. 148
  Destiny woven as spider his, ii. 364
  Father-mother spin a, i. 148
  Light, of, i. 130
  World stuff or, i. 149
WEBER, Prof., referred to, i. 119; ii. 154, 373;
  iii. 61, 62, 78, 229, 320; iv. 140, 177;
  v. 398, 406
WEBER, Akad Vorles, of, quoted, ii. 182
WEBHARA of the Pali MSS., i. 44
WEBS of Māyā, the, iv. 185
WEBSTER'S definition of empirical and evolu-
  tion, iv. 223, 234, 240
WEDNESDAY, Mercury, day of, ii. 378;
  v. 437, 441, 506
  Thot and Hermes, sacred to, iii. 366
WEEK(S), Days of the, v. 432, 438
  Roman, v. 433
  Represent Sub-races, v. 102
  Septenary, v. 433
  System of, in the Bible, iv. 195
  Years of, Hebrew, iii. 394
WEI PA YANG, referred to, iv. 124
WEISSMANN, Prof., referred to, iv. 280
WELCKER, referred to, iii. 362, 391
WELL, Knowledge, of, iv. 33
  Syene of, i. 257
WENGEL, anatonist, v. 183
WEST, Correspondences of, v. 444
  Defunct arrives in, i. 274
  East and, conventional terms, ii. 329
  England, of, iii. 342
  Evil comes from, i. 181
  Miraculous births in, iv. 120
  Mystic, iii. 59
  Mythology of, iv. 405
  Sidereal, i. 181
  Spirit of, ii. 398
  Views of consciousness in, v. 546, 547
  Wise men of, iii. 279
WESTERN, Astrology, v. 443
  Churches, v. 246
  Gnosticism, Founder of, v. 132
  Heaven, v. 392, 409, 410
  Kabalist, v. 230
  Occultism Eastern and, v. 226-236
  Occultists, v. 193, 436, 461

Religion, v. 111
  Scriptures, Esotericism of, v. 407
WESTMINSTER, Abbey, ii. 15
WESTMINSTER, the famous stone at, iii. 332
WESTROPP, referred to, iv. 322
WHALE(S) in Genesis, iii. 187
  Jonah, of, v. 67
WHEAT ear of Virgo, ii. 388, 389; iii. 433
WHEAT, food of divine justice, i. 268
  Inventors discovered, iii. 372
  Isis and, iii. 373
  Origin of, unknown, iii. 372
  Production of, iii. 363
WHEEL, age of small, i. 64
  Animals of, before, iii. 193
  Anupādaka was great, i. 113, 119, 123
  Central, i. 175
  Chain of spheres, small, our, i. 254
  Chakra, i. 262
  Crores, whirled for thirty, iii. 28, 63
  Divine Being with appearance of, iii. 142
  Enoch, of, v. 112
  Ezekiel, of, iii. 137; iv. 123
  Flame spark, and, i. 309
  Fohat, of, i. 180
  Life cycle one revolution of, i. 278
  Lipika in middle of, i. 177
  Mahākalpa, great, i. 113
  Men of, before, iii. 31
  Nemesis, of, ii. 367
  Potter's, i. 309
  Present, i. 309
  Rate, runs at usual, iii. 324
  Son had not yet awakened for new, i. 113
  Sons of Lord sent to people new, iii. 40
  Third round, or, iii. 187
  Tilted axle of, iii. 329
  Time, of, iii. 123; iv. 116; v. 365
  World, globe or, i. 113
WHEEL-emblem is cross and circle in one, iv. 116
WHEELS, Auphanim or, v. 192, 214
  Celestial, v. 321, 322
  Centres of force or, i. 176
  Chakras, or, v. 483
  Cyclic, ii. 366
  Divining, v. 123
  Eternity, rotated for an, i. 254
  Ezekiel, of, v. 460
  Fiery, i. 185
  Germs of, i. 175
  Life, ii. 358
  Living, v. 214
  Lucifer, v. 55
  Manvantaras or, i. 114
  Mysterious, v. 322
  Older, i. 248
  Planetary chain, and, i. 200
  Prismatic, v. 459
  Revolution of, iv. 159
  Ring watched by, i. 187
  Rotae, called, i. 176
  Sephiroth represented by, v. 116
  Seven small, i. 113, 196, 200, 242
  Solid watery, i. 294
  Symbol of the Hierarchies, v. 459
  Time, of, v. 365
  Time's, are worlds, iv. 183

WHEELS (*Contd.*)
World, of, ii. 157; v. 322
World-spheres or, i. 155
WHELP, Lion's, ii. 377
WHEVA or Bone, iii. 199
WHEWELL, Dr., referred to, ii. 331; iii.157; iv.193
WHIRLING souls, ii. 291
WHIRLWIND, Actions raised a, ii. 364
Breath becomes, i. 160, 273
Deity becomes, i. 176
Ezekiel, of, iv. 123
Fiery, i. 86, 166, 168
Motion or, one, i. 165
That called, i. 144
WHISTON, quoted, iii. 394
WHITE, Atlanteans, iii. 431
Central point of, in boundless darkness, ii. 41
Chiefs, savage, iv. 313
Colour Correspondences of, v. 437
Corpuscles in blood, v. 553
Deity, iv. 79
Devil, Demon of terror, iii. 401
    ,,   White island, of, iii. 405
    ,,   Wilford and, iii. 154
Dvipa, iii. 289
Head, Nation not in likeness of, iv. 275
    ,,   or Resha Hiv'rah, iii. 93
    ,,   Will of, ii. 52
Horse, Kalki, i. 151
Island, the, Atlantis Atala or, iii. 322, 401
    ,,   Black with sin, became, iii. 78
    ,,   British Islands and, iii. 401
    ,,   Child of, iii. 319
    ,,   Daityas and, iii. 406
    ,,   Ruta was, iii. 154
    ,,   Shaka-dvipa or, iii. 322
    ,,   Shvetadvipa, iii. 322, 401, 402; iv. 156
Magic, adept of, iii. 425
Magic black and, iii. 363; v. 38, 49, 244, 249, 254, 441, 468, 469, 487, 489
Mother, children of, iii. 117
Mother, moon, iii. 30
Pyramid, ii. 141
Races, iii. 251; iv. 349
Ray, iv. 60; v. 455
Regions, Dhyāni from, iii. 28
Swan from starry vault, iii. 30, 139
Tiger constellations of, ii. 125
Yajur Veda, Rudra in the, iv. 118
Zohar and Hidden Fire, ii. 52
WHITECHAPEL murderer, the, iv. 76
WHITED, sepulchre, a, iii. 234
'WHO' The God, v. 408
WHOLE, Universal, v. 419
WHYDAH, serpent beliefs among Africans of, iii. 214
WICKS, four, i. 282, 283
Sparks, i. 282
WIDBLAIN, heaven called, iii. 109
WIDOW, Son of, v. 103, 272, 273, 283
WIGRED, the field of, i. 251
WILDER, Prof. A., referred to, iii. 37, 142, 207; v. 34, 65, 68, 130, 298, 299, 304
WILDERNESS, Azazel and, iii. 375
Jews of, v. 71
Serpents of, iii. 127
Water, where there was no, ii. 79

WILFORD, Col., referred to, i. 53, 54; ii. 85, 380; iii. 150, 320, 400, 401, 404, 405
WILKINS and a universal language, ii. 22
WILKINSON, Sir J. G., iii. 429
WILKINSON, Rev. W. F., referred to, ii. 214
WILL, Absolute, ii. 69; iii. 171
Act, and, i. 318
Action and, v. 452
Ah-hi vehicle of divine, i. 111
Animals have, iv. 240
Architects, divine of, ii. 303
Atoms first moved by, ii. 57
Being from, of all father, ii. 145
Beings born through, iii. 129
Body of personal, iii. 244
Brahmā, of, i. 170
Cosmic, ii. 357
Creation by, iii. 180; iv. 355; v. 535
Creation of women by, iii. 148
Creators before fall propagated by, i. 243
Deity that acts, of, iv. 97
Desire, and, v. 510, 532, 557
Divine power latent in every man's, iii. 180
Effort called Satanic, iii. 248
Existence and, ii. 365
Fohat and, i. 169, 171
Gods of, iii. 68
Harmony of universal, ii. 357
Karmic, iii. 235
King, of, ii. 71
Kriyashakti and, v. 535
Messenger of their, i. 168
Mind and, v. 532
Motion and, ii. 227
Occultists on, iv. 241
Perception and, v. 548
Physical, ii. 226
Power or, iii. 70
Principle, v. 533
Procreation by, iii. 183
Progeny through, of Brahma, iii. 69
Purification by effort of, ii. 363
Schopenhauer on, v. 383
Sons of, and Yoga, v. 262
Thought, feeling and, i. 111
White head, of, ii. 52
Yoga and, sons of, i. 255, 258; iii. 31, 179, 180, 188, 204, 230, 277, 283, 319; iv. 340
Yogi of the, iv. 185
WILL-begotten offspring iii. 198
WILL-born, Chhandajas or, iv. 156
Daksha, progeny of, iii. 277
Lords, iii. 29, 95
Mind-born and iii. 164
WILL-less, host, iv. 53
WILL O' THE WISP, i. 317; ii. 394; iii. 211; iv.17
WILL-power, ii. 285; v. 47
Ichchhashakti or, iii. 180
Stones moved by, iii. 342
WILLI son of Ymir, ii. 145
WILLIAM of Salisbury and the Mona stone, iii. 345
WILLIAMS, Sir Monier, quoted, i. 119; ii. 95
WILLIAMS, W. Mattieu, quoted, i. 164; ii. 309
WILLIOW-LEAF theory of Nasmyth, ii. 254, 264, 315
WILSON'S Prehistoric Man, iv. 297

WINCHELL, Prof., Egypt, on, iii. 334
    Globe, on cooling of the, iv. 264
    referred to, ii. 217, 221, 222, 252, 316, 331, 362;
        iii. 22, 82, 157, 324, 325
WIND, Ahi Vritra hot, iii. 383
    Atma and, i. 273
    Boreas North, iv. 340
    Demon of, ii. 189
    Desert, iii. 384
    Dominator of, v. 61
    Ether or, iii. 113, 118
    Light, and, ii. 88
    Messenger, his, ii. 51
    North, cursing, i. 181
    Pravaha, iv. 183
    Rudimentary man nursed by, iii. 121
    Samvarta, iii. 308
    Spirit of God, or, ii. 182
    Sweat, fed, iii. 30
    Synonyms of, ii. 56
    Toom, north, ii. 398
    Vayu God of, i. 241
    Waters dissolved by hot, ii. 83
    Years, blows for a hundred divine, ii. 87
WINDING form of mundane God, ii. 62
WINDOW, within, self shining, iii. 292
WINDS, Karma, agents of, i. 181
    Seven, iv. 139
WINE, inventors discovered, iii. 372
    Merry God of, iii. 362
    Sea of, iii. 320
WING, shadow became, iii. 30, 130
WINGED, dragons, iii. 407
    Globes of occultists, i. 185
    Races of Plato, iii. 66, 105, 266
    Steed of Tahmurath, iii. 396
WINGED wheels, avengers and, i. 185
    Fohat, of, i. 180
WINGS, Cherubim, of, iv. 87
    Cherubs, of, ii. 377; v. 316
    Eternal bird, of, iii. 294
    Globe with two, iv. 122
    Great serpent with twelve, ii. 135
    Men with, iii. 65
    Mercury, of, iii. 41
WINTERS, Yima's reign of three hundred,
        iv. 181
WISDOM, Abhra and, v. 111
    Abode of sons of, iii. 209
    Above, which is not from, iii. 277
    Absolute, i. 43; ii. 127; iii. 383
    Absolute light or, iii. 169
    Abyss abode of, iv. 71
    Adept in secret, iv. 101
    Adi-Buddha, first primeval, i. 124, 170
    Aditi is, v. 215
    Agathodaemon endowed with divine, iii. 215
    Alhim, of, iii. 51
    Ancestors, of, iii. 109
    Ancient, i. 62; ii. 370, 400; v. 472
    Ancients, of, i. 59; iii. 199; ii. 310; v. 51, 303
    Apollo God of oracular, iii. 115
    Archaic, iv. 220, 228; v. 75, 215, 331
    Aryan, v. 306
    Āryan key to, iv. 16
    Astral light, male part of, i. 246
    Ātmā-Vidyā, true spiritual divine, i. 222

    Beams of light falling on paths of, iii. 197
    Bird of, iii. 294
    Bo-tree of, ii. 247
    Brahmanical, i. 315
    Buddha incarnate, i. 216
    Buddhism or Esoteric, i. 192
    Budha, iii. 56, 147, 236; iv. 66
    Celestial flock or occult, iii. 41
    Chaos and, i. 140
    Chokmah, i. 284; iii. 93; iv. 97; v. 211, 438
    Circle of, in infinity, iv. 122
    Creations, before all, iv. 58
    Crest jewel of, ii. 297
    Crystalline waters of primeval, ii. 118
    Dark, ii. 118
    Devas of, v. 102
    Divine, v. 127, 299, 306, 407, 449, 493
        ,,   and creative powers, iii. 408
        ,,   and Dhyān Chohanic, iv. 219
        ,,   and Karma, iii. 409
        ,,   incarnating on earth, iii. 133
        ,,   ones, of, iv. 208
        ,,   or Nous, iii. 375
        ,,   self, of, iv. 139
        ,,   symbolised by a swan, i. 145
    Dragon (s) of, i. 139, 166, 187, 266; ii. 192,
        194; iii. 35, 39, 103, 236, 352, 378, 423
    Dragon which feeds in water, of, iii. 364
    Dual power of secret, iii. 363
    Ea God of, iii. 64, 71, 124, 147
    Earth receives, from heaven, iii. 285
    East, came from, iv. 93
    Eastern Archaic, iv. 160
    Echoes of misunderstood, iv. 52
    Egypt, of priests, of, iii. 43
    Egyptian God of, iv. 99
    Elohim of, iii. 187
    Enoch represents secret, iv. 102
    Esoteric, v. 74
    Esoteric Budhism, or, i. 192; iii. 109
    Esoteric, of Egypt, iv. 130
    Esoteric, Vach goddess of, i. 158
    Essence of manifested, i. 139
    Ever-incomprehensible, iii. 238
    Eye of, v. 438
    Fallen angel teaches man, iv. 82
    Fathers of, iii. 393
    Fiery dragons of, iii. 216, 282
    Fire of, iv. 137
    Fragment of Grecian, ii. 369
    Fruit with kernel of, iv. 334
    Garden inhabited by dragons of, iii. 208
    Garden of, iii. 208
    Generations of men, of, iii. 145
    Germs of night and day and dragon of, iv. 76
    Gian-ben-Gian or, son of, iii. 393
    Gnosis, of true, iv. 137
    God of, iii. 19; v. 302
    Goddess of hidden, iii. 204; v. 165
    Gods of secret, iv. 68; v. 65, 287
    Great dragon and serpents of, iii. 350
    Gyan or occult, iii. 393
    Hanuman, of, iv. 250
    Hea or Nebo, God of, iv. 45
    Hermes and his, i. 140, 322; iii. 379
    Hermetic, on Smaragdine tablet, iv. 126; v. 464
    Hidden, v. 86

WISDOM (*Contd.*)
Highest God of, ii. 65
Idā wife of Budha, or, iii. 148
Impersonal divine, iii. 300
Indian origin of Gnostic, iv. 140
Intelligence and, union, of, iii. 143
Jah or, v. 192
Jesus accepted serpent as synonym of, i. 141
Jewels of, cast to enemy, i. 221
Jewish, iv. 36
Jnāna, or Logos, i. 131
John Baptist, of, iv. 136
Kabalah, of, iv. 55
Key of, iv. 365
Keys of secret, iv. 156
Knowledge hedged from, i. 219
Krita age by Vishnu, imparted in, iv. 51
Kurios signifies pure nature of, ii. 68
Lemuro-Atlantean, ii. 392
Light of lights or true, ii. 127
Living tree of divine, i. 259
Logos as, iii. 233, 234
Lord of, iii. 40, 357
Lords of, i. 258; iii. 372
Lotus, and, iv. 149
Love, of, v. 265
Magic great science of, iii. 319
Mahat or manifested, i. 170; iii. 233
Male and female, i. 161
Man spirit of divine, iii. 283
Masters of, i. 60; iii. 435, 442
Meditate on tree of, iv. 86
Mercury and, ii. 195; iii. 41, 56
Metis divine, ii. 99
Mind which hath, iv. 189, 317
Mirror of eternal, iv. 52, 85
Moses and, of, Egypt, i. 140, 175
Mother of Ogdoad, i. 139
Mystery of, iv. 102
Mystic speech, communicated by, ii. 148
Nāga serpent of, iv. 143
Names of, iv. 58
Nebo God of, iv. 22, 23; v. 272
Occult, on earth or Satan, iii. 376
Occult, or Dzyu, i. 168
Ophis divine, ii. 179; iii. 219
Oriental Secrets of, v. 29
Oviparous serpent, symbol of, ii. 79
Pagan, ii. 367; v. 302
Parabrahman, of, ii. 147
Parent of Esoteric, iv. 69
Paths of, thirty-two, iii. 51
Peacock bird of, iv. 190
Personal lives, gained from, iii. 187
Personifications of, v. 74
Philosophy and, ii. 129
Plunged in waters of, iv. 63
Power and, v. 128
Prakriti, mother of, iv. 97
Primeval, i. 65, 256; v. 350, 434
Primeval, Atlantean, iii. 371
Primeval people, in synonyms, of, ii. 56
Primitive, v. 91
Prometheus endowed man with, iii. 411
Purānas and *Bible*, in fables of, ii. 50
Pythagoras, of, Quaternary of, iv. 153
Rasit or, iv. 28

Recorders of Occult, iv. 98
Records of serpents of, iii. 351
Relics, of ancient, ii. 336
Root of, iv. 155
Secret, i. 65; iv. 23, 104, 153; v. 74, 109, 246, 443
Secret, in *Upanishads*, iv. 162
Seeds of Trinity of, iii. 278
Sephira, acts through, ii. 69
Serpent emblem of, i. 134, 140; ii. 383; iii. 186, 385; v. 43
Serpent embodiment of Divine, i. 140
Serpent of, iii. 107, 414
Serpents of, iii. 106, 233, 357
Seven pillars of house of, ii. 71, 124; iv. 212
Siddhas of, iv. 208
Solomon, of, v. 74
Soma, father of, i. 275
Sons of, i. 255, 259; iii. 175, 191, 197, 204, 238, 269, 274, 421, 426; iv. 180; v. 438, 471
Sons of Brahma, of, iii. 87
Sons of Dark, iii. 250, 284; iv. 63
Sons of Flame, of, iii. 410
Sons of God, of, iv. 231
Sophia Achamoth, daughter of, ii. 167
Sophia or Female, i. 247; ii. 67; v. 127, 215
Spark of Divine, iii. 283
Spirit of Divine, iii. 283; iv. 110
Spiritual, v. 497
Stream, called, i. 284
Supreme, i. 157, 190
Supreme, or Adi, i. 43
Sun, and verbum of, iv. 49; v. 277
Symbol of omniscience of, iii. 338
Synthesis of universal, i. 139
Terrestrial, iv. 210
Third race, in, v. 91
Thirty two ways of, v. 107
Thot or Thoth, God of, ii. 100; iv. 128
Tree of occult and spiritual, iii. 384
Truths of primitive, iv. 84
Unit body of, i. 321
Universal, i. 65, 139; v. 216, 374
Universal traditions of, iii. 141
Universe of nature of, ii. 138
Vedantic, iv. 97
Vehicle of divine, iii. 143
Virtue and, ii. 64
Vishnu taught, iv. 142
Voice of Secret, ii. 380
Word, or the, iv. 273
Workings of Dhyān Chohanic, iv. 305
Yogism of, iv. 138
Zohar on, v. 284
WISDOM-EYE, One eye or, iv. 339
WISDOM-GOD and angel of evil, iv 45
WISDOM-LANGUAGE, v. 185
WISDOM-OCEAN, the, iv. 71
WISDOM-PHILOSOPHY, v. 138
WISDOM-PRINCIPLE, v. 365
WISDOM-RELIGION, the, i. 42; ii. 91; iii. 41, 234, 377; iv. 37, 207, 325; v. 91, 181, 302, 305, 306, 364, 463
WISDOM-SCIENCE, Archaic system known as sacred, ii. 22
Religions show traces of, ii. 22
Universal language of, ii. 22

WISDOM-WORD, v. 180
WISE, Budha the, iv. 66
　　Demon, Tāraka, iii. 382
　　Lord, Ahura Mazda or, iv. 180
　　Manasvin, iii. 99
　　Men, Balaam taught by, iii. 407
　　　,,　Dragons or, iii. 354
　　　,,　Fifth race of, i. 316
　　　,,　Hierarchies of living, iv. 202
　　　,,　Keys to symbols passed to, ii. 337
　　　,,　Nāgas and, iii. 215
　　　,,　Pyramids, living under, iii. 350
　　　,,　Sages or, iii. 198
　　One, Dionysius heavenly, iii. 418
　　Ones, Adepts or, ii 120
　　　,,　Seven, iii. 197
　　Race, Asuramaya a descendant of, iii. 78
WISEMAN, Cardinal, referred to, ii. 331; iv. 273
WITCHCRAFT, Laws against, ii. 190
WITCHES' SABBATH, goat of, iv. 79; v. 172
WITCHES, Satan said to be head of, iii. 388
　　Thessaly, of, i. 211
WITHERING trees or left path Adepts, iv. 64
WITNESS, Divine, v. 503
WIVES, Atlanteans, of, iii. 288
WIZARDS, Simon Magus and Apollonius, v. 124
WODEN one of the Buddhas, iii. 421
WOGAN, referred to, ii. 359
WOLF, C., referred to, ii. 225, 314, 320, 321,
　　322, 323, 325
WOLF, Darkness, who comes out of, iii. 385
　　Dog and, iii. 289
WOLUSPA, Poem of, ii. 83
WOMAN, Alchemy, in, v. 430
　　Beast, and, iv. 317
　　Cow with head of, ii. 105
　　Curse and, iii. 220
　　Deluge, after, ii. 247
　　Fatal gift, iii. 272
　　Image of God, in, ii. 105
　　Light of shadow, ii. 118
　　Man born from, ii. 161
　　Matter serpent or, iii. 207
　　Moon and, iv. 29
　　Purple and scarlet, in, iv. 317
　　Son of the, v. 131
　　Sun, clothed with, iv. 340
　　Tempter of man, iii. 386
　　White man above a black, iii. 359
WOMB, Ark typified by, iii. 147
　　Astral body, first in, v. 532
　　Brass a symbol of, ii. 79
　　Creatures born from, iii. 189
　　Diti, of, iv. 184
　　Golden, of Absolute, ii. 129; v. 472
　　Hé or, iv. 28, 41
　　Heavenly Matrix and human, iii. 94
　　Holy of Holies or, iv. 34
　　Human, iv. 40; v. 422
　　Isis, of earth, iv. 155
　　Liquor amnii of, iii. 194
　　Mother, earth begotten in, of, ii. 338
　　Mundane egg and, ii. 69
　　Nature of, ii. 88; iii. 236; iv. 29; v. 422
　　Paradise as, v. 449
　　Symbol of, i. 308; ii. 162
　　Temple, Symbols of, v. 308

Universe, of, iii. 194
World of, ii. 306; iii. 116
WOODWARD, Dr. Henry, on the increase of
　　ice, iv. 294
WOOLLY-haired race, a, iii. 328
WORD, the absolute ALL manifesting in, iv. 123
　　Androgynous, iv. 107
　　Beginning, in, ii. 192
　　Breath crystallized into, i. 145
　　Energy of manifested, ii. 89
　　Flesh made, ii. 64; v. 76
　　God, of, iv. 17
　　　,,　Mercury and, iii. 41
　　　,,　Revelation in, i. 151
　　　,,　Sound or, iii. 115
　　　,,　Speech of Hermes, interpreted as,
　　　　　iv. 112
　　Hermes emblem of, iv. 112
　　Image of, iv. 106
　　Initiates received the, v. 271, 276
　　Kabalist, of, iv. 114
　　Kwan-Shi-Yin, or, ii. 194
　　Limbus from, of God, i. 326
　　Logos or, i. 161; ii. 125; iii. 48, 170; v. 215,
　　　229, 234, 327, 442, 475
　　Lost, iii. 224; v. 395, 406
　　Memrab or, ii. 60
　　Mercury, iv. 112
　　Mimra, ii. 99
　　Mystery-, v. 140
　　Mysterious, v. 309, 502
　　Names of wisdom or, iv. 273
　　Paul, leader of, iv. 49
　　Plural becomes, ii. 65
　　Sacred, v. 109, 395
　　Six highest aspects of, iii. 357
　　Sophia the Living, v. 199
　　Sound or, exists alone, ii. 88; v. 234, 442, 502
　　Speech or Logos, iii. 38
　　-Spirit, v. 218
　　Sun, or the, v. 277, 314
　　Symbols, iii. 335
　　Thought produced through its, iv. 57
　　Unspoken, v. 455
　　Voice a synonym for, i. 194
　　Voice, spirit and, i. 165; ii. 166
　　Wisdom and, iv. 243
　　Word that is no, ii. 156; iii. 224
　　Words synthesized by, ii. 148
WORDS, Evolution by, iii. 53
　　Speech, intelligence which does not under-
　　　stand, i. 157
WORDSWORTH, Bishop, referred to, iii. 136
WORDSWORTH, William referred to, v. 228
WORK(S) Secret, v. 258
　　Seventh Magic or, v. 326
WORKER'S HAMMER or Svastika, iii. 107
WORKSHOP, Processes in nature's, ii. 337
WORKSHOPS, Our terrestrial, ii 350
WORLD, Absolute, v. 418
　　Annals of, v. 155
　　Archetypal, v. 73, 418
　　Astral, v. 73, 208, 418
　　Celestial, v. 208
　　Egg of, i. 133, 134; v. 421
　　Elemental, v. 418
　　Elementary, v. 73, 208

WORLD (*Contd.*)
  Germs i. 250; ii. 397
  God of, v. 215
  Guardians of, v. 88
  -Holders of Tertullian, ii. 44
  Intelligible, v. 208
  Internal, v. 208
  Kosmos, Man and, v. 421
  Manasic, v. 418
  Middle, v. 446
  Nether, v. 153
  Original, v. 208
  Plane or, v. 448
  Planetary, v. 222
  Psychic, v. 418
  Rector of, v. 215
  Religions, Exoteric scriptures of, i. 218
        ,,   Symbolism of, iv. 15
  Saviours, ii. 379; v. 232, 289, 336
        ,,   Periodical births of, ii. 383; v. 350
  Soul, i. 76, 82, 252; iv. 125; v. 558
  -Spirit, Avataras incarnations of, i. 123
        ,,   Hegel and, ii. 365
  Spirit and Reality, of, v. 154, 456
  Spiritual, v. 73, 365, 418
  -Stuff, ii. 246, 303, 319, 322
  Temporal, v. 208
  Third, v. 447, 448
  Virgins, v. 293
  Year, Secret, of, v. 200
WORLDS, Four of Trismegistus, v. 73
  Seven, v. 208
  Universe of, v. 209
WORSHIP, Anthropomorphic idol, ii. 113
  Astoreth, of, iv. 30
  Baal and Bacchus, of, iv. 39
  Ceremonial of Egyptian, i. 52
  Ceremonial, profitless, iii. 102
  Culture God, of, iii. 148
  Dead letter, iv. 67
  Divinites, of false, iii. 281
  Dragon, iii. 354
  Earth's business a kind of, i. 259
  Exoteric, of Lares, iii. 359
  Form, of, v. 260
  God in the ark, of, iv. 37
  Heliolatrous, iii. 378
  Hercules, of, v. 258
  Hero, iii. 283
  Hindu intellectual classes, of, ii. 39
  History of, iii. 275
  Idol, iv. 292
  Isis, Astarte and Venus, of, iv. 29
  Kabirim, of, iii. 363
  Lunar and Solar, ii. 103
  Magi of, iii. 233
  Monotheistic, i. 72
  Nature of noumenal, ii. 97
  Phallic, i. 308; iv. 39
  Physical generation, of God of, iv. 160
  Primitive, establishment of, iii. 366
  Principles, of male and female, ii. 112
  Quadrumanic ancestors, of, iv. 231
  Ring position of body during, iv. 122
  Sabaean, iv. 29
  Serpent and crocodile, ii. 120
  Sexual, iii. 286, 335; iv. 159

Shemesh, ii. 112
Stars of, v. 219, 318-323
Stones, of, iii. 341
Sun and fire, i. 179
Sun and moon, of, ii. 117
Sun of, v. 316, 317
Tantrika, i. 222
Virgin Mary and Lunar Goddesses, of, ii. 116
WRAITH, iii. 211
WREN, Sir Christopher, ii. 144
WRIT, Holy, v. 90
WRITING, Art of, v. 275
  Babylonian art of, iii. 229
  Cipher-, v. 274
  Early men had rudiments of, iv. 297
  Hebrew, v. 205
  Hesiod and Homer said to be ignorant of, iii. 437
  Hieratic, of Egypt, v. 249
  Indian knowledge of, iii. 229
  . Inventor of, iv. 98
  Milleniums ago, known, iii. 437
  Pānini and, v. 217, 375
  Stone age, in, iii. 439
WU-LIANG-SHUW the boundless age, ii. 71; v. 391
WU WANG, of Chow dynasty, iii. 303

X

XANTHOCHROICS, of Huxley, iii. 315
XANTHOCHREATININE of Gautier, i. 305
XENCRATES, Philosophy of, v. 383
XENOPHANES and superstitions of Greece, iv. 333
XENOPHANTES, referred to, iv. 104
XERXES, Magi of, ii. 188; v. 44
  Oracle on approach of, ii. 188
XISUTHRUS, the Chaldean Noah, iii. 18, 147, 149, 226, 267, 309, 310; iv. 21, 343

Y

YaH, son of, iii. 94
YAH, Jah or, iii. 134, 138
  Duad, the, v. 211
YAH-HOVAH, Eve and Hé or, ii. 109
YAHO, ancient name of, God, iv. 111
  Hebrew, iv. 111
YAHO-Lah or Jaho-Jah, iii. 138
YAHO of Jews, iii. 138; iv. 33
YAHOUDI, or Jews, iii. 135, 205
YAHVA, Iabé or, iv. 33
  Samaritans, of, iii. 138
YAJNA, or Sacrifice, v. 542
YAJNA-Vidya, i. 222
YAKSH, to eat, iii. 172
YAKSHA-loka, v. 537
YAKSHAS, Brahma's fright at seeing, iii. 188
  Gandharvas, and, iii. 99
  Gods or minor, iii. 215
  Lanka of, iii. 80
  Spirits of heaven, or, iii. 369
YAMA, God of death, iii. 56
  God of Earth, ii. 183
  Heart becomes an open book before, i. 166
  South deity of, i. 186

YAMA (*Contd.*)
  Spirit of the earth, ii. 184
  Vaivasvata Manu, son of, iv. 180
YAMABOOSHI, the Buddhist mystics of Japan, i. 226
YĀNA, or vehicle, i. 112
YANG, iv. 124
YANG SUN of the Ming dynasty, iii. 65
YAO and deluge, Chinese, iii. 150
YARAB, Arabic of, v. 197
YARD, Jared in British Y. R. D. hence, iv. 169
YASKA, Predecessor of Pānini, v. 275
YASNA, Neryosangha translator of the, iv. 327
YASODHARĀ, a mystic power, v. 378
YATIS, Images nine, high, iii. 33
  Race of nine, high, iii. 35
YATUDHANAS, the sun's attendants, iii. 215
YAVANAS, v. 41
YAVE, Jehovah, iv. 32
YAZATAS, fire and water, iii. 399
  Men conversed with pure, iii. 355
YEAR, Brahma, of, i. 110; iii. 80
  Chandrāyana or lunar, i. 110
  Circles of sidereal, iii. 355
  Climacteric, of humanity, ii. 382
  Cyclic periods of great tropical, iv. 73
  Dhruva, of, iii. 308
  Duration, of two months, iv. 192
  Enquinoxes, and precession of, ii. 157
  Hindu, v. 191, 192
  Leap, iv. 99
  Length of divine, ii. 136
  Lunar, ii. 380; iv. 34, 109, 110, 155
  Mithras ruler of, iv. 42
  Mortals, of, iv. 191
  Nativity, of, ii. 381
  Numbers of solar, iv. 154
  Osiris, of, 365 Days, iv. 155
  Rishis, of seven, iii. 308
  Schemal meant, ii. 135
  Sidereal, ii. 153; iii. 430, 433; iv. 339
  Solar, iv. 192; v. 101, 129
  Tropical, iii. 444; iv. 73
  Wind of, v. 200
YEARS, Book of Enoch predicts a shortening of, iv. 103
  Brahma, 100 years of, i. 110, 254
  Creation, 12,000, in, ii. 53
  Cycle, in, ii. 152
  Divine and common, of Kali Yuga, iv. 120
  Indian wisdom and 6,000, ii. 91
  Naros, of, iv. 190
  Rain for 100 divine, ii. 87
  Sidereal, iii. 332, 356
  Week of, iv. 195
YECHIDA, of the Kabalah, iv. 205
YE-HOU-VIH, Jeve or, iii. 138
YEHOVAH, Jehovah or, iv. 41
YEHUDAH Ibn Gebirol, ii. 157, 166; see Book Index
YELLOW, Atlanteans, iii. 431
  Caps, Gelukpas or, i. 169
  Colour Correspondences of, v. 456, 457, 458, 461, 478, 507, 508
  Face (s), iii. 185, 425
  Father, children of, iii. 30, 117
  Gold, second was like, iii. 33, 230

-Golden, v. 437
  Hue, forefathers of, iii. 423
  Race, iii. 252; iv. 349
  Races, iii. 204, 350; iv. 313
  Saved from fourth, iii. 33
  Venus and, v. 441
  War between, and black men, iii. 227
YELLOW-Dragon, the, iii. 364
YELLOW-faced, fifth race, nations of, iii. 426
  Giants of post Atlantean days, iii. 423
YERED, Hanokh, son of, iv. 101
YESOD or globe C, i. 249
YEW, tree in Greenland, iii. 24
YEZIDI, the Persian, iv. 22
YEZIDIS worship Lord Peacock, iv. 83
YEZOD, foundation, i. 285
YGGDRASIL, Norse, iii. 106
  Universe of Time and life, tree of, ii. 145
Y H V H, ii. 343; iv. 19
YIHIGCHING, Lāmasery of, v. 394
YIMA, Adam or, iv. 182
  Ahura-Mazda and, iii. 292; iv. 181
  First man in Vendīdād, iv. 180
  Vara made by, iii. 19, 293
YIN Binary, iv. 124
  Etymology of, ii. 194
  Hia to, flight of, iii. 65
YIN-SIN not for speculations, ii. 360
YLIASTER, Magnus Limbus, or, i. 325
  Paracelsus, of, 325
YMIR, Giant, ii. 83, 145; iii. 106, 107
YO, Heavens or, i. 264
  Male ethereal principle, i. 264
YOD, Argha of, iv. 35
  Hook, phallic, ii. 61
  Jehovah, first letters of, iv. 146
  Jod or, iii. 137
  Letter, ii. 109
  Phallus or, iv. 41; v. 206
  Ten or, perfect number, iv. 121
YODCHEVA, Adam Kadmon or, iii. 137
YOD-Heva, Father of, iii. 136
YODS in Pythagorean triangle, ten, iii. 120
YOGA, Ālaya, one strong in, merges his soul in, i. 119, 121
  Brahmā, power, of, ii. 175; iii. 69, 98
  Contemplation of, state, i. 255
  Defined by Wilson, v. 404
  Deity, and union with, iii. 240
  Devarishis sons of, iv. 70
  Dharma or, iv. 70
  Esoteric teaching of, v. 411
  Evolution by, iii. 181
  Hatha, i. 119, 158; iv. 139; v. 399, 468, 476, 477, 479, 480
  Inhalation, i. 159
  Maru, son of Shighra by, is still living, ii. 93
  Philosophy, v. 476
  Power, iii. 297; v. 270, 378
  Kriyashakti, or, iii. 70
  Prānayāma in, practices, r. 158
  Rāja, i. 158, 211, 213; iv. 174; v. 361, 403, 451, 452, 476, 479, 480, 485, 497, 515
  Rite of Shukra, iii. 45
  Schlagintweit on, v. 403
  Siddha, iv. 129; v. 270
  Sons of Passive, i. 255; iii. 173, 277

YOGA (*Contd.*)
  Sons of Will and, i. 255, 258; iii. 31, 170, 179, 188, 204, 224, 283, 319; iv. 340; v. 262
  Supreme wisdom acquired by, i. 190
  Tāraka, iii. 381; iv. 164; v. 361
  Training, iii. 180
  Vidya, iii. 381
  Western Orientalists and, v. 403, 404
YOGĀCHĀRYA School, i. 115, 120, 121; iv. 208; v. 399, 400, 401, 402, 411, 412
YOGĀCHĀRYAS, Madhyamikas, and, i. 116
YOGI, above castes, v. 354
  Consciousness of, v. 542, 544, 545
  Divine will of, iv. 185
  Hatha, v. 542
  Indian, v. 468, 544
  Kandu, iii. 181
  Knowledge of initiated, ii. 241
  Kundalini shakti must be subjgated by, i. 333
  Rāja, v. 542
  Shiva Rudra Patron, iv. 186
  Striat gate, must pass, iv. 119
  Trance, in, v. 458, 555
  Wonders of, i. 333; iii. 180
YOGINI, defined by Jennings, ii. 194
YOGIS, Allegories of, iii. 88
  Brahmā, praise, to, ii. 138
  Brahman, or, i. 150
  Chit, a synonym of Mahat with, i. 330
  Demons sometimes great, ii. 133
  Doctrines of, v. 145
  Esotericism, are five in, iv. 149
  Fakirs and, v. 399
  Female demons and, iv. 185
  Initiates, v. 27, 395
  Kumāras described as, ii. 177; iii. 254; iv. 147
  Mantaras, of previous, iii. 103
  Modern, of Indra, v. 479, 480
  Passion, exempt from, iv. 149
  Perfect Svāmis, v. 137
  Rāja, v. 480, 520
  Rākshasas are, iii. 172
  Shiva, patron of, ii. 178; iii. 283; iv. 184
  Sushumna ray cherished by, ii. 240
  Svāmis or, v. 137
  System of, iii. 97
  Tibet, of, ii. 193
  Victims, voluntary, iii. 248
YOGISM, Wisdom of, iv. 138
YONG Grub, absolute perfection or, i. 114
  Stanzas, term used in the Senzar version of the, i. 87
  Tibetan for Mahāmanvantara, i. 115
YONI, Ark of covenant and, iv. 28
  Hindus, of, iv. 31, 41
  Lingam and, v. 292
  N' Cabvah means, ii. 106; iv. 34
  Perfect female, iii. 134
  Phallic symbol, iv. 33
  Shakti, or, ii. 194
  Shiva worship with its, iv. 159
  Symbols of Hinduism, i. 308
YOUNG, referred to, i. 319; ii. 265, 302
YOUNGER, Oeaohoo the, i. 138
YOUSSOUFZIC sons of Joseph, iii. 205
YOUTHS, Holy, i. 243
  Shiva reborn as four, iii. 283

YUCATAN, Calendar forms of, ii. 106
  Chinese meaning of, i. 130
  Remains of, iv. 361
YUDHISHTHIRA, King of Sacae or Shakas, ii. 85
  Yudhister or, v. 345, 346, 347
YUGA, Chatur, v. 259
  Dvāpara, iii. 155; v. 229
  Interval preceding each, iii. 309
  Kali, i. 64, 65; iii. 155; v. 229, 260, 338, 339, 396, 466, 563
  Mahā, v. 339, 346
  Revolutions, iv. 119
  Round or root race, may mean, iii. 155
  Satya, i. 309; v. 260, 324
  Treta, iv. 196; v. 91
YUGAS, Age of our small, i. 254
  Based on astronomy, v. 345
  Cycles or, iii. 68
  Duration of, iv. 191
  Esoteric and Brahmanical doctrine of, ii. 382
  Four, v. 259
  Hindus, of, ii. 362; iv. 195; v. 345, 346, 347
  Kalpas and, iii. 59, 80, 308
  Names of five, v. 340
  Racial cycles and, iii. 80
  Seven periods of humanity, i. 64
  Succession of four, iii. 322
  Third root race, of, iv. 89
YULE, Colonel, referred to, v. 39
YVES d'Alveydre, Marquis St., referred to, iv. 119

Z

ZABULON, Piscis in sphere of, ii. 377
ZACHAR va nakobeh, male and female, iii. 136
ZADKIEL, referred to, v. 314
ZAGREUS, or Bacchus, v. 278, 412
ZALIWSKY, Theory on electricity of, v. 220
ZALMAT, qaqadi, a dark race, iii. 18
ZAMA Zama Ozza Rachma Ozari, iv. 152
ZAMIA, in ancient Greenland, iii. 24
ZAMYAD YASHT on the Immortal Benefactors, iii. 357
ZANONI, face to face with his Augoeides, iii. 296
ZARATHUSHTA, Grotto of, iii. 185
ZARATHUSHTRA, Address to, iv. 341
  Ahura Mazda and, iii. 293, 384
  First, iii. 322
  Lord and ruler of Vara, iii. 19
  Zertusts or, iii. 19
ZARPANITU, Nebo son of, ii. 215; iv. 23
ZAO, I live, iv. 154
ZECHARIAH, iv. 198
ZEDEK, sons of, iii. 391
ZENANAS, women in Vedic period not in, ii. 97
ZENDS, i. 184; iii. 214
ZENITH Nadir and, iv. 163
  Svastika, and, iv. 158
ZENO, quoted, i. 143; iii. 167
ZERO, cipher or, ii. 76
  Circle or, ii. 47
  Egg-shaped, i. 155
  Electricity, state of, ii. 242
  Line, matter beyond the, ii. 246
  ,, Laya condition beyond, of action, ii. 313

ZERO (*Contd.*)
  Matter, state of, ii. 268
  Point (s), the, ii. 274
  ,, Chemist stops at, of matter, i. 189
  ,, Condition, i. 200
  ,, Laya or, i. 188, 205
  ,, Science, of, ii. 345
  ,, Seven Laya centres or, i. 195
  Unity within, iv. 152
ZEROĀNA, Chakra or circle of Vishnu, i. 173
ZERTUST or Zarathushtra, iii. 19
ZERUAN (Saturn) v. 181
ZERUĀNA AKERNE, boundless cirlce of unknown time, i. 172, 173; iii. 236; iv. 56, 57
ZEUS, Adas and, v. 316
  Allegory of, iii. 131
  Androgynes, and, iii. 184
  Barnabas called, iv. 49
  Beautiful virgin, said to be, i. 139
  Character of, iii. 417
  Deus, written, iv. 154
  Dodona and, v. 254
  Father of all living, iv. 154
  Fourth race, deity of, iv. 345
  Fourth race, reigns over, iv. 335
  Ganymedes, and, iv. 353
  Highest God, not, ii. 143
  Jehovah and, v. 278
  Jupiter or, i. 139; iii. 271
  Kronos and, ii. 145
  Male and an Immortal maid, iii. 143
  Night, reverencing, ii. 143
  Osiris and, v. 278
  Passions of, iii. 417
  Pater, iv. 145
  Pausanias, of, ii. 52
  Plato's banquet, in, iii. 142
  Pollux calls on, iii. 131
  Prometheus, and, iii. 247, 282, 410, 412, 413
  Race of men commanded by, iv. 88
  Son of, v. 278
  Supreme being, or, ii. 396
  Telchines destroyed by deluge from, iii. 390
  Third race of, iii. 188
  Thracian by, v. 305
  Triopis the three-eyed, iii. 296
  Unknown Deity, is not, iii. 411
ZEUS, Belos of Herodotus, iii. 215
ZEUS-ZEN, or Aether, ii. 54; iii. 139
ZI, God, iii. 18
  Spirit of Akkadians, or, iii. 65
ZIGZAG diagram, the, ii. 274
ZI-KU, the God, iii. 18
ZINC, ii. 250, 276
ZIPPORAH wife of Moses, ii. 32; v. 180
  City of Sippara, same name as, ii. 32; v. 180
ZIRCONIUM, an element, ii. 276
ZIRTUSHT, Desātir in, v. 281
ZODH or Cain, iii. 55
ZODIACAL, allegory, iii. 352
  Authority of, records, ii. 371
  Calculations, iii. 434
  Circle, Cardinal points of, ii. 78; v. 273
  Constellations, i. 166; ii. 106; iii. 330
  Egypt, calculations in, iii. 352
  Exigencies, ii. 382
  Flood, iii. 352

Gods, iii. 356; v. 332
Leo, sign, i. 261
Monad, and signs, ii. 391
Monuments, v. 332
Mysteries, i. 60
Relic of earthly ring, iv. 71
ZODIACS, Akkadian months and, ii. 375
  Ancients knew, ii. 372; iii. 76
  Antiquity of, ii. 373, 376; v. 331, 332
  Architects of, ii. 382
  Assyrian tablets and, iii. 352
  Bible in, ii. 374
  Cain and, v. 165
  Capricornus, tenth sign of, iv. 147
  Celestial Virgin in, iii. 213
  Changes in, iii. 433
  Chinese, iv. 191
  Christian era, before, ii. 383
  Circle Dance and, iv. 28, v. 310, 311
  Circular, iii. 430
  Correspondences of, v. 331, 430
  Dendera, iii. 367, 373, 430; v. 332
  Denon, given by, iii. 431
  Draco and, iii. 44
  Egyptian, iii. 429, 433, 434; v. 322
  Elements of, the, v. 241
  Figures of, i. 184; ii. 384
  Giants, a witness to, iii. 279
  Gods Counsellors of, v. 332
  Greeks, iii. 434
  Heliopolis at, ii. 110
  Hindu, ii. 384, 388, 389; iii. 62, 229, 331, 433
  History recorded in, iii. 436
  Horizon, North Pole, and, iv. 354
  Interpretation of, ii. 390
  Kanyā sixth sign of, i. 333
  Luna, ii. 124
  Mackey on, iii. 434
  Makara and, i. 266, 268; ii. 91; iii. 102, 271
  Māyā Indians, of, iii. 62
  Moon at first point of, ii. 389
  Music of spheres, and, iv. 172
  Mysteries of, v. 429
  Origin of, ii. 376
  Patriarchs, and, ii. 377
  Pisces sign of, i. 307
  Prophecies of, ii. 379
  Records preserved through, ii. 371; iii. 61, 332, 367, 436
  Reformation of, v. 430
  Sacred animals and signs of, i. 156; ii. 165; iii. 187
  Science of, ii. 378
  Shepherd of, v. 315
  Signs of, i. 145, 261; ii. 116, 374, 377, 383; iii. 15, 36, 121, 205, 352, 353, 357, 428; iv. 190; v. 142, 152, 164, 241, 332, 430
  Solar blaze, reddened with, iii. 356
  Spheres, and Lords of, ii. 301
  Stonehenge and, iii. 344
  Sun at first point of, at epoch of 1491, ii. 386
  Syro-Chaldean, ii. 131
  Theogonies related to, ii. 378
  True Mysteries of, v. 426
  Twelve Stones and, v. 241
  Western Astronomers and, v. 344

ZODMANAS ZHIBA in Senzar version of Stanzas, i. 87
ZOGEE or Jogee, ii. 194
ZOHAR, Compilers, of, v. 67, 216
  Creation, on, v. 205-215
  Infinite, on, v. 386
  Referred to, v. 176, 177, 214
  Sounds, on, v. 439
  Wisdom of, v. 216
  Worlds, on, v. 301
ZOLLNER, Prof., referred to, i. 295; ii. 244
ZONE, American, iii. 443
  Bauddhist's seventh, iii. 401
  Dvipa, or, iii. 402
  Frigid, formerly in east, iv. 104
  Luminous, iii. 408
  Men separated each in his own, iii. 29, 95
  Nebulae, outer of, ii. 316
ZONES, Climates and, iii. 252
  Geology traces, strata or, iii. 82
  Plane above all, ii. 127
  Seven, i. 301; ii. 88, 127; iii. 33, 47, 87, 100, 120, 230, 399, 401; iv. 184, 188, 301
ZONOPLACENTAL mammals, iv. 238, 283
ZOOLATRY, Egyptian, iii. 145
  Evangelical, ii. 78
  Risk of being charged with, ii. 101
ZOOLOGICAL, Development, iii. 300
  Discoveries, ii. 362
  Dragon Nāga and serpent, meaning of, iii. 212
  Primordial life, iii. 82
  Sclater's theory of a lost continent, iii. 20
  Teaching, iii. 190
ZOOLOGIST(S), Darwinian theory and, iv. 251
  Huxley, iii. 172
  Maximum time claimed by, iii. 23
  Psychologists and, iv. 240
  Soul, and, iv. 219
ZOOLOGY, Ancient, iii. 255
  Animals unknown to, i. 241
  Anticipated, iii. 255

Ape-man and, iv. 239
Botany and, iii. 125
Cycles and, iv. 302
Esoteric teaching confirmed by, iii. 202
ZOROASTER, Airyana Vaējō birthplace of, iii. 19
  Ātmā or Christos of, iv. 49
  Birds, slaughter of, forbidden by, ii. 78
  Ether, injunctions of, with regard to, ii. 45
  Founder of Magian rites, v. 42
  Magical and Philosophical precepts of, v. 42, 55
  Period of, iii. 358
  Precepts of, v. 55
ZOROASTRIAN, Ahura, iii. 69; iv. 68
  Caves, i. 184
  Creation, iv. 56
  Demons, iii. 102
  Dogma, v. 315
  Esotericism, iii. 355
  I am that I am, i. 144
  Meru, iii. 209
  Rebirth and religion, i. 284
  Sacred fire, ii. 52
  Scriptures, iii. 355, 357
  Teaching, iii. 418
ZOROASTRIANISM, v. 36
ZOROASTRIANS, Ahura Mazda of, i. 170
  Airyana-Varsedya of, iii. 414
  Allegorical dual system of, i. 246
  Amshaspends of, i. 186, 281
  Devas of, i. 140; v. 315, 316
  Evils or darkness not believed in by early, iv. 56
  Gabiri of, iii. 362
  Sacred fires of modern, iv. 329
  Seven Devs of, ii. 300
  Sun worship of, ii. 117
  Taurus sacred to, ii. 383
ZU, Babylonian God, iii. 285
ZUNG, Mantra, v. 374, 404
ZUNI, seven priests of, Indians, iv. 199

BOOK INDEX

A

Ab Angelis Opus Divinum de Quinta Essentia (R. Lully), v. 114

Abhidharma, v. 81

Abydos (Mariette), i. 142, 275

Académie des Inscriptions (Layard), i. 184; iii. 341; iv. 85

Academy, The, ii. 26

Achaica (Pausanias), iii. 340

Acts of the Apostles, i. 151; ii. 41, 94; iv. 49; v. 79, 99, 100, 126, 136, 160, 444

Add. MSS. (Brit. Mus.), iii. 48

Address (Duncan), i. 164

Address, to the British Association (W. Grove), i. 164

Adonais (Shelley), i. 283

Adrian (Lampridius), v. 148

Adv. Celsum (Origen), v. 126

Ad. Haeres. (Epiphanius), ii. 121; iv. 25, v. 126, 160

Adv. Med. (Grading), v. 483

Æneid (Virgil), iv. 166; v. 154

Against Apion (Josephus), i. 175

Age and Origin of Man, The, (Pfaff), iv. 92, 231

Agriculture of the Nabatheans, The (Chwolsohn) iv. 22

Ain-i-Akbari (Trans. Blockmann), i. 47

Aitareya Brāhmana, i. 141, 163; iii. 58, 416

Aitareya Upanishad, i. 73

Akad Vorles(Weber), ii. 81, 182

Alberti Parvi Lucii Libellus de Mirabilibus Naturae Arcanis, v. 122

Al Chazari (Jehuda-ha-Levi), iii. 51, 53

Allégories d' Orient (Gebelin), iv. 338

Almaq (Riccioli), ii. 391

Amida Sutra, v. 410

Amer. and Oriental Lit. Rec. (Trübner's), v. 385

American Journal of Science, i. 149; iii. 149, 323

American Naturalist, iii. 325

Analecta (Bruck), iii. 306

Analysis of Ancient Mythology, An (Bryant), ii. 74; ii. 390; iv. 169

Anatomy (Quan), iii. 298

Ancient Faiths Embodied in Ancient Names (Inman), iii. 50

Ancient Fragments (Cory), i. 137; ii. 54, 57, 62, 183; iii. 65, 196; v. 30, 56

Ancient Stone Implements (Evans), iv. 291

Anfänge zu einer physiologischen Schöpfungsgeschichte der Pflanzen-und Thierwelt (Baumgartner), iv. 287

Annales de Philosophie (de Sacy), iv. 103

Annales de Philosophie Chrétienne (de Rougé), iii. 367; iv. 21; v. 325

Annales des Soc. Nat. iv. 261

Annals of Rajāsthān (Tod), iv. 258

Anthropogeny (Haeckel), iii. 196; iv. 229, 233, 235

Anthropological Review, iv. 313

Anthropology (Topinard), iii. 252

Antiquitates (Pseudo-Berosus), iii. 151

Antiquités Celtiques (Cambry), iii. 343

Antiquités Celtiques et Antédiluviennes (de Perthes), iv. 308

Antiquités de France, iii. 346

Antiquities (Berosus), iii. 152

Antiquities (Josephus), i. 184; iv. 101

Antiquity of Man (Lyell), ii. 37; iv. 257, 290, 294, 296, 297, 352

Antiquity of Man Historically Considered (Rawlinson), iv. 290

Antiquity of Man in Western Europe, The, iv. 280

Ανθρωπος, i. 271

Anugīta, i. 136, 142, 151, 157, 159, 163; ii. 258, 259, 260, 269; iv. 64, 139, 140, 209, 211

Aphorisms of Sāndilya, The, i. 73

Aphorisms of the Bodhisattvas, i. 120

Apocalypse (St. John), iv. 85, 106, 133; v. 131, 132, 160, 314

Apocalypse (Kenealy), iv. 31, 189

Apocrypha, ii. 117; v. 126, 143, 313

Apollodorus, iii. 131, 272; iv. 88

Append. de Cabiris ap. Orig. Gent., iii. 392

Approaching End of the Age (Guinness), iv. 193, 194; v. 200

Archaeological Notes on Ancient Sculpturing on Rocks in Kumaon, India, etc., (Rivett-Carnac), iii. 346

Archaeology, iii. 378

Archeologie de la Vierge Mère, ii. 108

Archaic Dictionary, ii. 60

Armenian Tales (Herbelot), iii. 397

Arte Chymiae (Bacon), ii. 305

Arth. Index (Ackerman), iii. 342

Ārya Magazine, iii. 79

Asgard and the Gods (Wagner and McDowall), ii. 118, 142, 143, 145; iii. 106, 108, 284, 346; v. 89

Asiatic Translations, v. 36

Asiatic Society's Journal, v. 178, 184
Asiatick Researches, i. 53, 282; ii. 85, 380;
    iii. 60, 150, 154, 401, 403, 404, 405, 407;
    v. 341, 346, 347
As regards Protoplasm (Stirling), ii. 362
Assyrian Antiquities (G. Smith), ii. 31
Assyrian Discoveriess (G. Smith), iii. 73, 385
Astra Vidyā, ii. 286
Astron. Poétique, iv. 339
Astronomie (Francoeur), ii. 252
Astronomie Ancienne (Bailly), ii. 374; iv. 104
Astronomie du Moyen Age (Delambre), ii. 222
Astronomy of the Ancients (Lewis), ii. 376
Atharva Veda, i. 165; iii. 183, 381; iv. 150,
    183, 394
Athenaeum, ii. 217; iii. 315; iv. 217
Atlantic Islands, The (Benjamin), iv. 359
Atlantis, the Antediluvian World (Donelly),
    iii. 225, 269, 278, 333, 334; iv. 310, 315,
    330, 351, 361
Auction (Lucian), iv. 174
Aurelianus (Vopiscus), v. 149
Aurora, iv. 206
Auszüge aus dem Zohar, i. 263; ii. 71
Avatamsaka Avatumsaka Sūtra, v. 287, 395

B

Babylon (Smith), v. 94
Babylonian Mythology (G. Smith), iii. 250
Bamboo Books, iii. 303
Banquet (Plato), iii. 105, 142, 185; v. 29
Beginnings of Life, The (Bastian), iii. 260, 262
Beiträge zur Descendenzlehre, i. 270
Beiträge zur Kenntniss (Seyffarth), iii. 151; v. 164
Bereschith Rabba, iii. 64; iv. 274
Bhagavad Gītā, i. 76, 80, 136, 150, 151, 157,
    188, 192, 195, 317; ii. 93, 94, 123, 136, 140,
    144, 148, 149, 259; iii. 38, 60, 99, 140, 311,
    318; v. 81, 232, 345, 351, 396
Bhagavatam (or tam), iv. 191
Bhāgavata Purāna, i. 145; ii. 87; iii. 172, 218,
    250, 380, 416; iv. 119, 120, 141, 142, 186;
    v. 259, 345
Bhavishya Purāna, iii. 323
Bhrigu, iii. 309
Bible, i. 54, 134, 138, 155, 186, 244, 261, 275,
    284, 308, 314, 334; ii. 17, 18, 25, 28, 30,
    31, 32, 36, 36, 37, 50, 54, 59, 60, 75, 80,
    103, 113, 133, 138, 159, 165, 171, 186, 188,
    216, 331, 374, 375, 377, 378, 382; iii. 15,
    17, 40, 48, 54, 71, 91, 134, 135, 142,
    153, 207, 210, 215, 232, 238, 254, 255, 266,
    268, 269, 272, 279, 280, 281, 282, 284, 335,
    336, 339, 342, 365, 373, 376, 381, 392, 394,
    395; iv. 19, 22, 28, 32, 34, 35, 39, 40, 49,
    54, 55, 59, 60, 62, 72, 80, 102, 106, 108,
    109, 115, 156, 167, 168, 175, 182, 194, 195,
    197, 228, 230, 260, 261, 262, 273, 275, 277,
    283, 316, 318, 326, 331, 333; v. 41, 66, 67,
    68, 69, 72, 87, 89, 90, 91, 97, 103, 105,
    106, 128, 158, 167, 174, 178, 181, 183,
    186, 187, 190, 192, 194, 195, 196, 197, 198,
    200, 201, 205, 206, 207, 208, 209, 211, 212,
    231, 234, 237, 267, 278, 314, 315, 316, 317,
    401

Bible de Vence, ii. 159
Bible in India (Jacolliot), iii. 439
Bibliotheca (Diodorus Siculus), iii. 151; iv. 342
Bibliotheca Indica, i. 141; iii. 321
Biographical and Critical Essay, iv. 75
Bodhimur, i. 73
Book of Ali, iv. 188
Book of Changes, the canonical, iii. 48
Book of Commentaries, v. 379
Book of Creation, ii. 166
Book of Druschim, ii. 156
Book of Dzyan, i. 23, 24, 46, 79, 82, 87, 134,
    142, 250, 302, 330, 398; iii. 58, 122, 223,
    244, 256, 374; iv. 328; v. 105, 205, 357, 389
Book of Enoch (Trans. Laurence), ii. 334;
    iii. 133, 153, 232, 233, 282, 284, 375; iv. 21,
    50, 51, 65, 75, 80, 98, 100, 101, 103, 104,
    105, 156, 331; v. 68, 85, 96, 99, 100, 101,
    102, 103, 105, 106, 109, 112, 131, 200, 202
Book of Genesis, v. 74
Book of God, The (Kenealy), i. 257; iii. 60,
    123, 382, 396; iv. 31, 41, 188, 189, 326, 329;
    v. 178, 179, 181, 182, 183, 184, 196, 266
Book of Hammannunah, iii. 40; iv. 342
Book of Hermes (Pymander), i. 141; iii. 49;
    iv. 21, 22; v. 89, 131
Book of Jasher, ii. 301
Book of Life, i. 165; ii. 259
Book of Mashalim (Proverbs), v. 74
Book of Moses, iv. 197
Book of Numbers (Chaldean), i. 64, 146, 246,
    261, 262, 271, 277, 284, 285, 286; ii. 50,
    51, 82, 151, 344; iii. 49, 94, 107, 119, 207,
    377, 396; iv. 29, 76, 197, 275; v. 114, 180,
    189, 192, 193, 205
Book of Rules, The, ii. 185
Book of Ruth and Schadash, iii. 374
Book of Sarparājni, i. 141
Book of Ser Marco Poio (Yule), v. 40
Book of Splendour (Shimon Ben Yohai), v. 175
Book of the Aphorisms of Tsong-kha-pa, ii. 360
Book of the Beginnings (Massey), iv. 202, 344
Book of the Concealed Mystery, iii. 92, 107
Book of the Dead (Egyptian), i. 134, 266, 267,
    273, 274, 275, 277, 282, 283; ii. 44, 75, 80,
    96, 118, 398, 399, 400; iii. 17, 42, 217,
    373, 384, 395; iv. 108, 116, 148, 150, 159,
    206; v. 89, 199, 202, 249, 289, 590
Book of the Generations of Adam, iii. 142
Book of the Golden Precepts, v. 489
Book of the Law (of the Sadducees), v. 185
Book of the Law of Moses, v. 185
Book of the Keys, i. 154; v. 115
Book of the Ten Thousand Precepts, i. 116
Book of the Various Names of the Nile (Ben
    Yusouf Eltiphas), iii. 365
Book of Wisdom, iii. 120; v. 86
Books of Hermes, v. 115
Books of Knowledge and Wisdom, iv. 275
Books of Thoth, iii. 17; v. 68, 105, 221
Brahma Purānas, iii. 277
Brahma Siddhanta, v. 344
Brahma Vaivarta, ii. 84; iii. 308
Brāhmanas, i. 23, 50, 218, 314, 315; ii. 170,
    iii. 286, 408; v. 73, 232
Brahmānda Purāna, ii. 83, 154; iii 402
Brihadaranyaka Upanishad, iv. 118, 210; iv. 269

Bucolica (Virgil), iv. 173
Buddhism (Davids), ii. 193
Buddhism in Christendom, or Jesus the Essene (A. Lillie), ii. 263
Buddhism in Tibet (Schlagintweit), i. 50; iii. 187, 286; v. 287, 373, 376, 377, 402, 403, 404
Buddhismus (Schott), v. 401
Buddhismus, (Wassilief), i. 112, 116; v. 402
Buddhist Catechism (Olcott), ii. 360, 361; v. 385, 386
Buddhist Cosmos (Bouze Jin-ch'on). v. 390
Buddhist Pilgrims (Müller), v. 40
Builder, ii. 34
Bundahish, iii. 19, 293, 294
Burham-i-Kati, iii. 366

C

Cabala (Reuchlin), iv. 171, 173
Cabbalah, its Doctrines, Developments and Literature, The (Ginsburg), v. 188
Cabiri(Faber), iii. 150, 359, 360, 364, 392
Caesar, v. 306
Cain and his Birth (Philo Judaeus), iv. 58
Calcutta Review, i. 75
Canadian Theosophist, The, i. 36
Cartas (de Bourbourg), iii. 379
Catechism, iii. 54, 68
Catechism (Calvin), iii. 305
Catechism of the Vishishtādvaita Philosophy, a, (Bhashyacharya), i. 190
Cavernes de Périgord (Lartet), iv. 315
Celepas Geraldinus, iii. 365
Celestial Chemistry from the time of Newton (Hunt), ii. 218
Chagpa Thogmed, v. 73
Chaire d'Hébreu au Collège de France, iii. 200
Chaldean account of Genesis (G. Smith), i. 49; ii. 32, 72; iii. 16, 18, 19, 72, 112, 113, 284, 383
Chaldean Oracles, ii. 62
Champaitehos-nga, v. 412
Chhandogya Upanishad, iv. 209
China Revealed, ii. 193
Chinese Buddhism (Edkins), i. 44, 51, 139, 184; ii. 158; iii. 186; v. 391, 392, 394, 408, 409 410, 412, 413
Chinesische Literatur (Schott), i. 59
Chips from a German Workshop (Müller), iii. 226; v. 269, 341, 385
Christianity and Greek Philosophy (Cocker), iv. 124
Chronicles, ii. 139, 386
Chronicon (Eusebius), i. 49
Civilization of the Eastern Iranians in Ancient Times (Geiger), iv. 327
Clef des Grands Mystères (Lévi), i. 286
Clementine Homilies, v. 161
Climate and Time (Croll), iii. 149; iv. 264, 265, 283
Codex Nazaraeus, i. 245, 246, 264, 293; ii. 184; iii. 105, 388; iv. 31; v. 81
Collect. Nova Patrum (quoting Indicopleustes) iii. 398
Collect. de Reb. Hibern. (Vallancey), ii. 366
Collected Works (Wilson), ii. 173

Collection of Persian Legends, iii. 393
Colossians, v. 488
Coming Race, The, (Lytton), ii. 286
Commentaries, v. 389, 390, 391
Commentaries on the Book of Moses, v. 33
Commentary, iv. 165
Comment. on the Yashna, ii. 155
Comptes Rendus (Faye), ii. 225; iv. 318
Comte de Gabalis (de Villars), ii. 330
Concepts and Theories of Modern Physics(Stallo), ii. 205, 206, 208, 209, 210, 211, 216, 235, 236, 237, 268
Concerning Divine Names (Darboy), ii. 186
Concordance (Cruden), i. 185, 285; ii. 132
Conservation of Solar Energy, On the (Siemens), i. 164
Contra Celsum (Origen), ii. 164; iv. 108
Contra Ebionitas (Epiphanius), v. 161
Contra Gentes (Arnobius), iii. 149, 151
Contra Haereses (Irenæus), ii. 166, 167; v. 199
Contributions of the Theory of Natural Selection (Wallace), ii. 53; iv. 266
Coptic Legends of the Crucifixion, v. 162
Corinthians, ii. 97, 186, 298; iii. 91, 120, 341; iv. 82; v. 81, 82, 130, 138, 370, 463
Cornelius à Lapide, v. 313
Correlation of Physical Forces, The (Sir W. Grove), i. 164; ii. 186, 207, 221, 233
Correspondence (Leibnitz), ii. 356
Correspondence of Spinoza, The (Wolf), iii. 15
Cosmic Philosophy (Fiske), iv. 348
Cosmogonie de la Révélation (Godefroy), ii. 223, 230
Cosmogonies Aryennes (Darmesteter), ii. 50
Cosmogony (Pherecydes), i. 246
Cosmographie, ii. 227
Cosmos (Humboldt), iv. 242
Countries of the World, The (R. Brown), iii. 317, 336
Cours Philosophique et Interprétatif des Initiations (Ragon), iv. 146
Crânes des Races Humaines (de Quatrefages), iv. 314
Cratylus (Plato), i. 70; ii. 69; v. 30
Creation or Evolution (Curtis), 253
Crest-Jewel of Wisdom, The (Chatterji), ii. 293, 297
Critias (Plato), iii. 393; iv. 312, 330, 334, 337
Critique de la Raison Pure (Kant), ii. 339
Cyropaedia (Xenophon), ii. 378

D

Dabistān, ii. 375, 378; iii. 19, 358
Daniel, v. 184, 245
Darwinism, a Critical Investigation of the Theory (Danilevsky), iv. 224
Darwin's Philosophy of Language (Müller), iv. 231
Day after Death, The (Figuier), iii. 145
De Acervulo Cerebri (Sœmmering), v. 482
De Anim. Procr. (Plutarch), iv. 171
De Anima, i. 176
De Arithmetica (Boëthius), ii. 76
De Astrologia (Lucian), v. 334
De Bello Judaico (Josephus), iii. 120
De Cælo (Aristotle), i. 176; ii. 216; iii. 161

De Caus. Ep. (Morgagni), v. 483
De Civitate Dei (St. Augustine), iii. 45; iv. 105
De Consensu Moysis et Jesu, v. 34
De Cultu Egypt (Abenephius), ii. 77
De Diis Syriis (Seldenus), ii. 110; v. 238
De Docta Ignorantia (Cusa), iv. 115; v. 355
De Fundamento Sapientiæ (Paracelsus), i. 334
De Generatione Hominis (Aristotle), v. 241
De Genesis ad litteram (St. Augustine), v. 209
De Gigantibus (Philo Judaeus), iii. 120
De Idol. (Vossius), iv. 49
De Incomprehensibli Natura Dei (John Chry-
    sostom), v. 327
De Iside et Osiride (Plutarch), i. 184; ii. 62
De la Croix Ansée (Rochette), etc., iv. 116
De Lapillis Glandulæ Pinealis in Quinque
    Ment. Alien. (Gum), v. 483
De Legibus (Cicero), v. 254
De Legibus (Plato), iii. 372
De Mensibus (Lydus), iv. 112
De Motibus Planetarium Harmonicis (Kepler),
    ii. 216
De Mysteriis (Iamblichus), i. 281; iii. 451, 452
De Natura Animalium (Ælianus), iii. 354
De Natura Deorum (Cornutus), ii. 111
De Off. (Cicero), v. 262
De Opificio Mundi (Philo Judaeus), ii. 124;
    iv. 173
De Placitio Philosophorum (Plutarch), ii. 339,
    347
De Religione Persarum (Hyde), iii. 362
De Rerum Natura (Lucretius), i. 74
De Secundus Deis (Trithemius), v. 207
De Senectute (Cicero), iii. 216
De Somniis (Philo), iii. 120
De Theologia Gentilii (Vossius), ii. 216
De Ventis (Theophrastus), iii. 132
De Viribus Membrorum, ii. 256
De Viris Illust. (St. Jerome), v. 143, 160
De Vita Apollonii (Philostratus), ii. 120
De Vita Pythag. (Porphyry), ii. 76; v. 113
Delle Grandezze del Archangelo Sancti Mikæle
    (Maragone), iv. 47
Democrit. Vitæ (Laërtius), v. 44
Denarius Pythagoricus (Meursius), v. 115
Denkmäler (Lepsius), i. 275
Des Initiations Anciennes et Modernes (Ragon),
    v. 261, 262, 264
Desâtîr, iii. 270; v. 281
Descent of Buddhas (Jones), v. 369
Descent of Man (Darwin), iii. 127; iv. 167, 236,
    243, 245
Description of Greece (Pausanias), ii. 111; iii. 41,
    362, 363; iv. 85
De Special. Legibus, v. 255
De Stella Nova in Pede Serpentarii (Kepler),
    ii. 314
Deuteronomy, i. 145, 146, 151, 180; ii. 187,
    300, 336; iv. 28, 46, 107; v. 182, 187
Deutsche Mythol. iii. 273
Devi Bhāgavata Purāna, i. 76
Dhammapada, iii. 119; v. 411
Diable et Satan, Le, (Baissac), iii. 248
Dialogues (Plato), v. 27, 33
Dialogues of Plato (trans. Jowett), v. 31
Dialogus cum Tryphone (Justin), v. 58
Diary (Olcott), i. 18, 24

Diatesseron, v. 34
Dictionary of Hindu Mythology (Dowson), i. 145
Dictionnaire des Religions (Bertrand), iii. 342
Dictionnaire Encyclopédique de France, v. 330
Dieu et les Dieux (des Mousseaux), iii. 345
Dion Cassius, v. 148
Dionysiacs (Nonnus), iii. 152
Dirghotamas, iii. 106
Discours (Herschel), ii. 227
Dissertation on the Mysteries of the Cabiri, A,
    (Faber), iii. 267
Dissertations relating to Asia (Wm. Jones),
    ii. 94
Divine Pymander, The (Everard), i. 141
Doctrine of Descent and Darwininism, The
    (Schmidt), iii. 21, 173, 179, 191; iv. 217,
    232, 236, 237, 304, 305, 348, 357, 360
Dogmatic Theology, v. 125
Dogme et Rituel de la Haute Magie (É. Lévi),
    iv. 124, 132; v. 48, 49, 86, 117, 282, 326, 335
Dramas of Æschylus, The (Swanwick), iii. 410,
    411, 414, 415, 417
Du Dragon de Metz (Lenoir), iii. 384

E

Earth's Earliest Ages (Pember), iii. 232
Ecclesiastes, iv. 123, 273; v. 234, 313
Ecclesiastical History (Mosheim), v. 126
Ecclestiasticus, v. 86, 313
Eclogae (Virgil), ii. 117; v. 338
Eclogæ Physicæ et Ethicæ (Stobæus), iii. 146
Eddas, iii. 248, 385
Edinburgh Encyclopædia, v. 303
Edinburgh Medical and Surgical Journal, iv. 194
Egypt's Place in Universal History, (Bunsen),
    i. 50; v. 111, 140, 296
Égypte Ancienne (Champollion-Figeac), iii. 366,
    369; v. 58
Egypte Moderne (Champollon-Figeac), v. 323,
    334
Egyptian Mysteries (Iamblicus), v. 254
Ekashloka Shāstra (Nāgārjuna), i. 130
Electric Science (Buckwell), ii. 234
Elements and Meta-Elements (Crookes), ii. 322
Élévations (Bossuet), iii. 281
Elohistic and Jehovistic Writers (Colenso),
    iv. 41
Eloim, Les (Lacour), iii. 219
Eleusinian and Bacchic Mysteries (Taylor),
    v. 130, 139, 280, 281
Enchainements du Monde Animal dans les temps
    Géologiques (Gandry), ¹v. 318
Enchiridium Leonis Papae, v. 122
Encyclopaedia, iv. 275
Encyclopædia Britannica, iii. 77, 81; iv. 256,
    268
Encyclopædia (Japanese), v. 407
Encyclopædia Londiniensis, iii. 361
Enoïchion, iv. 98
Ephesians, ii. 45
Epipsychidion (Shelley), ii. 102
Ep. ad Paulinum (Jerome), v. 149
Epistle to Timothy (Paul), v. 138
Epistles (Paul), iii. 91; v. 99, 129, 136, 176, 215,
    301, 312
Epoch of the Mammoth (Southall), iv. 309

Esoteric Buddhism (Sinnett), i. 18, 19, 20, 41, 42
168, 181, 206, 207, 210, 211, 215, 216, 217,
218, 223, 228, 242, 277, 278; ii. 18, 62, 263;
iii. 21, 163, 185, 193, 201, 253, 267, 282, 309,
314, 318, 332, 333, 424, 431, 434; iv. 65,
169, 204, 206, 207, 211, 284, 285, 319, 320,
343, 347, 348; v. 25, 230, 300, 350, 365, 426,
427, 440, 455, 486, 496
Esoteric Catechism, ii. 344; v. 425
Esoteric Treatise on the Doctrine of Gilgul
(Valentinus), ii. 291
Esprits, Des (de Mirville), ii. 108, 116, 117, 158,
159, 186, 188, 228, 230, 374, 375, 378, 379,
380, 381, 383, 384; iii. 209, 210, 211, 212, 213,
214, 225, 280, 282, 337, 340, 341, 344, 345, 346,
347, 366, 367, 368, 369, 370, 371, 372, 374;
iv. 20, 47, 48, 49, 50, 99, 100, 101, 102, 104,
191; v. 55, 58, 61, 62, 63, 71, 95, 128, 132,
134, 143, 146, 149, 170, 209, 213, 217, 220,
221, 224, 225, 237, 246, 247, 250, 253, 254,
255, 256, 277, 312, 327
Esprits Tombés des Paiens, iv. 84
Essais Historiques sur la Franc-Maçonnerie,
(Laurens), v. 263, 264
Essias Orientaux, (Darmesteter), ii. 50
Essays (Freppel), v. 146
Essays (Montaigne), iii. 340
Essays on Physiology (Spencer), iii. 348
Eternal Wisdom (Huschenk), iii. 395
Ethnographische Skizzen über die Völker des
Russischen Amerika (Holmberg), iii. 227
Études Égyptologiques (Pierret), i. 275
Études Historiques (Renan), v. 53
Études Religeuses (Renan), v. 53
Evening Telegraph, iii. 439
Evolution, v. 136
Evolution of Christianity, iv. 50; v. 96, 99
Evolution without Natural Selection (Dixon),
ɪv. 217, 218
Evolutionary Psychology (Bourges), iv. 224
Examen des Principes de Malebranche, ii. 356
Exodus, i. 184; ii. 32, 100, 139, 216; iii. 424,
426; iv. 46, 108, 109, 127; v. 92, 114, 191,
278, 375, 439
Exposition du vrai Système du Monde (Laplace),
ii. 224, 315
Ezekiel, i. 186; ii. 113; iv. 60, 61, 62, 63, 70,
102, 122, 123, 127
Ezour Veda, iii. 440

F

Fa-hwa-King, ii. 192
Fallacies of Darwinism (Bree), iv. 266, 296
297, 298
Families of Speech (Farrar), iv. 358
Faraday Lectures (Helmholtz), i. 171; ii. 304
Faraday's Life and Letters (Airy), ii. 308
Fasti (Ovid), iii. 130
Fils de Dieu, Les, (Jacolliot), ii. 92
Finer Forces of Nature (Prasad), v. 85
First Principles (Spencer), i. 78
Five years of Theosophy, i. 195, 198, 212, 229,
230, 231, 300, 313, 334; ii. 93, 174, 251, 255,
264, 307, 314, 318, 321, 335; iii. 180, 327;
iv. 67, 147, 148, 168, 170, 241, 242, 312; v. 79,
275, 283, 364, 367, 368, 377, 384, 460

Flora Tertiaria Helvetiae (Heer), iv. 352
Florilegium (Stobæus), i. 328
Fluid Theory of Light and Heat (Leslie), ii. 240
Foe-Koue-ki, ou Relations des Royaumes
Bouddhiques (Chy-Fa-hian), iii. 208
Force and Matter (Büchner), ii. 364; iii. 162;
iv. 265, 287
Forces Non-définies (de Rochat), iv. 352
Fortnightly Review, iv. 257
Fourth Book of Esdras, iv. 21
Fragments (Pindarus), v. 254
Frag. of Styg., ap Stob. v. 255
French Encylopædia, ii. 223
Fuel of the sun, The, (W. M. Williams), i. 164;
ii. 309
Fundamental Conceptions of Psychology and
Physiology (Strachof), iv. 224

G

Galatians, v. 67
Garuda Purāna, iv. 135
Gemara Sanhedrin, iv. 41; v. 67
General Report, i. 24, 26, 29
Genesis, i. 72, 75, 77, 185, 263, 291, 308; ii. 32,
36, 44, 50, 60, 71, 72, 96, 130, 132, 139,
149, 171, 216, 247, 331, 377; iii. 15, 16,
19, 55, 56, 57, 69, 71, 85, 91, 103, 121, 132,
133, 134, 135, 136, 137, 142, 161, 187, 199,
215, 216, 217, 219, 232, 238, 246, 268, 275,
281, 284, 293, 357, 360, 373, 376, 379, 386,
387, 389, 390, 391, 393, 409; iv. 20, 28,
34, 37, 45, 59, 69, 77, 99, 153, 169, 203,
230, 260, 275, 283, 344; v. 66, 90, 101, 106,
107, 111, 165, 176, 178, 184, 187, 190,
198, 199, 200, 201, 206, 208, 231, 237, 239,
319, 439
Genesis of Enoch, iii. 270
Genesis of Species, The, (Mivart), iv. 267
Genesis of the Elements (Crookes), ii. 305, 347,
349, 350, 353; iii. 114
Geographica, lib. iv. (Strabo), iv. 329
Geographical Distribution of Animals (Wallace),
iii. 199
Géographie Ancienne, iv. 338
Geological Evidences of the Antiquity of Man
(Lyell), ii. 36
Geological Magazine, iv. 352
Geometry in Religion, v. 178
Georgica (Virgil), ii. 45
Gnostics and their Remains (King), ii. 76, 91, 126,
127, 167, 300, 391; iii. 246; iv. 42, 49, 87,
108, 111, 133, 135, 136; iv. 139, 140, 152,
162, 176; v. 111, 163, 169
God and His Book (" Saladin "), iv. 277
God in History (Bunsen), iii. 91
God of Moses, The (Lacour), v. 318
Goladhyaya of the Siddhanta-shiromani, iii. 321
Gospels, v. 100, 103, 125, 232
Gravitation par l'Electricité, La, (Zaliwsky),
v. 220
Great Book of the Mysteries, iii. 217
Great Pyramid, The (Wake), iii. 39, 44, 91, 351,
365, 429; v. 110
Greater Holy Assembly, The, iv. 196
Greek and English Lexicon (Liddell and Scott),
iv. 176

Griech. Götterlehre (Welcker), iii. 391
Grimoires des Sorciers (Lévi), v. 251
Guide au Musée de Boulaq (Maspero), ii. 24, 68, 101, 399; iv. 32; v. 246
Guide to the Perplexed (Maimonides), ii. 110
Gyut, v. 404

H

Ha Idra Rabba Qadisha (or Greater Holy Assembly), iv. 196
Ha Idra Zuta Qadisha (or Lesser Holy Assembly), i. 285; iii. 92, 93, 94; iv. 196
Handbook of the History of Philosophy (Schwegler), i. 122
Harivamsha, iii. 45, 85, 98, 154, 183, 277; iv. 143, 150, 184
Harmonie entre l'Église et la Synagogue (Drach), v. 217
Heart of Africa (Schweinfurth), iv. 235
Heathen Religion, The (Grass), i. 127
Heaven and Earth, ii. 229
Hebrew and Other Creations, The, (Massey), v. 199, 200
Hebrews, i. 285; iii. 391; iv. 100, 273; v. 131, 160
Herabkunft des Feuers und des Göttertranks, Die, (Kuhn), iv. 95
Heracles (Euripides), v. 153
Hercule et Cacus (Bréal), iii. 271
Hercules Furens (Euripides), iv. 333
Hermes, iii. 284; v. 309
Herodotus, iii. 365, 394
Herodotus (Rawlinson), iii. 429
Hermes Trismegistus, iv. 201
Heroica (Philostratus), iii. 280
Hesiod, iii. 188
Hibbert Lectures, iii. 64, 124, 230, 250; iv. 23, 30, 45, 262, 263; v. 199, 203
Hierarch. (St. Denys), v. 209
Hindu Classical Dictionary (Dowson), i. 175; ii. 176; iii. 155; iv. 66, 67, 118, 129, 184; v. 140
Hindu Pantheon (Moor), iii. 43; iv. 118, 130, 131; v. 288
Hippolytus (Euripides), ii. 111
Hisai Sûtra, etc., v. 390
Hist. (Diodorus), v. 334
Hist. Eccles., (Eusebius), v. 451
Hist. Nat. (Pliny), iii. 280, 342, 344, 346; iv. 191, 192, 342; v. 306
Histoire Critique du Gnosticisme (Matter), v. 36
Historie de l'Astronomie Ancienne (Bailly), ii. 374; iii. 368; iv. 104, 312
Historie de la Magie (É. Lévi), i. 156; iii. 241, 358; iv. 76, 80, 106; v. 231, 232
Histoire de la Réligion de la Grèce (Maury), v. 54
Histoire des Vierges, les Peuples et les Continents Disparus (Jacolliot), iii. 226; iv. 353, 356
Histoire des trois Premiers Siècles de L'Eglise (de Pressensé), v. 132
Historia Ante-Islamitica (Abul Feda), iii. 215, 365
Histoira Antiqua de la Nueva Espana (Daran), iii. 278
Historical and Experimental Researches, ii. 370
Historical View of the Hindu Astronomy (Bentley), iv. 68, 120; v. 201, 344

History (Herodotus), " Euterpe ", ii. 77; " Polymnia ", ii 188; " Thalia ", iii. 359
History of Ancient Sanskrit Literature (Müller), ii. 93
History of Civilization (Buckle), i. 337; ii. 240
History of Creation (Haeckel), iv. 281, 297
History of Magic (Ennemoser), v. 297
History of English Literature (Taine), iii. 334
History of Indian Literature, The (Weber), iii. 61
History of Paganism in Caledonia (Wise), iii. 342, 346
History of Persia (Malcolm), ii. 375
History of the Conflict between Religion and Science (Draper), i. 165; v. 271
Homilies, Clementine, v. 169
Homme Rouge des Tuileries, L' (Christian) i. 156
Homoiomeria (Anaxagoras), ii. 303
Horae Biblicae (Butler), iii. 205
Horae Hebraicae (Schoettgen), iii. 169
Hosea, iii. 138
Human Faculty, (Galton), v. 442
Human Species, The, (de Quatrefages), ii. 263; iii. 128, 222, 315, 442; iv. 216, 235, 237, 238, 282, 314, 315, 318, 349
Hymn. Nemes (Mesomed), iii. 306
Hymns to Minerva (Pindar), ii. 116
Hypoth. (Newton), i. 79
Hypothèses Cosmogoniques Les (Wolf), ii. 314, 320, 321, 322, 323

I

Ice Age Climate and Time, The, iv. 265
Ideen (Schelling), ii. 235
Idolat (Vossius), iii. 41
Idyll of the White Lotus, The, (Collins), ii. 298
Ilaid (Homer), ii. 374; iii. 189, 382; iv. 335, 340, 343, 345
Ilios (Schliemann), iii. 438
Illustrations of the Rock-cut Temples of India (Fergusson), iii. 224
In Matrem Deorum (Julian), iii. 47
Inde des Brahmes, L' (Jacolliot), ii. 92
India in Greece (Pococke), v. 110
India, What can it Teach us? (Müller), iv. 290
Indian Antiquities (Borlase), iv. 325
Indische Alterthumskunde (Lassen), i. 51; v. 405
Individuality in the Light of Biology and Modern Philosophy (Hellenbach), iv. 224
Indra Rabbah, iii. 64
In Quint. Lib. Euclid. (Proclus), iv. 122
Inst. Div. (Lactantius), iii. 170
Institutes of Justinian, ii. 190
Intellectual System (Cudworth), iii. 167
Introduction à l'Étude des Races Humaines (de Quatrefages), iii. 67, 163; iv. 251
Introduction to the Literature of Europe (Hallam), iv. 297
Introduction to the Old Testament (Horne), iv. 41
Introduction to the Parmenides of Plato (Taylor), ii. 143
Introduction to the Science of Religion (Müller), i. 47; ii. 194; iii. 199
Introduction to the Study of Foraminifera (Carpenter), iii. 260
Irenaeus, ii. 168; iv. 182

Isaiah, i. 138; iii. 74, 210; iv. 48, 60, 64, 69, 160; v. 309, 326, 375

Isis Unveiled (Blavatsky), i. 14, 18, 19, 20, 22, 24, 25, 42, 46, 60, 63, 64, 66, 71, 117, 164, 172, 175, 236, 237, 238, 245, 246, 247, 251, 258, 278, 280, 291, 293; ii. 15, 25, 29, 31, 32, 33, 46, 51, 52, 54, 57, 59, 77, 81, 91, 96, 134, 167, 183, 184, 213, 222, 292, 303, 304, 305, 350, 366, 382, 383, 395; iii. 14, 49, 62, 83, 84, 94, 100, 105, 133, 137, 138, 139, 152, 153, 160, 174, 194, 195, 196, 207, 208, 216, 218, 219, 223, 224, 225, 227, 232, 261, 262, 264, 330, 376, 378, 379, 388, 415, 427, 428, 438; iv. 22, 29, 33, 46, 65, 70, 78, 102, 111, 123, 124, 125, 126, 127, 146, 201, 211, 261, 290, 316; v. 29, 30, 40, 41, 42, 43, 44, 46, 51, 55, 56, 58, 67, 72, 76, 77, 80, 87, 89, 108, 112, 113, 130, 136, 137, 138, 139, 142, 143, 145, 161, 163, 164, 204, 205, 247, 248, 249, 255, 271, 275, 278, 279, 280, 281, 286, 293, 300, 305, 306, 307, 311, 322, 357, 358, 369, 382, 383, 384, 387, 388, 406, 411, 430, 486, 489, 491, 502

Island Life (Wallace), iv. 351

J

James, i. 247; ii. 131, 132
Japan (Kaempfer), iii. 364
Jeremiah, iii. 137; v. 179
Jewish Antiquities (Jennings), v. 187
Jnāna-bhāskara, iii. 78
Job, i. 138; ii. 59, 130, 139, 373, 374; iii. 374, 376; iv. 54; v. 143, 290
John, i. 138, 272, 308; ii. 294, 298, 302; iii. 102; v. 83, 84, 96, 360, 369
Josephus (Burder's trans), v. 185
Joshua, iv. 98, 128; v. 185
Journal (Wolff), v. 179
Journal Asiatique, iii. 209
Journal des Colonies (Lavoisier), ii. 189
Journal des Savants, iii. 398
Journal of Microscopical Science, iii. 161
Journal of the Anthropological Institute, iv. 324
Journal of the Asiatic Society of Bengal, v. 401, 402, 403
Journal of Royal Asiatic Society, ii. 140; iv. 116
Journal of Royal Microscopical Society, iv. 217
Journal of Science, i. 149; ii. 207; iii. 149, 324
Judaism and Paganism (Döllinger), v. 255
Jude, iii. 233; iv. 46, 59; v. 100
Judges, iv. 28; v. 238, 239, 277, 311
Justinian, Institutes of, ii. 190

K

Kabala(h), See Zohar
Kabbala Denudata (Rosenroth), i. 176; ii. 106, 230
Kabalah Unveiled (Mathers's trans.), i. 286; ii. 67; iii. 93, 294, 313; iv. 196, 197, 199
Kabbale, La, (Franck), i. 64; ii. 65; iii. 16; iv. 29; v. 85, 108, 305, 439
Kabiri (Faber), iii. 150
Kala Chakra, i. 123; v. 365, 366, 375
Kala Sankelita (Warren), v. 340
Kalevala, The (Crawford), iii. 26, 39, 130

Kanjur, i. 50, 123; v. 375, 404
Katha Upanishad, i. 136; ii. 81, 149, 182
Kaushitaki Brāhmana, Dās, i. 141; iii. 58
Kether Malkhuth (Ibn Gebirol), ii. 157
Key of Urania, The, ii. 381
Key to Theosophy, The (Blavatsky), v. 473, 490
Kià-yü, ii. 159
Kiddusheem, iv. 46
King (Confucius), i. 49
Kings, ii. 80, 374, 375; iii. 85, 341, 386; iv. 28; v. 277, 311
Kin-kwang-ming-King, ii. 192
Kioo-tche, iv. 192
Kiu-te, i. 64; v. 389
Knowledge, ii. 26; iii. 144, 159, 160, 352, 429; iv. 225, 255, 280, 282, 283
Kuku-ma, v. 122
Kurma Purāna, ii. 177; iv. 149, 183

L

Lalita-Vistara, i. 119
Lāmaism, or The Buddhism of Tibet (Waddell), v. 398
Lancet, iv. 194
Land and Water (Bartlett), iv. 167
Laws of Manu, iv. 144, 317
Lecture on Protoplasm (Huxley), ii. 394
Lectures (Massey), ii. 103, 108, 117
Lectures (Max Müller), i. 51, 52, 53
Lectures in Sweden (von Bergen), v. 337
Lectures on Heroes (Carlyle), i. 260
Lectures on the Bhagavad Gita, i. 170
Lectures on the Origin and Growth of Religion (Sayce), iv. 263
Lectures on the Philosophy of History (Hegel), ii. 366
Légendes Persanes (Herbelot), iii. 393, 395
Legends and Theories of the Buddhists (Hardy), i. 50
Letters of H. P. Blavatsky to A. P. Sinnett, i. 19, 20, 23, 24, 27
Letters from the Masters of Wisdom, 2nd Series, i. 21, 30
Letters from North America (Hodson), iii. 342
Letters on Magic (Lévi), v. 486
Lettres à Lettrone, v. 332
Lettres Persanes (Montesquieu), ii. 401
Lettres sur l'Atlantide (Bailly), iii. 267, 268, 396; iv. 311, 312, 341
Leviticus, i. 146; ii. 375; iv. 135, 189, 316, 317; v. 66, 265
Lexicon (Peter), iv. 177
Liber Mysterii (Rosenroth), i. 262
Library of Contemporary Sciences, iv. 255
Life and Teachings of Confucius (J. Legge), i. 59; iv. 59
Life of Apollonius of Tyana (Philostratus), v. 151
Life of Numa (Plutarch), iv. 192
Life of Paracelsus (Hartmann), ii. 256
Life of Pythagoras (Iamblichus), v. 279
Life of Sulla (Plutarch), ii. 376
Light of Asia, The (Arnold), iii. 232; v. 218, 412
Limestone as an Index of Geological Time (Reade), iii. 23

Linga Purāna i. 301; ii. 36, 170, 173, 177, 235; iii. 251, 252, 283, 308; iv. 183, 185

Lives (Laertius), iii. 376

Lives (Plutarch), " Caius Marius ", iv. 342

Lives of Alchemystical Philosophers, iv. 332

Livre des Morts, Le, (Pierret), i. 192

Logic (Bain), i. 180, 296; ii. 39

Longman's Magazine, iv. 257

Lucifer, i. 21, 31, 32, 33, 34, 36, 222; v. 427, 466, 486

Luke, i. 285; ii. 189; iii. 233, 234; iv. 40, 54; v. 84, 150, 211

Luniolatry, Ancient and Modern (Massey), iv. 122

M

Maccabees, Third Book of the (Hanneberg), iv. 10

Maçonnerie Occulte, (Ragon), i. 162; iv. 363, 364; v. 115, 116, 118

Magasin Pittoresque (Charton), iii. 346

Magic, White and Black (Hartmann), iv. 211

Magie (Maury), ii. 116

Magie au XIXe Siècle, La (des Mousseaux), v. 321

Magie der Zahlen (Hellenbach), iv. 198, 199

Mahābhārata, i. 154, 157; ii. 154; iii. 52, 55, 59, 78, 88, 147, 154, 163, 189, 218, 235, 277, 381, 424; iv. 64, 137, 200; v. 258, 288

Mahā-Prajnā-Pāramitā, v. 407

Mahātmā Letters to A. P. Sinnett, The, i. 214, 217, 218, 221, 239, 240; iii. 235, 427; iv. 347, 348; v. 440, 465

Mahāvanso, ii. 93

Malay Archipelago (Wallace), iv. 357

Man and Apes (Mivart), iv. 250

Man before Metals (Joly), iii. 109; iv. 231, 316, 318, 319, 320, 358

Man:Fragments of Forgotten History (Two Chelas), i. 206, 215; iii. 230; iv. 211

Mānava-Dharma-Shastra, i. 300; iii. 68, 98, 100; v. 382

Māndūkya Upanishad, i. 73, 79, 148; v. 79

Mani Kumbum, i. 116; v. 392

Man's Place in Nature (Huxley), iii. 160; iv. 226, 245, 247, 251, 256, 267, 287

Mantuan Codex, i. 284

Mantra Shāstra, i. 333

Manu, i. 136, 139, 194, 293; ii. 46, 47, 48, 75, 150, 166, 168, 177; iii. 77, 134, 135, 250, 309, 311; iv. 145

Manual of Geology (Jukes), iii. 202, 223

Manubhasya, ii. 47

Mark, iii. 234; v. 64

Markandeya Purāna, ii. 177

Masonic Review, The, i. 154; ii. 147, iii. 49, 51, 52, 53, 86; v. 90

Matériaux pour l'Histoire de l'Homme (de Morbillet), iv. 280

Mathematica (Theon of Smyrna), v. 280

Matsya Purāna, ii. 93; iii. 59, 98; iv. 121, 183, 185, 335

Matthew, i. 323; ii. 30, 132, 160, 298, 302, 380; iii. 234; iv. 54, 64, 136; v. 64, 65, 82, 125, 159, 160

Measure for Measure (Shakespeare), iv. 225

Medical Review, iv. 193

Melelwa Nahil, iii. 365

Members of Ārya Samāj, etc. To, (Lane Fox), v. 133

Mémoire of Dr. Bourges, iv. 224

Mémoire sur la Dispersion de la Lumière (Cauchy), ii. 209

Memoires (Danville), iii. 393

Memoires de l'Académie des Inscriptions, iv. 192, 332; v. 94

Mémoires de l'Académie des Sciences de Montpellier, ii. 230

Mémoires de l'Académie Royale de Belgique, ii. 205

Mémoires de la Société de la Linguistique, iv. 93

Mémoires de la Société des Antiquaires de France, v. 42

Memoirs (Della Penna), v. 389

Mère d'Apis, La, (Champollion), v. 215, 276

Meropis, iii. 370; iv. 333

Metamorphoses (Ovid), ii. 103; iii. 272; iv. 88, 341

Metaphysics (Aristotle), ii. 59, 77

Mexique (de Bourbourg), iii. 218

Midraschim, v. 177

Midraish (Rabbi Abaku), iii. 64; iv. 274; v. 91, 177

Mind, iii. 287

Miracle in Stone, A (Lundy), v. 95

Mirror of Futurity, iii. 61

Miscellaneous Essays (Colebrooke), iv. 195

Mishna Hagiga, v. 67, 179, 189

Mishna Sanhedrin, v. 162

Mission des Juifs, La (d'Alveydre), ii. 192; iv. 119

Mitākshara (Vignānesvara), ii. 150

Modern Chemistry (Cooke), ii. 304

Modern Genesis, The (Slaughter), i. 160

Modern Materialism (Wilkinson), ii. 214

Modern Science and Modern Thought (Laing), i. 209; ii. 228, 394; iii. 81, 82, 125, 163, 255, 256, 257, 261, 288, 289; iv. 79, 227, 245, 246, 247, 248, 285, 286, 292, 300, 301

Modern Thought, iv. 293

Modern Zoroastrian, A (Laing), iii. 173, 179; iv. 91, 227, 230, 231, 232, 241, 242, 243

Mokshadharma Parvan, iii. 88

Monadologie (Leibnitz), ii. 354, 356

Monthly Magazine, The, ii. 143, 144

Monumental Christianity (Lundy), iv. 50, 131; v. 95, 288, 311

Monuments Celtiques (Cambry), iii. 211, 342

Moral Essays, (Plutarch), iii. 132

Moreh Nebhuchim (Maimonides), ii. 110; iii. 209, 375; iv. 34; v. 238

MS. (Skinner), ii. 26, 34, 106, 107

MS. (St. Germain), iv. 154, 155

Muntakhāb at Tawārikh, i. 47

Musée des Sciences (Le Couturier), ii. 226, 328; v. 325, 335

Mystère et la Science, Le (Père Felix), ii. 395

Mystères de l'Horoscope (Ely Star), i. 166

Mystères de la Vie Humaine (Montlosier), iv. 124

Mysteries of Magic, The (Waite), i. 299

Mysteries of Magic, The (Lévi), iv. 75

Mysteries of Rostan, i. 283

Mystery of the Ages, The (Duchesse de Pomar), iii. 232

Mythical Monsters (Baring-Gould), iii. 21, 24, 65, 66, 221, 222, 223, 281, 295, 311, 364, 427, 438, 439; iv. 257, 265, 283, 284, 289

Mythological Astronomy of the Ancients demonstrated, The (Mackey), ii. 381; iii. 356, 357, 361, 429, 431, 435; v. 348

Mythological Geography (Volcker), iii. 20

Mythologie de la Grèce Antique (Decharme), iii. 130, 132, 271, 272, 273, 306, 361, 390; iv. 88, 89, 90, 91, 332, 346

Mythologie des Indous (Polier), ii. 59

Mythology (Murray), iv. 323, 339

Myths and Marvels of Astronomy (Proctor), ii. 375

Myths and Myth-Makers (Fiske), iv. 355

N

Nabathean Agriculture (Chwolsohn), ii. 110, 117, 135; iv. 19, 20, 21, 22

Nachweis der Echtheit der Sammtlichen Schriften des Neuen Test. (Olshausen), v. 160

Nārada-Pancha-Ratra, iii. 92

Nāradiya Purāna, iii. 92

Nation (New York), ii. 206

National Reformer, i. 337

Natural Geneis, The (Massey), ii. 103, 121, 122, 124, 125, 153, 376; iv. 116, 117, 158, 159, 174, 201, 202, 205

Natural History, i. 176

Natural History Review, iv. 296

Natural Philosophy (Herschel), v. 224

Natural Philosophy (Thomson and Tait), ii. 225; iii. 22, 23; iv. 264

Naturalist, ii. 34; iii. 325

Nature, i. 164; ii. 210; iii. 75; iv. 297, 350

Nature's Finer Forces (Prasad), v. 468, 469, 470, 474, 476, 479

Nem. (Pindar), iii. 131, 272

Nero (Suetonius), v. 134

New Aspects of Life and Religion (Pratt), i. 74, 76, 244, 272, 280; ii. 56, 340; iii. 242, 244, 248; iv. 77, 78

New Chemistry, The (Cooke), ii. 237

New Encyclopaedia (Rees), iii. 390

New Philosophy, The (Bloomfield-Moore), ii. 288

New Platonism and Alchemy, (Wilder), v. 34, 36, 65, 68, 74, 151, 298, 299, 301, 305, 308

New Testament, i. 54, 174, 244; ii. 50, 78, 87, 99, 331; iii. 120, 233, 376; iv. 50, 72, 195, 273, 316; v. 71, 83, 99, 101, 126, 136, 150, 151, 165, 184, 211, 249, 271, 337, 369, 450

Nimrod (Ælian), v. 181

Nineteenth Century, The, iii. 254, 352, iv. 335, 339

Nirukta, v. 270

Nobeleth 'Hokhmah, iii. 135

Noctes Atticae (Aulus Gellius), ii. 112

Non-Defined Forces, Historical and Experimental, Researches, The (de Rochas), ii. 370

Notes and Observations upon several Passages in Scripture (Gregorie), iv. 35

Notes on Aristotle's Psychology in Relation to Modern Thought, iii. 287

Notes on the Bhagavad Gita (T. Subba Row), ii. 346

Notice sur la Calendrer (Ragon), v. 433

Nouvelles Recherches, etc., iv. 261

Nuchthemeron of the Hebrews, The (Rabbi Simeon), ii. 168

Numbers, ii. 79, 80; iii. 336, 386

O

Observations of Bel, iv. 263

Observatory, The, iii. 320

Occult Catechism, i. 28

Occult World, The (Sinnett), i. 18, 183; ii. 239; iii. 295; v. 496

Odyssey (Homer), ii. 374; iii. 130, 382; iv. 163, 176, 331, 339

Œdipus Ægyptiacus (Kircher), ii. 80, 153; iii. 211, 370; v. 239, 293, 386

Œdipus Judiacus (Drummond), v. 292

Œuvres d' Arago, v. 225

Old Diary Leaves (Olcott), i. 18, 20, 24

Old Testament, i. 54; ii. 50, 54, 97, 99, 109, 132, 134, 331, 375; iii. 138, 394; iv. 115, 131, 316; v. 66, 71, 72, 101, 103, 150, 158, 163, 164, 179, 196, 197, 198, 239, 249, 265, 439, 562

On Amos (St. Ambrose), i. 181

On First Principles (Damascius), ii. 143

On Rosencranz (Hudd), i. 137

On the Good and Bad Demons (Porphyry), v. 240

On the Philosophy of Mythology (Müller), iv. 333

On Truth (Bacon), ii. 203

On Vortex Atoms (Thomson), i. 177

Opera et Dies (Hesiod), iii. 108; iv. 89, 341

Operations at the Pyramid of Gizeh (Vyse), iii. 361, 365

Optics (Newton), iv. 275; ii. 218

Opus de Lapide (F. Arnolphinus), v. 114

Opusc. X, iii (Aquinas), v. 321

Oracles of Zoroaster, ii. 45

Orestes (Euripides), iii. 131

Oriental Collections, iii. 396; iv. 189

Oriental Traditions, iii. 396

Origin and Growth of Religion as Illustrated by the Religion of the Ancient Babylonians (Sayce), iv. 263

Origin and Significance of the Great Pyramid, The (Wake), ii. 26, 27, 30

Origin of Nations (Rawlinson), iv. 290

Origin of Species (Darwin), iii. 196, 262

Origin of the Stars, The (Ennis), ii. 224

Origin of the World (Dawson), iv. 288, 297

Origine de tous les Cultes, (Dupuis Huet), ii. 379

Origeniana, v. 67

Origines de la Terre et de I'Homme, Les (Fabre), iv. 316

Origins of Christianity (Renan), iv. 24

Orlando Furioso (Ariosto), v. 73

Orphic Hymns, ii. 81

Orthodoxie Maçonnique (Ragon), iv. 146, 163, 164, 364; v. 272, 273, 282, 293, 294, 295

P

Padma Purāna, i. 282; ii. 132, 171; iii. 98, 319; iv. 141

Paganism and Judaism (Döllinger), v. 240

Pagan Idolatry (Faber), iv. 39
Panorama des Mondes (Ie Couturier), ii. 215, 225, 226
Panthéon Égyptien (J. F. Champollion), ii. 194, iii. 214, 215, 385
Papyrus d'Orbiney apud Grébaut, v. 462
Papyrus Magique Haris, La (Chabas), iii. 217; v. 244, 249, 250, 251, 256
Paracelsus (Hartmann), i. 324, 325; iv. 81
Paradise Lost (Milton), ii. 203, 204, 347, 370; iv. 53
Paragranum: Life of Paracelsus (Hartmann), ii. 256
Parmenides (Plato), v. 30
Pasigraphie (Demaimieux), ii. 22
Past and Present (Carlyle), i. 259, 260
Path, The, i. 30; ii. 348, 355, 357
Patrol Grecque (Anastasius), v. 134
Pedigree of Man, The (Haeckel), iii. 96, 172, 178, 195, 199, 298, 300, 327, 328; iv. 220, 222, 223, 229, 231, 232, 233, 234, 235, 237, 238, 240, 241, 250, 348, 357
Pentateuch, i. 64, 77, 174; ii. 33; iii. 16, 382; iv. 41, 46, 107, 115, 344; v. 74, 89, 103, 176, 178, 179, 181, 185, 186, 195
Penteglott (Schindler), iii. 216
Perfect Way, The, (Kingsford), iii. 232, 236, 237
Periodicity of Vital Phenomena (Laycock), iv. 194
Personal and Impersonal God (T. Subba Row), i. 195; iv. 168
Petemenoph Papyrus, v. 331
Peter, iv. 54, 198, 326; v. 267, 285
Peuple Primitif (de Rougemont), iii. 370
Peuples et les Continents Disparus, Les (Jacolliot), iii. 226
Phaedrus (Plato), iii. 105; v. 30, 92, 279, 281
Phallicism (Jennings), ii. 193, 194; iii. 241; iv. 35, 41; v. 55, 136, 292
Philebus (Plato), i. 144
Philosophical Magazine, ii. 236, 238
Philosophical Transactions (Halley), ii. 314
Philosophical Transactions (Herschel), ii. 314
Philosophical Writings of Leibnitz, The (Morris), ii. 354
Philosophie Naturelle, ii. 252
Philosophumena (Hippolytus), ii. 66; iii. 17; iv. 133, 148, 149; v. 133, 445, 447, 448, 449, 450
Philosophy (Lefèvre), iii. 76, 176, 193
Philosophy Historical and Critical (Lefèvre), iv. 255, 279, 282, 310, 349, 351
Philosophy of History (Hegel), i. 123
Philosophy of Language (Darwin), iv. 231
Philosophy of the Bhagavad Gita, The (T. Subba Rao), i. 76, 80, 170, 188, 193
Philosophy of the Inductive Sciences (Whewell), iv. 193
Philosophy of the Unconscious (Schöpenhauer), i. 324
Phönizier, Die (Movers), ii. 62, 81, 82, 181 iii. 378
Phoroneidae, iv. 88
Phreno-Kosmo-Biology, i. 337
Physical Basis of Life (Huxley), ii. 394
Physical Eclogues (Stobæus), i. 328
Physician's Hymn, iii. 63

Physics (Aristotle), ii. 315, 319
Physics (Ganot), ii. 394
Physiological Selection (Romanes), iii. 423
Pirkah, iv. 102
Pistis Sophia, i. 190; ii. 126, 127, 168, 301; i. 30, 81, 105, 132, 134, 140, 175, 189
Platonist, ii. 144
Pluralité des Mondes Habités, La (Flammarion), ii. 330, 331; iii. 144; iv. 272
Plurality of Worlds, The (Whewell), ii. 331; iii. 157
Polynesian Researches (Ellis), iii. 199
Popol Vuh, iii. 47, 66, 105, 106, 168, 188
Popular Astronomy (Newcomb), i. 149; ii. 267; iii. 157; iv. 264
Popular Science Monthly, iii. 438
Popular Science Review, ii. 233, 248, 254, 255, 256, 257, 262, 324, 327; iv. 265, 294, 348, 349
Posthumous Humanity (d'Assier), iii. 156
Praelectiones Theol. (Péronne), iii. 374
Precepts for Yoga, i. 128
Précis Élémentaire de Physiologie (Magendie), iii. 140
Preface to St. Mathew's Gospel (St. Jerome), v. 143
Prehistoric Antiquity of Man (de Mortillet), iv. 280, 289
Prehistoric Europe (Geikie), iv. 284
Prehistoric Man (Lubbock), iv. 291
Preparat. Evang. (Cornutus), iv. 112
Preparatio Evangelica (Eusebius), i. 126; iii. 391
Present Position of Evolution (Haeckel), iv. 220
Presidential Address to the Royal Society of Chemists (Crookes), ii. 306, 308
Primeval Man Unveiled; or the Anthropology of the Bible, ii. 36, 37
Primitive Principles (Damascius), v. 202
Principia, The (Newton), ii. 213, 214, 235; iv. 242
Principia Rerum Naturalium (Swedenborg), i. 177
Principles of Biology (Spencer), iii. 348; iv. 299
Principles of Geology, The (Lyell), iv. 295, 347, 353, 354
Principles of Human Knowledge, i. 70
Principles of Psychology (Spencer), iv. 59
Principles of Science (Jevons and Babbage), i. 166, 182
Principles of Zoology (Agassiz), iii. 177
Proceedings (Royal Institution), iii. 23, 258
Progress of Religious Ideas (Child), ii. 73
Progymnasmata (Brahé), ii. 314
Prolegomena, v. 179
Promenades au Musée de St. Germain (de Mortillet), iv. 318
Prometheus Bound (Swanwick), iii. 410, 411, 414, 415
Prometheus Vinctus (Æschylus), iv. 92, 332
Protagoras (Plato), iii. 411
Proverbs, ii. 71; iii. 143; iv. 212; v. 74
Psalms, i. 167; ii. 184; iii. 143, 216; iv. 28, 77; v. 96, 148, 159, 179, 180, 184, 214, 234, 316
Psammites, i. 176
Psychic Force and Etheric Force (Bloomfield-Moore), ii. 283

Puissance des Nombres d'après Pythagore, iv. 146

Purāna(s), i. 23, 64, 125, 134, 139, 174, 175, 218, 222, 251, 300, 301, 316, 327; ii. 18, 19, 28, 44, 50, 58, 62, 63, 75, 84, 96, 113, 132, 136, 137, 138, 139, 141, 154, 160, 165, 166, 170, 175, 177, 245, 311, 326, 348, 381; iii. 24, 36, 43, 47, 49, 59, 60, 62, 64, 69, 77, 85, 88, 100, 105, 110, 115, 129, 134, 145, 153, 154, 155, 156, 172, 178, 180, 181, 188, 189, 228, 229, 230, 235, 253, 254, 255, 266, 285, 286, 292, 295, 309, 310, 319, 323, 324, 365, 377, 380, 401, 402, 403, 404, 405, 408; iv. 22, 66, 73, 93, 96, 97, 133, 136, 141, 142, 143, 144, 147, 149, 156, 168, 182, 183, 184, 185, 186, 187, 188, 192, 200, 203, 227, 329; v. 27, 72, 95, 121, 188, 190, 199, 232, 258, 270, 339, 493, 517

Pushkara Mahātmya, iii. 277

Pymander, The Divine (Hermes), i. 141, 327; ii. 134; iii. 62, 105, 106, 113, 115, 123, 217, 234, 235, 238, 269, 270, 277; iv. 56, 57, 59, 60, 61, 112; v. 198

Pyramid, The Great, etc. (Wake), iii. 39, 44, 91, 351, 361, 365, 429; v. 110

Pyramids and Temples of Gizeh, The (Petrie), ii. 27

Pythagorean Triangle, The (Oliver), i. 173; ii. 338, 341, 342; iv. 171, 172, 173, 174, 175, 211, 212

Pythian Odes (Pindar), v. 332

Q

Qabbalah (Myer's), ii. 61, 67, 90, 91, 108, 109, 156, 166, 343, 344; iii. 40, 64, 65, 93, 94, 124, 135, 145, 170, 294, 315; iv. 19, 24, 25, 29, 46, 72, 109, 114, 342; v. 68

Quadrature of the Circle (Parker), ii. 28

Quæst, et Solut. (Philo), ii. 65

Quæstiones Græcæ, (Plutarch), iii. 131

Qu'rān, iv. 21, 31, 32, 188

R

Rabba Battra, iii. 387

Rāmāyana, ii. 95, 286; iii. 171, 235, 392; iv. 63, 141, 184, 185, 201, 250; v. 121

Rapports de St. Paul avec Sénèque (Fleury), v. 134

Rational Refutation, i. 336

Rechereches, etc., des Mammifères, iii. 223

Recueil de I'Académie des Inscriptions (Erard-Mollien, ii. 384

Réflexions Critiques sur I'Origine des Anciens Peuples (Fourmont), iii. 374

Règne des Dieux (Boulanger), iii. 371

Religion and Science (Temple), iv. 215

Religions of India, The, (Barth), iv. 17

Remarks on the Nutrition of the Foetus (Anderson), v. 449

Reminiscences of H. P. Blavatsky and the " Secret Doctrine " (Wachtmeister), i. 19, 20, 21, 22, 27, 28, 29, 31, 32

Republic (Plato), iv. 333; v. 215, 327

Researches on Light in its Chemical Relations (Hunt), ii. 304

Revelation, i. 136, 138, 151; ii. 116, 127; iii. 85, 213, 215, 232, 234, 347, 355, 382, 383; iv. 53, 65, 66, 75, 102, 110, 127, 133, 135, 189, 190, 340, 341; v. 133, 138, 160, 162, 200, 202, 212, 309, 375

Revelation (Marcus), ii. 66

Revelation, The Great, etc. (Simon Magus), v. 446

Révolution du Globe, (Cuvier), iii. 210

Révue Archéologique Eckstein), iii. 272, 344, 356; iv. 65

Revue des Deux Mondes, ii. 227, 400; iv. 308; v. 221

Revue Germanique, ii. 221; iv. 21, 93, 95

Rh Ya, iii. 303

Rig Veda, i. 50, 73, 90, 136, 153, 171, 172, 179, 194, 245, 314; ii. 60, 100, 144, 148, 150, 162, 398; iii. 57, 146, 183, 197, 249, 272, 377, 383; iv. 16, 17, 52, 67, 68, 118, 129, 150, 177, 178, 179, 183, 184, 185, 193, 327; v. 154, 232, 233, 269, 270, 370, 381

Rig Veda Brahmanas (Keith), i. 141, 160; iii. 58, 63, 69, 101, 110

Rigveda Samhita, v. 343

Rig Vidhana, ii. 154

Ritual Funéraire des Anciens Égyptiens (de Rougé), i. 192

Rivers of Life (Forlong), ii. 121

Roma Sotteranea (de Rossi), v. 286

Roman History (Mommsen), v. 256

Romance of Natural History (Gosse), iii. 438

Romeo and Juliet (Shakespeare), iii. 40

Rosarium Philosoph (de Villanova), v. 114

Round Towers of Ireland (O'Brien), ii. 194

Royal Masonic Cyclopaedia, The (Mackenzie), i 173, 186; ii. 17, 291, 292; iii. 120; iv. 98, 100, 126; v. 46, 93, 114, 226, 273, 284, 285

Ruins of Empires, (Volney), ii. 384; iii. 434

S

Sacred Books of the East, i. 67, 151, 158; ii. 258, 295; iii. 101, 292, 383; iv. 48, 64, 68, 85, 137, 138, 179, 209; v. 367

Sacred Mysteries among the Māyās and Quiches (le Plongeon), i. 310; iii. 47, 48, 232; iv. 75

Sādah Vendīdād, iv. 86

Saddharmalankara, i. 50

Sadducismus Triumphatus (Scot, Adie, and Webster), v. 51

Sagra Scrittura (Lanci), iii. 375

Salm (Cedrenus), iii. 151

Sam-Sam (Sabean), v. 181

Samuel, The Book of, ii. 187, 188, 386; iv. 28, iii; v. 311

Sānkhya Bhāshya, v. 320

Sānkhya Kārika, i. 300; ii. 44, 49, 176; v. 81

Sānkhya Sāra, i. 141

Sanskrit Dictionary (Goldstücker), iv. 93

Sartor Resartus (Carlyle), ii. 15

Satan ou le Diable (Baissac), iv. 78

Saturday Review, ii. 15

Saturnalia, (Macrobius), iii. 363; v. 310

Satyricon (Petronius), ii. 73; v. 44

Science and the Emotions (Clodd), i. 70

Science of Language (Hovelacque), iii. 176, 440

Science of Serpents, iii. 39
Sciences Occultes (Salverte), iii. 210
Scientific American, iv. 361
Scientific Arena, i. 201
Scientific Letters (Butlerov), ii. 242, 243, 244
Schlawische Myth., iii. 273
Schol. Vatic. ad Eurip. Troad., iii. 296
Secret Book, iii. 225
Secret Doctrine, The (Blavatsky), i. 10, 11, 12, 16, 17, 19, 20, 21, 22, 23, 24, 26, 27, 29, 30, 31, 32, 33, 34, 36, 41, 49, 60, 63, 239; iii. 438, 439; iv. 366; v. 72
Select Specimens of the Theatre of the Hindus (Wilson), iii. 425; iv. 200
Senzar Catechism, i. 75
Sepher Yetzireth, or Jetzirah, i. 64, 155, 157, 188, 338; ii. 51, 166; iii. 49, 51; iv. 106, 107; v. 85, 89, 91, 107, 108, 174, 177, 189, 205, 211
Sepher Toledoth Yeshu, v. 140
Sept Lecons de Physique Générale (Cauchy), ii. 212
Septem contra Thebas (Aeschylus), iii. 273
Septuagint, ii. 300; iii. 205; iv. 128; v. 183, 184, 239, 317
Sepultures des Tartares (Tooke), iii. 343
Sermon (St. Augustine), iv. 160
Sermon sur la Sainte Vièrge (St. Bernard), ii. 116
Sesha Jyotisha (Somākara), v. 341, 343
Seven Souls of Man, The (Massey), v. 274
Shaiva Purānas, ii. 117
Shākhyāyana Brāhmana, v. 343
Shan-Hai-King (Kwoh P'oh), iii. 65, 223, 303
Shastras, i. 174
Shatapatha Brāhmana, i. 135; ii. 149, 165; iii. 147, 148, 154, 155, 257; v. 343
Shing-Tau-ki, etc. (Wang Puk), v. 390
Shivāgama, v. 468, 469, 477
Shoo-King (Shu-King), i. 64; ii. 282, 337
Shu (Confucius), i. 49
Shvetāshvatara Upanishad, i. 76; iv. 208; v. 401
Sibylline Oracles, v. 21
Signatura Rerum (Böhme), iv. 205
Silliman's Journal, ii. 209
Siphra Dtzenioutha (Dzenioutha), i. 64, 284; ii. 52, 56, 90, 91; iii. 16, 64; iv. 73, 74, 275
Skanda Purāna, iii. 189
Smaragdine Tablet (Hermes), iii. 108, 122
Smithsonian Contributions to Knowledge, ii. 312; iii. 149
Smithsonian Report, iv. 360
Society of Antiquaries of London, iii. 379
Sōd: The Mysteries of Adoni (Dunlap), ii. 68; iii. 216; iv. 28
Sōd: The Son of Man (Dunlap), i. 245; iii. 158, 241; v. 54, 108, 160, 188
Soirées (de Maistre), ii. 207, 227
Soleil, Le (Secchi), ii. 265
Soul of Things, The (Denton), i. 250
Source of Measures, The (Key to the Hebrew Egypt. Mysteries) (Ralston Skinner), i. 72, 129, 154, 308; ii. 20, 25, 29, 31, 34, 35, 97, 99, 161, 162; iii. 48, 49, 50, 134, 136, 152, 220, 387, 389, 391; iv. 32, 35, 36, 37, 68, 112, 113, 127, 130, 131, 153, 169, 171; v. 66, 69, 72, 89, 90, 110, 111, 137, 150, 151, 158, 161, 164, 166, 183, 186, 190, 194, 195, 197, 201, 206, 286

Spinoza's Letters, iii. 15
Sphinx, iv. 204
Sphinxiad (Mackey), iii. 406
Spiritismus (Von Hartmann), i. 191
Ssabier und der Ssabismus, Die (Chwolsohn), iv. 22
Stichometry (Nicephorus), v. 160
Stonehenge (Petrie), iii. 344
Strange Case of Dr. Jekyll and Mr. Hyde, The (Stevenson), iii. 317; v. 500
Stromata (Clemens Alexandrinus), i. 184; ii. 182; iii. 417; iv. 14, 88; v. 58, 59, 61, 66, 92, 108, 183, 241, 313, 316
Study in Consciousness, A (Besant), i. 82
Suggestion Mentale et la Calcul des Probabilités, La (Richet), ii. 365
Summa (Thomas Aquinas), v. 331
" Sun " (New York newspaper), ii. 29
Supernatural Religion, v. 94, 129, 161
Sur la Distinction des Forces, ii. 230
Surya-Siddhanta, ii. 391; iii. 324, 325, 400, 402; v. 344
Symbolik (Creuzer), ii. 378; v. 54
Symbols of the Bonzes, ii. 40
System of Logic (Mill), ii. 312
Système du Monde (Laplace), ii. 225
Système Nouveau (Erdmann), ii. 355, 356

T

Tabula Smaragdina (Hermes Trismegistos) iii. 118; v. 114
Tittirīya Brahmana, iii. 183; iv. 68
Taittirīya Upanishad, ii. 44
Tales and Traditions of our Northern Ancestors, ii, 142
Tales of Derbent, iii. 396
Talmud, ii. 65, 135, 156, 157, 179, 384, 387; iv. 21, 46, 73; v. 163, 176, 179, 191, 305
Talmud (Babylonian), i. 64; v. 162
Talmud (Jerusalem), i. 64; ii. 33
Tanjur, i. 50
Tao-te-King, i. 48; ii. 194
Targum of Jonathan, iv. 128
Tchoon-Tsieoo (Chuan-Hsueh-pien), iv. 55
Temple de Jérusalem (Villalpandus), ii. 375
Terre et Ciel (Reynaud), ii. 227; v. 225
Terre et l'Homme, La (Maury), v. 222
Tesmophoriazusae (Aristophanes), iv. 176
Testaments, i. 33
Testimony of the Sea, iv. 351
Tetrabiblos (Ptolemy), v. 331
Text book of Physiology (Foster), iii. 140
Theogony (Damascius), i. 137; ii. 57
Theogony (Hesiod), ii. 136, 143
Theogony (Mochus), ii. 181
Theol. Cir. (Vossius), i. 182
Theological and Philosophical Works of Hermes Trismegistus, Christian Neoplatonist (Chambers), iii. 16
Theology of Plato (Proclus), v. 280
Theorie der Materie, Die (Wundt), ii. 238
Théorie du Monde (Huygens), iii. 45
Théorie Mécanique de l'Univers (Hirn), ii. 236
Theosophical Siftings, ii. 283, 284, 285

Theosophist, The, i. 18, 19, 20, 21, 23, 24, 25, 26, 29, 31, 33, 34, 42, 76, 80, 170, 188, 193, 212, 313; ii. 18, 146, 149, 150, 264, 283, 293, 297, 298, 346; iii. 38, 99, 142, 148, 248, 293, 311, 318, 425; iv. 83, 207, 356; v. 197, 226, 341, 342, 344, 360, 393, 440, 468, 469, 471, 480, 486, 493, 494, 500, 501, 502, 503

Thermochemie (Nazemann), ii. 238

Thessalonians, i. 151

Third Book of the Maccabees, iv. 101

Third Letter to Bentley (Newton), ii. 214

Tibet (Markham), v. 389

Timæum, Comm. in (Proclus), ii. 126, 376; iii. 151; iv. 175

Timæus, The (Plato), ii. 53, 165, 290, 291, 304; iii. 103, 106, 141, 393; iv. 88, 312, 353; v. 27, 29, 30, 32, 35

Times, The, ii. 15; v. 385

Timothy, v. 369

Tirukkanda Panchanga (Raghanāchārya), iii. 62, 77

Toledoth, iii. 142

Tongshaktchi Sangye Songa, iii. 421

Torah, v. 179

Traces de Bouddhisme en Norvége (Holmboe), iii. 421 ·

Tractatus de Transmutatione Metallorum (Hermes Tris.), v. 114

Tradition (Molitor), v. 120

Traité de l'Astronomie Indienne et Orientale (Bailly), ii. 391; iii. 433; iv. 192

Transactions of the Geological Society of Glasgow, iii. 260

Transactions of the Royal Asiatic Society, v. 37

Transactions of the Royal Society, Edinburgh, iii. 22

Transactions of the Royal Society, London, iv. 91

Transactions of the Society of Biblical Archæology, ii. 32

Traüme eines Geistersehers (Kant), i. 191

Travels in Egypt (Denon), iii. 429

Treatise on Colour (Newton), ii. 219

Treatise on Electricity (Maxwell), ii. 209

Treatise on Idolatry (Maimonides), v. 252

Treatise on Natural Philosophy (Thomson), ii. 208

Treatise on Optics (Brewster), ii. 304

Trinité Chrétienne Dévoilée (Lizeray), iii. 354

Tripitāka, i. 60

Trübner's Oriental Series, iii. 61

T'sang-t'ung-ky (Wei-Pa-Yang), iv. 124

Tusculan Disputations (Cicero), iii. 417

Twan-ying-t'u, iii. 364

Twelve Signs of Zodiac, i. 334; ii. 373; iii. 180; iv. 147, 148, 149

Types of Mankind (Nott and Gliddon), iv. 182

U

Ueber die Auflösung der Arten durch Natürliche Zuchtwahl, i. 236

Ueber ide Grenzen des Naturerkennens (Reymond), ii. 208

Unicorn, The, a Mythological Investigation (R. Brown), iii. 222

Unity of Nature (Argyle), iii. 372

Univers expliqué par la Révélation, L' (Chaubard), ii. 230

Unseen Universe, The (Tait and Stewart), ii. 183, 208

Upanishads, i. 74, 119 157, 194, 218, 259, 311, 313, 314, 315; iii. 39; iv. 52, 133, 136, 162; v. 27, 73, 89, 232, 353, 565

Uranographie Chinoise (Schlegel), ii. 384

V

Vāchaspattya, ii. 93

Vāhan, The, i. 33, 65

Varia Historia (Aelian), iii. 417

Vayu Purāna, i. 121, 301; ii. 84, 87, 93, 154, 173, 177, 245; iii. 68, 91, 98, 99, 100, 189, 380, 402; iv. 63, 143, 184, 185

Vedānta Sāra (Jacob), i. 73, 74; v. 380

Vedanta Sutras, v. 367

Vedas, i. 43, 52, 60, 87, 109, 115, 218, 314, 336; ii. 44, 133, 136, 139, 140, 178, 180, 247, 248; iii. 70, 111, 154, 250, 271; iv. 52, 93, 96, 156, 178, 179, 180, 184, 187, 284; v. 33, 68, 73, 81, 87, 91, 154, 293, 341, 342, 425

Vendīdād, The, iii. 19, 41, 71, 106, 272, 292, 355, 356, 383, 384, 408; iv. 44, 68, 86, 178, 328

Versunkene Insel Atlantis, Die (Ünger), iv. 352

Vestiges of the Spirit History of Man (Dunlap), ii. 62

Vie de Jésus (Renan), i. 67; iv. 21

View of the Levant (Parry), iii. 359

Vir, Illust. (Jerome), v. 34

Virgin of the Magi and Chaldeans, The (Albumazar), v. 293

Virgin of the World, The (Hermes), i. 323, 327, 335, 396

Vishnu Purāna (Wilson's trans.), i. 84, 109, 118, 121, 125, 134, 142, 253, 266, 300, 301, 326, 328, 331; ii. 50, 62, 63, 75, 83, 86, 87, 89, 91, 92, 93, 133, 136, 137, 138, 139, 140, 141, 164, 165, 166, 167, 169, 171, 172, 173, 174, 175, 176, 177, 179, 246, 266, 269, 286; iii. 59, 68, 69, 83, 86, 87, 98, 99, 106, 110, 116, 117, 135, 154, 162, 163, 170, 171, 172, 180, 181, 182, 183, 188, 189, 190, 218, 228, 235, 249, 277, 308, 309, 310, 319, 320, 321, 322, 323, 326, 368, 380, 381, 399, 400, 402; iv. 48, 51, 57, 63, 93, 97, 118, 119, 120, 135, 141, 142, 149, 157, 162, 183, 184, 185, 186, 187, 188, 195, 196, 228; v. 188, 189, 197, 203, 239, 259, 260, 339, 422, 469, 475

Vit. Pythag. (Diogenes Laërtius), ii. 152

Viveka Chudamani (Chatterji), ii. 293

Voice of the Silence, The (Blavatsky), i. 15; v. 467, 496, 502, 503, 506, 519

Volcans de la Grèce, Les (Pègues), iii. 280

Vortex Atoms, On (Sir W. Thomson), i. 177

Voyage dans le Comté de Cornouailles sur les Traces des Géants, iii. 342

Voyage de Rénard en Laponie, iv. 343

Voyage des Pèlerins Bouddhistes (Julien), v. 39

Voyage en Sibérie (Chappe), iv. 192

Voyageurs Anciens et Modernes (Charton), iii. 343

Vriddha Garga, iv. 195

Vulgate, v. 167, 238, 317, 319

W

Weltaether als Kosmiche Kraft, Der (Spiller) ii. 232
Westminster Review, ii. 324
What is Matter and what is Force, ii. 283
Wheel (Parcha), iii. 396
Wisdom of Solomon, v. 74
Wonders by Land and Sea, iii. 65, 223
" World " (New York newspaper), ii. 29
World Life or Comprative Geology (Winchell), i. 149, 160, 164, 176, 210; ii. 217, 218, 219, 221, 222, 223, 224, 225, 230, 252, 265, 316, 323, 324, 332, 333, 363; iii. 22, 82, 157, 324, 325; iv. 264
Wu-liang-Sheu-King, v. 410

Y

Yājnavālkya-Smriti, ii. 150
Yajur Veda, iv. 118
Yamyangshapda, v. 403
Yashna, Comment on the (Burnouf), ii. 155
Yasna, iv. 327
Ya-Yakav, v. 89
Yeast, (Huxley), ii. 362
Yih-shu-kia-lun, i. 130
Y-king, iii. 373; iv. 54
Yi-king, ii. 158, 159; iii. 48
Yoga Sastra, iii. 97

Z

Zachariah, iv. 198
Zamyad Yasht, iii. 357
Zanoni (Bulwer Lytton), ii. 296; v. 500
Zeitschrift für Vergleichende Sprachforschung, v. 54
Zem-Zem (Arabic), v. 181
Zend Avesta, i. 60; ii. 19; iii. 47, 71, 101, 209, 272; iv. 44, 48, 85, 327; v. 33, 81
Zends, i. 184
Zohar (Moses de Leon), i. 72, 77, 83, 84, 110, 124, 129, 134, 144, 154, 155, 156, 160, 161, 166, 172, 173, 174, 176, 187, 246, 247, 248, 261, 263, 271, 276, 277, 284, 286, 291; 314; ii. 50, 51, 52, 58, 60, 64, 65, 67, 70, 71, 89, 106, 109, 148, 150, 151, 156, 157, 162, 230; iii. 16, 17, 22, 38, 40, 44, 55, 56, 64, 93, 94, 119, 120, 121, 122, 129, 136, 145, 169, 209, 211, 219, 220, 232, 236, 238, 240, 242, 243, 248, 249, 265, 270, 283, 285, 291, 292, 293, 294, 313, 316, 373, 374, 375, 377, 387, 407, 408; iv. 14, 24, 25, 29, 35, 37, 45, 46, 48, 55, 56, 59, 70, 102, 106, 107, 109, 110, 114, 115, 121, 123, 147, 170, 175, 195, 196, 197, 240, 273, 274, 275, 342; v. 67, 68, 72, 85, 86, 89, 90, 91, 105, 107, 108, 112, 113, 114, 116, 118, 120, 123, 131, 138, 163, 165, 174, 175, 176, 177, 180, 181, 186, 187, 188, 189, 192, 198, 201, 206, 208, 209, 210, 212, 214, 215, 216, 217, 226, 230. 232, 271, 301, 310, 356, 386, 390, 418, 439
Zur Geschichte des Kanons (Gredner), v. 160

A SHORT GLOSSARY OF SANSKRIT AND OTHER TERMS

ALL words are Sanskrit, unless otherwise noted. Abbreviations are as follows:

[ ]=literal		Chal. = Chaldean	
(?)=uncertain		Chin. = Chinese	
der.=derivation		Egy. = Egyptian	
Cf.=Compare		Fin. = Finnish	
Occult.=in Occultism		Fr. = French	
pop.=popular		Ger. = German	
pos.=possible		Gn. = Gnostic	
q.v.=which see		Gr. = Greek	
S. D.=Secret Doctrine		Heb. = Hebrew	
Theos. = Theosophical		Icel. = Icelandic	
trans.=translated		Jap. = Japanese	
Akkad.=Akkadian		Kab. = Kabalistic	
Arab.=Arabian		Per. = Persian	
Ass.=Assyrian		Phoen. = Phoenician	
Bab.=Babylonian		Scan. = Scandinavian	
Cel.=Celtic		Tib. = Tibetan	

This Glossary has been prepared by Mrs. Adeltha Henry Peterson, with the assistance of the Adyar Library pandits for the Sanskrit.

HOW TO USE THE GLOSSARY

An endeavour has been made to cross-reference the *Glossary* adequately. For example, if, after reading the word *Ahriman*, the student wishes to follow further the idea of Duality, he is referred to that heading. There he will find references to other aspects of Duality to be found in the *Glossary*. If a student is particulary interested in the occult significance of *Numbers*, he is referred to that heading with its cross-references. While the word *Trinity* has many cross-references, the student is especially advised to check *Brahmā, Vishnu, Shiva*, as embodying the three aspects of the Logos.

Where possible, when a series of seven and twelve is mentioned, meanings are also given for correlative purposes.

Where a word is adequately defined in *The Secret Doctrine*, and there are only one or two references thereto, the word is not redefined in the *Glossary*, unless *The Secret Doctrine* definition differs from the usual connotation. As *The Secret Doctrine*

is our most monumental treatise on Theosophy, the *Glossary* is a fairly adequate one even for the student of other works.

Definitions in brackets are meant to show literal and root meanings. Where the derivation is uncertain, this is indicated by " der. (?)." The philologist's guess is indicated as " pos." for *possible*. Every effort has been made to trace all words back to the root of the root, as terms used in occultism are generally of ancient origin, and are usually nearer in accord with root than with derived meanings. The student is advised in this connection to note the word *Theosophy*.

To avoid duplication, when *The Secret Doctrine* definition is given in the *Glossary*, *S.D.* is used. If the generally accepted Theosophical connotation is given, " *Theos.*" is used. Otherwise, the student can rely on the material as being in accord with commonly understood meanings.

While this work has been carefully checked by pandits and reliable encyclo-paedias, further suggestions for emendation in future editions will be welcome. Where differences of opinion are found (and there are many among accepted authorities), weight has been given to original sources. For example, *The Jewish Encyclopaedia* has been found very helpful in tracing the origin of such words as YHVH. The *Catholic Encyclopaedia* and *Hastings* have been freely used for words of later Christian origin. We also acknowledge indebtedness to the *Encyclopaedia of Religion and Ethics*; Rose, *Handbook of Greek Mythology*; Fuerst, *Hebrew and Chaldee Lexicon*; White, *Latin-English Dictionary*; Chambers, *Etymological Dictionary*; Webster, *International English Dictionary*; Liddell and Scott, *Greek Lexicon*; Monier Williams, and Apte, *Sanskrit-English Dictionaries*, and the many Sanskrit dictionaries and encyclopaedias used by the pandits.

Many common terms are herein included, for example, *Noah*, which any western person would know, and *Prāna*, which any Indian would know, for the complier has stood with *The Secret Doctrine* on an imaginary line of Avidyā (lack of knowledge) between East and West, and has attempted to produce a *Glossary* which will be of service to both.

1938   A. H. P.

A

AANROO, Egy. A purgatorial domain of Amenti.

ABEL, Heb. [once trans, breath; later Son, or Shepherd]. *S.D.* " life-bearing soil ". Cf. Cain, Adam, Eve.

ABHAYAM [without fear], *S.D.* " There is no fear."

ABHIMĀNIN [abhi=towards; mānin=thinking of the Self]. *S.D.* Agni, (fire) eldest son of Brahmā and of Svāhā.

ĀBHŪTARAJASAS [existing endowed with Passion or Rajas].

ABJAYONI [abja=born in water; yoni=womb] Padmayoni.

ABRAHAM, Heb. [der. uncertain, pop.=Father of a Multitude]. Cf. Abram, Hagar, Melchizedek, Sarah, Ur.

ABRAM, Heb. [my Father is exalted]. *S.D.*, the historical character, forefather to the Jewish race, an ex-Brāhman who, having repudiated his caste, became A-Bram (A-bra (h) m), or " no-Brahman." Abram said also to be derived from Arba or Abhra, the " clouds," or the bosom of the Eternal ONE.

ABRAXAS, Gn. Supreme Deity, whose name equals 365, the number of His heavens. *S.D.* A generative and creative Deity. Cf. Unity.

ACHIT [not Chit, Perception or Wisdom].

ACHYUTA [that which does not give way or fall]. Vishnu, the Immutable, Imperishable, Firm, Fixed.

ADAM, Heb. [der. (?) three possible roots: earth-born, blood-red, to build or produce]. *S.D.* red " dust " or blood, the sign of the first " fleshly " man. Cf. Abel, Cain, Eden, Earth, Eve, Lilith, Meshia, Paradise, Prithvī, Seth.

ADAM KADMON or KADMONI, Heb. [First or Original Man-Woman], *S.D.* The First or Heavenly Man, the Manifested Logos, the

Divine Androgyne. Cf. Unity, Duality, Adon, Kaimurath.

ADBHUTAM [a wonder, marvel, or prodigy; pos. der. ati-bhūta=exceeding that which is] Name of Indra, of 8th Manvantara.

ADEPT [one skilled]. *Theos.* A fifth Initiate, *q.v.*, one who has achieved union with the Third Logos, *q.v.*, and uses Nirvānic waking consciousness. Cf. Dangma, Mahātmā, Nirmā-nakāya, Nirvāna, Pentecost, Tirthankara.

ADHI BUDHA [adhi=Supreme; budh=to know pos. original sense " to fathom a depth "]. *S.D.* Supreme Wisdom. Cf. Unity, Vishnu.

ĀDI [First beginning, Prime Cause]. *S.D.* First or Foundation Plane. Cf. Amida, Unity, Bhūtādi.

ĀDI-BHŪTA [First-born or Primeval Being].

ĀDI-BUDDHA [First Enlightened or Wise One] Chief Deity of Northern Buddhists: *S.D.* Primeval Wisdom; the First Logos; or Abstract Principle of all the Buddhas. Cf. Amitābha. Vishnu.

ĀDI-BUDDHI [First Perception or Understanding]. *S.D.* Absolute Consciousness.

ĀDI-BUDHA [First Wisdom]. Cf. Vishnu.

ĀDI-KRIT [Ādi=First; Krit=doer, maker; also to divide, cut, spin, surround, encompass]. The Creator.

ĀDI-NĀTH [Ādi=First; Nāth=to have power, to give boons or blessing]. *S.D.* First Lord.

ĀDI-NIDĀNA SVABHĀVAT [Ādi=First; Nidāna=the rope which binds, or first or original Cause; Svabhāva=Essential Nature or Being]. *S.D.* the Circle. Cf. Ring-Pass-Not.

ĀDI-SANAT [Primeval Ancient]. Cf. Sanat.

ĀDI-SHAKTI [Primeval Power or Energy]. Cf. Shakti.

ĀD-ĪSHVARA (Ādhīshvara) [First Supreme Lord].

ADITI [a=not; diti=cut, torn, or bound. The Boundless Whole, Aditi, Mother of the Gods, Eternal Space. *S.D.* Infinite, or Cosmic Space. Cf. Unity, Diti, Kashyapa.

ĀDITYA [son of Aditi, *q.v.*] *S.D.* the eight sons of Aditi, *i.e.*, the seven planets and Mārtānda, the Sun. (See also, Amsha, Aryaman, Bhaga, Daksha, Mitra, and Varuna). Sometimes listed as twelve. Cf. Sevens, Duality, Daitya, Shakra, Ushas, Vivasvat.

ĀDI-VARSHA [Ādi=first; Varsha=Place or Country; one of the divisions of the world]. *S.D.* Garden of Eden.

ADON, ADONAI, ADONAY, ADONIM, Chaldeo-Heb. [Adonai is plural form of Adon or Lord]. The perpetual substitute word to be read in place of YHVH or Jehovah in Hebrew script. ADONIS, the Divine Lover of Aphrodite, *q.v.* in Greek mythology, is a derivation. *S.D.* Adam-Kadmon, Cf. Amen.

ADVAITA [a=not; dvaita=dual]. Of one nature, unchanging; a philosophy stressing Unity, absolute monism, of Shankara. Cf. Dvaita, Duality, Unity.

ADYTUM, Gr. der. [not to be entered]. The sanctuary where only priests were permitted, and from which oracles were delivered. *S.D.* Adyta, Halls of Initiation. Cf. Tabernacle, Arcana.

VI–32

AEOLUS, Gr. [God of the Wind]. Cf. Breath, Vāyu.

ÆON, Gr. [an age or an infinitely long period of time]. *S.D.* a manvantara, or period of manifestation *not* eternity. Also, Æon and Æons are Gnostic terms designating a Series of Spiritual Creative Powers, or Emanations, proceeding progressively from Incomprehensible Potentiality, the Fulness of Pleroma, the Absolute. Time (Aion) is the First-Born Æon. All Æons are generated from an Eternal Divine Pair of Æons. Cf. Duality, Eternity, Kronos, Ogdoad, Pistis Sophia, Yuga.

ÆTHER, Gr. [the burning or shinning thing; the upper air or abode of the Gods; the God Æther, son of Chaos]. *S.D.* Third differentiation of evolving substance. (Ākāsha, Chaos). Though the word *Æther* in its higher aspects is often used as synonymous with *Ākāsha*, and *Ākāsha* manifested as *Æther*, it more properly applies to matter of the Ātmic, Nirvānic, or " Spiritual " Plane. If the planes be considered as horizontal, it is also one of the great perpendicular divisions of Elemental Life. Cf. Archacus, Ether, Indra.

AGASTYA [pos. der. aga=the immovable or mountain+asti = thrower; or aga=pitcher, asti=he exists, both referring to traditions, one that the Rishi Agastya compelled the Vindhya mountains to prostrate themselves; the other that he was born in a pitcher or water-jar]. The Father of South Indian civilization.

AGATHODÆMON [Agatho=Good; Dæmon= Divine Spirit]. Gr. a Gnostic term for the Serpent-emblem of Wisdom and Eternity from which emanates two serpents, one "The Good ", again *Agathodæmon*, as contrasted with *Kakodæmon*, Evil, its shadow. Cf. Serpent, Unity, Duality.

ĀGNEYA [belonging to or consecrated to Fire]. Agni.

ĀGNEYĀSTRA, AGNYASTRA [weapon presided over by Fire]. Agni.

AGNI [der. (?) pos. roots: ang=to walk around; ag=to move tortuously or wind; anj=to anoint with oil, making to shine or beautiful]. Fire. One of the oldest and most prominent deities of the *Rig Veda*. Cf. Abhimānin, Bhrigu, Gabriel, Havyavāhana, Kavyavāhana, Saharaksha, Hephaistos, Janaka, Kabarim, Manojava, Marut-vat, Molech, Muspel, Nergal-Serezer, Nirmathya, Pārvaka, Pavaka, Pavamāna, Pentecost, Phlogiston, Phoenix, Phoroneus, Pramantha, Prometheus, Purūravas, Seraphim, Sūrya, Svāhā, Svastika, Taijasa, Tapas, Vaidyuta, Vaishvānara, Vibhāvasu, Vulcan, Fiery Breaths under Zodiac.

AGNI-BĀHU [smoke]. Name of son of first Manu, and of grandson of first Manu. Cf. Agni.

ĀGNĪ-BHŪ [fire-born]. Name of Kārtikeya, the Son-God, Second Son of Shiva. Cf. Agni.

ĀGNĪDHRA [Agni=Fire; Dhri=to bear and/or idh=indh=to kindle]. Priest of the Sacrifice whose duty it is to see that the Sacred Fire is not extinguished.

AGNIHOTRI [Agni=Fire; Hotri=He who makes an offering, from root *hu* and/or *hve*, to

invoke]. One who performs morning and evening the Agnihotra Homa, a duty laid upon the householder.

AGNI-PUTRA [Agni=Fire; Putra=Son].

AGNI-RATHA [Agni=Fire; Ratha=Chariot]. Vehicle of the Gods.

AGNISHVATTA [consumed by the fires]. *Theos.* "Fire Dhyānis," "Heart of the Dhyān-Chohanic Body." Though this term is applied to all incorporeal creative Hierarchies as contrasted with Barhishads, technically it designates Sixth Rupa, *q.v.* Creative Order, fruitage of 2nd Planetary Chain. Cf. Agni, Pitris, Zodiac.

AGNUS DEI, Lat. [Agnus=lamb; Deus=God, root Deva], Lamb of God. Cf. Deity.

AHAM [I], Ego, Self.

AHAMKĀRA [Aham=Self; Kāra=the Maker]. *S.D.* "*I*-am-ness" or first shadowy outline of Selfhood, the tendency toward definiteness, origin of all manifestation. Reflected, it becomes great delusion of Separateness, Egoism. Cf. Unity, Duality, Mahāmaya, Mahat, Zodiac.

AHAM-SA [Aham=I (am) sa=He (*Tat* or *That* is actual base for Sa)]. Affirmation of identity of individual and Universal. Cf. Duality, Unity.

AH-HI, Senzar. See *Dhyān Chohans. S.D.* the Hierarchy of Spiritual Beings through which the Divine Mind comes into action. Cf. Creative Gods.

AHI [Der. (?) anh=to press together or strangle in original meaning; han (with ā prefixed and shortened) one that destroys on all sides]. Serpent.

AHRIMAN, Per. *S.D.* The impersonal opposing Power to Light (Ahura Mazda), the Negative and Positive Duality behind manifestation. Cf. Satan, Shishupāla, Svoyator.

AHURA MAZDA Zend. [Ahura=Breath, or Lord; Mazda=Wise] *S.D.* The Eternal Creative and Generative Light of Zoroastrianism. Cf. Zarathustra, Ahriman, Amesha Spentas.

AIN SOPH, Ensoph, Heb. [No-Thing]. *S.D.* the Kabalistic Boundless Absolute. Cf. Unity Qabbalah.

AION, See Æon.

AIRYAMAN, Zend. *S.D.* Bestower of Weal, see Ahura Mazda. Cf. Aryaman, Zarathustra.

AIRYANA VAÊJÔ, Zend. *S.D.* Garden of Eden or Imperishable Sacred Land of Zoroastrians.

AJA [A=not+ja=born] existing for all Eternity, a term especially applied to Brahmā, Vishnu, Shiva, Kāma, the Spirit or Jiva. Cf. Unity.

AJITAS [unconquered] one of the twelve classes of great Gods.

AJNA CHAKRA [ājnā=to command, to know +chakra=wheel]. *S.D.* The force centre between the eyebrows, or Brow Chakra.

AKĀSHA [To Shine, to be Bright]. *S.D.* The Second Differentiation of evolving substance Chaos, Æther. Matter of the Monadic Plane. Ākāsha is often used when Chaos or Æther more exactly would be indicated, but always in such cases the Ākāshic element therein is stressed. It is the substratum and cause of Sound. In Ākāsha all auras find their essence, and therein is the root of Duality. Cf. Anupādaka, Chidākāsham, Pashyanti, Vāch.

AKĀSHIC RECORDS. *S.D.* The Memory of Nature reflected in the Ākāshic element of the various planes.

AKTA [Anointed]. Cf. Christos, Messiah.

ĀLAYA [āli=to settle down upon, to melt, to unite with] an abode, a refuge. *S.D.* The Universal Soul or Self of all beings—"man its crystal ray." Cf. Unity, Anima Mundi, Khoom, Nyingpo, Pachacamac.

ALCHEMY [Arabic al]=the; Gr. cheo=to pour, smelt, dissolve]. *S.D.* the search for the Mysterium Magnum, the Universal Solvent, Elixir of Life, and the transmutation of base metal into gold. Cf. Amrita, Spagyrization.

ALHIM, Heb. *S.D.* Mystic name for *Elohim, q.v.* which read anagrammatically yields 31415, the Greek, *pi.* Cf. Numbers.

AM [at one time in nearly every language the Divine or Deity].

AMEN, Heb. [pop. aman=to strengthen or confirm]. *S.D.* der. from AUM, an invocation to Light. In Heb., its numerical value is 90 or that of YHVH, 25 plus ADoNaY, 65, the affirmation of being or sexless Lord within Man. Its Gr. numerical value is 99, and it is often used in mystic spells. Cf. Ammon, Numbers.

AMENTI, Egy. *S.D.* Is used not only for the purgatorial or immediate after-death region but also for that highest realm in which the Self becomes pure spirit for Eternity. Cf. Aanroo, Hades, Hel, Kāmaloka.

AMESHA SPENTAS, Zend. [amesha or amereta =undying + spenta = bountiful, beneficent. (from root su=to increase or benefit) Pahlavi as AMHRASPAND; Persian as AMSHA-SPEND]. *S.D.* with their Chief and Synthesis Ahura Mazda, *q.v.*, they are the Seven Planetary Logoi, as well as the Creative Hosts who carry out their will. Their names: Vohu Manah=Good Thought; Asha Vahishta =Perfect Righteousness; Khshathra Vairya= Wished-for Kingdom; Spenta Armaitī=Holy Harmony; Haurvatāt and Ameretāt=Saving Health and Immortality. Cf. Æon, Sevens, Karshvare, Sravah, Zarathustra.

AMEYATMAN [a-meya=immeasurable; Atman =Self].

AMIDA, Senzar. [Adi]. Cf. a-mi-toFo, Amitāpha.

AMITĀBHA [a-mita=unmeasurable, ābhā= irradiant blazing splendour]. *S.D.* very much the connotations given to Adi-Buddha, as well as title of one of Seven Dhyāni Buddhas, who is particularly the heavenly prototype of Lord Gautama Buddha. Cf. Nāgārjuna.

AMMON, AMMON-RA, AMUN sometimes AMEN. Egy. *S.D.* Concealed God, Hidden Supreme Spirit; AMOON-RA, the Generator or Wisdom God. With degeneration into phallicism. Ammon became the Creative God. Cf. Mendes, Neïth, Phoenix, Ra, Unity.

AMRITA [a-mrita=imperishable, immortal]. Elixir of Life. Cf. Alchemy, Rasa, Soma, Haoma, Hesperides.

AMSHA [the sharer or distributer, from amsh= to divide or distribute]. An Āditya.

AMSHASPENDS, see *Amesha Spentas*.

ANĀGĀMIN [am=not+āgāmin=subject to returning]. Buddhist term for Third Initiate.

ĀNANDA [bliss]. A Trinity, with Chit and Sat. Beloved disciple of Lord Gautama Buddha.

ĀNANDAMAYAKOSHA [ĀNANDA=Bliss+Maya=full of+kosha=shell, wrapper, sheath]. Bliss-Body.

ANANTA-SHESHA [Ananta=infinite, eternal, inexhaustible+Sesha=end, termination, death, destruction, also Servant, Remainder]. The name of the thousand-headed serpent who forms the couch of Vishnu and supports the entire world on his head. Cf. Unity.

ANDROGYNE, Gr. [andro=man+gyne=woman]. A dual-sexed Man-Woman. Adam-Kadmon. Cf. Ishtar, Sudyumna, Virāj, Duality.

ANGEL, Gr. [angelos=a messenger or envoy, one who announces; from Hebrew root=a divine or human messenger]. A non-human agent of the Creative Logos. The nine recognized orders of Angels are divided by St. Thomas into three Hierarchies: 1 Seraphim, Cherubim, Thrones; 2. Dominations, Virtues and Powers; 3. Principalities or Princedoms, Archangels, and Angels. (Trinity). This agrees with an old occult classification that placed Seraphim and Cherubim as above the seven great Archangels. Hebrew Angelology gives many classifications and sub-classifications. One is: Cherubim, Seraphim, Ophanim, Auphanim, [wheels], Power Angels, Principalities, The Elect One or Messiah, Elementary Powers of Earth and Water. Enoch classifies them: 1. Uriel; 2. Raphael; 3. Raguel [Ra'uel, the Terrifier] who chastizes the world and luminaries; 4. Michael; 5. Sariel [Sarakiel, Suriel=God turneth (?)] set over the spirits who seduce to sin; 6. Gabriel; 7. Jerahmeel [God is Merciful] Angel of the Resurrection. Maimonides gives: Over all Metatron-Enoch, Flaming Angel of the Fiery Presence. Then 1. Hayyot [living creature]Angels of the Silence and bearers of God's Throne. 2. Ophanim [wheels of Fire, Lipika, Watchfulness]. One of Guardians and bearers of Throne. Raphael; 3. Arelim with Michael, as Chief; 4. Hashmallim [silent when HE speaks, and then speaking]; 5. Seraphim; 6. Malakim; 7. Elohim; 8. Bene Elohim [children of Elohim] with Hofniel as Chief. Cf. Nephilim; 9. Cherubim; 10. Ishim [manlike beings] with Zephaniah or Zephaniel as Chief. One classification omits the Hayyots and the Elohim and substitutes the Shinannim with Zadkiel or Zedekiel and Gabriel as Chief; and the Tarshinim with Tarshish and Gabriel as Chief. Cf. Planetary Spirits, Samael, Anūnaki, Apsaras, Azael, Daemons, Devas, Gandharvas, Creative Gods, Peri, Rector, Rephaim, Sephira, Uzza.

ANGIRAS. (See Rishis).

ANIMA MUNDI, Lat. [Anima=that which breathes or blows, from Sanskrit an=to breathe; akin to Greek anemos=wind+Mundi=world. Soul of the World; the Life Principle pervading all. Cf. Unity, Breath, Ālaya, Khoom.

ANIMA-SUPRA-MUNDI, Lat. [See Anima Mundi+Supra=Over]. *S.D.* the Universal Ego. Cf. Uuity.

ANKH, see Tau.

ANNAMAYAKOSHA [anna from *ad*=eaten, means food in the mystical sense+maya=having the form made of, or sustained by+kosha=shell, wrapper, sheath]. The gross or dense physical body.

ANNAPŪRNĀ [Anna=food+Pura=possessed by or filled with]. Wife of Shiva. Cf. Devi, Mother.

ANTAHKARANA [antar=middle or interior+karana=cause, instrument, doing]. *S.D.* technical use: the bridge between lower and higher Manas.

ANU [minute, an atom] (Chaldean). See Ea, Trimūrti.

ANUGRAHA [A favour or kindness]. In the *Purānas*, the Eighth, a Special Creation.

ANŪNAKI [an=not+ūnaki=inferior; having full power]. Hindu Apsaras; *S.D.* Chaldean Angels of the Earth.

ANUPĀDAKA, *Theos.* The second plane of matter. See Ākāsha. In *S.D.* applied to those Great Beings "parentless" or "self-born of the Divine Essence."

ĀPAS [Water].

APĀNA [Expiration]. Of the five vital airs that which goes downwards and out at anus. Cf. Vāyu.

APHRODITE, Der. ? [related to Greek *Aphors* or foam, but the Goddess and the Name are very ancient. Born from the sea-foam gathered around the sundered generative organ of Uranus]. Goddess of Love and Beauty. Cf, Venus, Ariadne, Cupid, Eros, Hephaistos. Mother, Ilmatar.

APOCALYPSE, Gr. [to reveal]. The last book in the Bible, *Revelation.*

APOLLO, Gr. [der. apollumi=lay waste, destroy]. Twin-son of Jupiter and Latona; ever-young God of song and music; later identified with Sun-God as Phoebus Apollo. Cf. Sūrya, Delphoi, Diana, Gandharvas, Hilaeira, Manjushri, Orpheus, Phorminx.

APOPHIS, Gr. *S.D.* The destructive dragon. Cf. Serpent.

APSARAS [ap=waters+sri=to flow, to blow]. Wives of the Gandharvas, Gods of Song, produced at the churning of the ocean, who reside in the waters of the clouds. Indra is their Lord. Cf. Anūnaki, Mārisha, Pramlocha.

ARANI [Wood used for kindling sacred fires].

ARBA. (See Abraham).

ARCANA, Lat. [from arca=that which encloses or conceals]. A Secret or Mystery. Cf. Sod, Adytum.

ARCHÆUS, Gr. [the Ancient]. *S.D.* Father-Æther.

ARCHANGEL, Gr. [Arch=the beginning, as to Time; to lead or command, as to station; also to gain mastery over. Is often used for subordinate rulers; angel=messenger or envoy], Cf. Sevens. Kabarim.

ARCHE, Gr. [Beginning, Origin, First Cause or Principle]. Cf. Unity.

ARCHETYPE, Gr. [First-Moulded or stamped]. A Pattern or Model. Cf. Tzure.

ARES, Gr. [from root Ar=manhood, bravery]. God of Destruction, Mars.

ARDHANĀRI [Ardha=half+nāri=woman]. *S. D.* The third or Androgynous Race. Ardhanārisa is a form of Shiva, half male, half female. Cf. Duality.

ĀRYABHATTA, (Arghabhatta)=a learned Hindu astronomer, inventor of Algebra.

ARGHA [a worth or worship]. *S.D.* uses as synonymous with Ark. Cf. *Arghya*, often an oblation of water in a small boat-shaped vessel.

ARGHYANĀTH [Arghya=valuable, venerable, libations respectfully offered+Nāth=Giver of Boons, Lord].

ARHAT, (Buddhist) [from root arh=worthy or deserving]. Title given to Fourth degree Initiates, those who have attained Nirvāna. Cf. Crucifixion, Resurrection.

ARIADNE, Gr. the Mother-Goddess whose thread guided Theseus from the Minotaur's labyrinth. Theseus deserted his benefactor, later Dionysos married her, and at Cyprus she was worshipped as Aphrodite-Ariadne.

ARJUNA [arj=to shine or be white, (a doubtful root); Arjuna, the white or day-colour, the third of the Pāndava princes, son of Indra and Kuntī, see *Bhagavad-Gītā*]. Cf. Ulipī.

ARTHA [from arth=to strive, to obtain, to desire, also ri=to strive upwards]. Used commonly as prefix, *e.g.* Artha-Vijnāna=comprehension, *S.D.* interpretation.

ARUNA [the ruddy colour of dawn]. The brother of Garuda, *q.v.*

ARŪPA [a=without; rūpa=form; formless.] Cf. Duality, Zodiac.

ARVĀKSROTAS [arvāk=downwards+srotas =stream or current]. A creation of beings in which the current of nutriment tends downwards. *S.D.* The Seventh Creation, Man.

ARYAMAN [bosom Friend, arya=devoted, kind, a standard, excellent, from root ri=to fly or tend upwards, to move, to excite+ma=to measure]. An Aditya. Commonly invoked with Varuna and Mitra. Cf. Airyaman.

ĀRYAN [loyal or devoted, faithful to the Gods; noble, honourable, venerable, from ārya, root ri=to rise or tend upwards]. Used now to apply to Hindus, Iranians and all Fifth Race peoples. See Rāmachandra, Vyāsa, Varshas, Manu.

ĀRYĀSANGA or SANGHA [the collective body of the Āryans]. Names of a renowned philosopher, founder of the Yogāchārya School.

ĀRYAVARTA [Ārya and varta=above]. The sacred land of the Āryans.

ASAT [A=non+sat=being]. The non-existent, a synonym of matter, prakriti. Cf. Duality.

ASHA, Avesta. [pop.=purity or righteousness; the Supreme Spiritual Truth or Dharma; identical with Rita in Vedas]. Cf. Unity Zarathustra.

ĀSHRAM [ā=moving towards, all around;+ shram=exertion, penance, austerity]. A hermitage. Cf. Vihāra.

ASHTADISHA [ashta=eight+dish=direction]. Eight cardinal points.

ASHVAMEDHA [ashva=horse+medha=sacrifice]. A very ancient sacrifice in which the horse was not always immolated.

ASHVATTHA [under which horses stand; ttha =stha]. The holy fig tree, Ficus Religiosa. *S.D.* the Bo Tree.

ASHVINS [possessed of horses]. Two divinities who appear in the sky before dawn in a golden carriage drawn by horses or birds; the physicians of heavens the twins of the Zodiac. Cf. Cheiron, Kimpurushas, Shabalāshvas.

ASITA [dark-coloured, black or dark blue;*s ita* or white said to derive from *Asita*, rather than *vice versa*]. Cf. Duality.

ASHOKA [a=without+shoka=hate or sorrow]. Name of a great King-Apostle of Buddhism, about 270-232 B.C.

ASTARTE, (Phoenician), ASHTART, ASHTO-RETH (Semitic), ATHTAR, (Arabian), ISHTAR (Babylonian) [very primitive Heb. Arabic, etc. der. (?) pos.=to be watered, the self-watering, or Spring]. Goddess of Fertility worshipped by Canaanites, Hebrews, Phoenicians, Babylonians, etc. Identified with sun and morning star in Sabæa, with Venus in Mecca and Assyria, with Moon in Zidon. Cf. Sūrya.

ASTRA [weapon]. Usually interpreted spiritually, also Ashtar. Cf. Shastra.

ASTRÆA, ASTRAIA, Gr. [Starry-Maid] Constellation of Virgo. Cf. Kanyā, Zodiac.

ASTRAL, Gr. [from aster, a star, shooting star, flame or fire; Cf. Skt. staras, tārā, star-strewn or light-strewn]. *Theos.* first type of matter or plane more subtle than physical.

ASU [Breath, Life, Spiritual Life].

ASURA [Vedic, living, alive, Spiritual, epithet of Supreme Spirit, incorporeal gods]. *S.D.* The Dynamic Gods as compared with the Suras.

ATALA [a=without+tala=surface or roof, bottomless]. Cf. *tal*=to be full, complete or established. *S.D.* one of the seven Islands belonging to the nether Lokas, or antipodes.

ATHENA, Gr. The Latin Minerva, Goddess of Wisdom and Skill in the Art of Living. Cf. *Sophia*, Sarasvatī. A very ancient Goddess, called Trito-born, because her cult is found in Lake Tritonis, Libya. Only later myths speak of her as springing from the head of Zeus-Jupiter. Cf. Mother, Metis.

ATLANTA, ATALANTA, Gr. the swift runner of Bœotia, possibly another title for Artemis, the chaste Huntress or Moon Goddess, twin-sister of Apollo.

ATLANTIS, Gr. [from Atlas], the lost Continent, Poseidonis, in the Atlantic Ocean, one of the last homes of the Fourth Root Race. Cf. Deluge, Lif, Manu, Nāga, Noah, Dvīpa, Phlegyan Island, Quetzo-cohuatl, Rota, Tau.

ATLAS, Gr. [tlao=to bear]. The God who bore the world on his shoulders. Cf. Elektra, Titans, Pleiades.

ĀTMĀ, ĀTMAN [der. (?); possible roots: an= to breathe, at=to go or eternal movement; ah =to pervade and connected with aham=I; avātman from root av=vā to satisfy one's

self. As ātman in sense of breath, occurs only in four passages of the *Rig Veda*, of more recent date, and, as frequently in the *Rig Veda*, it occurs in the abridged form *tman*, some think der. from two pronominal stems a (in *a-ham*) and *ta*=this, meaning *this my own self*]. The Innermost essence of the individual as well as the Universal. Cf. Unity, Bhūtātman, Hamsa, Indriyātman, Jīvātman, Kāranātman, Kshet-rajna, Monad, Nara, Parabrahman, Paramāt-man, Pums, Quetzo-Cohuatl, Sarvātman, Spiritus, Sūtrātmā.

ĀTMAMĀTRA=[Ātma=Self; mātra=Mother Measure].

ATOM, Gr. [a=not+temnō=to cut]. Used in occultism to indicate individual lives from the greatest to the most minute. Cf. Unity, anu.

ATRI [devourer]. One of the seven stars of Great Bear. Cf. Prajāpati, Rishis.

ATYANTIKA [root atya-anta=perpetual, abso-lute, perfect, abundant, supreme; aty=trans-gressing+anta=limit]. Cf. Unity.

AUGOEIDES, Gr. [augo=radiant sunlight+eidos or eide=form or shape, sometimes as ideal form]. *Theos.* The Causal or Egoic Body with its aura, the permanent body of the Self as man.

AUM, OM,—Pranava, the sacred syllable in its triple form, denoting the Hindu Trimurti. While most authorities agree that M=Shiva, some place A as Vishnu the Self and U as Brahmā, the Not-Self, while others reverse this order. Cf. OM. Mani Padme Hūm, Amen, Tau.

AUPHANIM, *S.D.* Informing Angels of *Wheels*, or Celestial Orbs.

AURA, Gr. [the atmosphere inhaled, the vital air or breath, a bright light or gleam, a sound, an odour or exhalation]. *Theos.* the vital and subtle emanations that surround the body of a living being. Cf. Ākāsha, Augoiedes.

AVALOKITESHVARA [Avalokita=to look down upon+Ishvara=the capable, the power-ful, the Supreme Lord]. "The Lord who looks down from on High with Compassionate Glances with Face turned in every Direction" is the popular Buddhist interpretation of this Celestial Buddha, or Lord, whom *S.D.* deems synonymous with Ādi-Buddha, *q.v.* He gave mankind the magical formula "Ōm mani padme hūm," through which is attained the "Adored One." Cf. Bodhisattva, Kwan-Shai-Yin, Padmapāni, Dhyāni-Buddhas.

AVASTHĀS [to remain standing]. Condition or state; *S.D.* Hypostases.

AVATĀRA [ava=to come down or become less +trī which has many meanings, among which are: to cross over a river, to fulfil, transport, save, liberate from, make a way through, pervade]. Divine Incarnation. Cf. Vishnu, Krishna.

AVESTA [der, (?) from Pazand avastā, Pahlavi, *q.v.* āpastāk or avistāk; possibly wisdom or knowledge; or from Av. upastā, the original text]. Sacred book of Iran. Cf. Vendīdād, Zarathustra, Zend.

AVIDYĀ [a=without+vidy=knowledge wis-dom]. Cf. Nidāna.

AVYAYA [a=not liable to+vyaya=change]. Imperishable, immutable, not to be torn to pieces. Epithet of Vishnu. Cf. Unity.

AYANA [especially at end of compound=going]. See Nārāyana.

AYANAM=sun's road north and south of equa-tor, the half year, the equinoctial and solstitial points.

AZAEL, AZAZEL, Arab. [der. (?) poss.=scape-goat or entire removal of guilt or entire for-giveness; a rough or rocky mountain; a so-called "fallen" angel]. Cf. Uzza.

B

BAAL, BEEL BEL (fem. BAALAT, BEELA, BELTU) also Marduk, Muli, Sem. [primitive meaning=the owner, possessor or proprietor; secondary=the Master or Lord; a DIVINITY]. Originally meaning only Deity, the worship of Baal became degraded into mere phallicism. Cf. EI, Ea, Zu, Berosus.

BACCHUS, Gr. [Inspirer of noble enthusiasm, poss. from *echeō* and *iache*=to sound joyous-ly]. A later name for the God Dionysus, also, Iacchus.

BALA-RĀMA [*Bala*=the strong, the vigorous, the mighty, from *bal*=to breathe, to live+*Rāma*=delight, rejoicing, from *ram*=to repose in calm tranquillity, to be happy and rejoice, to sport, etc.]. The strong Rāma, a Hindu Hercules, born in the third Age, seventh son of Vasu-deva and elder brother of Krishna. Sometimes called *Halāyudha*=armed with a plough, or *Musalin*=club-armed. Considered by some as Vishnu's Eighth Avatāra, by others as an incarnation of the great serpent, Sesha. Cf. Ananta-Shesha.

BAL-I-LU (Senzar?) [pos. *bal*=strong+i=to go towards+lū=to destroy], Mārtānda.

BANDHA [tying a knot or bondage, joining, uniting].

BANYAN [from Banyā, a great merchant caste, most of whom are followers of Vishnu]. A wide spreading tree which sends down aerial roots. Ficus Bengalensis. A tree under which Shiva, as Dakshinamurti, taught His disciples in silence. One of the world's largest and finest Banyans is the great Banyan Tree of Adyar.

BARHISHAD [barhis=on a layer of kusha grass (Light, splendour, sacrifice)+sad=seated on; Cf. also barhishada=largest or strongest]. The corporeal pitris or progenitors as contrasted with Agnishvatta. See *Manu*, iii. 196, 199.

BEELZEBUB or BAALZEBŪB, a Philistine god of Accaron (Ekron) later confused with BEELZEBOUL, Prince of the lower regions or Demons. [Baalzebūb or Beelzebub means lord of the flies, or pos. lord of the mansion]. Cf. Satan, Bel, El.

BENE, BENI, Heb. [as a prefix=children of, more correctly rendered B'nei]. See Angels.

BEROSUS=a Chaldean priest in the temple of Bel (Marduk) at Babylon, said by Eusebius and Tatian to have been a contemporary of

Alexander the Great. He compiled in Greek a *History of Babylonia* which is only known through fragmentary quotations.

BHAGA [beauty, loveliness, adoration, affection from root *bhaj* to dispense, grant or bestow, worship, adore, be devoted to, etc.]. Name of an Āditya, regarded in the Veda as bestowing wealth and instituting or presiding over love and marriage.

BHAGAVAT, BHAGAVĀN [the adored, venerable, blessed, sacred or holy One]. Cf. below.

BHAGAVAD-GĪTA [the Song of the Bhagavān Krishna, admonishing Arjuna, his devotee]. An episode in the Sixth Book of the *Mahābhārata*.

BHĀGAVATA [a worshipper of BHAGAVĀN].

BHAKTI [has all the significance of its root *Bhaj* (see *Bhaga*) including that of allotment, division, separation, but is commonly translated in its meaning of love, reverence, devotion which is only possible when there is the māya of separation]. Cf. Yoga.

BHĀRATA [descended from Bharata, a famous King. *Bharata*=potter or servant from *bhri*= to bear, carry, sustain, nourish, cherish, protect]. Commonly refers to India, the country of Bharata and his descendants. Cf. Sumati, Varshas.

BHĀRGAVA [related or belong to Bhrigu, *q.v.*]

BHĀSKARA [bhās=light or lustre+kara=to cause].

BHĀVA [from root bhū=to be or become] becoming, being, existing. Cf. Nidāna.

BHRIGU [from root bhrā=to shine, illuminate, irradiate; Cf. root bhrajj=to apply intense heat or scorch]. A race of beings frequently mentioned in Vedas with Agni, described in *Rig-veda*, as cherishing and kindling Fire. Bhrigu is variously identified as father of this race, as Prajāpati, Mahārishi, adopted son of Varuna and author of *Rig-Veda*. Cf. Krishna, Sukrā or Venus, etc.

BHŪMI [earth from root bhū=to be or become; also the base, as of a geometrical figure].

BHŪTA [the produced or formed from *Bhū*]. Used especially of disembodied spirits, and also the elements.

BHŪTĀDI [bhūt=beings or being+Ādi=origin of source]. An epithet of Mahā-Purusha or the Supreme Spirit. Cf. Unity.

BHŪTA-SARGA [bhūta=beings+sarga=creation]. The second creation of the elements.

BHŪTĀTMAN [bhūt=beings+Ātman=Self]. Self of all Beings, epithet of Brahman. Cf. Unity.

BHŪTESHA [bhūt=beings+Īsa=Lord. Cf. Īshvara]. Lord of all Beings, an epithet applied to Brahmā, Vishnu, Krishna. Cf. Unity.

BHUVAS, BHUVAH, BHUVAR [the second syllable of invocation used beore Gāyatrī, referring to the Intermediate world, Astral, between the physical and Heaven or Mental World]. Cf. Plane, Loka.

BĪJA [seed or germ, in classical Sanskrit usually written vīja=seed, semen, germ or origin pos. from vi=to disjoin, scatter, separate+jan=to generate, produce, be born; some link with vī =to go in different directions, diffuse].

BINAH, Heb. [a feminie noun=understanding, insight]. Third Person of Kabalistic Trinity. Cf. Kepher, Chokmah, Neshmah, Sephira.

BIRDS. Many of the Gods take the form of Birds. Cf. Cygnus, Farcher, Garuda, Hamsa. Jatāyu, Leda, Mārtanda, Mercabah, Phoenix, Pyrrha, Quetzo-cohuatl, Ra, Tāmrā, Thoth. Vishvāmitra, Zu.

B'NE=Bene.

BODHA [knowing, understanding, perception, wisdom, to become awake, to blossom and bloom; from budh].

BODHI [the illuminated or enlightened intellect of a Buddha or Jīva]. Perfect wisdom, budh.

BODHISATTVA [Bodhi=wisdom+sattva=true essence, life, breath, consciousness, goodness, harmony]. The Heavenly Boddhisattvas such as Avalokiteshvara, are the " Essence of Wisdom." The earthly Buddhas-to-be or BODHISATTVAS, their reflections, are so resolved to become, *e.g.*, Maitreya]. Cf. Christos, Hermes Trismegistus, Jesus, Krishna, Kwan-Shai-Yin, Manjushri, Orpheus, Pāramitas, Vyāsa, Zarathustra.

BO-TREE, BODHI TREE [Ficus Religiosa]. The famous tree in Buddha Gayā under which Gautama Buddha attained his enlightenment, Cf. Ashvattha.

BRAHMA (Neuter) [from root brith=increase; Cf. brinh=to maintain or preserve].

BRAHMAN, the Absolute, the Supreme Spirit, the Causeless Cause. Cf. Unity, Bhūtatman, Parabrahman.

BRAHMĀ, *S.D.* (Masculine) the Creator, Divine Architect, corresponds to Third Person of Christian Trinity, the Holy Spirit or Divine Creativity. Cf. Trimūrti, Abhimānin, Aja, Aum, Bhūtesha, Chatur Mukham, Creative Gods, Fohat, Hamsa, Hiranya-Garbha, Jyotsnā, Padma, Padmapāni, Padmayoni, Parārdha, Pratisarga, Vaidhātra, Virāj, Vishvakarmān, Yuga.

BRAHMACHĀRI [Brahma, *q.v.*+chārya= practice, performance, austerity, from *char*=to move, to undertake]. The religious austerity, particularly as regards chastity, of the young Brāhman student.

BRAHMA-DANDA [Brahma, *q.v.*+danda= staff or mace, from *dam*=to subdue, tame, conquer, restrain and quiet]. Staff of Brahma symbolized by the ascetic's actual danda. Cf. Tridandin.

BRAHMA-LOKA [loka=abode]. Abode or World of Brahma.

BRĀHMAN, Brāhmana [belonging to or pertaining to Brahman]. The Priestly Caste of India, worshippers of Brahman. Cf. Smārta, Vashishtha, Vishvāmitra.

BRĀHMANASPATI, see Brihaspati.

BRAHMĀNDIKA [Brāhman, *q.v.*]. *S.D.* Solar and Lunar Pitris. Cf. Sūrya, Moon.

BRAHMAPUTRA [Brahma, *q.v.*+putra=son].

BRAHMA-RANDHRA [Brahma+randra, a slit, fissure, or hole, from root *radh*=to subdue. Cf. *rad*=to split]. The suture or aperture in the top of the head through which the soul passes at death. Cf. Nādī, Kundalinī.

BRAHMARISHI [Brahma+rishi, root ri=to rise or tend upwards]. Cf. Rishi; a great Sage, considered higher than Maharishi. Cf. Vishvāmitra.

BRAHMA VIDYA [Brahma+Vidyā, Knowledge or Wisdom]. The Knowledge of the Supreme Self. Cf. Unity.

BRAHMS, see ABRAHAM.

BREATH or AIR, always a symbol of the informing spirit. Cf. Aleous, Ahura Mazda, Anima Mundi, Asu, Asura, Ātmā, Aura, Hamsa, Hatha-Yoga, Nephesh, Neshamah, Pneuma, Prāna, Pranāyāma, Psyche, Quetzo-Cohuatl, Ruach, Pani under Sādhya, Samāna, Spiritus, Ūrjā, Vāyu, Vaikharī, Fiery Breaths under Zodiac.

BRIHASPATI, BRAHMANASPATI [Vedic, Lord of Brahman, the heavenly Brahman, later to mean the planet Jupiter]. Cf. Guru, Tārā.

BUDDHA [from budh=to know, to fathom a depth, der.(?) pos. bhū, existence, becoming; Cf. budhna=depth]. The Wise or Perfectly Enlightened One, free from the necessity of all phenomenal existence, yet broods over mankind to bring all to the Way of Righteousness and Liberation. An Initiate, of the Eighth Degree. See Gautama, the last Buddha; also Dhyāni-Buddhas. Cf. Bodhi and see below. Cf. Amitabha, Avalokiteshvara, Kashyapa, Nirvāna, Pratyeka.

BUDDHI [see Buddha, Bodhi, etc. Direct Perception, Intuition, Understanding]. Cf. Centrifugal, Christos, Heyah, Manas, Sparsha, Sūtrātma, Taijasa, Zodiac.

BUDDHIC PLANE, the middle or Intuitional plane of Solar System. Cf. Loka.

BUDH [SEE Buddha].

BUDHA [root Budh] the Wise. Cf. Bodha.

BUDHISM, the following of Wisdom as contrasted with Buddhism, the religion of the Buddha.

BYTHOS, Gn. S.D. the first Father of unfathomable nature, the Second Logos. Cf. Chaos, Duality, Vishnu.

C

CABBALAH, see Qaballah, Kabala, etc.

CABIRI, see Kabirim and Titans.

CADUCEUS, Lat. [caduceum=a herald's staff; the staff of Mercury, or Hermes, messenger of the Gods. Cf. (Gr.) kerukeion, the caduceus of Hermes, from root=to cry aloud]. As a physical symbol, it is the spinal column wherein are intertwined the Idā and Pingalā, female and male forces, and forms a channel through which pours the sexless Sushumnā power. Philosophical symbol of Spirit-Matter, intertwined in manifested universe. Cf. Serpent, Kundalini, Duality, Trinity.

CAIN, Heb. [Kayin, Qai-yin der. (?) pop. der.= kanah=to possess because of words uttered by his mother Eve, "I have possessed a man by the favour of the Lord." Kayin was originally the name of the Kenite tribe; in Masoretic text II Sam. xxi, 16 trans. "lance"; corresponding words in Arabic and Syriac mean "smith." S.D. quotes as correct der. "I have measured a man, even Jehovah."] The First-Born son of Adam and Eve who slew his brother Abel. S.D. Tiller of the Soil. Cf. Enoïchion.

CAPRICORN, Lat. [having a goat's horn]. The tenth sign of the Zodiac. Cf. Makara. Occult: tenth Creative Hierarchy, fifth remaining.

CASTOR AND POLLUX, Gr. Kastor and Polydeukes, the Twins identified by late writers with the Constellation Gemini and its Zodiacal Sign; the mortal Kastor saia. to be the son of the mortal King Tyndareus of Sparta and his wife Leda; his twin, the son of Zeus, the immortal Polydeukes, eventually persuaded Zeus to permit him to share his immortality with his brother. The two represent Spirit-Matter, the Immortal and Mortal of the Self. Cf. Duality, Dioskouroi, Jupiter, Zodiac. Note that Jupiter appears to Leda in the form of a Swan. Cf. Hamsa, the Swan of Brahmā.

CHAIN, Theos.=the incarnation of a Planetary Logos, through a seven-globed form, round which he successively passes his life-streams of evolving forms and consciousness seven times, stopping for a world-period of seven races on each globe. At most three only of the globes are physical, the remainder having as their densest form the subtler matters. Cf. Agnishvātta, Ring, Cycle, Yuga.

CHAKRA [from root kram=to step, walk, go towards; Cf. kri=to do, make, perform, accomplish]. A wheel or circle; the discus of Vishnu, which Dr. Besant says is the "whirling disc . . . . the svastika . . . symbol of creation in time or succession;" in Theos. a force centre in vital-etheric or subtler bodies; in the etheric to be found on the surface of the physical body. Cf. Ajna, Kundalini, Nādī, Od, Zeroana.

CHAKRAVARTIN [chakra=wheel, circle, disc, multitude, troop, army+vartin=abiding in]. Universal Monarch; one whose chariot wheels rool everywhere without obstruction, a ruler of a chakra or country extending from sea to sea.

CHANDĀLA [der. (?) chanda=fierce, violent]. Outcaste.

CHĀNDOGYA [the doctrine of the Chandogas. Chanters of the Sāma-veda or Udgātri priests]. [Belonging to Sāma Veda]. One of the Major Upanisads. Cf. Veda.

CHANDRA-BHĀGĀ [chandra=glittering, shining golden, the moon+Bhāga]. The River Chenāb, one of the Punjab or five streams. Punj=5+āb=stream.

CHANDRAGUPTA [Chandra=Moon,+gupta =protected]. Kings of the Gupta Dynasty.

CHAOS, Lat. [a yawning gulf]. Gr. [Chāos= Space, the first state of the Universe, a Void and Formless Infinite]. S.D. the root of matter on the Adi Plane, in its first remove from the Unknown Absolute, the impenetrable Veil between the Incognizable and the LOGOS, the Waters of Life, the Unawakened or only stirring Virgin Mother, to become Ākāsha when the Creative Potency sleeping or breathing within her bosom fructifies her. Cf. Unity, Duality,

Trimūrti, Ilus, Kosmos, Nārāyana, Noot, Ru, Ymir.

CHATUR-MUKHAM [chatur=four+mukham =face]. A cube. A name of Brahmā, Chatur-Mukha.

CHEIRON, Gr. [inferior]. One of the Centaurs, horse-men, son of Kronos and Philyra, author of the Art of Medicine. Accidentally wounded by Hercules, he gave up his immortality and was transformed into the constellation Sagittarius, ninth Zodiacal sign. Cf. Aesculapius, Ashvins.

CHELA [Cf. cheluka, a Buddhist novice]. Disciple. Cf. Lanoo.

CHENRESI, Tib. see Avalokiteshvara.

CHERUB, CHERUBIM, Heb. QERUB, QERUBIM [authorities differ as to der.; pos. borrowed from Assyrian kirubu from karābu=to be near, because of the nearness of these Heavenly Spirits to the Throne of the Most High; connected by metathesis with Xeref (Egyptian)=K-r-bh; also Kerub and Rakub=to ride and Merkeba=chariot]. CHERUBIM and SERAPHIM take highest place in the Angelic Hierarchies followed by Thrones. CHERUBIM are associated with Omniscience of the Divine. " Like blooming youth ", Says St. Augustine " Cherubim means the Seat of the Glory of God and is interpreted: Fulness of Knowledge." The Chariot of God. Depicted as winged children's heads. Cf. Angels, Garbiel, Merkabah.

CHESED. See Sephira.

CHHANDAJAS [chhanda=pleasing, delightful, free will, arbitrary choice+ja=born]. S.D.= " will-born." Used of Gandharvas, q.v.

CHHĀYĀ [from chho=to cut off the light; pos. a corruption of chhadyā from chhad=to conceal]. Cf. Saravanā.

CHIDĀKĀSHAM [chit=consciousness, perception+ākasham, q.v.]. S.D. field for Universal Consciousness. Cf. Unity.

CHINMĀTRA [Chit=consciousness+Mātra= complete]. Supreme consciousness of Parabrahman.

CHIT [to understand, know, become conscious, perceive, attend, design]. A trimūrti, with Anānda and Sat. Cf. Achit, Vishnu.

CHITKALA [chit, q.v.+Kala=the dumb, hoarse through sobbing or tears, tone]. The Voice of Wisdom. S.D. compares Kwan-Yin, q.v. Cf. Vishnu.

CHITRAGUPTA [chitra=perceptible, visible+ gupta=protected]. The recorder of the vices and virtues of mankind in Yama's world.

CHITRASHIKANDINAS [chitra=bright+ shikhandin=crested, from root shi=to make sharp or pointed]. Used of the Seven Rishis.

CHOHANS, Tib. ?[Lord]. Seven Mighty Beings who, having passed the Sixth Initiation, have the power to focus within themselves the Ray-Streams or Attributes of Logoic Consciousness. Cf. Dhyān Chohans.

CHOKMAH, CHOCHMAH, HOKMAH, Heb. S.D. the male Wisdom, the Second Person of the Kabalistic Trinity; see Kepher and Binah.

Cf. in the Christian Trinity the Son or Manifested Word, Hindu, Jnāna, Vishnu, Sephira.

CHRĒSTOS, Chrēsts, Gr. [chréstes=one who expounds oracles; chrēstos=auspicious; working for good]. " The terms Christ and Christians, spelt originally Chrēst and Chrēstians were borrowed from the Temple vocabulary of the Pagans. Chrēstos meant . . . a disciple on probation, a candidate for hierophantship; who, when he had attained it, through Initiation, long trials and suffering and had been anointed . . . was changed into Christos ", q.v.—The Kety to Theosophy.

CHRISTOS, Gr. trans. Hebrew Messiah [the Anointed (with oil). See Chrēstos]. " Christos —the ' purified ' in esoteric or mystery language. In mystic symbology . . . Christes or Christos meant that the ' way ', the Path, was already trodden and the goal reached . . . Occult=(1) the Buddhi in man born at the First Initiation; (2) the Cosmic Buddhi, or Second Principle of the Triune Logos; and (3) the World Teacher, or Bodhisattva, the Christ who is anointed by and at one with his Cosmic Father in Cosmic Wisdom-Love, the Second Principle. Cf. Maitreya, Trinity, Vishnu, Jesus, John, Akta, Easter, Horus, Quetzo-cohuatl.

CIRCE, Gr. daughter of the Sun and the Perseis, sea nymph and sorceress, fabled for her charm and magic arts. Cf. Apollo.

CIS-HIMĀLAYAN [this side of the Himālayas].

CONATUS, Lat. [an attempt, effort, undertaking, impulse or incitement to action].

CONSCIOUSNESS, Lat. [to know with one's self]. The act of Awareness, Perception of Otherness or of You as apart from I. Cf. Duality, Unity.

CONTEMPLATION, Lat. [to mark out a temple wherein one could survey or vision the inner worlds in time and space, Cf. contemplor]. The fourth stage of mental process in which an object is visioned with the stilled mind. Samādhi.

COSMOCRATORES, Gr. [Kosmo=universe+ krator=bodily strength, might, a Lord in authority]. The strong Lords of the Universe. Cf. Dhyān Chohans, Creative Gods.

COSMOS. See Kosmos.

CREATE, CREATION, Lat. etc. [though the present meaning of creation is to bring forth out of nothing, this derived meaning is not upheld by its roots; the Greek Kra or Kran=to fufil or accomplish, to bring to an end, to reign over, and is der. from Skt. kri], Cf. Ādi-Krit. The etymological meaning of Heb. briah is " to cut out and put into shape," signifying a preexisting material]. Cf. Duality.

CREATIONS. See Anugraha, Arvāksrotas, Bhūta-Sarga, Indriya, Kumāra, Mahat-tattva, Mukhya, Panchadasha, Prākrita, Pratisarga, Ūrdhva-srotas.

CREATIVE and GENERATIVE. For Gods representing this principle, see first Brahmā and Duality. Then compare: Abraxas, Ādi-Krit, Aeon, Agnishvatta, Ah-hi, Ahura Mazda, Amesha Spentas, Ammon, Angels, Aphrodité, Bija, Cosmocratores, Daksha, Dbrim, Demiourgos,

Dhyān-Chohan, Elohim, Eros, Ferho, Fetahil, Gaea, Ishtar, Kneph, Kriyashakti, Narāyana, Ophite, Pasht, Phallus, Pitris, Prajāpati, Priapus Propator, Purusha, Rasa Mandala, Scar', Scarabeus, Sephira, Shankha, Ūrjā, Vāch, Vaidhātra, Virāj, Vishvakarman, Zodiac. See also the goddesses listed under the term *Mother*.

CRORE=ten million in Hindu measurements.

CRUCIFIXION, Lat. [only in Ecclesiastical Latin is *crucio* used=to fix upon the cross; pop. to torture, torment]. In Occultism the crucifixion stands for the conflict-point or mid-period between involution and evolution, when the spirit of a Universe or an individual completely stretched out upon the cross of, or immersed in matter, strives to mould it into an instrument for expression. Cf. Arhat, Resurrection, Easter, Calvary, Tau.

CYCLOPES, Gr. [kuklos=circle+ōps=eye a race of Lemurian giants with the third eye awake in the middle of the forehead]. Cf. Pineal Gland, Uranus.

D

DABAR, Heb. [Word or Logos].

DBRIM, plural of Dabar, pronounced *Dabarim*, in Qabballah (Kabala) signifying the Creative Hosts.

DAEMON, DAIMON, Gr. [Divine Spirit or Power as contrasted with *Theos.* in person or manifest]. Though used also of actual disembodied angels, the word was often used to indicate " a flood of Divine Inspiration." Cf. Agathodaemon.

DAĒVAS, Per. [=Devas or Asuras].

DAG, DĀGŌN, Chal. Cf. *Matsya* [root=to be fruitful, manifold, self-increasing like the fish; also of. Heb. Dagan=corn; Arabic *dagn*= copious rain. Skt. dā=to purify or wash] the Philistine or Chaldean Fish-God of Procreation and Growth, closely associated with the god of the earth. Cf. Creative Gods, Water, Oan.

DAITYA [son of diti=a Divine Being who, in contrast to Aditi, *q.v.*, is the infinitely divided one, the principle of differentiation, disintegration, or liberality personified. From root dā= to give, or do=to loosen, cut, unbind]. The Daityas are always at war with the Gods. Cf. Asura and Sura. Cf. Duality, Adityas, Dānava, Hiranyakashipu, Hiranyāksha, Tāradaitya.

DAIVĪPRAKRITI [Daivī from Devi=Divine+ prakriti=original or natural form, primary essence or substance]. *S.D.* the Light of the Logos. Cf. Unity.

DĀKINI [Dā=to give, share, distribute]. The Five Incarnations of the Mother Goddess, Devī.

DAKSHA [the capable, competent, skilful, strong, and powerful]. An epithet applied to Shiva and other Gods. A Prajāpati, placed at the head of the Creative-Powers. An Āditya, *q.v.* Cf. Danu, Diti, Hari-ashvas, Kadrū, Kashyapa, Mārisha, Prāchetasas, Sambhūti, Shabalāshvas, Surasā, Tāmrā, Vishvas, Vīrabhadra, Vinatā.

DALAI-LĀMA—the Temporal Head of the Tibetan hierarchy of Lāmas.

DAMARU, DAMRU [from root da=the sound of drums]. The hour-glass drum of Shiva, the God of Time. Cf. Kronos, Dhvani under Vishvas.

DAMBHOBI, DAMBHOLI [from root *dabh*, *dambh*=to strike down, destroy, Indra's thunderbolt or a diamond]. *S.D.* variant of Dattoli.

DAN, Old Chinese [=Janna=Dhyāna, *q.v.*]. *S.D* " *Dan* in modern Chinese and Tibetan phonetics *Chhan*, is the general term for the esoteric schools and their literature. In the old books, the world *Janna* is defined as ' reforming one's self by meditation and knowledge,' a second *inner* birth. Hence *Dzan*, *Djan* phonetically; the *Book of Dzyan*." [Cf. *dan*, a Vedic root= to be striaght or straighten; *jan*=to be born; na=as it were (in early Vedic lit.)].

DĀNAVA, Cf. Asura Daitya [from root dā=to cut, divide, destroy; children of Danu]. Giants, Titans.

DANGMA, Senzar? *S.D.* " a purified soul . . . Jivanmukta . . . Adept."

DANIEL, Heb. [El]=God+Dani=my Judge; God is my Judge], the prophet and interpreter of dreams in the Chaldean court of Nebuchadnezzar (where he was named Baltassar=Bel protect his life), author of the *Book of Daniel* in the Bible.

DANU; daughter of Daksha, wife of Kasyapa, mother of the demons called Dānavas.

DARSHANAS [seeing or sight, insight, perception, vision; showing the way.] Technically the six recognized systems of Indian philosophy: *Pūrva*; *Uttara-mīmāmsā* (*Vedānta*); the *Sānkhya* and *Yoga*; the *Nyāya* and *Vaishesika*.

DEITY, Lat.-Skt. [through deus=god to Skt. deva-div=toshine]. Divinity, a SupremeBeing, the godhead, a god or goddess. [Cf. Avesta *daēva*, Lith. *deva*, Gael. and Irish, *dia*, O. Teut. *tiu*; Anglo-Saxon *Tiw*; Gr. *Zeus*, genitive *Dios*, Lat. *Jupiter* (i.e., *Jov-pater*) also Lat. *Diana*, *Janus*, *Juno*, Dis, genitive *Jovis* (*Diovis*), and *dies*]. Cf. Baal, El, Unity.

DELPHOI, DELPHI, Gr. A famous oracle of Apollo, in Phocis at the foot of Parnassus.

DEMETER, Gr. [Lat. Ceres; name for bread]. Goddess of fertility, agriculture and rural life and mother of Persephone, the Goddess of Spring, Cf. Hekate, Rhea.

DEMIOURGOS, Gr. [one who works for the people, a skilled workman, a handicarftsman]. Derived meaning, the Maker of the World; the Neo-Platonic Fabricator as opposed to a Creat-or-out-of-nothing. Cf. Creative etc.

DERVISH, Per. [darwish=mendicant]. The zāhid ascetics of Islam (" satisfied with little ") whose devotional acts take the form of whirling circular dances. Cf. Chakra.

DEVA, Dev. [root=div=to shine, be bright or splendid; pos. originally=to shoot forth as a ray of light; to sport, to play]. A Shining One, a Divine Being, God or Devī, Goddess. See below. Cf. Daēvas, Deity, Duality, Angels, Genii, Hanuman, Theos. Trinity, Vāmadeva, Vasudeva.

DEVACHAN [Deva, *q.v.*+Chan, Tib.=home or abode]. Home or abode of the Gods; that protected area of the mental plane reserved for those who are building faculty between incarnations and enjoying the fruits of good deeds done in the previous incarnation. Cf. Paradise, Tiaou.

DEVANĀGARĪ [Deva, *q.v.*+nāgarī=that which pertains to a city]. The script of the Gods, generally used for Sanskrit.

DEVATĀ [divine dignity or power]. See Deva.

DEVAYĀNA [deva, *q.v.*+yāna=car, vehicle, way]. Way of or to the Gods, the Path.

DEVĪ [feminine of Deva, *q.v.*]. Cf. Duality as "Every Deva has associated with him his Devī." Name of the wife of Shiva, she who is variously named Uma=light; Gaurī=the yellow or brilliant one; Pārvatī or Haimavatī=born of the Himālayas, child of the Mountain God; Jaganmāta=Mother of the world; Bhavānī, the excellent, the happy; Durga, the inaccessible; Kālī or Shyāmā=the dark one; Chandika, the fierce; Bhairavī=the terrible. Cf. Annapūrna, Dākinī, Kundalinī, Satī, Trilochana, Umā.

DEVIL, Gr. [diabolos=to traduce or accuse]. Cf. the Hebrew Satan, also the accuser and adversary of the brethren, pop.=the personification of Evil; philosophic, the principle of resistance to Divine Will for the purpose of manifestation and evolution. Cf. Duality, Yezidi.

DHAIVATA [sung by the wise men] sixth swara or tone of the Hindu gamut.

DHARMA [from root dhri=to hold, support, sustain, maintain, carry on, restrain, preserve; pos. (?) from old form bhri=to bear, nourish, foster, cherish, suffer]. Duty, Justice, Rightcousness, Order, Law, Truth, Virtue, Innate Nature or Condition, Sacrifice. Cf. Yama, Dhruva, Kuntī, Prashraya, Samnatī, Satya, etc., Sva-Samvedāna, Yudhishthira.

DHARMAKĀYA [Dharma, *q.v.*+kāya=vesture]. The Vesture of Truth. One of the Seven Paths open to the Adept, on which he drops all vehicles, atomic centres, and vestures lower than the Monadic plane and its triplicity of consciousness. The two other great vestures of Northern Buddhism are the Sambhogakāya and Nirmānakāya vestures. Cf. Trimūrti.

DHĀTU [that which is placed or laid, a deposit, a constituent or essential part]. The five (six or seven) principal elements, or substances of primitive matter. Cf. Prakriti.

DHRUVA [fixed, firm, immovable, stable, perpetual; Cf. dhri, see Dharma]. The Pole Star; the devoted devotee of Vishnu.

DHYĀNA [root dhyāni=meditation, reflection, contemplation, older form of *dhī*]. Profound abstract religious contemplation, divine intuition and discernment. The four stages are: Analysis (Vitarka); Reflection (Vichara); Fondness (Prīti); Bliss (Sukha). Cf. Dan (Old Chinese).

DHYĀN CHOHAN [Dhyān, Chohan, *q.v.*]. Lords of Contemplation—the Divine Intelligences charged with the supervision of the Kosmos. Cf. Agnishvātta, Ah-hi, Cosmocratores, Creative Gods, Nārada.

DHYĀNI-BUDDHA [dhyāna, *q.v.*+Buddha, *q.v.* The five (or seven) Buddhas of Contemplation, or Reflection: *Vairochana*, Manifester of Phenomena or Source, Lord of the All-Pervading Wisdom; *Akshobhya* of the Mirror-like Wisdom, whose reflex *Vajra-Sattva* is "The Trimuphant One of Divine Heroic Mind; *Dorjesempa*; *Ratna-Sambhava* [Born of a Jewel]. The Beautifier, Lord of the Wisdom of Equality; *Amitābha* [or boundless or Incomprehensible Light]. Lord of the Discriminating Wisdom; *Amogha-Siddhi*. [Almighty Transcendent Conqueror of manifested Existence]. Lord of the All-Performing or All-Fulfilling Wisdom. Cf. Quinary, Sevens, Vishnu, Maitreya, Manusha. Sambhogakāya, Tien-Hoang, Zodiac.

DIANA, Lat. the chaste Moon-Goddess, sister of Apollo, daughter of Jupiter and Latona, regarded as identical with Greek Artemis. Cf. Hekate, Nemesis, Phoebe.

DIANOIA [thought, intention, purpose, intelligence, understanding] *S.D.*: synonymous with Logos.

DIG-AMBARA [space-clothed]. A Jain or other mendicant who has forsaken worldly possessions, even clothes. Cf. Shiva.

DII MAGNI [Deus, *q.v.*+magnus=great]. The Great Gods.

DIONYSOS, DIONYSUS, Cf. Bacchus, Ariadne [Cf. dios=divine].

DIOSKOUROI, DIOSCORI, DIOSCURI, Gr. Castor and Pollux, the Heavenly Twins.

DISH [to point out or show; direction]. Lord of the Quarters.

DITI, Cf. Aditi [cutting, splitting, dividing]. Daughter of Daksha, mother of the Daityas. Cf. Duality.

DJIN, Per. [an elemental, *q.v.*].

DORJESEMPA, see Vajrasattva under Dhyāni-Buddhas.

DRAUPADI [or Drupada=pillar]. Wife of the Pāndu princes. Cf. Pāndavas.

DRUIDS, Celtic. [from *drew*=an oak; Cf. Greek *drys* or Dru-uids=the highly knowing]. Priest-Initiates of ancient Celts of Britain, Gaul, and Germany. Their ceremonies were celebrated under oak trees. Cf. Ogham, Initiation.

DRUSES, A Mohammedan Sect in Syria, characterized by a belief in a God above all attributes. Cf. Vedāntin.

DUALITY, Explained under Trimūrti and its references, *q.v.* Cf. Āditi, Diti; Āditya, Daitya; Adam Kadmon; Advaita, Dvaita; Aeon; Agathodaemon, Kakodaemon; Ahriman, Ahura Mazda; Ākāsha, the root of all Duality; Androgyne; Ardhanāri; Asat, Sat; Ashvins; Asita, Sītā; Asura, Sura; Castor and Pollux; Chhāya; Crucifixion; Demon; Devil; Deva, Devī; Dvi-ja; Echath, Echod; Adam, Eve; Evolution, Involution; Hiranyāksha, Hiranyapura; In, Yo; Lingayoni; Mother; N'cabvah, Sacr'; Nephthys; Ōm mani Padme Hūm; Set, Osiris; Syzygy; Arūpa, Rūpa; Yang, Yin; Idā, Pingalā; Isis, Nephthys; Loki, Odin; Macroprosopus, Microprosopus; Sephira; etc.

DURGĀ, Devī, *q.v.*

DVĀDASHA-KARA [possessed of twelve rays or hands]. A name of Kārtikeya, q.v.

DVAITA [Duality]. School of Indian Philosophy, stessing the Duality of Manifestation, Jivātma and Paramātma, Spirit-Matter, Life-Form, Dark-Light, etc. Cf. Advaita, Duality. "Pluralistic Realism"

DVĀPARA YUGA [dvāpara=the two-pointed die]. The Third Age in which the number two is noted: 2,400 years, i.e., 2,000 years with 2 twilights. Cf. Yuga.

DVI-JA [the twice-born]. In Brāhmanism, the three higher castes, entitled to be invested with the sacred thread. S.D. an Initiate.

DVĪPA [an Island]. Zones of the terrestrial world, situated around the mountain Meru, like the leaves of the Lotus flower. Each Dvīpa is separated from the next by a distinct circumambient ocean, their names being Jambu, Plaksha or Gomedaka [a precious stone, pos. an agate]. Shālmalī, Kusha, Krauncha [a heron], Shāka, and Pūshkara. Cf. Nāga, Dvīpa, Olympus, Sevens, Shveta, Varsha.

DZYAN, DZAN, DJAN, Book of=Book of Real Knowledge obtained through Contemplation; the oldest book in the world, a Manual of Creation in its earlier portions. Cf. Dan (old Chinese), etc.

E

EA, Chaldean. Also Hea. The Second Person of the Babylonian Trinity, composed of Anu, Hea, and Bel. The "Maker of Fate," "Lord of the Deep," "God of Wisdom and Knowledge." Cf. Oan, Vishnu, Mater.

EARTH. For Gods which represent the Elemental spirit of Earth, compare: Adam, Anūnaki, Bhūmi, Dag, Gaea, Gnomes, Hel, Idā, Ilus, Kuvera, Marut, Merodach, Orion, Prithivī, Pyrrha, Seb, Surabhi, Vasu, and Taurus under Zodiac.

EASTER, Teutonic [Eōstre, Ostara]. Goddess of the rising day, particularly of spring. The principal Feast of the Ecclesiastical Christian Calendar, celebrating the rise of the Christ in all its aspects from crucifixion, q.v.. Cf. Persephone.

ECHATH, Heb. [the "One" Feminine].

ECHOD, Heb. [the "One," Masculine].

EDDA, Icel. [great-grandmother]. The very oldest of the Scandinavian Lays or Sagas.

EDEN, Heb. [delight; pleasure]. The home of primeval man. In Kabala a place of initiation into the mysteries. [Cf. Adn, Arabic=fixed residence]. Cf. Olympus, Adam, Eve, Paradise.

EKA [One, Single, Alone, Only, the Same, Chief, Supreme, Peerless or Matchless; said to be from i=to go towards]. Cf. Unity.

EL, very old Semitic [the Highest and One God, used not only for Jehovah, but for the Gods of other Nations. Translated as the Mighty, it is considered as rooted in the verb ol=to be strong]. See also plural form ELOHIM. Cf. Angels, Unity, Deity, YHVH, Bel, Daniel, Gabriel, Michael, Samael, Uriel.

ELECTRA, ELEKTRA Gr. [from electron, shining or splendid, amber or gold, Cf. Skt. arkas (sol) arkis (splendour)]. Daughter of Atlas and Pleione, one of the seven Pleiades, and mother of Dardanus.

ELEMENTALS, Lat. Theos. Creatures evolving in the Hierarchies of Earth, Water, Air, Fire, Æther, and two other Elements. Gnomes are the lowest spirits of the earth line, undines of the water, salamanders of the fire, and sylphs of the air. Cf. Angels, Sevens, Bhūta, Bhūta-Sarga, Dhātu, Djin, Hiquet, Indra, Lhamayin, Lilith, Nymph.

ELEMENTARIES, Theos., remnants of the cast-off subtle bodies of disembodied spirits. Cf. Klippoth, Shell, Tselem.

ELIAS Heb. [ELIAHU, ELIJAH="Yahveh is God" one of the greatest prophets in the Old Testament].

ELOAH, ELOHA, ELOHI, see ELOHIM.

ELOHIM, Heb. see EL, ALHIM [Plural. Formed by adding a masculine plural ending im to the feminine noun Eloah, ALH]. The Male-Female Creative "Gods" or Hierarchies of Beings who bring a Universe into being. In Genesis, mistranslated as "God" in referring to the creation of the Universe. Cf. Alhim, Duality, Uzza.

ELOHISTIC—the Hebrew critical schools hold that only a fragment has been preserved of that very ancient portion of the Bible written by the author who uses Elohim, for God, as compared with the author who uses the term YHVH. Decided linguistic differences indicate plainly the two authors.

ELOÏ, Gnos. the Planetary Spirit of Jupiter.

ENOÏCHION, Gr. [the inner Eye, the Seer] S.D. the true name for Enoch, son of Cain, disfigured from Chanoch. The apocryphal Books of Enoch are esoteric in nature.

EPAPHOS, Gr. [he of the touch]. Son of Zeus and Io, who became pregnant when Zeus touched her with his hand. Epaphos became Father of Northern Africa. Cf. Jupiter.

EPIMETHEUS, Gr. [Afterthought]. Brother of Prometheus, Forethought. Cf. Pyrrha, Titans.

EROS, Gr. [desire, love in its creative aspect]. Held by Hesiod to be the oldest of the Gods. Third Person of the Trinity, Ūranos, Gaea, an attendant of Aphrodite. Later this God degenerated into the mischievous child Cupid, son of the Goddess. Cf. Kāma, Metis, Phanes, Protogonos, Psyche.

ESAU, Heb. [the red or hairy]. Twin brother of Jacob. Became almost a synonym for evil, as his brother was considered the good. Cf. Duality.

ESSENES, Gr.- Heb. [der (?) pos. hasaya=the modest, humble, or pious; kshim, "the silent"; asa=the healers; asah=those who do wonders; haza=the seers; ashen=the strong; seha=those who bathe, the pure]. A mysterious sect of Jewish Yogis.

ETERNITY, Gr. [æternum, originally aviternum =æon-long. Æon, q.v.]. The true meaning of eternity i.e., for a great age, has become warped, into everlasting. S.D. Eternity=the

seventh part of 311,040,000,000,000 years or an Age of Brahmā, taken after eliminating 6,220,880,000,000 years of twilights, or a final total of 43,547,600,000,000 years. Cf. Cycle, Garuda, Kalpa, Oulam, Serpent, Yggdrasil, Zeroana.

ETHER [der. from æther, *q.v.*]. Technically the four most subtle sub-states of physical matter through which the finer forces of that plane are made manifest. *Not* Æther. Cf. Linga Sharira.

EUA, EUE, EVA, EVE, HAVAH, HAUVAH, HEVE, HAWWAH, HAYAH. Chal-Heb, [to fall down into generation; Life, Living to be or to continue]. The wife of Adam, and the Mother of all created beings. Cf. Chaos, Duality, Cain, Abel, Hayah, Eden, Paradise.

F

FAFNIR, Scand. The Dragon of Wisdom. Cf. Serpent, Sigurd.

FAROHER, FEROUER, FRAVASHI, Per. A human body rising out of a winged solar disc, typifying the dual aspect of the One Life, as manifest in the lower and Higher Selves of man. The outspread wings and tail, a triple Sun-rayed symbol, shows the triplicity of its expression. Cf. Trimūrti, Unity, Bird, Sūrya.

FERHO, Gn. Highest Creative Power with the Nazarene Gnostics.

FETAHIL, Gn. Of the Creative Orders or Pitris, *q.v.*

FOHAT, Tib. *S.D.* " the constructive Force of Cosmic Electricity . . . polarized . . . into positive and negative electricity " born at any point of friction or union as the relation between polar opposites. The Forthgoing Power of The Third Logos, *q.v.* Cf. Duality, Brahmā, Oi-ha-hou, Pramatih, Toom.

G

GABRIEL, Heb. [El=God; Gab=the Strong God, the Hero, the Valiant]. Second in rank of the Archangels; on the left hand of Deity. Seat of all Powers, The Serpents, Seraphim and Cherubim. As Fire is Prince of Ripening Fruits. When Michael is Fire, He is Water. Messenger and Envoy of the Annunciation. Angel of Gold. Intercedes for earth. One of the Quaternary of Angels. Cf. Agni.

GAEA, GAIA, GE [Earth]. Mother Earth, spouse of Uranus. The first Creative Gods, who with Eros made up the first Trinity. Cf. Titans, Phoebe, Rhea, Tityos.

GĀNDHARA [Name of a people; Gā=words, dhr=bear. Cf. Gandharva; gandha=fragrance]. The third of the Hindu Svaras or Scale Tones, one of great power. Also name of a Vidyā-Devī.

GĀNDHARVA [gandha=fragrance]. Angels of Song, the Chief of whom was regarded as parent of the first pair of human beings. Assistants of Indra. Cf. Angels, Apollo, Apsaras, Chandajas, Creative Gods, Orpheus.

GANGĀ [pos. der=to go]. The sacred River Ganges in India, which is said to purify all it touches. Cf. Himavat.

GANYMEDE, Gr. The beautiful mortal stolen by the Gods to be their cup-bearer. Cf. Hebe.

GARUDA [from root grī=to swallow or consume, because of identification with the fire of the sun's rays]. Vāhan or vehicle of Vishnu, the winged Eagle or Kite-God, half bird, half man, the Great Cycle of Manifestation, with its down-and up-soaring expression, which Vishnu bestrides as Time. Considered by some as the Sāttvic Guna, *q.v.* Cf. Jatāyu, Aruna, Kronos, Eternity.

GĀTRA [instrument of moving]. Limb.

GAUTAMA—the sacerdotal name of the Buddha or Shakyamuni, founder of the Buddhist religion. Avatar of Vishnu. Cf. With Gotama under Rishis. Cf. Hermes Trismegistus, Orpheus, Vyāsa, Zarathustra, Bo-Tree, Kapila-vastu, Ananda, Kāshyapa, Mārīchi, Sammā Sambuddha, Shankarāchārya, Tathāgata.

GĀYATRĪ—the holiest of Hindu mantrams; invocation to the Divine Savitur or Sun-God, that he quicken the intuition of His worshippers [from gai=to relate in metrical language, especially to sing as do the Gods]. Cf. Sūrya, Sanjnā, Sāvitrī.

GENIUS, GENII, Lat. [gigno, genitus=to beget, to produce]. Good and Evil Spirits of Destiny, Karma-Devas, *q.v.* Cf. Duality.

GNOMES, Gk. [gnome=intelligence]. Primitive spirits. Cf. Elementals.

GNOSIS, Gr. [knowledge or inner Wisdom]. Cf. Jyān, Vishnu.

GNOSTIC, Gr. [the proficient in the knowledge, gnosis, *q.v.*]. A philosophical sect who taught much of the inner wisdom in the first three centuries of the Christian era.

GOPĀ [Go=cow, pāla=protector; Or go= speech, earth, wealth, etc.] Esoterically, a spiritual mystic power. Cf. Utpala, Varna and Yasodharā.

GRAHA-RĀJA [king of the planets]. The sun; the moon; the Planet Jupiter or its Regent. Cf. Sūrya.

GRIHASTHA [griha=house or habitation]. The householder stage in the cycle of life.

GUHYA VIDYĀ [the mysterious or secret knowledge or wisdom]. Cf. Vidyā, Upanishads.

GUPTA VIDYĀ [the guarded or protected knowledge or wisdom]. Cf. Vidyā.

GUNAS, GUNAMS [a thread or strand, from grah=to seize or take captive]. Three qualities of matter: sattva *q.v.*=goodness or balance (being, existence, essence, true life); rajas= passion or activity [from ranj=to colour; emotion, feeling]; tamas=darkness, inertia (tam=to gasp for breath, to become immovable, to desire, a heavy tendency). Cf. Tattvas Ichchhāshakti.

GURU [from grī=to announce or proclaim, to promulgate]. A Spiritual Teacher; Cf. Chela, the Planet Jupiter or its regent Brihaspati, considered as the preceptor of the Gods. Cf. Yugāchārya.

GURUDEVA [the Divine Guru, one's highest Guru, a term of Invocation.

GYĀN, GNAN, JNĀNA [knowledge, the hidden or inner Gnosis or Wisdom].

H

HADES, Gr. [haïdes, pos. from a=not+idein= to see; the unseen]. The immediate after-death region. Cf. Amenti, Hel, Kamaloka, Lethe, Limbo, Myalba, Naraka, Niflheim, Orcus, Pluto, Rhea, Tantalus, Tityous, Yama.

HAGAR, Heb. [Ha-Agar=this is reward]. In rabbinical literature considered to be a daughter of a Pharaoh who preferred to be a bondswoman in the house of Abraham, later his second wife. Esoterically: the yearly lunar cycle. Cf. Moon, Mother, Sarah.

HAM, Heb. [pos. abbreviation from 'yham, places of giants; critical Hebrew analysis places as Egypt, one of the names of which was "Chemi" or black]. Son of Noah. Some hold Ham to be Father of the Ethiopian Race, Lemurian.

HAMSA, HANSA [the eternal breath which ever "goes", from han; aham sa="I am That"]. Vāhan or vehicle of Brahmā who rides the Swan, an illusion to his function as divider or maker of atoms. The eternal Rajas of the breath. "Jīva (Ātmā) comes out with the letter ha and goes in with the letter sa."

HANUMĀN [pos. the long or large-jawed one; root han=to overcome, conquer]. The strong and powerful deva ally of Rāma, incarnate with thirty crores of Devas, in monkey form, to gain experience in mortal animal life and to assist Rāma in his war with Ravana, the apotheosis of Evil, who could not be killed by a celestial. Occultly, Hanumān, Son of Vāyu, the Wind God, represents variously the Supreme Ray of the Divine, the God of Thought, the Prānic Vital Force. Cf. Tārā.

HAOMA [Skt. soma, Persian hom, from an old Āryan root hu=su, to pound, to squeeze]. A plant used in a Persian ceremony of purification. Said to confer great vitality and spiritual happiness, if taken only by the pure. Cf. Amrita.

HARI [golden-green]. Name of Vishnu, and the Soma Juice. The Sun-Rayed One. The Haris are one of the twelve classes of great Gods. Cf. Sūrya-Vamsha.

HARI-ASHVAS, HARYASHVAS [Horses of Hari, q.v.]. S.D. sons of Daksha.

HARI-KESHA [yellow-haired]. One of the Seven Rays. Dispeller of Darkness.

HARPOCRATES, Gr. The Child Horus, God of Silence.

HATHA-YOGA [various der. Ha=the Sun (swara); tha=the Moon (swara) or a union of sun and moon breath, the positive with the negative; hatha=by violence or force+yoga, pop. hatha=health]. A form of yoga which aims at gaining mastery over the breath and other bodily processes, so that the physical body, both dense and vital, may be wholly under control. Cf. Rāja Yoga, Tantra, Prānāyāma.

HAVYAVĀHANA [oblations-bearing] the Fire of the Gods. Cf. Kavyavāhana, Saharaksha, Trimūrti, Agni.

HAY-YAH, in Kab.=Buddhi.

HE, Heb. Fifth letter of alphabet, ān article and demonstrative pronoun. A symbol of the Tetragrammaton. S.D. means an "opening," symbol of feminine principle. Cf. Mother.

HEBE, Gr. [youth]. Daughter of Zeus-Jupiter and Hera-Juno, wife of Hercules, cupbearer of the Gods, Goddess of Youth. Cf. Ganymede.

HECATE, HEKATE, Gr. [the far-shooting]. A Goddess often identified with Artemis-Diana, sometimes with Demeter and Rhea on earth, Luna in heaven, and Proserpine, in the lower world. Represented with three heads. Presided over purification and atoning rites; giver of riches, honour, victory and fair voyages, protectress of newborn babes. Cf. Trimūrti, Moon, Mother.

HEL, HELA, Scand. Goddess-Queen of the Land of the Dead, Helheim and Niflheim. In earlier mythology, the earth-goddess, the good and beneficent mother, nourisher of the weary and hungry. Cf. Persephone, Hades, Yggdrasil.

HELIOS, Gr. the SUN-GOD. Cf. Titans, Apollo, Sūrya, Phaethon.

HEPHAISTOS, Gr. the Planet Vulcan; the lame son of Zeus and Hera; God of Fire-Craft and all Arts needing Fire, God of the Forge, the Blacksmith, Husband of Aphrodite. [pos. from root aph which appears in apro=to kindle fire]. Cf. Agni, Tubal Cain.

HERACLES, HERCULES, Gr. [Hera's glory, so named from the power the Queen of Heaven obtained over Hercules at birth]. The most famous of the Greek heroes, son of Zeus-Jupiter, and Alcmena, noted for his twelve labours. Cf. Bala-Rāma, Cheiron, Hebe.

HERMES, Gr. Messenger of the gods, son of Zeus and Maia, God of Skill, God of Wisdom. Lat. Mercury, Cf. Caduceus, his magic rod, Vishnu, Michael, Psychopomp, Sephira.

HESPERIDES, Gr. Daughters of Night (Hesperos). They dwell in an island on the western verge of the world, guarding a garden of golden mystic apples. Cf. Amrita, Moon, Mother.

HILAEIRA, Gr. [Ilaeira; mildly shining]. Daughter of Apollo, wife of Pollux, Goddess of Twilight. Cf. Mother.

HIMĀLAYA [abode of hima=snow]. The range of mountains on the Northern border of India, said in S.D., to girdle the globe either above or below water. Cf. Himavat, Kailāsa, Varshas.

HIMAVAT [Lord of the Himālayas]. Father of Gangā, the Ganges; also of Devī, as Pārvati.

HĪNAYĀNA [smaller vehicle]. Used to denote that form of Southern Buddhism which holds more strictly to the Buddha's written teachings. Cf. Mahāyāna.

HIQUET, HIQIT, Egy. The frog-goddess; a symbol of immortality and of the Element Water. Cf. Āpas.

HIRAM ABIFF, Heb. a skilful builder and a "Widow's Son" whom King Solomon procured from Tyre to superintend the works of the Temple, later one of its Hierophants.

HIRANYA-GARBHA [shining, resplendent, or golden egg of the first nuclear Universe from which Brahmā was born, its creator]. Cf. Unity, Ildabaoth, Mārtānda, Urjā.

HIRANYAKASHIPU [clothed in gold]. A Daitya, destroyed by the Avatāra Vishnu as Narasimha (man-lion) to save his devotee Prahlāda, the Daitya's son. Cf. Hiranyāksha.

HIRANYĀKSHA [golden-eyed]. Twin Daitya of Hiranyakashipu, slain by the Avatāra Vishnu as a Boar, Shri Varāha. Cf. Duality.

HIRANYAPURA [golden city]. An abode of the Asuras.

HOD, HUD, See Sephira.

HORUS, Egy. That person of the Trinity Osiris, Horus, Isis, comparable to the Christ Principle of the Christian Trinity. A Sun-God. Cf. Sūrya. Vishnu, Harpocrates.

HRISHĪKESA [hrishīka=a sense organ from hrish=to thrill with rapture]. Lord of the organs of sense, Vishnu or Krishna. S.D. Spiritual or Intellectual Soul.

HYPERBOREAN, Gr. a region around the North Pole in the Arctic Circle, said to be inhabited by a joyous, music-loving race of immortals. Cf. Olympus, Meru.

I

IALDABAOTH, ILDABAOTH, Gn. [ilda=child; baoth=egg]. Cf. Hiranya-Garbha, Mārtānda; son of Sophia, and emanator of the six stellar Spirits. Cf. Planetary Spirits, Sevens.

IAŌ, Gn. YHVH, q.v., Phœn, the light conceivable only by intellect, the male Essence of Wisdom. Cf. Planetary Spirits, Vishnu.

ICHCHHĀSHAKTI [ichchhā=desire from ish =to endeavour to obtain, seek, or strive for + shakti=energy]. Will or Desire Power. Cf. Gunas.

IDA, Scand. The field of peace and rest on which the Gods assemble to hold counsel in the Edda.

IDĀ, ILĀ, the androgynous daughter of Manu. Occultly, the Second Race. [idā=offering, oblation; ilā=flow, speech, the earth]. Mother of Kuvera; also a name of Devī, feminine Force which flows up spine. Cf. Pingalā, Sushumnā, Vāch, Mother, Sudyumnā, Vāyu.

IKSHVĀKU, progenitor of the Solar Tribe (the Suryavamsas) in India and Son of Vaivasvata Manu.

ILMATAR (Fin. Kalevala). The Virgin who falls from heaven into the sea before creation. Daughter of the air, she becomes the mother of the seven forces of nature, as sons. Cf. Sevens, Water, Aphrodite, Vāyu.

ILUS, ILLUS, Gr. Primordial mud or slime. Cf. Chaos, Earth, Water.

IMHOT-POU, IMHOTEP, Egy. God of learning Cf. Greek Imouthes. Son of Ptah, and a solar God. [God of the handsome face]. Cf. Sūrya.

IN, Jap. female principle of matter or the Universe. Cf. Yo, Duality.

INDRĀ [der. (?) pos. in=to advance, press or drive upon; id=even, just; ind=to be powerful]. Lord of the Elements and cosmogenetic processes of the Heavens, Eastern Quarter and Æther. Cf. Adbhutam, Apsara, Dambhobi. Gandharvas, Jnānendryas, Jishnu, Kuntī, Marut, Marut-Van, Pulomā, Shakra, Shāmba, Surādhipa, Tāradaitya, Thor, Uriel, Vajradhara, Vāyu, Vishvakarman.

INDRĀNI, wife of Indra, q.v.

INDRIYA [belonging to Indra, q.v.]. Organs or powers; the third Creation.

INDRIYĀTMAN, name of Vishnu. Cf. Indirya and Ātman.

INITIATE, INITIATION, Lat. [a beginning or commencement]. To admit to secret religious rites. Theos. Great Stages on the Path of Superhumanity, to which a man who would serve the world is admitted, before the rest of his fellows. Cf. Adept, Adytum, Anāgāmin, Arhat, Bodhisattva, Buddha, Chohan, Chrestos, Christos, Crucifixion, Druid, Dvija, Job, Mahātmā, Mārga, Moses, Naga Dvīpa, Narthex, Neophyte, Orphic, Paul, Pentecost, Pratyeka, Sakridāgāmin, Sanat Kumāra, Serpent, Sigurd, Siloam, Srotāpanna, Tao, Uraeus.

IO, Gr. Daughter of Inachus, beloved by Jupiter, and changed through fear of Juno into a cow. The Greeks held Io was worshipped in Egypt as Isis. [Exclamation of triumph or suffering]. Cf. Mother, Epaphos.

ISAIAH, Heb. One of the great prophets of Isreal. Cf. Serphim.

ISHTAR, ISTAR, see also Ashtoreth, etc. Bab. the old Semetic mother Goddess, in Phoenicia= Ashtarte, Arabia=Athtar (an Androgyne). In Sabæa identified with the Sun and Morning Star; in Mecca and Assyria with Venus, and in Zidon with the Moon. She is Giver of Vegetation and Goddess of Spring, Creatrix of animals, Goddess of Wedlock and Maternity, Mother of Mankind, Giver of Revelations, Destroyer of Life, Storm and War Goddess; sometimes the star Sirius. Cf. Shakti, Sūrya, Duality, Creative Gods.

ISHVARA [THE SUPREME LORD; the Capable, the Powerful]. Cf. Unity, Avalokiteshvara, Bhūtesha.

ISIS, Egy. Third Person of Trinity, the Great Mother Goddess, Osiris, Horus. Daughter of Seb, god of the earth and Nut, goddess of the sky, she marries her brother Osiris, and gives birth to Horus, the Sun-God. Cf. Duality, Io.

ISRAEL Heb. [the people who walk in the law of the Omnipotent Righteousness]. Children of Israel, the Jewish or Hebrew people.

J

JACOB, Heb. [the supplanter, as he supplanted his brother Esau, q.v.]. Later his name became Israel, the father of the Israelites. His twelve sons stand for the Signs of the Zodiac. Cf. Dan, Issachar, Joseph, Levi, Napthali, Rachel, Rebekah, Zabulon.

JAGANNĀTHA [Jagat=world+nātha=giver of blessings; Lord]. Lord of the World. Cf. Sanat.

JACHIN, JAKIN, Heb. [he establishes] The right-hand of the two brazen pillars set up in the

porch of the Temple of Solomon, that on the left or North being called Boaz [in strength]; symbols of Heaven and Earth. Cf. Duality.

JAMBU-DVĪPA [jambu=rose-apple from jam= to eat+dvīpa=continent or island.] Cf. Varshas.

JANA-LOKA [jana=gives birth to all+loka= place]. The lowest third division of the Buddhic plane, fifth loka; counting from below.

JANAKA [generative]. A name of a prince produced miraculously through friction of sacred fires. Cf. Agni, Creation.

JANĀRDANA [he who excites or agitates men]. An epithet of several of the Gods.

JANGAMA [the movable from jagat=gamgam =to go].

JĀTA [the born, the arisen]. One of seven Kumāras.

JATĀYU [from jata=matted hair]. The King of the Birds, by some considered a son of Garuda, q.v. Cf. Yuga, Kalpa.

JĀTI [birth, tribe, rank, caste, lineage].

JAVO, JEVO, JEHO, JAH, IAH, JEHOVAH, see YHVH.

JEREMIAH, Heb. ["Lofty is Jahweh"]. A prophet who was called to his office about 627 B.C.

JESUS, Lat. [Jesus is the Latin form of the Greek Iesous, which is in turn the Hebrew Jeshua, Joshua, or Jehoshua=Jehovah is salvation]. Theos. The disciple of the World-Teacher, Christ, the Bodhisattva Maitreya, who gave his body at the time of the Baptism for the use of the Great One. Became the Head of the Christian Church. Cf. Calvary, Essenes, Joseph, Nazarene, Apollonius, Rāmānujāchārya.

JISHNU [from ji=to win by conquest]. The victorious, trimuphant; the sun; Indra, etc. Cf. Sūrya.

JĪVA [from jīv=to be alive, vivify, support life, to nourish, nurture]. A living being; The ensouling or informing spirit. Cf. Aja, Hamsa, Kshetrajna.

JĪVANMUKTA [mukta=loosened from+jīvan =manifested existence]. The liberated Adept. Cf. Dangma, Moksha.

JĪVĀTMAN, JĪVĀTMĀ [see Jīvā+Ātmā]. The Supreme Spiritual Principle incarnate in manifested existence, particularly the Self of man. Cf. Unity.

JNĀNASHAKTI [the power of understanding cognition]. Cf. Gyān, Shakti.

JNĀNENDRYAS [jnāna=perception+indryas =sense organs, lit. that which belongs to Indra, q.v.]. Organs of perception, the senses.

JNĀTA [it is known, the comprehended, the perceived]. The First Logos, S.D.

JOD, YOD, Heb. The tenth letter of the alphabet. Signifies a hand. As a numeral=10.

JOHN, ST., Gr. [Ioannes, Hebrew Yohanan]. Two St. Johns are closely associated with the coming of the Christ; John, the Baptist prepared the way for his Master by proclaiming his advent; John, the Beloved Disciple, supposed author of the Fourth *Gospel* and the *Book of Revelation*

JOSEPH, Heb. [shall add=The Lord shall add to me another son]. The favourite and eleventh son of Jacob who rose to power in Pharaoh's Court as Viceroy of Egypt. Also the name of the foster father of Jesus.

JOSHUA, Heb. [helped by YHVH]. Servent and successor of Moses. Also Heb. name for *Jesus*.

JUNO, Lat. [Gr.=Hera]. Daughter of Saturn, sister and wife of Jupiter, Queen of Heaven and guardian deity of women. Cf. Deity, Heba, Hephaistos, Heracles, Io, Mars, Rhea, Tithys, under Titans.

JUPITER, JOVE, Lat. [cf. Skt. *dyo* or *dyu*= heaven and Gr. Zeus+pater=father]. Heaven's Father, son of Saturn. Supreme Ruler of Olympus, home of the Gods. Apollo, Brihaspati, Castor, Deity, Diana, Eloi, Graha-Rāja, Guru, Hebe, Hephaistos, Heracles, Hermes, Io, Latona, Leda, Pater Aether, Sephira, Tantalus, Thor, Titans, Tityos.

JYOTISHA [from jyotis=light]. Petaining to the heavenly bodies. Astrology.

JYOTSNĀ [moonlight, splendour]. One of the bodies of Brahmā.

K

KA'ABAH, Arab. [house]. Famous Mohammedan temple at Mecca, a place of pilgrimage.

KABĀLA, see QABBALAH

KABARIM, KĀBEIRA, KABIRI, Gr.-Phoen. [from kaio=to burn; the Powerful through Fire]. Mighty Gods with the ancient nations; Archangels. Cf. Agni, Titans.

KADESH, KADOSH, KODESH, Heb. [consecrated, holy]. Term later degenerated into phallicism.

KADRU [from root kad=to colour; tawny]. Daughter of Daksha, wife of Kashyapa and mother of the Nāgas or Serpent-Race.

KĀILĀSA, the famous mountain north of the Mānasa Lake in the Himālayas, reputed to be the home of the God Kuvera and the paradise of Shiva. Cf. Olympus, Sinai.

KAIMURATH, Per. Last of the race of prehuman kings. A fabulous Persian hero. Cf. Adam Kadmon.

KĀLA [from root kala=to impel, incite, urge on, accomplish]. Time, Season. Cf. Kronos, Vishvas.

KĀLAHAMSA, see Hamsa. [the Swan of Time].

KALĀPA, KATAPA, [that which holds together single parts]. Residence of the immortals. Cf. Olympus.

KALEVALA, Fin. Epic Poem concerning the Scandinavian Gods and Heroes. [Kalevala= land of the heroes]. Cf. Svoyator.

KALI [from root kal=to impel, incite, urge on, bear]. Name of a die marked with one point, and of that age which is said to be the Kali Yuga of strife, conflict, and dissension, the shortest of the Yugas, *i.e.*, 1200 years of the Gods or 232,000 years of men, beginning 18 February 3102 B.C. When written Kali= black.

KĀLĪYA, Name of a Nāga or serpent slain by Krishna.

KALKI AVATĀRA [said to be from root kal=to incite, impel, urge on, bear; kalki refers to all that is wicked and mean]. The Avatar of Vishnu who is to rid the world of all evil and lead to purer ages. Represented by symbol of Horse-man. Cf. Ashvins, Kimpurusha, Shamballa.

KALPA [practical, feasible, possible from klrip= to order or arrange well]. A cycle of time; usually a day or day and night of Brahmā, each one of which is 4,320,000,000 years. Cf. Eternity, Yuga.

KĀMA [from root kam=to wish, desire, long for]. The principle of Desire, either Cosmic or Individual. Cf. Aja, Cupid, Eros, Karabtanos, Makara-Ketu, Māra, Nephesh, Vaidhātra.

KĀMA LOKA, immediate after-death or purgatorial condition [place of desire].

KANDU [pos. from root skand=to leap, jump, spring]. Name of a Yogi of the Second Root Race. Cf. Pramlocha.

KANYĀ [from kana=small]. A Virgin; Fifth Sign of the Zodiac, Virgo. Cf. Astraea, Mother.

KAPILA [of tawny colour]. Name of an ancient sage, identified with Vishnu, considered by some to be the founder of the Sānkhya system of philosophy. Name of one of the seven and three Kumāras.

KAPILAVASTU, the ancestral home of Gautama the Buddha, Prince Siddartha.

KARABTANOS, Gr. In the Nazarene Codex the Spirit of Blind Desire. Cf. Kāma.

KĀRANA SHARĪRA [Causal Body]. The immortal body of the human reincarnating ego.

KĀRANĀTMAN [the Causal Spirit or Soul]. Cf. Ātman.

KARATALA [that which can be taken into the hand]. Identical with Talatala. Cf. Tala.

KARMA [from root kri, action, deed, work]. The Law of Causation, Balance, Compensation by which every action begets a reaction; the actor becomes the attractor for a similar action. Cf. Duality, Devachan, Lipika, Satan, Saturn, Skandhas, Yoga.

KARMENDRIYAS [organs of action]. Cf. Jnānendryas, Karma.

KARSHVARE (Zend), the seven earths over which rule the Amesha Spentas. Cf. Zarathustra, Plane.

KĀRTIKEYA [from krittikā, the Pleiades, his nurses]. So-called God of War, identified with Mars. Son of Siva, his Outgoing Energy, as contrasted with Ganesha, the Inward-turned Energy. Cf. Dvādasha, Kara, Lohita, Skanda, Sanatkumara, Tāradaitya.

KASHYAPA, " the self-born who sprang from Time " (Atharva Veda), the father through Aditi and twelve other daughters of Daksha, of gods, demons, men, fish, reptiles and all animals. Name of the Buddha preceding Lord Gautama. Cf. Danu, Kadrū, Surasā, Tāmrā, Vinatā.

KAUMĀRI, the shakti of Kumāra.

KAVYA-VĀHANA [an offering to sages]. Electric Fire of Pitris. Cf. Havyavāhana and Saharaksha, Trimūrti, Agni.

KEPHER, KETHER, Heb. [the Crown]. The First Person of the Kabalistic Trinity. Binah, Chochmah. Cf. Trimūrti, Macroprosopus, Sephira.

KHAMISM, KHAMI, the ancient language of Egypt.

KHANDA [broken, torn asunder]. Multitides, numbers, assemblages.

KHOOM, KNOOPH, KHNOOM, Egy. Solu of the World. Cf. Ālaya, Anima Mundi, Unit.

KIMPURUSHA, KINNARA, a celestial being, represented as having a human figure with the head of a horse (the horse in Hinduism symbolizes knowledge). Cf. Ashivins, etc., Kalki, Cheiron, Purusha, Varsha.

KLIPPOTH, Q'lippoth, Heb. shells; evil spirits; remanants of departed personalities. Cf. Elementaries.

KNEPH, Egy. Also CNEPH, NEF. One of the Gods of Creative Force. By some identified with the Logos.

KOOTHOOMI, Tib. One of the Two Chohan Adepts responsible for the formation of The Theosophical Society. Cf. Dhruva, Vishnu, Nāgārjuna, Pythagoras, Rāja Yoga.

KOSHA [shell, wrapper, sheath; kosha, pos. from root kush=to embrace, enfold]. Man's various bodies are called koshas. Cf. Ānandamaya-, Annamaya-, Manomaya-, Pranamaya-, Vijnānamaya-.

KRISHNA [the dark one, pos. from root krish =to draw or attract to one's self, to draw into oneself and become master of]. The Eighth Avatāra of Vishnu; Teacher of the Bhagavad-Gītā and hero of the Bhāgavat; Lord of Devotion, the lodestar of Indian hearts. Cf. Bala-Rāma, Bhrigu, Bhūtesha, Hrishīkesa, Mādhva, Madhu-Sūdana, Rāsa-Mandala, Vaikuntha-Loka, Vasudeva.

KRISHNA-KIRANA [Krishna+Kirana, a ray or beam of light]. A son of the Sun-God who gave even his immortality to those who asked of him.

KRITA AGE [krita=accomplished, well-done, good]. The Good Age, the first or Golden Yuga, q.v.. Krita=the name of a die-face marked with four points, indicating the length of the age, according to the Purānas, 4,800 years of the gods=1,728,000 years of men. Cf. Satya.

KRITTIKĀ [from krit=to cut, divide]. The Pleiades, sometimes represented as a flame, or razor-edged knife; nymphs who nursed the god Kārtikeya.

KRIYĀ-SHAKTI [kriya=activity; action+ shakti=energy or power]. Technically, the power of creative thought or divine activity, one of the seven great potencies used by Yogis, and one of the five powers of the Divine.

KRONOS, Gr. [Time]. The God who swallows his children when born. Applied also to Saturn, son of Uranus, and father of Zeus-Jupiter, who dethroned him, Philologists, not realizing that child-races are taught by Divine Sages who incarnate for this purpose, find it difficult to believe the God Kronos, worshipped by a primitive people, stood for the abstraction

Time. Cf. Trimūrti, Cheiron, Cycle, Eternity Garuda, Kāla, Peshhun, Rhea, Titan.

KSHATRIYA [pos. from root kshi=to possess, have power over, rule]. The second or princely caste of India. Cf. Maru, Parashurāma.

KSHETRAJNA [kshetra=the soil+jna=knowing]. "Knowing the body," the soul or conscious principle in the corporeal frame. Cf. Ātmā, Jīva.

KUMĀRA [pos. from root kam=to wish or long for]. A Virgin Youth. *Theos.* Applied to the Eternal Virgin Youth and his Disciples, Venusian Adepts, who founded and head the Occult Hierarchy. See Sānat and Sevens. This term is also applied to certain higher classes of Pitris born from the limbs of Brahmā in the Ninth or special Creation, who refused to enter into generation, thus remaining virgin. Cf. Unity, Jāta, Ribhu, Shamballa, Shankarāchārya, Shukra, Vishnu, Vodhu.

KUMBHA-KARNA [the pitcher ear]. An epithet of a Rākshasa, brother of Rāvana. Also a name of Shiva.

KUNDALINI SHAKTI [kundalini=circular, spiral, coiling, pos. from root kun=to sound]. A form of Devī. *Theos.* The seven-layered power residing in the base of the spine which has its origin from the ascending force of the Third Logos, coming from the earth; it has three aspects Idā, Pingalā, and Sushumnā; in its milder form it is nerve force; its deepest layers quicken the body chakras. Cf. Caduceus, Sevens, Mother.

KUNTĪ, wife of Pāndu, the virgin mother of the Pāndavas, who through an incantation taught her by the sage Durvāsas, had a child by Sūrya, Krishna-Karna; by Dharma, Yudhishthira; by Vāyu, Bhīma; and by Indra, Arjuna; all Pandu Princes.

KŪRMA, the Tortoise Avatāra of Vishnu on whose back the mountain Mandara was supported at the churning of the ocean in the Amphibian Age.

KURUKSHETRA [field of the Kurus]. A region or extensive plain near Delhi, the scene of the great battles between the Kurus and Pāndus. The battle-ground of the Self in striving to gain control of matter. Hindu tradition places the body-field of Kurukshetra at the brow chakra. Cf. Duality, Vishvas.

KUSHA, a sacred fragrant grass; one of the great Dvīpas or continents.

KUVERA, KUBERA, [pos. from kumb=to cover; or ku=the earth+vera=body]. Lord of the earth, originally God of Dark Spirits, then God of riches and treasure, regent of the Northern quarter of the world. Cf. Idā, Kailāsa, Quaternary, Rāvana, Yakshas.

KWAN-SHAI-YIN, KWAN-SHI-YIN, KWAN-YIN, Chin. KWAN-NON or KWAN-JE-ON (Jap.) 33 Bodhisattvas, both male and female incarnations, all Gods of Mercy and Compassion, the chief of which was Avalokiteshvara. [Kuan=one who looks+yin=supplicatory sound+shi=world]. Cf. Vishnu, Chitkala.

L

LAKSHMI [a mark, sign or token, good fortune; der. (?) pos. root lag=to cling to or clasp, unite; or lanj=to shine or manifest. Wife or Shakti of Vishnu, Goddess of Prosperity and of the Lotus. Cf. Shrī, Trimūrti, Mother, Māhadevī, Padma.

LAMA, Tib. [the superior one]. Gurus or priests of equal rank in Northern Buddhist Monasteries. Cf. Dalai and Teshu Lamas.

LAMECH, Heb. [vigorous youth]. Descendant of Seth and father of Noah and Tubal-Cain.

LAMRIN, Tib. a sacred volume of precepts and rules, written by Tsong-Kha-Pa, "for the advancement of knowledge."

LANKĀ, pos. the island of Ceylon, though some accounts make this chief city of Rāvana famed in the Rāmāyana much larger than the present island. The first meridian of longitude passes through Lankā.

LANOO, Tib? Disciple or Chela.

LAO TZE or TZU, Chin. [the old-young]. The Chinese philosopher, born 604 B.C., who taught the Tao, the way of the Inner Life.

LAR, LARES (LASES), Lat. [akin to Skt. root las=to shine, glitter, dance, play, sound]. Tutelary deities, household gods whose images were placed in an interior shrine. Cf. Penates.

LATONA, Lat., LATO, LETO, Gr. daughter of the Titan Cœus and of Phœbe, and mother by Zeus of Apollo and Diana, sun and moon gods.

LAYA [Lī=to adhere, dissolve]. The act of union, sticking, adherence, embrace, melting, dissolution. A Laya Centre is a neutral or zero point of equilibrium where substance becomes homogeneous and static. Cf. Ālaya.

LEDA, LEDE, Gr. Mother by Jupiter in the form of a swan of Pollux and Helen, and Castor and Clytemnestra. Cf. Bird.

LEMURIA, The continent now submerged in the Pacific which, with portions of land still extant, was the home of the Third Race, remnants of whose architecture are to be seen on Easter Island. Cf. Cyclopes, Ham.

LETHE, Gr. [forgetfulness]. A river in the infernal regions whose waters gave forgetfulness of the past. Cf. Hades.

LEVIATHAN, Heb. [from Arab. Lawa=to bend or twist]. A huge aquatic animal; esoterically a creature of the deep, Deity as good and evil. Cf. Duality, Water.

LHA, Tib. Spirits of the highest spheres; given also as a term of respect to yogis, and saints.

LHAKANG, Tib. A temple or crypt for mystic ceremonies.

LHAMAYIN, Tib. Elemental sprites of lower terrestrial plane.

LIF and LIFTHRESIR in the Scandinavian *Edda* are the only sinless and innocent humans, allowed to survive in the world's renewal. Occult refers to sinking of Atlantis. Cf. Deluge, Noah.

LĪLĀ [der. (?) pos. from las=to shine, flash, coruscate, sound, play; or from lelāya=to quiver, move to and fro; or corrupted from krida=frolic or gambol]. The sport of the

Gods, particularly that of Shiva in his creative and destructive dance.

LILITH or LILATU, Ass. Heb. Lilu, Lilit and Ardat Lilit were three Assyrian storm demons. Later her character was changed from the "Holy dame," Lalla of the Arabs, to the maleficent demon of Hebrew lore, first wife of Adam, by whom spirits, devil, and *lilin* were procreated, half-human demons. Cf. Mother, Elementals.

LIMBO, Lat. [limbus=border]. According to Roman Catholic theology, the borders of hell in which pious souls who died before Christ's coming and unbaptised infants remain. Cf Hades.

LINGA, LINGAM [a mark, sign or token, Cf. lag=to cling to, clasp, unit]. Symbol of the Divine generative power of Shiva. Cf. Phallus Sacr'.

LINGA SHARIRA, the subtle or vital physical body, matrix of the gross visible body. The Etheric double, though sometimes applied to the astral body. Cf. Sthūla.

LINGYONI [linga+yoni, *q.v.*]. Cf. Duality.

LIPIKA [from lipī=to write]. The Four (and seven Great Scribes, Lords of Karma who assess man's deeds, and adjust his karma that the utmost advantage may be therefrom derived. Cf. Angels, Quaternary, Sevens.

LOGOS, Gr. [No exact equivalent in any language. Latin theology wavered between Sermo=a connected thing, speaking or talking; atio=reason (calculation or planning); and verbum=a word; finally accepting the latter for an orthodox translation. In Greek, Logos never refers to "word" as the name, but rather the innate substance or idea either expressible or expressed through the creative word]. The manifested Deity, who speaks the creative Word whereby universes spring into being and life. In *Theos.*, the three aspects of the Trimūrti, are spoken of as the *First Logos*, the Father or Power Aspect, the Three-in-One. Cf. Shiva; the *Second Logos*, the Dual Positive-Negative Power of Wisdom-Love, Cf Vishnu; the *Third Logos*, the One-in-Three, the Creator, Divine Intelligence or Activity, Cf. Brahmā. Though the order given in the Hindu Trimūrti varies from the above, the principles correspond.

LOHAN, LAHAN, Chin. Buddhist Hermit-Monks advanced on the Path of Holiness. Cf. Arhats.

LOHITA [red]. An epithet of Kārtikeya.

LOKA [open space, world, sky, heaven, a plane or division of the universe]. The seven lokas or planes of matter and consciousness, invoked in Gayatri, *q.v.*, are Bhūr-loka=the earth; Bhuvar-=the astral world; Svar-=the Heaven world or lower mental plane; Mahar-=causal or higher mental plane; janar-, tapar-, and satya-, considered by Dr. Besant to be divisions of the buddhic world. Some authorities consider the above lokas to correspond respectively to the seven planes or worlds, physical, astral, mental, buddhic, atmic or nirvanic, monadic, divine or ādi.

LOKI, Scand. the dark mischief-making God, shadow of Odin, Lord of Heaven. Cf. Ahriman. Typifies force or resistance.

LOTUS, a water-lily held sacred in the earliest scriptures of India and Egypt. Symbol of Perfect Manifestation both in Ideality and Expression. Cf. Padma, etc., Pundarīkaksha, Lakshmī, Pushkara.

LUCIFER, Lat. [light-bearer]. The planet Venus. Christian Theology, the principal fallen angel. Cf. Duality, Satan, Phosphoros, Prometheus.

LUNAR PITRIS [moon fathers]. Those beings who, having achieved mind on the Moon, assisted Earth in form-building.

M

MĀ [mother, measure, light, Lakshmī, etc.]

MA, MOOT, MŪT, Egy. Isis, the Eternal Mother, as Goddess of the Lower World.

MACROPROSOPUS, Kab. [compound Gr. word=Vast or Great Countenance]. Kether, *q.v.* Cf. Microposopus, Duality.

MĀDHAVA [Mā+Dhava=husband, or Lord of, honey-like, through madhu from mad=to be drunk with joy; vernal, spring-like]. An epithet of Krishna.

MADHU-SŪDANA [see above]. Destroyer of honey, a bee; Krishna as destroyer of the Demon Madhu.

MADHYA [midmost] "That whose commencement and end are unknown" *S.D.* Cf. Unity.

MADHYAMĀ [midmost, central]. The fourth swara of the Hindu tonal gamut. *S.D.* Beginningless, Endless. Cf. Unity.

MĀDHYAMIKAS, a sect of Buddhist atheists.

MAGA, Per. [magian, priest of Surya, the Sun-God].

MĀGHA [gift, wealth, power]. Geart Bear Constellation. Cf. Rishis.

MAGI, plural of MAGUS, Lat. Magian Persian Priests and Wise men [der. (?) pos. from Skt. Mahā, corrupted to mog or magu, in Pehlevi=great]. Astrologers and workers of magic.

MAHA [substitute for Mahat=great, mighty, strong, from MAH=to be great]. Cf. Chohan.

MAHĀCHOHAN [mighty lord; Chohan, *q.v.*]. Title applied to the Over-Lord of Rays. Commander-in-Chelf of Nature's Forces. Cf. Trimūrti, Arghyanāth.

MAHĀBHĀRATA [The Great War of the Bhāratas]. An epic poem which includes the *Bhagavad-Gītā, q.v.*

MAHĀMĀYĀ [great illusion]. Of separateness; also that which makes the phenomenal universe appear as reality to the senses. Cf. Māyā, Ahamkara.

MAHĀRĀJĀS—Four great Beings, agents of the Lipika, *q.v.* and Lords of Form. Cf. Quaternary.

MAHAT [see Mahā]. Universal Intelligence and Consciousness, the producer of "I-am-I" or a sense of separated existence. Cf. Egoism, Ahamkāra, Duality, Mahāt-tatva, Nous.

MAHĀTALA [tala, *q.v.*] 2nd Infernal Loka.

MAHATMĀ [Ātmā *q.v.*]. An Adept.

MAHĀT-TATTVA CREATION [the great state of being]. First creation, " self-evolution of Mahat." Cf. Tattva.

MAHĀVISHNU, the One Supreme Lord above the trinitarian expression of Shiva, Vishnu, Brahmā.

MAHĀYĀNA [greater vehicle]. Applied to Northern Buddhism because it includes a greater range of teaching than the Hīnayāna.

MAIA, MAYA, MARIA, MARY, all names applied to Goddesses who have typified the mother principle. Cf. Māyā, Mūlaprakriti, Chaos.

MAIMONIDES, Heb. (Moses ben Maimon). Talmudist, philosopher and physician, 1135-1204 A.D.

MAITREYA [from mitra, *q.v.*]. The Compassionate and Friendly Lord, the present Bodhisattva. In Northern Buddhism regarded as one of the Bodhisattvas under the Dhyāni Buddha, Vajra-Sattva.

MAKARA [a sea monster or crocodile regarded as emblem of Kāma-deva, god of love]. Tenth Sign of the Zodiac Capricorn, and Tenth Creative Hierarchy.

MAKARA-KETU [having a fish on his banner]. Kāma, see Makara.

MALACHIM, Heb. Messengers or Angels. Cf. Urion.

MALKUTH, Heb. Queen of Heaven, tenth Sephira. Cf. Mother.

MANAS [from man=to think or believe, mind, intelligence, understanding]. Regarded in Hindu philosophy as a 5th or synthesizing sense. *Theos.* the third highest of man's principles. Cf. Antahkarana, Psyche, Taijasa.

MĀNASAPUTRAS [sons of mind]. A term applied to the Monads and others. Cf. Putras.

MANDALA [from root mand=to clothe, surround, etc.] Circle, globe, wheel; a mystical diagram in which are drawn symbols representing aspects of Divinity and used in invoking the Gods. Cf. Yoga, Rāsa Mandala, Sarva-Mandala, Zodiac.

MĀNES, Lat. [akin to Skt. Mah=to be great]. The worshipped ones: the benevolent ones; deified souls of departed; also Gods of the Lower World; ghosts, shades, spirits of dead.

MANETHO [Mā-en-Tehuti=Gift of Thoth]. A Greco-Egyptian writer whose history of Egypt was written after 271 B.C.

MANICHÆANS, Lat. A sect of the third century which believed in two eternal principles —Good and Evil. Cf. Duality.

MANJUSRI [through manju=beautiful from manj=to purify or sound; of Gentle Glory; fuller form is Manjughosha=Glorious Gentle-Voiced One, Tibetan Hgam-dpal (pron. Jampal) co-Bodhisattva with Avalokiteshvara under the Dhyāni Buddha, Amitābha]. God of Mystic Wisdom, Buddhist Apollo. Cf. Vishnu.

MANOJAVA [swift as thought]. Name of Indra in the sixth Manvantara. Name of one of the seven tongues of flame. Cf. Agni.

MANOMAYAKOSHA [mental sheath]. The middle sheath or body of the Vedānta classification. Cf. Kosha.

MANTRA, MANTRAM[instrument of thought, sacred speech; der. (?) pos. from man=to think or create+tra=to protect. Cf. also man=to sound]. A series of syllables which, when correctly intoned, unleash potent forces. Cf. Om, and also OM, MANI PADME HŪM! Gāyatri. Cf. Oeaohoo, Svāhā, Sādhya, Sepher-Yetzirah, Veda, Yajur-Veda.

MANU[from man=to think or create].The MAN par excellence, Father of the Human Race. The term in occultism is generic and is applied to " creators and fashioners " of each racial type; the seven root-Manus and seven seed-Manus; Chain-Manus, etc., up to the LOGOS Himself. Vaivasvata Manu, of the Fifth or Aryan Race gave the code of laws and ethics still followed in India. The Manu, Chakshusha, is still the leader of the Fourth Atlantean or Mongolian Race. Cf. Pitris, Manvantara, Agastya, Agnibāhu, Prāchetasas, Priyavratā, Raivata, Sarvanā, Svarnchisha.

MĀNUSHA, MĀNUSHI, MĀNUSHYA [belonging to or propitious to mankind]. A Mānushī Buddha, as contrasted with a Dhyāni-Buddha, *q.v.*, is one who incarnates on earth to teach mankind.

MANVANTARA [the period presided over by a Manu]. According to *Manu*, I. 79, this period comprises 71 great Yugas held equal to 12,000 years of the gods or 4,320,000 human years, or 1/14th of a day of Brahmā. Cf. Parārdha, Cycle, Sandhya, Ūrja, Pralāya.

MAQUOM, Chal.[secret place]. Kabalistic for Shrine, Womb of the World, the human womb, etc. Cf. N'cabvah, Mother.

MĀRA[through mār=killer to root Mri=to die]. The embodiment of Desire, Kāma, which causes birth and death. The Tempter.

MĀRGA [the search, the seeking; Cf. mrig=to pursue, investigate]. The Path of Holiness, through which man attains expression of Divinity. Cf. Christos, initiation, Pāramitās, Tao.

MARĪCHI [ray of light] Name of a Prajāpati, (*Manu*, I. 35) first of the ten lords engendered by the first Manu Svayambhuva. Cf. Rishis, Sambhūti.

MARĪCHI [pertaining to Marīchi]. Son of, etc. A Buddhist Goddess, Queen of Heaven, mother of Shākyamuni. Cf. Gautama.

MĀRISHA, MĀRSHA, [respectful mode of address to a venerable person]. Mother of Daksha, an Apsara.

MARK, ST., Gr. Evangelist and author of one of the *New Testament* gospels.

MARS [Cf. Māra]. The Gr. Ares, the old Roman god of war, son of Jupiter and Juno. The Sanskrit planet Kuja. Cf. Planetary Spirits, Kārtikeya, Nergal-Serezer, Phobos, Sabaoth, Sephira, Set. Thor.

MĀRTANDA [Mārttanda, Mārtānda from mrit-anda=a seemingly lifeless egg, *i.e.*, a bird produced from seemingly lifeless egg]. *S.D.* the Eighth or Central Aditya, the Sun-God. Cf. Bal-i-lu, Sūrya, Hiranya-Garbha, Ialdabaoth.

MARU [the desert wilderness, asceticism]. Son of King Shīgra, the Speedy One. *S.D.* a corruption of the name of Morya, he who is to restore the Kshatriya race of the Solar Dynasty.

MARUT [der. (?) pos. root mri=to die or kill; or obsolete root mar=to shine]. Gods of the winds and storms, sons and brothers of Indra, or sons of Rudra and Prishni (the many-coloured earth).

MARUT-VAT, MARUT-VAN, etc. [attended by the Maruts]. A term applied to Indra, Vāyu, Vishnu, Sarasvatī, Agni, Soma, etc.

MASORETIC POINTS, Heb. a system of symbols used to indicate the vowel sounds to be given the vowelless Hebrew consonantal words.

MASSORAH, Masorah, Heb. [der.(?) from root =to bind or root=to hand down]. Traditional system of registration of words, consonants, vowels, etc.

MĀTRI-PADMĀ [Mother-Lotus]. The Great Feminine Receptive or Mother Principle.

MĀYĀ [der. (?) pos. from mā=to measure, form, create; or man=to think or create+ya=air, wind, he who moves]. The principle of illusion, philosophically matter as veiling spirit. Cf. Mahāmāyā, Duality, Mother, Mūlaprakriti.

MĀYĀVI RŪPA [illusory form]. A temporary vehicle created for use in the subtle worlds.

MAZDA, MAZDĀO, MAZDEAN, MAZDHĀ, see Ahura Mazda.

MELCHIZEDEK, Heb. [king of righteousness]. King of Salem and priest of the Most High in the time of Abraham, to whom the Father of the Jews gave homage.

MELEK, Heb. [singular of Malachim].

MEMRA, MEMRAB, MIMRA, Heb. [= Ma'amar or Dibbur]. The Logos, or creative and directive Word.

MENDES, MENDESIUS, Egy. Ram-headed god Ammon, later in Christian theology erroneously held to be a demon-goat worshipped by Masons. Cf. Aries under Zodiac, Pan, Satyras, Kreios under Titans.

MERCABAH, MERKABAH, MERCAVAH, Heb. [chariot]. The cherubim, or fiery cloud-birds, heavenly Throne-Chariot on which YHVH, rode; those Hierarchies of Beings through whom the Divine came into manifestation. Cf. Vahan, Birds, Metatron, Shekinah, Vimāna.

MERCURY, Lat. see Hermes, and Planetary Logoi.

MERODACH, Chal. God of Babylon, son of Davkina, goddess of the nether regions and earth and Hea God of the Seas and Hades. Esoterically, God of Wisdom. Cf. Oannes. Vishnu, Water.

MEROPE, Gr. One of the Pleiades.

MERU [from mi=to throw out light]. The cup or lotus seed-vessel, each of whose leaves are the Dvīpas; Mystic Mount, Home of the Gods. Its height is 84,000 Yojanas, 16,000 of which are rooted in the earth. Cf. Olympus, Vaikuntha-Loka.

MESHIA and MESHIANE, Zend. The first human couple of the early Persian system. Cf. Adam and Eve.

METATRON, Heb.; METATOR, Gr. [palace or Holy Place, metator=guide]. Divine Charioteer Youth, Archangel of the Presence, identified with both Enoch and Michael. To man he imparted knowledge of heaven, the past and future. Cf. Mithra, Angels.

METEMPSYCHOSIS, Gr. [meta=change+empsychosis=of the animating soul]. The transmigration of the soul after death into some other body. Vulgarly thought to be rebirth from human into animal form.

METHUSHAEL, METHUSELAH, Heb. [man of the dart. Bab. man of God]. Probably both are symbols of a long-lived patriarch, actually referring to an epoch.

METIS, Gr. [Wisdom, Skill]. One of the primal Gods identified with the bi-sexual Eros, God of Love, child of Chaos. Also the first wife of Zeus, destined to bear first Athena, and then a Super-Lord. Zeus swallowed Metis, and himself gave birth to Athena. Cf. Duality, Mother, Jupiter, Vishnu.

MICHAEL, MIKAEL, Heb. [Who is like El?]. Chief Archangel, Viceroy of God, sitting on the right of God's throne. (Gabriel, *q.v.*). He is Prince of Snow, in which is the element fo Water; the Angel of Silver, and of the South Wind. In one passage he is identified with Fire. In some Hebrew MSS. he is identified with the presiding deity of Mercury; in others with Saturn. Swiftest and most powerful of the Angels, he was held by Israel as its guardiane One of the holy Four who will survive the destruction of all other creatures. Cf. Thraetona, Quaternary, Hermes, Planetary Spirits.

MICROPROSOPUS, Kab. [compound Gr. word=small countenance]. Cf. Macroprosopus, Microcosm, Duality.

MIDGARD, Scan. The great snake in the *Eddas* which gnaws roots of Yggdrasil, the Tree of Life and the Universe. Cf. Serpent, Nidhog.

MIDRASHIM, Heb. [studies or investigations]. The ancient Scriptures of Hebraism.

MIMIR, Scan. The guardian giant or Titan of the well of Primeval Wisdom through which Odin acquired Supreme Knowledge of Past, Present and Future, Vishnu.-

MĪNA, MĪNAM [a fish, pos. from mī=to lessen, diminish, reduce, annihilate]. 12th sign of Zodiac, Pisces.

MISHNA, MISHNAH, Heb. [oral teaching]. Now applied particularly to collection made by R. Judah ha-Nasi which constitues the basis of the Talmud.

MITHRA, MITHRAS, MITRA, old form MITTRA [friend, from mid=to melt, love, expand; or from mith=to unite or pair as polar opposites]. Mitra in the Vedic Pantheon was one of the seven earliest Āditya, presiding over Day, calling all to activity, beholding all with unwinking eye, sustaining earth and sky, Primordial Light. The Persian Mithra is a Sevens-Rayed Saviour Sun-God of Justice who destroys the forces of darkness. The Mysteries of Mithra, having their origin in esoteric teachings of the first Zarathustra, 29,700 B.C., became in later millennia

the secret Masonry of the Roman soldier, the initiates of which were bound into a mystic body as ascetic soldiers of Light and Truth. Cf. Duality, Metatron, Ray, Sudyumna, Sūrya.

MIZRAIM, Egy. Ancient name of Egypt. A very old Masonic rite.

MLECHCHHA [root mlechh=to speak confusedly or unintelligibly]. Foreigner, barbarian, non-Āryan.

MOBED, Zend. Parsi or Zoroastrian Priest. Cf. Magi.

MOKSHA, MUKTA, MUKTI [from much through moksh=to loosen, set free, liberate]. Regarded as deliverance from the thraldom of life in form. Cf. Jīvanmukta.

MOLECH, MOLOCH, MELECH, Heb. [King]. An early Semitic God, whose rites finally degenerated into child sacrifice by fire; the ordeal of fire originally meant for the trials of initiation of the " little children", initiates. Cf. Agni.

MONAD, MONAS, Gr. [monas=alone, solitary, single, a unit]. A unitary element assumed by Leibnitz. In occultism, the one indivisible Self, the integral sparks from the Parent flame or MONAD. Used also of any unit of consciousness from an atom to a Solar System. Cf. Mānasaputras, Ātmā, Ego, Zodiac.

MOON, [through Anglo-Saxon mona=the measurer from mā=to measure, make, form, produce, create, the base for Mātā, Mother, the Moon]. Occultism recognizes the Moon as a former living planet, the literal mother of the Planet Earth, from which its substance was derived. Cf. Astarte, Atalanta, Brahmāndika, Chandrabhāgā, Chandragupta, Diana, Graha-Rāja, Hagar, Hatha-Yoga, Hekate, Hesperides, Ishtar, Latona, Lunar Pitris, Mooth, Nakshatras, Nanak, Phœbe, Purūravas, Qū'tāmy, Rāhu, Rāma, Riksha, Sabbath, Sabean, Samael, Sephira, Serapis, Sin, Sinai, Tao (1), Selene under Titan, Zarpanitu.

MOOTH, MOUT, MUT, Egy. Mother, q.v. primordial Goddess. Astronomically, the Moon.

MORYA. Cf. Maru. A Dynasty of Indian Princes. A Chohan heading the First Ray or Ray of Will.

MOSES, Egy.-Heb. [if the name is Egyptian pos. from mesh=child; if Hebrew=deliverer, saviour]. Law-giver and Initiate; adopted prince of Egypt who led his people from the land of Egyptian (materiality) into the heavenly land of Canaan.

MŌT (Tyrrhenian, Phœn.) Chaos, q.v.

MOTHER or feminine shakti aspect of theDivine is to be found in the following Goddesses: Aditī, Annapurna, Aphrodite, Astarte, Athena, Ātmamātra, Chaos, Demeter, Eva, Eve, etc., He, Hekate, Hera, Hesperides, Ida, Ilmatar, Io, Ishtar, Isis, Kanyā,Kuntī,Lakshmi,Latona, Leda, Lilith, Ma, Maia, Malkuth, Maquom, Mārichi,Mārisha, Mater, Mātri-Padmā, Māyā, Metis, Moon, Mooth, N'cabvah, Neïth, Nemesis, Nephthys, Noot, Norn, Nux, Pasht, Prakriti, Prithivī, Pyrrha, Rhea, Ru, Sarasvathī, Sarva-Mandala, Sati, Savarnā, Shakti and references, Shrī, Surasā, Svāsā, Umā,

Ushas, Vāch, Venus, Vesta, Vinatā, Yoni, Zarpanitu, Zipporah. Cf. also the Creative Gods, and Duality.

MUKHYA [originating from the mouth or head, Chief, primary]. S.D. Fourth Creation, " Fundamental Creation of perceptible things, . . . things immovable."

MŪLAPRAKRITI [mūla=root+prakriti, q.v.]. The original root or germ out of which all matter or form was evolved. Cf. Unity, Māyā, Plane, Prima Materia, Protomateria, Protyle, Shekinah.

MUSPEL, Scan. The Fire-god in the Edda. Cf. Agni.

MYALBA, Tib. exoterically=Hell; esoterically =the earth for those who must reincarnate. Cf. Hell, Hades.

N

NABATHEANS, NABATAEAN, an ancient kingdom to the east and southeast of Palestine, lasting from about 312 B.C. to 106 A.D.

NABHASTALA [nabhas=sky, atmosphere from nabh=to bind, connect (heaven and earth) tala=the lower part of]. Lower atmosphere.

NĀBHI [pos. from nabh=to bind or connect], Any navel-like cavity, point of concentration, or of focus. Grandson of Priyavratā, son of Agnīdhara and Father of Rishabha, Bhārata.

NĀDI [root nada=a species of hollow reed]. A hollow stalk or tubular organ, applied not only to physical but ethero-psychic channels for force. Cf. Chakra, Od, Brahmarandhra.

NĀGA [pos. from dah=to burn or consume by fire. Cf. naga=mountain, seven, serpent, sun; nagna=naked]. A Serpent, human-faced, under the rule of Sesha, q.v. Esoterically, wise Adepts or Rishis, as the Serpent is ever a symbol of Wisdom. Cf. Kadrū, Kāliya, Parāshara, Pulastya, Sutala, Ulūpī.

NĀGA DVIPA [see nāga and dvipa]. Said to be Nagpur and its environs in ancient days, wherein were the early Atlantean initiate Rajputs, " half-men, half-demons " which the Brahmans found when first coming to India.

NĀGĀRJUNA [nāga, q.v.+arjuna=to shine]. The first great Buddhist teacher of the Amitābha, doctrine. Born 223 B.C.

NAHUATLS, a very old civilization of Central Mexico including the Aztecs.

NAKSHATRAS [naksha=to approach+tra=to guard]. the 27 or (28?) lunar asterisms, considered to be the abodes of the gods and their devotees. Cf. Moon, Olympus, Pūrvāshādhā.

NANNAK, NANNAR, Ass. [the illuminator]. The moon god Sin, Lord of wisdom, dispeller of darkness, giver of dreams, worshipped in Ur and Harran, Babylonia. Vishnu, Name of the founder and first Guru of the Sikh religion.

NANDĪ [root nand=to be or cause joy]. The sacred Bull, vāhan of Shiva and Parvati, vehicle of the God's Bliss. Cf. Zodiac sign Taurus, q.v. The sacred AUM, the Guna Tamas. Cf. Serapis, Surabhi, Rishabha.

NARA [der. nri=leader from nī=to guide]. Man, male, the original or eternal Man, divine imperishable Spirit. Cf. Ātmā, Unity, Sādhya.

NĀRA [from nara, *q.v.* relating to men]. Also primordial waters. Nārāyana, *q.v.*

NĀRADA [Der. (?) Cf. Nāra and da=to give.] One of the seven great Rishis, and ten great Prajāpatis, regarded as inventor of the Vīnā. *S.D.* a Dhyān Chohan, *q.v.* Cf. Pesh-hun.

NARAKA [said to be from nri=to lead]. A purgatorial state of torment. Cf. Hades.

NARA-SIMHA [man-lion]. The fourth Avatāra of Vishnu, when he descended to war with Hiranyakashipu. That transition period in which Divine Life passed from Mammal to Man. Cf. Panchāshikha, Ra, Leo under Zodiac.

NĀRĀYANA [nāra, *q.v.*+ayana=going to]. Vishnu, the primordial Saviour, or Creative-Preservative Spirit or Life-Principle, moving toward expression in form out of the waters of Chaos.

NAROS, NEROS, Heb. an occult cycle of six hundred years, each of which was an epoch of time.

NARTHEX, Gr. [a tall umbelliferous plant with a hollow pithy stalk, by means of which Prometheus conveyed the spark of fire from heaven to earth]. A wand given to candidates for initiation, symbol of the spinal column. Cf Caduceus.

NĀSTIKA [na-asti or non-existence]. Atheist.

NĀTH [to ask for and have power to give boons; to be master, refuge, protector, helper]. Lord.

NAYA [from root nī=to lead, guide, direct, govern]. Orderly conduct of life. *S.D.* harmony.

NAZAR, NAZARITE, Heb. Set apart, dedicated, either for life or for a definite period of yoga.

NAZARENE, an early Christian-Jewish Sect, considered heretical by both Jews and Christians.

N'CABVAH, Heb. [n'cab=to hollow]. Female genital organ, Feminine Principle. Cf. Duality, Maquom, Mother, Yoni.

NEBO, NABU, Ass. [the announcer]. God of Wisdom and Agriculture. From the God was derived the name of Mount Nebo from which Moses first saw the promised land, Canaan.

NEBUCHADNEZZAR, NEBUCHADREZZAR II, Bab. [more correctly Nabuchodonosor, originally Nabu-kudurri-usur-Bab=O Nebo, defend my crown (empire or work)]. King of Babylon from 604 to 561 B.C., capturing Jerusalem, invading Egypt, and rebuliding Babylon.

NEÏTH, Egy. a goddess armed with bow and arrows, mother of Ra. Worshipped also in Sais and Libya. Cf. Ammon.

NEO-PLATONISM, Gr. [new-Platonism]. A philosophy which attempted to connect the teachings of Plato and Aristotle with the Eastern Wisdom. The Theosophy of the early Christian era, founded by Ammonius Saccas 175-250 A.D. with such representatives as Plotinus, Iamblichus, Proclus, Porphyry, etc.

NEPHESH, Heb. [soul, divine breath of life]. *H.P.B.* "This term is used very loosely in the *Bible.* It generally means Prana "life"; in

the *Kabalah* it is the animal passions and the animal Soul." Cf. Kāma.

NEPHILIM, Heb. [singular Nephal]. Giant demi-gods produced by union of Bene Elohim or Sons of God with "the daughters of men." Hence the "fallen ones." Cf. Angels, Titans.

NEPHTHYS, Egy. [Nebt-het=lady of the house]. Daughter of Seb and Nut, sister and wife of Set, the dark-shadow brother of Osiris. Nephthys is likewise the dark aspect of Isis, with whom she is often identified. Cf. Duality, Mother.

NEPTUNE, Lat. [akin to neptomai=to bathe]. Son of Saturn and Ops; God of the Waters, especially the Sea. Identified with Poseidon, Cf. Varuna, Oannes. The Planet farthest away from the Sun, held by science and some occultists to be a Solar Planet. In *S.D.* said to have some extra-solar function. Cf. Proteus, Triton.

NEREID, NEREUS, Gr. [neros=water. Cf. Skt. nāra]. Nereids, daughters of Nereus, a Water God, fifty or one hundred in number were water nymphs, attendants of Poseidon.

NERGAL-SEREZER, NERGAS, Bab-Ass. Title of Nergal, one of the great gods. Lord of the Midsummer sun, destructive fire, supreme lord of Death, God of the chase. Cf. Mars, Yama, Agni.

NESHAMAH, Heb. [breath, wind, soul or source of intelligence, spiritual inspiration of God in man]. *Kabalah,* one of three highest essences of Human Soul corresponding to Binah. Cf. Trimūrti.

NIDĀNA [ni-dā=to give out correctly].Primary cause of essence. In Buddhism, the twelve causes of finite existence; each one arising out of the other progressively: Avidyā, Ignorance; Samskāra, forms; Vijnāna, consciousness; Nāmarūpa, name and bodiness; Chadayātana, the senses and their objects; Sparsa, contact; Vedanā, feeling; Trishnā, thirst; Upādāna, clinging; Bhava, becoming; Jāti, birth; Jarāmarana, age and sorrow. These are sometimes given in reverse order. Cf. Adi-Nidāna Svabhāvat, Tanhā, Skandhas.

NIDHOG, NIDHOGGR, NITHHOGG, Icel. the serpent that gnaws at the root of Yggdrasil. Cf. Midgard.

NIFLHEIM, Icel. Cold Hell of the Scandinavian Eddas. Cf. Hades.

NĪLAKANTHA [blue-throated]. Name applied to Shiva, who took the posion of the world into Himself, for its transmutation.

NĪLA-LOHITA [purple or blue+red.] A name of Rudra-Shiva.

NIMROD, Heb. [der. (?) pos. Namra Udu= shining light.] Two principal theories are prevalent: 1. That Nimrod is the Babylonian hero Izdubar; 2. that Nimrod is the Babylonian Mercury, Marduk-Bel. Others think he represents the constellation of Orion; others a tribe. Always he is the prototype of the rebel. Cf. Duality, Hermes.

NIRGUNA [stringless, as a bow]. Without attributes, the Supreme Being. Cf. Unity.

NIRMĀNAKĀYA [nirmāna=measuring, producing, creating; with Buddhist, transformation+kāya=body]. The third great vesture in Northern Buddhism assumed by Buddhas who would incarnate to save the world. *Occult.* the path of those Adepts who remain as the guardian-wall of humanity to fill the spiritual reservoir of power for its use. As they do not give up Their permanent atoms (nuclei of the bodies of the various planes), They can, if needed, come into physical incarnation. This term is also loosely used of the whole Hierarchy of Adepts who remain in physical incarnation to help and guide the world. Cf. Dharmakāya and Sambhogakāya, Trimūrti.

NIR-MATHYA [to be rubbed or agitated; fire produced by friction]. One of the three great fire Gods. Cf. Pavamāna, Agni.

NIRUKTA [uttered, explained, defined]. A Vedic Glossary.

NIRVĀNA [nir (nis)=out, forth, away from+vā =to blow (as the wind) to move, to be agitated. By some vā is said to be from av-ā=to desire or satisfy; by others vai=to be languid, weary, extinguished]. With the uncertain derivation, many meanings are given: blowing out, cooling, disappearance, refreshment, comfort, repose, serenity. The teaching of obtaining liberation from the thraldom of sensual existence in a state of Nirvāna, given by the Lord Buddha, is not a doctrine of annihilation but fulfilment whereby the Nirvāni reaching the consciousness of the plane of Divine Causation (variously called "Spiritual," "Ātmic," and "Nirvānic,") *knows* himself as the One and all its effect, thereby forever losing the illusion of the existence of a separated personality, *q.v.* Instead of being annihilation, such a state is one of supreme conscious Bliss. Cf. Paranirvāna, Unity, Adept, Arhat, Sambhogakāya, Tārakā, Rājayoga, Yong Grüb.

NISHĀDA [sitting at the altar (inactive); root nishad=to sink down into, the time of rest, or night]. The seventh movable swara or tone in the Hindu gamut=ti of western sol-fa system.

NĪTI [guidance, direction, Prudence].

NITYA [own; Vedic=perpetual, eternal, everlasting].

NOAH, Heb. [rest, comfort]. A patriarch who at God's command built an ark to save himself and family from a universal deluge. *Theos.* the fathers of the Fifth or Āryan race saved at the time the remnants of Atlantis were submerged. Cf. Shem, Ham, Lamech, Lif, Pyrrha.

NOOT, Egy. Heavenly abyss. Cf. Aditi, Chaos, Isis, Seb, Toom.

MORN, Icel. [plural nornir]. One of the three demi-goddesses, giantesses, spinners, presiding over the past, present, and future fate of mankind. Cf. Karma.

NOUS, Gr. [mind]. A Platonic term for the Supreme Intelligence; in man the Spirit or Conscious Self. Cf. Unity, Mahat, Psyche, Pymander.

NUMBERS, See Unity, Duality, Trinity, Tetraktys, Quaternary, Tetragrammaton, Sesquitertia, Sesquialtera, Quinary, Pentacle, Senary, Sapta, Sevens, Ogdoad, Jod, Alhim, Amen, Senzar.

NUNTIUS, Lat. Messenger, name given to Mercury. Cf. Hermes.

NUX, NYX, Gr. [Night]. Daughter of Chaos, and mother of Day and Light. Cf. Duality.

NYĀYA [method, rule, doctrine, logic]. A celebrated system of Hindu philosophy delivered by Gautama or Gotama in a set of aphorisms. The Logical School. Cf. Darshanas, Rishis, Vidyā.

NYINGPO, see Ālaya, for which it is the Tibetan equivalent.

O

OAN, OANNES, Bab. Dagon, *q.v.* A deity, Fish-Man, who taught the Babylonians their civilization. Probably Ea, *q.v.* Cf. Matsya Avatar under Vishnu, Water.

ŌB Heb. [root ūb=to be hollow]. The hollow belly of conjurers in which it was believed the conjuring spirit Ōb resided. The evil currents in the astral light *q.v.* Cf. Duality.

OD [coined by Reichenbach from the Gr. odos =pathway or channel]. Various electric and magnetic forces in their passage. Cf. Chakra, Nādī.

ODIN, Scan. Supreme Deity of Norse Pantheon. Especially a God of Wisdom. Cf. Woden. Vishnu, Loki, Mimir, Valhalla, Unity, Duality.

OEAOHOO, OEAOHU, Occult mantram, name for the seven-vowelled Universal Principle. (see Stanzas, Vol. 1). See Oi-ha-hou, Sevens, Parināmin.

OG, Heb. Giant King of Bashan conquered by Moses.

OGDOAD, Gr. [eight]. A Gnostic term for Eight Divine Æons or Spiritual Powers. Cf. Numbers.

OGHAM Cel. A runic alphabet developed by the Druids for a sacred cipher. Each character consists of from one to five thin straight lines or strokes symmetrically arranged with regard to a common transverse line.

OI-HA-HOU, *S.D.* "permutation of Oeaohoo, [*q.v.*] Literal signification . . . among Eastern Occultists of the North, a circular wind, whirlwind . . . ceaseless and eternal Cosmic Motion, or rather the Force that moves it . . . the eternal Kārana, the ever-acting Cause." Cf. Mantram, Chakra, Creative, Vāyu, Fohat, Unity.

OLYMPUS, Gr. A mountain in Thessaly believed by the ancient Greeks to be the abode of the high Gods. Cf. Eden, Hyperborean, Kailasa, Kalāpa, Meru, Nakshatras, Parnassus, Plenum, Sinai, Vaikuntha-Loka, Dvīpas and Varshas, Jupiter.

ŌM MANI PADME HŪM! [ŌM, see Aum; MANI=the Jewel; also the positive Male Principle, from root man=to sound; PADME =Padma, the Lotus, der. (?) from padmat=rich in stalks or pad=to fall, to attain; HŪM=a mantram syllable of power. Many six-syllabled Tibetan mantrams begin with Ōm and end with Hūm]. "Hail to the Jewel in

the Lotus! " or " Hail to Him who is the Jewel in the Lotus! " The essence mantra of Chenresi (Avalokiteshvara, *q.v.*), the patron-god of Tibet, said to liberate even those who recite it in ignorance of its hidden significances. But see *S.D.* Vol. 5, pp. 418 *et seq.* Cf. Duality.

OMOROKA, Chal. The divine Waters and their Goddess, reflection of Wisdom. Cf. Chaos.

OPHIOMORPHOS, Gr. [having the form of a Serpent]. The embodied Serpent of Wisdom or Serpent Christ, Ophis-Christos, Christos.

OPHIS, Gr. [the Serpent of Wisdom]. Agathodaemon. Wisdom in Eternity.

OPHIS-CHRESTOS. Gr. [Ophis + Chrestos, *q.v.*].

OPHITE, OPHIDEAN, Gr. [like a serpent]. A group of sects, including the Naassenes (Naaseni) and Perates, of Gnostics, who revered the serpent as the symbol of Divine Creative Wisdom. Also Peratae.

ORCUS, Lat. [that hems in or confines]. The Lower World, Purgatory, Abode of the Dead, and its God Pluto. Cf. Hades.

ORIGEN of Alexandria, who lived in the 3rd century, one of the most learned of the Greek Fathers. He believed in the threefold interpretation of Scripture, in the pre-existence or reincarnation of spirit, and ultimate salvation.

ORION, Gr. [Urion=from the water of the Gods, later corrupted to Orion]. Born of the Earth, he was a celebrated hunter, killed by Artemis. The Constellation Orion. Cf. Nimrod, Diana.

ORMAZD, Zend. [Pahlavi corruption of Auharmazd or Ahura Mazda, *q.v.*].

ORPHEUS, Gr. A great teacher about 7,000 B.C., who gave to the Ancient Greeks the teaching of Harmony. It was said his lyre could charm the savage beasts and cause the rocks and trees to move.

ORPHIC MYSTERIES, orginated by Orpheus, though gradually becoming corrupted, survived to the time of hisotrical Greece where their essential teaching was that the initiate might by pure life and asceticism achieve mystic identification with the Divine Nature. Cf. Apollo, Phorminx.

OSIRIS, Egy. Lord of Light and Resurrection (hence called by some Lord of the Dead). First Person of the Egyptian Trinity, Osiris-Isis-Horus. The Cult of Osiris dates from the time of Hermes Thrice-greatest. 40,000 B.C. Cf. Set, Duality.

OTZ, Heb. [tree]. Otz-Chiim=the Tree of Life showing the progression of the Potencies known as the Ten Sephiroth.

OULAM, OULOM, Heb. An indefinite time of extended duration. Cf. Eternity.

·P·

PACHACAMAC, Peru. [Pacha=the world + camac der. camar=to animate]. " Soul of the Universe," " the One who gives life to the Universe and causes it to subsist ", " the one adored in the heart "—de la Vega. Cf. Ālayā, Unity.

PADMA [der. (?) pos. from pad-mat=rich in stalks; said to be from pad=to fall, go, attain, participate in, turn one's self toward; a foot. Cf. pada=step]. The Lotous Flower, a symbol of Perfection in Manifestation of the Divine. Cf. " Ōm Mani Padme Hūm," Lakshmi, Padmayoni, Paranishpanna.

PADMAPĀNI [Padma, *q.v.* Lotus-handed or bearing a Lotus Flower]. Cf. Avalokiteshvara, Brahmā, Vishnu.

PADMAYONI [padma=lotus + yoni=womb]. Cf. Abjayoni. Lotus-born; Sprung from a Lotus; an epithet of Brahmā.

PAHLAVI, PEHLEVI [Persian Pahlavi from Old Persian Parthava, Parthia]. The middle-Persian language from 3rd to 10th century A.D.

PĀLI [row, line, series of Buddhist sacred texts]. An ancient dialect of Sanskrit preserved as a medium of sacred Buddhist writings.

PALINGENESIS, Gr. [palin=again + genesis=born]. Regeneration, rebirth.

PAN, Gr. [All]. An ancient God represented with the ears, horns and feet of a goat, symbol of the All-ensouling Spirit of Nature. Cf. Mendes, Unity.

PANCHADASHA [fifteen]. Half month, full or new moon; certain Vedic hymns uttered by Brahmā at creation, from the five vowels. Cf. Quinary.

PANCHAMA [the fifth]. Beautiful, brilliant, pleasing; the fifth swara or tone of the Hindu gamut, so-called because its tone is produced from air drawn from five parts of the body—navel, breast, throat, heart and forehead. It is the one tone whose relationship is constant to the keynote *Sa*. Cf. Quinary.

PANCHA-SHIKHA [five-crested]. Having five tufts of hair on the forehead, a lion. Exoteric Name of one of the Kumāras. Alias with Ribhu for Sana and Sanatsujāta. Cf. Narasimha under Vishnu.

PĀNDAVAS [sons of Pandu, *q.v.*]. The five Children of Kuntī and Mādrī, the wives of Pāndu, *i.e.*, Yudhishthira, Bhīma, Arjuna, Nakula, and Sahadeva. Cf. Draupadī, Quinary.

PANDORA, Gr. [pan=all + doron=a gift]. Giver of all or Earth; the All-endowed one who received presents from all the Gods to win the heart of Epimetheus. Through her the Gods sent a box containing all the ills (and also the blessings) to which earth is subject, to punish the race for acquiring the sacred fire stolen by Prometheus from heaven. Cf. Pyrrha.

PĀNDU [yellowish white or pale]. A princely son of Vyasa, Levirate or niyogic son of Vichitravirya, foster father of the Pāndavas, who, as did the biblical Joseph, cherishes the five, divine Levirate or niyogic children of his wives. Cf. Kuntī.

PĀNINI—a celebrated Rishi Grammarian of India, generally placed in 4th century B.C.

PANTHEISM, Gr. [God in all]. A philosophy which regards the Divine as an indwelling and immanent Presence in every atom of Nature. Cf. Unity.

PANTOMORPHOS, Gr. [panto=all'+¯morphos]. Assuming all forms, an epithet of Proteus.

PARA [distant, remote, ancient, supreme, principal, etc.].

PARABRAHMAN [Para, *q.v.*+Brahman, *q.v.*]. The Supreme Self or the Absolute. Cf. Unity, Chinmātra, Ātman, Protologos.

PARACELSUS, a symbolical name adopted by the Swiss physician-philosopher, Philip Bombaste Aureolus Theophrastus von Hohenheim, born in Zurich in 1493. To him Physics is indebted for the discovery of Nitrogen or *Azote*.

PARARDHA [the more remote half]. A number equal, in mortal days, to half the term of Brahmā's life, fifty Divine years. Cf. Manvantara.

PARADISE, Gr. [originally from Avestan pairidæza, an inclosure]. The garden of Eden in which Adam and Eve were first placed. An after-death state where after purgation of grosser desires, more innocent selfish desires fall away through satiety, preliminary to the real "heaven" or "devachan" between incarnations. Cf. Hades.

PARAMAPADA [the Supreme Step]. Abode of Vishnu.

PARAMĀRTHA [the most sublime Truth]. Reality.

PARAMĀRTHASATYA [the truth of truths; Paramārtha+satya, *q.v.*]. Absolute Truth.

PARAMĀTMĀ, PARAMĀTMAN [the Supreme Ātmā or Ātman, *q.v.*]

PĀRAMITĀS [pāra=the further shore+mita= moving (beyond) by measured steps]. The six or ten perfections or paths belonging to a Bodhisattva. Cf. Mārga.

PARANIRVĀNA, PARINIRVĀNA [the highest Nirvāna, *q.v.*]. The supreme state of consciousness recognized to be attainable by Buddhists.

PARANISHPANNA [para, *q.v.*+nish=out of, forth from+panna from pad=having fallen down]. That which comes or issues forth from the Absolute. Cf. Padma, Unity.

PARĀSHARA [parā=inverted order, back, over +shara from shrī=to kill or repel]. A destroyer or repeller of evil. Name of a Nāga; father of Vyāsa, author of certain Rig-vedic hymns.

PARASHURĀMA [parashu from shrī+para= hurting another=an axe, a thunderbolt, etc. =Rāma, *q.v.*]. Rāma with the axe, the 6th Avatara of Vishnu. The ideal Avenger who came to punish the Kshatriyas for oppressing the people. *Theos.* the developed Fourth Race, whose power passes into the hands of Rāmachandra. Cf. Madhava.

PARINĀMIN [that which is subject to transformation (the nāmin are all the vowels or potent forces except *a*, the inherent vowel)+pari= round about]. Cf. Mantram, Oeaohoo.

PARNASSUS, Gr. A mountain in ancient Phocis sacred to Apollo and the Muses. Cf. Delphoi, Olympus.

PARSĪS, PARSEES [Pars=Fars, a province in Persia]. The hundred thousand remaining worshippers of Fire, following the teachings of Zoroaster. Exiled of old from their native land, most of them dwell in Bombay and Gujerat. Cf. Agni.

PARTHENOGENESIS, Gr. [partheno=virgin +genesis=reproduction]. Birth or generation by females through eggs without male fertilization. Cf. Mother.

PĀRVAKA—Sacrificial Fire, one of the three great fires, the other two of which were the Household and the Funeral Fires. Cf. Agni, Pāvaka, Trimūrti.

PĀSHA [pāsha from pash=to bind; a noose]. The sacred noose of Shiva that strangles all the unworthy elements in the yogi's nature, and is constantly shown in one of the left-hands of the ten-armed Shiva. Cf. Yogi.

PASHT, PACHT, PAKHT, Egy. Variations of the cat-headed Moon-Goddess Bast, female aspect of Ptah, the creative principle. "Lady of Life."

PASHYANTĪ [visible or observable]. Second differentiation of sound. Akāsha manifested.

PĀTĀLA [lowest infernal regions]. Cf. Tala.

PATANJALI, PATANJALA [pata=falling+ anjali=the joined hands. This refers to the falling of Patanjali as a small snake into the reverential hands of the grammarian Pānini]. The great authority on Yoga and Concentration, founder of an Indian School of Philosophy, Patanjala. Cf. Serpent.

PATER AETHER, Lat. [Father-Æther, *q.v.*] A name of Jupiter.

PAUL, ST., Gr. [originally Sāh'ūl, or Saul, a Rabbi Pharisee, *q.v.*, his name was changed to Paulos=resting point, completion, on becoming a Christian Prophet]. An Initiate and biblical author.

PĀVAKA, Pārvaka, *q.v.* [shining, brilliant, bright, purifying, a social fire, root pū=to cleanse]. *S.D.* Electric Fire, Father of Kavya-Vāhana. Cf. Agni, Pavamāna, Suchi, Trimūrti, Vasu.

PAVAMĀNA [purifying fire, associated within it the element of wind, winnowing, being strained, storm, thunderbolt]. *S.D.* Fire by friction. Cf. Agni, Pāvaka, Shuchi, Trimurti.

PAVANA [householder's sacred fire]. The Wind-God. Cf. Agni.

PELAGUS, PELAGOS, Gr. [The High Sea, a God of vast distances; root, plat=breadth or extension; or plak=flat or plane surface]. Cf. Water.

PELASGIAN, Gr. [Pelasgos; der. (?) pos. Per or Pera=from beyond, across, emigrant+pel= dark-coloured, or men from the East]. Pre-Hellenic settlers in Greece, and environs.

PENATES, Lat. [penus=the feeding thing]. Old Gaurdian Deities of the household and of the State (in the temple of Vesta), as the aggregate of Households. Cf. Lares.

PENTECOST, Gr. [fiftieth day after second day of Passover when the offering of the first fruits of the Harvest was made]. A solemn festival of the Jews; observed by Christians in Commemoration of the descent of the Fire of the Holy Spirit upon the Apostles described in *Acts*. A symbol of the descent of the Fire of

the third Logos, q.v., at the Adept, q.v. or Fifth Initiation.

PERI, Per. [a female genius or fairy]. Descendants of fallen angels, excluded from Paradise till penance is accomplished. On the whole benevolent. Cf. Satan, Lucifer.

PERSEPHONE, Gr.- Lat. PROSERPINA, Daughter of Zeus and Demeter, abducted by Hades, but allowed to spend two-thirds of the year with her mother. Goddess of Spring. Cf. Crucifixion, Easter, Hel Jupiter, Pluto, Resurrection.

PERSEUS, Gr. [fish]. A famous Greek hero, son of Zeus and Danaë, who slew the Gorgon Medusa. A constellation. Cf. Jupiter.

PESH-HUN, Tib. [skt. root pisuna=the meddlesome or betraying one]. An epithet of Nārada (the messenger and informant of the Gods). S.D. " the mysterious, guiding intelligent power, which gives the impulse to, and regulates the impetus of Cycles, Kalpas and universal events." Cf. Kronos.

PETER, St., Gr. Symeon (Heb. Shimon) [petros =a rock; Shimo=to get knowledge or to hear a call]. The great apostle and disciple of the Christ, considered to be the " rock " on which the Church of Rome is founded.

PHAETHON, PHAETON, Gr. [beaming, radiant]. One of the light-bringing steeds of Eos, the Dawn, son of Helios and Clymene, famous for his reckless driving of his father's chariot. The Sun-God Himself in the hottest months. Cf. Sūrya.

PHALLUS, Gr. [phallos=a symbol of the male generative organ, used as a symbol of the principle of generation in the Dionysian mysteries]. Cf. Duality, Lingam, Sacr', Creative Gods.

PHANES, Gr. A mystic Divinity in the Orphic Triad of Phanes, Chaos, and Kronos, q.v. Cf. Eros, Trimūrti.

PHARAOH, Egy. [pr'o=great house or place]. A sovereign of ancient Egypt. Cf. Uraeus.

PHARISEE, Heb. [Perushim=separatists from all that was considered unholy]. A school of ancient Jews, noted for strict observance of rites and ceremonies, pledged to levitical purity. Cf. Paul, Saducee.

PHILALETHES, Gr. [philo=lover+aletheia= truth]. Eugenius Philalethes was Rosicrucian name assumed by Thomas Vaughan, an eighteenth century English occultist and alchemist. Cf. Initiate.

PHILO, Gr. [lover]. An Alexandrian philosopher who sought to harmonize the western Greek and eastern Hebrew religions.

PHILOSTRATUS, Gr. [philo+stratus=outspreading]. A biographer of Apollonius of Tyanā.

PHOEBE, Gr. [fem. of Phoebus, q.v.]. A daughter of Uranus and Gaia, who bore Leto and Asterie to Coius. Titans, q.v. Common Epithet of Artemis-Diana, Moon-Goddess. Cf. Latona.

PHOEBUS, PHOIBUS, Gr. [pure, bright, radiant, referring particularly to the radiance of youth]. Later applied to Apollo. Cf. Sūrya.

PHOENICIANS, Gr. [land that produced purple]. The Canaanites of Bible times, inhabiting a Semitic country at the eastern end of Mediterranean.

PHOENIX, PHENIX, Gr. [phoinix=date palm]. The ancestor of the Phœnicians and father of Europa. In Egyptian religion an embodiment of Ra, the sun god, viewed as heron-like, later as an eagle. Fabled to live for 500 years, to be consumed by fire by its own act, and to rise in youthful freshness from its own ashes. Symbol of resurrection, rebirth, and regeneration. Cf. Unity, Ammon-Ra, Reincarnation, Agni, Bird, Sūrya.

PHORMINX, Gr. Oldest stringed instrument of the Greeks, Apollo's lyre. Seven-stringed after Terpander's time. Cf. Orpheus, Sevens.

PHORONEUS, Gr. [phora=motion]. A Titan; an ancestor and generator of mankind. Identified withPrometheus as the fire-bringer.Cf. Agni.

PHOSPHOROS, Gr. [phos=light+pherein=to bring]. The Bringer of Light, Lucifer, Venus, the Morning Star.

PHRYGIA, Gr. An ancient country of central and northern Asia Minor.

PHTAH, Egy. God of Death; in later times a Sun-God. Cf. Ptah, Sūrya, Yama.

PINEAL GLAND,Lat. [resembling a pine cone]. Aconical reddish gray gland-like body attached to the roof of the third ventricle, from which it rises as a hollow outgrowth, lying between the anterior corpora quadrigemina. In some reptilian forms, it is raised on a stalk, bringing it near the upper surface of the head in the median line, and has the structure of an eye with a more or less distinct retina and lens, and is then called the pineal or median eye. Physiologists recognize it to be " a remnant of an important sense organ in ancestral forms." Thoes. a connecting link between the physical and mental consciousness; when developed, an organ of thought-transference. The " third eye " of mental perception in the past, it will be revivified with racial progress. Cf. Trilochana, Cyclops.

PINGALĀ [reddish-brown]. The positive or righthand (in males) spinal force. See Caduceus.

PISHĀCHĀ [an eater of raw flesh]. A female demon.

PISTIS SOPHIA, Gr. [pistis=faith, Sophia, q.v.]. An early Christian Gnostic text, teaching the doctrine of the Æons.

PITARAS, PITRIS [from pā=to watch, guard, protect, shelter, rule, govern]. The Fathers who set the types for mankind at the beginning of the various great epochs, races, chains, rounds etc. Cf. Manu, Agnishvātta, Barhishad; Brahmāndika, creative Gods, Fetah, Kumāra, Propator, Svāhā, Yama Zodiac.

PITUITARY BODY, Lat. [pituita=phlegm. This organ was once erroneously supposed to secrete nasal mucus]. A small, oval, reddish gray vascular body attached to the infundibulum of the brain and occupying a depression in the middle line of the superior surface of the sphenoid bone. A ductless master-gland which plays an important part in body processes,

particularly as regards growth, sexual and reproductive functions, and the balancing and control of other glands. Pituitrin from the posterior lobe causes a strong direct contractive effect on all muscles, and maintains tone of blood vessels. *Theos.* it " focuses the astral vibrations much as a burning-glass focuses the rays of the sun " thus rendering possible the transfer of astral consciousness to the brain (A. Besant).

PLAKSHA [the waved-leaf fig tree, from root plush=to burn]. One of the seven Dvīpas.

PLANE, Lat. [planus=level]. *Theos.*=a type of matter created by the impress of Logoic consciousness on root matter. The seven "planes" or types of matter in the Solar System are Physical; Astral (Feeling, Emotional or Desire); Mental; Intuitional, (Buddhic, Love-Wisdom); Atmic (Nirvānic, Spiritual, or Will); Monadic (Anupādaka); Divine or Ādi. Cf. also Chaos, Ākāsha, Æther, Mūlaprakriti. The word "plane" was used, though "globe" or "world" in some ways would be more expressive, because a cross-section of the seven " planes " of a globe or solar system shows each subtler type of matter interpenetrating the grosser and extending beyond it in a definite " plane." Cf. Sevens, Dharmakāya, Bhuvas, Ether, Loka, Karshvare, Sānkhya, Tattvas.

PLANETARY LOGOI or SPIRITS, Lords of the Seven Great Planetary Systems of the Solar System, each of which is a channel for one of the Seven Rays or Aspects of Logoic Temperament, and to one of which each living thing belongs. *Theos.* given as Venus, Vulcan, Jupiter, Saturn, Neptune and two other as yet unknown planets, Uranus, the Earth with Mars and Mercury. Given in Hinduism as Surya, Sun; Budha [Wisdom]; Mercury; Shukra, Venus; Shani, Saturn; Chandra, Moon; Kuja [born of the earth or hell], Mars; Guru or Jupiter. One Gnostic classification is Ildabaoth=Saturn; Astaphaios=Venus; Adonaios, the Sun. Cf. Sūrya; Jao, Iao, Jahu, Jahveh=Jupiter, Sabaoth=Mars; Ailoaios, Ailoein, Elohim= Mercury; Oraios, Jareach [Light]=the Moon. Cf. Krittikā; Amesha Spentas; Angels; Dev, Sevens, Eloi, Sephira, Vishvakarman, Zodiac.

PLEIADES, Gr. [der. (?) pos. pleo=to sail]. The seven daughters of Atlas and the nymph Pleione: Alcyone=kingfisher, halcyon; Celæno=the black; Elektra=shining, splendour; Maia=mother, nurse, mother of Hermes; Merope=human, mortal, endowed with speech (having loved a mortal, she is the invisible seventh, with star dimmed she conceals herself for shame); Sterope or Asterope=lightning; Taygeta=a mountain. See Riksha, Kārttikeya.

PLENUM, Lat. PLERŌMA, Gr. [fulness]. Gnostic term for the Absolute. Also the abode of the Gods. Cf. Unity, Aeon, Olympus, Sod.

PNEUMA, Gr. [wind, air, breath, *q.v.* of life]. Divine afflatus or inspiration; Holy Spirit.

POPOL VUH (Gautemalan) [book of bark; collection of written leaves]. Mystic and heroic Saga of the Quiche Indians of Guatemala in which Gucumatz is identical with Quetzo-Cohuatl.

PORPHYRION, Gr. [rolling or dark-gleaming sea; purple, crimson]. A Titan.

POSEIDON, Gr. Son of Kronos and Rhea. Cf. Neptune, Nereid, Titan, Water, Rhea.

POSEIDONIS, Atlantis.

PRACHETĀS [coming forth from the deep]. The Wise or Esoteric Wisdom. An epithet of Varuna. Cf. Water, Vishnu.

PRĀCHETASAS [the ten sons of Prachetas, *q.v.*]. Also patronymic of Manu, Daksha, etc. One of names of the Sage Vālmīki. Cf. Rishis.

PRADHĀNA [fundamental or primeval substance]. Prakriti, *q.v.* PRĀDHĀNIKA [pradhāna, *q.v.*]. Pre-eminent, related to primary matter, in the Sānkhya Philosophy.

PRAJĀPATI [Lord of Generation of Birth; Lord of Creatures]. One of the Lords who superintend the creative processes of the Universe. Cf. Rishis and references. Daksha, Pratisarga.

PRAJĀ [wisdom, perception]. Cf. Vishnu.

PRĀKRITA [completed, made]. Primary creation.

PRĀKRITI [original or natural formfrom primary substance as opposed to vi-kriti or modified, changed substance]. Personified Female, Energies or Shaktis, Nature. Cf. Daivīprakriti, Dhātu, Mūlaprakriti, Pradhāna, Pūrvaja, Shuddha Sattva, Svabhāvat.

PRĀKRITIKA [of or belonging to Prakriti]. The name of a Pralaya, when all is resolved into the primal element.

PRALAYA [pra-lī=to dissolve, vanish, be absorbed]. A period of rest as opposed to Manvantara. Cf. Cycle, Prākrita, Samvārta, Yuga.

PRAMANTHA, stick used by Hindu priests to kindle fire by rotary motion. Cf. Agni.

PRAMATIH [protector]. Son of Fohat.

PRAMLOCHĀ [locha=sight or tears+pra=towards]. A nymph or Apsaras who beguiled Kandu.

PRĀNA [prā=to be filled]. Breathing, breath, spirit, vital air. *Theos.* The life-breath of the various vehicles. Cf. Nephesh, Sādhya, Vāyu, VII under Zodiac.

PRĀNAMAYAKOSHA [prāna, *q.v.*+maya= full of+kosha, *q.v.*]. Body of Prāna.

PRANAVA [PRA-NAVA=that which renovates, rejuvenates; or pra-nu=to praise]. The sacred word, AUM.

PRĀNĀYĀMA [suspension of breath]. A Hatha Yogic process.

PRĀSANGA MĀDHYAMIKA [devtion (to) the middle path]. A Tibetan Buddhist School of Philosophy.

PRASHRAYA [devotion or worship to]. Modesty, a son of Dharma and Hrī.

PRATISARGA [continued creation out of primitive matter from prati=towards, back, down upon=srij=to let loose, emit, pour out, procreate etc.]. Secondary creation by Brahmā and the Prajāpatis.

PRATYĀHĀRA [drawing back or retreat]. Used in many senses. One of the Yogāngas described by Patanjali.

PRATYEKA [singly, solitary, each]. Used in Occultism to designate those great Beings at the level of the Buddha (eighth initiation) who act as transmitters of the Will or Power Element, which path is solitary, as compared with that of a Buddha.

PRAVAHA [hearing forward]. One of the seven winds said to cause motion of planets. Cf. Vāyu.

PRIAPUS, Gr. [Priapos=Male generative principle personified]. God of Gardens and Vineyards. Fructifying Principle in Nature.

PRITHĪ [prith=to throw, cast, extend]. The first anointed sovereign of men, ruler of the lower animals, author of the *Rig-veda*. Cf. Adam, Prithu.

PRITHIVĪ [feminine of prithu] The Earth personified as the mother of all.

PRITHU [broad, wide, spacious]. Prithivī, *q.v.*

PRIYAVRATA [lover of vrata or religious observance]. A King, son of Manu and Shatarūpā.

PROCLUS, Gr. The last great exponent of Neoplatonism, the man whose influence overshadowed the whole medieval Christian Church.

PROMETHEUS, Gr. [Forethought or Provident]. A Titan, son of Iapetus and Clymene, grieved at the Gods' neglect of humanity stole the sacred fire from heaven. Cf. Skt. Pramantha, Epimetheus, Agni, Lucifer, Narthex, Pandora, Phoroneus, Titans.

PROPATŌR, Gn. [first founder of a family]. Forefather. Cf. Pitris.

PROTEUS, Gr. A prophesying sea-god in the service of Neptune who, when seized, would assume different shapes to try to escape making prophecies. Cf. Pantomorphos.

PROTOGONOS, Gr. [first-born]. Eros, *q.v.* In Orphism, conceived of as the generator of the universe. Cf. Unity.

PROTOLOGOS, PROTOLOGOI, plural [proto=primordial+Logos, *q.v.*]. Supreme Creator, Cf. Parabrahman, Unity.

PROTOMATERIA [primeval matter]. Cf. Unity, Mūlaprakriti.

PROTYLE, Gr. [primeval stuff]. Primordial undifferentiated matter. Cf. Unity, Mūlaprakriti.

PSYCHE, Gr. [breath, life, spirit, appetite, desire, organ of nous or mind, vital principle]. A lovely maiden, personification of the soul, represented with the wings of a butterfly, emblem of immortality. Through doubt of her lover Eros, she is separated from him for many wanderings and labours. Cf. Manas, Kāma, Reincarnation.

PSYCHOPOMP, Gr. [psyche=the soul+pempein=to send]. Hermes, the conductor or guide of souls.

PTAH, Egy. Cf. Phtah. The chief God of Memphis, worshipped from the first dynasty, a Father of Gods and Men, and shaper of the world in whom is Life, Strength and Stability. Cf. Imhoz-Pou, Unity.

PTOLEMY, Gr. [Geographer and astronomer of Alexandria about 130 A.D.].

PŪJĀ [pūj=adore, honour, reverence, worship] An act of pūj.

PULAHA [pul=to be lofty or high]. An ancient Rishi, one of the mind-born sons of Brahmā, enumerated among the Prajāpatis and seven sages. An epithet of Siva.

PULASTYA. Description of Pulaha applies also to Pulastya, another mind-born son of Brahmā Father of Nāgas.

PULOMĀ, daughter of a demon. Though loved by the demon father-in-law of Indra, she married Bhrigu.

PUMS [said to be from root pā=to guard, protect]. Human being, soul, spirit.

PUNARJANMAN [new or second birth, regeneration]. Cf. Reincarnation.

PUNDARĪKĀKSHA [lotus-eyed]. Epithet of Vishnu. The Supreme or Imperishable Glory, Lotus, *q.v.* Cf. Unity.

PURĀNAS [belonging to ancient times]. Sacred Hindu poetical works treating of the creation, destruction and renovation of worlds; the genealogy and deeds of gods and heroes; the reigns of the Manus and the deeds of their descendants. There are 18 principal Purānas and 18 supplementary *Upa Purānas*. Cf. Vidyā.

PURŪRAVAS [crying loudly]. A celebrated prince of the lunar race, son of Buddha, grandson of the Moon, who is said to have instituted the three sacrificial fires. Cf. Agni.

PURUSHA [root pur=to go before, to lead]. Mankind, the Male, the Spirit, the Supreme Being. Cf. Unity, Sānkhya.

PURUSHOTTAMA [Purusha, *q.v.* uttama=best of men]. Supreme Spirit, epithet of Vishnu or Krishna. Name of the fourth, black Vāsudeva, or son of Soma. Name of an Arhat. Cf. Unity

PŪRVAJA [ancient, primeval or elder]. Nature. Cf. Unity, Prakriti.

PŪRVĀRDHA, first half. [Pūrva=first+ardha =half].

PŪRVĀSHĀDHĀ, the first of two constellations called Ashādhā, the eighteenth or twentieth Nakshatra or lunar asterism containing two stars, one of which is Delta Sagittarii.

PUSHKARA [blue lotus flower]. A Dvīpa, *q.v.*

PUTRA [der. (?) pos. Pū=to cleanse; push=to nourish; pop.=preserving from the Hell of Put to which childless ones are condemned]. Progeny or Son. Cf. Agni-putra, Brahmaputra, Manasaputras.

PYGMALION. A king and sculptor of ancient Cyprus whose statue of a maiden was, through his love, changed into a living being.

PYMANDER, Gr. [The Thought Divine]. A work by Hermes Trismegistus.

PYRRHA, Gr. [red-earth, red-coloured bird]. Daughter of Epimetheus and Pandora, married Deucalion. After the deluge the mother of the new race. Cf. Noah, Earth.

PYTHAGORAS. The famous Greek philosopher, mathematician, musician, born about 582 B.C. in Samos. This Adept brought the Eastern mysteries, in India known as Yavanāchārya or Ionian teaching, to aid the west in the birth of its new civilization. Cf. Apollonius of Tyana.

PYTHON, Gr. Serpent slain by Apollo. The Spirit of Divination.

Q

QABBALAH, KABBALAH, CABBALAH, KABALA, etc. Heb. [quabal=to receive; the traditional or received lore]. The esoteric or mystic doctrine concerning God and the universe, asserted to have come down as a revelation to the elect from a remote past, and preserved by a privileged few. Called also hokmah nistarah=the hidden wisdom. Cf. Ain Soph, Kepher, Chokmah, Binah, Lévi, Sephira, Zohar.

QUATERNARY, Lat. [four]. A Group of Four. *Theos.* the four lower principles, a square of influence which with the three higher aspects of Spirit make the sacred Seven. Cf. Numbers and references, Tetraktys Sesquitertia, Tetragrammaton, Mahārājahs, Lipikas; Michael, Gabriel, Raphael, Uriel; Indra, Yama, Varuna, Zodiac.

QUETZO-COHUATL, Mex. [the Green Feathered Serpent]. In Aztect tradition a King from the East, (Atlantis, *q.v.*). Into a land rife with human ceremonial sacrifice, he introduced a cult of purification and penitential sacrifice. He is also the God of whom he taught, the Immortal Self, the Wind, the Giver of Breath and Life, the Water, the Sun, Saviour of Mankind. Cf. Serpent, Popol Vuh, Ātmā, Vāyu, Sūrya, Christos.

QUICHÉ, Mayan. An ancient Mayan nation of western Guatemala. See *Popol Vuh.*

QUINARY. The fivefold principles of manifested man. Cf. Numbers, Pentacle, Panchama, Skandas, Sesquitertia, Tapas, Panchadasha, Pāndavas.

QŪ-TĀMY, Chal. The mystic recipient of the revelations of the moon-goddess in *Nabathean Agriculture,* an ancient Chaldean work. Cf. Moon.

R

RA, Egy. The Sun-God, son of Nut, the Sky, variously represented by the lion, cat, and hawk. Cf. Ammon-Ra, Sūrya, Bird, Narasimha, Shoo.

RABBI, RABBIN, RABBAN, Heb. [fulness of might and grace; Rabban=Master; Rabbi= My Master]. A Jewish teacher and priest. Cf. Tanaim.

RAHASYA [secret essence of knowledge]. One of the Upanishads.

RĀHU [the seizer]. Serpent-headed ascending Node of Moon, *q.v.* Cf. Serpent.

RAIVATA [rich, shining, beautiful]. Fifth of the fourteen Manus, the root-Manu of the third Round.

RĀJA YOGA [kingly Yoga, *q.v.*]. The control of the lower vehicles by developing higher aspects of consciousness, the Mind and Will. The Yoga of the Second or Wisdom Ray. Cf. Hatha Yoga.

RĀJAGRIHA [king's house]. Residence of Buddhist Kings from Bimbisara to Ashoka; seat of the first Buddhist Council, held 510 B.C.

RAJAH, RAJAMSI [respectively nominative singular and plural forms of Rajas, *q.v.*] Vedic =World; modern=Dust. Cf. Earth.

RAJAS [see Gunas]. Cf. Duality.

RĀJASA(S) [endowed with rajas, passion or feeling]. See Gunas, Ābūtarajasas.

RĀKSHASA [to hold, guard, protect, preserve]. Embodiments of force of Evil or Resistance. Servents of Rāvana. Cf. Duality, Kumbhakarna.

RĀMA RAMACHANDRA [delight, rejoicing from ram=to repose in calm tranquillity, to be happy, rejoice, sport, etc., chandra=the moon]. The Seventh Avatar of Vishnu. Ideal of the Fifth Race or Developed Humanity. The Perfect Man, the true Āryan. "Moon" in the case of Rāma has an occult significance as Rāma is of the Solar Dynasty. Cf. Rāvana, Hanuman, Rāmāyana, Āitā, Sārya-varshas.

RĀMĀNUJĀCHĀRYA [" younger brother " of Rāma+Āchārya=one to whom one must have recourse as Spiritual Guide]. A South Indian philosopher in 1070 A.D. Instituted the great Vishishtādvaita Vedāntic System.

RĀMĀYANA [Rāma's goings or adventures]. A famous epic poem in seven books on the life of Rāma by Vālmīki. Cf. Lankā.

RAMSES, Egy. The name of a number of Kings, the most noted being Ramses II (1324-1258 B.C.) and Ramses III (about 1230 B.C.)

RAPHAEL, RAGUEL, Heb. [God has healed]. Generally, the third Archangel in the Jewish Pantheon. An Angel of the Presence; Western Angel of the Cardinal Points, Angel of Healing both physical and moral, he can bind even Death. Represented as Lord of the Serpents or Ophanim.

RASA [ras=taste, perceive, fell, love]. Essence, sap, elixir. Cf. Amrita, Water.

RASA MANDALA [Rāsa=sound, connected with ras, *q.v.*+Mandala, *q.v.*]. The magic circle in which Krishna danced with the Gopis. The Heavenly Circle of Creation.

RASĀ TALA, RĀPATALA [rasā, *q.v.*]. The third Tala. See "explanation of States of Consciousness," *S.D.* Vo . 5. p. 539.

RAUMAS—Gods or Devas said to have originated from the pores of Virabhadra's skin. Cf. Shiva-Gharamajā.

RĀVANA [rāva=a cry or a roar from ru]. Ruler of Lankā. Chief of the Rākshasas, younger half-brother of Kuvera, personification of evil or resistance. Cf. Duality, Hanuman, Kumbha-Karna, Rāma.

RAYS, SEVEN: *Theos.* Seven Aspects of Divine Consciousness. Planetary Spirits; Ray 1. Will or Purpose; 2. Wisdom; 3. Higher Creative Activity, Adaptability; 4. the Bridge between life and form, Ray of Harmony; 5. Scientific; 6. Fiery Devotion; 7 Ceremonial or Action Ray. Cf. also the Hindu names Sushumna, Harikesha, Vishvakarman, Vishvatryarchās, Sannaddha, Sarvavasu.

RECTOR [to lead or rule]. The Chief Angel. Term used in *Pymander* of the seven Archangels or RECTORES. Cf. Sevens.

REPHAIM, Heb. [reph=shadowy forms of death]. Primitive Giants or Titans. Cf Angel, Yama.

RHEA, Gr. [Rea=lightly, easily]. Daughter of Uranus and Gaea, wife of Kronos-Saturn, and of the Olympian Gods, Zeus, Hades, Poseidon. Cf. Hekate, Titans, Jupiter, Hera, Hestia and Demeter.

RIBHU [root, rabh=seize, embrace, desire]. Clever, skilful, artistic, an alias, for a Kumāra, and his descendants. Panchāshikha.

RIG VEDA [rich, rig=lustre, splendour, a hymn, or a single verse+Veda]. The oldest of the Vedas, Hymns of Praise.

RIKSHA [der. (?) from riksh=to kill or hurt, or from rich]. The seven stars, the Pleiades; in later times the seven Rishis. The particular star in the twenty-seven mansions of the moon under which one is born. Cf. Sevens.

RIMMON, Ass. [to roar or thunder]. A deity worshipped at Damascus, identified with Ramman, god of thunder and storms. Cf. Marut, Indra.

RISHABHA [to sprinkle or impregnate, a young and noble bull, or any male animal; the most excellent; root rish=to flow quickly, glide]. The second of the seven tones or svaras of the Hindu gamut. One of the seven Rishis of the second Manvantara. Cf. Nandi.

RISHI [der. (?) pos. from driseh=to see; Rish, q.v. Cf. Arch or rich=to praise]. A singer of sacred hymns; an inspired poet or sage; the seven ancient sages, born of Brahmā's mind, to whom the Vedic hymns are attributed. In the *Shatapatha-Brāhmana*, their names are given as: Gotama [Go=cow, speech, earth], Bharadvaja [bringing or bearing food], etc. Vishvāmitra, Jamadagni [blazing fire]. Vasistha, Kashyapa, and Atri; in the *Mahābhārata*: Marīchi, Atri, An-giras [to mark, to go around], Pulaha, Kratu [plan, determination]. Pulastya, Vasishtha. In *Manu* they are called Prajāpatis, and are reckoned as ten, the additional three being - Prachetas or Daksha, Bhrigu, and Nārada. They represent the Constellation of the Great Bear to which it is said they were translated.

ROSICRUCIANS, ROSY CROSS, Ger. [Rose-Cross]. Name given to followers of Christian Rosenkreuz, an Adept who founded an Order in Germany about 1460. Popularly supposed to have been the invention of a German theologian, Johann Valentin Andrea who in the 17th-18th century wrote anonymous pamphlets about the Order, calling himself a Knight of the Rose-Cross. The true Order of Rosicrucians has remained secret. Cf. Philalethes, Roger Bacon, Comte de St. Germain.

RU, RO, Egy. [gate or outlet]. Spot in the heavens whence proceeded primeval light. Cosmic Womb. Cf. Mother, Chaos, Unity.

RUACH, Heb. [to blow, breathe, draw in air, breath, life, spiritual force, passion, restlessness. Cf. rajas. Generally used as a spiritual direction of life or will]. Kabala: Second degree of the soul, knowledge of good and evil. Cf. Duality.

RUDRA [der. (?) pos. rud=to roar, weep, lament; or ru=to cry, to hum, to sound, to praise+dra from dru=to run]. The Roarer or Howler, Epithet of the God of Tempests, Raging Storm and Fire, Father of the Rudras or Maruts. The embodiment of the destructive, regenerative force of Shiva.

RUNE, Anglo-Saxon [a secret]. The magic signs used by early Teutons in ceremonies, which later became their alphabet.

RŪPA [a visible form, formal]. Cf. Arūpa, Duality. Agnishvātta, Barhishads, Skandhas.

RUTA [broken to pieces, divided sound]. The Sanskrit name of one of the last islands of Atlantis to succumb to the deluge.

S

SABAO, SABAOTH, Heb. [tsebā'ōth, plural of tsābā, an army or host; to go forth to war]. Armies or hosts in plural; the God of War. Lord of the Hosts of Heaven. Cf. Mars.

SABBATH, Heb. [shabbath; der. (?) pos. from shabb=cessation, to break off, desist]. " Probably originally connected with cult of moon " —*Jewish Encyc.* The seventh day of the week (Saturday) observed by Jewish people as a day of rest and worship. Early Christians observed two days, later dropping the Sabbath in favour of Sunday, a day of commemoration of the Christ's resurrection.

SABEAN, Sem. [Saba (Biblical=Sheba)]. An ancient kingdom of Southern Arabia, fifth century B.C., the religion of which was sun, moon and star worship. Cf. Sūrya, Planetary Logos.

SABHĀ [bhā=to shine, be conspicuous, manifest +sa=together]. An assembly, society.

SACR', Heb. [to be awake, nimble, watchful, the male organ of generation, the almond tree; also Cf. sacr=to burn, lighten, shine, the shining dawn or Lucifer]. *S.D.* the root of sacred. Cf. Lingam, Phallus, Duality.

SADAIKA-RŪPA [sadā=perpetually+eka, one +rupa, q.v.]. Changeless Essence.

SADDUCEE, Heb. [Tseduqim from Tsādoq=the just one, the name of the founder of the sect]. A Jewish sect, 2nd century B.C.-1st century A.D., composed largely of priestly aristocracy who rejected dogma and postulated freedom of the will. Cf. Pharisee.

SĀDHU, SĀDDHU [straight, pure, holy saint or sage, from sādh=to complete, finish, accomplish]. Cf. Rishi.

SĀDHYA [cf. above; =to be accomplished or effected]. Also used of " the pure and holy ones " celestial beings said to occupy Bhuvarloka. In *Manu*, iii. 195, they are said to be children of the Soma-sads, grandchildren of Virāj. Their names are sometimes given as: Manas=Mind; Mantri=sage, Cf. mantra; Prāna=life principle; Nara=man; Prāna=breath; Vinirbhaya=he who is wide apart from fear; Daya=guiding, reason, wisdom or prudence; Dansa=marvellous or shining power; Nārāyana=Spirit of the Deep; Vrisha=raining forth, generating, male, young, strong, a bull; Prabhu=surpassing all, multiplying, increasing over all. All sacred twelves can be compared with Zodiac.

SADIC, SADIK, SYDIC, Heb. [the Just or Right One]. See Melchi-zedek.

SAGARA [having poison]. A mystic King of the solar race, whose sixty thousand sons were reduced to ashes for showing disrespect to the sage Kapila.

SAHARAKSHA [saha=patient, bearing or enduring+raksha=strength: "preserving strength"]. Fire of the Asuras, son of the Fire called Pavamāna, *q.v.* Cf. Havyavāhana, Kavyavāhana, Trimūrti, Agni.

SAIS, the famous ancient capital of Lower Egypt, in Nile delta, celebrated for its temple of Isis-Neith. SAITIC=pertaining to Sais.

SAKRIDĀGĀMIN, SAKARADĀGĀMIN [he will receive birth (only) once more]. The Buddhist term for the second degree Initiate, he who need return but once more to birth.

SAMĀDHI [samādh=to place or hold together, to unite or compose differences, to adjust, set right, solve difficulties]. Profound contemplation and perfect absorption in the One, the eighth and last stage of Yoga; ecstatic apperception; the highest point or focus of consciousness. Cf. Unity, Turīya.

SAMAEL, SHAMAEL, Heb. [Venom of God; the veiled dark North or left]. The twelve-winged angel of Death, said to preside over Tuesday, and be associated with the Moon. Cf. Yama.

SAMĀNA [sam-an=to breathe again or come to life]. One of the five vital airs; that which circulates about the navel and aids digestion.

SAMBHOGAKĀYA [Sam=together with+bhoga=fruition, understanding, perception, cherishing, nourishing+kāya=vesture. Cf. Nirmāna-kāya and Dharmakāya]. The second great vesture in Buddhism, the body of those Dhyāni-Buddhas who overshadow but do not incarnate. *Occult.* That path open to the Adept who chooses to drop all but his nirvānic nucleus. Cf. Trimūrti.

SAMBHŪTI [being together, combination; suitability, fitness]. Daughter of Daksha and wife of Marīchi. Aslo birth, origin, production, power.

SAMMĀ SAMBUDDHA, Pali. [the thoroughly awakened Lord; also the power of recollection of past lives]. Title of Gautama, the Buddha.

SAMNATĪ, SANNATĪ [san-nam=to bow in reverence]. Humility personified as daughter of Daksha and wife of Dharma. Cf. Mother.

SAMSĀRA[sam-sri=to pass through a succession of states or revolve]. The wheel of birth and death or mundane existence.

SAM-VARTA [turning towards, crumpling up]. One of the seven clouds particularly one abounding in water, found at the periodical destruction or dissolution of the universe. Cf. Pralaya.

SAMVRITI [covering up, concealment, compression, contraction, suppression, secret purpose]. *S.D.* False Conception.

SAMVRITISATYA [covered, compressed or contracted truth, see Satya]. *S.D.* Relative Truth.

SANA [the Ancient]. SANAKA [the lesser Ancient] SANANDA[joy-possessing]. SANANDANA [full of rejoicings]. SANATKUMĀRA [the Eternal Virgin Youth]. SANATSUJĀTA [the nobly-born and perpetually beautiful]. These, with Kapila, are names of the seven Kumāras. Ribhu and Panchāshikha are exoteric names in place of Sana and Sanatsujāta, above given. Sanatkumāra, one of the four sons of Brahmā and oldest of the progenitors of mankind, is to esotericists known as the Head of the Occult Hierarchy or Inner Government of the World, and a self-taken Initiate, of the Ninth Degree. Known as Kartikeya. Cf. Sevens, Vaidhātra, Ādi-Sanat, Jagannatha, Sanakadikas.

SANAKADIKAS [the Ancients of the Space Diretions]. See Sanaka, above; the Seven Kumaras.

SANCHONIATHON, Gr. A pre-Christian writer on Phœnician Cosmogony, whose works are no longer extant. Fragments are given by Philo Byblus.

SANDHIS [to join or unite, bridge, combine]. Intervals between Manvantaras.

SANDHYĀ [see foregoing]. Boundary, limit, morning and evening twilight, dusk and daybreak or dawn, either of a day or an age.

SANDHYĀMSHA [a portion of twilight]. Cf. Sandhya. The period that follows each Yuga.

SANJNĀ [to be of the same mind; harmony, understanding; spiritual consciousness]. Name of Gāyatrī; name of a daughter of Vishvakarman, wife of the Sun. Cf. Sūrya, Skandhas.

SĀNKHYA [calculating, deliberating, reasoning] Oldest Indian philosophy, founded by Kapila. A system dealing with the causes of manifestation, the various planes and vehicles in which consciousness expresses itself, and the Supreme Purusha viewed as an onlooker. Cf. Prādhānika.

SANNADDHA [girded for the battle, prepared for action; clothed for expression]. One of the seven Rays.

SANSKRIT [carefully and accurately fabricated, polished, finished]. A refined or polished language. The ancient Aryan language of India, from which are derived the modern Āryan tongues. Called "The language of the Gods," because of its hidden potencies.

SANTATI [spreading out, uninterrupted succession, progeny].

SAPTA [rt. sap=to connect, join]. Seven. A sacred number with the Hindus, many compounds proceeding therefrom. Cf. Numbers.

SAPTAPARNA [seven-leaved]. The tree Alstonia, the sensitive plant. *S.D.* The heart of the man-plant is so called.

SAPTARISHI [seven Rishis, *q.v.*].

SARAH, Heb. [princess]. SARAI [der. (?) pos. =my princess; or is abridged from Jah is Ruler]. Wife of Abram whose name was changed from Sarai to Sarah. Said to be an eponym of Israel.

SARAMĀ [the runner]. A dog of Indra, mother of the SĀRAMEYAS, the two four-eyed brindled watch-dogs of Yama; thought by some to

have been originally Indra and Agni. Some scholars think Saramā is a name of Ushas, Dawn, who rescued the cows representing sun-rays stolen by Night. Sārameya is also identified with Hermes, and Saramā with the Wind, as conductor of the souls of the departed ones. Cf. Vāyu.

SARAPH, Heb. Singular for SERAPHIM.

SARASVATĪ [like flowing water]. Goddess of speech and learning, in later mythology regarded as the shakti or wife of Brahmā; sometimes identified with Vāch. Invoked, as was Minerva in Rome, as partroness of science; inventress of Sanskrit; mother of the Vedas, goddess of invention and industry, eloquence and art; goddess of fertility; Mother of Rivers, she is sevenfold in expression: Su-prabhā [the brilliant, a tongue of Fire]; Kānchanākshī [of shining or golden eye]; Vishāla [the broad or illustrious]; Manoramā [mind-rejoicing]; Oghavatī [like a torrent]; Su-renu [like an atom, having beautiful sand]; Vimalodikā [pure, transparent, beautiful]. Cf. Sophia, Sevens, Trinity, Marut-vat, Water, Mother, Shrī.

SARGON II, King of Assyria (B.C. 722-705) founder of a powerful dynasty.

SARĪSRIPA [crawling, creeping things]. Snakes.

SAROS, Gr. [sixty sixties=3,600]. A Chaldean cycle of cycles used both of years and days.

SARPA [from srip=creeping or serpentine, tortuous motion, sliding, twining, going, flowing]. A Serpent, Nāga.

SARPA-RĀJNĪ [Serpent-Queen].

SARVA-MANDALA [sarva=universal+mandala, q.v.]. The matrix of the universe. Cf. Mother.

SARVA-MEDHA [sarva=whole or universal+medha, marrow or essence]. Said of a sacrifice or sacrificial victim.

SARVAGA [all-pervading, omnipresent]. Cf Unity.

SARVĀTMAN [sarva=all, universal+Ātman, q.v.]. Cf. Unity.

SARVAVASU [Universal Riches]. Giver of all Life, one of the seven Rays.

SARVESHA [sarva=all+isha=lords, Lord of All]. The Supreme. Cf. Unity.

SAT [present participle of as=being, existing, real, true]. H.P.B. Be-ness. Cf. Asat, Sat, with Ananda and Chit forms a primordial Trimūrti.

SATAN, Heb. [from hassātān=adversary or accuser at law]. Shaitan, Arab. Originally with the significance of a Kārmic deity. Satan is now considered as a personification of the principle of Evil. Cf. Duality, Ahriman, Beelzebub, Peri, Lucifer, Shaitān, Shishupāla, Zohak.

SATĪ [virtuous, true; feminine of Sat]. Truth personified; the wife of Shiva. Cf. Devi. Used in later times of a wife who immolates herself on her husband's funeral pyre.

SATI, Egy. Queen of the gods and of Egypt, depicted with cow's horns, wearing crown of upper Egypt. Cf. Mother.

SATTVA [from sat, q.v.]. Being, existence, essence, principle of being, breath, spirit, mind, consciousness, goodness, virtue, truth, pure,

clean, etc., balanced. Cf. Gunas, Shankha, Shuddha Sattva.

SATURN, Lat. [the sower from satum=to sow]. An ancient God of seed-sowing, whose temple in Rome, 497 B.C., was a state treasury. Father with Rhea of the Olympian Gods. In 217 B.C. this God was identified with the Greek Kronos. The ringed, so-called malefic, planet next in magnitude to Jupiter. Cf. Shani, Michael, Neptune, Sephira.

SATYA [from sat, q.v.]. True, real, genuine, good, virtuous, etc. Cf. Dharma. Epithet of many of the Gods. Satyas are one of the twelve classes of great Gods. Cf. Vishvas, Loka.

SATYA YUGA [satya, q.v.+yuga, q.v.]. The first of the four Yugas, best or golden age.

SATYĀNNĀSTI PARODHARMAH [Than Sat, q.v., there is no higher Dharma, q.v.]. This, the family motto of the Maharajas of Benares, is found in an inverted form in the Mahābhārata, Santiparva, Chapter 160, Stanza 24. Translated since 1880 as "There is no religion higher than Truth." Many other interpretations are possible.

SATYA-VRATĀ [True to a vow, sincere]. Name of the 25th King of the Solar Dynasty in the second age; Name of Manu Vaivasvata.

SATYRS, Gr. [Satyroi or Tityroi from root ty=to swell; symbols of budding, germinating fertile plant and animal life]. Represented as part man and part horse or goat. Cf. Mendes and references.

SAVARNĀ [being of the same colour]. Said to have been substituted by Saranyū (the fleet-running one, or Darkness) for herself as wife of the Sun, from which union Manu, was born. Her other name is Chhāya, q.v. Cf. Sūrya, Mother.

SĀVITRI [relating to or belonging to the sun]. Gāyatri, q.v. Wife of Brahma, also of Siva, and epithet of many Goddesses. Cf. Mother, Sūrya.

SĀYANĀ. A learned Brāhman commentator on the Vedas, about A.D. 1370.

SCARABAEUS, Egy. The conventionalized stone representation of the large black dung-beetle, regarded as symbolic of resurrection and immortality. Symbol of the sun-god, man; the only-begotten, father, generation. Cf. Sūrya.

SEB, Egy. [the earth]. The consort was Nut, the sky, their children including Osiris, Isis, Nephthys and Set.

SENĀ [der. (?) pos. from si=bind; or from sena=having a lord or leader]. An army or armed force, the wife of Kārtikeya. Cf. Mother.

SENARY, Lat. [six]. The sacred Six represented by permutations and combinations of the Trinity e.g. SHIVA, VISHNU, BRAHMĀ and the three Shaktis. Cf. Shadja, Seraphim, Shrī-Āntara, Numbers, Twelves, Sevens, Titans.

SENZAR, the "Mother-Sanskrit" reported of have been brought from Venus by the great Kumāras. Such age-old symbols as the Circle, Cross. Tau, Svastika, Triangle, Quaternary, Pentagon, etc., were important characters of this universal script. Before the confusion of the "Tower of Babel," produced to protect

the Mysteries from an untrustworthy humanity, Senzar was universal. From it the *Stanzas of Dzyan* were translated. Cf. Dan, Numbers, etc.

SEPHER JETZIRAH or YETZIREH, Heb. [Book of Creation]. Two esoteric books dealing with sound and other occult potencies. Cf. Mantram.

SEPHIRA, plural **SEPHIROTH**, Heb. [der. (?) pos. to pierce, deepen, hollow; to shine or be beautiful]. In the *Kabalah* ten potencies or agencies through which the Divine produces the manifested Universe. They come forth in successive emanations from the Divine Light, some male, some female. From Ain Soph or the Absolute, emanates the Trinity (1) *Kepher* (Kaither=Crown, I-am-that-I-am with the Seraphim; (2) *Chochmah* (Wisdom), Jah, with the Ophanim or perhaps the Cherubim, *q.v.*; (3) *Binah* (Understanding), YHVH, *q.v.* Then follow the seven: (4) *Chaised* [grace or mercy] or Gedoolah male, active, [greatness], EI or Power, with the Chashmalim or amber angels, and the planet Saturn; (5) *Geburah* [strength, severity, power], female, passive, Eloah, with, some say the Seraphim, others the Chashmalim, the planet Jupiter; (6) *Tiphaireth*, Tiphereth [ornament, beauty or glory], Elohim or omnipotence, with the Malachim, or some say the Shinanim or angels, Mars; (7) *Naitsach* [victory, or eternity] male, active, Jehovah Zebaoth (Lord of hosts) with the beryl Tarsheeshim, and the Sun; (8) *Hod* [majesty splendour] female, passive, Elohim Zebaoth (might of hosts) with the B'ne Elohim [sons of God] the Planet Venus; (9) *Yesod* (Foundation), EI Chay [the power of life], with the Cherubim, *q.v.*, or perhaps the Ishim, and Mercury; (10) *Malchuth* [Kingdom or Government], Adonai, with the Isheem or some say the Malachim, the Moon. Cf. Trimūrti, Sevens, Angels, Creative Gods, Planetary Spirits, Otz, Sūrya, Tens, Numbers, Unity, Duality.

SERAPHIM, plural of **SARAPH or SERAPH** [der. (?) pos. fiery flying serpent; to consume with fire. Cf. Babylonian Sharrapu, a name for Nergal, the fire God, and Serif, Egyptian Guardian of Graves]. The Six-winged Servants of the Presence, proclaiming the Glory. They touched Isaiah's lips with a burning coal from their altar that his lips might be consecrated to prophesy. Cf. Angel, Gabriel, Agni, Senary.

SERAPIS (Gr. name for Egyptian Deity), the sacred bull Apis, moonbeam engendered, perpetually reincarnating. Cf. Nandi.

SERPENT, Lat. [from root=to creep. Cf. Sarpa]. The Serpent swallowing his own tail, as in the seal of The Theosophical Society, is the ancient symbol of Eternity, the Chakra-Circle without beginning or ending within which all universes grow and decay, Cf. Unity. The serpent is likewise the symbol of Eternal Wisdom, Initiates being so designated. Cf. Aesculapius, Agathodaemon, Ahi, Ananta-Shesha, Apophis, Bala-Rāma, Caduceus, Fafnir, Gabriel, Kadrū, Kāliya, Kundalinī, Midgard, Nāga, Nidhog,

Ophiomorphos, Ophis, Ophite, Python, Quetzo-Cohuatl, Rāhu, Raphael, Sarpa, Seraphim, Thraetaona, Uraeus, Vāsuki.

SESQUIALTERA, Lat. [sesqui=one-halfmore+altera=other]. The ratio of three to two which in music forms the perfect fifth (seven steps by semitones), basis of all harmonic progression, as it is the first *different* harmonic tone appearing when a given tone is struck, *e.g.*, C to G; ष, sa to ч, pa. Numbers, *q.v.*

SESQUITERTIA, Lat. [containing one and a third]. The ratio of four to three, or a perfect musical fourth (five steps by semitones). Next most important harmonic interval to the Sesquialtera its inversion, *e.g.* G to C; ч, pa to ष, sa. Cf. Numbers.

SET, Egy. The evil shadow of Osiris, his brother. Cf. Duality. In early Egypt regarded only as a War-God Cf. Mars, Nephthys, Seb, Typhon.

SEVEN. A Number sacred in Occultism as it is the natural outgrowth of the Trinity, *i.e.*, three factors may be combined in seven possible ways in order of dominance: ABC; ACB; BAC; BCA; CAB; CBA; with a final three in which there is complete balance. Cf. Ogdoad, Āditya, Amesha Spentas, Angels, Archangels, Chohan, Dhyāni-Buddha, Dvīpa, Ilmatar, Kumāra, Loka, Manu, Mithra, Manojava, Oeaohoo, Planetary Spirits, Phorminx, Pleiades, Pravaha, Rays, Riksha, Rishis, Sana, Sanakādikas, Sapta, Saptarishi, Sarasvatī, Sesquialtera, Skandhas, Sephira, Svaras, Talas, Titans.

SHABALĀSHVAS [shabala=variegated+āshvas relating to horses]. *S.D.* sons of Daksha.

SHABDA BRAHMAN [shabda=Sound or Word (Cf. Logos) from shap=to cry aloud+da=giving+Brahman]. The Supreme Spirit, Logos, Īshvara, or the Veda, considered as a revealed Word or Sound. Cf. Unity.

SHADDAI, Heb. [orig. significance=overmastering or overpowering strength. Pos=he who is sufficient]. The Almighty. Cf. Unity.

SHADJA [six-born or produced from six]. Epithet of the Keynote or *Do* of the seven svaras, sounds, of the Hindu gamut. So called because produced from tongue, teeth, palate, nose, throat and chest. Cf. Senary.

SHĀKA [root shak=to be competent, powerful, to bear, give]. Strong, mighty, powerful; the Teak tree, sixth of the Dvipas.

SHAKRA [root shak, see above]. The Powerful One, Name of the God Indra, and of one of the twelve Ādityas. Cf. Unity.

SHAKTI [root shak, see above]. Ability, power, capability, faculty, strength. The outgoing energy of a God is spoken of as his wife or shakti. See Devi, Sarasvati, Lakshmi, etc., Mother, Vāhan. Cf. Duality, Ādi-Shakti, Ïchchhāshakti, Ishtar, Jnānashakti, Kaumāri, Kundalinī.

SHĀKYAMUNI [root shak. Shāk, *q.v.*+muni=saint]. The powerful Saint, Gautama, the Lord Buddha.

SHĀLMAI [from root shal=to flow, run, shake. tremble, praise]. The silk-cotton tree; one of the Dvīpas where the wicked are tormented by

the thorns or prickles of the Shālmali. Cf. Hades.

SHĀMBA [Cf. shamba=Indra's thunderbolt]. Son of Krishna and Jāmbavatī, condemned to produce offspring in the shape of an iron club for the destruction of the race of Vrishni and Andhaka.

SHAMBALLA [pos. from root sham=quiet or tranquillity]. In 70,000 B.C. and for many thousands of years thereafter the "sacred white island" surrounded by the City of Manoa in Central Asia in the Gobi Desert. On this Island lived the Head of the Occult Hierarchy and His Lieutenants, the Kūmaras. Occultists still recognize His Presence there.

SHANI [slow-moving]. The regent of the Planet Saturn. Also a name of Shiva. Shani is held to be a planet of suffering and purging. See Planetary Spirits. Cf. Karma.

SHANKARA [see below]. Epithet of Shiva.

SHANKARĀCHĀRYA [shan-kara=causing happiness+ācharya=one to whom one must have recourse=spiritual guide]. One of the Kumāras, lieutenant of the Head of the Occult Hierarchy who incarnated, using the highly magnetized abandoned subtle vehicles of Gautama Buddha. He corrected certain misunderstandings which had arisen over the Buddha's teachings. (See Vol. 5, S.D.). Also, a celebrated teacher of the Vedānta philosophy reported to have lived anywhere between 200 B.C. and 740 A.D. Founder of one of the principal Shaiva sects, the Dashnāmī-Dandins. Cf. Smārta.

SHANKHA [root sham=happiness]. The conch shell of Vishnu; "the conch has been selected as the symbol of creative activity by sound." Sattvic Ahamkāra, the usual interpretation. Name of Datya who conquered the gods, stole the Vedas, hid them at the bottom of the sea, whence Vishnu, as the Fish Avatar, rescued them.

SHARĪRA [that which easily moulders or is dissolved]. The body, bodily strength. Cf. Upādhi, Sthūla, Sūkshma.

SHASTRA [from shas=to cut or wound, a weapon or sharp tool]. Cf. Astra, Agneyastra.

SHASTRAS [shās=to rule, govern, train, correct, proclaim, implore+tra=protect]. A sacred book or religious or scientific treatise.

SHEKINAH, Heb. [dwelling]. Manifestation of God as Light, Glory; the Indwelling Presence. Veil of the Divine. Cf. Mūlaprakriti, Merkabah, Vāhan.

SHELL, Theos. The cast-off remnants of subtle bodies that retain a certain likeness to the former wearer, influencing mediums in séances. Cf. elementaries.

SHEM, Heb. [man of fame, renown, shining, internal essence]. Eldest son of Noah; by biblical students held to be the type of the Mongolian Race (or Atlantean Race) as Ham was the type of the Nergo (or Lemurian) race, and Japheth was the type of the Āryans.

SHINTO, Chin. [shen=god+tao=The Way]. The ethnic and national cult of the Japanese, not considered by them as incompatible with other religions. It is a way essentially of channelship in which after purification its devotees invoke the Powers through Kami-oroshi or the "bringing-down-of-the Gods." Cf. Theurgy.

SHISHUMĀRA [shishu=child+māra=killer]. The Heavenly porpoise, a form of Vishnu, the tail of Ursa Minor. Cf. Water.

SHISHUPĀLA [child-cherisher]. The reincarnation of the spirit of evil, ignorance or resistance, which the Avatar Krishna killed. Cf. Satan, Duality, Ahriman, Vishnu.

SHISTA [Cf. Shāstra]. Ordered, commanded, chiefs, courtiers, counsellors, examples of good conduct.

SHIVA [der. (?) shī=to rest, repose, sleep, says Unādi-s. I, 153. Cf. shvi=to swell, grow, thrive, and shavas=power, strength, vigour from shav=to transform]. The Regenerator of all; Supreme Bliss. With Brahmā and Vishnu, the Hindu Trimūrti. Cf. Nīlakantha, Rudra, Nandi. Also Ardhanari, Aum, Damaru, Digambara, Kailāsa, Kārtikeya, Lilā, Linga, Nīla-Lohita, Pāsha, Pulaha, Satī, Sāvitrī, Shankara, Shiva, Gharmaja, Trilochana, Trishūla, Vāmadeva, Vīrabhadra.

SHIVA-GHARMAJĀ [born from the perspiration of Shiva, q.v.]. Epithet of the planet Mars. Cf. Raumas.

SHOO, Egy. the god Ra, represented as the "great cat of the Basin of Persea in An."

SHRAMANA [one who makes effort]. Jain ascetic, devotee, beggar. Cf. Yoga.

SHRĀVAKA [root shru=to hear or be attentive and obedient]. A hearer, pupil, disciple, class of Buddhist saints or ascetics. Cf. Shruti.

SHRĪ [prosperity, well-being, wealth, rank, sacredness, majesty, royalty, glory, renown, splendour, lustre, beauty]. Lakshmī; also used of Sarasvatī. Cf. Mother.

SHRĪ-ĀNTARA [antara=near, intimate, soul, heart]. Solomon's Seal or Double-Triangle; in its closely interwoven Triangles, a symbol of Spirit-Matter. Cf. Senary.

SHRUTI [anything heard. Cf. Shrāvaka]. Revelation. Smallest tone in music, etc.

SHUCHI [bright, resplendent, pure, white, virtuous, true, gentle, accuracy]. Name of the Fire of Purification. Cf. Agni, Pāvaka, Pavamāna, Trimūrti.

SHUDDHA SATTVA [shūddha=pure+sattva, q.v.]. Essence of matter. Cf. Prakriti.

SHUKRA [bright, resplendent, white, pure]. The regent of the Planet Venus. Cf. Planetary Spirits, Kūmāra, Brigu, Shveta.

SHVETA [dressed in white]. The Planet Shukra. Venus. Also one of the minor Dvīpas. Often translated as "the White Island." Cf. Shamballah, Shveta.

SIDDHA [sidh=to be accomplished, fulfilled, established, attained]. Semi-divine being of great purity and holiness, specially characterized by possession of the eight siddhis. Sometimes confused with the Sādhyas, q.v. Cf. Siddhapura.

SIDDHA-PURA [city of the Siddhas, q.v.]. Said to be located in the southern or lower regions.

SIDDHIS [powers of the Self]. Cf. Siddha. The eight usually enumerated are: animan=the power to become as small as an atom; mahiman=the power of increasing size at will; laghiman or levitation=the power to make the body as light as cottonwool; gariman=the power to make oneself heavy at will; prāpti=the power to obtain anything desired; prākāmya=an irresistible will; īshi-tva=superiority and supremacy; vashi-tva=the power to hold others in subjection to one's will. The above are considered as especial attributes of Shiva. To these are added Kāmā, vasāyi-tva=the power of suppressing desire at will; the power of flight and permeability; strength like Nārāyana. Bodily suppleness, smoothness and immunity to fire; ability to transmute and disperse all substances, or alchemy; transparency of the body which casts no shadow; the power of making the body invisible to others; and the transmutation of the body into vari-coloured rainbow radiances. Cf. Vibhūtayah, Yoga.

SIDZANG, Chin. Tibet.

SIGURD, Icel. Hero of the Volsunga Sāga who slays the dragon Fafnir, and, eating his heart, becomes the wisest of men—symbol of Initiation. Cf. Serpent.

SILOAM [canal, to conduct or send]. The sleep of Siloam was that of Initiation.

SIN, Ass. The Moon-God, variously conceived of as lord of wisdom, dispeller of darkness, giver of dreams and oracles. Cf. Vishnu, Sinai.

SINAI, Heb. [der. (?) pos. desert; or from Sin. Some rabbis say this mount is identical with Horeb.] The Holy Mountain wherein the power of the Lord dwells, and whereon Moses received the Ten Commandments. Occult, Lunar cycles. Cf. Mount Everest, Mount Kailāsa in India where Shiva dwells, Olympus, etc.

SĪTĀ [pos. from si=to bind; a furrow representing agriculture]. Wife of Rāma. Some take her as a symbol of the soul. Cf. Asita, Duality.

SKANDHAS, Buddhist. [skand=to rise]. Five, esoterically seven, Kārmic and innate attributes of the finite: 1. rūpa=form; 2. vidāna=perception; 3. sanjnā=consciousness; 4. samskāra=action; 5. vidyāna=knowledge. Cf. Vidyā. The essence of the attributes endures between incarnations, uniting at birth to form the personality. Cf. Quinary, Sevens, Reincarnation, Nidāna. Also used for a King or Prince; and the division of an Army. Name for Kārtikeya.

SMARAGDINE, Lat. der. [of or pertaining to an emerald]. In S.D. refers to the famous Tablet of Hermes Trismegistus, said by Éliphas Levi, to contain " the whole of magic in a single page."

SMĀRTAVA [smriti=remembrance, thought, traditional law]. A sect of Brāhmans skilled in jurisprudence, especially those belonging to a sect founded by Shankarāchārya, whose chief establishment is at Shringa-giri.

SOD, Heb. [breast, fulness that pours itself out]. An " Arcanum," or religious mystery. Cf. Plenum, Sodales.

SODALES, Lat. Initiates and members of the Priest-colleges of the Sod.

SOMA [root su=to distil, extract or sprinkle; Cf. su=to generate]. The mystic soma juice is supposed to have been pressed from a climbing plant Sarcostema Viminalis or Asclepias Acida which grows abundantly on the mountains of India and Persia, and whose exhilarating properties were used in ceremonial rites. The Soma God was all-powerful, all pervading, healing all diseases, lord of all other gods, and the Supreme Being. Soma is identified with the Moon, Amrita, etc. Cf. Amrita, Haoma, Hari, Maru-Vat, Purushottama, Sādhya, Unity, Tārā, Veda.

SOMA-PA [a drinker of soma juice].

SOPHIA, Gr. [primary and general meaning=craft, skill, artistic ability, especially in the fine arts, medicine, sports, etc]. From this grew the secondary meaning of skill in living, sage and sound judgment, political wisdom, knowledge of sciences, wisdom, philosophy. To Aristotle, Sophia was the Supreme Science, the Science of Causes. To the Gnostics, Sophia was the female Logos, the Universal Mind, Wisdom incarnate. Cf. Athenā, Sarasvatī, also Goddesses of Wisdom and Artistic Expression. Theosophy, Ildabaoth, Pistis Sophia, Sophia Achamoth.

SOPHIA ACHAMOTH, Gr. Daughter of Sophia. The reflection of Sophia in the Astral Light or lower plane of Ether.

SPAGYRIZATION (Eng. obsolete) [to separate and assemble]. Alchemical process.

SPARSHA [sprish=to touch or contact]. The quality inherent in Buddhic matter which gives to all beings the power of contact. Cf. Sūtrātma, Nidāna.

SRAVAH, Mazdean. Higher aspects of Amesha Spentas, q.v.

SROTĀPANNA, SROTĀPATTI, Bud. [he who has entered the stream]. The First Initiation which plunges the Initiate into the stream of the One Life. Cf. Unity.

STHŪLA [stout, bulky, thick, gross]. The grosser physical, as used with sharira, etc.

SUDYUMMA [very bright. The female child of Manu Vaivasvata born under the name of Ida, changed to a male by favour of Mitra and Varuna, S.D., q.v. Cf. Duality, Androgyne.

SŪFI, Arab. [der, (?) wool; pos. wise, pure, devout]. Mohammedan mystic who gains insight into the Divine Being through ecstasy and contemplation.

SŪKSHMA [subtle, minute, atomic, delicate]. Epithet of Shiva; the all-pervading-spirit. When used with sharira=subtle body or bodies. Sūkshmopādhi has same meaning as with sharira.

SUMATI [of good mind, benevolence]. Son of Bhārata, q.v.

SUOYATOR, Fin. Primordial Spirit of Evil in the Kalevala. Cf. Ahriman, Duality.

SURA [by some thought to be from su=to pour out or extract juice; but according to some formed from asura; also thought to be from svar=heaven. Cf. sur=to possess supreme or superhuman power]. Heavenly beings. The Gods, always thought of as beneficent and giving gifts, as contrasted with the dynamic asuras who often embodied the spirit of resistance.

SURABHI [root sura, *q.v.* sweet-smelling, charming, friendly]. The earth as a symbolic cow of plenty.

SURADHIPA [sovereign of the suras, *q.v.*]. Indra.

SURASA [the good taste]. A daughter of Daksha, Kashyapa's wife and the mother of a thousand many-headed serpents and dragons.

SURTUR, Scand. The leader of the fiery sons of Muspel in the *Eddas*. Cf. Agni.

SURYA [pos. originally sur-ya=heavenly one; or savan from root su. Cf. sura; pos. from sri=to move, to blow]. The Sun-God, all-creating, all-seeing son of Dyaus, the wide-spreading Sky. Cf. Agni, Apollo, Astrarte, Brahmandika, Faroher, Gayatri, Graha-Raja, Helios, Horus, Imhot-Pou, Ishtar, Jishnu, Martanda, Mithra, Phaethon, Phoebus, Phoenix, Phtah, Quetzo-Cohuatl, Ra, Sanjna, Savarna, Savitri, Scarabaeus, Sephira, Sol, Titans, Ushas, Vikartana, Vishvakarman, Vishvanara.

SURYA-VAMSHAS [the solar dynasty of Ramachandra, who was descended from Ikshvaku, son of Vaivasvata Manu, son of the Sun].

SUSHUMNA [rich in happiness, highly blessed]. The central sexless vital air, aspect of kundalini in the spinal column. Cf.Caduceus,Ida,Pingala, Trinity, Vayu.

SUSHUPTI [the good or deep sleep; profound repose].

SUTALA [immense depth]. One of the seven divisions of the lower regions, peopled by the Nagas. In some classifications sixth. Cf. Tala.

SUTRA [from root siv=to sew. Cf. sutr=to tie, thread]. A short rule or precept, axiom. aphorism.

SUTRATMA [thread-self. Cf. sutr]. So-called because the permanent atoms or nuclei of the various bodies are strung on a buddhic life-web. Cf. Buddhi, sparsha, Atma.

SVA-BHAVA [own state]. Essential or inherent property; natural state. Cf. Unity.

SVABHAVAT [see sva-bhava]. Plastic substance, or essential matter. Cf. Mulaprakriti, Unity.

SVABHAVIKA [see Sva-bhava]. Oldest existing school of Buddhism, which assigned manifestation to Svabhava.

SVAHA. [Cf. sv-adha=a good offering to the Pitris through fire]. Oblation personified, the wife of Agni, sometimes Rudra. A mystic word meaning " So be it," uttered with a rising inflection at the end of many mantrams to the Gods.

SVAMI [possessing proprietary rights]. Master, Lord, Sovereign, Spiritual Preceptor, a learned Brahman, or an ascetic. Title of many of the Gods, especially of Kartikeya, Vishnu, Siva.

SVARA [svri=to sound]. The seven tones of Hindu gamut: shadja, rishaba, gandhara, madhyama, panchama, dhaivata, nishada.

SVARAJ [sva=self+raj=resplendent or luminous]. An epithet of many of the Gods. The Ray, which is said to be the outermost cover, self-manifesting.

SVARGA [originally survar. Cf. sura and surya, thought to be from lost root svar=to shine]. Heaven, paradise, the abode of Indra and the Gods. Also called SVARLOKA.

SVAROCHISHA [sva-rochis=self-luminous]. Name of the second Manu.

SVA-SAMVEDANA [self-perception]. Truth of Truths. Cf. Dharma.

SVASTIKA [sv-asti=health, welfare, joy, bliss]. An auspicious object, especially used of the fiery cross whose extemities trail flames. Symbol of the Creative Fire of the Third Logos or Holy Spirit, Brahma. Its right arm points down in positive blessing, its left arm up in receptivity, as viewed in the Theosophical seal. It was one of the mystic symbols of the ancient Senzar and is found universally. Cf. Chakra, Agni.

SVAYAM-BHU, SVAYAMBHUVA [Self-Existent]. Universal Spirit. Cf. Unity.

SYLPH. A name given by Paracelsus to the elemental spirits of the air.

T

T'AGATHON [To Agathon=the highest good]. The Supreme Self; Atma. Cf. Unity.

TAIJASA [tejas=sharp point of flame]. Bright, luminous, fiery, shining. Used of Manas when it is overshadowed by Buddhi.

TALA [level surface, flat covering]. Hole pit, chasm, division of hell or the lower regions. Diagram V, vol. v. *S.D.*, *q.v.* Cf. Atala, Karatala, Patala, Rasatala, Rupatala, Sutala, Vitala.

TALISMAN, Arab. [tilism=a magical image]. An object charged with definite and strong etheric and more subtle vibrations which through their overtones tend to awaken in whoever comes in contact corresponding octaves of emotional and mental response. Talismans are *general*, *adapted* for a particular individual; *ensouled* as a indefinite centre of radiation; or *linked* with the maker as an outpost of his consciousness.

TALMUD, Heb. [lamad=to learn; limned=to teach]. Body of Jewish civil and canonical law. Cf. Mishnah.

TAMAS See Gunas. TAMASA=pertaining to Tamas.

TAMRA [coppery red]. Daughter of Daksha, a wife of Kashyapa, mother of various birds.

TANAIM, Aramic. [teachers]. A name applied to the rabbis.

TANHA, Pali. [thirst]. Desire to live and manifest in phenomenal existence. Cf. Nidana.

TANMATRAS [tan for tad=That+matra= measure]. A measure of THAT; one of the changes in the Divine Consciousness producing a plane or tattva.

TANTALUS, Gr. son of Zeus, whose punishment by the Gods for an atrocious sin stands as a symbol of the after-death experiences of the soul chained to sensual desire, for whenever Tantalus stretched out his hand for the desired object within his grasp, it eluded him. Cf. Hades.

TANTRA [the warp or threads from tan=to extend or stretch out]. An uninterrupted series; a religious treatise teaching magical and mystical formularies for the worship of the deities, treating five subjects: 1. creation; 2. world destruction; 3. worship of the gods; 4. attainment of the siddhis; 5. modes of union with the Supreme by meditation. TĀN-TRIKA [relating to the Tantras].

TAO ORI.=genius of the Moon.

TAO, Chin. [thought to be closely linked with Tau, the Sacred Word of the Atlantean root race]. The Way, the Path, Nature, Reason, Occult. The Inner Way or Flame of Life. The teaching given by Lao Tze in China in the 6th century B.C. in the TAO-TE-KING [te=action or manifestation+King=Classic]. The Class of the Manifested Source. Cf. Shinto, Mārga, Initiation, Tīrthankara.

TAPAR-or TAPO-LOKA, Loka, q.v.

TAPAS [tap=to heat or shine]. Tapas is the five fires to which an ascetic is exposed in the summer, i.e., four fires lighted in the four quarters and the sun overhead. Its derived meaning is any religious austerity involving self-denial, penance, suffering. Cf. Yoga.

TĀRĀ [trī=shining, star; or pos. for stāra from stri=to scatter rays of light; or possibly from as=to shine]. All-pervading, radiating, conquering; a pearl. The wife of one of Rāma's monkey-generals; the wife of Brihaspati, who was carried off by Soma.

TĀRADAITYA, TĀRAKA [root tāra, q.v. Tāraka=one who helps another through a difficulty, belonging to the stars]. Name of a Daitya, conquered by Indra, with the assistance of Kārtikeya.

TĀRAKĀ-MAYA [on account of Tārā]. The war waged by gods and demons for her rescue.

TĀRAKA RĀJA YOGA=S.D. One of the Brāhminical Yoga systems for the development of purely spiritual powers, and the attainment of Nirvāna. See above.

TĀRANA [that which enables another cross]. Name of the third year of the fourth Jupiter cycle.

TARGUM, Heb. [interpretation]. An oral translation of sacred texts.

TARTARUS, Gr. the infernal regions, situated as far below Hades or Purgatory as heaven is above earth. Cf. Uriel.

TAT, Egy. a symbol of male and female generation, made of an upright standard on which is a horizontal equilateral cross. Emblem of stability. Cf. Duality.

TATHĀGATA [of such a quality or nature; some translate tatha as "beyond", making the whole " he who has gone beyond "]. "One who is like those gone before" or "He who follows in the footsteps of his Buddha predecessors." An epithet of Gautama the Buddha.

TATTVA [state of being, reality as opposed to the illusory; essential nature]. States of matter. Cf. Tanmātras, Mahat-tattva creation, Planes.

TAU. Cf. Tao. Egy, Like the letter T, the Tau is a vertical standard on which rests a horizontal bar. With the circle resting thereon, it becomes the Crux Ansata or Egyptian Ankh in the centre of the Theosophical seal, symbol of Spirit which has descended into matter, been crucified therein, risen from death, and now rests triumphant on the two poles of manifestation, the vertical positive and horizontal receptive. Cross of Life or Immortality. Tau is the sacred word of the Atlanteans. Cf. Aum. Unity, Duality, Crucifixion, Resurrection.

TEMURA, T'MURA, Heb. [change]. The science by which Kabalists trace hidden analogies between words through transposition of letters.

TERAPHIM, Heb. Household images used in divination in ancient Jewish families.

TESHU LĀMA [Tehu Lunpo, the place where Lama had his origin]. The spiritual head of the Lamaic hierarchical order of Tibet, as the Dalai Lamai is the temporal head.

TETRAKTYS, TETRACTYS, Gr. [Four]. The Pythagorean symbol representing the principle of manifestation, in which is to be found the Unity, the Duality, and the Trinity, as well as the Quaternary. Cf. Numbers.

TETRAGRAMMATON=the four consonants YHVH, forming the incommunicable word of the Hebrew Supreme Being. Cf. Hè, Quaternary, Numbers.

THALASSA, THALATTH, THAVATTH, Chal. the God of the sea. Identical with the Assyrian Tiamat. Cf. Water.

THEOSOPHY, Gr. [Theos. manifested God+Sophia, q.v.]. As within the word Sophia is implied Creative Art, both in form and in life, which is the Supreme Wisdom, so Theosophy might be defined as the Art of God-Craft, that Ancient Wisdom which through every Mystery School of old taught its Initiates the Art of Arts—the release of the Shining Self.

THLINKITHIANS, TLINKITHIANS=Indian of a sea-faring group of Southern Alaska.

THOR, Icel. God of Thunder, Strength, War, Defence. Thor's Day or Thursday is said to be Jupiter's Day. Cf. Mars, Indra, Uriel.

THORAH, Heb. [Torah=Law]. Pentateuch. The Law of Moses.

THOTH, THOT, Egy. [Greek form of Egyptian Tehuti]. Scribe of the Gods, measurer of time, inventor of numbers; God of wisdom and magic, represented with the head of an ibis. Cf. Hermes Trismegistus, Bird.

THRÆTAOMA, Mazdean. The Persian Michael, who contended with Zohak, the destroying serpent.

THUMMIM, Bab. [complete whole, free from blemish]. Used with the Urim as tablets of destiny, through which YHVH communicated his will to his chosen people, the Hebrews. By some thought to be the stones in the high

priest's breastplate, by some the sacred dice, and by others, the little images of Truth and Justice such as are found round the neck of a mummy of an Egyptian priest. [Urim=urtu or fires, while thummin=tamitu=oracle].

TIAMAT, Thalassa, q.v.

TIAOU, Egy. a Devachanic after-death state.

TIEN-HOANG, Chin, Twelve Hierarchies of Dhyānis.

TĪRTHANKARA [tīrtha=the Way, the Ford, the Descent, the Shrine+kara=the doing or making of]. The Jain Adept, he who has become the Way; the Bridge over which the devotee passes.

TITAN, Gr. [der. (?) pos. titainō=he who stretches or strives; titas=avengers; titaz=kings or chiefs]. Primeval Deities, the six sons and daughters of Uranus and Gaia, from whom were born all the hierarchies of Gods, also sometimes called Titans. The six couples are: (1) Okeanos (great water girdle of the world) and his wife Tethys (the lovely), nurse of Hera; (2) Kronos (time), who with Rhea (ease, lightness, the fertile earth), bore Zeus and the Olympian Gods; (3) Iapetos (speed), who with Themis (she who makes fast, the lawgiver), bore Emimetheus, Prometheus, Atlas, Maia (Pleiades) and Dione (held by some to be mother by Zeus of Aphrodite). Themis in union with Zeus begot the seasons. (4) Koios (Number) who with Phoebe, (gold-crowned) bore Asterie and Leto, Latona; (5) Hyperion (sun-God), who with Theia (from Div=shining, Divine), bore Helios, the Sun, Selene, the Moon; and Eos, the Dawn Goddess; Cf. Sūrya, Ushas. (6) Kre (i) os (a ram). Cf. Mendes who with Mnemosyne (memory), bore Perse, the official consort of Helios. Mnemosyne by Zeus bore the nine muses or arts and crafts. Mention is also made of Phoreg a Mystery or Seventh Titan. Both the Gods and their descendants are spoken of as Titans. Cf. Angels, Senary, Twelves, Dānava, Kabarim, Nephilim, Phoroneus, Nimir Porphyrion, Rephaim, Water, Uranides.

TITYOS, TITYUS, a giant son of Gaea or of Zeus who for offering violence to Latona, was slain by her son Apollo. His punishment in Hades, to have vultures gnaw his liver, is a symbol of after-death purification.

TO ON, Gr. [" the ineffable all "]. Of Plato.

TOOM, Egy. A Protean God, emanation from the great deep Noot. S.D. links with Fohat.

TRETĀ YUGA [Treta=a die marked with three spots]. The second or silver age consisting of 1,296,000 years. Cf. Yuga.

TRIBHUJAM [Tri=three+bhujam arms]. A triangle.

TRIDANDIN [triple staved]. The interwoven staff of the sannyasi. Trinity. Cf. Brahmananda.

TRIDASHA [thirty].

TRIGUNAS. Gunas, q.v.

TRILOCHANA [three-eyed]. Epithet of Shiva, the third eye bursting forth to save the world from annihilation when Parvatī (matter) his wife playfully blinded him. Cf. Pineal Gland.

TRIMŪRTI [three-formed]. TRINITY. Within all Unity there is a Positive and Negative aspect, a Duality of Light and Darkness, Spirit-matter, Silence-Sound, Life-Form, etc. Out of manifestation, this is balanced in stable equilibrium. The act of manifestation throws it out of its static equilibrium into instability. An " unstable or dynamic equilibrium " is established by the immediate lightening flashing forth of the relation between the opposite poles, the Duality thus becoming a Trinity without which manifestation is impossible. " The One (Deity becomes Two (Deva or Angel) and Two becomes Three (or Man)." Cf. Number, Unity. Aum, Brahmā, Vishnu, Shiva; Kepher, Chokmah, Binah; Devi, Lakshmī, Sarasvatī; Dharmakāya, Sambhogakāya, Nirmanakāya; Eros, Gaea, Uranus, Phanes, Chaos, Kronos, Gunas, Isis, Horus, Osiris; Pāvaka, Pāvamāna, Shuchi; Kavyavāhana, Havyavāhana, Saharaksha; Tetrad; Tribhujam, Tridandin, Trigunas, Trilochana, Trishūla, Faroher, Neshamah; Ānanda, Chit, Sat; Idā, Pingala, Sushumna; Anu, Ea, Bel.

TRIPITAKA [three baskets]. The Buddhist canon composed of—1. the Doctrine; 2. the Rules and laws for the priesthood and ascetics; 3. Philosophical dissertations and metaphysics.

TRISHŪLA [trident of Shiva, q.v.].

TRISUPARNA [tri=three+suparna=beautiful winged or leaved]. Title of certain hymns of the Rig and Yajur Vedas; one who is conversant therewith being called a tri-suparnaka.

TRITON, Gr. Sea-god, son of Poseidon-Neptune, and Amphitrite. Later represented as a race of mermen.

TSABA, Heb. [Army or Host of Heaven].

TSELEM, TZELEM, Heb. [shade, phantom, image, likeness]. Cf. Elementaries.

TUBAL-CAIN, Heb. [Tubhal-qayin=beauty, external welfare, riches]. Son of Lamech and Zillah, " the first forger of every cutting instrument of brass and iron, and instructor of his art to every artificer." Cf. Hephaestus Asura-Maya, Vishvakarman, Vulcan.

TURĪYA [fourth; whose power extends on all four sides]. A state of oneness with the universal spirit; the fourth state of the soul. Cf. Samādhi.

TVASHTRI [carpenter, generator, builder, workman]. Identified with the later deity Vishvakarman. The Vulcan, of the Hindus.

TYPHŌEUS, Gr. Son of Tartarus and Gaea, or of Hera alone. A hundred-headed father of the Winds who made war upon the gods. Cf. Duality, Typhon, Vāyu. The word has a connotation of volcanic agency.

TYPHON, Egy. identified with Set. (Greek) son of Typhoeus, q.v., and father of Cerberus, the Chimaera, the Sphinx and other monsters.

TZALA, Heb. [shadow; veiling, fleeting image, Māya, q.v.].

TZURE, Heb. Prototype of the Image or Tselem, q.v., the Eternal Divine Individual. Cf. Archetype.

U

UDĀNA [to breathe upwards]. That vital air which rises up the throat and passes into the head. With Buddhists, an expression of joy or praise. Cf. Prānāyāma.

ULŪPĪ [a spreading creeper]. Name of a daughter of Nāga Kauravya, married to Arjuna.

ULYSSES, ULIXES, Lat. [a hater]. Gr.= Odysseus. King of Ithaca, famed among the Grecian heroes of the Torjan war. Husband of the faithful Penelope.

UMĀ [root ve=to weave, braid, plait]. Flax, light, splendour, quiet, tranquillity, night. A name of a wife of Shiva. Cf. Mother.

UNDINE. Paracelsus so named the elemental spirits of water.

UNITY, [one-ness]. Cf. Monad. The one absolute Reality behind the multiplications of that Unity in numbered manifestation. Cf. Numbers Trimūrti, Abraxas, Adam Kadmon, Ādi, and its compounds, Aditi, Advaita, Aham-sa, Ain Suph, Aja, Ālaya, Ammon, Ananta-Shesha, Anima Mundi, Anupādaka, Arche, Asha, Asura, Atom, Atyantika Avyaya, Bhūtādi, Bhūtātman, Bhūtesha, Brahma, Chidākāsham, Chinmātra, Echath, Echod, Eka, El, Hamsa, Īshvara, Jīvātman, Jupiter, Khoom, Logos, Madhya, Madhyamā, Mahāvishnu, Mūlaprakriti, Nara, Nārāyana, Nirguna, Odin, Pachacamac, Parabrahman, Paramārtha, etc., Plenum, Pradhāna, Prima Materia, Protogonos, Protologos, Protomateria, Protyle, Ptah, Purushottama, Pūrvaja, Ru, Sana, Sarvaga, Sarvātman, Sarvāvasu, Sarvesha, Sat, Sattva, Sephira, Shabda Brahman, Shaddai, Shakra, Shiva, Sophia, Spiritus, Sva-bhāva, Sva-Samvedanā, Svayam-Bhū, T'Agathon, Tao, Tau, *Theos*, To On, Young Grüb, Zeroana.

UPĀDĀNA [taking, acquiring, appropriating, including, containing, withdrawal, material cause, effort]. Particularly used in connection with assuming a form or manifestation. Cf. Nidāna, Upadhi.

UPĀDHI [upā=near+dhā=to place, offer, keep hold]. Disguise, body, limitation. Cf. Sharīra.

UPANISHADS [sad with upa+ni=sitting at the feet of another to learn how " to destroy ignorance by revealing the knowledge of the supreme spirit "]. Esoteric doctrine—mystical writings revealing the secret sense of the Veda. Cf. Rahasya, Guhya Vidyā, Vedānta.

URAEUS, Lat. [with a tail]. The Egyptian sacred serpent shown on the forehead crest, symbol of the vision held by the Pharoah. Initiates.

URANIDES [descendants of Uranus]. Titans.

URANUS, OURANOS, Gr. [Ouranos=Heavens, the Sky, identical with Varuna, or the firmament at night]. Son or husband of Gæa and father of the Titans, the Hecatoncheires [threehundred-handed giants or crashing waves], the Cyclops, the giants, the Furies. A Primeval God or Cause from whom came Kronos, who dethroned him, and was in turn dethroned by Jupiter. With Gæa and Eros, formed one of the oldest Trimūrtis. Cf. Planetary Spirits, Aphrodite, Phoebe, Rhea.

ŪRDHVA-SROTAS= Creation of beings whose stream of life or current of nutriment tends upwards.

URIEL, UZZIEL, Heb. [fire of God]. The fourth of the Angels of the Cardinal Points. See Michael, Gabriel, Raphael, though in *Enoc* he is listed as first of the seven archangels. He is Lord of Tartaruś, Head of the Malakim, Lord of Earthquake and Thunder. Said by some to be the Angel of Sunday and copper. Later authorities identified Uriel with Light. Cf. El, Thor, Indra.

ŪRJĀ [ūrj=food, strength, vigour, sap]. Procreative power; effort, like, breath. Name of several of the Gods, especially of the sons of Hiranya-garbha, reckoned among the seven Rishis of the third Manvantara.

USH [to shine]; USHAS [morning light or dawn] Daughter of Heaven and sister of the Ādityas. Cf. Eos. Titans, Sūrya, Vasu.

UTPALA VARNA [coloured as a blue lotus flower or to burst upwards as blossom]. One of the three esoteric forces. Cf. Gopā, Yasodharā.

UTTARA [upper, higher]. KHANDA. Last section.

UZZA, Heb. An angel, *q.v.*, who, together with Azrael opposed the creation of man by the Elohim, for which the latter annihilated both, according to the *Zohar, q.v.*

V

VĀCH [to speak, proclaim, etc.] The Goddess of the Creative Tone. Cf. Ākāsha, Idā, Vaikharī.

VĀHAN, VĀHANA [vāha=bearing or carrying] A vehicle, chariot, animal which can be ridden. In Hindu occultism, every God has His Shaktī, and every God and Goddess His or Her Vāhan, the God expressed in matter or form. The Vāhan is that type of form in which the power can be most readily embodied, symbolized or expressed, usually some form of animal, etc. which typifies the particular quality of the God's manifestation. *e.g.*, Nandi, Hamsa, Garuda, Ibis, Makara, Scarabeus, Eagle, Lamb, Cow, etc. Cf. Merkabah, Shekinah, Vimanā, Yama.

VAIDHĀTRA [from vidhātri=arranging, disposing, making, creating]. Vidhātri is a name of Brahmā, the creator, Vishvakarman, Kāma. Vaidhātra is a name for Sanatkumāra.

VAIDYUTA [vidyut=lightning]. Proceeding from lightning; electrical. Cf. Agni.

VAIKHARĪ=speech in the fourth of its four stages, from the first stirring of the air or breath, articulate utterance, that utterance of sounds or words complete in intelligible sentences. The Goddess of Speech. Cf. Vāch.

VAIKUNTHA-LOKA [vi-kuntha=not worn out, ever fresh]. Name of Vishnu, Krishna, and with the word Loka becomes the Heaven of these Gods, on the Eastern peak of Mount Meru. Cf. Olympus, Kailās, etc.

VAISHVĀNARA [Vishvānara, *q.v.*]. Relating to or fit for all men and benefiting all mankind. Son of Vishvā-nara, epithet of Agni. The fire

of digestion. The Spirit of Humanity. The fire of intellect or general consciousness.

VAIVASVATA [patronymic from vivasvat=the Brilliant One, a name of the Sun]. Vaivasvata Manu, is the present Manu, literally Father of the Āryan Race, whose work of race-building after many preliminary millennia was definitely established through an incarnation in Central Asia 60,000 B.C. The name Vaivasvata is also generic. Cf. Ikshvāku, Satya-Vrata, Sudyumna, Sūrya, Sūrya-vamshas.

VAJRADHARA [Vajra=adamantine, hard, impenetrable, forked, zigzag, thunderbolt, diamond, lightning, from vaj=to go, roam, increase, be hard or strong, to prepare the way+dhara=holder]. Usually translated Diamond or Thunderbot-Holder, an epithet of Indra. Cf. Dorje-sempa.

VAJRAPĀNI [vajra+handed. See above].

VAJRASATTVAS [vajra=sattva]. Usually translated " with adamant or diamond soul or heart." Dorjesempa and Maitreya, Dhyāni-Buddhas.

VALHALLA, WALHALLA, Icel. [hell of the slain]. Hall of Odin, in which he receives the souls of heroes slain in battle. Cf. Hades, Yggdrasil

VĀMADEVA [vāma=opposite or contrary and translated as the pairs of opposites, ugly-handsome, etc. A name of many of the Gods]. Name of a Vedic Rishi, author of the hymns Rig Veda IV, 1-41, 45-48. Name of Shiva.

VARA, Per. Creations of Yima.

VARĀHA [vrih=to tear up roots]. A boar. Superiority, Pre-eminence. Avatar of Vishnu who, as a boar, raised the earth from the bottom of the sea with his tusks. Symbol of the Mammalian Period.

VARNA [colour, covering, class, order, caste].

VARSHAS [der. (?) vrish=to rain; vri=to surround]. Rain, place or country. Continents of the world, the names of which are: Kuru (from kri=to do or make, probably a country above the Himālayas, one of everlasting happiness, home of the Āryan race): Hiranmaya (=made of gold; epithet of Brahmā, said to be between mountainous ranges Shveta and Shringavat) ;Ramyaka [the delightful]; Ilāvrita [ilā=flow, speech, the earth, the highest and most central part of the old continent]; Hari (Home of Vishnu); Ketu-mālā (ketu=brightness, light, chief+mālā=garland); western portion of Jambu-dvīpa, dvīpā; Bhadrāshva (honoured), some say the Eastern one of the four Mahādvīpas; Kinnara (country between the Himāchala and Hemakūta mountains); Bhārata (India).

VARUNA. Cf. Uranus. [universal encompasser; all-enveloper]. An Āditya. One of the oldest of the Vedic gods, sometimes regarded as the Supreme Deity. He fashions and upholds heaven and earth, is Incarnate Wisdom. God of all the Waters of the firmament; Regent of the Western quarter; King of the Nāgas, Presides over night as Mitra; presides over day. Cf. Vishnu, Bhrigu, Prachetās, Sudgumna, Vratāna.

VASISHTHA or VASHISHTHA [the most self-subdued; or the most wealthy]. A celebrated Vedic Rishi, q.v. owner of the cow of plenty. Typical representative of the Brahman or priestly caste. Cf. Surabhi.

VASU [wealthy, sweet-flavoured] celestial beings, the names of which according to Vishnu-purāna are: Āpa [from water]; Dhruva, q.v.; Soma, q.v.; Dhava or Dhara [bearer or supporter, the earth; Anila [Wind]; Anala or Pāvaka, q.v. [Fire]; Pratyūsha [the Dawn]; Prabhāsa [Light]. Sometimes Ahan [Day] is substituted for Āpa. Cf. Sarvāvasu, Sūrya, Ushas, Vāyu, Agni, Vishva. See below.

VASUDEVA [vasu+deva, q.v.]. Name of the father of Krishna, and Bala-Rāma, q.v. VĀSU-DEVA, LORD of ALL. Cf. Purushottama-Vishnu.

VĀSUKI [vāsu=dwelling in all beings]. Sovereign of the Serpents, q.v.

VAU=sixth letter of the Hebrew alphabet; and the numeral six.

VĀYU [vā=to blow, move, pierce, dry]. The God of the Wind. Often associated with Indra in the Rig-veda. Regent of the North-west quarter; and of the vital airs: prāna, apāna, samāna, vyāna. Cf. Aeolus, Breath, Hanuman, Idā, Ilmatar, Marut-Van, Pingalā, Pravaha, Sushumnā.

VEDA [vid=knowing]. The true or divine knowledge. The three-fold knowledge being given in the Rig-veda, from the fire the Yajur-veda, from air (cf. Vāyu) the Sāma-veda [song-veda] from the sun. (Cf. Sūrya). Then was added the Atharva-veda [fire and soma-veda], a veda of mantras, and formulae as to sacrifice. Vedic, pertaining to the Veda. Cf. Chandogya, Shabda Brahman, Shankha, Agni, Soma-Vidyā, Vyāsa.

VEDĀNTA [end of the Veda]. That portion of the Upanishads, which teaches the knowledge of Brahma or Universal Spirit, Paramātman, the material cause of all; Ātman, as identical with the Supreme, and their existence in manifestation as only the result of Ajnāna, or assumed ignorance of the Supreme who is Creator and Creation, Actor and Act, Existence, Knowledge, Joy, and above the gunas. The goal of the Vedāntist (Vedantin) is liberation of the human soul from the wheel of birth and rebirth, and re-identification with Paramatman. Cf. Darshanas, Druses, Shankarāchārya.

VEDHĀS [arranging, creating, wise, learned]. Names of many of the Gods.

VENDĪDĀD, Per. [from Pahlavī vī-dævō-dātem =law created against the devas or demons]. An account of creation, historical and other matter; a portion of the Avesta or sacred books of the Zoroastrian religion.

VENUS. Lat. Goddess of Love; one of the great Planetary Spirits. Later identified with Greek Aphrodite, q.v. Cf. Mother, Shukra, Astarte, Ishtar, Lucifer, Phosphoros, Senzar, Shveta, Vishvakārya, Vulcan.

VESTA, Lat. [akin to Gr. Hestia, the hearth, and Skt. vas=to dwell]. Goddess of the earth and its fire; hence of the preparation of food.

Her attendants were virgins, dedicated to watching the perpetually burning sacred fire of the altar. Cf. Penates, Agni.

VIBHĀVASU [vibhūs-vasu=having mighty treasures or wealth, from vibhu=pervading all things]. An epithet of the Trinity.

VIBHŪTAYAH [vibhūti=great or superhuman power, the siddhis, q.v.].

VIDYĀ [kinwoledge from vid=to see, perceive, understand, know, experience, feel, name, etc.]. The four Vidyās are: trayī=the triple Veda; ānvikshikī=logic and metaphysics; danda-nīti=the science of government; vārttā =the arts. Manu, VII, 43 adds a fifth, i.e., Ātma-vidyā, [the sicence of Ātmā], and a Sixth Vidyā, Guhya. The Vishnu Purāna mentions a Sixth, Guhya Vidyā. There is also in vogue another classification: 4 Vedas, 6 Vedangas, Mimamsa, Nyāya, the Purānas and Dharma-Shāstra or a total of fourteen.

VIDYĀ-DHARA [magical-knowledge holder]. A type of genius attendant on the Gods.

VIHĀRAS [vi-hri=to take away, walk or saunter about]. Pleasure-garden; a Buddhist or Jaina temple or convent where the Buddhist priests met or walked about. Cf. Āshram.

VIJNĀNAM [vijnā=to distinguish, discern, understand, investigate, etc.]. The act of vijnā. VIJNĀNA-MAYA [full of vijnā].

VIJNĀNAMAYA-KOSHA [the sheath of intelligence or understanding]. Cf. Kosha.

VI-KARTANA [vi-krit=to cut into or divide]. The Sun. Cf. Sūrya.

VIMĀNA [vi-mā=to measure out, traverse a course, pervade]. The chariot of the gods; the aircraft of old. Cf. Vāhan, Merkabah.

VINATĀ [bent down, humble]. One of the wives of Kashyapa and mother of Aruna and Garuda, daughter of Daksha.

VĪRABHADRA [vīra=strength, heroism+bhadra=auspicious]. Avatāra or son of Shiva, created from His (mouth) in order to spoil the sacrifice of Daksha; thousand-headed, thousand-eyed, with appearance fierce and terrific. Said in another Purāna to be produced from a drop of Shiva's sweat.

VIRĀJ [shining, radiant, beauty, splendour; of regal or military class]. First progeny of Brahmā. Having become male and female, Brahmā produced from the female the male power Virāj, who then produced the first Manu. The creative or male generative principle, Vairajas, descendants of Viraj. Cf. Sādhya, Vairāja, Androgyne.

VISHISHTĀDVAITA [vi-shish=to distinguish or define+advaita, q.v.]. A Hindu philosophy preached by Rāmanujācarya.

VISHNU [either from vish=to pervade, penetrate, embrace, convey, accomplish; or from vish=to enter, pierce, pervade, settle down, undertake]. The all-pervading, encompassing penetrating Preserver of the Hindu Trimūrti, the Second Logos, Mahavishnu, Shiva, Brahmā. Often identified with Nārāyana. His shakti is Lakshmi; his vāhan, Garuda. His Ten Great Avatāras: 1. Matsya, the Fish, Divine Life incarnate in the watery period with first dawnings of animal life; 2. Kūrma, the Tortoise, the Amphibian period; 3. Varāha, the Boar, the Mammalian period; 4. Narasimha, the Lionman, the transitional period from Mammal to Man; 5. Vāmana, the dwarf, Infant Humanity, whose future kingdom is the earth, the heavens, and the innermost heart; 6. Parashu-rāma, Rāma with the axe, the Avenger, the developed Fourth Race: 7. Rāmachandra, the ideal Āryan Race or developed Humanity; 8. Shri Krishna, type of Superhumanity; to be achieved in the Sixth Race; 9. Gautama, q.v., the Buddha, the Supremely Enlightened One, who, having touched the threshold of Godhood, overshadows, rather than incarnates; to be foreshadowed in the Seventh race and achieved in the Seventh Round; 10. the Kalki Avatār yet to come, type of the Supreme Kingship only achieved by such as the Kumaras. Cf. Avatāras, Bala-Rāma, Bhūtesha, Bythos, Chitkala, Chokmah, Christos, Dhruva, Dhyāni-Buddha, Ea, Hari, Hermes, Horus, Hrishīkesa, Iaō, Kwan-Sha-Yin, Mādhava, Manjusri, Merodach, Odin, Omorōka, Padmapāni, Paramapada, Prajna, Purushottama, Serpent, and references Shankha, Shishumārā, Sophia, Thoth, Vaikuntha-Loka, Varuna, Vāsudeva, Vishva, Vishvarūpa.

VISHVAS [pos. from vish=to pervade or shvi= to cause to swell]. All, every one, universal. A term used of all the Gods but particularly of the following ten: Vasu, Satya, Kratu(purpose, resolution, determination); Daksha, Kāla, Kāma, Dhriti (holding fast, seizing, maintaining); Kuru (from kri=to do or make); Purūravas (possessing much light); Mādravas (belonging to the madras=happiness). Occasionally are added Rochaka (brightening, enlightening) or Lochana (brightening, etc.); and Dhvani [tone or thunder, drum sound].

VISHVAKARMA, VISHVAKARMAN [vishva, q.v.+karman=the doer or creator]. One who does universal acts, the all-creator, all-maker. Architect and artist of the Gods. Son of Brahmā. Later identified with Tvashtri. An epithet of Indra and Sūrya; and of the Sun-Ray, supposed to bear heat to the planet Mercury. Cf. Sanjna, Vaidhātra, Planetary Logos.

VISHVAKĀRYA [vishva, q.v.+kārya=the accomplished or perfected]. That which has perfected All. The Sun-Ray, supposed to bear heat to Venus.

VISHVĀMITRA [vishva+amitra=no friend to all, but more probably vishva+mitra=friend to all]. A celebrated Kshatriya who elevated himself to Brāhman caste through rigid tapas earning the titles of Rājarishi, Rishi, Maharishi, and Brahmarishi. Finally the Gods sent the nymph Menakā [speech Cf. Vach] to tempt him. Their daughter Shakuntalā (a bird) is the heroine of a celebrated drama.

VISHVĀNARA [ruling all men, benefiting all men. Vishva, q.v.]. Epithet of the Sun. Cf. Sūrya.

VISHVARŪPA [present in all forms]. An epithet of Vishnu.

VISHVATRYARCHĀS [vish=all-encompassing +trya=three+archās, archi=flame or fire; archā=worship, adoration]. The threefold, balanced, all pervading Ray, Cf. Agni.

VISHVA-VEDAS [omniscient].

VITALA [vi=division, privation, or separation +tala, q.v.]. One of the nether regions.

VIVASVAT [the brilliant one]. Name of the Sun, sometimes regarded as an Āditya. Cf. Vaivasvata Manu, Sūrya.

VODHU [the one who is borne or carried]. Name of one of the seven Kumāras.

VOHU-MANŌ. Amesha-Spentas, q.v.

VRATA [anything enclosed or settled; a law or rite]. A vow.

VRATĀNI [Varuna's dynamic laws]. Rig-Vedic Hymns, X, 90-1.

VRITRA [pos. root vri=screen, conceal, cover]. The coverer and hider of rain with whom Indra continually battles, as Vritra-han.

VULCAIN, VULCAN [firebrand, meteor]. God of Fire, Agni. Identified with the Greek Hephaistos, consort of Venus. His earlier consort was Maja [the majestic one]. Cf. Hephaistos, Planetary Spirits, Tvashtri.

VYAKTA [adorned, decorated, manifested, differentiated].

VYĀKRITIS [grammar, grammarians, analysis].

VYĀNA [circulating or diffused through the body]. One of the vital airs. Cf. Vāyu, Prāna, Prānāyāma.

VYĀSA [distributing, expanding, amplifying, arranging, compiling]. The original arranger of the Vedas. A generic title given to any compiler or author. The great Vyāsa was he who gave the teaching of unity to the Āryan root race.

W

WATER. Gods and Goddesses embodying the elemental spirit of Water are: Chaos, Dag, Ea, Gabriel, Hiquet, Ilmatar, Ilus, Leviathan, Merodach, Michæl, Nārā, Nārāyana, Neptune, Nereid, Oan, Omorōka, Pelagus, Poseidon, Prachetās, Quetzo-cohautl, Rasa, Samvarta, Sarasvatī, Shishumāra, Thalassa, Oceanos and Tethys under Titans, Toom, Triton, Undine, Varshas, Varuna, Vasu, Ymir, the Hierarchies of Water under Zodiac.

WODEN, WODAN, Icel. [wind or air in motion] Odin. Wednesday or Woden's Day is derived therefrom. Cf. Vāyu.

X

XISUTHRUS [Gr. corruption of Atra-Khasis= very clever or pious]. Ephithet applied to Ut-napishtim, a hero of Babylonia, who secured immortal life, and who with his household were the sole survivors of the deluge. Cf. Atlantis, Noah.

Y

YAH, YAHO, YĀHO, YAHWEH. See YHVH.

YAJNA [prayer, devotion, homage, praise]. In later literature=any act of sacrifice or worship.

YAJUR-VEDA. See above and Veda. That text which contains mantras to be used at sacrifices. "The sacrificial Veda."

YAKSHAS [connected with yaj=to worship with sacrifices, through yaksh=to move or stir, to honour and worship]. A class of celestials who attend on Kuvera. One account says that they were produced by Brahmā crying "let us eat" from [jaksh=to eat] and are cruel and voracious. Others know them as harmless creatures delighting in song and dance.

YAMA [yam=to sustain, support, restrain, govern]. Rein, curb, bridle. Lord of the Pitris, and Judge and Lord of the dead; as King of Justice, Dharma, Lord of the Southern Quarter. Some hold that he and his twin sister Yamī are the first pair of beings born from Vivasvat, the Sun. The name of the seventh Manu. Cf. Hades and references, Chitragupta, Phtah, Pluto, Rephaim, Saramā.

YĀNA [act of going, moving, riding]. A carriage, chariot, vehicle, Vāhan.

YANG, Chin. S.D. Unity, q.v. The active male principle of Duality, q.v. Yang-yin.

YASODHARĀ [maintaining or preserving glory]. Name of an occult force. Cf. Gopa, Utpala, Varna, Trimūrti, Shakti.

YĀTU-DHĀNA [yātu=a goer, traveller, wind sorcery, witchcraft]. Rākshasas.

YESOD, YESUD, YEZUD, Heb. Sephira, q.v.

YEZIDI, Per. A sect of reputed Devil-worshippers of Armenia and Caucasus, who believe in the reinstatement of Satan.

YGGDRASIL, Icel. The tree which supports the universe. Cf. Midgard, Nithhogg. With its roots in cold Hel and its highest branches overshadowing Valhalla, q.v., it is a symbol of Eternity in manifestation.

YHVH, JAH, YAH, YAHO, YAHWEH, etc., Heb. [der. (?) pos, from root=to fall, to cause to fall, to be, to blow; the Ineffable Name of the eternal and everlasting Existence, embodied in a Being of the Past, the Present and the Future]. Mispronounced Jehovah by German theologians in olden days, the inserted vowels being derived from Adonay. This sacred Tetragrammaton is said by learned Jewish theologians to take the pronunciation YAHWEH, or YOD HE WAW (VAU) HE though no one has been sure as to its accuracy since the destruction of the Second Temple of Jerusalem. Cf. Aum, Tau, Amen, El, Elohistic, Iao, Javo, Joshua, Merkabah, Thummin.

YIMA, Per. An Avestan Hero and Demigod. Ruler of the Realm of Death. Cf. Yama, Pluto.

YIN, Chin. Feminine passive principle of Yang, Yin, or Duality.

YMIR, ÖRGELMIR, Icel. The primeval giant from whose body the Gods created the world. Personifies primeval waters or Chaos.

YO, Jap. Male active principle of Duality. Yo-In, q.v..

YOGA [the act of yoking, joining, uniting]. Applied to practices designed to achieve the Supreme Union with Ātmā, Rāja and Hatha Yoga. Some other forms of Yoga are Bhakti, Mantra and Yantra (diagrams and symbols.

Cf. Mandala), Jnana, Karma [action], Laya [the arousing of kundalinī]. Cf. Essenes, Kandū, Kriyashakti, Nazar, Samādhi, Shramana, Siddhis, Tapas, Tārakā Raja Yoga.

YOGĀCHĀRYA [yoga+ācharya=one to whom one must have recourse or Spiritual Guru or Guide].

YOJANA [yoga, q.v.]. Act of joining, yoking. A distance of about nine English miles, according to others about 2½ English miles. A Path, an Exertion. Cf. Mārga, Meru.

YOUNG CRŪB, Senzar. [absolute perfection or rest]. Cf. Nirvāna, Unity.

YONI [Yu=to bind, fasten, mix, betow]. Womb and female organs of generation. Cf. N'cabvah, Mother.

YUDHIS-THIRA [yudhi, locative+sthira=firm or steady in battle]. Eldest of the "sons" of Pāndu, son of Dharma or Yama, and Kuntī. Cf. Pāndavas.

YUGA [a yoke]. An age. While the exoteric classification gives only four yugas; Krita or Satya, Treta, Dvāpara, and Kali, the eosteric cycles regard Kali as the turning or balancing point of greatest materiality in a series of seven cycles, retracing the Yugas until the age of regained or conscious innocence, Satya, is realized. Technically a Yuga is a very small part of a Kalpa. A half-round is 306,720,000 years or 71 Mahā Yugas; a Chain or Day of Brahma with its round-twilights is 4,320,000,000 years with an equal length pralaya or Night of Brahmā. An age of Brahmā or Mahā Kalpa equals 100 years of Brahmā at 3,110,400,000,000 each, the total being the period of a (Solar?) Universe during its Manvantara, with probably a period of equal dissolution or rest. It is said we are only about 5,000 years advanced in the Kali Yuga of the Fifth Race, with 427,000 years pending. The periods spent in the snbtler ages are enormously longer than those spent in the grosser. The Yugas apply to every division of manifestation from a Chain to a nation. There is a definite overlapping of racial yugas. Ages, cycles, yugas are not measured by Nature but by stages of consciousness, and many factors may affect their duration. All exoteric figures must be approximations, even if correctly interpreted. Cf. Cycle, Chain, Eternity, Kalpa Manvantara, Round, Sandhyāmsha.

Z

ZARATHUSTRA, ZOROASTER [Lord of the Golden Shining]. The Founder of the Parsī faith. He gave the teaching of the Fire of Purity through which flamed the Joy of the Supreme. Cf. Mithra, Ahura Mazda, Ahriman, Airyaman. Airyana-Vaējō, Amesha-Spentas, Asha, Avesta.

ZARPANITU, Akkad. Moon-goddess, mother, by Merodach, of Nebo, god of Wisdom. Cf. Soma.

ZEND AVESTA [sacred text and its zend or interpretation in Pahlavi, q.v.]. The sacred Zoroastrian teachings. See Zarathustra, Avesta.

ZEROANA, ZERVANA, AKARNA (Akerne), Pahlavi. [boundless or limitless time; duration in a circle]. The Beginningless and Endless Unity. Cf. Chakra, Eternity.

ZEUS, Gr. [root Dis. Z=dy or j. Cf. Dyaus, Skt. for sky]. Jupiter. Cf. Deus, Deity.

ZIPPORAH, Heb. [the shining or radiant]. Spiritual Light, one of the seven daughters of Jethro, the Initiator of Moses, "wife" of Moses who marries her near the "well" (of occult knowledge).

ZODIAC, Gr. [of for animals, akin to zōos=living]. An astronomical belt in the heavens 16° broad, including the paths of the moon, and all the principal planets and, as its middle line, the ecliptic, or sun's path. *Occult*. An astrological mandala within which are marked by symbols the Twelve Creative Hierarchies, through which the Seven Planetary Logoi or Spirits work. While the Tenth Creative Hierarchy is stated to be identical with the Tenth Sign of the Zodiac, no exoteric information is given as to whether the other Creative Hierarchies can be correlated in their exact order with the signs of the Zodiac as usually given. The first four of the Hierarchies have passed away from work in our world, and the Fifth is on the threshold of liberation. The seven remaining are: 1. Formless Fiery Breaths, Fiery Lions of the Kosmic Will; 2. Two-fold units of Fire and Ether, Manifested Reason, Wisdom or Kosmic Buddhi; 3. Mahat, the Triads, of Fire-Ether-Water, Kosmic Activity. The above are Arūpa Creative Orders; 4. The Human Monads, Kosmic Form builders; 5 or 10 of the Twelve. The Asuras of Ahamkara, who link the Ātmic centre in man with his Will aspect. 6. The sixfold Dhyānis, or Agnishvattas who give to man his five middle human principles. 7. Barhishad Pitris, who give man his animal principles, prāna and body. The twelve signs of the Zodiac which are also correlated with the twelve Sons of Jacob, are: 1. *Aries*, the Ram, "slain from the foundation of the world" (Cf. Mendes), or Sanskrit *Mesam* [mish=to wink forth without any sense of identification or attachment. Actionless but full of potency for action]. 2 *Taurus*, the Young Bull (Nandi),or *Vrishabham* [vrsh=to outflow or outpour, Pranava, the ever-new]. 3. *Genini*, the Twins of Duality, or *Mithunam* (mith=to unite or twofol dmanifestation.) Cf. Castor and Pollux. 4. *Cancer*, the Crab of memory or tenacious imagination, archetypal ideation or *Karkatakam* (the Sacred Quaternary) 5. *Leo*, the Lion, or *Simham* (the limited Self). Cf. Nara-Simha. Many Hindu occultists consider signs six and eight as dual to be followed by sign seven. 6. *Virgo*, the Virgin, or *Kanyā* [kan=to desire]. Virgin Mother of Sakti. 7. *Libra*, or Balance, or *Tula* [the 36 tattvas, born of Avidya]. 8. *Scorpio*, the Scorpion or *Vrishchikam* [vrich=to cut, inflict pain or karma]. 9. *Sagittarius*, (the Archer) or Truth-Seeker, or *Dhanus* [the nine Prajāpatis. Cf. Cheiron, etc. 10. *Capricorn*, the Goat, or *Makara*, the Crocodile (fifth stage

of life which is death). Cf. Napthali. 11. *Aquarius*, the One who bears the Waters of Life, or *Kumbham* [Kum+bhah=illusion, error, the phenomenal world which is nothingness]; 12. *Pisces*, the Fishes of Balance or *Minam* [mi=to merge the individual into the universal]. Cf. Sādhyas.

ZOHAK, Azhi Dāhaka, Per. [the three-headed serpent]. Allegorical symbol of the Assyrian dynasty. Satan, *q.v.*

ZOHAR, SOHAR, [Splendour, light]. A revelation of Kabala, given in the 13th century by Moses de Leon, who attributed it to Simeon ben Jochai, a 2nd century teacher.

ZU, Bab. A storm bird god, who snatches the tablets of fate from Bel, in turn losing them to Marduk, who thus become supreme. Cf. Karma.

ZUNI, Red Indians of New Mexico, United States.

ERRATA

Vol. 1, p. 130, line 20:   After " good; " insert *sva*, self;

    p. 275, line 5:   for " Dankmoe " read "Denkmäler "

    p. 275, footnote[2]:   insert " Lepsius " before the reference

Vol. 2, p. 62, footnote[4]:   for " Phoinizer " read " Phönizier "

    p. 375, line 15:   for " Villapandus " read " Villalpandus "

Vol. 4, p. 276. line 11:   for " Argueil " read " Orgueil "

    p. 276, line 12:   for " 1857 " read " 1864 "

Vol. 6, Index, p. 70   Before CHERUBIM insert
    CHERCHEN, in Tibet, i. 55, 56
    CHERCHEN-DARYA, river, i. 55, 56

———

ADDENDUM

Vol. 3, p. 329, footnote[3]:   [In 1888 edition the word " three " occurs before " occasioned " in line 16.]

———